INCREASING MANAGEMENT RELEVANCE AND COMPETITIVENESS

PROCEEDINGS OF THE 2ND GLOBAL CONFERENCE ON BUSINESS, MANAGEMENT AND ENTREPRENEURSHIP (GC-BME 2017), AUGUST 9, 2017, UNIVERSITAS AIRLANGGA, SURABAYA, INDONESIA

Increasing Management Relevance and Competitiveness

Editors

Badri Munir Sukoco, Rahmat Heru Setianto & Nidya Ayu Arina
Universitas Airlangga, Indonesia

Ade Gafar Abdullah, Asep Bayu Nandiyanto & Ratih Hurriyati
Universitas Pendidikan, Indonesia

CRC Press
Taylor & Francis Group
Boca Raton London New York

CRC Press is an imprint of the
Taylor & Francis Group, an **informa** business
A BALKEMA BOOK

Published by:
CRC Press/Balkema
P.O. Box 447, 2300 AK Leiden, The Netherlands
e-mail: Pub.NL@taylorandfrancis.com
www.crcpress.com – www.taylorandfrancis.com

First issued in paperback 2020

Typeset by V Publishing Solutions Pvt Ltd., Chennai, India

ISBN 13: 978-0-367-73485-5 (pbk)
ISBN 13: 978-0-815-37455-8 (hbk)

Visit the Taylor & Francis Web site at
http://www.taylorandfrancis.com

and the CRC Press Web site at
http://www.crcpress.com

Increasing Management Relevance and Competitiveness – Sukoco et al. (Eds)
© 2018 Taylor & Francis Group, London, ISBN 978-0-8153-7455-8

Table of contents

Marketing management

Management and economics education

Increasing Management Relevance and Competitiveness – Sukoco et al. (Eds)
© 2018 Taylor & Francis Group, London, ISBN 978-0-8153-7455-8

Preface

International Conferences provide an excellent opportunity to bring together academics from different countries and backgrounds for the purpose of presenting their research results, critically discussing methodology and findings and improving the quality of research and the impact of the research on society and science. Furthermore, conferences enable the scientific community to create new networks, to foster relationships and extend their visibility.

The 2nd Global Conference on Business Management and Entrepreneurship (GCBME) 2017 is an annual conference co-hosted by Department of Management, Faculty of Economics & Business, Universitas Airlangga and Business Management Education Program, Faculty of Business and Economics Education, Universitas Pendidikan Indonesia. The theme of GCBME 2017 is increasing management relevance and competitiveness.

The theme inspired by the concern of Sumantra Ghoshal that bad management theories are destroying good management practices. Before that, the dichotomy between rigor and relevance is always becoming a hot topic in the management field. This conference aims to answer the following question: How might we accomplish a reconciliation of rigor (academic) and relevance (practitioner) standards to offer organizational competitiveness?

I expect this conference raises two important things in the discussion room and proceedings (based on Corley and Gioia, 2011): First, theories used in this conference should be problem driven—that is addressing a problem of direct, indirect, or long-linked relevance to practice, rather than narrowly addressing the (theoretical) "problem." Second, the fact that we are a profession (academia) studying another profession (management), therefore it needs balancing between theoretical contribution managerial implications. By doing that, I believe that our research and discussion in this conference could offer something useful for practitioners (thus increase its competitiveness) while at the same time contribute to the development of our management field.

I am looking forward to seeing you in GCBME in the near future.

With warmest regards,
Prof. Badri Munir Sukoco, PhD
GC-BME 2017 Conference Chair

 ISBN 978-0-8153-7455-8

Acknowledgements

Badri Munir Sukoco, *Universitas Airlangga, Indonesia*
Ratih Hurriyati, *Universitas Pendidikan Indonesia*
Ade Gafar Abdullah, *Universitas Pendidikan Indonesia*
Praptini Yulianti, *Universitas Airlangga, Indonesia*
Muhammad Madyan, *Universitas Airlangga, Indonesia*
Didi Sukyadi, *Universitas Pendidikan Indonesia*
Wann-Yih Wu, *Nanhua University, Taiwan*
John Nowland, *Illinois State University, USA*
Ikuro Yamamoto, *Kinjo Gakuin University Nagoya, Japan*
Jon Lovett, *University of Leeds, UK*
John Paul, *Kedge Business School, France*
Ranbir Malik Singh, *Curtin University, Australia*
Nobuhide Otomo, *Kanazawa University, Japan*
Mohamed Dahlan Ibrahim, *Universiti Malaysia Kelantan, Malaysia*
Dadang Kurnia, *GIZ, Germany*

 ISBN 978-0-8153-7455-8

Organizing committees

ADVISORS

Prof. John Paul
Prof. Ranbir Malik Singh
Prof. Dr. Nobuhide Otomo
Prof. Dr. Mohamed Dahlan Ibrahim
Prof. Dr. Anis Eliyana
Prof. Dr. Muslich Anshari
Prof. Dr. Fendy Suhariadi
Prof. Dr. Sri Iswati
Prof. Dr. Bambang Tjahjadi
Prof. Dr. Nanang Fattah
Prof. Dr.Agus Rahayu
Prof. Dr. Tjutju Yuniarsih
Prof. Dr. Disman
Prof. Dr. Suryana
Prof. Dr. Eeng Ahman
Prof. Dr. Ratih Hurriyati
Prof. Ina Primiana
Prof. Lincoln Arsyad
Prof. Gunawan Sumodiningrat
Dr. Phil Dadang Kurnia
Assoc. Prof. Arry Akhmad Arman
Assoc. Prof. Dwilarso
Assoc. Prof. Hardianto Iristidi
Assoc. Prof. Rachmawaty Wangsaputra
Assoc. Prof. Teungku Ezni Balkiah
Assoc. Prof. Ruslan Priyadi
Assoc. Prof. Sri Gunawan,
Assoc. Prof. Dr. Indrianawati Usman
Assoc. Prof. Yudi Aziz
Assoc. Prof. Lili Adiwibowo
Assoc. Prof. Vanessa Gaffar
Assoc. Prof. Chaerul Furqon
Vina Andriany MEd, PhD
Tutin Ariyanti, PhD

CONFERENCE CHAIR

Prof. Badri Munir Sukoco, Ph.D

COMMITTEES

Dr. Tanti Handriana
Rahmat Heru Setianto, SE, M.Sc.
Nidya Ayu Arina, SM, MSM.
Dr. Masmira Kurniawati
Made Gitanadya, SE, MSM.
Ratri Amelia Aisyah, SM, MSM.

Strategic management, entrepreneurship and contemporary issues

Increasing Management Relevance and Competitiveness – Sukoco et al. (Eds)
© 2018 Taylor & Francis Group, London, ISBN 978-0-8153-7455-8

Governance of financial intangible success factors: An option in building business resilience and sustainability

Pudjo Sugito
University of Merdeka Malang, Malang, Indonesia

ABSTRACT: The aim of this research is to analyze the financial intangible success factors related to business resilience and sustainability. The research population consists of small and medium sized enterprises in the Probolinggo region, East Java, Indonesia. The sampling technique is proportional random sampling. The number of respondents is 100, which is the minimum requirement needed for the data analysis techniques of structural equation models. Primary data was collected by a questionnaire. Further, it will be analyzed by using a structural equation model technique. Based on the results of the data analysis, it is revealed that financial intangible success factors significantly influence business resilience. Also, financial intangible success factors significantly influence business sustainability. In addition, business resilience also affects business sustainability. This means that the governance of financial intangible assets are extremely important for developing small and medium sized enterprises. In other words, this will be an option for building business resilience as well as for sustainability.

Keywords: Financial Intangible Success Factors, Resilience, Sustainability

1 INTRODUCTION

Several researches have revealed that there is currently a significant shift in the utilization of corporate assets. Evidently, more and more intangible assets are being utilized in order to realize organization targets (Zigan & Zeglat, 2010). This is due to the huge benefits of intangible assets to organizational performance. Reynoso (2008) and Durst (2015) also confirm that the intangible assets, such as collaborations, skills, knowledge, innovation, patents and other intellectual property, leadership, image and reputation, and culture, are now the essence of competitive advantage.

Interestingly, according to Feindt, Jeffcoate, and Chappell (2002), the Financial Intangible Success Factors (FISFs) are important components in achieving the vision and mission of the corporation. Moreover, Wiley (2012) and Olavarrieta and Friedmann (1999) support this idea. There are four dimensions that are dictated by financial intangible assets, namely, knowledge, image, brand value, and other immaterial assets. Therefore, current finance managers should concern themselves with the financial intangible assets in order to improve competitiveness and profitability. In Short, the financial intangible success factors play a significant role in meeting the business organization goals. Therefore, the purpose of this research is to analyze the effect of the governance of the FISFs on the resilience and business sustainability of Small and Medium Enterprises (SMEs) in Probolinggo.

The classification of the key success factors of small enterprises is based on the governance of the utilization of tangible assets and intangible assets, and also according to financial and non-financial factors. Interestingly, the successes of the small enterprises are also built through the utilization of financial intangible assets. These assets consist of brand value, goodwill and the value of immaterial properties. Therefore, the study of the utilization of financial intangible assets becomes really important, due to the given assets that are owned by many small enterprises.

Subsequently, Li and Wang (2014) proposed a framework that includes the corporate success of the marketing concept, a good management approach and ethics organizations to meet the needs and desires of various public organizations. Furthermore, in the long term, it may ensure the satisfaction of the needs of the organization itself. Flamholtz and Aksehirli (2000) found that there is a significant relationship among the development of the six critical success factors, which are the market, products and services, resource management, operating systems, corporate culture, and the overall financial success of the organization.

Meanwhile, Lonnqvist (2004) stated that the factor of business success is determined by the tangible and intangible assets. Hence, this explains why the intangible success factor is classified into financial and non-financial. The financial intangible success factors include brand value, goodwill, and the value of immaterial properties. On the other hand, the non-financial factors consist of competencies, customer satisfaction, customer retention, innovation, motivation, and personnel satisfaction. It should be noted that the majority of SMEs did not have any tangible assets of great value. Therefore, these potential assets can be optimized to improve the business sustainability by optimizing the governance of financial intangible success factors.

Burnard and Bhamra (2014) stated that business resilience is the ability to adapt and respond to a variety of business interruptions for the purpose of maintaining the continuity of its operations, to be reliable and to enable the entity to continue growing and developing. Carmeli and Tishler (2014), supported by Chang and Hsieh, (2011), explained that true business resilience originated from its ability to understand correctly how to run a business based on the performance of the business.

Management should not only focus on the issues that cause organizations to work defensively, but must also use a proactive approach to face unexpected problems. In this way, the resilience of the business will be effective and efficient. Linnenluecke (2017) revealed that there are six elements of business resilience. They consist of integrated risk management, business continuity, regulatory compliance, security data protection, knowledge and skills, and market readiness.

According to Ciarelo et al. (2014), the disclosure of financial intangible assets has turned out to have had a major contribution to the achievement of profit and business continuity beyond the contribution of physical assets. In addition, Husnah (2013) stated that the reinforcement of financial intangible assets, which produces a larger company because of the company's earnings, is relatively higher. Therefore, the research hypotheses are (1) financial intangible success factors significantly influence the resilience of the business; (2) financial intangible success factors significantly influence sustainability; and (3) business resilience has a significant effect on sustainability.

2 METHOD

This research is an explanatory research with quantitative methods. Data collection was achieved by using a survey. The research population consists of small and medium sized enterprises in Probolinggo. The research variables consist of exogenous and endogenous variables. In this study, FISFs are exogenous variables. The endogenous variables are business resilience and sustainability. Based on the literary review, the research variables include the FISFs, business resilience, and sustainability. By definition, the FISFs are financial intangible factors that become the key reasons for the success of business continuity. The indicators that the FISFs cover are brand value, goodwill, and the value of immaterial properties. Meanwhile, business resilience is the ability not only to adapt and respond to interruptions to the business quickly in order to sustain its operations, but also to become a reliable partner that allows it to continue growing. Sustainability indicates a business continuity that is apparent from positive asset growth. The indicators of the research variables are as follows.

Table 1. Indicators of research variables.

Variables	Indicators	Notation
Financial Intangible Success Factors (FISFs) (Lonnqvist, 2004)	Brand value	X1
	Goodwill	X2
	Value of immaterial properties	X3
Business resilience (Linnenluecke, 2017)	Adaptability	X4
	Responsive	X5
	Collaborative	X6
	Market readiness	X7
	Survivability	X8
Business sustainability (Shapiro, 2013)	Market growth	X9
	Customer growth	X10
	Profit growth	X11
	Asset growth	X12

The research population consists of small and medium sized enterprises in Probolinggo. Based on the results of the survey, there are 385 SMEs in this region, of which 100 SMEs have been the respondents. The number of respondents is in accordance with the requirements of the structural equation model (Ferdinand, 2013). This research uses a valid and reliable questionnaire for collecting data. Further, the primary data was analyzed by a Structural Equation Model (SEM).

3 RESULTS

The small and medium sized enterprises in Probolinggo consist of the timber industry, non-metallic minerals, manufacture of metal goods, food and beverages, textiles, leather, and the ceramics industry. Based on the primary data analysis by the structural equation model, the path diagram is demonstrated in Figure 1.

As is seen in Figure 1, there is linkage between the financial intangible success factors, business resilience and sustainability. Based on this Figure, the

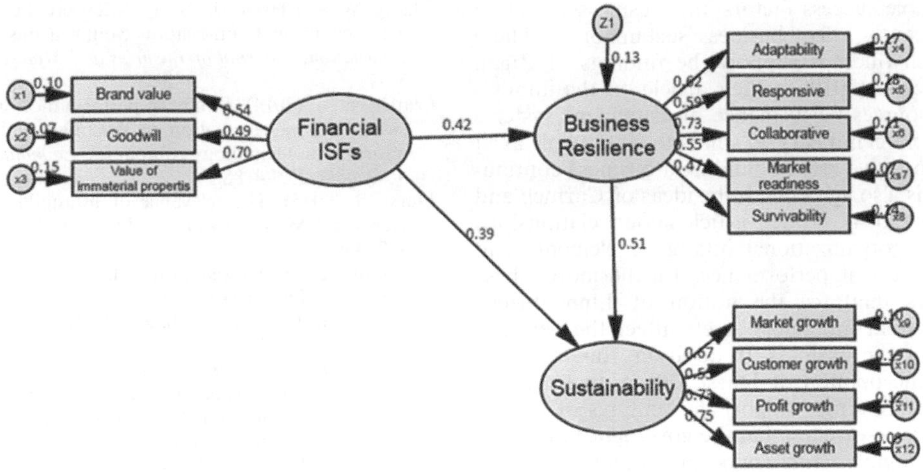

Figure 1. Linkage of FISFs, business resilience and sustainability.

financial intangible success factors affect business resilience, and also directly affect sustainability by a coefficient of 0.42 and 0.33. Then, business resilience affects sustainability by a coefficient of 0.51.

Subsequently, the test is done to determine whether the research variables can be utilized in order to confirm those variables that can be shared with other variables. The latent variables are assessed using analysis phases. The loading factors should be greater than or equal to 0.40. If the loading factor is lower than 0.40, it will be deemed that the dimensionless variables, together with other variables, will explain a latent variable. The loading factors for the variables in this confirmatory analysis are 0.54; 0.49; and 0.70. Thus, it can be concluded that these variables are jointly presenting undimensionality for latent variables.

Further, weight regression analysis was conducted to determine the strength of the dimensions that form its latent factor by utilizing the test of the regression weight generated by the model. Judging from this result, each indicator of each latent variable has already qualified, so it can be accepted. It has a value of loading factor (coefficient λ) or regression weight or standardized estimate significant to the value critical ratio (cr) of above or equal to 2.0. The results of this latent variable regression weight can be seen in Table 2. From these results, it can be seen that each of the indicators of each dimension has a value loading factor or standardized regression weight or significant estimate to the value of critical ratio > 2.0. In short, all of the indicators are eligible. Further, due to the probability values are less than 0.05. It can be concluded that the indicators forming latent variables have shown unidimensionality.

Table 2. Regression weights.

	Estimate	s.e	c.r.	p
Business resilience <--- Financial intangible success factors	0.42	0.14	3.00	0.009
Sustainability <--- Financial intangible success factors	0.39	0.10	2.60	0.004
Sustainability <--- Business resilience	0.51	0.11	4.63	0.000

Source: Primary Data, 2017.

4 DISCUSSION

Before discussing the research results, a research hypothesis test was done. The hypothesis testing was based on primary data analysis by using the structural equation model technique. The result is shown in Table 2. Hypothesis testing was done by analyzing the value of the critical ratio (cr) and the value of probability (p) on the results by regression weights, compared with the required statistical limits. The value must be greater than 2.00 for the critical ratio and below 0.05 for the probability. Table 2 describe the regression weights.

As shown in Table 2, the financial intangible success factors significantly affect the business resilience; the financial intangible success factors significantly affect the sustainability; and the business resilience significantly affects the sustainability. This is due to the fact that the critical ratio values are more than 2.00 and the p values are less than 0.05. This means that the financial intangible success factors and business resilience significantly affect business sustainability. These research findings support the findings of Zigan and Zeglat (2010) in their article on the intangible resources performance measurement systems of the hotel industry, in which the intangible asset has a positive role in building a business continuity. This also agrees with the ideas of Carmeli and Tishler (2004), in their article about relationships between organizational intangible elements and organizational performance. Furthermore, these findings reinforce the notion of Linnenluecke (2017), that intangible assets affect the development of the business. In addition, this also supports the opinion of Durst (2015). In brief, the research findings support the findings of several previous researches, that the governance of financial intangible assets can be an option in achieving business continuity.

5 CONCLUSION

Based on the discussion, it can be concluded that the financial intangible success factors significantly influence the business resilience and sustainability. Furthermore, the business resilience influences business sustainability. This means that when a business entity wants to build their resilience and sustainability, the manager should optimize the utilization of financial intangible assets such as brand value, goodwill and the value of immaterial properties. In this way, the small and medium sized industries will have better prospects.

REFERENCES

Burnard, K. & Bhamra, R. (2014). Organisational resilience: Development of a conceptual framework for organisational responses. *International Journal of Production Research,* 49, 5581–5599.

Carmeli, A. & Tishler, A. (2004). The relationships between intangible organizational elements and organizational performance. *Strategic Management Journal,* 25, 1257–1278.

Chang, W. S & Hsieh, J. (2011). Intellectual capital and value creation: Is innovation capital a missing link? *International Journal of Business and Management,* 6, 3–12.

Ciarelo, et al. (2014). Financial performance, intangible assets and value creation in Brazilian and Chilean information technology companies. *Economic Review of Galicia,* 23, 74–88.

Durst, S. (2015). The relevance of intangible assets in German SMEs. *Journal of Intellectual Capital,* 9, 437–446.

Ferdinand. 2013. A research for management (4th ed.). Semarang: Diponegoro University.

Flamholtz, E. G. & Aksehirli, Z. (2000). Organizational success and failure: An empirical test of a holistic model. *European Management Journal,* 18, 488–498.

Feindt, S., Jeffcoate, J., & Chappell, C., (2002), Identifying Success Factors for Rapid Growth in SME, *Small Business Economics*, 19(1): 51–62.

Husnah, et al. (2013). Intangible assets, competitive strategy and financial performance: Study on Rattan SMEs, IOSR. *Journal of Business and Management (IOSR-JBM),* 7, 14–27.

Li, H. & Wang, W. (2014). Impact of intangible assets on profitability of Hong Kong listed information technology companies, *Business and Economic Research Journal,* 4, 98–113.

Linnenluecke, M. K. (2017). Resilience in business and management research: A review of influential publications and a research agenda. *International Journal of Management Reviews,* 19, 4–30.

Lönnqvist, A. (2004). Measurement of intangible success factors: Case studies on the design, implementation and use of measures (Unpublished PhD Thesis). Tampere University of Technology, Tampere, Finland.

Olavarrieta, S. & Friedmann, R. (1999). Market-oriented culture, knowledge-related resources, reputational assets and superior performance: A conceptual framework. *Journal of Strategic Marketing,* 7, 215–228.

Reynoso, C. F. (2008). Role of intangible assets in the success of small and medium sized businesses. *Global Journal of Business Research,* 2, 53–68.

Shapiro, C. (2013). Theory of business strategy. RAND *Journal of Economics,* 2. 125–137.

Wiley, B. (2012). Success factors for high-technology SMEs: A case study from Australia. *Australian Business Journal,* 10, 86–91.

Zigan, K. & Zeglat, D. (2010). Intangible resources in performance measurement systems of the hotel industry. *Facilities Journal,* 28, 597–610.

Increasing Management Relevance and Competitiveness – Sukoco et al. (Eds)
© 2018 Taylor & Francis Group, London, ISBN 978-0-8153-7455-8

The influences of the alliance learning process and entrepreneurial orientation on the strategic alliance performance of Indonesian construction companies

R. Handayani & R. Dyah Kusumastuti
Universitas Indonesia, Depok, West Java, Indonesia

ABSTRACT: This study explores strategic alliances in the Indonesian construction sector, especially in terms of the impacts of the learning process and entrepreneurial orientation in their alliance organizations. The study aims to provide insights concerning the critical part of the learning process in the organization, which is implemented in four procedures: articulation, codification, sharing, and internalization. This is to guarantee that the motivation behind the establishment of an alliance can be fulfilled and that it will gain a competitive advantage. Moreover, this study will also give an outline of the entrepreneurial orientation that is required to change operational propensities or routines that are instilled inside the rigid structure of the organization, and thus, can overcome the issue of inertia by creating initiatives, implementing higher risk-taking and becoming more proactive in entering the new market. A survey with 62 respondents, representing alliances in construction companies in Jakarta, is conducted. The survey data is analyzed using structural equation modeling, and the results show that the alliance learning process and entrepreneurial orientation influence alliance performance.

Keywords: Strategic alliance, alliance learning process, entrepreneurial orientation, alliance performance

1 INTRODUCTION

The Indonesian government is currently focusing on infrastructure development in all regions of Indonesia. This policy has opened up a great business opportunity for the Indonesian construction sector. On the other hand, high demand for residences in urban areas that are not supported by the availability of sufficient land causes state-owned enterprises and private companies to race to construct buildings in strategic locations.

The construction sector is a high-risk business because it involves a large investment value with high safety standards. Then again, tight rivalry forces the businesses to compete with low costs and new innovations so that they can beat the competition in different ways. One of the strategies used to beat the competition is through the distribution of risks. A construction company may co-operate with a few different companies in its supply chain or process network, and use them as subcontractors (Chung & Ng, 2006).

Companies need a variety of resources and the ability to compete effectively. Resources and capabilities can be obtained through the acquisition, either developed internally or by establishing co-operative relationships with other companies through strategic alliances (Mudambi & Tallman, 2010; Bierly & Gallagher, 2007).

The objective of this research is to gain insights regarding the relationship between strategic alliances, entrepreneurial orientation and alliance performance within the context of strategic alliances in Indonesian construction companies.

2 THEORY AND HYPOTHESES

Researchers in strategic management start to develop the concept of strategic alliance by integrating the perspective of the resource-based view (Barney, 1991) with the perspective of the economic transaction costs (Williamson, 1989), as well as the knowledge-based view of the firm (Kale et al., 2002; Mudambi & Tallman, 2010; Emden et al., 2005).

One basic premise of the strategic alliance is that firms should concentrate on internal strategic activities that are important to them, while other activities can be outsourced to companies with specific expertise or a company that has a focus on those activities, which can offer economies of scale, as well as the benefits of wider organizational learning. This premise refers to the viewpoint of economic transaction costs (Williamson, 1989), whereby the company uses alliances to reduce their risks and costs (Franco & Haase, 2015). By utilizing this alliance, companies can reduce the costs of negotiation, co-ordination, and the monitoring of inter-company transactions and corporate governance (Williamson, 1989).

Strategic alliance is a relationship that is deliberately constructed between two or more independent companies, with activities involving the exchange, sharing, or co-development of the resources or capabilities to achieve mutual benefits (Gulati, 1995; Kale et al., 2002; Kale & Singh, 2007). A strategic alliance can be formed by developing one or more value chains, and has a variety of organizational configurations that are based on the inclusion of equity in the relationship, such as a joint venture, which is one kind of partnership based on equity or investment (Kale & Singh, 2009).

As a reliable strategy for achieving a competitive advantage in a dynamic environment (Bierly & Gallagher, 2007), it is not easy to have a successful alliance. For that reason, we need to understand how learning occurs in a successful alliance and how entrepreneurial orientation will address the problem of inertia, so that routines that are embedded in the company, as well as a rigid structure, will not hinder the learning process.

Strategic alliance can be seen as a formal agreement that could configure a contractual arrangement (not involving capital sharing) or establish an equity arrangement (involving capital sharing). The alliance may also initiate a new corporate entity or just form a joint operation without the establishment of a new corporate entity (Yoshino & Rangan, 1995).

2.1 *Alliance Learning Process (ALP)*

This study utilizes the alliance learning process in order to conceptualize the process that the firms undertake to learn, accumulate, and leverage alliance management know-how. By doing so, firms are able to develop or improve their partnering skills and thereby achieve a better alliance performance. These partnering skills are routines or practices that are used to better manage different phases in the life cycle of any alliance they engage in, for example, alliance formation and partner selection, alliance negotiation, formulation of alliance design, post-formation alliance management, and so on. The alliance learning process can help firms to develop alliance capability and have greater alliance success (Kale & Singh, 2007).

Based on the perspective view of a company's knowledge base, Kale and Singh (2007) indicate that organizations can improve their skills in managing tasks assigned to them by gathering and applying knowledge that is relevant to the task. Here, the company conducts the alliance learning process by applying four processes (the articulation of knowledge, codification of knowledge, sharing of knowledge, and the internalization of knowledge). With these activities, the company studies, accumulates, and spreads the influence of alliance management knowledge gained through the alliance, as well as from others.

Using this concept, the manager of the company in an alliance serves as the main storage of important experiences of alliance management, as well as knowledge gained from the experience of previous or ongoing alliances. Companies can take measures to help individual managers in an alliance to articulate their knowledge of alliance management. Thus, the company captures and externalizes the necessary alliance knowledge, so that other managers in the company can learn from these experiences (Kale & Singh, 2009).

A company can go a step further by arranging the accumulated knowledge of alliance management in the form of a knowledge object that can also be used by others, such as alliance management guidelines, checklists, and manuals, which incorporate best practices for managing different phases and decisions in the alliance life cycle. These codification tools and templates can help managers to assess the suitability of a prospective alliance partner, develop an alliance agreement, assess the performance of the alliance, and so on. The codification process of alliances facilitates the replication and transfer of best practice within the company by creating a toolkit for managers (Kale & Singh, 2007).

Companies can affect the alliance know-how by conducting the process of knowledge sharing in order to exchange tacit knowledge and individual knowledge (possessed by each manager in the alliance) so that they can be spread throughout the organization. This can be in the form of group or personal interactions in the alliance committee, task forces or a special forum for the exchange of experience and best practice among managers in the alliance (Kale & Singh, 2007; Kale & Singh, 2009).

The fourth process that needs to be undertaken in this learning process is to internalize and absorb the relevant knowledge of the alliance management in various parts of the company through formal and informal means. This internalization process emphasizes whether tasks are associated with a particular alliance, and also the process of apprenticeship, where a new manager will work with an experienced manager in the alliance to gain useful knowledge. Alternatively, the companies send their managers on a formal alliance training program conducted either by the company internally or by external parties (Kale & Singh, 2009).

Siren et al., (2016) explain that the strategic acquisition of knowledge is a process of exploration that allows individuals within an organization to gather strategic information from their environment in order to expand their current knowledge. The most feasible initiative eventually becomes a formal strategy and generates new products, new services, or new processes. Therefore, we draw the following hypothesis.

H1: An alliance learning process has a positive influence on alliance performance

2.2 *Entrepreneurial Orientation (EO)*

The concept of EO was originally conceived by Miller (1983). EO is a strategic construct that reflects the extent to which firms are innovative, proactive, and risk-taking in their behavior and management philosophies; or, stated more concisely, are entrepreneurial in their strategic posture (Covin & Slevin, 1989). The rapid development of the EO literature reflects its centrality to both the strategic management and entrepreneurship fields (Anderson et al., 2009).

In particular, innovativeness is a tendency to create and introduce new products, new production processes, or new organizational systems. Risk-taking is the tendency of companies to take a higher level of risk to try and venture into previously unknown areas by making a strong commitment, while proactiveness is the involvement in an opportunistic expansion in order to seize the opportunities for entering new markets and dealing with competitors (Li et al., 2017).

Previous studies find that EO is associated with the internal resources of the company, can be regarded as intangible resources embedded in an organization's routines, and is spread among members of the organization (Li et al., 2017). Furthermore, the company cannot purchase EO from the market, but they have to invest a lot of time to cultivate the culture so that EO can be a source of sustainable competitive advantage (Li et al., 2017).

The level of EO is higher when companies are more open to interaction with the external environment, thereby improving their ability to obtain knowledge-based resources that lead to a higher level of learning. Likewise, the tendency of companies showing a higher level of EO is to experiment with combining new resources, thereby facilitating the internalization of knowledge-based resources that will result in an increased level of experiential learning (Kreiser, 2011).

Companies can increase the level of EO to produce high performances when they are involved in alliances. When a company enters a certain alliance, EO will help the alliance to understand the learning process and give them the opportunities to look for resources in the collaboration (Sarkar et al., 2001; Teng, 2007; Li et al., 2017).

Compared to conservative firms, companies with a high level of EO tend to have a better understanding of the importance of the resources contributed by all of the alliance partners. The company may identify the entrepreneurial process and procedures that are effective in managing complex resource integration activities with uncertain outcomes (Li et al., 2017). They can also develop their superior resource management capabilities through the entrepreneurial learning process (Li et al., 2017), which will increase the yield of the alliance as a whole. In particular, corporate alliances with innovative ideas may have more insights into the creative aspects and can produce promising ideas and new ways of thinking. Innovative companies tend to favor the renewal, creation, and introduction of appropriate co-operative mechanisms in the alliance, which facilitates more effective control over the process of resource integration. In this way, innovation achieves a competitive advantage for the formed alliance, as well as for all of the companies involved (Li et al., 2017).

Conversely, when a company with a low level of EO is involved in the alliance, they may be more concerned with protecting their own resources rather than with providing sufficient resources to share (Teng, 2007). This will limit the opportunity to integrate resources in the alliance, which in turn can undermine its success (Li et al., 2017).

According to Siren et al., (2016), EO is needed to overcome the problem of inertia and routines that are ingrained in the company, as well as a rigid structure, which will cause a significant threat to the adaptability of the company in the long term. Companies that have a high level of entrepreneurship are considered to be better equipped to adapt to a dynamic competitive environment.

The success of the alliances of construction companies may also be affected by EO, which can change the habits involved in running operations, minimize organization inertia by building initiative, and increase the willingness to take risks and be more proactive (Siren et al., 2016). Based on the above explanations, we draw the following hypothesis.

H2: Entrepreneurial orientation has a positive influence on alliance performance

3 METHODOLOGY

We have two major research questions. First is to find out how far the alliance learning process influences the performance of the alliance. Second, whether the EO also has a positive influence on the performance of the alliance. We conducted a survey of persons in charge of managing alliances in construction companies in Jakarta, and the results are analyzed using Structural Equation Modeling (SEM). To simplify the model, we also use second order confirmatory factor analysis using a latent variable score technique. The research model is presented in Figure 1.

This study focuses on alliances in Indonesian construction companies in Jakarta that have been formed within five years. Referring to the unit of analysis that is being used in this study (the alliance), we involve project managers, project coordinators, project directors or persons in charge in consortiums or alliances as respondents in the survey. The total number of respondents in this study is 62, representing 62 strategic alliances from 34 construction companies in Jakarta. Whereby nine companies are state-owned enterprises (26%) and 25 companies are private national companies (74%). Variables, dimensions of each variable and the number of indicators in each dimension can be seen in Table 1.

In the pretest, questionnaires with six Likert-scale questions are distributed to 20 respondents with the same qualifications. We also interview all respondents to collect information on issues of interest. This pretest is important in order to get feedback for the questions posed in the questionnaire and to ensure that the respondents understand the questions.

In order to determine the sample in this study, we first identify construction companies that have conducted strategic alliances in their businesses. Then, we identify the right persons to be respondents, based on two criteria: 1) the persons must be responsible for the alliance management, such as the project director, project manager, manager of corporate development, or team coordinator for certain alliance projects; and 2) the persons have the ability to answer the questionnaire.

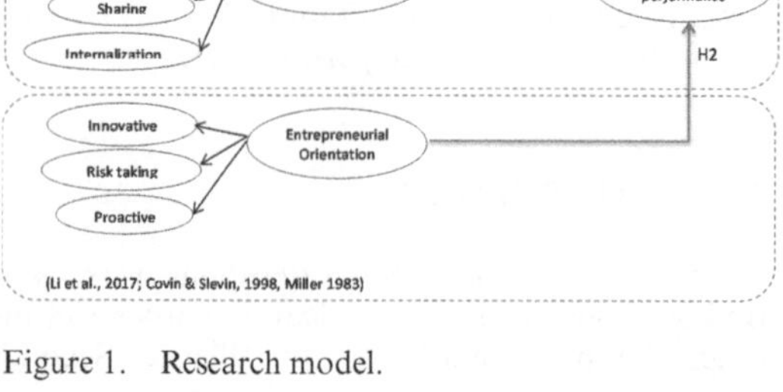

Figure 1. Research model.

Table 1. Operationalization of variables.

Latent variables	Dimensions	No. of Indicators per Dimension	References
Alliance Learning Process	Articulation	5	Kale & Singh (2007)
	Codification	4	Kale et al. (2000)
	Sharing	6	
	Internalization	4	
Entrepreunerial Orientation	Innovativeness	3	Covin and Slevin (1989)
	Pro-activeness	3	Li et al. (2017)
	Risk-Taking	3	Miller (1983)
Alliance Performance		5	Kale & Singh (2007) Kale et al. (2000) Li et al. (2017)
Total No. of Indicators		33	

4 RESULTS

The analysis and interpretation of the model using SEM requires two stages: 1) analysis of validity and reliability through the measurement model, and 2) analysis of the structural model.

4.1 *Measurement model*

Assessment of the measurement model entails examining the reliability of individual items to analyze internal consistency and validity tests to analyze latent constructs with reflective

The result of the reliability test shows that all indicators and dimension variables have a Cronbach Alpha coefficient above 0.7 and Variance Extracted (VE) above 0.5; which means that all of the variables in this model have internal consistency. The result of the validity test shows that all question items have loading factors above 0.5. This means that all items are valid to measure the abovementioned constructs.

4.2 *Structural model*

This research uses seven Goodness-of-Fit (GoFI) indicators to give information about the GoFI of the model, namely p-value = 0,04112 (marginal fit), RMSEA = 0,079 ($\leq$ 0,08: good fit), GFI ($\geq$ 0,90: good fit), AGFI ($\geq$ 0,90: good fit), CFI ($\geq$ 0,90: good fit), NFI ($\geq$ 0,90: good fit), RFI ($\geq$ 0,90: good fit) (Wijanto, 2015).

The empirical data shows that 6 out of 7 GoFI indices have higher values than the cut-off values. Only the p-value indicates marginal rate of fit. Thus, it can be concluded that the overall fit of the model is good.

Empirical data explained by chi-square = 66.29; Degree of freedom = 48; P-value = 0,04112 yields T-values for the relations of dimensions to latent variables are in the range between 6.39 to 14.34 or all are above 1.96. Thus, it can be said that all dimensions in this whole model have significant influence on the latent variables.

The T-values between the alliance learning process and alliance performance is 2.48, and between EO and alliance performance is 1.98. These indicate that H1 and H2 are supported by the data.

5 DISCUSSIONS

The empirical study proves that alliance performance at construction companies in Jakarta is directly influenced by the four stages of the learning process that occurs in alliances (Alliance Learning Process). This is in accordance with the results of previous research (Kale & Singh, 2002), that in order to understand the things that happen during the process of upgrading the alliance management skills, companies can focus their attention on the accumulation of knowledge and the four stages of the alliance learning process.

In the case of construction companies in Jakarta, they make deliberate efforts to learn, accumulate knowledge, and disseminate knowledge and internalize knowledge management alliances, so that all companies are able to develop their alliance capabilities and to achieve the goal of alliance, which is to complete the project on time through innovation breakthrough in the form of the utilization of the latest technology in the field of construction.

Empirical studies in this study also prove that EO has a direct influence on alliance performance, which is in accordance with previous studies (Li et al., 2017). So, it can be concluded that construction companies with high levels of EO, through deliberate efforts to take risks, to proactively compete and to continuously develop new ways or new mechanisms for creating innovation, will be able to produce a better alliance performance.

Out of the three dimensions that reflect EO, the most influential dimension for the entrepreneurial orientation mindset of construction companies in Jakarta is proactiveness. This is because construction companies in Jakarta have a mindset to always initiate newer and different actions compared to their competitors. The companies also face uncertainties, so they have the mindset to always apply an active and adventurous attitude and to try new things.

Meanwhile, the performance of the construction company alliance in Jakarta is reflected more by the level of corporate satisfaction with the alliance in general, in the hope that the company can improve its competitive position and can achieve its main goal through alliance.

This study provides useful implications for alliance managers on how they can achieve optimal results from established alliances by performing articulation, codification, sharing and internalization processes.

In addition, alliance managers can also take advantage of EO and their relationship with partners in order to maximize the performance of the alliance. Practitioners must recognize the importance of EO in managing the alliance. The result of this study also reinforces the belief that companies with strong EO tend to be better at finding opportunities for entrepreneurial alliances and in collaborating with those opportunities. Therefore, to achieve superior alliance performance, managers need to take steps that encourage efforts to create entrepreneurial attitudes in each of their actions and develop their own EO capabilities, such as encouraging companies to take unconventional actions and improve their innovative skills.

REFERENCES

Anderson, B. S., Covin, J. G. & Slevin, D. P. (2009). Understanding the relationship between entrepreneurial orientation and strategic learning capability: An empirical investigation. *Strategic Entrepreneurship Journal*, *3*(3), 218–240.

Avlonitis, G. J. & Salavou, H. E. (2007). Entrepreneurial orientation of SMEs, product innovativeness, and performance. *Journal of Business Research*, *60*(5), 566–575.

Barney, J. (1991). Firm resources and sustained competitive advantage. *Journal of Management*, *17*(1), 99–120.

Bierly, P. E. & Gallagher, S. (2007). Explaining alliance partner selection: Fit, trust and strategic expediency. *Long Range Planning*, *40*(2), 134–153.

Chung, A. S. Y. & Ng, S. T. (2006). The practice of subcontractor appraisal in the construction industry of Hong Kong. In *Proceedings, CIB-W107 International Symposium Construction in Developing Economies: New Issues and Challenges* (pp. 18–20).

Covin, J. G. & Slevin, D. P. (1989). Strategic management of small firms in hostile and benign environments. *Strategic Management Journal*, *10*(1), 75–87.

Emden, Z., Yaprak, A. & Cavusgil, S. T. (2005). Learning from experience in international alliances: Antecedents and firm performance implications. *Journal of Business Research*, *58*(7), 883–892.

Franco, M. & Haase, H. (2015). Interfirm alliances: A taxonomy for SMEs. *Long Range Planning*, *48*(3), 168–181.

Gulati, R. (1995). Does familiarity breed trust? The implications of repeated ties for contractual choice in alliances. *Academy of Management Journal*, *38*(1), 85–112.

Kale, P., Dyer, J. H. & Singh, H. (2002). Alliance capability, stock market response, and long-term alliance success: The role of the alliance function. *Strategic Management Journal*, *23*(8), 747–767.

Kale, P. & Singh, H. (2007). Building firm capabilities through learning: The role of the alliance learning process in alliance capability and firm-level alliance success. *Strategic Management Journal*, *28*(10), 981–1000.

Kale, P. & Singh, H. (2009). Managing strategic alliances: What do we know now, and where do we go from here? *The Academy of Management Perspectives*, August: 45–62.

Kreiser, P. M. (2011). Entrepreneurial orientation and organizational learning: The impact of network range and network closure. *Entrepreneurship Theory and Practice*, *35*(5), 1025–1050.

Li, L., Jiang, F., Pei, Y. & Jiang, N. (2017). Entrepreneurial orientation and strategic alliance success: The contingency role of relational factor. *Journal of Business Research*, *72*, 46–56.

Miller, D. (1983). The correlates of entrepreneurship in three types of firm. *Management Science*, *29*(7), 770–791.

Mudambi, S. M. & Tallman, S. (2010). Make, buy or ally? Theoretical perspectives on knowledge process outsourcing through alliances. *Journal of Management Studies*, *47*(8), 1434–1456.

Sarkar, M. B., Echambadi, R. A. J. & Harrison, J. S. (2001). Alliance entrepreneurship and firm market performance. *Strategic Management Journal*, *22*(6-7), 701–711.

Sirén, C., Hakala, H., Wincent, J. & Grichnik, D. (2017). Breaking the routines: Entrepreneurial orientation, strategic learning, firm size, and age. *Long Range Planning*, *50*(2), 145–167.

Teng, B. (2007). Corporate entrepreneurship activities through strategic alliances: A resource-based approach toward competitive advantage. *Journal of Management Studies*, *44*(1), 119–142.

Wijanto, S. H. (2015). *Metode Penelitian menggunakan Structural Equation Modeling dengan LISREL 9*. Jakarta: Lembaga Penerbit Fakultas Ekonomi Universitas Indonesia.

Williamson, O. (1985). *The economic institutions of capitalism: Firms, markets, relational contracting*. New York: Free Press.

Yoshino, M. & Rangan., S. (1995). *Strategic alliances: An entrepreneurial approach to globalization*. Boston: Harvard Business School Press.

Increasing Management Relevance and Competitiveness – Sukoco et al. (Eds)
© 2018 Taylor & Francis Group, London, ISBN 978-0-8153-7455-8

Assessing necessity and opportunity-based entrepreneurship: An analysis of demographic characteristics, propensity for new ventures and entrepreneurial motivation (a study of labor forces and entrepreneurs in Padang, Indonesia)

H. Rahman
Universitas Andalas, Padang, Indonesia

D. Lesmana
Dinas Tenaga Kerja dan Transmigrasi Provinsi Sumatra, Utara, Indonesia

ABSTRACT: This paper aims to discuss and to give an overview of entrepreneurship in Padang in Indonesia by analyzing demographic characteristics and the propensity of the labor force to start a new venture and, further, to understand the motivation of entrepreneurs when entering into entrepreneurship. Analysis is based on an empirical research, using members of the labor force and entrepreneurs in Padang as samples. The study is a quantitative study, which uses logistic regression and descriptive analysis to analyze data and information. Logistic regression is used to analyze and to predict the influence of demographic characteristics on the propensity of the samples to enter into entrepreneurship, while descriptive analysis is used to understand the tendency of the entrepreneurial motives of nascent entrepreneurs to be either necessity-based or opportunity-based. To support the analysis, indicators of entrepreneurship as introduced by the Global Entrepreneurship Monitor (GEM) are used in the study. The study found that, to a greater or lesser degree, demographic characteristics have influenced the propensity of the labor force to enter into entrepreneurship. The study also found that most of the nascent entrepreneurs in Padang (around 66.67% of the Total Early-stage Entrepreneurial Activities (TEA)) are categorized as necessity-based entrepreneurs.

Keywords: Entrepreneurial Motivation, Total Early-Stage Entrepreneurial Activities, Necessity-Opportunity Based Entrepreneurs, Nascent Entrepreneurs

1 INTRODUCTION

Entrepreneurship has become an economic panacea that is seen as generating both employment and economic prosperity in developed and developing countries (Kuratko, 2005). The entrepreneurship theories viewed show that preparing people to become an entrepreneur is not only a matter of knowing and mastering management and business skills (Kuratko, 2005), but that personality considerations, as have been studied and mostly emphasized in the traits and characteristics of entrepreneurs (McClelland, 1961, 1987; Rotter, 1966; Dyer, 1994; Grant, 1996), should also be considered. Research into entrepreneurial personality showed that the motivation to become an entrepreneur is mainly based on push and pull situational factors (Campbell 1992), such as frustration with present time lifestyle, childhood dreams, family business environment, education, entrepreneurial role models, work history, and support network (Hisrich, 1990; Krueger, 1993; Mueller & Thomas, 2000; McMullen, 2007). Analyzing entrepreneurs from their demographic characteristics and motivation will give us particular knowledge and understanding about the current situation and the type of entrepreneurs who engage in business activities in one area—so that we can suggest possible government policies and interventions to promote and foster entrepreneurship, especially for nascent entrepreneurs.

2 LITERATURE REVIEW

Most of the studies to identify the reasons why people enter into an entrepreneurial career and the propensity of individuals to start a new venture have been done in the field of entrepreneurial intentions, in which Ajzen's Theory of Planned Behavior (Ajzen, 1991) was mostly used as the foundation of the analysis. The study on entrepreneurial motivation can be found in Gilad and Levine (1986), Frese and de Kruif (2000), Shane et al. (2003), Rahman (2013) and Rahman and Day (2014). We believe that motivation and intention are different approaches. Even though it is debatable, we suggest that motivation is the first predictor in entrepreneurial processes and the propensity to start a new venture, which might further be developed into entrepreneurial intention.

Our study centers on entrepreneurial motivation and the propensity of an individual to start a business. Motivation per se, as defined by Cambridge Advance Learner's Dictionary is "enthusiasm for doing something" (p. 462). Shane et al. (2003) viewed this as "willingness". If we look back to the definition of entrepreneurial motivation, Shane et al. (2003) stated that entrepreneurial motivation is the willingness of people to become an entrepreneur. The willingness is abstract and it comes from 'inside' of people, which they called 'human motivation'. This human motivation is viewed as important and should also be considered, when determining the entrepreneurial motivation of people, alongside the other determinants from the quantitative and qualitative points of view.

Another argument regarding entrepreneurial motivation was made by Gilad and Levine (1986), who outlined two components of entrepreneurial motivation, which are the push theory and the pull theory. The push theory states that people enter into entrepreneurship because of negative forces, which could be job dissatisfaction, difficult employment opportunities, unmet expectations about salary, and inflexible working conditions. The push theory is closely related to 'necessity-based entrepreneurship', which argues that people tend to enter into entrepreneurship because they do not have any other work or life choices. Necessity entrepreneurship, as discussed by Reynolds et al. (2001), is a form of entrepreneurship in which necessity (for example, lack of choice in work, poverty, and survival) is the prime motivation to start the business.

On other hand, the pull theory argues that people enter into entrepreneurship because they need and want to achieve an 'outcome' from their entrepreneurial activities. These outcomes can be in the form of financial achievement, independence, self-fulfillment, status, and social position. The concept of the pull theory is closely related to the concept of opportunity-based entrepreneurship, which argues that people tend to enter into entrepreneurship because of existing profitable entrepreneurial opportunities and with the intention of creating and seizing opportunities (Timmons, 1999; Shane & Venkataraman, 2000). The presence of both enterprising individuals and lucrative opportunities have convinced people to exploit entrepreneurial opportunities (Shane, 2003). In short, the heart of opportunity-based entrepreneurship lies in the existence of opportunity, the decisions of enterprising people to enter into entrepreneurship, and the fact that people exploited these opportunities.

3 METHODOLOGY

This study is an empirical study that mainly uses the quantitative approach, in terms of *logistic regression* and *descriptive analysis*, as the method of analysis. The study sample is identified as members of the labor force and entrepreneurs in Padang. Data and information were collected by using a questionnaire and the Indonesian national census data and were further analyzed by using the statistical tools SPSS and STATA.

Logistic regression is used in this study to analyze and to predict the influence of age, gender, education, marital status, and the type of building belonging to the labor force, and to show the probability of people becoming an entrepreneur. This probability is based on the assumption that the random variable of the study is in the form of the logistic distribution function model—in which the equation shows the following (Gujarati, 1995):

$$P_i = \frac{1}{1 + e^{(-\beta_0 + \beta_1 x_1 + \beta_2 x_2 + \cdots + \beta_p x_p)}} \tag{1}$$

Equation 1 is further simplified into the following equation:

$$P_i = \frac{1}{1 + e^{-Z_i}} \tag{2}$$

where:

$$Z_i = Z(x_i) = \beta_0 + \beta_1 x_1 + \beta_2 x_2 + \cdots + \beta_p x_p$$

In order to estimate Equation 2, it is manipulated by multiplying $1 + e^{-zi}$ to both of its sides—so finally the equation is:

$$\frac{(1 + e^{-Z_i})P_i}{P_i^{-1}} = \frac{1}{P_i^{-1}} \tag{3}$$

$$(1 + e^{-Z_i})P_i = \frac{1}{1 + e^{-Z_i}} \cdot (1 + e^{-Z_i}) \quad \text{or } (1 + e^{-Z_i})P_i = 1 \tag{4}$$

So,

$$e^{Z_i} = \frac{P_i}{1 - P_i} \tag{5}$$

Equation 5 is further transformed into a natural logarithm model below:

$$Li = ln\left(\frac{P_i}{1 - P_i}\right) = Z_i = Z(x_i). \tag{6}$$

where:

$$\left(\frac{P}{1-P}\right) = \text{The possibility in a certain condition}$$

Descriptive analysis in this study is used to understand the tendency of entrepreneurial types, either in the form of necessity-based or opportunity-based nascent entrepreneurs. To support this, the study uses some indicators of entrepreneurship that were introduced by the Global Entrepreneurship Monitor (GEM).

4 FINDINGS AND DISCUSSION

Using the 2013 labor force figure, according to the status of occupation, the study uses 1,192 members of the labor force in Padang as its samples. We firstly undertake our study by measuring the demographic characteristics of our samples and relate them to the propensity to enter into entrepreneurship. Our findings are as follows.

4.1 *The influence of age*

The combination of the estimation of the coefficient model, the Wald examination scores, significance, and the odds ratio of the Logistic Regression Model regarding the status of the main occupations of the sample has resulted in the coefficient of variable of age 0.854—which means that members of the labor force who are above 30 years old have greater possibilities and chances to become self-employed (to become entrepreneurs) compared with members of the labor force who are under 30 years old. Given that the odds ratio (exp.B) is 2.349, this means that the possibilities and chances for members of the labor force who are above 30 years old to become entrepreneurs is 2.349 times higher than those who are under 30 years old. We believe that the age of entrepreneurs tends to be significantly affected by the age of the labor force,—which means that the older the individuals are, the higher the tendency for them to enter into an entrepreneurial career. There are some reasons to explain this, one of which is that there are more difficulties in finding a suitable job as individuals get older.

4.2 *The influence of gender status*

The result of the logistic test of the gender variable with a level of significance of $\alpha = 5\%$ is –0.183. This shows that the male labor force has smaller possibilities and chances to become self-employed compared to the female labor force. The result of odds ratio 0.833 has further shown us that the amount of the male labor force to become self-employed is only 0.833 times that of the female labor force. The result of our study further reflects that the tendency of the male labor force to become entrepreneurs is smaller compared with the female labor force.

4.3 *The influence of the status of education*

The education status variable shows a coefficient of –1,293, which means that those members of the labor force who are senior high school graduates and above have smaller possibilities and chances to enter into entrepreneurship compared to those who are lower than senior high school graduates. The odds ratio 0.274 in this analysis means that the probability of entering into entrepreneurship and self-employment of the members of the labor force who are senior high school graduates and above is 0.274 times those who are lower than senior high school graduates. We completely agree with this finding, as we believe that the lower an individual's education level, the more difficult it is for them to find jobs. As a consequence, the members of the labor force who have a lower level of education tend to enter into entrepreneurship or become self-employed in order to fulfill their daily needs, more so than do those who have a higher level of education.

4.4 *The influence of marital status*

The logistic regression for marital status of the sample also shows a positive coefficient of 0.635. This means that the probability of the married members of the labor force entering into entrepreneurship is bigger compared with those who are not (yet) married. The probability of the married members of the labor force entering into entrepreneurship is 1.886 times those who are not (yet) married. Implicitly, the married members of the labor force have more courage to start their own business and to face risks in business compared with those who are not (yet) married. The logical reason for this seems to be clear, which is that married couples need to secure their daily needs on their own—so, in the conditions of limited employment opportunities, the best possible alternative to fulfill their daily needs is by entering into entrepreneurship and self-employment. Maturity and responsibility are other possible reasons why married couples tend to enter into entrepreneurship rather than those who are not (yet) married.

4.5 *The influence of property possession*

In terms of whether or not the property belongs to the member of the labor force, the regression coefficient also shows a positive result of 0.356. This means that the probability of being self-employed of the members of the labor force who are living in mixed-property is greater than those who are living in residential property. The probability of those members of the labor force who live in mixed-property entering into entrepreneurship and self-employment is 1.427 times that of those who live in residential property. The findings of the study show that there is a tendency for the labor force in Padang to mix their residential location with the location of their business.

4.6 *Entrepreneurial motivation*

Apart from assessing the propensity of our samples to enter into entrepreneurship, we secondly analyze the entrepreneurial motivation of 100 respondents who have an entrepreneurial career.

Our study found that 58% of the sample are males and the rest are females. Using the Total Early-stage Entrepreneurial Activity (TEA) indicator from GEM, we found that Padang has a TEA of 30%, which inferred that there are 30% of the population who are aged 18–64 years old who become nascent entrepreneurs.

From this TEA value, we found 66.67% were necessity-driven TEA entrepreneurs. We can further understand that the greatest entrepreneurial motivation for entrepreneurs in Padang is in the form of necessity-based entrepreneurship. We further relate our findings above to the characteristics of entrepreneurs in Padang, which are: [a] above 30 years old, [b] below senior high school education, and [c] married—and found that out of the 66.67% necessity-driven TEA, 90% of the samples are above 30 years old.

5 SUMMARY

Our study found an entrepreneurship model that is based on the status of the main occupation of the labor force in Padang. Using logistic regression, we firstly conclude that the significant influencing variables in the status of the main occupation (self-employed or not) are: [a] age, [b] level of education, [c] marital status, and [d] type of residential property.

Meanwhile, the gender status does not significantly influence it. We also further discovered that the members of the labor force who have bigger chances, probabilities and propensities to become self-employed are females whose age is 30 and above, have a senior high school level of education, are married and are living in mixed-property. Based on the analysis of the entrepreneurial motivation of the entrepreneurs in Padang and relating it to the concept of necessity-based and opportunity-based entrepreneurship, we secondly conclude that entrepreneurship in Padang is mostly triggered by the needs of the individuals (necessity-based entrepreneurship).

REFERENCES

Ajzen, I. (1991). The theory of planned behaviour. *Organizational and Human Decision Processes, 50*, 179–217.

Campbell, C. A. (1992). A decision theory model for entrepreneurial acts. *Entrepreneurship Theory and Practice, 17*(1), 21–27.

Dyer, W. G. (1994). Toward a theory of entrepreneurial careers, *Entrepreneurship Theory and Practice, 19*(21), 7–21.

Frese, M. &. de Kruif, M. (2000). Psychological success factors of entrepreneurship in Africa: A selective literature review. In M. Frese (Ed.), *Success and failure of microbusiness owners in Africa: A psychological approach* (pp. 1–30). Westport, Connecticut: Quorum Books.

Gilad, B. & Levine, P. (1986). A behavioural model of entrepreneurial supply, *Journal of Small Business Management, 24*(4), 45–54.

Grant, R. M. (1996). Toward a knowledge based theory of the firms, *Strategic Management Journal, 17*(2), 109–122.

Gujarati, D. (1995). *Basic Economietrics*, New York: McGraw-Hill Inc.

Hisrich, R. D. (1990). Entrepreneurship/intrapreneurship. *American Psychologist, 45*, 209–222.

Krueger, N. (1993). The impact of prior entrepreneurial exposure on perceptions of new venture feasibility and desirability. *Entrepreneurship Theory and Practice, 18*(1), 521–538.

Kuratko, D. F. (2005). The emergence of entrepreneurship education. *Entrepreneurship: Theory and Practice, 29*(5), 577–598.

McClelland, D. (1961). *The achieving society*. Princeton, NJ: Van Nostrand,.

McClelland, D.C. (1987). *Human Motivation*. Cambridge: Cambridge University Press.

McMullen, J. S., Plummer, L. A. & Acs, Z. J. (2007). What is an entrepreneurial opportunity. *Small Business Economics, 28*, 273–283.

Mueller, S. & Thomas, A. (2000). Culture and entrepreneurial potential: A nine country study of locus of control and innovativeness. *Journal of Business Venturing, 16*, 51–75.

Rahman, H. (2013). The Influence of the Entrepreneurial Role Model on the Influence of Entrepreneurial Role Models on Entrepreneurial Motivation (A Study of Indonesian Undergraduate Students at the Faculty of Economics of Andalas University in Padang—Indonesia). Dissertation submitted to the University of Huddersfield for PhD Degree, Huddersfield: University of Huddersfield.

Rahman, H. & Day, J. (2014). Involving the entrepreneurial role model: A possible development for entrepreneurship education. *Journal of Entrepreneurship Education, 17*(2), 163–171.

Reynolds, P. D., Camp, S. M., Bygrave, W. D., Autio, E. & Hayet, M. (2001). *Global entrepreneurship monitor 2001* (Summary Report). London: London Business School & Babson College.

Rotter, J. B. (1966). Generalized expectations for internal and external control of reinforcement. *Psychological Monographs-General and Applied, 80*(1), 1–28.

Shane, S. (2003). *A general theory of entrepreneurship: The individual opportunity nexus*. Cheltenham: Edward Elgar Publishing.

Shane, S., Locke, E. A. & Collins, C. J. (2003). Entrepreneurial motivation. *Human Resource Management Review, 13*, 257–279.

Shane, S. & Venkataraman, S. (2000). The promise of entrepreneurship as a field of research. *Academy of Management Review, 25*(1), 217–226.

Timmons, J. (1999). *New venture creation*. Burr Ridge, IL: Irwin.

Increasing Management Relevance and Competitiveness – Sukoco et al. (Eds)
© 2018 Taylor & Francis Group, London, ISBN 978-0-8153-7455-8

Critical assessment on zakat management: Zakat scorecard model

T. Widiastuti, S. Herianingrum & I. Mawardi
Universitas Airlangga, Surabaya, Indonesia

ABSTRACT: Poverty still remains a global problem. Previous studies have been widely conducted into this issue, and these have used various perspectives related to aspects of poverty, such as fundamental and macroeconomic aspects. However, research that focuses on methods to manage zakat institutions still does not exist, despite zakat's role as a tool to alleviate poverty in Islam. This study used a qualitative approach through multiple cases study, and aims to determine the zakat fund management strategies at the National Zakat Agency (*BAZNAS*) and the Institute of National Zakat Al-Azhar (*LAZNAS* Al-Azhar) in East Java. In this research, the most fundamental aspects in *Lembaga Amil Zakat* (*LAZ*) and *Badan Amil Zakat* (*BAZ*) in the internal management and control development category of a Zakat Scorecard Model were addressed. The stage of development and optimal control, if implemented, will affect the performance of *LAZ* and *BAZ*, directly related to *muzakki* trust. *Muzakki* confidence on the performance of *LAZ* and *BAZ* determines the size of the funds that can be collected. Then, in the next stage will affect the financial control of the funds collected. *LAZ* and *BAZ* have support, so that they can carry out the operations of the institution or enter the operational phase control, which is the stage of the distribution of funds to *mustahik*.

1 INTRODUCTION

Poverty is a classic problem faced by every country the world. If measured using the World Bank poverty standard of US$1.25 per day per person, then as of 2014, there was 29% of the world population living in poverty, or as many as 1.6 billion people. Problems of poverty also occur in Indonesia. However, poverty in Indonesia from 2002 to 2016 was steadily declining, which means that there is positive progress in poverty alleviation. This amounted to 18.20% in 2002 to 10.86% in 2016, and Indonesia experienced a significant decline in poverty of 7.34% for the 14 years from 2002 to 2016 (*Badan Pusat Statistik*, 2016).

Since the second half of 2014 to 2016, East Java has been in the first rank of provinces with the highest number of people suffering from poverty. BPS data show that, as of 2016, the number of poor in East Java reached 11.85%, which amounted to 4,638,530 inhabitants (*Badan Pusat Statistik Provinsi Jawa Timur*, 2017. Islam, as a religion, has a poverty alleviation concept. It is mentioned in the Holy *Quran* in chapter *At-Taubah*, verse 103, which discusses the obligation of zakat as a means of allocating certain wealth from the rich to the poor as a religious duty, and as being the religious right of the poor.

Various researches demonstrate zakat's role in the economy. Ahmed (2002) and Kahf (1999) describe the implementation of zakat, which is also capable of providing microfinance to the poor. Both of these are in line with research results from Kusuma and Sukmana (2010) which states that charity is able to provide a positive impact for the consumption and investment variables in the economy.

1.1 *Zakat scorecard model*

Zakat management organizations in Indonesia are generally divided into two types, namely *Badan Amil Zakat* (*BAZ*) and *Lembaga Amil Zakat* (*LAZ*). *BAZ* is a zakat management organization established under the government's consent, while *LAZ* is a zakat management organization established by the community and is equivalent to a Non-Governmental Organization (NGO). Both institutions share the same spirit, namely to reduce poverty by channeling zakat (obligatory charity), infak (alms) and shadaqah (donation), both for consumptive and productive purposes.

This study uses a balanced scorecard framework approach that is divided into several perspectives (Kaplan & Norton, 2004). Firstly, the related learning and growth perspective, which are respectively the organizational strategy that manages a managerial system to continue to reform, and the growth towards a vision and mission. Secondly, the internal perspective that focuses on the management processes of an organization to operationalize the company. Third, the operational results of a customer-oriented perspective.

The third perspective focuses on how to provide satisfaction to customers through a variety of aspects, including the price, quality, and services. The final result of the balanced scorecard is a financial perspective. Therefore, this research focuses on methods to manage zakat as a tool to alleviate poverty in Islam. This research led to the concept in managing zakat institutions using four perspectives of a balanced scorecard, which provide a variety of comprehensive managerial processes.

1.2 *Research method*

This research uses a qualitative approach with the case study of Robert K. Yin, and aims to determine the zakat fund management strategies at the National Zakat Agency (*BAZNAS*) and the Institute of National Zakat Al-Ahzar (*LAZNAS* Al-Azhar) in East Java. Data was collected through individual depth interviews.

2 RESULT AND DISCUSSION

2.1 *Result*

There are some themes constructed for the Zakat Scorecard Model, which are derived from interviews with zakat managers in *BAZ* and *LAZ* Al-Azhar in East Java as well as some previous studies. The themes are as follows.

Theme 1. Organization

1. External Teamwork
Previous research states the necessary alternative cross-agency cooperation, namely Takaful with *BAZ* and *LAZ*, as an example of external cooperation. The alternative could be developed as an Islamic insurance company cooperating with the *BAZ* and *LAZ* that is of great help in the development of MSEs (Micro and Small Enterprises) from poor families or *mustahik*. Zakat institutions allocating part of zakat, pay a premium *tabarru mustahik* to protect from risk of loss (IZDR, 2009). It shows the cooperation between institutions or units outside zakat institutions. In *LAZ*, it has cooperation with units of volunteers in the implementation of disaster management. Meanwhile, *BAZ* uses a partner in conducting its programs.

2. Inter-Agency Cooperation
Given the importance of monitoring the integrity of its zakat institution, it should ensure that the direct supervision teams have the highest leadership level coordination. If needed, a team of supervisors could be coordinating with the founder and the zakat institution (Khofsah, 2011). *LAZ* tends to use a centralized system in the collection of zakat funds. Meanwhile, *BAZ* uses a decentralized style of fundraiser. It depends on each agency's procedure.

Theme 2. Information

1. Effective Transaction Process
Each zakat management institution that can effectively reduce poverty should have an effective method of information system that effectively manages the transaction process. Each *BAZ* and *LAZ* uses technological innovation to improve their operation.

2. Management Oversight
Some matters in professional management involve a system of supervision, and control the distribution of zakat (outstanding *Zakat Infaq Shadaqah* funds), the Internal Control System (SPI), Accounting Information Systems (AIS), Systems and Mechanisms Inspection (auditing), as well as accountability mechanisms (accountability) (Nikmatuniayah, 2014). *LAZ* and *BAZ* conduct surveillance through the flow of funds from *muzakki* income.

Theme 3. Human

1. Periodic Training
Zakat institutions have to initiate various programs, such as those which offer training, as well as giving business and marketing guidance, so the recipients of zakat can become self-reliant and own a formal business (Hassan & Kabir, 2015). *BAZ* holds regular training in financial management, while *LAZ* gives training to da'i, who will be deployed to become Islamic preachers to the public.

2. *Amil*'s Values
The results of field research provide an understanding of administrative control mechanisms, rules, and normative prominence in charity governance practices (collection, distribution and utilization), and the most dominant controls the incentive compensation practices. In terms of incentives, agents perceive relatively minor economic incentives, whereby agents see that optimizing the performance of institutions of *BAZNAS* into organizational change for *mustahik* is regarded as the highest value of the core mission of *BAZNAS* (Syawaluddin et al., 2016). Values that must be owned by zakat collectors, both in *BAZ* and *LAZ*, include the character development of the attitudes required to collect zakat. Among them are honesty and trust.

Theme 4. Financial

1. Improve Cash Flow
The development of financial performance, customer perspective performance, internal busi-

ness process, and learning and growth of zakat institutions will upgrade the performance of zakat institutions (Lestari, 2010). Each institution is involved in developing the financial aspects of utilizing the branding strategy. *LAZ* Al-Azhar uses Egypt's Al-Azhar greatness in Indonesia, while the *BAZ* has a branding as a government agency of zakat.

2. Customer Value Initiative
Zakat institution activities try to increased satisfaction and confidence in *muzakki* against *BAZ/LAZ* (IZDR, 2009). Customer (*muzakki*) Initiative in giving value to *muzakki* is very important for increasing the acquisition of zakat funds. *LAZ* provides customer benefit as an invitation to a zakat funded village that is empowered from *muzakki*'s zakat funds. Meanwhile, *BAZ* exploits the potential zakat fund through tax deduction.

Theme 5. Operation

1. Real-Sector Orientation
Zakat is able to reduce poverty and grow the real sector. First, it can relieve budget categories targeted for poverty alleviation for other budgetary needs. Second, it can increase the taxation potential through improvement of productivity, employment, and output (Hassan & Kabir, 2015). The process of reducing poverty in *LAZ* Al-Azhar is conducted via the production house *Gemilang* Indonesia. Meanwhile, *BAZNAS* of East Jawa creates empowerment through scholarships and capital assistance for the micro society, as well as by conducting social programs, such as those involved with disaster recovery and routine donations to the poor.

2. Equal 'in-out' Distribution
Similarly, trust in zakat institutions is predicted to be an important element that will boost zakat collection and mediate the relationship between zakat service quality and intention to pay zakat. In line with the literature discussed above, provision of excellent service quality may enhance the activity of zakat organizations (Lestari, 2010), (Firdaus & Muhammad, 2012). Zakat institutions should be able to distribute above the acquisition of *muzakki* after deducting operating expenses. Each *LAZ* and *BAZ* performs effective operation and coordination between agencies.

3. Risk Management
Internal controls are in the *BAZDA* (Regional Zakat Agency) form of control by supervisory elements, in this case the commission supervisor (internal auditor) in charge of monitoring and controlling the performance of the executing agency (*BAZ*). This includes the implementation of administrative and technical collection, distribution, utilization, and development (Khofsah, 2011). Strategies to manage risks are carried out through maintaining the stability of institutions, and periodic audits of all managerial sectors in *BAZ* and *LAZ*.

4. Voting System
Zakat institutions are responsible for collecting, managing and distributing zakat, and being a public organization. Zakat institutions are subjected to intense public scrutiny on their efficiency and effectiveness in managing zakat affairs (Wahab et al., 2011). The scheme of community funds becomes crucial. *LAZ* facilitates the personal touch by telephone. On the other hand, *BAZ* exploits the potential that is already available in the social culture of society.

Theme 6. Customer

1. Specific Selection
With regards to these implementations, the concept of localization could be considered as the best concept of zakat distribution; however, today's implementation cannot set aside the importance of government role while the rapid development in technology that supports any human activity can also be adopted to optimize the effectiveness and efficiency in collection and distribution of zakat (Lubis et al., 2011). Then the selection of *mustahik muzakki* must be specific to be effective and efficient. *LAZ* Al-Azhar uses a Standard Operating Procedure (SOP) in selecting *mustahik*. Meanwhile, *BAZNAS* of East Java has special models for *muzakki* which pledge to provide funds infaq.

2. Growth
This objective will be achieved through accelerated economic growth during the plan period to bring about a noticeable improvement in the standard of living (Hassan et al., 2012). The growth process can be conducted in three ways. First, increase the amount of funding through education (*LAZ*) and take advantage of the momentum (*BAZ*). Second, increase the number of employees targeted as *muzakki* through government agencies (*BAZ*). Third, distribute ZIS funds effectively through RGI (*LAZ*) and cooperation with partners through the monitoring mechanism (*BAZ*).

Theme 7. Innovation

1. Initiative Acceleration
Zakat management requires initiative in improving acquisition, including determining the target *muzakki*, and the presence of zakat in a macro model leads to higher growth rate, higher return on capital, and more equitable distribution of wealth (Kahf, 1999). In addition to determining the *muzakki* initiatives, strategies to help *mustahik* can be done through the formation of self-help groups.

2. Public Education
Success in educating people through the mosque, especially in aspects of religion, will not only increase the level of religious understanding of zakat recipients, but also will increase the awareness and changes the attitudes having more positive gradually (Wahid et al., 2011). One other important part is the process of dissemination to the public. *LAZ* do personal amyl, while *BAZ* programs go through the facility.

3. Tax Principle
The principle of appropriation of certain revenues to specific objectives is yet another principle that can benefit our tax systems (Kahf, 1999). Each institution has to facilitate the administration of the tax reduction system.

Theme 8. Social

1. Islamic Community Building
One example occurring in *BAZ* and *LAZ* is formed to *muzakki* coaching, and building a community for *mustahik*, giving ongoing training and religious knowledge.

2. Communication
Zakat payment to zakat institutions, in many Muslim countries is the choice of the zakat payer to either pay to the zakat institution or not. Based on this reason, the survival of the zakat institution has a direct relationship with the level of trust vested in zakat institutions by contributors of zakat fund (Firdaus & Muhammad, 2012). Communication takes place routinely with *muzakki* and *mustahik* to maintain intense interaction, which will have an impact on improving public confidence.

Theme 9. *Mustahik*

1. Evaluation
In other words, the optimization of zakat is affected by the management of zakat, in this case an effective internal control system, which may contribute to the realization of good governance zakat (alms good governance) (Zulfayani, 2011). Evaluations are conducted by dalah to assess the needs of zakat funds. This can be done through cross zakat to the needy areas. Evaluation on *BAZ* is done once a year for the entire national management.

2. Maintaining Relationship
The advantages of the *amil* include: payment discipline, keep the feeling *mustahik*, efficiency and effectiveness of the mobilization, and allocation of zakat funds (Qardawi, 2011). Keeping feelings *mustahik* is an important part in the distribution of zakat.

Theme 10. *Muzakki*

1. Service Innovation
With the changing times, many *amil* in Indonesia even provide service facilities that can be provided for the convenience of paying zakat, such as zakat distribution services via ATM, or credit card. Some even provide a shuttle service to the *Muzakki* charity, and there are others which seek to ease the amyl, which means that many people are willing to pay zakat. In *amil* zakat today, many have a personal website that can provide information about the *amil* institutions, and even provide application functions such as a zakat calculator (Siska & Siswantoro, 2012). Innovation through ease of service is done through bank deposits, and takes advantage of the zakat counter and the event.

2. Supporting Partner
The focus will be on how the zakat fund is used to finance economic activities or projects, run by poor and needy people as part of a long-term rehabilitation program (Abdullah, 2012). Supporting partner *muzakki* is achieved through mentoring and collaboration partners.

3. Reporting
Based on the analysis above, it can be stated that the internal control system and *amil* competence prove to have significant influence on financial reporting quality, both partially and simultaneously. To increase public trust, *amil* zakat should focus on increasing financial reporting quality, by increasing the effectiveness of internal control systems and *amil* competence (Naz'aina, 2015). Each uses a bulletin publishing strategy to provide financial reporting. In addition, the *LAZ* also displays the report through the website.

2.2 *Discussion*

The aforementioned sub-themes are the first-order data categories in the Zakat Scorecard Model. There are 30 categories of first-order data from information obtained in the field. Results of the first-order data categories are then classified into ten second-order data categories. Some categories will form a dimension. The first dimension formed is the development and growth control which consists of three themes, namely organization, information and human. The information theme describes how to use the information that is used to collect funds from *muzakki*. Meanwhile, the human theme is a method to do the training and development of human capital in the organization.

The second dimension is the financial control dimension. The financial aspects are a constituent of the Zakat Model Scorecard. However, social organizations, such as the *BAZ* and *LAZ*, do not use the financial as the destination. The aim of *LAZ* and *BAZ* is to bring welfare to *mustahik* through economic empowerment and other social programs. The fourth dimension is *muzakki* and *mustahik* control, which explains that the final orientation is to provide value to both parties.

LAZ and *BAZ* give value to *muzakki*, which may include services such as zakat calculation, recitals, and other Islamic services relating to zakat. The ability of fulfilling this orientation is conducted through the third dimension, namely aggregate operational control. In operational control, *LAZ* and *BAZ* must be able to effectively manage operations, providing value to customers in the form of zakat services in a transparent and effective way. Innovation in obtaining funding from zakat, donation and alms is necessary, as well as innovation in utilizing funds from *muzakki* to *mustahik*. The fourth theme is operational control, and the social value means that *BAZ* and *LAZ* should also become a bridge to reduce the social gap between *muzakki* and *mustahik* through their programs.

3 CONCLUSIONS

In this study, data is processed through categorical analysis to produce representative essential quotes from management of zakat in *LAZ* and *BAZ*. The main points are arranged in several categories and form the first phase and the most fundamental aspects in *LAZ* and *BAZ* in the internal management and control development category of the Zakat Scorecard Model. The stage of development and optimal control, if implemented, will affect the performance of *LAZ* and *BAZ* directly related to trust in *muzakki*. *Muzakki* confidence on the performance of *LAZ* and *BAZ* determines the size of the funds that can be collected. The next stage will then affect the financial control in the financial aspect of the funds collected in this financial aspect. *LAZ* and *BAZ* get support so that they can carry out the operations of the institution or enter the operational phase control, which is the stage of the distribution of funds to *mustahik*. Further operational control will affect the *muzakki* and *mustahik* control stage, which becomes the final stage and the main purpose of the existence of *LAZ* and *BAZ*—*mustahik LAZ* and *BAZ*—to provide funding and empowerment. As for *muzakki*, they can receive additional value on participation in paying zakat in the *LAZ* and *BAZ*.

4 IMPLICATIONS

4.1 *Academic implication*

This concept is the academic implications of the balanced scorecard created by Kaplan and Norton (2004). The critical point in the findings of this research is the change in orientation of the organization.

4.2 *Managerial implication*

This study is expected to be a recommendation for *LAZ* and *BAZ* in devising strategy in the management of zakat, donation, and alms. It is also a recommendation to improve the efficient, effective and competitive advantages in the sustainability of the organization.

REFERENCES

Abdullah, R. (2012). Zakat management in Brunei Darussalam: Funding the economic activities of the poor. Universiti Islam Sultan Sharif Ali.

Ali, A.F.M., Rashid, Z.A., Johari, F. and Aziz, M.R.A., (2002). The effectiveness of zakat in reducing poverty incident: An analysis in Kelantan, Malaysia. *Journal of Asian Social Science*, *11*(21), 2015 (ISSN 1911–2017).

Badan Pusat Statistik (2016) *perhitungan dan analisis kemiskinan makro Indonesia 2016*. calculation and analysis of Indonesian macro poverty 2016. bps.go.id. January 14, 2018 (15.58).

Badan Pusat Statistik Provinsi Jawa Timur (2017) *Profil Kemiskinan di Jawa Timur September 2017*. Profile of Poverty in East Java September 2017. jatim.bps.go.id. January 14, 2018 (16.05).

Firdaus, D. & Muhammad, I.S. (2012). Economic estimation and determinations of zakat potential in Indonesia. IRTI Working Paper Series.

Hassan, A., Shahid, M.A. & Abdus, M. (2010). Management and development of the awqaf assets. Seventh International Conference—The Tawhidi Epistemology: Zakat and Waqf Economy, Bangi: 315.

Hassan, M. & Kabir, J.M. (2015). Zakat, external debt, and poverty reduction: Strategy in Bangladesh. *Journal of Economic Cooperation*, *28*(4), 1–38.

Hassan, N.M., Bin, A.M.N. & Rom, N.M. (2012). Embracing microfinance: Proposed collaboration between zakat institution and microfinance institutions. *3rd International Conference on Business and Economic Research Proceeding (3rd ICBER 2012)*, Proceeding Bandung, 1–13 March 2012.

Ibrahim, M. (2015). Exploring the motivational factors for corporate zakat payments sheriff. *International Journal of Management and Commerce* Innovations, 3(1), 429–436.

Indonesia Zakat Development Report (IZDR). (2009). *Zakat dan Pembangunan: Era Baru Zakat menuju Kesejahteraan Umat*. Zakat and Development: The New Era of Zakat towards the Welfare of the People Jakarta: IMZ and PEBS UI.

Kahf, M. (1999). The performance of the institution of zakah in theory and practice. International Conference on Islamic Economics towards 21st Century. Kuala Lumpur.

Kaplan, R.S. & Norton, D.P. (2004). *Strategy maps: Converting intangible assets into tangible outcomes*. Massachusetts: Harvard Business Press.

Khofsah, S. (2011). *Pengawasan terhadap Pendayagunaan Dana Zakat, Infaq dan Shadaqah di Badan Amil Zakat Daerah (BAZDA) Kabupaten Demak pada Tahun 2010–2011*. Supervision on the Utilization of

Zakat, Infaq and Shadaqah Funds in the Regional Amil Zakat Agency (BAZDA) of Demak Regency in 2010–2011 (Thesis). Semarang Faculty of Da'wah State Islamic Institute (IAIN) Walisongo.

Kusuma, D.B.W. & Sukmana, R. (2010). 'Seventh International Conference' The Tawhidi Epistemology: Zakat and waqf economy sponsored by The Faculty of Economics, University Kebangsaan Malaysia, Bangi Selangor, Malaysia.

Lestari, P., 2010. *Pengukuran Kinerja Badan Amil Zakat Daerah (BAZDA) Kabupaten X di Wilayah Eks Karesidenan Banyumas dalam Perspektif Balanced Scorecard.* Performance Measurement of Regional Amil Zakat Agency (BAZDA) District X in Banyumas Residency Area in Balanced Scorecard Perspective. *InFestasi*, 6(1), pp.1–13.

Lubis, M., Yaacob, N.I., Omar, Y., Dahlan, A. & Rahman, A. (2011). Enhancement of zakat distribution management system: Case study in Malaysia. International Islamic University of Malaysia (IIUM).

Naz'aina. (2015). The Effect of Internal Control System and Amil Competence on the Financial Reporting Quality at Zakat Management Institution Active Member of Zakat Forum in Special Capital City Region Jakarta and West Java Provinces. *Procedia—Social and Behavioral Sciences*, 211, 753–760.

Nikmatuniayah, N., 2014. *Penerapan teknologi laporan keuangan berdasarkan sak etap dan psak 45 iai pada yayasan daruttaqwa kota semarang.* Implementation of financial report technology based on sak etap and psak 45 iai on the foundation daruttaqwa semarang. *Prosiding SNaPP: Sosial, Ekonomi dan Humaniora*, *4*(1), pp. 273–280.

Nugroho, E. (2016). *Pertumbuhan, Ketimpangan dan Kemiskinan di Indonesia: Analisis Dekomposisi Kemiskinan 2008–2014.* Growth, Inequality and Poverty in Indonesia: Poverty Decomposition Analysis 2008–2014. The material is presented in the Cooperation Forum of Gadjah Mada University (UGM) Yogyakarta with Badan Pusat Statistik (BPS)..

Nugroho, F. (2016). *Faktor Yang Berperan Terhadap Jumlah Penerimaan Dana Zakat (Studi pada Sembilan Lembaga Zakat di Kota Surabaya).* Factors Affecting Number of Zakah Fund Receipts (Study on Nine Zakat Institutions in Surabaya). Thesis. Surabaya: Airlangga University.

Qardawi, Y. (2011). Hukum Zakat. Jakarta: Pustaka Litera Antar Nusa.

Siska, H. & Siswantoro, D. (2012). Analysis of zakat on income payers preference in Indonesia (potency of double zakat). *The 3rd International Conference on Business and Economic Research (3rd ICBER 2012) Proceeding*, 12–13 March 2012.

Syawaluddin, S., Ananda, C.F., Manzilati, A. & Hoetoro, A. (2016). Principle agent relationship on zakat institution in Indonesia. *International Journal of Scientific and Technology Research*, *5*(6), 204.

Wahab, N.A. & Rahman, A.R.A. (2011). A framework to analyse the efficiency and governance of zakat institutions. *Journal of Islamic Accounting and Business Research*, *2*(1), 43–62.

Wahab, N.A. & Rahman, A.R.A. (2012). Efficiency of zakah institution in Malaysia: An application of data envelopment analysis. *Journal of Economic Cooperation and Development*, *33*(1), 95–112.

Wahid, H., Kader, R.A. and Ahmad, S., 2011, July. Localization of zakat distribution and the role of Mosque: perceptions of amil and zakat recipients in Malaysia. In *International Zakat Conference: Sustainable Zakat Development in the Poverty Alleviation and Improvement of Welfare of the Ummah.*

Zulfayani, A. (2011). *Studi Evaluatif atas Sistem Pengendalian Intern Pengelolaan Zakat pada Lembaga Amil Zakat Nasional Baitul Maal Hidayatullah (BMH) Cabang Makassar.* Evaluative Study on Internal Control System of Zakat Management at National Amil Zakat Institute Baitul Maal Hidayatullah (BMH) Makassar Branch (Thesis). Makassar: Faculty of Economics and Business Hasanuddin University.

Increasing Management Relevance and Competitiveness – Sukoco et al. (Eds)
 ISBN 978-0-8153-7455-8

Investigating entrepreneurial orientation impact on project performance in highly regulated industry: A case of renewable power industry in Indonesia

F.A. Firman, R.D. Kusumastuti & H.T. Kurniawan
Department of Management, Faculty of Economics and Business, Universitas Indonesia, Depok, West Java, Indonesia

I.M. Ruky
Department of Economics, Faculty of Economics and Business, Universitas Indonesia, Depok, West Java, Indonesia

ABSTRACT: Previous research on entrepreneurship has shown that Entrepreneurial Orientation (EO) has a positive relationship with firm performance. However, this research does not explain how EO achieves the performance. By introducing the concept of strategic entrepreneurship, this study argues that there is a need to link EO to capabilities in a certain industry in order to achieve the performance. Thus, this paper aims to empirically investigate the relationship between EO and firm performance in highly regulated industry by identifying specific capabilities as strategic actions to achieve the performance. The proposed model was measured using questionnaire. The units of analysis are Independent Power Producers (IPPs) – project based companies. There were 80 IPPs participating in the survey. The data was analyzed by using Structural Equation Modeling (SEM) LISREL 8.70. The results show that EO has significant influence on network capability, and that capability has significant influence on both project management capability and project performance. Interestingly, EO has less impact on project management capability, and that capability makes no significant contribution to the project performance. Finally, this paper also presents a discussion on implications and directions for future research.

1 INTRODUCTION

Research on entrepreneurship has centrally focused on the Entrepreneurial Orientation (EO) concept, both in theoretical and empirical studies (Covin et al., 2006). EO as a construct has been conceptualized in many different ways, such as by entrepreneurial intensity, entrepreneurial style, entrepreneurial posture, and entrepreneurial proclivity (Covin & Wales, 2012). Moreover, EO has many definitions, which mostly refer to Miller's work in 1983 on entrepreneurial firm.

An entrepreneurial firm is a firm that highly engages with proactivity, innovativeness, and risk-taking behaviors (Miller, 1983). EO is also about processes, practices and activities which are characterized by a degree to act autonomously and aggressively to competitors (Lumpkin & Dess, 1996). Some research has shown how EO influences the performance of a firm with different paths. It is found that EO has a positive relationship with the firm performance, and it becomes stronger over time (Wiklund, 1999). Another study shows that there is a mediating effect of firm capability between EO and a new entrant's performance in the international market (Zhou et al., 2010). It is also shown that an interaction between EO and knowledge-based resource is also important to achieve a good firm performance (Wiklund & Shepherd, 2003). Those different results have motivated further investigation on a relationship between EO and firm performance.

Further, most of the time, entrepreneurship is driven by the government through its policies and actions. That statement can be seen, for example, in the United States where anti-trust policies and deregulation in some sectors (e.g. telecommunication, airlines, railroads, banking, and natural gas) have brought entrepreneurial opportunities (Winston, 1998).

Specifically, in the power industry, the government can also create entrepreneurial opportunities (Joskow, 1997; Sine et al., 2005). Through its policies and actions, the government can create markets and can even regulate a return on capital (Eckhardt & Shane, 2003). This kind of industry is defined as being a highly regulated industry, where project based companies are usually developed to run the projects related to the government initiatives. For example, Independent Power Producers (IPPs).

IPPs are companies which are dedicated to developing, building, owning and operating the power plants to produce electricity (PLN, 2013). In this regard, project performance measured in those companies can be seen as a reflection of their business performance. Thus, it is interesting to investigate further on a relationship between EO and project performance.

Considering the motivations mentioned earlier, this paper has the objective to empirically investigate a relationship between EO and project performance in a highly regulated industry through a framework of strategic entrepreneurship. In order to gain the objective, this paper is organized as follows. Introduction is presented in Section 1. It is followed by the theoretical development in Section 2, while Section 3 discusses on method and result. Finally, discussion on the results and directions for future research is presented in Section 4.

2 THEORETICAL DEVELOPMENT

The conceptual model is developed by reviewing literature in three major areas of management research as follows: entrepreneurship, strategic management (i.e. institutional theory, strategic entrepreneurship), and project management (the strategic management school of thought). In addition, a specific context is chosen to clearly see a relationship between government policies and entrepreneurship. The reason is that government policies are very specific to the context.

The renewable energy-based power sector industry in Indonesia is selected in this research. This industry is a highly regulated industry where the government creates and shapes the market. Therefore, a review is also conducted of energy policy literature, and documents published by the Government of Indonesia. Based on both literature and contextual review, four variables are identified as follows: EO, network capability, project management capability, and project performance.

Relationships among those variables are developed based on the 'input-process-output' model of the strategic entrepreneurship framework developed by Hitt et al. (2011). This paper argues that EO can be seen as a both product and process of resource accumulation as part of resource structuring. Based on resource orchestration concept (Sirmon et al., 2011) which is defined as the process in the strategic entrepreneurship framework, EO as resource should be translated into specific capabilities to achieve the performance. It is identified

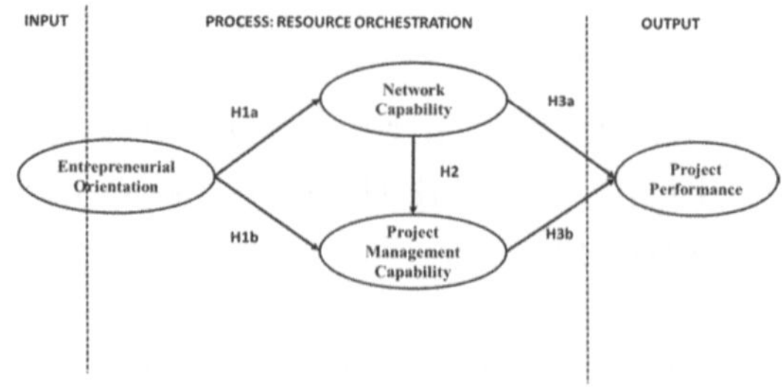

Figure 1. Proposed research model.

that network capability and project management capability are two critical capabilities in renewable power generation industry in emerging economies. The relationships among variables are presented in Figure 1.

EO can be defined as resources, an input for the strategy formulation. It can also be defined as a process in providing a firm with important direction on how entrepreneurs act in pursuing their opportunities (Rauch et al., 2009), which is needed to be translated into a strategic action. In pursuing the opportunities, both internal and external resources will be needed. EO is argued to have a role in stimulating a firm in managing its resources to seek and gain resources externally. That process is associated with a network capability of the firm (Chen & Tan, 2009; Mitrega et al., 2012; Walter et al., 2006). Thus, it can be stated:

Hypothesis 1a: Entrepreneurial orientation will positively affect network capability.

Furthermore, it is argued that EO will also affect the capability of the firm at project level. In this regard, it can be stated that:

Hypothesis 1b: Entrepreneurial orientation will positively affect project management capability.

Further, it is argued that there is a positive relationship between network capability and project management capability. Network capability is conceptualized as a firm-level capability (Kale et al., 2000) to gain, seek, and exploit external resources (Walter et al., 2006). It is argued that the network capability can influence the time and cost reduction in gaining the needed resources from markets. Thus:

Hypothesis 2: Network capability will positively affect project management capability.

Lastly, referring to the resource orchestration framework, both network capability and project management capability are argued as capabilities generated from persistent efforts to bundle and leverage resources and capabilities. Those two capabilities are expected to influence project performance.

Previous studies show that network capability has positive relationships with performance, such as supplier and buyer performances (Henseler, 2009), sales growth, customer orientation and financial performance (Human & Naudé, 2009), and innovation performance (Zeng et al., 2010). This paper argues that network capability will also influence the performance of a project in the firm, and it can be stated as follows:

Hypothesis 3a: Network capability will positively affect project performance.

Some previous studies also find that project management capability has a positive relationship with project performance (e.g. Ethiraj et al., 2005; Jugdev & Thomas, 2002; Jurisch & Palka, 2014; Zwikael et al., 2005). A higher project management capability leads to a higher success of the project. Thus, it is argued that:

Hypothesis 3b: Project management capability will positively affect project performance.

3 METHOD AND RESULTS

The model was empirically measured by distributing questionnaires as tools. Six Likert-scale was used to avoid the neutral position of the respondent (Wakita et al., 2012). The questionnaires were fulfilled through self-administer technique. There were 83 indicators used to measure the constructs of the model: EO (14 indicators), network capability (25 indicators), project management capability (19 indicators), and project performance (25 indicators).

The EO variable was measured by the dimension of proactiveness (PRO), risk-taking (RT) and innovativeness (INN) (Covin & Slevin, 1991; Hughes & Morgan, 2007), while network capability was measured by dimensions of coordination skills, relational skills, partner knowledge, and internal communication (Walter et al., 2006). The dimensions development were enriched by other literature (Peng & Luo, 2000; Uzzi, 1997, 1999; Uzzi & Lancaster, 2003).

The dimensions of project management capability were developed based on previous work of Erickson & Ranganathan (2006), and other literature (Grant & Pennypacker, 2006; Hillson, 2003; Jugdev & Thomas, 2002). Project performance was measured by the dimensions of project efficiency (PE), impact on consumer, business success (BS), and preparing the future (PF) (Shenhar et al., 2001).

The units of analysis were renewable energy-based IPPs in Indonesia. Eighty questionnaires

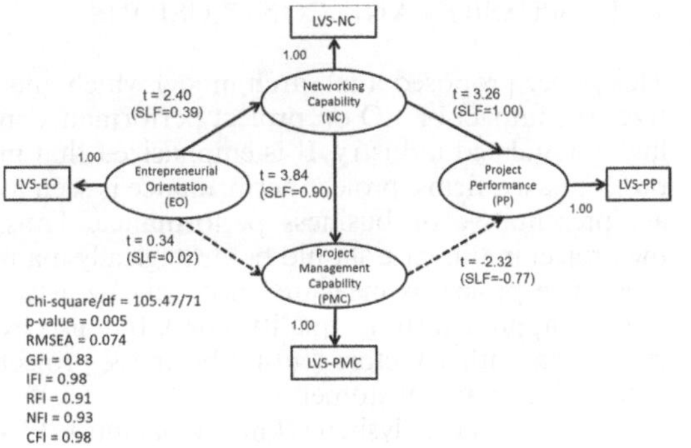

Figure 2. The structural model.

were successfully gathered between March and May 2017. The questionnaires were distributed through special events (IPPs workshops), email, mail, and directly delivered. The participants were IPPs on hydro (70%), bioenergy (10%), geothermal (12.5%), and wind and solar (7.5%). The respondents consisted of directors (37.5%), project managers (23.75%), and others (38.75%). Only two females participated in this study, and the rest were male.

The model was measured using a multivariate statistical technique, Structural Equation Modeling (SEM). The technique supports a series of regressions for variables which act as both dependent and independent variables (Diamantopoulos, 1994; Hair Jr. et al., 2014). It is also practical, since it combines structural and measurement model in one statistical test (Garver & Mentzer, 1999). The data analysis used SEM LISREL 8.70 with Latent Variable Score (LVS) method. The model has a moderate fitness, as can be seen in Figure 2. The RMSEA is 0.074 and the GFI is 0.83.

The solid line in Figure 2 shows that there is a significant influence between two constructs ($t \geq 1.96$). The less significant of the relationships ($t \leq 1.96$) is shown by the dash line. It can be seen from the Figure that only three hypotheses are accepted.

The model confirms that EO has a significant impact on networking capability (hypothesis 1a). Yet, EO has a lesser impact on project management capability (hypothesis 1b). The model shows that network capability has a significant impact on project management capability (hypothesis 2). Further, the network capability has a significant impact on project performance (hypothesis 3a).

However, EO has less impact on project management capability (hypothesis 2b). Finally, this project management capability is also seen to have no significant relationship with the project performance (hypothesis 3b).

4 DISCUSSION AND CONCLUSIONS

This paper proposed a research model which analyzes the impact of EO on project performance in highly regulated industry. It is emphasized that in project based firms, project performance is seen as a representative of business performance. Thus, the project in this case should be strategically managed. The project is measured not only by a traditional approach (time, quality, cost), but also by considering other factors (future business, project sustainability, and customers).

From the data analysis, it is known that most IPPs in the industry have good innovativeness (Standardized Factor Loading (SFL) of innovativeness is 0.96). The situation is according to industry conditions which motivate the IPPs to always find new ways in the business. The renewable energy market is relatively new compared to fossil energy. Both government and private sector are still in the learning phase to figure out and overcome some barriers in the process of industry development. The loading factor of the RT dimension (SFL = 0.39) is the lowest one among other dimensions.

Based on the model measurement, it is identified that network capability has a more important role to achieve the project performance compared to the project management capability in the IPPs industry, and it is shown that internal communication (SFL = 0.95) and knowledge about partners (SFL = 0.86) are the most essential firm abilities.

As operational level capability, project management capability is less influenced by EO (t = 0.34). Conceptually, following the resource orchestration process (Hitt et al., 2011; Sirmon et al., 2011), EO as firm resources should be translated into capabilities to achieve the performance. However, this study shows that not all capabilities can be directly influenced by EO. It might be that only capabilities at the business level can be directly influenced by EO. Then, those capabilities will have significant impact on project level capabilities, as can be seen in this study.

Further, project management capability does not have a significant impact on performance (t = −2.32), while network capability is significant (t = 3.26). This finding actually highlights that project performance here is not only measuring the performance of a project, but also the business process conducted by IPPs. The definition of project performance is broader than a traditional one, which cannot be achieved only by operational abilities of the firms. Most of the time, the project has to be postponed due to resources limitation, where network capability can reduce that obstacle.

Following the analysis, this paper gives a challenge on the role of project management capability in the industry to the project performance. It is expected that capability has a role to strengthen the relationship between network capability and project performance. Future research is expected to prove that presumption.

Further, it is also expected that future research can provide knowledge on how government policies influence the entrepreneurial orientation of the corporate. In addition, further research is expected to explain the influence of government policies on corporate strategy in providing resources for their project development. The study will be of benefit to both policy and managerial aspects. It will also benefit by filling the gap of knowledge on how the institutional context can improve the performance of the project.

REFERENCES

Chen, W. & Tan, J. (2009). Understanding transnational entrepreneurship through a network lens: Theoretical) and methodological considerations. *Entrepreneurship Theory and Practice*, *33*(5), 1079–1091.

Covin, J.G., Green, K.M. & Slevin, D.P. (2006). Strategic process effects on the entrepreneurial orientation–sales growth rate relationship. *Entrepreneurship Theory and Practice*, *30*(1), 57–81.

Covin, J.G. & Slevin, D.P. (1991). A conceptual model of entrepreneurship as firm behavior. *Entrepreneurship Theory and Practice*, 7–25.

Covin, J.G. & Wales, W.J. (2012). The measurement of entrepreneurial orientation. *Entrepreneurship Theory and Practice*, *36*(4), 677–702.

Diamantopoulos, A. (1994). Modelling with LISREL: A guide for the uninitiated. *Journal of Marketing Management*, *10*(1–3), 105–136.

Eckhardt, J.T. & Shane, S. (2003). Opportunities and Entrepreneurship. *Journal of Management*, *29*(3), 333–349.

Erickson, J.M. & Ranganathan, C. (2006). Project management capabilities: Key to application development offshore outsourcing. *Proceedings of the 39th Annual Hawaii International Conference on System Sciences (HICSS'06)*, *8*(C): 1–10.

Ethiraj, S.K., Kale, P., Krishnan, M.S. & Singh, J.V. (2005). Where do capabilities come from and how do they matter? A study in the software services industry. *Strategic Management Journal*, *26*(1), 25–45.

Garver, M. & Mentzer, J. (1999). Logistics research methods: Employing structural equation modeling to test for construct validity. *Journal of Business Logistics*, *20*(1), 33–57.

Grant, K.P. & Pennypacker, J.S. (2006). Project management maturity: An assessment of project management capabilities among and between selected industries. *IEEE Transactions on Engineering Management*, *53*(1), 59–68.

Hair Jr., J.F., William, B.C., Babin, B.J. & Anderson, R.E. (2014). *Multivariate Data Analysis* (7th ed.). Pearson Education Limited.

Henseler, G.W.Z.J. (2009). Inter-Firm network capability: How it affects buyer-supplier performance. *British Food Journal*, *111*(8), 794–810.

Hillson, D. (2003). Assessing organisational project management capability. *Journal of Facilities Management, 2*(3), 298–311.
Hitt, M.A., Ireland, R.D., Sirmon, D.G. & Trahms, C.A. (2011). Creating value for individuals, organizations, and society. *Academy of Management Executive, 25*(2), 57–75.
Hughes, M. & Morgan, R.E. (2007). Deconstructing the relationship between entrepreneurial orientation and business performance at the embryonic stage of firm growth. *Industrial Marketing Management, 36*(5), 651–661.
Human, G. & Naudé, P. (2009). Exploring the relationship between network competence, network capability, and firm performance: A resource based perspective in an emerging economy. *Management Dynamics, 18*(1), 2–14.
Joskow, P.L. (1997). Restructuring, competition and regulatory reform in the US electricity sector. *Journal of Economic Perspectives, 11*(3), 119–138.
Jugdev, K. & Thomas, J. (2002). Project management maturity models: The silver bullets of competitive advantage? *Project Management Journal, 33*(4), 4–14.
Jurisch, M. & Palka, W. (2014). Which capabilities matter for successful business process change? *Business Process Management Journal, 20*(1), 47–67.
Kale, P., Singh, H. & Perlmutter, H. (2000). Learning and protection of proprietary assets in strategic alliances: Building relational capital. *Strategic Management Journal, 3*(21): 217–237.
Lumpkin, G.T. & Dess, G.G. (1996). Enriching the entrepreneurial orientation construct—A reply to 'entrepreneurial orientation or pioneer advantage'. *The Academy of Management Review, 21*(3), 605–607.
Miller, D. (1983). The correlates of entrepreneurship in three types of firms. *Management Sciences, 29*(7), 770–791.
Mitrega, M., Forkmann, S., Ramos, C. & Henneberg, S.C. (2012). Networking capability in business relationships—Concept and scale development. *Industrial Marketing Management, 41*(5), 739–751.
Peng, M.W. & Luo, Y. (2000). Managerial ties and firm performance in a transition economy: The nature of a micro-macro link. *The Academy of Management Journal, 43*(3), 486–501.
PLN. (2013). Independent power producers' business in PT PLN (Persero). PLN.
Rauch, A., Wiklund, J., Lumpkin, G.T. & Frese, M. (2009). Entrepreneurial orientation and business performance: An assessment of past research and suggestions for the future. *Entrepreneurship: Theory and Practice, 33*(3), 761–787.
Shenhar, A.J., Dvir, D., Ofer, L. & Maltz, A.C. (2001). Project success: A multidimensional strategic concept. *Long Range Planning, 34*(6), 699–725.
Sine, W.D., Haveman, H.A. & Tolbert, P.S. (2005). Risky business? Entrepreneurship in the new independent-power sector. *Administrative Science Quarterly, 50*(2), 200–232.
Sirmon, D.G., Hitt, M.A., Ireland, R.D., & Gilbert, B.A. (2011). Resource Orchestration to Create Competitive Advantage: Breadth, Depth, and Life Cycle Effects. *Journal of Management*, 37 (5), 1390–1412.
Uzzi, B. (1997). Social structure and competition in interfirm networks: The paradox of embeddedness. *Administrative Science Quarterly, 42*(1), 35–67.
Uzzi, B. (1999). Embeddedness in the making of financial capital: How social relations and networks benefit firms seeking financing. *American Sociological Review, 64*(4), 481.
Uzzi, B. & Lancaster, R. (2003). Relational embeddedness and learning: The case of bank loan managers and their clients. *Management Science, 49*(4), 383–399.
Wakita, T., Ueshima, N. & Noguchi, H. (2012). Psychological distance between categories in the Likert Scale: Comparing different numbers of options. *Educational and Psychological Measurement, 72*(4), 533–546.
Walter, A., Auer, M. & Ritter, T. (2006). The impact of network capabilities and entrepreneurial orientation on university spin-off performance. *Journal of Business Venturing, 21*(4), 541–567.
Wiklund, J. (1999). The sustainability of the entrepreneurial orientation–performance relationship. *Entrepreneurship Theory and Practice, 24*(1), 39–50.
Wiklund, J. & Shepherd, D. (2003). Knowledge-based resources, EO, and the performance of small and medium-sized businesses. *Strategic Management Journal, 24*(13), 1307–1314.
Winston, C. (1998). US industry adjustment to economic deregulation. *The Journal of Economic Perspectives, 12*(3), 89–110.
Zeng, S.X., Xie, X.M. & Tam, C.M. (2010). Relationship between cooperation networks and innovation performance of SMEs. *Technovation, 30*(3), 181–194.
Zhou, L., Barnes, B.R., & Lu, Y. (2010). Entrepreneurial proclivity, capability upgrading and performance advantage of newness among international new ventures. *Journal of International Business Studies, 41*(5), 882–905.
Zwikael, O., Shimizu, K. & Globerson, S. (2005). Cultural differences in project management capabilities: A field study. *International Journal of Project Management, 23*(6), 454–462.

Increasing Management Relevance and Competitiveness – Sukoco et al. (Eds)
© 2018 Taylor & Francis Group, London, ISBN 978-0-8153-7455-8

How to survive in the modern era: Integrated local entrepreneurs, the traditional market and the modern store

P.P.D. Astuti, Y. Setyowati & A.A.G.S. Utama
Universitas Airlangga, Surabaya, Indonesia

ABSTRACT: The aim of this research is to increase the chances of developing SMEs (Small and Medium Enterprise) by creating a system design that integrates local business SMEs, the traditional market and the modern store. The method used is qualitative with a system design approach. Data was collected through observation of the existing system and through interviews with SMEs and traditional traders. The result of this research is system integration. System integration is the contribution between the modern market and the traditional market, and will have a wider impact, not only on economic growth of Banyuwangi Regency, but also on society as an economic agent. For the government of Banyuwangi Regency, it will have two benefits: in ensuring that the trend of economic growth continues to be positive, and also in protecting local entrepreneurs and traders in the traditional market. The hope is that Banyuwangi Regency can be a role model for other regions if it is able to implement the integration of a modern market system with the traditional market.

Keywords: Modern Era, Integrated, Local Entrepreneur, Traditional Market, Modern Store, SMEs, Banyuwangi

1 INTRODUCTION

Modern stores and traditional markets have an important role in the economic growth of Banyuwangi. Based on the Badan Pusat Statistik data of Banyuwangi, the number of SMEs (Small and Medium Enterprise) comprises of 269,267 business actors. This is evidence of the economic growth trend of Banyuwangi Regency, which is 5.91% higher than East Java, which remains at 5.86%. The average economic growth of Banyuwangi in the last five years is higher than the East Java growth of 0.32% (www.banyuwangikab.go.id).

In 2016, Banyuwangi also received a 'government award' for having the best economic growth of all regions in Indonesia. The award is given to the performance of the economic sector that is able to synergize in improving economic growth, including between modern stores and traditional markets.

E-commerce is considered to make traditional markets more advanced, with the help of technology and without abandoning cultural values. E-commerce can be implemented in Banyuwangi, supported by the existence of 'Smart Kampung'. There are 41 villages that are pilot projects in the 'Smart Kampung' program and will soon be followed by 172 other villages in Banyuwangi. The local government of Banyuwangi realizes that high economic growth also means retaining the SMEs and traditional market traders. In order to protect the traders of traditional markets and local entrepreneurs, Banyuwangi Regulation Number 4 Year 2016 about Public Order and Public Peace has been issued. One part of the local regulation is that the establishment of modern shops or franchises around traditional markets is prohibited. The government's good intentions in maintaining local business actors and traditional traders will have an impact on the integration with less modern markets.

E-commerce today is more complicated than others. Although the system's website 'Banyuwangi mall' already has a guide, it will be too difficult and too time consuming for the general public who only have the ability to call, and for the SMSs. The 'Banyuwangi mall' e-commerce system has not been fully accepted, because the value is too complicated. Thus, identification of the system replication, based on study by Bunker and Yin (2005) about the issue, will be addressed by evaluating the effect of SME e-commerce adoption in terms of changes to the SMEs' industry structure and competitive advantage. Application of the system in the region should pay attention to the human resources of the area.

2 LITERATURE REVIEW

2.1 *Traditional market*

The traditional market in the Precidential Decree of Indonesia Number 112 Year 2007 about Structuring and Fostering of Traditional Markets, Shopping Centers, and Modern Store is defined as a building owned and managed by the government, local government, private sector, state-owned enterprises and regional government-owned enterprises, including private partnerships in the form of shops, kiosks, stalls and tents owned or rented by small, medium, community or cooperative traders with small-scale business, small capital, and the process of buying merchandize by way of bargaining (Republik Indonesia, 2016). Traditional markets are a place where sellers and buyers meet directly. The market gives the buyer an advantage regarding the income of his merchandise, and the buyer benefits from provision of his needs for satisfaction and fulfillment (Sutami, 2012).

2.2 *Modern store*

Modern markets are often referred to as modern stores. Based on Precidential Decree of Indonesia Number 112 Year 2007 about Structuring and Fostering of Traditional Markets, Shopping Centers, and Modern Store, it is explained that the modern store is a building that is used to make sales transactions of goods by a single seller. There are various forms of modern stores, including minimarket, supermarket, department store, hypermarket and wholesale.

2.3 *Entrepreneurship*

Entrepreneurship theory is a logical and verifiable coherent relationship formulation or base principle regarding entrepreneurship. This principle describes entrepreneur activity or provides normative guidance. Entrepreneurship consists of doing something that is not a part of daily activities. It is essentially a phenomenon that is related to leadership. Entrepreneurship is a tool to connect between all societies in a non-authoritarian, and especially non-economic way, and is a tool that profit-oriented institutions can use to establish, satisfy, and take advantage of economic endowments (Frederick et al., 2016).

2.4 *Small and medium enterprise*

SMEs in particular have been regulated in Law of The Republic of Indonesia Number 20 Year 2008 about SMEs article 1, where there is a definition and criteria related to SMEs. A small business has a definition as being a stand-alone productive economic enterprise, carried out by an individual or a business entity, and not a subsidiary or a branch of a company owned, controlled, or partaken, either directly or indirectly, with a medium-sized or large enterprise with net worth or annual sales in accordance with the criteria provided for in this Law. A medium-sized enterprise is a productive and stand-alone economic enterprise, carried out by an individual or business entity that is not a subsidiary or a branch of a company owned, controlled, or incurred, either directly or indirectly, by a small business or a large business with a net amount of wealth or proceeds in annual sales as set forth in Law No. 20 of 2008.

2.5 *Information system design*

According to Romney and Steinbart (2012), conceptual system design system developers create a common concept framework in order to implement user requirements and solve identified problems, and ultimately to continue in the system analysis phase. System design consists of various basic activities of information systems that will produce a system specification that will meet the functional requirements to be developed in the business analysis process, so that it can be used by the user (O'Brien & Marakas, 2011). System design includes a variety of process identification subsystems contained in an information system, in the development of the system which is still in need of special attention (Bodnar & Hopwood, 2010).

2.6 *E-commerce*

E-commerce is a part of electronic business that makes transactions of buying and selling goods and services through the Internet media (Laudon & Laudon, 2016). O'Brien and Marakas (2011) further explain that e-commerce is the speed of an action, and interaction in accordance with the product, and payment from customers to companies and from companies to suppliers. E-commerce has become a very significant element in the increasingly modern global economic environment. E-commerce can increase efficiency, and cost incurred by the company will be lower (Radovilsky, 2015).

3 RESEARCH METHODOLOGY

The research methodology uses a qualitative approach in which data is obtained through interviews, observation and literature review. Interviews are conducted with employees in modern stores, the owners of SMEs and traders

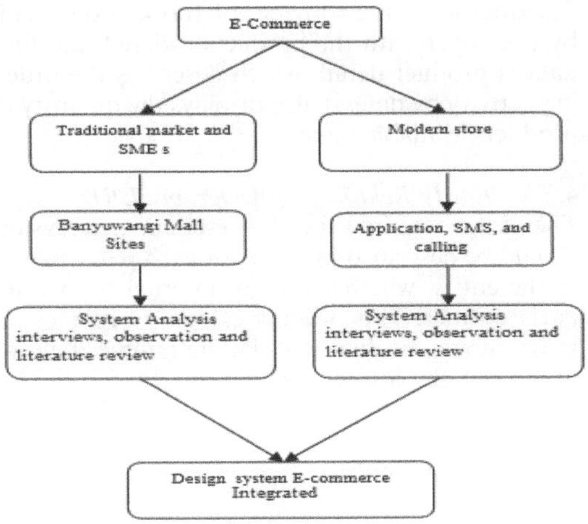

Figure 1. Conceptual framework.
Source: Processed, 2017.

in the traditional market 'Blambangan' in Banyuwangi. Interviews also involve the general public as consumers in the practice of buying and selling. The observations were conducted on the e-commerce system of SMEs and local products of Banyuwangi through the www.banyuwangi-mall.com website, and on an e-commerce system contained in two modern stores in Jalan Hos Cokroaminoto. Further data from library reviews were obtained from international jurisdiction and related books relating to e-commerce systems. Analytical techniques in this study use an input-process-output approach. Based on the literature review, an integrated system model design for e-commerce will be implemented.

4 RESULT AND DISCUSSION

4.1 *System analysis*

The development of information technology is currently very rapid and aims to improve efficiency and effectiveness of performance in work. This is needed in business processes, especially in marketing products, and both goods and services. Currently, there are two systems. They are the modern store, and 'Banyuwangi Mall' which is managed by the Banyuwangi local government. E-commerce systems in local government can be viewed on the website www.banyuwangi-mall.com. The e-commerce system managed by the local government contains local Banyuwangi products and services for tourists. Interviews conducted with traditional market traders and SME business actors around Banjarsari village in Glagah district have shown that the e-commerce system in 'Banyuwangi Mall' still does not cover all SMEs in Banyuwangi.

Based on the results of the interview, it can be concluded that the e-commerce system in 'Banyuwangi Mall' requires greater socialization and is not in accordance with the ability of the users of the Banyuwangi community.

4.2 *System requirement*

An information system is required today that has been adapted to cater for the level of ability of users in Banyuwangi society, in terms of SMEs as the owners of goods and services, consumers as users of products, and local governments as managers of e-commerce information systems as a whole, ranging from management to internal control. This system can be supported by SMEs as users who play a role in overseeing the number of products and services offered.

A study of Wright et al. (2006) about integrated marketing in the global marketplace and Internet-based communication, showed that many SMEs in the UK have not altered their mindset about marketing. They still export their products to traditional overseas markets. The study of Kartiwi and MacGregor (2007) about e-commerce adoption in SMEs in developed and developing countries found that two locations, Sweden and Indonesia, have different barriers. The Swedish are more concerned with technical issues and the Indonesians are more concerned with organizational barriers. A study by Coman and Coman (2013) about the integration of TIC in the Accounting Information System (AIS) of SMEs found that many SMEs still do not use AIS in their business. This study engaged not only SMEs in developing countries (in this case Banyuwangi Regency in Indonesia), but also traditional markets and modern stores in their surrounding area. The case discussed the importance of e-commerce being able to survive in the modern era.

4.3 *System design*

4.3.1 *Context diagram*

E-commerce that must be applied in Banyuwangi must involve four parties, namely (1) SMEs as product owner, (2) Consumer as product user, (3) Cashier as financial manager in buying and selling transactions, and (4) Local Government as manager as a whole.

This system will integrate all parties, so that management and control will be easier to do.

4.3.2 *Database*

There are four kinds of databases that should exist in e-commerce information systems, namely (1) Products, (2) Buyers, (3) Transactions, and

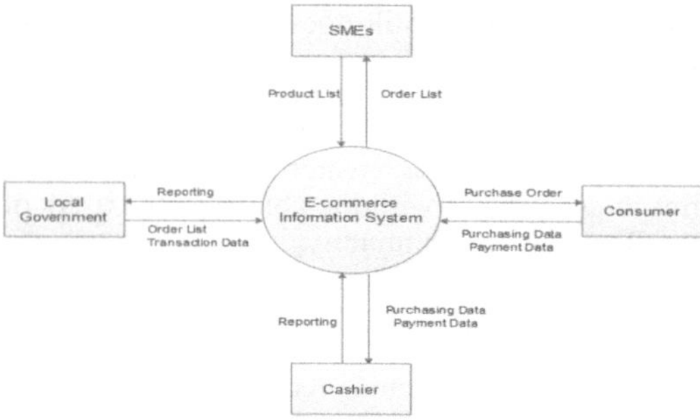

Figure 2. Context diagram.
Source: Processed, 2017.

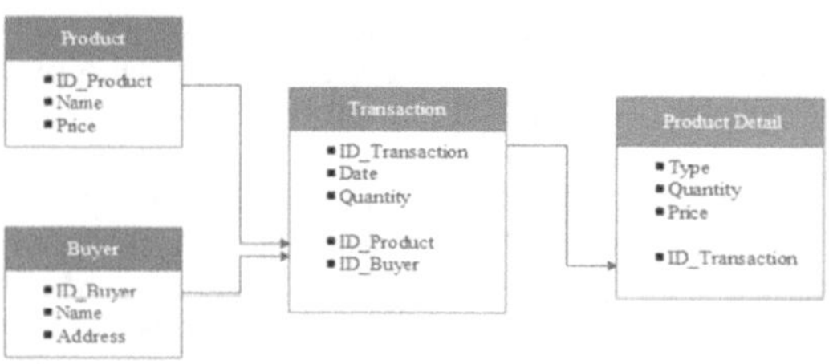

Figure 3. Database.
Source: Processed, 2017.

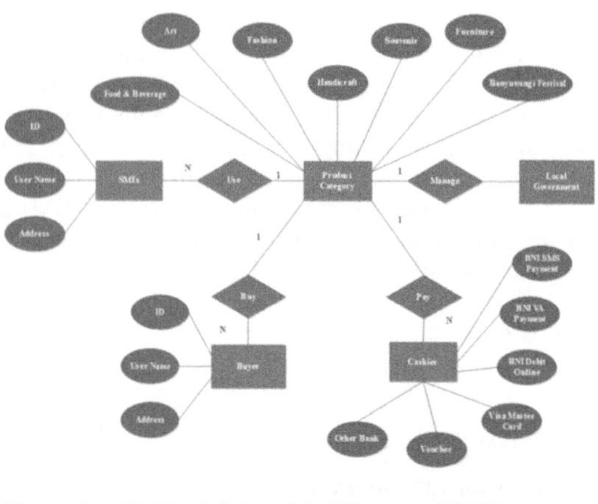

Figure 4. Entity Relationship Diagram (ERD).
Source: Processed, 2017.

(4) Product Details. The product presented should contain basic information that differentiates it from other products. The most important thing is the ID or product identity. This ID will be something that consumers first see when they buy a product. In the buyer's data, the ID will show the frequency of the buyer activity in ordering the product he wants. What should not be overlooked is the buyer's name and address. While the data on this transaction describes more the activities of transactions made by the buyer with the products ordered, the final data is product detail, which describes the ordering activity by date. It also displays the quantity of products available today.

4.3.3 *Entity Relationship Diagram (ERD)*

The data required in this e-commerce system should be described in detail for each party related to the entity, whether it is for internal or external party entities. This product category becomes the most important data that will determine the integration of all parties.

5 CONCLUSION

E-commerce is a very useful and powerful tool to increase competitive advantage, especially for the SMEs, which includes traditional markets. With e-commerce, SMEs can survive in the modern era. SMEs have more competitive advantages than the modern store, as shown by 'Banyuwangi Mall'. On the website, SMEs can sell and display their products, goods and services. However, it has some problems. The existing process in the 'Banyuwangi Mall' system takes too long and is inefficient. Nowadays, information systems need to be adapted to the ability of users, in this case the society of Banyuwangi, both in terms of SMEs as the owner of goods and services, consumers as users of the products, and local governments as managers of e-commerce information systems as a whole, including management and internal control.

REFERENCES

Badan Pusat Statistik. (2017). Accessed April 27, 2017. Retrieved from https://banyuwangikab.bps.go.id.

Banyuwangi Mall. (2017). Accessed April 27, 2017. Retrieved from https://www.banyuwangi-mall.com

Bodnar, G.H. & Hopwood, W.S. (2010). *Accounting information systems* (10th ed.). USA: Pearson Education, Inc.

Bunker, D. & Yin, L. (2005). The effect of e-commerce adoption on small/medium enterprise industry structure, competitive advantage and long-term profitability. *Australian Accounting Review*, *15*(3), 55.

Coman, M. & Coman, M.D. (2013). The integration of TIC in the Accounting Information System (AIS) of SMEs. *Valahian Journal of Economic Studies*, *4*(18), 7–14.

Frederick, H., O'Connor, A. & Kuratko, D.F. (2016). *Entrepreneurship: Theory/Process/Practice* (4th ed.). Australia: Cengage Learning.

Kartiwi, M. & MacGregor, R.C. (2007). E-commerce adoption in SMEs in developed and developing countries: A cross-country comparison. *Journal of Electronic Commerce in Organization*, *5*(3), 35–51.

Laudon, K.C. & Laudon. J.P. (2016). *Management information system—Managing the digital firm* (14th ed.). England: Pearson Education Limited.

O'Brien, J.A. & Marakas, G.M. (2011). *Management information systems* (9th ed.). New York: McGraw-Hill Companies, Inc.

Pemerintah Kabupaten Banyuwangi. (2017a). *Pertumbuhan Ekonomi Dinilai Terbaik, Banyuwangi Peroleh government awards 2016*. Accessed April 27, 2017. Retrieved from www.banyuwangikab.go.id/berita-daerah/pertumbuhan-ekonomi-dinilai-terbaik-banyuwangi-peroleh-goverment-awards–2016.html.

Pemerintah Kabupaten Banyuwangi. (2017b). *Pertumbuhan Ekonomi Banyuwangi Lampaui Rata-rata Provinsi Jawa Timur*. Accessed April 27, 2017. Retrieved from http://www.banyuwangikab.go.id/berita-daerah/pertumbuhan-ekonomi-banyuwangi-lampaui-rata-rata-provinsi-jawa-timur.htmlRepublik Indonesia. *Banyuwangi Regulation Number 4 Year 2016 about Public Order and Public Peace*. Accessed April 27, 2017. Retrieved from http://jdih.banyuwangikab.go.id/dokumen/perda/PERUBAHAN_KETERTIBAN_UMUM.pdf.

Radovilsky, Z. (2015). *Application models for e-commerce*. Chennai, India: Cognella Academy Publishing.

Republik Indonesia. *Law of The Republic of Indonesia Number 20 Year 2008 about SMEs*. Accessed April 27, 2017. Retrieved from http://www.bi.go.id/id/tentang-bi/uu-bi/Documents/UU20Tahun2008UMKM.pdf.

Republik Indonesia. *Precidential Decree of Indonesia Number 112 Year 2007 about Structuring and Fostering of Traditional Markets, Shopping Centers, and Modern Store*. Accessed April 27, 2017. Retrieved from http://koperindag.karokab.go.id/images/regulasi/inpres/perpres112_2007.pdf.

Romney, M.B. & Steinbart, P.J. (2012). *Accounting information systems* (12th ed.). England: Pearson Education Limited.

Sutami, W.D. (2012). Rational Strategy by Trader of Traditional Market. *Biokultur*, *1*(2), 127–148.

Wright, L.T., ul-Haq, R. & Oktemgil, M. (2006). Integrated marketing in the global marketplace. *Journal of Direct, Data and Digital Marketing Practice*, *7*(3), 216–238.

Increasing Management Relevance and Competitiveness – Sukoco et al. (Eds)
© 2018 Taylor & Francis Group, London, ISBN 978-0-8153-7455-8

The influence of Islamic service quality toward bank customer loyalty and satisfaction of BRI*Syariah* Surabaya

M.Q. Fauzi, S. Herianingrum, T. Widiastuti & R.P. Putra
Universitas Airlangga, Surabaya, Indonesia

ABSTRACT: This study aims to determine the influence of Islamic service quality on customer satisfaction and loyalty switching intentions, moderated by the religious knowledge level among customers of BRISyariah Bank in Surabaya. The research method used is quantitative approach. This research used a total of 96 customers of BRISyariah Surabaya. Customer characteristics used are Moslem, and registered as a funding or deposit customer for at least a year. The sampling technique is purposive sampling. This research uses the PLS (Partial Least Square) method. The results showed that Islamic service quality has a positive and significant impact on customer satisfaction. Other results showed that customer satisfaction has significant impact on customer loyalty and that Islamic service quality has a significant effect on customer loyalty. A suggestion for the BRISyariah Bank in Surabaya is to maintain and improve the quality of services provided in order to improve satisfaction and gain loyal customers. Further research could add another variable which affects customer satisfaction and loyalty.

Keywords: Islamic Service Quality, Customer Satisfaction and Customer Loyalty

1 INTRODUCTION

Islamic banking has entered the global competition, whereby according to statistics published by the Financial Services Authority, in Indonesia, as of January 2017, there are 13 Islamic public banks, 21 conventional banks having a syariah business unit, and 166 Islamic people's financing banks.The latest data shows that the total assets of PIFB and BSU reached 344,290 trillion rupiah (www.ojk.go.id).

The increase in assets shows the growing number of Islamic banking service users in Indonesia. An increasing number of Islamic banks must be offset by an increase in the quality of Islamic banks in serving customers. Islamic banks have recognized the importance of the quality of service, to retain existing clients and to attract new customers in a competitive environment (Wang et al., 2003). Abedniya and Zaeim (2011) state that service quality has become one of the factors that are important to the success of a business. This is a reason to improve the quality of Islamic banks in serving customers.

Quality, according to Kotler and Keller (2009:143), is the totality of features and characteristics of a product or service that relies on its ability to satisfy needs, expressed or implied. There are several approaches regarding the dimensions of service quality, among others using a method based on the 'Gap Model' developed by Parasuraman et al. (1985), where there are five dimensions designed to measure the quality of service based on the difference between the value of expectation and the value of the performance perceived by the customer, namely: Responsiveness, Reliability, Assurance, Empathy and Tangible. Zeithmal and Bitner (2000) suggest that the service quality has five dimensions, or SERVQUAL, by which these instruments can be used generally by service companies, which consist of Tangible, Reliability, Responsiveness, Assurance, and Empathy. But while the five dimensions of quality of service are common, there is need for adjustment when applied to companies that have special characteristics, such as in the case of Islamic banking.

To cover weaknesses that exist, Othman and Owen (2001) add the element of Compliance to the dimensions of service quality examined by Parasuraman et al. (1985), commonly known as Compliance with Islamic law (adherence to Islamic law). Additional dimensions of Compliance in SERVQUAL are better known as CARTER. In granting services, any related activities should be based on adherence to the Sharia, which is full of moral values and ethics (Othman & Owen, 2001).

Islam teaches to give good business results in the form of goods or services, which should provide good quality, and no one should receive bad quality. The higher the quality of service provided, the higher is the level of customer satisfaction also produced (Kotler and Keller, 2009:144).

Islamic banks are required to provide services of higher quality than competitors on a consistent basis and offer differentiation services in order to create customer satisfaction. The goal is to obtain customer loyalty when situations of competition between banks are increasingly tight. One strategy that can be applied as a differentiation from conventional banks is by emphasizing the values of Islam in his Ministry. It is expected to provide the satisfaction of making the customer loyal.

BRISyariah, as one of Islamic banks operating in Surabaya, gained several achievements in 2012. It continues in 2013 with awards obtained from the related ministries. For example, BRISyariah was ranked first in terms of The availabilyty of ATM, ranked third in teller service and ranked fifth in terms of performance. In the same year BRI-Syariah also gained Excellent Service Experience awards i.e. awards over the granting of a positive experience to customers (www.brisyariah.co.id).

Based on the above, it can be said that quality of service is important in an organization to create customer satisfaction, which will encourage them to become loyal customers. Therefore, the formulation of the problem in this research is: What is the Islamic quality of service influence on satisfaction?; What is the satisfaction influence on loyalty?; and also, What is the Islamic quality of service influence on loyalty?

2 FOUNDATION OF THEORY

2.1 *Influence of Islamic service quality on the satisfaction and loyalty of consumers*

Research conducted by Osman et al. (2009) strongly supports that service quality is indispensable for the realization of customer satisfaction and loyalty of consumers. From their studies of 'consumer satisfaction in a Malaysian Islamic Bank', it suggests that Islamic financial institutions are very able to provide consumer satisfaction with the service provided, with the resulting dimension of reliability (Reliability) as the most important attribute. Such is the case with research titled 'The influence of product attributes Islam, religious commitment, the quality of services and the trust of customer satisfaction and loyalty of customer bank Muamalat Semarang', which shows that the higher the quality of the service, then the higher the perceived customer satisfaction.

Othman and Owen (2001) state that there is a strong relationship between the quality of the services from an Islamic perspective with consumer satisfaction. The research has been defined as a system of CARTER-items, processing input and output overall satisfaction. In addition, Wong and Sohal (2003) stated that one of the effective strategies to keep consumers loyal to the service organizations, including Islamic banking, is to provide services of high quality to the consumer.

This research parallels with previous studies in which variable X is used (i.e. Islamic service quality (CARTER)), while the difference is in the analysis techniques and variables, where:

- Consumer Satisfaction Variable as moderating variable
- analytical techniques used are Partial Least Square (PLS).

2.2 *Hypothesis and analysis model*

Based on the outline of the problem and the foundation of the theory presented, then the hypotheses presented in this study are:

H1: Islamic service quality influences positively and significantly the customer satisfaction in Bank BRISyariah Surabaya.

H2: Consumer satisfaction influences positively and significantly customer loyalty among customers of Bank BRISyariah Surabaya.

H3: Islamic service quality influences positively and significantly customer loyalty of customers of Bank BRISyariah Surabaya.

3 RESEARCH METHOD

This research uses a quantitative approach that focuses on testing hypotheses from data that has been processed. Research on variable quality of service includes, among others, Islamic quality of service (X1), customer satisfaction (Y1) and consumer loyalty (Y2). The Islamic quality of service variable consists of six indicators: compliance with three rounds of questions; assurance with four rounds of questions; reliability with four rounds of questions; tangible with four rounds of questions; empathy with four rounds of questions; and responsiveness with four rounds of questions. The consumer satisfaction variable consists of six indicators which are also used as grain question items; likewise, the consumer loyalty variable consists of six indicators which are also used as grain question items.

Test reliability uses Cronbach's Alpha and Compositing Reliability with construct reliability above 0.7. Testing of the validity is by generating one item in Islamic quality of service indicators, namely item X, 1.3.4, and one item from loyalty indicators (i.e. Y 2.4 invalid (invalid)), so that the item should be deleted so as not to generate error data.

Measurement scale in this study is the ordinal scale with a Likert scale model using four answers: 4 (SS) Strongly agree; 3 (S) Agree; 2 (TS) Disagree; 1 (STS) Strongly disagree. The type of data used is the primary data obtained through questionnaires that have been completed by the respondents, and the secondary data as supporting in the form of corporate documents, such as the BRISyariah company profile, and supporting data such as journals, photo documentation, the Internet and literature-related problems that have been examined.

The subject or the population in this research is the entire clientele of BRISyariah Surabaya.

Because the populations in the study sample is infinite, then this study follows the formula by Zainuddin (2000:89).

Sampling techniques in the study are non-probability sampling techniques because they do not provide the same opportunity for every element (member) of the population to be elected to the sample. Whereas the determination of the sample is in using purposive sampling, namely the determination of the sampling with particular considerations (Sugiyono, 2012:84–85). Characteristics of the sample used are a customer who has registered to become a customer deposits/bank depositor at BRISyariah in Surabaya for at least one year and who is Muslim.

4 RESULTS OF THE RESEARCH AND DISCUSSION

4.1 *Relationship of quality of Islamic service to customer satisfaction*

The results show that the quality of the Islamic service influences significantly customer satisfaction with a t value calculated at 11.84 > 1.96. This shows that the first hypothesis is acceptable. These results are consistent with the research results presented by Othman and Owen (2001), which state that there is a strong link between service quality and Islamic consumer satisfaction. The research has been described as a system of CARTER-items, processing input and output overall satisfaction. In addition, these results are reinforced by research conducted by Osman et al. (2009), stating that Islamic financial institutions are very able to meet consumers' satisfaction with the service provided and generate the dimension of reliability (Reliability), which has the highest level of significance against satisfaction.

In addition to the relationship between the Islamic quality of the service and satisfaction of Bank BRISyariah Surabaya customers, previously carried out research shows that the quality of service has a positive relationship with consumer satisfaction (Parasuraman et al., 1985). Research findings suggest that establishment of a high level of quality service will lead to high customer satisfaction.

The study results also correspond to the values of Islam which are applied in Bank BRISyariah Surabaya, which hold that to provide good business results in the form of goods or services, good quality should be provided, and no one should receive bad quality. As stated in the Qur'an surat al-Baqarah [2] verse: 267:

'People—believers, spend (the way of Allah) most of the good of yourselves—good and most of what we take out of the Earth for you, and you shall not choose the bad—bad then you spend away from him but you didn't want to pick it up but with the narrow eyes to him. And know that Allah is Rich again Most Commendable.' (QS. Al-Baqarah: 267).

4.2 *The relationship between customer satisfaction and customer loyalty*

The results show that customer satisfaction has significant influence on customer loyalty with a t value calculated at 2.05 > 1.96. These results are corroborated by previous research by Isaac and Zhafiri (2011), stating that the loyalty of consumers is affected by the satisfaction and confidence of service providers. Likewise, researchers states that customer satisfaction has a positive and significant effect on the loyalty of consumers.

4.3 *The relationship of Islamic service quality to customer loyalty*

The results show a significant influence of Islamic service quality over customer loyalty with a t value calculated at 2.619 > 1.96. These results are in accordance with research by Badara et al. (2013) which state that the quality of service has a positive and significant effect toward loyalty.

The results of this research are also in accordance with the Islamic teaching that service providers in this Bank BRISyariah Surabaya have to provide the best quality of service to every consumer so that the consumers remain loyal to using their service. It is also stated in the verses of the Qur'an surat an-Nisa [4] verse 36, namely:

'Worship God and do not partner him with nothing. and did all right to two parents, Carib-kin, orphans, the poor, neighbors near and far neighbors, and his colleague, Ibn sabil, and the servant of sahaya. Verily, Allah does not like people who are arrogant and proud of yourself.' (QS. An-Nisa: 36).

The above paragraph describes the Islamic argument for keeping in touch with various groups by providing good service. The same can also be applied to Bank BRISyariah Surabaya by maintaining good relations with its customers through a variety of client groups, in order to create a good long-term relationship and establish their loyalty. The customers consider that the overall quality of services provided by Islamic banks is already good, but this does not guarantee that they are loyal. Therefore, Islamic banks need to continuously improve their service quality, providing innovation in the service of the product, thus ensuring that customer satisfaction is met and that their loyalty will be gained to continue using the services of Islamic banks.

5 CONCLUSION

Conclusions drawn from the results of research using statistical tests are as follows:

1. The quality of the Islamic service positively and significantly influences customer satisfaction with BRISyariah Surabaya. This is evidenced by the results of the research where the t value calculated for the Islamic quality of service against satisfaction is 11.84 > 1.96, which shows that the higher the quality of the service, then the higher the perceived customer satisfaction.
2. Customer satisfaction has positive and significant influence on customer loyalty of the Bank of BRISyariah Surabaya. This is evidenced by the results of the research using the t value to calculate the satisfaction against the loyalty, which is 2.05 > 1.96, indicating that the consumers' loyalty is influenced by their satisfaction toward the service providers.
3. The quality of the Islamic service positively and significantly influences BRISyariah Surabaya customer loyalty. This is evidenced by the results of the research where the t value calculated the quality of Islamic service against loyalty as 2.619 > 1.96, which illustrates that the quality of service has a strong effect on consumer purchase decision.

ABBREVIATIONS

People's Islamic Financing Bank (PIFB)
Bank Syariah Units (BSU)

REFERENCES

Abedniya, A. & Zaeim, M.N. (2011). Measuring the perceive service quality in the Islamic banking system in Malaysia. *International Journal of Business and Social Science*, *2*(13).

Al Qur'an and Terjemahannya. (2005). Syamil Al Qur'an. Bandung: PT. Syaamil Cipta Media.

Badara, M.A.S., Mat, N.K.N., Mujtaba, A.M., Al-Refai, A.N., Badara, A.M. & Abubakar, F.M. (2013). Direct effect of service quality dimensions on customer satisfaction and customer loyalty in Nigerian Islamic bank. *Management*, *3*(1), 6–11.

Ishak, A. & Luthfi, Z. (2011). Pengaruh kepuasan dan kepercayaan konsumen terhadap loyalitas: Studi tentang peran mediasi switching costs. *Siasat Bisnis*, *15*(1), 55–66.

Kotler, P. & Keller, K. (2008). *Manajemen Pemasaran, Edisi Ketiga Belas*. Jakarta: Erlangga.

Osman, I., Ali, H., Zainuddin, A., Rashid, W.E.W. & Jusoff, K. (2009). Customers satisfaction in Malaysian Islamic banking. *International Journal of Economics and Finance*, *1*(1), 197.

Othman, A., Owen L., 2001, *Adopting and Measuring Customer service Quality (SQ) in Islamic Banks: A Case Study in Kuwait Finance House.* International Journal of Islamic Financial Services Vol. 3 No. 4.

Parasuraman, A., Zeithaml, V.A. & Berry, L.L. (1985). A conceptual model of service quality and its implications for future research. *Journal of Marketing*, *49*: 41–50.

Peter, P. & Olson, J. (2002). *Consumer behavior: Perilaku Konsumen dan Strategi Pemasaran.* Jakarta: Erlangga.

Priyanti, D.R. (2005). *Analisis Mutu Pelayanan Di Bank Syariah (Studi Kasus Pada Unit Usaha Syariah–Bank Permata).* Tesis Program Magister Manajemen, Universitas Gunadarma: tidak diterbitkan.

Sugiyono. 2012. *Metode Penelitian Kuantitatif Kualitatif dan R&D.* Bandung: Alfabeta.

Wang, Y., Lo, H. and Hui, Y.V. 2003. *The antecedents of service quality and product quality and their influences on bank reputation: evidence from banking industry in China,* Manag. Serv. Qualit., Vol. 13 No. 1, pp. 72–83.

Wijaya, T. (2011). *Manajemen Kualitas Jasa*. Jakarta: Indeks.

Wong, A. and Sohal, A. 2003. *Service quality and customer loyalty perspectives on two levels of retail relationships*, Journal of Services Marketing, Vol. 17 No. 5, pp. 495–513.

Zainuddin, Muhamad. 2000. *Metodologi Penelitian.* Surabaya: BP AIRLANGGA.

Zeithaml, V. A., and Marry Jo Bitner. 2000. *Services Marketing: Integrating Customer Focus Across the Firm.* Second Edition. Boston: Irwin McGraw-Hill, Inc.

Increasing Management Relevance and Competitiveness – Sukoco et al. (Eds)
© 2018 Taylor & Francis Group, London, ISBN 978-0-8153-7455-8

Management accounting practices in micro enterprises in the Sleman Regency, Daerah Istimewa Yogyakarta

A.C. Laksmi & A.P. Putra
Universitas Islam Indonesia, Indonesia

ABSTRACT: Medium, Small and Micro Enterprises (MSMEs) are an important type of business in every country. Micro enterprises which are part of MSMEs deserve more attention from the government because these businesses still need help and support, especially in their management accounting practices. Management accounting is the process associated with planning, providing help in decision-making, controlling and providing feedback to the planning unit. Good management accounting practices can support micro enterprises in developing their businesses. This study uses a qualitative research methodology by using semi-structured interviews as the data collecting method to investigate the management accounting practices in micro enterprises in the Sleman Regency in Yogyakarta. The results show that management accounting practices in micro enterprises are still far from the required standards and this could potentially inhibit the growth and development of the businesses.

1 INTRODUCTION

Indonesia is a developing country in Southeast Asia and Medium, Small and Micro Enterprises (MSMEs) are the backbone of its economy. Around 99% of businesses operating in Indonesia are MSMEs and this type of business has provided employment for about 107.6 million people (WIEF, 2016). In addition, MSMEs also contributed to 60.6% of Indonesia's gross domestic product (GDP). All of these facts indicate the importance of the existence of MSMEs for Indonesia. In fact, it cannot be denied that MSMEs can protect the country's economy in the event of shock or crisis (WIEF, 2016).

The micro enterprise component of MSMEs deserve more attention from the government because these types of businesses still need a lot of help and support. Furthermore, quite often mistakes made by management or micro enterprise owners can result in bankruptcy (Tarmidi, 2005). Mistakes that occur in micro enterprises are usually derived from the response to daily activities. This indicates that business operational activity takes a lot of time and there is no longer time for future business-oriented management as well as decision-making (Wiedemann, 2014).

The Sleman Regency was chosen as the location for this study since it is one of the regencies in Daerah Istimewa Yogyakarta with a large number of MSMEs. The Sleman Regency government strives to continue to encourage MSMEs to improve the quality of human resources to face the free market of the Association of Southeast Asian Nations (ASEAN) Economic Community. In 2009, the number of people working for MSMEs in Sleman Regency area was 63,255 and the value of small industrial production reached Rp 610.32 billion. Small industries in the Sleman Regency in 2009 reached 15,112 business units consisting of 15,012 small industries and 100 large and medium industries. The number of MSMEs in the Sleman Regency increased significantly by around 25,000 businesses in 2011 (Deperindagkop, 2011). From the aforementioned facts, it can be assumed that the existence of MSMEs—especially micro enterprises—has an important role for the economy of Indonesia in general and the economy of the Sleman Regency in particular. Therefore, it is important that the micro enterprises in the Sleman Regency are further investigated.

2 RESEARCH QUESTIONS AND OBJECTIVES

In relation to the increasing importance of MSMEs in Indonesia's economic development, an investigation of management accounting systems applied to micro enterprises is required. Based on the literature review conducted, the research questions raised in this study are:

1. What are the management accounting practices in micro enterprises of the Sleman Regency?
2. Are the management accounting practices in the micro enterprises of the Sleman Regency consistent with existing theories?

The purpose of this study is to understand the application of management accounting in micro enterprises. Such an understanding will be obtained from the investigation undertaken to see if the micro enterprises have applied management accounting and if so, how much its application and how the practice of management accounting is aligned to existing theories.

3 LITERATURE REVIEW

3.1 *Management accounting*

Management accounting is the provision of accounting information for internal company interests and the three main objectives of management accounting are providing information for: (1) planning, (2) control and (3) decision-making (Mowen, Hansen & Heitger, 2016). Management accounting activities identify each action, analyze and accumulate accounting information which is passed on to management, ultimately serving to evaluate and control the company's resources.

3.2 *Contingency theory*

This study uses contingency theory as its theoretical basis. Contingency theory has been widely used in research investigating performance measurement and organizational effectiveness (Otley, 1980; Moorthy et al., 2012). Every company faces its own internal and external limitations as well as an environment that can affect the uncertainty of its business. This results in the absence of optimal organizational design for each company because each company has its own organizational culture and a different perspective on risk.

Meanwhile, contingency theory has been used extensively in the context of managerial accounting. Contingency theory is applied in management accounting research to answer the following three types of questions: (1) compatibility between organizational and structural controls; (2) the impact of such suitability on performance; (3) investigations of multiple contingencies and their impact on organizational design (Islam & Hu, 2012).

3.3 *Management control system theory*

This study also uses management control system theory since management accounting practices are closely related to the management control system. Management control is a must to be applied in every organization or business unit (Anthony & Govindarajan, 2007). The activities of management control consist of: planning, coordinating, communicating, evaluating, decision-making and influencing people to change their behavior in harmony with organizational goals with the aim of achieving goal congruence.

3.4 *Previous studies on management accounting practices in MSMEs*

Most previous studies regarding management accounting practices in MSMEs focus more on the small and medium enterprises than on the micro enterprises. López and Hiebl (2015) found that the use of management accounting is lower in SMEs compared to larger enterprises and economy downturn can adversely affect the SMEs' business. Meanwhile, Ahmad (2012) found weak support for the positive relationship between the use of management accounting practices and organizational performance of SMEs.

Previous studies also demonstrate the use of information technology in MSMEs. Email, online purchases and research related to online business are frequently used by micro enterprises (Burke, 2009) and the Internet and e-business are also used to advance business (Davis & Vlandica, 2005).

4 RESEARCH METHODOLOGY

This study employs a qualitative research methodology. A qualitative methodology in accounting research is strongly recommended given that current accounting is a pluralistic discipline, leading many researchers to use qualitative methods to explore broad ranging issues (Lee & Humphrey, 2006).

The population in this research encompasses all micro enterprises in the Sleman Regency, Daerah Istimewa Yogyakarta. Samples were taken by using purposive sampling. They were selected by using the criteria obtained from the definition of micro enterprises in Indonesia, namely: 1) enterprises with assets of less than 50 million rupiah or 2) income generated within a year of less than 300 million rupiah. The samples in this study consists of seven micro enterprises. Semi-structured interviews were conducted using questions from Wiedemann (2014). Thematic analysis was employed to analyze the data using guidelines from Miles, Huberman and Saldana (2014). Thematic analysis was chosen for this study because of the power of this analysis in uncovering themes contained in interview answers (Jones & Forshaw, 2012).

5 RESULTS AND DISCUSSION

The responses of participants to the general questions will be discussed first. All participants in this study belong to the owner–manager type of business, in which business owners are also business managers and the main worker. Only a few participants have some employees and even then, the number is small. This may be caused by a very small organization size. This particular finding supports the contingency theory that states that firm size can influence management accounting practices.

In terms of competition, most participants know who their competitors are. However, micro entrepreneurs seem to rarely make competitive efforts toward their competitors. Moreover, participants also rarely have access to the Internet. The use of MS Excel and other software is also absent in the micro enterprises studied.

Furthermore, all the participants are still using manual bookkeeping methods and have not utilized any information technology for promotion or selling, except for one participant. Thus, the results of this study contradict previous work by Davis and Vlandica (2005) and Burke (2009) who found that information technology is widely used by micro enterprises.

In addition to general management accounting, this study also highlights operational management accounting. With regard to pricing, most participants do not have a specific formula. The pricing process is still very simple by determining the desired profit percentage, with less attention being given to the total cost of production. The participants also have no knowledge whatsoever about cost classification. This finding is contrary to management accounting principles that state that cost behavior classification is important and indeed the core of management accounting (Hansen, Mowen & Heitger, 2016).

For employment, most of the study participants do not have employees so they could not answer questions about employees. Participants who did have employees explained that their employees work full-time and were paid in cash. However, the employees' salary payrolls were not accompanied by written documents containing how many hours they had worked, so that payments become less powerful because they were not supported by proof of payment.

The participants also had little understanding regarding target costing even though the target was not achieved. Participants also did not really care whether the actual cost was higher than the budgeted cost or not. They also seemed to pay less attention to the amount of sales that have been achieved and this is demonstrated by the absence of clear daily sales records and also the way in which customers pay them. The cash-handling control system also underperformed and this is evidenced by only one participant claiming to have a money safe. Most participants did not have a specific person who checks the daily cash balance or cash balance when finished selling. Again, this is not in line with the management control system which states that control is necessary if an organization wants to achieve its objectives (Anthony & Govindarajan, 2007). Anthony and Govindarajan (2007) also explain that business units should always measure and control their assets. The assets in question include cash, receivables, inventories, working capital, property, plant and equipment. Cash is necessary for day-to-day operations and also in preparation for unexpected events. Therefore, control of cash balances and cash inflows and outflows is very important for a business unit. In addition to cash, accounts receivable are other assets that must be controlled by micro entrepreneurs to avoid the risk of uncollectible debts that will eventually harm the business.

The participants are also less worried about customers who owe money to them on the grounds that the customer is a regular. Correspondingly, if these participants are indebted to a supplier or the bank they also did not record their debts. This finding cannot be separated from Javanese culture which is quite prevalent in the Sleman Regency.

Meanwhile, regarding inventory, micro entrepreneurs in this study know quite well that checking the inventory on a regular basis is indispensable. According to the participants, checking the inventory is important in order to fulfill orders from customers and also for the smooth running of the business. Some participants can clearly remember their business capital and others do not know exactly the business capital they have expended up to the time of the interview. Nevertheless, none of the participants had a calculation of their respective capital ratios compared to the trade accounts payable. This demonstrates that management accounting practices in micro enterprises are not in accordance with the principle of management control as described by Anthony and Govindarajan (2007), who explain the importance of control of working capital in order to provide useful information in making decisions about the assets used and to motivate managers to make decisions that are appropriate to the interests of the organization.

The findings of this study also show that micro enterprises are very vulnerable to their business environment. From the participants' answers it can be seen that there are months where sales are rising and months where sales go down. This greatly affects their business income and also influences their accounting practices. This proves that a decline in economic activity in the end will also negatively affect the intensity of application of management accounting practices (López & Hiebl, 2015).

According to management control system theory, performance measurement cannot be done through financial performance alone. Excessive obsession with financial performance will be bad for an organization because the incentives for members of the organization to act are not in accordance with the objectives of the organization (moral hazard). Since the participants of this study do not measure their non-financial performance, it can be concluded that the practices of micro enterprises in this study are not in accordance with management control system theory.

6 CONCLUSION AND RECOMMENDATIONS

This study aims to determine the practice of management accounting in micro enterprises in the Sleman Regency, Daerah Istimewa Yogyakarta and compare existing practices with the theories employed in this study. The theoretical basis used in this research is contingency theory and management control system theory. Micro enterprises are selected as the focus of this study because this type of business still requires extensive supports and encouragement from the Indonesian government compared to small and medium enterprises that are also MSMEs. The results demonstrate that the practices of management accounting in micro enterprises are still far from the required standards and this can hamper the growth and development of the business. Without the application of good management accounting, micro enterprises cannot survive in the midst of increasingly tight business competition. Micro enterprises are important for the Indonesian economy, especially since the number of this type of business is quite significant, in that it could become the backbone of the country's economy in the event of a financial crisis. Therefore, the improvement of management accounting practices through business owner training and workshops needs to be done immediately and could be initiated by the government together with educational institutions.

REFERENCES

Ahmad, K. (2012). *The use of management accounting practices in Malaysian SMEs* (Doctoral thesis, University of Exeter). Retrieved from: https://ore.exeter.ac.uk/repository/bitstream/handle/10036/3758/AhmadK.pdf?sequence = 3.

Anthony, R.N. & Govindarajan, V. (2007). *Management control systems*, 12th ed. New York, NY: McGraw Hill.

Burke, K. (2009). Internet ICT use in agriculture: Micro-enterprises and SMEs. *Journal of Developmental Entrepreneurship, 14*(3), 233–254.

Davis, C.H. & Vlandica, F. (2005). Adoption and use of Internet technologies and e-business solutions by Canadian micro-enterprises. *Proceedings of the Conference of the International Association for Management of Technology (IAMOT)*, Vienna.

Deperindagkop. (2011). *Micro, small, and medium-sized enterprises directory*. Daerah Istimewa Yogyakarta: The Industry, Trade Services and Cooperation Department of Sleman Regency.

Islam, J. & Hu, H. (2012). A review of literature on contingency theory in managerial accounting. *African Journal of Business and Management, 6*(15), 5159–5164.

Jones, S. & Forshaw, M. (2012). *Research methods in psychology*. Harlow, Essex: Pearson Prentice Hall.

Lee, B. & Humphrey, C. (2006). More than a numbers game: Qualitative research in accounting. *Management Decision, 44*(2), 180–197.

López, O.L. & Hiebl, M.R.W. (2015). Management accounting in small and medium-sized enterprises: Current knowledge and avenues for further research. *Journal of Management Accounting Research, 27*(1), 81–119.

Miles, M.B., Huberman, A.M. & Saldana, J. (2014). *Qualitative data analysis: A methods sourcebook*. Thousand, Oaks, California: SAGE Publications, Inc.

Moorthy, M.K., Tan, A., Choo, C., Wei, C.C., Ping, J.T.Y. & Leong, T.K. (2012). A study on factors affecting the performance of SMEs in Malaysia. *International Journal of Academic Research in Business and Social Sciences, 2*(4), 224–239.

Mowen, M.M., Hansen, D.R., & Heitger, D.L. (2016). *Cornerstones of managerial accounting*. Boston, MA: CENGAGE Learning.

Otley, D.T. (1980). The contingency theory of management accounting: achievement and prognosis. *Accounting, Organizations and Society, 5*(4), 413–428.

Tarmidi, L.T. (2005). *The importance of MSEs in economic development of developing APEC countries*. Retrieved from: http://www.apec.org.au/docs/korea-papers2/svii-lt-paper.pdf.

Wiedemann, D. 2014. *Characteristics of management accounting practices in small and medium sized enterprises. Case Rantalinna Oy* (Double degree thesis, Saimaa University of Applied Sciences). Retrieved from: https://www.theseus.fi/bitstream/handle/10024/86259/Wiedemann_Daniela.pdf?sequence=1.

World Islamic Economic Forum (WIEF). 2016. *Indonesian economy: Micro, small, medium sized enterprises*. Retrieved from: http://www.indonesia-investments.com/news/todays-headlines/indonesian-economy-micro-small-medium-sized-enterprises/item7068.

Increasing Management Relevance and Competitiveness – Sukoco et al. (Eds)
© 2018 Taylor & Francis Group, London, ISBN 978-0-8153-7455-8

The power of finance: The dynamics of female entrepreneurs in fulfilling their financial needs

M.R. Rita
Faculty of Economics and Business, Diponegoro University, Semarang, Indonesia
Satya Wacana Christian University, Salatiga, Indonesia

S. Wahyudi & H. Muharam
Faculty of Economics and Business, Diponegoro University, Semarang, Indonesia

ABSTRACT: The purpose of this research is to explore how an individual, in beginning a business, assembles resources, including financial capital, as well as constructs funding strength in developing a batik enterprise. A descriptive qualitative research was conducted using case studies. Six participants were chosen from three different locations using a purposive sampling method with a specific sampling quota. The results show that an individual who has the power of thought possesses a strong desire to be independent and more developed, so that they can take advantage of business opportunities and funding that were previously not known. In addition, funds are beneficial in that they facilitate entrepreneurs to recognize, utilize opportunities, develop their businesses, and improve the scale of their business in order to achieve a successful business cycle. This research produces a proposition in the form of a funding model for small and medium enterprises. In the future, empirical testing is needed, in order that a model generalization can be attained. There are two funding perspectives; the funding provider (supply) and funding recipient (demand). Up until now, there is no known in-depth research that discusses this aspect.

1 INTRODUCTION

Several previous research studies have not exposed the differences between males and females in their respective approaches to starting a business. As females are different from males, there is a possibility that there will be differences between males and females when starting an enterprise. Bakan (1966) revealed that there are personality differences between males and females in their orientation toward achieving results (agentic) as well as differences in characteristics that are oriented toward service and social activities.

The current business world is identified as being more appropriate for men (Marlow & Patton, 2005). The business world can be analogous as an organization that is full of challenges, has various risks, and demands quick responses when faced with numerous opportunities. Nevertheless, based on field observations conducted by researchers that was found in the Lasem and Gemawang batik villages, Central Java Indonesia, actually reveals that many women have become entrepreneurs. There are gender and cultural background differences that can provide color and dynamics to conducting a business (Lerner & Malach-Pines, 2011). These aspects influence how an entrepreneur analyzes a company's needs before eventually making a business decision (Tinkler et al., 2015).

Various previous research has shown that the family factor, especially parents, has a dominant role in determining the speed of business successors. (Çaliyurt, 2011) stated that the majority of female entrepreneurs in Turkey place more trust in business advice from their families than consultants/business experts, because they have previous business experience.

In the financing aspect, there are variations in financing based on gender (Garwe & Fatoki, 2012; Tinkler et al., 2015). This can be explained by the discouraged borrower theory (Kon & Storey, 2003); women are reluctant to make credit requests because they are worried that they will be rejected by creditors.

Based on the above explanation, there are still variations, or insufficient information regarding how female entrepreneurs start their businesses, how they compile resources and financial capital, and how financing plays a role in developing their businesses. It is interesting to explore how they begin their businesses, starting from the initial intention to become an entrepreneur up until how they consider and take advantage of financial capital to start a business.

2 THEORETICAL FRAMEWORK

2.1 *Behavioral finance theory*

Behavioral finance is a study which influences how a psychological phenomenon influences its financial behavior (Shefrin, 2007). Financial behavior teaches how humans in actual terms behave in making financial decisions (Nofsinger and Wang, 2011). This means that in financial problems, besides its own funds, there is a behavioral factor that influences financial decision making. It was found that entrepreneurs have several irrationality symptoms in decision-making with regard to funding including overconfidence, over optimism, self-serving attribution, illusion of control, the law of small numbers, similarity, availability, representativeness, status quo, planning fallacy, and commitment escalation (Zhang & Cueto, 2017). Companies that were classified as having high growth found that through debt, companies obtain advantages, such as a high accrual discretion compared to funding in the form of their own financial capital (Marciukaityte & Szewczyk, 2011). Bias in funding was also researched by Estwick (2013), who found that entrepreneurs have a preference for using their own financial capital in order to maintain control of the company so that it can be inherited to their successors.

2.2 *Entrepreneurial Finance (EF) theory*

King and Levine (1993) had already tried to connect the relationship between funding and entrepreneurship as well as see its effects on economic growth. The EF concept is also referred to in research by Ennew and Binks (1995), who discussed the connection between banks and businesses. Several early research studies connected EF with funding for small and medium enterprises during the start-up stage (Cassar, 2004, Allers, 2011, Buckley, 1997), or early stage (Kim & Wagman, 2016) as well as young firms (Koch et al., 2010; Takahashi, 2015). There are also those who defined EF in general as a funding activity for small and medium enterprises (SME) (Rocca et al., 2011; Urim & Imhonopi, 2015). Moreover, a study about EF explained the relationship between fund providers and entrepreneurs in providing alternative funding to increase a company's work performance that comes from: venture financial capital and angel investors (Mitter & Kraus, 2011); the bank, venture financial capital, angel investors, and crowdfunding (Chemmanur & Fulghieri, 2014); debt, asset-based funding, crowdfunding, a hybrid instrument, as well as its own financial capital/equity (OECD, 2015).

2.3 *Entrepreneurship theory*

The entrepreneurship process involves all functions, activities, and actions that are related to a perception about opportunity, and in creating an organization to bring that opportunity into realization (Bygrave & Hofer, 1991). According to Maine et al. (2015), the creativity process of a person can be done through a process of effectuation and causation. Effectuation places more emphasis on selecting various business opportunities that can be executed by an individual based on the available resources (logic of control). Shane et al. (2003) stated that the ability to assemble resources is greatly influenced by the entrepreneurial motivation and cognitive factor. Individuals who possess a need for achievement and a desire for independence will be able to recognize opportunities, develop ideas, and follow through on those ideas.

3 RESEARCH METHODS

This research used a descriptive qualitative study with a case study method. Related to this, six participants were chosen from three different locations, who were considered as reflecting the conditions/variations of shoreline (Lasem Rembang and Pekalongan) and non-shoreline (Gemawang in Semarang Regency) batik regions. To obtain the respondents, purposive sampling was done with a quota type of sampling. In-depth interview techniques were conducted to collect the data. The data was then analyzed by using a descriptive qualitative technique, by narrating the field data.

4 RESULTS, ANALYSIS, AND DISCUSSION

4.1 *Funds as an antecedent*

Every phase that occurs in the lifecycle of a company will determine the fund fulfillment strategies, and availability of financial resources, as well as financial costs (Rocca et al., 2011). When funds become a stimulus to be able to conduct a business, then an entrepreneur will engage in various funding patterns. Although they have similarities, no funding pattern is exactly the same in the small and medium enterprises (SME) researched.

In the early stages of starting a business, most of the respondents used their own financial capital obtained from their salaries as employees, holiday bonus money, and personal funds that they had saved over time. They only started to access bank credit when they felt their funds were insufficient to cover the business needs. When their businesses started to develop, they needed additional funds to meet their work capital needs or investments. Early capital that is used to start a business, whether its own financial capital or debt, can be considered as entrepreneurial funds. The presence of these funds is considered as still being insufficient to acquire bigger business opportunities. Then a need arises to increase the funding amount, in order that the production scale increases.

Capital is positioned as the beginning and becomes the antecedent of a business. This viewpoint is followed by the majority of individuals who agree that even to start a business there should be capital or money available first. In this context, financial capital has the power to facilitate someone in starting a business and developing it (Cook, 2001; Denis, 2004; Markova & Petkovska-Mirčevska, 2010). However, when SMEs have difficulty accessing funds, then the growth and development of the company will be hampered (Levy, 1993). When funds are available, oftentimes SMEs increase their work performance continuously. Meanwhile, other non-bank financial institutions can also play a role in accommodating business funding needs but with a lower credit quality (Denis, 2004).

Bank debt is perceived positively for a number of companies because there is a belief that they are sufficiently trusted by the bank to receive additional capital, which gives them more motivation and enthusiasm to operate the businesses (Oranburg, 2016). Besides that, funds from debt can be used to increase investments or add to work capital. Using debt can cause a leverage effect that facilitates a company's competitive superiority (Campello, 2006).

4.2 *Funds as a consequence*

To operate a business, it will certainly take financial capital. However, capital limitations do not become a barrier to starting a business. They consider the business first, and then they think about what is needed to run the business. They do not have expertise or money as capital. They usually work in cooperation with others or with people who have competencies in making batik and/or business capital. Initially, the business starts on a small scale, then extends to a wider range (Keats & Bracker, 1988; Drucker, 1964). They trust themselves to be able to run the business, thus they already have an internal locus of control in conducting their businesses (Boone et al., 2000, Shane et al., 2003).

4.3 *The power of finance*

There is already much understanding about the role of money in a business, but there is not much insight into the power of finance. If one has sufficient financial capital, then the entrepreneur can use it to innovate on a high scale to overcome market problems, efficiency obstacles, and productivity issues. In an entrepreneurial theoretical context, with the availability of funding, a need for achievement, independence, creativity, and innovation will increase. They will also be brave to try to develop their business ideas and implement them to solve their business problems.

With funding, the business cycle will develop to the growth stage and head toward a maturity stage. In the theory of financing lifecycle, every business cycle has different finance structures Fluck (2000). Fluck (2000) states that there are funding decision influences from one cycle to the next cycle. However, this paper mentions that funds have the power to drive the growth of the business cycle.

By funding, a production factor can be bought, whether it is supplemental raw materials, the ability to hire workers, or utilizing technology to develop a business. Proper working capital management will support the growth and sustainability of a small business (Kargar & Blumenthal, 1994). In this context, it shows that funds have the power as working capital to support business operations.

Funding also has the strength of expanding the business scale. With a greater capacity, more raw materials, and other production factors are necessary. Zeebaree and Siron (2017) showed that funding moderates the relationship between the entrepreneurial orientation and competitive advantage of small and medium enterprises. That result confirms that funding has the power as a moderator to increase competitiveness. Related to this, funding has the power to increase competition.

5 CONCLUSION

Previous research showed that funds seems to be a production factor (Denis, 2004; Kargar & Blumenthal, 1994; Markova & Petkovska-Mirčevska, 2010; Sarasvathy (2001). From this research, it reveals that funds have an extraordinary power in fostering and increasing a business to become bigger, more advanced, and expansive. Funds have the power to facilitate an entrepreneur in recognizing and taking advantage of opportunities as well as developing one's business. But, in a very competitive business environment, business culture and the proper setting mean that an entrepreneur is not just looking for funds when starting a business. An entrepreneur's background and characteristics, such as parents, society, desire to be successful and advance, bravery, unending desire to succeed, independent-free to create, and having a life vision all play a great role in triggering funds to become an important production factor in a business. Actually, under these conditions, fund providers are more likely to have a positive response by providing funds for the entrepreneur if needed.

This research produced a proposition in the form of a financing model for SMEs. In the future, empirical testing needs to be conducted, in order that a generalized model can be created. There are two funding perspectives; supply and demand. To date, there is no known in-depth study of this issue.

ACKNOWLEDGEMENT

This paper is arranged to fulfill the requirements for obtaining a doctoral degree in the Management Study Program, at the Faculty of Economics and Business, Diponegoro University of Semarang. I would like to thank Lembaga Pengelola Dana Pendidikan (LPDP), Ministry of Finance, Republic of Indonesia, which funded my tuition fee through the BUDI-DN 2016scholarship until completion of the study.

REFERENCES

Allers, K.S. 2011. Start-up Success: How to Finance a Small Business. *New York Amsterdam News*. New York Amsterdam News.

Bakan, D. 1966. *The duality of human existence: An essay on psychology and religion,* Oxford, England Rand Mcnally.

Boone, C., De Brabander, B. & Hellemans, J. 2000. Research note: CEO locus of control and small firm performance. *Organization Studies,* 21, 641–646.

Buckley, G. 1997. Microfinance in Africa: Is it either the problem or the solution? *World development,* 25, 1081–1093.

Bygrave, W.D. & Hofer, C.W. (1991). Theorizing about entrepreneurship. *Entrepreneurship Theory and Practice*, *16*, 13–22.

Çaliyurt, K.T. (2011). Importance of financial management knowledge of SMEs managing by women. *Trakya Üniversitesi Sosyal Bilimler Dergisi*, *13*, 327–354.

Campello, M. (2006). Debt financing: Does it boost or hurt firm performance in product markets? *Journal of Financial Economics*, *82*, 135–172.

Cassar, G. 2004. The financing of business start-ups. *Journal of business venturing,* 19, 261–283.

Chemmanur, T.J. & Fulghieri, P. (2014). Entrepreneurial finance and innovation: An introduction and agenda for future research. *Review of Financial Studies*, *27*, 1–19.

Cook, P. (2001). Finance and small and medium-sized enterprise in developing countries. *Journal of Developmental Entrepreneurship*, *6*, 17–40.

Denis, D.J. (2004). Entrepreneurial finance: An overview of the issues and evidence. *Journal of Corporate Finance*, *10*, 301–326.

Drucker, P.F. (1964). The big power of little ideas. *Harvard Business Review*, *42*, 6–182.

Ennew, C.T. & Binks, M.R. (1995). The provision of finance to small businesses: Does the banking relationship constrain performance. *Journal of Entrepreneurial Finance*, *4*, 57–73.

Estwick, S. (2013). The small business finance dilemma: An exploratory study of Barbadian firms. *Journal of Eastern Carribean Studies*, *38*, 1–28.

Fluck, Z. 2000. Capital structure decisions in small and large firms: a life-cycle theory of financing. https://archive.nyu.edu/jspui/bitstream/2451/26694/2/FIN-00–028.pdf (Access Date: April 28 2017).

Garwe, D.K. & Fatoki, O. (2012). The impact of gender on SME characteristics and access to debt finance in South Africa. *Development Southern Africa*, *29*, 448–461.

Kargar, J. & Blumenthal, R.A. (1994). Leverage impact on working capital in small businesses. *TMA Journal*, *14*, 46–53.

Keats, B.W. & Bracker, J.S. (1988). Toward a theory of small firm performance: A conceptual model. *American Journal of Small Business*, *12*, 41–58.

Kim, J-H. & Wagman, L. (2016). Early-stage entrepreneurial financing: A signaling perspective. *Journal of Banking and Finance*, *67*, 12–22.

King, R.G. & Levine, R. (1993). Finance, entrepreneurship, and growth. Theory and evidence. *Journal of Monetary Economics*, *32*, 513–542.

Koch, L.T., Kuhn, W., Gruenhagen, M. & Hisrich, R.D. (2010). The 'irrelevance of irrelevance' in entrepreneurial finance: Modeling the cost of capital in start-ups beyond Modigliani–Miller. *Strategic Change: Briefings in Entrepreneurial Finance*, *19*, 29–43.

Kon, Y. & Storey, D.J. (2003). A theory of discouraged borrowers. *Small Business Economics*, *21*, 37–49.

Lerner, M. & Malach-Pines, A. (2011). Gender and culture in family business: A ten-nation study. *International Journal of Cross Cultural Management*, *11*, 113–131.

Levy, B. (1993). Obstacles to developing indigenous small and medium enterprises: An empirical assessment. *The World Bank Economic Review*, *7*, 65–83.

Maine, E., Soh, P-H. & Dos Santos, N. (2015). The role of entrepreneurial decision-making in opportunity creation and recognition. *Technovation*, *39–40*, 53–72.

Marciukaityte, D. & Szewczyk, S.H. (2011). Financing decisions and discretionary accruals: Managerial manipulation or managerial overoptimism. *Review of Behavioral Finance*, *3*, 91–114.

Markova, S. & Petkovska-Mirčevska, T. (2010). Entrepreneurial finance: Angel investing as a source of funding high-growth start-up firms. *Annals of the University of Petrosani, Economics*, *10*, 217–224.

Marlow, S. & Patton, D. (2005). All credit to men? Entrepreneurship, finance, and gender. *Entrepreneurship Theory and Practice*, *29*, 717–735.

Mitter, C. & Kraus, S. (2011). Entrepreneurial finance—issues and evidence, revisited. *International Journal of Entrepreneurship and Innovation Management*, *14*, 132–150.

Nofsinger, J.R. & Wang, W. 2011. Determinants of start-up firm external financing worldwide. *Journal of Banking and Finance,* 35, 2282–2294.

OECD. (2015). *New approaches to SME and entrepreneurship financing: Broadening the range of instruments.* Paris, France: OECD.

Oranburg, S.C. (2016). 4 – Start-up financing. In *Start-Up creation* (pp. 57–73). Duxford, UK: Woodhead Publishing.

Rocca, M.L., Rocca, T.L. & Cariola, A. (2011). Capital structure decisions during a firm's life cycle. *Small Business Economics, 37*, 107–130.

Sarasvathy, S.D. 2001. Causation and effectuation: Toward a theoretical shift from economic inevitability to entrepreneurial contingency. *Academy of management Review,* 26, 243–263.

Shane, S., Locke, E.A. & Collins, C.J. (2003). Entrepreneurial motivation. *Human Resource Management Review, 13*, 257–279.

Shefrin, H. 2007. *Behavioral corporate finance: Decisions that create value,* New York, McGraw-Hill.

Takahashi, H. (2015). Dynamics of bank relationships in entrepreneurial finance. *Journal of Corporate Finance, 34*, 23–31.

Tinkler, J.E., Bunker Whittington, K., Ku, M.C. & Davies, A.R. (2015). Gender and venture capital decision-making: The effects of technical background and social capital on entrepreneurial evaluations. *Social Science Research, 51*, 1–16.

Urim, U.M. & Imhonopi, D. (2015). Operationalising financing windows for entrepreneurship development in Nigeria: An appraisal. *Research Journal of Finance and Accounting, 6*, 58–68.

Zeebaree, M.R.Y. & Siron, R.B. 2017. The Impact of Entrepreneurial Orientation on Competitive Advantage Moderated by Financing Support in SMEs. *International Review of Management and Marketing,* 7.

Zhang, S.X. & Cueto, J. (2017). The study of bias in entrepreneurship. *Entrepreneurship Theory and Practice, 41*(3), 419–454.

APPENDIX: MAIN INTERVIEW PROTOCOLS

1. Please explain the process of starting your business in the past. Where did you get the idea? What was the background behind it?
2. Please explain how you then developed this business and kept it going. Did you encounter any difficulties?
3. What is the condition of your company now? What are the prospects like for your business?
4. Please explain how you fulfill your financial capital needs. Where do you acquire it? What are the conditions?
5. What are the advantages of that financial capital toward your company? What kinds of obstacles do you often have to face with this financing?
6. Do you have any problems selling your product(s)? What have you done to overcome this problem?
7. Have you had any problems with production? What actions have you taken to resolve these problems?

Increasing Management Relevance and Competitiveness – Sukoco et al. (Eds)
© 2018 Taylor & Francis Group, London, ISBN 978-0-8153-7455-8

Entrepreneurial orientation in a family business group: The role of the corporate center and its effect on business unit performance

O. Pendrian, K.A. Karnen, R. Rachmawati & R.D. Kusumastuti
Department of Management, Faculty of Economics and Business, Universitas Indonesia, Indonesia

ABSTRACT: The number of studies on strategic management practices and their influence on entrepreneurship in family business has been on the rise lately. Yet, there have been few studies that investigate their relationships to large family business groups, where corporate management needs to ensure alignment between the corporate level strategy and the business unit level strategy. This paper aims to examine and analyze the influence of corporate parenting style played by the corporate center in the form of strategic planning, strategic control, and financial control on business unit Entrepreneurial Orientation (EO), which, in turn, affects a business unit's strategic initiative and performance. The study used a structural equation model involving 106 respondents who are CEOs and senior management officers in business units managed by 16 corporate centers of family business groups in Indonesia. The study results show that the presence of a corporate center affects business unit performances through the influences on the EO level. Corporate centers that follow a strategic planning and strategic control approach have a positive influence on the EO level in business units. On the other hand, the financial control approach has a negative influence on the EO level in business units. At the business unit level, it was found that the EO level does not have a direct relationship to performance, but its influence on performance will be positive whenever EO has been implemented in the form of strategic initiatives. The study's implication and future research directions for family business groups are discussed.

Keywords: Family business groups, strategic planning, strategic control, financial control, entrepreneurial orientation, business unit strategic initiatives

1 INTRODUCTION

The presence of family business groups has played an important role in global economic growth and has been the driving force behind industrialization in many countries (Yabushita & Suehiro, 2014; Piana et al., 2012). In recent, stiffer business competition environments, family business groups not only thrive, but also prospered and grew by entering various industries (Yabushita & Suehiro, 2014). In order to sustain such growth, a family business group should be able to adapt its strategies and modernize its management style to overcome management resources limitations (Yabushita & Suehiro, 2014); it also needs to have a corporate strategy that can drive business units to run entrepreneurial activities.

As is commonly found in multi-business companies, the management of corporate strategy in family business groups is managed by a corporate center (Ramachandran et al., 2013), and, according to Zahra et al. (2000), in multi-business companies, the corporate center context, comprising business unit mandates, and the control system, is an important determinant of business unit entrepreneurship. Furthermore, a business unit's entrepreneurial activities are the implementation forms of Entrepreneurial Orientation (EO) and are positively connected to the company's performance achievement (Lumpkin & Dess, 1996; Zahra et al., 1999).

Studies on corporate center roles that increase added value for business units, including increasing EO in the unit, have been carried out by other researchers in the past, however, these were conducted using the multinational company as their analytical unit (Zahra et al., 2000; Menz et al., 2013), and have been limited in terms of testing the roles in family business groups. Therefore, this study was conducted to close such research gaps, and to provide some answers to research questions, such as whether the presence of a corporate center affects the EO level of business units along with its influence on the performance of family business groups.

In analyzing the corporate center's role on a business unit's EO, this study combined the corporate center framework of Ramachandran et al.

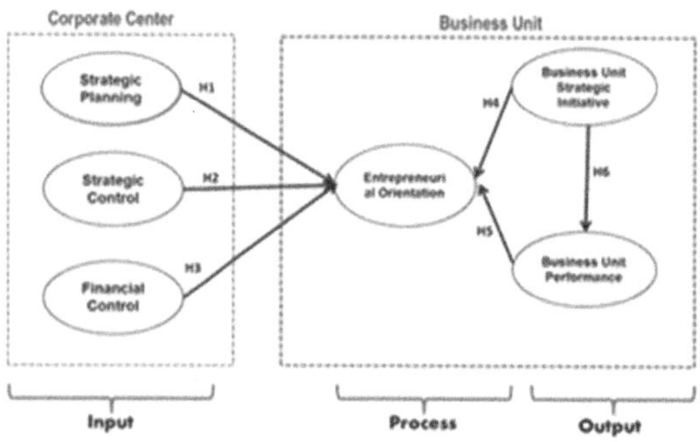

Figure 1. Proposed research model.

(2013) and the strategic entrepreneurship concept (input-process-output) of Hitt et al. (2011), and uses the concept of corporate parenting style developed by Goold and Campbell (1987) and Goold et al. (1994), that is, a corporate center's approach in managing business units through strategic management practice in the form of strategic planning, strategic control, and financial control. Complete inter-variable relationships are depicted in Figure 1.

This study contributes to strategic management and entrepreneurship literature by investigating the implementation of the corporate parenting role in family business groups that is commonly applied in multinational companies, as well as its relationship to business unit entrepreneurial activities. The measurement criteria of the corporate parenting style developed by Goold and Luchs (1996) has been extended by adding some additional indicators for the planning and control influence dimensions.

2 LITERATURE REVIEW

2.1 *Role of the corporate center in family business groups*

A family business group is a business entity consisting of several affiliated companies that are diversified and inter-connected by multiple common factors such as ownership structure, inter-company transactions within the group, and the presence of social relationships such as family connections and friendships (Khanna & Rivkin, 2001; Yiu et al., 2007).

According to Ramachandran et al. (2013), family business groups are managed by a corporate center that serves the role through strategy and identity work activities. The strategy work is performed by the corporate center by constructing and developing strategic frames for business units. Meanwhile, the identity work is one of the corporate center's tasks in managing the brand, identity, and group reputation as a whole. As an organization at the corporate level, a corporate center has two main functions: as a loss prevention and value creation for the business units (Luo et al, 2012), which can serve in value creation for the business units, or in contrary, in their value destructions (Buchanan & Sands, 1994; Goold et al., 1994).

2.2 *Business unit entrepreneurial orientation & strategic initiatives*

An entrepreneurial company is one that "engages in product market innovation, undertakes somewhat risky ventures, and is first to come up with proactive, innovations, beating competitors to the punch" (Miller, 1983). Based on such a definition, EO is a concept developed at the corporate level, reflecting a company's tendencies toward product innovation, pro-activeness, and risk-taking behaviors (Covin & Slevin, 1991; Wiklund & Shepherd, 2003).

In the context of multi-business companies (including family business groups), business unit strategic initiatives are implementation forms of EO. Business unit strategic initiative is defined as "entrepreneurial undertaking that allows the business unit to tap into new opportunities" outside of the corporate center (Ambos & Birkinshaw, 2010), capturing often autonomous 'under the radar' (Delany, 2000) development of products and technologies by the business unit operation (Birkinshaw, 1997).

3 HYPHOTHESES DEVELOPMENT

Goold & Campbell (1987) and Goold et al. (1994) introduce the concept of corporate parenting style, that is, the roles played by the corporate center in managing business units by executing strategic management practice approaches differentiated by corporate center involvement in the planning process (planning influence) and in the controlling process (control influence) of business units. Based on the level of these influences, there are eight possible types of corporate center's strategic management roles, wherein the following three are commonly used: strategic planning, strategic control, and financial control.

The strategic planning approach is a corporate center approach in running the strategic management practice by being heavily involved in the formulation process and strategy implementation in business units, and controlling them while flexibly observing operational performance based on set strategic plans (Goold et al, 1994; Goold & Luchs, 1996). The strategic planning approach is expected to enhance the entrepreneurial intensity in business units for several reasons. Firstly, the budget and target defined by the corporate center for business units tend to be more flexible, and reviewed within the context of strategic as well as financial performance (Goold & Campbell, 1987), which can encourage great innovation within the business unit. Secondly, interaction among business units within a multi-business company enables the opportunity of knowledge exchange among business units which, in turn, can increase innovation (Hitt et al., 1997). Based on the explanations above, one can form the following hypotheses:

***Hypothesis 1**: Strategic planning implementation by a corporate center will have positive effects on business units' entrepreneurial orientation*

The strategic control is a corporate center approach in executing strategic management practices by providing strategic directives to business units in the strategy development process, and in coordinating strategic organizational functions' management, along with performing control on business units while observing strategic performance achievements (Goold et al., 1994; Goold & Luchs, 1996). Barringer and Bluedorn (1999) explain that strategic control provides support and recognition to the creativity and opportunity-seeking processes through innovation (as a form of strategic initiative) within the company's organization. When strategic control is implemented, it will lead business unit managers' behavior toward the risk of taking on new ventures to confront uncertainties in business environments (Hitt et al., 1990, 1996). Therefore, the following hypothesis can be formulated:

***Hypothesis 2**: Strategic control implementation by a corporate center will have positive effects on business units' entrepreneurial orientation*

In the financial control approach, business units are treated as stand-alone units in which a business unit's strategy is self-formulated by each unit, and the corporate center has a tight control of the units with an emphasis on short term financial performance (Goold et al., 1994; Goold & Luchs, 1996). A corporate center implementing financial control always monitors and evaluates business units' performance based on business quantitative objectives and targets by focusing its judgments on the objectives and targets' achievements against preset numbers (Goold & Campbell, 1987; Hitt et al., 1990). Such conditions make the business units focus on business targets already set by the corporate center and thus the business units tend not to take initiatives to create innovation or business development beyond what has been set by the corporate center, which in turn, indicates a weakened level of EO in business units (Zahra et al., 2000). Based on the analyses above, the following hypothesis is proposed:

***Hypothesis 3**: Financial control implementation by a corporate center will have negative effects on business units' entrepreneurial orientation*

At the business unit level, according to Scott et al. (2009), there is a positive relationship between EO and strategic initiatives in business units. A company with a strong EO is predicted to be likely to create new product concepts fulfilling both existing and potential customers' needs. Zahra and Covin (1995) state that a company with a strong EO can attain a higher market target and position than those of its competitors. Based on the analysis, the following hypothesis is proposed:

***Hypothesis 4**: Entrepreneurial orientation has positive effects on strategic initiatives in business units*

EO is a concept at the corporate level, which is strongly linked to strategic management and decision-making (Covin & Slevin, 1991; Lumpkin & Dess, 1996). Many researchers have proven that EO has positive effects on increased business performance in general (e.g. Miller, 1983; Zahra & Covin, 1995; Wiklund & Shepherd, 2005). Moreover, several researchers have carried out longitudinal studies, and have found positive effects of EO on increased business performance throughout (e.g. Zahra & Covin, 1995; Wiklund, 1999). Based on the narratives above, the following is proposed:

***Hypothesis 5**: Entrepreneurial orientation has positive effects on business units' performance*

Previous studies have shown that strategic initiative programs as an implementation of EO in business units have positive effects on business units' performance in multi-business companies (Schmid et al., 2014; Liouka, 2007; Ambos & Birkinshaw, 2010). Thus, the following proposed hypothesis:

***Hypothesis 6**: Strategic initiative programs have positive effects on business units' performance*

4 RESEARCH METHODOLOGY

4.1 *Sample and data collection*

Data for this study were collected with a survey of business units that are part of family business groups in Indonesia. These business units are managed by a corporate center that has a majority shareholding. Out of 171 questionnaires distributed, 117 (68%) were returned, and 106 (71%) had all questions answered. Eleven questionnaires were eliminated because respondents left some questions blank and business units were not directly under a corporate center. These 106 valid questionnaires were used as the sample for this study.

4.2 *Measures of construct*

The data analysis proceeds using Structural Equation Modeling (SEM) and used a "two-stage approach". The first stage is analysis of the measurement model, which consists of validity and reliability analyses of the model, and then involves parceling (Rhemtulla, 2016; Bandalos, 2002) using Latent Variable Score (LVS) to simplify the measurement model from a second-order Confirmatory Factor Analysis model (second CFA) into a first CFA. The second stage is the analysis of the structural model, which includes a significance test of path coefficient between two research latent variables, followed by research hypothesis testing. The analysis using SEM is supported by LISREL 8.8 software.

Corporate parenting style in the form of strategic planning, strategic control and financial approach were operationalized as the degree of a corporate center's involvement in the planning process (planning influence) and controlling process (control influence). The scale developed by Goold and Luchs (1996), and Couto et al. (2008), was adapted and modified for this study.

EO was operationalized as business unit management's tendencies toward product innovation, pro-activeness, and risk-taking behaviors. The scale for EO was adapted from Miller (1983) and Kellermanns and Eddleston (2006), and modified for this study. Business unit strategic initiative was measured in accordance with Bindl and Parker (2011) and Zeng (2007), and operationalized as initiative or strategic activities executed by the business unit as a result of implementing EO in the form of innovation and entrepreneurship programs. Finally, business unit performance was defined as perception of a business unit's level of success through financial and non-financial indicators. The measure was adapted from Venkatraman and Ramanujam (1986) and Trapczynski (2013), and modified for this study.

4.3 *Results*

Based on analysis of the measurement model, the fitness test results of the overall model refer to the Goodness of Fit Index (GOFI) values which indicate good fit. Therefore, it can be concluded that the overall fit of the measurement model is good. In addition to GOFI, all dimensions have good validity (t value > = 1.96 and standardized loading factor > = 0.50) and all latent variables have good reliability (construct reliability = 0.70 and variable extracted > = 0.50). The hypotheses summary of proposed structural model is shown in Figure 2.

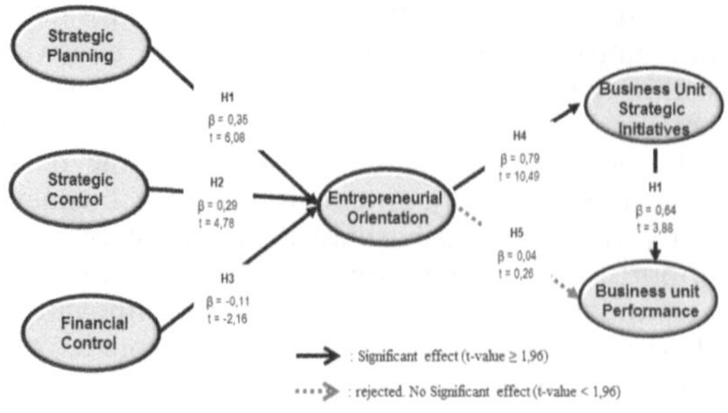

Figure 2. Hypotheses summary of structural model.

5 DISCUSSION

The study results show that in family business groups, strategic management practices applied by a corporate center have an effect on the EO level in business units. The results prove that corporate parenting style implementation generally applied by multinational companies can be applied in family business groups. Corporate parenting style implementation with different emphases will have an effect on the management's strategic behavior in business units, especially on the EO level. Corporate centers that manage business units with strategic planning and strategic control approaches will have positive effects on the EO level in business units, while corporate centers emphasizing the financial control approach will have negative effects on EO level in business units.

Thus, in essence, corporate parenting style implementation in family business groups in Indonesia must observe two important factors. Firstly, the business and organizational structures in family business groups that are independent are different legally from the divisional structures in multinational companies. These differences will impact different influences of corporate centers on strategy formulation and implementation processes in business units, including that of the strategic behavior of management related to entrepreneurial activities and innovation projects in business units. Secondly, specific characteristics in family business groups in which a family influence factor is present in the strategic decision-making process both at the corporate center level and at the business unit level that ultimately affects the magnitude of influence of the corporate center toward entrepreneurial activities in business units. Observing the results of this study that support the main hypotheses of the research, the authors believe that the two aforementioned important factors turn out not to make any significant difference on corporate parenting style influence toward the EO level in business units in family business groups and in multi-business companies in general.

Another interesting finding is that there is no direct relationship between the EO level and business units' performance. Nevertheless, the research finding supports reports of past researchers that they could not find any significant relationship between EO and performance (George et al., 2001; Covin et al., 1994). Empirical studies show that EO positive influence is heavily affected by many external environmental types (Covin & Slevin, 1989; Zahra & Covin, 1995) and internal company resources (Brush et al., 2001). Therefore, the study concludes that EO level affects the performance when the entrepreneurial intensity is realized in the form of strategic initiatives through innovation and market development programs.

6 CONCLUSIONS, LIMITATIONS, AND FUTURE RESEARCH

In general, the concept and literature on corporate parenting style, which was developed by Goold and Campbell (1987) and Goold et al. (1994), commonly run by multinational companies, can be implemented in family business groups. Yet, the implementation needs to consider a business unit structure with legally independent entities as specific characteristics of business units owned by family business groups in developing countries. Corporate parenting style implementation played by corporate centers in family business groups will have different effects on the EO level in business units, wherein a corporate center emphasizing strategic planning and strategic control approaches will have a positive influence on the EO level in business units, while emphasis on financial control approach has a negative influence on the EO level in business units.

Meanwhile, this research confirms that EO has indirect influences on business units' performance, and it is also affected by internal and external factors in business units, including the presence of strategic initiative programs as part of EO implementation owned by business unit leaders and employees.

There are some limitations in this study that should be taken into consideration in future research. First, family influence factor as a specific characteristic in family business groups that will affect the corporate center role and its influence on entrepreneurial activities in business units was not investigated. Therefore further research needs to be undertaken to measure the family influence on business unit's EO level. Secondly, in this research, the study was restricted to the influence of corporate parenting style toward EO that illustrates the tendency of strategic behaviors of business units, but not in the form of entrepreneurial activities. Therefore, the effects of corporate parenting style toward business units' strategic initiatives warrant further investigations.

REFERENCES

Ambos, T.C. & Birkinshaw, J. (2010). Headquarters' attention and its effect on subsidiary performance. *Management International Review*, *50*, 449–469.

Bandalos, D. (2002). The effects of item parceling on goodness-of-fit and parameter estimate bias in structural equation modeling. *Structural Equation Modeling*, *9*(1), 78–102.

Barringer, B.R. & Bluedorn, A.C. (1999). The relationship between corporate entrepreneurship and strategic management. *Strategic Management Journal*, *20*(5), 421–444.

Bartlett, C.A. & Ghoshal, S. (1997). The myth of the generic manager: New personal competencies for new management roles. *California Management Review*, *40*(1), 92–116.

Bindl, U.K. & Parker, S.K. (2011). Proactive work behavior: Forward-thinking and change-oriented action in organizations. *APA Handbook of Industrial and Organizational Psychology*, *2*(2), 567–598.

Birkinshaw, J. (1997). Entrepreneurship in multinational corporations: The characteristics of subsidiary initiatives. *Strategic Management Journal*, *18*(3), 207–229.

Brush, G., Greene, P. & Hart, M. (2001). From initial idea to unique advantage: The entrepreneurial challenge of constructing a resource base. *Academy of Management Perspectives*, *15*, 64–78.

Buchanan, R. & Sands, R. (1994). Creating an effective corporate centre: The influence of strategy on head office role. *European Business Journal*, *6*(4), 17–27.

Couto, V., Karlsson, P.O. & Neilson, G. (2008). *Putting headquarters in its place: A lean, global corporate core*. New York, NY: Booz & Company.

Covin, J.G. & Slevin, D.P. (1989). Strategic management of small firms in hostile and benign environments. *Strategic Management Journal*, *10*, 75–87.

Covin, J.G. & Slevin, D.P. (1991). A conceptual model of entrepreneurship as firm behavior. *Entrepreneurship Theory and Practice*, *16*, 7–25.

Covin, J.G., Slevin, D.P. & Schultz, R.L. (1994). Implementing strategic missions: Effective strategic, structural, and tactical choices. *Journal of Management Studies*, *31*(4), 481–503.

Delany, E. (2000). Strategic development of the multinational subsidiary through subsidiary initiative-taking. *Long Range Planning*, *33*, 220–244.

George, G., Wood, D.R., Jr., & Khan, R. (2001). Networking strategy of boards: Implications for small and medium-sized enterprises. *Entrepreneurship and Regional Development*, *13*(3), 269–285.

Goold, M. & Campbell, A. (1987). *Strategies and styles*. Oxford, UK: Blackwell.

Goold, M., Campbell, A. & Alexander, A. (1994). *Corporate-level strategy: Creating value in the multi-business company*. New York, NY: John Wiley & Sons.

Goold, M.A. & Luchs, K.S. (1996). *Managing the multibusiness company: Strategic issues for diversified groups.* London, UK: Routledge.
Hitt, M.A., Hoskisson, R.E. & Ireland, R.D. (1990). Mergers and acquisitions and managerial commitment to innovation in M-form firms. *Strategic Management Journal*, 11, 29–47.
Hitt, M.A., Hoskisson, R.E., Johnson, R.A. & Moesel, D.D. (1996). The market for corporate control and firm innovation. *Academy of Management Journal, 39*, 1084–1119.
Hitt, M., Hosskison, R. & Kim, H. (1997). International diversification: Effects on innovation and firm performance in product-diversified firms. *Academy of Management Journal, 40*, 767–798.
Hitt, M.A., Ireland, R.D., Sirmon, D.G. & Trahms, C.A. (2011). Strategic entrepreneurship: Creating value for individuals, organizations, and society. *Academy of Management Perspectives, 25*(2), 57–75.
Kellermanns, F.W. & Eddleston, K. (2006). Corporate venturing in family firms: Does the family matter? *Entrepreneurship Theory and Practice, 30*(6), 809–830.
Khanna, T. & Rivkin, J.W. (2001). Estimating the performance effects of business groups in emerging markets. *Strategic Management Journal, 22*, 45–74.
Liouka, I. (2007). *Opportunity identification in MNC subsidiaries: Context and performance implications* (Dissertation, University of Glasgow, UK).
Lumpkin, G.T. & Dess, G.G. (1996). Clarifying the entrepreneurial orientation construct and linking it to performance. *Academy of Management Review, 21*(1), 135–172.
Luo, B., Yu, J.J. & Ji, H.M. (2012). Empirical analysis of interactive control's effectiveness: A parent-subsidiary company's interdependence perspective. *iBusiness, 4*(3), 198–207.
Menz, M., Kunisch, S. & Collis, D. (2013). *What do we know about corporate headquarters? A review, integration, and research agenda.* Working Paper, Harvard Business School.
Miller, D. (1983). The correlates of entrepreneurship in three types of firms. *Management Science, 27*, 770–792.
Piana, D., Vecchi, A. & Cacia, C. (2012). Towards a better understanding of family business groups and their key dimensions. *Journal of Family Business Strategy, 3*(3), 174–192.
Ramachandran, J., Manikandan, K.S. & Pant, A. (2013). Why conglomerates thrive (outside the U.S.). *Harvard Business Review, December*, 110–119.
Rhemtulla, M. (2016). Population performance of SEM parceling strategies under measurement and structural model misspecification. *Psychological Methods, 21*(3), 348–368.
Schmid, S., Dzedek, L.R. & Lehre, M. (2014). From rocking the boat to wagging the dog: A literature review of subsidiary initiative research and integrative framework. *Journal of International Management, 20*, 201–218.
Scott, P.S., Gibbons, P.T. & Coughland, J. (2009). Developing subsidiary contribution on the MNC: Subsidiary entrepreneurship and strategy creativity. *Journal of International Management, 16*, 328–339.
Trapczynski, P. (2013). Does foreign direct investment theory explain subsidiary performance? A critical literature review. *Poznan University of Economic Review, 13*(2), 47–64.
Venkatraman, N. & Ramanujam, V. (1986). Measurement of business performance in strategy research: A comparison of approaches. *The Academy of Management Review, 11*(4), 801–814.
Wiklund, J. (1999). The sustainability of the entrepreneurial orientation–performance relationship. *Entrepreneurship Theory and Practice, 24*(1), 37–48.
Wiklund, J. & Shepherd, D. (2003). Knowledge-based resources, entrepreneurial orientation, and the performance of small and medium-sized businesses. *Strategic Management Journal, 24*, 1307–1314.
Wiklund, J. & Shepherd, D. (2005). Entrepreneurial orientation and small business performance: A configurational approach. *Journal of Business Venturing, 20*, 71–91.
Yabushita, N.W. & Suehiro, A. (2014). Family business groups in Thailand: Coping with management critical points. *Asia Pacific Journal of Management, 31*(4), 997–1018.
Yiu, D., Lu, Y., Bruton, G.D. & Hoskisson, R.E. (2007). Business groups: An integrated model to focus future research. *Journal of Management Studies, 44*, 1551–1579.
Zahra, S. & Covin, J.G. (1995). Contextual influences on the corporate entrepreneurship-performance relationship: A longitudinal analysis. *Journal of Business Venturing, 10*, 43–58.
Zahra, S.A., Dharwadkar, R. & George, G. (2000). *Entrepreneurship in multinational subsidiaries. The effect of corporate and local environmental contexts.* Department of Management, J. Mack Robinson College of Business, Georgia State University, Atlanta.
Zahra, S.A., Jennings, D.F. & Kuratko, D.F. (1999). The antecedents and consequences of firm-level entrepreneurship: The state of the field. *Entrepreneurship Theory and Practice, 24*(2), 45–65.
Zeng, Z.H. (2007). *The determinants of MNC subsidiary's autonomy and initiative: An empirical study of MNC subsidiary in Taiwan* (PhD thesis, National Sun Yat-sen University, Kaohsiung, Taiwan).

Increasing Management Relevance and Competitiveness – Sukoco et al. (Eds)
© 2018 Taylor & Francis Group, London, ISBN 978-0-8153-7455-8

Developing entrepreneurship for the performing arts community through an art incubation model

J. Masunah & R. Milyartini
Universitas Pendidikan Indonesia, Bandung, Indonesia

ABSTRACT: The purpose of this article is to explore entrepreneurship development for the performing arts community through an art incubation model. The aim of the art incubation model is to search for a strategy in developing entrepreneurship, increase the quality of performing arts production, and access the performing arts market. A project-based research method was used to analyze, create the art incubation model, implement and evaluate it. This research involved 15 participants in the first phase. In the second phase, the activity involved eight communities in creating their professional identity and productions. This research finds that the art incubation model fits arts incubator typology. In this model, there are the roles of the accelerator, the institution, the mentors, and the program initiatives in nurturing the communities to change their world view of the performing arts industry and accelerate their productions to be market-driven.

1 INTRODUCTION

The background of the research project was concern about the problems for the performing arts in entering the era of the creative economy. The main problem is the weakness of its ecosystem (Masunah, 2014). The ecosystem of performing arts begins with education, creation, production, distribution, consumption, and appreciation. Most higher education facilities that educate prospective art performers offer courses on how to lead students to create and produce their performing art, but, how to distribute and market their production is still a problem. Therefore, the purpose of this research is to seek a strategy to increase the quality of production and to access the performing arts market in order to distribute the performing arts productions to the stakeholders appropriately.

The Ministry of Tourism and Creative Economy facilitated an event to market Indonesia's performing arts productions in 2013 which is called the Indonesia Performing Arts Market (IPAM). According to Masunah (2017), there were 31 groups of art performers from Bogor, Jakarta, Bali, Surakarta, Jogjakarta, Aceh, Padang, and Riau. The ministry also invited buyers from many countries, including Indonesia, Korea, Japan, the USA, the United Kingdom, China, Finland, and Australia. Unfortunately, the performers from Bandung did not participate in the event. It is known that Bandung has a lot of artists and creative performer communities. The research project was conducted from May to October 2016 to develop entrepreneurship involving performing arts communities in Bandung, West Java.

The President's regulation Number 27 Year 2013, about entrepreneurship incubator development, regulates the mechanism for the institutions that will develop entrepreneurship programs (Yudhoyono, 2013). However, the regulation does not guide the incubation process. In this research, the use of art incubation models to nurture performing arts communities to build the capacity of entrepreneurs was explored. The goal is for the performing arts communities in Bandung to gain value-add in their business.

2 LITERATURE REVIEW

The Ministry of Tourism and Creative Economy 2012–2014, along with the National Statistics Board of Indonesia (NSBI), created the standard classification of entrepreneurship field for the creative industry sector. The field of performing arts entrepreneurship is categorized as "arts, entertainment, and recreation" and "entertainment, arts, and creativity" (BPS, 2014). In this case, entrepreneurship incubator development regulated by the Government of Indonesia is related to the efforts to build and maintain entrepreneurship start-up to meet the standard classification.

According to Pauwels et al. (2015), the accelerator is similar in concept to the role of the Intermediation Institution that is regulated by the Indonesian Government. Pauwels et al. explained that the new generation of incubation model is an organization that serves to mentor start-up entrepreneurs. This organization has mentors, programs, and locations for conducting the activities. The mentors are those who are capable of delivering a consultation for the start-up entrepreneurs. The location is the place for people to run the activities of incubation. The viewpoint of Pauwels et al. changed the concept of the traditional incubation model which provides physical and funding assistance for the tenants. In the new generation of incubation model, the accelerator serves as a consultant and mentor for the start-up entrepreneurs to connect with stakeholders.

Essig (2014) discussed the arts incubator typology. The arts incubator is defined as an organizational form or programmatic initiative concerning artistic production and entrepreneurship. The arts incubator typologies are: art incubator, community development incubator, commercial incubator, and student venture incubator. The art incubator is a type of institution which provides assistance to individual artists and art organizations to develop and sustain their artistic work. The community development incubator works with artists, art organizations, craft people, and small business owners to build and sustain a vibrant, diverse, engaging, inclusive, and safe community. The commercial incubator relates to creative industry entrepreneurs and aims to help arts-oriented businesses to start and grow. The student venture incubator works for student artists as education through investment in student creativity and innovation.

While Pauwel and Essig discussed the institutions which conduct the incubation activity, Klerk (2015) discussed the activity as an entrepreneurial bricolage. The bricolage contains a strategy to construct the behavior of the creative industry actors. The concept of bricolage regards the collaboration and relation among the actors as an effort to gain a short-term goal. The ideas, skills, attitudes, and vision of the individual actors will be blended in the collaborative activity to sustain creativity and network. To implement the concept of entrepreneurial bricolage appropriate education and training for the actors is needed.

Education and training are also important for the actors to strengthen their "professional identity" (Lindgren & Packendorff, 2007). In this effort, there is the institution which conducts the incubation activity as a process of educating and training the actors in the field of performing arts.

3 RESEARCH METHODOLOGY

This research adopted the qualitative paradigm, in which the project-based research method was implemented. According to Stoecker (2005), one of the characteristics of this method focuses on social change of individuals, organizations, communities, regions, and even society. The important point of the project is to help people in making a difference to their lives. The procedure of the method begins with diagnosing some problems after which the change agents develop a prescription or plan, which is implemented, and the final step is an evaluation.

The participants of the research included the tenants, mentors, and the researchers. The mentors were experts who were invited by the Intermediation Institution. The researchers actively worked for the Intermediation Institution and served the tenants during the incubation process. The tenants were the individual performers and representatives of performing arts communities in Bandung who applied for incubation activity.

The location of the research was in *Universitas Pendidikan Indonesia* (UPI), 229 Setiabudi Street, Bandung 40154. The Center of Women Studies, Arts and Culture at UPI had the role as the Intermediation Institution or the accelerator which conducted the incubation process.

For data collection, participatory observation, interview, documentary analysis, and Focus Group Discussion (FGD) was used. In the analysis, the data from interview, observation, and documentation was triangulated, with data from the FGD used to strengthen the triangulation analysis. After this the data was interpreted to answer the research questions.

4 FINDINGS AND DISCUSSION

The research was conducted in the form of a project with two phases of activities. Because the first phase of the activities has already been reported by Masunah and Milyartini (2016), in this article the data of the previous article is elaborated with that of the second phase of activity.

4.1 *Diagnosing the problems of the tenants*

The first step of the project was to analyze the tenants and learn about their problems. We analyzed the data from the 15 participants who participated in the first phase of the activities. These 15 people consisted of individual artists and performers, as well as the representatives of arts organizations, who have a background in the field of dance, music, theater, fine arts, and literature. Their problems were concerned with their lack of understanding of the values of the creative industry sector, in particular, how to distribute their works to the market. In addition, they lacked experience in accessing the performing arts markets, both nationally and internationally.

In the second phase, the eight tenants who already had business plans were diagnosed. The plans were for ideas or works of performing arts. There were five people representing arts organizations: Irwan Fitriawan from the Bintara Art and Education Company; Wildan Kurnia from the Shocking Rajah Performing Arts Community; the Leader or *Lurah* of Bumi Siliwangi Big Family, or *Keluarga Besar Bumi Siliwangi* (KABUMI) *Universitas Pendidikan Indonesia* (UPI); Ayo Sunaryo from Arga Studio; and Tono Rachmat from Semar Arts House Studio. There were also three individual artists, namely, Indra Gandara, E. Dikara Jawad, and Asep Kusmana.

Through the process of discussion with the experts and the tenants, three main problems for the tenants were found: a lack of reference for their ideas, no in-depth research, and a lack of execution for implementing their ideas. Funding to increase the quality of their performing arts productions also remained a problem for all tenants.

4.2 *Creating a prescription for solving the problems*

For solving the problems of the tenants, the art incubation model offered by Essig (2014) was developed. There are four components in this model: the institution, mentors, the program initiative, and funding.

The program initiatives have three steps of activities, namely discussion, collaboration, and presentation. The purpose of discussion is to increase the tenants' knowledge about the performing arts industry, the quality of performing arts productions, and their market. Also, the discussion activity served as a medium for sharing knowledge and experiences about the production process, as well as distribution to the markets.

The collaborative activities were arranged to achieve the short-term goals of the arts performers, that is, to build a group of entrepreneurs and create high-quality productions. Klerk's ideas about bricolage (2015) led to the collaborative activity among individual performers to produce works of performing arts. The target was to present the performing arts productions at the Bandung Isola Performing Arts Festival (BIPAF). BIPAF is one of the local performing arts markets conducted by the Faculty of Arts and Design Education, UPI.

The presentation activity first exposed the business planning, such as the tenants' creative ideas and/or their creative works of performing arts. The mentors evaluated the works in terms of whether they met the criteria for artistic and aesthetic demands, and if so, the tenants then recreated their works to be performed at the festival.

4.3 *Implementing the art incubation model*

The first phase to implement the art incubation model was from 20–21 May 2016. The form of activity was similar to a workshop. It was a very short time in comparison to the second phase which lasted from June to October, 2016.

4.3.1 *The discussion session*

The discussion activity began on 20 May 2016. The accelerator facilitated this activity for sharing knowledge and experiences between the five experts and the 15 tenants. The experts were Rama Thaharani, Eki Puradireja, Eko Supriyanto, Wiwied C59, and Juju Masunah. Rama Thaharani is the Director of the "*Seni Sini Sana*" (literally, Arts Here There) community; an independent producer who worked for IPAM 2013, and one of the organizers for the UK National Tour 2015. Thaharani discussed national and international performing arts markets. Eki Puradireja is a Creative Director and Consultant for Electric Ocean in Jakarta, and a producer, and was one of the curators for the Java Jazz Festival in 2004–2014. Puradireja discussed the music industry, and then shared his experiences in producing, distributing, and marketing his music. Eko Supriyanto is a choreographer and a dance educator at the Indonesia Arts Institute in Surakarta. He talked about his experiences creating the "*Jailolo*" festival and contemporary performing arts based on in-depth research of local cultures, in particular for the "Cry Jailolo" piece. Wiwied C59 presented his experiences on how to build entrepreneurship and become a successful entrepreneur in the T-Shirt industry in Bandung. Juju Masunah is the leader of the Center for Women, Arts, and Culture Studies, and a dance educator in the Department of Dance Education, UPI, as well as the team leader of this research. Masunah initiated BIPAF in Bandung and shared the concept of 'festival' as the local market for the works of performing arts created by the tenants.

The second discussion was held in two sessions, which were on 15–16 June and 26 August, 2016. The researchers discussed the follow-up of the incubation activity in the first phase with the tenants. The experts recommended implementing the business plan of the eight tenants. The researchers explored the appropriate venues for the festival at UPI in Jalan Setiabudi 229 Bandung and Institut Seni dan Budaya Indonesia (ISBI), or Indonesia Arts and Culture Institute Bandung, located on Jalan Buah Batu 212 Bandung.

Based on the characteristic of the tenants' works, the researchers offered both outdoor and indoor stages for BIPAF 2016. UPI's venue had the outdoor stages in front of the National Museum of Education, "Isola Heritage Building", and amphitheater, while the indoor stages were in the Amphitheater of UPI and the Sunan Ambu Auditorium in ISBI Bandung. In this discussion, four tenants were directed to the indoor stage, and the other four tenants explored the outdoor stages.

4.3.2 *Collaboration session*

The first collaboration session was on 21 May 2016, in the first phase of the art incubation activity. The researchers encouraged the 15 tenants to collaborate with each other to form groups and discuss the business plans. At the end of the art incubation activity in the first phase, eight tenants who would continue attending the art incubation in the second phase were chosen.

Klerk's ideas about bricolage were mentioned by the eight tenants in the second collaboration session from June to October, 2016. They collaborated with individual artists and other arts groups outside of those who had participated in the art incubation activity. The purpose of their collaboration was to produce the works of performing arts for BIPAF 2016.

Fitriawan worked with other musicians. Wildan Kurnia collaborated with a music group called "Wirahma" and the individual dancers from UPI. The Wirahma music group also worked with Indra Gandara. Asep Kusmana worked with Hendra Permana and two other artists to form a group. Tono Rachmat worked with Riau's community in Bandung. E. Dikara explored his music with a pianist, and he invited four musicians to work on another music piece. KABUMI UPI was the biggest group of angklung music in the art incubation activity. They worked with their own group to produce *angklung* music. Ayo Sunaryo focused on children's dance.

4.3.3 *Presentation session*

The goal of presentation activity is to showcase the tenants' pre-production or the business plan as well as the final production. The accelerator invited three mentors who were experienced with national and the international performing arts markets, namely Rama Thaharani, Eko Supriyanto, and Eki Puradireja. The mentors had the important role of reviewing the tenants' works conceptually and aesthetically, in particular, how to attract public audiences for their performances. In this project, the target audiences were also the venue presenters, festival directors, and other stakeholders who have events.

In the first phase of art incubation activity, Tono Rachmat, Asep Kusmana, and E. Dikara Jawad presented their creative ideas, while the five tenants presented their works of performing arts. According to the mentors, the three musicians had a specific problem in expressing their ideas, while the five tenants' works of performing art needed to be recreated because they remained too safe. The mentors also suggested the tenants conduct in-depth research and watch other performances as references. They commented that although the ideas of the tenants were strong, they were weak in execution.

On 20 September 2016, three mentors were invited. Eko Supriyanto and Eki Puradireja were present; however, Rama Thaharani was absent. The eight tenants presented the progress of their productions in front of the two mentors. One month later, on October 21–23, 2016, the eight performing arts productions were performed at BIPAF. They had two forms of presentation: a tourism package and a showcase of performing arts.

Soedarsono's criteria of arts tourism (1999) includes variation of the repertoires at the same time. Therefore, the performance included *angklung* music from KABUMI UPI, a children's dance created by Ayo Sunaryo, and other pieces of the repertoire, such as *Kroncong* music, Shaman, and *Piring* dances. On October 21, 2016, the showcase presented Irwan Fitriawan and Wildan Kurnia. On the same stage, there were poetry, and Parkpark's group. On October 22, 2016, Indra Gandara, Asep Kusmana, and E. Dikara Jawad performed in the Sunan Ambu Auditorium, ISBI Bandung, while Tono Rachmat performed in the amphitheater of UPI.

Eki Puradiredja was the only mentor who watched the performances at BIPAF 2016. He was surprised that the performing arts productions resulting from the art incubation activity had a lot of changes, in which compared to the first and second presentations, the works were performed even better and more artistically at BIPAF.

4.4 *Evaluation of the project*

During the six months of the art incubation project, the exchange of ideas and behavior of the eight tenants was very dynamic. Their changes can be identified in three aspects: their worldview of the performing arts market, professional identity of the performing arts communities, and their productions.

The evaluation of the first phase of the art incubation activity was focused on the 15 tenants. The result of the interviews showed that initially 70% of the tenants had no knowledge about the performing arts market, while 30% of the tenants understood how to distribute their works, but they had limited access to the market for performing arts. After the art incubation activity, all the tenants gained knowledge about the performing arts market. Eight of the tenants worked intensively to increase the quality of their productions, and worked collaboratively with other artists and performers to build start-up entrepreneurs.

Asep Kusmana (32). Kusmana created a piece of performance art and built a group as a start-up entrepreneur called the "Ulin Theater Community." This community involved four people: Hendra Permana as an actor, Erice Mantri as a multimedia person, Ali Nurdin as the person responsible for the artistic elements, and Asep Kusmana as a manager and artistic director. They created a piece of theater called "*Kelas Dua* [The Second Class]". This work of performance art raises the social issue of the impact of garments' industrialization in Subang. Kusmana used a film with screen media to represent the changing social situation from an agricultural to an industrial one. This piece was done with body images and multimedia to create symbols. The monologue of "*Kelas Dua*" was distributed on Facebook and YouTube.

Indra Gandara (24). For his incubation activity, he presented "*Jagat Suwung*". Gandara received a good response from the mentors in terms of the research, however, the mentors also commented that Gandara's piece was weak in execution. Gandara combined two styles of traditional movements represented by female dancers and movement explorations by three male dancers. The female dancers represented the agricultural contexts, while the male dancers represented the change in atmosphere to the industrial context through representation of the empty feeling of an individualistic situation. The mentors asked Gandara to stay with the contemporary issue, particularly "with how people feel empty as an effect of the industrialization in Sukabumi, West Java", said Thaharani. Gandara also formed a start-up dance company called *Warangka*.

E. Dikara Jawas (23). Dikara explored the sound of *kacapi* to be transferred to Western instruments like the cello and piano. The first exploration lasted for four minutes. During the incubation process, it was extended to 14 minutes. Dikara had a personal consultant work on his piece, in addition to the mentors who were invited by the institution. Then, Dikara worked on another piece with another composer, Bani Ambara. Afterwards, Dikara built a group called *Sauyunan Music Company* (*Sauyunan* is a word from Sundanese language that means working together with peace). This company presented two pieces at the BIPAF festival. Dikara explained that becoming a participant in the incubation activity had helped him create the music and build the music company.

Irwan Fitriawan (35). Fitriawan created many choreographies based on traditional dance movements, including the *Belekok* dance. This dance is inspired by the wild white birds which are usually found in the rice fields or swamp areas. The population of the birds is diminishing because the ecosystem of Belekok in Rancabiyawak, Rancaekek, Bandung has been destroyed. During the incubation process, Fitriawan created a new piece of *Belekok*, called "*belekok gugat*" (the word *gugat* originates from Sundanese and means asking for help). Fitriawan performed as a solo dancer using the pool as the outdoor stage. The movements expressed the critical environmental issue. Fitriawan was very proud of the "*Belekok Gugat*" dance, because he could change the traditional style to a contemporary one. He also received an invitation from a person in Bandung Barat to create a dance for a festival.

Wildan Kurnia (30). Kurnia created a piece called "*Sinom Barataning Rasa*". This work was inspired by the literary work created by Ali Haji. This work is an interdisciplinary dance theater. When this piece was presented on May 21, 2016, the mentors were impressed by his research. However, the mentors suggested he pay attention to the symbols, because they were different in meanings and interpretation from Kurnia's expectation. During the incubation process, Kurnia stuck to the previous concept. When he staged the dance in the front of Isola Heritage building for BIPAF, Kurnia developed the structure of its choreography to fit the unique outdoor stage with its gate, sculpture, and big tree. The gamelan music with Cirebonan and Sundanese flute was mixed artistically with lighting composition. The atmosphere was mystical. There was no distance between the dancers and the audiences. According to Kurnia, "the responses of audiences also were part of the performance".

KABUMI UPI (31). KABUMI presented a variety of songs, including how to play *angklung*. KABUMI had 40 minutes each day for its performance at BIPAF, from 21 until 23 October 2016, with the songs *Lalajo Wayang*, *Es Lilin*, and "Phantom of The Opera". The performance included the dances from Aceh and Minang as well as children's dances. After the performances, audiences from Malaysia immediately asked KABUMI to go to Malaysia to perform, because they were impressed.

Tono Rachmat (54). In the incubation activity, Rachmat presented an idea to create music and dance inspired by the style of Malay from West Sumatera. The concept is related to the destroyed green forests in Riau caused by fire. Rachmat explained that the music and dance contain symbols that represent Malay Culture. The mentors recommended Rachmat and his colleagues restructure the choreography based on Rachmat's ideas about the concepts of the universe. The collaborative work of music and dance was finally performed at BIPAF October 22, 2016. Surprisingly, after the performance, Rachmat's piece was invited to perform at the festival of *Anak Bunga Bandung* 206 in Citylink and for the event of the Bandung Declaration for NKRI held by the National Intelligence Board.

Ayo Sunaryo (39). For the art incubation activity Sunaryo explored a children's dance with an indoor stage. The mentors suggested that Sunaryo present the children's dance in a natural setting in order to get the original expression of the children's dance. Then, the children's dance was presented at BIPAF together with KABUMI's presentation in a tourism event on October 21, 2016.

Through the art incubation model, a change of viewpoints and responsive behaviors of the tenants and increased quality of the works was evident. Three tenants, Asep Kusmana, Indra Gandara, and E. Dikara, only had ideas at the beginning of the incubation activity. Surprisingly, they changed their viewpoint from being individual performers to building community entrepreneurship and creating performing arts productions. Two tenants, Indra Gandara, and Irwan Fitriawan, who created a mixture between traditional movements and contemporary ones, changed their works into fully contemporary movements. Three tenants, Asep Kusmana, Tono Rachmat, and Dikara, changed their ideas into performing arts productions which the audiences could enjoy for 30–40 minutes. Wildan Kurnia and Ayo Sunaryo changed the context of the performance because they had an outdoor stage. The eight performing arts communities presented their works at BIPAF 2016 and built networking with stakeholders.

5 SUMMARY

This project-based research has constructed the art incubation model. There are important components in this model, namely: 1) the institution; 2) the mentors who have knowledge and experience in the performing arts industry and who can nurture the tenants; 3) program initiatives based on the tenants' problems; 4) the target for performance; and 5) funding. The mentors nurtured the tenants to be open to the world, to focus their ideas based on research, and to rework their performing arts based on reflection and critiques. The tenants were also motivated to work collaboratively to improve and gain new visions. Mentoring the tenants based on their problems helped to improve the quality of their works. The goal of presenting the performing arts at the festival motivated the tenants in two ways: to produce the work in a timely manner and to widely broaden their markets. The concept of bricolage grew in the limited time and funding, but the tenants' visions were realized in the target of the festival. In other words, the five components are related to each other in the process of art incubation.

The art incubation model involves four activities which are: 1) selecting the tenants, 2) conducting the workshop, 3) mentoring the tenants to create the works consistently, and 4) evaluating the works in the festival. The implementation of this model has resulted in the creation of professional identities as start-up entrepreneurs in the performing arts industry. This model has enriched the arts incubator typology offered by Essig (2014), which has strength in the artistic performance of performing arts.

REFERENCES

BPS. (2014). *Klasifikasi Baku Lapangan Usaha Indonesia (KBLI) Bidang Ekonomi Kreatif.* Jakarta, Indonesia: The Ministry of Tourism and Creative Economy & The Central Statistics Board.

Essig, L. (2014). Arts incubators: A typology. *The Journal of Arts Management, Law, and Society*, *44*, 169–180.

Klerk, S.D. (2015). The creative industries: An entrepreneurial bricolage perspective. *Management Decision*, *53*(4), 828–842. doi:10.1108/MD-03-2014-0169.

Lindgren, M. & Packendorff, J. (2007). Performing arts and the art of performing – On co-construction of project work and professional identities in theater. *International Journal of Project Management*, *25*(4), 354–364.

Masunah, J. (2014). *Program dan Kegiatan Direktorat Pengembangan Seni Pertunjukan dan Industri Musik 2014* [*Programs and Activities of Directorate of Performing Arts and Music Industry Development 2014*]. Jakarta, Indonesia: Directorate of Performing Arts and Music Industry Development.

Masunah, J. (2017). Creative industry: Two cases of performing arts market in Indonesia and South Korea. *Humaniora*, *29*(1), 108–118.

Masunah, J. & Milyartini, R. (2016). Building entrepreneurship in performing arts industry through the incubation model. In *Creating innovation, and value added business: 1st global conference on business management, and entrepreneurship, Universitas Pendidikan Indonesia, Bandung, Indonesia* (pp. 838–843). Paris, France: Atlantis Press.

Pauwels, C., Clarysse, B., Wright, M. & Van Hove, J. (2015). Understanding a new generation incubation model: The accelerator. *Technovation, 50–51*, 13–24. doi:10.1016/j.technovation.2015.09.003.

Soedarsono, R.M. (1999). *Seni Pertunjukan dan Pariwisata* [*Performing Arts and Tourism*]. Jogjakarta, Indonesia: MSPI.

Stoecker, S. (2005). *Research methods for community change*. Thousand Oaks, CA: Sage Publications.

Yudhoyono. S.B. (2013). *Peraturan Presiden Nomor 27 Tahun 2013 Tentang Pengembangan Inkubator Wirausaha* [*President's Regulation Number 27 Year 2013 about Entrepreneurship Incubator Development*]. Jakarta, Indonesia.

Increasing Management Relevance and Competitiveness – Sukoco et al. (Eds)
© 2018 Taylor & Francis Group, London, ISBN 978-0-8153-7455-8

Capability to contest on market performance

B.M. Sukoco & R.R. Maulana
Universitas Airlangga, Sarabaya, Indonesia

ABSTRACT: Competitive asymmetry—the notion that two firms may not view their relationship or interaction in the marketplace equally—is very prevalent in business competition. Simply put, a firm's managers and outside stakeholders will perceive the rival with the resource profile most similar to the firm's own and/or with the highest salience regarding the resources critical to the firm's operations as posing the greatest challenge to the firm's operational capability and, therefore, as imposing the greatest competitive tension. This study examines the effect of capability to contest, similarity and salience, on market performance in a broadcasting industry. Based on the secondary data released by Nielsen Research, this study adopted conceptualizations of competitive dynamics. The results indicate that greater similarity among TV stations leads to higher TV ratings, while the opposite effect applies on salience. Further analysis indicates that there is an interaction effect between similarity and salience. There is a slight difference between high and low salience when the similarity between the two TV stations exists, while low similarity indicates that greater salience leads to lower TV ratings. Academic and managerial implications are further discussed in this study.

Keywords: Capability to Contest, Salience, Similarity, Competitive Dynamics and Broadcasting Industry

1 INTRODUCTION

Competitor analysis occupies a central place in strategy and organizational research (Smith et al. 2001; Hitt et al. 2007). Scholars have investigated various definitions of a firm's competitors (Reger & Huff 1993; Porac et al. 1995). Defining or identifying competitors is an important, but complicated task that involves careful evaluation of the tension between a focal firm and each of its competitors (Chen et al. 2007). Without such evaluation, a firm may underestimate the threat posed by a competitor or inadvertently allow a rival to go unnoticed (Zajac & Bazerman 1991). Important contributions have been made in refining competitor definitions and identifications, however, the literature continues to be constrained by an approach that centers on the focal firm.

Based on competitive dynamics as the study of interfirm rivalry based on specific competitive actions and reactions, their strategic and organizational contexts, and their drivers and consequences are addressed (Baum & Korn 1996). The identification of a firm's rivals are based either on objective criteria (e.g. industry or group affiliation, size or market share, customer overlap) (Ang 2008; Baum & Lant 2003) or on perceptions or opinions of the firm's strategies (Chen, Su et al. 2007; Tsai et al 2011). This study employs objective criteria to examine the effect of competitive interaction on action-level studies to determine market performance. An action is defined as a specific and detectable market move initiated by a firm, such as introducing a new product or entering a new market; such actions may erode a rival's market share or reduce its anticipated returns. A response is a specific and datable countermove, prompted by an initial action that a firm takes to defend or improve its share or profit position in its industry (Lee et al 2003; Boyd & Bresser 2008).

In the context of interfirm competition, the most salient relationship is *market engagement*, which reflects the extent to which the members of a pair of firms interact and engage in each other's markets as well as the strategic importance of these markets from both a focal firm and the target rival's perspectives (Chen 1996). As many studies have suggested, two firms come to know one another through competitive interactions in different markets and, more importantly, the way they engage in each other's markets shapes their respective perceptions and behaviors in the competitive arena (Baum & Korn 1996; Gimeno 1999).

Competitive asymmetry—the notion that two firms may not view their relationship or interaction in the marketplace equally—is very prevalent in business competition (Chen 1996; DeSarbo et al. 2006). It is unlikely, for example, that two rivals will perceive every competitive action or relationship in the same way. Due to differences in assumptions about industry outlook and disparate organizational arrangements and preferences, rivals may differ in their views of their competitive relationship (Tsai et al. 2011), which might result in different outcomes for the competing firms.

Simply put, a firm's managers and outside stakeholders will perceive the rival with the resource profile most similar to the firm's own and/or with the highest salience regarding the resources critical to the firm's operations as posing the greatest challenge to the firm's operational capability - and, therefore, as imposing the greatest competitive tension (Chen et al. 2007). The inclusion of similarity and salience considerations in the conceptualization of this construct is in line with Porac and Thomas's observation: "Two organizations are similar if they share important attributes and hence tap the same resources in the task environment. Because critical resources are usually scarce, similar organizations are usually competitively interdependent" (Porac & Thomas 1990).

The awareness motivation capability (AMC) framework of competitive dynamics provides an integrative model of the three key behavioral drivers that shape a competitor's actions and responses (Chen 1996; Smith et al. 2001; Grimm et al. 2006; Yu & Cannella 2007). Simply stated, a competitor will not be able to respond to an action unless it is aware of the action, motivated to react and capable of responding (Chen et al. 2007). This study focuses on capability to respond, in which capability is signaled by a rival's capability to contest (defined as the operational ability of a given rival to challenge a focal firm in the marketplace) and describes the rival's relative resource-deployment ability (compared with the focal firm's); this ability, in turn, influences assessments of the intensity of the competitive relationship by both the firm's managers and industry stakeholders (Chen et al. 2007).

Baum and Korn (1996, 1999) showed that for competitors in a dyad, rates of competitive market entry and exit increased with the degree of overlap between their market domains. Researchers were able to demonstrate empirically that these attributes of response were functions of three different characteristics: (1) attributes of the attack, such as difficulty of implementation, the amount of effort and time required for execution, and the visibility or degree of industry attention (Young et al. 1996); (2) characteristics of the attacker, such as the degree of organizational commitment to the attack (Chen et al. 1992); and (3) characteristics of the defender, such as a competitor's dependence or a defender's stake in the market under attack (Baum & Korn 1999). The research also demonstrated the performance consequences of different types of competitive interactions (Young et al. 1996; Smith et al. 2001; Boyd & Bresser 2008).

Given the role of perceived tension in competitor analysis, it is essential to identify its key antecedents. According to the awareness-motivation-capability perspective, three behavioral drivers influence a firm's decision to act or respond: awareness, motivation and capability (Chen 1996). In competitive dynamics research (Smith et al. 2001), individual awareness-motivation-capability components are manifested in a range of variables, including action visibility and firm size (Chen & Miller 1994) for awareness; territorial interests in different markets (Gimeno 1999) for motivation; and execution difficulty and information processing (Smith et al. 1991) for capability. This study focuses on the role of capability to contest, which is stated under explored in many studies (Chen & Miller 2012) and also the original dimension of competitive dynamics (Chen 1996). In addition, Chen and Miller (1994) found positive interaction effects between various triggers of competitive response, in this case capability to contest, which needs further investigation in this study.

2 HYPOTHESES DEVELOPMENT

The extent to which a rival's operational capability potentially challenges a focal firm in the marketplace (either with an attack or by responding to the focal firm's action) is a critical factor influencing market performance (Tsai et al. 2011). Each of a focal firm's rivals is endowed with various types and amounts of resources that are vital for its operation; consequently, each is equipped with different capabilities, in the eyes of the firm's managers and industry stakeholders, in its engagements with the firm. A rival's capability to contest derives mainly from two distinct, but closely related, circumstances (Chen et al. 2007). Similarity refers to when the rival and the focal firm have highly similar resource profiles, while salience occurs when the rival is a significant player in terms of the resource(s) the focal firm values most for its operation.

To elaborate, firms with similar resource profiles are likely to have comparable capabilities and competitive stances (Miller & Shamsie 1996), and competitors with similar strategies and structures impose great pressure on each other (Heil & Robertson 1991). Consequently, a focal firm's managers and industry stakeholders are likely to consider a rival with a similar operations resource profile to be a direct competitor. These arguments are in line with Gimeno and Woo's (1996) finding of a positive relationship between the strategic similarity of firms and the degree of their rivalry, and with Chen's (1996) prediction that the greater the resource similarity between a rival and a focal firm, the greater the likelihood that the rival will attack (or retaliate against) the firm. In the case of market performance in a TV industry, similarity resources lead a focal TV station which uses a similar program to its rival to generate better TV ratings. The better TV ratings generated by its rival indicate that viewers are familiar with and enjoy the show. Consequently, TV ratings will increase due to familiarity of the viewers with particular TV shows. Thus:

H_1: *Greater similarity between two TV stations increases the level of TV ratings, while smaller similarity reduces TV ratings.*

Resources that are essential for operational and competitive success are generally limited and scarce within an industry (Barney 1991). A rival's capability to contest a focal firm is determined by how salient the rival is in relation to resources that a focal firm values for its operation. Therefore, capability to contest is conditioned both by the strategic importance of a given resource to the focal firm's operation and by the rival's strength in this resource. Two firms which are head-on opponents will experience, in the eyes of their internal and external stakeholders, great tension if they rely on similar resources for operation and, more fundamentally, if each is a salient player in competing for the resources that are vital to the other (Chen 1996). When the TV program is salient for a focal TV station, it might endanger its TV ratings when a similar TV program also has salience for its rival. In the supply side, they will compete to get the best talent (when they produce in-house, such as actresses or producers) or TV programs (when they outsource to production houses). As a result, the production costs will increase and, at the same time, viewers have alternatives to watch the best TV programs at a similar time. Consequently, their TV ratings might reduce due to fierce competition between the two. Therefore:

H_2: *Greater salience between two TV stations reduces the level of TV ratings, while smaller salience increases TV ratings.*

In addition to the independent effect each salience and similarity has on market performance, there are likely to be interaction effects. Drawing on Vroom's (1964) expectancy-valence theory, Chen and Miller (1994) found positive interaction effects between various triggers of competitive response. Obviously, the high similarity and lower salience leads to higher TV ratings than any other conditions. On the contrary, low similarity and high salience leads to lower TV ratings than any other conditions. Therefore:

H_3: *There is an interaction between salience and similarity. High similarity and low salience level lead to higher TV ratings, while high salience and low similarity lead to lower TV ratings.*

3 RESEARCH METHOD

3.1 *Research context*

Our sample included ten private TV stations competing against each other during the period 2013. The broadcasting industry was an ideal research context because of the rich sources of public information, well-defined markets, and acknowledged intense competition among major players (Smith et al. 1991; Gimeno 1999). We chose this period because it was characterized by the rapid entry of new private TV stations, either national or local ones, and by the expansion of existing TV stations into new routes, followed by an industry consolidation through mergers and acquisitions (Morrison & Winston 1995). The period was also prior to the drop of TV advertising expenditure due to the sudden increase in Internet advertising expenditure beginning in 2014. In addition, this study mainly focused on prime time, which is from 6 pm until 10 pm. The reason is that, since this time frame attracts more than 50% of viewers and therefore also greater advertising expenditure.

The advertisement expenditure in Indonesia is dominated by TV (for about 64%) in which it grows 15.2% annually (emarketer.com 2013). In 2014, it reached $11.18 billion and increased to $14.21 billion in 2016 (zenithoptimedia.com 2014). Since the market penetration of cable TV is not big, about 5%, (Nugroho et al. 2012), then the money is mostly taken up among the ten free-to-air TV stations and distributed based on their rating (market share).

The television industry in Indonesia first aired on August 24, 1962 (with the help of NHK Japan), to broadcast Asian Games which were held in Jakarta (Ishadi 2014). After Soeharto took up the presidential position in 1966, TVRI (Television of the Republic of Indonesia) under the Ministry of Information, enjoyed a monopoly status to unite and inspire people to support the government's development programs. Sequentially, the government allowed five commercial TV stations to be established and aired nationally: RCTI (1987), SCTV (1989), TPI (1990), ANTV (1993), and Indosiar (1995). These were the first wave of commercial TV stations in Indonesia.

As the number of TV sets increased rapidly from 7.6 million in 1990 to about 20 million in 1997 (d'Haenens et al. 2000), the five recently-launched commercial TV stations aggressively competed for a share of the growing audience and an expanding advertising market (Hollander et al. 2009).

Without commercial revenues, the conventional TVRI could not compete to attract audiences, particularly when the five new stations offered combinations of drama series, sitcoms, and "soft news".

Transparency in media came into force when the new government issued deregulation that changed the landscape dramatically (Kitley 2003), through issuing 1200 new printing licenses, 900 new commercial radio licenses, and five newcomers to national commercial TV (Metro TV, Trans TV, Global TV, TV7, and LaTivi). Unlike the first wave, the owners of the new TV stations had no direct relationships with the regime and came from diverse backgrounds. For example, Bakrie Group owned ANTV and acquired LaTivi (which became TV One in 2008) with no background in the media industry. A banker owned Trans TV and Kompas Gramedia Group, which owned TV7, was a big publishing company which had twice been closed down by Soeharto's regime, before being taken over by Trans TV in 2006. Besides these five new national TV stations, the Act also attracted many broadcasters to develop local TV (more than 240 local TV stations, of which only 41 stations joined the local TV associations). Although the number is vast, their share remains insignificant (2–3%) (Nugroho et al. 2012) compared to national TV.

3.2 *Research variables*

1. *TV Rating.* To assess TV ratings, we used the Nielsen databases that record TV ratings for TV stations in Indonesia. TV rating, $RTV_{ij} = RTV_i / RTV_j$, where TVR_{ij} is the rating of TV_i relative to TV_j.
2. *Similarity* captured the extent to which two TV stations had the same profile in terms of program structure. To measure similarity, we followed the formula used by Chen et al. (2007) to calculate the Euclidean distance, D_{ij}, between two TV stations (see the formula below). A zero distance indicated that two TV stations had exactly the same distribution of different types of TV programs, and a high degree of distance indicated that two TV stations had very different programs. We then reverse-coded D_{ij} to arrive at a measure of similarity:

$$D_{ij} = \sqrt{\sum_{m=1}^{n}[(P_{im}/P_i) - (P_{jm}/P_j)]^2}$$

where P_{im} = the total number of type m programs aired by TV_i, P_i = the total number of programs operated by TV_i overall, P_{jm} = the total number of type m programs aired by TV_j, P_j = the total number of programs operated by TV_j overall, and m = types of programs operated by both TV_i and TV_j.

3. *Salience* captured the extent to which a rival was a dominant player in flying the aircraft that were vital to a focal firm's operations. It was calculated by following the modified formula used by Chen et al. (2007) as follows:

$$S_{ij} = \sum_{m=1}^{n}[(P_{im}/P_i)] \times (P_{jm}/P_m)]$$

where P_m = the total number of type m programs operated by all TV stations. In the calculation of salience index, S_{ij}, the first term, P_{im}/P_i, captured the strategic importance of a given type of program, for example telenovela or sport, to focal TV_i. The second term, P_{jm}/P_m, reflected the share of a given type of program owned by rival TV_j. We normalized the results so that the sum of the salience indexes for all given TV competitors was equal to 1.

4 ANALYSIS

For prime time in 2013, there were four TV stations that outsourced TV programs from domestic production houses by more than 85%: RCTI, SCTV, INDOSIAR, and MNCTV. Three TV stations produced programs in-house for more than 90%, which were Trans7, TV One and Metro TV. At the same time, four TV stations used more than 90% of their prime time by airing movies programs (RCTI, SCTV, MNCTV and Global TV). Variety shows dominated the TV programs of Trans7 and ANTV with more than 70%, and news was heavily used by TV One and Metro TV for more than 59%. In terms of movies, four TV stations (RCTI, Trans7, INDOSIAR and MNCTV) aired Indonesian movies, the largest being SCTV with 100% Indonesian movies. TV One and Global TV aired more than 85% Hollywood movies, followed by TransTV with about 46.47%. Miniseries were used dominantly by RCTI (60.83%) and SCTV (53.27%), while drama was aired extensively by Global TV and Metro TV (both 100%) and ANTV (81.81%).

In terms of ratings, RCTI had the highest TV ratings (4.203, followed by SCTV (2,889) and Trans TV (2,516) (Figure 1). Based on the formula RTV_{ij}, the average of TV rating is $\bar{X}_{TVR} = 1.691$ with SD = 2.078. To establish the group of salience and similarity, we used average value as the cut off, in which salience has $\bar{X}_{Sa} = 0.304$ and SD = 0.128, and similarity $\bar{X}_{Si} = 0.146$ and SD = 0.327. The value 1 represents value above the mean, while 0 refers to value below the mean. This study also employs day as the covariate. Hypothesis 1 posits that greater similarity between two TV stations reduces the level of TV rating (TVR), while smaller similarity produces a higher TVR. The results of one-way ANCOVA indicate that greater similarity of a focal firm to its rival leads to higher TVR

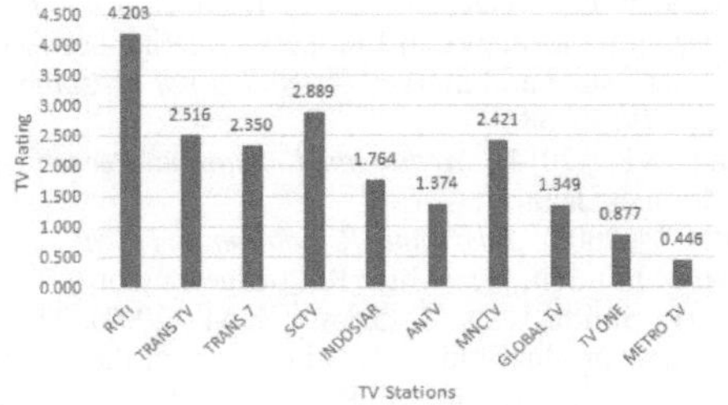

Figure 1. TV rating in Indonesia.

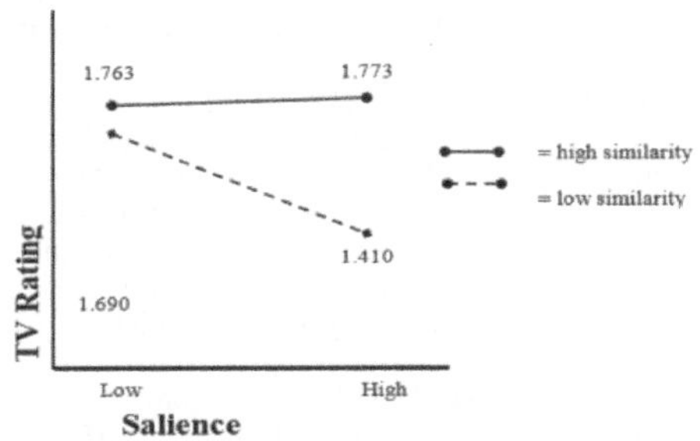

Figure 2. The moderating effect of relationship conflict.

($\bar{X}_{HSi}=1.769$) than smaller salience ($\bar{X}_{LSi}=1.507$), significantly ($F=109.755$, $sig=0.000$). Therefore, H_1 is supported. Hypothesis 2 predicts that greater salience between two TV stations reduces the level of TVR, while smaller salience produces greater TVR. By using one-way ANCOVA, the results indicate that greater salience of a focal firm to its rival leads to lower TVR ($\bar{X}_{HSa}=1.655$) than smaller salience ($\bar{X}_{LSa}=1.744$), significantly ($F=14.502$, $sig=0.000$). Therefore, H_2 is supported. Hypothesis 3 predicts that smaller salience and greater similarity lead to higher TVR, while greater salience and smaller similarity lead to lower TVR. By using two-way ANCOVA, the interaction effect is significant ($F=31.021$, $sig=0.000$). When the salience is low, the difference between high and low similarity is less marked ($\bar{X}_{LSaHSi}=1.763$) and ($\bar{X}_{LSaLSi}=1.690$). In contrast, when the salience is high, low similarity generates a low level of TV ratings ($\bar{X}_{HSaLSi}=1.410$). When the similarity is high, TV ratings reach the highest level ($\bar{X}_{HSaHSi}=1.773$). Even though the interaction effect is significant, the predicted value is not revealed and, thus, H_3 is not supported. The effect of day as covariate (Sunday as the baseline) is not significant ($F=1.028$, $sig=0.321$).

5 CONCLUSION

This study intentionally examines the effects of capability to contest of each TV station on their market performance in Indonesia. The results indicate that greater similarity, in the case of resources or TV program (Chen 1996), increases the overall market performance in the industry due to the increase of viewers' familiarity on a particular TV program. On the contrary, when each firm targets similar markets and uses similar TV programs—salience - then the market performance decreases (Chen 1996; Chen et al. 2007). This study further exhibits that there is an interaction between similarity and salience, in which high similarity and high salience reaches the greater market performance, while low similarity and high salience leads to lower performance. This further validates the idea of Chen and Miller (1994) about the interaction of salience and similarity in the industry.

There are several managerial implications that can be suggested. First, the manager should be aware that airing similar TV programs could increase the familiarity of viewers on a particular program (Alvarez et al. 2005), and thus increase the overall market performance. Second, managers should cautiously execute the first recommendation. When there is high similarity and salience among TV stations, this might increase the market performance in general. However, when the salience is high and similarity is low, this could reduce the industry's market performance in general (Chen & Miller 1994).

We expect that this study contributes to the competitive dynamics literature in a number of ways. First, this study uses the TV industry as a context to study competitive dynamics which is mainly dominated by the airline industry (Chen 1996; Chen et al. 2007). Second, this study empirically tests the interaction effect of similarity and salience as the dimensions of capability to contests as suggested the original idea of Chen (1996). Third, this study extends the prediction of AMC, which primarily influences the competitive tension (Chen et al. 2007; Tsai et al. 2011) to market performance, as the ultimate variable to be competed in the industry.

The results of this study must be considered in the light of some limitations. First, this study mainly uses data from 2003, which might limit the explanation of the competitive dynamics within the broadcasting industry in Indonesia. Second, this study employs the formula of Chen et al. (2007) to represent capability to contest on overall TV programs. However, the data can be broken down into more detailed analysis, such as movie TV programs into miniseries, cartoons, etc., which needs further analysis to provide precise results and recommendations.

REFERENCES

Ang, S.H. (2008). Competitive intensity and collaboration: Impact on firm growth across technological environments. *Strategic Management Journal, 29*, 1057–1075.

Alvarez, J.L., Mazza, C., Pedersen, J.S., & Svejenova, S. (2005). Shielding idiosyncrasy from isomorphic

pressures: Towards optimal distinctiveness in European filmmaking. *Organization, 12*, 863–888.
Barney, J.B. (1991). Firm resources and sustained competitive advantage. *Journal of Management, 17*, 99–120.
Baum, J.A., & Korn, H.J. (1996). Competitive dynamics of interfirm rivalry: Linking structural conditions of competition to patterns of market entry and exit. *Academy of Management Journal, 39*, 255–291.
Baum, J.A., & Korn, H.J. (1999). Dynamics of dyadic competitive interaction. *Strategic Management Journal, 20*, 251–278.
Baum, J.A., & Lant, T.K. (2003). Hits and misses: Managers' (mis)categorization of competitors in the Manhattan hotel industry. In *Advances in Strategic Management*, edited by J.A.C. Baum, and O. Sorenson, *20*, 119–156. Greenwich, CT: JAI.
Boyd, J.L., & Bresser, R.K.F. (2008). Performance implications of delayed competitive responses: Evidence from the U.S. retail industry. *Strategic Management Journal, 29*, 1077–1096.
Chen, M.-J., Smith, K.G., & Grimm, C.M. (1992). Action characteristics as predictors of competitive responses. *Management Science, 38*, 439–455.
Chen, M.-J., & Miller, D. (1994). Competitive attack, retaliation and performance: An expectancy-valence framework. *Strategic Management Journal, 15*, 85–102.
Chen, M.-J. (1996). Competitor analysis and inter-firm rivalry: Towards a theoretical integration. *Academy of Management Review, 21*, 100–134.
Chen, M.-J., Su, K.-H., & Tsai, W. (2007). Competitive tension: The awareness-motivation-capability perspective. *Academy of Management Journal, 50*, 101–118.
Chen, M.-J., & Miller, D. (2012). Competitive dynamics: themes trends and a prospective research platform. *Academy of Management Annals, 6*, 1–76.
d'Haenens, L., Verelst, C., & Gazali, E. (2000). In search of quality measures for Indonesian television news. In *Television in contemporary Asia*, edited by D. French, and M. Richards. 197–232. New Delhi, Thousand Oaks, CA, London: Sage.
DeSarbo, W.S., Grewal, R., & Wind, J. (2006). Who competes with whom? A demand-based perspective for identifying and representing asymmetric competition. *Strategic Management Journal, 27*, 101–129.
emarketer.com. 2013. Total Media Ad Spent Rising Steadily in Indonesia. Retrieved from: http://www.emarketer.com/Article/Total-Media-Ad-Spending-Rising-Steadily-Indonesia/1009246.
Gimeno, J. (1999). Reciprocal threats in multimarket rivalry: Staking out "spheres of influence" in the U.S. airlines industry. *Strategic Management Journal, 20*, 101–128.
Gimeno, J., & Woo, C.Y. (1996). *Do similar firms really compete less? Strategic distance and multimarket contact as predictors of rivalry among heterogeneous firms*. Working paper, Texas A&M University, College Station.
Grimm, C.M., Lee, H., & Smith, K.G. (2006). *Strategy as action: Competitive dynamics and competitive advantage*. Oxford, UK: Oxford University Press.
Heil, O., & Robertson, T.S. (1991). Toward a theory of competitive market signaling: A research agenda. *Strategic Management Journal, 12*, 403–418.
Hitt, M.A., Ireland, R.D., and Hoskisson, R.E. (2007). *Strategic management: Globalization and competitiveness*. Mason, OH: Thomson South-Western.
Hollander, E., d'Haenens, L., & Bardoel, J. (2009). Television performance in Indonesia: steering between civil society, state and market. *Asian Journal of Communication, 19*, 39–58.
Ishadi, S.K. (2014). *Media dan Kekuasaan*. Penerbit Buku Kompas: Jakarta.
Kitley, P. (2003). *Television, Regulation and Civil Society in Asia*. London, New York: Routledge Curzon.
Lee, H., Smith, K.G., & Grimm, C.M. (2003). The effect of new product radicality and scope on the extent and speed of innovation diffusion. *Journal of Management*, 29, 753–768.
Miller, D., & Shamsie, J. (1996). The resource-based view of the firm in two environments: The Hollywood film studios from 1936 to 1965. *Academy of Management Journal, 39*, 519–543.
Morrison, S., & Winston, C. (1995). *The evolution of the US airline industry*. Washington, DC: Brookings Institution.
Nugroho, Y., Putri, D.A., & Laksmi, S. (2012). *Mapping the landscape of the media industry in contemporary Indonesia*. Research collaboration of Centre for Innovation Policy and Governance and HIVOS Regional Office Southeast Asia, funded by Ford Foundation. Jakarta: CIPG and HIVOS.
Porac, J.F., & Thomas, H. (1990). Taxonomic mental models in competitor definition. *Academy of Management Review, 15*, 224–240.
Porac, J.F., Thomas, H., Wilson, F., Paton, D., & Kanfer, A. (1995). Rivalry and the industry model of Scottish knitwear producers. *Administrative Science Quarterly, 40*, 203–227.
Reger, R.K., & Huff, A.S. (1993). Strategic groups: A cognitive perspective. *Strategic Management Journal, 14*, 103–124.
Smith, K.G., Grimm, C.M., Gannon, M.J., & Chen, M.-J. (1991). Organizational information processing, competitive responses and performance in the U.S. domestic airline industry. *Academy of Management Journal, 34*, 60–85.
Smith, K.G., Ferrier, W., & Ndofor, H. (2001). Competitive dynamics research: Critique and future directions. In *Handbook of Strategic Management*, edited by M. Hitt, R. Freeman, and J. Harrison. 315–361. London: Blackwell.
Tsai, W., Su, K.-H., & Chen, M.-J. (2011). Seeing through the eyes of a rival: Competitor acumen based on rival-centric perceptions. *Academy of Management Journal, 54*, 761–778.
Vroom, V.H. (1964). *Work and Motivation*. New York: Wiley.
Young, G., Smith, K.G., & Grimm, C.C. (1996). "Austrian" and industrial organization perspectives on firm-level competitive activity and performance. *Organization Science, 7*, 243–254.
Yu, T., & Cannella, A. (2007). Rivalry between multinational enterprises: An event history approach. *Academy of Management Journal, 50*, 663–684.
Zajac, E., & Bazerman, M. (1991). Blind spots in industry and competitor analysis: Implications of interfirm (mis) perception to strategic decisions. *Academy of Management Review, 16*, 37–46.
zenithoptimedia.com. 2014. Executive summary: Advertising expenditure forecasts April 2014. Retrieved from: http://www.zenithoptimedia.com/wp-content/uploads/2014/04/Adspend-forecasts-April-2014-executive-summary.pdf.

Increasing Management Relevance and Competitiveness – Sukoco et al. (Eds)
© 2018 Taylor & Francis Group, London, ISBN 978-0-8153-7455-8

The influence of the socio-economic status of parents toward entrepreneurial attitudes

Hari Mulyadi, M. Arief Ramdhany & S. Sulastri
Universitas Pendidikan Indonesia, Bandung, Indonesia

ABSTRACT: The purpose of this paper is to find out the influence the socio-economic status of parents has on the entrepreneurial attitudes of students. The design of the research is cross-sectional and uses verificative approach, with survey methodology. A total of 71 respondents were chosen as a sample using non-probability sampling from Vocational High School (SMKN 11) Bandung, Indonesia. A questionnaire survey was used to collect data from the sample and linear regression was used to analyze the data. In conclusion, it can be said that the socio-economic status of the parents is not the main factor affecting the entrepreneurial attitudes of students. This paper provides a basis for understanding the socio-economic status of parents as one of the factors that influence the entrepreneurial attitude. The difference of this study with previous research is on objects that are used, the variable used, supporting the theory as well as the different references used by previous researchers.

Keywords: economic status of parents, entrepreneurial attitudes

1 INTRODUCTION

In a developing country, the role of the entrepreneur cannot be ignored, especially in carrying out a development. A nation will develop faster when people have an interest in being an entrepreneur; a person who can be creative, innovative, and ultimately realize new ideas into practical actions in business. Not many people are interested in becoming entrepreneurs. The limitation to becoming one is influenced by many things and people need to be given supplies and enlightenment so that there will be a desire to become an entrepreneur (Drucker, 2014).

People tend to work as employees than to open their own business. Lack of entrepreneurial spirit among the younger generation has become one of the factors behind the high unemployment rate in Indonesia (Purnomo, 2005). One effort to increase the number of entrepreneurs is through education. Education has a strategic role in improving the quality of human resources, tackling unemployment, fostering interest, intention and entrepreneurial talent, as well as a mean to realize the ideals of the Indonesian nation in developing common prosperity and intellectual life. The government is expected to strive to provide education policies in order to make students better prepared for entrepreneurship and that graduates not only become employees (Kirby, 2004).

The topic of socio-economic factors and the entrepreneurial attitudes have been analyzed by several authors. Socio-economic status may influence the degree of success in entrepreneurship, the entrepreneurial attitudes and entrepreneurial interests (Wang & Wong, 2004; Henry, et al., 2005; Nair & Pandey, 2006). This paper aims to confirm the findings and find out the influence the socio-economic status of parents has on the entrepreneurial attitudes of students.

2 LITERATURE REVIEW

Many experts have put forward the concept of entrepreneurship based on their opinions. Entrepreneurship has a basis that refers to nature, character, and traits inherent in a person who has the willpower to realize innovative ideas into the real business world, and can develop it (Suryana, 2013). It is a discipline that studies the value, capacity (ability), and a person's behavior in the face of life's challenges, and how to create an opportunity together with various risks that may be encountered. Entrepreneurship is the process of creating something new, that the value of using time and effort is necessary, that financial, physical, and social risks can be taken, a monetary reward is produced, as well as personal satisfaction and success (Hisrich et al, 2008). Entrepreneurship is a process of creativity and innovation with high risk, with the aim to generate added value for products that benefit society and bring prosperity to entrepreneurs (Buchari, 2011). In brief, entrepreneurship is an entrepreneurial attitude and behavior (Kao, 1991). In general, entrepreneurship is a mental attitude and a 'nature of the soul' that is always active in trying to promote its works of devotion in an effort to increase revenue in its business activities.

Entrepreneurship can be learned, although there are certain people who have talent in entrepreneurship. An entrepreneur must have task-oriented and strong confidence, attitude and confidence to initiate, and conduct and complete the task or the job at hand. An entrepreneur must have the attitude that has meaning for him or her. The determination of success of a being an entrepreneur is influenced by the attitude of the actor. The indicators of entrepreneurial attitudes are confident, task-oriented and result-oriented, demonstrate originality, have leadership, risk-taking, and future-oriented processes (Meredith, 2005).

The theory of entrepreneurship is divided into six categories (Kwabena, 2011) which are namely: economic entrepreneurship theory; psychology entrepreneurship theory (personal traits theory and achievement theory); sociological entrepreneurship theory (social networks, characteristics of the individuals, ethnic identification of the family and population ecology); anthropological entrepreneurship theory; opportunity-based entrepreneurship theory; and resource-based entrepreneurship theory. In this sense, the socio-economic status of parents is in the scope of the ethnic identification of the family. Several factors of socio-economic status of parents are education, income and work (employment).

This study was conducted to determine the effect of the socio-economic status of parents on the entrepreneurial attitudes of Class X students of the Marketing Department in SMKN 11 Bandung, Indonesia. The independent variable is the economic status of the parents, consisting of education, income and work. The dependent variable is the entrepreneurial attitude, consisting of confidence, task and result orientation, risk-taking, leadership, originality, and future orientation.

3 METHOD

The type of research used in this study is descriptive-verification, with the method of explanatory surveys to explore the problem situation, which is to get the ideas and insights into the problems faced by management or researchers. The population and the sample of this research was 71 students at Class X of Marketing Department in SMKN 11 Bandung. A survey questionnaire was used as a research instrument to collect the data from the sample.

4 RESULTS AND DISCUSSION

It was found that the parents' socio-economic status had a positive influence on the entrepreneurial attitude of the Class X Students of SMKN 11 in Bandung. This result is in line with the statement that socio-economic status has the meaning of a 'state' (good, sufficient or poor standard) that shows financial capability and the family-owned material supplies (Basrowi, 2005).

From the indicators of the socio-economic status of parents, it can be identified that:

- Education is defined as an activity where effort is made to improve the student's personality so as to foster the potential of conscious personality, and to create an atmosphere of learning. Students are actively developed to have the spiritual power of religion, self-control, personality, intelligence, noble characteristics and skills needed for them, society, nation and state;
- Income level is the sum of all the heads of household income or other family members in the form of money and goods. It is argued that the income received by the population will be affected by the level of education they have. With higher education, they will be able to obtain broader opportunities to get better jobs with greater revenue. As for the 'low-educated' population, they will get jobs with lower incomes; and
- The employment rate will determine the socio-economic status because when in work all human needs will be met. Employment not only has an economic value, but allows society to obtain satisfaction and earn rewards in the form of goods and services, that will meet their needs.

It was found that the socio-economic status of parents of Class X students of the Marketing Department in SMKN 11 Bandung, Indonesia, was relatively high and well established. An overview of the parents' socio-economic status showed that 72.9% were categorized as having high status.

Based on empirical results, it was found that entrepreneurial attitudes of the students of Marketing Department in SMKN 11 Bandung was relatively high (namely 75.0%) and was therefore categorized as high.

It was also found that the parents' socio-economic status had a positive influence on the entrepreneurial attitudes of the students of Marketing Department in SMKN 11 Bandung. The coefficient of determination was 0,477 or 47.7%. The influence was therefore categorized as high.

5 CONCLUSIONS AND RECOMMENDATIONS

Based on the results and discussion, it can be summarized that overall the socio-economic status of parents was considered high. The education level of parents was the highest indicator, while the indicator of employment rate (work) had the lowest value. The entrepreneurial attitude of the students was categorized as high. Risk-taking was the highest indicator, while the indicator of confidence was the lowest. Parents' socio-economic status had a positive and strong influence on entrepreneurial attitude. This shows that the better the socio-economic status of parents, the greater the entrepreneurial attitudes of the students.

Based on this conclusion, the authors recommend that the lowest indicator of socio-economic status of parents is the level of employment. To increase employment and eliminate unemployment, the government should offer job training. Job training can be done by the setting up a vocational training center in various regions. The lowest indicator of entrepreneurial attitude is the aspect of self-confidence. To increase confidence, the school teaching methods could encourage the exchange of opinions and problem solving. Entrepreneurship training, such as the holding of seminars, competitions in school or out of school would help develop talent. Socio-economic status of parents positively influences entrepreneurial attitude, so the authors of this study recommend that schools keep, maintain, monitor and improve entrepreneurial attitude through training, education, and seminars. Other forms of knowledge and skills also need to be improved in order to support the development of business.

REFERENCES

Basrowi, B. (2005). *Pengantar sosiologi (Introduction to sociology)*. Yogyakarta, Indonesia: Insan Cendekia.

Buchari, A. (2011). *Manajemen pemasaran dan pemasaran jasa (Management of marketing and marketing services)*. Bandung, Indonesia: Penerbit Alfabeta.

Drucker, P. (2014). *Innovation and entrepreneurship*. Routledge.

Henry, C., Hill, F. & Leitch, C. (2005). Entrepreneurship education and training: Can entrepreneurship be taught? Part I. *Education+ Training*, Feb 1, *47*(2), 98–111.

Hisrich, R.D., Peters, M.P. & Spepherd, D.A. (2008). *Kewirausahaan (Entrepreneurship)* (7th ed.). Jakarta, Indonesia: Salemba Empat.

Kao, J.J. (1991). *The entrepreneurial organization*. New York, New York: Macmillan Publishing Co., Inc.

Kirby, D.A. (2004). Entrepreneurship education: Can business schools meet the challenge? *Education+ training*, Oct 1, *46*(8/9), 510–519.

Kwabena, N.S. (2011). Entrepreneurship theories and empirical research: A summary review of literature. *European Journal of Business Management*, *3*(6). Retrieved from www.iiste.org.

Meredith, G.G. (2005). *Kewirausahaan, teori dan praktek (Entrepreneurship: Theory and practice)* Jakarta, Indonesia: PT. Pustaka Binaman Pressindo.

Nair, K.R. & Pandey, A. (2006). Characteristics of entrepreneurs: An empirical analysis. *Journal of Entrepreneurship*, Jan 1, *15*(1), 47–61.

Purnomo, B.H. (2005). *Membangun semangat kewirausahaan (Build entrepreneurial spirit)*. Yogyakarta, Indonesia: Pustak a Pelajar Offset.

Suryana, S. (2013). *Kewirausahaan pedoman praktis: Kiat dan proses menuju sukses (Entrepreneurship practical guidance: Tips and processes to succeed)*. Jakarta, Indonesia: Salemba Empat.

Wang, C.K. & Wong, P.K. (2004). Entrepreneurial interest of university students in Singapore. *Technovation*, Feb 29, *24*(2), 163–172.

Increasing Management Relevance and Competitiveness – Sukoco et al. (Eds)
© 2018 Taylor & Francis Group, London, ISBN 978-0-8153-7455-8

Analysis of the factors affecting the elected mode of transportation for workers using an analytical hierarchy process

E. Mahpudin & H. Sulistiyo
Universitas Pendidikan Indonesia, Bandung, Indonesia

ABSTRACT: The rapid growth in the industrial sector of Cikarang is impacting on many areas of life such as population migration of those of working age. This has led to a situation where workers and companies have not thought to bridge the transportation problems of workers (which will ultimately have an impact on the effectiveness of the company's business). Some companies have provided buses or shuttle vehicles for its employees and a few workers have taken the risk of buying two-wheeled vehicles (motorcycles). The problems that arise in choosing a mode of transportation that will be used for work, are of interest to this study. Factors that affect a person's choice of mode of transportation, be it travel time, security, comfort as well as costs incurred, will be analyzed using the method of Analytic Hierarchy Process (AHP).

Keywords: Analytic Hierarchy Process, analysis of factors, modes of transport

1 INTRODUCTION

According to data collected by the Greater Jakarta Transportation Agency (BPTJ) (2016), in 2014 there were nearly 25 million vehicles in Jabodetabek of which: 18.5 million were motorcycles and 6.4 million were vehicles (including passenger cars, trucks, and buses). In addition, the average number of motorcycles (74%) almost tripled that of cars (26%), except in South Tangerang City where the average proportion of motorcycles was 25% and cars 75%. The number of vehicles in Greater Jakarta was found to be about a quarter of the total vehicles in the whole of Indonesia (114 million).

Urban population growth has been increasing all over the world primarily due to the greater economic opportunities available in cities than in rural areas, but this has occurred generally without a corresponding upgrade in urban transport infrastructure. However, the diverse groups of city dwellers have different transport needs, but transport options in the city are often not so diverse. As a result, the transport systems in cities around the world are facing challenges, such as congestion, pollution and traffic accidents (Pareekha et al., 2016). Striving for satisfaction of the needs of clients is the principal task in any sector of the economy, including transportation by road vehicles. In the course of the growth in demand for transportation services, the number of enterprises offering transportation services grew increasingly in national and international markets (Matijošius et al., 2015).

Any modification to the transportation system serving a given area (whether it be the creation of a new infrastructure, the implementation of a traffic control system, the supply of a public transportation system, etc.) aims to attain specific goals. Such goals can usually be achieved in a number of different ways (Ferrari, 2003). The core factors important for transport service choice are cost, time, reliability, and quality (Floden, 2017). Ensuring the efficiency and competitiveness of the transport sector as well as providing a high quality of transportation service is one of the key tasks in the development of a national economy (Matijošiusa et al., 2015).

Additional means of transport as well as widening the streets, is not an adequate solution. Taking into account the increasing needs of the community, alternative solutions that divert people from vehicle use need to be researched

The purpose of this study was to:

1. determine the dominant factor in choosing a mode of transportation; and
2. determine what kind of mode of transport was used by the workers.

For this research, the Analytic Hierarchy Process (AHP), developed by Saaty (1993), was used.

2 LITERATURE REVIEW

2.1 *Transportation*

Transportation is the movement of people or goods from one place to the other or from the place of origin to a destination using a vehicle driven by a human, animal or machine (Sani, 2010). Transportation plays a role in improving the economy by providing access to trade and services in various sectors. Transportation systems have an influence on the population dynamics, urbanization, urban form, economic growth, and environmental quality (Sjafruddin, 2009; Wahidi, as cited in Buwana et al., 2015). The goal of using transportation is the fast and easy movement of people or goods from their point of origin to a destination. The transport function is not only an individual need, but also of public interest.

Pareekha (2016) quantified the concept of "transport diversity" by developing variables which reflect the concept. He extracted the research data from samples of cities and analyzed the association among the variables employing exploratory factor analysis. On the other hand, Ma (2016) evaluated the urban green transportation planning using a new method based on the central point triangle whiten weight function and entropy-AHP.

2.2 *Analytic Hierarchy Process (AHP)*

Analytic Hierarchy Process (AHP) is a mathematically-based procedure which is very good and appropriate for the evaluation of the condition of these attributes. Mathematically quantified in a set of pairwise comparisons, AHP was used for forming relationships within the structure. The results of these pairwise comparisons form a matrix wherein the ratio scale is derived in the form of principal vectors. AHP excess is compared to the others for their hierarchical structure, and as a consequence of the selected criteria, to the most detailed parts criteria, taking into account the tolerance limit of validity up to the inconsistency of various criteria and alternatives selected by the decision maker (Saaty, 1993).

3 RESEARCH METHODS

As a case study, data on the factors of interest that influence how the population travel to their place of work, was collected. Respondents were selected using simple random sampling from a percentage of a district working population.

For the district North Cikarang, Bekasi, paired comparison analysis of the data was undertaken with the scale of 1–9. The data collected was analyzed with the AHP method, the geometric average to get the matrix comparison pairs was calculated, and then the data was tested with a consistency ratio (CR). If the CR value is less than 10% then the data is considered consistent. To get the result expected, a sensitivity analysis to prioritize the elected alternative mode of transport was undertaken. This analysis was done with a way trial and error on each factor.

Data was also analyzed later with the Expert Choice program which helped the calculation of the AHP for 100 respondents working in the district of North Cikarang, Bekasi. With this software, analysis of sensitivity, charts and tables could be made.

4 RESULTS AND DISCUSSION

Transportation modes selected by workers (in order of priority) were as follows:

From the AHP analysis, respondents in North Cikarang District think that the factor of time was their main priority (40.6%), followed by cost, security and comfortableness (last factor of priority). The Top priority mode of transport used by respondents to head to their workplace was a motorcycle (38.3%), followed by a bus (27%), then a car (25.1%), and lastly, public transportation (such as trains) with 9.6%.

5 CONCLUSIONS AND RECOMMENDATIONS

5.1 *Conclusions*

Based on the results of data analysis through using AHP and with the help of the software, Expert Choice, a number of conclusions were found:

1. top priority in the selection of the mode of transportation for respondents to their place of work was the time factor. The next factor selected as the most influential in their choice of transport mode was the cost factor with safety and convenience as the last factor;
2. the dominant mode of transport selected for traveling to work was the motorcycle. The second selection was the bus shuttle,

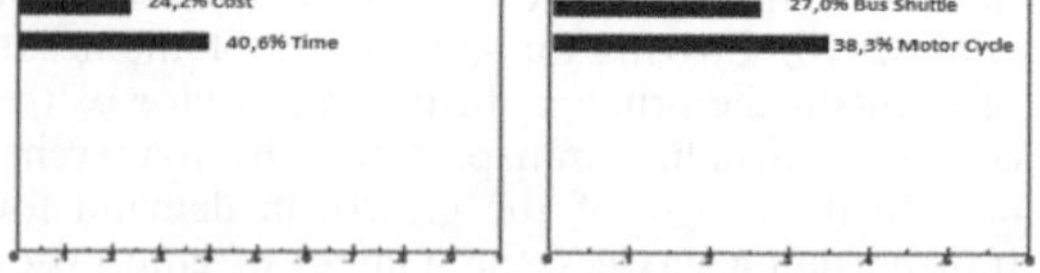

Figure 1. Dynamic sensitivity for alternative transportation modes.

a private car the third, and the urban transportation the fourth.

5.2 *Recommendations*

1. further development in taking samples that are more equal, consideration to other modes of transportation and building a structured hierarchy with more than three levels, would improve the analysis;
2. an appraisal of the comparison pairs must pay attention to the concepts of AHP so that the comparison pairs mentioned could made more consistent; and
3. research is necessary for other sub-districts in Bekasi.

REFERENCES

Buwana, E., Hasibuan, H.S. & Abdini, C. (2015). Alternatives selection for sustainable transportation system in Kasongan City. *Procedia-Social and Behavioral Sciences, 227* (2016), 11–18.

Ferrari, P. (2003). A method for choosing from among alternative transportation projects. *European Journal of Operational Research, 150* (2003), 194–203.

Floden, J., Barthel, F. & Sorkina, E. (2017). Transport buyers choice of transport service—A literature review of empirical results. *Research in Transportation Business and Management, 23* (2017), 35–45.

Ma, F., He, J., Ma, J. & Xia, S. (2016). Evaluation of urban green transportation planning based on central point triangle whiten weight function and entropy-AHP. *Transportation Research Procedia, 25C*(2017), 3638–3648.

Matijošiusa, J., Vasiliauskas, A.V., Vasilienė-Vasiliauskienė, V. & Krasodomskis, Z. (2015). The assessment of importance of the factors that predetermine the quality of a service of transportation by road vehicles. *Procedia Engineering, 134*(2016), 422–429.

Pareekha, P., Mitra, S. & Majumdarc, B.B. (2016). Quantifying dimensions of transportation diversity: A city-based comparative approach. *Transportation Research Procedia, 25C*(2017), 3178–3191.

Saaty, T.L. (1993). Pengambilan keputusan bagi para pemimpin: proses hirarki analitik untuk pengambilan keputusan dalam situasi yang kompleks [Decision Making for Leaders: Hierarchical-Analytical Process for Decision Making in Complex Situations]. Jakarta, Indonesia: Pustaka Binama Press.

Sani, Z. (2010). *Transportasi suatu pengantar*. [An Introduction to Transportation]. Jakarta, Indonesia: Universitas Indonesia Press.

The Greater Jakarta Transportation Agency (BPTJ). (2016, August 24). *The National Transportation Seminar.* Jakarta, Indonesia. Universitas Trisakti.

Increasing Management Relevance and Competitiveness – Sukoco et al. (Eds)
© 2018 Taylor & Francis Group, London, ISBN 978-0-8153-7455-8

Multidimensional approach for assessing service quality in the service industry

Y.D. Lestari
Universitas Airlangga, Surabaya, Indonesia

ABSTRACT: Globalization leads to greater market dynamics with increasingly fierce competition. Changes that have occurred must be responded to by companies in an effort to obtain and retain customers in the face of dynamic competition. Each company will make every effort through its competence to create something that is different from its competitors. The actions that are taken by the company should enable them to compete in the global market. The service industry has unique characteristics; high contact with the consumers and competitors are difficult to recognize and identify. Service companies should always seek to offer the most appropriate services and consumer satisfaction, to make them survive or win the competition. Some models reveal different dimensions to measure the service quality, but every dimension in general has something in common, and every kind of industry has different needs and dimensions. The influencing factor of concern in relation to improvements needs to be differentiated according to the company's needs.

Keywords: dimensions, service quality, service industry

1 INTRODUCTION

In recent years, the service industry has faced more dynamic competition compared to the previous decade (Kumar, 2010). More developed economies around the globe have evolved into service economies. Now consumers spend more for services than for tangible goods (Martin, 1999). The growth of the service sector can be seen from the increase of service industry variety, such as banking, retail, and professional service firms, such as accounting firms, consultants and lawyers.

During the past two to three decades, the unique differences between services and goods have been highlighted, and the resulting challenges faced by firms whose core products are services have come into focus (Martin, 1999; Zeithaml, 1988). Service quality issues are an important part and are a serious concern for any company if they want to survive in a business environment (Asubonteng et al, 1996). Today it is believed that the key to winning the fierce competition in the service industry is by providing value and satisfaction to consumers through excellent service delivery and quality. The paradigm change has forced every national and international service company to undergo service quality improvements. Service quality is important for both marketers and management, because service quality evaluations from the customer and the level of satisfaction as a result determine repurchase and ultimately affects the bottom line measures of business success (Iacobucci et al., 1994). It is important for management to understand what service quality consists of, its definition, and how it can be measured. If management take action to improve quality, then a clear conception of quality is great value (Asubonteng et al., 1996).

The problem in depicting and measuring service quality is that it cannot be studied like goods quality that can be described and measured objectively using several indicators, such as the amount of defects. Services are broadly defined at an abstract level and may be operationalized and interpreted in a number of different ways. Services at an empirical level include many different offerings, organizations, and customers (Edvardsson et al., 2005). Lovelock (1991) defined a service as 'a process or performance rather than a thing'.

The unique characteristic of an offered service is the high amount of contact between the service provider and the consumer. This means that the consumer becomes an important subject in determining the quality of the service itself. Consumers are highly varied, both in their perception and in their expectations. It is difficult for companies to judge the right quality in the services provided, so the company must take appropriate quality measurements to provide appropriate services to their customers.

2 LITERATURE BACKGROUND

2.1 *Service characteristics*

Services are basically something that can be characterized as follows: something intangible (Lehtinen & Raija, 2015) that can meet the needs of consumers. The production process can use the service itself or not, because the service can help a physical product in a complementary manner to increase the customer satisfaction in the product. Services do not result in the transfer of rights or ownerships. There is no interaction between the providers and the users of the services (Kotler in Rao, 2011). Categories of supply in the service context can be put in to five types, among others including pure tangible goods, that deal solely with a physical product. This product types does not need any attached service at all. For example, soap, toothpaste, shampoo and others. Second, are tangible goods with support services (or tangible good with accompanying services). Third, are tangible goods with an offer of support services, which consist of a tangible goods offer followed by one or several types of service to enhance the consumer appeal. For example, a car salesman representation or warranty one year free from any service damage. Fourth, is a service mixture that consists of an offer of goods and services in the same proportion. An example of this is food on offer in a restaurant with an impressive service. Fifth, are basic services with goods and additional services (major services with minor accompanying goods and services) that consist of basic service together with supplementary services (complementary) and or luggage support. For example, a passenger who buys transport services (transportation) during a journey. There are some physical products involved, such as food, newspapers and others. Services that only offer a pure form of service include massage parlors and psychological counselling.

There are several qualities that relate to the nature of services. Services have the nature of intangible because they may not be seen, felt, heard, touched or kissed before the purchase transaction. This is a form of service that cannot be separated from its source, whether that source is a person or machine, whether the source is present or not, and the physical tangible product remains. Change (variability) services are actually very easy to change because this service depends on who is present, when, and where it is presented. For perishability, the durability of a service is not a problem if there is always a steady demand for the service revenue in advance with ease. When a request is cancelled or the supply down, then difficult problems will soon appear.

2.2 *Dynamic competition*

The era of globalization has made the competition-based climate increasingly stringent. The competitive landscape that most businesses face is becoming more intense and dynamic than ever before (Rodie & Martin, 2001). Rapid changes in environmental conditions have an impact on consumers. The internet presence has made it even easier for consumers to obtain information such as advertisements or information related to the service industry, which makes consumers more informed. This makes the consumers more selective in choosing a service industry that has the quality as required. Good quality is different from the perception of the individual. This causes the company problems in determining the best quality of the services provided. According to their characteristics, a service is also intangible and cannot be stored. The services that have been granted not in accordance with the desired quality that the customers wants cannot be readily replaced.

Every company should make every effort to analyze their competitors and consumers with the intention of creating interesting innovations in the production process. In service, the quality should correspond to the customer's expectations and satisfy their needs and requirements (Edvardsson, Gustafsson and Roos, 2005). Current conditions are likely to change, and the change is often rapid. Service company management should be able to adapt, integrate and reconfigure the appropriate internal and external organizational skills, resources and functional competence to adjust to the changes. Companies must update their competence to adapt to the changing business environment. The dynamics of the competition are the result of activities in a series and are also in response to the competition between companies that compete in a given industry. The competitive actions taken by the company should be able to allow them to take part in the global competition in conditions that can easily change the paradigm shift. The situation that must be realized and requires a proactive attitude. In order to exist, a company needs to have a vision, mission and competitive strategy that is sturdy so that it will not oscillate or be run over by the changing times. In competitive rivalry, it is common to tend to follow the actions and responses other companies make in relation to competitive actions.

2.3 *Multi dimensions of service quality*

The dimensions of the service quality have been identified by marketing researchers studying several different service categories: appliance repair, retail banking, long distance telephone service, security brokerage and credit card companies (Fitzsimmons, Fitzimmons and Bordoloi, 2014). Good quality is not from the service provider's viewpoint or perception, but comes from consumers. Customers have the role as co-producers by carrying out activities as well as being part of the interactions influencing both the process quality and outcome (Edvardsson et al, 2005). There is no general agreement as to the nature or content of the service quality dimensions (Brady & Cronin, 2001). Therefore, there is the general perspective that service quality is a multi-dimensional or multi-attribute construct (Cronin & Taylor, 1992; Gronroos, 1990; Parasuraman et al., 1985, 1988). This makes service quality studies seemingly focused on the service delivery process. Additional aspects that have to be considered have already been suggested.

Sasser et al. (1978) in Yarimouglu (2014) stated that service quality can be improved through paying attention to factors such as security, consistency, attitude, completeness, condition, availability, and the training of the service providers. Lehtinen & Lehtinen (1982) added factors such a physical quality, interactive quality, and corporate quality.

According to Gronroos (1982) in Du Kang Gi and Jeffrey James (2014), two service quality dimensions were identified; the technical aspect (outcome) that emphasized "what" service was provided and the functional aspect (process) that emphasized in "how" the service was provided. The customers perceive what they receive as the outcome of the process in which the resources are used. This is the technical or outcome quality of the process. They also and often more importantly, perceive how the process itself functions. To facilitate the dynamic aspects of this perception, Gronroos also stressed the importance of corporate image. Image is important for service companies, and image can be formed mainly of the technical and functional quality of service including the other factors. An example of this is word of mouth and public relations (Nitin et al. 2005).

According to Parasuraman (1988) in Haksever (2013), by way of exploratory research, they refined their subsequent scale named SERVQUAL. In the beginning, 10 dimensions were found and then reduced to five dimensions; reliability, responsiveness, tangibles, assurance (communication, competence, credibility, courtesy, and security) and empathy.

Physical facilities, processes and procedures, people behavior and conviviality, and professional judgment are the basic attributes in the service quality model (Haywood-Farmer, 1988). The attributes proposed by Haywood Farmer in relation to Parasuraman's service quality determinants were as follows:

Physical facilities, processes and procedures including location, layout, size, decor, facility reliability, process flow and flexibility, capacity balance, control of flow and the range of services, the same as with Parasuraman, Zeithaml and Berry, 1985. People's behavior and conviviality, timeliness, speed, communication, warmth, friendliness, attitude, tone of voice, dress, neatness, politeness, anticipation, handling complaints and solving problems is the same as with Parasuraman, Zeithaml and Berry, 1985. Reliability, responsiveness, access, courtesy, communication are also the same. This is the same as professional judgment, diagnosis, advice, guidance, innovation, honesty, confidentiality, discretion, knowledge, skill, which is again, the same with Parasuraman, Zeithaml and Berry, 1985. Competence, credibility, security, and understanding the consumer is the last (Yaglu, Yarimoglu 2014).

One criticism of SERVQUAL has been the point that the instrument mainly focuses on the service delivery process. For measuring the service quality performance, Cronin & Taylor (1992) developed the SERVPERF model which explained more of the variations in the service quality than SERVQUAL (Yarimouglu, 2014). Rust & Oliver (1994) also proposed a model for measuring service quality. It included the service product, service delivery and service environment, but this model has not been formally tested. Frost & Kumar (2000) introduced the INTSERVQUAL model that measured the service quality of internal customers this model based on the GAP Model by Parasuraman.

3 DISCUSSION

Dynamic conditions, fierce competition and the unique characteristics of services give a company the challenge of winning against the competition in the global market. Knowing the competition is one of the most critical business principles according to Bagozzi et al. (1998) in Rodie & Martin (2001). Companies must make changes to get customers in order to survive the in-market competition. The changes that are made are to be adapted to consumer desires, especially those related to quality. High-level contact with consumers in the delivery process is an important factor in determining the basis of service quality improvement. On the other hand, competitors in the services sector are difficult to identify and the amount of resources to commit to this is often limited (Rodie & Martin, 2001).

There are many kinds of service companies and each company has its own unique characteristics to note, both in terms of management and customer types. Therefore, if the company wanted to make a change or innovation (Lehtinen & Jarvinen, 2015) in the form of improved quality in accordance with customer needs to enable the company to compete in the market, it takes on the exact same dimensions as when evaluating other quality services. Each service company has different characteristics and consumers, so that the accuracy of the use of models in the measurement of the quality of services determines the company's success in the provision of services in accordance with the consumer. Consumers do their evaluation based on sub-dimensions to shape their perceptions about the quality of the services (Brady & Cronin 2001). Several models with different approaches underlying the dimensions as the benchmark for quality repair services have been carried out. Many studies have been conducted to test the model associated with service quality, and the strength of the effect of each different dimension to the service industry. Reliability is the most important dimension in determining service quality (Yarimouglu, 2014). Tangibles is the other important critical variable for mixed services. Empathy is a critical variable for quasi-manufacturing services (Gupta & Chen, 1995). The perceptions on the factors of tangibility and convenience are significantly higher in conventional banks compared to Islamic Banks (Kumar et al., 2009).

Each service industry has different characteristics and through the internet, consumers are finding it increasingly easy to obtain a comparison when assessing the quality of the services of the company they are interested in. Therefore, companies must adapt quickly to anticipate the rapidly changing conditions and intense competition. The precise measurement of the competencies required to improve the quality of service for which the consumer is seeking is very important. This suggests that in order to face the dynamic conditions necessary to determine the exact dimensions to measure to improve the quality of service, the use of the proper dimensions can bring in results in accordance with the company's expectations.

4 CONCLUSION

Globalization has led to increasing dynamic conditions and competition in the service industry that is getting continually tougher. Every company must have a strategy to survive. Quality definition is abstract in the service industry and is difficult to know precisely. Every service industry must have something that makes their existence acceptable for the customer. The service industry has unique characteristics that need to identify their customers and their competitors. All services firms need to measure their quality continuously to find out how they are performing compared with other companies.

The service quality dimensions are commonly used for this measurement, and there are several approaches that can be used. One other have a common understanding related to the research of Parasuraman, 1985 and Haywood-Farmer, 1988. The provision of appropriate services in accordance with the consumer's expectations means winning the competition in the market. Many models are already being offered, and every industry has a different effect on each of the dimensions. The selection of the service quality measurement model with the correct dimensions can improve a company's ability to know the improvements that must be made.

ACKNOWLEDGMENT

The use of service quality varies greatly and needs to be tailored to the type of service that is offered by the company. Measuring the quality of services with the right dimensions will be useful for companies to make significant improvements. It will allow the company to survive in fierce competition.

REFERENCES

Asubonteng, P., Karl J., McCleary J. & Swan, E. (1996). SERVQUAL: Revisited a critical review of service quality. *Journal of Services Marketing. 10*(6), 62–81.

Babakus, E. & Boller, (1992). An empirical assessment of the SERVQUAL scale. *Journal of Business Research, 24*, 253–268.

Brady, M.K. & Cronin Jr, J.J. (2001). Some new thoughts on conceptualizing perceived service quality: a hierarchical approach. *Journal of Marketing, 65*(3), 34–49.

Cronin, J.J. & Taylor, S.A. (1992). Measuring service quality: a reexamination and extension. *Journal of Marketing, 56,* 1992, 55–68.

Du Kang-Gi, Jeffrey J. (2004). Service quality dimensions: an examination of Grönroos's service quality model: Managing service quality. *An International Journal, 14*(4), 266–277.

Edvardsson, B. (1997). Quality in new service development—key concepts and a frame of reference, *International Journal of Production Economics, 52*(1–2).

Edvardsson, B., Gustafsson, A. & Roos, I. (2005). Service portraits in service research a critical review. *International Journal of Service Industry Management, 16*(1), 107–121.

Edvardsson, B. (1997). Service quality; beyond cognitive assessment, managing service quality. *An International Journal, 15*(2), 127–131.

Edvardsson, B. (1997). Quality in new service development—key concepts and a frame of reference. International *Journal of Production Economics, 52*(1–2), pp. 31–46.

Fitzsimmons, J.A., Fitzsimmons, M.J., & Bordoloi, S.K. (2014). *Service Management*. London: McGraw Hill Higher Education, International Edition.

Frost, F.A., & Kumar, M. (2000). INTSERVQUAL—an internal adaptation of the GAP model in a large service organisation. *Journal of Services Marketing, 14*(5), 358–377.

Gronroos, C. in Fisk, R.P., Grove, S.J. & John, J. (Eds), (2000). *Services marketing self-portraits: Introspections, reflections, and glimpses from the experts*. Chicago IL: American Marketing Association, pp. 71–108.

Gupta, A. & Chen, I. (1995). Service quality; Implication for management development. *International Journal of quality and reliability management, 12*(7), 28–35.

Haksever, C. & Render, B. (2013). *Service management: An integrated approach to supply chain management and operations*. New Jersey: Pearson Education.

Haywood-Farmer, J. (1988). A conceptual model of service quality. *International Journal of Operations & Production Management, 8*(6), 19–29.

Kumar, M., Kee, F.T. & Charles, V. (2009). Comparative evaluation of critical factors in delivering service quality of banks. *International Journal of Quality and Reliability management, 27*(3), 351–377.

Lacobucci, D., Grayson, K. & Ostrom, A. (1994). Customer satisfaction fables. *Sloan Management Review, 35*(4), 93–6.

Lehtinen, U., & Jarvinen, R. (2015). The role of service characteristics in service innovations, *NJB, 64*(3), pp. 3–15.

Martin, C.N. (1999). The History, evolution and principles of services marketing: poised for the new millennium. *Marketing Intelligence & Planning, 17*(7), 324–328.

Nitin S. et al., (2005), Service quality models: a review, *International Journal of Quality & Reliability Management*, Vol. 22(9), pp. 913–949.

Parasuraman, A., Zeithaml, V.A. & Berry, L.L. (1985). A conceptual model of service quality and its implications for future research. *Journal of Marketing, 49*, 41–50.

Parasuraman, A., Zeithaml, V.A. & Berry, L.L. (1988). SERVQUAL: a multi-item scale for measuring consumer perceptions of the service quality. *Journal of Retailing, 64*(1), 12–40.

Parasuraman A., Zeithaml, A.V. & Berry L.L. (1994). Reassesment of expectations as a comparison standard in measuring service quality: Implications for further research. *Journal of Marketing, 9*, 111–124.

Philip, G. & Hazlett, S.A. (1997). The measurement of service quality: a new PCP attributes model. *International Journal of Quality & Reliability Management, 14*(3), 260–286.

Rao, K. (2011). *Services Marketing* (2nd ed.). New Delhi: Dorling Kindesley.

Rodie, A., & Martin, C.L. (2001). Competing in the service sector—The entrepreneurial challenge. *International Journal of Entrepreneurial Behavior & Research, 7*(1), 5–21.

Rust, R.T. and Oliver, R.L. (1994). *Service Quality: Insights and Managerial Implications from the Frontier*. In: Rust, R.T. and Oliver, R.L., Eds., *Service Quality: New Directions in Theory and Practice*, Sage Publications, Thousand Oaks, 1–19.

Seth, N., Deskmukh, S.G., & Vrath, P. (2005). Service quality models: a review. *International Journal of Quality and Reliability Management, 22*(9), 913–949.

Yarimouglu, E.K. (2014). Review on dimensions of service quality models. *Journal of Marketing, 2*(2), 2014, 79–93.

Zeithaml V.A., Berry, L.L. & Parasuraman, A. (1988). Communication and control processes in the delivery of service quality. *Journal of Marketing 52*(2), pp. 35–48.

Increasing Management Relevance and Competitiveness – Sukoco et al. (Eds)
© 2018 Taylor & Francis Group, London, ISBN 978-0-8153-7455-8

The influence of entrepreneurship orientation and management capability on performance of small and medium enterprises in Bogor

Agus Setyo Pranowo
Doctoral Management Science, Universitas Pendidikan Indonesia, Bandung, Indonesia

H. Hari Mulyadi
Universitas Pendidikan Indonesia, Bandung, Indonesia

Zulkifli Musannip Efendi Siregar
Doctoral Management Science, Universitas Pendidikan Indonesia, Bandung, Indonesia
Sekolah Tinggi Ilmu Ekonomi Labuhan Batu, Labuhan Batu, Indonesia

Yayan Hendayana
Doctoral Management Science, Universitas Pendidikan Indonesia, Bandung, Indonesia

ABSTRACT: The purpose of this research is to know the influence of entrepreneurship orientation and management capability on the performance of Small and Medium Enterprises (SMEs) in Bogor, Indonesia. The population in this study is all SMEs in Bogor that are registered with the Indonesian Chamber of Commerce and Industry: the total number is 78 SMEs. The data collection technique used in this study is a questionnaire. The data analysis technique used in this research is path analysis processed by the AMOS software, version 23. The results showed that entrepreneurship orientation variables have a positive and significant effect on the management capability of SMEs. The entrepreneurship orientation and management capability have a positive and significant effect on the performance of SMEs in Bogor. The direct influence of entrepreneurship orientation has the greatest influence on performance of SMEs in Bogor.

Keywords: Performance, Entrepreneurship Orientation and Management Capability

1 INTRODUCTION

Small and Medium Enterprises (SMEs) have an important role in the Indonesian economy. The SMEs sector, can help reduce unemployment in Indonesia. The SMEs has proven to be a pillar of a tough economy. During the crisis of 1998, the sector was able to survive and did not suffer serious consequences due to the crisis.

SMEs sector are also regarded as an activity that dominates more than 95% of the structure of the Indonesian economy. This sector has a very strategic role, both socioeconomic and political social. Economic functions of this sector include providing goods and services for consumers with low to medium purchasing power, contributing to more than half the economic growth and to the acquisition of foreign exchange. Socially and politically, the function of this sector is also very important, especially in the absorption of labor and efforts to eradicate poverty. In addition, small business is a fundamental requirement for Indonesia, a country that embraces the populist system.

With such a large role and potential, it is reasonable to develop small and medium businesses as much as possible in order to improve the welfare of the community while supporting the regional economy (Ratnawati & Hikmah, 2012). Based on searches conducted by the authors there are 78 SMEs registered with the Indonesia Chamber of Commerce and Industry. The types of SMEs in Table 1.

Many factors affect the performance of SMEs. This research discuss related to entrepreneurship orientation and management capability.

Entrepreneurial orientation has an important role in business success and a firm's performance. It refers to the attitude of an entrepreneur to be proactive, innovate, and have the courage to take risks with a strong calculation. This is in accordance with previous research showing that a firm can be said to use entrepreneurship orientation if

Table 1. Types of SMEs in Bogor.

Number	Types of SMEs	Total
1	Footwear	6
2	Electronic	1
3	Craft	30
4	Metal	2
5	Food and drink	10
6	Textiles and garment	9
7	Leather goods and imitation	2
8	Furniture	3
9	Chemical and rubber	10
10	Children's toys	3
11	Plants and ornamental fish	2
Total		78

the firm has characteristics such as product innovation, risk-taking, and being proactive in innovation. Thus, entrepreneurial orientation refers to processes, practices, and activities that use product innovation, take risks, and strive to proactively innovate in order to defeat competitors. A focus on innovation, proactive behavior, and risk-taking is used to guide entrepreneurship orientation (Andiningtyas & Ratna, 2014).

Previous research about the effect of entrepreneurship on performance as proposed by Barney et al (in Murni et al, 2014) suggests that the performance of the organization is essentially determined by internal resources, especially those related to intangible assets such as entrepreneurial orientation, managerial capabilities, and innovation. Barney et al. (in Murni et al., 2014) examines and analyzes the effect of entrepreneurial orientation on sustainable innovation with the management capability as an intervening variable.

Lumpkin Eisner (in Nur & Salim, 2014) examines entrepreneurship orientation by stating that there are 5 dimensions of entrepreneurship orientation, namely autonomy, inovativeness, risk taking, proactiveness, and competitive aggressiveness. Entrepreneurship orientation show significant effect on performance.

Entrepreneurial orientation, management capabilities, and innovations are direct positive influences and significant to the business performance SMEs in Aceh, Indonesia (Nurlina, 2014).

2 LITERATURE REVIEW

2.1 *Performance of SMEs*

According to Jauch and Glueck (in Soares, 2014) company performance can be seen from the level of sales, profit rate, return on capital, turnover and market share. SMEs not overcoming growth constraints arises from inherent weaknesses in SMEs, such as lack of knowledge and technology for production, lack of marketing knowledge and skill constraints in resources (human and financial), and lack of knowledge in management capabilities (Tambunan, 2009).

2.2 *Entrepreneurship orientation*

The concept of entrepreneurship as an organizational orientation was first used by Miller (in Nurlina, 2014) to capture the risk-taking, innovative and proactive dimension of entrepreneurial behavior. Entrepreneurship orientation is an organization desire to promote and support creativity, flexibility and risk considerations. It demonstrates the entrepreneurial process and attempts to answer the question of how an activity is implemented. Developments in strategic management experience a shift in the entrepreneurial process, in which the methods, practices, and decision-making styles of managers use entrepreneurial action, according to Lumpkin and Dess (in Wardi & Susanto, 2015).

According to Fatoki (in Nayda, 2016), entrepreneurship orientation refers to the tendency of organizational decision-making to support entrepreneurial activities. Entrepreneurship orientation is also an individual process in pursuit of entrepreneurship opportunities based on the level and nature of available resources reflected through innovative, risk-taking, and proactive attitudes.

2.3 *Management capability*

Roman & Soliman, (2016) emphasized the importance of different skills, talents, and competence that constitute managerial capability and of human resource actions that require managerial capability all in a bid to increase performance and foster a firm's growth.

Studies by Jantunen et al., (2005); Gastro, (2007); Balkundi and Harrison, (2006); Ireland et al., (2009); Yang, (2010); Jusoh et al., (2011) and Khalili, 2012 (in Roman and Soliman, 2016) include human relations skills encompassing emotional intelligence, self-management, flexibility, synergy, conflict resolution, time management, employee coaching, team work and learning.

According to Nur and Salim (2014) the management capability of an entrepreneur is a set of administrative and operative skill and competencies required to carry out management functions, such as the ability to plan, organize, direct, supervise, or carry out assignment. This is consistent with the notion that achievement of performance can not be separated from the proper execution of management functions. This is consistent with the approach proposed by (Mintzberg, 2014), in which managerial behavior consists of (a) interpersonal roles, (b) Informational roles and (c) decisional roles.

3 RESEARCH METHODS

The population in this study is all SMEs in Bogor, Indonesian that are registered with the Indonesia Chamber of Commerce and Industry; the total number is 78 SMEs. All populations were sampled. Data collection techniques in this study a questionnaire. The research questionnaires distributed to the respondents contained statements related to the performance of SMEs, entrepreneurship orientation and management capability of SMEs in Bogor. Data analysis technique in this research is by path analysis use proses by the AMOS sofware, version 23.

4 RESULT AND DISCUSSION

4.1 *Result*

4.1.1 *Normality test*

The normality assumption test is shown in Table 2:

Based on Table 2 the multivariate data distribution pattern of research variables tends to follow the normal distribution model. The multivariate critical ratio value of 0.178, Critical ratio ≤ 2.58.

4.1.2 *Hypothesis test*

Hypothesis test results are presented in the Table 3:

Table 2. Normality test.

Variable	Skewness	Critical ratio	Kurtosis	Critical ratio
Entrepreneurship	–	–	0,097	0,175
E_Orientation	0,062	0,225		
Management_ Capability	0,006	0,022	0,265	0,478
Performance	0,301	1,084	0,084	0,151
Multivariate			0,221	0,178

Table 3. Hypothesis test.

Relationship between variables			P-value
Management_ capability orientation	<---	O_Entrepreneurship	0,024
Performance	<---	Management_ Capability	0,040
Performance	<---	O_Entrepreneurship orientation	0,003

Table 3 shows that all exogenous variables have the significant effect on endogenous variables. This can be seen from the significant value of all exegenous variables on endegonous variables where $p \leq 0.05$.

4.2 *Discussion*

The results of this research showed that entrepreneurship orientation variables have a positive and significant influence on management capability with a coefficient of 0.249. In other words, every additional one unit of entrepreneurship orientation will will increase management capability by 0,249%.

The results also showed that entrepreneurship orientation has a positive and significant impact on the performance of SMEs with a path coefficient of 0.314. The path coefficient indicates a positive direction, indicating that if the entrepreneurial orientation increases then the company's performance will also increase. Conversely, if the entrepreneurial orientation decreases, then the performance of the company will also decrease. This shows that we can improve the performance of SMEs in Bogor by increasing the entrepreneurial orientation of business owners. The path coefficient of 0.314 indicates that every one unit increase of entrepreneurship orientation will improve the performance of SMEs by 0.314%.

Furthermore, management capability also has a positive and significant influence on the performance of SMEs with a coefficient of 0.219. The path coefficient shows a positive direction, indicating that if the management capability of business owners in Bogor increased then the performance of the company will also increase. The results of the study are in accordance with the results of the present study are in accordance with the results of the study by Nurlina (2014), showing that Entrepreneurial orientation, management capabilities, and innovations are positive and influence business.

The direct effect of entrepreneurship orientation toward management capability is given by $0{,}2491 \times 0{,}2491 = 0{,}0620$. This shows that the direct effect of entrepreneurship orientation on management capability is 6.20%. The direct effect of entrepreneurship orientation on the performance of SMEs in Bogor is given by $0.3141 \times 0.3141 = 0.0986$. This shows that the direct influence of entrepreneurship orientation on the performance of SMEs in Bogor is 9.86%. The direct effect of management capability on the performance of SMEs in Bogor is given by $0.2187 \times 0.2187 = 0.0478$. This shows that the direct effect between management capability on the performance of SMEs is 4.78%. The indirect effect of entrepreneurship orientation through management capability on the performance of SMEs in Bogor is given by $0{,}2491 \times 2187 = 0{,}054$. This shows that indirect influence of entrepreneurship orientation through management capability on the performance of SMEs in Bogor is 5,4%.

The calculation of direct and indirect effects of exogenous variables on endogenous variables found that the direct effect of entrepreneurship orientation has the greatest effect on the performance of SMEs in Bogor. In other words, entrepreneurship orientation has an important role in improving the performance of SMEs in Bogor.

5 CONCLUSION

The results showed that entrepreneurship orientation variables have a positive and significant effect on management capability of SMEs in Bogor. Entrepreneurship orientation and management capability also have a positive and significant effect on the performance of SMEs in Bogor. The calculations of direct and indirect effects of exogenous variables on endogenous variables found that the direct influence of entrepreneurship orientation has the greatest influence on the performance of SMEs in Bogor.

6 RECOMMENDATION

The authors provide recommendations to improve the performance of SMEs by increasing risks, taking and innovation and by expanding the network. Entrepreneurs also need to improve management capabilities in both planning and processes.

ACKNOWLEDGMENT

The authors would like to thank the Indonesian University of Education (Universitas Pendidikan Indonesia, Bandung) and the Airlangga University that has facilitated international conferences on the framework of the development of science, for a positive impact on the progress of the Indonesian nation. The authors also thanks the Indonesia Endowment Fund for Education (Lembaga Pengelola Dana Pendidikan) for sponsoring the publication of this paper.

REFERENCES

Andiningtyas R.S., & Nughroho. (2014). The Influence of Entrepreneurship Orientation on Small and Medium Enterprise Performance, *Jurnal Manajemen Indonesia* 14(1), 37–46.

Chinchang, P. 2015. Knowledge management capability and goal achievement: An empirical investigation of ISO 9000 certified firms in Thailand, *The Business and Management Review*, *7*(1), 9–10.

Chuang, H., Liu, M., & Chen, Y. (2015). The Effects of Human Resource Capability and Internal Customer Satisfaction on Organizational Effectiveness. *International Journal of Distributed Sensor Networks*, *2015*, 10. https://doi.org/10.1155/2015/83519.

Mintzberg, H. (2004). Managers, Not MBAs: A Hard Look at the Soft Practice of Managing and Management Development. San Francisco: Berrett-Koehler Publisher.

Murni, T., Alhansji, T., Idrus, M.S., & Arifin, Z. (2014). The Effect of Entrepreneurial Orientation on the Management Capability and Sustainable Innovation (Study on Batik Small and Medium Enterprises in East Java Indonesia). *IOSR Journal of Business and Management*, 16(4), 16–20.

Nayda, N. (2016). Innovation Capabiliy Mediate the Effect of Entrepreneurship Orientation on Product Performance of Food Industry Sector in Makassar. *E-Jurnal Manajemen Unud*, Vol. 5, No. 3, 2016: 1915–1941, 5(3).

Nur, N., & Salim, U. 2014. Entrepreneurship Orientation, Market Orientation, Business Strategy, Management Capabilities on Business Performance; Study at Small and Medium Enterprise Printing in Kendari International *Journal of Business and Management Invention* ISSN (Online, 3(12), 8–17).

Nurlina. (2014). The Effect of Management Capabilities and Entrepreneurship Orientation to Innovation and Implication on Business Performance: Study at Embroidery Motifs SMEs in Aceh-Indonesia. *Journal of Economics and Sustainable Development*, 5(26), 57–62.

Ratnawati, T., & Hikmah. (2012). Factors that Influence SME's Performance. *Jurnal Ilmiah Untag Semarang* 2(1), 102–114.

Roman & Soliman, A. (2016). A Phenomenological Analysis of Managerial Capability in SMEs in Nigeria. Mediterranean Journal of Social Sciences, 7(3), 125–137. https://doi.org/10.5901/mjss.2016.v7n3p125.

Soares, C. (2014). Effect of Entrepreneurial orientation on business performance moderated by Government Policy (Study On SMEs In Timor Leste). *International Journal of Business and Management Invention,* 3(8), 64–71.

Sugiyono. (2012). Qualitative and Quantitative Research Methods R & D. Bandung: Alfabeta.

Tambunan, Tulus, 2009, Export-Oriented Small and Medium Industry Clusters in Indonesia, *Journal of Enterprising Communities,* Vol.3, No.1, pp.25–58.

Wardi, Y., & Susanto, P. (2015), Analysis of Entrepreneurship Orientarion on Corporate Performance: Empirical Studies on Small and Medium Enterprises (SMEs) in West Sumatera. SNEMA-Padang. Indonesia.

Increasing Management Relevance and Competitiveness – Sukoco et al. (Eds)
© 2018 Taylor & Francis Group, London, ISBN 978-0-8153-7455-8

The influence of family factors on expatriate performance

N. Kartika
Universitas Airlangga, Surabaya, Indonesia

ABSTRACT: This research has been conducted to get more understanding about expatriate adjustment. Expatriate adjustment is a very important factor for the expatriate and also for the organization. As previous studies about expatriate adjustment have explained, family factors are significantly related to expatriate performance. Therefore, this research framework proposes to integrate expatriate adjustment into various theoretical constructs, such as expatriate performance. The results of this study explain that family factors, consisting of family support, family adaptability, and family-to-work conflict, have a positive influence on expatriate adjustment. Moreover, this study finds that expatriate adjustment has a positive influence on expatriate performance.

1 INTRODUCTION

Previous studies about expatriate adjustment have been popular due to the globalization of the business environment. This study adopted a research framework from Takeuchi (2010). A large number of empirical studies stated that family factors in expatriation can serve as an important role for the expatriate adjustment process (Caligiuri et al., 1998; Takeuchi et al., 2007). Although family and spouse are the major expatriate stresses on foreign assignment (Caligiuri et al., 1999; Shaffer & Harrison, 2001), family support, especially from the spouse, can provide assistance for expatriates to adjust in the stressful new environment (Kraimer et al., 2001). Furthermore, the adaptation of expatriate families to a host country seems to be a crucial aspect of international business assignments (De Leon & McPartlin, 1995). Similarly, the adaptation ability of a family is a critical stress response, both within the family and in the external environment (Caligiuri et al., 1998).

However, an important stressor for families on international assignment is from family-to-work conflict and parental demand (Parasuraman & Simmers, 2001). Another insight from the perspective of family-to-work conflict and the effect of expatriate adjustment is that an expatriate may not be able to meet family responsibilities (Takeuchi et al., 2005).

Many studies have stated that the success of expatriates resulted from expatriate adjustment, commitment, performance of work, completing an assignment, knowledge transfer, and successful business performance (Kraimer & Wayne, 2004; Pulakos et al., 2000). Expatriate performance has meaning in international assignments (Kraimer et al., 2001). Expatriates who can adapt in their foreign assignment have correlation with expatriate job performance and the facilities to support their job performance (Shaffer & Harrison, 2001). Thus, innovation is one of the most powerful sources of competitive advantage and successful business performance (Ireland & Hitt, 1999). Continuing innovation and generating and implementing new ideas are the keys to the success of multinational corporations in the global market (Gupta & Govindarajan, 2000).

This study may be helpful in examining various issues associated with expatriates' adjustment that have not yet been fully investigated. This study also expects the empirical validation of the research framework to develop into a new broader framework for the understanding of expatriate adjustment and performance.

2 LITERATURE REVIEW

2.1 *Family support*

Family support provides assistance for expatriates while adjusting in the stressful new environment (Kraimer et al., 2001). The number of intercultural traits is related to successful adjustment of expatriate spouses, cultural empathy, open-mindedness, emotional stability, flexibility, and social initiative (Van der Zee & Van Oudenhoven, 2000, 2001). Expatriates adapt to their unfamiliar work life and living environment. Family issues are one major source of stress among expatriates and their spouses while on assignment (Caligiuri et al., 1998; Shaffer & Harrison, 2001). Moreover, family support and personal peer networks have also been found to be important predictors of expatriate success in previous studies (Caligiuri et al., 1998; Shaffer & Harrison, 2001).

2.2 *Family adaptability*

Family or spouses can influence expatriate adjustment and provide further evidence of crossover effects (Takeuchi et al., 2007). Family adaptability is the perceived level of comfort and familiarity of the expatriate's family/spouse in the new host culture (Palthe, 2004). A spouse who is unfamiliar with the host culture can have an impact on the expatriate's adjustment process. A spouse who is well-adjusted to the general environment and the host culture may be available to support the expatriate (Takeuchi et al., 2002). On the other hand, the spillover theory, which suggests that the family can affect a worker's performance, provides a better understanding of the relationship between family adjustment and expatriate adjustment (Caliguiri, 1998).

2.3 *Family-to-work conflict*

In the international environment, expatriates feel unfamiliar with both their work and their living environments. Researchers have stated that an important factor affecting expatriate performance is the expatriate's family (Dowling and Welch, 2004). Expatriates have to understand the potential unexpected conflict between family and work. Another prior study examined the direct relationship between the availability of family benefits and outcomes of interest, such as organizational commitment or job satisfaction (Tammy, 2001). For an expatriate's adjustment to be successful, the implementation of family benefits can help employees manage multiple work and non-work responsibilities; it also can inhibit employees from successfully balancing career and family.

2.4 *Expatriate performance*

Expatriate success is often defined in terms of expatriate adjustment, commitment, job performance, and intentions to complete the assignment (Kraimer & Wayne, 2004). Employees who feel well-adjusted to the work environment will be able to perform at higher levels and will have greater reserves of personal resources (time, effort, and emotional investment) available to spend on their behaviors (Shaffer et al., 1999; Shaffer & Harrison, 2001). Expatriate performance can be explained using a four-stage process, which consists of cognitive, affective, co-native, and behavioral components (Lazarova et al., 2010).

3 HYPOTHESES DEVELOPMENT

3.1 *Family support and expatriate adjustment*

Previous studies have shown that spousal support and family adjustment are positively related to work and general adjustment of expatriates (Caligiuri et al., 1998, 1999; Hechnova, 2003; Palthe, 2004). Likewise, spousal support in particular has been identified as a critical source of support for expatriates because of the spillover effect that family support can have on work outcomes (Tung, 1981; Guzzo, 1994). From this discussion, the following hypothesis is proposed:

H1: Family support has a positive effect on expatriate adjustment.

3.2 *Family adaptability and expatriate adjustment*

A good adjustment of spouses in the host country may support and help expatriates to concentrate on their job, which can improve the quality of the foreign assignment (Takeuchi et al., 2002, 2007). A study by Forster (1997) showed that there were clear indications that family relationships, in terms of flexibility/adaptability, cohesion, and communication, played an important role in the outcomes of international assignments. From this discussion, the following hypothesis is proposed:

H2: Family adaptability has a positive effect on expatriate adjustment.

3.3 *Family-to-work conflict and expatriate adjustment*

From previous studies, it is recognized that family members can impact and be influenced by expatriates (Edwards & Rothbard, 2000; Greenhause & Powell, 2003). Moreover, workers who fail to adequately balance role requirements between work and family were found to have negatively influenced job satisfaction and performance (Aryee et al., 1999). Hence, the following hypothesis is proposed:

H3: Family-to-work conflict has a negative effect on expatriate adjustment.

3.4 *Expatriate adjustment and expatriate performance*

Individuals who are well-adjusted to work and to the general environment will be able to perform at higher levels. Moreover, well-adjusted expatriates will have greater reserves of personal resources (time, effort, and emotional investment) available to spend on the behaviors that facilitate their job performance (Shaffer & Harrison, 1999, 2001). The maladjustment of expatriates can result in poor performance (Caligiuri, 1997). It was expected by Takeuchi et al.

(2005) that expatriates' work adjustment is strongly correlated to their performance. From this discussion, the following hypothesis is proposed:

H4: Expatriate adjustment has a positive effect on expatriate performance.

4 RESEARCH METHODOLOGY

This research acquired 287 responses from expatriates in Taiwan and Mainland China, with an effective response rate of 15.9%. In order to achieve the purposes of this study and to test the hypotheses, SPSS 18 software was used to analyze the collected data. Questionnaire design was measured on a seven-point rating scale to indicate level of agreement toward each statement, from 1 = strongly disagree to 7 = strongly agree.

5 DISCUSSIONS AND RESULTS

This section explains the results (Table 1). Regression model M1 presents the testing of hypothesis H1. The result shows that family support has significant positive influence on expatriate adjustment ($\beta = 0.588$, $R^2 = 0.346$, F-value = 184.583, P-value = 0.000). This result is in line with previous studies showing that spousal support and family adjustment is positively related to work and general adjustment of expatriates (Caligiuri et al., 1998, 1999; Harvey, 1998; Hechnova, 2003; Palthe, 2004). Thus, the result supports hypothesis Hl that family support has significant positive influence on expatriate adjustment.

Regression model M2 presents the testing of hypothesis H2. The result shows that family adaptability has significant positive influence on expatriate adjustment ($\beta = 0.844$, $R^2 = 0.712$, F-value = 705.893, P-value = 0.000). This result is in line with prior study which explained that the good adjustment of spouses in the host country may support and help expatriates to concentrate on their job and can improve the quality of the foreign assignment (Takeuchi et al., 2002, 2007). Thus, the result supports hypothesis H2 that family adaptability has significant positive influence on expatriate adjustment.

Regression model M3 presents the testing of hypothesis H3. The result shows that family-to-work conflict has significant positive influence on expatriate adjustment ($\beta = 0.570$, F-value = 137.170, P-value = 0.000). The result does not support hypothesis H3 that family-to-work conflict has significant negative impact on expatriate adjustment. This result can be related to the spillover theory in that the condition concerns the transmission of states of well-being from one domain of life to another (Westman, 2002). In this study, family domains may have an effect on expatriates' work, and the demands of work and family collide.

Furthermore, the spillover theory postulates the conditions under which the spillover between work and family is positive (Hill et al., 2003). The overlap between work and family enables individuals (i.e., expatriates) to integrate responsibility in time and space for achieving a healthy work and family balance. It can be inferred that the expatriates with healthy work and family balance more easily adjust to their new work environment. Furthermore, by adopting the U theory, this positive influence of family-to-work conflict on expatriate adjustment may only be feasible if the conflict is low to medium. When the conflict is extremely high, then negative influence may result.

Regression model M4 presents the testing of hypothesis H4. The result shows that expatriate adjustment has significant positive influence on expatriate performance ($\beta = 0.626$, F-value = 183.826, P-value = 0.000). This result is in line with prior studies showing that expatriates' work adjustment is strongly correlated to expatriates' performance and has positive relationship with job performance (Kraimer & Wayne, 2004; Takeuchi et al., 2005). Low expatriate adjustment and expatriate maladjustment can result in poor performance (Caligiuri, 1997; Kraimer et al., 2001; Mol et al., 2005). This result implies that, when expatriates are well-adjusted in the new environment, it is easier for them to interact with/adjust to the work environment. Thus, this result supports hypothesis H4 that expatriate adjustment has significant positive impact on expatriate performance.

There are several implications of this research for multinational companies, especially for human resource departments, which always arrange and manage the expatriation process. Moreover, this study can become a reference for organizations to be aware of the crossover factors of expatriate adjustment. Knowing and understanding the factors that can influence and be influenced by

Table 1. Regression analyses of antecedents on expatriate adjustment.

Variable	M1	M2	M3	M4
Family support	0.588***			
Family adaptability		0.844***		
Family-to-work conflict			0.570***	
Expatriate performance				0.626***
R^2	0.346	0.712	0.325	0.392
Adjusted R^2	0.343	0.711	0.323	0.39
F-value	150.508	705.893	137.17	183.826
P-value	0.000	0.000	0.000	0.000

Notes: *$P < 0.1$, **$P < 0.05$, ***$P < 0.01$.

expatriate adjustment is very important for organizations. The findings of this study have also provided practical implications and suggested the need for multinationals to provide more support for expatriates in order to increase adjustment. For instance, the parent company or foreign subsidiary could offer a support structure for expatriates. Multinationals centering training on problems will help the work adjustment of expatriates.

REFERENCES

Aldous, J. (1969). Occupational characteristics and males' role performance in the family. *Journal of Marriage and Family, 31*, 707–712.

Ali, A., Van der Zee, K., & Sanders, G. (2003). Determinants of intercultural adjustment among expatriate spouses. *International Journal of Intercultural Relations, 27*(5), 563–580.

Argote, L.P. & Ingram, P. (2000). Knowledge transfer: A basis for competitive advantage in firms. *Organizational Behavior and Human Decision Processes, 82*(1), 150–169.

Aryee, S., Luk, V., Leung, A., & Lo, S. (1999). Role stressors, interrole conflict, and well-being: The moderating influence of spousal support and coping behaviors among employed parents in Hong Kong. *Journal of Vocational Behavior, 54*(2), 259–278.

Black, J.S. & Stephens, G. (1989). The influence of the spouse on American expatriate adjustment and intent to stay in Pacific Rim overseas assignments. *Journal of Management, 15*(4), 529–544.

Black, J.S. & Porter, L.W. (1991). Managerial behaviors and job performance: A successful manager in Los Angeles may not succeed in Hong Kong. *Journal of International Business Studies, 22*(1), 99–113.

Caligiuri, P.M., Hyland, M., Joshi, A., & Bross, A. (1998). A theoretical framework for examining the relationship between family adjustment and expatriate adjustment to working in the host country. *Journal of Applied Psychology, 83*(4), 598–614.

Caligiuri, P.M., Joshi, A., & Lazarova, M. (1999). Factors influencing the adjustment of women on global assignments. *International Journal of Human Resource Management, 10*(2), 163–179.

Canty-Mitchell, J. & Zimet, G.D. (2000). Psychometric properties of the multidimensional scale of perceived social support in urban adolescents. *American Journal of Community Psychology, 28*, 391–400.

Carraher, S.M., Sullivan, S.E., & Crocitto, M.M. (2008). Mentoring across global boundaries: An empirical examination of home- and host-country mentors on expatriate career outcomes. *Journal of International Business Studies, 39*(8), 1310–1326.

Collings, D.G. & Mellahi, K. (2009). Strategic talent management: A review and research agenda. *Human Resource Management Review, 19*(4), 304–313.

De Leon, C.T. & McPartlin, D. (1995). Adjustment of expatriate children. In J. Selmerpp (Ed.), *Expatriate management: New ideas for international business* (pp. 197–214). Connecticut: Quorum Books.

Dean, M.A., Russell, C.J., & Muchinsky, P.M. (1999). Life experiences and performance prediction: Toward a theory of biodata. *Research in Personnel and Human Resources Management, 17*, 245–283.

Dicken, C. (1969). Predicting the success of peace corps community development workers. *Journal of Consulting and Clinical Psychology, 33*, 597–606.

Dowling, P.J. & Welch, D.E. (2004). *International human resource management. Managing people in a multinational context* (4th ed.). London: Thomson.

Earley, P.C. & Peterson, R.S. (2004). The elusive cultural chameleon: Cultural intelligence as a new approach to intercultural training for the global manager. *Academy of Management Learning & Education, 3*(1), 100–115.

Eby, L.T., W.J., Casper, Lockwood, A., Bordeaux, C., & Brinley, A. (2005). A twenty-year retrospective on work and family research in IO/OB: A review of the literature. *Journal of Vocational Behavior, 66*, 124–197.

Edwards, T. & Ferner, A. (2004). Multinationals, reverse diffusion and national business systems. *Management International Review*, 49–79.

Eiadat, Y., Kelly, A., Roche, F.F., & Eyadat, H. (2008). Green and competitive? An empirical test of the mediating role of environmental innovation strategy. *Journal of World Business*, 43(2), 131–145.

Ensher, E.A., Grant-Vallone, E.J., & Donaldson, S.I. (2001). Effects of perceived discrimination on job satisfaction, organizational commitment, organizational citizenship behavior, and grievances. *Human Resource Development Quarterly*.

Eschbach, D.M., Parker, G.E., & Stoeberl, P.A. (2001). American repatriate employees' retrospective assessments of the effects of cross-cultural training on their adaptation to international assignments. *International Journal of Human Resource Management, 12*(2), 270–287.

Grant-Vallone, E.J. & Ensher, E.A. (2001). An examination of work and personal life conflict, organizational support, and employee health among international expatriates. *International Journal of Intercultural Relations, 25*(3), 261–278.

Hechanova, R., Beehr, T.A., & Christiansen, N.D. (2003). Antecedents and consequences of employees' adjustment to overseas assignment: A meta-analytic review. *Applied Psychology, 52*(2), 213–236.

Hill, E.J., Ferris, M., & Märtinson, V. (2003). Does it matter where you work? A comparison of how three work venues (traditional office, virtual office, and home office) influence aspects of work and personal/family life. *Journal of Vocational Behavior, 63*(2): 220–241.

Hitt, M.A., Tihanyi L., Miller, L.T., & Connelly, B. (2006). International diversification: Antecedents, outcomes, and moderators. *Journal of Management, 32*(6), 831–867.

Huang, T.J., Chi, S.C., & Lawler, J.J. (2005). The relationship between expatriates' personality traits and their adjustment to international assignments. *The International Journal of Human Resource Management, 16*(9), 1656–1670.

Ireland, R.D. & Hitt, M.A. (1999). Achieving and maintaining strategic competitiveness in the 21st century: The role of strategic leadership. *The Academy of Management Executive, 13*(1), 43–57.

Janssen, O. (2000). Job demands, perceptions of effort-reward fairness and innovative work behaviour. *Journal*

of Occupational and Organizational Psychology, *73*(3), 287–302.
Jensen, R. & Szulanski, G. (2004). Stickiness and the adaptation of organizational practices in cross-border knowledge transfers. *Journal of International Business Studies*, *35*(6), 508–523.
Jassawalla, A.R., Asgary, N., & Sashittal, H.C. (2006). Managing expatriate: The role of mentors. *International Journal of Commerce and Management*, *16*(2), 130–140.
Kraimer, M.L., Wayne, S.J., & Jaworski, R.A.A. (2001). Sources of support and expatriate performance: The mediating role of expatriate adjustment. *Personnel Psychology*, *54*(1), 71–99.
Kraimer, M.L. & Wayne, S.J. (2004). An examination of perceived organizational support as a multidimensional construct in the context of an expatriate assignment. *Journal of Management*, *30*(2), 209–237.
Lambert, S.J. (1990). Processes linking work and family: A critical review and research agenda. *Human Relations*, *43*(3), 239–257.
Lashbrook, W.B. (1997). Business performance, employee satisfaction, and leadership practices. *Performance Improvement*, *36*(5), 29–33.
Lazarova, M., Westman M. & Shaffer, M.A. (2010). Elucidating the positive side of the work-family interface on international assignments: A model of expatriate work and family performance. *Academy of Management Review*, *35*(1), 93–117.
Liden, R.C. & Maslyn, J.M. (1998). Multidimensionality of leader-member exchange: An empirical assessment through scale development. *Journal of Management*, *24*(1), 43–72.
Lii, S.Y. & Wong, S.Y. (2008). The antecedents of overseas adjustment and commitment of expatriates. *The International Journal of Human Resource Management*, *19*(2), 296–313.
Lin, N. (2001). *Social capital*. Cambridge, UK: Cambridge University Press.
Liu, X. & Shaffer, M.A. (2005). An investigation of expatriate adjustment and performance: A social capital perspective. *International Journal of Cross Cultural Management*, *5*(3), 235–254.
Lubinski, D. (2004). Introduction to the special section on cognitive abilities: 100 years after Spearman's (1904) "general intelligence," objectively determined and measured. *Journal of Personality and Social Psychology*, *86*(1): 96–111.
Martin, D.C. & Bartol, K.M. (2003). Factors influencing expatriate performance appraisal system success: An organizational perspective. *Journal of International Management*, *9*(2), 115–132.
McNulty, Y., De Cieri, H., & Hutchings, K. (2009). Do global firms measure expatriate return on investment? An empirical examination of measures, barriers and variables influencing global staffing practices. *The International Journal of Human Resource Management*, 20(6).
Shaffer, M.A. & Harrison, D.A. (1998). Expatriates' psychological withdrawal from international assignments: work, nonwork, and family influences. *Personnel Psychology*, *51*(1), 87–118.
Shaffer, M.A., Harrison, D.A., & Gilley, K.M. (1999). Dimensions, determinants, and differences in the expatriate adjustment process. *Journal of International Business Studies*, 557–581.
Shaffer, M.A. & Harrison, D.A. (2001). Forgotten partners of international assignments: development and test of a model of spouse adjustment. *Journal of Applied Psychology*, *86*(2), 238.
Shay, J.P. & Baack, S.A. (2004). Expatriate assignment, adjustment and effectiveness: an empirical examination of the big picture. *Journal of International Business Studies*, *35*(3), 216–232.
Shay, J.P. & Baack, S. (2006). An empirical investigation of the relationships between modes and degree of expatriate adjustment and multiple measures of performance. *International Journal of Cross Cultural Management*, *6*(3), 275–294.
Small, S.A. & Riley, D. (1990). Toward a multidimensional assessment of work spillover into family life. *Journal of Marriage and the Family*, 51–61.
Sonnentag, S. & Frese, M. (2003). Stress in organisations. In W.C. Borman, D.R. Ilgen, & R.J. Klimoski (Eds.), *Comprehensive handbook of psychology* (Vol. 12, pp. 453–491). Hoboken, NJ: Wiley.
Takeuchi, R. (2010). A critical review of expatriate adjustment research through a multiple stakeholder view: Progress, emerging trends, and prospects. *Journal of Management*, *36*(4), 1040–1064.
Takeuchi, R., Lepak, D.P., Marinova, S.V., & Yun, S. (2007). Nonlinear influences of stressors on general adjustment: the case of Japanese expatriates and their spouses. *Journal of International Business Studies*, *38*(6), 928–943.
Takeuchi, R., Shay, J.P., & Jiatao, L. (2008). When does decision autonomy increase expatriate managers' adjustment? An empirical test. *Academy of Management Journal*, *51*(1), 45–60.
Tarique, I. & Schuler, R.S. (2010). Global talent management: Literature review, integrative framework, and suggestions for further research. *Journal of World Business*, *45*(2), 122–133.
Thomas, D.C. & Inkson, K. (2004). *Cultural intelligence: People skills for global business*. San Francisco, CA: Berrett-Koehler Publishers.
Tucker, M.F., Bonial, R. & Lahti, K. (2004). The definition, measurement and prediction of intercultural adjustment and job performance among corporate expatriates. *International Journal of Intercultural Relations*, *28*(3), 221–251.
Tung, R. (1981). Selecting and training of personnel for overseas assignments. *Columbia Journal of World Business*, *16*, 68–78.
Van der Zee, K.I. & Van Oudenhoven, J.P. (2000). The Multicultural Personality Questionnaire: A multidimensional instrument of multicultural effectiveness. *European Journal of Personality*, *14*(4), 291–309.
Van der Bank, M. & Rothmann, S. (2006). Correlates of expatriates' cross-cultural adjustment. *Management Dynamics*, *15*(4), 29–39.
Wang, S., Tong, T.W., Chen, G., & Kim, H. (2009). Expatriate utilization and foreign direct investment performance: The mediating role of knowledge transfer. *Journal of Management*, *35*(5), 1181–1206.
Westman, M. (2002). Gender asymmetry in crossover research. In D.L. Nelson & R.J. Burke (Eds.), *Gender, work stress, and health* (pp. 129–149). Washington, DC: American Psychological Association.

Increasing Management Relevance and Competitiveness – Sukoco et al. (Eds)
© 2018 Taylor & Francis Group, London, ISBN 978-0-8153-7455-8

Is firm size an important determinant for firms in establishing political connections?

N.N. Amorita, D. Agustia & I. Harymawan
Universitas Airlangga, Surabaya, Indonesia

ABSTRACT: The purpose of this study is to investigate whether the size of firms affects the relationship between political connections and firm value in Indonesia. The sample of this study is firms listed on the Indonesian Stock Exchange in the period 2008–10. This study uses regression analysis. Results show that politically connected firms with size above the median have a positive impact on firm value. Interestingly, results show that politically connected firms with size below the median are associated with negative firm value. These findings indicate that the size of firms can help us to differentiate the outcome of connected firms. Therefore, the results of this study imply that the size of connected firms is an important determinant to define the motivation of these firms in establishing political connections.

1 INTRODUCTION

Prior studies have found that political connections can provide preferential benefit to business connections (Agrawal and Knoeber, 2001; Backman, 2001; Blau et al., 2013). However, there is still need for further investigation on several determinants that could affect the level of benefits or outcomes of politically connected firms. This study examines the role of firm size on the relationship between political connections and firm value in Indonesia.

The data used in this study are taken from all firms listed on the Indonesian Stock Exchange (IDX) spanning the period 2008–10. The final observation of this study is 828 firm-year observations. This study employs a regression method to test the hypotheses.

First, we examine how political connections affect firm value. We find that politically connected firms do not significantly associate with firm value. Since size is an important determinant of firms being politically connected, we further examine how firm size can affect the relationship between political connections and firm value.

To do so, we construct an interaction variable that relates political connections to firm size and add this variable into our baseline regression model. Interestingly, our finding shows that connected firms with firm size above the median are significantly associated with higher firm performance. In contrast, connected firms with firm size below the median are significantly associated with lower firm performance.

This study contributes to the extant literature by investigating the role of firm size as an important determinant in the outcome of politically connected firms. We argue that this finding reveals the different motivations of firms in establishing political connections depending on firm size. The remainder of this paper is structured as follows. Section 2 describes the literature and develops the hypotheses. Section 3 describes the sample and method. Section 4 presents the main result and the result of sensitivity tests. Section 5 presents concluding remarks.

2 LITERATURE REVIEW AND HYPOTHESES

This study uses the rent-seeking theory (Krueger, 1974) in testing the hypotheses. Rent-seeking is a way to obtain economic rents by manipulating the social or political environment in which economic activity takes place. A simple example of the practice of rent-seeking in a modern economy is bribing a politician to lobby the government to gain an advantage for private interest or to tighten the rules for competitors for private benefit.

Several prior studies have examined how political connections in Indonesia affect business decisions and outcomes. Fisman (2001) found that firms connected to President Suharto experienced a negative market reaction when there was bad news related to the health of the president. Furthermore, Leuz and Oberholzer-Gee (2006) found that politically connected firms experienced difficulties gaining financial access when their connections fell from power. Their finding is consistent with those of Goldman et al. (2009), who showed that in the United States firms connected to the Republican Party increased in value whereas those connected to the Democratic Party decreased in value when the Republicans won the 2000 presidential election.

Harymawan and Nowland (2016) found that increased government effectiveness reduces the benefits of political connections, requiring politically connected firms to be more responsive to market pressures and resulting in higher earnings quality. Interestingly, increased political stability enhances the certainty of benefits from political connections, reducing the need for politically connected firms to respond to market pressures and resulting in lower earnings quality.

Bebchuk and Neeman (2005) argued that politicians play a role in determining the level of investor protection (through regulation and policy) for outside investors. This protection determines the extent to which corporate insiders, or in this case managers and shareholders, who have control in company decisions gain advantages for their private interest.

Goldman et al. (2009) examined the effect of political connections on countries with a strong legal system in the United States. They found that firms' abnormal stock return is positive after the announcement of the nomination of politically connected individuals to the company board. In contrast, Gray et al. (2016) found that, in Australia, the market reacts negatively following the appointment of politically connected directors. Niessen and Ruenzi (2010) examined the relationship between political connections and firm performance in Germany. They found that stock market returns of connected firms are significantly higher than those of non-connected ones. In addition, Hillman (2005) found that the performance of connected firms, proxied by an adjusted market capitalization and the market adjusted to book, is significantly higher than that of non-politically connected firms. Based on the above discussion, we expect that firms with political connections in Indonesia will have higher firm performance than non-politically connected firms. The formal statement of hypothesis 1 is as follows:

H1: Politically connected firms will have positive associations with firm value.

Prior research found that firm size is positively associated with political connections. This indicates that larger firms are more likely to become politically connected. However, in being a politically connected firm it is not necessary to be a larger firm. We predict that the size of the firm is an indicator to differentiate the motivation of the firm in being politically connected, which also results in different outcomes for the firms. Therefore, we propose hypothesis 2 as follows:

H2: Politically connected firms with larger (smaller) firm size will have positive (negative) association with firm value.

3 DATA AND METHOD

The data used in this study were obtained from the financial statements of all companies listed on the IDX in the period 2008–10. We imposed the following selection criteria to construct the sample. First, we dropped all firms with missing data. Second, we dropped all firms in the financial industry (Standard Industrial Classification 6) due to the different nature of the financial statements. Third, we required all firms included in this study to have their financial statement end on December 31. Thus, we obtained 828 firm-year observations as our final sample. Table 1 presents the distributions of firms, with and without political connections, by year.

The data source of political connections is a list of companies that have political connections obtained from previous research by Basuki (2012). That study defines politically connected firms as those firms having at least one politically exposed person on their boards. Table 1 presents the distribution of connected and non-connected firms for each year.

The dependent variable is firm value (Tobin's *Q*). The institutional variable examined in this study is *PCON* versus *non-PCON*. *PCON* is defined as perceptions of the likelihood of the firm which is politically connected such as with government, while *non-PCON* is conversely not politically connected. A dummy variable is constructed to indicate whether or not a firm has political connections. This study also includes several control variables that are found to influence firm value (*ROA*, *LEVERAGE*, *SIZE*). This study employed Ordinary Least Square (OLS) and robust regression on testing the hypotheses.

Table 1. Firms' distribution by year.

Year	Connections	No connections	Total
2008	98	180	278
2009	97	178	275
2010	97	178	275
Total	292	536	828

4 RESULTS

Table 2 presents the descriptive statistics of the sample. About 35.3% of firms from total observations are politically connected. On average, the firm value of the firm is 4.133. The mean of total debt over total assets is 59.5%.

Table 3 provides the results of regression in this study. Specification model 1 tests the hypotheses using the OLS method. The coefficient of *PCON* is 0.027. Although all control variables are found to be significant, *PCON* is statistically insignificant. Specification model 2 re-examines the hypotheses using the robust regression method. The result is similar to specification model 1. This finding shows that political connections do not significantly affect the firm value.

Next, we test whether or not the size of firms affects the relationship between political connections and firm value. Table 4 reports the regression result of political connections, firm size, and firm value. Similar to Table 3, in this table we also employ two analyses to test the hypothesis. In specification model 1, using regression analysis, we find that the coefficient of the interaction variable between political connections and firm size (*PCON* × *SIZE*) is 8.342 and statistically significant at the 1% level (*t*-value = 2.73). Interestingly, the coefficient of *PCON* is –4.903 and statistically significant at the 5% level (*t*-value = 2.01).

Specification model 2 re-estimates specification model 1 using robust regression. Similar to model 1, we find that variable *PCON* × *SIZE* and *PCON* are positively and negatively (both significant) associated with firm value, respectively. It suggests that politically connected firms with a larger firm size are associated with a higher firm value. In contrast, those with a smaller firm size are associated with a smaller firm value.

These findings indicate that different sizes of politically connected firms lead to different firm outcomes. These could also indicate that there are motivational differences for large and small firms in establishing political connections.

Table 2. Descriptive statistics.

Variables	Mean	Median	Minimum	Maximum
Tobin's *Q*	4.133	0.975	0.193	220.314
PCON	0.353	0	0	1
ROA	0.059	0.048	–0.44	0.568
LEVERAGE	0.595	0.535	15	2.984
SIZE	27.547	27598	20620	32.234

ROA, Return on Assets.

Table 3. Results of regression of political connections on firm value.

	Predicted sign	*Tobin's Q* [1]	*Tobin's Q* [2]
Variables			
PCON	+	0.027	0.027
		(0.02)	(0.02)
ROA	+	23.082***	23.082*
		(–4.29)	(–1.93)
LEVERAGE	+	12.430***	12.430***
		(–7.16)	(–2.75)
SIZE	–	–3.775***	–3.775***
		(–8.58)	(–3.63)
Fixed effects			
Industry		Included	Included
Year		Included	Included
R-squared		0.165	0.165
N		828	828

Table 4. Results of regression of political connections and firm size on firm value.

	Predicted sign	*Tobin's Q* [1]	*Tobin's Q* [2]
Variables			
PCON × SIZE	+	8.342***	8.342***
		(2.73)	(2.60)
PCON	–	–4.903**	–4.903*
		(–2.01)	(–1.79)
ROA	+	22.747***	22.747*
		(4.24)	(–1.91)
LEVERAGE	+	12.098***	12.098***
		(6.98)	(2.71)
SIZE	–	–4.367***	–4.367***
		(–8.93)	(–3.67)
Fixed effects			
Industry		Included	Included
Year		Included	Included
R-squared		0.172	0.172
N		828	828

5 CONCLUSION

This paper reveals firm size is an important determinant that leads to different outcomes of politically connected firms. We find that connected firms with firm size above the average are significantly associated with higher firm performance. In contrast, connected firms with firm size below the median are significantly associated with lower firm performance. Based on these findings, we argue that firms have different motivations in establishing political connections based on their firm size.

For large firms, the reason to establish political connections is more related to increase in firm value, such as expanding market share by obtaining a special license from their connections (e.g., import, export, forestry concession licenses). In contrast, small firms are more likely to be politically connected to gain benefits that can help them to escape their financial difficulties. This study contributes to the political connection literature by explaining that firm size is an important determinant of the firm value of politically connected firms.

REFERENCES

Agrawal, A., & Knoeber, C. (2001). Do some outside directors play a political role? *Journal of Law and Economics*, *44*, 179–198.

Backman, M. (2001). *Asian eclipse: Exposing the dark side of business in Asia* (Revised Edition). Singapore: John Wiley & Sons.

Bebchuk, L., & Neeman, Z. (2005). A political economy models of investor protection. Incomplete Working Draft. Cambridge, MA: Harvard Law School.

Blau, B., Brough, T., & Thomas, D. (2013). Corporate lobbying, political connections and the bailout of banks. *Journal of Banking and Finance*, *37*, 3007–3017.

Faccio, M. (2006). Politically connected firms. *The American Economic Review*, *96*(1), 369–386.

Fisman, R. (2001). Estimating the value of political connections. *The American Economic Review*, *91*(4), 1095–1102.

Gray, S., Harymawan, I., & Nowland, J. (2016). Political and government connections on corporate boards in Australia: Good for business? *Australian Journal of Management*, *41*(1), 3–26.

Goldman, E., Rocholl, J., & So, J. (2009). Do politically connected firm affect firm value? *Review of Financial Studies*, *22*(6), 2331–2360.

Harymawan, I., & Nowland, J.E. (2016). Political connections and earnings quality: How do connected firms respond to changes in the political stability and government effectiveness? *International Journal of Accounting & Information Management*, *24*(4), 339–356.

Hillman, A.J. (2005). Politicians on the board of directors: Do connections affect the bottom line? *Journal of Management*, *31*(3), 464–481.

Krueger, A.O. (1974). The political economy of the rent-seeking society. *The American Economic Review*, *64*(3), 291–303.

Leuz, C., & Oberholzer-Gee, F. (2006). Political relationships, global financing, and corporate transparency: Evidence from Indonesia. *Journal of Financial Economics*, *81*(2), 411–439.

Niessen, A., & Ruenzi, S. (2010). Political connectedness and firm performance: Evidence from Germany. *German Economic Review*, *11*(4), 441–464.

Sobel, R.S., & Graefe-Anderson, R.L. (2014). The relationship between political connections and the financial performance of industries and firms. *Mercatus Center Working Paper*, pp. 14–18.

Sudiyatno, B., & Puspitasari, E. (2010). Tobin's Q and Altman Z-score as an indicator of firms' performance measurement. *Journal of Scientific Accounting Review*, *2*(1), 9–21.

Tjondro, E., & Basuki. (2012). Studies about political tie, its influence on decision to grant credit bank in Indonesia. *Journal of Accounting and Finance*, *14*(2), 116–134.

Increasing Management Relevance and Competitiveness – Sukoco et al. (Eds)
© 2018 Taylor & Francis Group, London, ISBN 978-0-8153-7455-8

Integration of corporate social responsibility and resource based theory to create and capture value

N. Nandang & H. Mulyadi
Universitas Pendidikan Indonesia, Bandung, Indonesia

ABSTRACT: This research aims to analyze the creation and capture of the value of social responsibility to a company, by connecting Corporate Social Responsibility (CSR) with Resource Based Theory (RBT). This study is entirely based on the results of literature studies. By integrating CSR, RBT, economic models, hedonic pricing, and contingent assessment models, this research found how RBT can provide a structure for determining the strategic value of CSR in building a Sustainable Competitive Advantage (SCA). This research implies that companies involved in CSR have enhanced reputations which can have a positive impact on reducing capital and labor costs. This paper systematically reviews the existing literature and reveals theoretically and determines how to measure the strategic value of CSR that can contribute to an organization's Sustainable Competitive Advantage and contribute positively to society.

1 INTRODUCTION

Corporate Social Responsibility (CSR) was first published by Bowen's "Social responsibilities of the businessman" in 1953. Over time, this topic was of interest to other scholars (Carroll, 1979; Wartick and Cochran, 1985). In this work Bowen argues that industry has an obligation "to pursue those policies, to make those decisions, or to follow those lines of actions which are desirable in terms of the objectives and values of society" (Bowen, 1953). Meanwhile Epstein (1987) found that a specific concept of business ethics can be traced even further to certain academics and entrepreneurs who announced the belief that "private business is a public trust". Bowen (1953) stipulates that the concept of corporate social responsibility, in particular, stressed that businesses exist at the pleasure of the public and their behavior and methods of operation must comply with the guidelines set by the community; businesses act as moral agents within society. Furthermore, Wood (1991) extends this idea and summarizes it into three principles driving social responsibility: first, the business is a social institution and, therefore, it is obliged to use power responsibly; second, the businesses are responsible for the outcomes relating to their areas of involvement with society; third, individual managers are moral agents who are obliged to exercise discretion in their decision making.

The focus of this CSR study is on the management literature about the relationship between CSR and corporate performance (Margolis & Walsh, 2001; McWilliams & Siegel, 2000; Orlitzky, Schmidt, & Rynes, 2003). From a theoretical point of view, there is little consideration of the influence of CSR strategy in creating and capturing the value to the company. But empirically, it is difficult to evaluate the benefits of CSR on their activities. This is usually because the resource capabilities are intangible. However, this study tries to integrate Resource Based Theory (RBT) with measuring the added value contributed by CSR activities.

2 METHODS

2.1 *Type of research*

This research is a concept article based entirely on the literature. This study focuses on how organizational values are formed through CSR and RBT so that strategies can efficiently produce and build a Sustainable Competitive Advantage (SCA) in improving the competitiveness of organizations.

2.2 *Data collection methods*

Types of data collected by authors in this study are secondary data, that is data that obtained from journals, books and documentation with database elements beeda, SABINET, EBSCOHost ProQuest and Emerald. From this research, writers like Bowen, Barney, Baron, Carroll, Donnet, Sharfman and many others, are identified.

2.3 *Data analysis methods*

The data obtained was then analyzed by the descriptive analysis method. This does not merely describe, but also provides understanding and explanations.

3 THEORETICAL DEVELOPMENT OF STRATEGIC CSR

The use of CSR to capture value for a firm was firstly referred to as "strategic" CSR by Baron (2001). This confirms that CSR is conceptualized as a responsible action and motivation for an action that identifies social interests, as opposed to the personal interests of the company. When the motivation is to serve the community, it will be treated as an action of social responsibility, but when the motivation is to serve the interests of the company or organization, then the actions are treated as personal responsibility.

Strategic CSR companies, according to McWilliams and Siegel (2001a), use a RBT framework for building a formal model of "maximization of profit" through CSR. A simple example is when two companies produce the same product, except that one firm adds an additional "social" attribute or feature to the product, which is valued by some consumers or, potentially, by other stakeholders. In this model, managers conduct a cost-benefit analysis to determine the level of resources to devote to CSR activities or attributes. That is, they assess the demand for CSR and also evaluate the cost of satisfying this demand. Up to the point where the marginal cost how to measure the value added by CSR to the firm, and to society, is much more difficult.

McWilliams and Siegel (2001a) describe the RBT framework for CSR as a strategy of differentiation. Several authors have developed the concept that there is a demand for CSR, so that CSR strategies can be formulated to achieve and maintain a competitive advantage. In particular, some authors (Bagnoli and Watts, 2003; Besley and Ghatak, 2007; Kotchen, 2006) see CSR as a provider of local public goods (e.g. social networks, community development) or the reduction of adverse effects to the public (e.g. pollution).

Others have focused attention on the role of information asymmetry in the provision of CSR (Siegel & Vitaliano, 2007). As noted by Bagnoli and Watts (2003), strategic CSR occurs when a company links the provision of a public good to the sale of its private goods or services (e.g., ecolabeling). Siegel and Vitaliano hypothesized that customers view a firm's CSR as a positive signal regarding the characteristics of the private good or service the firm is selling. Thus, one would expect that firms selling experience or credence goods or services (where quality is highly uncertain to the consumer, so the consumer must rely heavily on the firm's reputation for quality) are more likely to engage in CSR than firms selling search goods or services. The authors confirm these hypotheses in their empirical analysis.

Furthermore, Manasakis, Mitrokostas, and Petrakis (2007) treat CSR as a strategic variable in oligopolistic competition. Nyborg and Brekke (2004) state that the granting of CSR enables companies to develop human resource capabilities. Specifically, they assert that CSR is a labor market screening strategy that allows companies to attract employees who are motivated and productive. Russo and Fouts (1997) consider CSR as a mechanism to develop the ability of environmental resources. Other strategic advantages that may be associated with CSR include the ability to attract investors (Baron & Diermeier, 2007) or the use of CSR interventions to preempt government regulation (Baron, 2001; Maxwell, Lyon, & Hackett, 2000).

3.1 *Theoretical framework integrating*

Kraaijenbrink, Spender, and Groen (2010) recently assessed critiques of the RBT and found some to be difficult to dismiss, therefore requiring more theoretical development. One of the problematic critiques they identified was the valuation of resources that can create SCA. McWilliams and Siegel (2011) analyzed the two concepts of different RBT values; the value to consumers and the value to the company. They also introduce two theories to determine the value of the company's product or service to consumers, namely hedonic prices and contingent assessment.

RBT has been widely accepted as a theory to explain the sources of competitive advantage and inform managers about how to identify these sources. Sources of competitive advantage will be controlled by the company, which is a valuable resource, rare, difficult to imitate, and are not substitutable (Barney, 1991). Related to RBT, Barney confirms how companies can determine the value of the resource and also how much the company should invest in resources. The first step in determining the source that can lead to SCA is by identifying valuable resources. A company creates value when the revenue (value) generated is higher than the cost of resources to the company. Thus, the value is the difference between revenue generated or contributed and the costs incurred by the company's resources.

There are two different types of resource; real resources (tangible) and intangible resources (intangible). Valuable resources (superior) are scarce, not easily imitated, and not substitutable. Thus, superior resources allow RBT to be a source of SCA for the organization.

Assuming these resources are not free, McWilliams and Siegel (2001a) integrate RBT with the previous theory to show that there is some level of optimization of resource investment that will maximize the company's profits. Resource optimization levels of CSR will demonstrate the level where the difference between total revenue and total costs, can be determined by a cost benefit analysis.

3.2 *Extending the RBT framework to CSR*

3.2.1 *Hedonic analysis*

Hedonic pricing (Rosen, 1974) is a technique that has been used to determine the value to consumers based on product attributes. Managers need to perform an analysis by determining when the added value exceeds the additional costs associated with the CSR attribute. The cost information and pricing information, is normally only available within an enterprise. This means that it is possible for a competitor to determine the value to consumers of the CSR attributes but they can't determine those "priceless" attributes as the source for the company's SCA, because they will not know the cost of information. This limits the ability of competitors to imitate SCA. Donnet, Weatherspoon, and Hoehn (2007) describe the managerial implications of learning how customers appreciate certain attributes that can influence business strategies. Meanwhile, McWilliams and Siegel (2011) noted that every segment has its own infrastructure and supply chain which allows managers to choose between segments of different qualities. This can also inform them about how to manage and allocate resources to respond to market opportunities and to manage the value chain (production, processing, and distribution).

3.2.2 *Contingent valuation*

Contingent valuation is using survey-based techniques to determine the value of social goods, or goods that are not traded in the market. The use of a contingent valuation method allows a company to estimate the social value of its CSR actions. The social value will also produce benefits for the company, as reflected in an increase in the company's reputation (Siegel, 2009). McWilliams and Siegel (2001a) captures that this value depends on the consumer understanding the company's CSR actions. Therefore, advertising plays an important role in capturing the value of CSR actions.

3.2.3 *The role of advertising*

The advertising literature distinguishes between two types of consumer goods, namely search goods and experience goods (Nelson, 1974). The quality of goods can be determined before consuming. For example, furniture, is categorized as search goods because consumers can check the quality before buying. Meanwhile, in terms of experience goods, these goods must be consumed before the true nature is determined. Examples are shampo and food.

For the category of consumer goods, companies cannot charge higher prices (generate higher income). However, there is another way to create value through CSR actions, as mentioned above. Value may come through lower costs resulting from an improved reputation of socially responsible companies (Fombrun & Shanley, 1990).

Companies can use ads about the actions and attributes of CSR in order to develop or enhance a brand's reputation. Advertising serves to distinguish between certain types of consumer goods. Therefore, the brand name becomes an important determinant of quality of goods that has been established and also as an extension of value creation for consumers.

3.3 *Determining the value of RBT resources: Lowering costs*

According to McWilliams and Siegel (2001a), a firm can use capital, materials and services, and labor to generate CSR actions and attributes. They proposed that the company should use RBT to find the level where the marginal cost of an additional resource is equal to the marginal revenue that would be generated (in a perfectly competitive market, this is equivalent to maximizing the difference between the total additional costs and the amount of additional revenue).

Sharfman and Fernando (2008) found that companies that adopt environmental risk management practices can lower their capital cost overall.

For many companies, especially in the service industry, human resources are a major component of the total cost (McWilliams & Siegel, 2011). Some experts argue that human resources are the main potential source of SCA (Wright et al., 1994). Thus, companies are constantly looking for ways to control the cost of the salaries of workers and to make employees more productive. Stuebs and Sun (2010) found that "the reputation associated with labor efficiency and labor productivity increases". Meanwhile, they found that the total cost of labor is no different with a reputation. This would imply that labor cost or productivity was lower for firms with better reputations. Willard (2002) found three human resource advantages to being socially responsible. These include enhanced recruitment, retention, and productivity, all of which imply lower labor costs or levels and quality of output.

These results imply that firms that engage in CSR have enhanced reputations and these enhanced reputations lower the cost of capital and labor that may more than offset the cost of extra resources required to engage in CSR. Thus, the cost of being involved in CSR activity can be offset by the cost efficiency in labor and capital.

The Chief Executive Officer (CEO), as a strategic resource, plays an important role in formulating and implementing CSR strategies. Waldman, Siegel, and Javidan (2006) found a strong positive correlation between the "intellectual stimulation" dimension of CEO transformational leadership and the tendency of companies to be socially responsible. Sully de Luque et al. (2008) identify a further dimension of strategic leadership, which they refer to as "the values of stakeholders".

3.4 *Sustainability of CSR's advantage*

McWilliams and Siegel (2011) convey that CSR can enhance product differentiation, so that the company cannot produce an "abnormal return" or SCA from this activity. However, increased attention to CSR and the long-term success of the company has, in fact, become a resource in understanding RBT.

CSR can be a co-specialized asset leading to other assets which can be more valuable. A clear example of this is that CSR can enhance a company's reputation in financial institutions and on the stock market. CSR can also increase brand value. For example, CSR can be a special asset for companies that produce goods and affect health, such as food and medicine. Specialized assets have been identified as the main source of SCA because CSR can be seen as a form of product innovation (i.e. the creation of new features for the category of socially responsible products) or process innovations (i.e. the social responsibility of the production process).

While Barney (1991) and Reinhardt (1998) stated that companies involved in CSR-based strategies may gain an "abnormal return", only if they manage to prevent competitors from imitating their strategy. This seems unlikely, because CSR is so transparent, that is easy for it to be imitated by competitors. But remember, CSR, as a special asset that is involved in the production process of a product can increase the value of the product itself while also enhancing the company's reputation. As exemplified by Barney and Reinhardt, generic brands of acetaminophen are much cheaper, but consumers prefer Tylenol despite having to pay a higher price. Thus, it can be a valuable CSR strategy (in the sense of RBT) for differentiation, to increase the value of the brand's reputation and/or of the company.

4 CONCLUSION

Strategic CSR is conceptualized as one of the "responsible" activities which allows an enterprise to achieve SCA. Furthermore, RBT combines the concepts and methods which allow managers to measure the strategic value of a company when engaging in CSR. RBT integrates with marketing, discussing the importance of advertising to make consumers aware of the attributes of the CSR process. Using advertising and the media to tell consumers about a company's "socially responsible" activities is very important for its reputation. Furthermore, employees including CEOs—as resources, can be a strategic RBT resource when they are more productive than the employees of other firms. Having employees who are more productive may be a result of better hiring or more motivated workers, both of which can result from CSR practices within the firm. Other RBT resources, such as human resource processes, may also result in employees who are more productive may be a result.

REFERENCES

Bagnoli, M. & Watts, S. (2003). Selling to socially responsible consumers: Competition and the private provision of public goods. *Journal of Economics and Management Strategy*, *12*, 419–445.

Barney, J. (1991). Firm resources and sustained competitive advantage. *Jurnal Manajemen*, *17*, 99–120.

Baron, D. (2001). Private politics, corporate social responsibility and integrated strategy. *Journal of Economics and Management Strategy*, *10*, 7–45.

Baron, D. & Diermeier, D. (2007). Strategic activism and nonmarket strategy. *Journal of Economics and Management Strategy*, *16*, 599–634.

Besley, T. & Ghatak, M. (2007). Retailing public goods: The economics of corporate social responsibility. *Journal of Public Economics*, *91*, 1645–1663.

Bowen, H.R. (1953). *Social Responsibilities of the Businessman.* Harper & Row, New York, NY.

Carroll, A.B. (1979). A three-dimensional model of corporate performance, *Academy of Management Review*, *4*(4), 497–505.

Donnet, M.L., Weatherspoon, D.D. & Hoehn, J.P. (2007). What adds value in specialty coffee? Managerial implications from hedonic price analysis of Central and South American e-auctions. *International Food and Agribusiness Management Review*, *10*, 1–18.

Epstein, E. (1987a). "The corporate social policy process and the process of corporate governance", American Business Law Journal, 25, 361–83.

Fombrun, C. & Shanley, M. (1990). What's in a name? Reputation building and corporate strategy. *Academy of Management Journal*, *33*, 233–258.

Kotchen, M. (2006). Green markets and private provision of public goods. *Journal of Political Economy*, *114*, 816–834.

Kraaijenbrink, J., Spender, J.C. & Groen, A.J. (2010). berbasis sumber daya pandangan: Sebuah tinjauan

dan penilaiannya. *kritik Jurnal Manajemen, 36,* 349–372.
Manasakis, C., Mitrokostas, E. & Petrakis, E. (2007). Corporate social responsibility in oligopoly. *Working paper no. 0707*, Department of Economics, University of Crete, Greece.
Margolis, J.D. & Walsh, J.P. (2001). People and profits? The search for a link between a company's social and financial performance. Mahwah, NJ: Lawrence Erlbaum.
Maxwell, J., Lyon, T. & Hackett, S. (2000). Self-regulation and social welfare: The political economy of corporate environmentalism. *Journal of Law and Economics*, *43*, 583–617.
McWilliams, A. & Siegel, D. (2000). Corporate social responsibility and financial performance: Correlation or misspecification? *Strategic Management Journal, 21*, 603–609.
McWilliams, A. & Siegel, D. (2001a). Corporate social responsibility: A theory of the firm perspective. *Academy of Management Review*, *26*, 117–127.
McWilliams, A. & Siegel, D.S. (2011). Creating and capturing value: Strategic corporate social responsibility, resource-based theory, and sustainable competitive advantage. *Journal of Management*, *37*(5), 1480–1495.
Nelson, P. (1974). Advertising as information. *Journal of Political Economy, 81*, 729–754.
Nyborg, K., & Brekke, K.A. (2004). *Moral hazard and moral motivation: Corporate social responsibility as labor market screening*. Working paper no. 25/2004, University of Oslo Economics. Retrieved from http://ssrn.com/abstract=645741.
Orlitzky, M., Schmidt, F.L. & Rynes, S.L. (2003). Corporate social and financial performance: A meta-analysis. *Organization Studies*, *24*, 403–441.
Reinhardt, F.L. (1998). Environmental product differentiation: Implications for corporate strategy. *California Management Review, 49*, 43–73.
Rosen, S. (1974). Hedonic prices and implicit markets. *Journal of Political Economy*, *82*, 34–55.
Russo, M. & Fouts, P. (1997). A resource-based perspective on corporate environmental performance and profitability. *Academy of Management Journal*, *40*, 534–559.
Sharfman, M.P. & Fernando, C.S. (2008). Environmental risk management and the cost of capital. *Strategic Management Journal*, *29*, 569–592.
Siegel, D.S. (2009). Green management matters only if it yields more green: An economic/strategic perspective. *Academy of Management Perspectives, 23*(3), 5–16.
Siegel, D. & Vitaliano, D. (2007). An empirical analysis of the strategic use of corporate social responsibility. *Journal of Economics and Management Strategy*, *17*, 773–792.
Stuebs, M. & Sun, L. (2010). Business reputation and labor efficiency, productivity and cost. *Journal of Business Ethics*, *96*, 265–283.
Sully de Luque, M., Washburn, N.T., Waldman, D.A. & House, R.J. (2008). Unrequited profit: How stakeholder and economic values relate to subordinates' perceptions of leadership and firm performance. *Administrative Science Quarterly, 53*, 626–654.
Waldman, D.A., Siegel, D. & Javidan, M. (2006). Components of CEO transformational leadership and corporate social responsibility. *Journal of Management Studies*, *43*, 1703–1725.
Wartick, S. & Cochran, P. (1985). The evolution of the corporate social performance model. *Academy of Management Review*, *10*(4), 758–69.
Willard, B. (2002). *The sustainability advantage: Seven business case benefits of a triple bottom line*. Gabriola Island, BC, Canada: New Society Publishers.
Wood, D. (1991). Corporate social performance revisited. *Academy of Management Review, 16*(4), 758–69.
Wright, P.M., McMahan, G. & McWilliams, A. (1994). Human resources and sustained competitive advantage: A resource-based perspective. *International Journal of Human Resource Management*, *5*, 301–326.

Organizational behavior, leadership and human resources management

Increasing Management Relevance and Competitiveness – Sukoco et al. (Eds)
© 2018 Taylor & Francis Group, London, ISBN 978-0-8153-7455-8

Superior performance model of human resources

T. Yuniarsih, Disman & M.D. Sugiharto
Universitas Pendidikan Indonesia, Bandung, Indonesia

ABSTRACT: The aim of this study is to examine the validity of a hypothetical model for the superior performance of human resources from a behavioral perspective. Referring to behavior theory, human resource performance is influenced by environmental and personal aspects. Based on the results of our three years of research, it is found that both of these aspects have a significant positive effect on gaining a high level of human resource performance, so it can therefore be transformed into a fixed model. The model is directed to encourage individual superior performance with a highly competitive attitude, through the development of an employee-oriented mindset to quality corporate culture. This study used a quantitative approach with SEM and path analysis. Thus, the hypothetical model, which was formulated in the second year of research, has been tested to become a fixed model that will enable human resources to perform with superior capabilities.

Keywords: Human Resource Management, Superior Performance

1 INTRODUCTION

This research is motivated by the need to test a hypothetical model concerning the superior performance of human resources, which was formulated based on previous research results. The model begins with empirical facts that indicate the low performance of human resources in various institutions in Indonesia (Yuniarsih et al., 2014). This is indicated by the character and mindset of human resources, which are still oriented to routine formal work obligations, and have not yet been oriented to the quality of culture. Human resource competencies have not been optimally empowered to face global competition. These conditions are very apprehensive, therefore there is a need to look for solutions to the existing conditions of human resources in order to allow them to produce a superior performance. The end of December 2015 is the beginning of the era of the Asean Economic Community (AEC), a new chapter in the world economy. The birth of the AEC era is a challenge for Indonesian human resources to improve their competence and seize opportunities in business competition. To respond to these challenges, the presence of skilled and knowledgeable human resources has become an inevitable primary need. Human resources have become the key factor that will determine the achievement and the quality of organizational performance. In other words, the growth of the organization must be preceded by the development and empowerment of human resources in order to be able to show a superior performance.

The ultimate goal of this research is to test the hypothetical model to enable it to become a fixed model that is capable of forming superior performance, and designing the implementation technique. The process of achieving these goals was done through three stages of research, which lasted for three years. The first year research successfully identified and analyzed the strengths of the environmental and personal factors, as a variable that constructed the performance of human resources within the organization. The second year research formulated a hypothetical model of human resource management to form superior performance, which was tested in a third year study and became a fixed model.

2 THEORETICAL REVIEW

A new phase in the world economy, marked by the birth of the Asean Economic Community (AEC), requires a positive response from every institution, both in business and community services. The level of competition in the AEC era is getting tighter, including the flow of foreign labor into Indonesia, which is becoming increasingly open. These conditions encourage institutions to compete to get well-skilled workers who are knowledgeable, in order to be able to show a superior performance.

The human resource management review conceptually focused on efforts to obtain qualified people to demonstrate superior performance with high productivity, in order to provide an opportunity to contribute optimally to the institutional growth and development (Yuniarsih et al., 2015).

Baron and Kreps (1999) said that the study of HRM is actually related to human behavior, which will ultimately shape organizational behavior. The behavior theory explained that superior performance is influenced by environmental and personal aspects (Robbin, 2009). Environmental aspects consist of leadership, job characteristics, communication patterns, reward systems, and work-life balance. Meanwhile, the study of personal aspects consists of motivation, discipline, employee engagement, job satisfaction, and organizational commitment (Yuniarsih et al., 2014, 2015, 2016).

In addition, the research findings, which were formulated into a fixed model to build superior performance, concluded that the performance of human resources within the organization is constructed and maintained through environmental and individual aspects, as illustrated in Figure 1 Yuniarsih dkk. (2015–2016).

3 RESEARCH METHOD

This research used a quantitative approach with SEM techniques and path analysis. The population is individual employees working in educational, business, and government institutions. Sources of data were obtained from a sample of 300 people, taken randomly.

4 SUPERIOR HUMAN RESOURCE PERFORMANCE MODEL

Based on the statistics tested, it can be found that each exogen variable has a positive and significant effect towards the endogen variable. Thus, the hypothetical model has been tested to become a fixed model. The model was directed to support superior performance, which has a high level of competitiveness, through being synergic to both personal and situational factors.

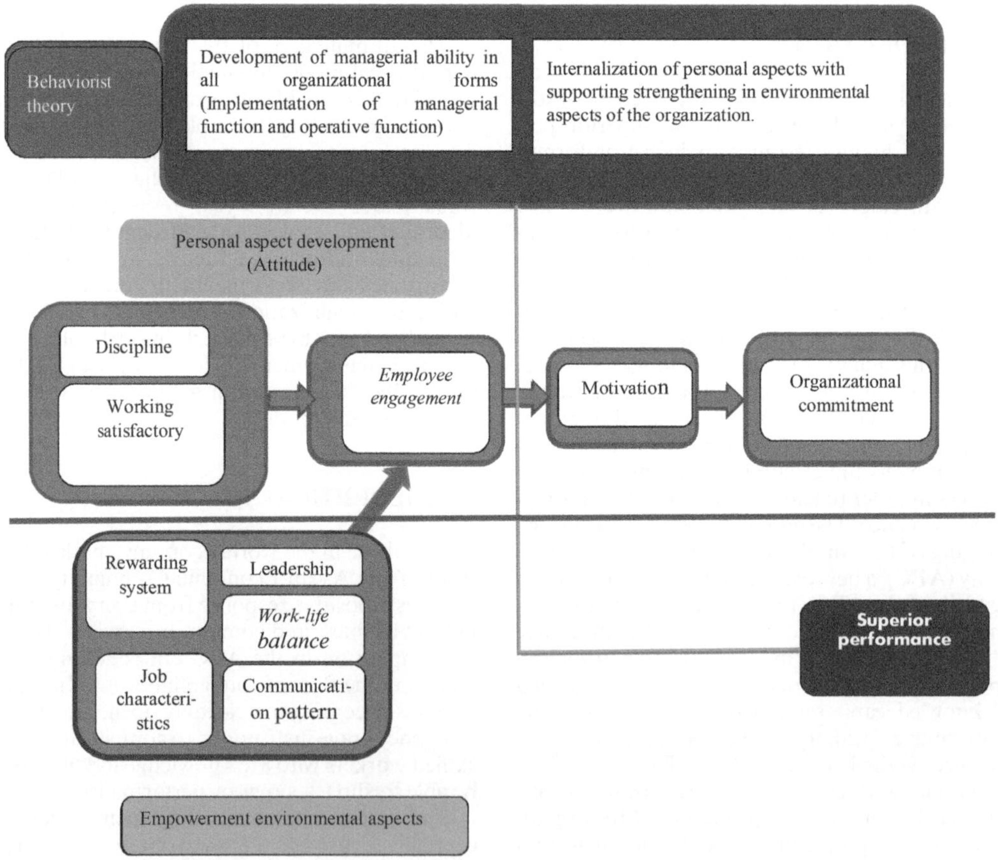

Figure 1. Human resource management model for building superior performance from a behavioral perspective.

To implement the model, firstly we have to understand the philosophical framework, then we determine the assumptions, and, finally, decide on the continual progress of the implementation.

4.1 *Superior performance philosophical basis*

From a behavior perspective, superior performance can be identified from personal characteristics, namely: the ability to work together co-operatively, communicate interactively, quality of work, mastery of the knowledge of the work, responsible, productive, adapt flexibly, and take the initiative in solving various problems. These characteristics could be used as an indicator to measure the performance of individual achievement. Therefore, the successful implementation of this model must be preceded by the strengthening and developing of managerial skills at all levels of the organization, both in terms of managerial functions and the operative functions of HRM. On the other hand, the implementation of the model must be accompanied by the internalization of the personal aspects and the strengthening of organizational support.

Schuler and Jackson in Millmore et al. (2007) stated that when human resource management functions are implemented in organizational development, it is necessary to set four strategic actions, as follows:

1. Engage in human resource planning;
2. Develop required employee competencies;
3. Ensure required role behaviors; and
4. Promote employee motivation.

These four actions reflect the importance of the special treatment of human resources, in particular the procurement planning process of human resources. The matery planning is the first step to obtaining appropriate human resources, both in terms of the adequacy of the amount and the relevance of the competence of the formations available. Every individual in the organization is expected to display strong commitment and behave in accordance with the norms of organizational life. Alignment of individual behavior with the demands of the organization will lead to a sense of comfort, satisfaction, and increased employee motivation.

The atmosphere of the work environment, built by the reward system, job characteristics, communication patterns, and work-life balance, under professional leadership, will strengthen the characteristics of the personal aspects of HR. This would appear to be through disciplined behavior and job satisfaction. In self-employees who are satisfied, it will foster engagement and encourage motivation for further commitment to the organization. With the synergy of support for both of these aspects, it will encourage employees to display behavior according to the demands of the organization, and ultimately superior optimal performance can be realized (Yuniarsih et al., 2016; Azeem, 2010, 2014; Gulbahar, 2014; Haar et al., 2014; Rice, et al., 2012; Irshad & Nas, 2011: dan Uche, 2011).

In line with the previous statement, Millmore et al. (2007) stated that one of the strategies that can form the superior performance of HR can be achieved by establishing an appropriate organizational structure and filling it with appropriate human resources. Specifically, Guest, cited in Millmore et al. (2007), identifies four outcomes as authentic proof of a successful organization, namely; "strategic integration, high commitment, high quality, high flexibility". Strategic integration is marked by HR integrity towards the organization strategy, which is formed through vertical, horizontal and diagonal co-operation among the job units in the organizational structure. High commitment is indicated by a high level of loyalty of the human resources to the organization, as well as the consistency of their motivation to achieve. With the devoted support of employees who have a strong motivation, it will lead to higher quality and flexibility of performance.

Based on these considerations, the purposes for which this model could be used are:

1. To build synergies between personal aspects and the environment to form superior performance;
2. To develop a working environment oriented to quality and excellence, not just about obligations and executing routines;
3. To strengthen the attachment and responsibility of the individual to the organization, which is manifested in strong organizational citizenship behavior;
4. To build the mindset and awareness of human resources in order to show superior performances consistently.

Referring to the intended use of the model as described above, the successful implementation of the model can be measured through the following indicators:

1. The creation of synergy between personal and environmental aspects in developing an organizational behavior-oriented culture of quality;
2. The development of a work environment oriented towards excellence, not just about obligations and executing routines;
3. Strengthening individual responsibility to the organization, which is manifested in a strong organizational commitment to deliver innovative works;
4. Creating a human resources mindset and consciousness that displays superior performance oriented towards vision, mission, policies, strategies, and the organizational program.

A superior performance implementation in the behavior perspective model requires the synergy of personal support and environmental aspects. Personal aspects are reflected in the behavior of individuals and can form the employee's characteristics, both in their personal life as well as when they are in their organization. Such personal behavior is shaped and colored by the characteristics of the environment in which they work.

4.2 *Assumption*

The implementation of this model is based on the following assumptions:

1. Organizations have a common vision and mission to be shared;
2. HR has the spirit to always show their best and be prepared for change;
3. Reciprocal communication is effectively established in order to build harmonious social interactions and social dynamics;
4. Leadership support that is empowering, responsible, and transparent.

4.3 *Strategy implementation*

The superior performance model can be implemented through the three stages of the strategy, namely: The first stage, implement the development strategy of managerial capabilities at all levels of the organization. At this stage, the leaders at every level of the organization apply managerial functions in a professional manner in all operative functions of human resource management. The second phase, strengthen the organizational culture and intensive socialization to all members of the organization. The third phase, the implementation of the superior performance model gives attention to personal and environmental aspects, to build and realize professional human resource management.

The three strategies above show the continuous stages of implementation. *The first stage* is a prerequisite for the implementation of the model. This indicates that the understanding and mastery of managerial competence by each level of the organization will determine the smoothness of the implementation process of the model. *The second stage* is the follow up after the managerial competencies have been mastered, namely training for strengthening personal aspects for each individual employee while monitoring the organization's support of the environment *The last stage* is to evaluate the success of the employee's performance, and whether or not it meets the institutional target.

HR is a key factor in improving the organization. Therefore, human behavior will determine organizational behavior, and vice versa, and organizational behavior will direct and regulate human behavior patterns. This is in line with the view of Stewart and Brown (2011), which is that organizational behavior is the meeting point of the contributions of human behavior when involved in an organizational situation. The study of organizational behavior cannot be separated from the analysis of human performance. Harmonious interrelationship among existing employees that has a strong engagement with a conducive organizational climate is a force in achieving the vision of the organization. Organizations open up opportunities for the development of personal competence and character building, while employees try to show their performance optimally. So it creates a win-win solution through mutualistic symbiotic co-operation. Both sides need each other and support each other "The individual is getting what he or she wants from the job, and the organization is getting what it needs from its employees" (Rice et al., 2012).

The quality of human resources within an organization will determine the level of performance of the organization, especially in improving competitiveness and responding to market changes. In this regard, the presence of competent human resources becomes a necessity. They are required to have technical skills in accordance with the demands and characteristics of their work, to understand the job description, display professional managerial skills, identify problems and develop innovative creative solutions, in order to support organizations to achieve a competitive advantage and a comparative advantage in the midst of increasing global competition.

The superior performance of human resources will be realized when they have strong engagement, motivation, and organizational commitment. Rice et al. (2012) stated "High levels of employee engagement drive high organizational performance". Their work orientation is not just reaching quantity targets and running program routines, but is coupled with an obsession and a strong spirit to meet quality targets (quality culture oriented). Thus, organizations must be able to select and sort out the truly competent and fully engaged human resources to be empowered continuously.

5 CONCLUSION AND RECOMMENDATION

5.1 *Conclusion*

A successful implementation of a superior performance model must be supported by synergetic interrelational forces between personal and environmental aspects. This is indicated by the occurrence of mutualistic symbiosis between employees and the organization. Employees are the spearhead of the organization in realizing the vision and the mission of the institution, while the organization becomes the focus of individual expectations for self-actualization. An individual's needs are met through rewards provided by the organization, and organizations benefit greatly from their employees' superior performance contribution.

The superior performance of human resources can be interpreted as a real contribution from the energy and mind of the employees, which is manifested in the form of responsibility for their work. These contributions are linked to efforts to realize the organization's targets and vision. In other words, the superior performance of human resources demonstrates individual success in encouraging increased organizational productivity.

5.2 *Recommendation*

The superior performance model in behavioral perspective can be considered by the leaders, engaged in both business and public service, to become one of the alternatives for building the human mindset to become corporate culture oriented.

REFERENCES

Azeem, S.M. (2010). Job satisfaction and organizational commitment among employees in the Sultanate of Oman. *Psychology*, 295–299. doi: 10.4236/psych.2010.14038.

Azeem, S.M. & Akhtar, N. (2014). The influence of work life balance and job satisfaction on organizational commitment of healthcare employees. *International Journal of Human Resource Studies*, *4*(2), 18–24.

Baron, J.N. & David M.K. (1999). *Strategic human resources. Frameworks for general manager. Organizations build ultimate competitive advantage*. United States of America: John Wiley & Sons, Inc.

Gulbahar, et al. (2014). Relationship between work-life balance and organizational commitment. *Research on Humanities and Social Sciences*, *4*(5), 1–7.

Haar, J.M., et al. (2014). Outcomes of work life balance on job satisfaction, life satisfaction and mental health: A study across seven cultures. *Journal of Vocational Behavior*. Accepted Manuscript.

Irshad, E. & Nas, S. (2011). Job satisfaction, organizational commitment, and personality traits: A relationship study. *Journal of Humanities and Social Science*, *XIX*(2), 37–60.

Millmore, M., Lewis, P., Saunders, M., Thornhill, A. & Morrow, T. (2007). *Strategic human resource management. Contemporary issues*. United Kingdom: Prentice Hall. @ Pearson Education Limited.

Rice, C., Marlow, F. & Masarech, M.A. (2012). *The engagement equation. Leadership strategies for an inspired workforce*. Hoboken, New Jersey: John Wiley & Sons, Inc.

Robbins, S.P. & Judge, T.A. (2009). *Organizational behavior* (12th ed.). Upper Saddle River, New Jersey: Pearson Education, Inc.

Stewart, G.L. & Brown, K.G. (2011). *Human resources management* (2nd ed.). USA: John Wiley and Sons, Inc.

Uche, A.L., Fiberesima, D. & Onwuchekwa, C.A. (2011). Relationship between motivational factors and teachers' performance on the job in Ogba/Egbema/Ndoni local government area of River State. *Mediterranean Journal of Social Sciences*.

Yuniarsih, T., Disman, & Suryadi, E. (2014). Model Manajemen Sumber Daya Manusia untuk Membentuk Kinerja Unggul. Laporan Penelitian Tahun Pertama. Bandung: LPPM UPI. Tidak diterbitkan.

Yuniarsih, T. & Sugiharto, M.D. (2015). Model Manajemen Sumber Daya Manusia untuk Membentuk Kinerja Unggul. Laporan Penelitian Tahun Kedua. Bandung: LPPM UPI. Tidak diterbitkan.

——. (2016). Human resource management model to create superior performance. *International Journal of Education*, *9*(1), 74–81. Bandung: Indonesia University of Education.

Yuniarsih, T., Disman, & Sugiharto, M.D. (2016). Model Manajemen Sumber Daya Manusia untuk Membentuk Kinerja Unggul. Laporan Penelitian Tahun Ketiga. Bandung: LPPM UPI. Tidak diterbitkan.

Increasing Management Relevance and Competitiveness – Sukoco et al. (Eds)
© 2018 Taylor & Francis Group, London, ISBN 978-0-8153-7455-8

The impact of fiscal decentralization on economic growth and manpower absorbed at districts/cities in South Kalimantan Province

Muzdalifah & R. Purwono
Universitas Airlangga, Surabaya, Indonesia

ABSTRACT: The focus of this research is to examine and analyze the impact of fiscal decentralization on economic growth and labor absorbed by variable instruments in the form of total investment, school average length, and life expectancy. This study uses panel data from 13 districts/cities in South Kalimantan Province in 2005–2015. Data analysis techniques use the simultaneous data panel Two Stage Least Squared (TSLS) and results show that the impact of fiscal decentralization together is significant. Individually, all variables have a positive and significant impact on economic growth. Hulu Sungai Tengah Regency shows the highest positive performance, while the impact of economic growth through fiscal decentralization on labor absorbed collectively is significant, but absorbed individually is only significant in the fiscal decentralization (t-1) variable, with Banjarmasin City recording the highest positive performance.

Keywords: Economic Growth, Fiscal Decentralization, Absorbed Labor

1 INTRODUCTION

The implications of fiscal decentralization policy mean that regions have the authority to seek funding sources, and allocate them in accordance with the delegation of powers granted by the central government. The quality of financial management in districts/cities is important because it will have an impact on economic growth and absorbed labor. Based on preliminary data collected by the researcher, it is known that districts/cities in South Kalimantan have a high dependence on balancing funds, which is reflected in the amount of contribution in regional income. At the beginning, implementation reached more than 80%, although in the last four years the dependence on the balance fund has begun to decline. The average economic growth of South Kalimantan Province in the last five years was 5.39%, below the Indonesian average of 5.52%. One of the causes is the decline in demand for mining commodities as the largest contributor in Gross Regional Domestic Product (GRDP), in terms of employment. Based on the National Labor Force Survey data from Central Bureau of Statistics (BPS) during 2007–2014, it is known that the number of absorbed workers experiences a varied trend and tends to fluctuate.

How is the impact of fiscal decentralization on economic growth and labor absorbed in the districts and cities in South Kalimantan? Through this research, the impact of the implementation of fiscal decentralization will be proxy with the degree of fiscal decentralization, in economic growth and labor absorbed in the districts and cities in South Kalimantan. The results of this study are expected to provide benefits for the development of science in the field of public finance, and also be used as a reference for policymakers.

2 LITERATURE REVIEW

The role of government in the economy, according to Musgrave (as quoted in Simanjuntak, 1998) and Rosen (2002), is the function of allocation, distribution and stabilization. The task that must be centralized is stabilization, and that which should be decentralized is the function of allocation and distribution. The political economy approach assumes that local people have relatively homogeneous preferences (such as those of individuals), so that local government choices are closer to, or better suited to, individual preferences than those made by the central government.

The most important economic authority, obtaining the largest portion for local government, is the allocation function, because it is closely linked to the allocation of economic resources to the community.

Government spending has a theoretical basis that can be seen from the identity of the national income balance of Keynes (1936) (that is, Y = C + I + G + (X – M)), which is a legitimate source of the Keynesian view of the relevance of government intervention in the economy. Keynes's analysis evolved as an attempt to explain that an economy will always face the problem of unemployment, and he believed that the government needs to implement policies to address this problem.

Wagner (as quoted in Mangkoesoebroto, 1997), says that if economic growth increases then government spending will also increase, whereby the analogy to Wagner's Law is that by increasing economic growth, then the need for public goods' supply will also increase, so that financing is required through government revenue. Ultimately, government spending will also increase or can be interpreted as high economic growth, which will also reflect the amount of government spending funds to finance the needs of government services. The Keynesian view supports that opinion, such that an increase in government spending will encourage an increase in demand for goods and services in aggregate, thereby promoting economic growth.

Decentralized revenues and expenditures can increase the efficiency of the public sector, reduce the budget deficit and encourage economic growth (Bahl & Linn, 1992; Bird, 1993; Gramlich, 1993; Oates, 1993), while fiscal decentralization tends to increase costs, reduce the efficiency of government services, distort the economy, and may possibly lead to more severe inequality between regions and macroeconomic instability (Prudhomme, 1995). Jin and Zou (2000), and Slinko (2002), point out the trade-off between fiscal decentralization and economic growth, indicating that fiscal decentralization in developing countries is problematic. Fiscal decentralization policies are designed poorly can also create a stimulus for local governments to undertake less responsible and unsustainable spending (Woller & Phillips, 1998).

3 DATA ANALYSIS METHOD

The approach used in this research is a positivist approach, with explanatory method because this study aims to test a theory or hypothesis to strengthen or even reject the existing theory/hypothesis. Through this method can be known the correlation between two or more variables in terms of pattern, direction, nature, form, and strength of relationship.

The research location consists of 13 districts/cities in the province of South Kalimantan, (11 districts and two cities): (1) Tanah Laut District, (2) Kotabaru, (3) Banjar, (4) Barito Kuala, (5) Tapin, (6) Hulu Sungai Selatan, (7) Hulu Sungai Tengah, (8) Hulu Sungai Utara, 9) Tabalong, (10) Balangan, and (11) Tanah Bumbu, and two cities: (1) Banjarmasin City, and (2) Banjarbaru. The type of data used in this study are secondary data in the form of panel data (combined between time series and cross section), including measurement of economic growth, degree of fiscal decentralization, absorbed labor, total investment, average length of schooling, and life expectancy.

These types of data have been documented and published officially by the competent agencies/institutions, including those sourced from the Central Bureau of Statistics (BPS), the National and Regional Development Planning Agency, Provincial Finance, and districts/cities in South Kalimantan.

The operational definitions of variables in this study are as follows:

1. *Fiscal Decentralization Variable (X1)*
   To measure the performance or financial capacity of the region, based on the concepts put forward by Musgrave and Musgrave (quoted in Sukanto, 2001), this study will use a proxy, which is the degree of fiscal decentralization between the central and local governments, a ratio that describes the level of regional independence seen from the source of regional income in the form of District Own Source Revenue (PAD), Tax Share and Non Tax Share (TSNTS), and Balance Budged (BB) to the total revenue area. The higher ratio, the greater degree of independence, which is calculated in percentages.
2. *Investment Variable (X2)*
   This is a summation of government investment and private investment.
3. *Life Expectancy (X3)*
   This is the average forecast of how many years a person can be expected to live; data sourced from BPS with units of year.
4. *Average Length of Schooling (X4)*
   This describes the number of years spent by people aged 15 years and above in formal education; data sourced from BPS with units of year.
5. *Economic Growth (Y1)*
   This is the percentage change of GRDP value of the current year from the GRDP of the previous year. GRDP is the amount of added value for goods and services produced by various production units' indistricts/cities (usually in one year). The calculation method on the basis of this constant price has eliminated the effect of inflation, so that it shows real value (real); data sourced from BPS with unit variable are expressed in percentage unit.
6. *Labor Absorbed (Y2)*
   This is the number of people conducting economic activities with the intent of obtaining, or

helping to earn, income or profits, for at least one hour in a row in the past week. These activities include unpaid worker activities that assist in an economic activity (BPS, 2016); with unit variable expressed in the unit of the Soul.

Data analysis used to answer the hypothesis in this research is simultaneous data panel 2SLS. Data processing is done using the Eviews software, version 8. There are two stages performed.

3.1 *First stage*

Regress endogenous left-tribe variables (Y_{11}) with exogenous variables, instrument variables, and predetermined variables to obtain $\hat{Y}1$:

$$Y_{11} = \alpha_{10} + \alpha_{11}Y_{21} + \alpha_{12}X_{11} + \alpha_{13}X_{12} + \varepsilon^*_1 \quad (1)$$

where Y_{11} = Economic growth in district/cities of South Kalimantan Province; X_{11} = District/cities fiscal decentralization in South Kalimantan Province; X_{12} = Total investment district/cities in South Kalimantan Province; Y_{21} = Manpower absorbed in district/cities of South Kalimantan Province; α_{10} = Constants; α_{11} = Regression coefficient of independent variables; ε^*_1 = Error term.

3.2 *Second stage regression*

This is followed by doing regression to Y_{21} by entering value $\hat{Y}_{11}$, which is the result of calculations at the first stage to get Y_{21}:

$$Y_{21} = \beta_{20} + \beta_{21}\hat{Y}_{11} + \beta_{22}X_{11} + \beta_{23}X_{23} + \beta_{24}X_{24}\varepsilon^*_2 \quad (2)$$

where Y_{21} = Manpower absorbed in district/cities of South Kalimantan Province; X_{23} = Life expectancy of district/cities in South Kalimantan Province; X_{24} = Average schooling length in district/cities of South Kalimantan Province; β_{20} = Constants; β_{21} = Regression coefficient of independent variables; ε^*_2 = Error term.

4 RESULTS AND DISCUSSION

In terms of the impact of fiscal decentralization on economic growth, from Table 1 it can be seen that R^2 reaches 1, and so the independent variable can explain the dependent variable perfectly. The F-statistic test is known with the trust value $\alpha = 0.05$. If independent variables have p-value 0.000 $<\alpha$, then H_0 is rejected, which means that the independent variable has a significant effect on the dependent variable, and that together, the variables fiscal decentralization, total investment, and absorbed labor are significant, and individual (t-statistical test) with value of trust $\alpha = 0.05$ and all free variables, fiscal decentralization, total investment, and absorbed labor, have positive and significant influence on economic growth.

Table 1. Panel data regression result method fixed effect.

Variable	Coefficient	Std. Error	t-Statistic	Prob.
C	−8.03E-06	2.16E-06	−3.715579	0.0003
X1	2.108934	4.85E-08	43,450,156	0.0000
INV	29.66906	5.20E-16	5.71E+16	0.0000
FY2	3.32E-17	1.58E-17	2.101816	0.0378

Effects Specification
Crosssection fixed (dummy variables)

R-squared	1.000000	Mean dependent var	1.42E+10
Adjusted R^2	1.000000	S.D. dependent var	3.02E+10
S.E. of regression	5.61E-06	Akaike info criterion	−21.22816
Sum squared Resid	3.59E-09	Schwarz criterion	−20.87523
Log likelihood	1,395.830	Hannan-Quinn criterion	−21.08475
F-statistic	2.49E+32	Durbin-Watson stat	2.002032
Prob. (F-statistic)	0.000000		

This result indicates that fiscal decentralization and instrument variable encourage economic growth of districts/cities in South Kalimantan Province, although not all impetus to economic growth in each district/city has positive performance, and some are negative, as seen in Table 2.

The performance of the independent variables on economic growth can be seen in Table 2. If the analysis is distributed in two areas of the city and district, then the impact of fiscal decentralization, total investment, and labor absorbed on economic growth, as shown in performance in the city area, is positive. This means that fiscal decentralization, total investment, and labor absorbed are able to encourage economic growth, with the highest performance in the city of Banjarbaru, while in the districts there are various positive and negative impacts. Positive performance districts are Banjar, Batola, Tapin, Hulu Sungai Selatan, Hulu River Central, Hulu Sungai Utara, and Balangan. The highest is in Hulu Sungai Tengah, while the negative performance in economic growth is found in Tanah Bumbu, Tabalong, Tanah Laut, and Kotabaru.

Table 2. Performance of dependent variable on economic growth in the district/cities of South Kalimantan Province.

	Region/District	Effect
1	District of Tanah Laut	−2.80E-06
2	District of Kota Baru	−4.05E-06
3	District of Banjar	2.47E-06
4	District of Barito Kuala	3.24E-06
5	District of Tapin	1.79E-06
6	District of Hulu Sungai Selatan	4.02E-06
7	District of Hulu Sungai Tengah	4.03E-06
8	District of Hulu Sungai Utara	2.90E-06
9	District of Tabalong	−3.18E-06
10	District of Tanah Bumbu	−7.15E-07
11	District of Balangan	1.00E-06
12	City of Banjarmasin	1.14E-06
13	City of Banjar Baru	2.97E-06

Table 3. Panel data regression result method fixed effect.

Variable	Coefficient	Std. Error	t-Statistic	Prob.
FY1	6.25E-08	4.05E-08	1.542849	0.1257
FD	677.8982	168.7344	4.017545	0.0001
X2	−1.49E-08	1.11E-06	−0.013504	0.9892
X3	2871.124	4,681.989	0.613227	0.5410
X4	658.9363	961.4448	0.685360	0.4945
C	40,813.84	55,529.92	0.734988	0.4639

Effects specification
Crosssection fixed (dummy variables)

R-squared	0.96442	Mean dependent var	134489
Adjusted R^2	0.95902	S.D. dependent var	61998.4
S.E. of regression	12550.2	Akaike info criterion	21.8407
Sum Squared Resid	1.76E+10	Schwarz criterion	22.2377
Log likelihood	−1401.649	Hannan-Quinn criterion	22.0020
F-statistic	178.5943	Durbin-Watson stat	0.668329
Prob. (F-statistic)	0.00000		

Regarding the impact of fiscal decentralization, total investment, average length of schooling, life expectancy, and economic growth of absorbed labor, from Table 3 it is seen that R^2 value reaches 0.964423. This means that the independent variable can explain the dependent variable of 96.44%. F statistics are known by the confidence level value

Table 4. Performance of dependent variable on manpower absorbed in the district/cities of South Kalimantan Province.

	Region/District	Effect
1	District of Tanah Laut	3,023.318
2	District of Kota Baru	−5,957.917
3	District of Banjar	113,510.1
4	District of Barito Kuala	27,582.67
5	District of Tapin	−51,755.95
6	District of Hulu Sungai Selatan	−19,169.63
7	District of Hulu Sungai Tengah	455.1023
8	District of Hulu Sungai Utara	−17,069.46
9	District of Tabalong	−28,591.11
10	District of Tanah Bumbu	−26,778.76
11	District of Balangan	−75,276.72
12	City of Banjarmasin	139,892.9
13	City of BanjarBaru	−59,864.51

$\alpha = 0.05$. If independent variables have p-value 0.000 $<\alpha$, then H_0 is rejected, it means that simultaneously, the variables of fiscal decentralization, total investment, the average length of schooling, life expectancy and economic growth significantly are explaining labor absorbed. Based on the individual test, only the lag of fiscal decentralization variable (t-1) has a positive.

These results indicate that fiscal decentralization will have a positive impact on labor absorbed by lag t-1, which means that at least in the second year of fiscal decentralization, there will be an increase in absorbed labor; this is reasonable given that the revolving funds will first then create labor demand.

Performance of fiscal decentralization, total investment, and average length of schooling, life expectancy and economic growth of absorbed labor can be seen in Table 4. The impacts in district/cities are positive in Banjarmasin, Tanah Laut, Banjar, Batola and Hulu Sungai Tengah, and are highest in Banjar, whereas performance is negative in Banjarbaru City, Tapin, Hulu Sungai Selatan, Hulu Sungai Utara and Balangan Hulu Sungai Tengah, Tanah Bumbu, Tabalong, and Kotabaru.

5 CONCLUSION

Based on the results of the analysis, it can be concluded that the impact of fiscal decentralization on economic growth and labor absorbed is that the implementation of fiscal decentralization encourages economic growth, with various effects in urban areas and some positive performance in districts, such as Banjarmasin and Banjarbaru, Banjar, Batola, Tapin, Hulu Sungai Selatan, Hulu

Sungai Tengah, Hulu Sungai Utara, and Balangan. This means that the existence of fiscal decentralization encourages economic growth.

The implementation of fiscal decentralization has a positive and significant impact on the workforce absorbed by a 1-year lag, and the effect that occurs in various districts/cities positively impacts Banjarmasin, Tanah Laut, Banjar, Batola, and Hulu Sungai Tengah, which means that the existence of fiscal decentralization encourages the increase of absorbed labor.

REFERENCES

Bahl, R.W. & Linn, J. (1992). *Urban Public Finance in Developing Countries.* New York: Oxford University Press.

Bird, R.M. (1993). Threading the Fiscal Labyrinth: Some Issues in Fiscal Decentralization. *National Tax Journal, 46*(2), 207–227.

Gramlich, E.M. (1993). A Policy Maker's Guide to Fiscal Decentralization. *National Tax Journal*, 46(2), 229–235.

Jin, Jing and Heng Fu Zou. (2000). Fiscal Decentralization and Economic Growth in China. *World Bank Working Paper Series 1452* Available http://www.worldbank.org.

Keynes, J.M. (1936). *The General Theory of Employment, Interest and Money.* Cambridge: King's College.

Mangkoesoebroto, G. (1997). *Public Economic.* Yogyakarta BPFE.

Oates, W. (1993). Fiscal Decentralization and Economic Development. *National Tax Journal, 46*(2), 237–243.

Prudhomme, R. (1995). On the Danger of Decentralization. *The World Bank, Policy Research Working Paper*, 1252. Washington DC.

Rosen, H.S. (2002). *Public finance*. New York: McGraw-Hill International Edition.

Simanjuntak, R. (1998). Regional Autonomy and Fiscal Decentralization of Thought *Contribution FE-UI on Economic Reform and Recovery* Jakarta LPEM-UI.

Slinko, I. (2002). *Fiscal decentralization on the budget revenue inequality among municipalities and growth of Russian regions.* Available http://pdc.ceu.hu/archive/00001992/.

Sukanto Reksohadiprojo. (2001). *Public Economica.* Yogyakarta. BPFE.

The Central Bureau of Statistik (2016). *Gross Regional Domestic Product (GDRP) of district/cities 2005–2015.* The Central Bureau of Statistik South Borneo Province.

The Central Bureau of Statistik (2016). *South Borneo in Figures 2005–2015.* The Central Bureau of Statistik South Borneo Province.

Woller, G.M. & Phillips, K. (1998). Fiscal Decentralization and ILDC Economic Growth: An empirical investigation. *The Journal of Development Studies, 34*(4), 139–148.

Increasing Management Relevance and Competitiveness – Sukoco et al. (Eds)
© 2018 Taylor & Francis Group, London, ISBN 978-0-8153-7455-8

Work-family conflict and satisfactions: A job demand-resources model perspective

J. Sulistiawan
Universitas Airlangga, Surabaya, Indonesia

ABSTRACT: One of the most demanding jobs, which requires great demands from the workplace and potentially leads to an imbalance between work and family life, is that of a police officer. This matter can, to some extent or another, affect the behavior and performance of police officers as public servants. The aim of this study is to examine the influence of job demand-resources on satisfaction outcomes through work-family conflict, as well as to determine the moderating role of social support on the job demand-resources and work-family conflict. Quantitative methods were used in this study with high-job-demand police officers as respondents. Our interesting finding is that family demand has insignificant influence on work-family conflict. In addition, work-family conflict has insignificant influence on family satisfaction. The moderating role of social support was only proved to moderate correlations between job demand and work-family conflict.

Keywords: Job Demand-Resources, Satisfaction Outcomes, Work-Family Conflict, Social Support

1 INTRODUCTION

Several studies have been conducted regarding work-life balance (Greenhaus & Beutell, 1985; Beutell & Wittig-Berman, 1999; Marcinkus, et al., 2007), and the association between job demand and family demand to the work/family interface, but most of these studies were only conducted in the United States or other Western countries (Lu et al., 2010). Although several studies related to Work-Family Conflict (WFC) have been conducted in Asia, such as in Singapore, Hong Kong, Japan and Taiwan, research related to the potential influence of work resource and family resource in Indonesia is still needed, because it seems that Indonesian people tend to spend more time at work rather than having quality time with family or colleagues.

Among the occupations that clearly appear to place great demands from the workplace, potentially causing an imbalance between work and family life, is that of the police officer. The fulfillment of job demand often leads to the absence of opportunity to meet family demand, causing conflict either within the family or at work (Demerouti et al., 2012).

Several antecedents of the WFC can be drawn from Job Demand-Resources (JD-R) (Demerouti et al., 2012). Drawing from JD-R, WFC occurs due to job demands which bring psychological effects to the individual. Those job demands could encompass longer working hours compared to normal, heavy workloads, as well as activities in the job that always involve deadlines (Demerouti et al., 2012). The JD-R model assumes that individuals tend to address two different matters at the same time, namely job demand and resources, i.e social supports (Bakker, 2003. Resources in JD-R refers to aspects in the job or the family that help individuals to fulfill either job or family demands (Demerouti et al., 2012). Those resources are social supports which come either from work or outside the work environment. The supports could diminish the effects of demand on WFCs. Since the employees get supports from both work and/or non-work, such as being permitted to be absent for a while to take care of their children, it will decrease the negative effects of job demand regarding WFC.

As argued by Marcinkus et al. (2007), intense WFC or Family-Work Conflict (FWC) would affect negatively on one's job satisfaction. Miller et al. (2009) argued that low satisfaction will affect the performance of police officers. Behavior is the most highlighted aspect of a police officer in public. Showcasing bad behavior/attitude will shape poor public perceptions pertaining to the organization and members of the Indonesian police. The contributions of this study are threefold. First, reviewing the WFC based on the JD-R model. Second, examining the influence of WFC on satisfaction outcomes. Third, examining the role of social support, either from work or outside the work environment, in influencing correlations between WFC and satisfaction outcomes.

2 HYPOTHESIS

Drawing on Job Demand-Resources (JD-R) (Demerouti et al., 2012), WFC might occur due to job demands which have a psychological effect on people. It could be manifested as longer working hours compared to normal, heavy workloads, as well as job activity that is always associated with deadlines (Demerouti et al., 2012).

Similarly, the cause of high level of FWC based on the JD-R model are the family demands that can disturb one's job role. Family demands correlate to a person's role in the family. When someone's role at the workplace becomes disrupted, he/she experiences FWC. As noted by Zhang and Liu (2011), a high family demand would affect a high level of FWC. Thus,

H1: Job demand has positive influence towards WFC;
H2: Family demand has positive influence towards FWC.

High levels of WFC and FWC also affect one's level of satisfaction outcomes. Satisfaction in this study encompasses job satisfaction, family satisfaction, and life satisfaction. When a person feels he/she encounters a high level of WFC, it will affect perceived job satisfaction. This is in line with prior study (e.g. Ford et al., 2007), that if one's roles in the family disrupt his/her roles at work, it will significantly reduce his/her level of job satisfaction. This is caused by conflicting roles in the family which interfere with one's roles at work, resulting in improperly unresolved tasks/duties which lessen job satisfaction. Thus,

H3: FWC has negative influence towards job satisfaction.

When employees perceive an endangering level of WFC, it will affect family satisfaction. Based on a prior study conducted in Taiwan, it was found that WFC has a negative influence on job satisfaction and family satisfaction (Lu et al., 2010). This is similar to the results acquired by Ford et al. (2007), in that if the role at work interferes with the family, it will degrade employees' perceived level of family satisfaction. As an employee experiences a conflicting role in his/her job, roles in the family become compromised, resulting in an improperly unresolved domestic situation, which leads to lower family satisfaction. Thus,

H4: WFC has negative influence towards family satisfaction.

According to Judge & Hulin (1993), there is significant positive correlation between job satisfaction and life satisfaction. A number of studies have examined the correlation between job satisfaction and family satisfaction towards life satisfaction, and it was found that there is a positive correlation between job satisfaction to life satisfaction, and between family satisfaction to life satisfaction (Chiu et al., 1998). When an employee feels happy with his/her family, it will contribute to increasing life satisfaction. Chiu et al. (1998) argued that marital satisfaction is one of the most important components of life satisfaction. Judge et al. (quoted in Beutell & Wittig-Berman, 1999) also found positive correlations between job satisfaction and life satisfaction. Thus,

H5a: Job satisfaction has positive influence towards life satisfaction;
H5b: Family satisfaction has positive influence towards life satisfaction.

Job and family demands can affect both WFC and FWC, but could be possibly minimized when someone obtains social support, both from work and personal support. Marcinkus et al. (2007 found that social support could play a significant role as an antecedent, a direct effect, mediator and moderator. Employees who perceive that companies are less supportive towards family issues were found to experience more WFC, less job satisfaction, less organizational commitment, and a higher desire to resign from the job, compared to those in a company that provides support to family matters. Similarly, when a person feels the support from his personal life, such as from his/her spouse/life partner, it motivates him/her to meet all the demands of the job, and therefore will reduce the FWC. This corresponds to Demerouti et al.'s (2012) description that, in order to balance job and family demands, frequent support from partners is needed to meet these demands, so as to minimize the possibility of FWC. Social support from family has negative influence towards family-work interference (dimension of WFC). Thus,

H6: Social support will moderate correlations between (a) job demand and WFC, as well as (b) family demand and FWC.

3 METHOD

3.1 *Sample and procedures*

We surveyed 470 police officers, from whom 198 questionnaires were returned, but of which only 178 were usable. The average range of respondents was 30–39 years old. The average range of respondents' tenure was 10–19 years.

3.2 *Measures*

All measures used a response scale from 1, which was 'strongly disagree', to 5 which was 'strongly agree'. Job demand was measured by Voydanoff's

(2004 three items; Family Demand was measured by Voydanoff's (2004) three items; Work-to-Family Conflict and Family-to-Work Conflict were measured by Grandey et al.'s (2005; 323) five items, respectively. Social support in this study was classified based on its domain, dividing it into two different types, namely work-related social support and non-work-related social support/personal support. Work-related social support was measured by Marcinkus et al.'s (2007 nine items, while non-work-related social support was measured by Foley et al.'s (2005) ten items. Job satisfaction was measured by Boyar et al.'s (2012) five items. Family satisfaction was measured by Mill et al.'s (1992) four items, and life satisfaction was measured by Diener et al.'s (1985) five items.

4 RESULTS

The study used Partial Least Square (PLS), as a means of analysis to examine the proposed hypotheses. Based on outer model analysis, there are some indicators that should be eliminated because they have values of less than 0.5. They involve two indicators of job and family demand, as well as five indicators of work-related social support and non-work-related social support. Composite reliability scores for all variables were above 0.7, including job demand (1), family demand (1), WFC (0.83), FWC (0.84), job satisfaction (0.89), family satisfaction (0.93), life satisfaction (0.94), work-related social support (0.79), and non-work-related social support (0.72).

Table 1. Table of PLS analysis.

	Original sample	Standard error	T Statistic	Note
JD -> WFC	−0.707	0.487	1.4519	H_1: Not Supported
FD -> FWC	0.321	0.857	0.3752	H_2: Not Supported
FWC -> JS	−0.300	0.107	2.7992**	H_3: Supported
WFC -> FS	0.059	0.117	0.5050	H_4: Not Supported
JS -> LS	0.285	0.156	1.8230*	H_5: Supported
FS -> LS	0.469	0.182	2.5765**	H_6: Supported
JD*WRSS -> WFC	1.123	0.498	2.2533*	H_7: Supported
FD*NWRSS -> FWC	0.025	0.868	0.0292	H_8: Not Supported

*Sig at p value 0.05 (one tail).
**Sig at p value 0.01 (one tail).
Notes: JD: Job Demand; WFC: Work-Family Conflict; FWC: Family-Work Conflict; JS: Job Satisfaction; FS: Family Satisfaction; LS: Life Satisfaction; WRSS: Work-Related Social Support; NWRSS: Non-Work-Related Social Support.

5 DISCUSSION

This study contributes to management literature, especially WFC, in several ways. First, the findings revealed that neither job nor family demand affected employees' work-family and FWC, respectively. One possible reason is because most respondents in this research were males (85.44%). Male employees have a higher tendency to find their own way of achieving given tasks at the workplace and securing their role accomplishment in the family, causing relatively fewer problems in both domains (Pleck, 1997).

Conversely, female employees tend to give more attention to their roles in the family (Cinnamon & Rich, 2002). This indicates that male employees would be able to keep all job demands fulfilled, enabling less propensity for employment issues. In addition, Lapierre et al. (2008) asserted that available family-friendly benefits for the employees will reduce WFC. Second, surprisingly, work-family conflict did not affect family satisfaction, drawing on the role demand concept, where most respondents are males and were likely to fulfill all job demands compared to female employees (Ford et al., 2007).

According to the role identification point of view, male employees would give more attention to their roles at work, while female employees would tend to give more attention to their roles in the family. It is even far more encouraging for male employees because males in the Indonesian culture tend to bear a responsibility to fulfill the economic needs of the family. Ford et al. (2007) also argued that family conditions also have a considerable influence on the employees' family satisfaction.

Family circumstances discussed in this context are the number of family members who generate incomes/revenues. In other words, when an employee and his/her partner both have a full-time job, time for family members will be reduced, unlike those whose partner is not employed. Therefore, when an employee and his/her partner are both employed, family satisfaction will be disrupted because both of them encounter pressure from job demands, and clearly would have very limited time to do home chores, and vice versa. Third, both family satisfaction and job satisfaction affect life satisfaction. This is also supported by data showing a considerably high level of family satisfaction and job satisfaction, as well as a high level of life satisfaction. The study supports Beutell et al.'s (1999) finding that satisfaction on life-related activities (job satisfaction and family satisfaction) will have a positive influence on life satisfaction. This is caused by life satisfaction as being a representation of overall quality of one's life, allowing job and family to become a subjective measurement related to life satisfaction.

6 CONCLUSION AND LIMITATIONS

There are several limitations of this study. First, our sample was only limited to police officers. Since there are several occupations susceptible to high work demand, such as doctor, nurse, or journalist, we suggest that the future research should examine these occupations. Second, individuals tend to experience different levels of WFC, depending on several things such as the employee's age, number of children, or age of children. We suggest that future research should group the respondents according to their family life stages (Demerouti et al., 2012).

REFERENCES

Allen, E. (2015). Labor and Social Trend in Indonesia. 2014–015. Retrieved from http://www.ilo.org/jakarta/whatwedo/publications/WCMS_381565/lang—en/index.htm.

Bakker, A.B., Demerouti, E., Tarsi, A.W., Schaufeli, W.B. & Schreurs, P.J. (2003). A multigroup analysis of the job demands resources model in four home care organizations. *International Journal of Stress Management*, *10*(1), 16–38.

Beutell, N.J. & Wittig-Berman, U. (1999). Predictors of work-family conflict and satisfaction with family, job, career and life. *Psychological Reports*, *85*(3). 893–903.

Boyar, S.L., Maertz Jr, C.P., Pearson, A.W. & Keough, S. (2003). Work-Family conflict: A model of linkages between work and family domain variables and turnover intentions. *Journal of Managerial Issues*, *15*(2), 175–179.

Carlson, D.S. & Perrewe, P.L. (1999). The role of social support in the stressor strain relationship: An examination of work family conflict. *Journal of Management*, *25*(4), 513–540.

Chiu, R. K., Man, J. S. W., & Thayer, J. (1998). Effects of roleconflicts and role satisfactions on stress of three professions in Hong Kong: A path analysis approach. *Journal of ManagerialPsychology*, 13(5/6), 318–333.

Cicek, I. (2013). Relationship between balance of job demands-control and shared mission/vision for blue-collar employees. *Journal of Social and Behavioral Science*, *99*, 1093–1104.

Cinnamon, R. G., & Rich, Y. (2002). Gender differences in the importance of work and family roles: Implications for work–family conflict. *Sex Roles*, 47, 531–541.

Demerouti, E., Peeters, M.C. & van der Heijden, B.I. (2012). Work-Family interface from a life and career stage perspective: The role of demands and resources. *International Journal of Psychology*, *47*(4), 241–258.

Diener, E.D., Emmons, R.A., Larsen, R.J. & Griffin, S. (1985). The satisfaction with life scale. *Journal of Personality Assessment*, *49*(1), 71–75.

Foley, S., Hang-Yue, N. & Lui, S. (2005). The effect of work stressors, perceived organizational support, and gender on work-family conflict in Hong Kong. *Asia Pacific Journal of Management*, *22*(3), 237–256.

Ford, M.T., Heinen, B.A. & Langkamer, K.L. (2007). Work and family satisfaction and conflict: A meta-analysis of cross-domain relations. *Journal of Applied Psychology*. *92*(1), 57–80.

George, J.M. & Jones, G.R. (2005). *Understanding and managing organizational behavior* (4th ed.). New Jersey: Pearson Prentice Hall.

Grandey, A.A., Cordeiro, B.L. & Crouter, A.C. (2005). A longitudinal and multi-source test of the work-family conflict and job satisfaction relationship. *Journal of Occupational and Organizational Psychology*, *78*(3), 305–323.

Greenhaus, H., Collins, K.M. & Shaw, J.D. (2002). The relation between work-family balance and quality of life. *Journal of Vocational Behavior*, *63*, 510–531.

Greenhaus, J.H. & Beutell, N.J. (1985). Sources of conflict between work and family roles. *Academy of Management*, *10*(1), 76–88.

Hall, G.B., Dollard, M.F., Tuckey, M.R., Winefield, A.H. & Thompson, B.M. (2010). Job demands, work-family conflict, and emotional exhaustion in police officers: A longitudinal test of competing theories. *Journal of Occupational and Organizational Psychology*, *83*(1), 237–250.

Hill, E.J., Jacob, J.I., Shannon, L.L., Brennan, R.T., Blanchard, V.L. & Martinengo, G. (2008). Exploring the relationship of workplace flexibility, gender, and life stage to family-to-work conflict, and stress and burnout. *Community, Work & Family*, *11*(2), 165–181.

Johnson, J.V. & Hall, E.M. (1988). Job strain, work place social support and cardiovascular disease: A cross-sectional study of a random sample of the Swedish working population. *American Journal of Public Health*, *78*(1), 1336–1342.

Judge, T.A., & Hulin, C.L. (1993), "Job satisfaction as a reflection of a disposition: amultiple source causal analysis", Organizational Behavior and Human Decisions Processes, Vol. 56, pp. 388–421.

Kahn, R.L., Wolfe, D.M., Quinn, R.P., Snoek, J.D. & Rosenthal, R.A. (1964). *Organizational stress*. New York, NY: Wiley.

Karasek, R.A. (1979). Job demands, job decision latitude and mental strain: Implications for job redesign. *Administrative Science Quarterly*, *24*, 285–308.

Lapierre, L. M. T. D. Allen, S. Poelmans, C. L. Cooper, M.P.O'Driscoll,J.I.Sanchez,P.Brough,andU.Kinnunen. (2008). Family-Supportive Organization Perceptions, Multiple Dimensions of Work-Family Conflict, and Employee Satisfaction: A Test of Model Across Five Samples." Journal of Vocational Behavior 73: 92–106.

Lirio, P., Lituchy, T.R., Monserrat, S.I., Olivas-Lujan, M.R., Duffy, J.A., Fox, S., ... Santos, N. (2007). Exploring career-life success and family social support of successful women in Canada, Argentina and Mexico. *Career Development International*, *12*(1), 28–50.

Lu, L., Cooper, C.L., Kao, S.F., Chang, T.T., Allen, T.D., Lapierre, L.M. ... Spector, P. (2010). Cross-cultural differences on work-to-family conflict and role satisfaction: A Taiwanese-British comparison. *Human Resource Management*, *49*(1),: 67–85.

Luthans, F. (1998). *Organizational behavior* (8th ed.). USA: Irwin/McGraw-Hill.

Marcinkus, W.C., Whelan-Berry, K.S. & Gordon, J.R. (2007. The relationship of social support to the work-family balance and work outcomes of midlife women. *Women in Management Review*, *22*(2), 86–111.

Miller, H. A., Mire, S., & Kim, B. (2009). Predictors of job satisfaction among police officers: Does personality matter? Journal of Criminal Justice, 37, 419–428.

Mills, R J, Grasmick, H.G., Morgan, C.S. & Wenk, D.A. (1992). The effects of gender, family satisfaction, and economic strain on psychological well-being. *Journal of Family Relation*, *41*, 440–445.

Namasivayam, K. & Zhao, X. (2007). An investigation of the moderating effects of organizational commitment on the relationship between work-family conflict and job satisfaction among hospitality employees in India. *Tourism Management*, *28*(5), 1212–1223.

Pavot, W. & Diener, E. (2008). The satisfaction with life scale and the emerging construct of life satisfaction. *Journal of Applied Psychology*, *3*(2), 137–152.

Pleck, J.H. (1997). *Paternal involvement: Levels, sources, and consequences.* In M.E. Lamb (Ed.), The role of the father in child development (3rd ed., pp. 66–103). New York: Wiley.

Sanne, B., Mykletun, A., Dahl, A.A., Moen, B.E. & Tell, G.S. (2005). Testing the job demand-control-support model with anxiety and depression as outcomes: The Hordaland Health Study. *Journal of Occupational Medicine*, *55*(6), 463–473.

Schaufeli, W.B. & Bakker, A.B. (2004). Job demands, job resources, and their relationship with burnout and engagement. *Journal of Organizational Behavior*, *25*(3), 293–315.

Survey shows Indonesians worry about work life balance. (2012). *The Jakarta Post*. Retrieved from http://www.thejakartapost.com/news/2012/11/01/survey-shows-indonesians-worry-about-work-life-balance.html.

The Impact of Moral Stress Compared to Other Stressors on Employee Fatigue, Job Satisfaction, and Turnover: An Empirical Investigation (PDF Download Available). Available from: https://www.researchgate.net/publication/257541648_The_Impact_of_Moral_Stress_Compared_to_Other_Stressors_on_Employee_Fatigue_Job_Satisfaction_and_Turnover_An_Empirical_Investigation [accessed Jan 15 2018].

Van Steenbergen, E.F., Kluwer, E.S. & Karney, B.R. (2014). Work-Family enrichment, work-family conflict, and marital satisfaction: A dyadic analysis. *Journal of Occupational Health Psychology*, *19*(2), 182–194.

Voydanoff, P. (2004). The effects of work demands and resources on work-to-family conflict and facilitation. *Journal of Marriage and Family*, *66*(2), 398–412.

Yang, N., Chen, C.C., Choi, J. & Zou, Y. (2000). Sources of work-family conflict: A Sino-US comparison of the effects of work and family demands. *Academy of Management Journal*, *43*(1), 113–123.

Zhang, J. & Liu, Y. (2011). Antecedents of work-family conflict: Review and prospect. *International Journal of Business and Management*, *6*(1), 89–103.

Increasing Management Relevance and Competitiveness – Sukoco et al. (Eds)
© 2018 Taylor & Francis Group, London, ISBN 978-0-8153-7455-8

Building employee engagement through transformational leadership, psychological empowerment and affective commitment

P. Yulianti & N. Hamidah
Airlangga University, Surabaya, Indonesia

ABSTRACT: Employee engagement in the workplace is very important, especially in pursuing competitive organizational advantages. It can be developed through transformational leadership, psychological empowerment and affective commitment. This study involves explanatory research that will explain the causal relationship between the variables through hypothesis testing. The sample in this study was collected from 132 respondents. The statistical method used was partial least squares regression. The results of this study indicate that transformational leadership is positively related to employee engagement, and that psychological empowerment and affective commitment partially mediate the relationship between transformational leadership and employee engagement.

Keywords: Transformational leadership, psychological empowerment, affective commitment, engagemen

1 INTRODUCTION

Employee engagement is used to achieve optimal company performance to gain a competitive advantage. A company not only recruits and retains employees who have talent, but also hopes that they have an emotional engagement towards the company and/or their jobs. The results of the measurement of employee engagement on a global level shows an increasing trend, but for the Asia Pacific region the level remains low (Hewitt, 2015). Employee engagement in Indonesia is still at a low level but is still better than in Malaysia (Hewitt, 2015). Employee engagement has a very strong influence on employee performance, more than intrinsic motivation, job involvement and being satisfied with work (Richman, 2006). High employee engagement is shown by saying, staying and striving according to employees (Hewitt, 2015). Saying is positive employee speak regarding the organizations by co-workers, potential employees or consumers. Staying is comparable with having a strong sense of belonging and wanting to be part of the organization. Striving is an employee behavior which motivates and implies an effort to succeed in relation to the working side of the organization. Employee engagement is not only physically apparent in organizations, but also more important is the emotional engagement which is shown by care and a focus on performance. Schaufeli et al. (2004) explained that an employee who is engaged in the workplace will feel energestic, enthusiastic, and happy when completing tasks. An employee who is engaged in their work will also have some initiative in working and can provide contributions towards improving innovations in their respective working unit (Hakanen et al., 2008).

Transformational leadership can facilitate the employee to take some initiative, to take on some risks, to stimulate innovation and to solve uncertainty (Spreitzer, 1995). Transformational leaders inspire, energize, and intellectually stimulate their employees (Bass & Avolio, 2004). Transformational leadership pushes and motivates followers to remain focused on the vision and goal of the organization so that the employee feels psychologically empowered. Psychological empowerment will allow the employee feel that they are involved and experience self-belonging in relation to the organization (Bell & Staw, 1989).

Psychological empowerment will provide intrinsic motivation that affects performance and allows the growth of positive feelings regarding their work. Positive feelings, which occurs from psychological empowerment, will have an effect on engagement from the employee to the organization and their work. Transformational leadership can improve psychological empowerment because the employee feels that they have intrinsic motivation regarding their work. Transformational leadership will improve self-confidence (Bass & Avolio, 2004). It can also help develop affective commitment. Meyer and Allen (1997) noted that affective commitment is the desire to be a part of the organization Transformational leadership communicates the hope of good performance regarding the organizations future, providing motivation for the employees to remain and be a part of the organization. PT. Bank Rakyat Indonesia (BRI) is a government bank in Indonesia which has demonstrated a good performance in facing the environmental challenges and uncertainty that has been encountered by transformational leadership. In the beginning BRI only focused on providing rural banking services and micro-credit, but as time went on there were many more competitors appearing in their business segment. BRI developed a market that offered different features, which involved new product innovations to provide more access for their customers. BRI says that it likes to go beyond customer expectations. The changes implemented by BRI also provide them with a competitive advantage. Employee engagement can achieve the expectation about their objectives which want to be achieved by BRI. Currently, BRI has become a government bank with the greatest profits of all of the banks owned by the government in Indonesia. Employee engagement can be stimulated by transformational leadership. Transformational leadership will help develop psychological empowerment and affective commitment, which will motivate employee's intrinsic engagement towards their work.

This research suggests achieving a competitive advantage, it is important to build employee engagement through transformational leadership and that employee engagement is built by psychological empowerment and affective commitment as the intrinsic motivation to achieve the best performance.

2 THEORY AND HYPOTHESES

2.1 *Transformational leadership*

According to Burns (1979), transformational leadership is a process in which a leader and follower help each other to achieve morality and motivation at a higher level. Transformational leadership focuses on gaining the engagement offollowers. According to Bass and Avolio (2004), transformational leadership acts as a bridge between the leader and follower to develop a clear opinion about the interests of the followers, their values and motivation. Bass and Avolio (2004) also said that there are four keys to the leadership dimension which can be used to achieve transformations inside organizations. A charismatic leader can inspire their followers with a clear vision, mission, pride, respect and trust of their followers, and they can also increase optimism (idealized influence or charisma). A leader communicates vision and high-level goals for the future, so that it will affect their enthusiasm and inspire employees to achieve the higher levelexpected (inspirational motivation). A leader stimulates employee creativity and innovation to encourage them to be more creative in doing their job and solving problems from a new perspective (intellectual stimulation) and the leader shows their consideration for their employees with responsiveness to their requests and needs, showing care for each employee and giving extra attention to the generation of the employee's career (individualized consideration).

2.2 *Psychological empowerment*

Conger and Kanungo (1988) defined psychological empowerment as a motivational concept to do with self-fulfillment, specifically as it can be said that the improvement of intrinsic task motivation occurs as a part of cognition which reflects the individual's orientation in relation to their working role. Intrinsic task motivation is defined as performing an action or behavior because you enjoy the task activity. According to Spreitzer (1995), psychological empowerment is cognitive motivation formed by the working environment, which is active in the working role. Menon (1999) defined psychological empowerment as a cognitive condition which is signaled by a sense of control, competency and goal internalization.

2.3 *Affective commitment*

Meyer and Allen (1997) defined affective commitment as occuring when an emotional individual within an organizations feels as if they are equivalent, are always involved and feels happy to be a part of the organizations. Meyer and Allen (1997) explained that affective commitment can be reflected by the employees with their attitudes as follows: spending their entire career with the organization, discussing the company with outsiders, feeling that the organization's problems are their problems, they are not easily engaged with other organizations, feel "part of the family" and feel emotionally engaged with the organization.

2.4 *Employee engagement*

Employee engagement is defined by Kahn (1990) as the effort by members of the organizations to bind themselves with the roles in which they are working. Employee engagement is not only an organizational commitment, but it is also their behavior as shown by giving their full consideration and affiliation with their jobs. (Saks, 2006). Schaufeli et al (2004) defined engagement as a positive motivational condition which is related to employement and is vary by vigor, dedication and absorption. Vigor is a high-level energy, ability or a strong mentality while working through various difficulties. Dedication is a sense that jobs have goals and means, where employees have a strong sense of involvement with enthusiasm, pride and inspiration. Absorption is a condition which makes someone feel happy in doing a job in which they feel that time goes by quickly and that they do not want to leave.

3 RELATIONSHIP BETWEEN VARIABLES

3.1 *The influence of transformational leadership on employee engagement*

The appearance of employee engagement is related to how the leader approaches the task, as the leader is the driver of employee engagement in working life. Transformational leadership gives extra consideration towards each employee, is responsible for their risks and creates a vision for the future which includes high expectations that are challenging to the employee and that will inspire and motivate them to achieve a higher level of performance. In the end, they will have a better degree of employee engagement in their jobs and the organization.

H1: Transformational leadership has positive influence to employee engagement

3.2 *The influence of transformational leadership on employee engagement through psychological empowerment*

Bass and Avolio (2004) found that transformational leadership influences the follower's perceptions about empowerment. The leader empowers the lower level employees by giving a clear orders and emphasizing the higher goals or values. The results are enthusiasm for achieving the organization's goals and providing challenges in their working time (Menon, 1999). According to the results, the employee will feel that their job has allowed them to complete a goal that equates with their personal standards. They will also feel more self-confident in their ability and competency in doing their jobs, which can lead to them feeling that they can make a decision which influences the organization. In the end, they will feel engaged to their job.

H2: Transformational leadership has positive influence to employee engagement through psychological empowerment.

3.3 *The influence of transformational leadership on employee engagement through affective commitment*

Leadership can be described as an important key of organizational commitment. (Bass & Avolio, 2004). Transformational leaders can influence affective commitment in their followers by improving the intrinsic value level of achieving the organization's goals. It will provide intrinsic motivation on employees. They will show work engagement with improved productivity.

H3: Transformational leadership has positive influence to employee engagement through affective commitment

4 RESEARCH METHODS

The population in this research include permanent employees of BRI Surabaya Office, amounting to 162 respondents. The sampling method involved acensus approach in which each data return that meets the requirements is used as a sample. From 162 questionnaires distributed, the return amount was 135 questionnaires and three questionnaires were not. This research uses the analytical technique with PLS (*Partial Least Square*). The instrument used to measure transformational leadership was the Multifactor Leadership Questionnaire (MLQ) which was developed by Bass and Avolio (2004). Psychological empowerment was determined the Psychological Empowerment Questionnaire (PEQ) which was developed by Spreitzer (1995). Affective commitment was investigated by Meyer and Allen (1997) using the Organizational Commitment Questionnaire (OCQ). Employee engagement was measured using the Utrecht Work Engagement Scale (UWES) involving indicators such as vigor, dedication, and absorption, Schaufeli et al. (2004).

5 RESULTS

The outer loading value of each indicator on the variables of transformational leadership, psychological empowerment, affective commitment and employee engagement were all valued by probability value > 0.50. The composite reliability values for the variables transformational leadership, psychological empowerment, affective commitment and employee engagement were all above 0.70. This shows that each variable meets the composite reliability requirements.

5.1 *The influence of transformational leadership on employee engagement*

The results of the first hypothesis show that there is a significant positive relationship between transformational leadership and employee engagement. In previous research by Tims, Bakker and Xanthopoulo (2011), a positive relationship between transformational leadership and employee engagement was found. The leader who adopts transformational leadership can influence employee engagement because transformational leadership can explain visions and missions clearly, using individual approaches to motivate employees to achieve the expected performance, allowing the

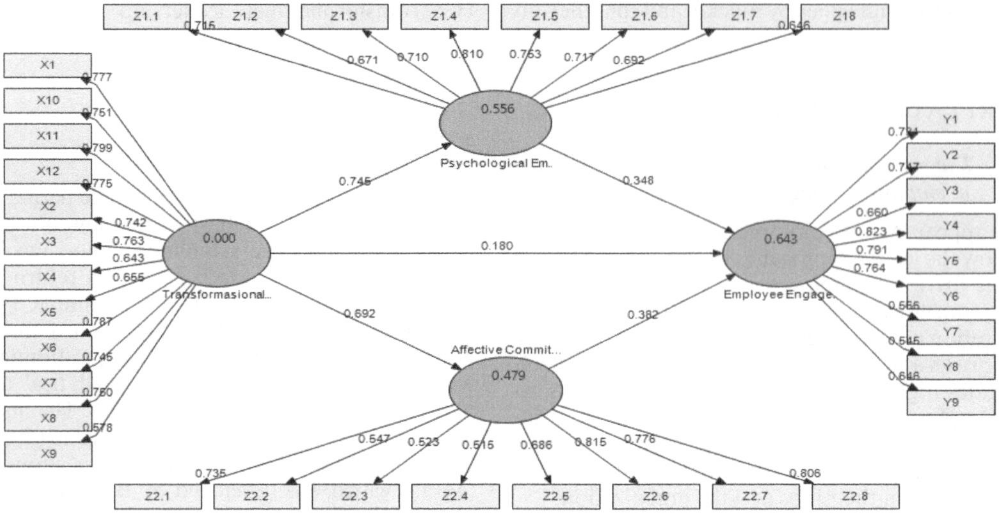

employee feel engaged with their job and aiming to do their best.

5.2 *The influence of transformational leadership on employee engagement through psychological empowerment*

There is a significant positive effect between transformational leadership and psychological empowerment, and between psychological empowerment and employee engagement. Avolio et al. (2004) demonstrated that transformational leadership influences the follower's perception of empowerment. Jose and Mampilly (2014) also proved that psychological empowerment is a significant influence on employee engagement. Transformational leadership influences the intrinsic motivation of the employee and help gain their trust.

5.3 *Transformational leadership to employee engagement through affective commitment*

There is a significant positive relationship between transformational leadership and affective commitment, and between affective commitment and employee engagement. Bass and Avolio (2004) showed that transformational leadership significantly influences affective commitment. Transformational leadership can influence affective commitment because the leader consider each individual and motivates them to improve their performance to the highest level to achieve the organization's goals. Someone who has affective commitment to their company will have a sense of engagement regarding their job and the organization (Niazi, 2015).

5.4 *Theoretical implications*

Transformational leadership has positively influences to employee engagement. Transformational leadership has positively influenced to psychological empowerment and also affective commitment. Psychological empowerment and affective commitment partially mediate the relationship between transformational leadership and employee engagement. According to the results, it can be concluded theoretically that employee engagement can be built up directly by transformational leadership or mediated by psychological empowerment and affective commitment.

5.5 *Practical implications*

The practical results are that the contribution of transformational leadership has little effect on employee engagement compared to the role of psychological empowerment. The leader of BRI has successfully adopted intrinsic employee motivation so that employees feel psychologically empowered and emotionally connected with their jobs. The other contribution of transformational leadership is that it does not have a greater value than affective commitment but affective commitment has a greater influence on employee engagement.

REFERENCES

Barroso C., Villegas Perinan, M.M. & Casillas Bueno, J.C. (2008). Transformational leadership and follower's attitudes: The mediating role of psychological empowerment. *International Journal of Human Resource Management,19*(10), 1842–1863.

Bass, B.M. & Avolio, B.J. (2004). *Improving organizational effectiveness through transformational leadership*. New York:Thousand Oaks Sage Publications.
Bell, N.E, & Staw, B.M. (1989) *People as sculptors versus sculpture.* (Cambridge University Press).
Burns, J.M. (1979). *Leadership*. NewYork, Harper & Row.
Conger, J.A. & Kanungo, R.N. (1988). The empowerment process: Integrating theory and practice. (*Academy of Management Review*).
Hakanen, J.J., Perhoniemi, R. & Toppinen-Tanner, S. (2008). Positive gain spirals at work: From job resources to work engagement, personal initiative and work-unit innovativeness. *Journal of Vocational Behavior*, *73*(1), 78–91.
Hewitt, A. (2015). *Trends in global employee engagement.*
Jose, Greetha. and Mampilly, Sebastian Rupert. Psychological empowerment as a predictor of employee engagement: An empirical attestation. *Global Business Review, 15*-(93).
Kahn, W.A. (1990). Psychological conditions of personal engagement and disengagement at work. *Academy of Management Journal*, *33*, 692–724.
Menon, S.T. (1999). Psychological empowerment: definition, measurement, and validation. *Canadian Journal of Behavioral Sciences*. *31*(3), 161–164.
Meyer, J. & Allen, N. (1997). *Commitment in the workplace: Theory, research, and application*. (Sage Publications).
Niazi, M.M.K. (2015). The role of affective commitment and person organization fit on overall satisfaction: Mediating role of Employee engagement. *Journal of Business and Management*, *5,* 17–23.
Richman, A. (2006). Everyone wants an engaged workforce how can you create it? *Workspan Journal*, *49*, 36–39.
Saks, A.M. (2006). Antecedents and consequences of employee engagement. *Journal of Managerial Psychology*, *21*-(6), 600–619.
Schaufeli, W.B., Salanova, M., Gonzalez-Romá, V. & Bakker, A.B. (2004). The measurement of engagement and burnout: A confirmative analytic approach. *Journal of Happiness Studies*, *3*, 71–92.
Spreitzer, G.M. (1995). Psychological empowerment in the workplace: Dimensions, measurement and validation. *Academy of Management Journal*, *38*, 1442–1465.
Tims M., Bakker, A.B. & Xanthopoulo D. (2011). Do transformational leaders enhance their followers' daily work engagement? *The Leadership Quarterly*, *22*, 121–131.

Increasing Management Relevance and Competitiveness – Sukoco et al. (Eds)
© 2018 Taylor & Francis Group, London, ISBN 978-0-8153-7455-8

The impact of transformational leadership, learning organization and job autonomy on creative self-efficacy

I.B.G.A. Permana & W. Astiti
Universitas Airlangga, Surabaya, Indonesia

ABSTRACT: The purpose of this study was to analyze the effect of transformational leadership, learning orientation and job autonomy on creative self-efficacy. Sixty-seven radio announcers were chosen as respondents. This research was designed with a quantitative approach using questionnaire distribution and a purposive sampling method. Data were analyzed using multiple linear regression analysis. The results show that transformational leadership, learning orientation and job autonomy have a simultaneous effect on creative self-efficacy. The significance of this study is to give a wide range of insights to owners or managers of a radio company about the predictors of creative self-efficacy.

1 INTRODUCTION

Creativity is the basis of an innovation process, as creativity is the first step in generating new thoughts or ideas that will be implemented in a real action, called innovation (Coelho, 2011). The existence of creativity and innovation is considered the most important source for the success of an organization's life (DiLiello, Houghton & Dawley, 2011). Creativity becomes necessary T every level or dimension, starting with the creation of ideas and continuing through the execution of several processes to achieve a certain goal. On an individual level, it can be seen that human resources have an important role to play in building creativity and running organizational activities.

Previous research, conducted by Wood and Bandura (1989), showed that self-efficacy could be an important factor in running an organization. Self-efficacy is the belief of being able to assemble the motivation, cognitive resources and actions that need to be completed to meet the demands of a particular situation. Related to the focus of this study, which examines creativity, the authors used a more specific concept of self-efficacy, which is creative self-efficacy. Creative self-efficacy is considered an important feature in the emergence of creativity in the workplace. A high level of confidence is necessary in order to take part in creative behavior (Tierney & Farmer, 2002).

In the creative industry, transformational leaders can behave supportively and trust their subordinates in ideas and daily activities. Moreover, leaders in the workplace with high creativity, as in creative industries, must be able to act directly, which will entail many direct orders specifically about how to finish the assigned task.

Radio Industry was chosen as context of this research because its has tremendous demand on creativity. That creativity become essential aspect in the world of radio. Radio focusing on delivering a good solid, fact based information towards to the listeners, but that activity will required a good communication skills from the announcers. Radios are also sensed to be closer to the listeners, cover a wider range, are simple and uncomplicated for both the administrators and listeners, acceptable to everyone, and without doubt, provide interaction that can happen at any time between the announcer and the listener, for instance, by providing information on a reciprocal basis. In addition, types of media other than radio, such as television, are limited by the means and process of delivering news to the public, which sometimes takes a long time to complete the process of shooting, editing and finally being broadcast to the audience. Against this background, the authors were interested in conducting research on "The influence of transformational leadership, learning orientation and job autonomy on creative self-efficacy of radio announcers in Surabaya".

2 LITERATURE

The theory of transformational or inspirational leadership is based on Burns (1978) ideas cited by Yukl (2010) stated that leadership occurs when one employs the available resources to awaken, engage and fulfill the motivation of followers. Burns argued that transformational leadership occurs when a leader deals with others and makes use of all his/her resources to be skilled in motivating subordinates to take responsibility beyond their expectations. In such conditions, the followers of transformational leadership will sense the trust, admiration, loyalty and respect of the leader. In addition, they will be motivated to do more than what was originally expected of them. The transformational leader will change and motivate his/her followers by: (1) making them aware of the importance of a task; (2) encouraging them to prioritize the interests of the company rather than self-interest; (3) increasing subordinates' need from the most basic level to higher levels.

Every individual has the ability to learn and through learning, they will adapt to changes and developments in the existing environment. Similarly, organizations must also have a learning process that is expected to adapt to all environmental changes occurring within themselves. By being able to maintain stability against existing changes, there will be a direct maintenance of the company's short-term and long-term competitive advantages (Liu, Luo & Shi, 2002). Kohli, Shervani and Challagalla (1998) argued that every organization would eventually perform learning through individuals within the organization; therefore, learning orientation will be directly influenced by individual learning. Learning orientation in individuals is considered as an important factor to achieve success (Porter & Tansky, 1999). Consequently, there will be reasons to focus on individual learning as a determining factor in creativity within an organization.

Job autonomy refers to a person's freedom and independence in performing tasks and determining how to perform such tasks. Job autonomy is associated with achieving basic human needs in work situations (Joo, Yang & Mclean, 2014). Job autonomy is an individual's freedom to choose the means or actions taken to start and perform tasks at work (Zhang & Bartol, 2010). Job autonomy includes the subjective evaluation of the level of control, responsibility and freedom concerning one's work situation.

Self-efficacy is one of the self-regulating abilities which are unique to each individual. The concept of self-efficacy was first proposed by Bandura. Self-efficacy refers to the perception of individuals' beliefs to organize and implement actions to present certain ability. Bandura (1997) also said that self-efficacy was essentially the result of cognitive processes in the form of decisions, beliefs or appreciations about the extent to which individuals estimate their abilities to perform tasks or specific actions needed to achieve desired outcomes.

There is a more specific concept in self-efficacy related to creativity, which is identified as creative self-efficacy. Creative self-efficacy can be defined as individual confidence in having the ability to produce something creative (Tierney & Farmer, 2002). In Bandura's proposed concept of self-efficacy (cited in DiLiello, Houghton & Dawley, 2011), which is a perception targeting a capacity within a person, the level of self-efficacy possessed by an individual can influence the development of his/her competence and activeness. This will be the same as the creative self-efficacy which leads to self-assessment on the creative potential possessed by each individual in generating and developing creative ideas and solutions within a particular condition.

The relationship between transformational leadership and creative self-efficacy will take place when there is a process whereby a leader with a transformational leadership style assumes that every employee is an individual who will enact positive behavior and mindset through his/her leadership attitudes (e.g. through intellectual considerations or stimulation). Transformational leadership can lead to a change within the employees' selves, giving them confidence in having the ability to produce something creative, namely creative self-efficacy (Bandura, 1997).

Learning orientation in the individual will relate to one's motivation to achieve something. The goals in learning orientation is to add a new competencies. Hirst et al. (2011) said that the individual's orientation will aid the development of one's interest in the tasks performed at work. The existence of learning orientation in the individual will also directly stimulate his/her motivation, which leads to the confidence to do something creative. The relationship between the two is the basis for the emergence of a creative self-efficacy, requiring the presence of adequate motivation and ability.

At work, every employee will be given responsibility for what is done. With these responsibilities, employees are expected to be able to freely determine everything that has a good impact on the outcome of the work itself. The responsibility given by the leader will resolve how much job autonomy will be felt by an employee. Wang and Netemeyer (2002, p. 219) said that a high level of job autonomy would occur when there was a message of trust from the leader about the ability of his/her workers. The higher level of job autonomy will also result in employees' confidence in doing their job to produce something creative. Hence, the relationship between the two is that the employees' positive perception of job autonomy will increase the emergence of creative self-efficacy at work and how they perform the task well each day.

3 RESEARCH METHODS

In this study, the target population was the radio announcers in Surabaya. The Indonesian Private Radio Broadcasters Association of East Java (*Persatuan Radio Siaran Swasta Nasional Indonesia Jawa Timur* - PRSSNI), on its official website www.radiojatim.com, stated that there are 33 radio stations in Surabaya, which includes six AM (Amplitude Modulation) radio stations and 27 FM (Frequency Modulation) radio stations. The sampling technique used was a census technique, which takes the entire population so that the total sample is the sum of all announcers from ten radio stations in Surabaya. In this study, the number of questionnaires distributed in accordance with the number of announcers from ten radio stations was 96.

4 RESULTS AND DISCUSSION

Transformational leadership has a significant influence on creative self-efficacy. This means that an increase in transformational leadership will also significantly enhance self-efficacy (Amabile, 2004; Hsu, Hou & Fan, 2011; Jaiswal & Dhar, 2015). This can happen when an announcer feels guided in doing his/her job and given given another perspective when he/she performs a gimmick on-air. This Perspective will get a positive response from his/her leader, including criticism and suggestions.

The influence of transformational leadership on creative self-efficacy also shows that the radio announcers in Surabaya, who are categorized in the segment of youth listeners, have positive perceptions regarding the leader's support in developing and training each announcer through a direct and specific approach. With the unstructured nature of the work, the potential of the announcer is expected to be high in order to perform confidently in any circumstances.

The result of this study also shows that learning orientation is part of a self-related approach that affects creative self-efficacy. In accordance with the statement, when radio announcers in Surabaya are accustomed to work in and face difficult conditions every day during the on-air broadcast process, their ability and confidence at work will increase automatically. Announcers become accustomed to being able to think creatively while interacting with both listeners and co-announcers.

Employee motivation that drive self-learning will effect commitment and eventually builds awareness. Radio announcers with limited goals in a part-time job still have a certain desire while working (Hackman & Oldham, 1975). This also proves that radio announcers also have an expectation for the quality of their work, for example by guiding a program, either off-air or on-air, or expecting a better position by, of course, facing competition fairly. However, not all announcers encompass the learning motivation to achieve certain goals with maximum effort; this is where the leader or direct supervisor has to be able to use another way to find the announcer's actual ability.

This can be done with a specific task or a particular program, which includes a discussion on a certain topic, so that later the ability of an announcer can be evaluated. Announcers are expected to learn from previous situations in order to improve. The process of learning orientation can also be done by seeing the success of others, such as the accomplishments or career journey of a direct superior or fellow announcers. The last independent variable that influences creative self-efficacy is job autonomy. The variables in the job-related category in the results of this study are also known to have a significant effect on the creative self-efficacy of radio announcers in Surabaya, with a regression coefficient of 0.524, indicating that job autonomy positively affects creative self-efficacy.

5 CONCLUSION

Consequently, if there is an increase in job autonomy, self-efficacy is also significantly enhanced. Job autonomy is seen as a consideration of freedom and responsibility when doing a job, and these findings are supported by both Gong, Huang and Farh (2009) and Slatten (2014). Radio announcers who have diverse or heterogeneous work are expected to have the responsibility to determine what kind of actions should be taken to face certain situations. Announcers need to take note that the freedom they have at work, comes with great deal of responsibility. For example, when there is an interaction between a listener and a fellow announcer in a program, the announcer must be able to determine how to place himself/herself to answer or respond to the interaction. With greater experience of self-control over the various situations that can be solved with varied and interesting solutions or ideas, radio announcers will be able to develop their creative behavior.

REFERENCES

Amabile, T.M. (2004). A model of creativity and innovation in organizations. In B. Staw & L.L. Cummings (Eds.), *Research in organizational behavior*, 10 (pp.)123–167. Greenwich, London: JAI Press.

Bandura, A. (1997). *Self-efficacy: The exercise of control*. New York, NY: W.H. Freeman.

Coelho, F., Augusto, M. & Lages, L.F. (2011). Contextual factors and the creativity of frontline employees: The mediating effects of role stress and intrinsic motivation. *Journal of Retailing*, *87*(1), 31–41.

DiLiello, T.C., Houghton, J.D. & Dawley, D. (2011). Narrowing the creativity gap: The moderating effects of perceived support for creativity. *The Journal of Psychology*, *145*(3), 151–172.

Gong, Y., Huang, J.-C. & Farh, J.-L. (2009). Employee learning orientation, transformational leadership, and employee creativity: The mediating role of employee creative self-efficacy. *Academy of Management Journal*, *52*(4), 765–778.

Hackman, J.R. & Oldham, G.R. (1975). Development of the job diagnostic survey. *Journal of Applied Psychology*, *60*(2), 159–170.

Hirst, G., Van Knippenberg, D., Chen, C.-H. & Sacramento, C.A. (2011). How does bureaucracy impact creativity? A cross-level investigation of team contextual influences on goal orientation-creativity relationships. *Academy of Management Journal*, *54*(3), 624–641.

Hsu, M.L.A., Hou, S.-T. & Fan, H.-L. (2011). Creative self-efficacy and innovative behavior in a service setting: Optimism as a moderator, *Journal of Creative Behavior*, *45*(4), 258–272.

Jaiswal, N.K. & Dhar, R.L. (2015). Transformational leadership, innovation climate, creative self-efficacy and employee creativity: A multilevel study. *International Journal of Hospitality Management*, *51*, 30–41.

Joo, B., Yang, B. & Mclean, G.N. (2014). Employee creativity: The effect of perceived learning culture, leader member exchange quality, job autonomy, and proactivity. *Human Resource Development International*, *17*(3), 297–317.

Kohli, A.K., Shervani, T.A. & Challagalla, G.N. (1998). Learning and performance orientation of salespeople: The role of supervisors. *Journal of Marketing Research*, *35*(2), 263–274.

Liu, S.S., Luo, X. & Shi, Y.Z. (2002). Integrating customer orientation, corporate entrepreneurship, and learning orientation in organization-in-transition: An empirical study. *International Journal of Research in Marketing*, *19*(4), 367–382.

Porter, G. & Tansky, J.W. (1999). Expatriate success may depend on a 'learning orientation': Considerations for selection and training. *Human Resource Management*, *38*(1), 47–60.

Slatten, T. (2014). Determinants and effects of employee's creative self-efficacy on innovative activities. *International Journal of Quality and Service Sciences*, *6*(4), 326–347.

Tierney, P. & Farmer, S.M. (2002). Creative self-efficacy: Its potential antecedents and relationship to creative performance. *Academy of Management Journal*, *45*(6), 1137–1148.

Wang, G. & Netemeyer, R.G. (2002). The effects of job autonomy, customer demandingness, and trait competitiveness on salesperson learning, self-efficacy, and performance. *Journal of Academy of Marketing Science*, *30*(3), 217–228.

Wood, R.E. & Bandura, A. (1989). Impact of conceptions of ability on self regulatory mechanism and complex decision making. *Journal of Personality and Social Psychology*, *56*(3), 407–415.

Yukl, G. (2010). *Leadership in organizations* (7th ed.). New Jersey: Pearson International Edition.

Zhang, X. & Bartol, K.M. (2010). Linking empowering leadership and employee creativity: The influence of psychological empowerment, intrinsic motivation and creative process engagement. *Academy of Management Journal*, *53*(1), 107–128.

Increasing Management Relevance and Competitiveness – Sukoco et al. (Eds)
© 2018 Taylor & Francis Group, London, ISBN 978-0-8153-7455-8

Enhancing commitment to organizational change initiative and performance outcomes

N.A. Arina & P. Yulianti
Universitas Airlangga, Surabaya, Indonesia

ABSTRACT: Support from salespersons is critical to corporate change initiatives. Their commitment to participate in the change needs to be taken into consideration if the company does not want its earnings to fall, especially if policy changes occur frequently. This research model was tested by a sample of 123 sales force employees of an Internet service provider company in Surabaya, Indonesia, by using Partial Least Squares (PLS). The study proved that job autonomy and self-efficacy can impact on three types of commitment: affective commitment, normative commitment and continuance commitment. These commitments affect their responsiveness to customer needs. In addition, interesting results indicate commitment has no significant effect on sales performance.

Keywords: Job Autonomy, Self-Efficacy, Commitment to Change, Customer Responsiveness, Performance

1 INTRODUCTION

It is not the strongest of the species that survives, nor the most intelligent, but the ones most responsive to change. Charles Darwin famously observed that adaption to change is the key for survival (Thomas and Hardy 2011). In a fast-paced dynamic environment, constant thing is change itself, so it will be easier for companies to learn to deal with change rather than avoid it. However, the challenges faced when they change is the risk of bankruptcy (Maurer 2005; Palmer 2009;). If companies want to succeed in the competition in the business environment, companies need to be flexible, adaptable, and able to perform continuous transformation (Jaramillo et al. 2012).

Employees must have a commitment to run organizational change initiatives for successful implementation of change. In this study, in particular, employees are those who served to provide an offer to customers for services provided by the company, or commonly referred to as salespersons. Support from a salesperson is important because salespersons are the spearhead of the company for profit. The presence of resistance to change initiatives in a salesperson can hamper a company's ability to meet the challenges of its competitors and rapidly changing markets. The resilience of salespersons to change can be a barrier to adopting new technologies, learning new sales techniques, embracing new customers, and responding to the diverse needs of dynamic customers, which ultimately affect their ability to work effectively (Jaramillo et al. 2012).

This study will take the respondents as salespersons in a telecommunication company. Companies in the service industry will be full of dynamics because the needs offered are tertiary and easily searchable substitutes. The dynamics of changing consumer needs and the number of competitors offering similar products makes working in the service industry to be very sensitive to existing changes. Service companies will generally respond to market dynamics quickly through frequently changing policies. This, for salespersons, can be a constraint to achieve the expected sales target, so that the possibility of resistance to change becomes greater. Furthermore, resistance to such change initiatives will affect their commitment to change. This, of course, will affect their ability to obtain targets that have been set by the company.

2 CONCEPTUAL BACKGROUND

2.1 *Commitment to change*

Employee support is a prerequisite for many types of successful change (Kanter 1983; Piderit 2000; Hornung and Rosseau 2007). In other words, successful organizational change initiatives will not work without the support of employees. Furthermore, the support provided by employees is that they are committed to participate in the planned changes of the company. Herscovitch and Meyer

(2002) define commitment to change, as a mind-set that binds individuals for a course of action deemed necessary for the successful implementation of a change initiative.

There has been a growing interest in understanding the experience of changes experienced by individual employees as well as research investigating the role of employee commitment to organizational change (Judge et al. 1999; Parish et al. 2008). In order for employees to be committed to organizational change, top management must seek the trigger from commitment to change as well as the role of commitment to change in the success of organizational change initiatives, because commitment to change is believed to be a predictor of employee support for change versus commitment to the organization (Parish et al. 2008).

According to Meyer and Allen (1991), commitment to the organization is translated through the three component models of affective, continuance and normative commitment. Affective commitment is defined as emotional attachment, identification with, and involvement in the organization. In other words, permanent employees are faithful to the organization because they "want it". Then, continuance commitment is defined as the commitment that arises because the employees are aware that, if out of the organization, there will be costs that arise, or, in other words, they "need it". The last type of commitment is the normative commitment whereby they feel that there is an obligation to work in the company or in other words a "necessity" for them.

Parish, et al. (2008) subsequently proposed the relevance of this type of commitment to changes, such as Herscovich and Meyer (2002): affective commitment to change (ACC), a desire to support change, continuance commitment to change (CCC) as recognition of costs that may arise if they resist Change and normative commitment to change (NCC) as feeling there is an obligation to support organizational change initiatives.

In Noble and Mokwa (1999), antecedents of employee commitment to organizational change from derived grounded theory work were divided into two categories: strategy factor and role factors (Perish et al. 2008). Based on this, this study proposed antecedents of employee commitment to organizational change based on two categories: individual internal factor (self-efficacy) and individual external factor (job autonomy).

2.2 *Job autonomy and commitment to change*

The definition of job autonomy is the extent to which the company provides substantial freedom, independence and discretion for individuals in job scheduling and determining procedures for use in performing their work (Jaramillo *et al.* 2012). Researchers have long held that individuals will resist change when they think that their autonomy is threatened. Employees who believe that organizations give them a high degree of autonomy usually achieve higher performance because they see themselves as responsible for their work (Jaramillo et al. 2012). Conversely, employees with low levels of autonomy often become frustrated with their work and are more likely to engage in cynical behavior such as apathy, high mistrust, suspicion and humiliation to others (Naus, Iterson, and Roe 2007).

The same thing was also proved by Parker (2006), who found that high-autonomous employees were

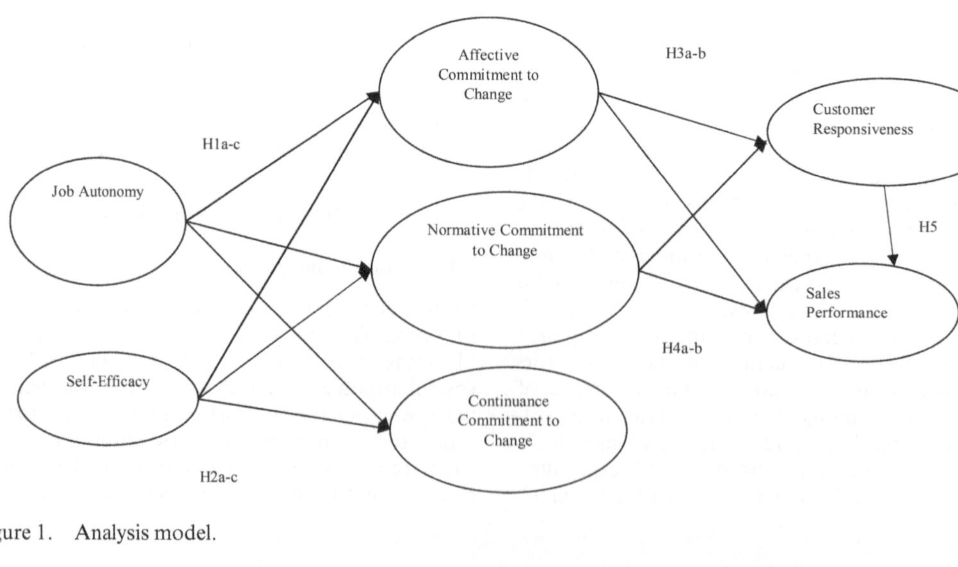

Figure 1. Analysis model.

more likely to think that managers believed them, and employees could have a more positive attitude toward changes made by the company. In addition to the positive influence of autonomy on employees, there is also a problem arising from the existence of autonomy for individuals, which is that not every employee prefers an autonomous job. But, in most findings, job autonomy accelerates higher level of liability and responsibility for behavior and conduct, which leads towards improving employees performance and commitment (Marchese and Ryan 2001; Shahrruddin and Ahmad 2015).

H1a: *Job autonomy has a significant positive effect on affective commitment to change*
H1b: *Job autonomy has a significant positive effect on normative commitment to change*
H1c: *Job autonomy has a significant negative effect on continuance commitment to change*

2.3 *Self-efficacy and commitment to change*

If employees do not believe they have the necessary skill to be successful in the new order or are heavily invested in the current order, then they will resist (Cook 2009; Waddell, et al. 2011). One reason employees refuse to change is because they do not believe in having enough skills to deal with their new jobs or they have invested heavily in the status quo.

Self-distrust of employees can be attributed to the concept of self-efficacy. The definition of self-efficacy according to Bandura (1997) is a person's belief in his ability to achieve a certain level of performance. High self-efficacy employees see complex work as a challenge to be faced and they tend to have low job stress. Employees with self-efficacy tend to have the confidence that they have control over the company's resources and the importance of responding to job-demand. According to Bandura's (1997) social cognitive theory, self-efficacy influences people's choices in creating and executing the actions they are addressing. Individuals with high self-efficacy can determine how much activity they can perform, and how tenaciously they work amid obstacles and existing work challenges. So, if a person experiences a problem or challenge, such as a change in the organization, they are expected to remain able to carry out their work well and remain confident enough to face the challenge of changing the job (Cho and Chang, 2008; Kauppila, Rajala and Jyrama 2010).

H2a: *Self-efficacy has a significant positive effect on affective commitment to change*
H2b: *Self-efficacy has a significant positive effect on normative commitment to change*
H2c: *Self-efficacy has a significant negative effect on continuance commitment to change*

2.4 *Commitment to change, customer-responsiveness and sales performance*

Organizational commitment is a vital part of the employee's psychosocial state as employees engaged in behavioral activities (Podsakoff et al. 2000; Naqfi et al. 2013;). Performance is the result obtained by the employee after performing the assigned task within the specified time period compared to the expectation (Casado-lumbreras, Colomo-Palacios, and Ordóñez de Pablos 2011). In this study, amid the changes that occur, salespersons are expected to have a commitment to respond to customer problems. Salespersons' rejection of change can be a barrier to achieving higher performance. They tend not to seek creative solutions if there is a complex customer demand (Jaramillo et al. 2012) and success in competitive business environments requires independent and out of the box thinking from salespersons (Wang and Netemeyer, 2004; Jaramillo, et al. 2012).

H3a: *Affective commitment to change has a significant positive effect on customer responsiveness*
H3b: *Normative commitment to change has a significant positive effect on customer responsiveness*

H4a: *Affective commitment to change has a significant positive effect on sales performance*
H4b: *Normative commitment to change has a significant positive effect on sales performance*

H5: *Customer responsiveness has a significant positive effect on sales performance*

3 METHOD

This research uses WarpPLS 3.0. This study uses Likert scale 1 to 5 to measure variables. Respondents are from an Internet service provider company in Surabaya, Indonesia. We approached their management teams and gained cooperation in surveying their salespersons. Salespersons in this sector have a need to deal directly with their customers and have company policies that change frequently. The competition between providers is so high, it makes corporate policies related to human resource management, such as salaries, incentives, etc., and policies on services sold, such as prices, promos, discounts, etc., change very quickly. Whereas, working in a service company requires salespersons to be responsive to requests from consumers and they should maintain customer relationships even after they have purchased their services (after-sales). In addition, salespersons in this sector are always given sales targets that they must achieve in the time period specified.

This survey was administered in Bahasa, Indonesia, but relied on items from published scales which

Table 1. Respondent profile.

Demographic		Freq.	Percent
Age	21–24 years	43	38%
	25–30 years	34	30%
	> 30 years	37	32%
Gender	Male	106	93%
	Female	8	7%
Tenure	0–1 years	41	36%
	2–3 years	62	54%
	> 3 years	11	10%
Education level	Senior High	85	75%
	Diploma	20	18%
	Bachelor	8	7%
	Master	1	1%

were translated into English in order to get consistency of meaning. The survey packet was sent to the Regional Sales Manager and was distributed to their District Supervisor and their sales team. This study used census method with 123 respondents. It took two weeks to collect data. Of the 123 questionnaires distributed, 114 (92.7%) were returned. Respondent profiles can see below (Table 1).

4 RESULT AND DISCUSSION

Based on the results of the statistical test tool output, in general, it can be said that the model has a good fit (see Table 2). AVIF and AFVIF values fall into the ideal category (below 3.3), which means there is no multicollinearity problem, while the resulting GoF is 0.586 included in the "Large" category. The result of the calculation of the structural model can be seen in Table 3 where it shows that JA has positive significant influence both to AC and NC, but significant negative effect to CC. It is not much different from the effect of SE on AC and NC. The difference lies in the effect of SE on the CC, which indicates a significant positive effect. This result supports previous research that job autonomy accelerates higher level of liability and responsibility for behavior and conduct, which leads towards improving employee performance and commitment (Marchese and Ryan 2001; Shahrruddin and Ahmad 2015).

Interesting results can be seen from the effect of the SE which can further increase the CC, counter to when compared with the hypothesis that has been built.

Regarding the outcome variables, AC was positively related to CR (H3a), but has no effect with SP (H4a). NC2C was related to CR, but not related to SP. Otherwise, the relationship between CR and SP was positively significant.

Table 2. General result.

Criterion	Result	Note
Average path coefficient (APC)	0.361, P < 0.001	Acceptable
Average R-squared (ARS)	0.485, P < 0.001	Acceptable
Average adjusted R-squared (AARS)	0.475, P < 0.001	Acceptable
Average block VIF (AVIF)	1.582	Acceptable
Average full collinearity VIF (AFVIF)	2.862	Acceptable
Tenenhaus GoF (GoF)	0.586	Large
Simpson's paradox ratio (SPR)	0.909	Acceptable
R-squared contribution ratio (RSCR)	0.997	Acceptable
Statistical suppression ratio (SSR)	0.909	Acceptable
Nonlinear bivariate causality direction ratio (NLBCDR)	0.909	Acceptable

Table 3. Result of structural model.

Hypothesis	Path coef.	P-values	R-square	
H1a: JA -> AC	0.576	<0.001*	AC	0.422
H1b: JA -> NC	0.597	<0.001*	NC	0.453
H1c: JA -> CC	–0.476	<0.001*	CC	0.220
H2a: SE -> AC	0.188	0.001*	CR	0.603
H2b: SE -> NC	0.195	0.002*	SP	0.726
H2c: SE -> CC	0.206	0.006*		
H3a: AC -> CR	0.368	<0.001*		
H3b: NC -> CR	0.476	<0.001*		
H4a: AC -> SP	–0.012	0.443		
H4b: NC -> SP	0.06	0.248		
H5: CR -> SP	0.816	<0.001*		

*Sig p < 0.05.

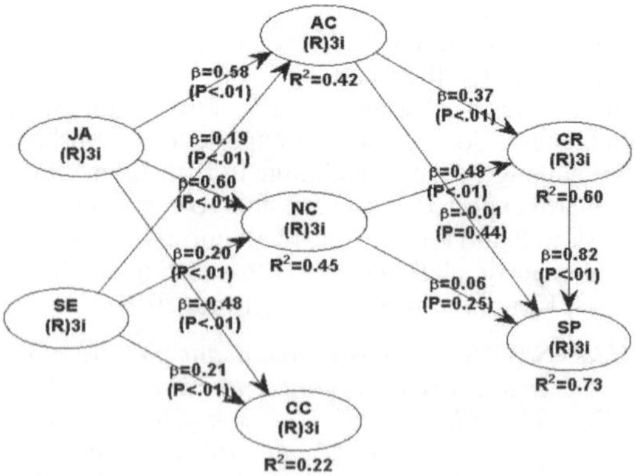

These results highlight the importance of CR as a mediated variable in the relationship between commitment and performance. Thus, of the hypothesized paths related to the proposed consequences of commitment, eight were supported and three were not (see Table 3). The mediated role of CR on relationship between AC, NC and SP has not been found in prior research.

5 CONCLUSION

Some important things can be obtained from this research: first, for companies that are making changes, they can consider the treatment to individual external factor salespersons by extending freedom in working, independence and discretion for individuals in job scheduling and determining procedures for use in performing their work. This allegedly can increase their affective commitment to change. Second, related to the internal individual factors of salespersons, the company can provide salespersons treatment so as to be more confident in completing the job well. Self-efficacy is considered to increase affective commitment that is needed by the company for change initiatives to succeed.

This study also contributes to the literature on change management, especially policy references to companies that have sales employees, as they spearhead the company to make a profit.

ACKNOWLEDGEMENT

This research project would not have been possible without the support of many people. The author would also like to convey thanks to the Faculty of Economic and Business, Universitas Airlangga for providing the financial means in HIBAH Fakultas program for funding this research project.

REFERENCES

Bandura, A. 1997. *Self-Efficacy: The Exercise of Control*. New York: W.H. Freeman and Company.

Casado-lumbreras, Pedro Soto-Acosta, Ricardo Colomo-Palacios, and Patricia Ordóñez de Pablos. 2011. Personnel Performance Assessment in Information Systems Outsourcing Environments. *The Journal of Workplace Learning,* 23 (7):468–482.

Cho, S.D., & Chang, D.R. 2008. Salesperson's Innovation Resistance and Job Satisfaction in Intra-organizational Diffusion of Sales Force Automation Technologies: The Case of South Korea. *Industrial Marketing Management*, 37.

Coelho, F., & Augusto, M. 2010. Job Characteristics and the Creativity of Frontline Service Employees. *Journal of Service Research*,13 (4): 426–438.

Giangreco A., & Peccei, R. 2005. The Nature and Antecedents of Middle Manager Resistance to Change: Evidence from an Italian Context. *International Journal of Human Resources Management,* 16 (10): 1812–1829.

Herscovitch, L., & Meyer, J.P. 2002. Commitment to Organizational Change: Extension of a Three-Component Model. *Journal of Applied Psychology*, 87:474–487.

Hornung, S., & Rousseau, D.M.. 2007. Active on the Job-proactive in Change: How Autonomy at Work Contributes to Employee Support for Organizational Change. *The Journal of Applied Behavioral Science*, 43 (4): 401–26.

Jaramillo, Fernando, Mulki, J.P., Onyemah, V. & Pesquera, M.R. 2012. Salesperson Resistance to Change: an Empirical Investigation of Antecedent and Outcomes. *International Journal of Bank Marketing*, 30 (7):548–566.

Kauppila, O., Rajala, R. & Jyrama, A. 2010. Antecedents of Salesperson's Reluctance to Sell Radically New Products. *Industrial Marketing Management,* 39 no. 2:308–16.

Marchese, M.C., & J. Ryan. 2001. Capitalizing on the benefits of utilizing part-time employees through job autonomy. *Journal of Business and Psychology*, 15 (4): 549–560.

Maurer, R. 2005. Sustaining Commitment to Change. The *Journal of Quality and Participation*, 28 no. 1L30–5.

Mulki, J.P., Lassk, F.G. & Jaramillo, F. 2008. The Effect of Self-efficacy on Salesperson Work Overload and Pay Satisfaction. *Journal of Personal Selling and Sales Management,* 28 (3): 283–95.

Naus, F., Iterson A.V. & Roe, R. 2007. Organizational Cynicism: Extending the Exit, Voice, Loyalty, and Neglect Model of Employees' Responses to Adverse Conditions in the Workplace. *Human Relations*, 60 (5): 683–718.

Palmer, I., R., Dunford, and Akin, G. 2009. *Managing Organizational Change: A Multiple Perspectives Approach.* 2nd ed. Boston: McGraw-Hill Irwin.

Parker, S.K., Williams, H.M. & Turner, N. 2006. Modeling the Antecedents of Proactive Behavior at Work. *Journal of Applied Psychology* 91 (3):636–652.

Piderit, S.K. 2000. Rethinking resistance and recognizing ambivalence: a multidimensional view of attitudes toward an organizational change. *Academy of Management Review*, 25 no. 4:783–794.

Podsakoff, P.M., MacKenzie, S.B., Paine, J.B., & Bachrach, D.G. 2000. Organizational Citizenship Behaviors: A Critical Review of the Theoretical and Empirical Literature and Suggestions for Future Research. *Journal of Management*, 26 (3): 513–563.

Shaharuddin, Sarah, & Ahmad, F. 2015. The Influence of Job Autonomy on Organizational Cynicism: The Reliability Test. *International Journal of Research in Business Studies and Management,* 2 (11): 91–100.

Increasing Management Relevance and Competitiveness – Sukoco et al. (Eds)
© 2018 Taylor & Francis Group, London, ISBN 978-0-8153-7455-8

The influence of Perception of Usefulness (PoU) and Perceived Ease of Use (PEU) on the perception of information system performance

F. Sayekti & L.E. Wijayanti
Universitas Teknologi Yogyakarta, Indonesia

ABSTRACT: This study analyzes factors influencing the information system performance and its acceptance based on the Technology Acceptance Model (TAM). TAM suggests that behavioral intention to use a system is controlled by two assumptions. The first is the Perception of Usefulness (PoU), the extent of the belief that engaging a certain system will increase the user's performance. The second is Perceived Ease of Use (PEU), the extent of the belief that it is easy to use a system. This study tries to identify factors that influence operators using Indonesia's Regional Financial Management Information System (SIPKD) and their perception of the performance of SIPKD, beyond their obligation to apply the system. The analysis focuses on the perception of using SIPKD. The perceptions being studied are the ease of applying the system and the benefit of using it for their work. When the users said that the system was easy to use, they accepted it. In addition, if users believed that a system helped them with their work, they accepted it. Furthermore, this study also identified the influence of users' perception of the system's performance. Thus, users assumed that the system worked well when they perceived it to be easy to use and to benefit their work accomplishment. The data were collected by distributing questionnaires to 100 respondents of which 67 were returned. The analysis shows that PEU influences the system's acceptance, while PoU does not influence the system's acceptance. Moreover, this research also found that, together, PoU and PEU do influence the perception of information system performance.

Keywords: Information systems, Perception of Usefulness, Perceived Ease of Use, performance of information systems, user acceptance

1 INTRODUCTION

The Indonesian government issued Government Regulation no. 56 of 2005 on Regional Financial Information Systems, and Minister of Finance Regulation no. 46 of 2006 on Procedures for the Submission of Regional Financial Information. Government form Letter no. SE.900/122/BAKD outlines the basis, development and coordination of a Regional Financial Management Information System (*Sistem Informasi Pengelolaan Keuangan Daerah,* SIPKD). The regulation aims to assist regional government in preparing reports on regional financial management accountability. Local government submits data/information relating to regional finance to the central government. Submission of data/information is made via the SIPKD. SIPKD is developed on the basis of information technology designed in such a way as to be a means of collecting, processing, presenting, and referencing, as well as the process of data communication/financial information, between the Ministry of Finance and the Ministry of Home Affairs with local government and the owners or users of other financial information.

Every financial manager of each SIPKD must understand SIPKD well so that the process of local financial administration is not hampered. The use of SIPKD in local financial reporting affects changes in the way civil servants work, especially SIPKD users. User acceptance of the Information System (IS) being used will affect the users' perceptions of the performance of information systems. This research will analyze the factors that influence user acceptance and user perception on SIPKD performance in Yogyakarta City Government. The analysis is based on the Technology Acceptance Model.

2 THEORETICAL BASIS

2.1 *Theoretical basis*

Information systems in an agency serve as a tool for the achievement of goals through the provision of information. The success of the information system is not only determined by how the system can process input and produce information well, but also by its conformity with the work environment, because although the information system uses advanced technology, the system cannot be said to succeed if the information system user cannot accept it or is reluctant even to use it (Jogiyanto, 2007).

The success of the information system can be measured by four types of measures, namely, user satisfaction, system usage, decision performance, and organizational performance. In this research, user satisfaction, and use of information systems were used to measure the success of an information system, such as that carried out by Barki (1994). The use of technology or information systems shows the individual's decision to use or not to use technology or information systems in completing a series of tasks (Goodhue, 1995).

The Technology Acceptance Model (TAM) was formulated by Ajzen and Fishbein (1980). This theory explains that in doing something someone is driven by two factors, namely, beliefs, and normative beliefs. These factors then encourage a person to have outcome evaluation and motivation to comply. Both of these will affect people's behavior (attitude) and personal norms (subjective norms). The state of attitude and subjective norms will affect the attention/focus of someone in the act (i.e. behavior intention). Ultimately, behavior intention will affect a person's behavior.

Davis (1989) developed TAM to examine the determinants of the use of information systems by users. The results indicated that the use of information systems is influenced by the intention to use the information system interest (intention) system utilization information, which is influenced by the perception of the usefulness of the technology (Perception of Usefulness), and perceptions of the ease of use of technology (Perceived Ease of Use). TAM also states that the impact of external variables (such as system characteristics, development process and training) on intention to use is mediated by Perception of Usefulness (PoU) and Perceived Ease of Use (PEU).

2.2 *Research hypotheses*

Research conducted by Sanjaya (2005) about the effect of benefit and ease on behavioral intention of students in using the Internet shows that the perceived benefits (PoU) may predispose a person to use the Internet, while the ease of use (PEU) does not influence someone to use the Internet. Other research on the acceptance of information technology was conducted by Kartika (2009). The results showed that self-efficacy had a positive relationship with PoU in the use of the information systems studied.

Research conducted by Muntianah (2012), which analyzed TAM against the behavior of the use of information systems on student learning activities at the Faculty of Administrative Sciences, Brawijaya, states that PEU of IT affects the perception of benefit, while the perception of benefit affects the interest in using IT. The research also found that interest in the use of IT affects the actual IT usage.

Based on the description of theory and the results of previous research, the following general hypothesis can be formulated: if SIPKD users have the perception that SIPKD is easy to use and facilitates their work, they will increasingly use SIPKD to complete their work. Thus, the proposed hypotheses are:

H1: PEU has a positive effect on the acceptance of SIPKD
H2: PoU has a positive effect on the acceptance of SIPKD
H3: PEU and PoU together have a positive effect on the acceptance of SIPKD
H4: User acceptance of SIPKD affects the perceived performance of the information system
H5: PoU and PEU directly or indirectly influence the perceived performance of the information system

3 RESEARCH METHODOLOGY

The research method used was the quantitative method. This research used three variables that are divided into two types, the first of which is the independent variable. The independent variables in this study are the usefulness of technology (Perception of Usefulness) and the ease of using the technology (Perceived Ease of Use). The second type is the dependent variable, which in this study is the variable of technology acceptance (IS Acceptance), in this case the acceptance of SIPKD.

3.1 *Research variables*

PEU illustrates SIPKD users' perceptions of the ease of use of SIPKD. The indicators used to measure variable PEU for SIPKD are: ease to learn (easy to learn), ease of reaching the destination (controllability), clear and easy to understand (clear and understandable), flexibility (flexible), free of difficulty (easy), and ease of becoming skillful (easy to use) (Davis, 1989).

PoU measures how respondents perceive the usefulness of SIPKD in their work. This variable is measured by asking about the following indicators: productivity, task performance or effectiveness, importance to job, and overall usefulness.

The acceptance of SIPKD (IS Acceptance) is measured by using an indicator of desire to continue using it in the future. This means how far the user would use the information system in daily work and tasks.

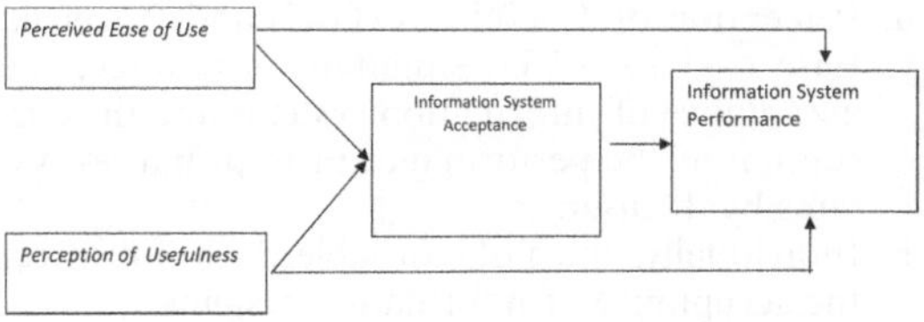

Figure 1. Research model.

The IS Performance variable was measured by 11 statements regarding each user's perception of the fulfillment of the work requirements by the system, the speed of use, the frequency of use, the accuracy of the funds and the resulting output.

3.2 *Research model*

The research model to be tested is shown in Figure 1.

3.3 *Data analysis method*

The data in the study was obtained by distributing questionnaires to SIPKD operators at government institutions in Yogyakarta City Region. The number of questionnaires distributed was 85; the number of questionnaires returned was 69 (response rate 81%). The number of questionnaires completely filled out that could be processed was 67 (usable rate 80%). Data analysis was over two stages, namely, to test the quality of data in the form of validity, and reliability tests.

The test for validity used Spearman's correlation, which correlates the value of each item statement with the total value, with the standard correlation coefficient above 0.5. Results of the validity test indicate all the data being used was valid. This is because the value of the correlation coefficient between each item of statement with the total value entirely above 5%.

The test for reliability used Cronbach's alpha, with a standard of 0.6. If the value of the Cronbach alpha is above 0.6 then the statement in the questionnaire is reliable. The hypotheses were tested by using multiple regression. Reliability test results show that the reliability value of all variables is above 0.6; thus all the data in this study is reliable.

Hypothesis testing was done using *F* tests, *t* tests, and coefficient determination tests with gradual regression.

4 RESULTS AND DISCUSSION

To determine the influence of PoU and PEU on IS Acceptance, we used the following equation:

$$X3 = a + b1X1 + b2X2 \quad (1)$$

The results of the data analysis are:

$$X3 = 0.416 + 0.714X1 + 0.166X2$$

The regression test for the influence of PoU and PEU on IS Acceptance are shown in Table 1.

Table 1 shows that PEU and PoU simultaneously influence the acceptance of the information system. The *F* value is positive with a significance level of 0.000. This means that, together, PoU and PEU variables have a significant positive effect on the acceptance of the IS. Thus Hypothesis 3 as proposed in this study is accepted.

The *t*-test result for Perception of Usefulness shows a positive value of 0.7 with significance of 0.194. A value of significance above 0.05 means that the Perception of Usefulness variable does not influence the acceptance of the information system. This means that the second hypothesis (H2) proposed is not accepted.

The *t*-test result for the PEU variable shows a positive value with a significance level of 0.000. It shows that PEU has a positive and significant influence on information system acceptance. This means that if a user has the perception that the system is easy to use then users will increasingly use that information system. An R-squared value of 0.624 means the independent variable is able to account for 62.4% of the changes in the dependent variable.

To determine the influence of IS Acceptance on IS Performance the following equation is used:

$$Y = a + b3X3 \quad (2)$$

The results of the data analysis are:

$$Y = 2.343 + 0.474X3$$

Table 2 shows that IS Acceptance has a positive and significant effect on the perception of IS Performance. This means that Hypothesis 4 proposed in this study is accepted. The implication of this research is that if the user is able to accept and use information systems effectively the user will

Table 1. The result of regression test 1.

Value *F*	53.318	Sig 0.000
R-squared	0.624	
Value *t* (PEU)	4.796	Sig 0.000
Value *t* (PoU)	1.313	Sig 0.194

Table 2. The results of regression test 2.

Value *F*	37.212	Sig 0.000
R-squared	0.375	
Value *t*	6.100	Sig 0.000

Table 3. The results of regression test 3.

Value *F*	54.702	Sig 0.000
R-squared	0.630	
Value *t* (PEU)	3.906	Sig 0.000
Value *t* (PoU)	2.362	Sig 0.012

Table 4. Comparison of regression coefficients.

Equation 1	PoU – IS Acceptance	0.714
	PEU – IS Acceptance	0.166
Equation 2	IS Acceptance – IS Performance	0.474
Equation 3	PoU – IS Performance	0.446
	PEU – IS Performance	0.229

have a positive perception of information system performance.

The results of *F* test, *t* test, and the coefficient of determination for Equation 3 are shown in Table 3.

Table 3 shows that the PEU and PoU variables simultaneously affect the perceived performance of information systems. If the user assumes that the information system is easy to use and useful in their work, they assume that the information system performance is good. The *t* value for PEU is 3.906 with a significance level of 0.000. This means if the user assumes that the information system is easy to use then the user assumes that the system performance is better. The *t* value for PoU is 2.362 with a significance level of 0.012, which means that if the user thinks the information system is useful in the job then the user also assumes the performance of the information system is good.

To determine whether the IS Acceptance variable mediates the association between PoU and PEU and perceived IS Performance, each of the regression coefficient equations is compared.

Table 4 shows that the relationship of the PoU variable to the acceptance of information systems is insignificant, so that the variable of IS Acceptance does not mediate the relationship between Perception of Usefulness and IS Performance. But PoU directly affects the perception of IS Performance. The PEU variable affects both the acceptance of information systems and their perceived performance.

Thus, PEU affects the perceived IS Performance directly. The implication is that perceived information system performance is influenced by user perceptions of the ease of use of the information system. Users consider the performance of information systems good if the information system is easy to use.

5 CONCLUSIONS

Based on the results of data analysis, the conclusions of this study are:

a. Perception of Usefulness (PoU) and Perceived Ease of Use (PEU) simultaneously affect the acceptance of information systems and the perception of the performance of information systems by the user.
b. Individually, the PoU variable does not affect the acceptance of information systems.
c. Individually, the PEU variable affects acceptance of information systems and perceived performance of information systems. Users also assume the performance of the information system is good.
d. The IS Acceptance variable does not mediate the relationships of PEU and PoU with system performance perceptions.

REFERENCES

Achjari, D. (2012). UGM Towards Financial Management of Public Service Agency Menuju Pengelolaan Keuangan Badan Layanan Umum (PK BLU). Paper presented at the Medical Faculty Meeting of Universitas Gadjah Mada, Salatiga, 28 January 2012.

Ajzen, I. & Fishbein. M. (1980). *Understanding attitudes and predicting social behavior*. Englewood Cliffs, NJ: Prentice Hall.

Barki, Henri and Hartwick, Jon. 1994. "Measuring User Participation, Use Involvement, and User Attitude," MIS Quarterly, (18: 1).

Davis, F.D. (1989). Perceived usefulness, perceived ease of use, and user acceptance of information technology. *MIS Quarterly*, *13*(3), 318–340.

Ghozali, I. (2005). *Application of Multivariate Analysis With SPSS Program.* Semarang, Indonesia: Badan Penerbitan Universitas Diponegoro.

Goodhue, Dale and Thompson, Ronald. 1995. "Task-Technology Fit and Individual Performance," MIS Quarterly, (19: 2). Jogiyanto. (2003). *Sistem Teknologi Informasi.* Yogyakarta, Indonesia: Penerbit Andi.

Jogiyanto. (2007). *Sistem Informasi Keperilakuan*. Yogyakarta, Indonesia: Penerbit Andi.

Kartika, S.E. (2009). Analysis of iCons Information System Acceptance Process Using Technology Acceptance Model on Employees of PT. Bank Negara Indonesia (Persero) Tbk in Semarang City. *Analisis Proses Penerimaan Sistem Informasi iCons dengan Menggunakan Techonology Acceptance Model pada Karyawan PT. Bank Negara Indonesia (Persero) Tbk di Kota Semarang*. Program Studi Magister Manajemen. Universitas Diponegoro.

Muntianah. (2012) The Influence of Behavioral Behavior to Actual Use of Information Technology with Approach of Teory Acceptance Model Pengaruh Minat Perilaku terhadap Actual Use Teknologi Informasi dengan Pendekatan Teory Acceptance Model. *Profit*, *6*(1).

Sanjaya, I.P.S. (2005). The Effect of Usefulness and Ease on Behavioral Intention In Internal Use Pengaruh Manfaat dan Kemudahan Pada Minat Berperilaku (behavioral intention) Dalam Penggunaan Internet. *Kinerja*, *9*, 146–156.

Increasing Management Relevance and Competitiveness – Sukoco et al. (Eds)
© 2018 Taylor & Francis Group, London, ISBN 978-0-8153-7455-8

Knowledge sharing benefits: The contingency effects of environmental contexts

A. Qomariyah
Universitas Airlangga, Surabaya, Indonesia

ABSTRACT: Nowadays, the nature of dynamism encourages organizations to focus more on knowledge as a strategic resource. In knowledge management, knowledge sharing is the most important activity. Even though many previous studies have discussed the benefits of knowledge sharing, only a few studies have examined the importance of the contingency factor. Thus, this study seeks to investigate the influence of environmental context on the relationship between knowledge sharing and its outcomes. The results of this study suggest that knowledge sharing is important to improve the innovative work behavior and job satisfaction of the expatriate. Also, environmental context has been proven to strengthen the influence of those relationships. These findings are expected to contribute new insight for academicians and management.

1 INTRODUCTION

Competitive advantage has become extremely important nowadays, which encourages organizations to focus more on knowledge as a strategic resource because it can help them to compete more effectively (Wang et al., 2014). Through knowledge sharing in the organization, several advantages can be obtained. For the consequences of knowledge sharing, this study adopts the knowledge-based theory (Grant & Baden-Fuller, 1995) that explains that knowledge is the key productive resource that a company has in order to create added value and as a contribution of strategic significance. It means that a company with valuable knowledge will generate more benefits than others. Thus, through knowledge sharing, a company will be able to transmit the knowledge to the whole organization, which further enhances the value added for the company. Based on that, many studies have explained the consequences of knowledge sharing or knowledge sharing performance, such as work performance, satisfaction, innovative work behavior, etc. (Radaelli et al., 2013, Trivellas et al., 2015). In this study, knowledge sharing performance consists of innovative work behavior and satisfaction.

Even though previous studies have discussed the benefits of knowledge sharing, those studies may have ignored the influence of environmental context. However, environmental context is a crucial factor that organizations need to consider because the rapid changing environment can create both opportunity and threat for them. Therefore, this study tries to explain this gap by applying environmental context as contingency or a moderating variable that influences the relationship between knowledge sharing and its outcomes. It is important because managers will understand whether environmental context can strengthen or weaken the positive impact of knowledge sharing on outcomes, so that they will have a better way to make decisions. Previous studies explained that environmental context, such as complexity, munificence and the dynamism of the environment need to be considered in the knowledge sharing and work performance (Li et al., 2013). As mentioned by Cummings (2003, p. 31), "the entrepreneurial, learning and innovation environments in which knowledge sharing take place can affect the parties and knowledge sharing in many ways." On the other hand, environmental factors can enhance the influence of exploratory and exploitative learning on firm performance (Li et al., 2013). Therefore, environmental context can be seen as the key moderator variable that influences the effects of organizational learning, such as knowledge sharing, on the performance and other outcomes.

As a summary, the objectives of this study are to examine the influence of knowledge sharing on innovative work behavior and job satisfaction as well as the moderating effects of environmental context on those relationships. The results of this study are expected to provide contributions for academicians and managers.

2 LITERATURE REVIEW

2.1 *Theoretical background*

Knowledge management as a tool to achieve competitive advantages refers to the process of collecting and identifying valuable information (knowledge acquisition), organizing the knowledge (organizing knowledge), exploiting and applying knowledge (knowledge leverage), sharing it to the whole organization (knowledge sharing) and finally, storing it in a repository (knowledge memory) (Trivellas et al., 2015). Knowledge management is the process of capturing firm knowledge and using it to maintain and create innovation through organizational learning (Kim & Lee, 2013).

Among several activities in knowledge management, knowledge sharing is the most crucial issue, yet the most difficult activity, especially for an organization that needs to share a lot of tacit knowledge (Trivellas et al., 2015). This is because knowledge sharing is defined as the provision of task information to help and collaborate employees in the organization, not only to implement the procedures, but also to solve the problems and to develop new ideas (Cummings, 2004). As explained by Lin (2007, p. 136), knowledge sharing is "a social interaction culture, involving the exchange of employee knowledge, experience, and skills through the whole department or organization." From that statement, it is clear that employees are required to engage in social interaction in order to get the knowledge. In the context of multinational operations, the interaction across cultures will be higher for Multinational Companies (MNCs) than a local company, because it consists of multiple countries as the subsidiaries.

2.2 *Knowledge sharing outcomes*

This study discusses two different outcomes of knowledge sharing; innovative work behavior and job satisfaction. It has been recognized that knowledge sharing leads to increased innovative work behavior of both senders and recipients (Radaelli et al., 2013). Innovative Work Behavior (IWB) refers to the intention of individuals to create, introduce and apply new ideas that have benefit for the organization (de Jong et al., 2010). IWB starts with developing a new idea (idea generation), then obtaining external support (idea promotion) and, finally, producing the prototype of the idea (idea application) (Radaelli et al., 2013). IWB can be innovations in products, services and/work processes. In this study, innovative work behavior is defined as the intention of individuals to create, introduce and apply new ideas for collective benefits.

Furthermore, job satisfaction is also an outcome of knowledge sharing (Almahamid et al., 2010). Job satisfaction refers to the individuals' positive or negative attitudes towards their job (Locke 1976). Job satisfaction also means a positive feeling, which can be the affective, cognitive and evaluative reactions that individuals have as the result of their jobs (Greenberg et al., 2003). In other words, job satisfaction relates to the feeling of fulfillment (Griffin et al., 2007). In terms of knowledge sharing, job satisfaction can be served as the positive feeling of sharing the knowledge with others and appreciating its value to the organization (Kostova, 1999). In this study, job satisfaction is defined as the positive feeling towards knowledge sharing success and its benefits for the organization.

2.3 *Environmental context*

The rapid environmental changes and high imitation by competitors have become crucial problems in globalization, which require firms or organizations to respond by continually generating superior knowledge to maintain competitive advantage (Chen & Lin, 2004). As explained by Pfeffer & Salancik (1978) in recourse dependence theory (RDT), an organization is an open system that will depend on contingencies in the external environment. It indicates that organizations are dependent on the external environment, which further forces them to find a way to deal with both conducive and unconducive environments. Furthermore, environmental factors have three dimensions; complexity, munificence and dynamism (Dess & Beard, 1984). According to Chen et al., (2015), these three dimensions can help to elaborate the environmental characteristics in relatively few classifications. In detail, a complex environment requires a combination of different kinds of knowledge in order to produce product development or other organizational benefits (Revilla, Manzoor, & Liu, 2008). Individuals in the complex environment are forced to engage in knowledge sharing that enhances their performance.

Furthermore, munificence refers to the availability of the critical resources from the environment. If the resource is difficult to be reached, it means that resource scarcity exists (Barney 1991). In contrast, high availability resource in the external environment increases the opportunities of the organization to achieve organizational benefits. As explained by Li et al., (2013), a munificence environment will generate more options for an organization because it creates alternative goals, strategies and organizational structures which become possible to reach. Thus, with effective knowledge sharing, individuals under a munificence environment will be able to perform well and innovate more because of the knowledge and other sources that are available for them.

Lastly, dynamism of the environment occurs when an environment changes unpredictably. Unpredictable changes of environment will increase the risk for firms (Keats & Hitt, 1988), which requires firms to be more flexible in terms of their strategy. Rapid changes in the external environment require continuity of learning in order to renew the existing knowledge (Revilla et al., 2008). This is important because, in the dynamic environment, existing knowledge will become obsolete in a short time. Thus, knowledge sharing as part of organizational learning will be more required more in the dynamic environment than in a static environment in order to create good performance and develop innovation. In this study, environmental context is defined as the external factors that can enhance or inhibit employees to do their jobs in the organization.

3 HYPOTHESES DEVELOPMENT

Based on the above explanations, this study proposes that:

H1: *Knowledge sharing has positive influence on innovative work behavior*

H2: *Knowledge sharing has positive influence on job satisfaction*

H3: *Environmental context will strengthen the influence of knowledge sharing on innovative work behavior*

H4: *Environmental context will strengthen the influence of knowledge sharing on job satisfaction*

4 METHODOLOGY

Based on the above explanation, the research framework is developed as shown in Figure 1. All of the items in this study were measured based on a seven-point Likert scale ranging from 1 = totally disagree to 7 = totally agree. Data were collected via both printed and online questionnaire surveys in Taiwan. This study collected 234 questionnaires that were used for further analysis. Furthermore, smart PLS (Partial Least Square) was applied to analyze the collected data.

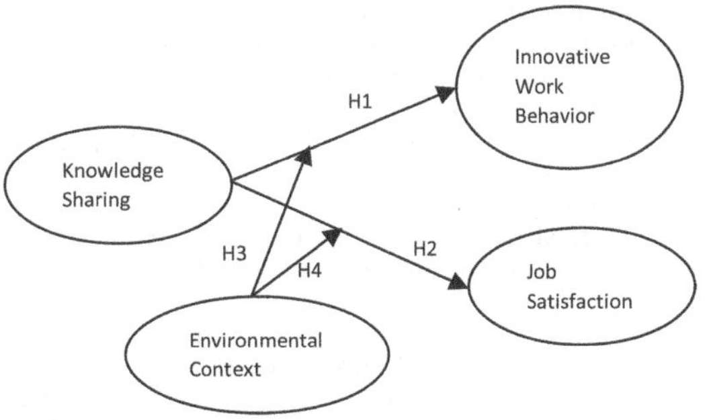

Figure 1. Research framework.

5 RESULTS AND ANALYSIS

The characteristics of respondents were gathered. For the 234 valid respondents, 104 were male (44.4%), and most of the respondents were aged between 36 and 45 years old (63.2%). In terms of working experience, most of the respondents had worked for less than five years and worked abroad for less than three years.

To verify the validity and reliability of constructs in this study, PLS has been applied. The results show that all variables have loadings higher than 0.700 and all of the Cronbach alpha values of the construct are higher than 0.7, which indicates that the constructs are satisfactory in reliability. In addition, the Composite Reliability (CR) values are also higher than 0.7, proving internal consistency.

Furthermore, Table 1 shows the results of hypotheses testing. The results show that, in the three models, knowledge sharing has a positive influence on innovative work behavior and job performance. In Model 1, which is the direct influence of knowledge sharing on the outcomes, the results show that knowledge sharing has positive influence on innovative work behavior ($\beta = 0.481$, $p < 0.001$). As stated by Radaelli et al., (2013), knowledge sharing will create a work environment that supports in generating ideas or innovations. Employees will be stimulated to be more innovative after they share their knowledge because they can elaborate, combine and translate

Table 1. Path coefficients of the moderating effects of environmental context.

Hyp.	Path	M1	M2	M3
H_1	KS → IWB	0.481***	0.263***	0.264***
H_2	KS → ST	0.469***	0.172***	0.222***
	ENV → IWB		0.513***	0.511***
	ENV → ST		0.701***	0.591***
H_3	KS*ENV → IWB			0.005
H_4	KS*ENV → ST			0.223***
		Construct R^2		
	Innovative work behavior	0.231	0.443	0.443
	Job satisfaction	0.220	0.621	0.660

Notes: *** $p < 0.001$.

the knowledge based on their ability. Therefore, hypothesis 1 is supported. Knowledge sharing also has a positive influence on job satisfaction ($\beta = 0.469$, $p < 0.001$). It also indicates that hypothesis 2 is supported. It is consistent with Almahamid et al., (2010) who stated that continued learning though knowledge will enhance job satisfaction. For the moderating effects, environmental context strengthens the influence of knowledge sharing on job satisfaction ($\beta = 0.223$, $p < 0.001$), but it is not significant to moderate the influence of knowledge sharing on innovative work behavior. Therefore, hypothesis 4 is supported, but hypothesis 3 is not supported.

6 CONCLUSION

Based on the results of this study, several conclusions can be drawn. Knowledge sharing has direct influence on innovative work behavior. According to Nonaka (1991, p. 98), "making personal knowledge available to others is the central activity of the knowledge-creating company." Thus, it is clear that, when expatriates are willing to share their personal knowledge and are subjective in the knowledge sharing process, it will create innovation and enhance their innovative work behavior. Furthermore, knowledge sharing is also served as a determinant of job satisfaction. This is because employees who share their knowledge will feel that they are making contributions to the organization.

Furthermore, environmental context is served as moderating variables to enhance the positive influence of knowledge sharing on innovative work behavior and job satisfaction. The results indicate that high levels of environmental context will strengthen the positive influence of knowledge sharing on job satisfaction. This is consistent with Revilla et al., (2008). According to resource dependence theory (Pfefer & Salancik, 1978), an organization will always depend on contingencies in the external environment in order to survive. This indicates that organizations have to consider the external environment to compete with others and gain more benefit than others. A high level of environmental context means the available resources are high, which indicates that employees will be enabled to use it to improve their knowledge sharing to develop job satisfaction. Meanwhile, a complex and dynamic environment requires employees to share their knowledge to manage and deal with the environment in order to generate innovation and make contributions to the organization. Thus, environmental context will be very useful in improving the impact of knowledge sharing on the outcomes.

Although these research results are compelling, several limitations need to be considered. These limitations suggest areas and directions for further research. Firstly, since this study conducts a cross-sectional research design, it may create unclear directional relationship. Thus, it is recommended that future study should use a longitudinal approach to further confirm the findings of this study. Secondly, the respondents of this study are limited to expatriates who work in Taiwan. The results of this study may not be applicable in other countries because cultural differences could influence expatriates in adjusting themselves, which further impacts on their performance (Johnson, Lenartowicz, & Apud, 2006). Furthermore, the respondents of this study were not classified based on the type of industry they are in. Therefore, future study may compare the scope of the study and consider the type of industry, because each industry may have different methods of knowledge sharing. Despite the limitations, this study will enrich knowledge sharing literature in general.

REFERENCES

Almahamid, S., McAdams, A. & Kalaldeh, T. (2010). The relationships among organizational knowledge sharing practices, employees' learning commitments, employees' adaptability, and employees' job satisfaction: An empirical investigation of the listed manufacturing companies in Jordan. *Interdisciplinary Journal of Information, Knowledge, and Management*, *5*, 327–356.

Barney, J. (1991). Firm resources and sustained competitive advantage. *Journal of Management, 17(1)*, 99–120.

Chen, C-J. & Lin, B-W. (2004). The effects of environment, knowledge attribute, organizational climate, and firm characteristics on knowledge sourcing decisions. *R&D Management*, *34*(2), 137–146.

Chen, H., Zeng, S., Lin, H. & Ma, H. (2015). Munificence, dynamism, and complexity: How industry context drives corporate sustainability. *Business Strategy and the Environment*, 1–17.

Cummings, J.L. & Ten, B-S. (2003). Transferring R&D knowledge: the key factors affecting knowledge transfer success. *Journal of Engineering and Technology Management, 20*, 39–68.

de Jong, J.P. & den Hartog, D. (2010). Measuring innovative work behaviour. *Creativity and Innovation Management*, *19*, 23–36.

Dess, G. & Beard, D. (1984). Dimensions of organizational task environments. *Administrative Science Quarterly*, *29*, 52–73.

Grant, R.M. & Baden-Fuller, C. (1995). A knowledge-based theory of inter-firm collaboration. *Academy of Management Journal,* 17–21.

Greenberg, M.T., Weissberg, R.P., O'Brien, M.U., Zins, J.E., Fredericks, L., Resnik, H., et al. (2003). Enhancing school-based prevention and youth development through coordinated social, emotional, and academic learning. *American Psychologist, 58*, 466–474.

Griffin, R., & Moorhead, G. (2007). *Organizational Behavior: Managing People and Organizations*. 18th edition, HoughtonMifflin Company, Boston.

Johnson, J.P., Lenartowicz, T., & Apud, S. (2006). Cross-cultural competence in international business: Toward a definition and a model. *Journal of International Business Studies, 37*, 525–534.

Keats, B.W. & Hitt, M.A. (1988). A causal model of linkages among environmental dimensions, macro organizational characteristics, and performance. *Academy of Management Journal, 31*, 570–598.

Kim, T.T. & Lee, G. (2013). Hospitality employee knowledge-sharing behaviors in the relationship between goal orientations and service innovative behavior. *International Journal of Hospitality Management, 34*, 324–337.

Kostova, T. (1999). Transnational transfer of strategic organizational practices: A contextual perspective. *Academy of Management Review, 24*(2), 308–324.

Li, Y., Wei, Z., Zhao, J., Zhang, C. & Liu, Y. (2013). Ambidextrous organizational learning, environmental munificence and new product performance: Moderating effect of managerial ties in China. *International Journal of Production Economics, 146*, 95–105.

Lin, H-F. (2007). Effects of extrinsic and intrinsic motivation on employee knowledge sharing intentions. *Journal of Information Science, 33*(2), 135–149.

Locke, E.A. (1976). *The nature and causes of job satisfaction*. In *Handbook of the industrial and organizational psychology* edited by M.F. Dunnette. Chicago: Rand McNally.

Nonaka, I. (1991). The knowledge-creating company. *Harvard Business Review, 69*(6), 96–104.

Pfeffer, J. & Salancik, G.R. (1978). *The external control of organizations: A resource dependence perspective*. New York: Harper & Row.

Radaelli, G., Lettieri, E., Mura, M. & Spiller, N. (2013). Knowledge sharing and innovative work behaviour in healthcare: A micro-level investigation of direct and indirect effects. *Creativity and Innovation Management, 23*(4), 400–414.

Revilla, M.A., Manzoor, S., & Liu, R. (2008). Competitive learning in informatics. The UVA online judge experience. *Olympiads in informatics, 2*, 131–148.

Trivellas, P., Akrivouli, Z., Tsifora, E. & Tsoutsa, P. (2015). The impact of knowledge sharing culture on job satisfaction in accounting firms. The mediating effect of general competencies. *Procedia Economics and Finance, 19*, 238–247.

Wang, Y., Gray, P.H. & Meister, D.B. (2014). Task-driven learning: The antecedents and outcomes of internal and external knowledge sourcing. *Information & Management, 51*, 939–951.

Increasing Management Relevance and Competitiveness – Sukoco et al. (Eds)
© 2018 Taylor & Francis Group, London, ISBN 978-0-8153-7455-8

The antecedents of entrepreneurial intentions in students of Airlangga university (A study of student participants in WEBS in the faculty of economics and business)

P. Yulianti & I.G.N.W.H. Saputra
Universitas Airlangga, Surabaya, Indonesia

ABSTRACT: The number of jobs in Indonesia nowadays is not comparable with the amount of labor, causing high levels of unemployment in the country. This situation has become one of the challenges that must be faced in order to pursue the country's development in a better direction. The government has rightly acknowledged the need to increase its efforts to reduce unemployment levels by creating new jobs or promoting entrepreneurship. The purpose of this research was to explore the influence of the antecedents of entrepreneurial intention among students of Airlangga University. The research used survey methods in relation to 68 student participants in the WEBS activity unit in the Faculty of Economics and Business at Airlangga University. Using a partial least square statistical tool (SmartPLS 2.0, SmartPLS GmbH, Boenningstedt, Germany), the results of the study showed that individual skills aligned with attitudes towards entrepreneurial behavior, perceived environmental dynamism aligned with perceived entrepreneurial behavior control, attitudes towards entrepreneurial behavior aligned with entrepreneurial intentions, and subjective norms aligned with entrepreneurial intentions in positive and statistically significant relationships. However, although the relationships between perceived environmental support and perceived entrepreneurial behavior control, and perceived entrepreneurial behavior control and entrepreneurial intentions were positive, they were not statistically significant.

Keywords: Entrepreneurial Intentions, Theory of Planned Behavior

1 INTRODUCTION

Nowadays, the number of jobs is not comparable with the amount of labor, which is causing a high level of unemployment in Indonesia. This has become one of the challenges that must be faced by the country in order to pursue the country's development in a better direction. The government has rightly acknowledged the need to increase its efforts in reducing unemployment by creating new jobs and promoting entrepreneurship.

Entrepreneurship is the process of creation and realizing value by entrepreneurs (Morris & Jones, 1999). Entrepreneurial activities play an important role in improving economic and social development. Entrepreneurship is known to reduce the level of unemployment and increase the welfare of the community through the creation of value in the economy. A country is said to be advanced when it has at least 2 percent of entrepreneurs from the total number of its population, but Indonesia has not yet been able to reach this level.

Becoming an entrepreneur can itself be interpreted as an effort by someone to create jobs by opening a business or creating something new: someone who has been improving the economy for themselves or for other people in the surroundings by becoming an entrepreneur. This course of action has meaningful and significant contributions to the greater good for themselves, those around them, the government and also the country.

Entrepreneurship education has recently become one of the alternative efforts undertaken by the Indonesian government to confront the reality of the current low levels in this area. Both at the school level and in universities, there is a curriculum or educational material related to entrepreneurship. There are also many other programs in addition to formal education, such as entrepreneurship training, seminars, workshops, and so on, which also aim to improve entrepreneurial intentions and the number of entrepreneurs who will later help in improving the economic development of the country.

Entrepreneurship programs implemented at university indirectly raise the young entrepreneurs of Indonesia. The programs were designed in such a way by the Ministry of National Education, through the curriculum and student creativity program with the purpose of creating college graduates who are ready to work and create jobs. One of the universities supporting and applying this program is Airlangga University. The university has been advancing the activities of entrepreneurship through supporting students who have talent and interest in the field. The Faculty of Economics and Business, especially, provides support for the entrepreneurship program through a student activity unit called webs through this unit, students get a variety of knowledge, training and motivation that can raise their entrepreneurial intentions.

In the field of entrepreneurship, intention models assume that entrepreneurial behavior is a behavior that is planned, which reflects some degree of cognitive processing, and where intentions are developed in the individual when they elaborate knowledge, trust, attitudes and experiences (Krueger et al., 2000). Many models have been used in previous research to explain and to learn about entrepreneurial intentions, but the most commonly used is the Theory of Planned Behavior (TPB). TPB (Ajzen, 1991) is one of the dominant theoretical frameworks used to analyze the formation of intention in various fields (Armitage & Conner, 2001), including that of entrepreneurship. There are three variables in TPB that form the factors in determining the intention or behavior: attitude towards the behavior, subjective norm, and perceived behavioral control.

This research will examine the factors that are associated with the formation of entrepreneurial intentions, especially in young people, to become entrepreneurs. The respondents in this research are students who are participants in the WEBS unit in the Faculty of Economics and Business at Airlangga University.

2 LITERATURE REVIEW

2.1 *Direct antecedents of entrepreneurial intentions*

The first antecedent of entrepreneurial intentions is attitude toward entrepreneurial behavior. Attitudes are what we feel for a concept (the object of the attitude), a people, brand, ideology, or any other entity that attracts a feeling. In other words, attitude is the evaluation (is it good or bad?) that we give to a certain concept. Attitude is developed from someone's belief, aligned with the object of the attitude. In general, beliefs are formed by associating an object with a specific characteristic or attribute. In relation to attitude towards entrepreneurial behavior, each belief is related to an action or behavior. From the assessment of whether an action is good or bad, we will then determine the extent of the attitude towards the behavior which we have, where, when someone feels that such behavior is beneficial for them, it is then translated into a strong intention to carry out the desired behavior.

The second antecedent of entrepreneurial intentions refers to subjective norms, related to the perception of an entrepreneur on the basis of approval of, or reference to, an individual or group that is important to them in relation to their involvement in the creation of new value through innovative, proactive or risky actions. If attitude illustrates the personal factors that affect the likelihood and willingness of a person to engage in certain behavior, subjective norms illustrate the social factors that affect the individual. In other words, subjective norms are the social pressure that a person feels and faces when he has to decide whether to take an action or behave in a certain way.

The third antecedent of entrepreneurial intentions is perceived entrepreneurial behavior control, namely individual beliefs related to how easy it is for them to create value through involvement in innovative, risky or proactive actions. In general, someone's behavior is influenced by their confidence in their ability to do something. Perceived behavioral control is developed from a belief about either having or lacking control of sufficient resources and opportunities. Such confidence may be based partly on past experience, but will also usually be influenced by secondhand information about the experience of friends and acquaintances, and by other factors that increase or decrease the perceived difficulty associated with performing the corresponding behavior. The more support that is acquired and the smaller it is felt that the obstacles are, the greater is someone's control over entrepreneurial behavior.

Theoretical and empirical results in psychology and sociology have widely confirmed that the attitudes, subjective norms and perceived behavioral control have the ability to predict intention (Armitage & Conner, 2001). TPB has also received strong support in the domain of management and entrepreneurship, wherein many successful contributions show the predictive validity of the theory in explaining intentions towards entrepreneurship (Kolvereid, 1996; Krueger et al., 2000). From the explanation above, we can draw hypotheses as follows:

H1a: Attitudes (ATT) toward entrepreneurial behavior have a significant effect on a person's entrepreneurial intention (EI).

H1b: Subjective norms (SN) have a significant effect on a person's entrepreneurial intentions.

H1c: Perceived entrepreneurial behavior control (PEBC) has a significant effect on a person's entrepreneurial intentions.

2.2 *Indirect antecedents of entrepreneurial intentions*

2.2.1 *Antecedents of attitude towards entrepreneurial behavior*

Individual skill. Attitudes can be predicted through cognitive factors such as skills and abilities. This is in line with the assertion by Ajzen and Fishbein (1980), which stated that competencies only impact indirectly on intention, with influences from the factors that closely align with intention (for example, attitudes). In addition, in line with TPB, a person's consciousness of skills and competencies does not directly determine their intention, but influences the degree to which a person develops an assessment (beneficial or otherwise) related to the corresponding behavior. Therefore, lack of awareness about competencies provides a better evaluation of focus on targeted behavior, which indirectly encourages the emergence of intention. Kolvereid (1996) shows that attitudes mediate the relationship between skill and entrepreneurial intentions. In addition, Shapero and Sokol (1982), and Souitaris et al. (2007) also support the premise that individual skills directly impact on attitudes and indirectly influence entrepreneurial intentions. On the basis of this explanation, we propose a hypothesis as follows:

H2: Individual skills (IS) have a significant effect on attitudes towards entrepreneurial behavior.

2.2.2 *Antecedents of perceived entrepreneurial behavior control*

Perceived environmental support. When entering the domain of entrepreneurship, some literature has described the importance of external environment in the support of entrepreneurial activity (Fini et al., 2009). Things such as government support, economic status, capital availability, and infrastructure and entrepreneurial support services are able to support and promote entrepreneurial activities. In addition, university support also triggers the emergence of entrepreneurial behavior, principally among students. The existence of environmental support has a positive effect on a person's perception of control in conducting entrepreneurial behavior and affects their confidence in success when applying such behavior.

Perceived environmental dynamism. In addition to the existence of the resources mentioned above, opportunities also influence a person's intentions and actions. The greater the number of opportunities that an individual experiences, the greater their control over the focal behavior (Ajzen, 1991). A dynamic and changing environment allows individuals to better understand, find, or create opportunities. In addition, an active and heterogeneous environment will hone individual innovative and proactive behaviors, and also generate the courage to take risks. From this explanation, we can draw hypotheses as follows:

H3a: Perceived environmental support (PES) has a significant effect on perceived entrepreneurial behavior control.

H3b: Perceived environmental dynamism (PED) has a significant effect on perceived entrepreneurial behavior control.

3 POPULATION

The population for this research was student participants in WEBS, a total of 68 people. This population was selected because, in the program, students were supplied with an understanding related to entrepreneurship, so that, in this case, they understand and have some vision related to entrepreneurship.

4 RESULTS AND DISCUSSION

4.1 *Relationship between individual skills and attitude toward entrepreneurial behavior*

The hypothesis test results (Table 1) show that there is a positive and significant relationship between individual skills (IS) and attitude (ATT) towards entrepreneurial behavior. In previous research, it has been mentioned that, when a person has awareness of the skills and competencies that they possess, it will have an effect on the degree to which a person develops their assessment (profitable or not profitable) in relation to the corresponding behavior. Therefore, when someone has awareness of their skills and competencies, it gives a better evaluation to focal behavior, which

Table 1. Path coefficients for hypotheses.

	Original sample (O)	Sample mean (M)	Standard deviation (STDEV)	Standard error (STERR)	T statistic (|O/STERR|)
ATT → EI	0.2745	0.2743	0.0865	0.0865	3.1743
IS → ATT	0.3538	0.3526	0.1341	0.1341	2.6378
PEBC → EI	0.0032	−0.0092	0.1252	0.1252	0.0254
PED → PEBC	0.3711	0.3949	0.1009	0.1009	3.6776
PES → PEBC	0.1592	0.1727	0.1063	0.1063	1.4980
SN → EI	0.5030	0.5107	0.0943	0.0943	5.3357

indirectly encourages the emergence of intention. Shapero and Sokol (1982), and Souitaris et al. (2007) also support the notion that individual skills have a direct effect on attitudes and an indirect effect on entrepreneurial intentions. When this result is associated with respondents' answers, we can also see that our respondents felt that they had good skills and competencies to take entrepreneurial action, especially in terms of leadership skills, managerial skills and their maturity to take entrepreneurial action.

4.2 *Relationship between perceived environmental support and perceived entrepreneurial behavior control*

The results of the study showed that the relationship between perceived environmental support (PES) and perceived entrepreneurial behavior control (PEBC) is positive, but not significantly so. This result does not support the theory expounded in previous research that stated that external environment support is very important to the support of entrepreneurial activities (Fini et al., 2009). However, when there is good environmental support, such as government support, economic status, capital availability, infrastructure, university support and other entrepreneurial support services, it can support and promote entrepreneurial activities.

4.3 *Relationship between perceived environmental dynamism and perceived entrepreneurial behavior control*

The results of the study showed that the relationship between perceived environmental dynamism (PED) and perceived entrepreneurial behavior control (PEBC) is both positive and significant. The existence of opportunity will affect a person's intent and actions. When a person experiences more opportunities, then they have more control over focal behavior (Ajzen, 1991).

4.4 *Relationship between attitudes toward entrepreneurial behaviour and entrepreneurial intentions*

The results of the study showed that the relationship between attitudes (ATT) towards entrepreneurial behaviour and entrepreneurial intentions (EI) is positive and significant. This result supports the theory expounded in previous research: Eagly and Chaiken (1993) stated that attitude is a psychological tendency of evaluative characteristics that certain parties have, both beneficial or otherwise, aligned with certain behavior, which includes cognitive, affective and conative aspects.

4.5 *Relationship between subjective norms and entrepreneurial intentions*

The results of the study showed that the relationship between subjective norms (SN) and entrepreneurial intentions (EI) is also positive and significant. This result is not in line with the research of Fini et al. (2012). On the other hand, the result supports previous research by Nilsson et al. (2004), which asserts that subjective norms are a construct which explain someone's belief with reference to the influence of other parties in behaving in a certain way, and that becomes the motivation to attain the particular reference behavior.

4.6 *Relationship between perceived entrepreneurial behavior control and entrepreneurial intentions*

The relationship between perceived entrepreneurial behavior control (PEBC) and entrepreneurial intentions (EI) is positive, but not significant. Behavioral control is based on how much someone is willing and able to control their behavior, such that the associated tendencies can be observed, regardless of whether such behavior provides ease or difficulty. If someone's behavioral control is high, then it affords a better opportunity, whereby the individual will be more ready, more optimistic, and more easily able to control the process to start and develop entrepreneurship, and vice versa.

4.7 *Recommendations*

On the basis of these results, researchers recommend the government be more proactive in encouraging and supporting entrepreneurial activities, especially for young people and students. We can see also from this research that government support is very important in increasing the younger generation's intention to become entrepreneurs. Some conditions that need to be revisited are how the government is able to provide assistance, either through ease of access to information, administration and capital assistance, and/or through funding for young people who want to become entrepreneurs. Meanwhile, our recommendations for educational institutions (universities) are to improve on the quality of programs and support, in both the academic and supporting infrastructure for students who show a high interest in entrepreneurship.

We also have recommendations for other academics/researchers who want to continue the research in this field with regard to the limitations of the present research. The small population here was a constraint, making it difficult to generalize. Researchers can also be further developed in future academic research is comparison of more concrete explanations related to the formation of entrepreneurial intentions among young people, adopting a wider scope than here by looking at different cultures, backgrounds, and so on. This would more clearly illuminate the formation of entrepreneurial intentions.

REFERENCES

Ajzen, I. (1991). The theory of planned behavior. *Organizational Behavior and Human Decision Processes, 50*(2), 179–211.

Ajzen, I. & Fishbein, M. (1980). *Understanding attitudes and predicting social behavior*. Englewood Cliffs, NJ: Prentice Hall.

Armitage, C.J. & Conner, M. (2001). Efficacy of the theory of planned behavior: A meta analytic review. *British Journal of Social Psychology, 40*, 471–499.

Eagly, A.H. & Chaiken, S. (1993). *The psychology of attitudes*. Fort Worth, TX: Harcourt Brace Jovanovich.

Fini, R., Grimaldi, R. & Sobrero, M. (2009). Factors fostering academics to start up new ventures: An assessment of Italian founders' incentives. *Journal of Technology Transfer, 34*, 380–402.

Fini, R., Grimaldi, R., Marzocchi, R.G.L. & Sobrero, M. (2012). The determinants of corporate entrepreneurial intention within small and newly established firms. *Entrepreneurship Theory and Practice, 36*(2), 387–414.

Kolvereid, L. (1996). Prediction of employment status choice intentions. *Entrepreneurship Theory and Practice, 21*(1), 47–57.

Krueger, N.F.J., Reilly, M.D. & Carsrud, A.L. (2000). Competing models of entrepreneurial intentions. *Journal of Business Venturing, 15*(5), 411–432.

Morris, M.H. & Jones, F.F. (1999). Entrepreneurship in established organizations: The case of the public sector. *Entrepreneurship Theory and Practice, 24*(1), 71–91.

Shapero, A. & Sokol, L. (1982). The social dimensions of entrepreneurship. In C. Kent, D.L. Sexton & K. Vesper (Eds.), *The encyclopedia of entrepreneurship* (pp. 72–90). Englewood Cliffs, NJ: Prentice Hall.

Souitaris, V., Zerbinati, S. & Al-Laham, A. (2007). Do entrepreneurship programmes raise entrepreneurial intention of science and engineering students? The effect of learning, inspiration and resources. *Journal of Business Venturing, 22*, 566–591.

Increasing Management Relevance and Competitiveness – Sukoco et al. (Eds)
© 2018 Taylor & Francis Group, London, ISBN 978-0-8153-7455-8

Effect of proactive personality and Organizational Support for Career Development (OSCD) on career satisfaction and job performance

V. Octia & D. Ratmawati
Universitas Airlangga, Surabaya, Indonesia

ABSTRACT: Career objective and career subjective is defined to be a career success. Career subjective is the perception of employees in terms of satisfaction with their careers. People who have talents are always wants a better career path. Both a proactive personality and Organizational Support for Career Development (OSCD), can affect career satisfaction, which is have an impact on improved job performance. The purpose of this study was to determine the effect of proactive personality and OSCD in relation to career satisfaction and job performance among 51 employees at PT Angkasa Pura I (Persero) Juanda Airport, Surabaya. The study variables were measured by a survey, followed by analysis using a partial least square statistical tool. The results showed that proactive personality has a significant effect on job performance. Although there was positive correlation between proactive personality and career satisfaction, it was not statistically significant, which means that career satisfaction is not a mediating influence between proactive personality and job performance. In contrast, OSCD had a significant effect on job performance and career satisfaction, which suggests that career satisfaction serves as a partial mediating factor between OSCD and job performance.

1 INTRODUCTION

PT Angkasa Pura I (Persero) Juanda Airport, Surabaya, is an international airport that constantly makes improvements as a world-class airport company. The use of a Human Capital Management System, implemented in the year 2011, resulted in a change in performance appraisal and support to employees' career development in the organization, and was expected to improve employee job performance. This research was intended to provide an overview to the company of employee performance after changes had been made.

A change in Human Capital Management System suggests that a company supports employee career development to achieve career satisfaction, and aims to influence employee performance for the better. Dessler (2003) states that organizations have an influence on HR processes, starting from recruitment, with selection, placement, training, appraisal, rewards, promotion, and some of employees all affecting a person's career, and, therefore, affecting career satisfaction and successful employee performance.

This research addressed permanent employees, also called organic employees, at PT Angkasa Pura I (Persero) Juanda Airport, Surabaya. Organic employees are employees who have opportunities for career development. The study also aimed to analyze whether these organic employees had a sufficiently proactive personality to determine their own career development.

1.1 *Proactive personality*

People with proactive personalities tend to identify opportunities and take actions, to discover the significance of changes that occur in their environment (Crant, quoted in Barnett & Bradley, 2007).

According to Bateman and Crant (1993), proactive personality is one of the motivators of proactive behavior in the workplace. Employees with proactive personality use initiative and persistence to try to shape their environment.

Greenhaus and Callanan (2006) define a proactive personality as a stable disposition to initiate various situations. People with high levels of proactive personality can be characterized as relatively unrestrained by situational force and can identify opportunities and persist until they provide meaningful change for the organization.

The study refers to the Bateman and Crant (1993) theory of proactive personality research, using two further factors derived from the "Big Five" personality theory: extraversion and conscientiousness, using the theory described by Robbins and Judge (2008).

1.2 *Organizational Support for Career Development*

Organizational Support for Career Development (OSCD) is also referred to as organizational career management or organizational sponsorship. It refers to the programs, processes and assistance provided by an organization to support and enhance employee career success (Orpen, quoted in Barnett & Bradley, 2007). OSCD includes the support environment and variables that are specific and relevant to the pursuit of individual career goals. OSCD consists of formal strategies (including career plans, training centers and performance appraisals) and informal support, such as providing mentoring, coaching and networking opportunities (Sturges et al., 2002; Barnett & Bradley, 2007).

According to Greenhaus and Callanan (2006), OSCD discusses career planning portfolio and management practices available to an organization and explores them in an organizational way using a career system to meet employee needs. Particular attention is given to the practice of career management and how it forms an integrative system for employee development within the organization.

This study uses the theory proposed by Sturges et al. (2002), namely that OSCD is an organizational environment that supports employees for career achievement. OSCD consists of both a formal and an informal strategy. Formal examples are career planning, training and assessment centers, while informal strategies provide mentors to employees, coaching, and networking opportunities.

1.3 *Career satisfaction*

According to Greenhaus and Callanan (2006), career satisfaction is an important variable in career development and other areas related to work, job dynamics and individual adjustment. Although career satisfaction is a rare topic for investigative research, it is often studied as an important criterion or variable in relation to many personal differences and organizational factors.

Career satisfaction is one of the variables of career success, subjectively referring to individual evaluations of employee career progress, achievement and the outcome of employee goals (Seibert & Kraimer, quoted in Barnett & Bradley, 2007). Subjective career success is always operationalized as job satisfaction or career satisfaction (Heslin, 2003; Erdogan & Bauer, 2005; Ng et al., 2005; Seibert & Kraimer, quoted in Barnett & Bradley, 2007).

This research uses the theory of Greenhaus et al. (1990), which suggests that career satisfaction is achieved by someone through intrinsic and extrinsic aspects, including salary satisfaction as well as satisfaction in career development.

1.4 *Job performance*

Job performance is a multidimensional construct that has been extensively researched in organizational psychology, and refers to the level of individual employee productivity, employment relationships with peers, and some work-related behaviors and outcomes (Babin & Boles, quoted in Trivellas et al., 2015).

According to Dessler (2003), performance assessment means evaluating current and/or past employee performance relative to a set of performance standards. Performance appraisals always assume that employees understand these performance standards, and that supervisors also provide employees with the necessary feedback, development and incentives to help the person eliminate poor performance or continue to perform well.

According to Mathis and Jackson (2009), the performance of individual employees is the main factor that determines organizational success. Many factors affect the performance of individual employees, including their ability, the effort invested and the support received from the organization.

Performance is basically what employees do or do not do. Employee performance that is common to most jobs includes the following elements:

1. Quantity of results
2. Quality of results
3. Timeliness of results
4. Presence
5. Ability to work with others.

2 METHODOLOGY

This research was conducted at Persero Juanda Airport, Surabaya, where the company endeavors to be very supportive and provide opportunities for employees to develop their expertise. This research uses the statistical test of Partial Least Squares (PLS) to address the problem formulation, and to test the hypotheses that have been proposed according to theoretical studies derived from previous research.

The type of research data used in this study is quantitative data, that is, data in the form of numbers or numbers that are the result of questionnaires distributed to employees of Persero Juanda Airport, Surabaya.

The data collected in this study represents the primary data. This was obtained from questionnaires that were prepared in the form of a series of statements and distributed by the researchers to 51 employees of Persero Juanda Airport, Surabaya.

The measurement scale used in this research is a Likert scale with an assessment interval for each respondent answer. This scale has five levels: 1 = Strongly disagree; 2 = Disagree; 3 = Quite agree; 4 = Agree; 5 = Strongly agree.

2.1 *Variables and definition of operational variables*

This research involved four variables, namely, proactive personality and OSCD as independent variables, career satisfaction as a mediation variable, and job performance as a dependent variable.

The proactive personality variable (X1) in the dimensions of this research is adapted from previous research. Bateman and Crant (1993) state that there are two factors that form proactive personality, extraversion and conscientiousness, on the basis of the definition of personality proposed by Robbins and Judge (2008).

1. Extraversion. A dimension that describes a person's comfort level in interacting with other individuals. Extraversion is measured by several indicators, as follows:
   a. Has the nature for living in groups;
   b. Is assertive;
   c. Has easy nature for socializing.
2. Conscientiousness. Defined as a trait that makes one trustworthy or reliable. Conscientiousness is measured by several indicators, as follows:
   a. Has a responsible nature;
   b. Has a persistent nature;
   c. Has natural discipline;
   d. Has a reliable character.

The definition of the OSCD variable (X2), according to Sturges et al. (2002), involves the support and resources of environmental variables specifically related to the pursuit of individual career pursuits. OSCD consists of formal strategies (e.g. career planning, training and assessment centers) and informal support, such as mentoring, coaching and networking opportunities.

This study was adapted from a previous study by Sturges et al. (2002). OSCD is divided into two dimensions: formal OSCD and informal OSCD.

1. Formal OSCD indicators:
   a. Provides training to help develop employee careers;
   b. Provides training to help develop employee skills;
   c. Provides direction to generate knowledge of careers within the organization;
   d. Provides personal development plans for employees;
   e. Provides clear feedback about employee performance.
2. Informal OSCD indicators:
   a. Advises on careers when employees need it;
   b. Introduces people ready to assist in employee career development;
   c. Provides mentors to assist employee career development.

The career satisfaction variable (X) is career success, subjectively referring to employee career evaluations related to their career goals (Seibert & Kraimer, quoted in Barnett & Bradley, 2007). Career satisfaction is typically measured using scales devised by Greenhaus et al. (1990).

The career satisfaction measurement indicator used here is adapted from the research of Greenhaus et al. (1990) and is as follows:

a. It is satisfaction with the success achieved in an employee's career;
b. It is satisfaction with the progress that has been made in realizing individual career goals;
c. It is satisfaction with the progress that has been made in realizing income objectives;
d. It is satisfaction with the progress that has been made in fulfilling improvement in higher career advancement;
e. It is satisfaction with the progress that has been made in meeting goals for the development of new skills.

The job performance variable (Y) is the result of an employee's work. This research uses the theory proposed by Mathis and Jackson (2009) to assess individual performance. The assessment consists of five aspects of performance criteria used for appropriate performance measures; the indicators used are as follows:

1. Quantity of work: able to complete the work in accordance with the target to be achieved;
2. Quality of work: able to complete the work given in accordance with the procedures and rules that apply to it;
3. Timeliness of the work: able to complete the job on time;
4. Attendance: has a level of attendance in accordance with the provisions of the organization;
5. Ability to cooperate: able to work with colleagues in completing the work, and to receive feedback from colleagues.

To generate objectivity in the assessment of job performance, this aspect of the data questionnaires was completed by the direct superiors of the respondents.

2.2 *Data analysis technique*

Test validity is performed to measure the extent of the validity of the questionnaire instrument used for data collection. The value of convergent validity is the value of the loading factor in the latent variable with its indicators. An indicator is valid or meets convergent validity if it has a loading factor above 0.5 in relation to the intended construct. The validity test for reflective indicator uses correlation between item score and construct score.

The measurement of reliability according Ghozali (2008) is intended to assess whether an indicator is truly reliable for measuring a construct. An indicator is said to be a good constructor when it has a correlation (loading) of 0.7. However, for the initial stage of the scale, loading values of 0.5–0.6 are considered sufficient.

2.3 *Result*

There were 51 respondents involved in the research, consisting of 30 men and 21 women. The age of respondents who are considered in development career was the most dominant in the age range, with 15 people aged 26–30, six people aged 31–35 years, and eight people aged 36–40. There were ten people characterized by a two-year working period, 20 people had a working period of 5–10 years, four people had a working period of 10–15 years, 13 people had a working period of 15–20 years, and for four people the working period was 20 years or more. In terms of most recent education, two respondents were high school graduates, seven people were diploma graduates, 37 people had a bachelor degree and five graduates had a masters degree. The departments involved in this research were: airport operations (one person); airport readiness (five people); airport security (nine people); Safety Management System, Quality Management & Customer Service (six people); finance & IT (eight people); shared services (16 people).

Based on Table 1, it can be seen that the value of the square root of the average variance extracted (AVE) for each latent variable is greater when compared to correlation with other variables, which is an indicator of good discriminant validity. Values of latent variables via the reliability test meet the rule of thumb requirement, that is, > 0.7. The results of this test indicate that all variables are reliable and can be used in the study.

The results of the path coefficients show that all latent variables have a positive effect (seen through the original sample values), and are deemed significant or not significant on the basis of whether the T-statistic has a value greater than 1.96. Based on the results contained in Table 1, it can be seen that proactive personality (PP) has a positive but not significant effect on career satisfaction (CS), because it has a T-statistic value below 1.96 (< 1.96).

Table 1. Fornell–Larcker criterion test results (AVE square root).

	CS	JP	OSCD	PP
CS	**0.863**			
JP	0.596	**0.727**		
OSCD	0.529	0.678	**0.797**	
PP	0.301	0.426	0.290	**0.729**

Figure 1 shows a bootstrapping research model created using SmartPLS 2.0 statistical software (SmartPLS GmbH, Boenningstedt, Germany). After performing validation testing of the model as a whole, the next step is to measure Goodness of Fit (GoF) by using calculation of the square root of multiplication of mean value of communality with mean value of R-squared.

Based on the value of GoF of 0.519, the performance fit between the model and the structural model is good. This means that the model in this study is correct and feasible for use.

On the basis of the hypothesis test results, three hypotheses are accepted and one is rejected, as follows:

1. Hypothesis 1 (H1) states that someone who has proactive personality will demonstrate good job performance. The result of calculation using SmartPLS 2.0 shows the value of the coefficient variable of proactive personality has a positive influence in relation to job performance (JP), with a beta coefficient value of 0.249 and a T-statistic value of 2.333, which indicates significance because the value is above 1.96 (> 1.96). This means that H1 is supported.
2. Hypothesis 2 (H2) states that a person's proactive personality will affect career satisfaction. The result of calculation using SmartPLS 2.0 shows that the value of the coefficient variable of proactive personality has a positive effect in relation to career satisfaction, with a beta coefficient value of 0.161 and a T-statistic value of 1.262. However, this T-statistic value is not significant because it is below 1.96 (< 1.96). This means that career satisfaction does not mediate proactive personality and job performance. Thus, H2 is not supported, which states that proactive personality is not positive significant to job performance through career satisfaction.
3. Hypothesis 3 (H3) states that OSCD affects employees' job performance. The result of calculation using SmartPLS 2.0 shows that the value of the OSCD coefficient variable has positive influence in relation to job performance, with a

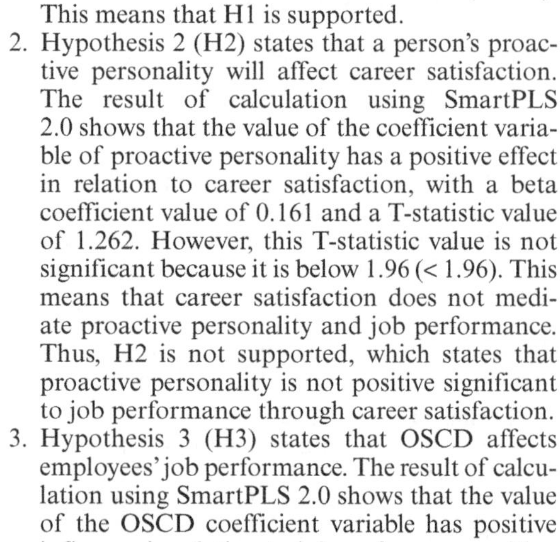

Figure 1. SmartPLS bootstrapping results research model.

beta coefficient value of 0.605 and a T-statistic value that is significant because it is greater than 1.96 (> 1.96). This means that H3, stating that OSCD has a significant positive effect on job performance, is supported.

4. Hypothesis 4 (H4) states that OSCD has an effect on career satisfaction. The result of calculation using SmartPLS 2.0 shows that the value of the OSCD coefficient variable has positive influence in relation to career satisfaction, with a beta coefficient of 0.481 and a T-statistic value of 3.743, which is significant because it is above 1.96 (>1.96). This means that career satisfaction mediates OSCD and job performance. Thus, H4, which states that OSCD has a significant positive effect on job performance through supporting career satisfaction, is supported.

2.4 *Discussion*

In terms of the first hypothesis, it can be said that employees who have a proactive personality like to work in teams and are also responsible in completing their work well. In this case, the company should provide or improve facilities to support the daily work of the employee; the employee performance will thus increase and have a positive influence on the company. Employees with a proactive personality will always find opportunities to improve their welfare by way of career advancement.

This result supports previous research conducted by Crant (2000), which stated that a person with proactive personality can create a situation consistent with effectiveness in employee job performance.

The second hypothesis tested the relationship between proactive personality and job performance through career satisfaction. The result of this study indicates that proactive personality has no significant effect on career satisfaction: career satisfaction does not mediate between proactive personality and job performance.

With a T-statistic value of 1.262, the influence of the proactive personality variable on career satisfaction is not significant. This could suggest that employees who have a proactive personality feel dissatisfied with their career, because the company is less able to provide them with opportunities to develop their career. In terms of the organizational structure, employees will rise to the level of the career above, which is the level of section head, and then the level of department head, but no higher up the career ladder. In company procedures for employees who want to attain a higher career, the employee must first be in rotation to another area, for a two-year working period with the same position; then, in the next two years, employees can rise to a higher position in the area of duty at that time.

The results of this study do not fit with research conducted by Barnett and Bradley (2007), who found that proactive personality significantly affects career satisfaction. Similarly, research conducted by Seibert, Crant, and Kraimer (2001) also found that proactive personality has a positive effect on career satisfaction, even after being examined in relation to several other career variables.

This difference is likely to arise because the research conducted by Seibert, Crant, and Kraimer (2001) considered respondents who were alumni from western universities and was derived from business school graduates and samples involving various jobs with comparable career outcomes, while the present study was conducted in one company with career results that cannot be compared with other companies.

In the test of the third hypothesis, the relationship between OSCD and job performance, the results of the study indicate that there is a significant relationship between OSCD and performance tracking. This suggests that OSCD can improve the job performance of employees because it can assist them in improving their skills in daily work.

This supports previous research by Kraimer et al. (2011), which states that for employees who feel that there is organizational support for both development and career opportunity, it can improve job performance. In addition, according to Hall (quoted in Kraimer et al., 2011), effective interpersonal relations and informal resources are important in supporting career development within the organization.

In the fourth hypothesis, that there is a relationship between OSCD and job performance through career satisfaction, the results of this research indicate that the relationship is a significant one. This shows that OSCD can improve employee career satisfaction, thereby impacting on employee job performance improvement.

The results of this study support previous research by Karatepe (2012), which states that employees who are satisfied with their careers, in terms of salary, development, and the achievement of career goals, as well as the development of new skills, will show good performance. Judge et al. (quoted in Karatepe, 2012) mention that there is good correlation between satisfaction and performance.

This is also supported by previous research conducted by Barnett and Bradley (2007), which stated that organizations can have an impact on employee experience of career success (both objectively and subjectively) by supporting employee career development.

The existence of a positive relationship between OSCD, career satisfaction and job performance supports previous research conducted by Zhang (quoted in Trivellas et al., 2015), which states that high performance can arise when the talents or competencies of employees are consistent with the personnel and organizational needs of the organization. People who have talents reflect values, visions, knowledge, competencies, and interest when career success and job demands are shaped by the roles of responsibilities and tasks. Then, career satisfaction facilitates new competencies in general or sharpens those already established. The progress of competence in general enhances the effectiveness of individuals in terms of increased job performance.

3 CONCLUSIONS AND RECOMMENDATIONS

3.1 *Conclusions*

Based on the foregoing analysis and discussion, the following may be concluded:

1. Proactive personality has a significant effect on job performance, such that H1 is accepted.
2. Proactive personality has no significant effect on career satisfaction and job performance, such that H2 is rejected.
3. Organizational support for career development has a significant influence on job performance, such that H3 is accepted.
4. Organizational support for career development has a significant influence on career satisfaction and job performance, such that H4 is accepted.

3.2 *Recommendations*

In terms of the characteristics of respondents, the company PT Angkasa Pura I (Persero) Juanda Airport, Surabaya, has a majority of employees in the age range of 26–30 years and they have proactive personalities; they have received training and direction for career development provided by the company. Employees of a younger age have a drive to move forward and develop both in terms of career and performance in the company. Employees are a valuable asset for the company, which should provide facilities to improve career satisfaction by providing a clear picture of the career ladder within the company in order to provide motivation to all employees of Persero Juanda Airport, Surabaya.

Theoretically, is able to know the influence of the relationship of each variable proactive personality, OSCD, career satisfaction and job performance. Based on the results obtained, it is shown that the proactive personality variable does not have a significant effect on job performance through career satisfaction, except through the variable of OSCD.

For researchers interested in conducting research in the same area, they should explore the context of different companies in the industry, to enrich the subject and to explore relationships among other variables in order to analyze the relationships between variables in more depth.

REFERENCES

Barnett, B.R. & Bradley, L. (2007). The impact of organizational support career development on career satisfaction. *Career Development International*, *12*(7), 617–636.

Bateman, T.S. & Crant, J.M. (1993). The proactive component of organizational behaviour: A measure and correlates. *Journal of Organizational Behaviour*, *14*, 103–118.

Crant, J.M. (2000). Proactive behaviour in organizations. *Journal of Management*, *26*(3), 435–462.

Dessler, G. (2003). *Human Resources Management* (10th ed.). Jakarta, Indonesia: PT Indeks.

Erdogan, B. & Bauer, T.N. (2005). Enhancing career benefit of employee proactive personality: The role of fit with jobs and organizations. *Personnel Psychology*, *58*, 859–891.

Ghozali, I. (2008). *Structural equation modelling: Alternative Method with Partial Least Square*. Semarang, Indonesia: Universitas Diponegoro.

Greenhaus, J.H. & Callanan, G.A. (2006). *Encyclopedia of career development* (Vol. 2). Thousand Oaks, CA: SAGE Publications.

Greenhaus, J.H., Pasuraman, S. & Wormley, W.M. (1990). Effect of race on organizational experiences, job performance evaluations, and career outcomes. *Academy of Management Journal*, *1*(1), 64–86.

Karatepe, O.M. (2012). Perceived organizational support, career satisfaction, and performance outcomes. *International Journal of Contemporary Hospitality Management*, *24*(5), 735–752.

Kaswan. (2014). *Career development*. Bandung, Indonesia: Alfabeta.

Kraimer, M.L., Seibert, S.E., Wayne, S.J., Liden, R.C. & Bravo, J. (2011). Antecedent and outcome of organizational support for development: The critical role of career opportunities. *Journal of Applied Psychology*, *96*(3), 485–500.

Lent, R.W. & Brown, S.D. (2006). Integrating person and situation perspectives on work satisfaction: A social-cognitive view. *Journal of Vocational Behaviour*, *69*, 236–247.

Mathis, R.L. & Jackson, J.H. (2009). *Human Resources Management* (10th ed.). Jakarta, Indonesia: Salemba Empat.

Orpen, C. (1994). The effects of organizational and individual career management on career success. *International Journal of Manpower*, *15*, 27–37.

Robbins, S.P. & Judge, T.A. (2008). *Organizational Behavior* (12th ed.). Jakarta, Indonesia: Salemba Empat.

Seibert, S,E. & Kraimer, M.L. (2001). The five-factor model of personality and career success. *Journal of Vocational Behavior*, *58*, 1–21.

Sturges, J., Guest, D., Conway, N. & Davey, M.K. (2002). A longitudinal study of the relationship between career management and organizational commitment among graduates in the first ten years at work. *Journal of Organizational Behavior*, *23*, 731–748.

Trivellas, P., Kakkos, N., Blanas, N.J. & Santouridis, I. (2015). The impact of career satisfaction on job performance in accounting firms. The mediating effect of general competencies. *Procedia Economics and Finance*, 33, 468–476.

Increasing Management Relevance and Competitiveness – Sukoco et al. (Eds)
© 2018 Taylor & Francis Group, London, ISBN 978-0-8153-7455-8

The effects of transformational and transactional leadership on work performance of middle-level leaders with organizational commitment as mediator: A study of state-owned company, Pelabuhan Indonesia III Inc.

A. Eliyana, S. Maarif & R.J. Sunarsono
Universitas Airlangga, Surabaya, Indonesia

ABSTRACT: Leadership as an antecedent of the success of an organization remains an interesting topic of study. We focus on a discussion of antecedent variables of transformational and transactional leadership in relation to their effect on work performance among middle-level leaders in the Pelabuhan Indonesia III (Persero) corporation. The variables used in this study are transformational and transactional leadership, organizational commitment, and work performance, and the sample was 30 respondents, which represented 75% of the total population. A questionnaire was used as the data collection technique in this study in order to minimize interpretation differences between respondents and researchers. Partial Least Squares (PLS) regression was selected to analyze the study data as a form of structural equation modeling, to ensure that the results were valid. The middle-leaders as the sample of this study demonstrate good transformational leadership style, and this leadership style does have a significant impact on employees' organizational commitment. Afterwards, this study also shows that the transactional leadership is better that transformational leadership. The significance of this study is to contribute theoretical ideas, empirically and practically, in the development of human resource knowledge.

Keywords: transactional leadership, transformational leadership, commitment, performance, human resource

1 INTRODUCTION

Nowadays, the human resources factor is heavily used to help fulfill the aspirations of an organization. Every organization or company seeks to be able to maximally manage and control the aspect of human resources. By managing this central factor through good human resource management, the goals and aspirations of an organization are more likely to be achieved. Human resource management is a means of improving these and, in this developing modern era, many preeminent aspects are needed by every organization in order to achieve its goals. The main quality required of human resources is to improve work performance and organizational productivity, so that there will be disciplined and high-performance employees.

The most important factor affecting work performance is leadership style. Leadership is an ability to affect a group to achieve goals, and transactional leadership is a leadership style used to focus on achieving goals or targets, but does not improve the responsibility and authority of subordinates for the better. The leadership styles broadly researched in relation to work performance are known as transformational and transactional leadership (Riaz & Haider, 2010). Some previous studies have shown that there is a significant effect from transformational leadership on employees' work performance. Almutairi (2016) found that organizational commitment had a mediating effect on the relationship between transformational leadership styles and employees' work performance. In its results, the study showed that a transformational leadership style was positively related to work performance.

An empirical study by Albion and Gagliardi (2007) also showed an effect of transactional leadership on employees' work performance, with which transactional leadership had a positive and significant relationship, while Paracha et al. (2012) described a similar relationship. Likewise, Bass et al. (2003), Pastor and Mayo (2006), and Sundi (2015) have all described study results that show a positive and significant relationship between transactional leadership and employees' work performance. In accordance with a theoretical approach and the empirical researches outlined above, both transformational and transactional leadership styles can affect employees' work performance. Transformational leadership is related to work satisfaction (Baltaci et al., 2012) and also has a relationship with organizational commitment (Bono & Judge, 2003; Almutairi, 2016). Transactional leadership also has a relationship with work satisfaction (Ali et al., 2014) and organizational commitment (Fasola et al., 2013).

2 THEORIES AND HYPOTHESES

2.1 *Transformational leadership*

According to Bass et al. (2003), *transformational leadership* is change-oriented leadership in which the organizational vision is not only formulated, but also implemented through: (1) the ideal influence of leaders with high levels of autonomy affects the subordinates; (2) inspirational motivation according to a leader's ability to inspire, motivate, emotionally encourage, and give compliments to the subordinates; (3) individualized consideration according to the ability and responsibility of a leader to satisfy and push the subordinates' productivity (such leaders tend to be friendly, informal, close to their subordinates, treating them fairly, advising, helping and giving support to the development of individuals); (4) intellectual stimulation, which reflects the ability of a leader to stimulate the intellect of the subordinates through motivation.

Transformational leadership theory began with the concepts of Burns (1978) and Bass (1985). According to Bass, transformational leaders stimulate their subordinates to create perceptions of leadership from new perspectives because there is intellectual stimulation. Leaders are perceived as individuals who can support and give care to their subordinates with individualized consideration, through inspirational motivation and charisma (Bass, 1985; Bass & Avolio, 2000).

2.2 *Transactional leadership*

Robbins and Judge (2008) described the theory of transactional leadership as one in which a leader guides and motivates subordinates with a set of goals to make their function and duty clear. Transactional leadership, according to Naidu and Van Der Walt (2005), is an exchange between leaders and employees, in which leaders exchange rewards or punishments for a task completed by employees, in return for which productivity, effort and loyalty is expected from employees. Transactional leadership style focuses on the importance of care on the part of employees and clarifies the ways in which needs are fulfilled with the purpose of improving employees' work performance to achieve desired goals (Bass & Avolio, 2000). Thite (2000) stated that transactional leadership style is a traditional view of leadership, which focuses on a contractual relationship between leaders and subordinates in the context of work performance for a given reward.

Transactional leadership theory explains leadership as motivating subordinates through contingent rewards and corrective actions until behaviors are formed that support the achievement of maximal work performance (Bass, 1985; Bass & Avolio, 2000). Transactional leadership theory focuses on the beneficial relationship between leaders and subordinates.

2.3 *Organizational commitment*

Robbins (2006) defined organizational commitment as a stage in which the employee recognizes a certain group and has goals and the desire to maintain their status as a group member. Moreover, Luthans (2006) stated that behaviors and organizational commitment are defined as: (1) strong willingness to remain a group member; (2) willingness to work hard as an organizational aspiration; (3) a certain willingness to accept the values and goals of the organization. In other words, these are behaviors that reflect employees' loyalty to the organization, and the next stage is one in which the organization's members express care for the organization's success and further development. Hettiararchchi and Jayarathna (2014) studied the effect of employees' behaviors related to work performance. The study results show that there is a positive and significant effect of organizational commitment on work performance.

2.4 *Work performance*

According to Rivai (2008), work performance is about working and achievements from that work, and also what to do and how to do it. Availability and skills are not sufficient to achieve something without a clear understanding about what to do and how to do it. As such, work performance is a real behavior shown by an employee as a work achievement based on his or her role in the organization. Hasibuan (2003) explained work performance as the accomplishment of work achievements by an individual in finishing their work according to their skills, experiences, capabilities, and also their work period.

3 SAMPLE AND RESEARCH METHOD

This study is a quantitative study and is designed to explain the effect or relationship between vari-

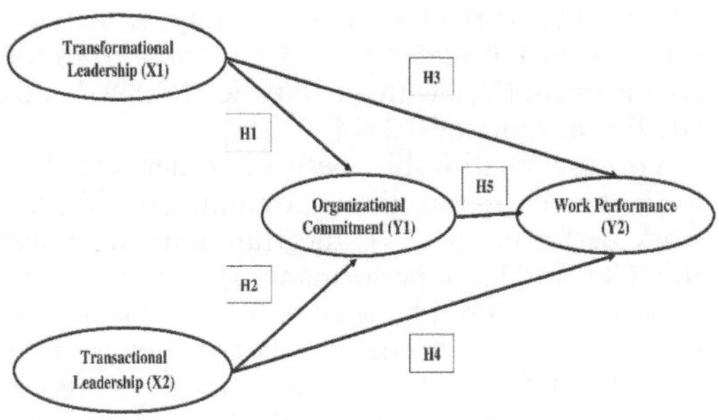

Figure 1. Conceptual framework.

ables through hypothesis testing or confirming the effect of the relationship between variables or constructs. It is also an explanatory study to prove whether there is a relationship between one variable and another or how one variable affects the other variables being studied. The population is 30 middle-level leaders in the state-owned seaport services company Pelabuhan Indonesia III (Persero) Inc. The variables in this study can be classified into exogenous and endogenous variables.

3.1 *Conceptual framework*

Based on the strong relationships that derive from theoretical and empirical study of the variables that form the focus of this study, the conceptual framework for the study is shown in Figure 1.

On the basis of these same theoretical and empirical studies, the hypotheses in this study were:

H1: Transformational leadership significantly affects the organizational commitment of middle-level leaders;

H2: Transactional leadership significantly affects the organizational commitment of middle-level leaders;

H3: Transformational leadership significantly affects the work performance of middle-level leaders;

H4: Transactional leadership significantly affects the work performance of middle-level leaders;

H5: Organizational commitment significantly affects the work performance of middle-level leaders.

4 FINDINGS

The characteristics of the 30 respondents in this study, broken down by gender, age and work period, are shown in Table 1.

Table 1. Respondents' characteristics.

Characteristic	Classification	Total	Percentage
Gender	Male	24	80
	Female	6	20
Age	<30 years	3	10
	30–41 years	12	40
	>41–50 years	13	43.3
	>50 years	2	6.7
Education	High School	1	3.3
	Diploma	2	6.7
	Bachelor	27	.90
Work period	1–5 year(s)	2	6.7
	>5–10 years	12	40
	>10 years	16	53.3
Position	Ass. Manager	17	56.7
	Supervisor	12	40
	Others	1	3.3
Position period	1–3 year(s)	16	53.3
	>3–6 years	9	30

4.1 *Model analysis measuring or outer model convergent validity and reliability*

Convergent validity testing in Partial Least Squares (PLS) regression is done by scoring loading factors (correlation between score items and construct scores), which reflects the relationship between each variable or indicator and the latent variable. Hair et al. (2010) stated that the rule of thumb is usually used for first identification in the matrix factor considered as practically significant. From the results of convergent validity analysis after eliminating some indicators shown in Table 1, it can be concluded that all remaining indicators have outer loading scores greater than 0.5. This shows that all indicators fulfill the rule of thumb in terms of their convergent validity scores (Chin, 1998). The test results show that almost all variables have composite reliability and Cronbach alpha scores that fulfill the typical rule of thumb, being >0.70 (Ghozali, 2008). However, one variable, transactional leadership, has a lower Cronbach alpha score of 0.5506.

Figure 2 shows the model figure created after validity and reliability testing.

4.2 *Structural model analysis (inner model)*

For this research model, the R-squared score of 0.3514 (moderate) for the work performance variable means that 35.14% of the effect of changing work performance can be explained by transformational leadership, transactional leadership and organizational commitment; the remainder can be explained by other variables not part of the

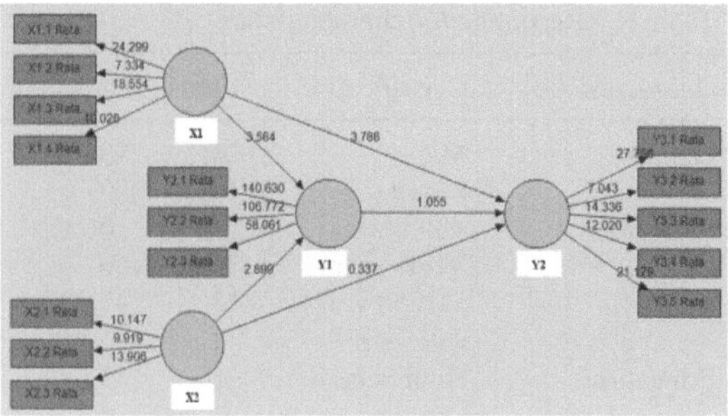

Figure 2. Inner model analysis results.

Table 2. R-squared values.

Variables	R-squared	Notes
Transformational leadership (X1)	0	–
Transactional leadership (X2)	0	–
Organizational commitment (Y1)	0.5385	Good
Work performance (Y2)	0.3514	Moderate

Table 3. Path coefficient scores.

	O	M	STDEV	STERR	(|O/STERR|)
$X_1 \rightarrow Y_1$	0.4344	0.4343	0.1212	0.1212	3.5842
$X_2 \rightarrow Y_1$	0.3414	0.3425	0.1178	0.1178	2.8987
$X_1 \rightarrow Y_2$	0.5363	0.5373	0.1416	0.1416	3.7884
$X_2 \rightarrow Y_2$	–0.0462	–0.0234	0.1371	0.1371	0.3369
$Y_1 \rightarrow Y_2$	0.1235	0.1129	0.1171	0.1171	1.0554

Note: O – Original sample; M – Sample mean; STDEV – Standard deviation; STERR – Standard error; |O/STERR| – T-statistic.

model measured in this study. The R-squared score of 0.5385 (good) for the organizational commitment variable means that as much as 53.85% of the changed organizational commitment can be explained by transformational leadership and transactional leadership, with the remainder explained by variables outside the model measured in this study.

From Table 3, it can be seen that there is a path relationship fulfilling significance with α 1%, which is between the variables of transformational leadership (X_1) and work performance (Y_2) with a t-statistic of 3.7884 and a coefficient score of 0.5363. Next, the relationship between the variables of transformational leadership (X_2) and organizational commitment (Y_1) give a t-statistic of 3.5842 and a coefficient score of 0.4344. After these, the last relationship with a high significance among the variables of this study is between transactional leadership (X_2) and organizational commitment (Y_1), with a t-statistic of 2.8987 and a coefficient score of 0.3414.

For the relationship between other variables, for instance organizational commitment (Y_1) and work performance (Y_2), and transactional leadership (X_2) and work performance (Y_2), a significant relationship cannot be seen; both relationships can only generate path coefficients with low t-statistics, of 1.0554 and 0.3369, respectively. Moreover, both of the latter relationships have a weak significance score, one having a negative coefficient score. However, because both variables are not significant, no further consideration is given to these relationships. Thus, there are three significant relationships, explained further in Section 5, and two insignificant ones.

4.3 *Hypothesis testing*

The PLS results show that the path coefficient score of the transformational leadership variable to that of organizational commitment ($X_1 \rightarrow Y_1$) has a positive effect, with a significant beta coefficient score of 0.4344 and a t-statistic score greater than 2.1, that is, 3.5842. This means that hypothesis H1 is accepted.

Testing of the second hypothesis, H2, shows that the path coefficient score for the variable of transactional leadership to organizational commitment ($X_2 \rightarrow Y_1$) also has a positive effect, with a beta coefficient score of 0.3414 and a t-statistic score greater than 2.1, that is, 2.8987. This means that hypothesis H2 is accepted too.

Testing of the third hypothesis, H3, shows that the path coefficient score for the variable of transformational leadership to work performance ($X_1 \rightarrow Y_2$) has a positive effect, with a positive beta coefficient score of 0.5363 and a t-statistic score greater than 2.1, that is, 3.7884. This means that hypothesis H3 is accepted.

Testing of the fourth hypothesis shows that the path coefficient score for the transactional leadership variable to work performance ($X_2 \rightarrow Y_2$) produces a negative effect, with a beta coefficient score of –0.0462 and a t-statistic score below 2.1, that is, 0.3369. This means that hypothesis H4 is rejected.

Finally, testing of the fifth hypothesis, H5, reveals that the path coefficient score for the variable of organizational commitment to that of work performance ($Y_1 \rightarrow Y_2$) has a positive effect, with a positive beta coefficient score of 0.1235 but an insufficiently high t-statistic score of 1.0554, which is below the minimum score α 1% (2.1). This means that hypothesis H5 is rejected.

5 DISCUSSION

Empirically, Jain and Duggal (2015) studied the role of transformational leadership style in the organizational commitment of employees. Our study shows that the leadership style experienced by employees does not significantly affect organizational commitment; the results of testing the relationship between the two varieties of leadership and organizational commitment are discussed above. Based on the order of indicators adopted from a study by Jones and George (2008), and according to the results of the interviews with the respondents, middle-level leaders in Pelabuhan Indonesia III demonstrate good transformational leadership style, and this leadership style does have a significant impact on employees' organizational commitment. A study by Almutairi (2016) explored the relationship between transformational leadership and work performance by analyzing the mediation effect of organizational commitment in this relationship. The results of the present study also demonstrate that a positive transformational leadership style has an effect on work performance. A study by Yeh and Hong (2012) shows a relationship between transformational leadership and organizational commitment in terms of the mediation of organizational commitment in the relationship between leadership styles and work performance.

Our results also show that a transactional leadership style positively and significantly affects organizational commitment. A study by Fasola et al. (2013) of the relationship between transformational and transactional leadership styles and organizational commitment showed that transactional leadership was more effective than transformational leadership in relation to organizational commitment. In terms of the relationship between transactional leadership and work performance, Bass et al. (2003) indicate that transactional leadership has a significant and positive impact on work performance. A study by Albion and Gagliardi (2007) found that transactional leadership had a positive and significant relationship with work satisfaction in a public organization in Queensland. In their study, Pastor and Mayo (2006) stated that there was a positive and significant relationship between transactional leadership and the work orientation of directors in a large-scale organization in Spain. A study by Paracha et al. (2012) showed that there was a positive and significant relationship between transactional leadership and work performance, and results in Sundi (2015) also show a positive relationship between transactional leadership and work performance. An empirical study by Tolentino (2013), who studied organizational commitment among selected administration and academic personnel in a university, showed a relationship between transformational leadership and work performance and indicated that affective commitment had a significant correlation with work performance in academic personnel. A study by Hettiararchchi and Jayarathna (2014) on the effect of work behaviors in relation to work performance showed that there was a positive and significant effect of organizational commitment on work performance. In the present research, we found the relationship to be positive but not significant (hypothesis H5).

6 CONCLUSION

This study aimed to investigate two antecedents of leadership that, to some extent, are able to positively affect some outcomes in the context of organizations, namely, work performance and organizational commitment. In the study, transformational leadership and transactional leadership were shown to make impacts in various ways: transformational leadership can have a positive impact on both work performance and organizational commitment, and transactional leadership had a positive and significant impact on organizational commitment but not on work performance. In addition, this study illustrates the impacts on work performance of middle-level leaders.

REFERENCES

Albion, M.J. & Gagliardi, R.E. (2007). A study of transformational leadership, organisational change and job satisfaction. *In 7th Industrial & Organisational Psychology Conference and 1st Asia Pacific Congress on Work and Organisational Psychology, 28 June – 1 July 2007, Adelaide, Australia.*

Ali, N., Ali, S., Ahsan, A., Rahman, W. & Kakakhel, S.J. (2014). Effect of leadership styles on job satisfaction, organizational citizenship behavior, commitment and turnover intention (Empirical study of private sector schools' teachers). *Life Science Journal, 11*(4 s), 78–86.

Almutairi, D.O. (2016). The mediating effects of organizational commitment on the relationship between transformational leadership style and job performance. *International Journal of Business and Management, 11*(1), 231–240.

Baltaci, F., Kara, E., Tascan, E. & Avsali, H. (2012). The effect of leadership on job satisfaction (Visionary leadership, transformational leadership, transactional leadership). In *3rd International Symposium on Sustainable Development, 31 May – 01 June 2012, Sarajevo.*

Bass, B.M. (1985). *Leadership and performance beyond expectations.* New York, NY: The Free Press.

Bass, B.M. & Avolio, B.J. (2000). *MLQ: Multifactor leadership questionnaire*. Menlo Park, CA: Mind Garden.

Bass, B.M, Avolio, B.J., Jung, D.I. & Berson, Y. (2003). Predicting unit performance by assessing transformational and transactional leadership. *Journal of Applied Psychology*, *88*, 207–218.

Bono, J.E. & Judge, T.A. (2003). Self-concordance at work: Toward understanding the motivational effects of transformational leaders. *Academy of Management Journal*, *46*, 554–571.

Burns, J.M. (1978). *Leadership.* New York, NY: Harper & Row.

Chin, W.W. (1998). The partial least squares approach for structural equation modeling. In G.A. Marcoulides (Ed.), *Modern methods for business research* (pp. 295–336). London, UK: Lawrence Erlbaum Associates.

Fasola, O.S., Adeyemi, M.A. & Olewe, F.T. (2013). Exploring the relationship between transformational, transactional leadership style and organizational commitment among Nigerian banks employees. *International Journal of Academic Research in Economics and Management Sciences*, *2*(6), 96–107.

Ghozali, I. (2008). *Model persamaan Struktural Konsep dan Aplikasi dengan Program Amos 16.0. Semarang, Indonesia: Badan Penerbit UNDIP.*

Hasibuan, M. (2003). *Organisasi dan motivasi*. Jakarta, Indonesia: PT Bumi Aksara.

Hair Jr., J.F., Black, W.C., Babin, B.J. and Anderson, R.E. (2010) Multivariate Data Analysis: A Global Perspective. 7th Edition, Pearson Education, Upper Saddle River.

Hettiararchchi, H.A.H. & Jayarathna, S.M.D.Y. (2014). The effect of employer work related attitudes on employee job performance: A study of tertiary and vocational education sector in Sri Lanka. *Journal of Business and Management*, *16*(4), 74–83.

Jain, P. & Duggal, T. (2015). The role of transformational leadership in organizational commitment. *International Journal of Business Quantitative Economics and Applied Management Research*, *2*(5),.

Jones, G.R. & George, M.J. (2008). *Understanding and managing organizational behavior*. Upper Saddle River, NJ: Pearson Education.

Luthans, F. (2006). *Perilaku Organisasi* (Bahasa Indonesia ed., V.A. Yuwono et al., Trans.). Yogyakarta, Indonesia: ANDI.

Naidu, J. & Van Der Walt, M.S. (2005). An exploration of the relationship between leadership styles and the implementation of transformation interventions. *SA Journal of Human Resource Management*, *3*(2), 1–10.

Paracha, M.U., Qamar, A., Mirza, A., Hassan, I. & Waqas, H. (2012). Impact of leadership style (transformational & transactional leadership) on employee performance & mediating role of job satisfaction: Study of private school (educator) in Pakistan. *Global Journal of Management and Business Research*, *12*(4), 55–65.

Pastor, J.C. & Mayo, M. (2006). *Transformational and transactional leadership: An examination of managerial cognition among Spanish upper echelons*. Instituto de Empresa Business School Working Paper No. WP06–13. doi:10.2139/ssrn.1015363

Riaz, A. & Haider, M.H. (2010). Role of transformational and transactional leadership on job satisfaction and career satisfaction. *Business and Economic Horizons*, *1*, 29–38.

Rivai, V. (2008). *Human resource management for corporations: Theory and practice*. Jakarta, Indonesia: PT Raja Grafindo Persada.

Robbins, S. (2006). *Organizational behavior*. Upper Saddle River, NJ: Prentice Hall.

Robbins, S.P. & Judge, T.A. (2008). *Organizational behavior* (Terjemahan). Jakarta, Indonesia: Salemba Empat.

Sundi, K. (2015). Effect of transformational leadership and transactional leadership on employee performance on Konawe Education Department at South East Sulawesi Province. *International Journal of Business and Management Invention*, *2*(12), 50–58.

Thite, M. (2000). Leadership styles in information technology projects. *International Journal of Project Management*, *18*, 235–241.

Tolentino, R.C. (2013). Organizational commitment and job performance of the academic and administrative personnel. *International Journal of Information Technology and Business Management*, *15*(1), 51–59.

Yeh, H. & D. Hong. (2012). The Mediating Effect of Organizational Commitment on Leadership Type and Job Performance. The Journal of Human Resource and Adult Learning, 8(2), 50–59.

Increasing Management Relevance and Competitiveness – Sukoco et al. (Eds)
© 2018 Taylor & Francis Group, London, ISBN 978-0-8153-7455-8

Transformational leadership style, team performance and team job satisfaction: Mediation by levels of cognitive trust and collective efficacy

P. Yulianti & R. Sanjaya
Universitas Airlangga, Surabaya, Indonesia

ABSTRACT: It is inevitable that the leadership of a team, if it is associated with the right team development process, will have a positive impact on the results of performance and job satisfaction in the team. The purpose of this study was to examine the relationship between transformational leadership and the performance of the team, as well as the level of team job satisfaction, the degree which is mediated by levels of cognitive trust in the team leader and among team members, and the collective efficacy of the team. The study was conducted in 12 branches of PT. Bank Mandiri Tbk, Surabaya, with research conducted with 86 departmental office staff and 32 divisional supervisors or managers of these staff. Partial least squares (via SmartPLS 3.0) was used as a statistical research tool. Based on the test results, transformational leadership was shown to have a positive and significant impact on cognitive trust in the team leader and among team members; cognitive trust in the team leader had a positive, but not significant, impact on collective efficacy, but cognitive trust among team members had as positive and significant impact on collective efficacy. Collective efficacy had a positive and significant impact on both team performance and team job satisfaction. In addition, the results showed that cognitive trust in the team leader was not a mediating variable between transformational leadership and collective efficacy; however, there was a different result with cognitive trust among team members, which was a mediating variable between transformational leadership and collective efficacy.

Keywords: Team, Transformational Leadership, Cognitive Trust, Collective Efficacy, Team Performance, Team Job Satisfaction

1 INTRODUCTION

Development in today's organizations is getting more and more complex, and there is a need for more effective ways of achieving goals and maximizing performance. One such way is the use of a team work system. Teamwork systems have become an important feature in various organizations (Cohen & Bailey, 1997). Cohen and Bailey (1997) stress the importance of team membership in achieving organizational success. The implementation of the team's working system has become an antecedent factor in team performance. The existence of the team has been an important factor in developments in the academic world and the practitioner community for some time. The performance of teamwork can be applied widely and is useful in various forms of organization and industry, one of which is the banking industry. The Executive Director of the Indonesian Bankers Association, in the book *Mengelola Kualitas Layanan Perbankan* (Managing Quality in Banking Services) (Sasmita, 2014), argues that if a task is done in the teamwork system, the team can perform its tasks and responsibilities well, and it will also have a positive impact on the performance results of the team and employees, as well as the level of employee satisfaction, both individually and at team level. This is in accordance with the results of research by Stewart & Barrick, (2000), found that the team can influence the results of the performance team, as well as the research results of Braun, et al. (2013), which described the influence on job satisfaction from teamwork. Good team performance is not fixed by the performance of a good and appropriate team leader and the processes that occur in the team. A team leader will play a central role in determining his or her group's work. According to Hartanto (2009), "transformational leadership is considered the right pattern to foster the passion and morale of members to respond to the challenges faced in the business world and contemporary workplace." Hartanto also states that "transformational leadership is briefly interpreted as a way of influencing others so that they want and have brought out their best virtues and capabilities in the process of value creation (performance or outcome). In addition to leadership factors that affect performance in the team, there are several other factors that also support the creation of performance in the team. The process is depicted in various forms, including the level of trust that members give to leaders and to fellow team members, and the emergence of a level of confidence in the ability of the team (collective efficacy). Among the process variables associated with the transformational leadership process, trust has been recognized as one of the most important factors that can mediate the effects of transformational leadership on team performance (Jung & Avolio, 2000; Braun et al., 2013; Zhu et al., 2013). With proper execution, the role of a transformational leader will result in a teamwork satisfaction level for transformational leadership (Belias & Koustelios, 2014). The influence of transformational leadership style on job satisfaction can be mediated by trust and collective efficacy (Walumbwa et al., 2004). The purpose of this study is to examine the relationship between a transformational leadership and team performance results and team job satisfaction level, mediated by trust in the team leader, as well as among the members, and by confidence in the joint ability (collective efficacy) of the team.

2 STUDY LITERATURE

2.1 *Transformational leadership style and cognitive trust*

Leadership is "the process of influencing individuals or groups to achieve group goals" (Hoyt & Blascovich, 2003). Transformational leadership affects subordinates by expanding and enhancing their goals and equipping them with confidence to accomplish achievements that exceed expectations, at least in accordance with acceptable expectations. Cognitive trust basically refers to an individual's belief in the reliability and dependence of their co-workers. Trust is a form of belief and a willingness to depend on others (McKnight, et al., 1998). When team members perceive a high level of trust in their interactions, they tend to devote more effort to cooperative behavior (Kramer et al., 1996). Therefore, trust is an important variable in explaining why team members are willing to complete their work together through teamwork.

H1a: Transformational leadership style has a positive and significant influence on the level of cognitive trust in the team leader.

H1b: Transformational leadership style has a positive and significant influence on the level of cognitive trust among team members.

2.2 *Cognitive trust and collective efficacy*

Collective efficacy is a shared belief among team members about the team's ability to complete an assigned task, which may arise from the creation of cognitive trust in the team. Several previous studies have examined trust and found that it is an antecedent variable to collective efficacy. Akgün et al. (2007) found that strong interpersonal trust increased collective efficacy in a team. They suggested that mutual trust among team members encourages them to collaborate more effectively. Kanawattanachai and Yoo (2007) suggest that cognitive trust underlies collective efficacy and other reliability to complete tasks.

H2a: Cognitive trust in the team leader has a positive and significant influence on collective efficacy.

H2b: Cognitive trust among team members has a positive and significant influence on collective efficacy.

2.3 *Transformational leadership style and collective efficacy are mediated by cognitive trust*

Researchers have shown that transformational leaders are associated with characteristics, such as ideal influences, intellectual stimulation, inspirational motivation and individual considerations, that can facilitate team members' trust in the leaders (Jung & Avolio, 2000) and mutual trust among team members (Zhu et al., 2013). When a team leader displays a transformational leadership style, team members will see a high level of cognitive trust within the team and will be more likely to understand others' 'ability and reliability' in performing the assigned tasks (McAllister, 1995; Kanawattanachai & Yoo, 2007). Thus, the cognitive trust team is associated with the collective success of the team in the transformational leadership process. In the study of leadership processes, belief in leaders is often found to mediate the relationship between leadership and outcomes (Jung & Avolio, 2000; Dirks & Ferrin, 2002; Dirks & Skarlicki, 2004). Dirks and Skarlicki (2004) argue that a team leader not only takes action to build team confidence in the team leadership, but also encourages the development of the necessary trust among team members to perform the tasks effectively.

H3a: Transformational leadership has an indirect effect on collective efficacy, mediated by cognitive trust in the team leader.

H3b: Transformational leadership has an indirect effect on collective efficacy, mediated by cognitive trust among team members.

2.4 *Collective efficacy and team performance; collective efficacy and team job satisfaction*

According to Hoegl and Gemuenden (2001), team performance refers to the extent to which teams can meet established goals of quality, cost and time. Jung and Avolio (2000) describe the concept of team performance as multidimensional and argue that there are three dimensions of team performance: quantity, quality and satisfaction.

Bandura, (1997) states that collective efficacy can be defined as the "sharing of group confidence in interrelated ability to organize and implement the program of action necessary to produce a certain level of achievement." In the transformational leadership process, as stated by Jung and Sosik (2002), collective efficacy has to do with team performance. Walumbwa et al. (2004) also showed that collective efficacy arose from the development of a team, and collective efficacy can mediate the impact of transformational leadership on performance.

Kozub and McDonnell (2000) argued that collective efficacy involves individual perceptions of the ability of the working group. When there is a strong level of collective efficacy, there will be a tendency for group members or organizations to be willing to devote more effort to achieving a common goal (Bandura, 1986). Previous research has shown that collective efficacy has a positive impact on team performance (Gully et al., 2002).

Several studies have also shown that team efficacy/collective efficacy are related to job satisfaction (Jex & Bliese, 1999; Jex & Thomas, 2003). It can be said that increasing collective efficacy in teams, marked by increased confidence and a sense of togetherness in the team, will have a positive impact on job satisfaction (team job satisfaction) in existing organizations or teams. A study conducted by Walumbwa et al. (2004) on collective efficacy found some factors that mediate the relationship between transformational leadership and satisfaction and commitment.

H4a: Collective efficacy has a positive and significant influence on team performance.
H4b: Collective efficacy has a positive and significant influence on team job satisfaction.

3 ANALYSIS MODEL

3.1 *Research methods*

The research method used was a quantitative one.

3.2 *Sample data*

Samples were taken from 12 branch offices of PT Bank Mandiri Tbk, Surabaya. The total sample was 32 teams, consisting of marketing teams, customer service teams and front office teams.

The respondent included 36 divisional leaders and 108 divisional staff. Returns were made by 32 divisional leaders and 86 divisional staff, giving response rates of 89% for divisional leaders and 79% for divisional staff. All of the returns were usable this research.

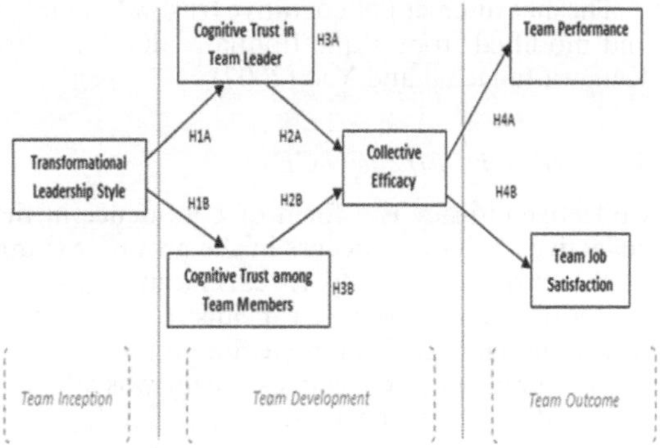

Figure 1. Research model.

3.2.1 *Analysis technique*

This research used the statistical analysis tool of Partial Least Squares (PLS), which is a method of Structural Equation Modeling (SEM) and is component and variable-based. The software used was SmartPLS.

4 MEASUREMENT

All measurements of the variables detailed below were assessed or measured using a 5-level Likert scale.

4.1 *Transformational Leadership Style (TL)*

The transformational leadership style is a leadership style involving leadership aspects that are charismatic, motivating or inspiring; leaders who create intellectual stimulation (problem solving).

The measurement of this transformational leadership style is adapted and modified from the Multifactor Leadership Questionnaire (MLQ) of Bass and Avolio (2000).

4.2 *Cognitive Trust (CT)*

Cognitive trust is a form of trust that is owned by an individual or team in relation to the existence and ability of someone. Cognitive trust is divided into two aspects: trust in a leader (CTL) and trust among fellow team members (CTM).

The measurement of cognitive trust was adapted and modified from a questionnaire developed by Kanawattanachai and Yoo (2007).

4.3 *Collective Efficacy (CE)*

Collective efficacy is a form of confidence in the collective ability that occurs in the group or team, in the effort and ability to carry out tasks and responsibilities, as well as a means to achieve and realize the same goals in the team.

Measurement of collective efficacy was adapted and modified from the questionnaire developed by Jung and Sosik (2002), and also from a questionnaire by Bandura (1986).

4.4 *Team Performance (TP)*

Team performance is the end result of what the team does in realizing team goals together. Team performance can be assessed in terms of efficiency and effectiveness. Efficiency refers to adherence to schedules and budgets. Effectiveness refers to the extent to which teams meet expectations about the quality of outcomes.

Measurement of team performance was adapted and modified from the questionnaire developed by Hoegl and Gemuenden (2001) and also that developed by Gemuenden and Lechler (1997).

4.5 *Team Job Satisfaction (TJS)*

Team job satisfaction is a manifestation of what has been done by the team and the performance produced. This is the sense of satisfaction and comfort in the work done, satisfaction with the work environment, and satisfaction with the results achieved in the team.

The measurement of job satisfaction was adapted and modified from the Job Diagnostic Survey questionnaire of the General Satisfaction dimension developed by Hackman and Oldham (1975).

5 MEASUREMENT RESULTS

5.1 *Convergent validity test, discriminant and model reliability*

A convergence validity test was conducted by looking at the factor loading of each indicator with a cutoff of >0.550. This was followed by a discriminant test using the result of the Average Variance Extracted (AVE) measurement with a cutoff of >0.50. We then reviewed the result of the cross-load factor for each indicator and the AVE root square value. After the convergence validity test and discriminant validity test were done, we continued with a reliability validity test by looking at the result of the composite reliability test. All test results could be described as valid and reliable in statistical terms.

5.2 *Hypothesis testing*

From the results shown in Tables 1 and 2, the results of the hypothesis test indicate five hypotheses (H1a, H1b, H2b, H4a, H4b) that have a positive relationship or influence (path coefficient) and have sufficient significance (t-statistic > 1.96 with p-value < 0.05). Basically, hypothesis H2a can also be said to be accepted because it has a positive relationship or influence, although the t-statistic is not significant (t-statistic < 1.96 with p-value > 0.05).

Thus we can say that: transformational leadership has a positive and significant influence on cognitive trust in team leader (H1a); transformational leadership has a positive and significant influence on cognitive trust among team members (H1b); cognitive trust among team members has a positive and significant influence on collective efficacy (H2b); collective efficacy has a positive and significant influence on team performance (H4a); collective efficacy has a positive and significant influence on team job satisfaction (H4b).

In the results of the PLS test shown in Table 3, it was found that there was no significant relationship between transformational leadership (TL) and collective efficacy (CE). Although there is an insignificant relationship between the variables of cognitive trust in team leader (CTL) and collective efficacy (CE), transformational leadership (TL) has a significant relationship to the cognitive trust in team leader (CTL) variable. Thus, it can be concluded that cognitive trust in team leader is not a mediating variable of the relationship between transformational leadership and collective efficacy (hypothesis H3a is rejected).

On the other hand, there was a significant relationship between cognitive trust among team members (CTM) and collective efficacy (CE), while transformational leadership (TL) has a significant relationship to cognitive trust in team

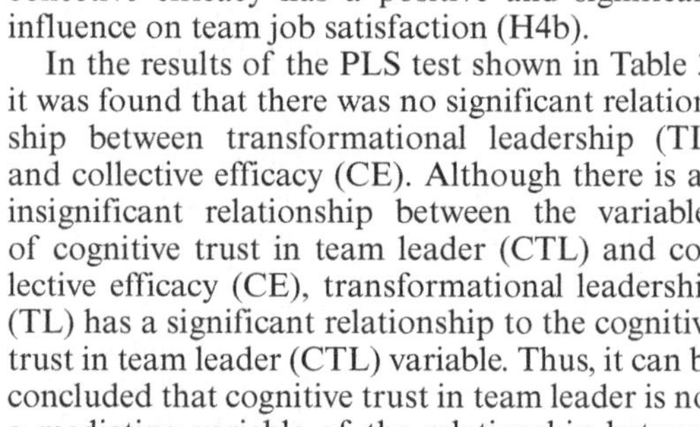

Figure 2. SmartPLS results.

Table 1. Path coefficient test results (Source: Processed from research data).

	Original sample (O)	Sample Mean (M)	Standard Deviation (STDEV)	T Statistics (|O/STDEV|)	P Values	Significant/ Not Significant
CE → TJS	0.544	0.555	0.126	4.323	0.000	Significant
CE → TP	0.345	0.382	0.110	3.126	0.000	Significant
CTL → CE	0.090	0.100	0.138	0.653	0.506	Not Significant
CTM → CE	0.546	0.534	0.142	3.851	0.000	Significant
TL → CTL	0.810	0.814	0.050	16.147	0.000	Significant
TL → CTM	0.585	0.593	0.078	7.510	0.000	Significant

Table 2. Hypothesis test results (Source: Processed from research data).

Hypothesis	Hypothesis influence among variables	Path coefficient	T Statistics (|O/STDEV|)	P values	Accepted/ Not Accepted
H4b	CE → TJS	0.544	4.953	0.000	Accepted
H4a	CE → TP	0.345	4.549	0.000	Accepted
H2a	CTL → CE	0.090	0.666	0.506	Not Accepted
H2b	CTM → CE	0.546	4.016	0.000	Accepted
H1a	TL → CTL	0.810	17.011	0.000	Accepted
H1b	TL → CTM	0.585	7.553	0.000	Accepted

Table 3. Path coefficient test results to determine mediation variables (Source: Processed from research data).

	Original sample (O)	Sample Mean (M)	Standard Deviation (STDEV)	T Statistics (|O/STDEV|)	P values	Significant/ Not Significant
CE → TJS	0.544	0.557	0.115	4.727	0.000	Significant
CE → TP	0.346	0.391	0.089	3.872	0.000	Significant
CTL → CE	−0.079	−0.069	0.139	0.567	0.571	Not Significant
CTM → CE	0.449	0.485	0.150	3.330	0.001	Significant
TL → CE	0.239	0.248	0.145	1.653	0.099	Not Significant
TL → CTL	0.809	0.814	0.047	17.248	0.000	Significant
TL → CTM	0.584	0.603	0.079	7.428	0.000	Significant

leader (CTL). Thus, it can be concluded that cognitive trust among team members (CTM) has become the mediation variable in the relationship between transformational leadership and collective efficacy (hypothesis H3b is accepted).

6 CONCLUSION

In summary: transformational leadership has a positive and significant influence on cognitive trust in the team leader; it also has a positive and significant influence on cognitive trust among team members. Cognitive trust in the team leader has a positive but insignificant effect on collective efficacy, whereas cognitive trust among team members has a positive and significant influence on collective efficacy. Collective efficacy has a positive and significant influence on both team performance and team job satisfaction. Cognitive trust in the team leader is not a variable that mediates the relationship between transformational leadership and collective efficacy, but cognitive trust among team members is.

REFERENCES

Akgün, A.E., Keskin, H., Byrne, J.C. & Imamoglu, S.Z. (2007). Antecedents and consequences of team potency in software development projects. *Information & Management*, *44*, 646–656.

Bandura, A. (1986). *Social foundations of thought and action*. Englewood Cliffs, NJ: Prentice Hall.

Bandura, A. (1997). *Self-efficacy: The exercise of control*. New York, NY: Freeman.

Bass, B.M. & Avolio, B.J. (2000). *MLQ: Multifactor leadership questionnaire*. Menlo Park, CA: Mind Garden.

Belias, D. & Koustelios, A. (2014). Transformational leadership and job satisfaction in the banking sector: A review. *International Review of Management and Marketing*, *4*(3), 187–200.
Braun, S., Peus, C., Weisweiler, S. & Frey, D. (2013). Transformational leadership, job satisfaction, and team performance: A multilevel mediation model of trust. *Leadership Quarterly*, *24*, 270–283.
Cohen, S.G. & Bailey, D.E. (1997). What makes teams work: Group effectiveness research from the shop floor to the executive, *Journal of Management*, *23*, 239–290.
Dirks, K.T. & Ferrin, D.L. (2001). The role of trust in organizational settings. *Organization Science*, *12*, 450–467.
Dirks, K.T. & Ferrin, D.L. (2002). Trust in leadership: Meta-analytic findings and implications for research and practice. *Journal of Applied Psychology*, *87*, 611–628.
Dirks, K.T. & Skarlicki, D.P. (2004). Trust in leaders: Existing research and emerging issues. In R.M. Kramer & K.S. Cook (Eds.), *Trust and distrust in organizations: Dilemmas and approaches* (pp. 21–40). New York, NY: Russell Sage.
Gemuenden, H.G. & Lechler, T. (1997). Success factors and project management: The critical few. In *Innovation in Technology Management—The Key to Global Leadership. PICMET '97: Portland International Conference on Management and Technology, Portland, OR, 27–31 July 1997* (pp. 375–377). doi:10.1109/PICMET.1997.653418.
Gully, S.M., Incalcaterra, K.A., Joshi, J.M. & Beaubien, J.M. (2002). A meta-analysis of team-efficacy, potency, and performance: Interdependence and level of analysis as moderators of observed relationships. *Journal of Applied Psychology*, *87*, 819–835.
Hackman, J.R. (1987). The design of work teams. In J.W. Lorsch (Ed.), *Handbook of organizational behavior* (pp. 315–342). Englewood Cliffs, NJ: Prentice Hall.
Hackman, J.R. (1990). Work teams in organizations: An orienting framework. In J.R. Hackman (Ed.), *Groups that work (and those that don't): Creating conditions for effective teamwork* (pp. 1–14). San Francisco, CA: Jossey-Bass.
Hackman, J.R. & Oldham, G.R. (1975). Development of the job diagnostic survey. *Journal of Applied Psychology*, *60*(2), 159–170.
Hartanto, F.M. (2009). The new paradigm Indonesian management. Bandung, Indonesia: Mizan Pustaka.
Hoegl, M. & Gemuenden, H.G. (2001). Teamwork quality and the success of innovative projects: A theoretical concept and empirical evidence. *Organization Science*, *12*, 435–449.
Hoyt, C.L. & Blascovich, J. (2003). Transformational and transactional leadership in virtual and physical environments. *Small Group Research*, *34*, 678–715.
Jex, S.M. & Bliese, P.D. (1999). Efficacy beliefs as a moderator of the impact of work-related stressors: A multilevel study. *Journal of Applied Psychology*, *84*, 349–361.
Jex, S.M. & Thomas, J.L. (2003). Relations between stressors and group perceptions: Main and mediating effects. *Work & Stress*, *17*, 158–169.
Jung, D.I. & Avolio, B.J. (2000). Opening the black box: An experimental investigation of the mediating effects of trust and value congruence on transformational and transactional leadership. *Journal of Organizational Behavior*, *21*, 949–964.
Jung, D.I. & Sosik, J.J. (2002). Transformational leadership in work groups: The role of empowerment, cohesiveness, and collective efficacy on perceived group performance. *Small Group Research*, *33*, 313–336.
Kanawattanachai, P. & Yoo, Y. (2007). The impact of knowledge coordination on virtual team performance over time. *MIS Quarterly*, *31*, 783–808.
Kozub, S.A. & McDonnell, J.F. (2000). Exploring the relationship between cohesive and collective efficacy in rugby teams. *Journal of Sport Behaviour*, *23*(2), 120–129.
Kramer, R.M., Brewer, M.B. & Hanna, B.A. (1996). Collective trust and collective action: The decision to trust as a social decision. In R.M. Kramer & T.R. Tyler (Eds.), *Trust in organizations: Frontiers of theory and research* (pp. 357–389). Thousand Oaks, CA: Sage.
McAllister, D. (1995). Affect- and cognition-based trust as foundations for interpersonal cooperation in organizations. *Academy of Management Journal*, *38*, 24–59.
McKnight, D.H., Cummings, L.L. & Cherany, N.L. (1998). Initial trust formation in new organizational relationships. *Academy of Management Review*, *23*, 473–490.
PT Bank Mandiri Tbk. (2013). *Annual report*. Surabaya, Indonesia: Bank Mandiri. Retrieved from http://ir.bankmandiri.co.id/phoenix.zhtml?c=146157&p=irol-reportsAnnual.
PT Bank Mandiri Tbk. (2015). *Annual report*. Surabaya, Indonesia: Bank Mandiri. Retrieved from http://ir.bankmandiri.co.id/phoenix.zhtml?c=146157&p=irol-reportsAnnual.
Sosik, J.J., Avolio, B.B. & Kahai, S. (1997). Effects of leadership style and anonymity on group potency and effectiveness in a group decision support system environment. *Journal of Applied Psychology*, *82*, 89–103.
Stewart, G.L. & Barrick, M.R. (2000). Team structure and performance: Assessing the mediating role of intrateam process and the moderating role task type. *Academy of Management Journal*, *43*, 135–148.
Walumbwa, F.O., Wang, P., Lawler, J.J. & Shi, K. (2004). The role of collective efficacy in the relations between transformational leadership and work outcomes. *Journal of Occupational and Organizational Psychology*, *77*, 515–530.
Zhu, W., Newman, A., Miao, Q. & Hooke, A. (2013). Revisiting the mediating role of trust in transformational leadership effects: Do different types of trust make a difference? *Leadership Quarterly*, *24*, 94–105.

Increasing Management Relevance and Competitiveness – Sukoco et al. (Eds)
© 2018 Taylor & Francis Group, London, ISBN 978-0-8153-7455-8

The impact of self-efficacy and perceived organizational support on operational managers' readiness to change

H. Prima & A. Eliyana
Universitas Airlangga, Surabaya, Indonesia

ABSTRACT: In the context of the Regional Water Supply Company in East Java, there should be efforts made to improve by way of organizational changes in order to build a sense of readiness for the operational managers to be the agents of change in the organization. This study will analyze the impact of self-efficacy and perceived organizational support on the operational managers' readiness to change in the Regional Water Supply Company. The inferential analysis used Structural Equation Modeling (SEM) with AMOS program version 19. The sample consisted of 130 operational managers in the Regional Water Supply Company in East Java, using census technique sampling. The data obtained from the questionnaire was withdrawn with a 5-point Likert scale. The research proved that self-efficacy had a positive impact on readiness to change. It also shows that perceived organizational support had an impact on readiness to change.

1 INTRODUCTION

Changes are important in an organization. They should be concerned with understanding the importance of change. Changes are one of the most critical aspects for effective management (Hussey: 2000). A change model is built from the observation that human behaviors are in accordance with the psychological balance, which sometimes comes from past observational learning and cultural effects, which tends to maintain the current behaviors.

Developing a complex organization dynamically creates challenges for the leaders. Leaders who act as agents for change in an organization are also known as managers. Mintzberg (1973) stated that there are ten roles of a manager in his or her workplace that are grouped into three categories: (1) Role between Individuals; (2) Informational Role and the (3) Decision-Making Role. Mintzberg then concluded that manager's activities are to interact with others.

The importance of the managers' readiness to change as agents of change becomes a measurement of the success of the changes in the organization itself. Rowden (2001) and Armenakis *et al.* (1993) stated that a key aspect of an effort of make changes in an organization, relating to the success or failure of the effort towards the changes, is related to the readiness to change between the organizational members. Lewin's Theory of Behaviors has been developed in to a function of the psychological behavior equation B = f (P, E) which explains that behavior is a function of a person and their environment as in Sansone's (2003) study. The equation function was developed by Bandura (1977), with a behavioral model formula, person, and environment that interact with one another as in the following Figure 1.

If social cognitive theory is combined with behavior theory, it can be concluded that the employees' readiness to change will be affected by the employees as individuals themselves and the organizational environment. The issue is also supported empirically in that readiness to change comes from a combination of personal characteristics and the organization (Madsen, 2003; George and Jones, 2001).

The Regional Water Supply Company in East Java is a Regionally-Owned Enterprise which has been demanded to improve in order to face the globalization era in the context of the ASEAN

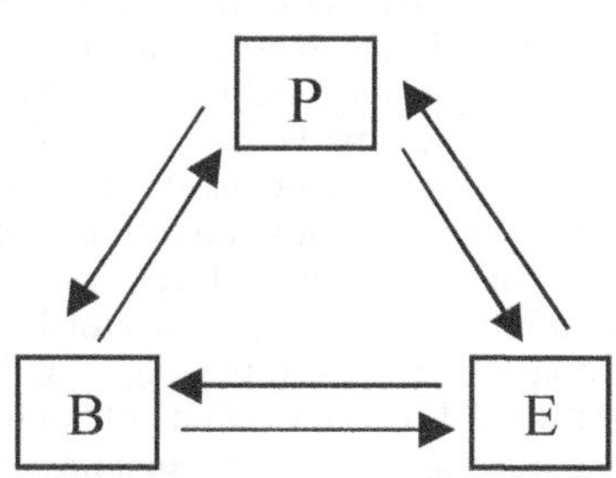

Figure 1. Triadic reciprocal determinism.
Source: Bandura, A. (2001). Social Cognitive Theory of Mass Communication. *Media Psychology*, 3(3), 265–299.

Economic Community (AEC) in 2015. In implementing the improvements in the organization and in the services in the Regional Water Supply Company especially in the East Java region, it needs to have readiness in its human resources and also in its organizational management system. This goal can be achieved if the managers have the role of being trainers, counselors, advisors, and agents for change. Operational managers are demanded by the wider community to be capable of facing organizational changes through their readiness to change, referencing the theory of behavior by Bandura (1977). Behaviors are formed by two factors which are the individual and the environment. Based on the discussion regarding the importance of the mangers' readiness for organizational changes as stated above, this research study hopes to describe the condition of the operational managers' readiness to change that happened in the Regional Water Supply Company in East Java. The focus of this research is the operational managers' readiness to change at the Regional Water Supply Company in East Java that is affected by the variable of self-efficacy and also the variable of perception of the organizational support available.

2 LITERATURE REVIEWS AND HYPOTHESES DEVELOPMENT

2.1 *Organizational changes*

Changes are global phenomena that are unpreventable, so every organization should make changes to follow and anticipate the changes in their external environment, both internally and externally. Organizational changes are not simple processes, since organizational changes are about changes in organizational performance. The changes are a transformation that is planned or unplanned in the organizational structure, technology, and/or a person (Greenberg and Baron, 2003). Agents of changes are people who act as a catalyst and have the responsibility to manage the changes (Robbins, 2009). It is hoped that they are capable to handle the problems happening, including resistance. Kurt Lewin is one of the experts that stated the idea that changes are a process that consists of three phases: unfreezing, changing, and refreezing. *Unfreezing* refers to create motivation and readiness to change in organization. *Changing* is a stage of learning in which employees are given new information, new behavioral model, or new means of seeing cases. *Refreezing* is a stage of changes that are stabilized. Schematically, the process of change model by Lewin can be developed in the following figure:

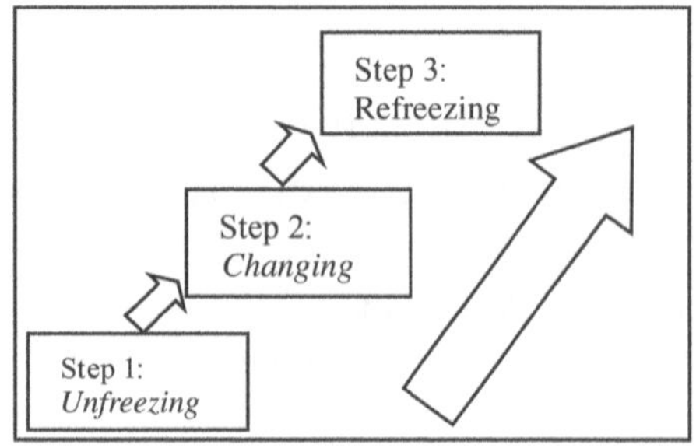

Figure 2. Lewin's change model.
Source: Greenberg and Baron, 2003, *Behavior in Organization*. New Jersey: Prentice Hall International, Inc.

Lewin's Change Model was developed through the observation that human behaviors are formed based on psychological balance, in which the behaviors are formed by past observational learning and cultural effects that tend to maintain the current behaviors.

2.2 *Readiness to change*

Readiness to change is the comprehensive attitude simultaneously affected by changing matters, how changes are made, a condition when changes happen, and a person's characteristics that demands to make changes together as a reflection of the cognitive aspects and also the individuals' emotions to prefer to accept and adopt changes made for handling current conditions (Holt *et al.*, 2007). The individual's readiness to change is defined as their willingness to be open to changes (Jones, Jimmieson, Griffiths: 2005; Eby *et al.*, 2002), cognitively and emotionally (Holt, Armenakis, Harris, and Field, 2006). The individual's readiness to change reflects their thoughts, feelings, and intentions that may or may not cause certain behaviors related to their attitudes (Desplaces, 2005). On the other hand, Armenakis et al. (1993) defined individual readiness for change as people's beliefs, attitudes and intentions regarding the extent to which changes are needed and their perception of the individual and organizational capacity to successfully make those changes. In the organizational context, the individual's readiness to change is defined as the individual's willingness to participate in an organization's activities during changes taking place within the organization (Huy, 1999).

2.3 *Self-efficacy*

The formal definition of self-efficacy that is commonly used is a statement by Bandura regarding the assessment or personal belief of "how good a person can act as needed to connect with prospective situation" (Bandura, 1982).

Self-efficacy and a more accurate understanding of positive organizational behaviors are stated by Stajkovic and Luthans to refer to the individual's belief in the capability to mobilize their motivation, cognitive resources, and actions as needed, so that he or she successfully executes their duties in a certain context (Stajkovic and Luthans, 1998). Then, it can be concluded that the leaders' self-efficacy is the individual's belief in their capabilities as leader, and also the trust of their leadership supported by senior leaders, colleagues, facilities, and the resources in the environment.

Bandura (1977) stated some dimensions of self-efficacy which are magnitude, generality, and strength. Magnitude is related to the level of difficulties in certain duties that are done. Generality, related to the field of duties, this is how deep an individual believes in doing the duties. Strength is related to how strong or how weak the individual's belief is. Some empirical studies have already examined self-efficacy as a precursor to building readiness for changes. Cunningham *et al.* (2002) showed that employees with a high level of self-efficacy have a high level of readiness to reverse engineer a hospital. Judge *et al.* (1999) studied generally on self-efficacy in the context of changes and found out that self-efficacy has a positive influence related to handling changes. Self-efficacy, as the capability for success in managing changes, has a mediator effect towards the individual's readiness (Prochaska *et al.*, 1997). Another research about the readiness of employees to change by Rafferty and Simons (2006) focused on self-efficacy, trust in their colleagues, logistics, and a support system. Holt *et al.* (2007) studied the employees' belief, self-efficacy, appropriateness, management support, and personal valence. The studies showed that self-efficacy has a positive influence towards employee readiness.

The researcher thus has made the following hypothesis:

H1: Self-Efficacy has positive and significant effect on readiness to change.

2.4 *Perception of organizational support*

The theory of organizational support explains the interactions between individuals and the organization, especially studies on how an organization treats their employees. Organizational support is a level of how deep the employees believe that the organization respects their contribution and cares about their welfare (Robbins and Judge: 2009).

Related to this case, Eisenberger *et al.* (1986); Shore and Shore (1995) and Rhoades and Eisenberger (2002) stated that in order to meet the needs of socio-emotions and to assess the benefits of an improvement in performance, the employees create a general perception to the extent of how an organization respects their contribution and cares about the employees' welfare, which is called organizational support.

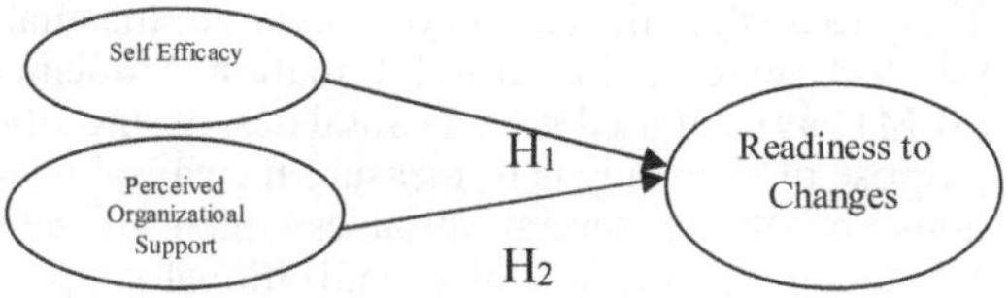

Figure 3. Conceptual research model.

A meta-analysis by Rhoades and Eisenberger (2002) indicated that there are three main categories of treatment that are viewed by the employees as having a relationships with the perception of organizational support.

The three main categories are as follows: *Justice,* stated that employees will evaluate organizational justice in relation to three classifications of different phenomena, which are the results that they get from the organization (distributive justice), formal policy or the process in which an achievement is allocated (procedural justice), and how the decision makers treat the personnel in an organization (interactional justice) (Cropanzano *et al.*, 2000). Second, *leaders' support*, employees develop their general view about how far the leaders assess their contributions and care about their welfare. And the last, *awards from an organization and condition* of a job.

In the context of changes, the individuals' belief assesses that an organization (leaders and colleagues) will give real support to the changes in the form of resources and information. This belief will provide a contribution towards the individuals' perception regarding their success or capability to apply the changes (Rafferty *et al.,* 2002). It can be concluded that the perception of organizational support has a contribution towards readiness to change.

Empirically, Rafferty and Simons (2005), and also Desplaces (2007), found out that perceived organizational support has a positive effect on readiness to change. Based on the above discussion, this research study has proposed the following hypotheses:

H2: Perceived organizational support has a positive significant effect on readiness to changes.

Figure 3 shows the proposed model based on the above literature review.

3 METHODOLOGY

This research study has been conducted to analyze and prove the effects of exogenous variables towards the endogenous variable. These variables are latent variables that are formed by several indicators.

Then, to analyze the data in this research, the analysis technique of Structural Equation Modeling (SEM) has been used with a causal design since the purpose of the study is to measure the causal relationship between several variables which are self-efficacy, the perception of organizational support and the operational managers' readiness in the city Regional Water Supply Company in East Java.

3.1 *Sample*

The sample in this research are operational managers, with the census sample method involving 130 operational managers who work in the Regional Water Supply Company in East Java. The data used in this research is primary data using the method of questionnaires to collect the data. A pilot study was conducted to ensure that all of the questions were understandable and to establish the content validity of the questionnaire. A total of 130 questionnaires were collected in the study and were usable in the analysis.

3.2 *Measurements*

The analysis technique used to test the hypotheses in this research study was Structural Equation Modeling (SEM) with the AMOS 5 method. All of the construct measurements involved in this study were adapted from the previous literatures. The questions of the constructs were measured using a 5-point Likert scale ranging from 1 (strongly disagree) to 5 (strongly agree). There were six items used to measure the self-efficacy of Bandura (1977). There were six items to measure the perceived organizational support of Rhoades and Eisenberger (2002), and six items to measure the readiness to change of Rafferty et al. (2012). The questionnaire items were based on the literature review with some modifications according to the objectives of this study.

4 RESULT AND DISCUSSIONS

The demographic analysis of the sample shows that it consisted of 96 (74%) males and 34 (26%) females. The respondents ranged in age from 26 to 35 years old (10%), 36 to 45 years old (46.92%) and 46 to 55 years old (43%) respectively. Almost all of the employees were of college or university education level. Moreover, more than 10 years working experience in PDAM was held by 86.92% of all of the respondents. Construct reliability was assessed using Cronbach's alpha coefficient. Table 1 presents the summary of the goodness of fit testing and the level of the goodness of the structural model. The Structural Equation Model (SEM) was employed

Table 1. Results of Goodness of Fit (GOF) testing and the level of good fit of structural model.

GOF standards	Targets of Good fit	Estimation results	Levels of Good fit
Chi Square	Lower than 13.848	$X^2 = 41.099$	Marginal fit
P	(p = 0.05, df = 24)	P = 0.016	Marginal fit
CMIN/DF	<5	1.712	Good fit
GFI	GFI ≥ 0.90	0.936	Good fit
RMSEA	RMSEA ≤ 0.08	0.074	Good fit
P (close fit)	P ≥ 0.05	0.146	Good fit
ECVI	Lower than ECVI saturated and independence	D* = 0.644 S* = 0.698 I* = 4.073	Good fit
TLI	TLI ≥ 0.90	0.946	Good fit
AGFI	AGFI ≥ 0.90	0.881	Marginal fit
IFI	IFI ≥ 0.90	0.965	Good fit
CFI	CFI ≥ 0.90	0.964	Good fit
AIC	Score which is lower than AIC saturated and independence	D* = 83.099 S* = 90.000 I* = 525.379	Good fit
CAIC	Score which is lower than CAIC saturated and independence	D* = 164.317 S* = 264.039 I* – 560.187	Good fit

(D* = Default, S* = Saturated, I* = Independence).
Sources: *Model Fit Summary.*

to test the overall model fit and the hypothesized relationships of all the variables in the entire model with the use of AMOS 5.0.

4.1 *Structural Equation Model (SEM)*

Structural equation model analysis was intended to test the model and hypotheses developed in this research study. Structural equation model testing is done through two tests which are model compatibility testing and quality significance testing in relation to regression co-efficiency. Structural model analysis is done to test the effect of self-efficacy and the perception of organizational support towards readiness to change.

Table 1 illustrates the structural equation model with parameter estimates. The fit indices adopted in this study were the comparative goodness of fit index (GFI), the adjusted goodness of fit index (AGFI), and the root mean square error of approximation (RMSEA). All of the goodness-of-fix indices in this study were based on the criteria recommended by Hair et al (2006). The results of the goodness of the fit testing of the structural model are as follows:

4.2 *Test of hypotheses*

The results of the structural model analysis in Figure 4 shows all of the impact included in the

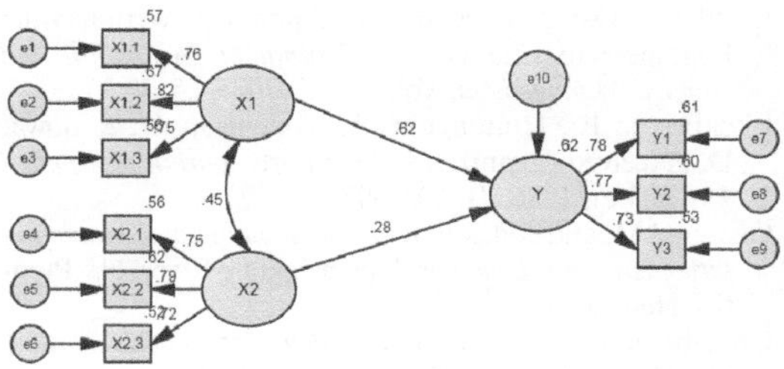

Figure 4. Results of structural equation model testing.

hypothesized direction. The impact of self-efficacy on readiness to change was positively significant (standardized regression weight score 0.619, $p < 0.05$). The results indicate that if operational managers have high self-efficacy, there is more readiness to change. The results was consistent with the previous literature studies of Cunningham *et al.* (2002), Judge *et al.* (1999), Prochaska *et al.* (1997), Rafferty and Simons (2006). The research showed that self-efficacy has a positive influence towards employee readiness. Thus hypothesis H_1 was supported. The study confirms that an employee with high self-efficacy (Magnitude is related to the level of difficulties in certain duties done. Generality is related to the field of the duties, and how deep an individual believes in doing their duties; and strength is related to how strong or weak the individual's belief is) is also a positively significant effect towards readiness to change. Moreover, the impact of perceived organizational support on readiness to changes was also positively significant (standardized regression weight score 0.282 and $p < 0.05$). The study confirms that if employees believe that their organization supports them and cares for their well-being, this will increase the readiness for changes. The results was consistent with the previous literature of Rafferty *et al.,* (2002), Rafferty and Simons (2005), and also Desplaces (2007). Empirically, it has already been found out that perceived organizational support has a positive effect on readiness to change. It can be concluded that the perception of organizational support has a contribution towards readiness to change.

4.3 *Research implications*

The importance of readiness to change for the employees' performance, when organizational changes happens, becomes a measurement towards the success of the organizational change. The case stated by Rowden (2001) and Armenakis *et al.* (1993) is a key aspect of the effort of organizational change which is related to the success or failure of the efforts of the changes themselves, in which it is readiness for change between organizational members that matters. Readiness to change is defined as how far employees tend to support changes (Zalno, 2008). The understanding of readiness to change according to Armenakis *et al.* (1993: 681) is that readiness for change is defined as the employees' beliefs and attitudes regarding the extent to which the changes are needed and the organization's ability to successfully complete the intended change.

From the understanding above, it is known that the employees' readiness to change is affected by the employees' individual factor and the organizational factor. Several research studies have already been done in the management context of change that discusses about the employees' readiness to change with the supporting factors that include individuals and the working environment, in which one of the research studies was done by Miller *et al.* (2006). They studied the management relationship between leaders, working knowledge, skill, and working demands; Rafferty and Simons (2006) focused on self-efficacy, trust in colleagues, logistics, and supporting system; the research by Holt *et al.* (2007) was about the employees' belief, self-efficacy, management support, and personal valence. In the research studies, all of the variables have a positive influence towards the employees' readiness to change.

This study proposes a simple and practical model that helps decision makers and senior managers to highlight the most influential factors to increase readiness to change in their operational managers as agents of change. The results of this study show that self-efficacy significantly affects the operational managers' readiness to change in the Regional Water Supply Company in East Java. The effect of self-efficacy towards the readiness to change is positive; it means that if self-efficacy improves, then the readiness to change improves as well. This is as the second hypothesis states that the perception of organizational support significantly affects the operational managers' readiness to change at the Regional Water Supply Company in East Java. The effect of the perception of organizational support is positive; it means that if the perception of organizational support improves, then the readiness to change improves as well. The paper may contribute towards the management teams in relation to making appropriate training schemes for operational managers to improve their self-efficacy. It will also help in determining the type of organizational support (justice, leader supports and reward system) that is needed for the operational managers as agents of change.

4.4 *Research limitations and future directions*

The research findings contribute to the aforementioned theoretical and practical implications. This study has suffered from a few limitations. The results are not generalizable since we examined only the operational managers in a regional water supply company in East Java and it might have a different result in relation to other positions and conditions. Therefore, some suggestions for future researchers have been provided. Firstly, besides the factors discussed in this study, there are other factors which may influence the employee's attitude, and the organization's commitment to job performance. The researcher can incorporate different factors such as social or psychological well-being to discuss in future research.

5 CONCLUSION

In this research, it can be concluded that the operational managers' readiness to change at the Regional Water Supply Company in East Java is affected by self-efficacy as an individual factor and the perception of organizational support as an environmental factor. Self-efficacy has the highest value related to the operational managers' capability to finish a job with a certain level of difficulty. On the other hand, the perception of organizational support has the highest value related to the operational managers' perception of awards from the organization. In line with this case study, it is known that to improve the operational managers' readiness in facing changes, it is necessary to have an individual factor which is the operational managers' self-efficacy and the environmental factor of the organization itself. It is also needed to improve the awards for employees, especially for the operational managers as the agents of change.

REFERENCES

Armenakis, A., Harris, S., & Mossholder, K. *Creating readiness for organizational change. Human Relations*, 46(6), 1993, 681–703.

Bandura, A. *Self-efficacy: Toward a unifying theory of behavioral change*. Psychological Review, 84(2), 191–215.

Bandura, A. 1982. "Self Efficacy Mechanism in Human Agency" American psychologist, Vol.37, 1977 hlm 122.

Bandura, A. Self Efficacy: The Exercise of control, op.cit., Social Cognitive Theory: An Agentic Perspective,"*Asian Journal of Sosial Psychology*, Vol. 2, 1999, hlm 21.

Cropanzano, R., Prehar, C.A., & Chen, P.Y. *Using social exchange theory to distinguish procedural from interactional justice*. Group & Organization Mangement, 2000.

Cunningham, C.E., Woodward, C.A., Shannon, H.S., MacIntosh, J., Lendrum, B., Rosenbloom, D., & Brown, J. Readiness for organizational change: A longitudinal study of workplace, psychological and behavioral correlates. *Journal of Occupational and Organizational Psychology*, 75, 2002, 377–392.

Desplaces, David. A Multilevel Approach to Individual Readiness to Change. *The Journal of Behavioral and Applied Management*, Vol. 7 No.1, 2005, 25–39.

Eisenberger, R., Huntington, R., Hutchison, S., & Sowa, D. Perceived organizational support. *Journal of Applied Psychology*, 1986, 71, 500–507.

George, J.M. and Jones. G.R. *Understanding and Managing Organizational Behavior*, Upper Saddle River. NJ: Prentice Hall, 2002.

Greenberg, J. and R.A. Baron. *Behavior in organization*. New Jersey: Prentice Hall International, Inc, 2003.

Hair, J.F., Black, W.C., Babin, B.J., Anderson, R.E., & Tatham, R.L. *Multivariate Data Analysis*, (6th ed.), Prentice Hall. Englewood Cliffs, NJ, 2006.

Holt, D., Armenakis, A., Harris, S., & Feild, H. Toward a comprehensive definition of readiness for change: A review of research and instrumentation. *In W. Pasmore & R. Woodman (Eds.), Research in organizational change and development* (Vol. 16). Oxford: Elsevier Science, 2006.

Hussey, D.E. *How to Manage Organizational Change*. London: Kogan Page, Ltd, 2000.

Judge, T., Higgins, C., Thoresen, C., & Barrick, M. 1999. The big five personality traits, general mental ability, and career success across the life span. *Personnel Psychology, 52, 621–652.*

Madsen, S. A Model for individual change: Exploring its application to human resource development. *Human Resource Development Review, 2(3), 2003, 229–251.*

Mintzberg, H. *The Nature of Managerial Work*. New York: Harper & Row, 1973.

Paul, JP. *Efficacy of Human Resources as Change Agents*, Walden University, 2002.

Prochaska, J.O., Redding. C.A., & Evers, K. The transtheoretical model of change. In K. Glanz, E.M., Lewis & B.K. Rimer (Eds), Health behewior and health education: Theory, research, and practice (pp. 60–84), San Erancisco: Jossey-Bass, 1997.

Rafferty, A.E., & Simons, R.H. An examination of readiness for fine-tuning and corporate transformation changes. *Journal of Business and Psychology*, 20, 2006, 325–350.

Robbins, Stephen P. & Judge Timothy A. Perilaku Organisasi, Edisi 12 Buku 1, salemba empat: Jakarta, 2009.

Rhoades, L., & Eisenberger, R. Perceived organizational support: A review of the literature. *Journal of Applied Psychology*, 87, 2002, 698–714.

Rowden, R. The learning organization and strategic change. *S.A.M. Advanced Management Journal*, 66(3), 2001, 11–24.

Sansone, C.; C.C. Morf, A.T. Panter. *The Sage Handbook of Methods in Social Psychology*. Sage. ISBN 0-7619-2535-X, 2003.

Shore, L.M., & Shore, T.H. *Perceived organizational support and organizational justice*. In R.S. Cropanzano & K.M. Kacmar (Eds.), *Organizational politics, justice, and support: Managing the social climate of the workplace* (pp. 149–164). Westport, CT: Quorum, 1995.

Stajkovic Alexander D dan Fred Luthans. "The Relationship between Self Efficacy and Work Reated Performance: A Meta-Analysis, *"Psychological Bulletin,"* Vol. 124, No. 2, hlm. 1998, 240–261.

Wanberg, C.R., & Banas, J.T. Predictors and outcomes of openness to changes in a reorganizing workplace. *Journal of Applied Psychology*, 85, 2000, 132–142.

Marketing management

Increasing Management Relevance and Competitiveness – Sukoco et al. (Eds)
© 2018 Taylor & Francis Group, London, ISBN 978-0-8153-7455-8

Factors affecting customer retention in a priority banking program

I.R. Aliyah, S. Soebandhi & A. Baktiono
Universitas Narotama, Surabaya, Indonesia

ABSTRACT: Free trade has touched the banking industry in the ASEAN region. Hence, the banking industries in Indonesia inevitably have to improve their performance in order to compete among ASEAN countries. One way to deal with this competition is to implement Customer Relationship Management (CRM) in order to maintain good relationships with customers, thereby winning their loyalty to the bank. This study was intended to analyze the effect of CRM, through bonding, empathy, reciprocity, trust and responsiveness variables, towards customer retention. The survey was conducted at one of the banks in Surabaya, specifically on priority banking customers. From the 66 questionnaires distributed, we obtained 49 valid data. The data were analyzed by multiple linear regression analysis using SPSS. The results showed that bonding, trust and responsiveness have a significant effect on customer retention. Meanwhile, empathy and reciprocity showed no significant effect on customer retention.

Keywords: Bonding, Customer Retention, Customer Relationship Management, Empathy, Reciprocity, Responsiveness, Trust

1 INTRODUCTION

In 1967, Indonesia joined the ASEAN (Association of South East Asian Nations), which involves co-operation among the countries of Southeast Asia (ASEAN, 2016). Co-operation between the countries in the ASEAN region continued with the implementation of the ASEAN Economic Community (AEC) in January 2016 (ASEAN, 2015). Therefore, the competition will now be more intense as the competition covers various ASEAN countries. Free trade in the ASEAN region also applies to the banking industry. The Indonesian banking sector should improve its performance in order to compete and the role of banks in creating products and services that are highly competitive is very important. In order to survive or to beat the competition in the AEC, banks need to elaborate their competences, mitigate their weaknesses, and identify opportunities and threats. For this purpose, banks have to be creative in conducting their business and seek new breakthroughs that can run alongside their core business strategy.

Under these conditions, Customer Relationship Management (CRM) needs to be implemented and managed seriously. CRM involves knowing each customer by creating a two-way communication and maintaining a mutually beneficial relationship between the customer and the company (Chan, 2003). Furthermore, Famiyeh et al. (2015) explain that CRM is a 'systematic relationship' to prevent our customers from dealing with our competitors, retain them and attract more potential customers. Banks that implement CRM consistently are expected to increase customer retention. Kotler and Keller (2012) state that CRM is closely related to customer retention. A higher level of CRM could lead to higher customer satisfaction, which could result in higher customer retention.

Furthermore, maintaining existing customers by establishing a good relationship with them is the essence of relationship marketing (Lo, 2012). Given the importance of corporate understanding of factors that may affect customer retention, this study aims to analyze the dimensions of CRM in relation to customer retention in the banking sector.

2 LITERATURE REVIEW

2.1 *Customer Relationship Management (CRM)*

Kotler and Keller (2012) define CRM as a process of managing detailed information on individual customer touchpoints in order to maximize customer loyalty. As for banks, the touchpoints may include their website, self-service machines, call centers, bank cards, customer assistants, mobile applications, and so on. This can provide an experience for customers with the services and service providers, and thus may affect their opinion of the service and service providers/company (Clatworthy, 2011). According to Famiyeh et al. (2015), CRM is a systematic relationship that aims to prevent existing customers from switching to another company and to attract new customers. This systematic relationship is described as an organized relationship, both implicit and explicit, within the company. Meanwhile, Chan (2003) stated that CRM involves knowing every customer more closely, by creating a two-way communication and maintaining a mutually beneficial relationship between the customer and the company.

Based on the explanation above, CRM can be defined as a marketing effort that creates a closer relationship between companies and consumers through a mutually beneficial relationship. This relationship can be fostered through a variety of physical facilities, particularly intensive communication between company and consumer.

2.2 *CRM dimension*

Ndubisi (2007) measures relationship marketing through the dimensions of trust, commitment, communication, and conflict handling. Trust is the belief that a partner's word or promise is trustworthy and he/she will fulfill his/her obligations in the relationship (Schurr & Ozanne, 1985). Calonius (1988) argued that marketing is responsible for not only making promises and persuading customers, but also for keeping its promises to maintain and enhance the evolving relationship. Commitment, as defined by Moorman et al. (1992), is the willingness to maintain a valuable relationship. Communication refers to the ability to present timely and reliable information (Ndubisi, 2007). It is an interactive dialog between the company and its customers during all stages of selling (Anderson & Narus, 1984). Conflict handling is related to the ability of suppliers to avoid possible conflicts, resolve conflicts, and discuss solutions to problems that arise (Rusbult et al., 1988).

Famiyeh et al. (2015) propose several dimensions derived from previous studies when describing CRM for customer retention. According to them, CRM consists of bonding, empathy, reciprocity, trust, and responsiveness. Bonding is a dynamic process that continues to evolve over time. Bonding significantly controls the social behavior of business in society. The bonding that exists between the organization and the customer helps to eliminate hesitance, boost confidence and foster a close relationship. Bonding is very good for establishing long-term relationships. Empathy is a situation where each party involved in a relationship is viewed from the viewpoint of the other with regards to thinking, feeling and emotion.

Meanwhile, according to Kotler and Keller (2012), empathy is the willingness to give depth and special attention to each customer. Reciprocity is based on the ability of each party to create pleasant conditions, so that each party can receive the same pleasure in the present and in the future. Trust is described as a belief or conviction that a party is interested in continuing the relationship. Trust is set as the degree to which each party can rely on the integrity and promises made by the other party in the relationship. Trust is widely recognized as an indicator to measure the business relationship. Responsiveness is a desire to help consumers and to provide services as soon as possible. Responsiveness is the dimension of CRM that is based on the organization's ability to respond to changing market conditions and to enhance the customer's choice, satisfaction, and loyalty. Responsiveness also means the willingness to help customers and provide immediate services (Kotler & Keller, 2012).

Based on the theoretical foundation and the conceptual framework described, we propose the following hypotheses:

H1: CRM that consists of bonding, empathy, reciprocity, trust, and responsiveness has a simultaneous influence on customer retention

H2: CRM that consists of bonding, empathy, reciprocity, trust, and responsiveness has a partial effect on customer retention

3 METHODOLOGY

This study was conducted at one branch office of the Regional Owned Enterprises (BUMD) in Surabaya. The respondents were all customers of the bank's priority programs, amounting to 66 customers. The sampling technique used was the census technique, due to the limited number of respondents (Kriyantono, 2008). Questionnaires were distributed to each priority customer who came to the branch office in the period from January to March 2017. Of the 66 questionnaires

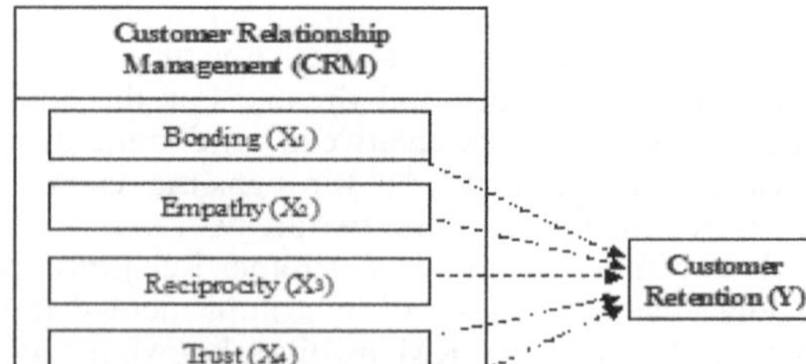

Figure 1. Conceptual framework.
Source: Famiyeh et al. (2015).

distributed, only 49 questionnaires were returned and can be processed further.

The data for a total of 24 items was analyzed using SPSS 23.0 statistical software. Variables were measured using a 5-point Likert scale, ranging from 1 (Strongly disagree) to 5 (Strongly agree). The hypotheses were tested with linear regression model analysis.

4 RESULT

The validity test indicates that each variable has a good validity. This is indicated by the r value, which is supported by the level of significance (p) < 0.05. In this study, the comprehensive reliability of all variables are between 0.603 and 0.759, which means that all of the variables had exceeded the minimum required level of coefficient (Cronbach $\alpha > 0.60$), which indicated that this scale has consistency reliability.

Table 1 presents the descriptive analysis of the respondents, indicating their gender, marital status, age, education, and occupation. The percentage of female customers is slightly different to that of male customers. The percentage of respondents aged between 36–45 years was 45%. They were mostly married, with 32% having an undergraduate/vocational education, and of the 49 respondents, 20 respondents or 40.8% are self-employed. And as shown in Table 2, it is inferred that each variable has a partial effect on customer retention, except for empathy (X2) and reciprocity (X3)

Table 3 showed that the H1 is rejected and H2 is accepted. This can be seen from the F value whose value is greater than the value of F distribution table (F value: 16.462; F distribution table: 2.432 at a significance level of 0.000). In other words, it is evident that simultaneously the independent variables in this study, which consist of bonding (X1), empathy (X2), reciprocity (X3), trust (X4), and responsiveness (X5), significantly affect the dependent variable, customer retention (Y).

Table 1. Demographic information of respondents.

Characteristics description		Frequency	Percentage
gender	male	23	47%
	female	26	53%
marital status	single	12	24%
	married	37	76%
age (years)	18–25	1	2%
	26–35	12	24%
	36–45	22	45%
	> 45	14	29%
education	high school	14	29%
	undergraduate/ vacational	32	65%
	post-graduate	3	6%
occupation	house wife	5	10,2%
	public sector	9	18,4%
	private sector	14	28,6%
	self-employed	20	40,8%
	student	1	2,0%

Table 2. Partial correlation test.

Model		t	Sig.
1	(constant)	2.562	0.014
	bonding (×1)	2.265	0.029
	empathy (×2)	1.641	0.108
	reciprocity (×3)	0.312	0.756
	trust (×4)	3.662	0.001
	responsiveness (×5)	3.465	0.001

[a]Dependent variable: Customer retention (y).

Table 3. Anova.

ANOVA[b]

Model		Sum of squares	df	Mean square	F	Sig.
1	regression	87.776	5	17.555	16.462	0.000[a]
	residual	45.857	43	1.066		
	total	133.633	48			

a. Predictors: (constant), responsiveness (×5), trust (×4), empathy (×2), bonding (×1), reciprocity (×3)
b. Dependent variable: customer retention (y).

5 DISCUSSION AND CONCLUSION

This finding implies that bonding, trust and responsiveness significantly affect customer retention. This is consistent with Famiyeh et al. (2015) and Yau et al. (2000). Contrary to the hypothesis, empathy and reciprocity have no significant effect on customer retention.

Research by Kuranchie (2010) argued that the empathy dimension is still questionable in building relationships between consumers and companies. This is because, from the beginning, consumers have been expecting companies to understand their problems and provide solutions. Therefore, they no longer expect special treatment from the company (Climis, 2016). Even further, in the study by Famiyeh et al. (2015), the validity test on empathy suggests that there is no internal consistency; therefore, empathy was not included in their research.

Although many previous studies have suggested that reciprocity is an important factor for determining long-term relationships with customers, studies by Kucukkancabas et al. (2009) and Serviere-munoz and Counts (2014) also found that reciprocity showed no significant effect on customer retention. This can be explained by the fact that if a consumer has felt the reciprocity with the company, then it can determine the satisfaction level of both parties (Blau, 1964; Gelbrich et al., 2016). Therefore, reciprocity is no longer an important factor in customer retention.

Although our research provides interesting results for understanding factors that may affect customer retention, this study also has its limitations. This research was conducted only in one branch office with a limited number of respondents; using more than one branch office or using several different banks for further research will be useful to analyze whether or not the results of this study can be generalized to the situation in other banks.

REFERENCES

Anderson, J.C. & Narus, J.A. (1984). A model of the distributor's perspective of distributor-manufacturer working relationships. *Journal of Marketing*, *48*(4), 62–74.

ASEAN. (2015). *ASEAN Economic Community (AEC)*. Jakarta: Association of Southeast Asian Nations (ASEAN).

ASEAN. (2016). *History: The founding of ASEAN*. Retrieved November 21 2016 from: http://asean.org/asean/about-asean/history/.

Blau, P.M. (1964). *Exchange and power in social life*. New York: John Wiley & Sons.

Calonius, H. (1988). A buying process model. In K. Blois & S. Parkinson (Eds.), *Innovative marketing–A European perspective, Proceedings from the XVIIth Annual Conference of the European Marketing Academy* (pp. 86–103). University of Bradford.

Chan, S. (2003). *Relationship marketing: Inovasi pemasaran yang membuat pelanggan bertekuk lutut [Marketing innovation that will make customer kneel before you]*. Jakarta: PT Gramedia Pustaka Utama.

Clatworthy, S. (2011). Service innovation through touch-points: Development of an innovation toolkit for the first stages of new service development. *International Journal of Design*, *5*(2), 15–28.

Climis, R. (2016). Factors affecting customer retention in the airline industry. *Journal of Management and Business Administration*, *24*(4), 49–69. Retrieved from http://doi.org/10.7206/jmba.ce.2450-7814.182.

Famiyeh, S., Ahafianyo, J.T. & Benneh, B. (2015). Customer relationship management and customer retention: Evidence from a bank in Ghana. *International Journal of Electronic Finance*, *8*(2/3/4), 202–217.

Gelbrich, K., Gäthke, J. & Grégoire, Y. (2016). How a firm's best versus normal customers react to compensation after a service failure. *Journal of Business Research*, *69*(10), 4331–4339. Retrieved from http://doi.org/10.1016/j.jbusres.2016.04.010.

Kotler, P. & Keller, K. (2012). *Marketing management* (14th ed.). Upper Saddle River, NJ: Prentice Hall.

Kriyantono, R. (2008). *Teknik praktis riset komunikasi [Practical techniques of communication research]*. Surabaya: Kencana Prenada Media Group.

Kucukkancabas, S., Akyol, A. & Ataman, B.M. (2009). Examination of the effects of the relationship marketing orientation on the company performance. *Quality and Quantity*, *43*, 441–450. Retrieved from http://doi.org/10.1007/s11135-007-9119-x.

Kuranchie, F.K. (2010). *The effect of customer relationship marketing on customer retention in the Ghanaian banking sector: A case of Intercontinental Bank Ghana Limited*, Blekinge Institute of Technology, Blekinge, Sweden Blekinge, Sweden.

Lo, S.C. (2012). A study of relationship marketing on customer satisfaction. *Journal of Social Sciences*, *8*(1), 91–94.

Moorman, C., Zaltman, G. & Deshpande, R. (1992). Relationships between providers and users of market research: The dynamics of trust within and between organizations. *Journal of Marketing Research*, *29*(3), 314–328.

Ndubisi, N.O. (2007). Relationship marketing and customer loyalty. *Marketing Intelligence & Planning*, *25*(1), 98–106.

Rusbult, C.E., Farrell, D., Rogers, G. & Mainous, A.G. (1988). Impact of exchange variables on exit, voice, loyalty, and neglect: An integrative model of responses. *Academy of Management Journal*, *31*(3), 599–627.

Schurr, P.H. & Ozanne, J.L. (1985). Influences buyers' on exchange processes: A preconceptions of seller's toughness trustworthiness and bargaining toughness. *Journal of Consumer Research*, *11*(4), 939–953.

Serviere-munoz, L. & Counts, R.W. (2014). Recruiting millennials into student organizations: Exploring Cialdini's Principles of Human Influence. *Journal of Business and Economics*, *5*(3), 306–315. Retrieved from http://doi.org/10.15341/jbe(2155-7950)/03.05.2014/002.

Yau, O.H.M., McFetridge, P.R., Chow, R.P.M., Lee, J.S.Y., Sin, L.Y.M. & Tse, A.C.B. (2000). Is relationship marketing for everyone? *European Journal of Marketing*, *34*(9/10), 1111–1127. Retrieved from http://doi.org/10.1108/03090560010342494.

Increasing Management Relevance and Competitiveness – Sukoco et al. (Eds)
© 2018 Taylor & Francis Group, London, ISBN 978-0-8153-7455-8

The impact of messages assertiveness on compliance with perceived importance as a moderation variable on the anti-cigarette campaign in Surabaya

Kristiningsih, R.S. Wuryaningrum & A. Trimarjono
University of Wijaya Kusuma Surabaya, Surabaya, Indonesia

ABSTRACT: Cigarettes consumption can cause diseases. The Ministry of Health launched Public Service Ads containings testimonials from former smokers who suffered from throat cancer, which were made in the context of the "Stop Enjoying Cigarettes before Cigarettes Enjoy You" campaign. The campaign's success or failure cannot be separated from the strategy of how to communicate the campaign program to the right targets. There are several ways that effective message delivery techniques can be applied in accordance with the targets market. Assertiveness communication is the ability to communicate what one wants, feels, and thinks, but still maintain and respect the rights and feelings of others. This research aims to find out the impact of assertive messages on consumers' compliance by seeing the moderate effect of perceived importance of the anti cigarette campaign in Surabaya. The population of this study is active smokers in Surabaya, people who are either still actively smoking now or who are trying to stop smoking, the statistical test used is Moderating Regression Analysis (MRA). The research results indicate that message assertiveness has a significant influence on levels of compliance and it also shows that perceived importance is the moderating variable that links message assertiveness and compliance.

Keywords: message assertiveness, compliance, perceived importance, moderating regression analysis

1 INTRODUCTION

Marketing communication is an important aspect of the overall marketing mission, as well as the determinant factor of marketing success. Marketing communications can also be understood by describing two basic elements, namely communication and marketing.

There are several effective message delivery techniques that can be applied, according to the target market. To build effective communication, the method of delivering messages or information needs to be carefully designed so that it can be adjusted to the characteristics of the person being informed as well as the circumstances of the social environment concerned. However, the success of communication is partially determined by the power of the message itself. With the message, one can control the attitude and behavior of the communicants. There are several ways to communicate the message; Aggressive Communication, Passive Communication (Submissive) and Assertive Communication.

Assertive communication is an open communication that stands up for one's point of view, while also respecting the rights and beliefs of others. Assertive communication is not merely concerned with to the final result, but also the emotion of the message receiver. Assertiveness is an ability to communicate what one wants, feels, and thinks; nevertheless it still maintains and respects the rights and feelings of others.

Many various communication researches have shown the weakness of assertive phrases used in persuasion, such as in the following researches; consumer behavior and psycholinguistics (e.g. Dillard & Sheen, 2005; Dillard et al., 1997; Edwards, Li & Lee, 2002; Gibbs, 1986; Holtgraves, 1991), the more people see a cause as important, the more they obey the message that promotes the cause (Clark, 1993; Clarck, 1998; Cleveland et al., 2005), compliance with messages that encourage environmentally responsible behavior is related to important consumer goals (Goldstein et al., 2008; Granzin & Olsen, 1991; Grinstein & Nisan, 2009).

Various forms of anti-smoking campaigns have been delivered in various ways; assertively, non-assertively, aggressively or passively. But the effectiveness of delivering messages to its target market still needs to be further evaluated. The purpose of this research is to find out the impact of assertive messages on consumers' compliance by seeing the moderate effect of perceived importance of an anti-cigarette campaign in Surabaya.

2 THEORETICAL BACKGROUND

2.1 *Message assertiveness*

Assertive communication is a way of communicating that shows one's self-respect, as well as respect for the rights of others, concern for others and empathy, but still refers to the ultimate goal (goals do not change). In the dictionary, the word assertive means firm and assertiveness is firmness. But in the literature of education, the word assertive itself is interpreted as the courage to state what is thought honestly and openly without disturbing the relationship. Assertive communication does not only concern the final result (Kronrod, 2012).

There are seven characteristics of assertive communication. They are being open and honest with the opinions of oneself and others, listening to other people's opinions and understanding them, expressing personal opinions without sacrificing other people's feelings, seeking joint solutions and decisions, respecting oneself and others, overcoming conflict, expressing personal feelings, being honest but being careful, and lastly, maintaining self-righteousness (Sarafino, 2007).

2.2 *Compliance*

Compliance is a form of indirect social influence by others. Compliance refers to how an individual affirms or rejects other people's requests. Compliance is one of the many psychological constraints studied in social psychology, especially prosocial behavior as introduced by Robert B. Cialdini, a professor of psychology and marketing who conducted the study through direct observation.

The definition of obedience comes from the basic obedient, which means discipline and obedience (Niven, 2002), whereas according to Bastable (2002), it is a term that describes obedience or surrender to a predetermined goal.

Normally, people more often affirm the requests of others, although actually they want to refuse them. What factors can increase or decrease an individual's compliance to perform the action requested? In several of Robert B. Cialdini's studies, he concludes that there are many compliance techniques that are actually based on the basic principles. The basic principles of compliance are as follows (Cialdiani in Sarwono, 2009): Friendship or likes, Commitment or consistency, Scarcity, Reciprocity, Social validation and Authority.

2.3 *Perceived importance*

Perceived importance is important in the delivery of marketing communications. Perceived importance indicates how important a certain problem is to the consumer and how much consumers are involved in it.

Perceived importance involves underpinning consumers' acceptance of communication messages. In the acceptance of the communication process, consumers sometimes comply to both important and unimportant messages. The findings on Kronrood's et al. (2012) research indicates that if the problem is not recognized as important, the communication receiver will see a message/communication and tend to stick with it.

2.4 *Hypothesis building*

Some literature shows that when a problem is considered as important, then the message becomes meaningful. However, on the other hand, when the problem is considered unimportant, the message becomes meaningless. The key idea is that issues that are perceived as important also affect linguistic expectations. Firmness can support perceived urgency and influence ideas that cover important issues. Therefore, the message's languages, expectations, and bold requests need to be more persuasive when the recipient also views the issues as important (Burgoon et al., 1994).

Fazio (1986, 1995) argues that strict language is more likely to be used in cases where it is in line with established attitudes. Conversely, weak and polite requests in this context may be considered irritating or "too polite" (Lakoff & Sachiko 2005; Tsuzuki, Miamoto, and Zhang 1999). This, in turn, reduces compliance because nonassertive languages are not in tune with the perceived importance of the problem.

H1: Message assertiveness has a significant effect on the level of customer compliance.
H2: Perceived importance has a significant effect on consumer compliance.
H3: Perceived importance moderates the influence of message assertiveness to consumer compliance.

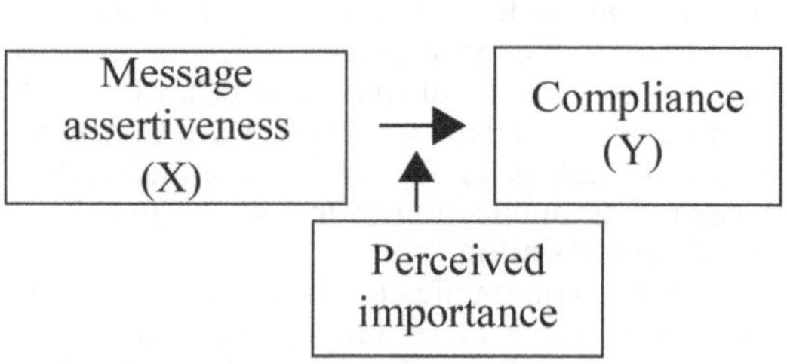

Figure 1. Conceptual framework.

3 RESEARCH METHOD

3.1 *Population and sample*

The population of this study is active smokers in Surabaya, who are either still actively smoking or who are trying to stop smoking. This research used non-probability sampling with a purposive sampling method, and a sample determination technique with certain consideration. So the data obtained are more representative due to conducting a competent research process in their field (Sugiyono, 2013). The sample criteria used are: active smokers, age of respondents 17 years and over, men, knowing the anti-smoking campaign program.

3.2 *Variables and their measurements*

1. *Message assertiveness (X)* is the consumer's assessment of anti-cigarette campaign messages conveyed in a strict language. It was measured by three indicators (Burgoon et al., 1994)
2. *Compliance l(Z)* refers to the extent to which a consumer accepts or rejects a request to comply with a message to quit smoking. It was measured by six indicators (Cialdiani, 2009)
3. *Perceived importance (Y)* is the consumers' perception of the importance of the issue in question. When the consumers feel that the problem is important to them and they have a high involvement in the problem then the consumers will tend to behave/respond to it. It was measured by two indicators.

When the questionnaires were distributed, the respondents were given cognitive treatment by given shown the examples of anti-smoking campaign scripts or taglines from the government in order to facilitate their understanding of the assertive message in question. The questions in the questionnaire were made using the Likert scale (1–5) which has five levels of preferences (5: Favourable to 1 Unfavorable).

3.3 *Analysis technique*

In accordance with the purpose of the research, which was finding out the impact of the independent variable, of message assertiveness on the level of compliance by looking at the moderation effects of the perceived importance variable, then the statistical test used is Moderating Regression Analysis (MRA).

4 RESULT OF RESEARCH

Of the 100 respondents who met the criteria specified in the study, only 94 respondents filled in the questionnaire completely. The remaining six respondents did not fill it in completely, so that the respondent's answer was cancelled for further processing in this study.

Table 1. Table of regression test result.

	Unstandardized coefficients		Standardized coefficients		
Model	B	Std. Error	Beta	t	Sig.
1 (Constant)	9.824	2.315		4.243	0.000
message	−2.060	0.572	−1.397	−3.604	0.001
importance	−1.487	0.748	−1.229	−1.987	0.050
xz	0.464	0.186	1.759	2.503	0.014

- Partially message assertiveness (X) variable has a significant effect on compliance (Y),
- Partially variable of perceived importance (Z) has a significant influence on compliance (Y),
- Partially multiplication between variable of message assertiveness (X) with variable of perceived importance (Z),
- The perceived importance (Z) variable is a moderation variable,
- It can be known that all the significant values are equal to or less than 0.05.

The R Square used in the test is 0.359, which shows that from the equation 35.9% of the compliance change value (Y) is influenced by both of the variables studied, while the rest, 0.641 or 64.1%, are influenced by other variables that are not in the research model.

The results of the moderation regression testing conducted with the help of the SPSS (Statistical Program for Social Science) computer program for Windows obtained the following regression equation:

$$Y = 9{,}824 - 2{,}060\ X - 1{,}487\ Z + 0{,}464\ XZ$$

5 IMPLICATION, CONCLUSION AND LIMITATION

5.1 *Implication*

From the results of this research in the previous sub-chapter, it can be seen that the message assertiveness (X) variable has a significant effect on compliance (Y), and that perceived importance (Z) variables significantly influence compliance (Y). This means that when the consumer sees an assertive advertising campaign with straightforward language prohibiting people from smoking, consumers are becoming less compliant. A call to force people to quit smoking makes consumers reluctant to comply with the invitation, even though they know that the invitation is for their own good. This is in accordance with the findings obtained in previous research which shows the weakness of assertive phrases used in persuasion, such as in the following researches; consumer behavior and psycholinguistics (e.g. Dillard & Sheen, 2005; Dillard et al., 1997; Edwards, Li & Lee, 2002; Gibbs, 1986; Holtgraves, 1991), and that messages/prohibitions that are open (assertive) tend to make people become reluctant to comply with the ban. Managerial implications that could be drawn from this research are that it is a good idea to ban coercive messages or to use a call to not smoke that is not assertive.

The perceived importance (Z) variable significantly affects the compliance (Y) and a negative value means that when a consumer considers himself to have no involvement with a cigarette problem or assumes a cigarette problem is not an issue that matters to him, he will obey the prohibition to quit smoking. On the other hand, if the consumer feels the cigarette problem is important to him and he is involved with the problem of cigarettes, then he becomes disobedient to the smoking ban.

Perceived importance is a moderating variable that links between the message assertiveness and compliance variables. It means that when the consumer sees an assertive advertisement message to ban smoking, the consumer becomes disobedient to the smoking cessation and the correlation becomes stronger when the consumer feels that the cigarette problem is not important to him and he is not involved in it.

This study supports the findings of Kronrood's (2012), which indicate that if the problem is not recognized as important, the communication receiver will see a message and stick with it. Someone will comply with an invitation/ban depending on how important the problem is to him/her.

5.2 *Conclusion*

From the research results and discussion described in the previous section, several conclusions can be drawn from the study as follows:

1. Message assertiveness significantly influences compliance on anti-smoking advertising campaigns in Surabaya.
2. It is found that perceived importance significantly influences compliance on anti-smoking campaigns.
3. It is found that perceived importance is the moderating variable that correlates the message assertiveness toward compliance in the anti-smoking campaigns.

5.3 *Limitations and further research*

From the study results, discussion and conclusions that have been described in the previous section, some suggestions can be given for further research. They are:

1. Further research should be able to examine the factors of the demographic characteristics of the respondents such as age, family and education background, as a valence moderator that affect compliance.
2. The subsequent research can also expand the objects of the research into two groups of consumers such as consumers, who are still actively smoking and those who have stopped smoking.
3. There is a limited data collection procedure in distributing questionnaires and showing video advertising campaigns directly to each consumer, so that the respondents were not treated equally or not conditioned in the same circumstances.

REFERENCES

Bastable. (2002). Nurse as Education. Jakarta: EGC.

Burgoon, M. Hunsaker, F.G. & Dawson, E.J. (1994). Approaches to gaining compliance. In Human Communication (3rd ed.) (pp. 203–217) Thousand Oaks, CA: Sage Publications.

Cialdini, R.B. & Goldstein, N.J. (2004). Social influence: Compliance and conformity. *Annual Review of Psychology, 55: 591–621.*

Clark, A.R. (1993) The impact of cost of compliance, deservingness of aid, and directness of request on reactions to the request, *Souther Communication Journal, 58(3), 215–26.*

Clark, T. (1998). The impact of candid versus legally defensible language on the persuasiveness of environmental self-assessments. *Journal of Business Communication, 35(3), 368–83.*

Cleveland, M., Kalamas, M. & Laroche, M. (2005). Shades of green: Linking environmental locus of control and pro-environmental behaviors. *Journal of Consumer Marketing, 22(4), 198–212.*

Dillard, J.P. & Shen, L (2005). On the nature of reactance and its role in persuasive health communication. *Communication Monographs, 72(2), 144–68.*

Fazio, R.H. (1986). How do attitudes guide behavior? in Handbook of motivation and cognition: Foundations of social behavior, Richard M. Sorrentino and Tory E. Higgins, eds. New York: Guilford Press, 204–243.

_____ (1995). Attitudes as object-evaluation associations: Determinants, consequences, and correlates of attitude accessibility in Attitude Strength: Antecedents and Consequences, Richard E. Petty and Jon A. Krosnick, eds. Hillsdale, NJ: Lawrence Erlbaum Associates, 247–82.

Gibbs, R.W. (1986). What makes some indirect speech acts conventional? Journal of Memory and Language, 25 (April), 181–96.

Goldstein, N.J., Cialdini, R.B. & Griskevicius, V. (2008). Norms to motivate environmental conservation in hotels. *Journal of Consumer Research, 35(3), 472–82.*
Government Regulation No 109/2012 About Anti-Cigarette Campaign.
Grandpre, J., Eusebio M.A., Burgoon, M., Miller, C.H., & Hall, J.R. (2003). Adolescent reactance and anti-smoking campaigns: A Theoretical approach. Health Communication, 15(3), 349–66.
Granzin, K. & Olsen, J. (1991). Characterizing participants in activities protecting the environment: A Focus on donating, recycling, and conservation behaviors. Journal of Public Policy & Marketing, 10 (Fall), 1–27.
Grinstein, A. & Nisan, U. (2009). Demarketing, minorities and marketing attachment. Journal of Marketing, 73 (April), 105–122.
Khasali, R. (2007). Advertising Management, Concepts and Application in Indonesia. Jakarta: Grafiti.
Kronrod A., Grinstein, A. & Wathieu, L. (2012). Go green! Should environmental messages be so assertive? *Journal of Marketing Vol. 76: 95–102.*
Lakoff, R.T. & Sachiko, I. (2005). *Broadening the horizon of linguistic politeness, Pragmatics and beyond New Series 139*. Amsterdam/Philadelphia: John Benjamins.
Li, H. & Lee J.H. (2002). Forced exposure and psychological reactance: Antecedents and consequences of the perceived instrusiveness of pop-up ads. Journal of Advertising, 31 (Fall), 83–95.
Niven, N. (2002). Health Psychology. Jakarta: EGC.
Sarafino & Slamet B. (2007). General Psychology. Bandung: PT Remaja Rosdakarya.
Sarwono, S.W., & Meinarno, E.A. (2009). Social Psychology, Salemba Humanika, Jakarta.
Shimp, T.A. (2003). Advertisement and Promotion, Erlangga, Jakarta.
Sugiyono (2013). Quantitative qualitative research method. Bandung: Alfabeta.
Tsuzuki, M., Miamoto, S., & Zhang, Q. (1999). Politeness degree of imperative and question request expressions: Japanese, English, Chinese. in Sixth International Colloquium on Cognitive Science–ICCS99. Tokyo: Japanese Cognitive Science Society, 519.

Increasing Management Relevance and Competitiveness – Sukoco et al. (Eds)
© 2018 Taylor & Francis Group, London, ISBN 978-0-8153-7455-8

Demographic variables and environmentally friendly behavior in a developing country

T. Handriana
Universitas Airlangga, Surabaya, Indonesia

ABSTRACT: The purpose of this study to examine and analyze the relationship between demographic variables and environmentally friendly behavior (buying environmentally friendly products; using environmentally friendly products; using own bags when shopping to the supermarket/market; sifting through garbage in the house; turning off the lights when leaving the room; switching from conventional products to environmentally friendly products; and inviting others to consume environmentally friendly products). This study uses a survey research approach. The number of samples is as many as 319 people, and analyzed with Chi-Square technique. The result of the study indicates the categories of age, sex, marital status, number of children, education level, occupation and, income and number of respondents indicates that the relationship varies on environmentally friendly behavior. Expected results of this study can be used as a reference by the government in environmental policymaking, as well as the benefits for the company/organization in offering products/services that are environmentally friendly.

1 INTRODUCTION

In this century, the threats to the environment on earth have soared, with the depletion of natural resources, the depletion of the ozone layer, and the further constriction of agricultural land. One of the solutions is that consumers begin to switch to environmentally friendly behavior, for example by using transportation and household products that are environmentally friendly. One type of environmentally conscious behaviors is called environmental consumerism or green buying.

The threat of environmental damage is felt by all the inhabitants of the earth; therefore, scientists and practitioners of marketing management have initiated the concept of green marketing and green buying. Ironically, in developing countries such as Indonesia, public awareness of environmental and health damage is still relatively low. Likewise, the research related to green marketing and green buying in developing countries are still relatively little.

Pride and Ferrell (1993) explained that green marketing is also known as sustainable marketing, which refers to organizational efforts on designing, promoting, pricing and distributing products that will not harm the environment. Meanwhile, Schlegelmilch, Bohlen, and Diamantopoulos (1996) classify green products into common green products, recycled paper products, animal-nontested products, environmentally-friendly detergents, organic fruits and vegetables, ozone-friendly aerosols, and energy-efficient products. Today, the green marketing strategy is a new mantra for marketers to produce recycled products, non-toxic products, and environmentally friendly products to meet customer need, and to make profit on a large scale (Patil, 2012).

The demographic factor is a characteristic inherent in human life, which will lead to one's knowledge, attitude and behavior. Demographic factors, which include age, gender, marital status, numbers of children, education level, occupation type and amount of income, are predicted to affect the behavior of purchasing green products, reflected in environmentally friendly behavior. Harris et al. quoted in Kaufmann, Panni, and Orphanidou (2012) revealed that environmentally conscious consumers are whites, women, professionals and young people. As for Ottman, Stafford, and Hartman (2006) explained that young people are better prepared than the older generation to receive new and innovative ideas. This is also strengthened by Schwepker and Cornwell (1991) who state that supporters of environmental protection tend to be younger in age. Therefore, this study focuses on the influence of demographic factors on environmentally friendly behavior.

The purpose of this study to analyze relationship between demographic variables and environmentally friendly behavior in a developing country.

2 LITERATURE REVIEW AND HYPOTHESIS DEVELOPMENT

2.1 *Green marketing*

Green marketing has been defined as all activities designed to generate and facilitate any exchange intended to meet human needs or desires, in order to provide satisfaction, with minimal adverse impact on the natural environment by Polonsky (2011). Meanwhile, Saini (2013) explained that green marketing is the process of selling goods and/or services based on environmental benefits, in which the goods or services themselves are environmentally friendly as well as products produced and/or packed in an environmentally friendly behavior.

The concept of green marketing has existed since at least the first Earth Day in 1970. However, despite reports that environmental concerns are one of the top public concerns, market growth for green products is disappointing, and far from marketers' expectations (Wong, Turner, and Stoneman, 1996). From the mid-1990s, consumers began to become more and more environmentally friendly and socially conscious (Strong, 1996). During this period, critical consumers began to emerge as a new force of green consumerism and social responsibility of a company (Gurau and Ranchhod, 2005). Meanwhile, green consumers are defined as people who avoid products that may endanger the health of consumers or others; cause significant damage to the environment during manufacture, disposal use, consuming a disproportionate amount of energy; and cause unnecessary waste, using materials from threatened environment or species (Strong, 1996). Sharma (2011) explains that green consumers focus on the following activities: product purchases, such as detergents, which have reduced environmental impacts; avoiding products with aerosols; purchase of recycled paper products (such as toilet paper and paper for writing); purchasing organic products; purchasing locally produced food; purchasing from local stores; looking for products that use less packaging; and using their own bags instead of using plastic ones supplied by the store.

2.2 *Green buying*

Green buying is defined as purchasing and consuming friendly/beneficial products for the environment. Elkington (1994) defines green consumers as a behavior that avoids products that are likely to harm the health of consumers or others, do not cause significant damage to the environment, use energy for advertising in proportionate amounts, are non-hazardous waste, and do not use ingredients derived from rare species or environments.

Kim and Choi quoted in Kaufmann, Panni, and Orphanidou (2012) explain that the public's attention to environmental issues slowly but surely has improved over the past three decades since the beginning of Earth Day, namely the interest of the people to conserve nature and biodiversity. Meanwhile, Cherian and Jacob (2012) revealed that raising awareness on various environmental issues has led to a shift in consumers' way of thinking about their lives. There has been a change in consumer attitudes towards a green life style. People are actively trying to reduce their impact on the environment. However, this is not widespread and is still developing. Organizations and business however have seen a change in consumer attitudes and strive to gain excellence in a competitive market by exploiting the potential in the green market industry. Green consumerism is described as a concept that can be seen from different perspectives, including environmental conservation, minimizing pollution, responsibility for the use of non-renewable resources, and the welfare of animal preservation and endangered species (McEachern and McClean, 2002).

2.3 *Demographic factors*

Research on environmentally friendly consumer behavior has been a major concern of researcher, based on the benefits of study findings for companies to understand the factors which influence consumer behavior. The findings of the study show that consumers have become more aware and concentrate on environmental impacts when they buy a product (Makeower, 2009). Meanwhile, Makeower (2009) finds that demographic factors, which include age, education level, and income level are closely related to perceptions of environmentally friendly products which will ultimately be needed by businessmen.

The relationship between demographic factors with behavior and environment (environmental behaviors) was studied in the 1970s, findings indicating that consumers' desire to buy environmentally friendly products is closely related to demographic factors (Fisher, Basyal, and Bachman, 2012). The findings of a study conducted by Diamantopoulos et al. (2003) indicate the inconsistency of the findings of a study which examined the relationship between demographic factors and environmentally friendly behaviors. Meanwhile, Robert (1990) explained that green behavior is influenced by age, education level, and income level.

2.4 *Research hypotheses*

H1: There are differences in people's behavior in consuming environmentally friendly products based on their age.

H2: There are differences in people's behavior in consuming environmentally friendly products based on their gender.

H3: There are differences in public behavior in consuming environmentally friendly products based on their marital status.

H4: There are differences in community behavior in consuming environmentally friendly products based on the number of children they have.

H5: There are differences in community behavior in consuming environmentally friendly products based on their level of education.

H6: There are differences in community behavior in consuming environmentally friendly products based on their type of work.

H7: There are differences in people's behavior in consuming environmentally friendly products based on their income.

3 METHODOLOGY

Independent variables include age, gender, marital status, number of children, education level, occupation type and amount of income. The dependent variable is environmentally friendly behavior. Independent variables and dependent variable in this research are measured by using nominal scale (categorical). The dependent variable is measured by two categories, namely 1 = Yes, and 2 = No. The sample unit in this study is an individual. The used sampling technique is purposive sampling. Data are collected by cross-sectional approach. Data were collected by survey by distributing questionnaires to a number of respondents directly. Chi-Square Technique is used as data analysis.

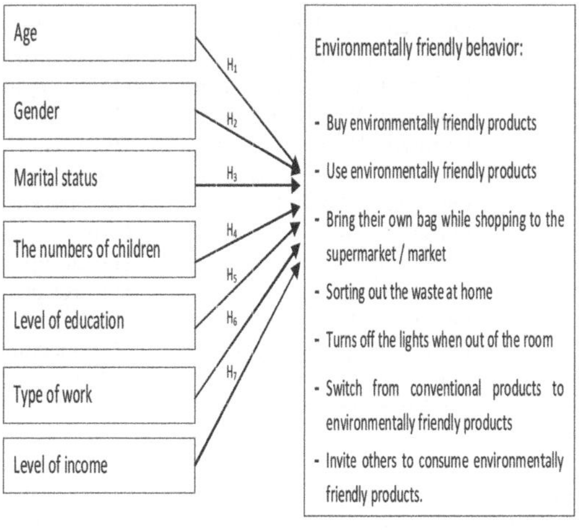

Figure 1. Research model.

4 FINDING AND DISCUSSION

After selecting the 330 questionnaires successfully distributed to the study respondents, only 319 questionnaires we eligible for processing or 96.67%. The findings using Chi Square with a significance level of 5% are as in Table 1.

From the table, it is seen that 37 supported/accepted hypotheses, meanwhile, there are 12 unsupported/rejected hypotheses. The accepted hypotheses are shown from the Chi-Square significance level of the findings if the data is <0.05. The correlation relationship between independent variable and dependent variable is seen from the value of contingency coefficient; if the value of contingency coefficient of >0.5 then a conclusion can be drawn of a strong relationship between the independent variable and the dependent variable.

In the relationship between age and environmentally friendly behavior variables, there are six supported hypotheses, namely the relationship between age with the purchase of environmentally friendly products, the use of environmentally friendly products, using their own bags while shopping, turning off the lights when leaving the room, and the intention to switch consumption from conventional products to green-friendly products. The strong relationship is seen in the age and the purchase of environmentally friendly products variables, as well as the relationship between age and the use of environmentally friendly products variables. Meanwhile, the hypothesis testing the relationship between age and willingness to invite others to make purchases of environmentally friendly products is not supported.

The findings of hypothesis testing above show that there are differences in community behavior in the use of environmentally friendly products, their own bags while shopping, sorting the waste before disposal, turning the lights off when leaving the room, switching from conventional products to green products, and willing to invite people (17 years - 20 years; 21 years - 30 years; 31 years - 40 years; 41 years - 50 years; and over 50 years). As for the action to invite others to behave in an environmentally friendly behavior, it appears that there is no difference between the respondents' age categories. In the hypothesis test findings to see the relationship between gender variables and environmentally friendly behavior, it appears that only five supported hypotheses, namely the relationship between respondents' gender with the purchase of environmentally friendly products, the use of environmentally friendly products, using their own bags while shopping, turning off the lights when going in and out of the room, and switching from conventional to environmentally friendly products. Meanwhile, there are two unsupported hypotheses

Table 1.

Hypothesis	Inter-variable relations	Level of Sig.	Coefficient-Contingency	Description	Conclusion
H1a	Age & Purchase	0.000	0.056	Different; Strong relationship	H1a accepted
H1b	Age & Use	0.000	0.591	Different; Strong relationship	H1b accepted
H1c	Age & Bag	0.000	0.494	Different; Weak relationship	H1c accepted
H1d	Age & Waste	0.000	0.266	Different; Weak relationship	H1g accepted
H1e	Age & Lights	0.000	0.494	Different; Weak relationship	H1e accepted
H1f	Age & Product	0.000	0.381	Different; Weak relationship	H1f accepted
H1g	Age & WoM	0.900	0.157	Not different	H1d rejected
H2a	Gender & Buy	0.000	0.381	Different; Weak relationship	H3a accepted
H2b	Gender & Use	0.001	0.181	Different; Weak relationship	H3b accepted
H2c	Gender & Bag	0.000	0.341	Different; Weak relationship	H3c accepted
H2d	Gender & Lights	0.000	0.264	Different; Weak relationship	H3e accepted
H2e	Gender & Waste	0.269	0.062	Not different	H3d rejected
H2f	Gender & Product	0.000	0.247	Different; Weak relationship	H3f accepted
H2g	Gender & WoM	0.165	0.078	Not different	H3g rejected
H3a	Marital & Buy	0.427	0.040	Not different	H2a rejected
H3b	Marital & Use	0.849	0.011	Not different	H2b rejected
H3c	Marital & Buy	0.016	0.134	Different; Weak relationship	H2e accepted
H3d	Marital & Waste	0.687	0.023	Not different	H2d rejected
H3e	Marital & Lights	0.963	0.003	Not different	H2c rejected
H3f	Marital & Product	0.307	0.057	Not different	H2f rejected
H3g	Marital & WoM	0.658	0.025	Not different	H2g rejected
H4a	Children & Buy	0.000	0.379	Different; Weak relationship	H4a accepted
H4b	Children & Use	0.002	0.207	Different; Weak relationship	H4b accepted
H4c	Children & Bag	0.000	0.320	Different; Weak relationship	H4c accepted
H4d	Children & Waste	0.018	0.175	Different; Weak relationship	H4d accepted
H4e	Children & Lights	0.000	0.298	Different; Weak relationship	H4e accepted
H4f	Children & Product	0.000	0.272	Different; Weak relationship	H4f accepted
H4g	Children & WoM	0.260	0.111	Not different	H4g rejected
H5a	Edu & Buy	0.000	0.237	Different; Weak relationship	H5a accepted
H5b	Edu & Use	0.008	0.203	Different; Weak relationship	H5b accepted
H5c	Edu & Bag	0.000	0.243	Different; Weak relationship	H5c accepted
H5d	Edu & Waste	0.030	0.180	Different; Weak relationship	H5g accepted
H5e	Edu & Lights	0.002	0.226	Different; Weak relationship	H5e accepted
H5f	Edu & Product	0.052	0.169	Not different	H5d rejected
H5g	Edu & WoM	0.062	0.162	Not different	H5f rejected
H6a	Work & Buy	0.000	0.395	Different; Weak relationship	H6a accepted
H6b	Work & Use	0.004	0.247	Different; Weak relationship	H6b accepted
H6c	Work & Bag	0.000	0.336	Different; Weak relationship	H6c accepted
H6d	Work & Waste	0.006	0.243	Different; Weak relationship	H6d accepted
H6e	Work & Lights	0.000	0.401	Different; Weak relationship	H6e accepted
H6f	Work & Product	0.024	0.220	Different; Weak relationship	H6f accepted
H6g	Work & WoM	0.038	0.211	Different; Weak relationship	H6g accepted
H7a	Income & Buy	0.000	0.389	Different; Weak relationship	H7a accepted
H7b	Income & Use	0.000	0.308	Different; Weak relationship	H7b accepted
H7c	Income & Bag	0.000	0.279	Different; Weak relationship	H7c accepted
H7d	Income & Waste	0.257	0.142	Not different	H7d rejected
H7e	Income & Light	0.000	0.447	Different; Weak relationship	H7e accepted
H7f	Income & Product	0.003	0.232	Different; Weak relationship	H7f accepted
H7g	Income & WoM	0.092	0.170	Not different	H7g rejected

in testing the relationship between sex and environmentally friendly behavior variables. These hypotheses are the relationships between sex and society's behavior to sort waste before disposal, and being willing to invite others to purchase environmentally friendly products. This indicates that males and females differ only in the action of sorting waste before disposal and a willingness to invite others to purchase environmentally friendly products. While both men and women are no different in purchasing environmentally friendly products, using environmentally friendly products, using their own bags while shopping, and switching consumption from conventional products to green-friendly products.

The next hypothesis is related to the relationship between marital status with environmentally friendly behavior. The results of the data show that there is only one supported hypothesis, namely the relationship between marital status with the habit of using their own bags while shopping. Meanwhile, the hypothesis examining the relationship between marital status and environmentally friendly behavior is the relationship between marital status variables with the purchase of environmentally friendly products, the use of environmentally friendly products, using their own bags while shopping, turning off the lights when going out of the room, and switching from conventional products to green products, and willingness to invite others to behave in an environmentally friendly behavior.

The findings of hypothesis testing on the relationship between the number of children owned by respondents with environmentally friendly behavior shows that six hypotheses are supported, which means that there are differences of consumer behavior in purchasing environmentally friendly product, environmentally friendly product use, using their own bag while shopping, sorting waste before disposing, turning off lights when exiting the room, and switching from conventional products to green products. The unsupported hypothesis is the relationship between the numbers of children with willingness to invite others to behave in an environmentally friendly behavior. This indicates that there is no difference in behavior to encourage others to behave in an environmentally friendly behavior based on the number of children owned by consumers.

The level of public education distinguishes environmentally friendly behavior, among other things in the purchase of environmentally friendly products, the use of environmentally friendly products, using their own bags while shopping, sorting waste before disposal, turning lights off when going out of the room, and switching from conventional products to green products. The unsupported hypothesis is the relationship between the number of children with willingness to invite others to behave in an environmentally friendly behavior.

When the type of community work is linked to environmentally friendly behavior, it indicates that the seven hypotheses are supported, which means that there are differences in environmentally friendly behavior (purchasing environmentally-friendly products, using environmentally friendly products, using their own bags while shopping, sorting waste before disposal, turning off lights when going out of the room). However, it appears that different levels of consumer education do not indicate differences in their behavior to switch from conventional products to green products, and a willingness to invite others in environmentally friendly behavior.

Finally, the test finding on the relationship between the amount of income and environmentally friendly behavior indicates that different levels of consumer income may differentiate their behavior in purchasing environmentally-friendly products, using environmentally friendly products, using their own bags while shopping, turning lights off when going out of the room, and switching from conventional products to green products. Meanwhile, the relationship between the level of income and the action of sorting waste before disposal, as well as the willingness to invite others to behave in an environmentally friendly behavior is not supported. This means that both low-educated consumers and highly educated consumers do not differ in the action of sorting waste before disposal, nor in willingness to invite others to behave in an environmentally friendly behavior.

Demographic factors are factors that play important roles in understanding consumer behavior (Kotler and Keller, 2016); therefore, to understand properly and correctly is the right step that businessmen need to take. Future business conditions will increasingly demand businessmen to think more about green marketing, and marketing social responsibility.

5 CONCLUSION

Based on the age of respondents, respondents with different age categories have differences in the behavior of purchasing environmentally-friendly products, using environmentally friendly products, using their own bags while shopping, turning off lights when going in and out of the room, and intention to switch consumption from conventional products to environmentally friendly products.

The current condition of society has begun to realize the importance of behaving in an environmentally friendly manner, so recommendation that can be presented to the government that it needs to promote a campaign about awareness of the importance of environmentally friendly behavior, through public service advertisements. Meanwhile, business people are advised to care more about the environment. One way that companies can do this is to produce products that are environmentally friendly, the companies can also implement social marketing responsibility.

Suggestions for future researchers are to conduct a comparative study of environmentally friendly behavior (green buying) between communities in developed countries and in developing countries. What can also be studied in the next research is the determinant factor of society in environmentally friendly behavior. Studies on the implementation of social marketing responsibility in developing countries can also be an option for future research.

REFERENCES

Cherian, J. & Jacob J. 2012. Green Marketing: A Study of Consumers' Attitude towards Environment Friendly Products. *Asian Social Science* 8 (12): 117–126.

Diamantopoulos, A., Schlegelmilch B.B., Sinkovics R.R. & Bohlen, G.M. 2003. Can Socio-Demographics Still Play A Role In Profiling Green Consumers? A Review of the Evidence and an Empirical Investigation. *Journal of Business Researchs* 56 (6): 456–480.

Fisher, C., Bashyal S. & Bachman B. 2012. Demographic Impacts on Environmentally Friendly Purchase Behaviors, *Journal of Targeting, Measurement and Analysis for Marketing* 20 (3): 172–184.

Gurau, C. & Ranchhod, A. 2005. International Green Marketing: A Comparative Study of British and Romanian Firms. *International Marketing Review* 2 2(5): 547–61.

Kaufmann, H. R., Panni M. F. A. K. & Orphanidou, Y. 2012, Factors Affecting Consumers' Green Purchasing Behavior: An Integrated Conceptual Framework, *Amfiteatru Economic*, 14 (31): 50–69.

Kotler, P. & Keller, K. L. 2016. *Marketing Management*. 15th ed., New York: Pearson.

Makeower, J. 2009. *Strategies for the Green Economy: Opportunities and Chalenges in the New World of Business*, New York: McGraw-Hill.

McEachern, M. & McClean, P. 2002. Organic Purchasing Motivations and Attitudes: Are they ethical? *International Journal of Consumer Studies* 26: 85–92.

Ottman, J. A., Stafford E. R. & Hartman, C. L. 2006. Avoiding Green Marketing Myopia: Ways to Improve Consumer Appeal for Environmentally Preferable Products. *Environment* 48 (5): 22–36.

Patil, V. G. 2012. Green Marketing: Myths & Facts. *Golden Research Thoughts* 1(VII): 1–8.

Polonsky, M. J. 2011. Transformative green marketing: Impediments and opportunities. *Journal of Business Research* 64 (12): 1311–1319.

Pride, W. M. & Ferrell, O. C. 1993. *Marketing: Concepts and Strategies*, 8th ed., Boston, MA: Houghton Mifflin.

Schlegelmilch, B. B., Bohlen G. M. & Diamantopoulos, A. 1996. The Link Between Green Purchasing Decisions and Measures of Environmental Consciousness. *European Journal of Marketing* 30 (5): 35–55.

Schwepker, C.H. Jr. & Cornwell T. B. 1991. An Examination of Ecologically Concerned Consumers and their Intention to Purchase Ecologically Packaged Products. *Journal of Public Policy & Marketing* 10: 77–101.

Strong, C. 1996. Features Contributing to the Growth of Ethical Consumerism: a Preliminary Investigation. *Marketing Intelligence & Planning* 14 (5): 5–13.

Wong, V., Turner, W. & Stoneman, P. 1996. Marketing strategies and Market Prospects for Environmentally-Friendly Consumer Products. *British Journal of Management* 7 (3): 263–81.

Increasing Management Relevance and Competitiveness – Sukoco et al. (Eds)
© 2018 Taylor & Francis Group, London, ISBN 978-0-8153-7455-8

Antecedents and consequences of ongoing search information

D.T. Firmansyah & D. Mardhiyah
Universitas Airlangga, Surabaya, Indonesia

ABSTRACT: This study aims to investigate the influence of developed product knowledge on the enjoyment of ongoing search information, and the influence of ongoing search information on future purchase efficiency, opinion leadership and impulse buying. The study involved 254 respondents. Respondents were Indonesian consumers who have ever watched a video review about a Smartphone on YouTube. Data was obtained through online questionnaire distributed via social media Line and WhatsApp, and screening conducted via Google-Form. Results of the study were processed using Structural Equation Modeling analysis, and show that in the model study developed product knowledge does not significantly influence the ongoing search information.

1 INTRODUCTION

Ongoing search information is the search for information that is not related to a particular decision or purchase requirement (Bloch et al., 1986). Consumers search for information, even when they are not going to make a purchase decision (Hoyer et al., 2008). An example of ongoing search information activity by consumers on automotive products is in subscribing to automotive magazines. Bloch et al. (1986) found that the level of involvement has a close relationship with ongoing search information. The ongoing search information activity becomes higher in a high involvement product (Bloch et al., 1986), which requires a lot of information when making a purchase decision, such as for a Smartphone.

Internet presence has changed the way consumers look for information, including when doing ongoing search information. Personal communication channels, such as word-of-mouth, are also a source of consumer information (Chakravarty et al.,2010). It should be considered by marketers, given that 89% of consumers in Indonesia trust more in the recommendations of friends and family when they want to buy a product (tribunnews.com, 2010).

The forms of electronic Words of Mouth communication are online discussion forums, product review sites, blogs, Social Networking Sites (SNS), and content communities such as YouTube and Wikipedia (Jansen et al., 2009). YouTube is a video sharing website. Videos on YouTube with the keyword 'Smartphone' were watched on average by 14,000 viewers per video, of which over 90% of the videos were uploaded by non-marketer sources (Marshall, 2015). Animoto's study about online and social video marketing, conducted on 1,051 consumers, revealed that consumers prefer watching videos compared to reading articles about a product (prnewswire.com, 2015). Based on these results, this study focuses on ongoing search information activities that use eWOM community content of a Smartphone video review on YouTube site as the source of information.

According to Bloch et al. (1986), search as recreation is also a consumer motivation in doing ongoing search information activity for enjoyment. Consumers do these activities without any reason other than to enjoy the activity itself (Van der Heijden, 2003). Enjoyment is the pleasure gained during the process of seeking information (Beatty & Ferrell, 1998).

The outcomes of ongoing search information are future purchase efficiency, opinion leadership, and impulse buying (Hoyer et al., 2008). Routinely in ongoing search information activities, consumers are constantly getting information that can develop product expertise, so that consumers become more efficient and rely on internal searches when consumption problems arise in the future (Bloch et al., 1986). Product information obtained from ongoing search information activities is likely to be spread by consumers to friends and family; this is because the skills of a product relate to opinion leadership (Schiffman & Kanuk, 2006). Ongoing search information can also lead to impulse buying. The more often a person searches for information about a product, the more awareness there is of the product and a better awareness that the product can provide solutions to the problems they face. Thereby, it increases impulsive purchase (Bloch et al., 1986).

Based on the explanation, this study tested the antecedents and consequences of ongoing search information. In other words, this study aims to investigate the influence of developed product knowledge and enjoyment on the ongoing search information, and the influence of ongoing search information on future purchase efficiency, opinion leadership and impulse buying.

2 LITERATURE REVIEW AND HYPOTHESES DEVELOPMENT

2.1 *Developed product knowledge and ongoing search information*

Chew and Palmer (1994) reveal that consumers seek information to meet the 'need to know'. Some researchers (Brucks, 1985; Selnes & Troye, 1989) have mentioned that consumer motivation in conducting pre-purchase and ongoing search information activities is to improve product knowledge. Ongoing search information is an information-seeking activity that is not related to a particular purchase decision (Bloch et al., 1986). These studies mentioned that consumers search information to improve the product knowledge that they own and to gain new product knowledge. According to Bloch et al. (1986), consumer motivation in doing ongoing search information is to get relevant information about products. The greater the desire of someone to develop his knowledge of a particular product, the more motivated the person is to do ongoing search information.

H1: Developed product knowledge has a positive effect on ongoing search information.

2.2 *Enjoyment and ongoing search information*

Consumers who do not have the desire to buy, but who still conduct ongoing search information activities, are motivated by enjoyment (Moe, 2003). Consumers are doing information search activities because they like the activity itself, without any other purpose. Bloch et al. (1986) concluded that the main motivation of consumers in conducting ongoing search information activities is to enjoy the process of seeking information itself. In the study by Bloch et al. (1986), enjoyment has a significant positive effect on ongoing search information activity. Punj and Staelin (1983) found that some consumers feel pleasure when looking for information on a product. Research shows that pleasure is the motivation of some behaviors, and in that situation, the activity undertaken does not aim to achieve a goal or outcome, but is done for the activity itself (Bloch et al., 1986).

H2: Enjoyment has a positive effect on ongoing search information.

2.3 *Ongoing search information and future purchase efficiency*

Consumers acquire product knowledge during ongoing search information activities, even though the activity is done for fun (Bloch et al., 1989). That knowledge can reduce the external search information before making a purchase (Srinivasan & Ratchford, 1991). Product knowledge gained from ongoing search information activities makes consumers more efficient by simply relying on internal information search when relevant consumption issues arise (Bloch et al., 1986). After consumption problems arise, consumers do not need to search for external information because consumers already have knowledge gained from ongoing search information activities (Beatty & Smith, 1987). Leemans and Stokmans (1992) said that from the results of ongoing search information, consumers already have knowledge on products and strategies when evaluating the product to be purchased in the future. This can reduce the effort of consumers in making purchases in the future.

H3: Ongoing search information has a positive effect on future purchase efficiency.

2.4 *Ongoing search information and opinion leadership*

Expertise and knowledge about a product can be obtained when regularly doing ongoing search information activities (Bloch et al., 1986). Consumers become more familiar and have more product knowledge than consumers who do not do ongoing search information activities. These consumers usually disseminate information to friends or family. Knowledge and skills about a product have a close relationship with opinion leadership (Bloch et al., 1986). Consumers usually provide information and advise people closest to them, influencing buying behavior through word-of-mouth communication. The results of research from Bloch et al. (1986) find that there is a significant positive relationship between ongoing search information and opinion leadership, because product expertise obtained from ongoing search information activities causes consumers to have the capacity to influence the opinions of other consumers.

H4: Ongoing search information has a positive effect on opinion leadership.

2.5 *Ongoing search information and impulse buying*

Han et al. (1991) stated that impulse purchase occurs when consumers engage in information search activity, in other words, when consumers

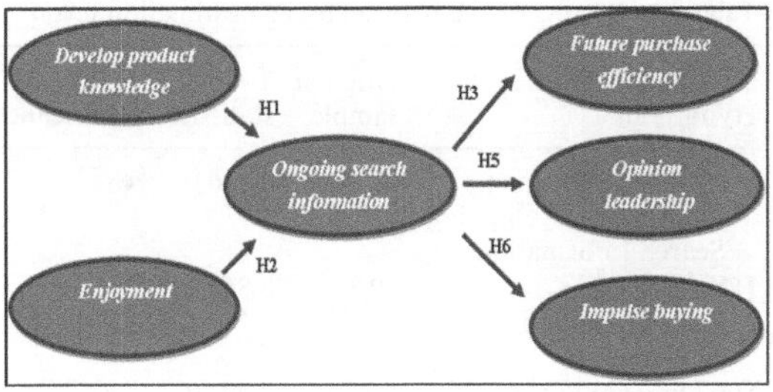

Figure 1. Research model.

search for product information by going to the mall or store and make a purchase impulsively. Rook (1987) found that one can sense a sudden urge and a mysterious impulse to make impulsive purchases when doing ongoing search information activities. The more often consumers do ongoing search information activities, the more it will increase impulse buying (Bloch et al., 1986). According to Beatty and Ferrell (1998), ongoing search information has a significant positive effect on impulse buying.

H5: Ongoing search information has a positive effect onimpulse buying.

The relationship between variables and hypotheses tested in this study can be seen in the following model study images.

3 RESEARCH METHODS

3.1 *Research design and data collection*

This research is a survey research, which uses a structured questionnaire with closed question as the main instrument of research to collect primary data. Back translation of the questionnaire was conducted to produce the instrument in Indonesian, which is the dominant language of the respondents. All measurements use a 5-point Likert scale. This research used 254 Indonesian respondents who have watched a video review of Smartphone products on the YouTube website when they have no desire to buy.

3.2 *Constructs and validity-reliability test*

The measurements used in this study were established, some of which were modified and adapted from previous studies and developed specifically for this study after reviewing the relevant literatures. Measurement of developed product knowledge variable was adopted from Ntoumanis's research (2001); enjoyment variable was adopted from the research of Chung and Koo (2015); the variable of ongoing search information was adopted from research by Bloch et al. (1986), Bloch et al. (1989) and Ono et al. (2012); the future purchase efficiency variables were adopted from Punj and Staelin (1983), and Park and Kim (2003); leadership opinion variables were adopted from Flynn et al. (1996); and impulse buying variables indicators were adopted from research by Rook and Fisher (1995).

All variables of this research passed the validity test with AVE value >0.5. It means all indicators of all the variables have high correlation with their each variables. Moreover each variable in model analysis had cross-loading correlation value of construct with their indicators higher than other constructs (discriminant validity). In addition, all variables in this study satisfied the assumption of reliability (Cronbach's alpha > 0.6 and composite reliability > 0.8).

3.3 *Structural testing (inner) model*

Predictive relevance was used to measure how well the observation values were generated by the model (Ghozali, 2006). From the value of predictive relevance, obtained through Q-square calculation involving R-square value, it shows that the model has a predictive relevance value of 0.289827. This result shows that the analysis model has a good predictive relevance.

3.4 *Results and discussion*

Hypothesis testing is done by using the Partial Least Square program. Based on the Table Results of Path Coefficient Estimation, it can be seen that the developed product knowledge has no significant effect on ongoing search information with the t-statistics value of 0.1103 (H1 not supported). Developed product knowledge is not a motivation in doing ongoing search information activities. Consumers are motivated by other things, such as enjoyment (Bloch et al., 1986). This means that consumers do ongoing search information activities, not because they want to develop product knowledge, but because of the urge to have fun while doing ongoing search information activities (H2 supported). These results can be caused by consumers having no intention to make a purchase during the ongoing search information activities. The results of this study are in accordance with research conducted by Bloch et al. (1986), who found that product knowledge development had no significant effect on ongoing search information activities.

Future purchase efficiency occurs when consumers are able to reduce the information retrieval process related to purchasing decisions to be made in the future (Sheth & Parvatiyar, 1995). Consumers conducting ongoing search information activities already have information about the product, so there is no need to search for product information again when there is a desire to purchase (Bloch et al., 1986).

Hypothesis testing results show that ongoing search information has a positive and significant influence on future purchase efficiency (H3 supported). This shows that consumers who do ongoing search information can improve the efficiency of purchasing products in the future. Consumers can shorten the time of purchase, reduce the effort to purchase of products, choose the best product type, and understand the benefits of products and lack of products, because consumers have knowledge when doing ongoing search information activities. Consumers simply search for internal information from long-term memory when they have a desire to buy sometime in the future.

In addition to its usefulness, knowledge of products obtained from ongoing search information activities can increase the capacity of consumers as a reliable source of information to those around them, and influence others who are taking purchase decision. It allows consumers to become opinion leaders (H4 supported). Descriptive statistics also support it with a composite mean value for the leadership opinion variable of 3.1. This shows that the majority of respondents are a source of information and able to influence the opinions of others about Smartphones.

Consumers who have a lot of product knowledge will be more familiar with the product, and cause the possibility of impulse buying to be greater (Bloch et al., 1986). It can also be applied to the setting of ongoing search information by watching a Smartphone review video on the YouTube website. The higher the intensity of watching a Smartphone review video on a YouTube site, the more likely the consumer is stimulated to purchase the product impulsively (H5 supported).

The mean value of the low composite of impulse buying can be caused by the intensity of watching a Smartphone video review on YouTube. When the intensity of consumers in watching a Smartphone video review on YouTube site increases, it will increase the value of the composite impulse buying variable, because there is positive and significant effect of ongoing search information activity on impulse buying. The results of this study are in accordance with the conceptual framework of Bloch et al. (1986) who found that ongoing search information activity has a positive effect on impulse buying.

According to Stern (1962), factors that can affect impulse purchases include low price, but Rook (1987) did not rule out that consumers make impulsive purchases on products with high price levels. This can be due to the ease of payment offered by the company in facilitating the purchases, such as installment facility and credit card usage.

Table 1. Results of the path coefficient estimation test.

Hypothesis	Original sample	T-statistics	Significance
H1: Develop Product Knowledge -> Ongoing Search Information	−0.0095	0.1103	No
H2: Enjoyment -> Ongoing Search Information	0.3801	4.8625	Yes
H3: Ongoing Search Information -> Future Purchase Efficiency	02285	3.2928	Yes
H4: Ongoing Search Information -> Opinion Leadership	0.2524	4.4200	Yes
H5: Ongoing Search Information -> Impulse Buying	0.2636	3.5957	Yes

4 CONCLUSIONS

The tests for the hypotheses supported by the research setting are: (1) the influence of enjoyment on ongoing search information; (2) the influence of ongoing search information towards future purchase efficiency; (3) the effect of ongoing search information on opinion leadership; and (4) ongoing search information on impulse buying. The hypothesis not supported is the hypothesis that examines the influence of developed product knowledge on ongoing search information.

Ongoing search information can make consumers more efficient in making purchases and can also encourage the occurrence of impulse buying. Companies should consider the use of information dissemination through Internet strategies that can stimulate consumers and potential customers to seek information about the product, even when the consumer has no intention to purchase the product, primarily by highlighting elements related to enjoyment, such as aesthetics, content, background selection of the corresponding narratives, interactive narration and interesting-looking sources. Furthermore, companies can take advantage of consumers who are uploading product review videos, as they are effective in reaching consumers and other potential customers at a more affordable cost; one strategy is by holding a competition to make a video review.

REFERENCES

Beatty, S. & Ferrell, E. (1998). Impulse buying: Modeling its precursors. *Journal of Retailing*, *72*(2), 169–191.

Beatty, S. & Smith, S. (1987). External search effort: An investigation across several product categories. *Journal of Consumer Research, 14*(1), 83–95.

Bloch, P., Ridgway, N. & Sherrell, D. (1989). Extending the concept of shopping: An investigation of browsing activity. *Journal of the Academy of Marketing Science*, *17*(1), 13–21.

Bloch, P., Sherrell, D. & Ridgway, N. (1986). Consumer search: An extended framework. *Journal of Consumer Research*, *13*(1), 119–126.

Brucks, M. (1985). The effect of product class knowledge on information search behavior. *Journal of Consumer Research*, *12*(1), 1–16.

Chakravarty, A., Yong, L. & Mazumdar, T. (2010). The differential effect of online word-of-mouth, and critics reviews on pre-release movie evaluation. *Journal of Interactive Marketing*, *24*(3), 350–362.

Chew, F. & Palmer, S. (1994). Interest, the knowledge gap, and television programming. *Journal of Broadcasting and Electronic Media*, *38*(3), 271–287.

Chung, N. & Koo, C. (2015). The use of social media in travel information search. *Telematics and Informatics*, *32*(2), 215–229.

Customers trust more to other recommendation than companies' advertising. (June, 2010). Retrieved from www.tribunnews.com/bisnis/2010/06/10/konsumen-lebih-percaya-rekomendasi-teman-daripada-iklan.

Flynn, L., Goldsmith, R. & Eastman, J. (1996). Opinion leaders and opinion seekers: Two new measurement scales. *Journal of the Academy of Marketing Science*, *24*(2), 137–147.

Ghozali, I. (2006). Application of Multivariate Analysis with SPSS. Fourth Edition. Semarang. Universitas Diponegoro Press.

Han, Y., Morgan, G., Kotsiopulo, A. & Kang-Park, J. (1991). Impulse buying behavior of apparel purchasers. *Clothing and Textiles Research Journal*, *9*(3), 15–21.

Hoyer, W., MacInnis, D. & Pieters, R. (2008). *Consumer Behavior* (6th ed.). Mason: Cengage Learning.

Jansen, B.J., Zhang, M., Sobel, K. & Chowdury, A. (2009). Twitter power: Tweets as electronic word of mouth. *Journal of the Association for Information Science and Technology*, *60*(11), 2169–2188.

Keller, K. (2008). *Strategy brand management (building, measuring, and managing brand equity)* (3rd ed.). New Jersey: Prentice Hall.

Leemans, H. & Stokmans, M.J.W. (1992). A descriptive model of the decision making process of buyers of books. *Journal of Cultural Economics*, *16*(2), 25–50.

Marshall, C. (2015). How many views does a YouTube video get? Average Views by Category. Retrieved from www.tubularinsights.com/average-youtube views/.

Moe, W. (2003). Buying, searching or browsing: Differentiation between online shoppers using in-store navigational clickstream. *Journal of Consumer Psychology*, *13*(2), 29–39.

Ntoumanis, N. (2001). A self-determination approach to the understanding of motivation in physical education. *British Journal of Education Psychology*, *71*(2), 225–242.

Ono, A., Nakamura, A., Okuno, A. & Sumikawa, M. (2012). Consumer motivations in browsing online stores with mobile devices. *International Journal of Electronic Commerce*, *16*(4), 153–178.

Park, C. & Kim, Y. (2003). Identifying key factors affecting consumer purchase behavior in an online shopping context. *International Journal of Retail & Distribution Management*, *31*(1), 16–29.

PR Newswire. (May, 2015). Animoto survey: Consumers want more video marketing on web social and email. Retrieved from http://www.prnewswire.com/news-releases/animoto-survey-consumers-want-more-video-marketing-on-web-social-and-email-300079377.html.

Punj, G. & Staelin, R. (1983). A model of consumer information search for new automobiles. *Journal of Consumer Research*, *9*, 366–380.

Rook, D. (1987). The buying impulse. *Journal of Consumer Research*, *14*(2), 189–199.

Rook, D. & Fisher, R. (1995). Normative influences on impulsive buying behavior. *Journal of Consumer Research*, *22*(3), 305–313.

Schiffman, L. & Kanuk, L. (2006). *Consumer Behavior* (7th ed.). New Jersey: Pearson Education Inc.

Selnes, F. & Troye, S. (1989). Buying expertise, information search, and problem solving. *Journal of Economic Psychology*, *10*(3), 411–428.

Sheth, J. & Parvatiyar, A. (1995). The evolution of relationship marketing. *International Business Review*, *4*(4), 397–418.

Smartphone Vendor Market Share, 2017 Q1. (n.d.). Retrieved from www.idc.com/prodserv/smartphone-market-share.jsp.

Srinivasan, N. & Ratchford, B. (1991). An empirical test of a model of external search for automobiles. *Journal of Consumer Research*, *18*(2), 233–242.

Stern, H. (1962). The significance of impulse buying today. *Journal of Marketing*, *26*(2), 59–62.

Van der Heijden, H. (2003). Factors influencing the usage of websites: The case of a generic portal in the Netherlands. *Information & Management*, *40*(6), 541–549.

Increasing Management Relevance and Competitiveness – Sukoco et al. (Eds)
© 2018 Taylor & Francis Group, London, ISBN 978-0-8153-7455-8

Role of negative brand name perception and religiosity on brand attitude

S. Gunawan & R.T. Ratnasari
Universitas Airlangga, Surabaya, Indonesia

ABSTRACT: This article investigates the role that negative brand name (as in Rawon Setan, the name of a restaurant meaning 'Satanic') and product quality play in influencing brand attitude and intention to buy, with religiosity as the moderator variable. This study uses quantitative research based on a survey. The data was collected from questionnaires distributed to 200 sample respondents. The respondents were students in the Faculty of Economics and Business, Universitas Airlangga, during April 2016. The respondents were aged between 17–22 years and were all familiar with Rawon Setan Restaurant. The analysis uses PLS (Partial Least Square). This is a study to investigate brand name with negative impact from an Islamic perspective, and how it can influence intention to buy with religiosity as the moderator variable. The influence of negative brand name is still largely unexplored. The hypotheses are: Religiosity strengthens the relationship between negative brand name with brand attitude; Religiosity strengthens the relationship between negative brand name with intention to buy; Product quality has a positive effect on brand attitude; Product quality has a positive effect on the intention to buy; and brand attitude has a positive effect on the intention to buy.

Keywords: Negative Brand Name, Product Quality, Religiosity, Brand Attitude, and Intention to Buy

1 INTRODUCTION

Muslims conduct their daily activities using Islamic Sharia as the basis in order to meet people's welfare. Islamic Sharia not only refers to practices of *mahdhah* worship, but also regulates the practice of human relationships. The issue of how we process valence has received much attention in psychology because negative/positive stimuli potentially signal a threat/reward. To ensure our survival, it is important that we react to potential threats. According to this automatic vigilance, negative information may have undesirable consequences for the perceivers' wellbeing and so is automatically, preferentially, and more efficiently processed. For instance, negative words capture and hold attention and induce larger neural responses than positive words. This automatic vigilance also influences memory. Relative to non-negative words, words with negative valence are better recognized and recalled. Moreover, besides capturing attention, it also takes longer to disengage attention from negative words. Based on this research, it seems possible then that using a negative word as a brand name may have distinct advantages in terms of attentional capture and memorability (Guest et al., 2016).

Religion has regulations about certain behavior. Religion is a belief wherein people could find the root of consumption behavior. Religion provides the rules to determine food consumption (Ambali & Bakar, 2014). Previous studies have found that there is a significant relationship between a consumer's religious affiliation and the number of consumption-related variables (Abou-Youssef et al., 2015).

What might the effect of negative brand names on product perception be? By their very nature, negative words will be associated with negative concepts and undesirable consequences, which will become activated when processing a negative brand name. Additionally, negative words are potentially threatening and can trigger an avoidance response. Utilizing a negative brand name might be expected to worsen product evaluations (Guest et al., 2016).

So, we need to more explore the role of religiosity in food consumption. This research seeks to examine the final impact of negative brand name (Rawon Setan Restaurant) and product quality on brand attitude and intention to buy, with religiosity as the moderator variable of the study.

2 CONCEPTUAL THEORY

Based on the Quran, Hadits, Islamic literature and the interviews conducted with religious Islamic scholars, the researcher can define Islamic marketing as being 'the wisdom of satisfying the needs of customers through the good conduct of delivering Halal, wholesome, pure and lawful products and services with the mutual consent of both seller and buyer for the purpose of achieving material and spiritual wellbeing in the world here and hereafter and making consumers aware of it through the good conduct of marketers and ethical advertising' (Quran, 4:29).

Religion, from a consumer behavior perspective, has an important role that may influence purchase decisions, advertising, and media usage in general (Fam et al., quoted in El-Bassiouny, 2014).

Brand is generally a name and a symbol. Brand has an important role in creating a positive image in customers' minds (Mirabi et al., 2015). Marketers need the proper strategy in order to attract consumers and make them understand, in order to drive consumer purchase intention of a brand (Mirabi et al., 2015).

Brand name is a critical part of the brand elements (Keller, quoted in Round & Roper, 2015). Negative words are potentially threatening and can trigger an avoidance response. Brand names tend to be the first point of contact with a brand. It is therefore important to consider the effects of negative brand name valence on product perception. Negative brand name has two impacts. First, customers respond to it slowly, and second, the negative brand name will be better remembered (Guest et al., 2016). Perceived quality is defined as a consumer's evaluation of a brand's overall excellence based on intrinsic (e.g. performance) and extrinsic (e.g. brand name) cues (Kirmani & Baumgartner, quoted in Faryabi et al., 2015).

The consumers' attitudes have a positive impact on their intentions to buy a product (Hasbullah et al., 2016). According to such definitions, it is understood that attitude towards an organizational brand is called brand attitude; therefore, brand attitude is an appraisal towards a brand from the consumers' point of view (Esmaeilpour, 2015). Basically, consumer attitude towards a brand is highly important, since brand attitude has a positive relationship on intentions to buy (Abzari et al., 2014). When the consumer meets a brand that fits their personality, it can lead to the positive attitude of the consumer towards the brand. Further, it will lead to the consumers' purchase intention (Adis et al., 2015). Brand attitude refers to the consumers' evaluation towards a brand (Davtyan & Cunningham, 2016). Brand attitude is the consumers' consideration, whether positive or negative, towards a brand (Shimp, quoted in Adis et al., 2015). According to Mirabi et al. (2015), brand name has significant and positive impact on purchase intention and indicates that a company should invest more in its brand name in order to increase their customers' brand awareness.

Religiosity is reported to have significant influences on various dimensions of consumer behavior. Religion is a set of righteous rules, which is trusted in or held as a belief. It depends on an individual's conscience, and such things cannot be created by force, pressure or compulsion (Karami et al., 2014). Religion provides some rules which can influence awareness towards consumer behavior (Muhamad et al., 2016). Religious teachings examine principles and norms in society, which are implemented in regard to business activity. So, religion affects consumer reactions towards questionable or unethical business practices (Karami et al., 2014).

Brand name has a significant effect on consumer attitude (Häubl, 1996:90, quoted in Fetscherin et al., 2015), and also influences intention to buy a product (Ahmed et al., 2004:102, quoted in Fetscherin et al., 2015). Attitude is also an influencer of consumer decision and leads to some behaviors (Abou-Yousef et al., 2015). Brand attitude is an appraisal towards a brand from the consumers' point of view (Esmaeilpour, 2015). Basically, consumer attitude towards a brand is highly important, since brand attitude has a positive relationship on intentions to buy (Abzari et al., 2014). When a consumer meets a brand that fits their personality, it can lead to the positive attitude of the consumer towards the brand. Further, it will lead to the consumer's purchasing intention (Adis et al., 2015).

Perceived quality is defined as 'a consumer's evaluation of a brand's overall excellence based on intrinsic (e.g. performance) and extrinsic cues (e.g. brand name)' (Kirmani & Baumgartner, 2000, quoted in Faryabi et al., 2015). Chi et al. (2008, quoted in Mirabi et al., 2015) stated that if the quality of a product is increased, consumers will be more interested to purchase it.

3 RESEARCH MODEL AND HYPOTHESES

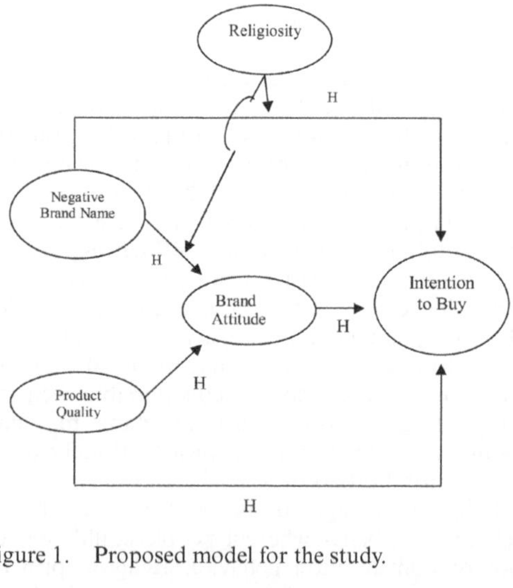

Figure 1. Proposed model for the study.

4 METHOD

This study uses quantitative research, based on a survey. Perceived quality is generally an intangible feeling towards a brand. Product quality is the consumers' appraisal towards overall products based on their performance, durability and brand name. Brand attitude is the consumers' appraisal, either positive or negative, towards a brand (Adis et al., 2015). Brand attitude may affect consumer behavior (Adis et al., 2015).

The data was collected from questionnaires distributed to 200 sample respondents. The respondents were students in the Faculty of Economics and Business, Universitas Airlangga, during April 2016. The reasons for selecting these respondents is that students are likely to buy new products that are eye-catching or ear-catching, including culinary products. The respondents were aged between 17–22 years and were familiar with Rawon Setan Restaurant. The analysis uses PLS (Partial Least Square) to test the hypotheses.

5 RESULT

5.1 *Hypothesis testing with Partial Least Square (PLS)*

The PLS test is an analytical method that is not based on many assumptions. PLS can be used to confirm the theory and explain whether there is any relationship between latent variables. The processing of PLS is done in two stages. The first stage is to test the outer models, and the second stage is to test the inner workings of the model. In this phase, it aims to determine whether there is any influence between variables. Tests were carried out using t-test.

5.2 *Outer model testing phase*

Tests were conducted on overall individual performance of each variable. Criteria indicators of the variable are said to construct a valid and reliable manner if they have a loading factor value greater than or equal to 0.5 and the value of its t-test > 1.96. Below is the outer test of the model.

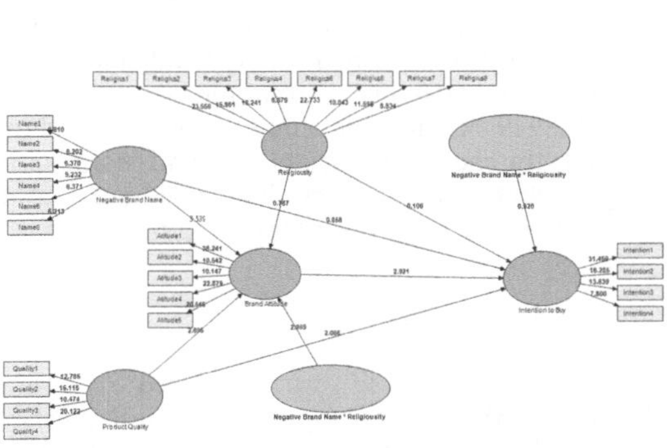

Figure 2. Model of measurement test.

5.3 *Inner phase or structural model*

This model of structural phase aims to determine whether there is influence between variables and to determine the effect of moderating variables. The moderating variable in this study is religiosity. This moderating influence occurs in the variable negative brand name on the brand attitude and purchase intention. Tests were carried out using t-test. A variable is said to have an influence when t is greater than t table, which in this study is 1.96. Likewise, if there is a relationship between the variables then the decision is negative if—t is smaller than—t table.

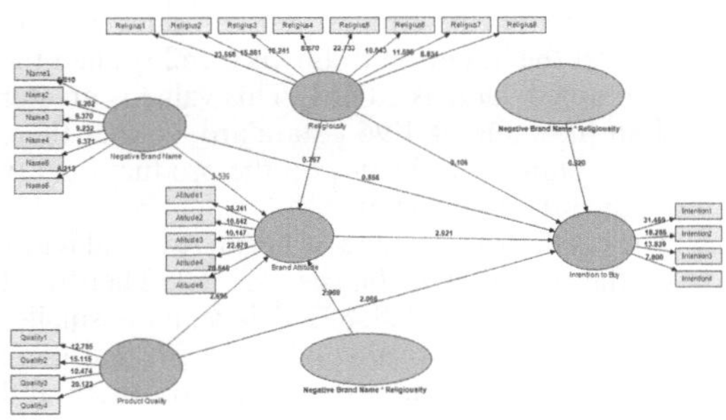

Figure 3. Structural test model moderation.

Table 1. Hypothesis results.

	Original Sample (O)	T Statistics (|O/STERR|)
Negative Brand Name -> Brand Attitude	–0.9186	3.5388
Product Quality -> Brand Attitude	0.1636	2.6953
Brand Attitude -> Intention to Buy	0.2490	2.9208
Product Quality -> Intention to Buy	0.1425	2.0661
Negative Brand Name -> Intention to Buy	–0.3569	0.8583
Negative Brand Name * Religiosity -> Brand Attitude	1.0743	2.9692
Negative Brand Name * Religiosity -> Intention to Buy	0.5310	0.9196

5.4 *Hypothesis testing*

Based on the above table, it can be interpreted as follows:

a. The coefficient estimate of negative brand name on brand attitude is –0.9186. Then the t obtained value is 3.5388. This value is greater than the value of 1.96 t standard, so that there is a significant negative impact on brand attitude and brand name.
b. The coefficient estimate of product quality to brand attitude is 0.1636. Then the t obtained value is 2.6953. This value is greater than the value of 1.96 t standard, so that there is a significant influence of product quality on brand attitude.
c. The coefficient estimate on the brand attitude of the intention to buy is 0.2490. Then the t obtained value is 2.9208. This value is greater than the value of 1.96 t standard, so that there is a significant influence on brand attitude of the intention to buy.
d. The coefficient estimate of product quality against the intention to buy is 0.1425. Then the t obtained value is 2.0661. This value is greater than the value of 1.96 t standard, so that there is a significant influence on the product quality of the intention to buy.
e. The coefficient estimate of negative brand name of the intention to buy is –0.3569. Then the t obtained value is 0.8583. This value is smaller than the standard value of 1.96 t, so that there is no significant negative impact on the brand name by the intention to buy.
f. The coefficient estimate of negative interaction with the brand name on brand attitude religiosity is 1.0743. Then the t obtained value is 2.9692. This value is greater than the value of 1.96 t standard, so that religiosity is significantly moderating the negative brand name on the brand attitude.
g. The coefficient estimate of negative interaction with the brand name religiosity of the intention to buy is 0.5310. The coefficient is positive, which means a negative influence of religiosity reinforces negative brand name on the intention to buy. Then the t obtained value is 0.9196. This value is smaller than the standard value of 1.96 t, so that religiosity is not significantly moderating the negative brand name of the intention to buy. The indirect negative influence of brand name and product quality on the intention to buy through brand attitude can be seen in the following Sobel test.

Table 2. Indirect influence by Sobel test.

Indirect influence path	Coefficient value	Significant value
Negative brand name towards *intention to buy* between *brand attitude*	–0.22876	0.0242
Product quality towards *intention to buy* between *brand attitude*	0.04074	0.0476

Table 3. Value of R square.

	R Square
Brand Attitude	0.6842
Intention to Buy	0.6609

The result of the calculation of the indirect effect indicates that there is an indirect effect of the variables negative brand name of the intention to buy through the brand attitude with significant value Sobel 0.0242. The coefficient of its indirect influence is –0.22876. Other results also show the same thing: that there is an indirect effect of the variable product quality intention to buy through the brand attitude, with significant value of Sobel 0.0476. The coefficient of indirect influence is 0.04074.

5.5 *Testing goodness of fit*

Evaluation of the inner model can be seen from several indicators, which include: R square explains how big an exogenous variable (independent/free) in the model is able to explain the endogenous variables (dependent/dependent).

a. R square shows that the influence of negative variables brand name and product quality on the brand attitude is 0.6842 or 68.42%. The negative variables influences brand name and the product quality and brand attitude on intention to buy is 0.6609 or 66.09%.
b. Predictive Relevance (Q-square)
   The value of Q-square can be calculated as follows: $Q2 = 1 - (1 - 0.6842)(1 - 0.6609) = 0.8929$. Based on the results of the calculation of Q-square, it can be seen that the Q-square value is 0.8929 because the value of $Q2 > 0$; it show that the negative variables brand name and product quality and brand attitude have a good prediction rate in the intention to buy.

5.6 *Goodness of fit index*

Unlike the CBSEM (Covarianc-Based Structural Equation Modelling), GoF value in PLS-SEM (Partial Least Squares-Structural Equation Modelling) must be searched manually. The formula is:

$GoF = \sqrt{\overline{AVE} \times \overline{R^2}}$....Tenenhaus (2004)

The results of calculation of value—average AVE is 0.515999, while the average—average R2 is 0.672538, such that the value of GoF is 0.589092. According to Tenenhau (2004), the value of small GoF = 0.1, GoF medium = 0.25 and GoF great = 0.38.

5.7 *Discussion*

Religious values can also influence perceptions and attitudes towards religious terms. Religious terms used in a brand name might lead to changes in consumer perception. In this sense, examining the relationships between religious orientation and attitude towards the use of a religious brand name and a religious brand image could make a significant contribution to the literature.

H1: Religiosity strengthens the relationship between negative brand name with brand attitude.

Religious orientation influences the way people choose products and brands (Rehman & Shabbir 2010; Alam et al., 2011). The respondents had several reasons for intending to buy food and beverages at the restaurant that has a negative brand name, as follows:

a. No need to worry because there is no hadith that prohibits or forbids.
b. Because it is just a name; in the presentation there is nothing that violates sharia.
c. Negative brand strategy was just about curiosity and promotional products.
d. Because it is only for the fulfillment of the desire for consumption, so did not see the brand.
e. The most important thing is simply lawful and *thayyib*, brand problem number 2.
f. Negative brand is not very influential; what is important is the quality of the products.
g. Because it could be that the product has a value that is more than just a name.
h. The unique name will have the possibility of unique products as well.
i. Today's consumers are interested in new and unique things.
j. Because you want to try.
k. Intrigued by a value-added products page.
l. Negative brand gives an impression to consumers.
m. Because of the sense of taste.

H2: Religiosity strengthens the relationship between negative brand name with intention to buy.

Attitude has been divided into four functions as: 'utilitarian', 'value-expression', 'ego defensive' and 'knowledge function'. Affect and cognition factors of attitude are believed to be a generalized concept of brand attitude, indicating that they could be influenced by different factors, such as quality.

H3: Product quality has a positive effect on brand attitude.

Product perceived quality directly influences purchase intention. Customers have some perceptions about the product quality, price and styles before going on to purchase the product. After using a product, purchase intention increases as well as decreases. If the quality is high, then customer purchase intention is also high.

H4: Product quality has a positive effect on intention to buy.

As proposed by Wu and Wang (2014:453, 457), this study views brand affection, purchase intention and brand trust as presenting the affective, behavioral and cognitive dimensions of brand attitude, respectively. Due to the definitional overlap between behavioral brand loyalty (Belaid & Behi, 2011:39) and brand purchase intention (Wu & Wang, 2014:453, 457), brand attitude was only measured in terms of brand affection and brand trust. In conclusion, the consumers' attitudes predict their purchase intention.

H5: Brand attitude has a positive effect on intention to buy.

6 CONCLUSION

Based on the research, this study finds some conclusions, that: religiosity strengthens the relationship between negative brand name with brand attitude; religiosity strengthens the relationship between negative brand name with intention to buy; product quality has a positive effect on brand attitude; product quality has a positive effect on intention to buy; and brand attitude has a positive effect on intention to buy.

ACKNOWLEDGMENT

This work was supported by Faculty of Economics and Business, Universitas Airlangga research grants.

REFERENCES

Abou-Youssef, M.M.H., Abou-Aish, E. & El-Bassiouny, N. (2015). Effects of religiosity on consumer attitudes toward Islamic banking in Egypt. *International Journal of Bank Marketing*, *33*(6), 786–807.

Abzari, M., Ghassemi, R.A. & Vosta, L.N. (2014). Analysing the effect of social media on brand attitude and purchase intention: The case of Iran Khodro Company. *Procedia-Social and Behavioral Sciences, 143*, 822–826.
Adis, A.A., Kim, H., Majid, M.R.A., Osman, Z., Razli, I.A. & Ing, G.P. (2015). Purchase behaviour in advergame and the effect of brand attitude as a mediator. *Asian Social Science,* 11(5), 249.
Amalia, I., Riani, W. & Julia, A. (2016). The influence of religiosity values on happiness with Islamic consuming ethics as moderator variable. *Procedia-Social and Behavioral Sciences, 219*, 76–83.
Davtyan, D. & Cunningham, I. (2016). An investigation of brand placement effects on brand attitudes and purchase intentions: Brand placements versus TV commercials. *Journal of Business Research*. Retrieved from http://dx.doi.org/10.1016/j.jbusres.2016.08.023.
El-Bassiouny, N. (2014). The one-billion-plus marginalization: Toward a scholarly understanding of Islamic consumers. *Journal of Business Research, 67*(2), 42–49.
Esmaeilpour, F. (2015). The role of functional and symbolic brand associations on brand loyalty. *Journal of Fashion Marketing and Management, 19*(4), 467–484.
Faryabi, M., Fesaghandis, K.S. & Saed, M. (2015). Brand name, sales promotion and consumers' online purchase intention for cell-phone brands. *International Journal of Marketing Studies, 7*(1), 167.
Fetscherin, M., Diamantopoulos, A., Chan, A. & Abbott, R. (2015). How are brand names of Chinese companies perceived by Americans? *Journal of Product & Brand Management, 24*(2), 110–123.
Guest, D., Estes, Z., Gibbert, M. & Mazursky, D. (2016). Brand suicide? Memory and liking of negative brand names. *PloS one. 11*(3), e0151628. doi:10.1371/journal.pone.0151628.
Hasbullaha, N.A., Osman, A., Abdullah, S., Salahuddin, S.N., Ramlee, N.F. & Soha, H.M. (2016). The relationship of attitude, subjective norm and website usability on consumer intention to purchase online: An evidence of Malaysian youth. *Procedia-Economics and Finance, 35*, 493–502.
Hashim, N. & Hamzah, M.I. (2014). 7P's: A literature review of Islamic marketing and contemporary marketing mix. *Procedia-Social and Behavioral Sciences, 130*, 155–159.
Karami, M., Olfati, O. & Dubinsky, A.J. (2014). Influence of religiosity on retail salespeople's ethical perceptions: The case in Iran. *Journal of Islamic Marketing, 5*(1), 144–172.
Mirabi, V., Akbariyeh, H. & Tahmasebifard, H. (2015). A study of factors affecting on customers purchase intention case study: The Agencies of Bono Brand Tile in Tehran. *Journal of Multidisciplinary Engineering Science and Technology, (JMEST)*, 2(1).
Muhamad, N., Leong, V.S. & Mizerski, D. (2016). Consumer knowledge and religious rulings on products. *Journal of Islamic Marketing, 7*(1), 74–94.
Round, G. & Roper, S. (2015). Untangling the brand name from the branded entity. *European Journal of Marketing, 49*(11/12), 1941–1960.
Wu, S. & Wang, W. (2014). Impact of CSR perception on brand image, brand attitude and buying willingness: A study of a global café. *International Journal of Marketing Studies, 6*(6), 43.
Zarrad, H. & Debabi, M. (2015). Islamic marketing ethics: A literature review. *International Journal of Management Research & Review, 5*(2), 60–66.

Increasing Management Relevance and Competitiveness – Sukoco et al. (Eds)
© 2018 Taylor & Francis Group, London, ISBN 978-0-8153-7455-8

The effects of good/bad news on consumer responses toward higher education

G.C. Premananto & M.H. Hanafiah
Management Master, Airlangga University, Surabaya, Indonesia

ABSTRACT: The aim of this research is to test the effect of publication in media, which it can be good and bad news, toward consumer response in higher education. Using experimental design, the news had been manipulated. The good and bad news had been set for institutional and individual domain. Consumer responses measured by trust, brand image and attitude toward university. Using 150 students of Senior High School as participants, it found that news contents have different effects on trust, brand image and attitude toward brand. The higher education needs to create and share their positiveness to media, and intense to cope the negativeness.

1 INTRODUCTION

Many research about higher education/universities, such as on brand image (Jiewanto et al., 2012); determinant of students selection (Polat, 2012; Noorafshan et al., 2014), had been conducted. But the effects of news about university still remain unexplored. Though, university has many news about their institution and individual performances. The existence of positive and negative news was able to portray the image of the institution's reputation.

Previous research has shown that social media shapes the views of the community involvement and the impact on the level of confidence (Warren et al., 2014). Other studies have also shown that the use of a website to get information is able to bring social trust (McLeod and Schell., 2001). Additionally, Go et al., (2016) states that interactive messages on a website is able to push the level of confidence of users in the community.

The good or bad news can be a source of interest for the research object. Given the news, of course, will influence the decision of a prospective student in determining the continued study of the electoral college. Referring to a market where the student is considered as a customer, the university must implement strategies to manage and improve competitiveness so that the reputation of the university is well formed and become the university choices for students. The higher the reputation of the university have, the higher the confidence and goodwill of prospective students for admission to the university.

According to research conducted by Balakrishnan, et al. (2014), marketing communications online, (especially electronic Words of Mouth/E-WOM), online communities and advertising online, have a very strong influence and are very effective in promoting the brand image of a product through a website and social media platform company.

This study will use the object in the form of an imaginary university with the aim to find out wider relevance of each study variable.

According to the background and problem identifications above, the problems of this research are, (1) Can news content affect trust toward a University?; (2) Can news content affect university's image?; and (3) Can news content affect attitude toward university?

H1: News Content (Positive and Negative News) affects Trust on University
H2: News Content (Positive and Negative News) affects University Image
H3: News Content (Positive and Negative News) affects Attitude Toward University

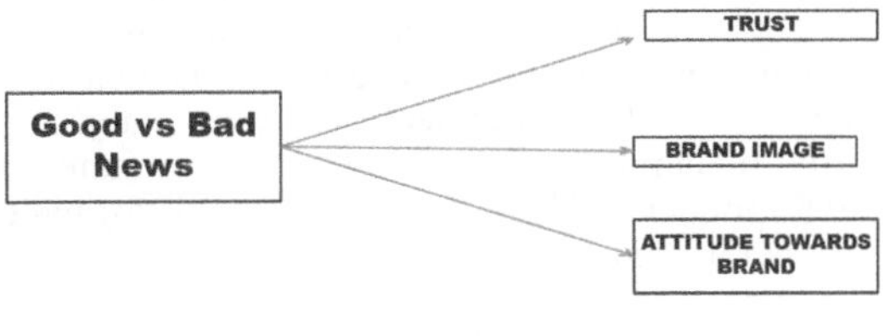

Figure 1. Research framework.

2 RESEARCH APPROACHES

According to Malhotra (2007) suggested that the experiment is the process of manipulating one or more independent variables and measure the influence of one or more of the dependent variable and then controlling for variables that are not connected. The use of the experimental method makes it possible to test the theory directly by implementing different treatments simultaneously while controlling factors that can blend in with this concept in real conditions (Agrawal, et al., 2010).

2.1 *Research design*

This experimental study will measure the difference in the average score (mean) of variable trust, brand image and attitude towards an university.

Experimental manipulations in the independent variable is create scenarios for the study of research that tells a fictional of an university and it positive/negative news. This scenario will be attached to a section of the initial questionnaire and be displayed as if it were a news online. At the end of the scenario will be a questionnaire about trust, brand image and attitude towards the brand.

2.2 *Population and sample*

The sample collection method using purposive sampling, whereby researchers determine the specific criteria to take samples that will be used as the respondents. Researchers determined that the population in this study was all students in senior high school (grade XII) Surabaya.

3 ANALYSIS AND DISCUSSION

Pretest process conducted on 20 students in SMA Negeri 5, Surabaya, especially on grade XII IPA 1 with the school's permission and consent. Treatments were given in the form of an article related to positive and negative news as if it came from the news online on the internet. There are four scenarios: positive news associated with individuals and institutions, and a negative news associated with individuals and institutions. Each scenario given to different respondents. One scenario given to respondents (between subjects). Total of number used at pretest was as many as 20 respondents. The total of participants for main test is 150 students.

3.1 *Validity and reliability*

Validity test is measured by calculating the value of item-to-total correlation of each indicator on each variable. The reliability test is measured by calculating the Cronbach's alpha value of each variable.

Table 1. Validity and reliability.

Variable		Item-to-total correlation	Cronbach's alpha
Trust	T1	0.808	0.923
	T2	0.868	
	T3	0.894	
Brand Image	BI1	0.775	0.872
	BI2	0.776	
	BI3	0.743	
Attitude Towards Brand	ATB1	0.699	0.887
	ATB2	0.831	
	ATB3	0.828	

Source: Processed data.

3.2 *Differential test (One-way ANOVA)*

ANOVA (Analysis of variance) was used to see it there is difference between the mean of the sample groups, between the control group and the experimental group consisting of a group of individuals' good news, institutions' good news, individual' bad news and institutions' bad news. This experimental study used two tabulation of data: the data for individual group and data for group institutions. Each tabulation will be processed in the average of mean from each variable (trust, brand image and attitude toward university). ANOVA analysis results can be seen on Table 2.

From the results of the different test on groups (Table 2), it can be concluded that: (1) accepting H1 or News Content (Good and Bad News) affects Trust toward University; (2) Accepting H2 or News Content (Good and Bad News) affects University Image; and (3) Accepting H3 or News Content (Good and Bad News) affects Attitude Toward University.

3.3 *Discussion*

This experimental study supports Polat's research (2012) that the rumors or news about the university, including the factors that affect the interest of a prospective students in choosing a university and department.

A study conducted by Keh and Xie (2009), stated that the profits of companies with a good reputation built on trust and identification among customers, are able to positively influence customer commitment to purchase intention.

In the group of good news when given the news that is positive, their image of the university they

Table 2. ANOVA between group test.

Group		Trust			Brand image			Attitude		
		Mean	F	Sig.	Mean	F	Sig.	Mean	F	Sig.
Individual	Control	4.5230	560.802	0.0000	4.0440	270.560	0.0000	3.6550	328.388	0.0000
	Individual Good News	4.5003		0.0000	4.4777		0.0000	4.4780		0.0000
	Individual Bad News	2.0333		0.0000	2.1557		0.0000	2.0783		0.0000
Institution	Control	4.5230	573.058	0.0000	4.0440	416.352	0.0000	3.6550	327.884	0.0000
	Institution Good News	4.5333		0.0000	4.4893		0.0000	4.5007		0.0000
	Institution Bad News	1.9673		0.0000	2.1003		0.0000	1.9110		0.0000

Source: Processed data.

want will tend to increase, while in the bad news groups, when given news that is negative, their image of the university they want will tend to decline.

4 IMPLICATIONS

This experimental study generates managerial implications that can be used by stakeholders in the university to enhance its role in education. In a market where the student is considered as a customer, and the competition does not only come from within the country but also from abroad, then the university must develop excellence unique competitive possessed by each university characteristics. The better a university in enhancing its reputation, the higher the intentions and interests of prospective students to choose and continue their studies at the university. It is also not independent of how a university to constantly develops and improves its performance, whether it is an individual accomplishment or institution. But in reality, there will always be cases involving negative news; the university needs to know how to manage this so as not to allow the negative publicity to affect the reputation of the university nor the intention of applicants to choose and continue his studies at the university.

REFERENCES

Agarwal, R., Croson, R. & Mahoney, J.T. (2010). The role of incentives and communication in strategic alliances: An experimental investigation. *Strategic Management Journal, 31*(4), 413–437.

Balakrishnan, B.K.P.D., Dahnil, M.I. & Yi, W.J. (2014). The impact of social media marketing medium toward purchase intention and brand loyalty among generation Y. *Procedia-Social and Behavioral Sciences, 148*, 177–185.

Go, E., You, K.H., Jung, E. & Shim, H. (2016). Why do we use different types of websites and assign them different levels of credibility? Structural relations among users' motives, types of websites, information credibility, and trust in the press. *Computers in Human Behavior, 54*, 231–239.

Jiewanto, A., Laurens, C. & Nelloh, L. (2012). Influence of service quality, university image, and student satisfaction toward WOM intention: A case study on Universitas Pelita Harapan Surabaya. *Procedia-Social and Behavioral Sciences, 40*, 16–23.

Keh, H.T. & Xie, Y. (2009). Corporate reputation and customer behavioral intentions: The roles of trust, identification and commitment. *Industrial Marketing Management, 38*(7), 732–742.

Malhotra, N. (2007). *Marketing research: An applied orientation* (5th ed.). New Jersey, USA: Pearson Education Inc.

McLeod, R. & Schell, G. (2001). *Management information systems* (8th ed.). Yogyakarta: Andi Offset.

Noorafshan, A., Pourahmad, S., Sagheb, M.M., Nazhvani, A.D., Abdollahi, M., Mohebbi, Z., Dousti, S.K. (2014). The students' intentions and satisfaction with the field of study and university. *Journal of Advances in Medical Education and Professionalism, 2*(4), 176–182.

Polat, S. (2012). The factors that students consider in university and department selection: A qualitative and quantitative study of Kocaeli University, faculty of education students. *Procedia-Social and Behavioral Sciences, 47*, 2140–2145.

Warren, R.P. (2014). *Who speaks for the negro?,* London, Yale University Press.

Increasing Management Relevance and Competitiveness – Sukoco et al. (Eds)
© 2018 Taylor & Francis Group, London, ISBN 978-0-8153-7455-8

Examining leadership style and advertising evaluation on employees' customer focus

R.A. Aisyah & N.A. Arina
Department of Management, Faculty of Economics and Business, Universitas Airlangga, Surabaya, Indonesia

ABSTRACT: This paper examines the links between leadership styles, organizational identification, advertising evaluations and employees' customer focus. Advertising contains information useful to employees in meeting customer needs. A model is proposed and tested using a sample of 65 salespersons from a service company. Data are analyzed through the use of Partial Least Squares (PLS). The results of this study showed that a transactional leadership stylesignificantly and positively influences organizational identification of salesperson. Organizational identification of salespersons significantly and positively influences advertising evaluations. Salespersons evaluate company's advertising significantly and positively influence judgments of advertising effectiveness and salespersons express their pride. Pride significantly and positively influences salespersons to support customer-focused.

Keywords: Leadership styles, organizational identification, promise accuracy, value congruence, salespersons' customer focus

1 INTRODUCTION

Leaders who do not have the competency to give direction and provide positive responses to subordinates will not create company growth. We discuss two leadership styles, transformational and transactional. These have been discussed in many previous studies and influence organizational identification. External customers view employees as internal customers. Moreover, a leader must motivate his employees, fulfilling their needs and wants as well as paying attention to the satisfaction of external customers.

The organizational identification of employees is especially relevant for companies because employees, such as salespersons, act as representatives of their organization by directly communicating and dealing with customers (Korschun, Bhattacharya and Swain, 2014). We expect that employees who strongly identify themselves with the company. This information reinforces their attitudes and beliefs and they can interprets this information to make it consistent with their beliefs. Employees are even encouraged to evaluate their company's advertising. Employees who lack confidence rarely indicate to a customer that they are part of the company, especially salespersons. They cannot identify with the company in the way that they identify themselves.

Celsi and Gilly (2010) researched employees who strongly identifiedwith a company and found they are likely to evaluate their company's advertising. As insiders, employees have a privileged position to interpret and assess communications of and about their organization. Moreover, employees who evaluate their company's advertisements are especially likely to evaluate the effectiveness of advertising with consumers (Gilly and Wolfinbarger, 1998).

Gilly and Wolfinbarger (1998) suggested that employees evaluate their organization's advertising on the dimensions of promise accuracy, value congruence and effectiveness. Gilly and Wolfinbarger (1998) found that employees often show their pride in a company through effective advertising. Michie (2009) found that pride is related to prosocial behaviors; for example,treating others with dignity and respect. Pride is a motivational component (White and Locke 1981) and employees become motivated to process and provide excellent service to customers when they are sufficiently proud of their company's advertising.These actions will result in greater customer focus (Fu 2013).

2 HYPOTHESIS DEVELOPMENT

2.1 *The influence of leadership style on organizational identification*

In this study, we have two leadership style approaches, transformational and transactional.

Transformational leadership is defined as a predictor of organizational identification and this type of style pays more attention to employees' high-order needs and provides motivation to employees through learning stimulation, achievement of needs and individual development (Epitropaki and Martin 2005). On the other hand, transactional leaders explain to subordinates about responsibilities, tasks that must be accomplished and performance objectives. The transactional leadership style provides a basis for self-categorization by enabling members to recognize and understand what the organization stands for (Epitropaki and Martin 2005). Therefore, transactional leadership will be positively related to employees' organizational identification. Thus, we predict that:

H1: Transformational leadership positively significant influences organizational leadership.
H2: Transactional leadership positively significant influences organizational leadership.

2.2 *The influence of organizational identification on advertisement evaluation*

Celsi and Gilly (2010) suggested that employees who are strongly identified with a company are likely to evaluate their company's advertising. Gilly and Wolfinbarger (1998) mentioned that employees commonly evaluate promise accuracy and the value congruence of advertisements. Employees are in a privileged position to evaluate promise accuracy and value congruence;in other words, how likely it is that the organization will consistently fulfill promises which were made in advertisements (Celsi and Gilly, 2010). As a result, value congruence in advertisements is likely to engage and motivate employees to support the vision of their organization portrayed in the advertisement (Celsi and Gilly, 2010). Therefore, we predict that:

H3: Organizational identification positively significant influences promise accuracy.
H4: Organizational identification positively significant influences value congruent.

2.3 *The influence of advertisement evaluation on effectiveness of advertising*

Celsi and Gilly (2010) defined the term effectiveness as being whether employees believe that advertising will be successful in gaining consumer attention. Gilly and Wolfinbarger (1998) suggested that employees link promise accuracy with effectiveness because employees are more likely to feel that their organization can fulfill promises when they are accurate. Advertising evaluation creates other responses to the company. Employees believe that the company should fulfill the promises that are portrayed in the advertisements, such as providing high quality services and high quality products to the consumerand not exaggerating statements to be displayed in the advertisements. Therefore, we predict that:

H5: Promise accuracy positively significant influences the effectiveness of advertisements.
H6: Value congruence positively significant influences the effectiveness of advertisements.

2.4 *The influence of effectiveness and pride on customer focus*

Michie (2009) defined pride as resulting from positive outcomes attributed to one's own or one's own group's efforts. Gilly and Wolfinbarger (1998) found that employees often express pride in effective advertising. When employees believe that an advertisement is effective, they indicatetheir group's success to both group and customers (Robert B. et al., 1976). On other hand, Michie (2009) showed that pride encourages behavior that conforms to social standards of what is valued or has merit in the organization. Michie (2009) found that pride is related to well-being behaviors, that is, treating others with dignity and respect. Because pride has a motivational component (White & Locke 1981), employees will be motivated to process and support customer-focused beliefs when they are proud of their firm's advertising.

H7: The effectiveness of advertisements positively significant influences employee pride.

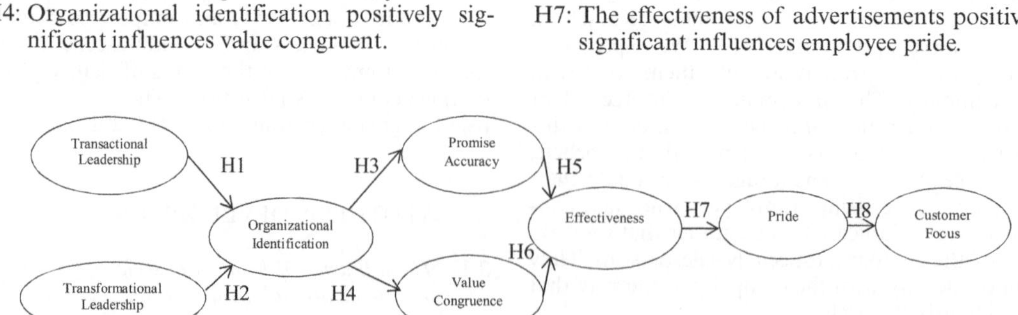

Figure 1. Research framework.

H8: Employee pride positively and significantly influences employees' customer focus.

3 METHODOLOGY

3.1 *Variables measurement*

To measure the different variables included in this study, a five-point Likert scale (0 = Strongly disagree; 5 = Strongly agree) was used. Transformational leadership was measured with seven items adapted from Carless, Wearing and Mann (2000). To capture transactional leadership, we used the measure of Avolio, Bass and Jung (1999) comprising of four items. Organizational identification was measured with four items from Smidts, Pruyn and van Riel (2001). Promise accuracy was measured with three items and value congruence was measured with three items from Gilly and Wolfinbarger (1998). Effectiveness was measured with four items from Celsi and Gilly (2010). Pride was measured with three items from Michie (2009). Customer focus was measured with four items from Celsi and Gilly (2010).

3.2 *Data collection*

Data were collected from salespersons at MyRepublic, an Internet service provider which is located in Surabaya. We initially collected 70 questionnaires. However, after discarding incomplete questionnaires, 65 were finally considered valid, giving a return rate of 92.86%. The demographic data showed that the sample generates annual sales of Rp.10 billion to 50 billion (58.30% of the respondents). The length of work between salesperson and company is 72.90% of the respondents having one year. The ownership resources capacity by buyer is 70.80% of the respondents have middle ownership resource capacity.

3.3 *Methods and data analysis*

To test the research model, partial least squares (PLS) are employed, modeling (Chin, 1998; Chin, Peterson & Brown, 2008; Hair, Ringle & Sarstedt, 2011), and used the SmartPLS 2.0 program (Ringle, Wende & Will, 2005). This choice was based on the fact that the primary concern of the study is the prediction of the dependent variable (Chin, 1998). To validate the measurement model, internal consistency and three types of validity were assessed: (1) content validity, (2) convergent validity and (3) discriminant validity. Content validity was confirmed by interviewing experts in the academic field and by pilot-testing the instrument.

4 ANALYSIS AND RESULTS

4.1 *Analysis of the measurement model*

The reliability, convergent and discriminant validity of the constructs were also assessed in the initial estimation. This analysis revealed that all items' outer loadings on their respective latent variables were above the critical threshold of 0.5 (Chin, 1998), with the exception of the indicator Transformational Leadership 7. Consequently, since this item did not present individual reliability, we decided to remove it and to estimate the first-order model again. The results revealed that this final first-order measurement model presents individual item reliability, since all the factor loadings exceed 0.5.

4.2 *Analysis of the structural model*

The measurement model analysis was conducted and verified the reliability and validity of the measurement items used in this study. The next stage, an assessment of the structural model, involved estimating the path coefficients and the R^2 value using PLS. For assessing the statistical significance of the model's path estimates, a bootstrapping method was used (Chin, 1998). The *t*-test value was 1.96 (when $p< 0.05$, using two-tailed tests). The results of the PLS analysis are shown in Table 1.

A bootstrapping method provides means, *t*-statistics and standard deviations for the path coefficients.

According to the results of the structural model, transactional leadership positively influences organizational identification ($\beta = 0.5512$; $t = 5.4721$), which supports hypothesis 2. Conversely, transformational leadership does not statistically significant influence organizational identification ($\beta = 0.1093$; $t = 1.0781$), leading to the rejection of hypothesis 1. Transactional leadership significantly and positively influences

Table 1. Results of the structural model.

Hypothesis	B	*t*-values	R^2
H1	0.1093	1.0781	R^2 (Organizational Identification) = 0.3955
H2	0.5512	5.4721	
H3	0.5484	6.9076	R^2 (Promisse Accuracy) = 0.3008
H4	0.4946	6.1707	R^2 (Value Congruence) = 0.2447
H5	0.4324	5.9208	R^2 (Effectiveness) = 0.5816
H6	0.4559	5.3963	
H7	0.6085	8.8558	R^2 (Pride) = 0.3702
H8	0.5315	5.989	R^2 (Customer Focus) = 0.2825

organizational identification. Transactional leaders can thus, provide a basis for self-categorization by enabling members to understand what the organization stands for and what it is like to be a typical member of it (Epitropaki & Martin 2005).

As expected, organizational identification positively and significantly influences promise accuracy ($\beta = 0.5484$; $t = 6.9076$), supporting hypothesis 3. Organizational identification positively and significantly influences value congruence ($\beta = 0.4946$; $t = 6.1707$), supporting hypothesis 4. Celsi and Gilly (2010) suggested that employees who strongly identified with the company are likely to evaluate their company's advertisements. Employees are in a privileged position to evaluate promise accuracy, in other words, how likely it is that the organization will consistently fulfill claims made in advertisements (Celsi & Gilly, 2010).

Promise accuracy positively influences effectiveness ($\beta = 0.4324$; $t = 5.9208$), supporting hypothesis 5. Value congruence positively influences effectiveness ($\beta = 0.4559$; $t = 5.3963$), supporting hypothesis 6. Employees who evaluate their company's advertisementsare especially likely to evaluate the effectiveness of advertising with consumers (Gilly & Wolfinbarger 1998). Gilly and Wolfinbarger (1998) suggested that employees evaluate their organization's advertising on the dimensions of accuracy, value congruence and effectiveness. Celsi and Gilly (2010) defined the term effectiveness as being whether employees believe that advertising will be successful in gaining consumer attention and generating sales.

Effectiveness positively influences pride ($\beta = 0.6085$; $t = 8.8558$), supporting hypothesis 7. Michie (2009) defined pride as resulting from positive outcomes attributed to one's own or one's own group's efforts. Gilly and Wolfinbarger (1998) found that employees often express pride in effective advertising.

Pride positively influences customer focus ($\beta = 0.5315$; $t = 5.989$), supporting hypothesis 8. Michie (2009) suggested that pride encourages behavior that conforms to social standards of what is valued or has merit in the organization. Pride has a motivational component (White & Locke 1981) and employees will be motivated to process and support customer-focused beliefs when they are proud of their firm's advertising.

5 MANAGERIAL IMPLICATIONS AND FUTURE RESEARCH

5.1 *Managerial implications*

Advertisements targeted at consumers also have effects on employees. It is particularly important to employees that advertisements effective and value congruent. Companies can leverage advertising internally, whenever advertisements are effective and value congruent, because such advertisements increase the salience of customer focus for employees. When campaigns are incongruent with employee values or perceived to be ineffective, organizations should limit employee exposure if possible or explain the strategy behind the advertisements to dampen negative effects on their internal audience.

Organizational communications should highlight the probable or actual effectiveness of advertisements when selling the campaign internally. It is particularly important to feature employees accurately in the eyes of most employees, as the judgment of employee portrayal accuracy has multiple effects on employee evaluations of advertisements. When employees are featured accurately, management has a golden opportunity to leverage advertising internally to increase organizational pride and customer focus. Evaluation of organizational advertising may both influence and be influenced by organizational identification. Therefore, the effects of advertising campaigns on organizational identity should also be examined. A research design that includes managerial assessment of employees' customer-focused behaviors would provide strong evidence between advertising and customer focus.

5.2 *Future research*

Future research might also analyzeemployee involvement in advertising as employees who are likely to feel more involved in their successful company will evaluate the advertisements more positively; and feel their contributions are valued. Advertisement is showing to the company that employees provide potentially even more compelling images with which other employees may identify (Celsi & Gilly, 2010). While merely featuring employees in advertisements has been shown to result in positive responses from employees in previous studies, evaluation of advertisements is, nevertheless, likely to be strongly influenced by employees' assessment of the similarity between the advertising portrayal and their perceptions of the actual characteristics and behaviors of employees of the company. (Bass 1990).

REFERENCES

Avolio, B.J., Bass, B.M. & Jung, D.I. (1999). Re-examining the components of transformational and transactional leadership using the multifactor leadership. *Journal of Occupational and Organizational Psychology*, *72*(4), 441–462.

Bass, B. & Avolio, B. (1997). *Full-range of leadership development: Manual for multifactor leadership questionnaire*. Palo Alto: CA Mind Garden.

Bass, B.M. (1990). From transactional to transformational leadership: Learning to share the vision. *Organizational Dynamics*, *18*(3), 19–31.

Bollen, K.A. & Stine, R.A. (1992). Bootstrapping goodness-of-fit measures in structural equation models. *Sociological Methods & Research*, *21*(2), 205–229.

Carless, S.A., Wearing, A.J. & Mann, L. (2000). A short measure of transformational leadership. *Journal of Business and Psychology VO - 14*, *14*(3), 389.

Celsi, M.W. & Gilly, M.C. (2010). Employees as internal audience: How advertising affects employees' customer focus. *Journal of the Academy of Marketing Science*, *38*(4), 520–529.

Chin, W. (1998). The partial least squares approach to structural equation modeling. *Modern Methods for Business Research*, *295*(2), 295–336.

Chin, W., Peterson, R. & Brown, S. (2008). Structural equation modeling in marketing: Some practical reminders. *The Journal of Marketing Theory and Practice*, *16*(4), 287–298. http://doi.org/10.2753/MTP1069-6679160402.

Dutton, J.E., Dukerich, J.M. & Harquail, C.V. (1994). Organizational images and member identification. *Administrative Science Quarterly*, *39*(2), 239–263.

Edwards, M.R., 2005. Organizational identification: A conceptual and operational review. *International Journal of Management Reviews*, 7(4), pp. 207–230.

Epitropaki, O. & Martin, R. (2005). From ideal to real: A longitudinal study of the role of implicit leadership theories on leader-member exchanges and employee outcomes. *Journal of Applied Psychology*, *90*(4), 659–676.

Fornell, C. & Larcker, D.F. (1981). Structural equation models with unobservable variables and measurement error: Algebra and statistics. *Journal of Marketing Research*, *18*(3), 382–388.

Friestad, M. & Wright, P. (1994). The persuasion knowledge model: How people cope with persuasion attempts. *Journal of Consumer Research*, *21*(1), 1–31.

Fu, Y.K. (2013). The influence of internal marketing by airlines on customer-oriented behavior: A test of the mediating effect of emotional labor. *Journal of Air Transport Management*, *32*, 49–57.

Gilly, M.C. & Wolfinbarger, M. (1998). Advertising's internal audience. *Journal of Marketing*, *62*(1), 69–88.

Grönroos, C. (1984). A service quality model and its marketing implications. *European Journal of Marketing*, *18*(4), 36–44.

Hair, J.F., Ringle, C.M. & Sarstedt, M. (2011). PLS-SEM: Indeed a silver bullet. *Journal of Marketing Theory and Practice*, *19*(2), 139–152.

Hair, J.F., Sarstedt, M., Ringle, C.M. & Mena, J.A. (2012). An assessment of the use of partial least squares structural equation modeling in marketing research. *Journal of the Academy of Marketing Science*, *40*(3), 414–433.

Homburg, C., Wieseke, J. & Hoyer, W.D. (2009). Social identity and the service–profit chain. *Journal of Marketing*, *73*(2), 38–54.

Korschun, D., Bhattacharya, C.B. & Swain, S.D. (2014). Corporate social responsibility, customer orientation, and the job performance of frontline employees. *Journal of Marketing*, *78*(3), 20–37.

Lings, I.N. (2004). Internal market orientation — Construct and consequences. *Journal of Business Research*, *57*(4), 405–413.

Mael, F. & Ashforth, B.E. (1992). Alumni and their alma mater: A partial test of the refomulated model of organizational identification. *Journal of Organizational Behavior*, *13*(2), 103–123.

Michie, S. (2009). Pride and gratitude: How positive emotions influence the prosocial behaviors of organizational leaders. *Journal of Leadership & Organizational Studies*, *15*(4), 393–403.

Mitchell, R.K., Mitchell, J.R. & Smith, J.B. (2008). Inside opportunity formation: Enterprise failure, cognition, and the creation of opportunities. *Strategic Entrepreneurship Journal*, *2*(3), 225–242.

Nunnally, J.C. & Bernstein, I. (1994). *Psychometric theory*. McGraw-Hill, New York, 3, 701.

Ringle, C.M., Wende, S. & Will, A. (2005). *SmartPLS 2.0.* Hamburg: University of Hamburg.

Robert B.,C., Richard J., B., Avril, T., Marcus Randall, W., Stephen, F. & Lloyd Reynolds, S. (1976). Basking in reflected glory: Three (football) field studies. *Journal of Personality and Social Psychology*, *34*(3), 366–375.

Sirén, C.A., Kohtamäki, M. & Kuckertz, A. (2012). Exploration and exploitation strategies, profit performance, and the mediating role of strategic learning: Escaping the exploitation trap. *Strategic Entrepreneurship Journal*, *6*(1), 18–41.

Smidts, A., Pruyn, A.T.H. & Van Riel, C.B.M. (2001). The impact of employee communication and perceived external prestige on organizational identification. *Academy of Management Journal*, *44*(5), 1051–1062.

Tracy, J.L. & Robins, R.W. (2004). Putting the self into self-conscious emotions: A theoretical model. *Psychological Inquiry*, *15*(2), 103–125.

van Knippenberg, D. (2000). Work motivation and performance: A social identity perspective. *Applied Psychology: An International Review*, *49*(3), 357.

van Knippenberg, D., van Knippenberg, B., De Cremer, D. & Hogg, M.A. (2004). Leadership, self, and identity: A review and research agenda. *The Leadership Quarterly*, *15*(6), 825–856.

Verplanken, B. & Holland, R.W. (2002). Motivated decision making: Effects of activation and self-centrality of values on choices and behavior. *Journal of Personality and Social Psychology*, *82*(3), 434–447.

Walumbwa, F.O., Avolio, B. & Zhu, W. (2008). Weaves Its influence on individual job performance : The role of identification and efficacy eeliefs. *Personnel Psychology*, *61*, 793–825.

White, F.M. & Locke, E.A. (1981). Perceived determinants of high and low productivity in three occupational groups: A critical incident study. *Journal of Management Studies*, *18*(4), 375–388.

Zagoršek, H., Dimovski, V. & Škerlavaj, M. (2009). Transactional and transformational leadership impacts on organizational learning. *Journal for East European Management Studies*, *14*(2), 144–165.

Increasing Management Relevance and Competitiveness – Sukoco et al. (Eds)
© 2018 Taylor & Francis Group, London, ISBN 978-0-8153-7455-8

The effect of airline sale promotion types on consumers' attitudes toward brand and purchase intentions

M. Kurniawati
Universitas Airlangga, Surabaya, Indonesia

ABSTRACT: The airline business is facing an increasing level of competition. In order to increase their sales volumes, marketers use sales promotions. Direct premium is one of the sales promotion techniques which can be categorized into two types; fit and non-fit direct premium. A direct premium will create positive attitudes toward the brand which ultimately affects the consumer's purchase intentions. This study investigates the differences in consumers' attitudes toward brands and purchase intention to do with the application of fit and non-fit direct premium, and its impact on consumers' purchase intentions. Using an experimental design approach, this study focuses on hypothesis testing by using one way ANOVA analysis techniques and simple linear regression. The managerial implications and suggestions for future research will then be delivered.

Keywords: Sales promotion, direct premium, attitude toward brand, consumer purchase intention

1 INTRODUCTION

Today's technological developments make it easier for consumers to buy products that they want, including airline tickets, whereas in the past, consumers had to employ a great deal of effort. This means that the consumer demand for airline tickets has increased. The International Air Transport Association (IATA) announced their full-year global passenger traffic results for 2016, showing that demand (revenue passenger kilometers or RPKs) rose by 6.3% compared to 2015 (or 6.0% if adjusted for the leap year). This strong performance was ahead of the ten-year estimated average annual growth rate of 5.5%. This high demand is set to continue. IATA even predicted that 7.2 billion passengers will travel in 2035, with 3.8 billion air travelers in 2016.

IATA also stated that the industry has changed; there is the increasing price of transparency, with deregulated markets and no frills increasing competition. Corporate travel buyers are becoming more price sensitive. One approach for companies to survive in this competition is by utilizing sales promotions. There are several methods of sales promotion that can be used. One of them is the premium method (gift-giving). A premium is an item offered at a relatively low or free price as an incentive to buy certain products (Kotler & Keller, 2016). Sales promotions in the form of premiums can be categorized into two types: direct premiums that are given directly (such as articles that are provided along with the main product) and delayed premiums (such as articles sent by mail to the consumers who have sent proof of purchase).

However, sales promotions do not always work effectively and consumers do not always respond positively. One of the factors affecting sales promotion effectiveness is the particular type of sales promotion used (DelVecchio et al., 2006). Hence, some types of sales promotion will be more effective than others. Thus, this research study seeks to analyze which types of premium-based sales promotion are the most effective at leading consumers to purchase an airline ticket.

2 LITERATURE REVIEW AND HYPOTHESIS

2.1 *Premium-based sales promotion*

D'Astous and Landreville (2003) defined premium-based sales promotions as being the goods or services offered for free or at a relatively low price on single or multiple purchases of products or services. The strength of premium-product conformance is likely to be accepted as natural and consistent, and consumers will respond positively. When premium-product conformity is weak, promotional offers tend to be regarded as being inconsistent and possibly opportunistic. In addition, the increasing perceived value of the promotional offers will be obtained when the premiums can actually be integrated with consumption or the use of the product (d'Astous & Landreville, 2003). So in this case, the fit and non-fit of the direct premium to the product category affects consumer attitude.

2.2 *Relationship between direct premium and consumer attitude toward brand*

D'Astous and Landreville (2003) posited that a premium can be regarded as a reward that leads to a positive reaction toward the product or brand purchased. Alternatively, it can be regarded as a persuasive trick set to make the product appear more attractive. D'Astous and Landreville's (2003) work suggests that unattractive premium offerings may affect brand image and consumer attitude toward the brand. This is also supported by Simonson et al. (1994), in that consumers react negatively toward brands that provide gimmicks like useless premiums in an attempt to attract potential customers.

Direct premiums as a sales promotion technique can be categorized into fit direct premium (premium that fits with the core products) and non-fit direct premium (premium that does not fit with the core product). Fit refers to the perceived level of proximity or conformity between a promoted product and an offered prize (Montaner, Chernatony & Buil, 2011). Chandon et al. (2000) stated that effective promotions are those that offer congruent benefits with the promoted products. Fit between product categories and premiums will have an effect if they are considered attractive by the consumers (d'Astous & Landreville, 2003). Montaner, Chernatony and Buil (2011) stated that consumers will respond positively when the fit between products and premiums is high, and vice versa. This is in line with the opinion of d'Astous and Landreville (2003) who said that when there is a low fit between the product and premium, promotional offers may be considered as being inconsistent or opportunistic.

H1: Consumer attitude toward the brand will be higher when there is a high fit rather than a low fit between product and premium.

2.3 *Relationship between direct premium and purchase intention*

Consumers show a positive response toward attractive premiums, i.e. premiums with a high fit with the product. A high fit between product and premium will increase consumer purchase intentions (Montaner et al., 2011). The fit between product and premium has a significant impact on the consumer's evaluation. In addition, a high fit between the product and premium offered will increase consumer purchase intentions (Montaner et al., 2011). The application of sales promotion techniques such as premiums will increase consumer satisfaction and purchase intention. This is evident in the Malaysian market where sales using such techniques are increased (Teck Weng & Cyril de Run, 2013).

H2: Consumer purchase intention will be higher when there is a high rather than a low fit between product and premium.

2.4 *Relationship between attitude toward brand and consumer purchase intention*

The attitude toward a particular brand often affects whether the consumer will buy or not. A positive attitude toward a particular brand will lead to the consumer repurchasing the brand. Conversely, a negative attitude will prevent the consumer from purchasing (Sutisna, 2002). These positive and negative feelings toward a brand will eventually affect the consumer's purchase intention. The higher the consumer attitude is toward the brand, the higher the purchase intention (Kurniawati, 2009).

H3: The attitude toward the brand will affect the consumer's purchase intentions.

3 RESEARCH METHODS

Using an experimental design, this study has manipulated the independent variables, namely the level of fit between the premium and the core product. The media used was a printed brochure for an airline ticket promotion. The best airline in Indonesia was chosen to avoid risk aversion bias. Illustrations in the brochure depict a direct premium with a fit direct premium (hotel voucher) and a non-fit direct premium (microwave oven). The stimulus was presented on the size of half a page of colored magazine. To avoid any confusing effect, the brochure displayed the image of the product and the premium in the same composition and within proportion to one another. The brochures were then presented to two different groups of participants. The first group of participants received the brochure containing the fit direct premium and the second group of participants received the brochure containing the non-fit direct premium. After the brochure was presented, the participants were then asked to answer questions about their attitude and purchase intention.

4 RESULTS AND DISCUSSION

Table 1 shows that the difference between brand attitudes on fit and non-fit direct premium is

Table 1. ANOVA analysis of attitude toward brand.

Direct premium	Attitude toward brand		
	Mean	*F*-value	Sig
Fit	4.834	8.921	0.003
Non-fit	3.450		

Table 2. ANOVA analysis of purchase intention.

Direct premium	Purchase intention		
	Mean	*F*-value	Sig
Fit	4.812	6.566	0.010
Non-fit	4.125		

Table 3. Simple linear regression analysis.

Variable	Regression coefficient	*t*-value	Sig.
Constant	–0.036		
Attitude toward brand (X)	0.874	9.247	0.000
$R^2 = 0.625$			
$R = 0.783$			

significant ($Mean_{fit}$: 4.834; $Mean_{non\text{-}fit}$: 3.450; F = 8.921; Sig = 0.003). In other words, there is a different attitude toward the brand in the two conditions. H1 is supported.

Table 2 shows that the difference in purchase intention between fit and non-fit direct premium is significant ($Mean_{fit}$: 4.812; $Mean_{non\text{-}fit}$: 4.125; F = 6.566; Sig = 0.010). In other words, there is a difference in purchase intention in the two conditions. H2 is supported. The next analysis uses a simple regression analysis to test the relationship between attitude toward the brand and purchase intention.

Table 3 shows that with a significant value of 0.010, the attitude toward the brand significantly affects the consumer's purchase intention. H3 is supported.

Support for H1 and H2 in the present research indicates that a fit direct premium is preferred by the consumer rather than non-fit direct premium. Montaner, Chernatony and Buil (2011) also found the same result, in that a fit direct premium will produce positive consumer responses whereas a non-fit direct premium will produce negative responses or rejection. Another study by d'Astous and Landreville (2003) also found that when a firm offers a non-fit direct premium, the promotional offerings may be considered as being inconsistent and opportunistic. Furthermore, a fit direct premium has a significant impact on consumer evaluation. In addition, a high fit between the product and the premium offered will increase the consumer purchase intention (Montaner, Chernatony & Buil, 2011). H3 indicates that the consumer attitude toward the brand affects the consumer purchase intention. This result is similar to Kurniawati's (2009) study which found that the positive and negative feelings that form the attitude toward a brand will ultimately create or negate the consumer purchase intention. The higher the attitude toward the brand, the higher the consumer purchase intention.

5 IMPLICATIONS

5.1 *Managerial implications*

It is recommended for marketers to use a fit direct premium instead of a non-fit direct premium. This is because a fit direct premium generates a positive response in relation to consumer brand attitudes and purchase intentions in contrast with a non-fit direct premium.

Marketers should understand what kind of direct premium consumers consider as fitting with the main product. In this case, the premium fit with the main product does not always mean that the premium should have the same or a strong relationship with the main product. It also means that the premium product has benefits or an effect on the main product such as when consumers buy cereals, a plastic box comes with the product as storage.

5.2 *Further research*

For future research, researchers could use fit and non-fit premiums with different prices or values to determine whether consumers will respond differently. This is because d'Astous and Jacob (2001) found that consumers will choose a fit over a non-fit premium even when the non-fit premium has a higher value.

Also, in this study, the researcher showed a premium product to participants without informing them of the price of the product. For further research, in addition to showing the type of premium offered, the value or price of the premium could also be delivered to determine whether the consumers will respond accordingly.

REFERENCES

Chandon, P., Wansink, B., & Laurent, G. (2000). A benefit congruency framework of sales promotion effectiveness. *Journal of marketing*, *64*(4), 65–81.

d'Astous, A. & Jacob, I. (2002). Understanding consumer reactions to premium-based promotional offers. *European Journal of Marketing, 36*(11/12), 1270–1286.

d'Astous, A. & Landreville, V. (2003). An experimental investigation of factors affecting consumers' perceptions of sales promotions. *European Journal of Marketing, 37*(11/12), 1746–1761.

DelVecchio, D., Henard, D.H. & Freling, T.H. (2006). The effect of sales promotion on post-promotion brand preference: A meta-analysis. *Journal of Retailing, 82*(3), 203–213.

Kotler, P., & Keller K.L. 2016. *Marketing Management.* 15 edition. Essex: Pearson Education.

Kurniawati, D. (2009). *Studi Tentang Sikap Terhadap Merek dan Implikasinya Pada Minat Beli Ulang.* Tesis tidak diterbitkan. Semarang Pasca Sarjana Universitas Diponegoro.

Montaner, T., de Chernatony, L. & Buil, I. (2011). Consumer response to gift promotions. *Journal of Product & Brand Management*, *20*(2), 101–110.

Simonson, I., Carmon, Z. & O'curry, S. (1994). Experimental evidence on the negative effect of product features and sales promotions on brand choice. *Marketing Science, 13*(1), 23–40.

Sutisna. (2002). *Perilaku Konsumen dan Komunikasi Pemasaran.* Bandung: PT Remaja Rosdakarya Offset.

Teck Weng, J. & Cyril de Run, E. (2013). Consumers' personal values and sales promotion preferences effect on behavioural intention and purchase satisfaction for consumer product. *Asia Pacific Journal of Marketing and Logistics, 25*(1), 70–101.

Increasing Management Relevance and Competitiveness – Sukoco et al. (Eds)
© 2018 Taylor & Francis Group, London, ISBN 978-0-8153-7455-8

The influence of celebgrams, e-WOM, and pictures on impulse buying

Hartini, Sri & Uswatun
Universitas Airlangga, Surabaya, Indonesia

ABSTRACT: In this research, the author proposes that social media has an effect on consumer behavior. This study aims to examine the relationship between celebgrams (celebrities on Instagram), electronic Word of Mouth (e-WOM), and pictures on impulse buying. A sample was obtained through purposive sampling and 116 samples used. The results showed that celebgrams have a positive, statistically significant influence on impulse buying. Neither pictures nor e-WOM had a significant influence on impulse buying.

Keywords: celebgram, e-WOM, pictures, impulse buying

1 INTRODUCTION

The variety of emerging adult social media also affects the mechanism of selling–purchasing in more diverse forms as well. Whereas in the 1960s buyers and sellers had to be able to meet physically to conduct transactions, in 2016 sellers and buyers no longer have to do this.

By utilizing the facilities provided by the Internet and social media the seller can promote to unlimited market segments, the cost allocated to the promotion budget can be minimized, and relatively small capital is required, along with a trimmed distribution chain. The inventory cost can be eliminated, which will, of course, lower the price. Principal sales can attract consumer interest so that the potential to achieve as much profit as possible will be easily achieved.

Individuals and groups have begun to use social media as a medium to support the delivery of messages. Businesses today have social media accounts like Twitter, Facebook, Instagram and others to introduce products or communicate with their customers (Purnomo, 2015). A social media with the main focus of visual content in the form of photos, and which has become one of the most popular media in Indonesia, is Instagram (maxmanroe, 2014).

Instagram can load the image of the product with complete and excellent image quality. Thousands and even up to millions of images can be stored that are at once accessible to both sellers and buyers. In social media, the seller can provide as much information as possible about the products offered. The information submitted is precise, accurate and has a fixed standard and it aims to provide uniform information about the product and thus reduce misunderstanding of product information to consumers.

Sellers no longer have to pay sales force personnel to simply explain product information or serve to help the payment process, especially given the fact, for various reasons, that the sales force is not always best placed to deal with consumers. Sellers and buyers do not need to conduct meetings for the transfer of knowledge, but information can be accessed anywhere at any time as long as there is an Internet connection, so as not to take up time for either sellers or buyers.

Surfing on the Internet is analogous to walking around the mall while looking at stores without buying anything. Online shopping can form a rational buying behavior. This is supported by the fact that the Internet has the characteristics of efficiency and a variety of information enabling consumers to make price comparisons as well as obtain other information about a product.

From here arose the expectation that consumers use logic as well as grounded reasons when making a purchase. However, the fact is that not all consumers act rationally and logically when transacting or making online purchases. Therefore, the term irrational buying or unregulated buying was devised. According to LaRose (2002), unregulated buying consists of impulse buying, compulsive buying, and addictive buying. These three types of purchase are a form of deviation from consumer behavior in the context of the shopping environment.

2 THEORETICAL FRAMEWORK AND HYPOTHESIS

Lovelock (2008) explains that word of mouth or testimony can consist of comments or recommendations distributed by the customer, based on their experience, which have a strong influence on the decision-making of others. Based on the above opinion, it can be concluded that testimony is a form of marketing that tends to include communication that can be delivered directly to provide information, and promote, or recommend a product or service.

H1: Electronic Word of Mouth (e-WOM) positively affects consumer impulse buying.

A 'celebgram' can be interpreted as a celebrity endorser on Instagram social media. According to Shimp (2002), an 'ad advocate', also known as an 'ad star', is someone who supports an advertised product. An endorser is a particular icon or figure who is often also referred to as a direct source to deliver a message and/or demonstrate a product or service through promotional activities aimed at supporting the effectiveness of the delivery of the product messages (Belch & Belch, 2004, p. 168) endorsers are divided into two types: typical-person endorsers are ordinary people not well-known who are used to advertise a product, whereas a celebrity endorser is a famous person used to support an advertisement. Both types of endorsers have the same attributes and characteristics.

H2: Celebgrams positively affect consumer impulse buying.

According to Sadiman (2006, pp. 28–29), images are part of visual graphics media as well as other media. Graphics media aims to channel messages from sources to message recipients through visual channels. Messages to be delivered are poured into visual communication symbols. These symbols need to be understood correctly as regards their meaning so that the message delivery process can be successful and efficient.

H3: Pictures positively affect consumer impulse buying.

3 RESEARCH METHOD

The population in this study is comprised of people who have an Instagram account and the study uses a purposive sampling method, whereby not all members of the population have the same opportunity to become a member of the sample. The population of individuals is virtually unlimited in number. Purposive sampling is a sample determination technique that enables anyone found and considered appropriate as a sample of a study to be a data source (Aaker et al., 1996). The sample size was 116 people who have an Instagram account and had never made a purchase of fashion products through the social medium of Instagram.

3.1 *Measurement*

Word of mouth or testimony is a comment or recommendation that a customer disseminates based on their own experience, indicators are number of likes and number of positive comments on the celebgram page uploader (Shimp, 2002). Picture images are visual graphics media that aim to deliver messages from sources to the message recipients (Sadiman et al., 2003, pp. 28–29). Solomon (2004, p. 408) describes impulse purchases as unplanned purchases which arise when one feels a sudden impulse buying. The data analysis technique used in this study is multiple linear regression analysis in statistics, a mathematical formula that shows the relationship between one or more variables whose value is known and a variable whose value is not known.

4 RESULT AND DISCUSSION

The research respondents consisted of mostly females (70%), while male respondents comprised 30%. The percentage of respondents aged between 20 and 24 years was 51%; those aged 24–29 was 21%; aged 30–34 was 11%; aged 34–39 was 10%; aged over 39 was 7%.

The educational background of respondents consisted of: postgraduate (S2) at 8%; undergraduate education (S1) at 41%; diploma education or equivalent at 30%; respondents with high school education at 21%. In terms of employment, 42% of respondents were students, while respondents with jobs as private employees accounted for 25%, respondents with entrepreneur jobs totaled 14%, and respondents with a job as a civil servant comprised 5%. Respondents having jobs other than those mentioned accounted for 13%. Those with an income between Rp. 2,500,000 and Rp. 4,990,000 accounted for 31%; respondents with an income between Rp. 1,000,000 and Rp. 2,490,0000 numbered 20%; respondents with a maximum income of 1,000,000, and those with an income between Rp. 5,000,000 and Rp. 6,990,000 each accounted for 18%; respondents with an income between Rp. 7,000,000 and Rp. 9,990,000 totaled 8%, while 5% of respondents had an income greater than Rp. 10,000,000.

Test results with SPSS used the 0.05 significance limit (i.e. if the significance value is smaller than the 5% level, it means the null hypothesis, H_0, is rejected and the alternative hypothesis, H_A, accepted). Test results obtained for testimonial variable t test equal to −1.168 with significance level 0.245, by using the 0.05 significance limit, the first hypothesis is rejected. This means testimony on Instagram does not affect consumer impulse buying. However, the second hypothesis is accepted. Test results show that celebgram obtained t test equal to 5,538 with level of significance, this means that if a better known celebgram is on, it will affect consumer impulse buying. The third hypothesis is rejected. This means a good picture of the product on Instagram has no effect on impulse buying.

Celebgram is found to significantly influence the impulse buying of consumers while the other independent variables of testimony and images are found to have no significant effect on impulse buying. This happens because the consumer familiar with the purchase online, so they understand that testimony is a marketing strategy, testimony made by the company. Consumers experienced that the product sent not in accordance with the image shown in on line.

The phenomenon of engineered testimony by producers or marketers is being used more frequently, both in terms of quantity and content, making consumers less trusting of the accuracy and validity of testimony submitted by the manufacturer.

The discovery of a commentary on the incompatibility of images with products received by consumers also led to high levels of consumer distrust of the images listed on Instagram. This was also supported by the sophistication of editing technology and camera resolution to improve image quality in terms of lighting, color combinations, and so on. Consequently, consumers feel unsure, and ultimately do not encourage other consumers to do impulse buying.

Whereas in the variable of the known celebgram, the result is significant, as a result of the tendency of the consumer to idolize the celebgram so that anything that is delivered by the celebgram is considered correct. Based on the definition of impulse buying described in the previous chapter, meaning that purchase is irrational or without intent, Consumers who feel positive about a particular celebgram, this will make the celebgram a reference in impulsively choosing a product.

5 CONCLUSION

Based on research about the influence of e-WOM, celebgrams, and pictures of fashion products on Instagram on impulse buying consumers, the following conclusions are drawn: the results of multiple linear regression and *t*-tests on the respondents' answers show that there is only one regression coefficient signified as positive and significant: celebgrams.

This means that celebgrams have a positive and significant influence on consumer impulse buying. This means the better the celebgram, the more positive and significant the impact on consumer impulse buying. The image/picture has a negative and not significant influence on consumer impulse buying. This means that any image on Instagram will not affect consumer impulse buying.

REFERENCES

Aaker, D., Batra, R. & Myers, J.G. (1996). *Advertising management* (5th ed.). Englewood Cliffs, NJ: Prentice Hall.

Ali, H. (2010). *Marketing dari Mulut ke Mulut* [*Word of mouth marketing*]. Yogyakarta, Indonesia: Media Presindo.

Belch, George E. Belch, Michael, A. (2009). *Advertising and Promotion: An Integrated Marketing Communication Perpectiv*. 8th Edition. New York: Mc Grow-Hill.

Cobb, C.J. & Hoyer, W.D. (1986). A planned versus impulse purchase behaviour. *Journal of Retailing*, *62*, 67–81.

Hu, Y., Manikonda, L. & Kambhampati, S. (2014). What we Instagram: A first analysis of Instagram photocontent and user types. In *Proceedings of the 8th International Conference on Weblogs and Social Media, ICWSM 2014* (pp. 595–598). Palo Alto, CA: The AAAI Press.

Larose, Robert; Eastin Mathew, Is Online Buying Out of Control? Electronic Commerce and Consumer Self-Regulation, Journal of Broadcasting & Electronic Media Volume 46, 2002 - Issue 4.

Lovelock, C. & Wright, L.K. (2011). *Service marketing, people, technology, strategy*. Upper Saddle River, NJ: Prentice Hall.

Maxmanroe (2014). 7 Fakta Unik Instagram yang Perlu Diketahui oleh Internet Marketer.

Mayfield, A. (2008). What is social media. *ICrossing*.

Muruganantham, G. & Bhakat, R.S. (2013). A review of impulse buying behaviour. *International Journal of Marketing Studies*, *5*(3), 149–160.

Nielsen, A.C. (2007). *Survey of consumer behaviour and perception toward modern retail and traditional trade channels*. Jakarta, Indonesia: Departemen Perdagangan Indonesia.

Purnomo, Wahyu D. (2015). Apa Itu Sosial Media Marketing? *http://semseomanagement.com/apa-itu-social-media-marketing/*.

Rook, D. & Fisher, J.R. (1995). Normative influences on impulsive buying behaviour. *Journal of Consumer Research*, *22*(3), 305–313.

Sadiman, 2006, Media Pendidikan, pengertian, pengembangan, dan Pemanfaatanya Jakarta: Pustekom. Dikbud, PT Raja Grafindo.

Shimp, Terence. (2002). Periklanan Promosi. Erlangga. Jakarta.

Shoham, A. & Brencis, M.M. (2003). Compulsive buying behaviour. *Journal of Marketing Research*, *20*, 127–138.

Solomon (2004), Consumer behavior, buying, having and being, Amazon.com.

Stern, H. (1962). The significance of impulse buying today. *Journal of Marketing*, *26*(2), 59–62.

Increasing Management Relevance and Competitiveness – Sukoco et al. (Eds)
 ISBN 978-0-8153-7455-8

Value propositions of supermarkets

R. Rinawati
Universitas Pendidikan Indonesia, Bandung, Indonesia

ABSTRACT: Customer loyalty is indicated by the consumers' repeat-purchase behavior. Such factors as price, quality of goods, services, location, and innovation, are some determinant factors affecting the consumers' purchase decision. A value proposition provides an overview of products and services that provides value for specific customer segments. This research investigated the customers' perception towards the value in general and, more specifically, in supermarkets, namely in Carrefour, Giant, Lottemart, Toserba Yogya, Borma, and Super Indo. The research method employed was qualitative method. This research aimed at indentifying consumers' behavior in shopping, selecting and acquiring their value from every supermarket. The results of this study revealed that the majority of customers become more loyal when their needs and desires were satisfied. This will give the company a competitive advantage.

Keywords: Marketing, value proposition, supermarket, Bandung

1 INTRODUCTION

The existence of supermarkets today provides another alternative for the community in accomodating their needs. The increasing number of supermarkets increases competitiveness in business. Customer satisfaction and loyalty are the objectives of every business. Every company wants high loyalty from its customers, and therefore must have an effective and efficient strategy. Companies should, as much as possible, accomodate the wants and needs of their customers. The customers' standard of value can provide the basis of comparative assessment. This assessment can provide an insight to the value proposition for a company. A value proposition describes the value creation process that is provided to customers by the products or services offered. A supermarket is a business organization which offers a wide range of consumption options to the community. Each supermarket has a different value proposition, due to the different factors considered by customers in the provision of value, such as price, quality, service, and innovation.

Kaplan and Norton (1996) explain that the value of propositions varies between industries and across different market segments within an industry. Different appraisals from each customer affect the buying decision until the purchase repeats in the same place. Capon and Hulbert (2007) describe a clear and effective value proposition as the basis for successful corporate, psychological, and organizational functionality when customers buy repeatedly. Each customer has different motives and behaviors for shopping; there are customers who look for quality, others prefer quantity, while others look for satisfaction in service, or desire to do it for themselves. Organizations must compete to attract more customers to buy and re-buy.

Customer loyalty is formed when a company consistently satisfies customers' needs. Ang and Buttle (2009) describe a value proposition as an explicit promise made by a company to the customer that will give a certain amount of value in benefit creation. Barnes et al. (2009) explain that creation of a value proposition is a process consisting of inputs (customer experience, offerings, benefits, costs and risks, prices, alternatives) and outputs (new and retained customers, favorable growth, increased supply, business through sales). This is similarly expressed by Anderson et al. (2006), who stated that there are three kinds of value proposition that involve all benefits, namely favorable points of difference and resonating focus. The value proposition of different companies is based on the customer's judgment of their shopping experience. Carbone and Haeckel (1994) in Rintamaki et al. (2007), describe the customer experience as a "takeaway" of impressions formed by people's encounters with products, services, and businesses—a perception that is generated when human consolidates sensory information. The company, as a provider of products and services, will generate a unavoidable pleasant or unpleasant sensation. Customer ratings that are built on a pleasant customer experience will provide competitive advantage for the customer.

This study aims at investigating the customer assessment on the companies' products and services in general and specifically the value proposition of the companies. This research employs qualitative method. It is a method that is systematic, focused and consistent on the data obtained in order to gain information from respondents to solve research problems. This method was used to obtain a detailed view of the customer's experience in shopping. Qualitative methods are preferred because it does not depend on a measurement but on the reasons behind the facts. To obtain the accurate required information as a data source, primary and secondary data were obtained through literature study and questionnaires. It was administered to respondents as the research samples. Meanwhile, the research was conducted on existing supermarkets in Bandung, namely, Carrefour, Yogya Shop (Riau Junction), Giant, Lottemart, Borma, and Super Indo.

The results of the research showed that in terms of price, Borma had the primary value proposition, followed by Super Indo, Yogya Shop, Lottemart, Giant, and Carrefour. For the second aspect, the quality of goods, the supermarket with the leading value proposition were the Yogya Department Store, followed by Lottemart, Carrefour, Giant, Super Indo, and Borma. The supermarkets with the leading value proposition in terms of the third aspect, service, were Yogya Department Store, followed by Borma, Super Indo, Lottemart, Giant and Carrefour. In terms of innovation, the supermarkets with the highest-rated value proposition were Yogya Department Store, followed by Carrefour, Lottemart, Giant, Super Indo, and Borma. Different values propositions from each supermarket imply different capabilities in creating value. Every supermarket had different ratings from customers on the basis of their experience.

2 RESEARCH RESULTS AND DISCUSSION

2.1 *Study results*

The questionnaires were randomly distributed to 30 respondents in order to obtain a subjective assessment of the supermarkets chosen to shop. There are six supermarkets in Bandung that became the objects of assessment in this research. The questionnaires aimed at establishing an assessment of the chosen supermarkets and the reasons behind. The respondents were grouped according to their type of work, as illustrated in Table 1.

Table 1. Respondent by job type.

Job	Riau Junction	Borma	Superindo	Lottemat	Carrefour	Giant	%
Housewife	2	1	1	–	1	–	16.66
Government employee	–	1	1	1	–	1	13.33
Private employee	2	3	–	–	–	1	20.00
Entrepreneur	2	1	2	1	–	–	20.00
Professional	2	4	1	–	1	–	26.66
College student	–	1	–	–	–	–	3.33

Of the six supermarkets, three (Riau Junction, Borma, and Super Indo) of them had different respondents on the basis of their type of work. This indicated that the supermarket sector had a degree of market segmentation. In this section, the findings in the context of value propositions will be identified. This is to clarify the general relationship between customers and supermarkets in Bandung. An important fact that the majority of customers became more loyal when their needs are met and what they want could be achieved. Satisfaction is something desired by customers when they are shopping. The research results indicated that customer assessments were influenced by several aspects, such as price, quality, service, and innovation, each of which creates a value proposition. Each supermarket made effort to create a value that results in customer loyalty. A slight change in the value that has been created can cause customers to shift to other supermarkets. It became very difficult for competitors to attract loyal customers.

Some of the findings that researchers obtained from research relating to the value propositions of supermarkets are presented in Figure 1. This identifies the main elements of the value propositions described by customers based on their shopping experience, and shows the relationship between the number of respondents and the perceived value. The majority of customers found that the highest value is that of store location, including distance to the store, other distribution channels such as internet delivery, and the availability of car-parking space. The second most important element is the quality of an item; almost half of the respondents mentioned quality as a value creator. Third is price: seven out of 30 customers see value in a cheaper price. Finally, elements such as promotion, product variety and loyalty cards produced the lowest values for prospective customers in this study.

Table 2 presents the description of the perception of value from the customer's point of view. It is clear that in general there are more than one

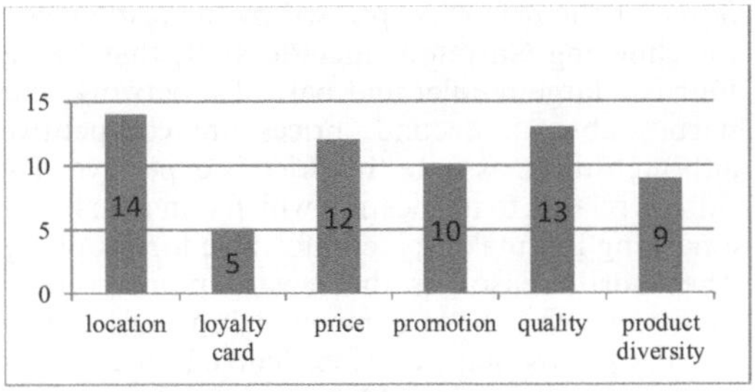

Figure 1. Chart of types of perceived value.

Table 2. Value perception per respondent.

Value perception	Riau Junction	Borma	Super Indo	Carrefour	Lottemart	Giant
Location	2	5	3	1	1	2
Loyalty card	3	–	1	–	–	–
Price	2	7	2	–	1	–
Promotion	2	4	1	1	1	1
Quality	4	2	2	1	1	1
Range of products	3	3	1	–	–	2

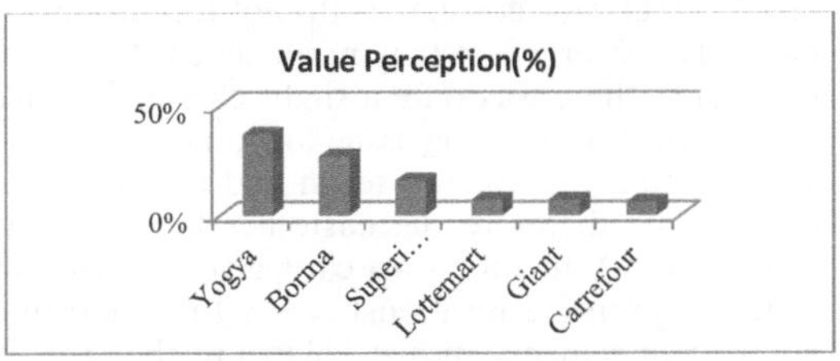

Figure 2. Perception value per supermarket.

sources of value for customers, such as a good location (good access to shops, Internet shopping, parking and proximity), loyalty cards, quality, and various products. Therefore, perception of supermarket value is based on the values attribute that are provided by the supermarket.

Figure 2 describes the confidence of respondents in their chosen supermarkets. 35.7% of respondents who shopped at Borma for location reasons and 58.3% due to price. Riau Junction shoppers choose the value proposition elements of goods quality (30.7%), loyalty card (60%) and goods price (16.66%). Similarly, Super Indo had various value proposition elements, such as competitive (16.66%), location (21.42%) and quality (15.3%), while Carrefour, Giant, and Lottemart had similar percentage value. Giant, Lottemart, and Carrefour had good locations, very competitive goods prices, and variety in their quality of goods.

2.2 *Discussion*

Riau Junction was part of the Yogya Department Store. This supermarket had a different perceived identity to other supermarkets. Its vision is to "remain at the top choice" and its mission is to "faithfully meet the needs of our society, always strive to present quality products, superior service, friendly and fun shopping atmosphere". Riau Junction as a place to shop is based on several things, including a not too big retail. The variety price of made the product sold competitive, because the valuation given by consumers for the price depends on what they expect in terms of the quality of goods. In the sale of its products, Riau Junction always emphasized the quality, and most consumers argued that the goods are very high quality, and sometimes consumers did not think the prevailing price was the most important but what they need as the customers. The market segments were local and imported goods. The location was easy to reach. The interest of people in shopping there was different; this is shown by the parking owned by Riau Junction, which as not broad yet was not a problem for customers. There are some customers who claimed that if the space was too broad, it would make them exhausted to find the items needed. In an effort to capture its customers, Riau Junction was enacting a membership card system. Customers who had this membership card get many benefits; for example, discounts on all items sold; in other words, loyal customers are rewarded. Good display or arrangement of goods makes it very easy for customers to get the items required; related to this, Riau Junction display goods in accordance with the category. Riau Junction is not in the mall, which is a corporate strategy to encourage people to focus on shopping in one store. All customer segments are addressed. This means that shopping there is not limited to a single market segment, and the revenue stream related to business development that Riau Junction offers is not limited to basic needs only; fashion, food court, and hotel also exist. The majority of respondents said that they were satisfied shopping there.

The second supermarket is Borma, which offers the concept of "One-stop shopping". This is related to the choice of diverse products, low prices, and also provides the best service, exceeding customer expectations. Some reasons people choose Borma as a place to shop is that it is a large retail store. The majority of respondents stated that comfortable place is important, but most importantly, they needs are fulfilled. Besides, the price of goods varies and cheapness makes them satisfied. This is an advantage for Borma in setting a low price, which is very reasonable because the goods sold come from local suppliers. With regard to its location, most respondents argued that it is easy to reach because of its strategic location, equipped with a parking area big enough to accommodate either two-wheeled or four-wheeled vehicles. Another aspect that could be a positive value is that the market segment is not limited, and the location is close to a residential area. Borma had more values in terms of range of goods sold, since they moved providing from the basic necessities and adding the non-essential, or unique necessities. In terms of the comfort factor, the majority of respondents say Borma was less comfortable; one of the reasons was the untidy arrangement of goods inappropriate display, unbalanced ratio between goods and the place. In general, the majority gave a positive assessment of Borma.

The third supermarket is Super Indo, which provides a variety of daily needs products with reliable quality, provided complete necessities, low prices, and convenient store location. The freshness and quality of the products is maintained through good source selection and handling, with standard operational procedures that are always monitored. This leads Super Indo to declare itself the shopping place that is always "Fresher", "More Efficient" and "Closer." In relation to the motto of Super Indo, the results from the majority of respondents agree, but not for all that it sells. The motto suits products sold such as vegetables, fruits, fish, and meat. The majority of respondents stated that shopping for vegetables, fruits, fish and meat was often done in Super Indo. This was because Super Indo had another favorable, namely 20% discount every Tuesday. This became a differentiator with other supermarkets. In relation to price, the majority of respondents agreed that Super Indo is competitive. For the quality of goods, the majority of respondents thought about local quality, easy-to-reach locations, spacious, and free parking lot: most other supermarkets charge for parking. The customers of Super Indo are varied. It means that all segments were gained, showed revenue stream, provided basic and varied necessities, unlike Borma, Super Indo did not structure goods well enough so that the customer did not feel comfortable in shopping.

The fourth supermarket, Carrefour, is one of the world's largest retailers. As part of a global company, PT. Carrefour Indonesia strives to deliver world class service standards in Indonesia's retail industry. Indonesia for Carrefour Indonesia customers. Carrefour offers the concept of "One-stop shopping", which offers a selection of places with diverse products, low prices, and also seeks to provide service to exceed customer expectations. Some of the reasons expressed by the respondents for choosing Carrefour include, first, that Carrefour is a large retailer and part of a network with parties abroad. Second, prices are competitive, although most assume the price is expensive. The third is related to its location which is in a mall with a parking lot, making it comfortable for shopping. The fourth reason is the reward points offered to buyers who have a membership card, which accrues points that can be exchanged for goods to the value of the points. Massive promotions are an attraction for buyers, and for the most part they were of the same opinion: they are happy with the promotions. The market segmentation of Carrefour consists of upper middle class customers.

The fifth supermarket, Lottemart, is one of the premier retail outlets and owns a vast shopping area. It is part of the Lotte group, becoming the first Korean company to penetrate the market in the wholesale and retail industry in Indonesia. Lottemart ran the business by applying good business ethics. The existence of Lottemart in Bandung got an assessment by its customer. The people in Bandung went shopping to Lottemart since it had competitive prices, Most respondents stated the prices were cheaper compared to other three supermarkets (Riau Junction, Borma, and Super Indo). Lottemart has been using a packaging strategy, such as the concepts "Buy 1, Get 2" and "Buy 2, Get 3"; that way, consumers do not feel disadvantaged. However, when they recalculated the actual unit price, there was only a slight change in price (10%), which is not a big issue for some customers. The location was easy to reach and had spacious parking lot therefore the customer felt comfortable to go. A membership card gives benefits in order to promote loyal customers. In structuring good arrangements means balancing the size of the shopping area by locating it in inside the mall so that consumers can visit many places. However, some of them argued because they had to visit mall just to go shopping Lottermart has gained all market segments became customers, had revenue streams, provided diversity of products sold ranging from basic needs, food court, sponsors. The overall assessment of Lottemart is quite good.

The sixth supermarket is Giant, which has many branches in Indonesia. In addition to department stores that sell clothing products, Giant also has a supermarket that sells clothing, necessities of life, and everyday items. In accordance with its motto "Many More Cheaper Prices", Giant provides around 35,000–50,000 items, of which 90% are local and ethnic products, as a strategy to gain loyal customers. This is certainly aligned with the operating philosophy of "Cheap Price Guarantee Every Day", because Giant wants to be known as a cheap, affordable, and trustworthy brand by providing more value for the price paid. The first attraction for the majority of respondents who choose Giant as a place to shop is that it is a vast store, with a great variety of goods sold. In terms of price, the majority of respondents claimed that their prices are competitive. This means that not all goods were sold at low prices, nor were members guaranteed cheap prices every day. The diversity of the items sold has received comment from many respondents. Finding similar or typical goods in the same area is easy to be done Locations are easy to reach, and a small proportion of respondents occasionally shop in Giant or by chance as needed. The size of the shopping area did not always attract customers attraction, since they would feel easily tired to wander in the aisles. Besides, the location of this supermarket, whether it is located inside and outside the mall, became another consideration for the customers. Most of the respondents who shop in Giant come from the middle to upper segment. Just like any other supermarket, Giant uses promotional media such as brochures and electronic media, and information related to the promotion continues to be submitted to the public. To try and gain loyal customers, Giant also offers a membership card.

3 CONCLUSION

Identifying customer behavior in shopping is complex, as there are various reasons, such as price, quality, location, product diversity, service, promotion, and innovation, for choosing a supermarket. The decision to buy in the same place is the greatest hope of a company. Getting customers to return to shop in the same place is not easy and needs the right strategy. Various efforts can be made by each supermarket with a high level of consistency, in the sense that the company should not change its business strategy. The most appropriate business strategy is that the company offers superior value. Having superior value does not only bring customers to the company, but a value proposition will be formed. A value proposition is the reason for customers to switch to other companies as it articulates all the benefits that the company offers to customers with respect to products and services. Value propositions become innovative and represent a new offer or alter an existing offer. The process of creating value is known as Creating Value for Customers (CVC), which is formed from the existence of customer value and operational excellence. Customer value is formed from the factors of benefit, effort, risk and price (Fifield, 2009). The value proposition of the company is influenced by factors such as price, quality, service, innovation, product diversity, location, and others. Value propositions can be achieved on the basis of a positive customer perception, where customers feel satisfaction in shopping. If the company is consistent in building value then customer loyalty will be created.

ACKNOWLEDGMENTS

I would like to thank the University of Education of Indonesia and the University of Airlangga who facilitated this international conference in order to increase the development of knowledge, which will have a positive impact on progress in Indonesia. I would also like to thank the LPDP (*Lembaga Pengelola Dana Pendidikan*), who sponsored the publication of this article.

REFERENCES

Anderson, J.C., Narus, J.A. & Van Rossum, W. (2006). Customer value propositions in business markets. *Harvard Business Review*, *84*(3), 90–99.

Ang, L. & Buttle, F. (2009). Customer development strategies for exceeding expectation: An exploratory study. *Journal of Data Base Marketing & Strategy Management*, *16*(4), 267–275.

Barnes, C., Blake, H. & Pinder, D. (2009). *Creating & delivering your value proposition: Managing customer experience for profit.* London, UK: Kogan Page.

Capon, N. & Hulbert, J.M. (2007). *Managing marketing in the 21st century: Developing & implementing the market strategy.* New York, NY: Wessex Press.

Carbone, L.P. & Haeckel, S.H. (1994). Engineering customer experiences. *Marketing Management*, *3*(3), 8–19.

Fifield, P. (2008). *Marketing strategy masterclass: Making marketing strategy happen.* Oxford, UK: Butterworth-Heinemann.

Fifield, P. (2009). *Strategic marketing decisions module.* Lecture Presentation, University of Southampton.

Hassan, A. (2012). The value proposition concept in marketing: How customers perceive the value delivered by firms—A study of customer perspectives on supermarkets in Southampton in the United Kingdom. *International Journal of Marketing Studies*, *4*(3), 68–87.

Kaplan, R. & Norton, D. (1996). *The balanced scorecard: Translating strategy into action.* Brighton, MA: Harvard Business School Press.

Rintamaki, T., Kuusela, H. & Mitronen, L. (2007). Identifying competitive customer value propositions in retailing. *Managing Service Quality International Journal*, *17*(6), 621–634.

Increasing Management Relevance and Competitiveness – Sukoco et al. (Eds)
© 2018 Taylor & Francis Group, London, ISBN 978-0-8153-7455-8

Empirical study of perceived quality information and perceived information security impact on online purchasing in Indonesia

L. Lisnawati, L.A. Wibowo & P. Andi
Universitas Pendidikan Indonesia, Bandung, Indonesia

ABSTRACT: The purpose of this study is to determine the effect of quality information and information security on online purchases. The research design used the verification approach with survey method. A total of 170 respondents were selected as a sample using nonprobability sampling. Survey questionnaires were used as research instruments to collect data from respondents. The analytical technique used is a path analysis tool. The findings of this study suggest that quality information and information security affects online purchasing decisions both simultaneously and partially. This research provides a basis for understanding the issues of online purchasing decisions to buy and sell on online sites in Indonesia.

Keywords: Information Quality; Information Security; E-Commerce; Online Purchasing

1 INTRODUCTION

The development of technology has a lot of influence in various fields. One of the areas progressing with technology is the field of marketing. Revolution in the field of marketing is able to produce marketing strategies that can utilize technology in order to help market the product to consumers. One of the most important issues studied in the field of marketing management is the low purchase decision. Many consumers are starting to use internet media solely to get information and not to buy products (Lim & Ting, 2012). Research on purchasing decisions has grown for over 300 years. When consumers cannot get complete transaction guidance, products are not delivered on time or not delivered at all, sellers do not respond to e-mails from consumers, and the desired information is inaccessible, the reputation of a site will be harmed and this will be bad for consumers (Oliveira, 2007; Parasuraman, Zeithaml, & Malhotra, 2005).

The tremendous growth of e-commerce systems since the early 1990s has changed the retail structure of the world and affects the shopping process for consumers. It makes the Internet an important medium for selling goods and services (Chen & Chang, 2003; Parasuraman, Zeithaml, & Malhotra, 2005a; Brown, Pope, & Voges, 2003; Lim & Ting 2012).

The importance of understanding consumer behavior when making online purchasing decisions must be considered in order for online buying and selling activities to continue to grow and be able to improve online business marketing. In addition to providing benefits to consumers by providing convenience and saving time in shopping activities, online purchasing decisions made by consumers will also affect their satisfaction and future purchase decisions, thus impacting on the sales and revenue of the company (Hennig-Thurau, Gwinner, Walsh, & Gremler, 2004; Lim & Ting, 2012).

The influence of purchasing decisions on the viability of a company makes low online purchasing decisions a critical issue to be addressed by the marketing management within the company. The impact of understanding consumer responses in an online shopping environment is essential for building marketing planning (Demangeot & Broderick, 2007; Aljukhadar & Senecal, 2011). Another impact that may be caused by lack of background research on consumer purchasing decisions is the failure of companies to compete in the global economy resulting in economic failure within the business (Smith & Rupp, 2003; Durmaz, 2014).

2 LITERATURE

The decision to purchase online is a decision made by consumers via the Internet, so it requires the technological ability of consumers in processing the information available to help him in making purchasing decisions online (Khalifa & Limayem, 2004; Akhlaq & Ahmed, 2015). In this study, the dimensions used to measure online purchasing decisions are; Merchandise, Customer Service and Promotion, Navigation and Convenience, and Transaction Security (Aljukhadar & Senecal 2011).

The quality of information as perceived by the consumer may be measured in terms of information about the product or service offered (with an assessment of the accuracy), correctness, frequency of renewal, ease of understanding, satisfying customer need and relevance of the information (Barnes & Vidgen, 2002; Park & Kim, 2003). The quality of information relates to the general perception that consumers have about the accuracy and completeness of site information in describing the product and explaining the transactional process. Dimensions used in this study to measure the quality of information are Accurate, Latest, and Relevant (Kim et al. 2008).

The consumer perception with regard to online transaction security, authentication and encryption of personal data is that information given by the consumer when conducting the transaction will not be misused by the online site in any way that could harm the consumer (Park & Kim, 2003; Kim et al., 2008; Eid, 2011; Mekovec & Hutinski, 2012). Consumers believe that their personal information will not be seen, stored or manipulated during transit or storage by inappropriate parties—this is how consumers perceive the security level of transactions on an online site. The dimensions used to measure transaction security in this study are Security policy of the transaction, Disclaimer of transaction security, Secure shopping guaranteed, Encryption, Protection, Authentication, and SSL (Secure Socket Layer) Technology (Chellappa & Pavlou, 2002).

3 RESEARCH METHOD

This study analyzes the effect of information quality and security information of the online purchases of consumers on online sites in Indonesia. The independent variable, or exogenous variable, contained in this study is the quality of information with dimensions; accuracy, up to date and relevancy. The second variable is the information security variable with the dimensions of security features and protection mechanisms. The dependent variable, or endogenous variable, in this research is the purchasing decision with dimensions; merchandise, promotion and service, ease of navigation and comfort, and security of information.

The units of analysis in this study are consumers of online trading sites in Indonesia. This research was conducted in less than one year, so the data collection technique used in this research is a cross-sectional method. The technique used in this research is the probability technique i.e. simple random sampling on a sample size of 170 consumers. The data collection techniques used were literature studies, field studies with the distribution of online questionnaires, and literature studies. The data analysis verification was conducted using path analysis with the help of SPSS software v.22.0 for windows.

4 FINDINGS AND DISCUSSIONS

Hypothesis testing in this study was conducted to determine the magnitude of the effect of information quality and security information on online purchasing decisions. The hypothesis of this research is that the quality of information and security of the information affect simultaneously, and partially, the decision to purchase online. This hypothesis is tested simultaneously, or partially, by using SPSS v.22.0 for windows. The results of this hypothesis testing as a whole (simultaneous) can be displayed in an ANOVA table with values of $F_{arithmetic} = 79.495$ and $F_{table} = 2.66$. The results show that if $F_{arithmetic}$ (79.495) > F_{table} (2.66) then the decision can be taken that the null hypothesis (H_0) is rejected and H_a accepted. It can then be said that there is a linear relationship between the quality of information and the security of the information to the decision of online purchase. The results also indicate that the regression model used is feasible and correct. The probability test (Sig) shows the result that the probability level value (Sig) = 0.000, because the value of Sig (0.000) ≤ 0.05 then the decision is H_0 rejected and H_a accepted, it means that simultaneously (whole) there is influence between the quality of information and the security of information against online purchasing decisions.

The tests both show significant results. In order to determine the independent variables that significantly affect the dependent variable, we can proceed with partial testing. The matrix of correlation between information quality and security information to purchasing decision can be displayed on a correlation table. The correlation between quality of information to decision of online purchase = 0.608, based on the interpretation of the correlation coefficient at a coefficient interval of (0.60–0.799) which means there is a strong correlation between the quality of information on online purchasing decisions. The result of the correlation between the security of the information to the online purchase decision is 0.677 and based on the interpretation of the correlation coefficient at a coefficient interval of (0.60–0.799) which means there is a strong correlation between the security of information to the decision of online purchase. The correlation result between information quality and security information is 0.724, based on the interpretation of the correlation coefficient at a coefficient interval of (0.60–0.799) meaning there is a strong correlation between information quality and security information.

From the SPSS results, partial tests and calculations can be displayed in a coefficients table. The table shows the result that $t_{arithmetic}$ from the quality of information to online purchase decision = 3.075 and t_{table} = 1.650, so it can be interpreted that $t_{arithmetic}$ (3.075) > t_{table} (1.650). Based on these results the decision can be taken that H_0 is rejected and H_1 accepted. This means there is a partial influence between the quality of information with the decision of purchasing online. A large influence can be seen based on the path coefficient of 0.247 with Sig value 0.002 < 0.005 which means a significant influence. The partial test between security information to online purchasing decision shows a result of t_{count} = 6.203 and t_{table} = 1.650, so t_{count} (6.203) > t_{table} (1.650), hence the decision can be taken that H_0 is refused and H_1 accepted. There is partial influence between security information and online purchase decision. Path coefficient of the security information to the online purchase decision is 0.498 with the Sig value 0.000 < 0.005 which means a significant influence.

Based on the above calculations, the path diagram of the hypothesis in the study can be shown as follows:

As can be seen from the figure, hypothesis calculations can be done to determine the direct and indirect effects between dimensions.

From the calculation on the quality of information with a value of path coefficient = 0.247 we can obtain the calculation of direct influence = 0.061 and the indirect effect through the security of the information = 0.089, so that, the overall effect of information quality on online purchase is 0.15. While the calculation on the security of information with the coefficient value = 0.498 obtained direct influence of 0.248 and indirect influence through quality information of 0.089, so that, the overall effect of information security on online purchase is 0.337. It can be seen that the total coefficient of the path between the quality of information and the security of information on online purchasing decisions with R^2 = 0.487. So it can be seen the value of the residual coefficient in this

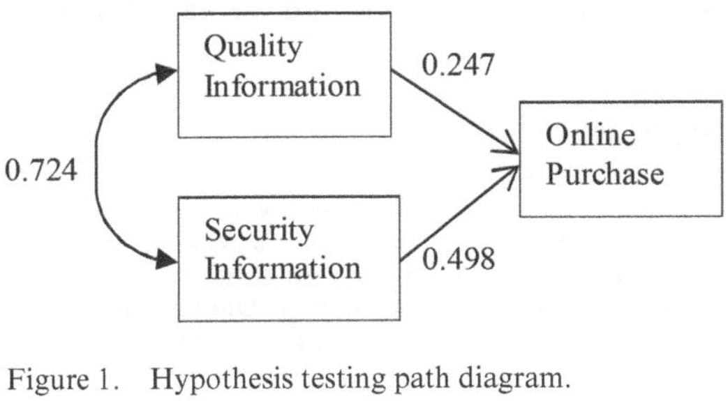

Figure 1. Hypothesis testing path diagram.

Table 1. The results of the direct and indirect effect test.

Variables	Path coefficient	Direct effect	Indirect influence through Quality information	Security information	R^2
Quality Information	0,247	0,061	–	0,089	0,15
Security Information	0,498	0,248	0,089	–	0,337
Total		0,309			0,487

study amounted to 0.751. These results indicate that the quality of information and security information simultaneously affect the decision of online purchasing with a large influence of 48.8%, while the influences from outside that are not examined are: $(0.715)^2 = 0.511 \times 100\% = 51.1\%$ influenced by other variables not included in the study.

Simultaneously the quality of information and security of the information affect the online purchase decision by 49% while the influence between the quality of information and the security of information to online purchasing decisions if calculated partially will get a 50% result of the influence between the security of information against purchasing decisions online and 25% for the effect quality of information has on online purchasing decisions. These results indicate that greater security information affects online purchasing decisions compared to the quality of information. Based on the calculations, if both variables between the quality of information and security information affect purchasing decisions simultaneously or simultaneously this will result in a greater value of influence than if the variables affect purchasing decisions partially or not simultaneously.

Online buying and selling activities, are in the condition of the buyer and seller not face to face directly, they can only communicate with each other through the site or other online communication. The limitations of such communications, is the reason that clear and complete product information on e-commerce websites becomes very helpful for consumers to know how the product is offered.

If the information provided by the site is qualified and can meet the needs of consumers, then consumers will follow through to the payment transaction process. A benefit that can be felt by the seller is the frequency of consumer purchasing decisions providing revenue for the company and the perceived satisfaction of consumers after shopping can lead to an interest in buying and a long-term relationship between the consumer and the seller. The impact if a site does not provide the quality of information and security information is a decrease in purchases made by consumers on the site, because it cannot provide what consumers need in helping them to make a buying decision.

The results of the study in accordance with the theory that suggests that the quality of information and security information becomes an important factor in influencing purchasing decisions online. The quality of information, the quality of the user interface, and the perception of security are significantly related to site commitment and purchasing decision behavior (Park & Kim, 2003). Factors such as trust, reputation, privacy issues, transaction security, the quality of information from websites and the reputation of companies have a strong effect on consumer purchasing decisions (Kim et al. 2008).

Based on the results of partial calculations, there is a direct influence on the variable quality of information to online purchase decision of 25%. Its mean that consumers need information about the product that will be purchased in shopping activities on the websites e-commerce. The consumer can not directly touch the products offered meaning the provision of quality information about the product is required in order to support consumer purchasing decisions. The lack of interaction that occurs between consumers and sellers means consumers can only utilize the information about the product to help make online purchasing decisions. So, the influence of quality information in making consumer purchasing decisions is very great.

The results are in accordance with the results of research (Alhasanah 2014) which shows that there is a significant influence between usability variables, quality information, and quality of service interaction to online purchasing decision variable simultaneously. Further research results show that the variables of quality of information, trust and easiness have a positive relation to the variable of purchase decision and the variable of quality of information has the biggest influence on consumer online purchasing decisions (Adityo 2011).

Based on the results of partial calculations, there is a direct influence on the variable quality of information on online purchasing decisions by 50%. This can be the effect of security information on partial purchasing decisions to make full online purchasing decisions—consumers will be faced with payment methods that require them to provide personal data about credit cards or personal financial data. The number of criminal or fraudulent actions that occur in online transaction activities mean consumers should be more vigilant in maintaining the security of their transactions. That's what makes consumers hesitant to make online purchases. One way to safeguard the personal data of consumers is to convert the information provided by consumers into codes that are not easy to read with the encryption process.

The process of encryption provided by the site can provide benefits for consumers to ensure no leakage of information or personal data to parties that are not responsible. If a site has a commitment to maintaining the security of information in online purchasing activities for consumers then, the consumers do not have to worry if they have to provide personal data for online transactions. This information security factor can be utilized in the ability to meet customer expectations. In addition to impacting on the lack of purchasing decisions made by consumers, the impact of the lack of security information is an inherent risk in the development of e-commerce. The information on online purchasing decisions is affected by 50%. There is a positive relationship between privacy and security of transactions on the website and the decision to purchase online (Azadavar & Teimouri 2011). In a very competitive business market, every website should try to have a competitive advantage and take care with customer profiles and personal information so that consumers can consider security an important factor in online purchasing. In other words, companies should try to attract consumers to visit their website by convincing consumers about security in addition to other factors such as price and quality. This study conducted on online consumers in Malaysia, found that transaction security factors have a positive and significant effect in influencing purchasing decisions online (Raman & Annamalai 2012).

5 CONCLUSION AND RECOMMENDATION

Based on the results of this research that has been done by using descriptive and verification analysis and the path analysis technique it can be concluded that the quality of information and transaction security influence simultaneously any online purchasing decision. The quality of information partially influences online purchasing decisions and transaction security partially influences online purchasing decisions.

This research is expected to help companies with online trading sites to pay more attention to information quality and transaction security factors to improve consumer online purchasing decisions.

REFERENCES

Adityo, B. (2011). Analysis of the Influence of Trust, Ease and Quality of Information Against Purchasing Decision Online On Kaskus Site, 53(9), 1689–99.

Akhlaq, A. & Ahmed, E. (2015). Digital commerce in emerging economies. *International Journal of Emerging Markets, 10*(4), 634–47.

Alhasanah, J.U. (2014). Quality of Information and Quality of E-Commerce Web Services Interaction to Online Sales Decision (Consumer Survey www.getscoop.com), 15(2).

Aljukhadar, M. & Senecal, S. (2011). Segmenting the online consumer market. *Marketing Intelligence & Planning, 29*(4), 421–35.

Azadavar, R. & Teimouri, M.E. (2011). The role of security as a customer perception on customers' online purchasing behavior. *International Conference on Software and Computer Applications, 9*, 174–81.

Barnes, S.J. & Vidgen, R.T. (2002). An integrative approach to the assessment of e-commerce quality. *Journal of Electronic Commerce Research, 3*, 114–27. Retrieved from http://opus.bath.ac.uk/11490/.

Brown, M., Pope, N. & Voges, K. (2003). Buying or browsing? *European Journal of Marketing, 37*(11/12), 1666–84. doi:10.1108/03090560310495401.

Chellappa, R.K. & Pavlou, P.A. (2002). Perceived information security, financial liability and consumer trust in electronic commerce transactions. *Logistics Information Management, 15*(5/6), 358–68.

Chen, S., & Chang, T. (2003). A descriptive model of online shopping process: Some empirical results. *International Journal of Service Industry Management, 14*(5), 556–69. doi:10.1108/09564230310500228.

Demangeot, C. & Broderick, A.J. (2007). Conceptualising consumer behaviour in online shopping environments. *International Journal of Retail and Distribution Management, 35*(11), 878–94. doi:10.1108/09590550710828218.

Durmaz, Y. (2014). The impact of psychological factors on consumer buying behavior and an empirical application in Turkey. *Asian Social Science, 10*(6), 194–204.

Eid, M. (2011). Determinants of e-commerce customer satisfaction, trust, and loyalty in Saudi Arabia. *Journal of Electronic Commerce Research, 12*(1), 141–9.

Hennig-Thurau, T., Gwinner, K.P., Walsh, G. & Gremler, D.D. (2004). Electronic word-of-mouth via consumer-opinion platforms: What motivates consumers to articulate themselves on the Internet? *Journal of Interactive Marketing, 18*(1), 38–52.

Khalifa, M. & Limayem, M. (2004). Drivers of internet shopping. *Communications of the ACM, 46*(12), 233–40.

Kim, D.J, Ferrin D.L. & Rao, H.R. (2008). A trust-based consumer decision-making model in electronic commerce: The role of trust, perceived risk, and their antecedents. *Decision Support Systems, 44*(2), 544–64.

Lim, W.M. & Ting, D.H. (2012). E-shopping: An analysis of the technology acceptance model. *Modern Applied Science, 6*(4), 49–62.

Mekovec, R. & Hutinski, Ž. (2012). The role of perceived privacy and perceived security in online market. *MIPRO, Proceedings of the 35th International Convention,* 1883–8.

Oliveira, A. (2007). A discussion of rational and psychological decision-making theories and models: The search for a cultural-ethical decision-making model. *Journal of Business Ethics and Organization Studies, 12*(2), 1478–82.

Parasuraman, A., Zeithaml, V.A. & Malhotra, A. (2005a). E-S-QUAL: A multiple-item scale for assessing electronic service quality. *Journal of Service Research, 7*(Feb.), 1–21.

Parasuraman, A., Zeithaml, V.A. & Malhotra, A. (2005b). E-S-QUAL. *Journal of Service Research, 7*(3), 213–33. doi:10.1177/1094670504271156.

Park, C.-H. & Kim, Y.-G. (2003). Identifying key factors affecting consumer purchase behavior in an online shopping context. *International Journal of Retail and Distribution Management, 31*(1), 16–29.

Raman, A. & Annamalai, I. (2012). E-marketing the lifeline of NetGeneration: An empirical study, *3*(2), 117–26.

Smith, A.D. & Rupp, W.T. (2003). Strategic online customer decision making: Leveraging the transformational power of the Internet. *Online Information Review, 27*(6), 418–32.

Increasing Management Relevance and Competitiveness – Sukoco et al. (Eds)
© 2018 Taylor & Francis Group, London, ISBN 978-0-8153-7455-8

Measuring religiosity and its effects on attitude and intention to wear a hijab: Revalidating the scale

H.A. Wibowo & M.R. Masitoh
Universitas Serang Raya, Kota Serang, Indonesia

ABSTRACT: This research aims to investigate the relationship pattern between religiosity, attitude and intention to wear a hijab. This research used purposive sampling from four cities and four regencies in the Banten Province of Indonesia. Data was collected through questionnaires, interviews, observations, and reviews of literature. The Latent Variable Score (LVS) was used to simplify the religiosity construct and structural equation modeling was chosen as the analytical tool. The results showed attitude is not proven to have an influence on the intention to wear a hijab—however, religiosity has quite a significant role in shaping attitude and intention. Fashionable Islamic public figures could be used to provide positive role models toward the wearing of hijabs. The results of this study should be considered for future research into religiosity, attitude and behavioral intention relationship patterns.

Keywords: religiosity, attitude, hijab-wearing intention, latent variable score, Muslim religiosity scale

1 INTRODUCTION

In society, the rise of the Islamic fashion business in Indonesia has been indicated by the emergence of several great hijab brands, for example, Rabbani, Uwais, Zenita, Zoya, Elzatta, Inayah, and Hijabstory. Unfortunately, empirical research conducted in Indonesia regarding religiosity and its impact on consumer behavior, is still lacking. Even though there has been international attention to religiosity and its role in changing consumer behavior, many empirical results have focused on the religiosity influence on consumer attitudes and behavior (Abou-Youssef et al., 2015; Ahrold et al., 2011; Alam et al., 2012; Al Jahwari, 2015; Barkan, 2014; Bodford & Hussong, 2013; Graafland, 2015; Lindridge, 2005; McKenzie, 2012; Schouten & Graafland, 2014; Shakona, 2013; Souiden & Rani, 2015).

Previous studies were conducted with diverse methods, contexts and outcomes. Nevertheless, there is a common pattern of relationships which consist of religiosity, attitude and intention, in which the pattern is either a full model or part of it. Souiden and Rani (2015) discussed the mediated pattern of religiosity influence on intention through attitude. Al Jahwari (2015) added the mediated pattern with actual behavior, while Shakona (2013), placed religiosity as an antecedent of the three predictors of Theory of Planned Behavior. Abouyoussef et al. (2015) employed a mixed method, but simplified it by deleting intention. Contradictly, Alam et al. (2012) put religiosity and attitude as a predictor of intention, and was supported by the work of Ahrold et al. (2011), Barkan (2014) and Bodford and Hussong (2013); they argued that religiosity has a direct effect on behavior intention.

Surprisingly, due to lack of consiousness of contradiction, there is no consensus about the right pattern that should be used. A question has emerged: did religiosity have a direct effect on behavioral intention or must it be mediated by attitude? This study tries to address this reoccurring problem and answer it by investigating the true relationship pattern of religiosity, attitude and intention regarding the hijab in Indonesia.

The proposed hypotheses are as follows:

H1. Religiosity positively affects attitude toward hijab-wearing behavior;
H2. Religiosity positively affects hijab-wearing intention; and
H3. Attitude positively affects hijab-wearing intention.

2 THEORETICAL BACKGROUND

2.1 *Religiosity effects on attitude and intention*

Past studies do not agree on whether religiosity is unidimensional or multidimensional, what the determinants are, and how to measure them. (Souiden & Rani, 2015). Religiosity is also a complex construct and defined differently based on the approach of the dicipline used, for instance, a theologian would define it as faith, a psychologist would call it piousnes and holines, and a sociologist would address membership and living with a faith (Holdcroft, 2006).

Problems occurred when Muslim religiosity was measured with a scale developed in a Christian based community. These problems are as follow, First a misconception that Islamic piety is a one-dimensional construct; Second, a one-to-one translation of Christian measures into Islamic terminology; Third, interpretation of research results within a framework of western or Christian concepts of religiosity; Forth, use of indicators measuring more than religiosity; and a lack of statistical estimates of reliability and validity (El-Menouar, 2014). This is why a Muslim based religiosity scale, from El-Menouar's work, was applied in this study instead.

Attitude is an evaluative tendency of hijab-wearing behavior based on the belief in the results obtained, and it lead to a certain direction in the form of judgment, agree-disagreeing or positives-negatives. It is a person's evaluation, whether positive or negative, and their beliefs or feelings (Fishbein & Ajzen, 1975). This study argues that one's religiosity provides input to one's belief in an object, for example, hijab-wearing behavior and/or its effects, and in which it becomes the basis of one's attitude. Empirical evidence that supports this argument can be found in: Abou-Youssef et al., (2015); Al Jahwari (2015); Graafland (2015); Schouten and Graafland (2014); Souiden and Rani (2015); Shakona 2013; (Wibowo, 2017).

On the other hand, the intention to behave is a person's subjective probability that he/she will perform an action (Fishbein & Ajzen, 1975). This study also agrees that one's religious conformance can lead to the intention to match behavior with the value, that is, wearing a hijab. Research that supports this idea can be found in: Ahrold et al. (2011); Alam et al. (2012); Al Jawhari (2015); Barkan (2014); Bodford and Hussong (2013); Lindridge (2005); and Schouten and Graafland (2014). However, McKenzie (2012) found the effect insignificant.

Some researchers, such as Souiden and Rani (2015) and Abou-Youssef et al. (2015) strictly treat religiosity as merely having an effect on attitude. They neglect the probability that it can also effect behavior intention. On the other hand, Alam et al. (2012) neglects the probability that religiosity can provide an input into one's belief in an object, as this study argued earlier. Other researchers (Ahrold et al., 2011; Al Jawhari, 2015; Bodford & Hussong, 2013; Graafland, 2015) do not pay enough attention to ensure that the theory relating to religiosity, attitude and behavior intention patterns in described human behavior, is robust.

2.2 *Influence of attitude on intention to wear a hijab*

This study also found a great deal of evidence regarding the relationship between attitude and behavior intention as being a part of the Theory of Reasoned Action and the Theory of Planned Behavior. In a diverse context, attitude proved to have a positive effect on: the intention to buy halal food (Lada, et al., 2009) in the Y generation intention (Khalek & Ismail, 2015); Islamic financing (Alam, et al., 2012); Islamic hotels (Shakona, 2013); Islamic banks (Souiden & Rani, 2015); and digital hijacking (Yoon, 2011). More specifically, Schouten and Graafland (2014) found that a number of attitude dimensions positively affected a number of Corporate Social Responsibility behaviors. However, Wibowo (2017) found the effect insignificant.

3 METHODS

Purposive sampling was used in this study and results from 367 validated respondents from Serang City and district, Cilegon City, Pandeglang District, Lebak District, Tangerang City and district and Tangsel City were analyzed. Data was collected through observations, interviews, questionnaires, and literature reviews. Religiosity was measured by El-Menouar's (2014) scale, attitude and the intention to wear a hijab was measured with the Likert's five point scale (Ajzen, 2010). The study manipulated the religiosity dimensions complexsity with the latent variable score (LVS) technique. The attitude scale was developed by conducting interviews on 20 higher education female students which resulted in seven indicators: increasing self esteem; honorable; elegant; increasing faith; obligation; keeping fashionable; and getting a healthy head skin. The intention to wear a hijab—was indicated by the statements: will wear a hijab; wants to wear a hijab; will decide to wear a hijab; tend to wears a hijab; and hopes to wear a hijab in the future.

We rigorously developed the questionaire by placing two trap statements: I pray at *pura* (temple) and my father wears a hijab. The first trap was placed 4th in the list of the statements in order to stimulate attention and interest. The second trap question was placed rather later to remind them to seriously read and respond.

Factor formation based on eigenvalues > 1. Analysis performed with 20 to 50 indicators and the eigenvalues > 1 can determine the number of factors formed that will be the most reliable (Hair, et al., 2006). The LVS is used to convert religiosity dimensions into indicators. Convergents and discriminants are tested. Construct reliability (CR) should be ≥ 0.70, with average variance extracted (AVE) cut off value of 0.5 (Hair et al., 2006; Wijanto, 2008) for the reliability test. The five goodness of fit (GoF) indexes were chosen. Acceptance of hypothesis was determined by the path significancies.

4 RESULTS AND DISCUSSION

4.1 *Demography*

All respondents were female and based on Worlh Health Organization, 68.05% of them were young women whose ages ranged from 17 to 24 years old. This age group is characterized by: transactional orientation; seeking an identity; emotionally developing; and have a high imagination. Our additional interview confirmed this characterization. Women of this age are still looking for fun rather than conforming to their religion. There is a need to do some further research to obtain more reasonable explanations.

4.2 *Dimensionality Results*

Samplingadequacymeasurementsshowed K Kaiser-Meyer-Olkin = 0.872 and the Bartlett test had significance below 0.01. Both results indicated that the all indicators had sufficient intercorrelation, so the factor analysis could proceed.

Satisfactory cumulative variant defined at 66.94%, and precisely formed seven (made up of five dimensions of religiosity plus attitude and intention) components based on eigenvalues > 1. All item communalities were greater than 0.5 meaning that items were eligible for inclusion in the analysis. Items deleted: tahajjud prayer (R3), Allah Watches (5), Jinn existence (R6), drink alcohol (R7), celebrate ied mubarak (R10), always halal food (R11), know Islam in general (R15), from the religiosity dimensions, and keeping fashionable (S6), healty head skin (S7) from the attitude variable.

4.3 *Validity and reliability results*

From Table 1, the confirmatory factor analysis yielded satisfactory results by deleting the indicators of: basic; orthopraxy; in the future, I wanna wear a hijab (I2) and I tend to wear hijab in the future (I5), due to convergence problems. The remaining indicators had a standardized loading factor (SLF) > 0.6 which meant very good convergence. The square correlation between constructs, entirely below the AVE of each construct, meant discriminant validity was achieved. All factors were reliable, based on CR values > 0.7. At the same time, its AVE was ≥ 0.5. These results are classed as very satisfactory.

Table 1. Validity and reliability.

No.	Variables	Items	SLF	Errors	CR	AVE
1	Religiosity	Cent Duti	0.77	0.41	0.78	0.55
		Experience	0.79	0.37		
		Knowledge	0.66	0.57		
2	Attitudes	S1	0.7	0.51	0.88	0.61
		S2	0.86	0.26		
		S3	0.86	0.26		
		S4	0.73	0.47		
		S5	0.73	0.46		
3	Hijab intention	I1	0.88	0.23	0.92	0.74
		I3	0.94	0.12		
		I4	0.86	0.27		
		I6	0.75	0.44		

4.4 *GoF and hypotheses results*

The five indexes of Root Mean Square Error of Approximation, Normed Fit Index, Comparative Fit Index, Incremental Fit Index, Relative Fit Index, Goodness of Fit Index from the structural model were found to be 0.051, 0.98, 0.99, 0.99, 0.97 and 0.96. All indexes indicated that the research model acquired GoF. Hypotheses results are shown in Table 2.

Table 2 shows that H1 and H2 are acceptable and H3 is not. All effects are positive.

4.5 *Discussion*

The discussion is divided into two sections. Firstly, previous research had contributed a lot of evidence, of which, became the underlying argument for both H1 and H2. This study has proven the effects of religiosity and strengthened the theory on shaping attitudes toward hijab-wearing behavior and intention to wear hijabs. Based on the standardized path coefficient, it can also be said that the effect religiosity has on attitude toward hijabs is greater than it has on the intention to wear a hijab. It means the first argument in this study, that is, one's religiosity provides input to one's belief in an object e.g. hijab-wearing behavior and/or its effects, in which it becomes the basis of one's attitude, is more important to consider in marketing action than second argument one's religion conformance will lead to match behavior with the value ie. hijab-wearing.

Secondly, it was proven that the attitude effect on intention to wear a hijab was insignificant. This is a big result and has great impact on theory and world practice. This result concides with the results

Table 2. Hypotheses test results.

Hypothesis	Paths	Estimates	Std. Solution	T value	Decision
H1	Religiosity ==> attitude	0.83	0.64	9.18	Accepted
H2	Religiosity ==> jijab-wearing intention	0.55	0.46	5.55	Accepted
H3	Attitude ==> hijab-wearing intention	0.13	0.14	1.94	Rejected

on positive attitude toward smoking and smoking behavior (Rahmadi et al., 2013). In business practice, it is reasonable to hire Islamic public figures to attract market attention, in order to shape a positive attitude and behavior toward a religious based product such as a hijab. Future research needs to investigate the effects dimensionally, and find out which dimension has the biggest effect on attitude and intention to behave. Furthermore, Wibowo (2014) suggests that bivariate correlation should be applied dimensionally to implement the theoretical results.

5 CONCLUSIONS

This research has proven the significant role of religiosity on shaping attitude and increasing the intention to wear a hijab. Influence on attitudes toward hijab-wearing is greater than influence on intention to wear a hijab. The dimensional effects of religiosity needs to be tested in future research.

REFERENCES

Abou-Youssef, M.M.H., Kortam, W., Abou-Aish, E. & El-Bassiouny, N. (2015). Effects of religiosity on consumer attitudes toward Islamic banking in Egypt. *International Journal of Bank Marketing*, *33*(6), 786–807. http://doi.org/10.1108/IJBM-02-2015-0024.

Ahrold, T.K., Farmer, M., Trapnell, P.D. & Meston, C.M. (2011). The relationship among sexual attitudes, sexual fantasy, and religiosity. *Journal of Sexual Behavior*, *40*(3), 619–630. http://doi.org/10.1007/s10508-010-9621-4.

Al Jahwari, D.S. (2015). *An integrative model of Muslim students' religiosity and travelling behavior to gaming destinations.* (Doctoral dissertation). University of South Carolina, South Carolina.

Alam, S.S., Janor, H., Aniza, C. & Wel, C. (2012). Is religiosity an important factor in influencing the intention to undertake Islamic home financing in Klang Valley? *World Applied Science Journal*, *19*(7), 1030–1041. http://doi.org/10.5829/idosi.wasj.2012.19.07.392.

Barkan, S. E. (2014). Gender and abortion attitudes: Religiosity as a suppressor variable. *Public Opinion Quarterly*, *78*(4), 940–950. http://doi.org/10.1093/poq/nfu047.

Bodford, J.E. & Hussong, A.M. (2013). Moderators of the relationship between religiosity and alcohol use in college students. *Journal of Psychology and Theology*, *41*(1), 78–93. Retrieved from https://ucd.idm.oclc.org/login?url=http://search.proquest.com/docview/1373443286?accountid=14507%5Cnhttp://jq6am9xs3s.search.serialssolutions.com/?ctx_ver=Z39.88-2004&ctx_enc=info:ofi/enc:UTF-8&rfr_id=info:sid/ProQ%3 Apsycinfo&rft_val_fmt=info:ofi/fmt:kev.

El-Menouar, Y. (2014). The Five Dimensions of Muslim Religiosity. Results of an Empirical Study. *Method, Data, Analyses*,8(1),53–78. http://doi.org/10.12758/mda.2014.003.

Fishbein, M. & Ajzen, I. (1975). Attitude formation. In (Olson, M & Kendrick, R), *Belief, Attitude, Intention, and Behavior, An Introduction to Theory and Research* (pp. 216–287). http://doi.org/10.1016/B978-0-12-375000-6.00041-0.

Graafland, J. (2015). Religiosity, attitude, and the demand for socially responsible products. *Journal of Business Ethics*. 144(1), 121–138. http://doi.org/10.1007/s10551-015-2796-9.

Hair, J., Black, W.C., Babin, B.J. & Anderson, R.E. (2006). *Multivariate Data Analysis* (6th ed.). Upper Saddle River. New Jersey: Pearson Education.

Holdcroft, B. (2006). What is religiosity? *Catholic Education: A Journal of Inquiry and Practice*, *10*(1), 89–103.

Khalek, A.A., & Ismail, S.H.S. (2015). Why are we eating halal—using the theory of planned behavior in predicting halal food consumption among generation Y in Malaysia. *International Journal of Social Science and Humanity*, *5*(7), 608–612. http://doi.org/10.7763/IJSSH.2015.V5.526.

Lada, S., Tanakinjal, G.H., & Amin, H. (2009). Predicting intention to choose halal products using theory of reasoned action. *International Journal of Islamic and Middle Eastern Finance and Management*, *2*(1), 66–76. http://doi.org/10.1108/17538390910946276.

Lindridge, A. (2005). Religiosity and the construction of a cultural-consumption identity. *The Journal of Consumer Marketing*, *22*(2/3), 142.

McKenzie, D. (2012). *Relationship between religiosity, violent behavior and gang activity among economically disadvantaged adolescents*. (Doctoral dissertation). Available from ProQuest Dissertations and Theses. University of Alabama, Birmingham. Retrieved from https://search.proquest.com/openview/2cb289b8c459fc76886765436f48d1a4/1?pq-origsite=gscholar&cbl=18750&diss=y.

Rahmadi, A., Lestari, Y. & Yenita, Y. (2013). Relationship of knowledge, attitude on cigarette and smoking habit of Junior High School student in Padang City. *Jurnal Kesehatan Andalas*, *2*(1), 25–28.

Schouten, C.M.D.D. & Graafland, J. (2014). Religiosity, CSR attitudes, and CSR behavior: An empirical study of executives' religiosity and CSR. *Journal of Business Ethics*, 123, 437–459. http://doi.org/10.1007/s10551-013-1847-3.

Shakona, M.Y. (2013). *The influence of religiosity on the intention of United States Muslim tourists to choose a shariah compliant hote*l. (Doctoral dissertation). Available from ProQuest Dissertations and Theses. Graduate School of Clemson University, South Carolina. Retrieved from http://search.proquest.com.ezaccess.library.uitm.edu.my/docview/1499232994?accountid=42518.

Souiden, N. & Rani, M. (2015). Consumer attitudes and purchase intentions toward Islamic banks: The influence of religiosity. *International Journal of Bank Marketing*, *33*(2), 143–161. http://doi.org/10.1108/IJBM-10-2013-0115.

Wibowo, H. A. (2014). Switching Costs Moderation on Service Quality and Satisfaction influence on Customer Loyalty (study at PTS X). *Jurnal Ilmiah Manajemen*, *IV*(3), 363–380.

Wibowo, H. A. (2017). The Effects of Indonesia Female Religiosity on Hijab-Wearing Behavior: An Extended of Theory of Reasoned Action. *International Review of Management and Business Research.* *6* (3) 2306–9007.

Wijanto, S.H. (2008). *Structural Equation Modeling Dengan Lisrel 8.8 Konsep & Tutorial* (1st ed.). Yogyakarta, Indonesia: Graha Ilmu.

Yoon, C. (2011). Theory of planned behavior and ethics theory in digital piracy: An integrated model. *Journal of Business Ethics*, *100*(3), 405–417. http://doi.org/10.1007/s10551-010-0687-7.

Management and economics education

Increasing Management Relevance and Competitiveness – Sukoco et al. (Eds)
© 2018 Taylor & Francis Group, London, ISBN 978-0-8153-7455-8

Communication skills of accountants and managers in Indonesia

Y.L. Rudianto & A.R. Sridadi
Universitas Airlangga, Surabaya, Indonesia

ABSTRACT: The aim of this study was to determine the communication skills necessary to practice successfully as an accountant and a manager. The elements included in the study are a discussion of the role of communication in the accounting process and the managerial process; and a discussion of the relationship of the accountant's and manager's writing ability in performance evaluations, salary raises, and promotions. Thirty individuals, eight public accountants, seven beginning accountants, eight senior managers, and seven junior managers, were interviewed; but more of the data for this report came from periodicals in the library at the Airlangga University. Analysis and interpretation of the data revealed that effective communication skills are important in promotions, salary raises, and performance evaluations. The ten most important (by rank ordering) communication skills in relation to job success are 1) nonverbal communication, 2) confidence, 3) friendliness, 4) clarity and concision, 5) empathy, 6) respect, 7) listening, 8) open-mindedness, 9) feedback, and 10) picking the right medium. And the ten most important (by rank ordering) writing skills in relation to job success are 1) letters, 2) analytical reports involving comparisons or evaluations, 3) narrative-audited and unaudited reports, 4) memoranda, 5) policy and procedures manuals, 6) systems analysis reports, 7) interim reports, 8) proposals-budgets or programs, 9) policy statements, and 10) compliance reports. The accounting student and the management student of today must be prepared to face up to communication challenges of his or her career. To meet these challenges, the student should obtain both oral and writing skills in undergraduate studies. Effective communication is a necessity for the accountant and the manager.

Keywords: communication skills, accountant, manager, promotions, salary raises, and performance evaluations

1 INTRODUCTION

The accountant and the manager of today has not only to measure economic data, but must also communicate this data in a meaningful way to various users of accounting information and management information. These users or receivers of the information include investors, creditors, the government, management, and others within the organization. The purpose of this study was to determine the communication skills that are necessary to practice successfully as an accountant and a manager in Indonesia.

Although an accountant and a manager can take numerous professional routes, this study analyzed the communication skills that are important to the accountant and the manager to practice successfully. Such factors are promotions, performance evaluations, and salary raises.

The sources of data for this study include articles in professional journals and handbooks. Thirty individuals, eight public accountants, seven beginning accountants, eight senior managers, and seven junior managers were interviewed.

2 LITERATURE REVIEW

Communication skills are a fundamental part of success in most human endeavors, particularly in leadership. Being in relationship with others can be rewarding, if challenging, and is a necessary and fundamental aspect of being human and having a healthy life. Communication is a cornerstone of relationships, yet most of us are not formally taught how to communicate effectively. Many of us have been taught how to be polite, but not necessarily how to communicate effectively beyond having generally civilized behavior. In order to develop a curriculum of communication skill practice for the purpose of personal growth, it is important to get a firm grasp on the nature of communication itself (Johnson, 2008).

Intrapersonal communication includes attitude towards the self, attitude towards life, and the way one speaks to oneself. Interpersonal communication is the complex dance between two or more people. It involves the quality of the connection between the people, the mechanics of the communication, such as clarity of speaking, airtime balance, and eye contact.

Interpersonal communication can be analyzed by distinguishing between quantitative communication, which assesses the number of people involved, and qualitative communication based on whether the communication is personal or impersonal. One can also distinguish between relationship-focused communication and content-focused communication. Another distinction that can be made is in looking at communication as being linear, where trading roles of speaker and listener occurs, or simultaneous, where messages are being conveyed at the same time. Both intentional and unintentional communication instances were also considered. There is also an aspect of nonverbal communication. Although interpersonal communication may have many aspects, the basic function seems to be an expression of the fundamental human need for connection to others. Johnson (2008) proposed a model consisting of seven basic elements:

1. Intentions. The ideas, and feelings of the sender and the way she decides to behave, all of which lead to her sending a message that carries some content.
2. Encoding. The sender translates her ideas, feelings and intentions into a message appropriate for sending.
3. Sending. The sender conveys the message to the counterpart.
4. Channel. The channels are the verbal and nonverbal means by which the message is sent.
5. Decoding. The receiver interprets its meaning. The receiver's interpretation depends on how well the receiver understands the content of the message and the intentions of the sender.
6. Internal response. The receiver responds internally to the way the decoded message strikes her.
7. Noise. Noise is any element that interferes with the communication process. For the sender, noise refers to such things as her attitudes, prejudices, and frame of reference, and the appropriateness of her language or other expression of the message.

The existing literature on communication skills primarily focuses on the importance of effective communication in a variety of specific settings. These settings include communication and hirability, communication skills in the college curriculum, airtime and influence in teams, how talk shapes interactions in teams, how narcissism appears in everyday conversational interaction, the effect stress has on communication in medical settings, teamwork and appreciative inquiry, communication skills and emotional intelligence in leadership settings, and decision-making. The research listed above has contributed significantly to provide greater understanding of how practicing communication skills may yield personal growth, and contribute to the developing leader's ability to be effective in the many settings that may present themselves to a leader.

Although there is much literature on communication, 'despite the ancient roots and growing profusion of theories about communication, communication theory as an identifiable field of study does not yet exist' (Craig, 1999, p. 119). Craig's claim that there is no field of study that can be identified as communication theory is based on his observation that there is no unified understanding among communication theorists. Whether or not there is a field of communication theory, there is abundant literature on the topic, including Craig's seven traditions of communication: rhetoric, semiotic, phenomenological, cybernetic, socio-psychological, socio-cultural, and critical.

Craig cites the lack of coherence among the theorists as one of the sources of the problem in communication theory. In other words, it seems that a lack of communication is one of the problems in the communication theory community.

Despite the assertion that there is no field of communication, communication in groups has been studied and discussed by many researchers including Katzenbach and Smith (1992). Katzenbach, an ex-McKinsey consultant, explained his ideas about teams by using business examples. Teams, the new approach to getting to better business solutions (as in, two heads are better than one), were *en vogue* starting in the 1990s. It is likely that this emphasis will persist, as team outcomes are often superior to individual outcomes, and considering that employees change jobs and locations rather frequently, a team can maintain continuity in projects in ways that work structured around individuals cannot. One issue that arises with communication in teams is that, along with cooperation, comes a variety of kinds of conflict. The trend towards teams makes the importance of effective communication skills even greater. Katzenbach and Smith offered suggestions as to how best to work with teams, as well as characteristics of good teams. Although the authors mentioned the importance of interpersonal and communication skills, they did not identify specific skills.

Teamwork skills and communication skills rank fourth of ten in the most important attributes for job candidates (Watson, 2000). Communication skills have also been cited as critical for the success of marketing majors (Young & Murphy, 2003). In fact, the Association to Advance Collegiate Schools of Business standards is now requiring business schools to document how communication skills goals are being accomplished. In a study on the development of life skills at Indiana Wesleyan University, graduates indicated that communication skills and problem-solving skills were, from their perspective, the most important skills to learn (Flowers, 2003). While patient care ranked highest in importance in a study of paramedics (Rae, 2000), the study identified communication skills as the second most important issue in effective paramedic work. The same study also revealed the importance of reflection and support among paramedics as they deal with the emotional stress of medical emergencies.

The role of communication in the accounting process and managerial process is analyzed in relation to its importance, and the accounting and managerial communication process. The American Accounting Association's Committee to Prepare a Statement of Basic Accounting Theory noted the importance of communication in accounting in the following paragraph:

'The development of accounting information is only part of the accounting function. A necessary companion aspect of the function is the development of the communication process so that information can be transmitted and so that those to whom information is provided understand it and its potential usefulness. Communication is a vital link in accounting activity. It is of no less importance than that of developing the information itself' (Golen, 1989, p. 37).

The accounting and managerial communication process. The communication process plays an integral part in the development of accounting and management information. The accountant and the manager must observe economic data and transmit the data in meaningful ways through quantitative accounting and management reports. The user of the accounting and management reports must convert the quantitative data into qualitative data by interpreting the facts provided. The accountant and the manager are responsible for preparing meaningful and understandable accounting and management reports for the reader.

H. Lon Addams conducted a study on communication skills of the beginning accountants working for the eight largest accounting firms in the United States. Addams mailed 303 questionnaires to accountants who had worked for a public accounting firm for approximately one year; he received a 54 percent return (Addams, 1989, p. 37).

Ninety percent of the accountants in the Addams study indicated that their supervisors, in year-end performance appraisals, placed at least some importance on writing ability. Of this 90 percent, 38.4 percent ranked writing ability to be of substantial importance and 8.5 percent ranked it to be of vital importance. In a personal interview, a beginning accountant stated that writing ability is of substantial importance in performance evaluations (Addams, 1989, p. 38).

Eighty-three percent of the respondents in Addams's study stated that writing ability was at least of some importance in salary raises; of these respondents, 18 percent felt it was of substantial importance, and 2 percent felt it was of vital importance. The beginning accountant felt writing ability was of substantial importance in receiving salary raises. The practicing accountant considered writing ability to be of vital importance in salary raises (Addams, 1989, p. 38).

Sixty percent of the beginning accountants considered writing ability to be at least of some importance in promotions. Approximately 12 percent of the respondents considered writing ability to be of substantial importance (Addams, 1989, p. 39).

In one study, a systematic sampling technique was used to select 400 names from a list of 3,035 Brigham Young University accounting graduates. Among the questions, the respondents were asked to rate each writing project they perform according to its importance to their job success, as defined by promotions, pay raises, performance appraisals, and personal goal achievements (Addams, 1990, p. 331).

3 RESULTS

The results of the survey, as seen in Table 1, reveal that the 15 most important writing assignments in relation to job success are 1) letters, 2) analytical reports involving comparisons or evaluations, 3) narrative-audited and unaudited reports, 4) memoranda, 5) policy and procedures manuals, 6) systems analysis reports, 7) interim reports, 8)

Table 1. Rank ordering by percent of responses regarding the importance of specific writing projects to job success.

Writing projects	Rank number	Percentage for job success
Letters	1	97
Analytical reports involving comparisons or evaluations	2	91
Narrative-audited and unaudited reports	3	88
Memoranda	4	85
Policy and procedures manuals	5	82
Systems analysis reports	6	82
Interim reports	7	79
Proposals-budgets or programs	8	76
Policy statements	9	76
Compliance reports	10	73
Proposals-new business	11	73
Narrative-special reports	12	70
Responses-associations	13	67
Newsletters, articles	14	64
Testimonial reports	15	61

proposals-budgets or programs, 9) policy statements, 10)compliancereports,11)proposals-newbusiness,12) narrative-special reports, 13) responses-associations, 14) newsletters or articles, and 15) testimonial reports.

The results of the survey, as seen in Table 2, reveal that the ten most important (by rank ordering) communication skills in relation to job success are 1) nonverbal communication. Your body language, eye contact, hand gestures, and tone all color the message you are trying to convey; 2) confidence. It is important to be confident in all of your interactions with others; 3) friendliness. Through a friendly tone, a personal question, or simply a smile, you will encourage your co-workers to engage in open and honest communication with you; 4) clarity and concision. Good communication means saying just enough—do not say too little or talk too much; 5) empathy. Even when you disagree with an employer, co-worker, or employee, it is important for you to understand and respect their point of view; 6) respect. People will be more open to communicating with you if you convey respect for them and their ideas; 7) listening. Being a good listener is one of the best ways to be a good communicator; 8) open-mindedness. A good communicator should enter any conversation with a flexible, open mind; 9) feedback. Being able to appropriately give and receive feedback is an important communication skill; 10) picking the right medium. An important communication skill is to simply know what form of communication to use.

Table 2. Rank ordering by percent of responses regarding the importance of communication skills to job success.

Communication skills	Rank number	Percentage for job success
Nonverbal Communication Your body language, eye contact, hand gestures, and tone all color the message you are trying to convey.	1	94
Confidence It is important to be confident in all of your interactions with others.	2	91
Friendliness Through a friendly tone, a personal question, or simply a smile, you will encourage your co-workers to engage in open and honest communication with you.	3	91
Clarity and Concision Good communication means saying just enough—do not say too little or talk too much.	4	88
Empathy Even when you disagree with an employer, co-worker, or employee, it is important for you to understand and respect their point of view.	5	88
Respect People will be more open to communicating with you if you convey respect for them and their ideas.	6	85
Listening Being a good listener is one of the best ways to be a good communicator.	7	82
Open-Mindedness A good communicator should enter any conversation with a flexible, open mind.	8	82
Feedback Being able to appropriately give and receive feedback is an important communication skill.	9	79
Picking the Right Medium An important communication skill is to simply know what form of communication to use.	10	76

The results of the survey, as seen in Table 3, reveal that the four most important writing ability skills in relation to job success are 1) writing ability and performance evaluations letters, 2) writing ability and salary raises analytical reports involving comparisons or evaluations, 3) writing ability and promotion narrative-audited and unaudited reports, and 4) writing assignments and overall job success.

The accountant as a manager is a dynamic profession, where one is expected to provide objective, meaningful quantitative information to the users of data and to communicate the information effectively in both written and oral expression. Sources reported in secondary data and sources interviewed for this report are that oral and written communication skills ability influences evaluations, salary increases, and promotions.

Table 3. Rank ordering by percent of responses regarding the importance of writing ability to overall job success.

Writing ability	Rank number	Percentage for job success
Writing ability and performance evaluations	1	91
Writing ability and salary raises	2	82
Writing ability and promotion	3	64
Writing assignments and overall job success	–	70

4 CONCLUSIONS

Communication skills affect evaluations, salary increases, and promotions. The ten most important (by rank ordering) communication skills in relation to job success are 1) nonverbal communication, 2) confidence, 3) friendliness, 4) clarity and concision, 5) empathy, 6) respect, 7) listening, 8) open-mindedness, 9) feedback, and 10) picking the right medium. The ten most important (by rank ordering) writing skills in relation to job success are 1) letters, 2) analytical reports involving comparisons or evaluations, 3) narrative-audited and unaudited reports, 4) memoranda, 5) policy and procedures manuals, 6) systems analysis reports, 7) interim reports, 8) proposals-budgets or programs, 9) policy statements, and 10) compliance reports.

5 RECOMMENDATIONS

Because of the relationship between effective communication skills and success as an accountant and manager, the accounting student and the management student should develop excellent oral and written communication skills.

REFERENCES

Addams, H.L. (1989). Should the Big 8 teach communication skills? *Management Accounting*, 62(11), 37–40.

Borin, N., Metcalf, L. & Tietje, B. (2007). A replicable, zero-based model for marketing curriculum innovation. *Journal of Marketing Education*, *20*(10), 1–11.

Bottger, P. (1984). Expertise and air time as bases of actual and perceived influence in problem-solving groups. *Journal of Applied Psychology*, *69*(2), 214–221.

Brown, M.E. & Trevino, L.K. (2006). Ethical leadership: A review and future directions. *Leadership Quarterly*, *17*(6), 595–616.

Burgo, J. (2012). *Why do I do that? Psychological defense mechanisms and the hidden ways that shape our lives.* Chapel Hill, NC: New Rise Press.

Craig, R. (1999). Communication theory as a field. *Communication Theory*, *9*(2), 119–161.

Flowers, J. (2003). *Developing life skills: Perceptions of graduates of the adults, non-traditional business and management programs at Indiana Wesleyan University* (Doctoral dissertation) UMI. No. 3098153.

Fry, L. & Kriger, M. (2009). *Towards a theory of being-centered leadership: Multiple levels of being as context for effective leadership.* Thousand Oaks, CA: Sage.

Gardner, W., Avolio, B. & Walumba, F. (2005). *Authentic leadership theory and practice: Origins, effects and development* (vol. 3). Bingley, UK: Emerald Group Publishing Ltd.

Golen, S. (1989). Communications: Its role in accounting education. *The ABCA Bulletin*, *44*(4), 37–40.

Johnson, D. (2008). *Reaching out: Interpersonal effectiveness and self-actualization.* Upper Saddle River, NJ: Pearson.

Katzenbach, J. & Smith, D. (1992) *The wisdom of teams: Creating the high-performance organization.* New York, NY: Harper Business.

Kouzes, J.M. & Posne, B.Z. (2002). *The leadership challenge.* San Francisco, CA: Jossey-Bass.

Kriger, M.P. & Seng, Y. (2005). Leadership with inner meaning: A contingency theory of leadership based on the worldviews of five religions. *The Leadership Quarterly*, *16*(5), 771–806.

Liden, R., Wayne, S.J., Zhao, H. & Henderson D. (2008). Servant leadership: Development of a multidimensional measure and multi-level assessment. *The Leadership Quarterly*, *19*(2): 161–177.

McKee, A., Boyatzis, R. & Johnston, F. (2008). *Becoming a resonant leader: Develop your emotional intelligence, renew your relationships, sustain your effectiveness.* Boston. MA: Harvard Business Press.

Meyers, R. (2008). *Examining conflict styles: How do you manage conflict?* Paper presented at the Colloquium of the Medical College of Wisconsin, Milwaukee.

Nicolescu, B. (Ed.). (2008). *Transdisciplinary: Theory and practice.* Cresskill, NJ: Hampton Press.

Rae., J. (2000). *Communication practices that constitute paramedic team effectiveness.* (Doctoral dissertation) UMI. No. 9973616.

Schaetti, B., Ramsay, S. & Watanabe, G. (2008). *Personal leadership: Making a world of difference: A methodology of two principles and six practices.* Crestone, CO: Flyingkite Publications.

Strozzi-Heckler, R. (2007). *The leadership dojo: Build your foundation as an exemplary leader.* Berkeley, CA: North Atlantic Books.

Tichy, N. (2007). *The leadership engine: How winning companies build leaders at every level.* New York, NY: Harper Collins.

Watson, P.G. (2000). *A hirability study: The characteristics that cause an engineering student to receive a job offer.* (Doctoral dissertation) UMI. No. 9972017.

Young, M.R. & Murphy, J.W. (2003). Integrating communications skills into the marketing curriculum: A case study. *Journal of Marketing Education*, *25*(1). 57–70.

Young, S. (2007). Micromessaging: *Why great leadership is beyond words.* New York, NY: McGraw-Hill.

Increasing Management Relevance and Competitiveness – Sukoco et al. (Eds)
© 2018 Taylor & Francis Group, London, ISBN 978-0-8153-7455-8

Factors knowledge management and the work motivation of lecturers

Rino
Doctoral Program of Management Science, School of Postgraduate Studies, Universitas Pendidikan Indonesia, Bandung, West Java, Indonesia

ABSTRACT: This study analyzes the influence of Information Technology (IT), implementation of ISO 9001:2008, and leadership on knowledge management of motivation and performance of lecturers'. The population was lecturers of Padang State University (UNP). The samples were 175 respondents selected by a proportional random sampling technique. Data were analyzed by structural equation modeling using AMOS19 software. Results show that IT has significant influence on knowledge management, leadership has significant influence on knowledge management and lecturers' performance, and work motivation has significant effect on lecturers' performance. There is no significant relation between motivation and information systems. It is recommended that knowledge management activities should be developed into whitin the academic culture, as well as the importance of lecturers' participation in the planning and implementation of ISO 9001:2008.

1 INTRODUCTION

To effectively manage resources, a superior organization should rely on intangible knowledge asset because it is a strategic advantageous resource (Solvatore, 2004), and the key to business success. (Enz & Davison 2011, Sangkala, 2007). To remain competitive, organizations must create, locate and share knowledge and expertise to solve problems and obtain opportunities. This is known as the knowledge Management concept introduced by Stankosky (Aldi, 2005; Satyagraha, 2010). Besides, the paradigm of exploiting physical capital should be shifted into human capital, knowledge and social capital (Yulhendri, 2011).

To be specific, organization and human resources performances are positively related. Work motivation, leadership effectiveness and work time management contributes to performance (Oluseyi Ayo 2009). Chailom and Mumi (2010) found that IT capability has a significant positive effect on competitive advantage and performance. Additionally, it is proven that there is a significant positive relationship between quality management systems, such as ISO 9000:2001 and organizational performance (Dharma 2007; Levine, and Toffel, 2010). Leadership is also proven to affect organizational performance (Andrews and Boyne, 2010; Chan, 2010).

Many studies on organizational and human resource performance address the variables of IT, quality management systems and leadership, and their impact on performance (Andrews and Boyne 2010; Chailom and Mumi 2010; Corbett, 2005; Dharma, 2007; Oluseyi and Ayo, 2009; Ying and Ramamurthy, 2011).

The relationship of IT, quality management, and leadership variables with the formation of knowledge management and work motivation as intervening variable is rarely studied (Aldi, 2005; Enz and Davison, 2011; Satyagraha, 2010; Yulhendri, 2011). Therefore, this study examines the formation of knowledge management and work motivation and the connection with academicians' performance.

2 LITERATURE REVIEW

2.1 *Performance*

Performance is an output generated by work or profession indicators within a certain time referring to the achievement action according to the requested work that is characterized by work evaluation (Gibson et al., 2009; Griffin, 2002; Rivai and Sagala, 2009; Rivai, 2005, 2009; Wirawan, 2009). Thus, performance is related to the measurement or evaluation of people's work within an organization as a whole representing the organization achievement.

3 METHOD

This study design is hypothesis testing (Indriantoro and Supomo, 2009; Sekaran, 2003). The data were obtained using questionnaire and research reports. The variables are smart IT campus, implementation of ISO 9001:2008, leadership skills, knowledge management, work motivation and performance of academicians at Padang State

University (UNP). This study explains the influence of IT and leadership on knowledge management, influence of IT and ISO 9001:2008, and leadership on lecturer's motivation, influence of knowledge management and work motivation on lecturers' performance.

The subjects were lecturers, on the t basis that their performance can be measured using a standard measurement tool, that is the lecturers' performance evaluation guideline; they were involved in the academic process using IT tools and for them, knowledge management is important for knowledge dissemination and better organizational development.

The population was all UNP lecturers in seven faculties that have been certified by ISO 9001:2008, which have applied smart IT campus for academic and learning purposes, including academic information system, e-learning application, research information systems and community service. The sample size was determined based on Structured Equation Modeling (SEM) analysis requirements. (Yulhendri, 2011). The number of observed variables is 38; hence the number of samples required is 175 lecturers from the Faculties of Engineering, Economics, Mathematics and Natural Sciences, and Social Sciences. The data were analyzed using descriptive statistical analysis to describe the characteristics of the variables, and inferential statistical analyses to describe the relationship between variables and the asymmetric relationship between groups of related variables. Thus, this study is a multivariate analysis using SEM analysis technique assisted by AMOS software.

4 FINDINGS AND DISCUSSION

4.1 *Findings*

4.1.1 *Respondent profile*

Questionnaires were given to all lecturers in four UNP faculties. 454 questionnaires were distributed over three weeks period, 175 were returned, only 155 were usable.

4.1.2 *Descriptive analysis*

Table 1 shows that the average perception of UNP lecturers of the use of IT, the implementation of ISO 9001:2008, leadership, knowledge management activities, and UNP lecturers' performance is fair. Only work motivation variable is considered good.

4.1.3 *Assumption tests of SEM analysis*

The results of data processing show that the data tend to be not normally distributed, thus out liers need to be found (Santoso, 2012). The highest Mahalanob is value was 70.174 and this lower than the Chi square of 577.49 at *df* 659 with probability 0.01, thus there is no multivariate outlier. Additionally, the results of a linearity test using the Ramsey method of comparing the calculated value of F and F table is that all built relationships are above the F table and linear.

Table 1. Variable description.

No	Observable variable	Mean	TCR (%)	Category
1	Information technology	3.59	71.85	fair
2	ISO 9001:2008 quality management system	3.57	71.47	fair
3	Leadership	3.67	73.32	fair
4	Knowledge management	3.68	73.65	fair
5	Work motivation	4.21	84.17	good
6	Lecturers' performance	3.70	73.97	fair

Source: Processed primary data 2013.

4.1.4 *Fit test of measurement model using confirmatory factor analysis*

The test was performed using confirmatory factor analysis (CFA), consisting of two fit tests namely partial CFA and overall CFA, which show that the overall model is acceptable.

4.1.5 *Structural model fit*

AMOS software was used to perform SEM analysis in order to see the fit of the initial model by generating some fit model requirements that are measured in the SEM analysis model after several stages of assumption test (normality, outlier, and linearity).

4.1.6 *Hypothesis testing*

Hypothesis testing was conducted determine the relationship between endogenous and exogenous variables with the proposed hypotheses. This study proposes ten hypotheses (see Table 2).

4.2 *Discussion*

Interestingly, knowledge management does not serve as a moderating variable in the relationship between IT and lecturers' performance. Knowledge management in an organization must be built with solid construction supported by main pillars: leadership, organization, technology and learning (Satyagraha, 2010).

There is no additional influence from work motivation to explain the relationship between leadership and lecturers' performance. However, on direct influence, leadership has a significant effect on lecturers' performance. The weak relationship

Table 2. Results of hypothesis testing.

Variable	Relationship	Variable	Estimate	S.E.	C.R.	P	Label	Description
KM	<---	TI_SK	0.285	0.099	2.876	0.004	par_33	Significant
WM	<---	TI_SK	0.204	0.152	1.340	0.180	par_35	Not Significant
WM	<---	SMM_ISO	0.045	0.157	0.287	0.774	par_37	Not Significant
KM	<---	Skil_Pimp	0.542	0.082	6.602	***	par_38	Significant
WM	<---	Skil_Pimp	0.064	0.115	0.554	0.580	par_40	Not Significant
Performance	<---	TI_SK	0.182	0.191	0.952	0.341	par_34	Not Significant
Performance	<---	SMM_ISO	0.010	0.195	0.049	0.961	par_36	Not Significant
Performance	<---	Skil_Pimp	–0.348	0.176	–1.974	0.048	par_39	Significant
Performance	<---	KM	–0.163	0.232	–0.702	0.483	par_41	Not Significant
Performance	<---	MK	0.569	0.136	4.191	***	par_42	Significant

between leadership and lecturers' performance, when mediated by the work motivation variable, indicates that lecturers' work motivation is not influenced by leadership. This finding contradicts with the theory that organizational performance is strongly influenced by organizational leadership (Andrews and Boyne, 2010; Chan, 2010).The lecturers perceive that the faculties needs leadership skills improvement. This indicates the importance of improving lecturer's performance with leaders who can motivate the lecturers'.

4.3 *Limitations of the study and suggestions for further study*

The study has several limitations; (1) it only tests the model fit between the theoretical model and the empirical model based on collected data, and does not produce a new model or make generalization; (2) proportional random sampling was quite difficult in the field due to the lecturers' activities; (3) it was problematic to fulfill theoretical studies of individual performance, particularly lecturers in universities since the literature review and empirical study in this study are mainly about organizational performance; (4) the instruments were standard instruments used in prior studies and thus failed to reveal the true nature of the situation, so the instrument needs to be modified to fit the conditions in the field; (5) smart IT campus instrument should have addressed respondent's knowledge about existing smart IT campus; (6) this study does not observe knowledge management activities at individual or institutional levels, and does not thoroughly examine the lecturers' motivation in carrying out their main duties; (7) the relationship between ISO 9001:2008 implementation and lecturers' performance seemed weak because knowledge management and work motivation activities were not seen in the implementation of ISO 9001:2008.

Taking the limitations into account, it is suggested that; (1) the sampling should consider the respondents' characteristics, timing, and situation; (2) performance measurement should avoid the use of the Likert scale; (3) the model could be improved by considering other factors affecting the lecturers' performance such as education level, experience, and other theoretically possible factors; other relationships constructs should considered the following variables: assessment on smart IT campus, the implementation of ISO 9001:2008, and leadership skills.

5 CONCLUSION AND IMPLICATIONS

5.1 *Conclusions*

The implementation of ISO 9001:2008 has no significant effect on motivation and the performance of UNP lecturers. Specifically, leadership has no significant effect on motivation, but it does have significant effect on performance. Knowledge management does not significantly affect the performance of UNP lecturers. Work motivation has a significant effect on the lecturers' performance. Work motivation can strengthen the relationship between the assessment of smart IT campus and lecturers' performance, as well as the relationship between the implementation of ISO 9001:2008 and lecturers' performance. Knowledge management can strengthen the relationship between leadership skills on lecturers' performance. This means that knowledge management plays a role in improving lecturers' performance in leadership skills.

5.2 *Academic and practical implications*

The academic or theoretical implications are (1) There should be efforts to build a more appropriate path of influence with adequate data and instruments to accept H_A and reject H_O; (2) The ISO 9001:2008 implementation variable should be maintained in the model of lecturers' performance framework, because work motivation plays an important role in improving and strengthening the relationship of ISO 9001:2008 implementation and lecturers' performance. In this case, the ISO 9001:2008 is an administrative process handled by administrative staff, while lecturers as the academic staff are not involved in the process. It will require align their perspective and improve their work motivation which in turn will improve the lecturer's performance; (3) It is recommended to formal path ways between the smart IT campus and lecturers' performance through knowledge management and work motivation, and the implementation of ISO 9001:2008 with performance and leadership skill.

The practical implications as follows. First, although this study found low knowledge of management activities among UNP lecturers, the leaders' concern about improving lecturers quality should be appreciated. Therefore, knowledge management should always be developed into a culture that will accelerate the dissemination of information and knowledge on substantial basis among lecturers. Second, viewed in terms of research and activity, writing articles for national and international scientific journals should be improved, and there should be policies that support lecturers to develop themselves. Third, UNP should reconsider the policy of performance improvement through ISO 9001:2008 certification, and efforts should be made to actively involve lecturers in its implementation to motivate them. Fourth, this study considers DIKTI's lecturers' performance evaluation (EKD) and lecturers' performance load (BKD) as reliable performance measurement tools.

REFERENCES

Aldi, B. (2005). "Menjadikan Manajemen Pengetahuan Sebagai Keunggulan Kompetitif Perusahaan Melalui Strategi Berbasis Pengetahuan." *Jurnal Studi Manajemen & Organisasi* 2.58–67.

Andrews, R., & Boyne, G.A. (2010). "capacity, leadership, and organizational performance testing the black box model of public management." *Public Administration Review*: 443–54.

Chailom, P., & Mumi, A. (2010). "The Effect of Information Technology Capability, Network Competency, and Organizational Learning on Logistics Innovation, Competitive Advantage and Performance of Food Business on Thailand." *International Journal of Business Strategy* 10.71–85.

Chan, S.H. (2010). "The Influence of Leadership Expertise and Experience on Organizational Performance: A Study of Amanah Ikhtiar Malaysia." *Asia Pacific Business Review* 16.: 59–77.

Corbett, C.J., Montes-Sancho, M.J., & Kirsch, D.A. 2005. "The Financial Impact of ISO 9000 Certification in The United States An Empirical Analysis." *Management Science* 51.1046–1059.

Dharma, C. (2007). "Analisis Pengaruh Penerapan Sistem Manajemen Mutu ISO 9001:2000 Terhadap Peningkatan Kinerja Pada PT. Jasa Raharja (Persero) Cabang Sumatera Utara." Universitas Sumatera Utara.

Enz, J.F., & Davison, B. (2011). *How to Measure Human Resources Management*. 3rd Ed. Jakarta: Kencana Prenada Media Group.

Gibson, J.L., Ivanceivich, J.M., Donnelly Jr, J.H., & Konopaske, R. (2009). *Organizations Behavior, Structure and Process*. Singapore: Mc Graw Hill.

Griffin, R.W. 2002. *Manajemen*. Translated version by *Gina Gania (2004)*. 7th Edition. Jakarta: Erlangga.

Indriantoro, N., & Supomo, B. 2009. *Etodologi Penelitian Bisnis Untuk Akuntansi dan Manajemen*. Yogyakarta: BPFE.

Levine, D.I., & Toffel, M.W. (2010). "Quality Management and Job Quality How The ISO 9001 Standard For Quality Management System Affect Employees And Employers." *Management Science* Vol.56 No.: 979–996.

Oluseyi, A.S., & T. Ayo, H. (2009). "Influence of Work Motivation, Leadership Effectiveness and Time Management on Employees' Performance in Some Selected Industries in Ibadan, Oyo State, Nigeria." *European Journal of Economics, Finance and Administrative Sciences* 16. 7–17.

Rivai, Veithzal. (2005). *Manajemem Sumber Daya Manusia Untuk Perusahaan, Dari Teori Ke Praktek*. Jakarta: Raja Grafindo Persada.

Sangkala. (2007). *Knowledge Management Suatu Pengantar Memahamai Bagaimana Organisasi Mengelola Pengetahuan Sehingga Menjadi Organisasi Yang Unggul*. Jakarta: Raja Grafindo Persada.

Santoso, S. (2012). *Analisis SEM Menggunakan AMOS*. Jakarta: Elex Media Komputindo.

Satyagraha, T. (2010). "Pengaruh Kepemimpinan Transformasional dan Budaya Organisasi Terhadap Implementasi Knowledge Management Pada Learning Centre Group PT. Bank Mandiri (Persero)Tbk. Studi Persepsional Pada Karyawan Learning Centre Group Bank Mandiri." Universitas Pendidikan Indonesia.

Sekaran, U. (2003). *Research Methods for Busines Metodologi Penelitian Untuk Bisnis. Translated version by Kwan Men Yon 2006*. Second Edition. Jakarta: Salemba Empat.

Solvatore. (2004). *Manajerial Economics Ekonomi Manajerial Dalam Perekonomian Global*. 1st Ed. Salemba Empat.

Wirawan. (2009). *Evaluasi Kinerja Sumber Daya Manusia Teori, Aplikasi, dan Penelitian*. Jakarta: Salemba Empat.

Ying, L., & Ramamurthy, K. (2011). "Understanding the Link Between Information Technology Capability and Organizationalagility: An Empirical Examination." *Mis Quarterly* 35.931–54.

Yulhendri. (2011). "Faktor Pembentuk Mutu Modal Manusia, Modal Sosial dan Pengaruhnya Terhadap Kesejahtearaan Rumah Tangga Keluarga Studi Padan Rumah Tangga Petani, Nelayan, dan Pedagang, Di Pedesaan dan Perkotaan Di Sumatera Barat." Universitas Malang.

Increasing Management Relevance and Competitiveness – Sukoco et al. (Eds)
© 2018 Taylor & Francis Group, London, ISBN 978-0-8153-7455-8

The role of talent management in student performance in higher education

D. Purwaningsih
Universitas Pendidikan Indonesia, Bandung, Indonesia

ABSTRACT: This research aims to determine the impact of Talent Management (TM) on student performance in higher education. Seven important success factors of TM have been identified selection, retention, training, rewards, development, succession planning and career management—in relation to students in both state and private universities. The research method used was a descriptive and exploratory survey. The questionnaires were randomly distributed among students of several universities in Indonesia, mainly in Jakarta city. SPSS 23 software was used to perform validity and reliability test, and regression analysis. The results of this study support the proposed hypotheses that there are significant relationships between TM and student performance. The implications of the results of this study are that if a student takes a course in a field appropriate to their talent then their success rate could be increased.

1 INTRODUCTION

In recent years the application of Talent Management (TM) in companies has become a hot topic. One of the goals of applying TM is to increase employee performance. Researchers such as Antonucci (2005) and Fegley (2006) have shown that organizations are increasingly focusing on TM.

The implementation of TM is not only carried out by companies, but lately by many universities too although until today the application of TM in colleges has been limited to employees and not applied to students. On the other hand, the responsibility of universities and colleges is to provide qualified graduates. Thus the ability to improve performance of students in higher education will become one of the key issues for universities across the globe.

This study is based on a desire to establish the influence of TM on student achievement and student performance.

2 LITERATURE REVIEW

2.1 *Talent management*

Today TM is the one of the most important elements in human resource development. In TM, the analysis of its relationship with work satisfaction is very important (Prati et al., 2003). The most important attributes of TM are: selection, retention, training, rewards, development, succession planning and career management. Talent management needs to continue for in term of the training and development of high performance for potential new roles, identifying the gaps in knowledge and executing plans to improve competency or abilities and ensure they are maintained (Ariss et al., 2014).

TM usually refers to sourcing, selecting, retaining, developing, establishing and renewing the workforce through analysis and planning. TM is also what occurs in relation to the recruitment, development and processing of the management workforce and can be alternatively described as talent optimization. There is no single compatible definition of TM (Tansley, 2011).

Managing of talent understanding is from static succession to action oriented activity by different levels of stress on substitution planning (Meayers & van Woerkom, 2014).

Any employees have an opportunity to have an individual plan and organizations create position actually and clearly for the future (Soans, 2015).

2.2 *Student performance*

Performance has some variables to measure (Chen & Lou, 2002). Personal performance is not only a basic unit of organizational behavior) but also an important subject of personnel research that deals with the subjects of compensation, promotion, training and feedback (Karakurum, 2005). Task performance is essential if an organization is to achieve its planned goals and activities (Campbell, 1983). McCrae and Costa (1996) stated that the impact of ability and personality on performance is affected by other variables. Raja and Johns (2010) found that there is a joint effect of personality and performance. An individual's performance

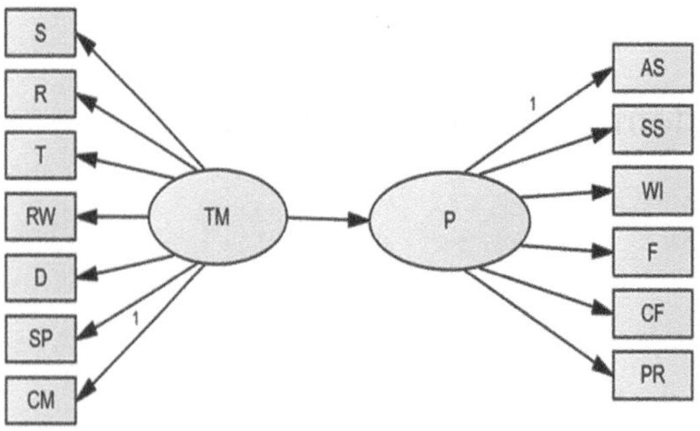

Figure 1. Conceptual model.
Legend: S – Selection; R – Retention; T – Training; RE – Rewards; D – Development; SP – Succession planning; CM – Career management; TM – Talent management; P – Performance; AS – Ability to complete study; SS – Spirit of study; WI – Working independently; F – Focus; CF – Cooperation with friends; PR – Forming positive relationship.

can be seen in their ability to complete studies, the spirit in which this occurs, independent working, focus, cooperation with friends and formation of positive relationships.

2.3 *The conceptual model*

In this model Talent Management (TM) is considered as the independent variables and student performance (P) as the dependent variables as shown in Figure 1.

In Figure 1, TM variables were observed through seven attributes, that is: Selection (S), Retention (R), Training (T), Rewards (RW), Development (D), Succession Planning (SP), and Career Management (CM). Performance (P) variables were observed through: Ability to complete Study (AS), the Spirit of Study (SS), Working Independently (WI), Focus (F), Cooperation with Friends (CF) and forming Positive Relationships (PR).

2.4 *Hypothesis development*

Hypothesis 1: TM has a direct and positive relationship with student performance.

Hypothesis 2: Selection, retention, training, rewards, development, succession planning and career management which are considered as attributes of TM together have a direct and positive relationship with student performance.

3 RESEARCH METHODOLOGY

The study was conducted in April 2017 by distributing questionnaires to students at several universities in Indonesia, mainly in Jakarta. The sampling used incidental sampling method, while data analysis was descriptive, qualitative and quantitative.

3.1 *Instruments and measures*

The research method used a descriptive and explanatory survey. The advantage of this strategy is that data gathering is very economical (Saunders et al., 2009). The questionnaires were randomly distributed among students of several universities in Indonesia, mainly in Jakarta city. The questionnaires consisted of questions about the demographic information of the respondents, and questions related to the research variables, namely, TM and student performance in higher education.

In order to measure the TM, seven attributes: – selection, retention, training, rewards, development, succession planning and career management —were used in the questionnaires. To measure student performance, 13 questions were asked in the questionnaires. These questions explored the ability to complete study, the spirit in which study was conducted, independent working, focus, cooperation with friends and the formation of positive relationships.

3.2 *Sample data*

The primary data was collected via questionnaires returned by 72 respondents. 59.7% of respondents were students of state universities, 13.9% were from private universities, while the remainders were from college or government institutions. 48.6% were males and 51.4% were females. 97.2% studied D4/S1 (Bachelor degree), while 1.4% each studied S2 (Master degree) or S3 (Doctoral degree).

3.3 *Data analysis process*

SPSS 23 software was used to perform validity, reliability, and regression analysis. The questionnaires were measured using a five-point Likert's scale. The answers were thus divided into five values: 1 – strongly disagree; 2 – disagree; 3 – neither agree nor disagree; 4 – agree; 5 – strongly agree. The relevance and clarity of the questionnaires was first tested through a pilot study.

The reliability of the research instrument was measured using Cronbach's alpha (α). After checking the validity and reliability tests for the trial questionnaire one question regarding student performance had to be removed to make the questionnaire valid and reliable.

After checking the data with SPSS software two data outliers were removed from the data set. The effects of TM on student performance were examined through regression analysis using SPSS software.

4 FINDINGS AND INTERPRETATION

Validity and reliability tests were conducted to ensure the questionnaires are valid and reliable. The questionnaires were distributed to 40 of the respondents ($n = 40$) with test level $\alpha = 0.05$. A validity test was performed using SPSS 23. The resultant values of *rxy* through SPSS were compared with the *r*-table. If *rxy* > *r*-table, this indicated that the attribute was valid.

The results of the validity test for both student performance (P) and for TM show that all attributes are valid because *rxy* > 0.321 (*r*-table).

The value of Cronbach's alpha of the two variables P and TM in the reliability test were 0.879 and 0. 897. These values were greater than the 0.6 critical value and they are thus reliable.

The resulst of the test for normality using the Kolmogoro-Smirnov test shows that the value of asymp. Sig. (= 0.078) is greater than 0.05, thus the study failed to reject H*o* and the conclusion was drawn that the student P variable was normal in distribution and, as a result, further analysis could be conducted.

The results of the goodness of fit test showed that R-squared for this regression model was 0.195; which means that only 19.5% of the student's performance could be explained by TM. Because the value of sig in Table 1 smaller than the test level of research α (0.000 < 0.05) H*o* was rejected and Ha accepted, which means that the value of R-squared is significant and the regression equation model can feasibly explain the effect of TM on P. Nevertheless, this result reinforced the statement by Stewart and Knowles (2007) that there is a relationship between selection of students and their performance.

The results of the Analysis Of Variance (ANOVA) indicated that the model has an *F* value = 16.460, and sig *F* <0.05. It explained the impact of TM on student performance in higher education.

The analysis was computed through SPSS 23. The coefficients of regression are shown in Table 1, where unstandardized coefficient β indicates the value of the numbers in the linear regression equation. The *t*-value shows the *t*-statistics in the *t*-test. The *p*-value or the significance in the table should be less than 0.05 to be significant. Table 1 shows analysis of the effect of TM on P, where it can be seen that there was a positive effect of TM on P that was significant at the 0.05 level, ($\beta = 2.656$, $t = 11.704$, sig. = 0.000). Thus, it can be concluded that there is a significant relationship between TM and P.

Table 1. Coefficient for regression between TM and P.

	Unstandardized coefficients		Standardized coefficients		
Model	B	Std. Error	Beta	T	Sig.
Constant	2.656	.227		11.704	.000
TM	.252	.062	.441	4.057	.000

The equation for the regression model can be derived on Table 1:

$$Y = 2.656 + 0.252\ X$$

where Y indicates P (performance) and X indicate TM (Talent Management).

The influence of the independent variable TM towars P was indicated by the β value of 0.252.

5 CONCLUSION

There are significant influences by TM on student performance (P) in higher education. Together, the seven attributes of TM: selection, retention, training, rewards, development, succession planning and career management—all influence student performance. This proves that student performance will be improved if the university makes selection tests based on the talent of students during the candidate admission process. The student's performance is also improved if they received training and rewards as students want to develop their knowledge and skills. Support by the university to help students get good jobs will increase student's motivation to do their best. An improvement in student performance will thus improve their ability to complete study, their spirit of study, their independent workingly, focus, cooperation with friends and formation of positive relationships. Based on the results of this study it is recommended that universities immediately apply TM to students.

ACKNOWLEDGEMENT

I would like to thank LPDP (*Lembaga Pengelola Dana Pendidikan*) for sponsoring my presentation in Surabaya. My compliments to the management of Universitas Pendidikan Indonesia (UPI) who provided us with great support.

REFERENCES

Antonucci, E.J. (2005). *The leadership benchstrength challenge: Building integrated talent management systems*. Oklahoma City, OK: Executive Development Associates, Retrieved from - http://www.executivedevelopment.com.

Ariss, A., Cascio, W. F, & Paauwe, J. (2014). Talent management: Current theories and future research directions. *Journal of World Business*, *49*, 173–179.

Campbell, J.P. (1983). Some possible implications of "modelling" for the conceptualization of measurement. In F. Landy, S. Zedeck, & J. Cleveland (Eds.), *Performance measurement and theory.* (pp. 277–298). Hillsdale, NJ: Lawrence Erlbaum Associates.

Chen, Y. & Lou, H. (2002). Toward an understanding of the behavioral intention to use a groupware application. *Journal of End User Computing 14*, 1–16.

Fegley, S. (2006). *2006 talent management survey report.* Alexandria, VA: Society for Human Resources Management. Retrieved from https://www.shrm.org/hr-today/trends-and-forecasting/research-and-surveys/documents/2006%20talent%20 management%20survey %20report.pdf

Karakurum, M. (2005). The effects of person-organization fit on employee job satisfaction, performance and organizational commitment in a Turkish public organization. (Unpublished doctoral dissertation, METU, Turkey).

McCrae, R.R., & Costa, P.T. (1996). Toward a new generation of personality theories: Theoretical contexts for the five-factor model. In J.S. Wiggins (Ed.), *The five-factor model of personaliy* (pp. 51–87). New York, NY: Guilford Press.

Meyers, M.C. & van Woerkom, M. (2014). The influence of underlying philosophies on talent management: theory implications for practice, and research agenda. *Journal of World Business*, *49*, 192–203.

Prati, L.M., Douglas, C., Ferris, G.R., Ammeter, A.P., & Buckley, M.R. (2003). "Emotional intelligence, leadership effectiveness and team outcomes". *International Journal of Organizational Analysis*, *11*, 21–41.

Raja, U. & Johns, G. (2010). The joint effects of personality and job scope on in-role performance, citizenship behaviors, and creativity. *Human Relations*, *63*(7), 981–991.

Saunders M., Lewis P. & Thornhill A. (2009). *Research Methods for Business Students* (5th ed.). Harlow, UK: Pearson Education.

Soans, F.S. (2015). Managing talent in the modern business world. *International Journal of Multidisciplinary and Current Research*, *3*, 1199–1203.

Stewart, J. & Knowles, V. (2007). Graduate recruitment and selection practices in small businesses. *Career Development International Review*, *5*(1), 21–38.

Tansley, C. (2011). What Do We Mean by the Term "Talent" in Talent Management? *Industrial and Commercial Training*, *43*(5), 266–274.

Increasing Management Relevance and Competitiveness – Sukoco et al. (Eds)
© 2018 Taylor & Francis Group, London, ISBN 978-0-8153-7455-8

Strategy to build universities

P. Dewi Dirgantari, B. Widjajanta & L. Lisnawati
Universitas Pendidikan Indonesia, Bandung, Indonesia

ABSTRACT: The purpose of this study is to create and choose alternative strategies and determine the best of these in helping universities achieving their goals. This study used a case study approach at Universitas Pendidikan Indonesia (UPI). The results of the study indicate that the generic strategy that can be applied by UPI is an intensive strategy with a choice of main strategies such as market penetration and, market and product development.

1 INTRODUCTION

In the 21st century, the trend of business orientation is changing so that it takes strategic management to address all the challenges faced by an organization, including the world of education. In Indonesia there are three types of Public Universities namely Work Unit, Public Service Agency and Legal Body. Public University of Legal Entity is the highest level including Cluster 1 because it is considered as a Public University that has grown and been able to meet government targets, which must be included in the Public University with accreditation (http://bem.fisip.ui.ac.id/notulensi-disikat/, accessed on 22 February 2017 at 12 pm).

All Public Universities in Indonesia are given a ranking for the purpose of coaching and in order to improve the quality. So, that the Public Universities will be spread into clusters. Coaching in Cluster 1 aims to master and achieve the World Class University ranks. However, there are some Public Universities that are thrown from the first cluster because the decreasing of the rank (http://bem.fisip.ui.ac.id/notulensi-disikat/, accessed on 22 February 2017 at 12 pm).

Between 2011 and 2015 there were various dynamic situations that had to be addressed by UPI, namely: (1) the transition to a university organized by the government from 2010 to 2012; (2) the implementation of the Public Service Body Financial Pattern from 2011 to 2013; And (3) the re-establishment of UPI as an autonomous university in the form of a Public University of Legal Entity based on Law Number 12, 2012, in Higher Education (Strategic Plan Universitas Pendidikan Indonesia 2016–2020). The UPI is continuously striving to prepare the organizational units and provision of State University of Legal Entity in order to maintain and stay in the first cluster.

Shawyun (2010), since the 1990s, education has been viewed from an appropriate management point of view in the sense that "education must deliver value to the end consumer", and "education must have a purpose". It is inevitable that education is seen through the management lens and guided by the principles of POC3 management (Planning, Organizing, Communicating, Coordinating and Controlling), PDCA Quality lenses (Plan, Do, Check and Act), ADLI Performance Lens (Approach, Deployment, Learning and Integration) and LeTCI performance level lenses (Level, Trend, Comparison and Integration). In order to meet the needs and requirements of the stakeholders in value creation and education, education must be strategically managed based on the institution's goals or mission.

Andersen et al (2006), contrary to the holistic approach of Shawyun (2010), takes advantage of the various tools and concepts into the overall framework within which the interrelationships can be understood when responding to internal and external challenges. Rouse and Putterill (2003) proposed a macro/micro relationship between: 1) organization and stakeholders, 2) capacity and resource capability, 3) planning, evaluation and resources, and achievements, 4) basic core elements of input, process, output. This approach moves from the organizational level (strategic plan) to the operational level (action plans) that support the main determinants of success. Franco-Santos et al (2007), Bernardin et al (1998), Kennerly and Neely (2002), Harrington (2005), Newkirk-Moore and Bracker (1998), Temporal (1990), Bolt (1993), Tovey (1991) and Mason (1993) have strengthened the success of management implementation from the strategic level to the operational level.

The increased risk error, loss, and even economic collapse, have led to current professional managers in all organizations to apply strategic management seriously, in order for their companies to remain competitive in an increasingly volatile environment. In order for the managers to strive to have a better deal within their ever-changing world, a company generally develops four phases of strategic management: basic financial planning, forecast-based planning, externally oriented (strategic) planning, and strategic management (Wheelen and Hunger, 2012).

Strategic management can be defined as art and science in formulating, implementing and evaluating cross-functional decisions that enable an organization to achieve its goals. As this definition implies, strategic management focuses on integrating management, marketing, finance and accounting, production and operations, research and development, and information systems to achieve organizational success (David and David, 2015). Strategic management is a set of managerial decisions and actions that determine the long-term performance of a company. These include environmental scanning (external and internal), strategy formulation (strategic or long-term planning), strategy implementation, and evaluation and control. The study of strategic management emphasizes the monitoring and evaluation of external opportunities and threats based on the strengths and weaknesses of the company. Originally called business policy, strategic management combines topics such as strategic planning, environmental scanning, and industry analysis (Wheelen and Hunger, 2012).

Figure 1, states that corporate strategy, among others, can be classified by type of company. For example, there is a corporate strategy for a conglomerate company that has several strategic business units and a company that has only one strategic business unit, which is usually a small company. In addition, it is also known that corporate strategy is classified on the basis of the task level. These strategies are generic strategies that will be translated into main strategies or master strategies (grand strategy). This master strategy is further developed into a strategy at the firm's functional level, often called a functional strategy (Umar, 2003).

Table 1 shows the generic strategic terms proposed by Porter, a strategy approach utilized by companies in order to outperform their competitors in similar industries. In practice, once the company knows the generic strategy, the implementation can be followed up with a more operational strategy step. Meanwhile, the main strategy (grand strategy) is a more operational strategy that is a follow-on of generic strategies (Umar, 2003). In conclusion, this study aims to utilize and create new and different opportunities for the future, long-term planning, and to optimize today's trends in order to achieve college goals.

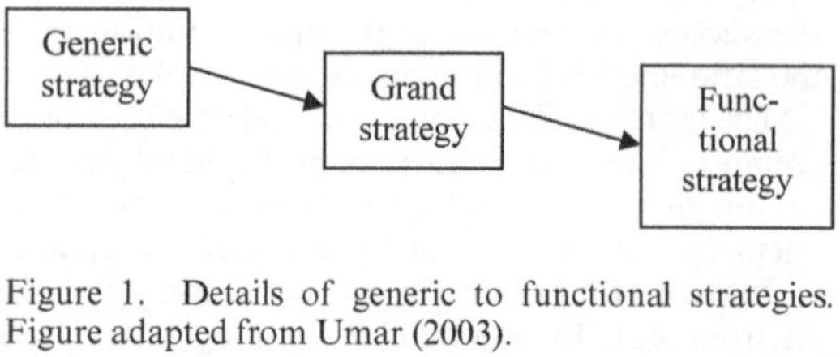

Figure 1. Details of generic to functional strategies. Figure adapted from Umar (2003).

Table 1. Generic and grand strategy. Table adapted from Umar (2003).

Wheelen and Hunger	David and David	Porter
1. Stability a. pause strategy b. no change strategy c. profit strategy	1. Vertical Integration Strategy a. Forward Integration Strategy b. Backward Integration Strategy c. Horizontal Integration Strategy	Differentiation
2. Growth a. concentration b. diversification	2. Intensive Strategy a. Market Dev. Strategy b. Product Dev. Strategy c. Market Penetration Strategy	Overall Cost Leadership
3. Retrenchment a. turnaround strategy b. captive company strategy c. sellout/ divestment strategy d. bankruptcy strategy/ liquidation strategy	3. Diversification Strategy a. Concentric Divers. Strategy b. Conglomerate Divers. Strategy c. Horizontal Divers. Strategy 4. Defensive Strategy a. Joint Venture Strategy b. Retrenchment Strategy c. Divestiture Strategy d. Liquidation Strategy	Focus

2 METHOD

This study used a case study approach at UPI. This study perfomed several steps as can be seen in Figure 2.

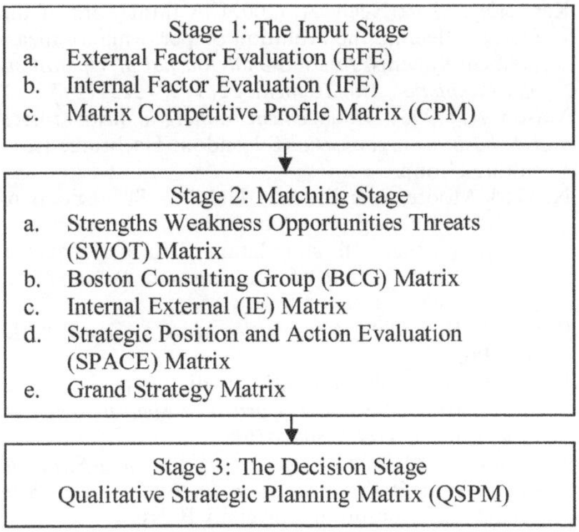

Figure 2. The strategy of formulation analytical framework. Figure adapted from Umar (2003).

2.1 *Stage 1: The input stage*

The External Factor Evaluation (EFE) Matrix is used to evaluate the company's external factors while the Internal Factor Evaluation (IFE) Matrix is used to determine the internal factors of the firm regarding the strengths and weaknesses that are considered important. The Competitive Profile Matrix (CPM) is used to identify key competitor companies and their major strengths and weaknesses in relation to the company's strategic position.

2.2 *Stage 2: Matching stage*

SWOT Analysis (Strengths, Weaknesses, Opportunities and Threats) is an important matching tool to help managers develop four types of strategies: SO, WO, ST, WT. The Strategic Position and Action Evaluation (SPACE) Matrix is used to map the company's condition using a model presented on a Cartesian diagram consisting of four quadrants of the same size scale. The Boston Consulting Group (BCG) Matrix describes the differences between divisions in terms of relative market share position and industry growth rate. The Internal External (IE) Matrix positions the various divisions of an organization in the form of nine cells. The Grand Strategy Matrix is based on two evaluative dimensions: competitive position and market growth (industry).

2.3 *Stage 3: The decision stage*

The Qualitative Strategic Planning Matrix (QSPM) is a technique that objectively shows which strategy is best.

3 RESULTS AND DISCUSSION

Based on the calculation results of the strategy formulation analysis, the following results are obtained:

3.1 *Stage 1: The input stage*

The EFE Matrix Acquisition Score of 3.320 shows that UPI already has a good strategy (strong enough) in anticipating internal threat. The IFE Matrix score of 2.715 shows that UPI already has a good enough strategy (average) in anticipating existing external threats. As compared with Pasundan University Bandung and Langlangbuana University of Bandung, UPI has a CPM score of 3.40.

3.2 *Stage 2: Matching stage*

The SPACE Matrix result shows that UPI is in the aggressive quadrant of the Cartesian diagram indicating that UPI is well positioned to harness its internal strengths to take advantage of opportunities, overcome internal problems, and avoid threats. The BCG Matrix has UPI with coordinates (0.39, 20) which are in the Question Marks position demonstrating a relatively low market share but competing with in a high growth industry. A strategy that can be used is an intensive strategy (market penetration, market development or product development). The IE Matrix has UPI with coordinates (3.320, 2.715) which are in quadrant IV so they are best controlled with growth and built strategies. The usual strategy is intensive strategy (market penetration, market development, and product development) or integrative (backward integration, forward integration, and horizontal integration). The Grand Strategy Matrix for UPI is in the first quadrant. This is an excellent position of strategy.

3.3 *Stage 3: The decision stage*

The UPI score of 6.035 means an intensive strategy is selected.

The generic strategy that UPI can implement is an intensive strategy with a choice of key strategies such as: (a) Market Penetration—to seek a greater market share for current products or services in existing markets through better marketing efforts. UPI improves its quality of service and promotes its resources such as sports facilities, hotels and so on; (b) Market Development—introducing the current product or service to a new geographic area. UPI cooperates with related agencies or consulates of Indonesia abroad to promote or introduce UPI products and services; (c) Product Development—helping to increase sales through improvement of current products or services or development of new products. In this case,

UPI could open new study programs or new faculties in response to market needs and wants.

4 CONCLUSIONS AND RECOMMENDATIONS

Universities, especially the University of Education Indonesia, can apply an intensive strategy to achieve the goals of the university, so that, the competitive position of university's current products and services can develop to a better higher standard.

REFERENCES

Andersen, B., Henriksen, B., & Aarseth, W. (2006). Holistic performance management: An integrated framework. *International Journal of Productivity and Performance Management, 55(1), 61–78.*

Bernardin, H.J., Hagan, C.M., Kane, J.S. & Villanova, P. (1998). Effective performance management: A focus on precision, customers and situational constraints. *Performance appraisal: State of the art in practice (pp 3–48).* San Francisco, CA: Jossey-Bass Inc.

Bolt, J. (1993). Achieving the CEO's agenda: Education for executives. *Management Review, 82(5), 44–49.*

David, F.R., & David, F.R. (2015). *Strategic management concepts and cases: A competitive advantage approach, 15th Edition.* Edinburgh Gate England: Pearson.

Franco-Santos, M., Kennerley, M., Michelli, P., Martinez, V., Mason, S., Marr, B, Neely, A. (2007). Towards a definition of a business performance measurement system. *International Journal of Operations and Production Management, 27(3), 784–801.*

Harrington, H.J. (2005). The five pillars of organizational excellence. *Handbook of Business Strategy (pp. 107–114). Emerald Group Publishing Ltd.*

Kennerley, M. & Neely, A. (2002). A framework of the factors affecting the evolution of performance measurement systems. *International Journal of Operations and Production Management, 22(11), 1222–1245.*

Mason, A. (1993). *Management training in medium sized UK business organizations.* London: Harbridge Consulting Group.

Newkirk-Moore, S. & Bracker, J. (1998). Strategic management training and commitment to planning: critical partners in stimulating firm performance. *International Journal of Training and Development, 2(2), 82–90.*

Porter, M.E. (1980). *Competitive strategy.* New York: Free Press.

Rouse, P. & Putterill, M. (2003). Predicting performance. *Special Issue: Business Performance Measurement and Management, 41(8), 806–816.*

Shawyun, T. (2010). *Developing and Actioning Strategic Planning In Higher Education Institutions.* Bangkok Thailand: Assumption University Press.

Strategic Plan (Renstra) Universitas Pendidikan Indonesia 2016–2020.

Temporal, P. (1990). Linking management development to the corporate future - the role of the professional. *Journal of Management Development, 9(5), 7–15.*

Tovey, L. (1991). *Management training and development in large UK business organizations.* London: Harbridge Consulting Group.

Umar, H. (2003). *Strategic Management In Action.* Jakarta: PT Gramedia Pustaka Utama.

Universitas Indonesia. (2016). Notulensi Disikat. http://bem.fisip.ui.ac.id/notulensi-disikat/, accessed on 22 February 2017 at 12 pm.

Wheelen, T.L. & Hunger, J.D. (2012). *Strategic management and business policy toward global sustainability.* New Jersey: Pearson Education Inc.

Increasing Management Relevance and Competitiveness – Sukoco et al. (Eds)
© 2018 Taylor & Francis Group, London, ISBN 978-0-8153-7455-8

Factors affecting the improvement of students' Grade Point Average (GPA)

A.B. Santoso, E.C.M. Simatupang & R.H. Sofyandi
University of Widyatama, Bandung, West Java, Indonesia

ABSTRACT: At the time of graduation, not all students have a satisfactory Grade Point Average (GPA) in accordance with the quality standards set by the university. The GPA itself is often used as a measurement by many companies or institutions during the recruitment process of prospective employees. This study is to determine the extent that internal and external factors have in influencing the improvement of a student's'—GPA. A survey method associative research was used in this study. The data was collected through a questionnaire distributed to Diploma students (D3) majoring in a-Management- Study course, in the classes of 2012, 2013, and 2014. Based on the research results, it can be concluded that there is significant influence from internal and external factors on students' GPA. In an effort to improve student's GPA, it is better for the university to pay attention to both internal and external factors.

Keywords: internal factors, external factors, Grade Point Average (GPA)

1 INTRODUCTION

In the increasingly competitive environment of today, businesses should have a strong competitiveness in order to maintain their sustainability. Therefore, it is important for a company to have a competent workforce capable of working well in order to achieve the objectives of the company. One of the requirements that is often set by a company or institution in recruiting and selecting a prospective workforce is the cumulative grade point average (GPA) of the prospective worker (Hendikawati, 2011). Thus, it is important for college graduates to have a satisfactory GPA score to make them more marketable when applying for work. Even though the GPA score is not the only indicator that can determine somebody's success at work, the company often requires the prospective employees to have a high GPA score in the recruitment process. This is because there are still many people who assume that college graduates with a high GPA are a the high achiever and so they will be able to perform better at work.

For universities, GPA itself is an indicator that can be used as a measurement in assessing student achievement during his or her study (Daely et al. 2013). When a student achieves a GPA above 3.00 at the time of graduation, it is an indication that he or she has an excellent academic record during his or her study. Widyatama University, as one of the best private universities in Bandung, Indonesia, has 'University Quality Goals', and one of them is: at least 75% of students can graduate on time with a very satisfactory achievement, i.e. GPA above 2.75.

Not all students are able to get a satisfactory GPA as set in the Widyatama University's quality goals. As an example, among 75 Diploma students of the class of 2014 majoring in their Management Study program in the odd semester (study year 2015–2016) or during one year of the study, only 36 students had a GPA below the average or set standard quality. This indicates that nearly 50% of students have a poor GPA score in the first year of their study. Therefore, it is necessary to find out the causes why some college students can have an unsatisfactory GPA.

Based on the background outlined earlier, the study aimed to understand the factors affecting the improvement of a GPA.

To identify the subject studied in this research, the following question was asked: "To what extent do the internal and external factors influence the improvement of students' GPA?".

2 LITERATURE REVIEW

2.1 *Definition of learning*

The definition of learning is presented here by some experts.

Learning is to be able to do something that has never been done before, or if the student behavior has changed when facing a situation, compared to before the learning experience (Hilgard & Bower, 1996).

Learning is a process that allows the emergence or change of a behavior as a result of the formation of the main response, provided that the change or the emergence of new behavior is not caused by a maturity or a temporary change due to a thing (Nasution, 2004).

Learning is an effort process undertaken by a person to gain a whole new behavioral change as a result of his own experience in interacting with his environment (Slameto, 2010).

Learning is a change that occurs within an organism, a human or an animal, caused by experiences that may affect the behavior of the organism (Hintzman, 1987).

Based on the definition proposed by those experts, it can be concluded that "to learn" is more directed to the changes in individual behavior, usually shown in the form of an improvement in the quality or quantity of an individual's behavior, caused by the existence of mental or psychological activities conducted by that individual. While the meaning of "learning" is a process of change in an individual, behavior as a process and is as a result of a person in experiencing, feeling, and learning something.

2.2 *Factors affecting learning outcomes*

Some factors that can affect the learning outcomes are as follows (Slameto, 2010):

1. internal factors, that is the factors coming from within a person which can affect the learning results of that person. These internal factors are as follows: a) physical factors including health and body defects; b) psychological factors including intelligence, attention, interest, talent, motive, maturity and readiness; and c) Fatigue Factor; and
2. external factors, that is the factors originating from outside of a person which may affect the learning achievement of that person. The external factors include: a) family factors (nurturing by their parents, relationships among family members, household atmosphere, and the family economic condition; b) school factors (learning methods, curriculum, relationships among the teachers, relationships among students, school discipline, teaching and school time, lesson standards, building condition and home work; and c) community factors (student activities in the community, mass media, social friends, and community life).

3 METHODS

3.1 *Research methodology*

This research is an associative research in which the information and data relating to the problems were collected through questionnaires distributed to respondents. The study sample was Diploma students (D3) majoring in a Management Study program in the class of years' 2012, 2013, and 2014.

3.2 *Operational variables*

In this research, there were three main variables studied, namely: internal factors (X1); external factors (X2); and student's GPA (Y). X1 and X2 are the independent variables while Y is the dependent variable.

3.3 *Population and sample*

The population in this study weres all active Diploma students (D3) majoring in a Management study program class of 2012–2014. The total number was 162 students with a sample taken of 115 students. In this research, probability sampling or random sample was used, while the sampling technique used was cluster sampling.

3.4 *Data collection technique*

Data collection was conduted through the questionnaires distributed to the students. The scale used in this questionnaire is an interval scale and the type of scale measurement was the Likert scale.

3.5 *Processing technique and data analysis*

For processing and analyzing the data, the multiple regression was determined by using SPPS version 17.0.

4 RESULT AND DISCUSSION

4.1 *Data collection results*

To know the correlation between the variables studied in this research, the measurement of variables was completed through a questionnaire distributed to the Diploma students (D3) majoring in a Management Study program. Of the 115 respondents, only 32 respondents were able to complete the questionnaire.

4.2 *Classic assumption tests*

The following table shows the results of the normality test using the Komogorov Smirnov test:

Table 1 shows that the data has a Normal Distribution because the Sig. value is above alpha 0.05, that is 0.687.

Table 2, shows that all variable data is free from multicollinearity because tolerance is above 0.1, that is, 0.187 and VIF below 10 (5.354).

Table 1. Normality test: One-sample Kolmogorov-Smirnov test.

		Unstandardized residual
N		32
Normal parameters[a,b]	Mean	0.0000000
	Std. deviation	3.05607501
Most extreme differences	Absolute	0.112
	Positive	0.102
	Negative	−0.112
Kolmogorov-Smirnov Z		0.714
Asymp. Sig. (2-tailed)		0.687

a. Test distribution is normal.
b. Calculated from data.

Table 2. Data multicollinearity test.

	Unstd. Coeff.		Std. Coeff.			Collinearity statistics	
Model	B	Std. Error	Beta	t	Sig.	Tolerance	VIF
1 (Constant)	−1.568	1.303		−1.204	0.238		
x1	0.182	0.069	0.302	2.640	0.513	0.187	5.354
x2	0.262	0.044	0.683	5.978	0.500	0.187	5,354

a. Dependent variable: y.

Table 3. Data autocorrelation.

Model	R	R^2	Adj. R^2	Std. Error	Durbin-Watson
1	,964[a]	,929	,924	1,24105	1,758

a. Predictors: (Constant), x2, x1.

Table 4. Heteroscedasticity test.

	Unstd. Coeff.		Std. Coeff.		
Model	B	Std. Error	Beta	t	Sig.
1 (Constant)	−1.568	1.303		−1.204	0.238
x1	0.182	0.069	0.302	2.640	0.513
x2	0.262	0.044	0.683	5.978	0.500

a. Dependent variable: y.

The data autocorrelation test uses the Durbin-Watson test and requires the value to be around 2 or between 1 and 3 to be free from autocorrelation. Table 3, shows that the Durbin-Watson value as 1.758, meaning there is no autocorrelation.

Table 4, shows that the Sig. value of X1 is 5.013 and the Sig. value of X2 is 5.000. Both are more than alpha 5%, meaning that the data is free from heteroscedasticity.

4.3 *Multiple linear regression analysis*

Table 5, shows that the R (correlation) value is 0.964. This number shows that the relationship between internal factors and external factors on the improvement of GPA is high. For contributions from both factors is 0.929, meaning that 92.9% of GPA can be explained by the independent variables in this study, while the rest, 7.1%, is explained by other factors outside of this research.

In Table 6 above, regarding the F test and significance, it is shown that the F count in the Analysis of Varian test or F test is 190.532 with a significance value of 0.000. Since the probability (p = 0.000) is much smaller than 0.05, it can be concluded that H0 is rejected and Ha is accepted, meaning that internal and external factors influence the improvement of a student's' GPA.

The regression equation used to predict the degree of variable X1 and X2 if Y is manipulated, is shown in Table 7.

Based on Table 7, the regression equation is shown in Equation 1:

$$Y = -1.568 - 0.182X_1 + 0.262X_2 + \varepsilon \quad (1)$$

Table 5. Result of multiple correlation analysis of X1 and X2 on Y.

Model	R	R^2	Adjusted R^2	Std. Error
1	0.964[a]	0.929	0.924	1.24105

Table 6. F test and significance of variable X1 and X2 on Y.

Model	Sum of squares	df	Mean square	F	Sig.
1 Regression	586.919	2	293.459	190.532	0.000[b]
Residual	44.666	29	1.540		
Total	631.585	31			

a. Dependent variable: y.
b. Predictors: (Constant), x2, x1.

Table 7. Multiple regression test.

	Unstd. Coeff.		Std. Coeff.		
Model	B	Std. Error	Beta	t	Sig.
1 (Constant)	−1.568	1.303		−1.204	0.238
x1	0.182	0.069	0.302	2.640	0.513
x2	0.262	0.044	0.683	5.978	0.500

5 CONCLUSION AND RECOMMENDATIONS

5.1 *Conclusion*

Referring to the test results, it was shown that the internal and external factors studied in this research influence the GPA. It is known that two factors have contributed to an 92,9% inprovement in GPA and the rest is influenced by other factors not examined in this study.

5.2 *Recommendation*

In an effort to improve student's GPA, it is better for the university to pay attention to both factors. In terms of external factors, it is better if the university can provide learning facilities that can motivate students to learn better or lecturers, who at the time of teaching, can use interesting learning methods, so that the students are triggered to wilingly study with more diligence.

There are some things that need to be undertaken in any further research on this subject matter such as increasing the sample size so the results may represent a grater population. In addition, similar research could be conducted in other study programs and faculties at Widyatama University so that the general learning factors influencing GPA can be found.

REFERENCES

Daely, K. et al. (2013). Analisis statistik faktor-faktor yang mempengaruhi indeks prestasi mahasiswa. Saintika Matematika, 1(5): 483–494.

Hariandja, M. (2006). *Perilaku organisasi: memahami dan mengelola perilaku dalam organisasi.* Bandung, Indonesia: Unpar Press.

Hendikawati, P. (2011). Analisis faktor yang mempengaruhi indeks prestasi mahasiswa. *Jurnal Matematika Kreatif-Inovatif*, 2(1): 27–35.

Hilgard, E.R., & Bower, G.H. (1996). *Theories of learning*. New York, New York: American Book Company, Meredith Publishing Company.

Hintzman, D.L. (1987). *The psychology of learning and memory*. Eugene, Oregon: Department of Psychology, University of Oregon.

Muhidin, A., Sambas dan Abdurahman, M. (2009). *Analisis korelasi, regresi, dan jalur dalam penelitian [dilengkapi aplikasi program SPSS]*. Bandung, Indonesia: Pustaka Setia.

Nasution, N. (2004). *Psikologi belajar*. Jakarta, Indonesia: Gramedia Pustaka Utama.

Robbins, S.P. (2006). *Organizational behavior* (10th ed.), Perilaku Keorganisasian Edisi Kesepuluh, Terjem. oleh. benyamin molan. Jakarta, Indonesia: PT. INDEKS, Kelompok Gramedia.

Slameto. (2010). *Belajar dan faktor-faktor yang mempengaruhinya*. Jakarta, Indonesia: PT. Rineka Cipta.

Innovation, operations and supply chain management

Increasing Management Relevance and Competitiveness – Sukoco et al. (Eds)
 ISBN 978-0-8153-7455-8

Analysis of the small segment credit business process at Bank ABC Indonesia

A.C. Saifullah & R.D. Kusumastuti
Universitas Indonesia, Depok, Indonesia

ABSTRACT: Banks function as the intermediary that collects funds from the public and channels it back in the form of credit loans to society. One credit segment that plays an important role in developing Small and Medium Enterprises (SMEs) is small segment credit. Bank ABC is a state-owned enterprise in Indonesia, and the management repeatedly changes the number of credit officers involved in processing small segment credit applications from two officers to only one officer. The objective of this study is to analyze which business process is better and propose ways to improve the process. We conduct interviews to gather primary data, and collect secondary data related to both business processes. We use flowcharts to compare both processes, and use three parameters (application processing time, percentage of realized target of debit balance, and non-performing loans) to determine which is the better process. The findings show that the current credit process (with one credit officer) has a higher realized target of debit balance and a shorter processing time than the previously applied process (with two credit officers). However, this results in a higher percentage of non-performing loans and, thus, we propose improvements by simplifying the business process, reorganizing the small credit segment division, and simplifying the credit analysis forms.

Keywords: business process analysis; small segment credit; bank

1 INTRODUCTION

Small and medium enterprises play a significant role in the Indonesian economy. According to data from the Indonesia Statistics Body (BPS), until December 2015, there were 3,385,581 micro enterprises and 283,022 small firms in Indonesia (BPS, 2016a), which contributed a value added of about IDR 220.7 trillion to the Indonesian economy in 2015 (BPS, 2016b).

Banks play an important role in financing the micro and small businesses, as small firms have a high dependency on financial institutions because they do not have access to public capital markets (Berger & Udell, 2002). According to the regulation issued by the Bank of Indonesia (BI) in 2015, commercial banks must allocate at least 20% of their total credit loans to micro, small and medium businesses by the year 2018.

Bank ABC** is a state-owned commercial bank, which also has a mission to support the growth of micro and small businesses by providing financing for them. In 2015, Bank ABC distributed around IDR 326 trillion of credit loans, and therefore IDR 65.2 trillion of it should have been allocated to small businesses (small credit segment). There are three segments of productive loans at Bank ABC, namely small, medium, and corporate segments. In the small segment, the amount of loans is in the range of IDR 1 to 15 billion. Credit loan applications for the small segment are processed by the Small Credit Centre (SKC), and Bank ABC has 51 SKCs nationwide.

According to Bank ABC's regulation, the length of the processing time for the application should not exceed 14 working days after all documents have been completed. However, in current conditions, the process takes about two months to complete. A longer application processing time means fewer numbers of approved debtors and, thus, lower revenue for Bank ABC.

In order to overcome the problem, the management has taken action to change the business process at the SKCs. Generally, SKCs conduct credit analysis to assess the business potential and risks. Prior to 2010, the credit application was processed by one person, a Relationship Manager (RM). In the year 2010, the business process was changed by implementing the four-eyes principle. In this setting, the credit application was processed by two people, namely the RM to assess the business potential and the Credit Analyst (CA) to assess the business risks. In the year 2015, the credit application process was changed back to the system prior to the year 2010,

**The name of the bank is not revealed for confidentialiy reasons.

whereby the credit analysis is conducted only by the RM. Since the system has been changed back and forth, it is important to know which business process is more effective and efficient, and to identify improvements that can be made at the SKCs, so that the Bank's revenue can be increased with a good quality of credit.

The remainder of the paper is organized as follows. Relevant literature is discussed in Section 2, research methodology is explained in Section 3, findings and discussions are presented in Section 4, and, lastly, conclusions and recommendations are explained in Section 5.

2 RELEVANT LITERATURE

Every bank should focus on innovation in order to increase their revenue, increase the number of customers and reduce their costs (Skinner, 2010), for instance, by improving their business process. A business process is a complete, dynamically co-ordinated set of activities or logically related tasks that must be performed in order to deliver value to customers or to fulfill other strategic goals (Guha et al., 1993).

Business Process Reengineering (BPR), introduced by Hammer in 1990 and Davenport and Short in 1990, is claimed to be able to produce radical improvements in performance (O'Neill & Sohal, 1999). Radical changes are needed as customers can be very diverse and segmented, the competition has been intensified, and changes have become pervasive, persistent and faster in some marketplaces (Hammer & Champy, 1993).

According to Lowenthal (1994), BPR is the fundamental rethinking and redesign of operating processes and organizational structure, with the focus on an organization's core competence to achieve dramatic improvements in organizational performance. Elements of BPR are refocus (a corporation's values should be customer oriented), redesign (the main business process, usually by using information technology to make improvements), reorganize (the business into cross-functional teams with end-to-end responsibility for a process), rethink (the organization's and people's issues), and improve (the business process organization-wide) (Rigby, 2015).

Tools for BPR are, namely, process visualization, process mapping/operational method study, change management, and benchmarking (O'Neill & Sohal, 1999).

3 RESEARCH METHODOLOGY

This research is conducted by using a combination of qualitative and quantitative approaches. In-Depth Interviews (IDIs) with five experts from the Bank are conducted in order to gain insights in to the story behind the changes in business process and the ideal business process that should be implemented at the SKCs.

Based on the IDIs results and the Bank's standard operations procedures, we develop flowcharts of both business processes, and compare them based on the application processing time, realized target of debit balance (representing the Bank's target), and Non-Performing Loans (NPL), which represents the quality of the credit loans. Loans are classified as NPL if debtors fail to pay installments for more than 90 days. The application processing time is determined based on interviews with three informants (head of the SKC in South Jakarta, a supervisor of RMs at the SKC in South Jakarta, and the RM of the SKC in South Jakarta) as the data is not well documented at Bank ABC. Data for the last two parameters are collected from a branch of Bank ABC located in South Jakarta, for the period of 6 months prior (December 2014-May 2015) and after the last business process change (June-November 2015). Improvements are then proposed to be implemented at the SKCs in order to increase the Bank's revenue.

4 FINDINGS AND DISCUSSIONS

As previously mentioned, in the year 2015 the business process at the SKCs was changed back, with an RM conducting both business potential and risk analyses, with a simplified application kit. According to the informant at the SKCs, the reason behind one-person credit analysis is to shorten the loan application processing time, because both analyses are carried out by one person, thus eliminating potential conflicts in the business process. Meanwhile the reason behind a two-person credit analysis is to ensure that the distributed credit loans will have a low level of NPL or high quality of credit.

In the two-person credit analysis, the process starts with the RM reviewing the prospects of future debtors. If they are deemed worthy of the credit loans, the RM will then gather initial data and documents to get their history and conduct pre-screening by checking their data at the Debtor Information System (SID), and the National Blacklist (DHN) of BI. If they have a clear history, the RM will ask future debtors to submit further documents, and then verify all the documents.

The CA will also verify all the submitted documents by visiting On The Spot (OTS), and also by telephoning future debtors' suppliers and buyers. After the documents are complete, the CA will then conduct an analysis of all aspects, namely marketing, production, finance, and management, as well as analyzing the risks. The analysis results will determine the future debtor's rating. Only those that are classified as Investment Grade can be considered to be given the loan. The CA will then prepare the loan structure according to the future debtor's needs, based on the analysis result and the future debtor's capability. Then, all the completed forms are bundled into a Credit Application File (PAK), which is then checked for compliance at the Compliance Unit.

The Committee will then decide whether or not to approve the credit application. The Committee consists of the RM, CA, CA supervisor, Head of Business Unit, and Head of Risk Unit. The decision will be made jointly by the Head of Business Unit and the Head of Risk Unit.

If the credit application is approved, then the Credit Administration Unit (ADC) will prepare a Credit Approval Letter (SKK). If the future debtor agrees with all of the terms and conditions, the ADC will prepare the Credit Contract (PK) that will later be signed by the future debtor and the Bank, otherwise the credit will not be given. Credit loan disbursement is then conducted according to contract.

Afterwards, the RM and the CA will monitor the debtor to check whether all payment conditions are fulfilled, and reassess the business feasibility to prevent any loss by the Bank. Monitoring of the debtor is conducted by evaluating the debtor's performance and the collateral. In certain conditions, the loan will be restructured to prevent any loss by the Bank (see Figure 1).

In one-person credit analysis (Figure 2), activities that were previously done by the RM and the CA, are now done by the RM alone.

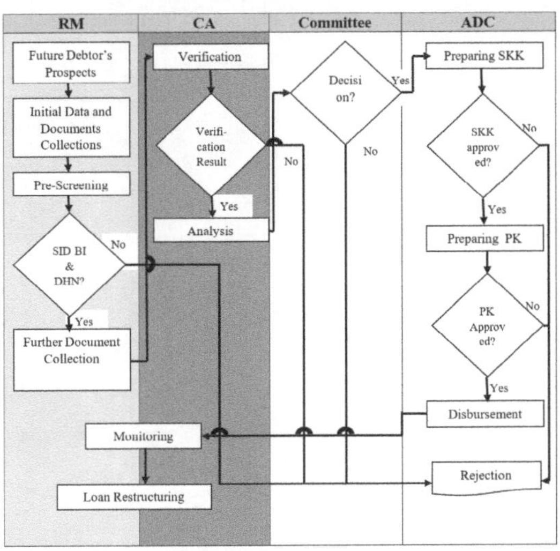

Figure 1. Two-person credit analysis.

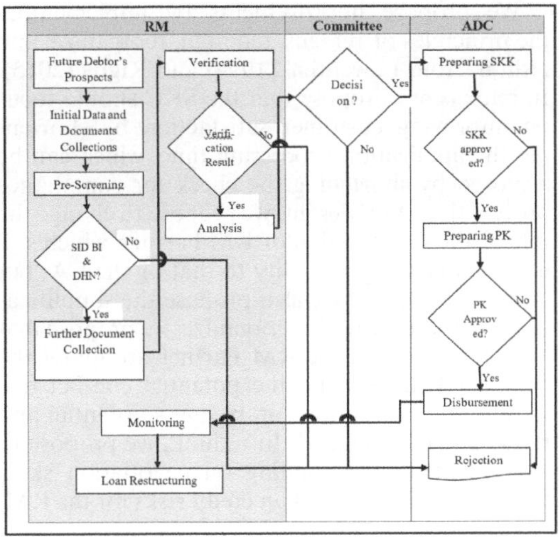

Figure 2. One-person credit analysis.

Table 1. Comparison of both business processes.

Parameters	Two-person credit analysis	One-person credit analysis
Average application processing time (Days)	24.7	12.3
Average realized target of debit balance	95.24%	108.14%
Average NPL	8.82%	9.42%

The average processing times of both processes are presented in Table 1. It can be seen that one-person credit analysis is more efficient, as the analysis only involves one person, thus eliminating any conflict that may happen in a two-person credit analysis.

In terms of the realized target of debit balance, it can also be seen in Table 1 that the average realized target in a two-person credit analysis is 95.24%, which is lower than in a one-person credit analysis (108.14%). The explanation for this is similar to that for the application processing time; with only one person conducting the analysis, conflict is eliminated, resulting in a higher realized target of debit balance. In terms of NPL, a one-person credit analysis has a higher NPL (9.42%) than a two-person credit analysis (8.82%), indicating that although reducing the number of people causes a shorter processing time and higher realized target, it also results in a lower quality of credit loans.

Thus, in terms of application processing time and realized target of debit balance, a one-person credit analysis is better than a two-person credit analysis. However, in terms of NPL, a two-person credit analysis is better than a one-person credit analysis.

We propose improvements by implementing the principles of refocus, redesign, reorganize, and rethink from Lowenthal (1994) and Rigby (2015). In refocus, we propose that the SKC should focus on improving customer satisfaction by shortening the application processing time, which can be achieved by shortening the check for compliance process time. In redesign, we propose to change the role of the CA into that of RM Partner, which still has a similar responsibility to that of the CA, but at the back office. We also propose the simplification of credit forms. In reorganize, we propose that both the RM and the RM Partner are under the Business Unit, so that the potential conflict due to different perceptions on business potential and risks can be eliminated. In rethink, we propose to provide additional training on negotiation skills for the RM Partner and on credit risks for the RM.

5 CONCLUSIONS

This paper presents a study on the business processes of credit applications that were previously and are currently applied at the small segment credit center at Bank ABC. The current process (one-person credit analysis) has a higher realized debit balance and shorter processing time, while the previous process (two-person credit analysis) has a higher quality of credit (lower NPL). We propose improvements by conducting BPR to shorten the business process and improve customer satisfaction.

REFERENCES

Berger, A. & Udell, G.F. (2002). Small business credit availability and relationship lending: The importance of bank organizational structure. *The Economic Journal, 112*, F32–F53.

BPS. (2016a). *Number of micro and small businesses by province, 2013–2015*. [Online] Available from: https://www.bps.go.id/linkTableDinamis/view/id/1004 [Accessed 1st March 2017].

BPS. (2016b). *Value added (at market price) of micro and small businesses by province, 2013–2015*. [Online] Available from: https://www.bps.go.id/linkTableDinamis/view/id/1009 [Accessed 1st March 2017].

Guha, S., Kettinger, W.J. & Teng, J.T.C. (1993). Business process reengineering: Building a comprehensive methodology. *Information Systems Management, 10*(3), 13–22.

Hammer, M. & Champy, J. (1993). *Reengineering the corporation: A manifesto for business revolution*. New York: Harper Business.

Lowenthal, J.M. (1994). *Reengineering the organization: A step-by-step approach to corporate revitalization*. Milwaukee: ASQC Quality Press.

O'Neill, P. & Sohal, A.S. (1999). Business process reengineering: A review of recent literature. *Technovation, 19*, 571–581.

Rigby, D.K. (2015). *Management tools 2015: An executive's guide*. Boston: Bain & Company Inc.

Skinner, C. (2010). *It's banking Jim, but not as we know it: Creating tomorrow's bank by identifying the most critical strategic changes and trends in banking today*. Cambridge: Searching Finance Limited.

Increasing Management Relevance and Competitiveness – Sukoco et al. (Eds)
© 2018 Taylor & Francis Group, London, ISBN 978-0-8153-7455-8

The identification of defects in rubber slipper production using the six sigma method

T.A. Auliandri & M.A. Setiani
Faculty of Economics and Business, Universitas Airlangga, Surabaya, Indonesia

ABSTRACT: "Rumpun Mas" (Rumpun Mas. UD) is a producer of Rubber Slippers, known in Indonesia as the "Sandal". Their main product is Rubber Slippers, and they also produce other products, such as shoes, shoe components, bottle caps, and clothes hangers. Unfortunately, during the production of Rubber Slippers, production failure in the form of product defects cannot be avoided. This research aims to find out about the Rubber Slipper production process, observe the cause of the defects and provide some suggestions to solve the Deproblem of defects during production at Rumpun Mas. UD by using the Define – Measure – Analyze – Improve – Control (DMAIC) *Six Sigma* method.

1 INTRODUCTION

The manufacturing industry plays an important role in countries such as Indonesia, where it has grown tremendously. The Central Bureau of Statistics (BPS) shows that, in 2015, the growth of medium and large manufacturing industries increased by 4.57 percent compared to its rate in 2014. Among the different types of industry, the footwear industry enjoyed a high rate of growth in its production for the fourth quarter of 2015 (7.22 percent). Under such conditions, footwear companies should exhibit a good performance and apply appropriate strategies to sustain themselves in the business world.

This concept is applicable for companies that aim to improve their product quality dramatically and record a zero defect rate. It can motivate the management of Rumpun Mas UD. to enhance their product quality. Rumpun Mas UD.'s problem is due to a low level of effectiveness and efficiency, which causes defective products to occur during their production process. The defect problems that occur in Rumpun Mas UD. happen during the production of the soles of Rubber Slippers.

2 LITERATURE REVIEW

Hansen and Mowen (2004:441) argued that quality represents excellence or a relative measure of goodness. Quality has a conventional definition and a strategic definition. The conventional definition of quality usually illustrates the direct characteristics of a product, namely performance, reliability, ease of use, aesthetic, and so on, while the strategic definition represents everything that meets the needs of customers (Gaspersz, 2002). The management of companies that compete in a global market must pay serious attention to the strategic definition in order to maintain their existence in the market.

3 RESEARCH METHOD

This research employs a qualitative-descriptive approach. The data are collected by interviews and direct observations of the research object in order to relevantly illustrate and/or describe the research findings based on a certain situation or phenomena. The data collection procedure is conducted through introduction, literature study, and field study. The data will be analyzed in accordance with the DMAIC stages of Six Sigma.

4 RESULTS AND DISCUSSION

To discover the cause of the defects, further reduce the defects of Rubber Slippers and enhance their quality, the Six Sigma method is employed. The success of this method is depicted through the increase in the capability of the production process towards a zero defect goal through a DMAIC cycle. The authors will discuss the five stages, namely (1) Define, (2) Measure, (3) Analyze, (4) Improve, and (5) Control.

4.1 *Define*

At this stage, the Six Sigma selection is conducted by analyzing the defective products' data at Rumpun Mas UD. From the data, it is found that Rubber Slippers recorded the highest production quantity (3,918,750 pairs), with a 5.22 percent defect rate in 2015. In this research, Six Sigma's quality enhancement is employed to find the causes of the defects in order to increase and improve the quality of the Rubber Slippers. As previously mentioned, the Rubber Slipper production (which records the highest demand) method will be analyzed and is expected to fulfill the demand for Rubber Slippers from Indonesia.

The selected Six Sigma project will define its key process, order and interaction. Before defining the key processes and consumers in Six Sigma projects, the SIPOC (Supplier, Input, Processes, Output, Customer) model first needs to be determined.

4.2 *Measure*

Based on direct observation, interviews with production staff and the SIPOC diagram, the authors determine three potential Critical to Quality (CTQ) in Rubber Slippers production at Rumpun Mas UD. Table 2 illustrates the defects that occur during the Rubber Slippers production process. The sample is taken from the company data in 2015. Output resulting from the production process is not the same each month, because the production process in Rumpun Mas UD. is conducted based on consumer orders.

After determining CTQ, the basic performance of the production process is measured by calculating Defects Per Million Opportunities (DPMO) and sigma value to discover whether there is any increase or decrease in monthly performance. The performance of the Rubber Slippers production in January 2015 is selected as the basic performance standard. It is found that the Rubber Slippers

Table 1. SIPOC diagram for rubber slippers products.

Suppliers	Inputs	Process	Outputs	Customers
Suppliers of raw material: PT. Nagasakti, the collectors of used PVC in Mojokerto, HMKI Margomulyo	1. Used PVC 2. DPO oil 3. Blowing agent 4. Patterned Stencil plastic 5. Plastic coloring 6. Plastic seed 7. Stabilizer 8. Packing plastic 9. Production machine 10. Human resources	Raw material acceptance and storage ↓ Soles-making process ↓ Shoelaces making process ↓ Assembly process ↓ Examining process ↓ Packing process	Rubber Slippers	All small and medium enterprises that order the Rubber Slippers at Rumpun Mas UD.

Source: Company data.

Table 2. Defect rate in the rubber slippers production process in 2015.

Months	Production (in pairs)	Defects (in pairs)	CTQ	Description of potential CTQ
January	294.000	17.640	3	1. Perfect stencil on Rubber Slippers soles.
February	294.000	20.580	3	2. The soles are not hard and clotted.
March	306.250	18.375	3	3. The soles' shapes fit the *molding*.
April	325.000	16.250	3	
May	299.000	17.940	3	
June	362.500	14.500	3	
July	227.500	6.825	3	
August	430.000	17.200	3	
September	400.000	20.000	3	
October	318.500	22.295	3	
November	331.250	19.875	3	
December	330.750	13.230	3	

Source: Company data.

sigma value from January to December 2015 is from 3.49 to 3.82.

4.3 *Analyze*

Using the Pareto diagram, the smallest to the largest causes of defects can be illustrated. The most frequent cause of defects is illustrated by the highest bar, then the bar size shrinks as the causes grow less frequent. This Pareto diagram is based on the Rubber Slippers defects, namely hard and clotted soles, imperfect stencil, molding mishap, incorrect weight and punctured soles.

The biggest cause of defect is recorded as hard and clotted soles at 43.2 percent, while the second is an imprecise stencil at 38.3 percent. The third cause of defect is molding mishap at 9.3 percent; incorrect weight is recorded in fourth place with 7.1 percent; and, lastly, a punctured sole is the lowest cause of defect with a rate of 2.1 percent. Based on such results, the most urgent defects to be solved are hard and clotted soles and imprecise stencils. The level of defects in Rubber Slippers in 2015 is shown by the Pareto diagram in Figure 1.

In order to enhance the understanding of the production of Rubber Slippers, uncover the cause of the defects and conduct repairs, this stage starts by illustrating the production process using a flowchart. Figure 2 illustrates the flowchart of the production process of Rubber Slippers.

4.4 *Improve*

At the "improve" stage, the repair plan is determined in order to reduce the defects. At this stage, the priority is handling the defect problem and the authors' recommendations will be provided by Failure Mode and Effects Analysis (FMEA) analysis. Based on the FMEA analysis, a repair solution will be determined by Risk Priority Number (RPN) ranking to discover which causes of defects should be solved first. After this, the

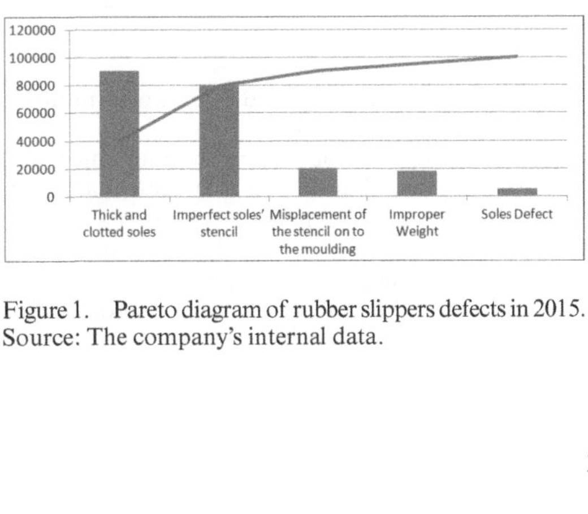

Figure 1. Pareto diagram of rubber slippers defects in 2015. Source: The company's internal data.

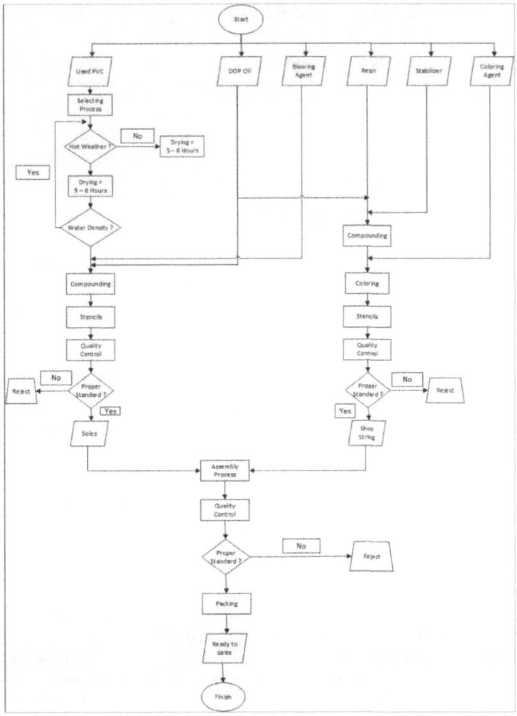

Figure 2. Rubber slippers production process flowchart. Source: The company's internal data.

highest cause of defects will be determined based on each mode of defect. Table 3 illustrates the RPN ranking for the causes of the defects in Rubber Slippers.

Based on the table above, the highest RPN value for hard and clotted soles is recorded by soggy raw material (RPN 192). Meanwhile, the highest RPN value for an imperfect stencil is caused by the less than optimal production process (RPN 80). Therefore, the recommendations for the company are listed as follows:

The recommendations above are conducted based on the highest RPN value for each mode of defect. Moreover, recommendations are also provided for the other causes of defect based on human, method, material and machinery factors. Table 4 depicts the RPN ranking based on human, method, material and machinery factors. Based on Table 4, the highest RPN value is recorded by the material category (RPN 423), followed by method (RPN 341).

4.5 *Control*

After devising the repair plan at the "improve" stage using FMEA analysis, this stage aims to

Table 3. The RPN ranking of the causes of defects.

Modes of defect	Cause of defect	RPN
Thick and clotted soles	Soggy raw material	192
	Imperfect drying process of PVC	120
	Inaccurate material volume	96
	Malfunctioned sensor	96
	Loose molding	72
	Negligence in control during production	72
	Improper installation	48
	Delayed time in taking the soles out of the mold	48
	Improper mixing of chemical material	48
Imperfect soles' stencil	Less than optimal production process	80
	Misplacement of the stencil on to the molding	75
	Wet and soggy raw material	75
	Dirty material	60
	Reversed placement of the stencil	30
	Imperfect drying process for PVC	20

Source: Processed data.

Table 4. RPN ranking based on human, machinery, material and methods.

Categorization for the causes of defects	Cause of failure	RPN
Human	Negligence in control during production	72
	Improper installation	48
	Less than optimal production process	80
	Total	**200**
Material	Soggy raw material	192
	Inaccurate material volume	96
	Dirty material	60
	Wet and soggy raw material	75
	Total	**423**
Machinery	Malfunctioned sensor	96
	Loose molding	72
	Total	**168**
Method	Imperfect drying process of PVC	120
	Delayed time in taking the soles out of the mold	48
	Improper mixing of chemical material	48
	Misplacement of the stencil on to the molding	75
	Imperfect drying process for PVC	20
	Reversed placement of the stencil	30
	Total	**341**

Source: Processed data.

maintain the sigma increase during the production process. Control is expected to prevent repeated mistakes. The steps required during this stage are as follows:

1. Ensuring that the quality of raw materials is fit for the company's standards.
2. Conducting regular training every six months, devising special supervision for production staff's performances, and holding a monthly evaluation for the staff.
3. Controlling the machinery maintenance and repairing any damage. In addition, machinery maintenance should be managed to prevent damage that could potentially cause an unfavorable optimum production process.
4. Controlling the production method and continuously evaluating it to remain efficient and effective.

5 CONCLUSION

After identifying the causes of defects in the production of Rubber Slippers in Rumpun Mas UD. and formulating the repair suggestions using the Six Sigma method, we can conclude that:

1. At the defining stage, the Six Sigma project is determined, objectives are stated according to SMART principles, the key process is defined using the SIPOC diagram, and the defects in Rubber Slippers are defined.
2. At the measuring stage, CTQ identification is conducted after determining that three CTQs in this research highly influence Rubber Slippers production, namely a perfect stencil on the sole, the sole is not hard and clotted, and the sole shape fits the molding.
3. At the "analyze" stage, the production process mapping is conducted through a flowchart. Then, the dominant cause is selected using a Pareto diagram, in which hard and clotted sole records the highest percentage with 43.2 percent, followed by an imperfect sole stencil in second place with 38.3 percent.
4. At the "improve" stage, alternative repair is identified using FMEA based on the highest RPN grade. The alternative repairs, which can be conducted by Rumpun Mas UD. to solve hard and clotted soles, are as follows:
   a. Sorting the raw material in accordance to the water content;
   b. Providing a special room to dry PVC materials;
   c. Altering the size of the shredded PVC to a smaller size.
5. At the controlling stage, activity control is conducted to prevent repeated mistakes, namely by conducting material control, regular training every six months, regular machine maintenance and repair, supervision of the production methods and evaluation of its effectiveness and efficiency.

ACKNOWLEDGMENT

This research activity is supported and fully funded by the Department of Management, Faculty of Economics and Business, Universitas Airlangga, Indonesia.

REFERENCES

Foster, S.T. (2007). *Managing quality integrating supply chain*. Canada: Pearson Prentice Hall.

Gaspersz, V. (2000). *Total Productivity Management*. Jakarta: PT. Gramedia Pustaka Utama.

Gaspersz, V. (2002). *Guidance of Implementation of Six Sigma Integration for ISO 9001:2000, MBNQA, and HACCP.* Jakarta: PT. Gramedia Pustaka Utama.

Gaspersz, V. (2007). *Lean Six Sigma for manufacturing and service industries.* Jakarta: Gramedia.

George, M.L., Rowlands, D.T. & Kastle, B. (2004). *What is Lean Six Sigma?* New York: McGraw-Hill.

Hansen, D.R. & Mowen, M.M. (2004). *Cost management: Accounting & control*. United States: Thomson South-Western.

Indonesian Central Bureau of Statistic (BPS—Badan Pusat Statistik). (2016). *Report on Growth Production of Large Medium Industry in Indonesia*. Accessed 5 May 2015. www.bps.go.id.

Increasing Management Relevance and Competitiveness – Sukoco et al. (Eds)
© 2018 Taylor & Francis Group, London, ISBN 978-0-8153-7455-8

The design of service quality improvement in a library by using LibQUAL model and fishbone diagram

F. Wurjaningrum & A. Kurniawan
Universitas Airlangga, Surabaya, Indonesia

ABSTRACT: The purpose of this research was to identify students' perceptions of quality attributes based on the LibQUAL model, identifying problems of the quality of library services by using the Fishbone Diagram and designing improvements that can be made by the head of the library. The approach used in this study was a qualitative approach with case study method. The qualitative approach allows researchers to conduct a fairly broad and in-depth discussion on a subject. The determination of dimensional attributes of the library services quality in this research was based on the LibQUAL model, consisting of library staff, library services, library collections and the library as a place. The next steps were to collect and analyze the results of a questionnaire distributed to the students, to conduct an in-depth interview with the head of the library as the decision-maker, to discuss the results of the analysis, and to find a solution using the Fishbone Diagram.

Through the results of the questionnaire data processing, it was found that only one attribute from 27 attributes had a positive value or otherwise satisfied, but 26 attributes were still in the tolerance zone. This meant that the library has been providing a quality service above the users' minimum expectations, but it has not been able to provide superior service quality, or indeed as per users' expectations. By interviewing the head of the library, it was found that the main factors lacking in the quality of library services were the quality of human resources and limited budget. The final result showed that the first proposed improvement was to provide training for improving the quality of human resources, and then to set up a performance measurement system for improving employee responsibilities. The second improvement was to meet the needs of the book collections with a limited budget.

Keywords: service quality, LibQUAL model, Fishbone Diagram, quality improvement, library services, quality management

1 INTRODUCTION

Interest in literacy reading in Indonesian society still very much lags behind other countries, with Indonesia ranked 60 out of 61 countries. This shows that the ability to read in Indonesian society is still equivalent to that in South Africa. The literacy value of reading in Indonesian society is still very low. Research of the Program for International Student Assessment (PISA) shows an average value of 493, while the value of Indonesian literacy is only 396-(www.gobekasi.pojoksatu.id).

The lack of interest in reading can be caused by low appeal, and lack of facilities and infrastructure that are feasible and comfortable in which to read. The quality of services provided by the institution to support increased interest in reading should be taken into account. One of the facilities provided to increase reading interest is the library. As mentioned in Indonesia Law No. 43 in 2007, the library is an institution managing the collection of papers, prints, and/or professional record work, with a standard system to meet the educational, research, conservation, informational and recreational needs of the library users. To increase the desire for the community to have a library, the library should be designed to attract and provide good service quality.

A library is an important element in a university because a good library will support the quality of education and research. In assessing the service quality, the perspectives of the recipients of the service are required, in this case from the library users. The perceptions of library users can be used as a reference to assess the quality of services provided by the library. In performing a service quality assessment, the SERVQUAL method is used to find the gap between the value of the service quality provided and the expectation of the recipient. However, for a library, there is a model of service quality assessment available called the LibQUAL model. This is a model developed from the SERVQUAL method to measure the quality of a library service, containing the attributes obtained from the dimensions devoted to the library. Furthermore, Fishbone Diagrams are used to determine the problems that affect the quality of services in the library.

The results of the Dahan study also mention the dimensions of LibQUAL; first, that the staff library is related to responsiveness and assurance; second, library services are related to reliability and empathy; third, is the library collections, which are related to the completeness of the literature and sources as a reference for the interests of students, based on the respective knowledge of their disciplines; and fourth, is the library as a place, in this case a place that has the ability to display something real. The indicators are tangibles, physical facilities, how libraries utilize space, equipment, furnishings, the availability of staffs or officers and communication equipments, as well as symbols, and convenient learning places (Dahan, 2016).

The LibQUAL model is used to determine the level of quality of library services by analyzing the gap between received services with minimum expectations (adequacy gap) and services received with a real expectation (superiority gap), based on LibQUAL dimensions. By calculating the value of the adequacy gap and superiority gap, the quality of a library service can be seen, based on user perception. According to Nadiri and Mayboudi (2010), consumers have a distance of expectations and it shows as a tolerance zone, with the desired level of service as the upper limit and the minimum service level as the lower limit. The distance is the distance of service performance that is still tolerable and acceptable to customers. If the customer service is above the minimum tolerated value, the customer will be satisfied. Zone tolerance is defined as the minimal distance between the level of acceptance and desire (Cook et al., 2003).

The Fishbone Diagram was developed in 1943 by Dr. Kaoru Ishikawa, a professor from the University of Tokyo. According to Scarvada, et al. (2004), the Fishbone Diagram is a visual tool for identifying, exploring, and graphically describing in detail all causes related to a problem. The basic concept of the Fishbone Diagram is that the fundamental problem is placed on the right side of the diagram or on the head of the skeleton of the fishbone. The cause of the problem is described in the fins and the thorns.

Hambleton (2007) suggests that the Fishbone Diagram can be used to analyze issues at the individual, team, or organizational level. There are many uses or benefits of using the Fishbone Diagram in problem analysis, for instance: focusing on individuals', teams', or organizations' key issues; making it easy to illustrate a brief overview of team or organizational problems; determining agreement on the cause of a problem; building team members' support to produce solutions; focusing the team on the cause of the problem; facilitating visualization of the relationship between cause and problem; and, facilitating team and team members to conduct discussions and become more focused on the discussion and the cause.

2 RESEARCH METHODOLOGY

The approach used in this research is qualitative approach with case study method. The qualitative approach allows the researcher to conduct a wide and in-depth discussion on a case. This approach aims to analyze a problem, find the cause, and find a solution to the problem of an object. Bogdan and Biklen (1982) add that the qualitative approach of case study is a detailed analysis of a problem, a document storage, or a specific event. The result of the study is a deep and specific knowledge, so it is not general.

Data collection techniques used were literature study, field study, observation, questionnaire distribution and triangulation. Researchers conducted direct interviews to find out all the information about the company and issues raised. In this study, unstructured interviews were used. Some interviews were conducted without recording, in order to dig deeper into the information. The observation was conducted by a direct review of the library owned by one of the government-owned universities located in Surabaya, to support the results of the interview in conducting the analysis of the discussion in the study. The distribution of questionnaires aims to determine the quality of university library services, based on the perceived acceptance by students and what the students expect from the actual service. Questionnaires were distributed to students who visited the library more than once a month. Triangulation is a technique done to check the validity of data that has been obtained. Hernon (2010) defines triangulation as a combination, or a combination of methods, used to study interrelated phenomena from different perspectives. This research used triangulation method and triangulation of data source. Therefore, using the data processing questionnaire, validity and reliability tests were also done in reviewing the results of this research data processing.

Stages of analysis used in solving problems in this research are: first, determining the attributes of service quality dimensions of the library based on the LibQUAL model, that is library staff, library services, library collection and library as place, through literature study and discussion with librarians; second, to collect and analyze the results of the LibQUAL model questionnaire; third, to make observations, and interview the head of the library to determine the factors that affect the quality of service; fourth, to analyze the results of observations and interview which have been obtained with the Fishbone Diagram, and discuss with the head of the library; fifth, to provide suggestions for improvements, conclusions and suggestions from the research that has been done.

3 FINDINGS

The results of the analysis of service quality gap are based on visitor perception of the university library, obtained from the LibQUAL model questionnaire, consisting of 27 service quality attributes that have been completed by 100 respondents. The obtained results were to find out the students' perceptions of the service gap received by the minimum expectation (adequacy gap) and the gap between the received service and the real expectation of service (superiority gap).

The adequacy gap is obtained by calculating the difference between the perceived value of the service received and the minimum expectation of the user. From the library staff's dimension, the highest gap value is owned by the attribute of "smiling library staff" with the adequacy gap of 0.55, while the lowest adequacy gap value is in attribute "librarian in rearranging the completed collections" with 0.38. In the library services dimension, the attribute that has the highest adequacy gap value is "the information provided in the website is easy to understand and clear (library profile, library condition, available services)" with 0.45, while for attributes that have the lowest adequacy gap available, these are in "library provides an easy-to-understand online catalog" and "library collection location according to available information" with a value of 0.34. From the library collection dimension, it can be seen that the highest adequacy gap value is in the attribute of "actual available collection" with the value of 0.59, while the lowest value is in the attribute "library collection in accordance with curriculum" with value 0.35. The attribute that occupies the highest adequacy gap value in the library as place dimension is "safe place storage" with a value of 0.34, while, for the lowest value, it is "room has good lighting" with 0.17. It can be seen from the data processing that the library user is quite satisfied, because the gap analysis shows the level of service received is greater than the minimum expectation level.

The superiority gap is obtained by calculating the difference between the perception of the service received and the visitors' actual expectations. From the library staff's dimension, the highest gap value is owned by the "polite officer library" attribute, with a superiority gap of 0.04, while the lowest value in the superiority gap is the attribute of "smiling library staff" with –0.16. In the library services dimension, the attribute that has the highest superiority gap value is the "library time library" with –0.16, while, for the attribute that has the lowest adequacy gap, this is found in the "library provides an easily understandable online catalog" attribute, with the value of –0.33. From the library collection dimension, it can be seen that the highest superiority gap value is in the attribute "library collection in accordance with the educational curriculum" with the value of –0.35, while the lowest value is in the attribute "actual available collection", with the value of –0.46. The attribute that occupies the highest superiority gap value in the library as place dimension is "safe storage of goods", with a value of –0.11, while the lowest value is "library provides adequate copier", with –0.54. From these results, the user feels that the library has not been able to provide a good level of service quality because the level of service received is still below the level of real expectations.

The results of data processing analysis state that the university library is able to make visitors quite satisfied with the services provided. However, the 'quite satisfied' in question is the satisfaction that is still in the zone of tolerance because it still cannot meet the real expectations of users. The tolerance zone is a value that is still between the minimum level of adequacy and the level of service desired (Cook et al., 2003).

According to Nadiri and Mayboudi (2010), the consumer has a distance of expectations, and this shows as a tolerance zone with the desired level of service as the upper limit and minimum service level as the lower limit. The distance is the range of service performance that is still tolerable and acceptable to customers. In other words, it can be said that the library is only able to meet the minimum satisfaction of visitors, has not been able to provide superior service to visitors of the university library, and requires an improvement in the quality of services provided.

To identify the problem, we will use interview method and also direct observations to know what caused the service quality of the library to be less good. Furthermore, these factors will be grouped and visualized using a Fishbone Diagram, so an alternative solution can be formulated that is the most appropriate to be applied by the university library. In identifying the cause of the lack of service quality, researchers used four categories tailored to the LibQUAL model dimensions: library staff, library services, library collections, and library atmosphere and facilities. Factors that cause lack of service quality in the dimension of library staff are less responsive officers, less rapid service, and library staff having less mastery of library science. Factors that cause lack of service quality in the dimensions of library services are the inappropriate operating hours, and book catalog and book layout that are less appropriate. Factors that led to the lack of service quality in collections were that collections are less complete, new collections are limited, and there are few journal subscriptions. Factors that cause lack of service quality in the dimensions of the atmosphere and facilities of the library are the difficulty of using existing facilities, and the lack of library cleanliness.

From interviews with the head of library, the department heads and some library staffs, the most dominant issue in library service quality is the root of all problems, with the criteria that the problem has a significant influence on the service quality of the library. If improvements are made to the dominant problem, many problems can be overcome and necessarily improve the quality of the university's library services. From the problems mentioned above, two dominant issues are highlighted, namely the limited quality of human resources and the budget. The problem of low quality of human resources must be considered. If the human resources are less qualified, then the quality of service cannot be provided. The next problem is the limited budget. In the fulfillment of all library needs, either the collection or facility would require a budget. The budget is very important to support the quality of services related to meeting the needs of the appropriate collection and the existing collection.

From the results of the discussions conducted, it was found that the root problem regarding the lack of human resources quality, is the lack of education, with a lack of staff with a basic knowledge of a library. Only three employees of the twelve employees, have basic library knowledge, while nine of them do not have a library background, with education levels, ranging between elementary, junior high, vocational, undergraduate, and magister. The lack of service quality is also due to the limited number of existing employees and the lack of responsibility each employee has in doing their job. From the results of the discussion, to solve the human resource performance problems, the proposal is to provide training to improve the quality of human resources, and then to establish a performance standard system to increase the responsibility of each employee, in addition to providing clear performance standards to be binding in order for employees to achieve the expected levels of performance.

For budgetary problems, this is an internal policy of the university, but there are still several things that can be done to meet the needs of students regarding the library collections. After discussion with the head of the library, the proposal is handling budget issues by using priorities. The intended priority is for the library to provide a book or literature when there is an urgent interest, such as for majors' accreditation. On that occasion, majors that have an interest for accreditation are prioritized in the fulfillment of collections, such as books and scientific journals. This priority is very important given the limited budget, while the latest collection of books and journals must also be fulfilled.

4 CONCLUSION

The theoretical implications of this research are, first, according to the result of the LibQUAL model analysis, that the attribute values of the questionnaire which obtained results, are still within the respondents' tolerance zone, which means the value of the adequacy gap is positive and, for the superiority gap, is positive and still within tolerable limits. This indicates that library users are quite satisfied with the services provided by the university library based on the research attributes used, because the values obtained from the adequacy gap and the superiority gap are still between the minimum level of adequacy and the level of service desired. So, it can be concluded that the respondents are satisfied with the library services because they have exceeded the minimum expectations of respondents. However, the library has not been able to provide a superior service that can impress the library visitors. Second, in identifying the cause of the lack of service quality, researchers used four categories tailored to the LibQUAL model dimensions, that is library staff, library services, library collections, and atmosphere and facilities. Furthermore, from these categories, the influential factors were searched and eleven factors were found that can affect the quality of the university library services. Third, there are two dominant problems in the university library that lessen the quality of library services. These problems are the quality of human resources and limited budgetary issues. The first suggested improvement is to provide training to raise the quality of human resources, and then to design a performance measurement system to improve employee responsibilities. The second improvement proposal is to use the priority scale to meet the needs of the collection with limited budget.

The practical implications of this research are, first, that much-needed support is required from all at the university library to achieve maximum service quality, both from the university and the management officers, so as to provide the best service for library visitors. The second is that both the university management and the managers of the university library should pay more attention to the improvement of the service quality attributes. Finally, it is better to improve the quality of this service continuously (continuous improvement) to see the development of the desires and needs of the library visitors, and to know the extent of the university library's ability to meet the needs of the library visitors.

The limitations of this study are that the results of this study cannot be generalized for all university libraries in Indonesia or in the world. Therefore, this research is a case study research, and the results of this study represent the actual situation and condition occurring at the government university library which is the subject of this research. Further research is suggested to use not only the Fishbone Diagram, but also other analytical methods.

REFERENCES

Bogdan, R.C. & Biklen, S.K. (1982). *Qualitative research for education: An introduction to theory and methods.* Boston: Allyn and Bacon Inc.

Cook, C., Heath F.M. & Thompson, B. (2003). "Zones of tolerance" in perceptions of library service quality: A LibQUAL+ TM study. *Libraries and the Academy*, 3(1): 113–123.

Dahan, S.M. (2016). Surveying user's perception of academic library services quality: A case study in Universiti Malaysia Pahang (UMP) library. *The Journal of Academic Librarianship*, 42(1): 38–43.

Hambleton, L. (2007). *Treasure chest of six sigma growth methods, tools, and best practices*. United States of America: Pearson Education, Inc.

Hernon, P. (2010). *Assessing service quality*. Chicago: American Library Association.

Nadiri, H. & Mayboudi, S.M.A. (2010). Diagnosing university students' zone of tolerance from university library services. *Malaysian Journal of Library and Information Science*. 15(1): 1–21.

Retrieved from http://gobekasi.pojoksatu.id/2016/05/19/survei-unesco-minat-baca-masyarakat-indonesia-0001-persen/.

Scarvada, A.J., Bouzdine-Chameeva, T., Goldstein, S.M., Hays, J.M. & Hill, A.V. (2004). A review of the causal mapping practice and research literature. *Second World Conference on POM and 15th Annual POM Conference, Cancun, Mexico.*

Increasing Management Relevance and Competitiveness – Sukoco et al. (Eds)
© 2018 Taylor & Francis Group, London, ISBN 978-0-8153-7455-8

The strategic role of Indonesia in Global Value Chains (GVC)

M.A. Esquivias
Escuela de Ciencias Económicas y Empresariales, Universidad Panamericana,, Guadalajara, México
Universitas Airlangga, Surabaya, Indonesia

D.W. Sari & R.D. Handoyo
Universitas Airlangga, Surabaya, Indonesia

ABSTRACT: This study looks at the participation of Indonesia in Global Value Chains (GVC) and the role it plays in fragmented structures. Through an international input-output database and by breaking up Gross Exports (GE) into different components of Value Added (VA), it traces the interaction of Indonesia within the global value chain to measure vertical specialization for Indonesia. The results show that Indonesia has significantly gained in integration with Asian value chains, both East Asia and ASEAN. Even though ASEAN as a single production region has gained little over time, Indonesia has gained presence within it. Indonesia lost share in VA trade with NAFTA and Europe and focused on Asia instead. The role of Indonesia across the GVC has experienced a structural change, moving from 50% exports of value added though final goods in 1997 to a supplier of intermediaries (59%) in 2012. Indonesia differs from ASEAN countries regarding foreign value added content in its exports as most of its value added is local (88%), is less globally integrated (12% of vertical trade vs. 35% in ASEAN), is more intra-Asian focused, and has less high-tech exports.

Keywords: vertical specialization, AFTA, production networks, value added trade, global input-output

1 INTRODUCTION

This article measures the "real" participation and temporal changes of Indonesia within fragmented structures by addressing three questions: 1) to what extent is the liberalization process of Indonesia affecting the way it produces goods-services? 2) how does Indonesia integrate (adds value) with the main trading hubs (ASEAN, East Asia, European Union and North America)? and 3) how important is the participation of Indonesia in fragmented structures?

To measure the participation of Indonesia in GVC requires assessing the achievement of Indonesian's liberalization efforts, to distinguish the role of the country in GVC, and its links with other regions. To answer those questions, an adjusted world input-output table is employed to decompose the value added of Indonesia's gross exports according to where the value of Indonesia's gross exports is created and where it is finally absorbed, either through intermediate goods (IPC) or final goods. The study looks at three years 1997, 2004 and 2012, and analyses the links with ASEAN, East Asia (hereafter EA), North America (NAFTA), and the European Union (EU).

2 METHODOLOGY

This paper falls within value added (VA) measurement and vertical specialization. This paper uses Koopman et al.'s (2010; 2012) methodology in which they include linear combinations of previous indicators on VA exports and vertical specialization (VS) such as those developed by Hummels et al. (2001) Daudin et al. (2011) and Johnson and Noguera (2012). While the above empirical methodologies rightly decomposed VA based on direct and some indirect degree, some miss shares of VA embedded in other countries' IPC that cross multiple borders (Wang et al. 2013). The contribution comes as it integrates regions and traces inter-temporal variations. The framework consists of breaking up a country's gross exports (GE) into exports of domestic value added (DV), VA that returns home, foreign VA and double counted terms, all terms according to the source of VA creation and the final destination of VA. The detailed model is depicted by Koopman et al. (2012). Total gross exports are split into nine terms, a further decomposition of Leontief input-output, as follows:

First, data are set as an ICIO Matrix. It is assumed that each G-country produces goods in N differentiated tradable sectors. Goods can be consumed as final goods or intermediate inputs, either exported or used/consumed at home.

$$X_s = \sum_{r}^{G} \left(A_{Sr} X_r + Y_{sr} \right), r, s.....G \qquad (1)$$

X_s is the Nx1 gross output vector of country s, Y_{sr} is the NxN final demand vector and A_{sr} is the NxN IO coefficient matrix (Koopman et al. 2012). Equation (1), the G-country, N-sector production and trade system is written as an ICIO matrix notation:

$$\begin{bmatrix} X_{11} & X_{11} & \cdots & X_{1G} \\ X_{21} & X_{22} & \cdots & X_{2G} \\ \vdots & \vdots & \ddots & \vdots \\ X_{G1} & X_{G2} & \cdots & X_{GG} \end{bmatrix} = \begin{bmatrix} B_{11} & B_{12} & \cdots & B_{1G} \\ B_{21} & B_{22} & \cdots & B_{2G} \\ \vdots & \vdots & \ddots & \vdots \\ B_{G1} & B_{G2} & \cdots & B_{GG} \end{bmatrix} = \begin{bmatrix} Y_{11} & Y_{12} & \cdots & Y_{1G} \\ Y_{21} & Y_{22} & \cdots & Y_{2G} \\ \vdots & \vdots & \ddots & \vdots \\ Y_{G1} & Y_{G2} & \cdots & Y_{GG} \end{bmatrix} \qquad (2)$$

B_{sr} denotes the total requirement matrix (Leontief inverse). Next, the VA share matrix by source is build. Vs is the correspondent 1 × N direct VA coefficient vector or GxGN matrix of direct domestic VA for G-countries. Multiplying these direct VA shares with the Leontief inverse matrices produces the G × GN VA share (VB). However, to obtain domestic VA in a country's gross output, a new VA coefficient matrix is created ($\hat{V}_s$), with a GN-by-GN dimension with the direct VA coefficients along the diagonal and exports of VA in the off-diagonal columns. This GNxGN matrix is multiplied by BY to obtain $\hat{V}BY$ matrix.

$$BY = \begin{bmatrix} \hat{V}_1 & 0 & \cdots & 0 \\ 0 & \hat{V}_1 & \cdots & 0 \\ \vdots & \vdots & \ddots & \vdots \\ 0 & 0 & \cdots & \hat{V}_G \end{bmatrix} = \begin{bmatrix} X_{11} & X_{12} & \cdots & X_{1G} \\ X_{21} & X_{22} & \cdots & X_{2G} \\ \vdots & \vdots & \ddots & \vdots \\ X_{G1} & X_{G2} & \cdots & X_{GG} \end{bmatrix}$$

$$= \begin{bmatrix} V_1 \sum_{r}^{G} B_{1r} Y_{r1} & V_1 \sum_{r}^{G} B_{1r} Y_{r2} & \cdots & V_1 \sum_{r}^{G} B_{1r} Y_{rG} \\ V_2 \sum_{r}^{G} B_{2r} Y_{r1} & V_2 \sum_{r}^{G} B_{2r} Y_{r2} & \cdots & V_2 \sum_{r}^{G} B_{2r} Y_{rG} \\ \vdots & \vdots & \ddots & \vdots \\ V_G \sum_{r}^{G} B_{Gr} Y_{r1} & V_G \sum_{r}^{G} B_{Gr} Y_{r2} & \cdots & V_G \sum_{r}^{G} B_{Gr} Y_{rG} \end{bmatrix} \qquad (3)$$

Next gross exports are decomposed. A country's total VA exports, denoted by $VT_{s*} = \sum_{r\neq s}^{G} VX_{sr} = V_s \sum_{r\neq s}^{G} \sum_{g=1}^{G} B_{sg} Y_{gr}$ are rewritten according to where and how the VA is absorbed.

$$VT_{s*} = V_s \sum_{r\neq s}^{G} B_{ss} Y_{sr} + V_s \sum_{r\neq s}^{G} B_{sr} Y_{rr} + V_s \sum_{r\neq s}^{G} \sum_{t\neq s,r}^{G} B_{sr} Y_{rt} \qquad (4)$$

Equation (4) is the VA export decomposition equation, including VA in a country's *s* final goods exports to *r*; 2nd VA in intermediate exports; 3rd VA in re-exports to *t* countries. Country's gross exports are defined as

$$E_{s*} = \sum_{r\neq s}^{G} E_{sr} = \sum_{r\neq s}^{G} A_{sr} X_r + Y_{sr} \qquad (5)$$

Equation (5) can be further decomposed according to where the intermediate and final goods are finally absorbed.

$$\begin{aligned} uE_{s*} &= V_s B_{SS} E_{s*} + \sum_{r\neq s}^{G} V_r B_{rs} E_{s*} \\ &= VT_{s*} + \left\{ V_s \sum_{r\neq s}^{G} B_{sr} Y_{rs} + V_s \sum_{r\neq s}^{G} B_{sr} A_{rs} X_s \right\} \\ &\quad + \left\{ \sum_{r\neq s}^{G} \sum_{r\neq s}^{G} V_t B_{ts} Y_{sr} + \sum_{r\neq s}^{G} \sum_{r\neq s}^{G} V_t B_{ts} A_{sr} X_r \right\} \end{aligned} \qquad (6)$$

VT_{s*} in equation (6) indicates the VA exports in final goods, and four different flows of the country's VA exports. Based on each country's gross output identity, $X_s = (I - A_{ss})^{-1} Y_{ss} + (I - A_{ss})^{-1} E_{s*}$ and $X_r = (I - A_{rr})^{-1} Y_{rr} + (I - A_{rr})^{-1} E_{r*}$ and substituting into equation (6) the new equation:

$$\begin{aligned} uE_{s*} = &\left\{ V_s \sum_{r\neq s}^{G} B_{ss} Y_{sr} + V_s \sum_{r\neq s}^{G} B_{sr} Y_{rr} \right. \\ &\left. + V_s \sum_{r\neq s}^{G} \sum_{r\neq s}^{G} B_{sr} Y_{rr} \right\} \\ &+ \left\{ V_s \sum_{r\neq s}^{G} B_{sr} Y_{rs} + V_s \sum_{r\neq s}^{G} B_{sr} A_{rs} (I - A_{ss})^{-1} Y_{ss} \right\} \\ &+ V_s \sum_{r\neq s}^{G} B_{sr} A_{rs} (I - A_{ss})^{-1} E_{s*} \\ &+ \left\{ \sum_{t\neq s}^{G} \sum_{t\neq s}^{G} V_t B_{ts} Y_{sr} \right. \\ &\left. + \sum_{t\neq s}^{G} \sum_{t\neq s}^{G} V_t B_{ts} A_{sr} (I - A_{rr})^{-1} Y_{rr} \right\} \\ &+ \sum_{t\neq s}^{G} V_t B_{ts} Y_{sr} \sum_{t\neq s}^{G} (I - A_{ss})^{-1} E_{r*} \end{aligned} \qquad (7)$$

Equation (7) contains nine different terms based on the sources of creation and destination. The first three terms represent the VA in exports; the fourth and fifth include VA initially being exported, but eventually returning home. The seventh and eighth terms include foreign VA in the home's country exports. The sixth and ninth terms are double counted terms.

Table 1. Accounting gross exports. 1997, 2004 and 2012 (Share of total gross exports).

Gross exports in billion of US doubts		Domestic Value added exports DV			Domestic value added returns home		Pure double counting	Foreign value added FV		Pure double counting			VA that crosses nations at least twice
		In direct final exports	In IPCs absorbed by direct importers	In IPCs re-exports to third countries	In final exports	In IPC exports	In IPC exports produced in home	in final exports	in IPC exports	In IPC exports produced abroad	Value added exports (VT)	Foreign Content Vs	
		(1)	(2)	(3)	(4)	(5)	(6)	(7)	(8)	(9)	(10)	(13)	(14)
1997													
EAST ASIA	$961	53.1%	28.5%	5.9%	0.4%	0.4%	0.1%	7.1%	3.5%	1.3%	87.5%	12.0%	12.8%
ASEAN	$449	37.5%	21.9%	5.6%	0.2%	0.1%	0.2%	19.8%	8.3%	4.3%	65.1%	32.4%	33.0%
Singapore	$170	27.4%	15.6%	3.2%	0.2%	0.1%	0.3%	31.2%	11.5%	4.6%	46.2%	47.3%	47.8%
Malaysia	$93	36.5%	22.5%	7.4%	0.4%	0.2%	0.3%	17.6%	8.1%	6.4%	66.4%	32.1%	33.1%
Thailand	$72	45.6%	24.9%	6.7%	0.1%	0.1%	0.1%	13.2%	7.2%	4.0%	77.2%	24.4%	24.7%
Indonesia	$63	50.9%	30.7%	7.5%	0.1%	0.1%	0.0%	6.1%	3.4%	1.7%	89.1%	11.1%	11.4%
Philippines	$38	45.2%	27.4%	6.3%	0.1%	0.1%	0.0%	11.9%	5.8%	2.6%	79.0%	20.4%	20.6%
Vietnam	$12	45.6%	26.1%	6.1%	0.0%	0.0%	0.0%	12.9%	6.7%	3.0%	77.9%	22.6%	22.6%
NAFTA	$1,336	55.3%	28.4%	4.3%	1.6%	1.2%	0.2%	5.5%	2.8%	0.8%	87.9%	9.1%	12.0%
EU	$2,472	50.0%	21.9%	5.0%	0.4%	0.2%	0.1%	14.4%	5.6%	2.3%	76.8%	22.3%	23.0%
2004													
EAST ASIA	$1,743	48.2%	29.1%	6.6%	0.5%	0.4%	0.1%	8.7%	4.9%	2.2%	83.9%	15.8%	16.8%
ASEAN	$662	31.6%	21.4%	6.5%	0.2%	0.1%	0.3%	21.3%	9.5%	6.4%	59.6%	37.2%	37.7%
Indonesia	$83	45.3%	32.2%	9.7%	0.1%	0.1%	0.0%	6.4%	3.8%	2.5%	87.3%	12.7%	13.0%
NAFTA	$1,767	52.5%	29.8%	4.7%	1.8%	1.3%	0.1%	5.7%	3.1%	0.9%	87.0%	9.7%	12.9%
EU	$4,021	46.5%	23.0%	5.5%	0.4%	0.3%	0.1%	14.7%	6.2%	2.9%	75.0%	23.9%	24.7%
2012													
EAST ASIA	$4,109	55.4%	21.7%	5.5%	0.5%	0.5%	0.1%	10.6%	4.1%	2.0%	82.6%	16.8%	17.9%
ASEAN	$1,504	30.5%	24.5%	7.1%	0.2%	0.1%	0.2%	19.4%	9.4%	5.7%	62.1%	34.5%	35.0%
Singapore	$555	22.9%	15.8%	4.0%	0.1%	0.0%	0.3%	30.2%	11.5%	5.9%	42.7%	47.5%	48.0%
Malaysia	$266	24.5%	30.1%	10.5%	0.3%	0.3%	0.4%	12.6%	13.1%	11.1%	65.1%	36.8%	37.7%
Thailand	$268	41.9%	22.3%	5.8%	0.1%	0.1%	0.1%	17.7%	7.6%	4.0%	69.9%	29.4%	29.7%
Indonesia	$213	28.5%	45.5%	14.1%	0.4%	0.3%	0.1%	3.6%	4.6%	3.1%	88.0%	11.3%	12.1%
Philippines	$77	45.2%	29.7%	8.5%	0.1%	0.1%	0.0%	8.9%	5.5%	3.2%	83.3%	17.6%	17.8%
Vietnam	$125	46.8%	16.5%	4.0%	0.0%	0.0%	0.0%	22.6%	6.7%	3.1%	67.3%	32.4%	32.5%
NAFTA	$3,130	50.6%	30.7%	6.0%	1.4%	1.2%	0.2%	5.3%	3.3%	1.2%	87.2%	9.8%	12.6%
EU	$6,132	46.8%	18.2%	5.9%	0.4%	0.2%	0.2%	18.2%	5.8%	3.7%	70.9%	27.6%	28.4%

[a] Notes: VT Column (10) = (1)+(2)+(3); VS column (13) = (7)+(8)+(9) Column (14) equal sum (4) through (9). East Asia (EA): Japan, China, Rep of Korea, Taiwan. ASEAN: Singapore, Malaysia, Thailand, Indonesia, Philippines, Vietnam. NAFTA: USA, Canada, and Mexico. EU: France, Germany, Austria, Belgium, Finland, Ireland, Italy, Luxembourg, Netherlands, Portugal, Spain, UK.

This research uses the YNU-GIO Table, Inter Country Input-Output table (ICIO) developed by the CESSA. It includes 29 endogenous countries, 59 exogenous countries and 35 industries. Sato and Shrestha (2014) carried out a series of harmonization in the data, linking OECD input-output tables with data on trade flows from UN COMTRADE.

3 RESULTS AND DISCUSSION

Table 1 presents the accounting of Indonesia versus East Asia (EA), ASEAN, NAFTA and the EU for 1997, 2004 and 2012. The column number indicates the order of each term in the equation (7). All figures are expressed as share of each region's gross exports (GE).

3.1 *Indonesia gross export decomposition*

Column 1 in Table 1 indicates that Indonesia increased its exports of domestic value added (DV) through final goods by 89% in value terms. However, as a share of gross exports, it fell from 51% in 1997 to 29% in 2012, a low DV through final goods versus Thailand, the Philippines and Vietnam, as well as with EA and NAFTA (more than 50%).

DV through intermediary goods (column 2) directly absorbed by importers reached 46% in 2012, an increase from 31% share in 1997, and 401% more in value terms. Re-exports concept of trade (col 3) reports growth of 525% versus 1997, a shift from 7% as share of GE in 1997 to 14% in 2012. VA through IPC accounts for nearly 60%, stating a strategic role of Indonesia as supplier of IPC within GVC.

Foreign content (FV) embedded in Indonesian exports (column 7 to 9) represents 11.8%, a low share versus ASEAN region (largest share with 35%). Out of the 22% of FV embedded in ASEAN exports, Indonesia supplies 2%, while FV from extra ASEAN accounts for 78%, 30% alone from East Asia.

Indonesia registered 2.6% of double counted VA (column 6 and 9), a small amount but a large change in value terms from 1997 to 2012, indicating a more dynamic Indonesia within vertical trade.

Indonesia experienced a small change in vertical trade, with only 12% of GE under it, half of ASEAN's level. Indonesian exports were highly supported by one-way trade (75%) with IPCs accounting for 45%.

3.2 *Interactions of Indonesian in GVC*

Table 2 presents the accounting of gross exports based on main blocs of value added aggregated at regional level. Column 10 indicates VA exports, specifying who exports (row) and who absorbs the VA (column). Since 1997, East Asia has accounted

Table 2. Accounting gross exports. 1997 and 2012 based on Origin-destination of value added.

Gross exports in billion of US dollars		Value-added exports (VT) (10)						VS Foreign content of region (VS) (11)						Domestic content in region's exports (13)					Value added that crosses nations at least twice (14)					
		EA	ASEAN	*IDN*	*NAFTA*	EU	OE	EA	ASEAN	*IDN*	*NAFTA*	EU	OE	EA	ASEAN	*IDN*	*NAFTA*	EU	EA	ASEAN	*IDN*	*NAFTA*	EU	OE
Region		Accounting of Gross Exports 1997																						
$960.73	EA	20%	12%	2%	24%	10%	20%	3%	1.81%	0.24%	3%	1%	3%	20%	12%	2%	24%	10%	3%	2%	0%	3%	1%	0%
$449.2	ASAAN	18%	12%	1%	13%	8%	13%	7%	7.41%	0.88%	6%	4%	7%	18%	12%	2%	13%	8%	7%	8%	1%	6%	4%	1%
$63.04	*IDN*	30%	12%	0%	15%	12%	21%	3%	2.01%	0.00%	2%	1%	3%	30%	12%	0%	15%	12%	4%	2%	0%	2%	1%	3%
$1,335.61	NAFTA	16%	4%	1%	33%	14%	18%	1%	0.39%	0.04%	5%	1%	2%	16%	5%	1%	35%	15%	1%	1%	0%	7%	1%	0%
$2,47.86	EU	4%	2%	0%	10%	38%	22%	1%	0.56%	0.07%	3%	17%	6%	4%	2%	0%	10%	49%	1%	1%	0%	3%	28%	0%
		Accounting of Gross Exports 2012																						
Region		EA	ASEAN	*IDN*	*NAFTA*	EU	OE	EA	ASEAN	*IDN*	*NAFTA*	EU	OE	EA	ASEAN	*IDN*	*NAFTA*	EU	EA	ASEAN	*IDN*	*NAFTA*	EU	OE
$4,109.13	EA	22%	9%	2%	19%	10%	20%	4%	2.08%	0.33%	4%	2%	5%	23%	9%	2%	19%	10%	5%	2%	0%	4%	2%	1%
$1,503.51	ASEAN	22%	11%	2%	8%	7%	10%	10%	7.52%	1.46%	4%	4%	9%	22%	12%	2%	8%	7%	10%	8%	1%	4%	4%	3%
$213	*IDN*	34%	17%	0%	11%	9%	16%	4%	3.09%	0.00%	1%	1%	3%	35%	18%	0%	11%	9%	4%	4%	0%	1%	1%	2%
$3,130.03	NAFTA	19%	4%	1%	34%	14%	15%	2%	0.53%	0.05%	5%	1%	2%	19%	5%	1%	35%	14%	2%	1%	0%	7%	2%	0%
$6,131.74	EU	8%	2%	0%	9%	34%	17%	3%	0.81%	0.07%	3%	18%	7%	8%	2%	0%	9%	40%	3%	1%	0%	3%	24%	1%

for the largest export target of Indonesian DV (34% in 2012), while DV to ASEAN countries accounted for 17% and NAFTA decreased from 15% to 11%. More than 50% of Indonesia's DV exports remained in Asia.

ASEAN significantly increased its participation in multiple cross border trade from 27% in 1997 to 35% in 2012 (col 14). Indonesia changed less than 1%, however, in value accounts for an increase in 256%.

The largest share of FV embedded in Indonesian exports comes from East Asia (4%), followed by ASEAN 3.09%, while only 3.87% of Indonesian VA is embedded in other regions. Indonesia exports more than 60% of its VA in parts and components.

Out of the 14% of VA created through exports of IPCs that will be further re-exported (col 3), 80% belongs to Asian countries. Indonesia shifted focus to EA rather than building ASEAN chains. Within ASEAN, Indonesia has the largest expansion to EA.

The Indonesian DV that crosses nations at least twice (MCB, 14) was kept at 4% of GE, increasing its share with ASEAN countries by 2% but lowering with NAFTA, the EU and OE. ASEAN levels have at least twice as much share of GE under (14) than Indonesia. However, Indonesia appears better integrated and producing more under vertical structures, increasing MCB trade from $7.2 billion US in 1997 to $25.6 in 2012 and increasing common GE with ASEAN from US$ 3.9 to more than US$ 22 billion in 2012, more than five-fold growth.

Indonesia has a small dependency (11%) with foreign supplies, but signals possible low sophisticated exports. Malaysia 32%, Vietnam 22.6%, and Thailand 17.7%, who are more engaged in manufacturing, tend to have larger levels of VS.

While East Asia offers a larger market and a channel for indirect exports (11% of VA), it also creates dependency, competition and potential risk.

3.3 *Participation of Indonesia in vertical trade*

Indonesia significantly increased its participation in fragmented structures in value terms; however, not in share from its gross exports. Vertical structures in Indonesia are expanding at a slower speed than other countries. Even though the participation of Indonesia in other regions exports has increased in the last 15 years (from US$ 9.2 to US$ 44.7) there is no sign of supply chain development in the country.

4 CONCLUSION

This study looks at the process of liberalization-integration of Indonesia and at the role it plays in vertical structures. Indonesia is a strong supplier of intermediate goods (59%) rather than of final goods. Indonesia has created a strong presence in Asia value chains, mainly East Asia and lowering trade with the EU and NAFTA.

Indonesia's participation in fragmented structures is increasing; however, it is still small (12% of GE) compared to other regions (ASEAN 35%). Its VA through re-exports is growing as well. Exports take mainly domestic VA, contrary to ASEAN high foreign VA. However, the larger GDP content in Indonesian exports does not necessarily mean better supply chain.

Finally, a fragmented production structure matters for Indonesian exports as it is helping to increase the value of exports; however, the participation is rather small. Indonesia is less dependent on vertical exports versus ASEAN.

REFERENCES

Ando, M. 2006. Fragmentation and Vertical Intra-Industry Trade in East Asia. *The North American Journal of Economics and Finance* 17 (3): 257–281. doi:10.1016/j.najef.2006.06.005.

Athukorala, P. & Yamashita, N. 2006. Production Fragmentation and Trade Integration: East Asia in a Global Context. *The North American Journal of Economics and Finance* 17 (3): 233–256. doi:10.1016/j.najef.2006.07.002.

Daudin, G., D. Schweisguth, and C. Rifflart. 2011. Who Produces for Whom in the World Economy? *The Canadian Journal of Economics* 44 (4): 1403–37. doi:10.1111/j.1540–5982.2011.01679.x.

Hummels, D., J. Ishii, and K. Yi. 2001. The Nature and Growth of Vertical Specialization in World Trade. *Journal of International Economics* 54 (1): 75–96. doi:10.2139/ssrn.163193.

Hummels, D., D. Rapoport, and K. Yi. 1998. Vertical Specialization and the Changing Nature of World Trade. *Economic Policy Review* 4 (2). doi:10.2139/ssrn.163193.

Johnson, R.C. & G. Noguera. 2012. Fragmentation and Trade in Value Added over Four Decades. National Bureau of Economic Research. https://doi.org/10.3386%2Fw18186.

Koopman, R., W. Powers, Z. Wang, and S. Wei. 2010. Give Credit Where Credit Is Due: Tracing Value Added in Global Production Chains. National Bureau of Economic Research. https://doi.org/10.3386%2Fw16426.

Koopman, R., Z. Wang, and S. Wei. 2012. Tracing Value-Added and Double Counting in Gross Exports. *American Economic Review* 104 (2): 459–94. doi:10.1257/aer.104.2.459.

Sato, K. & N. Shrestha. 2014. Global and Regional Shock Transmission—An Asian Perspective-. *Center for Economic and Social Studies in Asia (CESSA) WP* 4. http://www.econ.ynu.ac.jp/cessa/publication/pdf/CESSA%20WP%202014–04.pdf.

Wang, Z., S. Wei, and K. Zhu. 2013. Quantifying International Production Sharing at the Bilateral and Sector Levels. Working Paper 19677. National Bureau of Economic Research. https://doi.org/10.3386%2Fw19677.

Increasing Management Relevance and Competitiveness – Sukoco et al. (Eds)
© 2018 Taylor & Francis Group, London, ISBN 978-0-8153-7455-8

Service innovation: The moderating effects of environmental contingencies

N. Anridho
Universitas Airlangga, Surabaya, Indonesia

ABSTRACT: This study aims to investigate first, the effect of service innovation on organizational performance, and second, the moderating effects of environmental contingencies on the relationship between service innovation and organizational performance. Survey study was conducted. Data were collected by both online and offline questionnaires. In total, 112 data from retail companies in Indonesia were used for analysis. The results show service innovation has a positive effect on organizational performance; environmental munificence and environmental dynamism positively moderate the relationship between service innovation and organizational performance, while environmental heterogeneity and environmental hostility negatively moderate that relationship. This study contributes to the current literature by proving that environmental contingencies may support co-producing and co-creating values activities as long as the company can overcome resistances resources and integrate those resources with other organizational resources.

Keywords: Service Innovation; Environmental Contingencies; Organizational Performance

1 INTRODUCTION

Service innovation is a complex field which represents various disciplines. Many scholars from different disciplines have been paying attention to service innovation research. Those disciplines include marketing (e.g., Berry et al. 2006; Nijssen et al. 2006; Oliveira and Von Hippel 2011), economics (e.g., Gallouj 2002; Cainelli et al. 2006; Gallouj and Savona 2008), information systems (e.g., Lyytinen and Rose 2003; Rai and Sambamurthy 2006; Alter, 2008), operations (e.g., Metters and Marucheck 2007; Oke 2007), and strategy (e.g., Dorner et al. 2011). They also have been exploring multiple dimensions of service innovation, following unique approaches, building various conceptual and analytical frameworks, and adopting distinct perspectives (Rubalcaba et al. 2012).

The link between innovation and performance has been widely studied especially on tangible products (Menor, Tatikonda and Sampson 2002). However, since the multidimensional service innovation by Janssen et al. (2015) is still new, empirical testing is needed. The increasing of organizational performance may imply that the company's service innovation is successful. Organizational performance can be measured from both financial and non-financial performance (Blazevic and Lievens 2004; Chen, Tsou and Huang, 2009). Chen, Tsou and Huang (2009) found that service delivery innovation contributes to firm performance. Ordanini and Parasuraman (2011) also found that radical service innovation and volume service innovation have a positive influence on firm performance. Therefore, this study proposes that service innovation has a positive influence on both financial and non-financial performance.

Furthermore, the dominant marketing paradigm assumes the external environments (i.e., legal, competitive, social, physical, technological and others) are largely uncontrollable and forces where the company needs to adapt (McCarthy 1960). Most businesses tend to view external environments as resistances and forces rather than resources. In contrast to this paradigm, S-D logic views the external environments as resources that the company needs (Lusch, Vargo and O'Brien 2007). The idea involves viewing the ecosystem as something to collaborate with in the co-creation of service as well as integrating firm, individual and public resources.

A company needs to overcome resistances and proactively co-create these environments. A truly S-D company would view the entire community as resources to collaborate with, which is the source of competitive advantage (Vargo and Lusch 2004). In the dynamic environment, the value propositions that a company offers depend on the collection of resources and competences which the company can continually renew, create, integrate and transform.

However, research that elaborates the environmental effects based on S-D logic is still rare. Therefore, this study proposes that environmental contingencies which consist of environmental munificence, environmental dynamism, environmental heterogeneity and environmental hostility positively moderate the relationship between service innovation and organizational performance.

Based on the above explanation, this study aims to investigate first, the effect of service innovation on organizational performance, and second, the moderating effects of environmental contingencies on the relationship between service innovation and organizational performance.

2 LITERATURE REVIEW

2.1 *The effects of service innovation on organizational performances*

According to Jannsen et al. (2015), multidimensional service innovation consists of new service concept, new customer interaction, new value system/business partners, new revenue model, new organizational delivery system and new technological delivery system. The link between innovation and performance is widely studied in the innovation literature, especially innovation on tangible products (Ordanini and Parasuraman 2011). Previous studies support the positive link between service innovation and organizational performance (e.g., Avlonitis, Papastathopoulou and Gounaris 2001; Chen, Tsou and Huang 2009; Ordanini Parasuraman 2011).

This study proposes that service innovation enhances organizational performance. Avlonitis, Papastathopoulou and Gounaris (2001) found that new delivery processes positively influence financial performance such as profitability and sales. Chen, Tsou and Huang (2009) revealed that service delivery innovation leads to better financial and non-financial performance. Furthermore, Ordanini and Parasuraman (2011) found that both innovation radicalness and innovation volume have positive effects on performance. Having new service concept, new customer interaction, new value system/business partners, new revenue model, new organizational delivery system, and new technological delivery system leads to greater financial and non-financial performance. Thus, this study hypothesizes:

H1: Service innovation has a positive effect on organizational performance.

2.2 *The moderating effects of environmental factors*

Environmental factors consist of environmental munificence, environmental dynamism, environmental heterogeneity and environmental hostility. According to S-D logic, external environments are resources that the company needed (Lusch, Vargo and O'Brien 2007). The ecosystem may be integrated and collaborated into value co-creation and a company needs to overcome resistances and proactively co-create these environments. A truly S-D company would view the entire community as resources to collaborate with, which is the source of competitive advantage (Vargo and Lusch 2004).

This study proposes that environmental munificence, environmental dynamism, environmental heterogeneity and environmental hostility positively moderate the effect of service innovation on organizational performances. The positive effect of service innovation on organizational performance will be stronger in higher environmental munificence, environmental dynamism, environmental heterogeneity and environmental hostility conditions. Better organizational performances are likely to be achieved through better service innovation when a company is able to integrate the scarcity of critical resources, the change of customer needs and of technology, the differences in competitive tactics and customer preferences as well as competition and demographic trends (Wong 2014). Therefore, this study hypothesizes:

H2: Environmental munificence positively moderates the effect of service innovation on organizational performance.

H3: Environmental dynamism positively moderates the effect of service innovation on organizational performance.

H4: Environmental heterogeneity positively moderates the effect of service innovation on organizational performance.

H5: Environmental hostility positively moderates the effect of service innovation on organizational performance.

3 METHODOLOGY

3.1 *Research model*

Based on the hypotheses developments above, the conceptual framework of this study is shown in Figure 1.

3.2 *Construct measurement*

This study employed quantitative method by using questionnaire to collect the data. As the questionnaire items were mainly adopted from English language journal papers they first needed to be translated into Bahasa and then translated back to English by a linguistic expert. Two academics were then consulted to check the face validity of the scales (Konuk, Rahman and Salo 2015). Scale

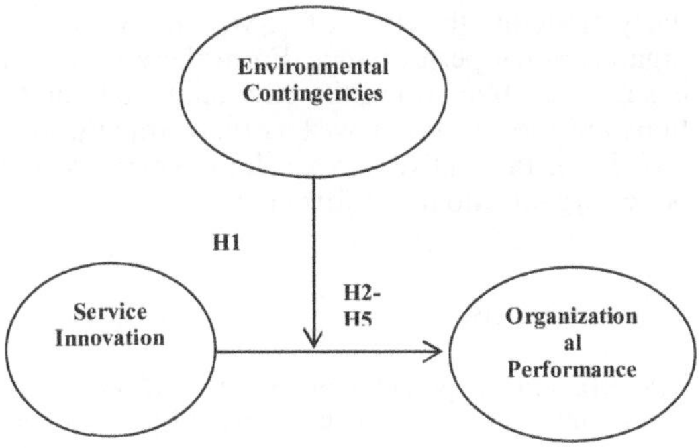

Figure 1. Research model.

items were adopted from previous studies' validated scales. The measurement scale items for service innovation were adopted from Janssen et al. (2015) (fourteen items); the scale items for organizational performance were adopted from Chen, Tsou and Huang (2009) (ten items); the scale items for environment munificence (three items), environmental dynamism (two items), environmental heterogeneity (four items) and environmental hostility (two items) were adopted from McGinnis and Kohn (2003). All scale items were measured by seven-point Likert-type scales, ranging from "strongly disagree = 1" to "strongly agree = 7."

4 RESULTS

4.1 *Demographic characteristics*

Questionnaires were distributed to 300 retail companies in Indonesia. From 300 questionnaires, 116 were returned, resulting in a 38.65% response rate. However, due to some missing data, only 112 data were used for further analysis. The demographic results for company information show that, among 112 data, 29% were convenience store, 23% were fashion store, 12% were drugstore, followed by banking, automotive retailer, home appliance store, supermarket, department store, bookstore, and apparel and footwear store. More than 50% of respondents' companies have operated more than 15 years and more than 60% of those companies had capital more than 751 million rupiah (1$US = 13,255 Rupiah). In terms of the distribution of number of employees, 45% had less than 50 employees.

The demographic characteristics of respondents' information show that approximately 58% of the 112 respondents were male. For age, 44% were between the ages of 26 and 35. With regards to their educational background, 64% of the respondents had obtained at least a bachelor's degree. In terms of working experience distribution, 44% of the respondents have worked for less than or equal to five years. More than 50% of the respondents were operational managers.

4.2 *Evaluation of measurement model*

The collected data were analyzed by Partial Least Squares (PLS) using SmartPLS software. PLS is appropriate for causal-predictive analysis when the research model is more complicated (Chin 1998). Both the measurement model and structural model can be simultaneously examined by PLS (Hair, Ringle and Sarstedt 2011). The measurement model was evaluated to ensure the reliability and validity of measurement scales. The test of the measurement model involves the estimation of reliability and validity of first-order and second-order constructs, which indicate the strength of measures used to test the proposed model (Fornell 1987). All the criteria for reliability and validity of the constructs were fulfilled.

4.3 *Common method bias*

In order to assess the issues of common method bias, firstly, a Harmon one-factor test was adopted and loaded all variables into a principal component factor analysis (Podsakoff et al. 2003). The explained variance of one-factor test is 32.57% in the un-rotated solution, which is less than 50%. Second, discriminated validity can also be used to identify common method bias. As explained above, discriminant validity also showed satisfactory results. All the AVE square root values are higher than the constructs' inter-correlations in the research model. These results suggested that the issues of common method bias are still under the accepted level.

4.4 *Evaluation of structural model*

The results show that service innovation has a positive influence on organizational performance ($\beta = 0.582$; $p < 0.001$). Furthermore, for the control variables, company age ($\beta = -0.100$; $p < 0.001$) and company capital ($\beta = 0.089$; $p < 0.001$) show significant effects on organizational performance. However, these influences not as strong as the effect of service innovation on organizational performance. Company size ($\beta = 0.001$; $p > 0.05$) shows non-statistically significant effect on organizational performance.

Furthermore, the results show that environmental munificence (EM) ($\beta = 0.028$; $p < 0.05$) and environmental dynamism (ED) ($\beta = 0.054$; $p < 0.01$) positively moderate the effect of service innovation on organizational performance, while environmental heterogeneity (EHE) (β = –0.125; $p < 0.001$) and environmental hostility (EHO) (β = –0.115; $p < 0.001$) negatively moderate the effect of service innovation on organizational performance.

The R^2 values of organizational performance for each hypothesis are as follows: 0.371, 0.442, 0.381, 0.527, and 0.451, respectively, which are higher than its critical value of 0.1 (Falk and Miller 1992). Therefore, H1, H2, H3 are supported while H4 and H4 are not supported.

5 DISCUSSIONS

The aims of this study are to investigate first, the effect of service innovation on organizational performance, and second, the moderating effects of environmental contingencies on the relationship between service innovation and organizational performance. From the results, it shows that service innovation has a positive influence on organizational performance. This result is in line with previous studies (e.g., Avlonitis, Papastathopoulou and Gounaris 2001; Chen, Tsou and Huang 2009; Ordanini and Parasuraman 2011). Better service innovation tends to enhance organizational performance. Avlonitis, Papastathopoulou and Gounaris (2001) found that new delivery processes positively influence financial performance such as profitability and sales. Chen, Tsou and Huang (2009) revealed that service delivery innovation leads to better financial and non-financial performance. Furthermore, Ordanini and Parasuraman (2011) found that both innovation radicalness and innovation volume have positive effects on performance.

Furthermore, this study examined the moderating effects of environmental factors, which consist of environmental munificence, environmental dynamism, environmental heterogeneity and environmental hostility on the relationship between service innovation and organizational performance. The results show that environmental munificence and environmental dynamism positively moderate the effect of service innovation on organizational performance. These results support the S-D logic perspective in viewing external environment as resources. According to S-D logic, the ecosystem is something to collaborate with in the co-creation of service as well as integrating firm, individual and public resources (Lusch, Vargo and O'Brien 2007).

It is suggested that, in the conditions of high environmental munificence and dynamism, when a company has better service innovation, better organizational performance may be achieved.

In contrast, the results show that environmental heterogeneity and environmental hostility negatively moderate the effect of service innovation on organizational performance. From these results, it is suggested that, when the environmental conditions are too diverse as well as the competition is too fierce, innovative service does not guarantee better organizational performance.

REFERENCES

Avlonitis, G.J., Papastathopoulou, P.G., & Gounaris, S.P. 2001. An empirically-based typology of product innovativeness for new financial services: Success and failure scenarios. *Journal of Product Innovation Management*, 18 no.5: 324–342.

Berry L.L., Shankar, V., Parish, J.T., Cadwallader, S., & Dotzel, T. 2006. Creating new markets through service innovation. *MIT Sloan Management Review*, 47 no.2: 56.

Blazevic, V. & Lievens, A. 2004. Learning during the new financial service innovation process: Antecedents and performance effects. *Journal of Business Research*, 57 no. 4: 374–391.

Cainelli, G., Evangelista, R., & Savona, M. 2006. Innovation and economic performance in services: A firm-level analysis. *Cambridge Journal of Economics*, 30: 435–458.

Chen, J.S., Tsou, H.T., & Huang, Y.H. 2009. Service delivery innovation. *Journal of Service Research*, 12 no.1: 36–55.

Chin, W.W. 1998. The partial least square approach for structural equation modeling. In *Modern methods for business research*, edited by G.A. Marcoulides. Mahwah, NJ: Erlbaum, pp. 295–336.

Dorner, N., Gassmann, O., & Gebauer, H. 2011. Service innovation: Why is it so difficult to accomplish? *Journal of Business Strategy*, 32 no. 3: 37–46.

Fornell, C. & Larcker, D.F. 1981. Evaluating structural equation models with unobservable variables and measurement error. *Journal of Marketing Research*, 18 no. 1: 39–50.

Gallouj, F. & Suvana, M. 2009. Innovation in services: Review of the debate and a research agenda. *Journal of Evolutionary Economics*, 19 no. 2: 149–172.

Gallouj, F. and O. Weinstein. 1997. Innovation in services. *Research Policy*, 26: 537–556.

Gallouj, F. 2002. *Innovation in the service Economy: The new wealth of nations*. Cheltenham, UK: Edward Elgar Publishing.

Hair, J.F., Ringle, C.M., & Sarstedt, M. 2011. PLS-SEM: Indeed a silver bullet. *Journal of Marketing Theory and Practice*, 25 no. 1: 107–120.

Hsieh, J.K. & Hsieh, Y.C. 2015. Dialogic co-creation and service innovation performance in high-tech companies. *Journal of Business Research*, 68: 2266–2271.

Hughes, A. & Wood, E. 1999. Rethinking innovation comparisons between manufacturing and services: The experience of the CBR SME surveys in the UK. *Working Paper No. 140*. ESRC Centre for Business Research, University of Cambridge: Cambridge.

Janssen, M.J., Castaldi, C., Alexiev, A., & den Hertog, P. 2015. Exploring a multidimensional approach to service innovation. In *Handbook of Service Innovation*,

edited by R. Agarwal, W. Selen and G. Roos, 91–108. Boston: Springer.
Karpen, I.O., Bove, L.L., & Lukas, B.A. 2012. Linking service-dominant logic and strategic business practice: A conceptual model of a service-dominant orientation. *Journal of Service Research,* 15 no. 1: 21–38.
Lusch, R.F. & Nambisan, S. 2015. Service innovation: A service-dominant logic perspective. *MIS Quarterly,* 39 no.1: 155–175.
Lusch, R.F. & Vargo, S.L. (2011). Service-dominant logic: A necessary step. *European Journal of Marketing,* 45 no. 7/8: 1298–1309.
Lusch, R.F., Vargo, S.L., & Malter, A.J. 2006. Taking a Leadership Role in Global Marketing Management. *Organizational Dynamics,* 35 no. 3: 264–278.
Lusch, R.F., Vargo, S.L., & O'Brien, M. 2007. Competing through service: Insights from service-dominant logic. *Journal of Retailing,* 83 no. 1: 5–18.
Lyytinen, K. & Rose, G. 2003. The disruptive nature of information technology innovations: The case of internet computing in systems development organizations. *MIS Quarterly,* 27 no. 4: 557–595.
McGinnis, M.A. & Kohn, J.W. 1993. Logistics strategy, organizational environment and time competitiveness. *Journal of Business Logistics*, 14 no. 2: 1–23.
Menor, L.J., Tatikonda, M.V., & Sampson, S.E. 2002. New service development: Areas for exploitation and exploration. *Journal of Operations Managements,* 20 no.2: 135–157.
Metters, R. & Marucheckm, A. 2007. Service management—Academic issues and scholarly reflections from operations management researchers. *Decision Sciences Journal,* 32 no. 2: 195–214.
Morgan, R.E. & Strong, C.A. 2003. Business performance and dimensions of strategic orientation. *Journal of Business Research,* 56: 163–176.
Nambisan, S. & Sawhney, M. 2007. *The global brain: Your roadmap for innovating faster and smarter in a networked world.* Upper Saddle River, NJ: Wharton School Publishing.
Navarro, S., Andreu, L., & Cervera, A. 2014. Value co-creation among hotels and disabled customers: An exploratory study. *Journal of Business Research,* 67: 813–818.
Nijssen, E.J., Hillebrand, B., Vermeulen, P., & Kemp, R. 2006. Exploring product and service innovation similarities and differences. *International Journal of Research in Marketing*, 23 no. 3: 241–251.
Oke, A. 2007. Innovation types and innovation management practices in service companies. *International Journal of Operations & Production Management,* 27 no. 6: 564–587.
Oliveira, P.E. & von Hippel, 2011. Users as service innovators: The case of banking services. *Research Policy*, 40: 806–818.
Ordanini, A. & Parasuraman, A. 2011. Service innovation viewed through a service-dominant logic lens: A conceptual framework and empirical analysis. *Journal of Service Research,* 14 no. 1: 3–23.
Podsakoff, P.M., MacKenzie, S.B., Lee, J.Y., & Podsakoff, N.P. 2003. Common method biases in behavioral research: A critical review of the literature and recommended remedies. *Journal of Applied Psychology*, 88: 879–903.
Rai, A. & Sambamurthy, V. 2006. The growth of interest in services management: Opportunities for information systems scholars. *Information Systems Research,* 17 no. 4: 327–331.
Vargo, S.L. & Akaka, M.A. 2009. Service-dominant logic as a foundation for service science: Clarifications. *Service Science,* 1 no. 1: 32–41.
Vargo, S.L. & Lusch, R.F. 2004. Evolving to a new dominant logic for marketing. *Journal of Marketing*, 68 no.1: 1–17.
Vargo, S.L. & Lusch, R.F. 2006. Service-dominant logic: Reactions, reflections, and refinements. *Journal of Marketing Theory,* 6 no. 3: 281–288.
Vargo, S.L. & Lusch, R.F. (2008). Service-dominant logic: Continuing the evolution. *Journal of the Academy of Marketing Science,* 36 (1): 1–10.
Wong, W.P., Ahmad, N.H., Nasurdin, A.M., & Mohamad, M.N. 2014. The impact of external environmental on business process management and organizational performance. *Service Business,* 8: 559–586.

Increasing Management Relevance and Competitiveness – Sukoco et al. (Eds)
© 2018 Taylor & Francis Group, London, ISBN 978-0-8153-7455-8

Efficiency and total-factor productivity in the manufacturing industry in 33 provinces of Indonesia

Muryani
Universitas Airlangga, Surabaya, Indonesia

ABSTRACT: This study emphasizes the importance of controlling escalation of emissions in the current decade. In addition, the study focuses on efficiency techniques and the Total-Factor Productivity (TFP) of manufacturing industry in 33 provinces in Indonesia. This research was conducted by utilizing Data Envelopment Analysis (DEA). The input variables were labor, energy consumption and investment, and the output variables were GDP, SO_2 and NO_2. The Malmquist–Luenberger (ML) productivity index was used to measure changes in productivity of observation data using undesirable variables as input or output. The result is based on operational efficiency; at the end of the observation (2015), 17 provinces were in a state of operational inefficiency with efficiency scores in the range of 0.750–0.999. Meanwhile, in the results for technical efficiency, there was a trend for increasing technical efficiency in manufacturing industry in 19 provinces. Thus, it can be concluded that the majority of manufacturing industries in Indonesia are efficient, while only a few provinces can increase their productivity by increasing desirable output while reducing the growth rate of undesirable output production.

Keywords: Efficiency, Productivity, Industry, DEA

1 INTRODUCTION

Energy use in the industrial sector contributes to emissions in many countries, especially developing countries. The greater the energy use, the greater the amount of emissions produced. At first, the relationship between this energy and the environment was not a major concern. Now, however, environmental conditions are making their own demand for all countries to pay attention to energy utilization in the process of economic development in order to achieve economic sustainability. Hence, all of them can be regarded as an integrated process, which will implicitly encourage growth in the production and consumption of energy.

Sustainable economic development itself is a balance between the factors of energy, economy and environment. Among these three factors, energy is the most influential factor in economic growth, and economic growth also depends on the use of energy for economic development of the country. When economic growth is accelerating and maximizing all possible energy sectors, then, in the process of this economic growth, natural resources, including energy resources, are used on a large scale and create emissions on a large scale too. Therefore, the existence of economic development policy that takes into account environmental conditions is very necessary.

Previous studies concerning energy have been varied: one area has been efficiency measurement. Thus, previous studies have attempted to measure the magnitude of energy efficiency in terms of output produced. However, the research, such as that by Korhonen and Luptacik (2004), Sueyoshi and Goto (2010), and Sueyoshi et al. (2010, 2013), has only covered particular provinces in some countries. Therefore, the study of energy efficiency in relation to output in each province in a country needs to be far more prolific.

The present research focuses on the operational efficiency and efficiency of technique in the manufacturing industry in 33 provinces in Indonesia. Analysis of an industry will be more effective if the Total-Factor Productivity (TFP) is also assessed. In essence, TFP is the growth in output that cannot be explained by the growth in inputs. TFP is assessed through the use of the Malmquist–Luenberger (ML) productivity index, which measures environmentally sensitive changes in productivity through the use of undesirable variables as inputs and/or outputs within Data Envelopment Analysis (DEA). The input variables are labor, energy consumption and investment, and the output variables are GDP, SO_2 and NO_2. Thus, this research formulates the following research questions: what are the operational efficiency levels, technical efficiency levels and TFP of manufacturing industries in 33 provinces in Indonesia when undesirable outputs exist?

2 RESEARCH METHODOLOGY

2.1 *Operational efficiency*

Operational Efficiency (OE) is designed using non-radial measurement models. Thus, the level of inefficiency is determined through the slack of each Decision-Making Unit (DMU). OE ignores the undesirable output in the measurement (Sueyoshi et al., 2013). The non-radial mathematical model used in the measurement of OE is as follows:

$$\begin{aligned}
&\text{Maximize} \sum_{j}^{m} = {}_{1}R_{i}^{x}\, d_{i}^{x} + \Sigma_{r}^{S} = {}_{1}R_{r}^{g} d_{r}^{g} \\
&\text{such that} \sum_{R}^{S} = {}_{1}X_{ij,g} + d_{j}^{x} = X_{ik} (i = 1,\ldots,m), \\
&\sum_{j}^{n} = {}_{1}g_{rj\,\lambda j} - d_{r}^{g} = g_{rk}\ (r = 1,\ldots,s), \\
&\sum_{j}^{n} = {}_{1}\lambda_{j} = 1, \\
&\lambda_{j} \geq 0\,(j = 1,\ldots,n),\ d_{i}^{x} \geq 0\,(i = 1,\ldots,m), \\
&d_{r}^{g} \geq 0\,(r = 1,\ldots,s)
\end{aligned} \tag{1}$$

After calculating Model (1), the OE can be obtained by the calculation:

$$OE = 1 - \left(\sum_{i=1}^{m} R_{i}^{x} d_{i}^{x*} + \sum_{r=1}^{s} R_{r}^{g} d_{r} g^{*}\right) \tag{2}$$

Thus, the slack of each DMU in OE measurement can be obtained by calculating Model (1). This model calculates the inputs and desirable outputs, but does not include undesirable output variables.

2.2 *Total-Factor Productivity Change (TFPC) and Technical Efficiency Change (TEC)*

The approach used in this research is a quantitative one using DEA and determining TFP Change (TFPC) and Technical Efficiency Change (TEC) of inputs and outputs in each country using the ML productivity index, which is the measurement of productivity and technical efficiency when DMUs produce undesirable output. Chung et al. (1997) used this index to measure marginal productivity from observational data that uses undesirable variables as input or output. If $ML > 1$ it means that efficiency increases and DMUs generate desirable output and reduce production of undesirable outputs. If $ML = 1$, the productivity is constant and there is no change; if $ML < 1$, it indicates declining levels of DMU productivity (Aparicio et al., 2013). Based on the model of previous research, the authors use a slightly adapted version of the model of Aparicio et al. (2013). The change involves adding the following element to the model:

$$Y^{1,b}\lambda \geq y^{2,b}{}_{o} - \beta y^{2,b}{}_{o}$$

Thus, the Malmquist model used in this study is:

$$\begin{aligned}
&\text{Maximize}\ \beta, \lambda \\
&\text{such that}\ X^{1}\lambda \leq X^{2}o \\
&Y^{1,g}\lambda \geq y^{2,g}{}_{o} + \beta y^{2,g}{}_{o} \\
&Y^{1,b}\lambda \geq y^{2,b}{}_{o} - \beta y^{2,b}{}_{o} \\
&\text{Max}\left\{ y^{t,u}{}_{i} \right\} \geq y^{2,b}{}_{o} - \beta y^{2,b}{}_{o} \\
&\lambda \geq 0
\end{aligned}$$

where $\text{Max}\{y^{t,u}{}_{i}\}$ is the maximum number of observations of each undesirable output (SO_2 and NO_2) during the observation period (Aparicio et al., 2013, 2015).

3 RESULT

Attachment 1 (Table 1) shows the distribution of OE scores of manufacturing industry for 33 provinces in Indonesia. The table shows the names of the provinces which had an efficiency score of 1, meaning that they were in operationally efficient condition. Provinces showed inefficiency if their score was less than one (< 1), assuming Variable Return to Scale (VRS).

Attachment 1 (Table 1) shows that, in 2012, 12 of the 33 provinces in Indonesia were in operationally efficient condition, while 17 of the provinces were in optimally efficient condition to the production of manufacturing industry. The table shows that another 17 provinces have not utilized their resources, capital and human, to achieve operational efficiency in their manufacturing industry sector. In 2015, the number of provinces experiencing improved efficiency increased to 16.

Attachment 1 (Table 2) shows the distribution of the changes of technical efficiency (index of technology) for 2012–2013 from the manufacturing sector of 33 provinces in Indonesia. In the Table 2 above, efficiency is divided into three classes, namely, efficient, inefficient and very inefficient. It can be seen that there were 14 provinces classified in the efficient group for 2012–2013, increasing to 19 provinces for 2013–2015. On the other hand, the number of provinces in the inefficient and very inefficient groups showed a decline during the period of observation, 2012–2015. For example, there was a decline in the number of provinces, from ten to nine, in the inefficient category (0.750–0.999), while the level of very inefficient (0.5–0.7499) provinces also experienced a decline too, which means that several provinces in the manufacturing industry sector managed to improve their technical efficiency score.

In 2012–2013, there were nine provinces with technically inefficient conditions in the manufacturing industry sector, but this reduced to four provinces in 2013–2014 and continued to decrease until the end of the observation, when only two provinces were inefficient in the manufacturing industry sector.

Table 1. Operational efficiency of manufacturing industry for 33 provinces in Indonesia.

Operational efficiency score	2012	2013	2014	2015
1.00 (Efficient)	1. Riau	1. Riau	1. Riau	1. West Sumatra
	2. Bengkulu	2. Jambi	2. Jambi	2. Riau
	3. Lampung	3. South Sumatra	3. Bengkulu	3. Bengkulu
	4. Jakarta	4. Bengkulu	4. Lampung	4. Lampung
	5. West Java	5. Lampung	5. Riau Islands	5. Jakarta
	6. Central Java	6. Riau Islands	6. Jakarta	6. West Java
	7. East Java	Jakarta	7. West Java	7. Central Java
	8. Banten	7. West Java	8. Central Java	8. East Java
	9. East Nusa Tenggara	8. Central Java	9. East Java	9. Banten
	10. North Sulawesi	9. Special Region of Yogyakarta	10. Banten	10. East Nusa Tenggara
	11. Gorontalo	10. East Java	11. East Nusa Tenggara	11. North Sulawesi
	12. West Sulawesi	11. Banten	12. Sulawesi Utara	12. Gorontalo
	13. Maluku	12. West Sulawesi	13. West Sulawesi	13. West Sulawesi
	14. North Maluku	13. Maluku	14. Maluku	14. Maluku
	15. West Papua	14. North Maluku	15. North Maluku	15. North Maluku
		15. West Papua	16. West Papua	16. West Papua
0.750–0.999 (Inefficient)	1. Aceh	1. Aceh	1. Aceh	1. Aceh
	2. North Sumatra	2. North Sumatra	2. North Sumatra	2. North Sumatra
	3. West Sumatra	3. West Sumatra	3. West Sumatra	3. Jambi
	4. Jambi	4. Bangka Belitung	4. South Sumatra	4. South Sumatra
	5. South Sumatra	5. Bali	5. Bangka Belitung	5. Bangka Belitung
	6. Bangka Belitung	6. West Nusa Tenggara	6. Special Region of Yogyakarta	6. Riau Islands
	7. Riau Islands	7. West Kalimantan	7. Bali	7. Special Region of Yogyakarta
	8. Special Region of Yogyakarta	8. Central Kalimantan	8. West Nusa Tenggara	8. Bali
	9. Bali	9. South Kalimantan	9. West Kalimantan	9. West Nusa Tenggara
	10. West Nusa Tenggara	10. East Kalimantan	10. Central Kalimantan	10. West Kalimantan
	11. West Kalimantan	11. Central Sulawesi	11. South Kalimantan	11. Central Kalimantan
	12. Central Kalimantan	12. South Sulawesi	12. East Kalimantan	12. South Kalimantan
	13. South Kalimantan	13. Sulawesi Tenggara	13. Central Sulawesi	13. East Kalimantan
	14. East Kalimantan	14. Papua	14. South Sulawesi	14. Central Sulawesi
	15. Central Sulawesi		15. Sulawesi Tenggara	15. South Sulawesi
	16. South Sulawesi		16. Papua	16. Sulawesi Tenggara
	17. Papua			17. Papua

In the observation year 2012–2013, North Sulawesi experienced technical inefficiency, but successfully increased its efficiency score in the 2013–2015 observation to become fully technically efficient with an efficiency score of 1. Aceh also experienced a similar trend; in 2012–2013, Aceh exhibited a very inefficient condition with an efficiency score of 0.5964, but massively improved its technical efficiency scores in 2013–2014 to score 1.1632 and 1.3793 in 2014–2015. The increasing trend in technical efficiency was experienced by several provinces in Indonesia and, among the members of the inefficient or very inefficient group that became efficient during the years of observation are DI Yogyakarta, North Sumatra, North Maluku, Sumatra Barat, East Java, West Kalimantan and Papua.

Other provinces seem able to increase their technical efficiency in the manufacturing industry sector too, but unfortunately this change was not significant and the provinces have remained technically inefficient. Such provinces include South Kalimantan, Central Kalimantan and Central Sulawesi. However, some provinces experienced a decrease in their technical efficiency score in the manufacturing industry sector. For example, in

Table 2. Technical Efficiency Change (TEC) of manufacturing industry for 33 provinces in Indonesia.

Operational efficiency score	Year 2012–2013	Year 2013–2014	Year 2014–2015
1.00 (Efficient)	1. Riau	1. Aceh	1. Aceh
	2. Jambi	2. North Sumatra	2. West Sumatra
	3. Bengkulu	3. Riau	3. Riau
	4. Lampung	4. Jambi	4. South Sumatra
	5. Riau Islands	5. Lampung	5. Lampung
	6. Jakarta	6. Bangka Belitung	6. Jakarta
	7. West Java	7. Riau Islands	7. West Java
	8. Central Java	8. Jakarta	8. Central Java
	9. Yogyakarta	9. West Java	9. Yogyakarta
	10. Banten	10. Central Java	10. East Java
	11. EastNusa Tenggara	11. East Java	11. Banten
	12. West Sulawesi	12. Banten	12. EastNusa Tenggara
	13. North Maluku	13. East Nusa Tenggara	13. North Sulawesi
	14. West Papua	14. North Sulawesi	14. South Sulawesi
		15. South Sulawesi	15. Gorontalo
		16. Gorontalo	16. North Maluku
		17. West Sulawesi	17. West Papua
		18. West Papua	18. Papua
		19. Papua	19. West Kalimantan
0.750–0.999 (Inefficiency)	1. South Sumatra	1. West Sumatra	1. Jambi
	2. East Java	2. Bengkulu	2. Bangka Belitung
	3. Bali	3. Jogyakarta	3. Bali
	4. West Nusa Tenggara	4. Bali	4. WestNusa Tenggara
	5. South Kalimantan	5. West Nusa Tenggara	5. Central Kalimantan
	6. East Kalimantan	6. West Kalimantan	6. South Kalimantan
	7. North Sulawesi	7. Central Kalimantan	7. East Kalimantan
	8. South east Sulawesi	8. East Kalimantan	8. Central Sulawesi
	9. Gorontalo	9. South east Sulawesi	9. SouthEast Sulawesi
	10. maluku	10. maluku	
0.5–0.7499 (very inefficient)	1. Aceh	1. South Sumatra	1. North Sumatra
	2. North Sumatra	2. South Kalimantan	2. Maluku
	3. West Sumatra	3. Central Sulawesi	
	4. Bangka Belitung	4. North Maluku	
	5. West Kalimantan		
	6. Central Kalimantan		
	7. Central Sulawesi		
	8. South Sulawesi		
	9. Papua		

observation year 2012–2013, North Sumatra was extremely inefficient with a score of 0.5015, but was classified as very inefficient for 2014–2015 with a score of 0.6479. This indicates that North Sumatra did not have a sustainable policy for determining the optimum input–output combination in the manufacturing industry production process. Had North Sumatra experienced an increasing score in 2013–2014 it would have indicated that, in these observations, the province had managed to combine the use of input–output in the manufacturing industry sector, so that it could achieve technical efficiency. However, unfortunately, in the years 2014–2015, there was a policy change by the managerial system in the use of input–output, such that it had the highest technical inefficiency. The same thing was experienced by the province of Maluku.

3.1 *The Total-Factor Productivity Change (TFPC) of manufacturing industry for 33 provinces in Indonesia*

The first TFP measurement result is technical efficiency change (TEC). TEC is the growth rate in efficiency of the DMU from the current year (t) to the next year ($t + 1$), as measured from the change in technical efficiency assuming Constant Returns to Scale (CRS). However, in the Malmquist models used

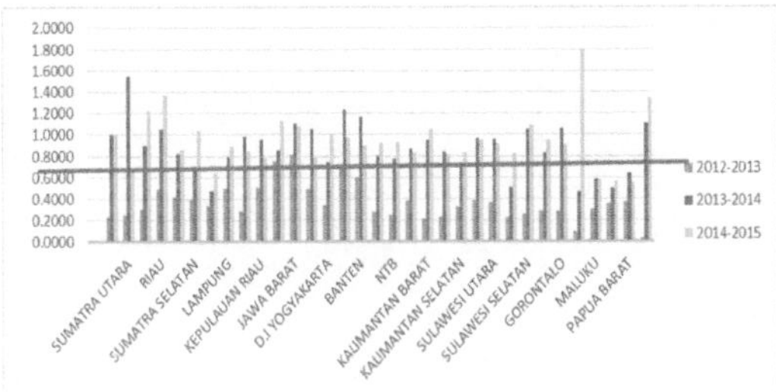

Figure 1. Total-factor productivity change (TFPC) in manufacturing industry for 33 provinces in Indonesia.

by the author, the results are divided into TFPC and TEC. In this study, the author used the Malmquist–Luenberger Index, which is a measurement of productivity and technical efficiency when a DMU produces undesirable output (Chung et al., 1997).

Figure 1 shows that for the period 2012–2013, none of the provinces in Indonesia could reach ML > 1. This means that, during the period, the Indonesian manufacturing industry was degraded, mainly in terms of suppressing the production of emissions. This was caused by incorrect use of technology to optimize productivity in Indonesia's manufacturing industry. In the period 2013–2014, eight provinces were able to increase productivity and achieve ML > 1; the best of these was North Sumatra with a ML score of 1.5395. This indicates that North Sumatra, in these observations, managed to increase productivity by suppressing the production of emissions and improving good outputs in its manufacturing industry.

Unfortunately, in the period 2014–2015, 23 provinces in Indonesia degraded their productivity in the manufacturing industry sector. North Sumatra was one of them, experiencing a drastic reduction in its ML with a final score of 0.6677. In contrast to Sumatra, West Sulawesi experienced a significant productivity improvement. In the period 2012–2013, West Sulawesi only achieved a score of 0.0966, but this rose to 0.4605 in the period 2013–2014, and then increased rapidly with the highest productivity score of all at 1.7978. This indicates that West Sulawesi has been precise in its use of technology in the production process of the manufacturing industry sector, as supported by the high ML index, which indicates that the province succeeded in increasing desirable output along with reducing undesirable output production.

4 CONCLUSION

There were 17 provinces observed in a state of operational inefficiency, with scores in the range 0.750–0.999. This indicates low optimal control of provincial governments in relation to the manufacturing sector. However, in technical terms, the majority of manufacturing industries are efficient; in fact, only a few provinces can increase their productivity by increasing desirable output while reducing undesirable output. This indicates that the implementation and control (law enforcement) by local government in relation to the implementation of environmental policy in the manufacturing industry need to be further improved.

This suggests that the government can encourage the majority of industries to achieve efficiency in technical issues by increasing the use of proper technology and environmentally friendly production processes. Furthermore, investment in the technology sphere is important. Nevertheless, capital insensitivity can diminish the volume of labor through dismissal; hence, investment is assumed be a balance between capital insensitivity and labor insensitivity. Ultimately, productivity can also be increased as well as reducing unemployment.

REFERENCES

Aparicio, J., Pastor, J.T. & Zofio, J.L. (2013). On the inconsistency of the Malmquist–Luenberger index. *European Journal of Operational Research*, *229*(3), 738–742.

Aparicio, J., Pastor, J.T. & Zofio, J.T. (2015). How to properly decompose economic efficiency using technical and allocative criteria with non-homothetic DEA technologies. *European Journal of Operational Research*, *240*(3), 882–891.

Charnes, A., Cooper, W. & Rhodes, E. (1978). Measuring the efficiency of decision making units. *European Journal of Operational Research*, *2*(6), 429–444.

Chung, Y, Fare, R. & Grosskopf, S. (1997). Productivity and undesirable outputs: A directional distance function approach. *Journal of Environmental Management*, *51*(3), 229–240.

Korhonen, P.J. & Luptacik, M. (2004). Eco-efficiency analysis of power plants: An extension of data envelopment analysis. *European Journal of Operational Research*, *154*(2), 437–446.

Kost, F.E. & Rosenwig, J.E. (1979). *Organization and management: A system and contingency approach*. New York, NY: McGraw-Hill.

Page, J.M. (1980). Technical efficiency and economic performance: Some evidence from Ghana. *Oxford Economic Papers*, *32*(2), 319–339.

Sueyoshi, T. & Goto, M. (2010). Should the US Clean Air Act include CO_2 emission control? Examination by data envelopment analysis. *Energy Policy*, *38*(10), 5902–5911.

Sueyoshi, T., Goto, M. & Ueno, T. (2010). Performance analysis of US coal-fired power plants by measuring three DEA efficiencies. *Energy Policy*, *38*(4), 1675–1688.

Sueyoshi, T., Goto, M. & Snell, M.A. (2013). DEA environmental assessment: Measurement of damages to scale with unified efficiency under managerial disposability or environmental efficiency. *Applied Mathematical Modelling*, *37*, 7300–7314.

Increasing Management Relevance and Competitiveness – Sukoco et al. (Eds)
© 2018 Taylor & Francis Group, London, ISBN 978-0-8153-7455-8

Academic excellence and total quality supply chain management in higher education

I. Usman & Windijarto
Management Department, Faculty of Economy and Business, Airlangga University, Indonesia

ABSTRACT: The purpose of this study was to analyze the concept of supply chain quality management to support the achievement of academic excellence in a higher education study program. Empirical studies were carried out to identify good practice in the management of study programs in terms of the concepts of supply chain quality management. Currently, most universities have a quality management department, but the quality culture that raises academic performance in the organization does not yet exist. The method in this study involved empirical review of multiple case studies among those study programs at the forefront of performance achievement in higher education, specifically, those study programs which have already been awarded the highest grade by the Indonesian National Accreditation institution. The results of this study are expected to provide a model of total supply chain quality management for a study program to achieve academic excellence and enhanced performance.

Keywords: Total Quality Management, Supply Chain Management, Total Quality Supply Chain Management

1 INTRODUCTION

This research will explore how to develop supply chain quality management in order to create academic excellence. A new, well-integrated framework should be developed to facilitate the implementation of Supply Chain Management (SCM) and Total Quality Management (TQM). The traditional approach to TQM emphasizes specification-based performance, while SCM tends to focus on time-based performance (Vanichchinchai & Igel, 2009). The interesting thing in conceptualizing the education system as a supply chain is that a supply chain will generally involve several entities that are directly related to each other, both upstream and downstream (Mentzer et al., 2001). Educational services have the same process in terms of operating functions, for instance, transforming inputs into outputs (Slack et al., 2012). Services account for 70% of the workforce in advanced economies, including the government sector and education. Overall, this will exceed manufacturing and agribusiness industries (Economist, 2014).

Considering these circumstances, it is time that Supply Chain Quality Management (SCQM) theory and practice were further developed. It is understood that education produces well-educated human resources, but has this sector been implemented in the most effective way, given that the management of educational systems is becoming so complex (Mason, 2008; Snyder, 2013)? Rashid and Aslam (2012) state that, currently, most universities have a quality management department, but the quality culture that raises academic performance in the organization does not yet exist.

The results of this study will form a basic foundation for the development of studies in the area of strategic management, operations management and SCQM, both theoretical and practical. The practical benefit of this research will be in providing a new practical concept for the management of study programs designed to achieve academic excellence through the application of the Total Quality Supply Chain Management (TQSCM) concept.

1.1 *Conceptual background*

The definition of supply chain management has evolved as part of modern business management concepts and SCM can enhance an organization's capacity to achieve its strategic objectives. This means that supply chain concepts are very useful in support of the management practices of an organization. SCM activities can be described as having three components: supply chain configuration; supply chain relationship, and supply chain coordination (see Figure 1).

Supply chain configuration consists of strategic decisions and concerns the construction of all participant organizations in the chain, also referred to

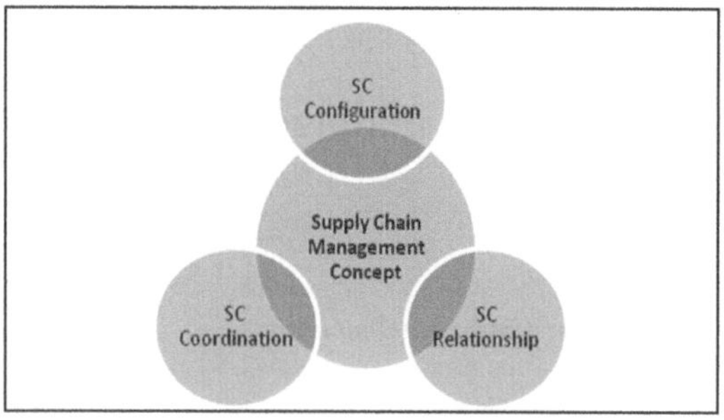

Figure 1. Supply Chain (SC) management conceptual model (Source:Storey, Emberson, Godsell, & Harrison, 2006).

as supply chain architecture. Supply chain relationship concerns the relationships between organizations in the supply chain. In terms of level, decisions associated with supply chain relationships can be strategic or operational. Supply chain coordination deals with coordination between organizations in the supply chain. Decisions about supply chain coordination are operational in nature. The conceptual model (Figure 1) also illustrates the interrelationship with managerial decision-making within the organization, which includes strategic, tactical and operational decisions.

1.2 *Total quality supply chain management*

The development of university audit efforts to attain academic excellence is concerned with quality assurance activities. TQM is a management philosophy intended to drive cost reduction, creation of high-quality goods and services, customer satisfaction, employee empowerment and measurement. SCM strategy focuses on developing strategic alliances according to core competencies. In a new economic era, companies operate manufacturing or services by integrating corporate partnership activities along the value chain. The fundamental challenge in applying TQM all the way to the base of the value chain in supply chain networks is the development of programs and techniques that encourage diverse cultures among human resources to make continuous improvements in all areas that reflect the ambitions of the organization.

Total Quality Supply Chain Management (TQSCM) is a combination of SCM and TQM activities: SCM is a paradigm aimed at adjusting the system to the supply chain so as to create harmony in all processes, while quality improvement is pursued to achieve given levels of achievement or better. These SCM and TQM activities need to be integrated, as they are closely related; better quality cannot be achieved without supply chain integration, and continuous quality improvement efforts also result in integration among supply chain partners. Therefore, we need a framework to manage quality throughout the supply chain. Previous research has been undertaken by Robinson and Malhotra (2005), and Foster and Ogden (2008), while a study of TQM and SCM practices was conducted by Sila et al. (2006). The purpose of this study is to identify TQM and SCM practices that are often used in organizations. We also compare and illustrate the relationship between TQM and SCM, using a review of literature from published papers that adopt different types of organization.

2 METHODOLOGY

This research uses qualitative exploratory research, and a multi-case study approach. The research design has several levels of analysis to improve the accuracy and richness of the resulting theory (Cheng, 1997) Eisenhardt, 1989), and focuses on the management of study programs that have implemented TQM. The research was conducted on undergraduate study programs in Indonesia that have been rated "A" by the National Accreditation Board of Higher Education. Data were collected through face-to-face and telephone interviews, and emails to track the strategies used through the media and materials owned by existing study programs and external databases. Researchers also conducted pilot interviews with university quality control leaders, in relation to faculty and study programs. The data obtained were processed and analyzed to formulate a Total Quality Supply Chain Management (TQSCM) model.

3 ANALYSIS AND RESULTS

In critical terms, top-management commitment in SCM is referred to by different levels and terms, such as changing corporate culture, management support, participative management, and cooperation, but the underlying concept is the same in the case of both TQM and SCM. Moreover, TQM and SCM can only succeed in achieving improved performance in an organization with the continuous support of senior management and their efforts towards never-ending improvement in customer services and customer satisfaction. TQM and SCM both play an important role in improving the competitiveness of an organization (Sila et al., 2006). The development of global competition today makes the situation even more complex and difficult. Existing challenges include a focus on the supply chain to determine timely and targeted shipments for product delivery (Chin et al., 2004; Robinson & Malhotra, 2005).

Although TQM and SCM are important for organizational performance, they are seldom studied simultaneously (Casadesus & Castro, 2005; Robinson & Malhotra, 2005). Some researchers (Vanichchinchai & Igel, 2009, 2011) have also stated that, although SCM and TQM are important management systems for achieving competitive advantage, the success rate of implementations in organizations is not the same. SCM is the coordination and integration of all supply chain activities to make a process run smoothly, this is demonstrated through improved supply chain performance. The synergy between quality management and SCM leads to improved supply chain performance (Robinson & Malhotra, 2005; Foster & Ogden, 2008; Kuei et al., 2001).

Initially, the development of synergy between quality management and SCM occurred in the manufacturing sector, and the wholesale and retail industries. Utilization of such integration is still low in service industries. The education sector is similar to other service operations; it involves the process of changing inputs into outputs (Slack et al., 2012). Habib and Jungthirapanich (2009) conducted research on supply chain education in universities. Through exploratory research, a new dimension for education management is provided, revealing the importance of the supply chain in contributing to the success of university operations. Contributions include human resources and research contributions to end customers, that is, communities. Effective education depends on the knowledge, experience and ethics of its personnel. (Sarrico & Rosa, 2016) conducted a study to introduce a supply chain quality management (SCQM) concept into education. This study found that education is an SCM system. SCQM in education presents a challenge, with respect to trust for information sharing, integration and leadership. Nevertheless, this study also found some good practices in a more systematic SCQM implementation. Based on the analysis of several study programs, we conclude that SCM serves to balance all parties involved in meeting the demands of consumers, ranging from those upstream to those downstream. The Supply Chain Operations Reference (SCOR) model, developed by the Supply Chain Council (TX, USA), can be implemented in the operational academic process to obtain high-quality graduates and research.

In Indonesia, study programs that obtain an "A" grade from the National Accreditation Board of Higher Education have generally run quality assurance. Based on observations of some of the "A"-rated management majors, all have performed quality assurance, yet no study program has taken advantage of the SCM concept in its design strategy to achieve its performance. Based on interviews, observations and references relating to the higher education value chain, SCM critical practices based on the SCOR model and TQM critical practices based on the Plan–Do–Check–Act (PDCA) cycle are applicable to study programs.

The result of semi-structured interviews with heads of study programs, lecturers, administrative staff and quality assurance managers resulted in a TQSCM design. The integration of both TQM and TQM in study program, call TQSCM design indicate that implementation of SCM and quality management practice integration will improve the achievements of study program's performance.

Table 1. TQM and SCM critical practices.

Critical practice	
SCOR model (SCM practice)	
Plan	The coordination plan of units related to the study programs
Source	Identification of the source qualification to support the academic operation of the study programs (incoming student, facilities, lecturer, etc.)
Make	Operational academic process of study program
Deliver	Relevance of graduate
Return	Organizing feedback from stakeholders
PDCA cycle (TQM practice)	
Plan	How the quality assurance (QA) activity is planned and practiced
Do	How the QA is organized
Check	QA activities processed
Act	Assessment process of teaching learning and research activities
	Continuity in assessment processes
	Consistency and reliability of the QA programs
	Converting/transforming feedback into program improvements

REFERENCES

Casadesus, M. & Castro, R. (2005). How improving quality improves supply chain management: Empirical study. *TQM Magazine*, *17*(4), 345–357.

Chin, K.S., Tummala, V.M.R., Leung, J.P.F. & Tang, X. (2004). A study on supply chain management practices: The Hong Kong manufacturing perspective. *International Journal of Physical Distribution & Logistics Management*, *34*(6), 505–524.

Cheng, Y.C.(1997). Quality assurance in Education "A framework for dimensions of quality in higher education", Quality Assurance in Quality assurance in education: internal, interface, and future. *Quality Assurance in Education Iss Quality Assurance in*

Education Iss Education, *11*(22), 202–213. Retrieved from http://dx.doi.org/10.1108/09684880310501386.

Economist. (2014, January 18). The onrushing wave. *The Economist*. Retrieved from https://www.economist.com/news/briefing/21594264-previous-technological-innovation-has-always-delivered-more-long-run-employment-not-less.

Eisenhardt, K.M. (1989). Building theories from case study research. *Academy of Management Review*, *14*(4), 532–550.

Foster, S.T., Jr. & Ogden, J. (2008). On differences in how operations and supply chain managers approach quality management. *International Journal of Production Research*, *46*(2), 6945–6961.

Gunasekaran, A. & McGaughey, R.E. (2003). TQM in supply chain management. *TQM Magazine*, *15*(6), 361–363.

Habib, M.M. & Jungthirapanich, C. (2009). Research framework of education supply chain, research supply chain and educational management for the universities. *International Journal of the Computer, the Internet and Management*, *17*(SP1), 24.1–24.8.

Kuei, C.H., Madu, N.C. & Lin. C. (2001). The relationship between supply chain quality management practices and organizational performance. *International Journal of Quality & Reliability Management*, *18*(8), 864–872.

Lau, A.K.W. (2007). Educational supply chain management: A case study. *On The Horizon*, *15*(1), 15–27.

Li, S., Ragu-Nathan, B., Ragu-Nathan, T.S. & Rao, S.S. (2006). The impact of supply chain management practices on competitive advantage and organizational performance. *Omega*, *34*, 107–124.

Mason, M. (Ed.). (2008). *Complexity theory and the philosophy of education*. Chichester, UK: Wiley-Blackwell.

Mentzer, J.T., DeWitt, W., Keebler, J.S., Min, S., Nix, N.W., Smith, N.C.D. & Zacharia, Z.G. (2001). Defining supply chain management. *Journal of Business Logistics*, *22*(2), 1–25.

Rashid, K. & Aslam, M.M.H. (2012). Business excellence through total supply chain quality management. *Asian Journal on Quality*, *13*(3), 309–324.

Robinson, C.J. & Malhotra, M.K. (2005). Defining the concept of supply chain quality management and its relevance to academic and industrial practice. *International Journal of Production Economics*, *96*, 315–337.

Sarrico, C.S. & Rosa, M.J. (2016). Supply chain management in education. *International Journal of Quality & Reliability Management*, *33*(4), 499–517.

Sila, I., Ebrahimpour, M. & Birkholz. C. (2006). Quality in supply chains: An empirical analysis. *Supply Chain Management: An International Journal*, *1*(6), 491–502.

Slack, N., Brandon-Jones, A., Johnston, R. & Betts, A. (2012). *Operations and process management*. Harlow, UK: Pearson.

Snyder, S. (2013). *The simple, the complicated, and the complex: Educational reform through the lens of complexity theory*. Paris, France: OECD.

Storey, J., Emberson, C., Godsell, J., & Harrison, A. (2006). International Journal of Operations & Production Management Supply chain management: theory, practice and future challenges "Supply chain management practices in toy supply chains", Supply Chain Management: An. *International Journal of Operations & Production Management An International Journal Iss International Journal*, *26*(5), 754–774. Retrieved from http://dx.doi.org/10.1108/01443570610672220.

Vanichchinchai, A. (2012). The relationship between employee involvement, partnership management and supply performance: Findings from a developing country. *International Journal of Productivity and Performance Management*, *61*(2), 157–172.

Vanichchinchai, A. & Igel, B. (2009). Total quality management and supply chain management: Similarities and differences. *TQM Journal*, *21*(3), 249–260.

Vanichchinchai, A. & Igel, B. (2011). The impact of total quality management on supply chain management and firm's supply performance. *International Journal of Production Research*, *49*(11), 3405–3424.

Financial management and accounting

Increasing Management Relevance and Competitiveness – Sukoco et al. (Eds)
© 2018 Taylor & Francis Group, London, ISBN 978-0-8153-7455-8

The influence of usage accounting information on small medium enterprise's perception

S. Mintarti, D.M. Sari & T. Fitriastuti
Universitas Mulawarman, Samarinda, Indonesia

ABSTRACT: This research examines the impact of the completed accounting process and the use of accounting information on the perception of Small and Medium Enterprises (SMEs) by using an experimental method. This method has been chosen with the purpose of seeing the alteration in the perception of SMEs who have 'negatively' perceived the value of accounting information. It is assumed that the negative perception basically comes from the closure mechanism, which shaped the whole perception through incomplete stimulation. Therefore, ignorance towards accounting information indirectly leads to the belief that accounting information could be something unreachable, complicated, and unimportant. The experiment is done by forming 2 (two) groups, which are the experiment group and the control group. Each group contains 30 SMEs. It is found that the implementation and the use of accounting information has no impact on the negative perception of the accounting information itself, which is proved by respondents who still believe that the Indonesia Accounting Standard Non-Publicly-Accountable Entities (SAK ETAP) and, similarly the International Financial Reporting Standard for Small and Medium Sized Entities (IFRS for SMEs), are still difficult to implement.

Keywords: Perception, Accounting Information, Experiment

1 INTRODUCTION

The existence of Small and Medium Enterprises (SMEs) in Indonesia is a vital asset for this nation. However, problems still occur at this business level, where they often face obstacles in product marketing, technology, financial management, human resources, and capitals. Most of the small scale business owners are unwilling to make a note on their business, since they have the perception that book keeping or accounting is a very complex procedure.

The limitation of the SMEs in undertaking accounting information based finance management is due to a perception that has been is shaped among the entrepreneurs which is that the accounting process is a series of complicated and unimportant activities (Pinasti, 2007; Lalin & Sabir, 2010; Smirat, 2013; Sofiah & Murniati, 2014). The perception regarding accounting information has been constructed by their experiences in implementing and using the accounting information (Pinasti, 2007). From one point of view, a perception occurs as a response to a stimulus. According to the previous researches, it is also difficult to find SMEs who have kept the accounting records, since most of the small scale business owners do not do book keeping (Idrus, 2000).

This research actually uses SAK ETAP (Standardized Entity Financial Accounting without Public Accountability – *Standar Akuntansi Keuangan Entitas Tanpa Akuntabilitas Publik*) as the form of treatment. SAK ETAP is the only alternative of standardized formal accounting that is used by SME entities because there is no standardized SME accounting that is applicable in Indonesia.

The strategic role of accounting in the development of a business unit is what initiates the proper steps to be taken in altering the SMEs perception on the implementation and the use of accounting information. Throughout an exploration on the needs of SMEs and the barriers that occurs in the accounting system-based financial management, there will be an accurate solution offered the relation to a simple accounting system that is applied effortlessly by SMEs but still meets the quality of financial statement needed.

2 LITERATURE REVIEW

2.1 *Concept of perception*

Solso, et al (2008) stated that perception involves cognition in interpreting the information. The events or the information are processed by conformingan individual's pre-understanding of the object of perception he interprets. Robbins (2002) adds that a positive perception is an individual appraising an object or information with a positive view or with an attitude that is expected towards the object of perception from the implied rules. According to Davidoff (1988), perception is a process done by a stimulus that is received by the sensory system which is then organized and interpreted so that the individual is aware of what his sensory system perceives.

2.2 *Accounting information*

Accounting results in information that can beused by a manager to operate a business and that can be provided to the stakeholders in order to acknowledge the economic performance and the financial condition of a business (Niswonger, et al 2002:6). The elements of the Accounting Information System are fundamentally coordinated to provide the information needed to facilitate the management of business.

2.3 *The effect of the experience of accounting information on the perception of accounting information*

The SMEs owner's perception of the accounting information is closely related to the experience gained when they use the accounting information. Most of the SMEs have never kept an accounting record, so therefore they have not achieved the benefits of accounting records. Due to this situation, they have a negative perception of accounting records. As stated by Robbins (2002), the trigger for this negative perception is an individual's dissatisfaction with the object of his perception and where there is a lack of knowledge in the individual about the perceived object. The construe of this negative perception is based on the *closure* mechanism towards the accounting information.

The findings in Pinasti's research (2001) show that the small scale traders in traditional markets in the Banyumas Region do not apply and use accounting information in their business management. Amdani (2009); Idrus (2000) also states that the small scale entrepreneurs view accounting as something complicated and unattainable. For them, the application of an accounting procedure is unnecessary. The previous findings prove that small scale business owners have a negative perception of the accounting information. This perception appears to be because they never implement and use the accounting information. Therefore, it is likely that the SME entrepreneurs tend to focus only on the things that satisfy their desires and ignore the things that are thought as a disadvantages or bothersome (Leavitt, 1997).

Therefore, the experience of implementing and using accounting information is needed wished to be able to change the small scale business entity's perception of accounting information which would later result in a positive perception which is the effect of individual's satisfaction on the object that becomes his object of perception. Based on this framework, a hypothesis is construed as:

The implementation and use of accounting information will affect the small scale entrepreneurs' perception of accounting information.

3 METHODOLOGY

3.1 *Variable and the measurement*

The implementation and the use of accounting information was the independent variable in this research, where the variable was measured by the knowledge and the experience of the respondent of accounting information. The given treatment was training on the accounting procedure, which was based on SAK ETAP with modification and adjustment.

The independent variable in this research was the SME's perception of accounting information. There were three types of perception (Pinasti, 2007) that could be measured; (1) the perception of the benefit of accounting information, (2) the perception of the comparison between the cost and benefit of accounting information, and (3) the readiness in implementing accounting information in the sustainable business management. These perceptions were measured within the Likert scale 1 to 5 in the initial assessment (pretest) and in the final assessment (posttest).

3.2 *Population and sampling*

The population in this research was the SMEs in Samarinda City. The samples in this research were chosen with a purposive sampling method under the following criteria:

1. SMEs with stability in business indicated by their sustainability through a number of years.
2. SMEs that have operated for a minimum of 2 (two) years.

3.3 *Experiment design*

The experiment design used in this research was a pretest-posttest control group design, as seen in Figure 1. This design employs a both pretest and posttest and uses samples that were randomly chosen (Hartono, 2008:105). The placement of the samples in 2 groups is done randomly to avoid and overcome the threat to internal validity.

The experiment group consisted of 30 (thirty) SMEs. This group received a treatment The

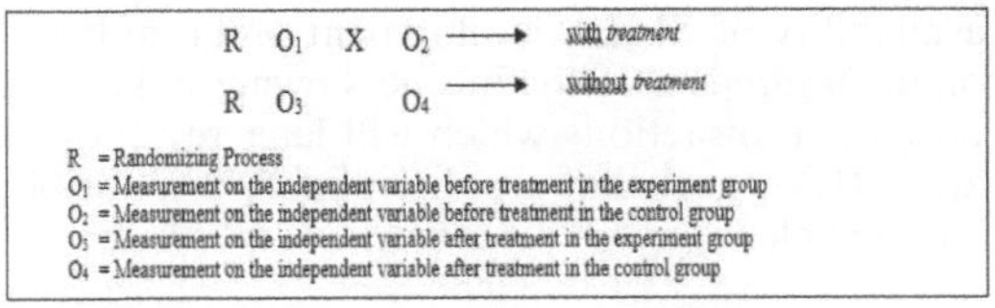

Figure 1. Pretest-posttest control group diagram.

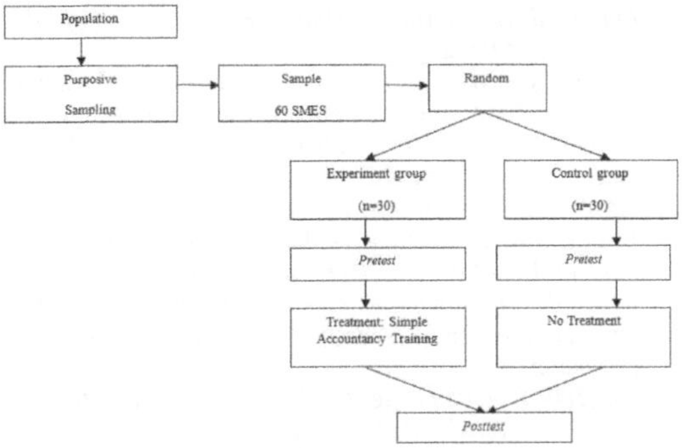

Figure 2. Experiment procedure.

treatment period for training had been decided for as from 6 (six) to 7 (seven) weeks. The control group consisted of 30 (thirty) SMEs. This group did not receive any treatment. The steps of pretest and posttest were undertaken in this research. The experiment procedure figured bellows:

3.4 *Data analysis*

The data analysis in this research was done by a non-parametric method. This method employed the t-test paired statistic to analyze the results gained from both the experiment group and the control group in the pretest and the posttest.

4 FINDINGS AND DISCUSSION

4.1 *Data description*

This research was done on the UKM Tenun Samarinda in Kampung Tenun Samarinda Seberang (Weaving Center). From 60 (sixty) samples of SMEs, the majority of respondents were between the ages of 31–39 years old 45%, they mostly Elementary School education (38%) and 45% of the owner had operated their business for 6–10 years. The respondents were divided into 2 (two) groups, the experiment and control groups.

4.2 *The experiment group and control group before and after receiving the training*

The examination to discover the transformation in the perception of accounting information was done by using a *Paired t-test,* and the result is shown in the table below:

The table shows that there is no change in the perception of accounting information by either the experiment or control group before and after the accounting training.

4.3 *Difference of the perception of accounting information between the experiment group and the control group*

To see the difference in perception between the experiment group and the control group, both before and after the accounting training was given to the experiment group an independent t-test was done and the result is shown in the table below:

From the table, it is known that there is no difference in the perception of accounting information between the experiment group both and the control group before and after treatment.

4.4 *The impact of accounting information implementation and its use SME's perception of accounting information in business management*

Based on the statistic test done on the 4 (four) sets of testing on the respondents, the evidence shows that the implementation and the use of accounting information measured by the application of knowl-

Table 1. Result of the statistic test on the experiment and control group.

	Experiment group	Control group
Mean before receiving accounting training	3.40325	3.42871
Mean after receiving accounting training	3.41581	3.42941
Signification (*p-value*)	0.113	0.142

Table 2. Result of the statistic test of the perception difference before accountancy training.

	Before treatment	After treatment
Mean in the experiment group	3.40325	3.41581
Mean in the control group	3.42871	3.42941
Signification (*p-value*)	0.734	0.332

edge and the experience of using the accounting information, had no impact on the SMEs business owners' perception of accounting information. The business owners who were already considered as having knowledge and experience of accountancy through the delivery of the SAK ETAP-based accountancy training and the given assistance could not change their negative perception on the accounting information.

This finding proves that the experience of implementing and using accounting information with more complicated standards was perceived as a negative experience, so that no change happened in perception before and after the treatment given, which was simple accountancy training. This was caused by the complicated process of accounting which changed from the cash basis to the full accrual basis accounting. This condition could be seen from SAK ETAP, which became complex because of the nature of its report, so that the respondents perceived that it was difficult to undertake accounting procedures. Generally, the small scale enterpriseshave neither had nor managed tight accounting and have not had the indiscipline to maintain proper book keeping whether in the form of daily, weekly, monthly, or annual book keeping. One of many reasons for this was the thought that adequate accounting is just a waste of time and money.

5 CONCLUSIONS AND IMPLICATIONS

5.1 *Conclusion*

Following the research and the analysis, the researcher concludes that there is no change in the perception of the SMEs (*experiment group*) on accounting information before and after receiving the accounting training. This result shows that the implementation of accrual basis accounting had not been fully understood and implemented by the SMEs although the treatment and the assistance were delivered.

5.2 *Research implication*

This research proves that the implementation and the use of accounting information with a SAK ETAP basis have not changed the negative perception of the SMEs of accounting information. This research can be a basic source and a consideration for the SMEs assistants and the related institutions in order to give more attention and create a real effort to raise the awareness of the SMEs in applying an accounting system that supports the development of their business. Furthermore, the result of this research hopefully implies the availability of SMEs development program based on the awareness of the business owner in keeping business transactions which will later resulting as an SME owners that are disciplined, responsible, and reliable.

REFERENCES

Amdani, S. (2009). *SMEs Requires Standardized Entity Financial Accounting without Public Accountability (SAK-ETAP)*. Jurnal Bogor.

Antaranews. SMEs in Samarinda recruit 50.327 Labor Market. http://www. antarakaltim.com/berita/4886/ukm-di-samarinda-serap-50327-tenaga-kerja. Accessed on 26 April 2014.

Davidoff, LL. (1988). *Introduction to Psychology*. Maria Juniati translated. Jakarta: Erlangga Publisher.

Hartono, J. (2008). *Information System Research Methods: A Handbook Conduct on Information System Technology Research Field.* Yogyakarta: Andi Publisher.

Idrus. (2000). *Accounting and Small Medium Enterprise.* Akuntansi (7/March/Yr.VII).

Ikatan Akuntan Indonesia. (2017). Indonesia Accounting Standard Non-Publicly-Accountable Entities (SAK ETAP). Jakarta: IAI Jakarta.

Lalin, H. dan Sabir, I. (2010). Research on usage and usefulness perception of financial accounting practices in a less developing country: A case of SMEs in Cambodia. *Proceedings of 7th International Conference on Innovation & Management*. China.

Leavitt, H.J. (1997). *Psikologi Manajemen,* (2nd ed). Translated by Muslichah Zarkasi. Jakarta: Erlangga.

Niswonger, R.C., Reeve, J.M and Fess, P.E (2002). *Accounting*. (19thed). Kansas: South-Western College Publishing.

Pinasti, M. (2001). Accounting Information applied in the Management of Small Traders in Traditional Market of Banyumas Regency. *Jurnal Ekonomi, Bisnis, dan Akuntansi, 1(3)*.

Pinasti, M. (2007). The Influence of Accounting Information applied on Small Medium Enterprises's perception: an Experiment Research. *Prosiding Simposium Nasional Akuntansi X*. Makassar.

President of Republic Indonesia. Act Number 20 year 2000 Small Medium Enterprises.

Robbins, S.P. (2002). *Prinsip-prinsip Perilaku Organisasi.* (5th ed). Jakarta: Erlangga.

Smirat, B.Y.A. (2013). The Applied of accounting information by small and medium enterprises in South District of Jordan (An empirical study). *Research Journal of Finance Accounting, 4(16) 169–175*.

Sofiah, N. & Murniati, A. (2014). SME's Perception on Accounting information based on the Indonesia Accounting Standard Non-Publicly-Accountable Entities (SAK ETAP). *Jurnal Jibeka 8(1)*.

Solso, R.L., Maclin, O.H. & Maclin. M.K. 2008. *Psikologi Kognitif.* Jakarta: Penerbit Erlangg Solso, R.L., Maclin, O.H. & Maclin, M.K. 2008. *Cognitive Psychology.* Jakarta: Erlangga Publisher.

Winarno, Y. (2014). http://tulisanantik.blogspot.com/2014/04/kajian-teori-persepsi-peserta-didik.html.

Increasing Management Relevance and Competitiveness – Sukoco et al. (Eds)
 ISBN 978-0-8153-7455-8

Determinants of banks' net interest margin in five South East Asian countries

M. Gitanadya & R. Setiawan
Airlangga University, Surabaya, Indonesia

ABSTRACT: South East Asian banking has different characteristics in each country and this affects the Net Interest Margin (NIM) acquired. Indonesian banks enjoy 5.4% NIM, while Singaporean banks only acquired 1.4% in the same period. This study aims to determine the various factors that affect NIM in five South East Asian countries, which are Indonesia, Malaysia, Thailand, Singapore and the Philippines. There will be 11 independent variables grouped into three factors, which are bank-specific, industry and macroeconomics. The study will use a linear regression model. The result shows that South East Asia's NIM is affected significantly by relative size, credit risk, capital adequacy, diversification, industry concentration, short-term interest rate volatility and stock market capitalization. The study also concludes that capital markets and banks are both financial intermediaries that substitute for each other when their roles should be complementary in order to improve the respective country's economic condition.

1 INTRODUCTION

Banks have an important role as an intermediary institution in society. For that intermediary service, banks get Net Interest Margin (NIM), or the spread between interest incomes received from debtors and interest expenses paid to depositors, as the reward. A fascinating trend about NIM is that, in developed countries, banks are no longer relying solely on interest as the main source of income. The difference in dependency on NIM will affect a bank's rate of charged NIM to its customers.

Figure 1 shows that Indonesia has consistently provided the highest NIM during this study's period, followed by the Philippines, while Malaysia, Singapore and Thailand have relatively low and constant NIM. So, it will be intriguing to discover what variables influenced these differences of NIM among South East Asian countries.

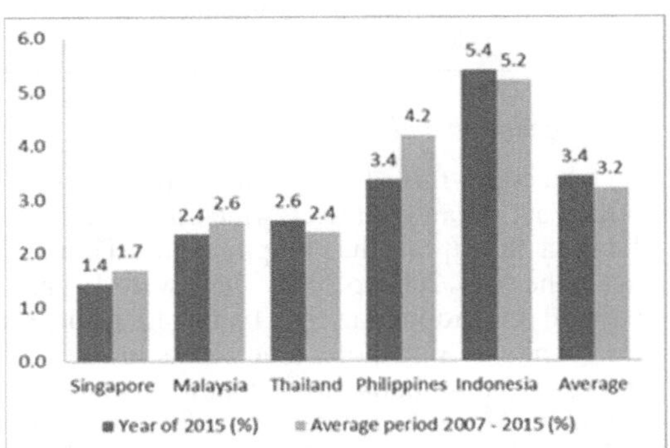

Figure 1. NIM data on five South East Asian banks for the year 2015 and the average in period 2007–2015.

Many previous researches have tried to outline NIM's determinants, with various countries and periods as objects. Those determinants can be categorized into three main factors, which are bank-specific, industry and macroeconomics factors. Those main factors have been researched independently, but not many have researched all three factors. One of those few was conducted by Islam and Nishiyama (2016) on the determinants of NIM in four South East Asian countries during 1997–2015. Its result showed that liquid assets, equity, required reserve and operational expenses, as bank-specific factors, impact NIM positively. Whereas both the bank's size and industry concentration have a negative influence. For the three variables from the macroeconomics factors tested, which were inflation, short-term interest rate and economic growth, this showed that only GDP growth affects NIM negatively and significantly.

Based on the background elaborated above, this research aims to see whether bank-specific factors, which consist of relative size, credit risk, liquidity, capital adequacy, operational risk and diversification; industry factors, which are represented by industry concentration; and macroeconomic factors, which consist of short-term interest rate volatility, inflation, PDB growth and stock market capitalization, influenced NIM in the five South East Asian countries, Indonesia, Malaysia, Thailand, Singapore and the Philippines, during 2007 to 2015. These five countries are chosen because their total banking assets are a combined worth of US$ 3.417 billion, representing 89% of the total South East Asian banking assets.

2 LITERATURE ON DETERMINANTS OF NET INTEREST MARGIN

2.1 *Net interest margin*

This research defines NIM according to Islam and Nishiyama (2016), which is the difference between interest income and cost divided by the bank's total assets to know the bank's net interest earning asset ability. Saunders (1997) investigated seven developed countries during 1988–1995 to see the effect of macroeconomic factors on the NIM acquired by banks. The result showed that the adjustment of reserve requirement from the central bank has a positive and significant relationship with NIM, where banks are exposed to the opportunity cost of reserves and set a higher loan rate to compensate. Saunders also found that a 1% increase in the short-term interest rate will see the NIM also surge by 0.2%.

Fungacova and Poghosyan (2008) stated that a trade-off occurred between a bank's net interest margin and economic growth. The higher the margin that banks charged, the fewer the loans disbursed, which was caused by higher loan interest rates, and this will affect economic growth from either consumption or real sectors driven by bank loans. But, on the other hand, banks need higher margins to strengthen their capital and act as a buffer from any possible external shocks.

Valverde (2007) researched seven European countries during 1994–2005 and found that credit, liquidity and operational risks affect NIM positively and significantly. This is explained by the fact that banks can reassign the cost from those risks to customers by setting a higher loan rate and a lower deposit rate. Meanwhile, diversification has a negative effect towards NIM, caused by non-interest income that can replace a bank's interest revenue.

The banking industry has been regulated strictly because of its important role in the economy and mostly has an oligopoly market system where it is dominated by a few big players. Four Indonesian banks own 46% of the industry's assets, while Singapore's three main banks dominate the industry by a staggering 78%.

There are many internal bank-specific factors that are determinants of NIM, such as a bank's relative size, credit risk, liquidity, capital adequacy, operational risk and income diversification. Industry factors are represented by industry competition or concentration that is measured with the Herfindahl Index. Macroeconomic factors that can influence NIM consist of short-term interest rate volatility, inflation rate, GDP growth and stock market capitalization from each country. These bank-specific, industry and macroeconomic factors are expected to comprehensively explain NIM.

3 RESEARCH METHODS

3.1 *Research model*

$$
\begin{aligned}
NIM_{i,j,t} = {} & c + \beta_1 RLSZ_{i,j,t} + \beta_2 NPL_{i,j,t} \\
& + \beta_3 LQTA_{i,j,t} + \beta_4 ETA_{i,j,t} + \beta_5 EXP_{i,j,t} \\
& + \beta_6 NII_{i,j,t} + \beta_7 HHI_{j,t} + \beta_8 VOL_{j,t} \\
& + \beta_9 INF_{j,t} + \beta_{10} PDB_{j,t} + \beta_{11} KAP_{j,t} + \varepsilon.
\end{aligned} \tag{1}
$$

3.2 *Variables*

Table 1. Description of variables used in the study.

Variable	Description
Dependent variable	
NIM	Difference between interest income and interest expense over total assets
Bank-specific independent variable	
RLSZ	Total assets of a bank compared to the country's banking industry assets
NPL	Non-performing loan to outstanding loan ratio
LQTA	Liquid assets to total assets ratio
ETA	Equity to total assets ratio
EXP	Operational expenses to gross income ratio
NII	Non-interest expense less non-interest revenue to total assets ratio
Industry-specific independent variable	
HHI	Sum of squared market share of bank in a country
Macroeconomics independent variable	
VOL	Annual standard deviation of monthly average of overnight interbank money market rate
INF	Annual inflation rate
PDB	Annual GDP growth
KAP	The value of stock market capitalization compared to the amount of money deposited in banks

3.3 *Population and sample*

The object of this study is the banking in five South East Asian countries, which are Indonesia, Malaysia, Singapore, the Philippines and Thailand, during the years 2007 to 2015. There were 21 banks observed in Indonesia, five banks in Malaysia, three banks in Singapore, nine banks in the Philippines and nine banks in Thailand, with a total sample of 47 banks across South East Asia. The banks used in this study should fulfill certain criteria, which are conventional commercial, non-sharia banks, own financial reports for every 31st

December, and already listed in its respective country's stock market.

4 RESULTS

The bank-specific data are obtained from each bank's financial report. For industry and macroeconomic data, these are attained through each country's central bank report and the World Bank. Table 2 confirms this study's background on the difference of each South East Asian country's NIM. The average NIM for the South East Asian area is 3.33%, in which Indonesia claims the highest NIM among these five countries with an average of 4.34%, followed by Thailand with 2.81% and the Philippines with 2.73%. Malaysian banks accomplish an average NIM of 2.1% and Singaporean banks have the lowest NIM with 1.31%.

The regression model used in this study has fulfilled all of the classical assumption tests for regression in which the data have been normally distributed, free from any symptoms of autocorrelation, heteroskedasticity and multicollinearity. H_0 proposed in this study means that there are no significant relationship between certain independent variable and NIM as the dependent one, and vice versa for H_1. This study uses a significance rate of 5%, so, if the regression result shows a significance of below 5% then H_0 is rejected and H_1 is accepted, and vice versa. Each independent variable will be discussed separately for its effect on NIM as a dependent variable for each country and South East Asia as whole.

NIM in Indonesian banking shows that it is significantly affected by relative size, liquidity, capital adequacy, operational risk and diversification. Meanwhile, the Malaysian banking industry indicates that relative size, credit risk, liquidity, capital adequacy, industry concentration and stock market capitalization affects NIM significantly.

Table 2. Descriptive statistics result for South East Asian banks.

	NIM	RLSZ	NPL	LQTA	ETA	EXP	NII
MEAN	0.033	0.070	0.032	0.105	0.106	0.335	0.014
MAX	0.094	0.375	0.161	0.326	0.248	0.877	0.056
MIN	0.010	0.001	0.002	0.008	0.000	0.123	0.001
STDEV	0.014	0.073	0.025	0.064	0.031	0.092	0.008

	HHI	VOL	INF	PDB	KAP
MEAN	0.064	0.394	4.378	5.000	1.176
MAX	0.152	1.112	11.060	15.240	2.471
MIN	0.007	0.006	–0.895	–1.514	0.507
STDEV	0.030	0.341	2.806	2.267	0.360

Independent variables that significantly affect Thailand's NIM are credit risk, liquidity, diversification and industry concentration.

Whereas Singaporean banks exhibit their NIM as being significantly affected by relative size, liquidity, capital adequacy, operational risk and diversification, NIM in the Philippines is significantly affected by credit risk and liquidity only. For South East Asian banking overall, NIM is significantly affected by relative size, credit risk, capital adequacy, diversification, industry concentration, short-term interest rate volatility and stock market capitalization.

The result of regression analysis on these five countries, and on South East Asia as a whole, shows the relationship of NIM with 11 independent variables, with six of them being bank-specific ones consisting of relative size, credit risk, liquidity, capital adequacy, operational risk and diversification; industry concentration is the only industry-specific variable. Four macroeconomics variables, which are short-term interest rate volatility, inflation, GDP growth and stock market capitalization, are detailed in the table on the next page.

Relative size shows a significant and positive effect towards NIM in Indonesia and Singapore, a significant and negative effect in Malaysia and the South East Asia region, but it is insignificant in Thailand and the Philippines. This result matches the banking system in each country, where Indonesian and Singaporean banks are an oligopoly market, where three to four major banks hold more than 50% of the industry assets. Four major banks own 54% of Indonesia's banking assets, while Singapore's three major banks account for 78% of the assets of their industry. Meanwhile, the three other countries and the region itself have no major player that dominates the industry. It is proven that a bigger bank can claim higher NIM for governing the market.

Credit risk is affecting NIM negatively and significantly in Thailand and the South East Asia region, and this can be explained by the fact that Thailand's banks hold the highest NPL ratio among other countries by 4.42%, resulting in detrimental effects on interest revenue and the banks' profit margins. Meanwhile, Malaysian and Philippine banks show a positive and significant relationship between NIM and credit risk. This is caused by these banks still being heavily dependent on NIM as a source of income, so the higher risk possessed by their loans will be transferred back as higher margins to their customers.

Most observations show that liquidity affects NIM positively, with the exception of the Philippine banks, which display a negative and significant result. This uniqueness is equivalent to the highest LQTA ratio in the Philippines as proxy for liquidity in the data collected. Bangko Sentra Ng Pilipinas, as its central bank, has set a bigger required reserve after the incidents in 2011 and 2012, when a massive shock hit the Philippine banks and forced 53 banks to go bankrupt. Even some major and old banks, such as Banco Pilipino (operating since 1964), Next Genesis Bank and Philippines Saving Bank, were closed or merged with other banks. This was caused by shortness in liquidity and internal fraud that had been ignored by the central banks for too long. Since then, Bangko Sentra Ng Pilipinas has undergone some major restructuring and improved the quality of Philippine banks. For the other four countries and the region, liquidity shows a positive effect towards NIM, which supports the results of Valverde and Fernandez's (2007) study, where the higher liquidity kept by banks allows them to set higher NIM for lowering the liquidity and solvency risk to their depositors.

All results for capital adequacy exhibited a positive relationship to NIM, in accordance with Fungacova and Poghosyan's (2008) study, which explained that the stronger the capital position owned, the less bankruptcy risk possessed by the banks, so they will be able to charge a higher risk premium to customers. Operational risks also indicated a constant and positive result in all of the countries researched. This agrees with Islam and Nishiyama (2016), who explained that all operational costs and risks will simply be switched as a higher profit margin for banks. But operational risk is only significant in Indonesia, while in the other countries it is not. This can be explained by the conventional banking system employed in Indonesia, which still relies heavily on ATM and branch service across the archipelago and does not maximize e-banking, unlike other countries.

Diversification affected NIM negatively in all of the observations. This result accords with Trinugroho's (2014) study, which found that diversification is a cross-subsidization strategy and results in a lower NIM being required with a higher rate of diversification. Even though this variable has the same direction, it differs in its significance across countries. Indonesia, Thailand, Singapore and the South East Asia region show a significant effect, but Malaysia and the Philippines do not. The significance dissimilarity can be traced from the proportion of NIM and NII across the countries, as shown in Table 4.

Table 3. Regression result.

Variable	Indonesia	Malaysia	Thailand	Singapore	Philippines	South East Asia region
Constanta	−0.031	0.039*	0.041*	0.023*	0.025*	0.032*
	(0.186)	(0.000)	(0.000)	(0.000)	(0.000)	(0.000)
Relative size	0.103*	−0.013**	−0.003	0.009**	0.003	−0.051*
	(0.000)	(0.026)	(0.761)	(0.048)	(0.788)	(0.000)
Credit risk	−0.040	0.051*	−0.069*	−0.004	0.055*	−0.039*
	(0.199)	(0.002)	(0.000)	(0.924)	(0.002)	(0.004)
Liquidity	0.034*	0.023*	0.170*	0.011	−0.024*	0.012***
	(0.001)	(0.007)	(0.002)	(0.148)	(0.002)	(0.063)
Capital adequacy	0.139*	0.067*	0.009	0.024	0.003	0.039*
	(0.000)	(0.009)	(0.592)	(0.301)	(0.835)	(0.001)
Operational risk	0.067*	0.00003	0.011***	0.000	0.003	0.004
	(0.000)	(0.996)	(0.057)	(0.977)	(0.560)	(0.320)
Diversification	−0.279*	−0.210	−0.294*	−0.224**	−0.029	−0.162*
	(0.000)	(0.272)	(0.000)	(0.030)	(0.570)	(0.001)
Industry concentration	0.623***	−0.020*	−0.085**	−0.550*	0.020	−0.027**
	(0.084)	(0.006)	(0.011)	(0.000)	(0.559)	(0.043)
Short-term interest rate volatility	0.000	−0.002	0.002	0.004*	−0.001	0.008*
	(0.926)	(0.287)	(0.464)	(0.004)	(0.729)	(0.000)
Inflation	0.00001	−0.001	0.000	0.000*	0.000	0.000*
	(0.954)	(0.185)	(0.176)	(0.000)	(0.255)	(0.000)
GDP growth	0.001	0.000	0.00007	0.00002	0.000	0.000
	(0.577)	(0.588)	(0.710)	(0.587)	(0.188)	(0.124)
Stock market capitalization	−0.003	−0.009**	−0.006	−0.002*	−0.003***	−0.007*
	(0.480)	(0.030)	(0.131)	(0.002)	(0.073)	(0.000)
R^2	0.604	0.761	0.620	0.903	0.608	0.607
Adjusted R^2	0.576	0.676	0.553	0.832	0.539	0.595

: Significant at 1%; **: Significant at 5%; *: Significant at 10%.*

Table 4. NIM and NII proportion comparison.

Country	%NIM	%NII
Indonesia	77,12%	22,88%
Malaysia	73,96%	26,04%
Thailand	68,87%	31,13%
Singapore	59,28%	40.72%
Philippines	59,13%	40.87%
South East Asian region	70.62%	29,38%

The industry-specific variable has the same effect as relative size, because they both use the comparison of a bank's assets with its industry in the respective country. Indonesia's and the Philippines' banking show a positive and significant effect towards NIM because there are more than 100 operating banks in each country, with a higher degree of competition among those banks. This is in line with Ho and Saunders (1981), in that the closer the market system is to a monopoly, the higher NIM it will be able to charge to customers. The anomaly happened in Singapore, where relative size had a positive effect, while industry concentration had an opposite one. Singaporean banks are highly competitive, with only three major banks dominating the industry and no banks able to set higher NIM. This is proven with the highest HHI score in Singapore among the other countries.

The movement of short-term interest rates has a positive and significant effect towards NIM in Singapore and the South East Asia region. This can be explained because the Singapore Interbank Overnight Rate (SIBOR) is mainly used as the standard for many securities and derivative transactions in Singapore, not only for conventional banking; as such, it greatly affects NIM in Singapore. The contrast is shown in Indonesia, where it has no effect on its NIM because it has the highest average volatility. If it is too volatile, banks can not anticipate its movement and redistribute its effect on NIM. Indonesia is also dominated by conventional banking, as mentioned in the background of this study.

Inflation shows a positive effect in all of the observations, but it is only significant in Singapore and the South East Asia region and is insignificant in the other countries observed. This result matches with Demirgüç-Kunt and Huizinga (1999), who stated that the government of a country will try to subdue inflation by increasing its interest rate and this will affect banks to set a higher NIM.

All observations showed an insignificant result for the effect of GDP growth towards NIM. It is a relief to see that South East Asian banks are resilient to shocks in macroeconomics because, in some of the years observed, recession occurred. Even if the GDP is decreasing, banks are still able to make a positive NIM. A strong and resilient banking system will support continuous economic growth, both from its financial and real assets.

Table 5. Stock market data for South East Asia in 2015.

Country and region	Stock market capitalization (Billions USD)	Comparison of stock market capitalization to GDP (%)
Indonesia	347	41
Malaysia	380	129
Thailand	368	81,7
Singapore	639	218,6
Philippines	238	88,3
South East Asia	2.022	78,4

The last variable observed is the capitalization of the stock market. All of the observations have confirmed that the stock market acts as a substitution for banks, meaning that companies are no longer dependent on banks for fresh funds. Companies have other options by issuing securities through the capital market. The role of the capital market as a bank's competitor will restrain a bank's ability to charge higher NIM in order to attract companies requesting loans.

Table 5, below, shows the data of each country's observed capital market in 2015, collected from the World Bank.

Table 5 strengthens this study's finding that the more significant the result, the higher the country's ratio of stock market capitalization to GDP. The least significant countries are Indonesia and Thailand, which matches the lowest ratio and signifies the much-needed development of the stock market in both countries.

The model used in this study has a particularly high goodness of fit score or R2. This model has successfully explained 60.7% of variability in NIM movements in the South East Asia region. The highest R2 score belongs to Singapore and it can be interpreted that the model only missed less than 10% of NIM's variability in Singapore.

5 CONCLUSION

Based on the study conducted in 47 commercial banks across five South East Asian countries during 2007–2015, it can be concluded that the bank-specific factors that significantly affect NIM in the region are relative size, credit risk and diversification inversely, while capital adequacy has a positive effect. Industry concentration also has a negative and significant effect towards NIM. The macroeconomic factor that has a positive and significant effect towards NIM is short-term interest rate volatility, while stock market capitalization has an inversely significant effect. Capital adequacy, operational risk and GDP growth affect NIM positively in all of the countries observed, but they differ in their significance rate. However, diversification and stock market capitalization are inversely affecting NIM, only differing in their significance rate among those observed countries.

The differences in the required return set by banks from their lending and saving activities across the South East Asian countries are caused by the dissimilarity in economic conditions, government regulation, a bank's leniency to govern its internal system, diversification strategy and the financial services that banks are allowed to enact. This study would like to notify South East Asian banks to pay more attention towards a bank's relative size, default loans, capital adequacy and diversification strategy, which have a significant effect towards their NIM. Banks with persistent profit and return will help to strengthen the economic system of a country.

Lastly, capital markets and banks are financial intermediaries that could serve as complementary to each other and improve the respective country's economic condition. Nowadays, the role is still substitutionary when it should be complementary in order to acquire more comprehensive information on prospective debtors or issuers.

For future research, it is advised to add more observations caused by the limitations of sampling procedure in this study. The higher observation numbers will increase the model's reliability to explain NIM in banking.

REFERENCES

Almarzoqi, R. & Naceur, S. B. (2015). *Determinants of bank interest margins in the Caucasus and Central Asia* (IMF Working Paper no. 15/87). Retrieved from https://www.imf.org/en/Publications/WP/Issues/2016/12/31.

Angbazo, L. (1988). The determinants of bank interest margin: Default risk, interest rate risk and off balance sheet banking. *Journal of Banking and Finance, 21*, 55–87.

Athanasoglou, P. P., Brissimisa, S. N. & Delisc, M. D. (2008). Bank-specific, industry specific and macro economic determinants of bank profitability. *Journal of International Financial Markets, Institutions and Money, 18*, 121–136.

Busch, R. & Memmel, C. (2015). *Bank's net interest margin and the level of interest rates* (Bundesbank Discussion Paper 16), Deutsche Bundesbank Research Center.

Chansarn, S. (2014). Total factor productivity of commercial banks in Thailand. *International Journal of Business and Society, 15*(2).

Covas, F. B., Rezende, M. & Vojtech, C. M. (2015). *Why are net interest margins of large banks so compressed?* Retrieved from https://www.federalreserve.gov/econresdata/notes/feds-notes/2015/why-are-net-interest-margins-of-large-banks-so-compressed-20151005.html.

Demirgüç-Kunt, A. & Huizinga, H. (1999). *Determinants of commercial bank interest margin and profitability: Some international evidence*. Development Research Group, The World Bank Volume Agustus 1998.

Deorukhar, S. & Xia, L. (2015). *ASEAN: Deciphering the region's banking sector* (BBVA Research on Asia Banking Watch December 2015). Retrieved from. http://www.bbvaresearch.com.

Fungacova, Z. & Poghosyan, T. (2008). Determinants of bank interest margins in Russia: Does bank ownership matter? *Research in International Business and Finance, 24*.

Hawtrey, K. & Liang, H. (2008). Bank interest margins in OECD Countries. *Journal of Economic Finance, 19*, 249–260.

Ho, T. S. Y. & Saunders, A. (1981). The determinants of bank interest margin: Theory and empirical evidence. *Journal of Financial Quantitative Analysis, 16*, 581–600.

Islam, M. S. & Nishiyama, S. (2016). The determinants of bank net interest margin: A panel evidence from South Asian Countries. *Research in International Business and Finance, 37*, 501–514.

Kosmidou, K., Tanna, S. & Pasiouras, F. (2012). *Determinants of profitability of domestic UK commercial banks: Panel evidence from the period 1995–2010* (Economics, Finance and Accounting Applied Research, Working Paper Series), Coventry University Business School.

Maudos, J. & Guevara, J. F. (2004). Factors explaining the interest margin in the banking sectors of the European Union. *Journal of Banking and Finance, 28*, 2259–2281.

Saunders, A. & Schumacher, L. (1997). *The determinants of bank interest rate margins: An international study.* NYU Stern Department of Finance Working Paper Series. South East Asia Network for Development. 2015. AFAS on Financial Services. Retrieved from http://www.seanet.com/.

Torres, T. (2012). *Fiasco in our banks: What went wrong?* Retrieved from http://philstar.com/headlines/2012/09/15/849205.

Trinugroho, I. A. A. & Tarazi, A. (2014). Why have bank interest margins been so high in Indonesia since the 1997/1998 financial crisis? *Research in International Business and Finance, 32*, 139–158.

Valverde, S. C. & Fernandez, F. R. (2007). *The determinants of bank margins in European banking*. FUNCAS Department of Economics, University of Granada Spain.

Williams, B. (2007). Factors determining net interest margins in Australia: Domestic and foreign banks. *Finance Markets Institutions and Instruments*, 16(3), pp. 145–156.

Increasing Management Relevance and Competitiveness – Sukoco et al. (Eds)
© 2018 Taylor & Francis Group, London, ISBN 978-0-8153-7455-8

The effect of monetary policy and macroeconomic variables on foreign portfolio investment in Indonesia

N.F. Anne & R. Purwono
Universitas Airlangga, Surabaya, Indonesia

ABSTRACT: This study aims to identify and analyze the effect of monetary policy and macroeconomic variables on foreign portfolio investment in Indonesia. Liberalization and the integration of world financial markets encourages the movement of capital between countries, one of them in the form of portfolio investment. Foreign portfolio investment in Indonesia has a high volatility, which, in turn, may have negative consequences for the stability of the domestic financial market, so it needs to be analyzed in order to establish the determinants of the movements of foreign portfolio investment. This study used time series data from July 2005 to December 2015. The variables used consist of external variables (push factor) and domestic variables (pull factor) and the analytical method used is Structural VAR (Vector Auto Regression). The results showed that foreign portfolio investment responds significantly to changes in the federal funds rate and the Bank Indonesia rate, while, on the other hand, foreign portfolio investments respond, but not significantly, to changes in the real effective exchange rate, the Industrial Production Index, the Composite Stock Price Index, and the Dow Jones Industrial Average. Results of the forecast error variance decomposition state that the federal funds rate gives the largest contribution of the external variables (push factor) to changes in foreign portfolio investments in Indonesia.

Keywords: Monetary Policy, Macroeconomic Variables, Foreign Portfolio Investment in Indonesia, SVAR

1 INTRODUCTION

The era of financial market integration, both nationally and globally, has been very dynamic, especially as it is supported by financial liberalization, technological progress, and globalization. The movement of capital between countries is generally realized in the form of foreign direct investment and foreign portfolio investment. Foreign portfolio investment has different characteristics from foreign direct investment, which is more volatile and sensitive to the factors that influence it, so it is better known as "hot money", where the flow of foreign funds can go in and out with movements and amounts that have high volatility (Waqas et al., 2015).

The increasing liquidity of the global market allows the flow of foreign capital to not only enter developed countries, but also to make emerging markets an investment destination. One of these is Indonesia. The phenomenon of foreign capital inflows into the country gives, on the one hand, a positive impact on capital market liquidity increase, but, on the other hand, the Indonesian economy becomes more vulnerable to shocks that come from investor sentiment, which is capital outflows, and this can cause economy instability.

The movement of foreign investment flows is influenced by two factors: the push factor and the pull factor. The push factor is a factor that encourages investors' decisions to transfer their capital to a country. The pull factor is a condition that attracts investors to invest in a country. As in the research of Kim (2000) and Byrne and Fiess (2011), it is explained that the decline in both interest rates and the economic growth of developed countries is a push factor, whereas, in research by the World Bank (1997) and Felicies and Orskaug (2008), it was found that the stock index, domestic reserves and a country's credit ratio are pull factors.

There are several studies that discuss the analysis of the determinants of foreign portfolio investment, with case studies in several countries. Garg and Pami (2014) examined the determinants of foreign portfolio investment in India, while Kaya and Ondes (2013) discussed the same topic using Turkish case studies, Chaudry et al. (2014) used Pakistan as a case study and Ekeocha et al. (2012) used Nigeria. This study examines the same topics as the determinants of foreign investment portfolios with different combinations of variables as determinants.

This research is different from previous research, using the case study of Indonesia during the period 2005: Q3-2016: Q2. The monetary policy used in this study is the BI rate and the macroeconomic variables in this study are the Jakarta Composite Index (IHSG), Real Effective Exchange Rate (REER), Industrial Production Index (IPI), federal funds rate and the Dow Jones Industrial Average (DJIA). It is viewed from both the external and domestic side, in other words, as both the driving factor (foreign factor) and the pull factor (domestic factor) of six variables. Federal funds interest rates and the DJIA are driving factors. The BI rate, IHSG, REER and IPI are not towing factors. The research method used is Structural VAR. This model is expected to explain the impulse response and the estimated variation of variance decomposition due to the movement of foreign portfolio investment in Indonesia as a shock to monetary policy and macroeconomic variables for the period 2005: Q3-2016: Q2.

2 LITERATURE REVIEW

Waqas et al. (2015) examine the effect of macroeconomic factors on the volatility of foreign portfolio investment flows using case studies of four South Asian countries, China, India, Pakistan and Sri Lanka. The method used is Generalized Autoregressive Conditional Heteroskedasticity (GARCH) to measure the volatility of high volatility foreign portfolio investment flows. The results shown may vary by country, however, all macroeconomic factors affect the volatility of foreign portfolio investment in China, except for interest rates; India is significantly influenced by inflation, FDI, interest rates and the stock price index; and in Pakistan, exchange rates and inflation have a significant effect. Meanwhile, in Sri Lanka, only economic growth, industrial production growth and stock price indexes have a significant effect.

Garg and Pami (2014) examine the related determinants of foreign portfolio investment flows in India using the Autoregressive Distributed Lag (ARDL) model. The results suggest that India can attract foreign portfolio investment by maintaining increased economic growth, lowering exchange rate volatility through currency intervention and by making their domestic financial market performance less vulnerable to global shocks by expanding the domestic investor base in financial markets.

Ekeocha et al. (2012) aimed to analyze the determinants of foreign portfolio investment flows in Nigeria for the period 1981–2010. Using the Vector Error Correction Model (VECM) method, they show that foreign portfolio investment correlates positively in the long term with market capitalization and the degree of transparency.

Kaya and Ondes (2013) examined the associated determinants of portfolio investment in Turkey from 1998 to 2010 using the Ordinary Least Square (OLS) method. The research consisted of many independent variables. The result was that the balance of trade, with a positive correlation, negative interest rate, positive consumer price index, and trade deficit, has a significant negative effect, and financial transparency, with positive investigation, a positive stock price index and significant negative economic risk, has a significant negative financial risk.

Chaudry et al. (2014) examined the same aspects as previous studies of factors affecting portfolio investment, but using Pakistani case studies from 1981–2012. The method used is OLS, while the independent variables used are market capitalization, trade openness, return on deposit rates, money supply (M2) and FDI. The results obtained showed that foreign portfolio investment is only influenced by market capitalization and is significantly positive, and the level of positive yield and FDI yield is significant with a negative relationship.

Saraogi (2008) used an Indian case study for the 2001–2007 period to see the determinants of foreign portfolio investment. The methods used are GLS and OLS. The results of the study found that investment in rising portfolios influenced by the Bombay Stock Exchange (BSE) was positively significant, the US stock indices were DJIA significant negative, the investment risk level in is significant, and the level of risk of investing in other countries is negatively significant.

Vita and Kyaw (2007) examined the determinants of the movement of investment to developing countries. Using the Structural VAR (SVAR) method in their research, the analysis focused on Impulse Response Function (IRF) and Variance Decomposition (VD). The variables defined as determinants of foreign portfolio investment are foreign output, foreign interest rate, domestic productivity and domestic money supply. The resulting IRF result, related to the foreign portfolio investment response, showed that foreign outputs generally have a negative effect, the interest rate generally gives a positive influence, and domestic productivity generally has a negative effect. The results of VD analysis are that foreign output and domestic productivity, while they influence the money supply and foreign interest rate, are not dominant.

3 METHODOLOGY

3.1 *Sampling and data collection*

The type of data used in this study is secondary data. Secondary data is data that is obtained indirectly, because the data already exists and can be obtained through publications or documentary data, either published or unpublished. The secondary data used are quarterly data comprising of Foreign Portfolio Investment (FPI), BI rate, IPI, REER, Jakarta Composite Index (IHSG), DJIA, and the Federal Funds Rate (FFR) for 2005: Q3-2016: Q2.

The sources of secondary data used in this study are, among others, FPI data taken from the official website of the International Monetary Fund (IMF), BI rate obtained from the official website of SEKI Bank Indonesia, IPI data obtained from the official website of the Central Bureau of Statistics (BPS), REER data obtained from the official website of the Bank of International Settlements, IHSG obtained from the official website of the Financial Services Authority, and FFR and DJIA obtained from the official Federal Reserve Economic data website.

3.2 *Variables measurement*

Foreign portfolio investment is foreign investment in the form of financial assets, such as stocks, bonds, and other commercial letters (Krugman et al., 2012). The foreign portfolio investment variables data in this study are in millions of USD. The interest rate of Bank Indonesia is the benchmark interest rate, commonly referred to as the BI rate, and is the policy rate reflecting the monetary policy stance. The interest rate or BI rate is obtained by using percentage units. The Jakarta Composite Index is a number that is a measure of the capital market situation, in other words, the value used to measure the combined performance of all shares listed on the stock exchange. JCI in this study uses the index unit.

REER is measured using the weighted average value of the domestic exchange rate against several major currencies that are converted to index numbers using the base year then adjusted to the price/inflation rate. REER in this study uses the index unit. The FFR is the interbank interest rate as a bank loan and the borrowing fee placed by commercial banks to the US central bank in overnight duration. The US interest rate uses a percentage unit. DJIA is the index used to measure the performance of industrial components in the American stock market. Dow Jones Industrial Average, commonly called DJIA, uses the index unit. IPI is an index that describes the development of production in the previous manufacturing sector. The index of industrial production is obtained from the survey results of large and medium industries. The IPI unit is the index.

3.3 *Econometric model*

The model used in this research is SVAR, which is a development of the VAR model. The VAR model has been criticized by various experts and researchers, primarily regarding the economic essence contained in the system, unless there is a strong theoretical foundation to justify the restriction. Because of this weakness, the SVAR model is also known as the theoretical VAR and is used as the estimation model in this study.

In this research, there are seven variables used with the SVAR model: BI Rate (BIR), IPI, IHSG, REER, DJIA, FFR, and FPI. Furthermore, based on the seven variables, it can formulate the vector of endogenous variables as follows:

$$X_t = [\text{FFR, DJIA, BIR, IPI, REER, IHSG, FPI}] \tag{1}$$

Based on the use of seven variables, as described earlier, the SVAR research in this study can be denoted as follows:

$$A_0 X_t = A(L) X_{t-1} + B_{\epsilon_t} \tag{2}$$

X_t = Vector with seven variables used
A_0 = Contemporaneous relation between variables
$A(L)$ = Finite-order matrix polynominal with operator lag L
ϵ_t = Vector structural disturbance
B = Matrix with non-zero diagonal

referring to the theory of economics and research of the precursor to the contemporaneity of structural parameters. The SVAR model mentioned above can be formulated as follows:

$$\begin{bmatrix} \varepsilon ffr \\ \varepsilon ldjia \\ \varepsilon bir \\ \varepsilon lipi \\ \varepsilon lreer \\ \varepsilon lihsg \\ \varepsilon lfpi \end{bmatrix} = \begin{bmatrix} 1 & 0 & 0 & 0 & 0 & 0 & 0 \\ A21 & 1 & 0 & 0 & 0 & 0 & 0 \\ A31 & 0 & 1 & 0 & 0 & 0 & 0 \\ A41 & 0 & A43 & 1 & 0 & 0 & 0 \\ A51 & 0 & A53 & A54 & 1 & 0 & 0 \\ A61 & A62 & A63 & A64 & A65 & 1 & 0 \\ A71 & A72 & A73 & A74 & A75 & A76 & 1 \end{bmatrix} \times \begin{bmatrix} \mu ffr \\ \mu ldjia \\ \mu bir \\ \mu lipi \\ \mu lreer \\ \mu lihsg \\ \mu lfpi \end{bmatrix}$$

Structural disturbance on the left side (t), as in the successive matrix, indicates $\in_{FFR}, \in_{LDJIA}, \in_{BIR}, \in_{LIPI}, \in_{LREER}, \in_{LIHSG}, \in_{LFPI}$ federal funds rate shock, DJIA, BI rate, IPI, REER, joint stock price index, and foreign portfolio investment. While the letter (μt) on the right side of the matrix is $\mu_{FFR}, \mu_{LDJIA}, \mu_{BIR}, \mu_{LIPI}, \mu_{LREER}, \mu_{LIHSG}, \mu_{LFPI}$ showing the residual shock (residual shock) of each variable.

4 RESULTS AND DISCUSSION

The SVAR model is a development of the atheoritical VAR model. SVAR is present as a restriction model, meaning that, in the SVAR model, the available variables are given restrictions according to the theoretical basis, so that the results of the SVAR estimation analysis can be analyzed and given restriction based on theories and aims of this study. This research is focused on the equation where foreign portfolio investment becomes a variable that is affected by the shock of other variables and the variable itself.

SVAR estimates are shown in Table 1, and also attachments for more detailed data results, indicating that the FFR, DJIA, BI rate, REER and Composite Stock Price Index are statistically significant on foreign portfolio investment. The FFR and DJIA give an influence with negative relations, and, vice versa, the BI rate, REER and Jakarta Composite Index have an influence with a positive relationship. For the IPI variable, this has a positive effect, but is not statistically significant. Evidence of the variables that give a significant influence can be seen from the value of a p-value below the level of significance of 5% and 10%, meaning that it has a significant effect. In this SVAR estimation, the analysis will only analyze the restriction of all variables on the model of the foreign portfolio investment variable. SVAR estimation results using STATA14 software are as follows:

Based on the IRF (Figure 1) after the first period, the shocks provided by the FFR were instantly responded to negatively by the foreign portfolio investment. The resulting conditions, as in Montiel and Reinhart (1999) and Byrne and Fiess (2011), indicate that the interest rate is regarded as the yield of capital investment carried out, so that, when the interest rate in another country is higher relative to a country (domestic), then the investor pours funds into a country with a higher yield. Furthermore, in the second period, the given response is positive. These results are the same as in Vita and Kyaw (2007), who found that, based on the impulse analysis of global interest rates, it responds positively,

Table 1. SVAR estimation results.

Variable	Coefficient	Std. Error	Z-statistic	P-value
FFR	–2,479112	1,343099	–1,85	0,065*
DJIA	–6.669634	0.0482105	–2.07	0.038**
BIR	0.3463345	0.1894432	1.83	0.068*
IPI	1.051535	3.010376	0.35	0.727
REER	0.0243923	0.0165782	–1.88	0.061*
IHSG	0.0254934	21.85613	2.44	0.015**

Description: 1%***, 5%**, 10*.

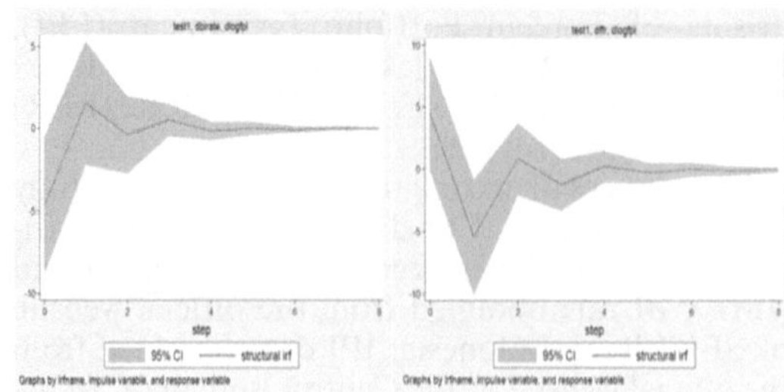

Figure 1. Response of foreign portfolio investment to shock of BI rate and federal funds rate.

then tends to fluctuate in some periods and return to the equilibrium point in the 6th period.

The IRF analysis (Figure 1) shows that, since the first foreign portfolio period, investment has been able to respond to BI rate shocks, and when there is a shock from the BI rate it will be positively responded to by foreign portfolio investment in the first period. Ghura and Godwin (2010) found that the higher the domestic interest rate, the more the global interest rate or the interest rate of another country will increase the foreign investment to the country. The foreign portfolio investment response to the BI rate shock turns into a negative response in the second period. In the third period it again gives a positive response, until after the fifth period of foreign portfolio investment response in Indonesia when it returns to its original balance. The results of IRF analysis also show a negative response. Waqas et al. (2015) conducted research in India and Pakistan and found that when interest rates rise, there is an increase in the volatility of foreign portfolio investment.

Based on the results of the IRF analysis (Figure 2), foreign portfolio investment since the first period has given a negative response. The DJIA is an indicator of US capital market performance so that, if the DJIA rises, then the US capital market is showing a good performance, and vice versa. So, when the DJIA rises, investors are interested in investing in US capital markets relative to other capital markets, so that the relationship is negative with the foreign portfolio investment in Indonesia (Rai & Bhanumurthy 2004; Indawan et al., 2013; Nugroho, 2014). Subsequently, having a positive response in the second period, the positive influence of the DJIA has implications for investor decision-making. The US stock market is the largest stock market and affects the world's stock markets so that, when the DJIA rises, then it influences most of the world's stock indices to also rise, and so serves as a signal increase in global and domestic stock market performance. After that it tends to fluctuate until it returns to the balance seen in the sixth period.

Based on the analysis of IRF shocks (Figure 2) provided by the JCI, it has also responded to foreign portfolio investment in Indonesia since the first period. In the first period of positive investment response, JCI is considered as an indicator of Indonesian capital market performance, so, primarily for investors who want to invest in the stock market, JCI is a signal. These results were also found by Rai and Banumurthy (2002), Richards (2002) and Egly et al. (2010) in their research. Further decline, in the second and third period of foreign portfolio investment consecutively, responded negatively. There are foreign investors who have a strategy to buy stocks

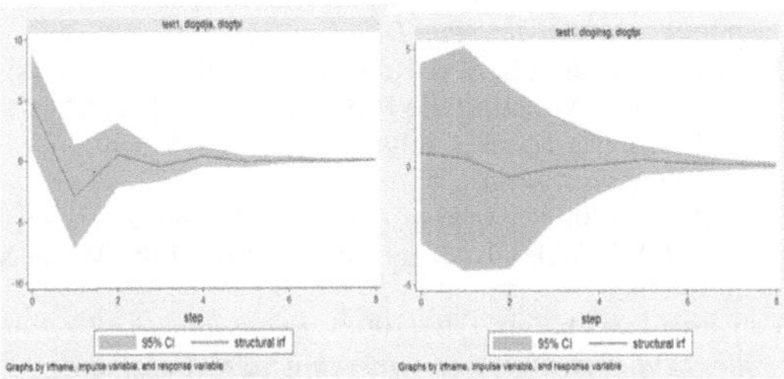

Figure 2. Response of foreign portfolio investment to shock of Dow Jones Industrial Average and Jakarta Composite Index.

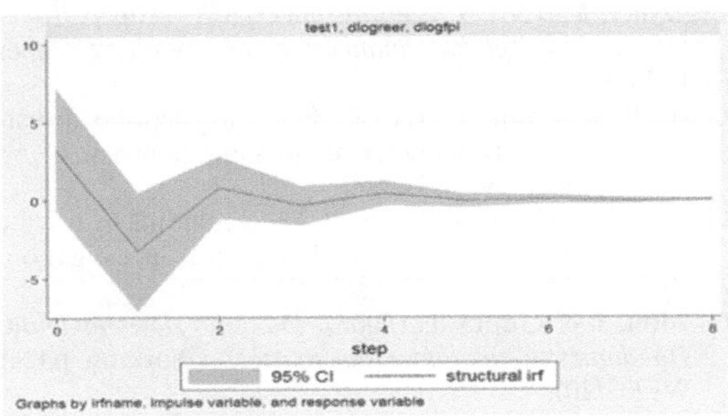

Figure 3. Response of foreign portfolio investment to shock of real effective exchange rate.

when prices are low (JCI goes down) by way of expecting high returns when JCI rises (Griffin et al., 2003). After that, the given response tends to be positive until it returns to the balance seen following the fifth period, when it starts to become stable.

Based on the IRF results (Figure 3), following the first period of shocks from REER, the response of foreign portfolio investment is negative. This action is caused by investors making profits and taking action so as to reduce (sell) their financial assets, which impacts on the decline of foreign portfolio investment (Waqas et al., 2015). Furthermore, Kandir (2008) stated that the exchange rate has a negative effect on portfolio investment as the depreciation of the rupiah exchange rate will increase the profit of export-based companies. The response of foreign portfolio investment to REER shocks up to the second period responded positively due to the belief in future rupiah stability, as in Garg and Pami's research (2014). It then fluctuates until reaching a balance at the start of the fifth period, which means foreign portfolio investment has not responded to REER shocks significantly.

In the changes of the contributions of innovative structural variables to foreign portfolio investment in Indonesia, with increasing periods until the eighth period, based on Table 2, It is seen that there is a major change in the contribution of each variable to foreign portfolio investment in Indonesia. If sorted according to the variable that gives the highest contribution to the variable that gives the lowest contribution in the eighth period then it gives 15.1% FFR, 9.5% DJIA, a BI rate of 7.2%, REER of 6.5% and JCI of 0.21%. The result of forecast error variance decomposition analysis shows that the push factor (external factor) on foreign portfolio investment in Indonesia has a more dominant influence compared with the pull factor (internal factor/domestic), which is reflected by the FFR and DJIA making a greater contribution when compared with other variables.

Table 2. Forecast error variance decomposition.

Period	FPI	BIR	FFR	IHSG	DJIA	REER
1	0,673481	0,091688	0,083784	0,001405	0,099013	0,044446
2	0,599633	0,07416	0,151068	0,001396	0,09818	0,065325
3	0,601884	0,072555	0,148972	0,001919	0,09614	0,065534
4	0,600063	0,072349	0,151585	0,001901	0,095747	0,065044
5	0,599728	0,072269	0,151401	0,001915	0,095798	0,06543
6	0,599562	0,072219	0,151524	0,002083	0,095755	0,065385
7	0,599525	0,072232	0,151503	0,002129	0,095742	0,065389
8	0,599485	0,072225	0,151537	0,002142	0,095746	0,065386

5 CONCLUSION AND RECOMMENDATIONS

The FFR, DJIA, BI rate, REER, and composite share price index significantly affect foreign portfolio investment in Indonesia. The IPI has no significant effect on foreign portfolio investment in Indonesia. The contribution of all of the variables to foreign portfolio investment increased during the eight-period analysis of forecast error variance decomposition, except for the BI rate. The contribution of the FFR shock was 15.54%, the DJIA was 7.44%, the BI rate was 7.23%, the REER was 6.62%, and the Composite Stock Price Index was 0.22%. It can be concluded that the overseas factor (push factor) gave the biggest shock to foreign portfolio investment in Indonesia, in line with the increase of the periods, compared to internal factors in the country (pull factor).

Considering that external factors have had a significant impact and contribution to foreign portfolio investment in Indonesia, based on the results of the research it is expected that policymakers will be able to find other solutions and alternatives that are offset by existing policies in order to allow domestic macroeconomic and monetary variables to be more stable and not too easily shaken by the movement of external factors, so that the flow of incoming and outgoing foreign funds does not fluctuate sharply, bringing further negative impact to the stability of financial markets in Indonesia. It is expected that further research can develop from this research by minimizing the existing limitations of the type of foreign investment portfolio in Indonesia, which is still lacking, and the addition of more variables could explain the foreign portfolio investment in Indonesia.

REFERENCES

Bakaert G. & Harvey, C. R. (2000). Capital flows and the behavior of emerging market equity returns. *Graduate School of Business, 1*(1), 1–81.

Bernanke, B. S. (1986). Alternative explanations of the money income correlation. *Cornegie Rochester Conferences Series on Public Policy, I*(25), 49–99.

Blanchard, O. & Johnson, D. R. (2006). *Macroeconomics.* United States of America: Pearson.

Byrne, J. P. & Fiess, N. (2011). International capital flows to emerging and developing countries: National and global determinants. Business School-Economics University of Glasglow, 4(2), 5–25.

Chaudry, I. S., Farook, F. & Mushtaq, A. (2014). Factors affecting portfolio investment in Pakistan: Evidence from time series analysis. *Pakistan Economic and Social Review, 52*(2), 141–158.

Cocris, V. & Nucu, A. E. (2013). Monetary policy and financial stability: Empirical evidence from Central and Eastern European countries. *Baltic Journals Economics, 13*(I), 75–98.

Culha, A. A. (2006). A structural VAR analysis of the determination of capital flow into Turkey. *Central Bank Review, 2*, 11–35.

Dornbusch, R., Fischer, S. & Starz, R. (2008). *Macroeconomics. Translated by: Roy Indra Mirazudin, SE.* Jakarta: PT. Media Global Edukasi.

Egly, P., Johnk, D. W. & Liston, D. P. (2010). Foreign portfolio investment inflows to the United States: The impact of investor risk aversion and US stock market performance. *North American Journal of Finance and Banking Research, 4*(4), 25–41.

Ekeocha, P., Ekeocha, C, S., Malaolu, V. A. & Oduh, M. O. (2012). Modelling the long run determinants of foreign portfolio investment in Nigeria. *Journal of Economics and Suistainable Development, 3*(8), 194–206.

Elfarij, A., Wahyudi, S. & Raharjo, S. T. (2016). Analysis of Factors Affecting the Flow of Foreign Investments in Indonesia Stock Exchange 2004–2015. *Universitas Diponegoro Journal, 5*(7), 1–20.

Enders, W. (2009). *Applied econometric time series* (3rd ed.). USA: Wiley International Edition: John Wiley & Sons, Inc.

Felicies, G. & Orskaug, B. (2008). *Estimating the determinants of capital flows to emerging market economies: A maximum likelihood disequilibrium approach* (Working Paper 354). Bank of England.

Forbes, K. J. & Warnock, F. E. (2011). *Capital flow waves: Surges, stops, flight, and retrenchment* (Working Paper 174351).

Fratzsher, M. (2011). *Capital flows, push versus pull factors and the global financial crisis* (Working Paper 17357).

Garg, R. & Pami, D. (2014). Foreign portfolio investment flows to India determinants and analysis. *World Development, 59*(1), 16–28.

Ghura, D. & Godwin, B. (2010). Determinants of private investment: A cross regional empirical investigation. *Applied Economics, 32*, 1819–1829.

Gordon, J. & Gupta, P. (2003). *Portfolio flows to India: Do domestic fundamentals matter?* (Working paper WP/03/20).

Gozgor, G. & Erzurumlu, Y. O. (2010). Causality relation between foreign direct investment and portfolio investment volatility. *Middle Eastern Finance and Economics, I*(8), 170–178.

Griffin. J. M, Nardari, F. & Stultz, R. M. (2003). *Daily cross border equity flows: Pushed or pulled?* (Working paper no. 9000).

Gujarati, D. N. & Porter, D. C. (2009). *Basic Econometrics* (5th ed.). New York: The McGraw-Hill Companies.

Handoyo, R. D., Jusoh, M. & Shah Zaidi, M. A. (2015). Impact of monetary policy and fiscal policy on Indonesian stock market. *Expert Journal of Economics, 3*(2), 113–126.

Indawan, F., Fitriani, S., Permata, M. I. & Karlina, I. (2013). Capital flows in Indonesia: The behavior, the role, and its optimality uses for the economy. *Bulletin of Monetary, Economics, and Banking, 13*(1), 1–20.

Jogiyanto. (2003). *Portfolio and Investment Theory and Applications.* First Edition. Yogyakarta: BPFE UGM.

Jogiyanto. (2013). *Portfolio Theory and Investment Analysis.* BPFE Yogyakarta. Sixth Edition. Yogyakarta.

Kandir, S. Y. (2008). An investigation of the invetsment choices of foreign investors in Turkey. *Journal of Accounting and Finance, 38*, 199–210.
Kaya, A. & Ondes, T. (2013). Determinants of foreign portfolio investment in Turkey. *The ISE Review, 13*(52), 17–37.
Kim, Y. (2000). Causes of capital flows in developing countries. *Journal of International Money and Finance*, 19(2), 235–253.
Krugman, P., Obstfeld, M. & Melitz, M. (2012). *International economics theory and policy.* England: Pearson Education Limited.
Lay, L. & Wickramanayake, J. (2007). Role of inward foreign portfolio investment in transition of Singapore to a hing income economy. First 25 years *The Icfai Journal of International Business, 2*(4), 55–108.
Mankiw, N. G. (2010). *Macroeconomics.* United States of America: Worth Publisher.
Markowitz, H. M. (1959). *Portofolio selection: Efficient diversification of investments. Cowles foundation monograph 16.* New York: John Wiley and Sons.
Mishkin, F. (2010). *The economics of money, banking, and financial market.* United States of America: Pearson Education.
Mishkin, F. S. & Eakins, S. G. (2012). *Financial markets and institutions.* United States of America: Pearson Education.
Montiel, P. & Reinhart, C. M. (1999). Do capital controls and macroeconomic policies influence the volume and composition of capital flows? Evidence from the 1990s. *Journal of International Money and Finance, 18*(4), 619–635.
Muntasir, Al. (2014). Cross border portfolio invetsment and the volatility of stock market index and Rupiah's rate. *Buletin Ekonomi Moneter dan Perbankan, 17*(4 L), 430–473.
Nugroho, M. N. (2014). The impact of capital reversal and the threshold of current account deficit to Rupiah. *Bulletin of Monetary and Banking, 14*(1), 315–367.
Parkin, M. (2010). *Macroeconomics.* United States of America: Pearson Education.
Rai, K. & Bhanumurthy, N. R. (2004). Determinants of foreign institutional investment in India: The role of return, risk, and inflation. *The Developing Economics, 15*(44), 479–493.
Richards, A. (2002). *Big fish in small ponds: The treading behaviour and price impact of foreign investor in Asian emerging equity markets* (Research Disscussion Paper 2004–2005). Sydney: Reserve Bank of Australia.
Salvatore, D. (2007). *International economics.* United States of America: John Wiley & Sons, Inc.
Saraogi, R. (2008). Determinants of FII inflows: India. *Munich Personal RePEc Archive, 22850*(5), 1–19.
Sims, C. A. & Zha, T. (2006). Macroeconomics and reality. *Econometrica, I*(48), 1–49.
Sunariyah (2006). *Introduction to Capital Market Knowledge.* Fifth Edition. UPP STIM YKPN, Yogyakarta.
Tandelilin, E. (2010). *Investment Analysis and Portfolio Management.* First Edition. Yogyakarta: BPFE.
The World Bank. (1997). *Private capital flows to developing countries: The road to financial integration* (World Bank Policy Research Report). USA: Oxford University Press.
Tobin, J. (1969). On stock market returns and monetary policy. *The Journal of Finance, 52*(2), 635–654.
Venska, D. A. K., Suhadak, & Handayani, S. R. (2014). The effect of global stock indexs (Dow Jones Industrial Average, Nikei 225, Hangseng, and Strait Times) on Jakarta composite index at Indonesian stock exchanges (Period of 2010–2012). *Journal Administrasi Bisnis, 9*(2) 205–234.
Vita, G. D. & Kyaw, K. S. (2007). Determinants of capital flows to developing countries: A structural VAR analysis. *Journal of Economic Studies, 35*(4), 304–332.
Waqas, Y., Haider, S., Muhammad, H. & Nazirb, I. (2015). Macroeconomics factor and foreign portfolio investment volatility: A case of South Asian countries. *Future Business Journal*, I (11) 305–350.

Increasing Management Relevance and Competitiveness – Sukoco et al. (Eds)
© 2018 Taylor & Francis Group, London, ISBN 978-0-8153-7455-8

Internal factors, external factors, and bank liquidity in Indonesia

I.M. Sudana & A.F. Akbar
Universitas Airlangga, Surabaya, Indonesia

ABSTRACT: This study aims to determine the influence of internal and external factors on bank liquidity in Indonesia. The measurement of liquidity in this study was done using two approaches, namely the ability of banks to meet the credit demand as measured by the assets to loans ratio (TA/TL), and the ability of banks to meet their obligations to depositors, measured by the liquid assets to deposits ratio (LA/Deposit). The study was conducted on a conventional commercial bank in Indonesia during the period from 2008–20014. This study used an unbalanced pool of data with 429 observations and used multiple linear regression analysis to determine the effect of internal and external factors on bank liquidity. The results of the analysis showed that capital adequacy, cost to income, the interest rate of JIBOR and GDP had a positive effect, but funding costs and credit risk had a negative effect on the bank's liquidity (TA/TL ratio). Capital adequacy, inflation and GDP growth had a positive effect, but funding cost, costs to income ratio and credit risk rate had a negative effect on the bank's liquidity (LA/Deposit).

1 INTRODUCTION

Banks are businesses that are formed of financial institutions which collect funds from people who have excess funds (surplus of funds), and distributed back to the community that lack funds (deficit of funds), as well as providing services. Banking services can be for profitable motives and social ones; i.e. improving the standard of living of the people. As intermediary institutions, banks should be able to manage the availability of the liquid assets owned, so there is no shortage or surplus funds. Banks with poor management of liquid assets will have difficulty in meeting the demands or withdrawals made by customers, which will affect their confidence. The management of liquid assets that are less good will cause idle funds which will lead to costs incurred by the bank greater than the revenue obtained, so the liquidity of banks is one aspect that is essential to run well for the smooth operation of the bank as a whole.

The Bank for International Settlements (2008) defines liquidity as the ability of banks to finance an increase in assets and to meet its obligations without incurring losses. The level of bank liquidity is an important concern, because the level of liquidity will affect the operations of a bank. As one of the parties that have an important role in the field of finance, the bank should pay attention to the current level of liquidity in order to avoid the risk of liquidity that could lead to bankruptcy.

Going from the data from the Directorate of Indonesian banks, the average liquidity of banks in Indonesia as measured by the ratio of total assets to total loans is in the amount of 159.74%, with the lowest value of 117.69% and the highest value reaching 277.17%. Liquidity is measured by comparing the amount of liquid assets held by the banks with third party funds showing an average value of 12.49%, with the lowest value of 4.13% and the highest value reaching 24.44%. Variations in the level of bank liquidity could be affected by the bank's internal factors, such as the adequacy of capital, credit risk, cost and operational efficiency, and external factors such as interest rates on the interbank money market, inflation and gross domestic product growth.

Roman and Sargu (2015), in a study of a bank's internal factors on the level of liquidity in banks in CEE countries, found that ROE has a positive effect on bank liquidity while the CAR, the impaired loans ratio, and funding costs negatively affected bank liquidity. Monteanu (2012) found different results where the CAR, impaired loans ratio, funding cost, inflation, interbank funding, and the unemployment rate had a positive effect on the liquidity of banks, while credit risk rate, cost to income and interbank interest rate had a negative effect on the liquidity of banks. Vodova (2012) found the results that CAR, credit risk rate, and inflation had a positive effect on liquidity, while interbank interest rate, unemployment rate, and ROE had a negative effect on bank liquidity. Asih (2012) found that BOPO had a negative effect on bank liquidity.

Based on this phenomenon, the problems examined in this study are whether internal factors (capital adequacy, funding cost, cost to income ratio, credit risk rate) and external factors (interest rate of JIBOR, inflation rate, GDP growth) have an effect on bank liquidity in Indonesia.

2 THEORETICAL AND HYPOTHESIS DEVELOPMENT

This study used two measures of liquidity. First, is the liquidity of banks to finance an increase in assets, and the second liquidity is used to measure the ability of the bank meet its obligations. The liquidity of banks in financing growth in their assets is measured by the ratio of total assets to total loans. The higher ratio result indicates that the banks have the ability to finance credit demands from the community, and vice versa. This is because even with the greater the amount of assets owned by banks compared to the loans that have been disbursed, there are still other assets that can be used to meet the credit demand by the debtor, such as cash, demand deposits at other banks, demand deposits at Bank Indonesia, and marketable securities.

Second, the liquidity of banks from the aspect of a bank's ability to meet its obligations is measured by ratio of liquid assets to deposits. The higher ratio result indicates the greater ability of the banks to meet their obligations to depositors if at any time they make a withdrawal. However, if this ratio is too high, it will reduce the bank's ability to generate profits, because the gains of investments in liquid assets will be relatively small.

The level of liquidity of a bank is influenced by several factors; factors are derived from the bank aka internal factors, and factors that come from outside the bank aka external factors.

2.1 *Capital adequacy*

Capital is money that comes from owners or shareholders plus the share premium and the results of operations that are derived from the direct operations of the bank (Hadinoto, 2008: 242). Sufficient capital will allow the bank to cover the assets that may be impaired as a result of bank losses caused by risky assets. The level of capital adequacy of a bank can be measured by using a capital adequacy ratio (CAR). A high capital adequacy ratio will increase the banks' ability to fund operations when there is a decline in value of their riskier assets, so that the operations of the bank to meet the demands for credit are not disturbed. In other words, the higher the CAR, the higher the liquidity of the banks, and vice versa. Research conducted by Vodova (2012), Roman and Sargu (2015), as well as Monteanu (2012) found that there is a positive effect to do with capital adequacy and bank liquidity.

H1: Capital adequacy has a positive effect on the liquidity of banks.

2.2 *Funding cost*

The cost of funds is the cost of the interest paid by banks on the overall funds raised from various sources. The cost of funds that should be covered by the bank for any funds raised from various sources, before deducting the mandatory minimum liquidity to be maintained by the respective banks (Siamat, 2004: 122). Cost of funds is measured by comparing the total interest expense divided by the total third-party funds collected by the bank. The higher the funding cost, the more the liquidity of banks will decrease, and vice versa. Roman and Sargu (2015) showed in their study results that funding costs negatively affect bank liquidity.

H2: Funding cost has a negative effect on the liquidity of banks.

2.3 *Cost to income ratio*

This ratio is used to measure the efficiency of the bank in conducting its operational activities (Dendawijaya, 2005: 120). The higher the cost to income ratio is, the more that the level of operational efficiency of the bank is getting worse. Poor operational efficiency makes banks tend to maintain a high level of liquidity to meet operational expenses so that the operations of the bank can keep running. Conversely, if the level of the efficiency or cost to income ratio is decreased, then the liquidity of the bank will also decrease, because they do not need to have large liquid assets to sustain their operations.

H3: Cost to income ratio has a positive effect on the liquidity of banks.

2.4 *Credit risk rate*

Credit risk is the risk of failure or the inability of the debtor to refund the amount of loans received from the banks and interest thereon in a predetermined time period (Siamat, 2004). One indicator of the magnitude of credit risk, is the amount of non-performing loans. Credit risk is measured by the ratio of non-performing loans divided by the total number of given loans.

The higher result of this ratio means a higher level of credit risk, which causes the level of bank liquidity to decline. Vodova (2012) found that credit risk had a negative effect on the level of bank liquidity.

H4: Credit risk rate has a negative affect the liquidity of banks in Indonesia.

2.5 *Interest rate of JIBOR*

Jakarta interbank offering rate (JIBOR) is the average rate indicative of unsecured loans, which is offered and is intended to be transacted by a bank to the bank's contributors. Vodova (2011) found that the interest rate on interbank transactions had a positive effect on the liquidity of banks.

H5: The interest rate of JIBOR has a positive effect on the liquidity of banks.

2.6 *Inflation rate*

Inflation according to Rosyidi (2014: 131) is a general price increase that is continuous in the economy. In other words, inflation is the decline in the purchasing power of a currency for goods and services. According to Downes & Goodman (1994) inflation is the rising prices of goods and services due to an increased demand for goods and services higher than the supply of goods and services available in the market. The higher the rate of inflation, so too will the risk of losses faced by banks be higher, so the banks are likely to increase their liquidity to guard against the possible risks faced. Monteanu (2012) showed that inflation has a positive effect on the liquidity of banks.

H6: Inflation has a positive effect on the liquidity of banks.

2.7 *Gross Domestic Product (GDP) growth*

Gross domestic product is the indicator used to assess a country's economy. The definition of GDP according to Mishkin (2011: 26) is the value of all final goods and services produced within a country in a given period. A better economic growth rate will create business opportunities and employment opportunities for the community, which will increase the income of the company and the community and will in turn impact on the decline in demand for credit. The higher the GDP growth, the higher the level of bank liquidity, and vice versa. Vodova (2012) found that real gross domestic product growth has a positive effect on bank liquidity.

H7: Real GDP growth has a positive effect on the liquidity of banks in Indonesia.

3 RESEARCH METHODS

The population used in this study was conventional commercial banks during the period 2008–2014. The sampling method used was the purposive sampling method. This study used unbalanced pool data. The analysis model used in this study was multiple regression analysis.

4 RESULTS AND DISCUSSION

Based on Table 1, the results showed that the variables of capital adequacy (CAR), cost to income ratio (CI), JIBOR, and GDP had a significant positive effect on the level of bank liquidity, while the variables of funding cost (FUND) and credit risk (CRISK) had a negative effect that was significant on the bank's liquidity as measured by the ratio of total assets to total liabilities (TA/TL). The rate of inflation (INF) had no effect on liquidity. Differences in the influence of the internal and external factors on liquidity occurs when the level of liquidity is measured by the ratio of liquid assets to total deposits (LA/Deposit). The variable cost to income ratio (CI) had a significant negative effect and inflation (INF) had a positive effect that was significant towards liquidity. The variable JIBOR had no effect on liquidity. The other variables that influenced were consistent with good liquidity as measured by the N/NE and LA/Deposit.

Table 1. Analysis of models and hypothesis testing.

	Liquidity (L1) = *TA/TL*		Liquidity (L2) = *LA/Deposit*	
Variable	Coefisien β	Sign	Coefisien β	Sign
(Constant)	78,968	0,000	13,383	0,000
CAR	0,932	0,000	0,033	0,017
FUND	–2,599	0,000	–0,288	0,000
CI	0,282	0,004	–0,046	0,000
CRISK	–1,317	0,003	–0,115	0,036
JIBOR	4,843	0,000	0,028	0,823
INF	–0,670	0,136	0,202	0,000
GDP	5,773	0,002	0,481	0,036
F(ANOVA)	**17,939**	**0,000**	**13,332**	**0,000**
$\mathbf{R^2}$	**0,230**		**0,181**	

Source: Data processing.

Capital adequacy has a significant positive effect on liquidity because the larger the bank's capital adequacy, the larger the ability of the banks to finance an increase in assets. The bank is therefore able to meet the demands for credit, and the ability of banks to anticipate losses from risky assets is increased, so that depositors do not withdraw funds that they do not have. The results are consistent with the research conducted by Monteanu (2012) who found the positive effect of capital adequacy on liquidity.

The cost of funds has a significant negative effect on the liquidity of banks in Indonesia. Due to the higher cost of funds, banks tend to reduce their liquidity, both in the bank's ability to finance an increase in assets or in the aspect of the bank's ability to meet their obligations to depositors. The greater cost of funds makes for a lower level of bank liquidity. The results are consistent with the research conducted by Roman and Sargu (2015) who found that funding costs negatively affect liquidity.

Cost to income ratio has a significant positive effect on bank liquidity in the aspect of the banks' ability to finance an increase in assets, and a negative effect on the liquidity of banks from the aspect of a bank's ability to meet its obligations to depositors. Cost to income ratio is a ratio used to measure the efficiency of the bank in conducting operations (Dendawijaya, 2005). A higher cost to income ratio will make banks less likely to hold liquid assets in large numbers because an investment in liquid assets has relatively small gains. They prefer to invest in productive assets to maintain profitability. The results are consistent with those found by Monteanu (2012).

Credit risk has a significant negative effect on liquidity. The greater the NPL ratio is, the bigger the growing number of problem loans that will reduce the value of the assets owned by the bank, thereby reducing the ability of the banks to meet the credit demands. The higher non-performing loans will make depositors assume that the bank's ability to meet its obligations will also decline, so that depositors will withdraw their funds from the bank which makes the level of the bank's liquidity decrease further. The results are consistent with the results of research conducted by Monteanu (2012) in that the credit risk negatively affects bank liquidity.

Interest rates on interbank offering rate Jakarta has a significant positive effect on bank liquidity from the aspect of the banks' ability to finance an increase in assets (L1), but has no significant positive influence on the liquidity of banks from the aspect of meeting their obligations to depositors (L2). Higher JIBOR magnifies tight liquidity among banks, so the banks will tend to lend in smaller amounts to keep the liquidity level. These results are consistent with the research conducted by Vodova (2011), who found that the interest rate on interbank transactions had a positive effect on the liquidity of the aspect of the banks' ability to finance growth in assets and had no effect on the liquidity of banks from the aspect of a bank's ability to meet its obligations to depositors.

Inflation does not have a significant negative effect on the liquidity of banks from the aspect of the banks' ability to finance an increase in assets (L1), and has a positive significant effect on the bank's liquidity from the aspect of the ability of banks to meet their obligations to depositors. These results are consistent with the research conducted by Monteanu (2012) who found that inflation does not affect the liquidity of banks from the aspect of the banks' ability to finance an increase in assets, and has a positive effect on the liquidity of banks from the aspect of a bank's ability to meet obligations to depositors.

Gross domestic product growth has a significant positive effect on the liquidity of banks in Indonesia. A better economic growth rate will create business opportunities and employment opportunities for the community, which will increase the income of the company and the community. Large public revenue will increase the amount of deposits going in to banks, and reduce the withdrawals from the depositors. The results of this study are consistent with the results found by Vodova (2012), in that gross domestic product growth has a positive effect on the liquidity of banks.

5 CONCLUSIONS

The results of the analysis showed that capital adequacy, cost to income, the interest rate of JIBOR and GDP has a positive effect, but funding cost and credit risk has a negative effect on a bank's liquidity (TA/TL ratio). Capital adequacy, inflation and GDP growth has a positive effect, but funding cost, costs to income ratio and credit risk rate has a negative effect on bank's liquidity (LA/Deposit).

The results indicate that the internal factors of CAR, funding cost and credit risk and external factor GDP has a consistent effect on both aspect of liquidity, but the internal factors of cost to income ratio, and external factors JIBOR and inflation have an inconsistent effect on both aspects of liquidity.

REFERENCES

Asih, B. 2012. Pengaruh Profitabilitas dan Tingkat Suku Bunga SBI terhadap Likuiditas Perbankan pada Bank Umum yang *Terdaftar di Bursa Efek Indonesia* (BEI) Periode 2009–2011.

Basel Committe on Banking Supervision. 2008. Liquidity Risk: Management and Supervisory Chalenges.

Dahlan, S. 2004. Manajemen Lembaga Keuangan. Edisi Keempat. Jakarta: Lembaga Penerbit Fakultas Ekonomi Universitas Indonesia,

Dendawijaya, L. 2005. *Manajemen Perbankan.* Edisi Kedua. Jakarta: Ghalia Indonesia,

Downes, J. & Goodman, J.E. 1994. *Kamus Istilah Keuangan dan Investasi.* Jakarta: PT. Elex Media Komputindo,

Hadinoto, S. 2008. *Bank Strategy on Funding and Liability/Treasury Management.* Jakarta: PT. Elex Media Komputindo.

Mishkin, F. S. 2011. *Ekonomi Uang, Perbankan, dan Pasar Keuangan.* Edisi 8 – Buku 1. Jakarta: Salemba Empat,

Munteanu, I. 2012. Bank Liquidity and Its Determinants in Romania. *Procedia Economics and Finance* 3 (2012): 993–998.

Rivai, V., Basir, S., Sudarto S. & Veithzal, A. P. 2013. *COMMERCIAL BANK MANAGEMENT* Manajemen Perbankan dari Teori ke Praktik. Jakarta: PT. Rajagrafindo Persada,

Roman, A. & Sargu, A.C. 2015. The Impact of Bank-Spesific Factors on The Commercial Banks Liquidity: Empirical Evidence from CEE Countries. *Procedia Economics and Finance* 20: 571–579.

Rosyidi, S. 2004. *Pengantar Teori Ekonomi Pendekatan Kepada Teori Ekonomi Mikro dan Makro.* Edisi Reisi. Jakarta: PT. Rajagrafindo Persada,

Samuelson, P.A. & Nordhaus, W.D. 2004. *Ilmu Makroekonomi.* Edisi Tujuh Belas. Terjemahan. Jakarta: PT. Media Global Edukasi,

Suyatno, T. M., Abdullah, D. T. A., Apono, J.T. Ananda, C.T.Y., & Chalik, H. A. 2005. *Kelembagaan Perbankan.* Edisi Ketiga. Jakarta: PT. Gramedia Pustaka Utama,

Vodova, P. 2011. Determinants of Commercial Banks' Liquidity in the Czech Republic. *International Journal of Mathematical Models and Methods in Applied Sciences* 6:1060–1067.

Vodova, P. 2012. Determinants of Commercial Banks' Liquidity in Poland. *Proceedings of 30th International Conference Mathematical Methods in Economics*: 962–967.

Increasing Management Relevance and Competitiveness – Sukoco et al. (Eds)
© 2018 Taylor & Francis Group, London, ISBN 978-0-8153-7455-8

The obstacles in developing Indonesia's sovereign *sukuk*

N. Laila, F.F. Hasib & M. Anshori
Universitas Airlangga, Surabaya, Indonesia

ABSTRACT: As sharia finance is growing in Indonesia, the sovereign *sukuk* has an important role in encouraging the growth of *sharia* finance. As a financial instrument, the sovereign *sukuk* is expected to enhance the government's capacity in infrastructure development. However, the development of the sovereign *sukuk* in Indonesia is relatively low compared to the global *sukuk* trend. This research study aims to find out the problems and the solutions in developing the sovereign *sukuk* in Indonesia. The method used in this research is a qualitative method using a case study. The research data is gathered from a literature review and in-depth interviews with Bank Indonesia, Islamic fiqh experts, academics, and practitioners. The results of this research are several strategies that can be used to enhance the development of the sovereign *sukuk* in Indonesia.

Keywords: Strategy Developing in Islamic Perspective; Sovereign Sukuk; Islamic Capital Market

1 INTRODUCTION

As the sharia finance industry grows in Indonesia, it also creates the concept of a sharia capital market and various related instruments. *Sukuk* is one of the instruments in the sharia capital market that is currently developing rapidly. In Indonesia, *sukuk* is commonly known as a sharia compliant bond. The Accounting and Auditing Organization for Islamic Financial Institution (AAOIFI) in the standard No.17 defines *sukuk* as securities of equal denomination representing an undivided share of an intangible asset, the value of the asset (*usufruct*), and the service or asset of a particular project/investment.

Nowadays, the issuance of *sukuk* is widely supported by various sharia finance institutions, so that there is rapid development in the aspects of issuing denominations and various structures of *sukuk*. There are currently various types of *sukuk* being developed, including hybrid *sukuk*, convertible *sukuk*, project financing *sukuk*, *sukuk* wakalah, and so on (IIFM, 2015). Sovereign *sukuk* in Indonesia does not only include *sukuk* issued by corporations, but also those published by the government. Moreover, the issuance of sovereign *sukuk* mostly encourages the development of the intersovereign *sukuk* market. In line with this, sovereign *sukuk* is used as one of the instruments of sovereign budget financing, which is in the form of government securities. As a sharia-based instrument, the issuance of sovereign *sukuk* requires the underlying asset to be either in the form of sovereign assets or a sovereign budget financing (*APBN/Anggaran Pembelanjaan Dalam Negeri*) project. In addition, it also requires sharia fatwa and opinion in each issuance.

The *sukuk* market began in 2002, when the Malaysian government issued *sukuk* worth $600 million, followed by Bahrain issuing sovereign *sukuk* with Ijarah and Salam contracts. The issuance of *sukuk* is centralized in the Middle Eastern countries incorporated in the Gulf Cooperation Countries (GCC), in addition to some Asian countries. According to the report by the Inter Sovereign Islamic Financial Market (IIFM, 2015), the 2012–2013 period has set the annual record for global *sukuk* issuance, which is in contrast to the 2014 period, when the *sukuk* market drastically decreased to over USD 100 billion, followed by the 2015 period, when the total global *sukuk* issuance was only about USD 60.6 billion, which drastically decreased by about 43% compared to the previous year, which can be seen in Figure 1 below.

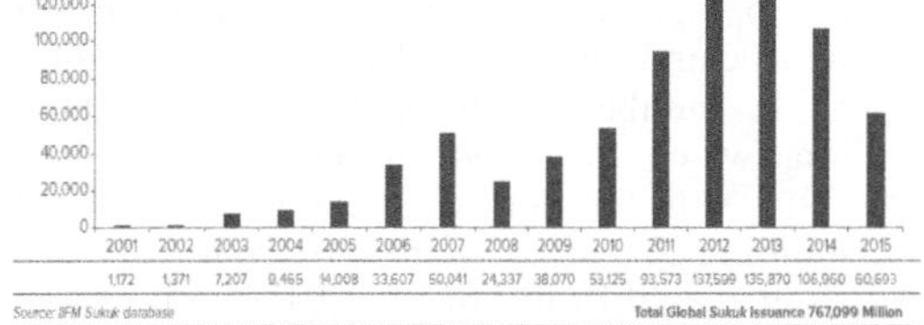

Figure 1. Total issuance of global *sukuk* 2001–2015.

Sukuk in Indonesia was first published in 2002 by PT. Indosat, which is a corporation based on a mudharabah contract with a value of USD 17.5 million. The subsequent issuances of *sukuk* were conducted in 2005 and 2007, both of which were based on ijarah contracts with a value of USD 28.5 million and USD 40 million respectively. Recently, the *sukuk* market has been dominated by the sovereign *sukuk* or Government Sharia Securities (*SBSN/Surat Berharga Sharia Negara*), both tradable and non-tradable.

According to the enactment of Law No. 19 Year 2008, the Indonesian government began to publish the sovereign *sukuk* regularly in both the domestic and international markets. The issuance of the sovereign *sukuk* series IFR (Islamic Fixed Rate) has successfully managed to obtain high interest rates from investors. In the following year, the government started to offer *sukuk* to Indonesian citizens individually through the instrument of Retail *Sukuk* SR-001. In 2009, in order to increase benefits in the management of pilgrim funding and the endowment of the community (*dana abadi umat*), the Indonesian government issued Indonesian *Sukuk* for Pilgrim Funding (*SDHI/Sukuk Dana Haji Indonesia*). Then, in 2011, the Indonesian government issued the Sharia Sovereign Treasury *Sukuk* to encourage the development of the sharia money market while providing liquidity instruments. The government issued the Sharia Sovereign Treasury *Sukuk* (*SPN-S/Sukuk Perbendaharaan Negara Sharia*) through an auction method. The number of *sukuk* issued by the government varies from the project financing *sukuk* to the global *sukuk*.

It is further described in the Sharia Capital Market Sovereign government report, published by the Financial Services Authority (OJK) in 2015 based on the total value and total issuance of *sukuk* and the amount of *sukuk* outstanding, that there has been a significant number year to year and showing that at the beginning of 2010, the total denomination of *sukuk* emission was 14.483 billion Rupiah, which is in line with the denomination of outstanding *sukuk* in 2010, which decreased to 6.121 billion Rupiah. Although several years, the outstanding *sukuk* will decreased in 2011 and 2014. The condition of outstanding *sukuk* still exists as shown in.

On the other hand, corporate *sukuk*, despite its development as an initiator in the country, still remains behind sovereign *sukuk*. As per September 2015, the number of *sukuk* issuances is Rp14.5 trillion, which increased by 11.8% from January 2015, with 80 total issuances. In addition, the outstanding corporate *sukuk* was Rp 8.28 trillion, which increased from January 2015, with 41 total issuances. This indicates that corporate *sukuk* only dominates the total domestic *sukuk* by 0.62%, based on the IIFM report.

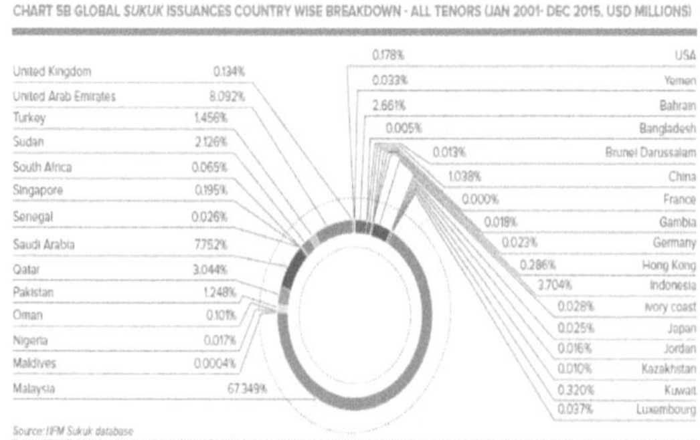

Figure 2. The country details of global *sukuk* issuers.

As the country with the largest Moslem population worldwide, Indonesia has great potential to be at the center of the development of global Islamic finance, including the sharia capital market. The development of *sukuk* has rapidly increased from year to year. As can be seen from the charts of the geographical distribution of *sukuk* issuance, there are already 30 countries that issue *sukuk* worldwide. Figure 2 shows that Malaysia dominates the *sukuk* market, as it has more than 67% of the total global *sukuk* emissions. By the end of 2015, Indonesia ranked fourth, after UAE (8.1%) and Kingdom of Saudi Arabia (7.8%), with 3.7%. However, we also know that our neighboring country, Malaysia, has claimed half of the total issuances, which is why the sovereign *sukuk* is not well developed in Indonesia.

The objective of this research is to find out the obstacles and solutions to developing the sovereign *sukuk* in Indonesia.

1. What are the obstacles to developing the sovereign *sukuk* in Indonesia?
2. What is the solution to developing the sovereign *sukuk* in Indonesia?

2 LITERATURE REVIEW

The first previous research, which was done by Ascarya and Yumanita (2007), entitled "Comparing the Development Islamic Financial/Bond Market in Malaysian and Indonesia", explained some of the problems of *sukuk* in Indonesia, which are: 1) the government's commitment to developing an Islamic financial system in Indonesia is still very low; 2) the regulatory frameworks that cover Islamic financial systems are also few and very weak 3) no sharia instrument has been issued by the government, which would be needed for basic policy, and also as benchmark for sharia financial institutions; and 4) the human resources development of the sharia economy is not yet well developed.

The second previous research, which was done by Al-Amine (2008), identified problems with *sukuk*, which are: 1) a warranty by a third party for *sukuk* ijarah has been debated by sharia experts; 2) the sale and lease back on *sukuk* ijarah is considered in a form of *bai al-wafa*, *bai al-istighlal*, or *bai al-inah*; 3) pricing on *sukuk* ijarah still refers to LIBOR (London Interbank Offered Rate); 4) there is a warranty of return by one party in *sukuk* musyarakah; and 5) there is no special rating model for *sukuk* itself.

According to Iqbal and Mirakhor (2007), there are several challenges and issues in developing the *sukuk* market, which are: (1) it is difficult for small scale institutions to issue *sukuk*; (2) the cost efficiency is a competitive disadvantage compared to conventional bonds; (3) pricing still refers to conventional benchmarks in the *sukuk* floating rate; (4) institutional and bank investors tend to hold *sukuk* until the maturity date, so that the *sukuk*'s secondary market is illiquid, which improves transaction costs; and (5) adverse selection causes additional costs.

The research of Jobst (2008), entitled "Islamic Bond Issuance-What Sovereign Debt Managers Need to Know", explains that the problems that are often faced by the *sukuk* market, particularly in countries that embrace a dual system, are legal aspects and regulatory frameworks, structure innovation design and externality from political aspects.

Another research was undertaken by Nazar (2011), which explains that the problems of *sukuk* in the sharia capital market are caused by the Western legal system, which is not suitable for protecting the rights of *sukuk* holders if a *sukuk* default happens.

According to Pramono (2006), the challenges in developing *sukuk* are: 1) operational aspects; 2) regulations and infrastructure; 3) fiqh provision and formal laws; and 4) integrity of Special Purpose Vehicle (SPV) legal status.

3 RESEARCH METHOD

This research study is a qualitative research with a case study approach, using a method that has been developed by Yin (2011). It aims to find out the obstacles to developing sovereign *sukuk* and to find out solutions and appropriate strategy implementation based on informants' opinions. It aims to answer the problems mentioned in this research.

Basically, a case study research aims to find out something deep and could provide a broad figure about a problem. Consistent with case study design, the data source used is primary data, which are in-depth interviews that have been held with many informants, which are Bank Indonesia, Islamic fiqih experts/theologians, practitioners and academics that have a good understanding about the problems discussed and have a deep knowledge of *sukuk* problems in Indonesia, and also other literature sources. The data from the informants' assessments about these problems are the objects of this research.

4 RESULT AND DISCUSSION

From the literature sources and the interviews with some of the experts and practitioners, the researcher can conclude that the problems with sovereign *sukuk* development in Indonesia can be divided into four aspects. They are:

1. Investor: 1) Lack of Moslem investors, based on a concept of halal investment. Halal investment is not yet included in Moslem investors' portfolios. There are many investors who still assume that Islamic investment is an opportunity cost; 2) Pricing still refers to LIBOR, so that the return reflects the interest rate. The development of the pricing policy, according to some experts, is rational because *sukuk* return has to be greater than that of conventional bonds and it is a midpoint between deposit return in a month and the interest rate of financing, particularly in the beginning of issuing *sukuk* as initial strategy so that people demands it. 3) Buy and Hold Strategy, which is performed by the majority of investors, is when the investor invests and then leaves it for long periods of time without being too concerned about any increase and decrease of prices in the market, by assuming that a long-term investment is profitable. This causes the secondary market to be illiquid and, until now, it is still Over the Counter (OTC).
2. Issues: 1) Cost efficiency becomes a competitive disadvantage compared to conventional bonds, and because the *sukuk* market is still small compared to conventional securities, it experiences diseconomies of scale; 2) Adverse Selection, which is a kind of asymmetry information where one party or more who makes or will make a business transaction or potential business transaction has more information than any other party; 3) Limitations of assets, which are securitized and not yet optimized. Considering sovereign assets, the condition can be classified into two categories: optimal and not yet optimal. The condition that is not yet optimal can be classified again into three conditions. First, idle usage status (not yet utilized or idle). There are so many assets, including land, buildings,

structures, and other assets that are idle, so that they do not give any value-added to the country's income. In fact, many assets in the form of the building thus draining the budget of sovereign budget for maintenance. So many assets, particularly vacant land and buildings, are managed unprofessionally so that it is not effective to use them to give an income to a country. Third, the cost of maintenance is greater than earned income.

3. Market: 1) The limitation of the number of human resources that meet the qualifications in the sharia capital market. This is because, in reality, human resources that exist in the Indonesian sharia financial institutions today are only capable of handling the conventional economy and there is still doubt about the basis of sharia (implementation of *ushul fiqh* and *fiqih muamalah*); 2) Lack of the level of knowledge and understanding needed by market participants about sharia financial instruments, caused by the limitations of information and education about sharia products in the capital market; 3) Lack of *sukuk* variant, because the investor tends to wish for a simple *akad* (contract or agreement) that provides safety, such as a fixed income, while *akad ijarah* is in demand in the market.
4. Legal: 1) Lack of regulatory support from the government. One of the main reasons for this inefficiency is that most of the markets in many Islamic countries, especially Indonesia, operate a legal system that is obedient to civil and common law, which is not always compatible with sharia/Islamic law; 2) Lack of suitability of *ulama* (Islamic theologians) opinions about *sukuk* product law; 3) A lack of academic support in research, training, and study about *sukuk* in the academic world.

Besides that, from the results of the interviews and the researcher's analysis, there are many alternative solutions to solve the problems in sovereign *sukuk* development in Indonesia, which are:

1. Investor: 1) Enhancing domestic investors or investors other than those from the Middle East and changing the mindset of investors to invest in the concept of sharia investment; 2) When the *sukuk* price competes directly with conventional bonds in the relative spread rate, then there are no inherent cost advantages that could be earned on the side of borrower. Thus, the formulation of a comprehensive rule is needed, and also a long-term and strategic view and plan about how to reduce costs, if the *sukuk* price wants to enter the Islamic financial market rather than focus on single transactions; and 3) Change the mindset of investors from the logical consequences of investing in the *sukuk* market, which tend to be held to the limit of its maturity.
2. Issues: 1) Evaluating the used contracts; 2) Giving education to the issuer, in this case, the government. The majority of issuers used to issue bonds to get big funds, so lack understanding about the benefits of *sukuk*, will make companies or enterprises do not concern with *sukuk* instrument. If issuing and buying *sukuk* does not add any value for them, then they will be reluctant to be active in the *sukuk* market. Education is needed to help them understand this paradigm; 3) Identifying the assets of the country, whether they are optimal or not, so that it can be rented in implementing various *sukuk* agreement (*akad sukuk*).
3. Market: 1) Providing human resources that are capable of expert knowledge of the sharia capital model. These human resources will be at the center of running the operational function strategy of *sukuk* in the future, so that the practice could make the best contribution to reaching the expected goals; 2) Providing intensive socialization and education about the sharia product to sharia capital market participants, with the expectation that the *sukuk* market could grow rapidly. Some practitioners know that people who understand about *sukuk*, from the aspects of both fiqih and finance, are still rare; 3) Variation of *sukuk* agreements/contracts. What makes Malaysia the country with the highest GIE (Global Islamic Economy) in the world is because they have an outstanding *sukuk* market. More than 50% of the world's *sukuk* market is in Malaysia. So, the existence of *sukuk* becomes very important in Indonesia. According to some experts, Indonesia has very few *sukuk* variants, whereas *sukuk* can be a very good alternative for companies in obtaining capital.
4. Legal: 1) Revising more comprehensive and complete regulations and rules. The existence of a strong legislative framework and rules are very important for the capital market. A framework has to ease transaction implementation without creating one of the technical problems that have lately become an issue in the regulations and rules. The necessity of comprehensively revising the legal system and making a serious effort to ensure the legality of the legal framework in accordance with sharia; 2) Uniting the Islamic theologians/*ulama's* perspective; 3) Co-operating and collaborating with academics. This can improve lecturers' and college students' knowledge about implementing sharia financial practice and can improve the quality of sharia financial lecturers and teachers in college.

From the solutions above, there are some strategies that are assumed to be appropriate to represent the problem of developing sovereign *sukuk* in Indonesia in accordance with the four aspects above, which are:

1. Investor: 1) Providing education and holding an exhibition about the products, especially *sukuk*, to sharia financial institutions *sukuk*; 2) Developing a supporting institution. A capital market is supported by many institutions, which perform an important function for the success of their performance. Some progressions have been made while such an intitution is built, such as the International Islamic Rating Agency (IIRA), which was founded to assess, evaluate, and give independent assessments and opinions about the possibility of future losses caused by sharia financial institutions, products and services; 3) Developing moral standards for investors. One of the important aspects in the business world is that of norms and ethics. Basically, ethics is a commitment to do what is right and to avoid what is not. In this case it is the damaging of the market conditions. All investors must have this ethic in order to keep the *sukuk* market liquid.
2. Issues: 1) Issues, investors and SPV need to take precise care of the *sukuk* market. Islamic transactions usually face competitive losses, more so than do conventional transactions. The problem that usually occurs is the cost requirement, which includes legal fees, higher documentation, and cost distribution, and also involves the examination of structural resilience in addition to evaluating the quality of the obligor credit. Standardization will reduce this problem; 2) Market driven strategy is a strategy that follows the market's demands and conditions. Therefore, it is expected that regulators will not make direct policies/regulations that contain elements of intervention that will disrupt the market. However, they can make regulations to make the market mechanism go well; 3) Optimizing the role of government in identifying sovereign assets. As we know, Indonesia has many airfields, public hospitals, universities, and so on, that can be rented.
3. Market: 1) Co-ordinating the provision of training on *sukuk*. For example, a college institution should prepare, as early as possible, excellent human resources in the field of economic and Islamic finance, especially regarding *sukuk*. Thus, the resources will be familiar when they come into practice; 2) Guidance by informal educational institutions. Informal education is a formal education that can be implemented in a structured way and step by step. Informal education serves to develop the potential of the capital market participants with an emphasis on the mastery of knowledge and functional skills, and the development of professional attitudes and personalities; 3) Developing innovative and simple *sukuk* products. Some experts argue that it is more important to develop *sukuk* mudharabah because of the clarity of financing a project, and also fairer because the benefits are to be shared.
4. Legal: 1) Approaching legislators to make technical regulations so that local governments do not need to worry about *sukuk* tenors that must adapting the positions of governors/mayors; 2) Focus Group Discussion (FGD) with the *ulama* to align the views on *sukuk* in accordance with AAOIFI. Sharia theologians/*ulama* can play an important role, because multidisciplinary expertise is developed through knowledge sharing and training in order to gain an understanding of market functions; 3) Undertaking studies and research about *sukuk* with scholars and academics; also undertaking studies and discussions with students, lecturers, and practitioners, or training that can provide insight about sharia financial practice in the field.

5 CONCLUSION

Based on the sovereign goverment of the problems, results and discussions, this research obtains several conclusions, which are:

1. There are commonly many challenges in developing sovereign *sukuk*, starting with investor aspects, issues, legal markets, which involve a buy and hold strategy that is done by investors, limitation of assets that are securitized, limitation of the number of human resources that meet the qualifications in the sharia capital model, and also the lack of regulatory support. This is something reasionable because *sukuk* can be categorized into new products that are integrated into the established conventional financial market.
2. From the problems above, there are some solutions to solve them with regards to sovereign *sukuk*, including investor aspects, issues, and legal markets, which are changing investors' mindsets and identifying assets.
3. Strategies that can be implemented to develop the *sukuk* market in this country are: developing the moral standard of investors, optimizing the role of the government in identifying assets, and co-ordinating the provision of training to legislators about the approach to *sukuk*.

ACKNOWLEDGMENT

Thank you to our research assistant, Karina Ayu.

REFERENCES

AAOIFI Accounting and Auditing Organization of Islamic Financial Institutions. (2005). *Shari'ah Standards.*

Abdul Wahid, N. (2010). *Sukuk, Memahami & Membedah Obligasi pada Perbankan Syariah.* Yogyakarta: Ar-Ruzz Media.

Al Bashir, M. & Al Amine, M. (2008). The Islamic bonds market: Possibilities and challenges. *International Journal of Islamic Financial Services, 3*(1).

Al-Amine, M.M.A. (2008). *Sukuk market: Innovations and challenges, Islamic research and training institute* (pp. 35–54). Islamic Development Bank.

Arsalan, T.A. (2004). *Managing financial risk of sukuk structure* (dissertation). Loughborough University, UK.

Ascarya & Yumanita, D. (2007). *Comparing the development Islamic financial/bond market in Malaysia and Indonesia.* Saudi Arabia: IRTI Publications.

Firdaus, (2005). *Konsep Dasar Obligasi Syariah.* Jakarta: PT Renaisan.

Global Investment House Report. (2008). *Sukuk: The new dawn of Islamic finance era.* Kuwait.

Huda, N. & Nasution, M.E. (2007). *Investasi pada Pasar Modal Syariah.* Jakarta: Kencana.

IIFM. (2015). *A comprehensive study of the globall sukuk market, International Islamic Financial Market* (5th ed.). Retrieved from www.iifm.net.

Iqbal, Z. & Mirakhor, A. (2007). *An introduction to Islamic finance theory and practice.* Singapore. John Wiley & Sons.

Islamic Financial Services Board. (2009). *Capital adequacy requirements for sukuk securitisations and real estate investment.*

Ismal, R. (2011). *The Indonesian Islamic banking, theory, and practices.* Depok, Jawa Barat: Gramata Publishing.

Jaffer, S. (2011). *Global growth, opportunities and challenges in sukuk market.* London, UK: Euromoney Institutional Investor PLC.

Jarkasih, M (2008). *Analisis Masalah dalam Pengembangan Sukuk Korporasi di Indonesia.* Skripsi Sarjana pada Jurusan Bisnis dan Manajemen Islam Sekolah Tinggi Ekonomi Islam (STEI) Tazkia, Bogor.

Nasution, M.P. (2006). *Indonesian sovereign sukuk: Prospect and policy.* Presented at the International Conference on Islamic Banking.

Nazar, J.K. (2011). *Regulatory & financial implications of sukuk's legal challenges for sustainable sukuk development in Islamic capital market.* Proceedings of 8th International Conference on Islamic Economics and Finance. Qatar.

Pramono, Sigit and Setiawan, Aziz. 2006. *Obligasi Syariah (Sukuk) untuk Pembiayaan Proyek Infrastruktur: Tantangan dan Inisiatif Strategis.* Tesis diterbitkan. Jakarta: Program Pascasarjana Universitas Indonesia.

Tariq, A.A. (2004). *Managing financial risks of sukuk structures* (Masters dissertation). Loughborough University, UK.

Yin, R.K. (2011). *Applications of case study research.* California, USA, Sage.

Increasing Management Relevance and Competitiveness – Sukoco et al. (Eds)
© 2018 Taylor & Francis Group, London, ISBN 978-0-8153-7455-8

The effect of trading volume changes on JKSE's market return

M. Madyan, S. Hasan & D.F. Putri
Universitas Airlangga, Surabaya, Indonesia

ABSTRACT: This research aims to examine the relationship between market returns and trading volume as well as market returns and changes in trading volume on the JKSE from January 1st, 2008 to September 30th, 2013. This research used GARCH (1, 2) to examine the relationship. The researchers found that market returns and trading volume were significantly positive, as well as market returns and the change of trading volume. The results showed that past information, such as trading volume, could provide new information to the market in the future.

1 INTRODUCTION

There were many threats of crisis contagion hitting Indonesia, particularly JKSE, in December 2008, which was the steepest plunge in the first half of 2008 and amounted to 2.627,3 points with the fall of capitalization market and a sharp decline in trading volume. The fall of stock prices in 2008 affected the prices in 2009. The steepest decline point in 2009 amounted to 1256,109 points, but this improved due to the re-entry of foreign investors into the market. At the end of 2009, JKSE increased and closed at 2.534,36 points.

After the crisis, JKSE increased gradually in 2010 and ended at 3.703,51 points, while 3.821,99 in 2011. In 2012, JKSE rocketed and ended at 4.316,69 and improved in August 2013. Unfortunately, it steeply declined again at 3.967,84. Throughout this volatile period, the investors needed more new information in the market as the analysis sources. The information is usually related with the trading volume. Since the information about shares cannot be received in the market simultaneously, the changes in trading volume are considered as a signal of the information of a stock.

The relationship between return and trading volume can be analyzed using Generalized Auto Regressive Conditional Heteroskedasticity (GARCH). GARCH is considered effective to be used for analyzing the data with high volatility obtained from a time series.

2 LITERATURE REVIEW

Floros (2007) suggests that there are some reasons why traders should pay attention to the trading volume. Theoretically, on the one hand, the low trading volume indicates that the market is not liquid or is in high volatility. On other hand, the high trading volume indicates high liquid market and, thus, results in low volatility price. That result can cut down the high trading effect. High volume can increase the revenue of broker, a market maker, who can generate return at high turnover.

In normal condition, trading volume will rise when the price increases. In other words, when the stock price drops, the volume will drop as well, because the investors hold their stocks. A change in trading volume is resulted from four reasons. First, when the volume increases unexpectedly (volume spike), second, if the stock price rises with small stable volume and the likelihood of sharp correction in the short term. Third, when the stock price drops and low price occurs when profit taking takes place. Four, when price change is followed by the high volume, then the price will decline and create a new balance with lower price.

2.1 *Relationship between market return and trading volume*

Karpoff (1987) investigated the relationship between stock prices and trading volume and argued that it is important to study this relationship because it provides insight into the structure of the financial market. Second, knowing the price-volume relationship is important for studies that use both the data of market price and trading volume. Third, the price-volume relation is also critical to the empirical distribution of speculative price. And, fourth, price-volume relationships have significant implications for research in future markets.

The relationship between return and trading volume has been of interest to economists and investors. In general, previous studies have noted a strong positive correlation between trading volume and price volatility returns (Karpoff 1987). Karpoff (1987) concluded that the trading volume is important in the information market because it describes the information about a change in market and investor's expectation (Harris and Raviv 1993).

2.2 *Previous research*

A study conducted by Darwish (2012) found that there is a significant positive relationship between trading volume and return. This finding indicates that the information about the content of volume affects the future stock return. Darwish (2012) also found evidence of bidirectional relationship between trading volume and return. The study also confirmed that the volume would add a predictive power of future returns, or vice versa. The suggestion is that the regulators and the investors could use past information for monitoring the stock price movement in the market. Attari, Rafiq, and Arwan (2012) found significant positive relationship between trading volume and return and change in trading volume and return.

Another study by Kamath and Wang (2006) conducted in the developing market from ASIA found that trading volume and return have positive relationship, except of those in Indonesia. Pathirawasam (2011), in the Colombo stock exchange, also found a significant positive relationship between return and the changes in trading volume. The different results obtained from the previous research from the same stock market are still interesting to be studied.

Pisedtasalasai and Gunasekarage (2008) showed a causal relation between market returns and trading volume in Indonesia, Malaysia, Singapore and Thailand, while, in the Philippines, there was no relation found. Harris and Raviv (1993) found that price change has a positive relation with volume. The data used ire the price change, which was not autocorrelation, while the volume was autocorrelation.

Also, Darwish (2012), in a study on the Palestinian stock market claimed that there is a causal relation between returns and trading volume using GARCH (1, 1). Kamath and Wang (2006) examined the relation of return and trading volume in six developing countries in Asia and showed a significant positive relation. There is a reciprocal causal relation directly among the four markets of the six markets studied.

Khan and Rizwan (2012) examined the relation of return and trading volume in the stock market of Pakistan. The results indicated a positive relation between trading volume and return, and a reciprocal relation between return and trading volume. Also, Paramitawati (2009) examined the relation of market return, return volatility and trading volume. The results showed that there is a reciprocal relation between market return and return volatility. There is also a positive relation between return and market trading volume as well as between return volatility and trading volume.

Ariani (2008) examined the relation of trading volume, return volatility and market returns. The results showed that trading volume and return volatility have a significant positive effect on market return. Meanwhile, Gursoy, Yuksel, and Yuksel (2008) studied 12 share markets from the period of 2000 to August 2006showing that the trading volume is good for stock analysis, but not good for the market analysis.

2.3 *ARCH and GARCH models*

The Auto Regressive Conditional Heteroscedasticity (ARCH) Model was developed by Robert Engle (1982) and then modified by Mills (1999). Between 1986–1994, Tim Bollerslev developed GARCH (Generalized Auto Regressive Conditional Heteroscedasticity) to improve the ARCH. GARCH is used for time series data in the financial sector, especially for rate of return (Bollerslev et al. (1994). The first probability distribution of returns is from fat tails (higher dissemination data) compared with the Gaussian distribution/Normal (data dissemination is not low or high), which have a greater tendency for the occurrence of extreme events modeled by a Gaussian distribution.

Second, volatility clustering will occur when the variability of the data at any given time is relatively high, so there will be a similar tendency in the period of the next, and vice versa. If the variability of the data is relatively small data, there will be the same tendency in the next period. This is often referred to as time-varying variance or heteroscedasticity.

2.4 *Hypotheses*

The hypotheses of this research are formulated as follows:

H1: There are relationships between market return and trading volume

H2: There are relationships between market return and change in trading volume

3 RESEARCH METHODOLOGY

This research uses sample stock price and trading volume of weekly Composite Stock Price Index (CSPI) from 1 January 2008 to 30 September 2013.

The three variables used in this study are market returns, trading volume and change in trading volume. Market return is the average daily market return in one week, which is obtained from the average daily closing index in one week. Market return can be calculated by using the formula below:

$$R_t = \ln(P_t / P_{t-1}) \quad (1)$$

where Pt is the average daily closing price of the index in one week.

Trading volume (V_t) is the average daily trading volume in one week JKSE. V_t can be calculated using the formula:

$$v_t = \frac{\sum_{h=1} V_{ht}}{\text{Trading Days}} \quad (2)$$

where V_{ht} is the daily trading volume

Changes in trading volume (ΔV_t) are the change in average daily trading volume in one week. This volume can be calculated by using the following formula:

$$\Delta V_t = \ln(V_t / V_{t-1}) \quad (3)$$

where V_t is the average daily trading volume in a week.

3.1 *Analysis model*

The following formulations are used to investigate the relationships between market return and trading volume, and between market return and change in trading volume:

$$R_t = \propto_1 + \beta_1 R_{t-1} + b_1 V_t + \in_{t1} \quad (4)$$

$$R_t = \propto_2 + \beta_2 R_{t-1} + b_2 \Delta V_t + \in_{t2} \quad (5)$$

where Rt = market return; α_1 = constant; β_1 = coefficient for market return at t–1; R_{t-1} = market return at t–1; b_1 = coefficient for trading volume; V_t = trading volume; $\in_{t1}$ = residual at t_{t1}; α_2 = constant; β_2 = coefficient for market return at t–1; b_2 = coefficient for change in trading volume; ΔV_t = change in trading volume; $\in_{t2}$ = residual at t_2

4 RESULTS AND DISCUSSION

Fluctuating changes in market returns will cause variability or volatility reflecting the size of the pace of the market in response to price changes. The market return movement experienced constant change (time-varying volatility) with a recent vulnerable time and the magnitude of change was huge. This random movement was caused by the crisis in 2008 and the strength of the rupiah against the dollar.

According to the table above, by late January 2009, JKSE still decreased due to the crisis of 2008. Positive standard deviation indicates that the risk is not too high. Moreover, the trading volume had the lowest value in 2008, which can be seen in the object 235 which stands at below 1000. This is due to the crisis in 2008 that led to the world markets, including Indonesia, to decrease. As a result, some investors were less interested in the market due to uncertainty and weak investor resilience in the market. But, in the following years, trading volumes started to increase. This means that investors were again interested in the market because market conditions had begun to improve.

The highest change of trading volume was 1.18493 that occurred in mid-week in April 2009 due to increased banking shares and infrastructure. Meanwhile, the lowest value was –1.17372, found at the end of 2008, due to the subprime mortgage crisis that occurred in America and Europe as well as developing countries, such as Asia, which began to feel the impact. Positive standard deviation indicates that the risk is not too high.

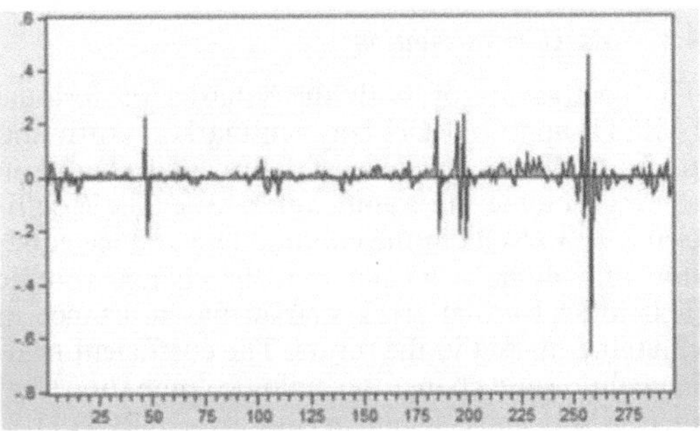

Figure 1. Market return movement.
Source: Indonesia Stock Exchange (data processing).

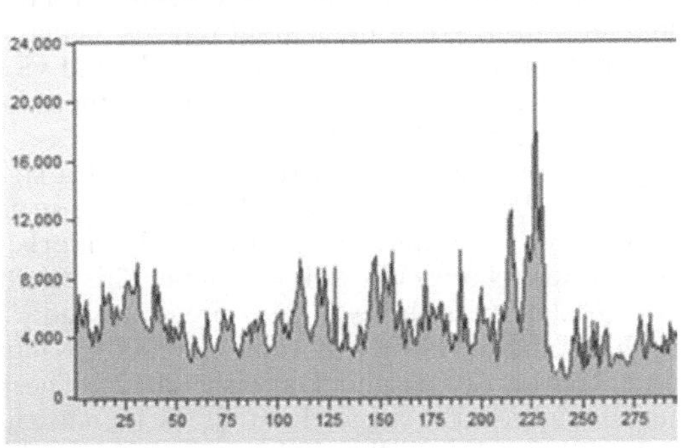

Figure 2. Trading volume movement.
Source: Indonesia Stock Exchange (data processing).

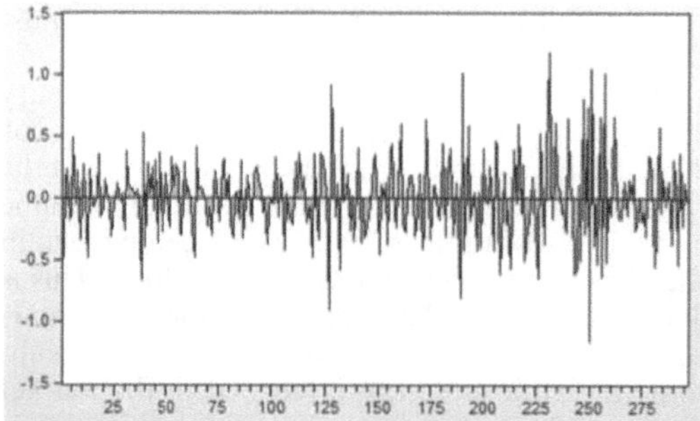

Figure 3. Trading volume change movement.
Source: Indonesia Stock Exchange (data processing).

The graph of trading volume change movement indicates that the changes had randomized movement. The object 235 had continuous changes in trading volume (time varying volatility). Meanwhile, the objects 100–200 which had changes in the trading volume began to stabilize. However, object 1–95 re-experienced volatility, but it is unlike in 2008 (object 235). Volatility occurred in object 235 caused by crisis condition of the markets.

Regression Eq.: $R\_t = \alpha_1 + \beta_1 R_{t-1} + b_1 V_t + \varepsilon_{t1}$.

Var.	Coeff.	Std. Err.	z-stat	Prob.
C	–0.0063	0.00213	–296.017	0.0031
Rt–1	–0.20335	0.01192	–1.706	0.0000
Vt	0.0000	0.0000	670.912	0.0000
Variance equation				
C	0.0001	0.00003	382.569	0.0001
ARCH	110.728	0.1773	624.531	0.0000
GARCH	0.27877	0.03964	703.243	0.0000

Regression Eq.: $R\_t = \alpha_2 + \beta_2 R_{t-1} + b_2\,\Delta V_t + \varepsilon_{t2}$

Var.	Coeff.	Std. Err.	z-stat.	prob.
C	0.00548	0.00093	589.373	0.0000
R_{t-1}	–0.1965	0.01213	–1.620	0.0000
ΔV_τ	0.0122	0.0029	420.534	0.0000
Variance equation				
C	0.00011	0.00003	361.748	0.0003
ARCH	117.1	0.1798	651.272	0.0000
GARCH	0.25211	0.04076	618.58	0.0000

4.1 *GARCH estimation*

The coefficients of both the squared of residual (ARCH) and GARCH between market return and trading volume and market return and change in trading volume are significant at 5%. The Coefficient of GARCH in the conditional variance equation of volume is greater that the change volume This indicates that stock market has resistance in changing market in the future. The coefficient trading volume and change in trading volume show that there is a positive significant use by GARCH (1.2) Model.

The probability of trading volume and change in trading volume is less than 5% and this indicates that the trading volume has a relationship with the market return. When the market returns increase, the trading volume will increase as well, and vice versa. When the market returns decrease, then the trading volume will also decline.

Based on the statistical results, there is a significant relationship between the market returns and trading volume and between the market returns and change in trading volume. This result is consistent with those of most previous studies, such as conducted by Lee and Rui (2000). Khan and Rizwan (2008) and Darwish (2012), These results support the suggestion that the increase in the market will be followed by an increase in the volume, and vice versa. The decline in the market will be followed by a decrease in the volume.

The trading volume, which implies information, leads to price change, and large positive price change, which implies higher capital gain, encourages transactions by traders, which, in turn, leads to increase in volume. This study also explains that regulators and investors can also use this past information to monitor the movement of stock prices in the market. This is consistent with the existing theory stating that information of the volume affects the market return in the future.

4.2 *Discussion*

The relation of market returns and trading volumes can be analyzed from multiple perspectives, such as a research on the relation of trading volume and stock returns in stock market of Pakistan (Khan and Rizwan 2008), a research on the relation of volatility and trading volume (Attari, Rafiq, and Awan 2012), a research on the relation of trading volume and market returns (Darwish 2012), as well as a research on the relation of price and trading volume (Karpoff 1987). Statistical calculations indicate that there are significant relations between market returns and trading volume as well as between market returns and changes in trading volume. These results are consistent with previous researches, such as Lee and Rui (2000). Khan and Rizwan (2008) and Darwish (2012).

These results, moreover, also support previous researches which claimed that the market's rise will be followed by an increase in volume, while a decline in market will be followed by a decrease in volume. GARCH Statistics show that current trends will occur within the next period, and the coefficient of GARCH trading volume greater than the change in trading volume will indicate that the market has a resilience in the future. The volume implies information about price changes, and a positive price change shows high capital gain. In other words, high capital gains will push the volume of transactions carried out by traders to be increased. This research also explains that regulators and investors can use past information to monitor share price movements in market. This is consistent with existing theory, in that the volume of information affects the market return in the future.

5 CONCLUSION

This study shows that there is a significant positive relationship between trading volume and market returns and between the changes in trading volume and market returns. This means that, if the trading volume increases, the market return will increase, and vice versa. If the trading volume decreases, the market return will also decrease. This study shows that historical data, such as market return and trading volume, can provide new information to the future market.

5.1 *Recommendation*

Further research is expected to analyze with a longer time so that the relation between market return and trading volume, as well as market returns and changes in trading volume, could be revealed more accurately. Therefore, further research needs to differentiate the condition of market, whether it is bear or bullish to determine the relation of market return and trading volume, as well as market returns and trading volume changes occurring in each market. For instance, further researches should differentiate between two distinct markets, such as developing countries (such as Indonesia, Malaysia and Taiwan) and developed countries (such as Japan, China and the United States) since the volatility of the markets in the developing countries is different from those in the developed countries. Thus, such research may have different results.

REFERENCES

Ariani, E. 2008. Pengaruh Trading Volume and Return Volatility terhadap Market Return Pada Bursa Effek Indonesia GARCH-M (1.1). *Disertasi.* Program Pasca Sarjana Universitas Airlangga. Surabaya.

Attari, M. I., Rafiq, J. S. & Awan, H. M. 2012. The Dynamic Relationship between Stock Volatility and Trading Volume. *Asian Economic and Financial Review* 2 (8): 1085–1097.

Darwish, M. 2012. Testing the Contemporaneous and Causal Relationship between Trading Volume and Return in the Palestine Exchange. *International Journal of Economics and Finance* 4 (4): 182–192.

Fahmi, I. 2006. *Analisis Investasi dalam Perspektif Ekonomi dan Politik.* Refika Aditama. Bandung.

Floros, C., and D.V.Vougas. 2007. Trading volume and returns relationship in Greek stock index futures market: GARCH vs. GMM. *International Research Journal of Finance and Economics*12: 98–115.

Gursoy G., Yuksel, A., & Yuksel. A. 2008. Trading Volume and Stock Market Volatility: Evidence from Emerging Stock Market. *Investment Management and Financial Innovations* 5 (4): 200–210.

Harris, M., & Raviv, A. 1993. Differences of Opinion Make a Horse Race. *Review of Financial Studies* 6 (3): 473–506.

Kamath, R. R., & Wang, Y. 2006. The causality between stock index returns and volumes in the Asian equity markets. *Journal of International Business Research* 2: 63–74.

Karpoff, J. M. 1987. The relation between price changes and trading volume: A survey. *The Journal of Financial and Quantitative Analysis* 22 (1): 109–126.

Khan, S. & Rizwan, F. 2008. Trading volume and stock returns: evidence from Pakistan's stock market. *International Review of Business Research* Pipersville 4 (2): 151–162.

Lee, C. F., & Rui, O.M. 2000. Does trading volume contain information to predict stock returns? Evidence from China's stock markets. *Review of quantitative finance and accounting* 14: 341–360.

Paramitawati, D. M. P. 2009. Hubungan klausa antara Return, Return Volatility dan Trading Volume Pada Bursa Efek Indonesia. *Disertasi.* Program Pascasarjana Universitas Airlangga. Surabaya.

Pathirawasam, C. 2011. The relationship between trading volume and stock returns. *Journal of Competitiveness* 3: 41–49.

Pisedtasalasai, A, & Gunasekarage, A. 2008. Causal and dynamic relationships among stock returns, return volatility and trading volume: Evidence from emerging markets in South-East Asia. *Asia-Pacific Finance Markets* 14: 277–29.

Increasing Management Relevance and Competitiveness – Sukoco et al. (Eds)
© 2018 Taylor & Francis Group, London, ISBN 978-0-8153-7455-8

The influence of the profitability indicator, capital and performing loans on the liquidity of the bank in the Indonesian stock exchange

O.V.B. Nainggolan
Sekolah Tinggi Ilmu Ekonomi Wiyatamandala, Jakarta, Indonesia

ABSTRACT: There are many factors that affect the Bank's Loan Deposit Ratio. The purpose of this research was to analyze the influence of Profit Growth, Return on Asset, Return on Equity, Capital Adequacy Ratio and Non-Performing Loan on the Bank's Loan Deposit Ratio. The sample used was 30 banks registered in the Indonesian Stock Exchange from 2011 to 2015. The samples were chosen by the purposive sampling technique. Tests were performed using multiple linear regression analysis. The research result proved that, simultaneously, Profit Growth, Return on Asset, Return on Equity, Capital Adequacy Ratio and Non-Performing Loan had an influence on the Bank's Loan Deposit Ratio. Non-Performing Loan and Return on Asset partially have a positive and significant effect on the Bank's Loan Deposit Ratio. Return on Equity partially has a negative and not significant effect on the Bank's Loan Deposit Ratio. Capital Adequacy Ratio and Profit Growth partially do not have enough evidence to influence the Bank's Loan Deposit Ratio.

Keywords: Loan Deposit Ratio, Capital Adequacy Ratio, Non-Performing Loan, Return on Asset, Return on Equity, and Profit Growth

1 INTRODUCTION

The Loan Deposit Ratio (LDR) is commonly used as a variable for assessing a bank's or a financial institution's liquidity, calculated by dividing the bank's total loans by its total deposits in rupiah and foreign currency. If the ratio is too high, this means that the bank may not have enough liquidity to cover any unforeseen fund requirements and, conversely, if the ratio is too low, the bank may not be earning as much as it could be. The important goal of the LDR equation is to find and assess how far the banks have a healthy condition when carrying out their operations. Previous research (Alper, 2012) found that bank liquidity is an essential determinant in a bank loan in Turkey and that monetary policy should be capable of manipulating the position of the liquidity. Based on the provisions of Bank Indonesia, the standard of the Bank's LDR, according to Bank Indonesia, is between 85%–100% (Bank Indonesia, 2015).

Table 1, above, represents the changes of LDRs between 2011 and 2015, and makes it easier to understand the trends for each bank with respect to its peers. The growth of LDR in Indonesia tended to slow down by about 14% from 2011 to 2015, which is indicated by bigger challenge liquidity funds, and is not in line with the growth of deposits, which was 37% in five years. This means that people chose to divert their funds into deposits.

Table 1. Comparison of LDR 2011–2015.

LDR	2011	2012	2013	2014	2015
LDR (%)	78.77	83.58	89.70	89.42	92.11
Total loans	2,117	2,597	3,158	3,526	3,904
Total deposits	2,688	3,107	3,520	3,944	4,238

This makes banking liquidity excessive, as the deposits collected were greater than the bank loans. This study uses fundamental analysis to examine the financial variables that have a significant influence in predicting LDR in the banking companies listed in the Indonesian Stock Exchange.

The Net Loans to Total Asset Ratio (NLTA) measures the percentage of assets that are tied up in loans. The NLTA is also another important ratio that measures the liquidity condition of the bank. Whereas the Loan to Deposits is a ratio in which the liquidity of the bank is measured in terms of its deposits, the NLTA measures the liquidity of the bank in terms of its total assets. That is, it gages the percentage of total assets that the bank has invested in loans (or financing). The higher the ratio, the less the liquidity is of the bank. Similar to LDR, banks with low NLTA are also considered to be more liquid compared to banks with higher NLTA. However, high NLTA is an indication of potentially higher profitability and, hence, more risk. The higher the ratio, the less liquid the bank is.

2 RESEARCH METHOD

This research uses a causal design to analyze the influence of the characteristics of financial banking, which are represented by Capital Adequacy Ratio (CAR), Non-Performing Loan (NPL), Return on Asset (ROA), Return on Equity (ROE) and Profit Growth. The study was conducted using secondary data obtained from the Indonesian Stock Exchange. The data collection uses pooling data. In addition, financial firms embrace specific regulations with different characteristics from those of non-financial corporations. The use of public banks in this study is as stated by previous researchers (Sugiarto & Nursiana, 2016) as follows:

1. Public banks in Indonesia must obey disclosure regulations required by Bank Indonesia (BI) and the Otoritas Jasa Keuangan (OJK), so public banks in Indonesia are considered more transparant than non-public banks. This condition makes the objectivity of the data higher.
2. Public banks in Indonesia are closely monitored by Bank Indonesia (BI) and the Otoritas Jasa Keuangan (OJK), so that their data quality is more reliable.

Data was collected from the Indonesian Stock Exchange, on the basis of the following criteria:

1. Public banks already listed as public banks in the Indonesian Stock Exchange.
2. Public banks that have the required financial statement data for the period of 2011–2015.
3. Public banks that reported variables analyzed in this study as follows:

   a. CAR = Capital Adequecy Ratio
   b. NPL = Non-Performing Loan
   c. ROA = Return on Asset
   d. ROE = Return on Equity
   e. Profit Growth

4. Public banks that did not have a loss during the research period.

The dependent variable in this study is public banks LDR in Indonesia. In connection with the time span of the data used in this study (2011–2015), there were 24 eligible public banks for analysis. In analyzing the data, simple and multiple regression analysis was used by first seeking the fulfillment of the assumption of the Ordinary Least Squares (OLS) regression analysis.

3 RESULT AND DISCUSSION

Partially, the influence of CAR, NPL, ROA, ROE and Profit Growth to LDR is shown in Table 2 below.

NPL partially has a positive and significant effect on the Bank's LDR. For the implications of this research, NPL reflects credit risk; the smaller the value of the NPL, the smaller the credit risk borne by the bank. A smaller credit risk borne by the bank will reduce liquidation because the credit is handled well. This research supports the previous research (Granita, 2011; Akbar & Mentayani, 2010; Nasaruddin, 2005), where NPL has a negative significance to LDR, while another research (Irwan, 2010) showed that NPL is positive and not significant to LDR.

ROA partially has a positive and significant effect on the Bank's LDR. Banks with a higher ROA value are more efficient for existing business activities. The more increasing amount of asset will affect the amount of revenue. The increase in total revenue will affect profit, so that financial performance will be better. This is contrary to previous research (Granita, 2011), which shows that ROA does not significantly affect the LDR.

ROE partially has a negative and significant effect on the Bank's LDR. The research showed that ROE is not in accordance with the underlying theory that the greater the ROE, the more efficient the bank is in running its business activities. This means that a higher capital requirement of the bank should show a smaller LDR, so the possibility of liquidity is also getting smaller.

The significance of the CAR and Profit Growth > 0.05, which means that CAR and Profit Growth partially do not have enough evidence to influence the Bank's LDR. The function of bank capital is to meet the minimum capital requirement. Capital adequacy is very important for banks in order to distribute loans. The higher the CAR value, which indicates a higher level of liquidity of the bank, means that the capital structure of the bank is getting stronger and the bank will have enough reserve funds if at any time there is a bad loan. This research showed that a good or bad capital adequacy level does not affect whether or not people take loans. The model of forecasting public banks LDR is shown below. Based on Anova calculations, the F-test value is 3.183, with 0.010 significance value.

$$LDR = 79.919 - 0.079\ CAR + 2.063\ NPL + 4.356\ ROA - 0.586\ ROE - 0.009\ PROFITGROWTH$$

The significance 0.010 < 0.05 showed that this model is reliable for predicting LDR in the banking companies listed in the Indonesian Stock Exchange.

The contribution of independent variables simultaneously on dependent variables can be seen from the coefficient determination.

Table 2. Collinearity statistics and T-test (in'000).

Model	Unstandardized coefficients		Standardized coefficients			Collineaity statistics	
	B	Std. Error	Beta	T	Sig	Tolerance	VIF
(Constant)	79.919	5.209		15.343	0.000		
CAR	–0.079	0.244	–0.029	–0.326	0.745	0.964	1.037
NPL	2.063	0.878	0.209	2.349	0.021	0.959	1.043
ROA	4.356	1.392	0.410	3.129	0.002	0.441	2.268
ROE	–0.586	0.191	–0.389	–3.069	0.003	0.472	2.118
PROFIT GROWTH	–0.009	0.027	–0.030	–0.324	0.747	0.864	1.157

Table 3. F-test.

Model		Sum of squares	df	Mean square	F	Sig.
1	Regression	1649.968	5	329.994	3.183	0.010b
	Residual	12025.872	116	103.671		
	Total	13675.839	121			

Table 4. Coefficients determination.

Model	R	R^2	Adjusted R^2	Std. error of estimate	Durbin-Watson
1	0.347[a]	0.121	0.083	10.1819108	1.636

The coefficient determination is a measure of the magnitude of the dependent variant described by the independent variable (Sugiarto, 2015). The determination coefficient is 0.121 or 12.1%, which means a 12.1% variable LDR. This can be explained by the variation of the independent variable (CAR, NPL, ROA, ROE, and Profit Growth), while the remaining 87.9% can be described by the other variables in the model research. This research showed that LDR is not only influenced by fundamental factors, which are represented by the CAR, NPL, ROA, ROE and Profit Growth, but also by other variables, such as inflation and other macro factors.

The impact of the crisis caused by Europe should mean that the economic prospects for Indonesia are growing, and many investors should come to invest their funds. According to the International Monetary Fund, (2011) research, the capital inflow for developing countries has a high correlation to global economic conditions. The funds will flow from crisis-stricken Europe and the United States, which have economic stagnation, to high yielding countries and stable economic conditions. The flow of foreign funds into Indonesia certainly brings its own impact on the government and Bank Indonesia (BI) as the authority of financial and monetary.

Previous research (Alper, 2012) found that the liquidity of the bank is an essential determinant in a bank loan in Turkey and monetary policy is capable of manipulating the position of the liquidity. In addition, in determining the loan, the bank considers not only the position of individual liquidity but also that of the entire banking system. Moreover, the significance of the interaction between the systemic liquidity and the liquidity of the bank shows that the more excess systemic liquidity that there is, the more irrelevant is the bank's liquidity position. This research is supported by another research (Katsios, 2006), which highlights the interaction between the economy and corruption. This research discusses Greek economic activities and focuses on certain Greek economic variables, such as expense, tax, national insurance and the intensity of the relevant rules in Greece. The research also showed that higher corruption and the problem of tax is one of the causes of the emergence of the crisis in Greece. This is compounded by the inability of the Greek government in dealing with economic activities and the relevant scale of corruption.

The amount of capital coming into Indonesia causes difficulties for Bank Indonesia in implementing monetary policy. Investment strengthens the rupiah, while outflow funds weaken the rupiah. Bank Indonesia must sterilize the incoming funds by buying dollars with rupiah. As a result, the money supply will be greater. Therefore, Bank Indonesia should withdraw money to prevent inflation. The amount of foreign investment (PMA) is also increasing the demand for dollars for capital expenditure and daily capital needs.

The growth of financial service providers in the form of loan cash without collateral or guarantees from personal asset ownership causes great competition between local banks and foreign banks, especially banks that are located in big cities, such as Jakarta. Indeed, there are many benefits that can be obtained by the competitive credit loan services of some banks. The more promotion that is given, the more comfortable the customers are. In conducting their business activities, banks need to manage credit risk, such as maintaining asset quality and the calculation of allowances for possible losses on assets, and applying prudential principles to ensure that bank liquidity can be achieved and maintained primarily by the increasingly widespread non-collateral credit.

4 CONCLUSION

Based on the results of the data analysis and discussion conducted by this research, the results proved that simultaneously Profit Growth, ROA, ROE, CAR and NPL had an influence on the Bank's LDR. This research showed that LDR is not only influenced by fundamental factors, which are represented by the CAR, NPL, ROA, ROE and Profit Growth, but also by other variables, such as inflation and other macro factors. NPL and ROA partially have a positive and significant effect on the Bank's LDR. ROE partially has a negative and significant effect on the Bank's LDR. CAR and Profit Growth partially do not have enough evidence to influence the Bank's LDR.

REFERENCES

Akbar, H.M. & Mentayani, I. (2010). *Faktor-Faktor Yang Mempengaruhi Intermediasi, Studi Pada Bank Umum Swasta Kalimantan Selatan Tahun 2007–2009 (Factors that Influences Intermediation, The Study in Banks in South Kalimantan from 2007–2009).* Jurnal Manajemen Dan Akuntansi Banjarmasin Sekolah Tinggi Ilmu Ekonomi Indonesia, 107–116.

Alper, K. (2012). *An Empirical Study on Liquidity and Bank Lending*, [Electronic Version]. Turkiye Cumhuriyet Merkez Bankasi, 12, 04).

Bank Indonesia. (2015). *Peraturan Bank Indonesia Nomor 17/11/PBI/2015 (Bank Indonesia Regulations No. 17/11/PBI/2015).* Jakarta: Bank Indonesia.

Granita, J.K. (2011). Analisis Pengaruh DPK, CAR, ROA, NPL, NIM, BOPO, Suku Bunga, Inflasi, Dan Kurs Terhadap LDR (Studi pada Bank Umum Swasta Nasional Devisa periode 2002–2009 (Analysis of DPK, CAR, ROA, NPL, NIM, BOPO, Interest, Inflation, and Kurs to LDR, Study of Commercial Banks Period of 2002–2009). Semarang: Universitas Diponegoro.

International Monetary Fund, 2011, World Economic Outlook, *International Capital Flows and Economic Growth*, September 2011.

Irwan, L.N.Q. (2010). *Tinjauan Terhadap Fungsi dan Faktor—Faktor yang Mempengaruhi Intermediasi Perbankan Nasional 2010 (Analysis of Functions and Factors Influence the Intermediation National Bank 2010).* Bandung: Universitas Pasundan.

Katsios, S. (2006). *The shadow economy and corruption in Greece*. South-Eastern Europe Journal of Economics 1, 61–80.

Nasaruddin, N. (2005). *Faktor Faktor yang Mempengaruhi Loan to Deposit Ratio (LDR) di BPR Wilayah Kerja Kantor Bank Indonesia Semarang (Factors that Affect Loan to Deposit Ratio (LDR) in BPR of the Bank of Indonesia Semarang District).* Semarang: Program Pasca Sarjana Manajemen UNDIP.

Sugiarto & Nursiana, A. (2016). *Determinants identification of public banks stock prices in Indonesia based on fundamental analysis. International Journal of Applied Business and Economic Research 2016*, 4705–4712.

Sugiarto. (2015). *Metode Statistika Bisnis (Bussiness Statistical).* Tangerang: PT. *Matana Publishing Utama.*

Increasing Management Relevance and Competitiveness – Sukoco et al. (Eds)
© 2018 Taylor & Francis Group, London, ISBN 978-0-8153-7455-8

Corporate governance performance evaluation of banks operating in Indonesia

Fongnawati Budhijono
Department of Accounting, Universitas Prasetiya Mulya, South Jakarta, Indonesia

ABSTRACT: This research focuses on corporate governance and its effect on the performance of banks operating in Indonesia. This research was conducted using secondary data obtained from Infobank (2015). Overall there were 99 banks evaluated. The research variables were Net Interest Margin (NIM), Good Corporate Governance composite profile (GCG_CG), Return on Assets (ROA), Return on Equity (ROE) and Profit Growth (PrGrowth). The independent variable was the bank's Good Corporate Governance composite profile (GCG_CG). The dependent variables were NIM, ROA, ROE, and PrGrowth. Tests were conducted on the hypotheses, which stated that corporate governance has a significant positive correlation on each of the dependent variables and corporate governance has a significant positive effect on each of the dependent variables. Tests were performed using Correlation Analysis and Simple Regression Analysis after seeking the fulfillment of the assumptions. The correlation coefficient obtained stated that Good Corporate Governance composite profile was significant negative correlated with variable NIM. Good Corporate Governance composite profile showed a significant negative effect on the NIM of banks at 10% Type I error. The research findings did not support the research hypotheses.

Keywords: Good Corporate Governance composite profile, Bank performance

1 INTRODUCTION

The financial performance of Indonesian banks in 2015 was not better than that of the previous year. If the liquidity condition in 2014 was very tight and bank credit rose by only 11%, then the liquidity condition in 2015 did not change much. Despite looser liquidity conditions, inflationary pressures sparked interest rates, and the rising prices of subsidized fuel oil, which was affecting the real sector, impacted on the performance of the banks. The weakening of the global economy has not fully recovered due to the Euro zone, the slowing down of economic growth in China and the threat of capital outflows if the US central bank raises the interest rates (Mohamad, 2015). In order for banks operating in Indonesia not to slip because of decreasing loans and decreasing earnings, the Indonesian banking authorities have considered corporate governance as one of the issues that can ensure the stability of the management of the banks operating in Indonesia with respect to the weakening economic conditions that they face (Bank Indonesia, 2011a). Good Corporate Governance (GCG) in banking is a bank governance that applies the principles of transparency, accountability, responsibility, independence, and fairness. GCG in banking is important because it can increase banks' profits and those of shareholders in the long term.

Corporate governance is becoming a major issue during the post-financial crisis period in the Asian emerging market, such as in Indonesia, Thailand, Philippines and Malaysia. In particular, the financial institutions have implemented corporate governance reforms in order to enhance the protection of shareholders and stakeholders interests. The consequence of this is that it allows for greater monitoring, especially by the shareholders. As noted by previous research (Praptiningsih, 2009), corporate governance remains a serious issue for the Indonesian banking regulatory authority. The Indonesian banking authorities boost banks operating in Indonesia so that they have a good composite ranking of GCG. Banks operating in Indonesia are required to conduct an assessment of the bank on an individual basis using a risk approach (risk-based bank rating) with coverage assessment of the factors of risk profile; GCG; profitability (earnings); and capital (Bank Indonesia, 2011b).

Good Corporate Governance composite profile (GCG_CG) reflects the bank's ability to implement the GCG basic principles of transparency, accountability, responsibility, independence and fairness. The bank's GCG_CG determination is based on a comprehensive and structured analysis of the implementation results of the bank's corporate governance principles and also other information related to the bank's GCG. There are five GCG composite rankings that reflect the extent to which the bank is able to implement the basic principles of corporate governance. Rating one is the best and rating five is the worst. A previous researcher (Sugiarto, 2016) converted the GCG_CG ratings to a scale of measurement that allows analysis of correlation and ANOVA based on the reference value used by the Infobank Research Bureau (2015). Based on the reference value, the higher the value of the GCG composite profile, the better the bank's performance in conducting GCG. This study used the conversion value of the GCG composite ranking, as used by previous research (Sugiarto, 2016).

The focus of this research is to evaluate whether or not the bank's corporate governance performance has a significant positive effect on the bank's performance. In this research, the bank's performance focuses on the bank's profitability and the bank's efficiency. The variables examined according to the bank's profitability were Return on Assets (ROA), Return on Equity (ROE) and earnings growth in the current year (PrGrowth). The banks' earnings growth in the current year were calculated based on the average of the industry and their group. The variable related to bank efficiency was Net Interest Margin (NIM). NIM is one of the key indicators of the bank's performance in respect to bank efficiency, as NIM indicates the bank's ability to generate income from interest by looking at the banks' lending performance.

2 RESEARCH METHOD

The study was conducted using secondary data obtained from the Infobank Research Bureau (2015). The research variables are ROA, ROE, PrGrowth, NIM, and GCG_CG. The study was conducted without considering the grouping of banks according to the rules of Bank Indonesia (BI) on commercial banks business activities.

The tests were performed using Correlation Analysis and Simple Regression Analysis after seeking the fulfillment of the assumptions. The independent variable is the bank's GCG composite profile. NIM, ROA, ROE, and PrGrowth were dependent variables that represent the bank's performance, which was affected by the variable corporate governance. The tests were conducted on these hypotheses:

1. Corporate governance has a significant positive correlation on each dependent variable studied in this research.
2. Corporate governance has a significant positive effect on each dependent variable studied in this research.

3 RESULTS AND DISCUSSION

Overall there were 99 banks belonging to the various classifications of books. From the 99 banks examined, the correlation coefficient and the significance of the relationship are shown in Table 1.

The correlation coefficient obtained stated that GCG is only correlated significantly with NIM (with a correlation coefficient –0.191 and sig of 0.029). Corporate governance was not significantly correlated with all of the other three variables.

Although GCG-CG was significantly correlated with the NIM variable, the sign of the correlation coefficient obtained was negative. Logically the expected sign of the correlation coefficient between GCG-CG and NIM should be positive due to the better management of the bank, which would be expected to increase the bank's NIM. The findings of this study are consistent with the findings of the previous study (Praptiningsih, 2009), which found that only the foreign shareholders, which represent the ownerships monitoring mechanisms, were significantly negatively related with corporate performance measures in the banking firms in the Asian emerging markets.

One argument that can be put forward is the possibility that the people in Indonesia have not been aware of the importance of corporate governance. People are much more appreciative of the high interest rates and ease of lending procedures, so that ultimately the banks that have low GCG_CG have high NIM. Banks with high GCG_CG will usually be more rigorous in their operational procedures and also provide lower interest rates.

People who are less aware of the importance of corporate governance will think that the bank's strict procedures and lower interest compensation are not attractive conditions, so they prefer to choose banks with high convenience and who offer high interest rewards, regardless of the bank's performance on their corporate governance. This condition is strengthened by the policy of savings being guaranteed by the Deposit Insurance Agency (*Lembaga Penjamin Simpanan, LPS*) up to the nominal value of IDR 2 billion, so banks customers who have savings of less than IDR 2 billion are not too concerned with the condition of a bank's GCG, because when banks fail, their funds in the bank are still guaranteed by the Deposit Insurance Agency (LPS). At this time, all of the banks operating in Indonesia are tightly controlled by Bank Indonesia, the Financial Services Authority (*Otoritas*

Table 1. The correlation coefficient and the significance of the relationship of research variables.

		GCG_CG	NIM	ROA	ROE	PrGrowth
Pearson correlation	GCG_CG	1.000	−0.191	0.092	0.091	−0.044
	NIM	−0.191	1.000	0.491	0.495	0.096
	ROA	0.092	0.491	1.000	0.917	0.347
	ROE	0.091	0.495	0.917	1.000	0.303
	PrGrowth	−0.044	0.096	0.347	0.303	1.000
Sig. (1-tailed)	GCG_CG	.	0.029	0.182	0.186	0.331
	NIM	0.029	.	0.000	0.000	0.173
	ROA	0.182	0.000	.	0.000	0.000
	ROE	0.186	0.000	0.000	.	0.001
	PrGrowth	0.331	0.173	0.000	0.001	.
N	GCG_CG	99	99	99	99	99
	NIM	99	99	99	99	99
	ROA	99	99	99	99	99
	ROE	99	99	99	99	99
	PrGrowth	99	99	99	99	99

Table 2. Simple regression analysis result.

Equation	Dependent variable	Constant	Unstandardized coefficients	R Square	ANOVA	
					F	Sig
1	NIM	11.827 (sig = 0.000)	−0.071 (Sig = 0.058)	0.036	3.669	0.058
2	ROA	−0.247 (Sig = 0.908)	0.023 (Sig = 0.363)	0.009	0.834	0.363
3	ROE	−4.658 (Sig = 0.781)	0.174 (sig = 0.373)	0.008	0.802	0.373
4	PrGrowth	41.680 (sig = 0.703)	−0.556 (sig = 0.662)	0.002	0.192	0.662

Jasa Keuangan, OJK) and the Deposit Insurance Agency (LPS), so that the bank's reputation for safety among that of the other banks does not differ much. A bank's customers choose to associate with any bank with which they feel comfortable and secure, so that customers can move from one bank to another bank without feeling anxious (Nursiana, 2015).

The results of a simple regression analysis of variable GCG as an independent variable with each of the four dependent variables studied is shown in Table 2.

By using a 5% Type I error, from the four equations set as shown in Table 2, it can be seen that the effect of GCG on each of the dependent variables is not significant. Of the four dependent variables studied, GCG_CG has most influence on NIM, despite the fact that its sig just reached 0.058 (which is still greater than 0.05). By using a 10% Type I error, the GCG_CG showed a significant negative effect on the NIM of the banks. Nevertheless, the contribution to variation changes of GCG_CG to NIM of the banks surveyed is not great. This condition is indicated by the determination coefficient of 0.036, which is the highest coefficient of determination of the other equations in the set.

From the magnitude of the coefficients of determination obtained, it can be seen that GCG variables contribute no more than 3.6%, which means that the bank's profitability and the bank's efficiency are influenced by other variables that are not examined in this study. Similar to the findings of the correlation coefficient, the regression coefficient sign obtained in the regression coefficient related to the dependent variables NIM and PrGrowth was also negative, which indicates that conditions differ from expectations. Logically, by increasing the value of GCG_CG, the better management of the bank will, in turn, enable the bank to generate an increased profit. According to these findings can be stated arguments as explained previously. The findings of this study do not support the previous research findings, which found that corporate governance indicated a significant impact on ROE and ROA (Siddique et al., 2014), although previous research found that ROA and ROE have a positive significant effect on public banks stock prices in Indonesia (Sugiarto & Nursiana, 2016).

4 CONCLUSIONS

1. The correlation coefficient obtained stated that the GCG_CG is only negative significantly correlated with the variable NIM. Corporate governance was not significantly correlated with any of the other three variables.
2. The regression coefficient obtained stated that GCG_CG showed a significant negative effect on the NIM of banks at 10% Type I error. Corporate governance did not have a significant effect on any of the other three variables.
3. There is no strong evidence that corporate governance affects bank performance.

REFERENCES

Bank Indonesia. (2011a). Peraturan Bank Indonesia No.13/1/PBI/2011 tanggal 5 Januari 2011 perihal Penilaian Tingkat Kesehatan Bank Umum, 4–10.

Bank Indonesia. (2011b). Surat Edaran Bank Indonesia No.13/ 24 /DPNP/2011 tanggal 25 Oktober 2011 perihal Penilaian Tingkat Kesehatan Bank Umum,1–28.

Infobank. (2015). Rating 118 Bank di Indonesia. *Infobank, no 437, XXXVII*(411), 32–37.

Mohamad, K. (2015). Menilai Angka dan Kualitatif Bank. *Infobank, no 437, XXXVII*(411), 26–31.

Nursiana, A. (2015). Pengaruh Internet Banking, Kualitas Layanan, Reputasi Produk, Lokasi Terhadap Loyalitas Nasabah Dengan Intermediasi Kepuasan Nasabah. *Jurnal Keuangan dan Perbankan, 19*(3), 450–462.

Praptiningsih, M. (2009). Corporate governance and performance of banking firms: Evidence from Indonesia, Thailand, Philippines, and Malaysia. *Jurnal Manajemen dan Kewirausahaan.*

Siddique, A., Afzal, M.A., Sajid, M. & Khan, S.M. (2014). Impact of corporate governance on banks performance. *International Journal of Research in Social Sciences, 4*, 378–391.

Sugiarto. (2016). Performance evaluation of Indonesian banks and foreign banks operating in Indonesia related to classification of capital. *Advances in economics, business and management research: Vol 15, 1st Global conference on business, management and entrepreneurship (GCBME-16)* (pp. 104–108). Atlantis Press.

Sugiarto. & Nursiana, A. (2016). Determinants identification of public banks stock prices in Indonesia based on fundamental analysis. *International Journal of Applied Business and Economic Research, 14*, 4705–4712.

Increasing Management Relevance and Competitiveness – Sukoco et al. (Eds)

What drives finance pattern debt companies to pay dividends in Indonesia?

L. Gestanti
Universitas Airlangga, Surabaya, Indonesia

G. Memarista
Universitas Kristen Petra, Surabaya, Indonesia

ABSTRACT: The purpose of this study is to investigate what drives firms to pay dividend, especially for those firms that have had finance pattern debt through a non-financial listed company on the Indonesia Stock Exchange between 2010–2014. The idea behind the research is that the researchers will investigate how the companies with higher default risk pay the dividend through the good mechanism of corporate governance. The results show that there is a significant relationship between finance pattern, blockholder ownership and company size towards dividend payment. On the other hand, there is no significant relationship between the Board of Directors (BOD) ownership and firm performance towards dividend payment. This paper uses the literature by extending the understanding of a country in an emerging market, so that this research will encourage the non-financial listed companies who have higher debt to create better performance through good corporate governance when paying dividend to the investors.

Keywords: Dividend Payment, Finance Pattern Debt, Good Corporate Governance, Company Size, Firm Performance

JEL Classification: G30, G32, G35, L25

1 INTRODUCTION

Every company has its own financial pattern (Corbett & Jenkinson, 1996; Moenaddin & Karimianrad, 2012). The finance pattern will show the primary source that is always used by the company and if it is consistent across several years. According to Meggison (1997), there are three financial sources of a company: retained earnings as the internal financial source, debt, and stock as the external financial source.

It has special attention in the emerging market, especially in Indonesia. The listing companies in the developing countries tended to borrow from the bank and another source to help their activities between 2010–2014, while the listing companies in countries like Thailand, India, South Korea, Poland and the Czech Republic, which were the emerging market, stopped issuing debt due to lesser borrowing needs. Those countries have improved credit quality and have become increasingly developed.

Based on the data from non-financial listed firms from the Indonesia Stock Exchange between 2010–2014, there are three financial patterns. The highest value and the most used financial pattern is finance pattern debt (60% of non-financial listed companies). However, the funding pattern of retained earnings and equity (stock) shows a very low funding pattern (31% and 9% of non-financial listed companies, respectively).

Finance pattern is indicated by the comparative value of the funding sources (retained earnings, debt, or stock) that will be compared with the total assets (Turkalj & Srzentic, 2011). The data from non- financial listed firms shows that the growth of finance pattern retained earnings, debt and equity is 0.74%, 1.25%, and –5.24%, respectively. This indicates that the companies have higher default risk. The higher value of finance pattern debt growth shows that managers always prefer to use debt as the primary source in Indonesia, especially for a larger company size. By using debt, it indicates a positive signal that companies have good management.

One of the indicators that the company still has good firm performance is the dividend payment. A higher dividend payment indicates that the company has good performance, even if the company has higher debt. The dividend payment is a residual decision for the company. For higher default risk companies, it is difficult to distribute the dividend payment because of the debt covenant.

Megginson (1997) stated that debt can be either a threat or a protection for investors. As a threat, higher debt means firms face a higher probability of bankruptcy. Thus, investors are threatened with not getting enough dividend. This creates a conflict of interest between investors and creditors. As a protection, managers will work hard to fulfill the debt payments (Meggison, 1997). Thus, investors are protected from free cash flow usage by managers. They will feel protected from a manager's bad behavior in seeking a safe position or higher salary (Memarista, 2016).

In order to see the function of finance pattern debt, whether as a threat or as a protection for the investor, this research uses finance pattern debt firms with positive net income to pay a dividend.

Agency conflict also occurs between the majority and the minority stockholders. Based on La Porta et al. (2000), better minority shareholder protection is associated with a higher dividend. The dividend will give certainty return to all investors, especially when the company has finance pattern debt. The dividend will reduce free cash flows that might be expropriated (Anderson & Reeb, 2004; Faccio et al., 2001; La Porta et al., 2000). Dividend decision is also determined by ownership pattern and the firm's characteristics (size and performance).

The ownership pattern shows how the firm has a Good Corporate Governance (GCG). It is shown by Board of Directors (BOD) as the minority shareholders, and by the blockholders as the majority shareholders. GCG can minimize agency problems by distributing a dividend to the investors. According to Berger et al. (1997), Abor (2007) and Memarista (2016), the BOD will act as investors who want a secure return, yet they also act as the manager to pay debt. Moreover, the blockholders have power at the General Meeting of Shareholders. The blockholders can have two behaviors: either become a risk taker (Alba et al., 1998) or to realize their positions (Harada & Nguyen, 2011).

Based on those phenomena, the researchers investigate what drives firms to pay dividend, especially for the companies that have finance pattern debt. This study will identify the effect of finance pattern debt, corporate governance (the BOD and blockholders share ownership), and a firm's characteristics towards dividend payment.

2 LITERATURE REVIEW

2.1 *Dividend payment*

Dividend can be distributed to the investor, either in cash or stock. As the bonding mechanism for managers, dividend will show the stability of firm performance. It indicates a positive signal to the shareholders. Therefore, dividend encourages and binds the manager to reach the stability of this payment. Dividend will be used to minimize the agency conflict between manager and shareholder. Dividend also reduces the opportunities for using risky financing, as well as the issues of the minority and majority ownership pattern (La Porta et al., 2000).

$$\text{Dividend Payout Ratio}_{it} = \frac{Dividend_{it}}{Earning\ After\ Tax_{it}} \quad (1)$$

2.2 *Finance pattern debt*

Myers (1984) stated that finance pattern indicates the managers' habits. It will reflect the behavior that the managers are more comfortable with, and that they do not change previous decisions. This research pays special attention to the finance pattern debt. Finance pattern debt reflects the use of debt as the largest proportion of funding, instead of the other financial sources (Moeinaddin & Karimianrad, 2012). By using finance pattern debt, it leads the firms to face the trade-off theory, whether to bear higher risk of bankruptcy or to save company taxes, as well as to secure bonding mechanisms. Jensen and Meckling (1976) stated that the increasing debt means that the manager is bonded to pay the principal and interest rate.

$$\text{Finance Pattern Debt}_{it} = \frac{Total\ Debt_{it}}{Total\ Asset_{it}} \quad (2)$$

When companies with finance pattern debt increase their debt, then those companies will need more funds. This means that the dividend payout cannot be increased. Jensen and Meckling (1976) stated that debt is a substitute of dividends payment. If debt increases, the company will bond to repay the debt. Thus, cash flow of the company cannot be used to increase dividends (La Porta et al., 2000).

H_1: Finance pattern debt affects dividend payment.

2.3 *Good corporate governance and dividend*

GCG will be reflected by the ownership through the minority and the majority of shareholders. BOD ownership represents the total share ownership of the BOD as the minority shareholder. Thus, the BOD has the same position of interests as the shareholders (Abor, 2007).

$$BOD_{it} = \frac{Board\ of\ Director\ Share\ Ownership_{it}}{Outstanding\ Share_{it}} \quad (3)$$

Companies with finance pattern debt will have higher default risk. Thus, if the BOD acts as shareholders, they will prefer dividend payment (Abor & Fiador, 2013). Conversely, if the BOD acts as managers, they will choose retained earnings instead of dividend. Therefore, managers can maintain the firm performance to be able to repay debt, by increasing retained earnings and by decreasing dividend.

H_2: BOD ownership affects dividend payment.

According to *Keputusan Direksi* PT Bursa Efek Jakarta number 305/BEJ/07/2004, in Indonesia, the investor will be stated as the blockholder (majority shareholder) if they hold stock at a minimum 25% of the outstanding share. Alba et al. (1998) stated that the higher ownership indicates that blockholders bear higher risk and tend to be a risk taker because they expect higher return.

$$\text{BLOCK}_{\text{it}} = \frac{\textit{Sum Shareholder Minimum } 25\%_{it}}{\textit{Outstanding Share}_{it}} \quad (4)$$

The risk taker blockholders will increase their investment, thereby reducing the dividends (Amidu & Abor, 2006) and increasing retained earnings. On the other hand, Harada and Nguyen (2011) also stated that when the blockholders realize the level of risk, they will choose dividend (Frank 1988).

H_3: Blockholders have an effect on dividend payment.

2.4 *Firm characteristics and dividend*

According to Abor (2007), and Moenaddin & Karimianrad (2012), the firm characteristics reflect the company's condition. This firm condition can explain the dividend payment. The firm characteristics that are used in this research are company size and firm performance.

$$\text{SIZE}_{\text{it}} = \textit{Ln Total Assets}_{it} \quad (5)$$

Company size describes the company's wealth (Abor, 2007). If the company's size is larger, thus the ability to complete the company's liabilities is also greater. The larger firm will be richer and have high liquidity, and so the ability to pay dividends will be higher (Rajan & Zingales, 1995; Redding, 1997).

H_4: Company size has an effect on dividend payment.

Furthermore, the other firm characteristic that is used in this study is company performance. Firm performance can be measured as the profitability of the firm. It will show the firm's ability to generate profits with all resources owned by the firm.

$$\text{ROA}_{\text{it}} = \frac{\textit{Earning after tax}_{it}}{\textit{Total Asset}_{it}} \quad (6)$$

Firm performance indicates the main factor for firm characteristic, and thus the company will be able to pay dividend to the investors (Amidu & Abor, 2006). The better the firm's performance, the greater the company's cash flow, and thus the investor receives a greater dividend payment (Rajan & Zingales, 1995).

H_5: Firm performance has an effect on dividend payment.

3 RESEARCH METHODOLOGY

The research will analyze the effect of finance pattern debt, corporate governance and firm characteristics towards dividend payment in 27 non-financial listed firms in the Indonesia Stock Exchange between 2011–2014. This study does not use financial companies because they have different policies, such as the account's name in the financial statements and the meaning of those accounts.

The research's sample selection uses purposive sampling technique which must fit with the criteria, such as having positive net income, having positive retained earnings, having long-term debt financing, and having finance pattern debt during the research period. This study will use linear multiple regression to investigate the research's goals. Furthermore, the following equation is the model analysis in this research.

$$\begin{aligned}\text{DPAY}_{\text{it}} = \alpha + b_1 FPDEBT_{it} + b_2 BODOWN_{it} + \\ b_3 BLOCKOWN_{it} + b_4 CSIZE_{it} + \\ b_5 FPERFO_{it} + \varepsilon_{it}\end{aligned} \quad (7)$$

where $DPAY_{it}$ = dividend payment; $FPDEBT_{\text{it}}$ = finance pattern debt; $BODOWN_{it}$ = BOD ownership; $BLOCKOWN_{it}$ = blockholder ownership; CSIZE_{it} = company size; and FPERFO_{it} = firm performance.

4 RESULT AND DISCUSSION

This research uses 27 non-financial listed firms on the Indonesia Stock Exchange between 2010–2014. Table 1 shows the statistics descriptive, which includes the value of minimum, maximum, mean and standard deviation (Std. Dev.).

The researchers test three regressions to investigate the consistency of the effect of independent variables towards the dependent variable. This research also uses diagnosis tests to get the BLUE Regression like normality, no autocorrelation, no or little multicollinearity, and homoscedacity. The following Table 2 shows the regression results.

The regression results show that finance pattern debt, blockholder ownership, company size and firm performance significantly affect dividend payment; however, the BOD ownership does not have a significant effect on dividend payment. Furthermore, the addition of independent variables

Table 1. Statistics descriptive.

Variables	N	Min	Max	Mean	Std. Dev.
DPAY	135	0.000	1.225	0.228	0.259
FPDEBT	135	0.410	0.811	0.591	0.082
BODOWN	135	0.000	0.082	0.008	0.230
BLOCKOWN	135	0.123	0.769	0.503	0.176
CSIZE	135	25.639	33.095	29.399	1.598
FPERFO	135	0.001	0.276	0.059	0.046

Table 2. Regression results.

Variables	Coefficient of regression		
(Constant)	−0.115**	−0.275**	−1.232***
	(−2.340)	(−2.543)	(−6.593)
FPDEBT	−0.410***		−0.318**
	(4.169)		(−2.578)
BODOWN	0.014		0.313
	(0.040)		(0.696)
BLOCKOWN	0.198***		0.175***
	(−4.181)		(2.963)
CSIZE		0.009**	0.048***
		(2.513)	(8.109)
FPERFO		0.913***	1.138***
		(6.077)	(4.843)
R-Square	0.297	0.444	0.539
Adj. R-Squares	0.261	0.425	0.516
F-Test Sig.	0.000***	0.000***	0.000***

Notes: ***, **, * *indicates level of significance of 1%, 5%, and 10%, respectively.*

will increase the ability to explain the dependent variable through the value of Adj. R^2 (51.6%).

Based on the regression results, the following equation is the model analysis for this research.

$$DPAY_{it} = -1.232 - 0.318 FPDEBT_{it} + 0.313 BODOWN_{it} + 0.715 BLOCKOWN_{it} + 0.048 CSIZE_{it} + 1.138 FPERFO_{it} + \varepsilon_{it} \quad (8)$$

Finance pattern debt has a significant effect on dividend payment. By increasing debt when having finance pattern debt, can decrease dividend payment. This is consistent with Jensen and Meckling (1976) who stated that debt is the substitution of dividend. When the debt value increases, the bonding mechanism is about the ability to repay debt. Thus, the free cash flow cannot be used to increase dividend (Rajan & Zingales, 1995).

BOD ownership has no significant effect on dividend payment. This means that increasing the BOD ownership does not always lead to higher dividend payouts. This is because the BOD as the minority shareholder will be bonded to a debt covenant (Berger et al., 1997; Frank, 1988).

Blockholders have a significant effect on dividend payment, which is consistent with Harada and Nguyen (2011). Blockholders will understand the firm's condition when they have higher debt. Thus, blockholders have rational behavior in asking for dividend, to be able to ensure that they still have earned profit should the company go bankrupt.

Company size has a significant effect on dividend payment. The larger the firm, the greater the increase in the wealth of the firm. This will encourage companies to have more ability to pay dividends. The large companies will find it easier to access funding, will be less dependent on internal financing and will pay more dividends (Memarista, 2016).

Firm performance has a significant effect on dividend payment. This indicates that increasing firm performance creates more profitability, and thus may lead to increased dividend payment (Amidu & Abor, 2006). However, not all companies with finance pattern debt have this ability, since to pay the value of debt, there first must be a debt covenant.

5 CONCLUSION AND IMPLICATION

This study investigates the factors that determine a company to pay dividend, especially for firms that have finance pattern debt through a non-financial listed company on the Indonesia Stock Exchange between 2010–2014. The research results show that there is a significant relationship between finance pattern, blockholder ownership and company size towards dividend payment. On the other hand, there is no significant relationship between BOD ownership and firm performance towards dividend payment.

The research used the literature by extending the understanding of countries in an emerging market. Thus, the implication of this research will help companies who have finance pattern debt and higher bankruptcy risk to create better performance through a bonding mechanism and GCG to distribute the dividend.

Moreover, this study will help shareholders to consider firm characteristics to support their investment decision regarding the firms with finance pattern debt. The firms will pay higher dividend if they have larger size, and better firm performance and a greater number of blockholders will help to realize this.

This study is expected to be a good reference for further research and can be investigated in more depth. Future researchers could add more variables (such as manager behavior) to determine the dividend payment, extend the sample period and add different sample research with another financing pattern.

REFERENCES

Abor, J., (2007). Corporate governance and financing decisions of Ghanaian listed firms. *Corporate Governance: The International Journal of Business in Society, 7*(1), 83–92.

Abor, J. & Fiador, V. (2013). Does corporate governance explain dividend policy in Sub-Saharan Africa? *International Journal of Law and Management, 55*(3), 201–225.

Amidu, M & Abor, J. (2006). Determinants of dividend payout ratios in Ghana. *The Journal of Risk Finance,* 7(2).

Alba, P., Claessens, S. & Djankov, S. (1998). *Thailand's corporate financing and governance structures (No. 2003)*. World Bank Publications.

Anderson, R.C. & Reeb, D.M. (2004). Board composition: Balancing family influence in S&P 500 firms. *Administrative Science Quarterly, 49*(2), 209–237.

Berger, P., Ofek, E. & Yermack, D.L. (1997). Managerial entrenchment and capital structure decisions. *The Journal of Finance, 52*(4) 1411–1438.

Corbett, J. & Jenkinson, T. (1996). The financing of industry, 1970–1989: An international comparison. *Journal of the Japanese and International Economies, 10*(1), 71–96.

Faccio, M., Lang, L.H.P. & Young, L. (2001). Dividends and expropriation. *American Economic Review, 91*(1), 54–78.

Frank, M. (1988). An intertemporal model of industrial exit. *Quarterly Journal of Economics, 103*(2), 333–344.

Harada, K., & Nguyen, P. (2011). Ownership concentration and dividend policy in Japan. *Managerial Finance, 37*(4), 362–379.

Jensen, M.C. & Meckling, W.H. (1976). Theory of the firm: Managerial behavior, agency costs, and ownership structure. *Journal of Financial Economics, 3*(4), 305–360.

Keputusan Direksi PT Bursa Efek Jakarta number 305/BEJ/07/2004. Minimum Blockholder's Share ownership in Indonesia.

La Porta, R., Lopez-De-Silanes, F., Shleifer, A. & Vishny, R. (2000). Investor Protection and Corporate Governance. *Journal of Financial Economics 58.*

Meggison, W.L. (1997). *Capital finance theory*. Addison-Wesley.

Memarista, G. (2016). Managerial optimism and debt financing: Case study on Indonesia's manufacturing listed firms. *Jurnal Keuangan dan Perbankan, 20*(3), 438–447.

Moeinaddin, M. & Karimianrad, M. (2012). The relationship between corporate governance and finance patterns of the listed companies. *Interdisciplinary Journal of Contemporary Research in Business, 4*(7), 489–500.

Myers, S.C. (1984). The capital structure puzzle. *The Journal of Finance, 39*(3), 574–592.

Rajan, R.G. & Zingales, L. (1995). What do we know about capital structure? Some evidence from international data. *The Journal of Finance, 50*(5), 1421–1460.

Redding, L.S. (1997). Firm size and dividend payouts. *Journal of Financial Intermediation, 6*(3), 224–248.

Turkalj, K.G. & Srzentic, N. (2011). Financing patterns of firms in transition countries and its implications: Evidence from Croatia. *Young Economists Seminar.* Dubrovnik.

Increasing Management Relevance and Competitiveness – Sukoco et al. (Eds)
© 2018 Taylor & Francis Group, London, ISBN 978-0-8153-7455-8

Diversification, firm value and government ownership

S.A. Usman & C. Sulistyowati
Universitas Airlangga, Surabaya, Indonesia

ABSTRACT: This paper examines the effect of diversification by using the Herfindahl-Hirschman Index (HHI) on firm value. This study uses a panel data set of 520 companies within the period 2011–2014. The results of multiple linear regression showed that the HHI has a significantly negative effect on firm value, or in other words, diversification has a significantly positive effect on firm value. The lower the HHI (the highest of diversification) of the company, the higher the firm value. Moreover, government ownership would weaken the positive effect of diversification on firm value.

1 INTRODUCTION

1.1 *Background*

One way in which companies grow is to diversify. According to Harto (2005), diversification is a business development strategy by expanding the business segment. Diversification can be done by opening new business lines and expanding existing product lines. Umrie and Yuliani (2011) stated that diversification is a natural process of company growth.

Diversification is important for a company because diversification can create value through lower production risks and lower consolidated tax liabilities. It can also create greater market forces and higher efficiency in resource allocation through internal capital markets. But diversification will also have a negative impact on the value of the company when its management is not going well, adversely affecting the value of the company. Diversification can degrade value because of asymmetric information between CEOs and division managers, conflicts of interest between managers and shareholders, and inefficient allocations between divisions in a diversified company.

The effect of diversification on firm value will become weaker when the company is owned by the government (Badan Usaha Milik Negara). The results of Lin and Su (2008) provide evidence that state-owned companies tend to diversify and have poor corporate value compared to companies owned by other entities. According to Siregar (2012), of the factors related to the bad value of state-owned companies, one of them is allegedly because the essence of State-Owned Enterprises (SOE) is different from non-government companies, in view of the largest share ownership in each company.

Non-governmental companies planning diversification tend to be more mature because their shares are openly owned by more parties and the directors become more responsible. State is own majority of the shares. While the ownership of state-owned shares is owned mostly by the state, then these companies tend to be less mature. In SOEs, there are also many cultures, such as corruption and nepotism, which compromise the performance of the directors or managers. Therefore, this study will discuss the influence of diversification on the value of the company with moderated government ownership on non-financial companies listed on the Indonesia Stock Exchange.

1.2 *Research problems*

Based on the background that has been described above, then the formulation of issues raised in this study is as follows:

1. Does diversification affect the value of the company?
2. What is the effect of diversification on corporate value moderated by government ownership?

2 LITERATURE REVIEW

2.1 *Market power*

The number and size of sales distribution can affect the price as measured by market power. According to Berger and Ofek (1995), (1992), market power is the company's ability to influence market prices to beat competitors.

2.2 *Diversification and firm value*

Diversification strategy is a strategy undertaken by the company to expand its business by extending the company from its core business into other products or services. Diversification is a form of business expansion by expanding the number of business segments, as well as by expanding existing market share or developing diverse products (Harto 2005). Diversification can be done in ways such as by opening new business lines, expanding existing product lines, mergers and acquisitions.

According to Lin and Su (2008), diversification can be measured using the Herfindahl-Hirschman Index (HHI), which measures the diversification rate of total business segment sales with the formula:

$$HHI_{i,t} = \sum_{i=1}^{n} \left(\frac{Sgsales_{i,i}}{\sum_{i} Sales_{i,i}} \right)^2 \tag{1}$$

$Sgsales_{i,t}$ = sales from each segment in company i at period t
$Sales_{i,t}$ = total sales company i at period t
n = total segment

The HHI equals 1 for a single-segment company and decreases as the rate of diversification increases.

2.2.1 *Firm value*

According to Berger and Ofek (1995) Hermuningsih (2013), the value of the company is the perception of investors to the success rate of companies associated with stock prices. High stock prices also make the value of the company high, and increase market confidence, not only in the company's current performance, but also in the future prospects of the company. Investors who judge a company to have good prospects in the future will tend to buy the company's shares. The main aspect that causes investors to give more value to the company is the performance of the company, which is reflected in the profit figure. In general, investors assess high profits as showing good prospects in the future. High profits show the effectiveness and efficiency in the management of the company.

The measurement of the firm's market value is done by adopting the measure of Tobin's Q. Tobin's Q ratio is defined as the ratio of the firm's market value relative to the replacement cost of its assets. Tobin's Q is written in the formula:

$$Tobin's\ Q_{i,t} = \frac{MVE_{i,t} + Total\ Debt_{i,t}}{Total\ Asset_{i,t}} \tag{2}$$

$MVE_{i,t}$ = *Market Value of Equity* firm i at period t
Total Debt = total debt firm i at period t
Total Asset = total asset firm i at period t

2.2.2 *Government ownership*

According to Umri and Yuliani (2011) Rahayu and Rokhman (2014), the status of a company is divided into state-owned and non-state enterprises. According to the Law of the Republic of Indonesia No. 19 of 2003 on SOEs (Badan saha Milik Negara), BUMN is a business entity which is wholly or partly owned by the state through direct participation derived from separated state assets. SOEs are divided into Limited Liability Companies (Persero), which are profit-oriented SOEs, and Public Companies (Perum), which are BUMNs that aim for general benefit. Meanwhile, a non-BUMN company is a business entity established and owned by a profit-oriented private entity. To quantify see the ownership of the company, it can be measured using a dummy with number 1 for SOE and 0 for non-SOE.

2.3 *The effect of diversification on corporate value*

According to Lin and Su (2008), diversification is important for a company because diversification can create value through lower production risks and lower consolidated tax liabilities, and can create greater market forces and higher efficiency in resource allocation through internal capital markets. The addition of segments in multi-segment companies is expected to increase market coverage, so that the company's profits will increase. High profit will attract investors to invest so that the value of the company will increase. In this study, the level of diversification was measured using the HHI, where the higher the indicated HHI value, the lower the diversification rate. Therefore, the higher the level of diversification (the lower the HHI), then the value of the company will also be higher. Thus, the level of diversification positively affects the value of the company, or in other words, the HHI negatively affects the value of the company.

2.3.1 *Government ownership moderates the effect of diversification on corporate value*

The results of Lin and Su (2008) provide evidence that diversification has an impact on corporate valuation. According to Siregar (2012), companies owned by the government tend to diversify and have poor corporate value compared to companies owned by other entities. This is because that in the government-owned companies there are many cultures, such as corruption and nepotism, which compromise the performance of the directors or managers. This is what makes investors reluctant to invest their capital into a company owned by the government. At the same time, the non-government companies are considered more effective at diversifying because they have mature planning, so that the level of losses that will be experienced by investors when the company diversifies will be smaller. Thus, state-controlled enterprises (BUMN) weaken the positive effect of diversification on firm value compared to non-government-controlled enterprises (Non-State-Owned

Enterprises). In other words, the negative impact of HHI on corporate value is weaker on government companies (SOEs) compared to companies controlled by non-government enterprises.

2.4 *Factors affecting firm value*

Firm size (firm Size) shows the size of the wealth owned by the company. Companies with large size generally have the flexibility and high access in funding issues; thus, the company's operational activities will be easier. Firm size (firm size) is measured using the natural logarithm (Ln) for total assets at the end of the year using the formula:

$$Size_{i,t} = \text{Ln } Total\ Asset_{i,t} \tag{3}$$

Firm Size$_{i,t}$ = size of the firm i at period t
Total Asset$_{i,t}$ = *Total asset* firm i at period t.

2.4.1 *Firm age*

Every company wants to go public, because they want to raise funds from the capital market. If the company decides to go public there are some benefits to be gained, such as reducing barriers to borrowing funds, portfolio diversification and liquidity. According to Umri and Yuliani (2011) in order to go public, companies have costs to be incurred, both cash outlay and non-cash outlay. According to Lin and Su (2008), the company's age can be measured from when the company goes public or listed on the Stock Exchange from the company going public or companies listing on the Stock Exchange.

$$Age = \text{firm age starts from IPO} \tag{4}$$

2.4.2 *Blockholder ownership*

Blockholder ownership is a large shareholder of a company's shares. Based on Umrie and Yuliani (2011) the decree of directors of BEJ No. Kep 305/BEJ/07–2004, open company controllers are parties owning 25% or more of shares that have the capability to directly or indirectly control the company rather than the smaller shareholders.

$$BLOCK = \text{percentage of the stock owned by stockholders} > 25\% \tag{5}$$

2.5 *Hypothesis and model analysis*

The hypotheses proposed in this study are:

H1 = Diversification has a positive effect on firm value. In other words, HHI negatively affects the firm value.
H2 = Government ownership weakens the positive influence of diversification confirm value.

The analysis model used is multiple linear regression.

Model 1:

$$\text{Tobin's } Q_{i,t} = \alpha + \beta_1 HHI_{i,t} + \beta_2 SIZE_{i,t} + \beta_3 AGE_{i,t} + \beta_4 BLOCK_{i,t} + \varepsilon_{i,t} \tag{6}$$

Model 2:

$$\text{Tobin's } Q_{i,t} = \alpha + \beta_1 HHI_{i,t} + \beta_2 GOV_{i,t} + \beta_3 HHI_{i,t} \times GOV_{i,t} + \beta_4 SIZE_{i,t} + \beta_5 AGE_{i,t} + \beta_6 BLOCK_{i,t} + \varepsilon_{i,t} \tag{7}$$

Tobin's Q = firm value
α = *konstanta*
$\beta_1 - \beta_6$ = *coefficient regression*
HHI = diversification
GOV = dummy government ownership
HHI × GOV = government ownership moderating
SIZE = firm size
AGE = firm age
BLOCK = blockholder ownership
$_{i,t}$ = *firm i, at year t*
ε = *standard error*

3 RESEARCH METHODS

3.1 *Types and data sources*

The data used in this study are obtained from the financial statements in rupiah of non-financial companies listed on the Indonesia Stock Exchange (BEI) in 2011–2014.

3.2 *Technique analysis*

This research uses two analytical techniques: multiple linear regression and moderated regression analysis.

4 DISCUSSION

4.1 *Testing the diversification hypothesis on corporate value*

Table 1. Results of multiple regression analysis Equation 6 (without moderation).

Dependent variable	Independent variable	Regression model		
		Coefficient	t	Sig.
Tobin's Q	HHI	−0.723	−8.714	0.000
	SIZE	0.083	7.140	0.000
	AGE	−0.007	−2.584	0.010
	BLOCK	0.403	6.158	0.000
	R square	0.293		
	F statistic	53.315		
	F Sig.	0.000		

The HHI variable has a significant negative coefficient, which means that HHI negatively affects Tobin's Q. In other words, the level of diversification has a significant positive effect on firm value. The SIZE variable has a significant positive coefficient, which means that SIZE positively affects Tobin's Q. The AGE variable has a significant negative coefficient, which means that AGE negatively affects Tobin's Q. The BLOCK variable has a significant positive coefficient, which means that BLOCK positively affects Tobin's Q.

4.2 *Testing the diversification hypothesis on corporate value by moderated government ownership*

The results of regression analysis show some results of a positive value and some that are negative. A coefficient marked positive indicates a unidirectional change between independent variables to the dependent variable. A coefficient marked negative means no unidirectional change between independent variables to the dependent variable. The HHI variable has a significant negative coefficient, which means that HHI negatively affects Tobin's Q. In other words, the level of diversification has a significant positive effect on firm value. HHI has a significant negative effect on firm value. In other words, diversification has a significant positive effect on firm value.

HHI variable * GOV has a significant positive coefficient, which means that government ownership weakens the negative impact of HHI on Tobin's Q. In other words, government ownership weakens the positive influence of diversification on corporate value. The SIZE variable has a significant positive coefficient, which means that SIZE positively affects Tobin's Q. The AGE variable has a significant negative coefficient, which means that AGE negatively affects Tobin's Q. The BLOCK variable has a significant positive coefficient.

4.3 *Effect of diversification on corporate value*

Diversification is measured by HHI; if the value of HHI decreases, the company will diversify. The results are in accordance with the hypothesis that the more companies diversify, the higher the value of the company.

The results of this study are in line with the research of Lin and Su (2008), which states that diversification has a significant negative effect on firm value. According to Lin and Su (2008), diversification can create value through lower risk, lower consolidated tax liabilities, create greater market forces, as well as higher efficiency in resource allocation through internal capital markets; thus, investors will be interested in investing in the company and this will increase the value of the company.

In developing countries like Indonesia, the process of allocating capital internally through diversification is more dominant, especially in conglomerate companies, so that conglomeration power will play a significant role in developing countries that do not yet have an advanced external capital market mechanism. The conglomerate company will transfer its excess resources to the subsidiary owned company subsidiary owned, and so the risk of failure of the subsidiary will be reduced.

4.4 *The effect of diversification on corporate value by moderated government ownership*

In Table 2, the moderate variable of government ownership has a significant positive value. It indicates that when a company is owned by the government, it will have a negative impact or weaken the diversification of a company, which will have an impact on the declining value of the company.

Siregar (2012) stated that state-owned companies tend to diversify and have poor corporate value compared to companies owned by other entities. Because of the government-owned companies, there are many cultures, such as corruption and nepotism, which cause the performance of the directors or managers to be compromised. Government-owned companies have inadequate planning to diversify, so that it will have the impact of increasing risk in each segment. This is what makes investors reluctant to invest their capital into a company owned by the government. On the other hand, the non-government companies are considered more effective to diversify, because they have a mature planning strategy, so that the level of losses that will be experienced by investors when the company diversifies will be smaller.

Table 2. Results of multiple regression analysis Equation 7 (with moderation).

	Regression model		
Independent variable	Coefficient	t	Sig.
HHI	−0.824	−9.878	0.000
GOV	−0.991	−2.801	0.005
HHI*GOV	1.900	3.753	0.000
SIZE	0.062	5.033	0.000
AGE	0.007	−2.714	0.007
BLOCK	0.361	5.509	0.000
R square	0.328		
F statistic	41.699		
F Sig.	0.000		

5 CONCLUSION

The level of diversification has a significant positive effect on the value of the company. The higher a company's HHI, the lower the company's diversification rate, resulting in lower corporate value. Government ownership weakens the significant negative impact of the HHI on corporate value. This shows that the positive effect of diversification on corporate value is weaker in companies with government ownership (BUMN) than in companies with non-government ownership.

REFERENCES

Berger, P.G. & Ofek, E. (1995). Diversification's effect on firm value. *Journal of Financial Economics, 37*(1), 39–65.

Chen, S.S. & Ho, K.W. (2000). corporate diversification, ownership structure, and firm value: The Singapore evidence. *International Review of Financial Analysis, 9*(3), 315–326.

Harto, P. (2005). Diversification policy and its impact to company performance Kebijakan Diversifikasi Perusahaan dan Pengaruhnya Terhadap Kinerja Studi Empiris Pada Perusahaan Publik Di Indonesia. *Forum Penelitian*, VII: 297–307.

Lin, C. & Su, D. (2008). Industrial diversification, partial privatization and firm valuation: Evidence from publicly listed firms in China. *Journal of Corporate Finance*, 14(4), 405–417.

Montgomery, C.A. (1994). Corporate diversification. *Journal of Economic Perspective*, 8 no. 3: 162–178.

Montgomery, C.A. & Wernerfelt, B. (1998). Diversification, Ricardian rents and Tobin's q. *Rand Journal of Economics*, 19 no. 4, 623–632.

Siregar, E.I. (2012). The impact of diversification poicy and Firm Characteristics to Firm Value Pengaruh Kebijakan Diversifikasi dan Karakteristik Perusahaan Terhadap Nilai Perusahaan BUMN Jasa Konstruksi. *Jurnal Etikonomi*, 11 no. 1.

Umrie, R.H.S. & Yuliani. Yl (2011). The Role of Financing Mix as Mediating Variable for Diversification Impact to Firm Value Peran Financing Mixsebagai Mediasi Pengaruh Diversifikasi Terhadap Nilai Perusahaan (Studi Empiris Secondary Sectorsdi Bursa Efek Indonesia). *Jurnal Manajemen & Bisnis Sriwijaya,* 9 no. 17: 13–32.

Increasing Management Relevance and Competitiveness – Sukoco et al. (Eds)
© 2018 Taylor & Francis Group, London, ISBN 978-0-8153-7455-8

Do operating costs, investment returns and claims have an effect on contributions?

D.F. Septiarini
Airlangga University, Surabaya, Indonesia

ABSTRACT: The slow and stagnant economic conditions in 2015 caused numerous sectors to decline. Sharia insurance was no exception. Sharia life insurance saw a higher claim growth than contribution growth in 2015. This also happened in the sharia life insurance industry. The objective of this research is to understand the influence, both partially and simultaneously, of Operating Cost, Investment Returns and Claim towards Contribution to sharia life insurance companies in Indonesia during the 2013–2015 period. This research uses a quantitative approach. The type and data source used are secondary data. The sample obtaining technique is by purposive sampling and is obtaining from 18 sharia life insurance companies in Indonesia, with three companies in the form of pure sharia companies (full–fledged) and 15 sharia units as the subject of the research. The analysis technique used is data panel regression by using the Fixed Effect Model (FEM). The result of this research shows that Operating Cost, Investment Returns and Claim simultaneously influence contribution partially. While simultaneously, Operating Cost, Investment Returns and Claims are also influenced significantly.

Keywords: Sharia Life Insurance, Operational Cost, Investment Result, Claim, Contribution

1 INTRODUCTION

Sharia insurance is an attempt at protecting and helping each other between a number of people or parties through investment in the form of an asset or *tabarru'*, which gives a returning pattern in order to face certain risks through a contract according to sharia (Sula 2004:28). According to Fatwa DSN MUI No. 21/DSN-MUI/X/2001 on General Guidelines of Sharia Insurance, the contract used needs to be in accordance with sharia. This means that it does not contain *ghahar* (fraud), *maysir* (gambling), *riba* (interest), *zhulm* (torment), *risywah* (bribe), or *haram* (forbidden and immoral goods).

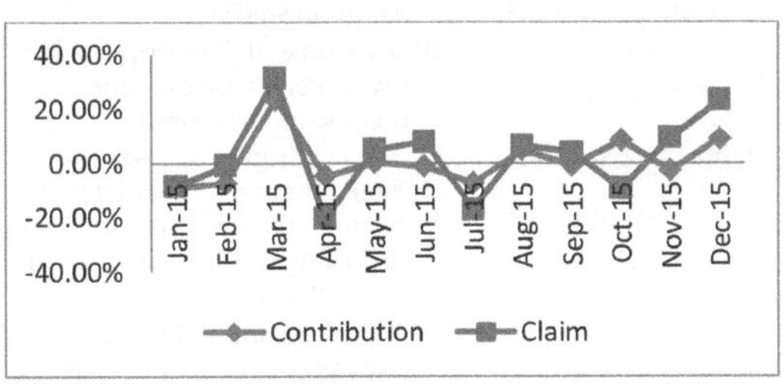

Figure 1. Growth of contribution and claim of sharia life insurance company in the period of January–December 2015.
Source: *Data Statistik IKNB Syariah* (www.ojk.go.id) cultivated data.

The growth of claims is higher compared to the growth of contributions collected by sharia insurance industries. Slow economic conditions, which tend to be stuck, causes many sectors to degenerate (OJK 2015).

The growth of claims which is higher than contribution growth of the participants is also experienced by sharia life insurance companies. The following Table 1 explains such phenomenon.

2 THEORETICAL FRAMEWORK

2.1 *Relationship between independent and dependent variables*

According to Fitriati (2009), the achievement of the Contribution (C) portfolio can break even using the assumptions of the costs and expenses of the company. Operational Cost (OC) has a significant positive relationship to contribution.

H_1: OC partially and significantly influences C.
H_2: Investment Research (IR) partially and significantly influences C.

Table 1. Table of difference between conventional insurance and sharia insurance.

No.	Principal	Sharia insurance	Conventional insurance
1.	Concept	A group of people who help, guarantee, and cooperate with each other with their own methods to generate *tabarru'* fund.	An agreement between two or more parties, in which the underwriters are bound to the insured by receiving premium to provide exchange.
2.	MAGHRIB (*Maysir, Gharar,* and *Riba* (Interest))	Clean from the practice of *maysir, gharar*, and *riba* (interest).	There are *maysir, gharar*, and *riba* (interest) which are forbidden by *muamalat*.
3.	DPS	Yes	No
4.	Contract	*Tabarru'* contract and *tijarah* contract (*mudharabah, wakalah*).	Buying and selling contract (*mu'awadah, idz'aan, gharar*, and *mulzim* contract).
5.	Guarantee/Risk	Sharing of risk	Transfer of risk
6.	Fund management	In the product of saving (life), there is fund separation, *tabarru'* (charity), and clients' fund.	There is no fund separation.
7.	Investment	According to Islamic sharia principal.	Free to be used and invested anywhere.
8.	Elements of contribution	Consists of *tabarru'* element and saving (which do not contain interest element). *Tabarru'* is also calculated from a mortality table, without calculating technical interest.	Elements of clients' contribution consist of mortality tables, interest, and cost of insurance.
9.	Source of claim payment	From *tabarru'* account, where the clients insure each other. If there is any client who experiences disaster, other clients will insure the risk together.	From the company saving, as the consequence of the underwriter's actions towards the insured. It is purely business and there is no spiritual nuance.

H_3: Claim (CLM) partially and significantly influences C.

H_4: OC, IR and CLM simultaneously and significantly influences C.

The regression equation is obtained is:

$$Y = a + b_1X_1 + b_2X_2 + b_3X_3 \quad (1)$$

3 RESEARCH METHODOLOGY

This research was conducted by using a quantitative approach.

Identification of Variable: (1) Exogenous Variables are Operational Cost (OC), Investment Result (IR) and Claim (CLM). (2) Endogenous Variable is the variable Contribution (C).

3.1 *Type and source of data*

The type of data is this research is secondary data. The source of the data is from the financial report of each sharia life insurance company in Indonesia. Using industrial population and sharia life insurance companies with purposive sampling, 19 companies were analyzed for three years, so there were a total number of 57 samples in this research.

3.2 *Operational definition of variable*

Table 2. Operational definition of variable.

Research variable	Type of variable	Operational definition
Operational cost	Endogenous	OC is the cost in the form of expense to carry out the primary activities of the company. OC = Amount of Expense or Cost paid by the Company.
Investment result	Exogenous	IR is the result from the clients' collected fund that is invested based on sharia. IR = Income of *Tabarru'* Fund Investment + Investment Income of the Company.
Claim	Exogenous	CLM is the rights of insurance clients that are obligated to be given by the insurance company according to the agreement in the contract. CLM = Amount of Insurance Expense or Net Claim Expense.
Contribution	Endogenous	C is the insurance clients' responsibility to give an amount of money to the insurance company according to the agreement in the contract. C = Gross Amount of Participant's Contribution.

Source: Cultivated from various sources.

3.3 *Hypothesis test*

3.3.1 *Simultaneous significance test (F test)*

If the significance of calculated F < 0.05 then H_0 is rejected, which means that there is a relation between variable X and variable Y. If the significance of calculated F > 0.05, then H_0 is accepted, which means that there is no relation between variable X and variable Y.

3.3.2 *Partial significance test (t-test)*

If the significance of calculated t < 0.05, it means that there is an influence between variable X towards variable Y and H_0 is accepted. If the significance of calculated t > 0.05 it means that there is no influence between variable X towards variable Y.

4 RESULTS AND DISCUSSION

Table 3. Result of estimation of Fixed Effect Model (FEM).

Included observations: 3
Cross-sections included: 19
Total pool (balanced) observations: 57

Variable	Coefficient	Std. Error	t-Statistic	Prob.
C	67,051.80	19,413.28	3.453913	0.0015
BO?	0.578102	0.191133	3.024598	0.0046
HI?	2.605768	0.295646	8.813814	0.0000
KLM?	1.427397	0.275073	5.189150	0.0000

Effects Specification

Cross-section fixed (dummy variables)

R-Squared	0.998753	Mean dependent var	221,329.1
Adjusted R-Squared	0.998004	S.D. dependent var	467,469.3
S.E. of Regression	20,883.48	Akaike info criterion	23.01553
Sum Squared Resid	1.53E+10	Schwarz criterion	23.80408
Log Likelihood	−633.9426	Hannan-Quinn criterion	23.32199
F-Statistic	1,334.527	Durbin-Watson stat	2.689246
Prob (F-Statistic)	0.000000		

The linear equation can be written as follows:

$$C = 67051.80 + 0.578102OC + 2.605768IR + 1.427397CLM$$

Therefore, the relation between the independent variable and the dependent variable as a **partial** can be shown as follows:

Result	Hypothesis	Regression	t-Statistic test	Explanation
OC to C	H_1	+0.5781	0.0046 < 0.0500	Significant
IR to C	H_2	+2.6057	0.0000 < 0.0500	Significant
CLM to C	H_3	+1.4273	0.0000 < 0.0500	Significant

Therefore, the relation between the independent variable and the dependent variable as a **simultan** can be shown as follows:

Result	Hypothesis	F-Statistic test	Explanation
OC, IR, CLM to C	H_4	0.0000 < 0.0500	Significant

5 DISCUSSION

5.1 *Influence of operational cost partially on the contribution*

The result of this research supports the research conducted by Fitriati (2009), which stated that OC significantly influences C. Therefore, if OC increases, the contribution fund also increases because the company needs to be able to cover the costs expended for the company's operations. The company is encouraged to keep increasing its efficiency. The efficiency itself is very useful for the company. The smaller the cost expended for operations, the better is the performance of the company, so that the company can concentrate more on other more productive sectors, such in creating a new product or renewing an old product, which will in turn increase the company's profit. The source of OC is taken from the profit sharing of surplus underwriting, investment profit sharing, shareholders' fund and clients' contribution (Sula 2004:181).

5.2 *Partial influence of investment result on the contribution*

The positive influence of IR on C is in accordance with a research conducted by Saksono (2006), which stated that the contribution will be influenced by the component of investment result if the company desires a certain amount of investment result from the clients' contribution. Of the 19 studied companies, there were 14 companies in which the IR increased, and the clients' contribution also increased. This means that if the company desires a high expected return, the invested fund also needs to be high. The target of investment result becomes the company's policy.

5.3 *Partial claim influence on clients' contribution*

The positive influence of CLM on C is according to the research conducted by Saksono (2006). One of the principals of sharia insurance is sharing risks between the insurance clients and providing protection for the clients. Therefore, if the claims of a sharia life insurance company increase, the clients' contributions also increase, because the company needs to be able to pay its obligations to the clients (i.e. the claim). In addition, if the clients' contribution increases, the more the clients who assist each other (*ta'awun*) using the *tabarru'* fund taken from each clients' contribution devoted to assist other clients who experience disaster.

5.4 *Influence of operational cost, investment result and claim on clients' contribution*

The positive influence of OC, IR and CLM on C is in line with the research conducted by Saksono (2006) and Fitriati (2009). Based on the research, the OC, IR and C have positive simultaneous influence on the clients' contribution. Therefore, if the sharia life insurance company needs to expend costs for the company's operations, while setting the target of IR that can reach the expected return and being able to pay the claims to the clients who experience loss, then it is expected that the sharia life insurance company will obtain the amount of the clients' contribution which can cover all expenses.

6 CONCLUSIONS

1. The OC partially has a significant and positive influence on the contribution.
2. The IR partially has a significant and positive influence on the contribution.
3. The Claim partially has a significant and positive influence on the contribution.
4. The OC, IR and Claim simultaneously have a significant and positive influence on the contribution.

REFERENCES

Archer, S., Karim, R.A.A. & Nienhaus, V. (Eds.). (2009). *Takaful Islamic Insurance Concepts and Regulatory Issues.* Singapore: John Wiley and Sons (Asia).

Herman, D. (2000). *Manajemen Asuransi.* Jakarta: Bumi Aksara.

Khoiril, A. (2007). *Asuransi Syariah Halal dan Maslahat.* Tiga Serangkai: Solo.

Increasing Management Relevance and Competitiveness – Sukoco et al. (Eds)
© 2018 Taylor & Francis Group, London, ISBN 978-0-8153-7455-8

Crowdfunding new paradigm for financing: Operational pattern of crowdfunding in Indonesia

S.R. Arifin & Wisudanto
Universitas Airlangga, Surabaya, Indonesia

ABSTRACT: This article aims to confirm crowdfunding as being a new phenomenon in funding, especially for a millennial business entrepreneur. The development of crowdfunding in Indonesia is facing challenges and opportunities because crowdfunding is a new type of intermediary funding which uses innovation in technology. This article explores Indonesian crowdfunding development, and the awareness of millennial business entrepreneurs to access this funding. Descriptive analysis method found that there are two operational patterns of crowdfunding platforms in Indonesia, and the lending-based is four times bigger than donation-based. In recent years, they collected 455 billion rupiahs and involved 304,467 entities users. The research is also resulting in potential development towards crowdfunding.

1 INTRODUCTION

In recent years, the world has been introduced to an alternative way to gain access to finance, known as crowdfunding. It raises funds from a large society or 'crowd', using Internet-based platforms involving a large number of people. In 2014, global crowdfunding collected $16.2 billion, almost three times more than in 2013 (Massolution, 2015). In Indonesia, the six leading crowdfunding platforms raised over 505.3 billion rupiahs.

The total funds raised by banking in Indonesia reached 4.334 trillion rupiahs, while the capital market raised a total fund of some 34.3 trillion rupiahs. Venture capital collected 8.15 trillion rupiahs, while crowdfunding only collected 0.5 trillion rupiahs. Despite some funds collected by crowdfunding being relatively small compared to existing funding models such as banking, capital markets, and venture capital, its potential is very likely to become larger in the future.

The crowdfunding model is readily available to anyone. Therefore, it will be able to reduce the market share of traditional financial institutions, such as banking and capital markets, in direct or indirect ways. The crowdfunding model can easily go viral on the Internet, so the funds collected from the Internet can reach a sizable amount. Compared to banking and capital markets, the crowdfunding model is more unregulated, and consequently the investment environment is more vulnerable and insecure.

On the one hand, crowdfunding can reach many people previously unreachable by traditional financial services. The ease of use that crowdfunding offers, allows it to reach non-bankable small to medium enterprises SMEs, and people with low literacyor uneducated in financial investment. It strongly supports the financial inclusion and financial literacy programs proclaimed by regulators, such as Indonesian Central Bank (BI) and Indonesian Financial Service Authority (OJK). Therefore, the funds collected by financial institutions are fully utilized by the business world.

The main focus in this article is on the operational pattern of crowdfunding in Indonesia. This article aims to form a big map of the operational pattern of crowdfunding in Indonesia, consisting of the types, sizes, regulations, and parties involved in the whole crowdfunding process and development. By knowing the map, it is expected to answer what issues are inherent in the new model of financial intermediation, such as the potential and the challenges faced.

2 LITERATURE REVIEW

2.1 *Crowdfunding*

Valančienė and (2014) define crowdfunding as being a method to connect entrepreneurs who want to increase capital, with new investors who have excess capital resources and want to invest small amounts through Internet-based intermediary entities.

Crowdfunding can be divided into four categories, according to the funding base offered by the crowdfunding platform. The four categories are donation, pre-selling, lending and equity crowdfunding (Vulkan et al., 2016).

Three main stakeholders in the crowdfunding process are entrepreneurs, crowdfunding platforms and investors (backers). Each stakeholder has its roles and interests. The first line starts from

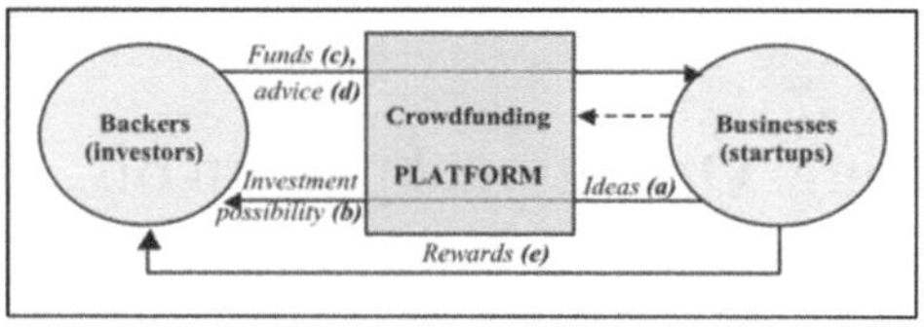

Figure 1. Crowdfunding process framework.
Source: Valančienė and Jegelevičiūtė (2014).

entrepreneurs (business or startups) proposing ideas, funding requests through the crowdfunding platform and promising returns to investors. Backers (investors) will see the investment opportunities offered by entrepreneurs, who can then give funding commitment or advice. The crowdfunding platform serves as an intermediary that connects investors and backers (Valančienė & Jegelevičiūtė, 2014).

2.2 *Financial intermediary institution and financial innovation*

The main function of the financial system is to collect funds from the surplus unit and distribute it to the deficit unit. One of the main parts of the financial system is the intermediary financial institutions, such as banks and capital markets (Boot & Thakor, 1997).

The development of the financial system demands a change known as the spiral of innovation (Merton & Bodie, 1995). Technological advancement makes it possible to achieve high efficiency, and it can be used to reduce transaction costs. Low transaction costs, in theory and practice, will encourage broad changes in the future of financial institutions (Merton & Bodie, 1995).

The new emerging type of funding entity in the millennial age is called crowdfunding. These entities have different characteristics from traditional financial institutions, such as banks and capital markets. Crowdfunding is not only an intermediary financial entity but also *loci* of social interaction that forms private social capital among supporters of crowdfunding. These characteristics distinguish between crowdfunding and other funding sources (Colombo et al., 2015). Internal social capital can also be obtained outside the crowdfunding supporters communities, such as from family and friends (Agrawal et al., 2011) and through social media (Mollick, 2014).

3 METHOD

3.1 *Descriptive method*

This article uses the descriptive research method to discover the operational pattern of crowdfunding in Indonesia. Descriptive research is a study aimed at describing events or situations. This type of research is not intended to prove correlation, testing hypotheses, forecasting and getting implications and meaning (Suryabrata, 2000).

Descriptive research to answer the research problem consists of three stages. Stage I is searching the crowdfunding platform websites using search engines, by entering certain search keywords to get a list of active crowdfunding platforms in Indonesia. Keywords used are 'crowdfunding in Indonesia' and 'P2P lending in Indonesia'. Stage II is conducting a content analysis on each platform site on the list that has been made. Stage III is to increase the objectivity of the result by surveying every crowdfunding platform site on the list. We simply confirm information about the operating base, the amount of funds collected and the total users on their platform.

3.2 *Research object and subject*

The research object in this article is the operational pattern of a crowdfunding platform and its development potential. Topics in this study are the content displayed by crowdfunding platforms and the crowdfunding platform managers.

3.3 *Operationalization of variables*

Operationalization of variables aims to know the measurement of variables at the level of practice and reality. The operational definitions of each variable in this study are as follows.

3.3.1 *Amount of crowdfunding*

Crowdfunding is an Internet-based intermediary entity (Valančienė & Jegelevičiūtė, 2014). The variable measured as one website address counts as one platform.

3.3.2 *Size*

Company size is the number of users involved in the financial institution. Users of crowfunding platform consist of investors and startups. Each entity who participate in crowdfunding platform whether as an investors or startups, counted as one user. The total amount of funds raised from funding activity is a proxy for company size.

3.3.3 *Type*

Crowdfunding type can be categorized as donation-based, pre-selling, lending and equity crowdfunding (Vulkan et al., 2016). It is identified from the funding and financing mechanisms offered by crowdfunding platforms. When, in the platform, it describes or mentions 'donate', it is identified as being donation-based crowdfunding. So that 'lend' is lending-based, or 'invest' and 'return' are equity-based crowdfunding.

4 RESULT

4.1 *Number of crowdfunding platforms in Indonesia*

The finding through search engines to collect a list of crowdfunding platforms in Indonesia indicates active and inactive crowdfunding platforms. Table 1 is a list of current crowdfunding in Indonesia.

The crowdfunding platforms that became inactive during this research—in 2017 - was 'Wujudkan', with the website address www.wujudkan.com, and 'Ayo Peduli' at www.ayopeduli.com. The closure of the 'Wujudkan' platform was due to an inability to collect complete funded projects of more than 12%. This made the manager feel unable to fulfill their responsibilities as a good funder. Therefore, the manager decided to close the site.

4.2 *Crowdfunding size*

The identified crowdfunding platforms were then analyzed regarding the content to determine the size of crowdfunding. The content of crowdfunding is used to measure its size, and also shows the number of participants involved, both as investors (backers) as well as accessing funds.

The total funds collected by each crowdfunding platform can also be a measure of the size of the crowdfunding platform, in addition to the number of people involved as users.

4.3 *Types of crowdfunding in Indonesia*

The identified crowdfunding platform was then analyzed as regards to its content, to determine the operational base of each platform. According to Vulkan et al. (2016), there are four crowdfunding types: donation, pre-selling, lending and equity crowdfunding. Referring to Vulkan's categories, then the type of crowdfunding in Indonesia today consists of only two kinds of categories—donations and lending. Pre-selling and equity-based schemes no longer exist.

The donation-based crowdfunding platform operates on a fundraising basis from the community in the form of voluntary donations, to distribute charitable projects or activities with the objective of bettering humanity. The lending-based crowdfunding platform operates as an intermediary party, just like a bank. The platform collects funds from the community as funds disbursed to the borrowers. The borrower is obligated to repay the principal and interest according to the contract. The crowdfunding platform will return the funds invested by the lender, along with the promised interest.

Table 1. Crowdfunding platforms in Indonesia.

Website address	Platform name
www.kitabisa.com	Kitabisa
www.gandengtangan.org	GandengTangan
www.modalku.co.id	Modalku
www.investree.id	Investree
www.koinworks.com	Koinworks
www.amartha.com	Amartha
www.crowdo.co.id	Crowdo

Source: Author's compilation.

Table 2. Crowdfunding platform size in Indonesia.

Total users	Total fund raised*	Platform name
103.8	289.981	Kitabisa
0.3	1.05	GandengTangan
151.2	1.072	Modalku
122	2.219	Investree
Unknown	8.059	Koinworks
78	3.2	Amartha
50	34	Crowdo

*In billion rupiah.
Source: Author's compilation.

Table 3. Crowdfunding types in Indonesia.

Type	Platform name
Donation-based	Kitabisa
Lending-based	GandengTangan
Lending-based	Modalku
Lending-based	Investree
Lending-based	Koinworks
Lending-based	Amartha
Lending-based	Crowdo

Source: Author's compilation.

4.4 *Potential development of crowdfunding in Indonesia*

4.4.1 *Growth of SMEs*

The result of content analysis on crowdfunding platforms in Indonesia shows that the main target of crowdfunding financing is SMEs. SMEs are the strategic market of the crowdfunding business model. If we look at the data of Indonesia's SMEs in 2013, it recorded as many as 57,895,721 units with an average annual growth of 2.41% per year since 2009. It has become a major opportunity for crowdfunding platforms to expand the market.

4.4.2 *Millennial generation in Indonesia*

The millennial generation is a generation born between 1980–2000. The millennial characteristics are closely related to the digital world. Millennials grow and evolve together with broadband, smartphones, laptops, and social media, which have become the norm, and millennials demand fast access to information and flexibility (PWC, 2011).

Based on the 2010 census, the millennial generation in Indonesia reached 36% of the total Indonesian population of 238 million. Currently, the main decision-makers are generation X. In 2020, the millennial generation is projected to be 31% of the total population of Indonesia. Someday, when a demographic transition occurs whereby millennials are the main decision-makers, crowdfunding as a digital platform will have major opportunities for the growth and will be increasingly needed as a means of investment.

4.4.3 *Regulation*

Lending-based crowdfunding platforms have been regulated by the Financial Services Authority of the Republic of Indonesia through the Financial Services Authority Regulation No. 77/POJK.01/2016 on Information Technology-Based Lending Services. The lending-based crowdfunding platform (known as P2P lending), is included in the regulation in the category of 'Other Financial Institutions', such as pawnshops, export financing institutions and secondary housing finance companies (OJK, 2016).

This rule ensures security for crowdfunding users. This regulation requires that crowdfunding platforms should be in the form of a limited liability company or a cooperative. The existence of this regulation further reinforces that there is support and supervision from the government concerning Internet-based financial services. The weakness of this rule is that it has not yet covered the donation-based crowdfunding platform. Moreover, the regulation does not consider that one day there may also be a crowdfunding platform that offers equity-based schemes.

5 CONCLUSION AND DISCUSSION

The results of this study show a big map of the operational pattern of crowdfunding in Indonesia. The crowdfunding type in Indonesia currently only consists of two kinds: crowdfunding based on donations, and lending-based. The total size of crowdfunding counted from total users is 304,467 entities. The size in total funds collected reached 455 billion rupiahs. This measure, compared to traditional financial intermediary institutions such as banking and the capital market, is relatively small and quite insignificant in amount.

The development of crowdfunding will continue to grow as the number of SMEs grows as the main market of the majority of crowdfunding platforms. Crowdfunding opportunities will also grow with the demographic shift in which X generation will changed by the millennial generation, who will subsequently become the major decision-makers in many sectors of life and business.

Regulation is necessary as a legal means to ensure the safety of the users of crowdfunding. With this support, the crowdfunding platform can still be well developed without ignoring the security and convenience aspects for the users. Those aspects can increase trust from users.

In the millennial age, crowdfunding has become the main topic of financial issue. Research on the risk of crowdfunding becomes necessary in the first place to complement existing regulations, so that the level of security when using crowdfunding is better, without hampering the development of innovation from the finance.

REFERENCES

Agrawal, A.K., Catalini, C. & Goldfarb, A. (2011). Geography of crowdfunding (No.W16820). National Bureau of Economic Research.

Boot, A.W. & Thakor, A.V. (1997). Financial system architecture. *The Review of Financial Studies*, *10*(3), 693–733.

Colombo, M.G., Franzoni, C. & RossiLamastra, C. (2015). Internal social capital and the attraction of early contributions in crowdfunding. *Entrepreneurship Theory and Practice*, *39*(1), 75–100.

Massolution, C.L. (2015). Crowdfunding industry report. Retrieved from http://reports.crowdsourcing.org/index.php?route1/4product/product&product_id1/454#oid1/41001_23_banner_38.

Merton, R.C. & Bodie, Z. (1995). A conceptual framework for analyzing the financial system. *The Global Financial System: A Functional Perspective*, 3–31.

Mollick, E. (2014). The dynamics of crowdfunding. An exploratory study. *Journal of Business Venturing*, *29*(1), 1–16.

OJK. (2016). *Salinan Peraturan Otoritas Jasa Keuangan No. 77/POJK.01/2016 tentang Layanan Pinjam Meminjam Uang Berbasis Teknologi Informasi* [Copy of Indonesian Financial Services Authority No.77/POJK.01/2016 about Financial Service based on Information Technology]. Retrieved from http://www.ojk.go.id/id/regulasi/otoritas-jasa-keuangan/peraturan-ojk/Documents/Pages/POJK-Nomor-77-POJK.01-2016/SAL%20%20POJK%20Fintech.pdf. Accessed at March 2nd 2017.

PWC. (2011). Millennial at work reshaping the workplace. Retrieved from http://www.pwc.com/en_M1/m1/services/consulting/documents/millennials-at-work.pdf. Accessed March 7th 2017.

Suryabrata, S. (2000). *Metode penelitian* [Research Method]. PT. Raja Grafindo Persada, Jakarta.

Valančienė, L. & Jegelevičiūtė, S. (2014). Crowdfunding for creating value: A stakeholder approach. *Procedia-Social and Behavioral Sciences, 156*, 599–604.

Vulkan, N., Åstebro, T. & Sierra, T.M.F. (2016). Equity crowdfunding: A new phenomena. *Journal of Business Venturing Insights*, *5*, 37–49.

Increasing Management Relevance and Competitiveness – Sukoco et al. (Eds)
© 2018 Taylor & Francis Group, London, ISBN 978-0-8153-7455-8

Different ways to solve the liquidity problem of Indonesian Islamic microfinance

I. Mawardi & T. Widiastuti
Universitas Airlangga, Surabaya, Indonesia

ABSTRACT: *Baitul Maal wa Tamwil* (BMT), which is a form of Islamic microfinance institution in Indonesia, faces liquidity problems. This study aims to map out the liquidity problems faced by BMTs, to discover how BMTs are addressing the different problems and to find a BMT model of liquidity management. This study used a qualitative approach using the case study analysis techniques of Robert K. Yin. Subjects of this study are BMTs in East Java, which were selected purposively with ten BMT managers as key informants. The results show that there are five different ways used by BMTs in overcoming liquidity. BMTs were established as formal securities guarantor institutions, in the form of a secondary cooperative that consists of BMTs, taking a standby loan from Islamic banks which can be taken when needing liquidity, establishing non-formal inter-BMT relations, borrowing from other financial institutions, and having individual backing that can be borrowed at any time. The best way to manage the liquidity of BMTs is to form a secondary cooperative, because it can also act as an alternative for BMTs to save funds when there is excess liquidity.

Keywords: Islamic microfinance, *baitul maal wa tamwil*, liquidity problem, cooperative

1 INTRODUCTION

An Islamic microfinance institution, *Baitul Maal wa Tamwil* (BMT), is an intermediary financial institution such as a bank, operating in the micro sector. BMTs receive deposits from surplus units and disburse them in the form of financing to customers in need (deficit units). As a sharia intermediary financial institution, the BMT runs it's operations according to Islamic sharia. From the financing side, BMTs will earn revenue, where some will be given to the depositor (*shahibul mal*) and some will be the income of the BMT (Ridwan, 2006, 34).

In BMTs, liquidity risk emerges as one of the most important risks, where BMTs need to handle it in order to avoid greater losses. As an intermediary institution that relies on trust, failure to regulate liquidity will impact on other risks. Liquidity risks are broadly defined as potential losses for financial institutions, arising from their inability to meet obligations or to fund asset increases when they mature without incurring unacceptable costs or losses (Dusuki, 2005; Greuning & Bratanovic, 1999). This risk occurs when depositors collectively decide to withdraw their funds in greater amounts than the funds owned by the institution (Hubbard, 2002, 323), or when borrowers fail to meet financial obligations.

In practice, one of the main objectives of liquidity management is to maintain assets and liabilities. Among these are managing financing and financing activities, estimating funding and financing requests, as well as maintaining a reserve fund to meet its financial obligations to third parties. Sharia intermediary financial institutions have unique characteristics because BMT operations must comply with sharia principles. Therefore, the arrangement of liquidity management mechanisms in these financial institutions requires extra effort and special attention. Liquidity risk in the intermediary financial institution arises when the business in the real sector decreases, resulting in a failure to perform proper liquidity management.

In principle, sharia intermediary financial institutions seek to provide good liquidity management on real business transactions. This is because each financing contract with a real asset in a sharia intermediary financial institution is unique, compared to that of a conventional one. Therefore, in operation, sharia intermediary financial institutions should consider business cycles, cooperation among business partners, and deal with stakeholders to avoid any liquidity risk arising from the disharmony of business partners or unfavorable business conditions.

The intermediary Islamic finance institution also acts as a financial intermediary, supporter and facilitator, as well as positioning itself as a trusted body for investors and business partners. Thus, liquidity management in BMTs is done based on trust, confidence and support from each other. In the context of banking in Indonesia, both sharia and conventional banks, in the case of solving liquidity problems, guarantees are provided by a third-party deposit guarantee institution (LPS) and are bound by the regulator to provide savings, such as the minimum reserve requirement in the banking system, so that the liquidity problem in the bank can be overcome.

As a financial intermediary institution like sharia banks, a BMT is faced with greater liquidity problems. In addition to having to consider profitability with more release financing, a BMT faces problems not faced by sharia banking. Firstly, BMTs do not have a third-party deposit guarantee institution; secondly, BMTs are not bound by regulators to provide savings, such as minimum statutory reserves in banks that function as a source of liquidity when experiencing problems. These reasons underlie this research to find the way or mechanism of a BMT in overcoming its liquidity problem.

1.1 *Function of liquidity*

Liquidity for intermediary financial institutions is very important. Therefore, the level of liquidity reflects the ability of intermediary financial institutions to meet financial obligations that must be met immediately. According to Kuncoro and Suhardjono (2002, 279), liquidity is the ability of the intermediary financial institution to provide sufficient funds to meet all its obligations, as well as commitments, which have been issued to its customers at any time. According to Wood et al (2004, 153), liquidity is the ability of intermediary financial institutions to meet all withdrawal of funds by the depositors, clients and liabilities that have matured, and to meet the demand for credit without any delay.

According to Taswan (2006, 97), liquidity may serve as follows: a) to indicate that the intermediary financial institution is a safe place to save money; b) to enable intermediary financial institutions to fulfill their credit commitments; c) to avoid the sale of unprofitable assets; and d) to minimize the risk assessment of the inability to pay the obligation to withdraw the funds.

1.2 *Liquidity management policy*

The liquidity management process begins with the establishment of a liquidity management policy by the Board of Directors as the primary guideline for all entities in the organization. For this purpose, there are at least three implementation requirements: a) the Board of Directors should understand the bank's liquidity risk profiles and internal/external business environment, and stimulate the liquidity risk tolerance; b) the Board of Directors shall determine and agree on liquidity risk management strategies, policies and practices; and c) the Board of Directors shall deploy, communicate and guide senior managers to manage liquidity effectively (BCBS, 2008).

Following liquidity management policies and the role of liability committees of assets and their peers, effective information systems need to support the liquidity management processes (BCBS, 2008). This system allows *Lembaga Keuangan Syariah* (LKS) to monitor, report and control liquidity risk exposures, and determine funding needs within and outside the organization. In general, an effective information system concerns two players, namely, decision-makers of liquidity management and decision-makers at the operational level.

In order to maintain the soundness of the liquidity management process, financial institutions must have an internal control system, to adhere to the processes undertaken by decision-makers with a single set of decision-makers (BCBS, 2008). This internal control system can be assigned to the Asset Liability Committee (ALCO) as a representative of the directors to bridge the gap between the decision-makers. However, regular functions of a comprehensive internal control system audit the liquidity management process, to evaluate liquidity positions, and if necessary, to propose revisions or improvements of the liquidity management process to the Board of Directors (decision-makers).

1.3 *Identification and measurement of liquidity risk*

Measurement of liquidity risk in a BMT can be done in four ways. First, the funding structure, namely the assessment of the structure of deposits by type, term, currency, interest rate, fund owner and concentration of funds ownership. Second, expected cash flow, which is the assessment of all cash inflows and cash outflows, including funding, needs to meet commitments on administrative account transactions to identify possible future funding shortages. Third, market access, in other words the assessment of the ability of intermediary institutions to obtain liquidity in the market, both under normal conditions and in abnormal conditions. Fourth, marketability asset, which is the assessment of liquid assets that can be converted into cash, especially in abnormal conditions (crisis), when the BMT is not able to fulfill all obligations by using positive cash flow owned and loaned from the money market.

Liquidity calculation can be done by arranging a maturity profile (maturity ladder) for each type of scenario, by arranging cash flow based on maturity or estimation using an assumption based on past experience. If the cash flow forecast is based on estimated statistical data, the accuracy and precision of the estimate should be periodically reassessed. In addition, the assumptions and variables used in these estimates should be reviewed in accordance with changing market conditions, competitive factors and changes in customer behavior (Muhamad, 2009, 74).

1.4 *Liquidity as sharia responsibility*

Good liquidity management shows good sharia implementation as well. Sharia implementation is a good consequence for sharia financial institutions that will get closer to the achievement of the goal of sharia, the *maslahah*. The better implementation of sharia will have a positive impact on BMTs. Therefore, Allah has promised a blessing that can be interpreted as achievement of performance and the better benefits of a BMT for anyone who implements Sharia properly. In surah Al A'raf (7) verse 96, Allah says that for anyone who believes and is cautious to Allah, which means to observe the sharia of Allah by doing what is commanded and away from what is forbidden by Allah, Allah will give blessings and prosperity.

This means that if the BMT implements Islamic sharia correctly, then the performance of the BMT will be good and will affect the benefit for all. Vice versa, if the implementation of sharia in the BMT is bad, then the difficulties will also hit the BMT. Allah has declared that if implementing the sharia of Allah is below par, Allah promises shame, as explained in Surah Al-Baqarah (2) verse 85. Both verses above show that the implementation of sharia is very important for BMT, because the implementation of sharia is closely related to the achievement of the purpose of implementation of sharia, namely maqashid sharia or *maslahah*.

2 RESEARCH METHOD

2.1 *Research approach*

This research uses qualitative approach with the case study approach of Robert K. Yin. Subjects of this study are BMTs in East Java that were selected purposively with ten BMT managers as key informants. A survey research design involves selecting respondents and receiver samples of questionnaires (McMillan & Schumacher, 1993). Primary data is collected by using structured interviews with the participation of BMT managers.

This study assumes that BMT managers are involved, either directly or indirectly, to solve liquidity problem in BMTs. Purposive sampling is used to select managers of BMTs in East Java that know exactly how to manage liquidity and solve liquidity problems. In addition, managers responsible for BMTs in the study area (i.e. the operations manager and BMT employees) are used as additional informants.

2.2 *Data analysis technique*

The data analysis technique of this research uses content analysis method. Content analysis methods are defined as techniques for drawing conclusions by identifying the specific characteristics of a message objectively, systematically and generally (Holsti, 1969, 14). This method is intended to analyze all discussion about the concept of solving BMTs' liquidity problems.

The author prepares the basic procedures for the design of research and the execution of content analysis studies, consisting of six steps for data analytics: a) stages of formulating research problems; b) arranging the conceptual framework of the research concept operationalization; c) data collection by sampling the selected data sources; d) creation of categories used in the analysis; e) data collection of selected documents; and f) interpretation of data obtained.

3 RESULT AND DISCUSSION

3.1 *Form of BMT liquidity risk*

As a business institution, a BMT acts as a financial intermediary institution. BMT receives deposits from third parties with surplus funds and then distributes these to parties who need funds (minus). The short-term nature of deposits and long-term financing make BMTs often experience liquidity difficulties. Of the 128 BMTs questioned, all claimed to have experienced liquidity difficulties.

Even so, according to the BMT managers, liquidity difficulties can be anticipated. Therefore, liquidity difficulties can be predicted as to when they occur, so they can be prepared for. The main cause of liquidity difficulties experienced by BMTs is the commemoration of religious holidays, such as Ramadhan and Idul Fitri, the new school year, and planting season. This is as revealed by Nyakdin, the director BMT Pahlawan Tulungagung: 'Historical data about customer behavior is an important lesson in regulating liquidity. Before Ramadan, we relax the financing to increase cash for withdrawals during Ramadan. So is July, because of the new school year.'

The importance of liquidity is well understood by BMTs. According to Abdul Madjid Umar, director BMT UGT Sidogiri, which is the largest BMT in Indonesia, as an intermediary institution, regulating liquidity is very important for BMTs. Therefore, liquidity is the pulse of intermediary financial institutions, so that if it fails to regulate liquidity, then the future of the BMT business will be destroyed.

Liquidity is a trade off of profitability, so it must be carefully arranged. If liquidity is good then generally profitability is disrupted, and vice versa, if profitability is good then liquidity is threatened. Because, to maintain liquidity, a BMT needs to reserve a certain amount of funds so that if at any time these are taken by the depositors, the BMT will have no liquidity problem. However, the reserve fund is idle, so it cannot be used to make profit.

From this study, it is found that 82 of 128 BMTs (64%) claim to be able to solve their own liquidity problems. BMTs that can overcome their own liquidity problems rely on customer deposits to do so (35 of 46 BMTs). In addition, by linkage with other financial institutions, either with sharia banks, other BMTs or other financial institutions, some BMTs rely on multiple sources at once.

From this fact, it appears that linkage becomes very important for BMTs. If they cannot rely on customer deposits to cope with the usually urgent liquidity, then they rely more on linkage with Islamic financial institutions. During this time, most BMTs in East Java are already doing linkage with Sharia banks. Meanwhile, of the BMTs that cannot cope with their own liquidity problems, 48% rely on ownership capital (first rank), other BMTs (13%), the government (13%), and on personal bank loans.

From this study, BMTs which can solve their own liquidity difficulties perform productivity improvement measures (36%), internal process optimization (32%), and productivity improvement (32%). These three are quite effective in overcoming liquidity difficulties independently. Generally, those who do this are BMTs which are experienced in performing their intermediary function, so they already know when liquidity difficulties will occur, such as before Idul Fitri, the new school year, and planting season for farmers.

Activities in addressing the need for liquidity independently in BMTs in East Java are very diverse. In optimizing the internal process, this is done by reducing the financing (40%) and increasing the capital (53%), while the efficiency step is done by reducing the operational cost (51%) and the optimization of working hours. In improving productivity, this is done to improve employee performance (47%) and billing (45%).

The various ways BMTs solve liquidity problems can be differentiated in five different ways. Firstly, BMTs establish a formal guarantor institution in the form of a secondary cooperative which consists of the BMT, namely the Center for Sharia Cooperatives and Parent Sharia Cooperatives.

In East Java, there are five secondary sharia cooperatives. This secondary cooperative consists of other institutions, namely the primary cooperative BMT. Primary BMTs that lack liquidity can obtain liquidity from secondary cooperatives. Likewise, the primary cooperative BMTs that have excess liquidity can place funds in secondary cooperatives. Thus, the secondary cooperative becomes a lender of last resort for the BMT. 'We set up a secondary cooperative, recognizing the importance of places to place excess liquidity or otherwise seek funding when there are liquidity shortages,' said Nyakdin, director of BMT Pahlawan in Tulungagung as informant.

BMT Pahlawan, along with 39 other BMTs in Tulungagung, Blitar and Trenggalek districts, form a secondary sharia cooperative called Center for Sharia Cooperatives (Puskopsyah). In addition, 40 BMTs affiliated with the Indonesian Islamic Da'wah Institution (LDII) form a secondary cooperative BMT. Similarly, 40 BMTs under Aisiyah Muhammadiyah East Java form a secondary cooperative Bueka As-sakinah East Java.

Second, BMTs adopt the financing of a standby loan at a sharia bank, which can be taken at any time when liquidity difficulties occur. In general, BMTs have assets and are bankable, so it is easy to obtain financing in sharia banks. In fact, many BMTs have linkage with sharia banks, not only in case of liquidity difficulties, but also to enlarge the reach of financing. This is done by BMT UGT Sidogiri, BMT Maslahah Sidogiri Pasuruan, and BMT Mandiri Sejahtera Gresik.

Third, in establishing non-formal inter-BMT relations. BMTs that are in one region generally have a close relationship that can help one another. Likewise, BMTs are affiliated in an organization's ties, such as Muhammadiyah, Nahdhatul Ulama, and the Indonesian Islamic Da'wah Institution (LDII). Therefore, they usually form non-formal relationships to help each other when needed, including in overcoming the lack of liquidity, or vice versa.

Fourth, by borrowing from other financial institutions, either other BMTs, sharia banks, or *Bank Perkreditan Rakyat Syariah* (BPRS). BMTs that use this method generally do not have a good relationship with other BMTs, so when faced with liquidity difficulties, they seek loans from other financial institutions.

Fifth, by having individual backing that can be borrowed at any time. This step is usually done by BMTs with relatively small assets. Usually, people who can lend to a BMT have an ongoing business relationship, such as customers or administrators. When experiencing liquidity difficulties, BMT management borrows short-term funds from them.

Table 1. Problem solving of liquidity risk in BMTs.

Problem of liquidity risk in BMTs	Result
Functional Activities of Credit (Provision of Funds), Treasury Investments, Financing Activities and Debt Instruments.	BMT doing linkage with other financial institutions, either linkage with sharia banks, linkage with other BMT or other financial institutions. BMTs that lack liquidity can obtain liquidity from secondary cooperatives. The primary cooperative BMTs that excess liquidity can place funds on secondary cooperatives. Thus, the secondary cooperative becomes a lender of last resort for the BMT. BMT takes the financing of a stand by loan at a sharia bank that can be taken at any time when liquidity difficulties occurred. Establishing non-formal inter-BMT relations. Have individual backing that can be borrowed at any time. To borrow to other financial institutions, both to other BMT, sharia banks, or BPRS.

The best way to overcome the liquidity problem of a BMT is to form a secondary cooperative, because it can also be an alternative for BMTs to place funds when there is excess liquidity.

4 CONCLUSION AND RECOMMENDATIONS

The main cause of liquidity difficulties that are often experienced by BMTs is the commemoration of religious holidays, such as Ramadan and Eid al-Fitr. In addition, other causes of liquidity difficulties are the new school year, and the planting season. Most BMTs can solve liquidity problems by relying on customer deposits to overcome their liquidity, linkage with other financial institutions, linkage with sharia banks, other BMTs, and with the *Bank Perkreditan Rakyat Syariah* (BPRS). BMTs that cannot cope with their own liquidity rely on ownership capital, from other BMTs, the government, and Islamic or personal bank loans. BMTs that can solve their own liquidity difficulties use productivity improvement measures, internal process optimization and increased productivity. These three things are quite effective in overcoming liquidity difficulties independently.

There are five ways in which BMTs can overcome liquidity difficulties. First, the BMT is established as a formal guarantor institution in the form of a secondary cooperative, which consists of the BMT, namely the Center for Sharia Cooperatives (Puskopsyah). There are at least five Puskopsyah in East Java. Second, BMTs cooperate with sharia banks by opening a standby loan which can be taken at any time when facing liquidity difficulties. Third, by establishing non-formal inter-BMT relations. Fourth, by borrowing from other financial institutions, be it from a BMT and or *Bank Perkreditan Rakyat Syariah* (BPRS). Fifth, in having individual backing that can be borrowed at any time. The best way to overcome the liquidity problems of a BMT is to form a secondary cooperative, because it can also be an alternative for BMTs to place funds when facing excess liquidity.

REFERENCES

Aggarwal, R.K. & Yousef, T. (2000). Islamic Banks and Investment Financing. *Journal of Money, Credit and Banking*, 32(1), 93–120.

Akhtar, M.F., Khizer, A. & Shama, S. (January 2011). Liquidity Risk Management: A Comparative Study Between Conventional and Islamic Banks of Pakistan. *Interdisciplinary Journal of Research in Business*, 1(1), 35–44.

Allen, F. & Santomero, A.M. (1998). The Theory of Financial Intermediation. *Journal of Finance and Banking*, 36(3), 454–480.

Arun, T.G. & Turner, J.D. (2002). Financial Sector Reform in Developing Countries: The Indian Experience. *The World Economy*, 25(3), 429–445.

Baker, M.P. & Wurgler, J. (2002). Market Timing and Capital Structure. *Journal of Finance*, 57(1), 1–32.

BCBS. (2008). *Principles for Sound Liquidity Management and Supervision*. Basel, Switzerland: Bank for International Settlement.

Campion, A. (2000). *Improving Internal Control: A Practical Guide for Microfinance Institutions*. Micro Finance Network.

De Franco, A. (2005). *Financial Management in Developing Countries*. Pearson Publishers.

Diamond, D.W. & Rajan, R.G. (2001). Liquidity Risk, Liquidity Creation, and Financial Fragility: A Theory of Banking. *Journal of Political Economy*, 109(2), 287–327.

Dusuki, A.W. (2005). Commodity Murabahah Programme (CMP): An Innovative Approach to Liquidity Management. *Journal of Islamic Banking*, 3(1), 1–23.

Freeman, R.E. (1984). *Strategic Management: A stakeholder Approach*. Boston: Pitman.

Greenbaum, S.I. & Thakor, A.V. (2007). *Contemporary Financial Intermediation* (2nd ed.). America: Elsevier Publications.

Greuning, H.V. & Bratanovic Sonja Brajoviv (2009). *Risks associated with liquidity in the Islamic financial*

services Paris, Industry (IIFS). Third Islamic Financial Forum: The European Challenge, France.
Holsti, O.R. (1969). *Content Analysis for Social Sciences and Humanities*. Reading, Mass.: Addison-Wesley.
Hubbard, G.R. (2002). *Money, the Financial System, and the Economy.* New Jersey: The Addison Wesley Series in Economics, Pearson Education Inc.
Ismal, R. (2010a). Assessment of Liquidity Management in Islamic Banking Industry. *International Journal of Islamic and Middle Eastern Finance and Management*, 3(2), 147–167.
Ismal, R. (2010b). The Management of Liquidity Risk in Islamic Banks: The Case Study of Indonesia. *Durham University Journal of Political Economy*, 91(3), 401–419.
Kuncoro, and Suhardjono. (2002). *Manajemen Perbankan: Teori dan Aplikasi. Banking Management: Theori and Application*. Yogyakarta: BPFE.
Miles, S. (2011). *Stakeholder definitions: Profusion and Confusion.* IESE EIASM 1st Interdisciplinary Conference on Stakeholder, Resources and Value Creation, Business School, University of Navarra, Barcelona.
Mugenda, O.M. & Mugenda, O.G. (1999). *Research Methods*. Kenya: Acts Press.
Muhamad. (2009). *Lembaga Keuangan Mikro Syariah. Islamic Microfinance Institutions*. Yogyakarta: Graha Ilmu.
Obwocha, G. (2003). *Financial Management Practices*. Macmillan Publishers.
Ridwan, M. (2006). *Baitul Maal wa Tamwil*. Jakarta: Prenada Media Group.
Simplice, A.A. (2013). Post-Crisis Bank Liquidity Risk Management Disclosure. *Qualitative Research in Financial Markets*, 5(1), 6–84.
Taswan. (2006). *Manajemen Perbankan. Banking Management*. Yogyakarta: UPP STIM YPKP.
Umer, C. (2001). *What is Islamic Economics*? Jeddah: Islamic Development Bank & IRTI.
Wood, Robert A. et al. (2004). Decimals and Liquidity: A Study of the Nyse. *Journal of Financial Research*.

Increasing Management Relevance and Competitiveness – Sukoco et al. (Eds)
© 2018 Taylor & Francis Group, London, ISBN 978-0-8153-7455-8

Determinant of banks stock risk in Indonesia

R. Setiawan & R. Anggraeni
Universitas Airlangga, Surabaya, Indonesia

ABSTRACT: The purpose of this study is to examine the determinant of bank's stock risks on the Indonesian Stock Exchange. This study uses a multiple linear regression analysis model, and the data was obtained from the bank's financial statements published during the 2006–2015 period. The dependent variable in this study is the bank's stock risk that is proxied by the standard deviation of the daily bank's stock risk. The independent variables in this study are the book value Equity to Total Asset (EQTA), Non-Performing Loan (NPL), Liquid Asset to Total Asset (LIQATA), and Standard Deviation of ROA (SDROA). The results showed that NPL and SDROA have a positive influence on bank stock risk, while EQTA and LIQATA have a negative influence on bank stock risk.

Keywords: bank's stock risk, book value Equity to Total Asset (EQTA), Non-Performing Loan (NPL), Liquid Asset to Total Asset (LIQATA), Standard Deviation of ROA (SDROA)

1 INTRODUCTION

The existence of the banking sector in the economy of a country has an important role, even in the daily life of the community mostly involving services from the banking sector. This is because the banking sector has the primary function as a financial intermediary between excessive economic units and underfunded economic units. Through a bank can be collected funds from the community in various forms of the subsequent deposits of funds that have been collected by the bank and channeled back in the form of credit to the business sector or other parties in need.

The globalization of the economy has made progress in the banking system, but on the other hand, it also poses various risks due to the world economy. In addition, the increasing complexity of the business activities of banks has the potential to lead to higher risks being faced. This increased risk needs to be followed by an increase in the capital required by banks to bear the likelihood of losses. Hanafi (2009) defined risk as a possible result of deviation other than what is expected.

All banking companies must be prepared against all kinds of risks faced. If the risk is not properly managed, the bank may fail and eventually end up in bankrupt. Risk in the business context does not always represent something bad. Risk can be an opportunity for those who can manage it well. Banking wherever it is located will not be separated from the risks arising from all activities undertaken. There is no other way for banks to avoid the risks in addition to implementing a strategy of reliable management in controlling the risks that it faces itself.

Banking risk management is very important for banks. It concerns the success and failure of the banks in running operations. If banks can manage the risk well, it is expected that the banks will increase their returns. However, if the bank is not able to handle the risks properly, then the probability of bankruptcy will also increase. The essence of the implementation of risk management is the risk management methodology used so that the bank's business activities can be controlled within acceptable limits and benefit the banks.

The banking industry is one of the industries selected by investors in which to invest their capital. The existence of a more predictable level of financial globalization poses new and complex risks that investors must confront. Generally, investments made by investors in the capital market are to earn returns, but investors also need to look at the risks that exist in the securities because of the uncertainty in the investment. The risk due to the uncertainty of stock prices or the returns obtained by investors in the capital market is called the risk of shares. According to Agusman et al. (2008), stock risk can be reflected in the fluctuation of stock prices in the capital market.

According to Sudana (2011), there are three types of investor behavior against risk, namely risk seeker, indifferent to risk, and risk averter. For investors who are risk seekers, a big risk will be preferred because of the amount of return that will be obtained. But there are also investors who are risk averters that try to minimize the risk but still expect a high return. Thus, risk is one of the parameters that is important for investors to use to determine the return and to identify the factors that affect risk. Agusman et al. (2008) stated that there are several types of financial ratios related to stock risk, among others, book value equity to total asset, non-performing loan, liquid asset to total asset, and standard deviation of ROA.

The four financial ratios related to stock risk are indicators of bank performance. By using the bank's performance indicators, it is expected that investors will be able to respond to whether the banks they are going to buy in to are worthy to make investments in line with the risk of the stocks that will be generated later on. Book value equity to total assets is the proportion of capital to the total assets owned by banks. If the bank has its own capital with an amount greater than the debt, it is expected to create a risk of bank stocks in the small capital market. A non-performing loan is how much problem loans are owned by the bank. If a bank has a large portion of bad loans, the losses are to be borne by the bank. This causes the risk towards the bank shares in the capital market. High liquid asset to total assets is how much of the bank's liquid assets can be used to maintain liquidity. If the bank can manage their assets until it can avoid a liquidity risk, then the bank is considered to be a healthy bank and this causes the risk of shares in the capital market to be low. The standard deviation of ROA illustrates the uncertainty of the profitability obtained by the bank. Jika's high profitability is uncertain, considering that the bank is not healthy and this causes the risk of bank shares in the capital market to also be high. Below is the risk of banking stock data from 2006–2015. It did not show any significant increases or decreases in trends. Below is the data of the banking stock risk from 2006–2015 as measured using the standard deviation of the daily stock returns.

Based on the above data, it can be seen that the risk level of banking stock is unstable. From this phenomenon, the researcher wanted to research about the effect of stock risk instability with five financial ratios, namely book value equity to total asset, non-performing loan, liquid asset to total asset, and the standard deviation of ROA. Aside from the phenomenon itself, the research was on the influence of banking risk with the five financial ratios mentioned. This is rarely done in Indonesia, so the researcher wanted to examine the effect of bank stock risk on book value equity to total asset, non performing loan, liquid asset to total asset, and the standard deviation of ROA. Based on the description of the above background, the formulation of the research problem is as follows:

1. Does book value equity to total asset negatively affect the risk of bank stock?
2. Does a non-performing loan positively affect the risk of bank stock?
3. Does liquid asset to total asset negatively affect the risk of bank stock?
4. Does the standard deviation of ROA positively affect the risk of bank stock?

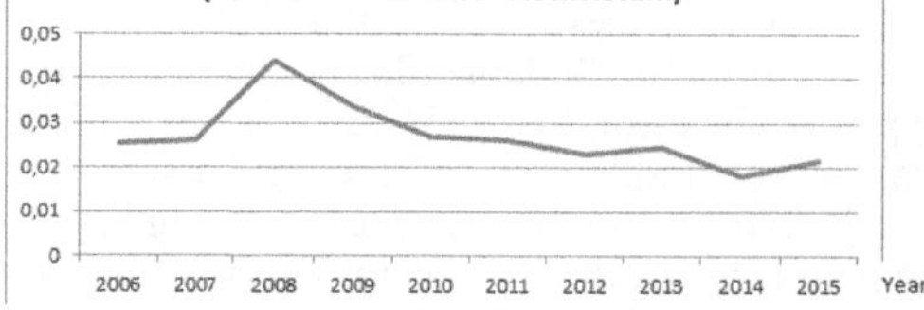

Figure 1. Risk data of banking stocks period 2006–2015.

2 THEORETICAL BASIS

2.1 *Understanding bank*

According to Law no. 10/1998 about banking, a bank is a business entity that collects funds from the public in the form of savings and distributes it to the community in the form of credit and/or in other forms in order to improve the standard of living of the community. The purpose of banking is explained in article 3 of Law no. 10/1998; to support the implementation of national developments in order to improve equity, economic growth, and national stability towards improving the welfare of the people.

2.2 *Bank stock risk*

Risk is the possibility of the results obtained that deviate from the expected (Hanafi, 2009). Meanwhile, according to Sudana (2011), risk is defined as the variability of the actual investment return on the expected investment results. So it can be concluded that the risk of the stocks is a possibility. The results obtained deviate from the expected, which are the results of the stock investments. Referring to Agusman et al (2008), the risk of bank stock in this study is measured using the standard deviation of daily stock return. The standard deviation indicates how far the probability of the value obtained deviates from the expected value. The greater the standard deviation value, the greater the probability that the true value deviates from the expected meaning. Therefore, the higher the risk. Referring to Agusman et al (2008) and Ehrhardt and Brigham (2001), stock risk is measured using the standard deviation of daily stock returns.

2.3 *Book value Equity to Total Asset (EQTA)*

The ratio of book value equity to total assets is a ratio that shows how much of the bank's equity portion is out of the total assets owned.

2.4 *Non-Performing Loans (NPLs)*

The non-performing loan ratio is the ratio between the total non-performing loans and the total loans granted to debtors (Rivai et al., 2012). The smaller the ratio, the smaller the risk of the possibility of uncollectible loans compared to the total amount of loans granted, which leads to bank profits (Rivai et al 2012). Banks are said to have a high ratio of non-performing loans if the number of credit problems are relatively large.

2.5 *Liquid Asset to Total Asset (LIQATA)*

The ratio of liquid assets to total assets is a comparison of a bank's liquid assets to their total assets (Agusman et al, 2008). Liquidity is one of the indicators used to measure the company's ability to meet its short-term liabilities. According to Rivai et al (2012), liquidity is the ability of the bank's management in providing sufficient funds to meet its obligations at any time. Management in terms of liquidity is very necessary, because if the bank lacks liquidity then it can disrupt not only the bank, but also the banking system as a whole.

2.6 *Standard Deviation of Return on Asset (SDROA)*

The standard deviation ratio of ROA is a risk of profitability generated by banks (Agusman, et al., 2008). Risk itself has the meaning of uncertainty, and ROA is the ability of banks in managing their assets to generate profit. It can be concluded that the standard deviation of ROA is the uncertainty to do with the earnings obtained by banks.

2.7 *The effect of book value equity to total asset on bank stock risk*

The ratio of book value equity to total asset negatively affects the risks to do with bank stock. This indicates that the higher the book value equity to the total asset ratio, the lower the risk of the stocks to be faced by the bank (Agusman, et al., 2008). This ratio is negatively related to the risk of bank shares because the percentage of the bank's operational activity is more funded by the bank's own equity than debt, where the debt itself will cause a fixed burden of interest (Pettway, 1976 in Salked, 2011). If the bank's debt is less than the equity, the interest on the bank will not be too large. Equity absorbs the possibility of losses and provides the basis for maintaining customer confidence. The greater the equity, the greater the financial resources that can be used for business development purposes and to anticipate potential losses, as a result of lending.

Banks with a large equity will face lower bankruptcy risks and may earn lower funding costs. People trust banks that have greater equity than debt, because they feel that the funds held in the bank will be safe with the equity of banks to protect their funds in the event of a loss. Investors will also trust banks that have greater equity than debt because investors believe that banks with greater equity can guarantee the value of their investments, at least with a value that remains stable. The risk of stocks on investments is subsequently low. The maximum bank equity will be able to improve the bank's management capabilities in identifying, measuring, controlling and controlling risks arising later. The higher the book value equity compared to the total asset ratio, the lower the risks to do with bank stock.

H1: Book value equity to total assets negatively affects the risk of bank stock.

2.8 *The effect of non-performing loans on bank stock risk*

The ratio of non-performing loans positively affects the risk of bank stock. This means that the higher the ratio of non-performing loan-giving banks, the higher the risk of stocks faced by the banks (Mamoghli, 2009). The non-performing loan ratio is the percentage of the number of non-performing loans faced by the bank. The high rate of non-performing loan as indicated by the higher ratio of non-performing loan indicates the low ability of the debtors to pay back all of their loan or credit provided by the bank. This can increase the cost (opportunity cost) resulting in potential losses in the banks. The high ratio of non-performing loans has been proven to cause the banks to suffer losses due to that magnitude of change. Banks should be careful in channeling credit in order to avoid high non-performing loans, or to deal with it in a more selective way when it comes to channeling credit to the community. Investors consider that banks with high non-performing loans are considered to be unhealthy and risky banks. The effect of the high non-performing loan ratio is that the bank will experience more credit risk. If the bank is exposed to credit risk, this will lead to the disruption of bank liquidity because it has to bear the losses due to the risk of default from the debtor. If bank liquidity gets disturbed and also has credit risk involved, investors will assume that the bank is unhealthy and investors will not trust to invest its shares in the bank. When no investors invests in the bank, the share price of the bank will fall, and the risk of the bank's shares will be high. Thus, the higher the ratio of non-performing loans, the higher the risk of bank stock.

H2: Non-performing loans positively affect the risk of bank stock.

2.9 *The effect of liquid asset to total asset on bank stock risk*

The ratio of liquid assets to total assets has a negative effect on bank stock risk. This means that the higher the bank's liquid assets, the lower the risk of stocks faced by the bank. If this ratio shows a high number, it indicates that the bank has a large liquid asset, thus has a relatively small liquidity risk. Banks with large liquid assets are expected to buffer unexpected losses in the short term, as the amount of available liquid assets is greater and avoids the liquidity risk. If the public wants to withdraw their funds by a large amount, the bank can serve them immediately. Investors consider banks with liquid assets of a considerable value to be rated as sound banks because they can avoid the liquidity risk. Investors will invest in the bank, so the stock price of the bank will rise, and the risk of its shares will fall. Thus, the higher the liquid asset to total asset, the lower the risk faced by the bank.

H3: Liquid asset to total assets negatively affects the risk of bank stock.

2.10 *The effect of standard deviation of ROA ratio on bank stock risk*

The standard deviation of ROA ratio positively affects the risk of bank stock. This means that the higher the standard deviation of the bank's ROA, the higher the risk of stocks faced by the bank. The high ROA variability value reflects the instability of bank management in managing its assets to generate profit, so that the profit generated also fluctuates. Banks that have not been able to manage their assets well cause operational activities to be undertaken by that banks that is not good. This causes the profit generated by the bank to fluctuate. Fluctuating earnings leads to uncertainty faced by banks. For investors, profit is one of the main elements of bank health information. When a bank's earnings are experiencing instability, this indicates that the performance of the bank is not maximized because it cannot maintain stability or even increase its profit. This phenomenon becomes a bad signal for investors, because the banks are considered to be unhealthy and this will be reflected in the stock price of the banks in the capital market. The resulting risk of capital faced by the banks will be high. This causes the higher risk of stock to be faced by the bank. Thus, the higher the standard deviation of ROA, the higher risk of shares faced by the bank.

H4: Standard deviation of ROA positively affects the risk of bank stock.

3 RESEARCH METHOD

3.1 *Sample*

The sample in this study was a banking company listed on the Indonesian Stock Exchange operating in the period 2006–2015. The sample firm has a financial report with complete data-related variables to be used. Sharia banks have not been included in the samples because sharia companies do not distribute community funds in the form of interest-based credit but in the form of financing based on the results so as not to face credit risks.

3.2 *Operational definition and variable measurement*

3.2.1 *Dependent variable*

Bank Stock Risk (RISK)

$$\mathrm{RISK}_{i,t} = \sqrt{\frac{\sum_{d=1}^{n}(\overline{r}_{i,d} - \overline{r}_{avg,i,d})^2}{n-1}} \quad (1)$$

$\overline{r}_{i,d}$ = daily stock return bank i at day t;
$\overline{r}_{avg,i,d}$ = average daily stock return bank i at day t.

3.2.2 *Independent variable*

1. Book value Equity to Total Asset (EQTA)

$$\mathrm{EQTA}_{i,t-1} = \frac{\text{Total Equity}_{i,t-1}}{\text{Total Asset}_{i,t-1}} \quad (2)$$

2. Non Performing Loan (NPL)

$$\mathrm{NPL}_{i,t-1} = \frac{\text{Non Performing Loan}_{i,t-1}}{\text{Total Loan}_{i,t-1}} \quad (3)$$

3. Liquid Asset to Total Asset (LIQATA)

$$\mathrm{LIQATA}_{i,t-1} = \frac{\text{Liquid Asset}_{i,t-1}}{\text{Total Asset}_{i,t-1}} \quad (4)$$

4. Standard Deviation of Return on Asset (SDROA)

$$\mathrm{SDROA}_{i,t-1} = \sqrt{\frac{\sum_{i=1}^{n}(\overline{\mathrm{ROA}_{1,t-1}} - \overline{\mathrm{ROA}_{avg,1,t-1}})^2}{n-1}} \quad (5)$$

3.3 *Data analysis method*

The model of analysis in this research is

$$RISK_{i,t} = \alpha + \beta_1 EQTA_{i,t-1} + \beta_2 NPL_{i,t-1} + \beta_3 LIQATA_{i,t-1} + \beta_4 SDROA_{i,t-1} + \varepsilon_{i,t-1} \quad (6)$$

where, $RISK_{it}$ is bank stock risk bank i year t, $EQTA_{i,t-1}$ is book value equity to total asset bank i year t-1, $NPL_{i,t-1}$ is non-performing loan bank i year t-1, $LIQATA_{i,t-1}$ is liquid asset to total asset bank i year t-1, $SDROA_{i,t-1}$ is standard deviation of ROA bank i year t-1.

4 RESULT AND DISCUSSION

4.1 *Results of the research analysis*

Table 1. Data description.

	N	Minimum	Maximum	Mean	Std. deviation
RISK	113	0,0111	0,0482	0,0244	0,0070
EQTA	113	0,0529	0,2601	0,1087	0,0314
NPL	113	0,0000	0,1050	0,0283	0,0165
LIQATA	113	0,0536	0,1434	0,0924	0,0190
SDROA	113	0,0002	0,0138	0,0038	0,0028
Valid N	113				

Source: Data processed.

Table 2. Regression analysis results.

Variable	Coefficient	Sig. t	Result
Konstanta	0,031	0,000	
EQTA	–0,044	0,030**	Significant
NPL	0,093	0,026**	Significant
LIQATA	–0,069	0,039**	Significant
SDROA	0,437	0,064*	Significant
R^2	0,207		

Dependent Variable: RISK.

** = Significant at 5%, * = Significant at 10%.

4.2 *The effect of book value equity to total asset on bank stock risk*

Book value Equity to Total Asset has a significant negative effect on bank stock risk. This means that the higher the book value equity to the total asset ratio, the lower the risk of stock to be faced by the bank (Agusman et al, 2008). This ratio is negatively related to the risk of bank stocks because the percentage of the bank's operational activities is funded by the bank's own equity rather than debt, whereas the debt itself will create a fixed burden of interest (Pettway, 1976). If the bank's debt is less than the equity, the interest on the bank will not be too large. Equity absorbs the possibility of losses and provides the basis for maintaining customer confidence. The greater the equity, the greater the financial resources that can be used for business development purposes and to anticipate potential losses, as a result of lending. Banks with large equity will face lower bankruptcy risks and may earn lower funding costs. People trust the banks that have greater equity than debt, because they feel that the funds held in the bank will be safe with the equity of the banks in place to protect their funds in the event of a loss. Investors will also trust banks that have greater equity than debt because investors believe that banks with greater equity can guarantee the value of their investments, at least with a value that remains stable, so the risk of stocks on investments is low. The maximum bank equity will be able to improve the bank's management capability in identifying, measuring, controlling and controlling risks arising later. The higher the book value equity to total asset ratio, the lower the risk of bank stock.

4.3 *The effect of non-performing loans on bank stock risk*

The ratio of non-performing loans has a significant positive effect on bank stock risk. The higher the ratio of non-performing loans in banks, the higher the risk of stocks faced by the aforementioned banks (Mamoghli, 2009). The non-performing loan ratio is the percentage of the number of non-performing loans faced by banks. The high rate of non-performing loans indicated by the high ratio of non-performing loans indicates the low ability of debtors to pay for all of the loans provided by the bank. This can increase the cost at the bank. The high ratio of non-performing loans has been proven to cause the bank to suffer losses that amount to change. Banks should be careful in channeling credit in order to avoid high non-performing loans. Investors consider that banks with high non-performing loans are considered to be unhealthy and risky banks. The effect of the high non-performing loan ratio is that the bank will experience more credit risk. If the bank is exposed to credit risk, this will lead to the disruption of the bank's liquidity because it has to bear the loss from the risk of the default of the debtor. If the bank liquidity gets disturbed and also involves credit risk, investors will assume that the bank is unhealthy and investors will not trust to invest their shares in the bank. When no investor invests in the bank, the share price of the bank will fall, and the risk of the bank's shares will be high. Thus the higher the ratio of non-performing loans, the higher the risk of bank stock.

4.4 *The effect of liquid asset to total asset on bank stock risk*

The ratio of liquid assets to total assets has a significant negative effect on bank stock risk. This means that the higher the bank's liquid assets, the lower the risk of stocks faced by the bank. If this ratio shows a high number, it indicates that the bank has a large liquid asset, and thus has a relatively small liquidity risk. Banks with large liquid assets are expected to buffer unexpected losses in the short term, as the amount of available liquid assets is greater. If the public wants to withdraw their funds in relation to a large amount, the bank can serve them immediately. Investors consider banks with liquid assets to be of considerable value to be rated as sound banks because they can avoid the liquidity risk. Investors will invest in the bank, so the stock price of the bank will rise, and the risk of its shares will fall. Thus, the higher the liquid asset to total asset ratio, the lower the risk faced by the bank.

4.5 *The effect of standard deviation of ROA ratio on bank stock risk*

The standard deviation ratio of ROA has a significant positive effect on bank stock risk. This means that the high standard deviation of ROA is owned by the bank, and affects the high risk of bank stocks. The high ROA variability value reflects the instability of the bank's management in managing its assets to generate profit, so that the profit generated also fluctuates. Banks that have not been able to manage their assets well cause the operational activities undertaken by the banks to not be so good. This causes the profit generated by the bank to fluctuate. Fluctuating earnings leads to uncertainty. For investors, profit is one of the main elements of bank health information that are looked at prior to making a decision. When a bank's earnings are experiencing instability, this indicates that the performance of the bank is not maximized because it can't maintain stability or even increase its profit. This phenomenon becomes a bad signal for investors, because the banks are considered to be unhealthy and this will be reflected in the stock price of the banks in the capital market. The risk of capital faced by banks will be high. This causes the higher risk of stock to be faced by the bank. Thus, the higher the standard deviation of ROA, the higher the risk of shares faced by the bank.

5 CONCLUSION

Based on the research conducted on 113 observations of bank research registered on Indonesian Exchange in 2006–2015, the following conclusions have been generated:

1. Book value equity to total asset and liquid asset to total assets has a significant negative effect on bank stock risk. This shows that the higher the ratio of book value equity to total asset and liquid assets to total assets, the lower the risk of bank stock.
2. Non-performing loans and standard deviation of ROA have a significant positive effect on bank stock risk. This shows that the higher the non performing loan ratio and standard deviation of ROA, the higher the risk of bank stock.

REFERENCES

Abdullah, A. M. A. 2003. The Relationship Between Commercial Banks Performance and Risk Measures. *A Case of Saudi Arabia Stock Market. Journal of KingFaisal University* 4 (2): 1424.

Agusman, A. et al. 2007. Accounting and Capital Market Measures of Risk: Evidence from Asian Banks during 1998–2003. *Journal of Banking & Finance* 32 (2008): 480–488.

Al-Jarrah, I. M. 2012. Evaluating the Riskiness of the Banking Sector of Jordan. *European Journal of Economics, Finance and Administrative Sciences* 48 (2012).

Bank Indonesia. 1998. Undang-undang No. 10 Tahun 1998.

—. 2015. Peraturan Bank Indonesia No. 17/11/PBI/2005.

Brigham, E. F. & Houston, J. F. 1998. Fundamentals of Financial Management. Eight Edition. New York: The Dryden Press. Harcourt Brace College Publishers.

Darmawi, H. 2011. *Manajemen Perbankan*. Jakarta: Bumi Aksara.

Dendawijaya, Lukman. 2005. *Manajemen Perbankan*. Edisi Kedua. Jakarta: Ghalia Indonesia.

Dhouibi, R. & Mamoghli, C. 2009. Accounting and Capital Market Measures of Risk: Evidence from an emerging market. *Banks and Bank Systems* 4 (4).

Elyasiani, E. & Mansur, I. 1998. Sensitivity of the bank stock returns distribution to changes in the level and volatility of interest rate: A GARCH-M model. *Journal of Banking and Finance* 22: 535–563.

Gozhali, I. 2007. SPSS. Analisis Multivariat dengan Program SPSS. Semarang: Badan Penerbit Universitas Diponegoro.

Hanafi, M. M. 2010. *Manajemen Risiko*. Edisi Kedua. Yogyakarta: UPP STIM YKPN.

Hartono, J. 2014. *Teori Portofolio dan Analisis Investasi. Edisi ke 9*. Yogyakarta: BPFE-Yogyakarta.

Jarvela, M., et al. 2009. The Relationship Between Market and Accounting Determined Risk Measures: Reviewing and Updating the Beaver, Kettler, Scholes (1970) Study. College Teaching Methods & Style Journal, Special edition 2009.

Rivai, V., Basir, S., Sudarto, S., & Veithzal, A. P. 2013. *Commercial Bank Management*. Jakarta: Raja Grafindo Persada.

Salked, M. 2011. Determinants of Bank's Total Risk: Accounting Ratios and Macroeconomics Indicators. Honors Projects 24.

Santoso, S. 2002. *Aplikasi SPSS pada Statistik Multivariat*. Jakarta: Elex Media Komputindo.

Sudana, I Made. 2011. *Manajemen Keuangan: Teori dan Praktik*. Surabaya: Erlangga.

Increasing Management Relevance and Competitiveness – Sukoco et al. (Eds)
© 2018 Taylor & Francis Group, London, ISBN 978-0-8153-7455-8

Degree of internationalization and firm financial performance

F. Ismiyanti
Universitas Airlangga, Surabaya, Indonesia

ABSTRACT: Previous empirical results on the relationship between internationalization and firm performance have been mixed. Both linear and non-linear relationships have been reported. The linear analysis that was used by previous studies shows different results. Most recent studies are focused on non-linear analysis to describe the relationship between internationalization and firm performance. This paper focuses on analyzing the relationship between Degree of Internationalization (DOI), measured by Foreign Sales to Total Sales (FSTS) ratio, and firm performance, measured by return on asset, return on equity, net profit margin and total assets turnover. Ordinary least square multiple regression and a curvilinear regression model were used to test the hypothesis. The result shows that the relationship between internationalization and firm performance is more significant in curvilinear regression analysis.

Keywords: internationalization, firm performance, linear and non-linear analysis

1 INTRODUCTION

1.1 *Background research*

With the enhancements of today's global economy and technology, international business practices are not bound only to market expansion by exports, but more to develop international cooperation and production bases in other countries, commonly known as Foreign Direct Investment (FDI). Global business improvement also influences domestic business behavior, generating cooperation programs between local and foreign companies, which induces direct and indirect investments, both to and from Indonesia.

The multinational companies expect diversification from asset exploration and market expansion, and decreasing risks from international diversification (Madura, 2003). Gaur and Kumar (2007) articulated that although international diversification, which is measured by Degree of Internationalization (DOI), has a positive effect on corporate performance, those that are affiliated with a certain business group tend to have a more negative effect than those that are not. This shows that international diversification using DOI will have a positive effect to certain conditions.

Several literatures comparing the relationship between DOI and corporate performance state that the pattern of the relationship is divided into two types: linear and curvilinear relations (Markowitz, 1952). Sambharya (1995) finds that the curvilinear relation is also divided into three: U-shaped, inverted U-shaped and multiple waves. These curves illustrate the relationship between corporate performance and DOI.

1.2 *Research question*

Based on the background of this paper, the research question is as follows: is there a relationship between DOI, measured using Foreign Sales to Total Sales (FSTS) ratio, and corporate performance, measured using return on asset (ROA), return on equity (ROE), net profit margin and total assets turnover?

2 LITERATURE REVIEW

2.1 *Internationalization and performance*

In order to enhance their scope of activity, companies tend to make decisions to internationalize as one of their strategies. This refers to income rate or operations located outside their country of origin. In general, internationalization is measured using the FSTS ratio (Gaur & Kumar, 2007; Elango, 2009). With abundant research on corporate operation internationalization and performance, Grant et al. (1988) and Geringer et al. (1989) examined international expansion and concluded that internationalization has a positive effect on corporate financial performance. Other research has different results, finding that internationalization has a negative effect on performance (Siddharthan & Lall, 1982; Collins, 1990).

During the second stage of internationalization, relationship becomes positive in line with increasing profit earned from the process. Larger expansion makes efficiency possible to increase the maximum use of resources. Another advantage in this stage is the corporation's ability to overcome global market power and develop the product cycle (Grant et al., 1988).

During the third stage, the relationship becomes negative. The decreasing performance when the value of international expansion is high is caused by the corporate decision to expand higher than its optimum potential. This is because the company must face different legal, cultural and environmental regulations (Gomes & Ramaswamy, 1999).

2.2 *Performance measurement*

Corporate business activity is categorized in three main actions: budgeting, investing and operation (Helfert, 2003). These three focuses are entirely binding and must move sustainably in order to keep the company running. The statement shows that to facilitate a smooth operational process, activities related to budgeting and investing cannot be separated. Investment decision on the appropriate asset affects operational activities in production and the sales process.

2.3 *Research hypotheses*

Based on research background, research question, theoretical basis and earlier research, the hypotheses advanced in this paper are as follows:

- H_1: Degree of internationalization measured using FSTS negatively affects ROA at the linear relationship level.
- H_2: There is an effect of degree of internationalization measured using FSTS on ROA at the quadratic relationship level, as shown by the U-curve.

The U-curve illustrates that at the initial to medium stage of internationalization, performance will decrease, but at the medium level (critical point) to the high level of internationalization, performance will increase.

- H_3: Degree of internationalization measured using FSTS negatively affects ROE at the linear relationship level.
- H_4: There is an effect of degree of internationalization measured using FSTS on ROE at the quadratic relationship level, as shown by the U-curve.

The U-curve illustrates that, at the initial to medium stage of internationalization, performance will decrease, but at the medium level (critical point) to the high level of internationalization, performance will increase.

- H_5: Degree of internationalization measured using FSTS negatively affects net profit margin at the linear relationship level.
- H_6: There is an effect of degree of internationalization measured using FSTS on NPM at the quadratic relationship level, as shown by the horizontal curve. The horizontal curve shows that no significant relationship exists between FSTS and NPM.
- H_7: Degree of internationalization measured by FSTS negatively affects total asset turn over at the linear relationship level.
- H_8: There is an effect of degree of internationalization measured by FSTS on TATO at the quadratic relationship level, as shown by the U-curve.

The U-curve shows that, within the initial stage of internationalization to the medium level, performance decreases. However, performance increases at the medium level of critical point to the high internationalization level.

3 RESEARCH METHOD

3.1 *Data*

Secondary data used in this paper covers financial reports, Indonesian Capital Market Directory (ICMD) period 2014–2016 and other required secondary data. This data is obtained from Indonesian Stock Exchange.

Based on the hypotheses, ordinary least square with multiple regression is used on linear and non-linear models, as follows:

Linear Model:

$$PERF = \beta_0 + \beta_1 FSTS_{it} + \beta_3 SIZE_{it} + \varepsilon_t \quad (1)$$

Non-Linear Model (quadratic):

$$PERF = \beta_0 + \beta_1 FSTS_{it} + \beta_2 (FSTS)^2_{it} + \beta_3 SIZE_{it} + \varepsilon_t \quad (2)$$

Key:
PERF: corporate performance
FSTS: foreign sales to total sales
SIZE: corporate size

3.2 *Research variable*

Variables used in this paper are as follows. Foreign sales to total asset, as measured by dividing foreign sales by total corporate sales. ROA is based on the comparison of net profit (after tax) and total assets of the company. ROE is based on the comparison of net profit and total equity. NPM is based on comparing net profit with sales. TATO is based on comparing sales with total asset. Firm size is measured using a sales algorithm.

4 RESULTS AND DISCUSSION

The results show that FSTS have an insignificant negative effect on ROA for the linear relationship

Table 1. Result on the effect of FSTS on ROA.

Linear				Non-linear		
Var	B	t	Sig	Var	B	t
FSTS	−0.02	−3.5	0.45	FSTS	−0.077	−2.8
LgSales	0.064	−0.7	0.00	$FSTS^2$	0.034	2.41
Kons	−0.87	3.95	0.00	LgSales	0.072	−4.87
				Kons	−0.86	−5.76
R	0.542			R	0.6662	
R^2	0.672			R^2	0.3562	
F	8.238			F	16.652	
Sig F	0.000			F table	2,48	

level, which means there is no effect of FSTS, to ROA. If the corporate internationalization level increases, then the ROA irrelevance to internationalization level.

The uniqueness of the research is in the form of the U-shaped curve, whereas in the earlier research, the relationship formed an inverted U shape. This is caused by differences in research settings, whereby this paper was conducted in Indonesia with its developing economy, whereas Hsu & Boggs (2003) conducted their research in Switzerland with an advanced economy.

For the non-linear relationship there is significant effect of internationalization to ROA and it is a U shape curve. The U-curve for the relationship between FSTS and performance showed that a decrease at the initial internationalization stage may be caused by a high transaction cost, due to the difference between the market characteristics of the country of origin with those of another country. A high learning cost will also have an effect, due to the importance of acquisition, and local acculturation and market knowledge, which require an alignment with the corporate culture. In turn, there will be considerable capital and expenditures for market fusion and corporate cultural synchronization, also with the existing system and local environment. Eventually, the company can correspond with the local market, and implement its management system so as to adapt it to the existing local market and enhance its investment. In the non-linear analysis, firm size has a significant positive effect, whereby if the score of firm size increases, so will the ROA.

5 CONCLUSION

Based on the calculation of linear and non-linear regression analyses, the relationship between the degree of internationalization and corporate performance shows that non-linear analysis has a more significant effect than linear analysis. This represents that non-linear analysis is more appropriate to explain the effects.

The pattern of the relationship between internationalization and performance (ROA, ROE, TATO) is illustrated as the U-curve in the non-linear analysis. This means that, during the initial stage of internationalization to the medium level, corporate performance tends to decrease, but at its critical point, performance will increase. The pattern of relationship between internationalization and performance (NPM) is illustrated as the horizontal curve in the non-linear analysis. This shows that there is no relationship between FSTS and NPM.

REFERENCES

Collins, J.M. (1990). A market performance comparison of us firms active in domestic, developed and developing countries. *Journal of International Business Studies, 21*(2), 271–287.

Elango, B. (2009). An exploration of the relationship between country of origin and the internationalization-performance paradigm. *Management International Review, 47*(3), 369–392.

Gaur, A.S. & Kumar, V. (2007). International diversification, business group affiliation and firm performance: empirical evidence from India. Accessed October 13th 2016. Retrieved from http://papers.ssrn.com.

Geringer, J.M., Beamish, P.W. & DaCosta, R.C. (1989). Diversification strategy and internationalization: Implications for MNE performance. *Strategic Management Journal, 10*, 109–119.

Gomes, L. & Ramaswamy, K. (1999). An empirical examination of the form of the relationship between multinationality and performance. *Journal of International Business Studies, 30*, 173–188.

Grant, R.M., Jammine, A. & Thomas, A. (1988). Diversity, diversification and profitability among British manufacturing companies, 1972–1984. *Academy of Management Journal, 31*(4), 771–801.

Helfert, E.A. (2003). *Techniques of financial analysis: A guide to value creation* (11th ed.). New York: McGraw-Hill.

Hsu, C. & Boggs D.J. (2003). Internationalization and performance: traditional measures and their decomposition. *Multinational Business Review, 11*(3), 23–50.

Madura, J. (2003). *Financial markets and institutions* (6th ed.). USA: South-Western.

Markowitz, H. (1952). Portfolio selection. *Journal of Finance, 7*(1), 77–91.

Sambharya, R.B. (1995). The combined effect of international diversification and product diversification strategies on the performance of US-based multinational corporations. *Management International Review. 3*, 197–218.

Siddharthan, N.S. & Lall, S. (1982). Recent growth of the largest US multinationals. *Oxford Bulletin of Economics and Statistics, 44*(1), 1–13.

Increasing Management Relevance and Competitiveness – Sukoco et al. (Eds)
© 2018 Taylor & Francis Group, London, ISBN 978-0-8153-7455-8

Cost efficiency of Indonesian banks over different groups of capital

M. Anwar
University of Padjadjaran, Bandung, Indonesia

ABSTRACT: This study aims to reveal the cost efficiency of Indonesian commercial banks during the period 2015–2016 using the parametric approach. The study employs stochastic frontier analysis to estimate banking cost efficiency with the extent of analyses covering the performance of different ownership, operation, and different groups of capital over the study period. The findings suggest that the average cost efficiency of Indonesian commercial banks has declined in 2016. Private Banks have emerged to be the most cost-efficient banks compared to their peers. Islamic banks are more cost-efficient than conventional banks. Banks of the first group of capital (BUKU 1) have experienced more cost efficiency than the other group of banks. Loans to Deposits Ratio (LDR), Return on Assets (ROA) and Other Operating Income, each has a positive impact on bank cost efficiency. Bank size also has a positive association with bank cost efficiency.

Keywords: stochastic frontier analysis, bank performance

JEL Code: G21, G28, D21, C1

1 INTRODUCTION

After Indonesia witnessed financial turmoil through the Asian Financial Crisis of 1997–98, Indonesian banking has been enjoying the recovery phase for about two decades. Although the number of commercial banks in Indonesia has reduced to only a half of the total banks in the 1990s, the current circumstances of Indonesian banking looks sound and more resilient to crisis. The development of Indonesian banks could be observed by pointing out several banking indicators (i.e. total assets and Return on Assets (ROA)).

Figure 1 demonstrates the total assets of the Indonesian banking sector, which have grown up from IDR3,009 trillion in 2010 to IDR5,793 trillion in 2015. The average ROA of Indonesian banks has decreased over the period of 2013–2015 but the ROA was still above 2%. The other indicators are presented in Figure 2.

Net Interest Margin (NIM) of Indonesian banks has tended to decline over the period 2010–2015 and their Non-Performing Loans (NPL) have fluctuated within the points under 5%.

Figure 3 demonstrate the Indonesian Banking Penetration Rate, where all indicators have increased during the period 2010–2014. Loan to Gross Domestic Product (GDP) has increased to 37% in 2014. Third Party Funds (TPF) also reached 41% of GDP in 2014.

All those indicators demonstrate the steady stance of Indonesian banks over the period, enjoying the

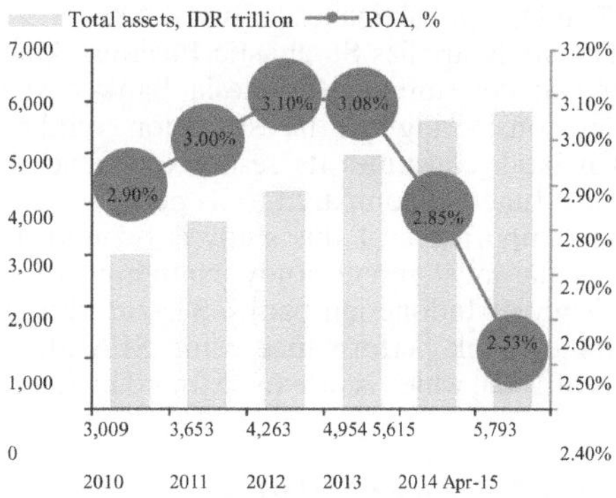

Figure 1. Total assets, ROA of Indonesian banks. Source: EY, 2015.

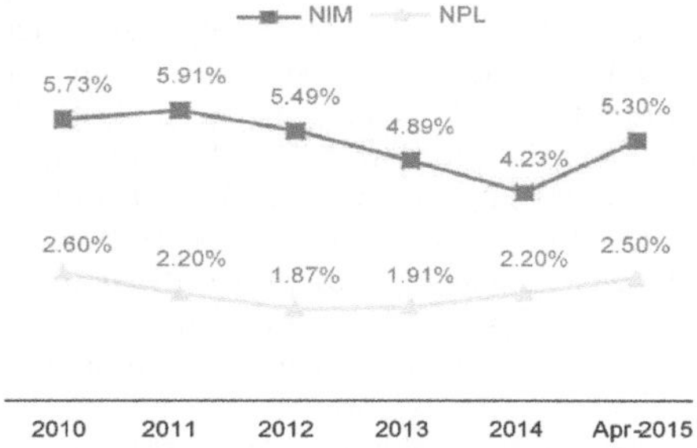

Figure 2. NIM and NPL of Indonesian commercial banking.
Source: EY, 2015.

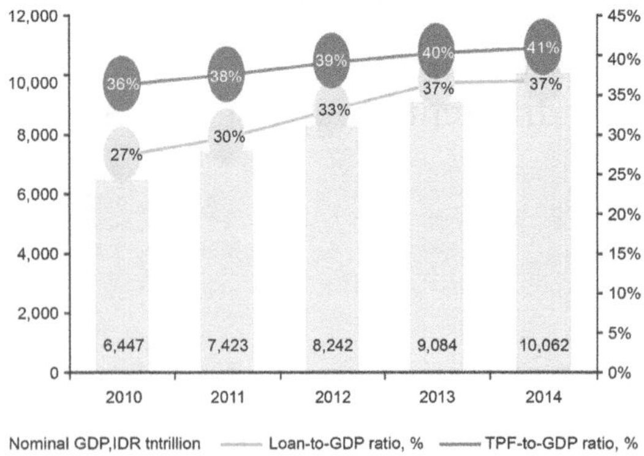

Figure 3. Nominal GDP (IDR Trillion), Loan to GDP, and Third Party Fund to Gross Domestic Product (TPF to GDP).
Source: EY, 2015.

growing assets, high net-interest margin, low level of NPLs, increasing Loan to GDP, and TPF to GDP. Although the banking indicators reveal sound condition, the evaluation of bank performance should always be undertaken over time to monitor the performance. This is to anticipate the possibility of another financial crises occurring, similar to AFC 1997 and the global financial crisis of 2008.

The study applies Stochastic Frontier Analysis (SFA) in determining Indonesia bank cost efficiency, considering that the estimation could reveal which bank consumes its resources efficiently in the cost function compared to its peers.

The importance of this study is twofold. First, this is the most recent study examining the cost efficiency of Indonesian banks. Second, this study examines bank performance using SFA after the crisis of 2008, which is rare to be found in literature.

2 LITERATURE STUDIES

Performance of commercial banks can be analyzed by two approaches: banking ratio analysis and bank efficiency analysis. These two analyses have been employed extensively by researchers to date. Bank efficiency analysis has attracted many authors for several decades, as the analysis can be applied to estimate how efficient a bank is in its operation in using its resources. In terms of analysis types, the analysis consists of technical efficiency, cost efficiency, and profit efficiency. Cost efficiency analysis is more interesting, in its ability to estimate cost efficiency of a company using output(s) and price of inputs.

There has been abundant research examining cost efficiency of commercial banks. Altunbas et al. (2000) examined risk and quality factors on bank cost efficiency, using the SFA method in Japan. Bonin et al. (2005) scrutinized the impact of ownership on SFA bank efficiency in Europe. Mamatzakis et al. (2008) employed SFA in estimating bank cost and profit efficiency in ten new European members. Hamilton et al. (2010) studied SFA cost and profit efficiency in Jordanian banks. Chan and Karim (2010) examined the influence of macroeconomic factors on SFA bank efficiency in 43 developing countries in Asia, the Middle East and Africa. Chunhachinda and Li (2010) compared the profit and cost efficiency of Thai commercial banks. Suhaemi et al. (2010) investigated the determinants of commercial banks' SFA profit efficiency in Malaysia. Andries (2011) examined bank efficiency in Central and Eastern European countries with SFA and Data Envelopment Analysis (DEA).

In the case of Indonesia, it is rare to find the papers examining bank cost efficiency using the SFA parametric technique. Margono et al. (2010) employed SFA in estimating cost efficiency, technological progress, and the productivity growth of Indonesian banks over the period 1993–2000. Besar (2011) examined the influence of foreign ownership on SFA bank cost efficiency over the period 2000–2009. Anwar (2015) examined Indonesian SFA bank cost efficiency and its determinants over the period 2002–2010.

3 DATA AND METHODOLOGY

This study includes all commercial banks in Indonesia over the study period 2015–2016. The data comprises 106 conventional banks and 12 Islamic banks. The banks are classified into four groups of banks, based on the equity size or *Bank Umum Klasifikasi Usaha* (BUKU). BUKU 1 are those banks with the equity of less than IDR1 trillion (32 banks); BUKU 2 are banks with the equity of IDR1 trillion to less than IDR5 trillion (53 banks); BUKU 3 are those with the equity of IDR5 trillion to less than IDR30 trillion (18 banks); BUKU 4 are those with the equity of IDR30 trillion or more (5 banks). In terms of ownership, the banks consist of seven State-Owned Banks (SOB), 28 Local Government-owned Banks (LGB), 10 Foreign-owned Banks (FB) and 73 Private Banks (PB).

The study uses the SFA parametric technique in estimating bank cost efficiency. The cost efficiency estimation was generated by the standard method with the specification of the components as follows. The left-hand side variable is *total costs* and the right-hand side variables are *outputs* (loans, interest income for Conventional banks or profit sharing income for Islamic Banks, and other operating income) and *prices* (price of funds, price of labor and price of capital). All variables are provided in natural logarithm form. The study also extends the analysis by revealing the determinants of cost efficiency of Indonesian banks over the period 2015–2016. The analysis of regressions is divided into two periods of the cross-sectional data with Tobit regression. The model is as follows:

$$\begin{aligned} CE_{it} = {} & b_0 + b_1 LNTA_{it} + b_2 CAR_{it} + b_3 NPL_{it} \\ & + b_4 LDR_{it} + b_5 ROA_{it} + b_6 INT\_INC_{it} \\ & + b_7 O\_OPINC_{it} b_6 NOPINC_{it} + \varepsilon_{it} \end{aligned} \tag{1}$$

where CE_{it} = SFA Cost efficiency of *i*-th bank in period-t; $LNTA_{it}$ = Natural Logarithm of Total Assets (LNTA) as a proxy for bank size; CAR_{it} = Capital Adequacy Ratio, which represents bank capital; NPL_{it} = Non-Performing Loans, which is a proxy of bank risk; LDR_{it} = Loans to Deposits Ratio (LDR), which is the proxy for bank liquidity; ROA_{it} = Return on Assets (ROA), which is the proxy for bank profit; INT_INC_{it} = Interest Income, as the representation of bank core operating-cost. Interest income is replaced by total revenue from the revenue sharing for Sharia banks; O_OPINC_{it} = Other Operating Income, which represents the bank's other operating income; $NOPINC_{it}$ = Non-Operating Income, which is the revenue generated by the bank from non-operating activities; and ε_{it} = Error term.

4 RESULTS

Table 1 reveals that all accounts increased in 2016 except for interest expense (int_exp).

Figure 4 shows that Capital Adequacy Ratio (CAR) of Indonesian banks has declined, NPL has increased, and LDR has increased. These findings indicate that the banks have enrolled the aggressive lending strategy by expanding lending facility to their customers. This policy has implications for the ratio of NPLs, which was also increasing during the period. The other findings reveal that the Indonesian banks have reduced their capital put in place during the period. All the policies taken by the banks' management have resulted in the decline of the average cost efficiency over the period.

Table 2 shows that PBs are evidenced as being the most cost-efficient banks. Meanwhile, SOBs are the least cost-efficient over the period. The results demonstrate a big improvement attained by the PBs during the period, considering that the banks were less efficient in the period 2002–2010 (Anwar, 2015; Hadad et al., 2011; Suzuki & Sastrosuwito, 2011).

Figure 5 demonstrates the performance of SHARIA (Islamic banks), which are more cost-efficient than conventional banks.

Figure 6 illustrates the cost efficiency attainment by different class of equity of those banks

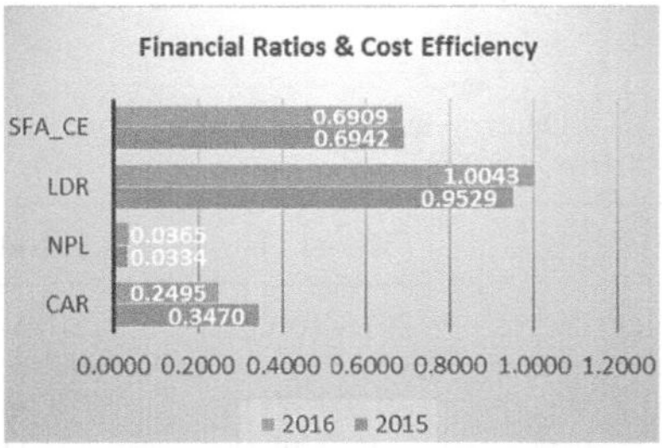

Figure 4. Financial ratios and cost efficiency (2015–2016).
Source: Data processed.

Table 2. The average cost efficiency of Indonesian banks (by different ownership).

	Foreign Banks (FB)	Local Government Owned Banks (LGOB)	Private Banks (PB)	State Owned Banks (SOB)	Total
2015	0.6172	0.6959	0.7148	0.5814	0.6942
2016	0.6530	0.7032	0.7051	0.5473	0.6909
Total	0.6351	0.6995	0.7100	0.5644	0.6925

Source: Data processed.

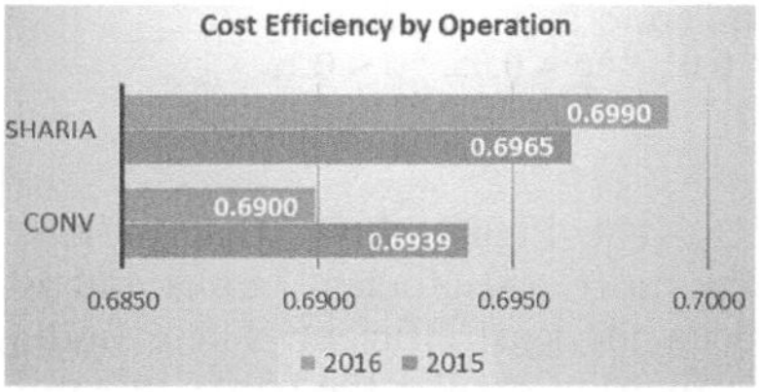

Figure 5. Average cost efficiency by different operation.
Source: Data processed.

Table 1. Highlights of Indonesian Banks (in IDR million).

	loans	int_inc	o_opinc	int_exp	o_opexp	tot_exp
2015	33,800	3,225.12	1,157.89	1,366.43	2,101.12	3,541.36
2016	36,000	3,424.60	1,305.02	1,322.42	2,554.59	3,869.45

Source: Data processed.

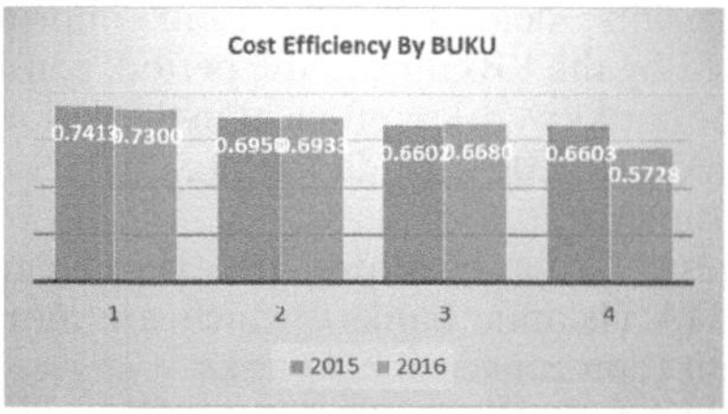

Figure 6. Average cost efficiency by different BUKU. Source: Data analysis by author.

Table 3. Determinants of bank cost efficiency (2015–2016).

	(Model 1)	(Model 2)
Variables	2015-Tobit	2016-Tobit
LNTA	–0.0253***	–0.00458
	(0.00903)	(0.00946)
CAR	–0.00806	0.0376
	(0.00843)	(0.0903)
NPL	–0.518*	–0.0881
	(0.282)	(0.326)
LDR	0.0822***	0.0667***
	(0.0245)	(0.0226)
ROA	2.094**	1.189***
	(0.857)	(0.360)
INT_INC	5.20e-09**	–1.85e-09
	(2.23e-09)	(1.92e-09)
O_OPINC	–1.15e-08**	–1.01e-08**
	(5.34e-09)	(3.91e-09)
NOPINC	–1.90e-07*	1.10e-07
	(1.05e-07)	(1.19e-07)
Constant	1.035***	0.697***
	(0.149)	(0.157)
Observations	118	118

Standard errors in parentheses.
***p < 0.01, **p < 0.05, *p < 0.1.

(BUKU). The Figure shows that BUKU 1 have been the most cost-efficient banks and BUKU 4 have been the least efficient. These findings also suggest that the smaller the banks in equity term, the better the banks.

The results show that there are three variables that conclusively and significantly affect Indonesian bank cost efficiency: LDR, ROA and O_OPINC. LDR has a very strong positive impact on bank cost efficiency, meaning that the bigger the loans provided to customers compared to deposits collected, the more cost-efficient the bank in the operation. It is very sensible that the sound loans facility can generate income from interest and that the amount is higher than the interest paid to depositors. ROA is also significant in determining cost efficiency of the banks with a positive association. The findings show that the return generated from the operation has covered the expenses paid. Meanwhile, other operating income has a negative significant impact on bank cost efficiency. The other result is that bank size (LNTA) has a negative association with bank cost efficiency in both models, with a very strong impact in model 1. The results confirm the findings that the smaller the banks the more cost-efficient the banks.

5 CONCLUSIONS

The study is to examine SFA bank cost efficiency of Indonesian banks over the period 2015–2016. The findings suggest that the average cost efficiency of Indonesian banks has declined in 2016. PBs emerged to be the most cost-efficient banks while SOBs are the least cost-efficient. Sharia banks are more cost-efficient than conventional banks. Banks of BUKU 1 (the smallest banks in equity) are the most cost-efficient banks. The regression results suggest that LDR, ROA and Other Operating Income conclusively and significantly affect Indonesian bank cost efficiency.

REFERENCES

Altunbas, Y., Liu, M.H., Molyneux, P. & Seth, R. (2000). Efficiency and risk in Japanese banking. *Journal of Banking and Finance*, *24*(10), 1605–1628.

Andries, A.M. (2011). The determinants of bank efficiency and productivity growth in the Central and Eastern European banking systems. *Eastern European Economics*, *49*(6): 38–59.

Anwar, M. (2015). *Bank efficiency and lending propensity: Evidence from commercial banks in Indonesia*. PhD Thesis, University of Leicester.

Besar, D.S. (2011). *Essays on Indonesian banking: Competition, efficiency, and its role in monetary policy transmission*. PhD Thesis, City University London.

Bonin, J.P., Hasan, I. & Wachtel, P. (2005). Bank performance, efficiency and ownership in transition countries. *Journal of Banking & Finance*, *29*(1), 31–53.

Chan, S.G. & Karim, M.Z.A. (2010). Bank efficiency and macro-economic factors: The case of developing countries. *Global Economic Review*, *39*(3), 269–289.

Chunhachinda, P. & Li, L. (2010). Efficiency of Thai commercial banks: Pre-vs. Post-1997 financial crisis. *Review of Pacific Basin Financial Markets and Policies*, *13*(03), 417–447.

Ernst and Young (EY) (2015). *Indonesian banking industry:* Challenging yet promising. http://www.ey.com/Publication/vwLUAssets/EY-Indonesian-banking-industry-challenging-yet-promising/%24FILE/EY-indonesian-banking-industry-challenging-yet-promising.pdf. Accessed 6 April 2017.

Fethi, M.D., Shaban, M. & Weyman-Jones, T. (2011). Liberalisation, privatisation, and the productivity of Egyptian banks: A non-parametric approach. *The Service Industries Journal*, *31*(7), 1143–1163.

Hadad, M.D., Hall, M.J.B., Kenjegalieva, K.A., Santoso, W., Satria, R. & Simper, R. (2011). Banking efficiency and stock market performance: An analysis of listed Indonesian banks. *Rev Quant Finan Acc*, *37*(1), 1–20.

Hamilton, R., Qasrawi, W. & Al-Jarrah, I.M. (2010). Cost and profit efficiency in the Jordan banking sector 1993–2006: A parametric approach. *International Research Journal of Finance and Economics*, *56*, 111–123.

Kao, C. & Liu, S.T. (2004). Predicting bank performance with financial forecasts: A case of Taiwan commercial banks. *Journal of Banking & Finance*, *28*(10), 2353–2368.

Mamatzakis, E, Staikouras, C. & Koutsomanoli-Filippaki, A. (2008). Bank efficiency in the New European Union member states: Is there convergence? *Int'l Review of Financial Analysis*, *17*(5), 1156–1172.

Margono, H., Sharma, S.C. & Melvin II, P.D. (2010). Cost efficiency, economies of scale, technological progress and productivity in Indonesian banks. *Journal of Asian Economics*, *21*(1), 53–65.

Sufian, F. (2010). The impact of the Asian financial crisis on bank efficiency: The 1997 experience of Malaysia and Thailand. *Journal of International Development*, *22*(7), 866–889.

Suhaemi, R., Abdullah, F. & Saban, G. (2010). Factors affecting profit efficiency of commercial banks in Malaysia. *International Conference on Science and Social Research, December 2010*, Kuala Lumpur, Malaysia.

Suzuki, Y. & Sastrosuwito, S. (2011). Efficiency and productivity change of the Indonesian commercial banks. *International Conference on Economics, Trade and Development* IPEDR, vol. 7, IACSIT, Singapore.

Increasing Management Relevance and Competitiveness – Sukoco et al. (Eds)
© 2018 Taylor & Francis Group, London, ISBN 978-0-8153-7455-8

Analysis of investor preference in investing on initial public offering

M. Sari
Universitas Pendidikan Indonesia, Bandung, Indonesia

ABSTRACT: This research aims to investigate the effects of reinforcement learning and risk averse level upon preference to investment on Initial Public Offering (IPO). Quasi experiment is used as research method, along with the participation of students from management department UPI, who have taken a financial management course and have knowledge in the capital market. The hypothesis tests used in this research are the *Mann-Whitney test* and *Two-way ANOVA test*. This research found there to be significantly different investment decisions between those participants who have positive reinforcement learning and those groups of participants who have negative reinforcement. There are significantly different investment decisions in a group of participants who have Less Risk Averse preference and a group of participants who have More Risk Averse preference. The research also found that there is no interaction between reinforcement learning and risk preference on IPO investment decision.

Keywords: Reinforcement Learning, Risk Preference, Risk Averse, IPO

1 INTRODUCTION

Corporation action through Initial Public Offering (IPO) is one determinant of the growing number of stocks listed on the Indonesian Stock Exchange. In IPO transactions, investors are faced with a condition of limited information as an impact from the existence of *asymmetric information* between issuer and investor, whereas *fundamental information* is a factor that is considered by the investor in investment decision. The limitation of information raises a question: if the fundamental information of IPO is relatively limited, then what other factors are taken into investor's consideration of decision in IPO?

Reinforcement Learning Theory explains that under a limited information condition, the investor will use experience as a reference when taking a financial decision. Awais (2016) explains that if behavior in the investment appraising process is just based firstly on publisher information, the investor's personal experience of investment in the past will be the primary consideration in the investment appraising process in the future.

Attitude toward risk is also one of the factors that influence investment preference. Research conducted by Vlaev et al. (2008) shows that the investor will be *Risk Averse* (RA) when they do invest in high risk financial products. In reality, that risk preference is not absolute, but it is a tendency, so the level of risk aversion from each investor will vary.

According to this knowledge background, this research will examine how Reinforcement Learning (RL) and risk aversion attitude influence the decision on IPO investment and how the relationship between the two factors is made.

2 LITERATURE REVIEW

2.1 *Initial public offering*

IPO is a corporate action of a company in order to gain funds from society. Welch (1989) explains that the use of IPO to capital expenditure for a company with good quality will be considered as an effort to increase company quality through product capacity enhancement, while for a bad quality company it does not mean anything. Gumanti, cited in Kristiantari (2012), explains that the first stock price application of a particular company is a relevant price. This happens because the company stock has never been traded before the implementation of the initial offering, resulting in difficulties in appraising and deciding a proper price.

2.2 *Reinforcement learning*

In solving a complex problem, every person experiences a limitation in thinking rationally. Rational behavior only plays a small part for humans, because there are a number of individual actions which are instead rather based on their emotional side. This kind of limitation is related to experience, and information processing, which are used to take decisions. The existence of those limitations and experience in the past is one of the shortcuts which could be useful, where experience becomes a booster for a person to take an action.

RL is the utilization of a person's experience to increase the performance in taking a decision. Results of research by Kaustia and Knüpfer (2008) found that there is a positive relationship between stock return IPO in the past and research findings from Nicolosi et al., cited in Baker & Nofsinger (2010), explaining that the ability to choose a financial product which is owned by an individual investor comes from their own transaction experience. Moreover, it is explained that an investor who has positive experience in the transaction tends to increase the volume of transaction in the future, compared with an individual investor who has a negative transaction experience.

2.3 *Investor preference toward risk*

Investor expectation in investment is in receiving maximum *expected return* from a number of funds which have been invested. But to receive the *expected return*, an investor is faced with uncertainty (*risk*), and yet in order to take an optimal decision for investment, both of those factors should be taken into consideration, because of the existence of *trade-off* between *expected return* and the *risk*. A rational person is someone who tends to be RA, but the level and characteristic of risk aversion is not absolute and is generally divided into two subdivisions: More Risk Averse (MRA) and Less Risk Averse (LRA). A person who tends to be More RA (MRA) is relatively unwilling to take the uncertain return rather than the certain one. However, the contrary happens in a person who tends not to be RA (LRA). An investor who is in the MRA category tends to choose the investment with the higher level of return certainty rather than the lower one.

2.4 *Reinforcement learning interaction and risk aversion in IPO stock transactions*

Bush and Mosteller (1955), cited in Börgers and Sarin (1997), claim that RL could be classified into RL positive and RL negative. RL positive is related to experience with positive *return* in the past, while RL negative is related to experience with negative *return* in the past. Groups with RL positive are supposed to do more in purchasing IPO compared with RL negative groups. By having risk preference, investors who have RL positive manage to maximize their own profit by decreasing the level to which they are RA, with the result that the investors will purchase more IPO. On the contrary, in a group of investors who have RL negative, in order to minimize the loss they have had, they will increase their risk preference to become MRA, resulting in fewer purchases of IPO. Therefore, in the process of making an investment decision, both RL and RA investors could interact with one another.

Denrell (2007) shows that when a person has had good rewards in the past, he/she will tend to use past reward estimation to make present decisions. Therefore, the probability that choosing security in the past gives positive reward, will increase according to experience. On the assumption that traders are rational, there will be interaction between RL and RA investors which will influence the investment decision in purchasing IPO stock.

3 RESEARCH HYPOTHESES

H1: The average volume of IPO transaction which is performed by an investor on a RL positive group, is different with the average of the volume of IPO transaction performed by an investor on a RL negative group.

H2: The average volume of IPO transaction which is performed by an investor who tends to be MRA, is different with the average of the volume of IPO transaction performed by an investor who tends to be less RA.

H3: There is interaction between RL and risk aversion in the decision of an IPO transaction.

4 RESEARCH METHODS

The method used in this research is *quasi experiment*, with 27 participants divided into 14 men and 13 women. Participants are students who have taken a financial management course and have a knowledge of transactions in the field of capital market. Participants are taken from the student population to represent the respondent from the investor group. This refers to the results of research by Kufepaksi (2008), that the student's participation as participant will give a valid result because it shows the actual phenomenon which is related to the lack of experience in transaction, as occurs in the actual investors when they are faced with IPO transaction.

Experiment design used in this research is based on the experiment done by Kufepaksi (2008). The fist IPO session is performed for two groups of participants. Group A is participants who get Positive RL, which is conditioned to be getting positive return from each IPO transaction. On the other side, group B is participants who get Negative RL, which is conditioned to be getting negative return.

The second and third IPO session are performed to determine the decision of IPO stock purchases, after getting an experience of stock purchases in the next session.

The hypothesis test used in this research are the Mann-Whitney and the two-way ANOVA test. Level of significance used in this research is 0.05 or 5% ($\alpha = 0.05$).

5 RESULT AND DISCUSSION

5.1 *Effect of RL differences toward IPO stock purchase decision*

The measurement result for the average volume of IPO transaction in the third session shows the average volume of IPO transaction in the participant group with Positive Reinforcement (16.96 lots), which is higher compared with the average volume of IPO transactions in the other group that obtains Negative Reinforcement (10.54 lots).

To test the first hypothesis, this research uses the Mann-Whitney test, where the results can be seen in Table 2. The Mann-Whitney test obtains the Asymp. Sig value of $0.032 < 0.05$, which shows that Ho is rejected, or that the average volume of IPO transaction from the investors with Positive RL has a different significance from that of the average volume of IPO transaction from investors with Negative RL.

This research explains that there is a different experience that will impact on the different financial decision taken. Thus the success in an IPO transaction, besides being affected by factors of the underwriter in determining the cost, is also affected by the factor of experience in previous IPO transactions to be the basic consideration in an IPO offer. An investor, initially (before having any experience) only considers the stock performance information, but will also consider his experiences (after having prior experience) before doing the transaction. In the case of IPO transaction, the investment decision is not purely based on the result of prospectus analysis, but also on the investor's experience in previous IPO transaction. This is done because the investor will need a long time to process the information, so that it will result in a high cost. Thus, the experience in previous IPO transaction can be used as guidance to make future transaction decisions.

Table 1. Average of volume of IPO transaction according to rank's RL.

	Reinforcement Learning (RL)	N	Mean rank	Sum of ranks
TOTAL IPO	Negative RL	14	10.54	147.50
	Positive RL	13	16.96	203.50
	Total	27		

Table 2. Mann-Whitney variable test.

Test Statistics[b]	
	TOTAL IPO
Mann-Whitney U	42.500
Wilcoxon W	147.500
Z	–2.143
Asymp. Sig. (2-tailed)	0.032
Exact Sig. [2*(1-tailed Sig.)]	0.031[a]

a. Not corrected for ties,
b. Variable: RISK AVERSION.

5.2 *The influence of difference in risk acceptance level to the average volume of IPO transactions*

In the third session of IPO experiment, the RA level measurement is taken from each participant, through the game of Deal or No Deal. The result shows that of the 13 participants from the Positive Reinforcement group, eight participants were identified as being in the LRA category, and the rest from the MRA category. While 14 participants were in the Negative Reinforcement group, nine were identified as being in the MRA group, while the rest were in the LRA category.

Table 3 explains the average volume of IPO transactions from each group, which has a different RA level. The average volume of IPO transactions from the group of investors with the LRA category is 16.73 lots. That volume of transaction is higher compared with the average volume of transactions from participants in the MRA category of 10.27 lots.

The results of the Mann-Whitney test, which is applied to the participants in the MRA category and the LRA category, obtains an Asymp. Sig value of $0.031 < 0.05$. This shows that the average volume of IPO transactions from investors in the MRA category that has different significance with

Table 3. Average of volume of IPO transactions according to rank's risk preference.

	Risk aversion	N	Mean rank	Sum of ranks
TOTAL IPO	More Risk Aversion	14	10.27	133.50
	Less Risk Aversion	13	16.73	217.50
	Total	27		

Table 4. The results of Mann-Whitney test in variable average volume of IPO transaction and variable risk aversion.

Test statistics[b]	
	TOTAL IPO
Mann-Whitney U	42.500
Wilcoxon W	133.500
Z	−2.162
Asymp. Sig. (2-tailed)	0.031
Exact Sig. [2*(1-tailed Sig.)]	0.029[a]

a. Not corrected for ties,
b. Variable: RISK AVERSION.

the average volume of IPO transactions which are made by investors in LRA.

The second result shows that, besides having a factor of past experience, the IPO investment decision is also influenced by the risk preference. Someone in the MRA category is unwilling to receive the *uncertain return* rather than the *certain return*. The opposite result happens with an individual who is in the LRA category, where the investor in the LRA group tends to receive the investment in stock compared to one who is in the More Averse group.

5.3 *The influence of learning reinforcement interaction with the risk aversion to the IPO stock purchase decision-making*

According to previous two researches, the Positive RL investor group will behave to bequests their RA because of the past experience, where it is favorable to maintain the advantage which has been obtained. On the other hand, the Negative RL group tends to increase the RA because of the adverse experiences in the past, to minimize the disadvantages being experienced. Thus, in processing of the investment decision-making, both RL and RA are connected in interaction. The result of the hypothesis shows that there is interaction between RL and Risk Aversion in the IPO purchase decision. This can be seen from the results of the two-way ANOVA test, as shown in Table 5.

In the *two-way ANOVA* test, there are two analyses performed: testing the different variable (RL and RA), and the interaction test between variable categories. The result of the F-test of average value of IPO transaction with RL variable shows the probability value. The result of the T-test is obtained, as shown in the following:

Table 5. The test results of two-way ANOVA interaction between RL and RA in IPO.

Source	Type III Sum of Squares	Df	Mean Square	F	Sig.
Corrected model	11,609.713[a]	3	3,869.904	3.426	0.035
Intercept	100,513.074	1	100,513.074	88.979	0.000
RA	3,856.875	1	3,856.875	3.414	0.078
RL	3,239.033	1	3,239.033	2.867	0.105
RA * RL	1,038.381	1	1,038.381	0.919	0.348
Error	24,851.825	22	1,129.628		
Total	138,650.000	26			
Corrected total	36,461.538	25			

a. R Squared = 0.318 (Adjusted R Squared = 0.225).

1. Probability based on RL variable is the different average test in average volume of IPO transactions with RL of 0.105 > 0.05, which means that the average volume of IPO transactions from respondents who have different RL is the same.
2. Probability based on RA variable is the different average test in average volume of IPO transaction of 0.078 > 0.05, which means the average volume of IPO transaction from respondents who have different RA is the same.
3. The results of RL and RA interaction test shows both variable of probability interaction of 0.348 > 0.05, which shows that Ho is accepted and that there is no interaction between RL and risk aversion in the average volume of IPO transaction.

6 CONCLUSIONS AND SUGGESTIONS

The average volume of IPO transactions in a group of participants with Positive RL is significantly different with the average volume of IPO transactions in a group of participants with Negative RL. The average volume of IPO transactions in a group of participants in the LRA category is significantly different with the average volume of IPO transactions through the group of participants through IPO in a group of participants in the MRA category. There is no interaction found between RL and Risk Preference Level in IPO investment decision-making.

The company should consider the experiences and risk preference from the investors when appraising and deciding a proper price for IPO. It is suggested to other researchers that they examine the disposition effect phenomena that happens in IPO stock when being in transaction in a secondary market, as is found to be the case in this research.

REFERENCES

Awais, M., Laber, M.F., Rasheed, N., & Khursheed, A. (2016). Impact of Financial Literacy and Investment Experience on Risk Tolerance and Investment Decisions: Empirical Evidence from Pakistan. *International Journal of Economics and Financial Issues*, *6*(1).

Baker, H.K., & Nofsinger, J.R. (Eds.). (2010). *Behavioral finance: investors, corporations, and markets* (Vol. 6). John Wiley & Sons.

Börgers, H.T. & Sarin, R. (1997). Learning through reinforcement and replicator dynamics. *Journal of Economic Theory*, *77*(1), 1–14.

Denrell J (2007) Adaptive learning and risk taking. Psych. Rev. 114(1):177–187.

Guiso, L., Sapienza, P. & Zingales, L. (2013). *Time varying risk aversion* (No. w19284). National Bureau of Economic Research.

Hoffmann, A.O., Post, T. & Pennings, J.M. (2013). Individual investor perceptions and behavior during the financial crisis. *Journal of Banking & Finance*, *37*(1), 60–74.

Kaustia, M. & Knüpfer, S. (2008). Do investors overweight personal experience? Evidence from IPO subscriptions. *The Journal of Finance*, *63*(6), 2679–2702.

Kristiantari, I.D. (2012). Analisis Faktor-Faktor Yang Mempengaruhi Underpricing Saham Pada Penawaran Perdana Di Bursa Efek Indonesia. *Jurnal Ilmiah Akuntansi Dan Humaka Jinah*, *2*(2).

Kufepaksi, M. (2008). The contribution of self-deceptive behavior on price discovery: An experimental approach. *Asia Pacific Management Review*, *13*(1), 419–434.

Lang, M.H. & Lundholm, R.J. (2000). Voluntary disclosure and equity offerings: Reducing information asymmetry or hyping the stock? *Contemporary Accounting Research*, *17*(4), 623–662.

Miller, J.A. & Olshavsky, R.W. (2016). Limits to optimal consumer problem solving: A framework for consumer protection policy. In *Proceedings of the 1979 Academy of Marketing Science (AMS) Annual Conference* (pp. 350–354). Springer International Publishing.

Vlaev, I., Stewart, N. & Chater, N. (2008). Risk preference discrepancy: A prospect relativity account of the discrepancy between risk preferences in laboratory gambles and real world investments. *The Journal of Behavioral Finance*, *9*(3), 132–148.

Welch, I. (1989). Seasoned offerings, imitation costs, and the underpricing of initial public offerings. *The Journal of Finance*, *44*(2), 421–449.

Increasing Management Relevance and Competitiveness – Sukoco et al. (Eds)
© 2018 Taylor & Francis Group, London, ISBN 978-0-8153-7455-8

Female directors, nationality diversity, and firm performance: Evidence from the mining industry in Indonesia

Y.S. Putri, M. Nasih & I. Harymawan
Universitas Airlangga, Surabaya, Indonesia

ABSTRACT: This study investigates how the presence of female directors and the nationality diversity affect firm performance in the mining industry in Indonesia. This study uses 186 firm year observations on mining industry listed on the Indonesian Stock Exchange (IDX) spanning the 2010–2015 period. The regression method is used to test the hypotheses using STATA software. The finding shows that the presence of female directors in the mining firms is associated with negative firm performance. Interestingly, the nationality diversity is positively associated with firm performance.

1 INTRODUCTION

Prior studies have found that the composition and characteristics of the board of directors of the company can affect the outcome of the company (Gray and Nowland 2015; Gray. Harymawan, and Nowland 2016; Harymawan and Nowland 2016). The composition of the board is also influenced by the diversity of board members. The diversity of board members illustrates the differences between individuals regarding measurable factors, such as age, religion, ethnicity, gender, socioeconomic, residence, formal qualifications and technical skills. It also may include factors such as the real-life experience, personal attitude or perspective (Committee, 2009).

This study focuses on examining two specific compositions of board directors, the prevalence of female directors and nationality diversity, on firm performance. Using 186 firm year observations listed in IDX for the period 2010–2015, the findings of this study show that, for firms in the mining industry, the presence of female directors is negatively associated with firm performance. Moreover, the results also show that firms with high nationality diversity are associated with better firm performance. These findings imply that the mining industry in Indonesia, which is more likely to have higher political pressure, demands specific requirements of a board director. Furthermore, the need of more complex operation and implementation of the latest advanced technology requires the company to involve directors from different nationalities. This study contributes to the literature by examining the role of female directors and nationality diversity in one of the more interesting industries, mining, in Indonesia.

2 LITERATURE REVIEW AND HYPOTHESES

Freeman (1984) defines stakeholders as any group or individual who can affect or be affected by the achievement of an organization's objective. Stakeholder theory states that the company is not just an entity that operates for its own account, but also must provide benefits to stakeholders. The higher the power of stakeholders in the company, the effort to adapt also increases. This theory explains the importance of the company to maximize the interest of the stakeholders.

As the primary key in the company's sustainability, board members are required to have a deeper retention regarding the company in accordance with the field of the mobile company. Tarus and Aime (2014) and Ararat, Aksu, and Cetin (2010) provide empirical evidence that educational background has a positive effect on the financial performance of the company. Taljaard, Ward, and Muller (2015) finds that the increase diversity of gender and firms in younger average age significantly influence the company's financial performance. Adams and Ferreira (2009) find that firms with larger business segment are associated with larger board composition. However, it has negative associations with firm performance. The above discussion proves that characteristics of board directors affect financial performance.

The issue of gender differences is very sensitive, especially in the mining industry, whereas high class lobbying is very important. Distribution of gender between male and female in top management positions is believed to increase diversity in the organization. The success of male directors is considered to be because of high ability (in terms of talent or intelligence), whereas female director success is considered more due to luck factor (Crawford 2006). Fidanoski, Simeonovski, and Mateska (2014) found that the average company with higher composition of women and foreign board members will reduce firm performance.

H1: In the mining industry, the presence of female directors is negatively associated with firm performance.

One of the consequences to meet the demand from investors to create an independent and competitive corporate environment becomes a major issue of the need to increase nationality diversity. Especially in the mining industry, the presence of nationality diversity is important to ensure that the company will maximize the firm performance in the interest of stakeholders. More specifically, the need to implement advanced technology is also a possible reason to increase nationality diversity for the firms in the mining industry. Nielsen and Nielsen (2013) found that nationality diversity has a positive and significant influence on the performance. Nationality diversity is stronger in longer tenure teams and more internationalized firms.

H2: In the mining industry, the nationality diversity is positively associated with firm performance.

3 DATA AND METHOD

The companies used in this study are firms in the mining industry listed on the IDX spanning the 2010–2015 period. Our final observation is 186 firm years. The data are obtained from the audited company's annual report. The firm performance is measured by Tobin's Q (Salinger, 1984). The interested variables are the presence of female directors (FEMALE) and nationality diversity (NAT). The control variables used in this study are educational background diversity of the board member (EDU); age diversity (AGE); size of the firm (SIZE); ownership (OWN); the proportion of independent commissioners (INDEPDIR); plant, property, and equipment (PPE); and firm leverage (LEV).

Table 1. Firm distribution by year.

Year	No. of firms
2010	20
2011	30
2012	33
2013	36
2014	36
2015	31
Total	**186**

All continuous variables used in this study are winsorized at 1 and 99 percent. To test the hypotheses, this study uses Ordinary Least Square (OLS) method and robust regression. Table 1 provides the detail distribution of the firms by year. The trend shows that number of mining firms is increasing.

4 RESULT

Table 2 presents the descriptive statistics of all variables used in this study. The mean of firm performance is 1.643 (million rupiah) with the minimum 0.30 and maximum 15.28. On average, each firm in mining industry appoints 7.2 percent of female directors from their total directors. For nationality diversity, on average, 14.9 percent of the directors of each firm are from overseas. The maximum of proportion of overseas directors in this sample is 4 percent. The mean of independent directors is 3.73 percent. The proportion of debt to total assets, on average is 48 percent.

Table 3 present the results of regression in this study. Specification model 1 tests the hypotheses using Ordinary Least Squares (OLS) method. The coefficient of *FEMALE* is –0.057 and statistically significant at the 10 percent level (t-value = –1.92). This finding shows that mining firms with higher percentage of female directors are more likely to have worse performance.

Interestingly, the coefficient of *NATION* is 0.005 and statistically significant at the 5 percent level (t-value = 2.48). It implies that higher diversity in nationality in mining firms is associated with better financial performance.

Specification model 2 re-examines the hypotheses using robust regression method. The coefficient of *FEMALE* is –0.024 and statistically significant at 10 percent level (t-value = –2.27). This finding reinforces the result from Specification model 1, that mining firms with higher percentage of female directors are more likely to have worse performance. Consistent with the finding in model 1,

Table 2. Descriptive statistics.

Variable	Mean	Std. Dev.	Min	Max
PERFORM	1.643	2.020	0.03	15.28
FEMALE	0.072	0.101	0	0.4
NATION	0.149	0.172	0	0.71
EDUCATION	0.575	0.123	0.25	0.81
AGE	0.220	0.100	0.05	0.52
SIZE	28.878	1.650	23.15	32
OWN	58.516	17.000	16.5	94.6
INDEPDIR	0.373	0.137	0	0.67
PPE	0.207	0.190	0	0.83
LEV	0.480	0.253	0.01	1.23

Table 3. Regression results.

Variables	Pred. sign	*PERFORM* [1]	[2]
FEMALE	–	–0.057*	–0.024**
		(–1.92)	(–2.27)
NATION	+	0.005**	0.011**
		(2.48)	(2.56)
EDU	+	0.492	0.454
		(0.69)	(0.75)
AGE	–	–0.915	–0.904
		(–0.11)	(–0.12)
SIZE	–	–0.116	–0.2
		(–1.58)	(–1.29)
OWN	–	0.027**	–0.058*
		(–2.22)	(–1.91)
INDEPDIR	+	0.052*	0.079*
		(1.96)	(1.77)
PPE	–	–0.145	–0.125
		(–1.46)	(–1.54)
LEV	–	–0.2	–0.203
		(–1.29)	(–1.28)
Year dummies		Included	Included
Adjusted R2		0.072	
R-Squared		0.152	0.152
N		186	186

the coefficient of *NATION* is 0.011 and statistically significant at a 5 percent level (t-value = 2.56), suggesting that higher diversity in nationality in mining firms is associated with better financial performance.

With respect to control variables, we find that ownership is negative and significantly associated with firm performance. The percentage of independent directors (INDEPDIR) is positive and significantly associated with firm performance. The remaining control variables are insignificant. In both specifications model, we also control the variance of the year by using year-fixed effects. The R-squared is about 15 percent.

5 CONCLUSION

In this study, we examine the prevalence of female directors and the level of nationality diversity of firms in the mining industry in Indonesia. We find that firms, on average, appoint 7.2 percent of female directors on their board. In our regression model, we find that the prevalence of female directors on the board is associated with worse firm performance. Furthermore, we find that firms with higher nationality diversity are associated with higher firm performance.

This study further enhances our knowledge on how the firms in the mining industry should manage their board composition, especially in the prevalence of the female director and the diversity of nationality of the board members. We acknowledge the limitation of this study that the samples used in this study are only limited to listed firms. Therefore, it might underestimate the result.

REFERENCES

Adams, R.B., & Ferreira, D. 2009. Women in the boardroom and their impact on governance and performance. *Journal of Financial Economics,* 94 no. 2: 291–309.

Ararat, M., Aksu, M., & Cetin, A.T. 2010. *Impact of Board Diversity on Boards Monitoring Intensity and Firm Performance: Evidence from the Istanbul Stock Exchange*. Working Paper. Available at SSRN Corporations and Markets Advisory Committee. *Diversity on Board of Directors, Report.* Australia: Australian Government.

Crawford, M.E. 2006. *Transformations: Women, Gender, and Psychology.* McGraw-Hill.

Fidanoski, F., Simeonovski, K., & Mateska, V. 2014. *The Impact of Board Diversity on Corporate Performance: New Evidence from Southeast Europe Corporate Governance in the US and Global Settings.* Emerald Group Publishing Limited.

Freeman, R.E. 1984. *Strategic Management: A Stakeholder Approach.* Boston: Pitman.

Gray, S., & Nowland, J. 2015. The diversity of expertise on corporate boards in Australia. *Accounting & Finance,* 57 no. 2:429–463.

Gray, S., Harymawan, I., & Nowland, J. 2016. Political and government connections on corporate boards in Australia: Good for business? *Australian Journal of Management*, 41 no. 1: 3–26.

Harymawan, I., & Nowland, J. 2016. Political connections and earnings quality: How do connected firms respond to changes in political stability and government effectiveness? *International Journal of Accounting & Information Management*, 24 no. 4:339–356.

Nielsen, B.B., & Nielsen, S. 2013. Top management team nationality diversity and firm performance: A multilevel study. *Strategic Management Journal*, 34 no. 3: 373–382.

Salinger, M.A. 1984. Tobin's q, unionization, and the concentration-profits relationship. *The Rand Journal of Economics*, 15 no. 2:159–170.

Stolk, D. 2011. *Demographic Diversity in the Boardroom and Firm Financial Performance.* Erasmus University.

Taljaard, C.C., Ward, M.J., & Muller, C.J. 2015. Board diversity and financial performance: A graphical time-series approach. *South African Journal of Economic and Management Sciences*, 18 no. 3: 425–447.

Tarus, D. K, & Aime, F. 2014. Board demographic diversity, firm performance and strategic change. *Management Research Review,* 37 no. 12: 1110.

Increasing Management Relevance and Competitiveness – Sukoco et al. (Eds)
© 2018 Taylor & Francis Group, London, ISBN 978-0-8153-7455-8

Sharia governance framework in Islamic banking and financial institutions in Indonesia: A proposed structure

M.I.S. Mihajat
Oman Arab Bank, Oman

ABSTRACT: The current sharia governance structure in Indonesia is far from ideal compared to international best practice. Therefore, the paper proposes a new sharia governance framework by involving a new higher sharia board authority, named, the Sharia Supervisory Board Authority (*Otoritas Dewan Pengawas Syariah*, ODPS), under the commissioners of the Indonesian Financial Services Authority (*Otoritas Jasa Keuangan*, OJK), to oversee, regulate and supervise sharia matters for Islamic banking and financial institutions in Indonesia. The paper concludes that the current shortcomings of a proper sharia governance framework for sharia supervision and regulation require a new sharia board authority under the commissioners of OJK that will have full authority over sharia matters.

Keywords: Sharia governance, Islamic banking and financial institutions, ODPS-OJK

1 INTRODUCTION

Islamic banking and financial institutions have a duty to ensure the full compliance of Islamic Financial Institutions (IFIs) with sharia rules and principles in all aspects of their products, instruments, business, operations, and practices by establishment of a proper sharia governance framework. In addition, regulatory authorities (such as the Central Bank and Financial Services Authority) should ensure the established regulation covers the proper sharia governance framework. The significance of sharia governance transpires via its role of ensuring and maintaining the confidence of the Islamic banking and finance industry in the eyes of stakeholders. The data and history have shown that improvement in the aspect of sharia governance would assist the impressive growth of the Islamic finance industry (Onagun & Mikail, 2013).

Currently, in Indonesia, the supervision and regulation of banking, capital market, insurance and other financial institutions including Islamic Banking and Financial Institutions (IBFIs) are regulated and supervised by the Indonesian Financial Services Authority (OJK) under the legal *Otoritas Jasa Keuangan* act, no. 21, 2011. There is an urgent need to develop effective sharia governance in the arena of sharia regulation and supervision as a tool to strengthen the resilience of the Islamic financial system in Indonesia because the current sharia governance structure in Indonesia is far from ideal compared to international best practice. Therefore, this paper will focus on the proposal of a new higher sharia supervisory board authority under the commissioners of OJK, named, the Sharia Supervisory Board Authority (ODPS-OJK). The paper also compares its functions with the National Shari'a Board of Indonesian Council of Ulama (DSN-MUI) and the Sharia Supervisory Board (SSB) in each individual Islamic financial institution.

2 THE IMPORTANCE OF SHARIA GOVERNANCE FOR IFIs

The importance of sharia governance has been stressed by the Islamic Financial Services Board (IFSB) in Principle 3.1 of the "IFSB Guiding Principles on Corporate Governance" (IFSB, 2006), which states that "an appropriate mechanism must be created to ensure the compliance with the sharia principles". Similarly, Principle 7.1 of the "IFSB Guiding Principles on Risk Management" (IFSB, 2005) states that "IFIs shall have in place adequate systems and controls, including sharia board/advisor, to ensure compliance with sharia principles".

Sharia governance can be defined as a system whereby an IFI attempts to comply with sharia in all its activities. According to IFSB-10 No. 3, a sharia governance system is "a set of institutional and organizational arrangements through which IFIs ensure that there is effective independent oversight of sharia compliance over the issuance of relevant sharia pronouncements, dissemination of information, an internal sharia compliance review/audit and annual sharia compliance review/audit" (IFSB, 2009).

Because sharia compliance is the backbone of IBFIs, it gives legitimacy to the practices of IBFIs. It also boosts the confidence of shareholders and the public that all the practices and activities comply with sharia at all times. Therefore, sharia governance is crucial to IBFIs to protect the interests of the stakeholders. In addition, the implementation of sharia governance is encouraged by international institutions of regulation, for example, the Accounting and Auditing Organization for Islamic Financial Institutions (AAOIFI) and the IFSB (Hamza, 2013). It is essential that IFIs comply with sharia to enhance the confidence of the stakeholders of IBFIs (Miskam & Nasrul, 2013).

3 THE FUTURE OF ISLAMIC BANKING AND FINANCE IN INDONESIA

In 2011, the Indonesian parliament has been endorsed the new act No 21 2011 regarding the supervision of financial institution would be took over by a new authority namely *Otoritas Jasa Keuangan* (OJK, Indonesian Financial Services Authority) from Bank Indonesia (Central Bank of Indonesia).

Prior to the endorsement of this act, the regulation and supervision of banking institutions fell under Bank Indonesia. However, after this endorsement, OJK took over this supervision that not only covers Islamic banking institutions but also takaful (Islamic insurance) companies, the Islamic capital market, and non-financial institutions such as Islamic leasing companies, BMTs (*Baitul Maal wa al-Tamwil*, Islamic microfinance institution) and cooperatives. These reforms aim to enhance the soundness of the financial system and improve the quality of supervision, thus broadening and deepening the financial system.

In addition, according to E&Y (2013), Indonesia, Malaysia, Saudi Arabia and the UAE are among the few countries that will become driving forces behind the next big wave of Islamic finance in the world, as well as being in a position to offer lessons to other nations seeking to build their own Islamic finance capacity. With the big of Muslims' population in the world, many countries in particular Muslim Countries expect Indonesia can become an Islamic finance Hub in the global.

4 A NEW PROPOSAL

The existing framework of Islamic finance in Indonesia is such that each Islamic financial institution is obliged to appoint a Sharia Supervisory Board (SSB). The SSB is appointed by the general assembly of shareholders and recommended by the Board of Commissioners in their meetings; SSB candidates require approval by the OJK and are recommended by the National Shari'a Board of Indonesian Council of Ulama (DSN-MUI). The SSB is an extension of the hand of DSN-MUI in maintaining and supervising sharia matters in each individual Islamic financial institution. The SSB is not only independent of the Board of Commissioners but also permitted to attend the Board of Commissioners' meeting to discuss the sharia aspects of their decisions (AAOIFI, 2005).

In general, the aims of the SSB are to guide the IBFIs in the setting of sharia policies and regulations; to approve Islamic banking and finance products and policies that are in accordance with sharia; and propose a proper Islamic contract that can be used by Islamic banks (Daoud, 1996; Hassan & Chachi, 2007). The SSB members represent the IBFIs in the general meeting and explain any sharia matters to the stakeholders. In addition, the SSB members will provide advice to the Board of Commissioners and top management on sharia issues.

The good point in the era of OJK is that, all IFIs regulated and supervised under one umbrella, OJK not only regulate and supervise Islamic banking like in the era of Bank Indonesia, but also Islamic capital markets, Islamic insurance, BMTs, Islamic cooperatives, and venture capital, etc. In the OJK era, there are three points that the author expected to happen, first, the development of IFIs will be more optimal, second, Indonesia could become the international hub for Islamic finance in Asian and Middle East Countries (AMED) and third, Indonesia has to be a trendsetter for Islamic finance industries globally.

Therefore, the paper suggested that OJK shall set up the Sharia body that regulate and supervise the Sharia matters for IFIs in Indonesia namely the SSB Authority of OJK (ODPS-OJK), under Board of Commissioners of OJK.

What is ODPS-OJK? What are the differentiations between ODPS-OJK and SSB and DSN-MUI? According to Mihajat (2012), ODPS-OJK is Sharia Supervisory Board Authority in Indonesia Financial Services Authority framework. This body is under line of the Board of Commissioners of OJK that has the duty to supervise and regulate Islamic banking and finance activities on sharia matters.

The role of ODPS-OJK is to help the development of the Islamic finance industry in Indonesia, ODPS-OJK also has to conduct a meeting on a weekly or monthly basis as per required. There are several point of discussions as the role and responsibilities of OJK, including as follows:

1. Review existing products that has been complied with Sharia to see either this product is able to disrupt the economic system in general or kill real sectors of the economy. ODSP-OJK will decide such as Gold Pawn Broking in Islamic banks that merely leads to speculation rather than investment.
2. Discuss the proposed products by IFIs either has been complied with sharia rules. If the proposed product is a normal product and easily understood, the ODPS-OJK will endorse quickly. If the proposed product is relatively new and using a new structure of 'aqad', ODPS-OJK will take time to endorse the proposed product, this endorsement shall be based on research and a proper *instinbatul ahkam* (deriving a Sharia rule from its sources).
3. Proposed a new product with a proper sharia structure that demanded by the Islamic finance market so that IBFIs can compete nationally and internationally. By endorsement of this product, international investor such as Asia, Europe, and Africa will invest their fund in Indonesia as Indonesia well known as International hub in Islamic finance.
4. Establish cooperation with International Sharia Standard, such as AAOIFI, IFSB, ISRA and the International Shari'a Board Association to exchange and share idea among Sharia Scholars in developing IBFIs in Indonesia so that become a trendsetter and international center for Islamic finance.

The paper suggested a new Sharia Governance Framework of OJK, as described in Figure 1. This framework shall support by special government regulations (*Peraturan Pemerintah*, PP) that describe the authority of ODPS-OJK in such a way that any decision issued by them is binding and far from the conflict of interest. The figure also indicates that ODPS-OJK oversees the department of Islamic capital market, Islamic bank, Islamic Insurance and other IFIs. Each department will regulate and take care of the IFIs under its line including product development. If one Islamic bank proposed one product to OJK, this product shall go first to Islamic Banking Department in OJK, Islamic Banking Department will review either the product is possible to go to the upper level (ODPS-OJK). If the product is worthy, the Islamic Banking Department will pass to ODPS-OJK, otherwise, it will return back to the respected Islamic bank that proposed the product to revise back and send back to Islamic Banking Department of OJK.

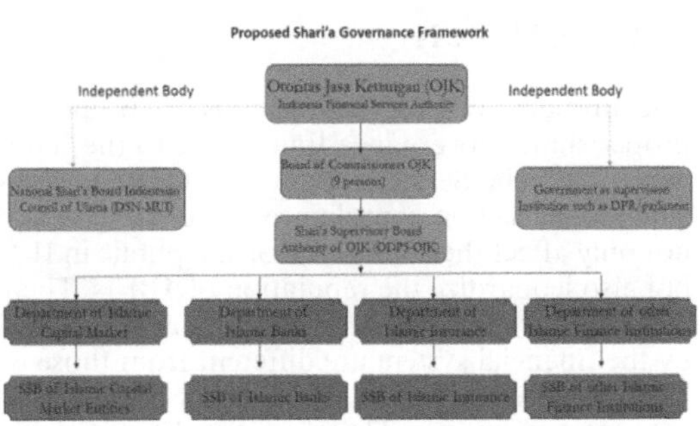

Figure 1. Sharia regulatory framework for Islamic finance in the OJK era.

1. *Top-down approach model*
   The first model, the product normally proposed by ODPS-OJK where they see that the product is seen to be important for the development of Islamic finance in Indonesia. First step, ODPS-OJK will proposed in the weekly/monthly meeting among the members and design the product so that it can be applied. For example, ODPS-OJK proposed Islamic structured product instrument that can be used by Islamic banks, Islamic capital market entities, Takaful companies to diversify their investment portfolio. If it is approved among the members, this product will be circulated among the IBFIs. The IBFIs can start to use the product without any new approval from ODPS-OJK, IBFIs just need to inform OJK to get its approval.
2. *Bottom-up approach model*
   The second model is that bottom-up approach; this model normally used by Islamic banking industries to Bank Indonesia. Sharia compliance unit will coordinate with the product development unit to structure a new product and then will go to SSB for discussion and approval. If in this meeting the SSB members approve the product, it will go to the Department of Islamic Banks of OJK for review, after which it goes to the ODPS-OJK meeting. ODPS-OJK will review and decide either the product is Sharia compliance or it will return back to Islamic bank for their rectification and revision in case if there is a Sharia issues. Islamic bank will submit back the proposed product until it is complied with Sharia and approved by ODPS-OJK.

4.1 *Is it possible for ODPS-OJK members to become SSB members in IFIs?*

There are would a lot of question come up from Islamic finance stakeholders, is it permissible for ODPS-OJK members to become SSB members in Islamic bank, Takaful companies, Islamic capital market entities and other IFIs. Therefore, the paper suggest that the government has to issue the regulation saying that it is not permissible for

ODPS-OJK members to be become a member of SSB in IBFIs to avoid a conflict of interest among ODPS-OJK members due to one of them is representing one of IBFI.

4.2 *Appointment of ODPS-OJK members*

The OJK is expected to regulate what the requirements are to become a member of ODPS-OJK, so that only a qualified person is appointed to this position. The criteria for the members of ODPS-OJK should be as follows:

1. Members of the ODPS-OJK have to be Muslim individuals.
2. Members of the ODPS-OJK must be holders of academic qualifications in the field of sharia—minimum bachelor degree—specialized in *Ushul Fiqh* (rules of Islamic jurisprudence) and *Fiqh al Muamalat* (Islamic commercial transactions) from a recognized institution. They should be able to demonstrate an adequate understanding of Islamic banking, Islamic capital markets, takaful and other IFIs.
3. Members of ODPS-OJK must have more than five years' experience in Islamic finance industries (teaching, research and fatwa issuance). They should be able to demonstrate strong proficiency in Arabic.
4. Members of ODPS-OJK must have a respectable character and be of good conduct and moral values, particularly in terms of honesty, integrity and reputation in their professional business and financial dealings.
5. Members of ODPS-OJK must have commitment to develop the IFIs industry.

The above requirements are proposed to maintain the reputation of OJK as the regulatory body of IFIs.

4.3 *The role of ODPS-OJK, DSN-MUI and SSB in the era of OJK*

As elaborate in the above discussion, the role of ODPS-OJK is different with DSN-MUI and SSB in each Islamic financial institution. ODPS-OJK has the authority to decide whether the product in IFIs in compliance with Sharia, review the proposed product from IFIs either to reject or to approve and the regulation issued by them are binding to all IFIs. While DSN-MUI is still stick with their rule which is issuing the fatwa for IFIs, and SSB is responsible for maintaining Sharia compliance of business activities, transactions and products in which they sit in a particular IFIs (please see Table 1).

From the above delineation of roles and responsibilities, each DSN-MUI and ODPS-OJK has their respective roles in the development of the Islamic finance industry without overlapping with one another. Thus, the emergence of ODPS-OJK is not something that should lead to dispute.

Table 1. The differences between ODPS-OJK, DSN-MUI and SSB.

	Institution	Authority	Fatwa/ Regulation issued
ODPS-OJK	OJK	Decide to approve or reject a proposed product from IFIs	Binding to all IFIs
DSN-MUI	Independent	Issue the fatwa of IFIs	Not binding in nature
SSB	Institutions offering Islamic financial products and services	– Approve a proposed product in a particular IFI – Ensure that a particular IFI is in compliance with sharia	Binding to a particular IFI where they sit as an SSB member

4.4 *Sharia supervisory boards*

The next issue to arise is whether the existence of ODPS-OJK will affect the role and responsibility of SSB in every Islamic banking and financial institution? Surely not, because their respective institution is very different one another, where SSB in each Islamic financial institution only entitled to supervise the products and regulations relating to Sharia of a particular Islamic financial institution, while ODPS-OJK has the authority to impose regulations generally for all IFIs in Indonesia.

5 CONCLUSION

The primary aim of the paper is to propose a proper sharia governance framework to the Indonesia Financial Services Authority (OJK) to mitigate the sharia non-compliance element that would not only affect the confidence of the public in IFIs but also jeopardize the reputation of IBFIs. There is strong recognition that some of the risks faced by the financial system are different from those of IFIs, because IBFIs have unique risks compared to conventional entities. Therefore, the sharia governance framework system in Indonesia in the era of OJK needs to be reformed.

REFERENCES

AAOIFI (Accounting and Auditing Organization for Islamic Financial Institutions). (2005). Accounting, Auditing and Governance Standards for Islamic Financial Institutions. Bahrain: AAOIFI.

Bank Indonesia. (2009). *Circular letter on good corporate governance for full-fledged Islamic bank and Islamic windows* (No. 11/33/PBI/2009).

Daoud, H. (1996). *Shari'a control in Islamic banks*. Herndon, VA: International Institute of Islamic Thought.

DSN-MUI. (2012). *Himpunan Fatwa Dewan Syariah Nasional MUI* (The Fatwas Compilation). Jakarta, Indonesia: Dewan Syariah Nasional and Bank Indonesia.

Ernst & Young. (2013). *The world Islamic banking competitiveness report, 2013–2014: Transition begins* (GIFR report 2013).

Hamza, H. (2013). Governance in Islamic banks: Effectiveness and supervision model. *International Journal of Middle Eastern Finance and Management*, *6*(3), 226–237.

Hassan, A. & Chachi, A. (2007). Corporate governance of the Islamic financial services industry in Brunei Darussalam. *Journal of Islamic Economics, Banking and Finance*, *4*, 39–59.

IFSB. (2005). *Guiding principles of risk management for institutions (other than insurance institutions) offering only Islamic financial services*. Kuala Lumpur, Malaysia: Islamic Financial Services Board.

IFSB. (2006). *Guiding principles on corporate governance for institutions offering only Islamic financial services (excluding Islamic insurance (Takaful) institutions and Islamic mutual funds)*. Kuala Lumpur, Malaysia: Islamic Financial Services Board.

IFSB. (2009). *Guiding principles on Shari'a governance systems for institutions offering Islamic financial services*. Kuala Lumpur, Malaysia: Islamic Financial Services Board.

Mihajat, M.I.S. (2012, March). Masa Depan Industri Keuangan Syariah di Era OJK (*the Future of Islamic Finance Industry in the OJK Era*). *Sharing Magazine, page 19–22*.

Miskam, S. & Nasrul, M.A. (2013). *Shari'a governance in Islamic finance: The effects of the Islamic Financial Services Act 2013*. Paper presented at the World Conference on Integration of Knowledge, 25–26 November 2013, Langkawi, Malaysia.

Onagun, A.I. & Mikail, A. (2013). Shari'a governance system: A need for professional approach. In *Proceedings of Shari'a economic conference, 29 February 2013, Hanover, Germany*.

Otoritas Jasa Keuangan (OJK). (2011). Act No. 21.

Increasing Management Relevance and Competitiveness – Sukoco et al. (Eds)
© 2018 Taylor & Francis Group, London, ISBN 978-0-8153-7455-8

Mediating role of Investment Opportunity Set (IOS) on diversification–corporate value relationship: Empirical study of manufacturing companies in the IDX, 2013–2015

D.W.I. Hartono, B. Tjahjadi, N. Soewarno & Y. Permatasari
Universitas Airlangga, Surabaya, Indonesia

ABSTRACT: Diversification is a company's strategic choice and has long-term implications. Previous studies show that there is still variation regarding the effect of diversification on a firm's value, and this is seen as an opportunity to conduct further research by using the Investment Opportunity Set (IOS) as a mediating variable. This study therefore aims to analyze the role of diversification on a firm's value with IOS as a mediating variable. The study was conducted on 224 companies in the manufacturing sector of the Indonesian Stock Exchange (IDX) for the period 2013–2015. Hypothesis testing was conducted using partial least squares and the results revealed that diversification had a positive, statistically significant impact on corporate value. It also had a positive, statistically significant effect on IOS. This study also proved that IOS had a positive, statistically significant effect on corporate value. Finally, this study proved that IOS partially mediated the diversification–corporate value relationship.

Keywords: diversification, corporate value, Investment Opportunity Set

1 INTRODUCTION

The ASEAN Economic Community (AEC) drives competition as well as cooperation among ASEAN countries on a more intense and global scale. This phenomenon requires corporates to improve corporate advantage and to increase corporate values. To be able to realize these goals, corporates must have good corporate strategies, one of which is diversification strategy, which can be conducted in the form of related diversification or unrelated diversification (conglomeration).

The diversification strategy is very common in practice because management of a corporation hope that they can eliminate or reduce investment risk of a single business. Elimination of investment risk is usually a good signal to both investors and companies. For investors, corporates that are able to avoid risk will be preferred, because losses in business units could trigger bankruptcy. For management, in addition to cross-subsidizing, diversification enables them to evaluate which business segments will be most profitable in the future. The level of investor confidence in corporates that have a profitable business line leading to improved corporate value will be higher.

As a corporate diversifies, there will be a number of investments involved. Empirical research on the effect of diversification on IOS was found in MacKay (2003) and Singh et al. (2003). The existence of diversification opportunities for companies will cause various investment opportunities to be implemented. The basis for decision-making that is undertaken by corporate management for the implementation of various investment opportunities is a high rate of return. A high rate of return means that the company is able to cover the cost of capital, which will eventually give rise to a surplus, which will result in higher corporate value.

Management of diversified companies believe that having business diversity will increase corporate value. Various studies have proven the impact of diversification strategy on corporate value. Research by Bohl and Pal (2006) revealed that diversification strategy can increase corporate value, thus creating a premium effect for the company's performance. The majority of companies implement diversification strategies to enable them to enhance strategic competitiveness. When diversification strategies increase strategic competitiveness, then total corporate value will increase as well.

However, there are also several researchers whose findings argued that the more business segments (the higher diversification level), the lower the corporate value. Furthermore, the higher the diversification level, the higher deficiency level of cross-subsidy between segments. Berger and Ofek (1995) also stated that diversification strategy decreased corporate value, thus delivering a discounted effect toward value and performance of the corporate. The statement above was based on agency theory, which states that, besides leveraging corporate value, business diversification can also destroy corporate value. In the latter context, there are two underlying factors: these are careless management decisions and worthless cross-subsidy. If a decision to diversify disrupts a corporate, this would be a burden for owners or shareholders, while the converse applies for managers, since they are managing enterprises with a broad scope. This is a conflict between managers and owners, which would emerge as a result of differences in the purpose of diversification.

Findings regarding the failure of diversification to create value are an issue that needs to be studied in the light of arguments against the theory of economies of scope. This theory explains that a corporation with multi-businesses could gain economic benefits, such as joint asset utilization, fund allocation with the aim to reduce business risk, or cheaper transfer pricing between business units (Nayyar, 1993). However, the phenomenon described above demonstrates that diversification can experience failure, given the fact of several corporations undertaking divestment and restructuring. This fact becomes an interesting topic for research. This illustration of diversification failure indicates that diversification does not always elevate corporate value, and can even, in this case, push corporate value down instead, which means decreasing the prosperity of owners. In order to minimize default risk, corporate diversification needs to consider some decisions that are related to several investments. The diversification concept involving a certain number of investments is perceived important for a firm when considering which type of investments will be performed by the management of the firm. Therefore, the concept of IOS is introduced as one of the methods for increasing corporate value.

Empirical research about the effect of diversification toward IOS was conducted by MacKay (2003) and Singh et al. (2003). When a corporate performs diversification, there are certain numbers of investments involved. The existence of diversification opportunity shows that various investment opportunities are taken. The basis for decision-making to be taken by corporate management to carry out various investment opportunities is a high rate of return. A high rate of return indicates that a firm is capable of covering the cost of capital, which eventually leads to a surplus in the firm.

An investment decision is one of the factors that affects corporate value, as it has an impact on the debit side of the balance sheet in the form of assets in place, either non-current, or current assets. The goal of corporate investment decisions is defined such that the wealth of a firm is increased if the decision is to increase Net Present Value (NPV), because a positive NPV reflects the real wealth of a firm (Husnan & Pudjiastuti, 2002, p. 209).

Research from Myers (1977) on investment decisions introduced several IOS. The fundamental of IOS is to provide broader guidance on how corporate value is expected to be determined by corporate expenditure in the future. This concept can be used to predict a firm's prospects in the expected future. The calculation of IOS is by combining the assets in place and investment opportunity in the expected future with positive NPV or higher than cost of capital; hence, its ability to forecast the anticipated value to shareholders.

Empirical research studying the effect of IOS toward corporate value has not yet presented consistent results. IOS affecting corporate value was found in publications by Fama (1978), and Hasnawati (2005a, 2005b). However, research by Suharli (2007) found that IOS did not affect corporate value. IOS affecting corporate value is defined as the situation in which investments will gain a surplus if a firm is capable of making appropriate investment decisions. The surplus gained will contribute to cash inflow, then accumulate into an increase in corporate profit. On the contrary, if IOS does not affect corporate value this would mean that a firm would have a deficit from several investments performed which will therefore decrease equity, and eventually decrease corporate value.

2 THEORETICAL REVIEW AND HYPOTHESES DEVELOPMENT

2.1 *Diversification and corporate value*

Diversification is the result of a firm's management decisions taken in order to maximize firm size and diversity, as well as efforts to increase corporate performance. If the effort to increase corporate performance succeeds, this will cause corporate value creation. In various literature, agency theory has a critical role in explaining the relationship between owner and agents in performing each of their respective functions. Agency conflict that emerges due to conflict of interest will bring out problems between related parties (Jensen & Meckling, 1976). The conflict mainly appears when a firm has a high level of free cash flow, agents tend to direct it into investments such as diversification that will increase corporate sales, while principals desire some dividend distribution. This is attributed to management performance appraisal that is related to sales level of a firm. This matches studies by Setionoputri et al. (2009) and Selçuk (2015) who found that corporate diversification significantly affects corporate value in a positive manner.

H1: *Diversification significantly affects corporate value*

2.2 *Diversification and investment opportunity set*

The diversification concept that involves several investments is perceived as urgent for a firm when considering which type of investment will be carried out by the corporate management. Therefore, IOS is introduced as one of the means to increase corporate value.

Empirical research studying the effects of diversification toward IOS can be found in studies by MacKay (2003) and Singh et al. (2003). When a firm performs diversification, this will involve several investments. The basis for decision-making used by corporate management for implementing various investment opportunities is a high rate of return. A high rate of return is defined as such that a firm is able to offset a certain amount of the cost of capital, which will eventually lead to a surplus in the firm.

H2: *Diversification significantly affects Investment Opportunity Set*

2.3 *Investment opportunity set and corporate value*

Investment opportunity is one of the focuses of investment decision goals. To achieve such goals, as explained by Fama (1978), a firm has to generate positive NPV; therefore, the corporate value is initially determined by investment decisions. Such a perspective suggests that investment decision-making is crucial, because corporate goal achievement is only made through a firm's investing activities. The implication is that IOS plays an important role in corporate finance in regard to corporate goal achievement.

Hasnawati (2005b) explained that variables used for investment decisions reveal either ones that have already been invested or expected investment opportunities in the future. Using a population target of 259 companies from 26 industry categories in year 2001, the study found a significant positive effect of investment decisions toward a firm.

H3: *Investment Opportunity Set significantly affects corporate value*

2.4 *Diversification, investment opportunity set, corporate value*

The diversification approach is performed in an effort to increase corporate performance and create corporate value. Diversification strategy is perceived as a business alternative to gain significant profit from the addition of business segments to a firm. This means that, with the addition of segment numbers, revenue is assumed to increase, due to corporates fulfilling growing diverse consumer needs. Corporates with a large number of segments could also create synergy among the segment units; therefore, a firm could gain benefits from the combination of activity value-chain relations to generate lower operating costs. Diversified corporates could also gain benefits from sharing skills, competency, knowledge, and technology to achieve competitive advantage for a company.

Various investment opportunities as investment options depend on managerial policy to perform discretionary expenditure in the expected future, which could be seen as growth option (Kole, 1991). Every growth option is affected by the particular business area and based on competitive advantage. Diversification can be performed by a firm if they have such an IOS. The existence of investment opportunity means that a firm will have value, either reflected in share price or by other indicators. The implication is that IOS plays a critical role in corporate finance in regard to corporate goal achievement.

Empirical research that studied the effect of diversification toward IOS was conducted by MacKay (2003) and Singh et al. (2003) and found that a firm performed diversification due to the existence of investment opportunities. The existing IOS is based on consideration of existing resources, strategical assets, and market share; therefore, when a firm performs diversification, it will contribute to an increase in corporate value. Diversification performed by a company is an immensity in diversifying business into some segments by involving several investments. Therefore, management is obliged to determine appropriate investments; hence, its impact on increasing corporate value. The tendency to engage in long-term investment means that return on investment would take a long time; hence, the importance for a firm to consider appropriate options before deciding on the investment. Therefore, this research predicts that IOS becomes a mediating influence on diversification in relation to corporate value, because when a firm operating in more than one business segment, it will involve several investments. The ability to choose from alternative sets of investment opportunities becomes a critical factor that eventually increases corporate value.

H4: *Investment Opportunity Set (IOS) has a mediating effect on the relationship between diversification and corporate value*

3 METHODOLOGY

3.1 *Research design*

The design of this study is quantitative using partial least squares; data on 224 manufacturing companies listed in the IDX were obtained and processed as sample data.

3.2 *Research model*

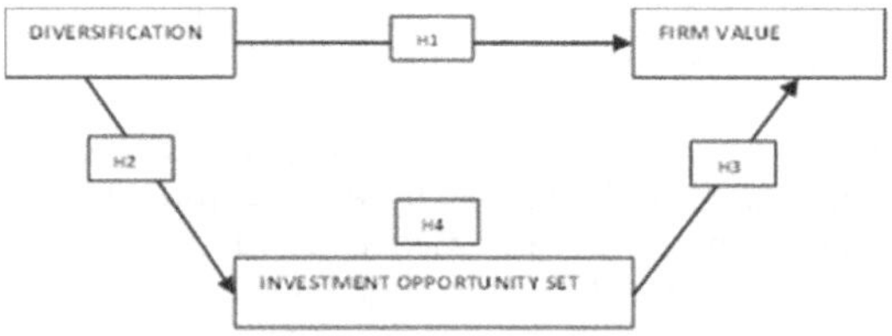

Figure 1. Research model.

4 RESULTS AND DISCUSSION

4.1 *Hypothesis tests*

Based on the results in Table 1, it can be concluded that Hypotheses 1, 2, and 3 are significantly proven. However, for the mediating effect, the results showed that IOS partially mediated the effect between diversification in relation to corporate value with a VAF (Value Adjustment Factor) score of 55.2 percent. It can be said that even without the intervening variable of IOS, the independent variable (diversification) still has an effect on the dependent variable (corporate value).

4.2 *Discussion*

Corporate diversification performed by a firm could lead an increase in corporate value as reflected in Tobin's Q with a partial influence of IOS. Corporate value will increase if the firm is able to see and determine the type of investment to be carried out. This finding for manufacturing companies listed in the IDX is consistent with research from Fama (1978). Direct and indirect influence of diversification on corporate value through IOS is the result generated by its investment activity itself through the choice of project or other policy, such as creating new products, or replacement of machinery with more efficient equipment, elaboration of research and development, and merging with other corporations (Myers, 1977).

When a firm brings about diversification, there will be several investments involved. Such investment opportunities for the firm create an obligation for various investment opportunities to be carried out. Investment opportunity is one of the focuses of the investment decision goal, because corporate goal achievement can only be made through the investment activities of a firm. Hence, the implication of IOS playing a critical role in corporate finance in relation to corporate goal achievement.

Therefore, each decision taken by management to carry out the investment of manufacturing companies listed in the IDX would consider the rate of return and risk of investment, thus choosing investments that result in the most benefits for the company. Corporates will choose an investment type that has a positive NPV and high return. An appropriate investment expenditure will give a positive signal regarding corporate growth in the future, thus increasing its share price as an indicator of the increase of corporate value.

Table 1. Results.

Correlation between variables	Coefficient of direct effect	Coefficient of indirect effect	VAF
Diversification → Corporate value	β_1 0.19		
Diversification → *Investment Opportunity Set*	β_2 0.35	–	–
Investment Opportunity Set → Corporate value	β_3 0.67	–	–
Diversification → *Investment Opportunity Set* → Corporate value		$\beta_2\,\beta_3$ (0.35 × 0.67) = 0.2345	0.2345/(0.19 + 0.2345) = 0.552 = 55.2%

**p*-value < 0.01.

5 CONCLUSION

From previous findings and discussions, it can be concluded as the following:

1. Diversification significantly affects corporate value.
2. Diversification significantly affects IOS.
3. IOS significantly affects corporate value.
4. IOS mediates the effect of diversification on corporate value.

REFERENCES

Berger, P.G. & Ofek, E. (1995). Diversification's effect on firm value. *Journal of Financial Economics, 37*, 39–65.

Bohl, T.M. & Pal, R.R. (2006). *Discount or premium? New evidence on corporate diversification of UK firms.* SSRN Working Paper Series.

Fama, E.F. (1978). The effect of a firm's investment and financing decision on the welfare of its security holders. *American Economic Review, 68*, 272–284.

Hasnawati, S. (2005a). Implication of investment decision, funding, and dividend on the public firm's value in Jakarta Stock Exchange. *Usahawan Indonesia, 9*(XXXIV), 33–41.

Hasnawati, S. (2005b). The impact of investment opportunity set on the public firm's value in Jakarta Stock Exchange. *Jurnal AAI, 9*(2), 117–126.

Husnan, S. & Pudjiastuti, E. (2002). The fundamentals of financial management. (3rd Edition). Yogyakarta, Indonesia: Penerbit UPP AMP YKPN.

Jensen, M.C. & Meckling, W.H. (1976). Theory of the firm: Managerial behavior, agency cost and ownership structure. *Journal of Financial Economics, 3*(4), 305–360.

Kole. S.R. (1991). A cross-sectional investigation of managerial compensation from an ex ante perspective, University of Rochester working paper.

MacKay, P. (2003). Real flexibility and financial structure: An empirical analysis. *Review of Financial Studies, 16*(4), 1131–1165.

Myers, S.C. (1977). Interactions of corporate financing and investment decisions implications for capital budgeting: Reply. *Journal of Finance, 32*(1), 218–220.

Nayyar, P.R. (1993). Performance effects of information asymmetry and economies of scope in diversified service firms. *Academy of Management Journal, 36*(1), 411–418.

Selçuk, E.A. (2015). Corporate diversification and firm value: Evidence from emerging markets. *International Journal of Emerging Markets, 10*(3), 294–310.

Setionoputri, A., Meiden, C. & Siagian, D. (2009). The influence of corporate diversification on the Excess Value of manufacturing, wholesale and retail, also property and real estate company listed on IDX 2005–2007. Simposium Nasional Akuntansi XII.

Singh, M., Davidson, W.N., III & Suchard, J-A. (2003). Corporate diversification strategies and capital structure. *Quarterly Review of Economics and Finance, 43*, 147–167.

Suharli, M. (2007). The influence of profitability and investment opportunity set on cash dividend policy with liquidity as moderating variable. (Study on the Firm Listed on Jakarta Stock Exchange 2002–2003). *Jurnal Akuntansi dan Keuangan, 9*(1), 9–17.

Increasing Management Relevance and Competitiveness – Sukoco et al. (Eds)
© 2018 Taylor & Francis Group, London, ISBN 978-0-8153-7455-8

Underpricing, operating performance, long-term market performance, and the probability of conducting seasoned equity offerings of IPO in Indonesian capital market

N. Sasikirono
Universitas Airlangga, Surabaya, Indonesia

Djumahir & A. Djazuli
Universitas Brawijaya, Malang, Indonesia

ABSTRACT: The signaling hypothesis (Welch 1989) suggests that high-quality issuers underprice their stocks to reveal signals about quality to investors and then undertake a subsequent financing through SEOs. Companies with high quality will then show high operating and market performance. Ritter (1991) argued that underwriters systematically set IPO prices too low in order to increase demand for IPO stocks. Hence, stocks with high initial return tend to have low long-term performance. This study aims to test whether there are differences in Operating Performance and Long-Term Market Performance of stocks with different level of underpricing, as well as to examine the relationship between underpricing with the probability of conducting SEOs and the long-term market performance of IPO. Results indicate that there are no differences in operating and long-term market performance of companies with high and low underpricing. The implication of this is that underpricing cannot be attributed to the signaling of a better issuer's quality.

Keywords: Signaling Hypothesis, Underpricing, Operating Performance, Long-Term Market Performance, Seos

1 INTRODUCTION

The signaling hypotheses of Allen and Faulhaber (1986), Welch (1989) and Welch (1996) suggest that high-quality issuers use underpricing as a mechanism to convey signals about their condition to investors. Such companies will make phases in collecting funds from the capital market. The initial stage of financing is the process of initial public offerings whereby the company sells shares to the public to raise funds with a relatively small value while sending signals about their quality to investors. In the next stage, additional fund raising is made through the mechanism of seasoned equity offerings (SEOs). Such quality signal delivery is done by underpricing IPO shares. The higher the quality of the issuer, the greater the level of IPO underpricing. Low-quality issuers are prevented from underpricing because of the high cost of underpricing. Therefore, signaling hypothesis basically states that firms with high underpricing levels should show better post-IPO performance. There are two performance measures in IPO activities, namely: operating performance and market performance. Operating performance measures can be grouped into several proxies, i.e. profitability (ROA, ROE and EPS), output (sales and sales growth), and leverage (debt and asset ratio) (Jing and Padgett 2006). Commonly used market performance is initial return, which is used as an underpricing proxy, and long-term market performance (Ritter 1991; Loughran and Ritter, 1995).

Jain and Kini (1994) conducted a study of operating performance in the context of IPO underpricing. They found a significant decrease in the company's operating performance after the IPO, but found no solid evidence of the relationship between changes in the company's operating performance and the level of underpricing of the firm. Wang (2005) found that, in the Chinese capital market stocks with greater underpricing, experienced a large decrease in operating performance as well. The study of long-term market performance can be seen in Ritter (1991). Ritter's findings show that, in the United States, stocks sold through IPOs perform lower than other stocks for a period of three to five years after the IPO. De Bond and Thaler (1987) show that stocks with low initial returns tend to have low long-term performance. Loughran et al. (1994), in research on international capital markets, found that the higher the issuer's risk, the lower the long-run performance of IPO stocks. Understanding of underpricing, operating performance, long-term performance and the relationship between underpricing with the probability of conducting SEO of stocks in the primary market is very important to investors. This study aims to examine whether there are differences in the operating performance and long-term market performance of stocks with different underpricing levels. The study also examines the relationship between the level of underpricing and the probability of doing Seasoned Equity Offerings as well as the long-term market performance of IPO stocks.

2 LITERATURE REVIEW

2.1 *Operating performance of IPOs*

Operating performance is a measure of firm performance based on accounting information widely used in measuring post-IPO performance (Barber and Lyon 1996; Alanazi 2013). Several studies examine the operational performance in the IPO context, such as Jain and Kini (1994), Jing and Padgett (2006) and Mayur (2014). The operating performance of companies conducting IPOs can be measured using a variety of dimensions. Commonly used measurement dimensions (Jain and Kini 1994; Khursed 2003; Jing and Padget 2006; Alanazi 2013) include profitability, output and leverage. Profitability shows the company's ability to generate profits. This can be measured by ratios: Return on Asset (ROA) and Return on Equity (ROE). ROA indicates the level of income for the company's investment. This can be expressed as a result of net income after taxes divided by total assets of the company.

$$ROA_t = \frac{NLAT_t}{TA_t} \tag{1}$$

The output dimension measures the company's ability to increase sales. A commonly used proxy for measuring the output dimension is sales growth (SG). This can be calculated by dividing the difference in the value of the sales in two years to the value of the base year sales. The higher the sales growth, the better the output performance.

$$SG_t = \frac{S_t - S_{t-1}}{S_{t-1}} \tag{2}$$

Leverage shows the size of the company's debt. The greater the level of corporate leverage, the higher the debt, the greater the fixed liabilities borne by the company. Leverage can be measured using the ratio of debt to assets (DTA); that is, by dividing the total debt with the value of assets.

$$DTA_t = \frac{D_t}{TA_t} \tag{3}$$

2.2 *IPOs long-term market performance*

Long-term market performance is the rate of stock return up to three years post IPO (Ritter 1991). In this study, the level of stock returns observed is monthly return. Long-term market performance of the IPO, measured by cumulative abnormal return (CAR) in the 36-month period. Cumulative abnormal return is an accumulation of abnormal return in a certain period. Abnormal return (AR) is calculated by subtracting the monthly return of shares with the market monthly return (also known as market adjusted abnormal return). The market return was obtained from the Indonesian Stock Exchange composite index during the 36-month observation period.

$$ARit = Rit - Rmt \tag{4}$$

$$CAR_{qs} = \sum_{t=q}^{s} AR_{it} \tag{5}$$

3 METHODOLOGY

3.1 *Variables*

Initial return measures the size of underpricing, i.e. the rate of return on stock on the first day of trading, post listing on the stock exchange board. The operating performance of an IPO company is firm performance measured based on accounting information. The period of accounting information used in the calculation of operating performance is between t–1 to t + 3, where t0 is the IPO year. Using the Jain and Kini research framework (1994), the average operating performance of t0, t + 1 and t + 1 is reduced by the performance of the t–1 operating period. There are several measures of operational performance utilized in this research, namely: Return on Assets, Debt to Total Assets and Sales Growth. Long-term market performance of IPO stock is the rate of IPO stock returns month 1 to 36 post-IPO. Long-term market performance is calculated using CAR36 formula. Probability of implementing SEO is a dummy variable that is worth 1 if the issuer does SEO and 0 if the issuer does not do SEO.

The control variables used in this study are commonly used variables in the analysis of market performance and SEO of IPO stock. Ln Total asset is the natural logarithm of the total asset value of the IPOs company, as indicated in the last annual financial statement before the company conducts the IPO. Ln Total sales is the total natural logarithm of net sales of the IPO company as indicated in the last annual financial statement before the company conducts the IPO. Ln Proceed is the natural logarithm of the amount of funds collected through the IPO. Proceed is obtained by multiplying the price per share of the IPO by the number of shares sold. Ln Age is the age-old natural logarithm of a company which is calculated from the date of establishment of the company until the first trading day of the IPO shares.

3.2 *Sample and data*

The population of this research is all companies that go public in the Indonesia capital market. The sample is taken by purposive sampling technique from all companies that conducted IPO between 2006 and 2010 in the Indonesian capital market. Sample selection criteria are:

1. Non-financial industry companies.
2. Firms submitting complete financial statements two years before and after the IPO year.
3. Firms with complete stock price information up to three years after the IPO date (after the first trading date on the secondary market).
4. IPO stocks which are directly listed on the Main Board on the Indonesia Stock Exchange.

Secondary data for this study are documented from Indonesia Stock Exchange (IDX), Indonesian Capital Market Directory (ICMD), Indonesian Capital Market Library (Icamel) and Yahoo Finance. The data used in this study include data of companies conducting IPO and SEO, stock prices, Composite Index during the period 2006 to 2013 (depending on IPO year), and audit financial statements required for the calculation of operating performance.

3.3 *Analysis technique and models*

Differences between operating and long-term market performance of issuers with different level of underpricing, i.e. high and low, are examined by test of differences with the following steps:

1. Calculating initial return. Grouping the company into two, based on the median initial return, to form an IPO stock group with high and low initial return.
2. Calculating values of ROA, DTA and SG on period t–1 to t + 2, where t0 equals IPO year. Averaging ROA, DTA and SG periods t0 to t + 2. Reduce the average ROA, DTA and SG with ROA, DTA and SG period t–1.
3. Calculating CAR36.6
4. Conducting a different test using Independent t test on ROA, DTA, SG and CAR36.

Relationship between variables is examined by multivariate analysis with the following models:

$$DFiSEO = \beta0 + \beta1IR + \beta2LnTA + \beta3LnSales + \beta4LnProceed + \beta5LnAge + e \quad (6)$$

$$CAR36\beta0 = \beta1IR + \beta2LnTA + \beta3LnSales + \beta4LnProceed + \beta5LnAge + e \quad (7)$$

where DFiSEO = Dummy SEO; CAR36 = Cumulative Abnormal Return up to the 36th month; IR = Initial Return; LnTA = Natural logarithm of total asset; LnSales = Natural logarithm of total sales; LnAge = Natural logarithm of firm's age; LnProceed = Natural logarithm of IPO proceeds (IPO price multiplied by IPO volume).

4 FINDINGS AND DISCUSSION

Table 1 shows the general description of the results of the research on the IPO companies being sampled. The average initial return of 31.44% with a minimum value of –18.12% illustrates the large number of IPOs with underpricing below the average. Post-IPO operating performance of listed companies tends to decrease, although, for ROA, the rate of decline is relatively low (–0.67%). This is in line with findings in previous studies (Jain and Kini 1994; Wong 2012). An increase in DTA with an average of 33.22% indicates access to larger debt for going public companies. The increase in sales growth shows better output performance after the company did go public. This is related to the increase in production and sales capability followed by the improvement of the company's reputation after implementing the IPO. The decline in CAR36 compared to the initial return also occurred in the Indonesian capital market. The average CAR36 of 13.86 is not unlike some previous studies in other countries (Ritter,

Table 1. Descriptive.

	N	Minimum	Maximum	Mean	Std. Deviation
IR	62	–18.1250	123.8100	31.442597	30.6852842
Δ ROA	62	–47.5200	15.4600	–.665726	7.5325843
Δ DTA	62	–73.2320	368.0000	33.220177	56.7193800
Δ SG	62	–918.5490	1351.5870	46.026032	223.2126765
CAR36	62	–175.0230	333.5730	13.863048	108.8496634
DFiSEO	62	0	1	.18	.385
LnAGE	62	.0920	4.0340	2.646694	.7533333
Lns	62	24.2730	30.3180	27.579726	1.4591524
LnTA	62	21.8020	30.4590	26.945097	1.8350185
LnPROC	62	23.8370	30.1370	26.438194	1.5043663

Table 2. Group statistics.

	CAT	N	Mean	Std. Deviation	Std. Error Mean
IR	Low IR	31	5.891194	11.8298456	2.1247030
	High IR	31	56.994000	20.6237958	3.7041431
ΔROA	Low IR	31	−1.449258	9.4309045	1.6938405
	High IR	31	.117805	5.0159989	.9009000
ΔDTA	Low IR	31	35.432226	68.7655870	12.3506640
	High IR	31	31.008129	42.4569657	7.6254961
ΔSG	Low IR	31	56.335226	71.4959649	12.8410544
	High IR	31	35.716839	309.8019969	55.6420812
CAR36	Low IR	31	9.477677	94.6137698	16.9931347
	High IR	31	18.248419	122.8817708	22.0702176

1991 Nurwati et al. 2007); there is a decline in long-term performance of IPO stocks.

Observations on two sub-samples (Table 2), the sub sample of high and low initial returns, indicated the decrease in operating performance, which was worse for firms in the low initial returns group. This can be seen in the decrease in ROA and the increase of higher debt ratios in the low initial return group. This means that companies in the low initial return group tend to decrease ROA after IPO implementation, with an average of 1.45%. Companies with low initial returns also tend to increase the higher debt ratio of 35.43% compared to high initial return group companies. Not all of the companies' operating performance of low initial return group decreased, the sales growth in this group was higher, i.e. 56.34%, compared to the 35.72% increase in the group of issuers with high initial return.

The operating performance of low initial return group companies is generally lower, but not in long-term market performance. Although the average CAR36 of low initial return group is lower (9.47%), when compared with the average initial return (5.89) there has been an increase. In contrast, the CAR36 of high initial return group (18.25%) actually indicates very bad long-term market performance, considering the average IR of this group reached 57%.

The different test results indicate that performance difference, both operating and market performance, between the two groups of issuers is not significant (Table 3). This is indicated by all performance measures showing p values above 10%. This result is in line with Jain and Kini (1994) who found a decline in the performance of post-IPO operations, but found no strong evidence of the relationship between changes in the companies' operating performance and the level of underpricing.

The results of regression analysis on the probability of implementing SEO show the coefficient of determination 0.023. There is no relationship between initial return with the probability of doing SEO. This indicates that the initial return does not act as a quality signal sent by the issuer as predicted by signaling theory (Jegadeesh et al. 1993; Welch 1996). The control variable that is utilized is also unable to explain the probability of the issuer doing SEO.

Table 3. Independent samples test.

Var	t	df	Sig. (2-tailed)
ΔROA	−0.817	60	0.417
ΔDTA	0.305	60	0.762
ΔSG	0.361	60	0.719
CAR36	−0.315	60	0.754

Table 4. Results of regression on probability of SEO and CAR36.

	Probability of SEO		CAR 36	
Var	B	Sig.	B	Sig.
(Constant)	0.498	ns	−72.958	ns
IR	0.00	ns	−0.325	ns
LnAGE	0.04	ns	−44.524	**
LnS	0.004	**	31.624	***
LnTA	0.012	ns	−3.168	ns
LnPROC	−0.033	ns	−21.633	ns

: Significant at 5%; *: Significant at 10%.

The result of regression analysis on CAR36 shows the coefficient of determination 0.156. The results show no relationship between initial return and CAR36. This shows that initial return cannot be used as a predictor of long-term performance of IPO stocks. The results also show that the company's age and sales have influence on CAR36. The age of the firm negatively affects CAR36; the older the company's age, the lower CAR36. This can happen because, with the increasing age of the company to the stage of maturity and even decline, then the growth prospect also decreases. In contrast, younger companies have higher growth prospects because they are constantly encouraged to aggressively take advantage of all the emerging business opportunities. This can lead to a negative relationship between the age of the company and the long-term market performance of IPO shares. Sales before IPO also appear to be used as a proxy for corporate risk. Companies with high sales rates in pre-IPO periods may be dealing with low risk. This has an impact on the long-term performance of IPO stocks.

Signaling theory assumes that the company has superior knowledge of its quality and uses underpricing at the IPO to inform the quality to the market. This study shows that, in the Indonesian capital market, underpricing is not a sign of quality that investors send to the market. Therefore, there is no link between underpricing and post-IPO operating and long-term market performance. This is possible for several reasons. First, the Indonesian capital market is a developing market, wherein the competence of market paticipants including issuers and underwriters still not good. This condition results in a weak understanding of the market, especially issuers, about their prospects. There is the possibility that issuers will seek to obtain information about their quality from other market participants, such as investment managers and foreign institutional investors who conduct transactions in the Indonesian capital market, which are considered to have higher competencies due to longer business experience in the capital markets with global geographic coverage. Second, the impresario hypothesis (Ritter 1991), which states that underpricing is "marketing cost" for IPO shares and may be in accordance with Indonesian capital market conditions. The low understanding of local investors pushes issuers and underwriters to undertake underpricing to boost IPO stock demand. This is very appropriate with the condition of the Indonesian capital market where the level of investor confidence in the stock market is still low. The low level of investor confidence cannot be separated from factors, such as knowledge of low capital markets and low investment culture. Third, in line with the low capacity of local investors, the evaluation of the prospects and risks of issuers is done by using benchmarks that are more easily observed and understood, such as the company's age and pre-IPO sales level.

5 CONCLUSION

Indonesia's emerging capital markets have not allowed issuers to truly have a superior understanding of the quality; thereby, underpricing cannot be attributed to better quality issuer cues. On the other hand, there is need to stimulate investor interest in buying stocks and low investor competence in investing, encouraging companies to undertake underpricing solely to increase stock demand.

In this study, the operating performance of the issuer is not compared to the performance of the benchmark company's operations. This makes it difficult to understand the "true" operating performance of the issuer. The use of benchmark is expected to give an idea of the real performance changes of the issuer over the size of the company. Finally, in order to have a better understanding of the underpricing phenomena in Indonesia, further studies can be directed to find other hypotheses capable of explaining the phenomena. In addition, it is also interesting to investigate other factors around IPO that can distinguish the quality of issuers.

REFERENCES

Aggarwal, R., Leal, R., & Hernandez, L. 1993. The Aftermarket Performance of Initial Public Offerings in Latin America. *Financial Management*, 2 no.1: 42–53.

Ahmad-Zaluki, N.A. & Campbell, K. 2007. The Long Run Share Price Performance of Malaysian Initial Public Offerings (IPOs). *Journal of Business Finance & Accounting,* 34 no. 1–2: 78–110.

Alanazi, A.S., & Liu, B. 2013. IPO Financial and Operating Performance: Evidence from the Six Countries of the GCC. *Department of Accounting, Finance and Economics Griffith University. Discussion Papers.*

Allen, F., & Faulhaber, G.R. 1989. Signaling by Underpricing in the IPO Market. *Journal of Financial Economics,* 23: 303–323.

Barber, B., & Lyon, J. 1996. Detecting Abnormal Operating Performance: The Empirical Power and Specification of Test- Statistic. *Journal of Financial Economics*, 41 no. 3: 359–399.

De Bondt, W., & Thaler, R. 1987. Further Evidence of Investor Overreaction and Stock Market Seasonality. *Journal of Finance*, 42: 557–581.

Espenlaub, S., Gregori, A., & Tonks, I. 2000. Re-assessing the Long-term Underperformance of UK Initial Public Offerings. *European Financial Management*, 6 no. 3: 319–342.

Ibbotson, R.G. 1975. Price Performance of Common Stock New Issues. *Journal of Financial Economics*, 2: 235–272.

Jain, Bharat, A., & Kini, O. 1994. The Post- Issue Operating Performance of IPO Firms. *Journal of Finance,* XLIX no. 5: 1699–1726.

Jegadeesh, N., Weinstein, M., & Welch, I. 1993. An Empirical Investigation Of IPO Returns And Subsequent Equity Offerings. *Journal of Financial Economics*, 34 no. 2: 153–175.

Jing, C., & Padgett, C. 2006. Operating Performance and Its Relationship to Market Performance of Chinese Initial Public Offerings. *The Chinese Economy*, 39 no. 5: 28–50.

Levis, M. 1993. The long-run performance of initial public offerings: The UK experience, 1980–1988. *Financial Management*, Spring: 28–41.

Loughran, T., Ritter, J.R., & Rydqvist, K. 1994. Initial Public Offerings: International Insights. *Pacific-Basin Finance Journal*, 2 no. 2–3: 165–199.

Loughran, T., & Ritter, J.R. 1995. The New Issues Puzzle. *Journal of Finance*, 50 no. 1: 23–51.

Mayur, M., & Mittal, S. 2014. Relationship between Underpricing and Post IPO Performance: Evidence from Indian IPOs. *Asia-Pacific Journal of Management Research and Innovation*, 10 no. 2: 129–136.

Ritter, J.R. 1991. The Long Run Performance of Initial Public Offerings. *Journal of Finance*, 46 no.1: 3–27.
Rock, K. 1986. Why New Issues Are Underpriced. *Journal of Financial Economics*, 15 no. 1–2: 187–212.
Tinic, S. 1988. Anatomy of Initial Public Offerings of Common Stock. *Journal of Finance*, 43 no. 4: 789–822.
Wang, C. 2005. Ownership and operating performance of Chinese IPOs. *Journal of Banking & Finance*, 29: 1835–1856. Welch, Ivo. 1989. Seasoned Offerings, Imitation Costs, and the Underpricing of Initial Public Offerings. *Journal of Finance*, 44: 421–449.
Welch, I. 1996. Equity Offering Following the IPO Theory and Evidence. *Journal of Corporate Finance*, 2: 227–259.
Wong, J. 2012. Operating Performance of Initial Public Offering Companies in Hong Kong. *Journal of Modern Accounting and Auditing*, 8 no. 1: 46–65.

Increasing Management Relevance and Competitiveness – Sukoco et al. (Eds)
 ISBN 978-0-8153-7455-8

The effects of firm size, good corporate governance, and business risk towards financial performance with corporate social responsibility as the moderating variable

N. Soewarno, E.S. Wulandari & B. Tjahjadi
Universitas Airlangga, Surabaya, Indonesia

ABSTRACT: The aim of this research was to prove empirically that firm size, good corporate governance, and business risk affects financial performance with corporate social responsibility as a moderating variable. The population were all of the manufacturing companies listed on the Indonesian Stock Exchange period 2014–2015; there were 108 samples in this research study. The variable used was firm size, good corporate governance, business risk, corporate social responsibility and financial performance. The analysis technique used was Partial Least Square (PLS). The results showed that 1) size, good corporate governance, and business risk had an effect on financial performance; 2) size had an effect on good corporate governance; 3) good corporate governance had an effect on business risk; 4) corporate social responsibility was proven as being the moderating variable; 5) and good corporate governance and business risk weren't intervening variables. This result might help companies to increase the implementation of good corporate governance and corporate social responsibility, and even might help investors to make an investment decision.

Keywords: Business Risk, CSR, Financial Performance, GCG, Size

1 INTRODUCTION

To achieve the company's objective, there will be a difference of interest between its owner (principal) and the management (agent) on making decisions that are called agency theory. The failure of good corporate governance implementation, which has happened to public companies such as Enron, Worldcom, Tyco, Poly Peck, Maxwell etc, is one effect of interest differentiation that causes distrust from investors. Bankruptcy of many companies is believed to cause economic crises in the Asia and USA ([1] Dainiri, 2005). A company needs to improve the implementation of GCG to prevent cases like the aforementioned from occurring in the future.

Good corporate governance (GCG) implementation is assessed by commitment, transparency, accountability, responsibility, independency, justice, leadership competence, vision-mission, collaboration, strategy, ethic, culture, risks, organizational capability, knowledge management and value creation ([2] Anonim, 2015). CSR based on [3] Undang-Undang Nomor 40 Tahun 2007 Pasal 1 ayat 3 about Perseroan Terbatas mentioned that social and environmental responsibility is the company's commitment to participate in sustainable economic development in order to improve the quality of life and the environment. This is beneficial, both for the company itself, the local community, and the community at large.

The rule is continued by the legalization of new policies about the Regulation of Corporate Social Responsibility and Limited Companies Environment Implementation on [4] Peraturan Pemerintah Nomor 47 Tahun 2012. With the policies, many companies begin implement CSR not only in the form of GCG, but also to fulfill the government's rules, even against their wish to achieve better performance.

Prior research about the effect of GCG on financial performance includes that conducted by [5] Waseem et al. (2011); [6] Jo and Maretno (2011); [7] Renny N et al. (2013); and [8] Ihsan, et al (2014). They found that there were positive effects between corporate governance and financial performance. But [9] Purwani (2010) found that GCG implementation didn't have a direct effect on financial performance when measured by way of EVA momentum. While the research about GCG and business risk done by [10] Li, et al. (2013) and [11] Lee et al. (2016) showed that GCG had a negative effect on business risk. Companies that have better management will decrease the company's business risk. But in contrast, [12] [12] Roziq and Herdian (2012) found that GCG had a positive effect on business risk.

[5] Waseem et al. (2011); [13] Kaptiana dan Diana (2013) showed that there was significant

relationship between business risk and financial performance. [12] Roziq and Herdian (2012) and [14] Izati and Farah (2014) showed that there was no relationship between business risk and financial performance. Research by [5] Waseem et al. (2011); [14] Izati and Farah (2014) and [15] Meilic and I Gede (2014) mentioned that firm size had a positive effect on financial performance. That result was against that founded by [16] Fachrudin (2011) in that firm size had no effect on financial performance. From the description above, this research aims to examine 1) the effect of firm size on financial performance; 2) the effect of firm size on GCG; 3) the effect of GCG on business risk; 4) the moderation effect of CSR on the relationship of GCG on business risk; 5) the effect of GCG toward financial performance; 6) the effect of business risk on financial performance; 7) the effect of firm size toward financial performance through GCG as the mediating variable; 8) the effect of GCG on financial performance through business risk as the mediating variable and the 9) the effect of firm size toward financial performance through GCG and business risk as the mediating variables.

2 THEORETICAL FRAMEWORK AND HYPOTHESIS DEVELOPMENT

2.1 *Theoritical framework*

2.1.1 *Agency theory*

Agency theory is a potential conflict that arises in an organization caused by interest differences. The relationship appears when an individual called the owner (principal) employs other individuals or organizations called agents to work by delegating the authorization of decision-making to the agent, which may cause the difference of interest between the agents, stockholder and also the potential creditors ([17] Brigham and Houston, 2004).

2.1.2 *Contingency theory*

Contingency theory reveals that organizational practices can be affected by the company's situation, and condition ([18] Schoech, 2006). Islam and Hui (2012) defined contingency theory as a research approach on organizational behavior which is explained by how factors like technology, culture, and external environment affect the design and function of an organization. Contingency theory is a tool which has full potential towards increasing the organization or company's performance ([19] Betss, 2003).

2.1.3 *Resource-based view theory*

A firm's performance is affected by firm-specific resources and capabilities (Barney, 1996:469). So in order to achieve an advantage that is competitive, the firm has to manage its resources. Jay Barney as the Father of The Modern Resource-based View said that RBV has a correlation with strategic choice, including delegating a manager to identify, develop, and use resources to get the best result.

2.1.4 *Financial performance*

[5] Waseem et al. (2011) defined performance as "the improvement which is done in the corporate that is reflected in the end of the year". Performance could be seen as every change in a company that could be seen at the end of the company's accounting period. Financial performance could be seen additionally by analyzing the information in the company's financial report. Stakeholders use the financial report to then make a decision ([21] Sudana, 2011).

Market to Book Ratio is the ratio between the market price of the company's shares to its book value. Market price is the value of equity that is seen by investors ([20] Harahap, 2009). [5] Waseem et al. (2011) define market to book ratio as an increase of the company's performance which is reflected by increasing the market price to book value.

Price Earning Ratio is a part of the market value analysis. [22] Gibson (1988) said that "E/P ratio express the relationship between market price per share and current earnings per share". [23] Wahyudiono and Bambang (2014) described that "Price Earning Ratio compares share price that got from stock market and earnings per share which obtained by the owners through its financial report". Price Earning Ratio reflects the profit growth expected by investors on their capital. Return on Asset is the ratio used for measuring the company's ability to do asset management to earn profit ([22] Gibson, 1988). ROA has become the most important ratio among other profitability ratios. This ratio is used to assess the effectiveness of management towards profit earning by managing the assets owned ([24] Gitman dan Zutter, 2012).

[21] Sudana (2011) declared that ROE shows the organization's ability to use its own capital. The higher this ratio, the more efficient the usage of its own capital by the management staff. Meanwhile [25] Brigham and Houston (2010) described "Return on Equity is the ratio net income to equity that measures the return of investor's investment."

2.1.5 *Corporate social responsibility*

CSR is a company's commitment to participate in sustainable economic development by focusing on balancing the economic, social, and environment aspect to prevent bad effects derived from the manufacturing process ([26] Budi, 2007).

There are two expressions about CSR. Rhey are that, one, companies do their business so it has no negative effect on certain communities. Or two, that companies do their business so it can create better a community and be prosperous at the same time, according to [36] Wahyudi dan busyra (2008). In a simpler way, CSR is defined as a concept that suggests that a company is concerned about the community's welfare actively ([17] Brigham and Houston, 2004).

2.1.6 *Good corporate governance*
[27] Martin et al. (2005) defined Corporate Governance as a system and process used to direct and control organizations to increase their performance and to achieve value for the stakeholders simultaneously.

The corporate governance principles established by The Organization for Economic Cooperation and Development (OECD) include the following: ([28] Pieris dan Nizam, 2007).

1. Ensure good corporate governance implementation;
2. Stockholder's rights and the function of the ownership towards shares or assets;
3. Fair treatment for stockholders;
4. Stakeholders can take on the corporate governance role;
5. Disclose information transparently;
6. The committee's obligations.

Or it can alternatively be summarized in to 4 points. They are 1) fairness; 2) transparency; 3) accountability; and 4) responsibility ([29] Sedarmayanti, 2007). See Figure 1 below.

2.1.7 *Firm size*
Firm Size is one of scales which can be classified based on how big or small the company is by the natural logarithm of the total assets, market stock value, etc. firm size divided to three categories such as 1) large firm; 2) medium firm; and 3) small firm ([30] Suwito dan Arlen, 2005).

2.1.8 *Business risk*
[27] Martin et al. (2005) stated that risks always relate to business failure, fraud and decreasing brand popularity that may ruin the value of the shareholders. According to Brigham and Houston (2013), risk can be divided in to two dimensions; financial risk and business risk. Financial risk is the risk faced by shareholders when the company has liabilities. Business risk is the risk that arises when the company uses liabilities in relation to their operating activities.

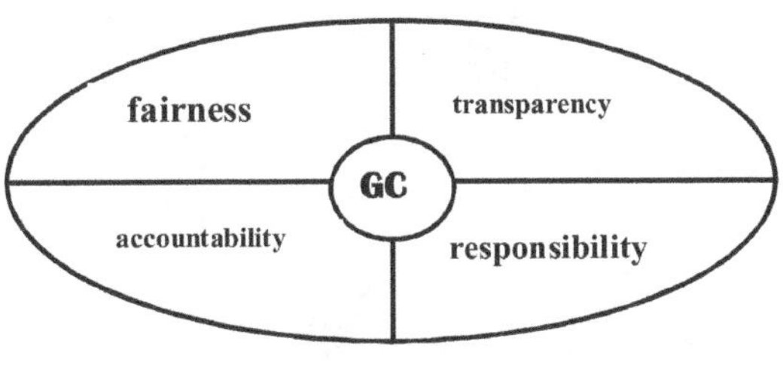

Figure 1. GCG principle.
Source: [29] Sedarmayanti (2007:55).

2.2 *Hypothesis development*

The aims of this research is to prove empirically that firm size, good corporate governance, and business risk affects financial performance with corporate social responsibility as a moderating variable.

2.2.1 *Firm size affects financial performance*
A bigger company has more resources to manage to get a return. A higher return from a firm will be responded to by a higher demand of the firm's stock that will cause a higher price of the stock in turn. Performance and effectiveness in its management is important ([14] Izati and Farah (2014); [32] Wiagustini and Ni Putu (2015)). While [5] Waseem et al (2011); [15] Meilic and I Gede (2014) stated that firm size had an effect on financial performance. This is against what was found by [16] Fachrudin (2011). From the description above, it can be defined in the hypothesis below:

H1: *Firm size affects financial performance.*

2.2.2 *Firm size affects good corporate governance*
Bigger companies tend to get more attention from society. Therefore the corporation will be concerned about stability and the other conditions that cause its financial performance. Research studies by [5] Waseem et al. (2011) and [8] Ihsan, et al. (2014) showed that firm size has a positive relationship with good corporate governance implementation. From that description can be defined the hypothesis below:

H2: *Firm size affects good corporate governance*

2.2.3 *GCG affects business risk with CSR as moderating variable*
When company the implement GCG, it will need to be sure of how it effects its business risks. Risks can be caused by external factors, therefore CSR is often used as factor arising from the implementation of GCG that also affects the relationship between GCG and the associated risks. The research conducted by [12] Roziq and Herdian (2012) found that GCG had a positive effect on business risk. [35] Alam and Syed (2013) and Lee Sewon (2016) stated that GCG effects business risk. Li Hao (2013) said that GCG had a negative effect on business risks. The research that used CSR as

a moderating variable between GCG and business risk done by Lee, et al. (2016) showed that CSR weakens the effect of GCG on business risk.

H3: *GCG affects business risk*

H4: *CSR moderates the effect of GCG on business risk*

2.2.4 *GCG Implementation affects financial performance*

Good corporate governance is believed to have a good effect on financial performance. That statement is supported by the research done by [5] Waseem et al (2011); [6] Jo and Maretno (2011); [7] Renny N et al. (2013); [12] Roziq and Herdian (2013); and [8] Ihsan, et al. (2014). While [15] Meilic and I Gede (2014); [31] Rahman, Arief et al (2015) said that GCG had an effect on financial performance. The opposite result was found by [9] Purwani (2010).

H5: *GCG affects financial performance*

2.2.5 *Business risk affects financial performance*

Business risk has a positive relationship on financial performance. When the company has higher risks, it will increase its financial performance. This was the result obtained by Kaptiana and Nadia (2013). Research by [5] Waseem et al. (2011) stated the same, in that there was a significant relationship between business risk and financial performance. But [12] Roziq and Herdian (2012) and [14] Izati and Farah (2014) concluded that there was no relationship between business risk and financial performance. [32] Wiagustini and Ni Putu (2015) found that business risk had a negative effect on financial performance.

H6: *Business risk affects financial performance*

2.2.6 *Firm size affects financial performance through GCG and business risk*

From research conducted by [5] Waseem et al. (2011); [15] Meilic and I Gede (2014); [14] Izati and Farah (2014); [32] Wiagustini and Ni Putu (2015) stated that the bigger the firm size, the higher the financial performance. Then research about how firm size affected GCG implementation was undertaken by [5] Waseem et al. (2011). [8] Ihsan (2014) found that the bigger firm sizes will force the company to keep up corporate stability by implementing corporate governance which is affected by society's attention. The results which stated that the better implementation of GCG will increase the financial performance were from studies by [5] Waseem et al. (2011); Renny et al. (2013) and [12] Roziq and Herdian (2013). From the discussion above that mentions how firm size affects financial performance, firm size therefore affects GCG implementation, and GCG implementation affects financial performance. This can be used to define the hypothesis below.

H7: *Firm size affects financial performance through GCG*

Higher GCG implementation will decrease the business risks faced by the company. A firm that has good corporate governance implementation will be confident when facing any business risks. [12] Roziq and Herdian (2012); Li Hao et al. (2013); [35] Alam and Syed (2013); and Lee Sewon et al. (2016) are the researchers who have examined the effect of GCG on business risk. Like "high risk high return", the company is expected to get a high return if it takes higher risks and this will have an effect on financial performance. This is the result of Nadia (2013) and [5] Waseem et al. (2011)'s study, but [32] Wiagustini and Ni Putu (2015) found the opposite result, in that business risk had a negative effect on financial performance. From the research gap above, the defined hypothesis is below.

H8: *GCG affects financial performance through business risk*

With the research conducted before that stated that firm size affects financial performance ([5] Waseem et al. (2011); Meilic dan I Gede (2014)), that firm size affected GCG implementation ([5] Waseem et al. (2011); and [8] Ihsan (2014), and then that GCG affected business risk ([12] Roziq and Herdian: 2012), it also stated that business risk affected financial performance (Nadia: 2013 dan [32] Wiagustini dan Ni Putu:2015). This can define the hypothesis below.

H9: *Firm size affects financial performance through GCG and business risk*

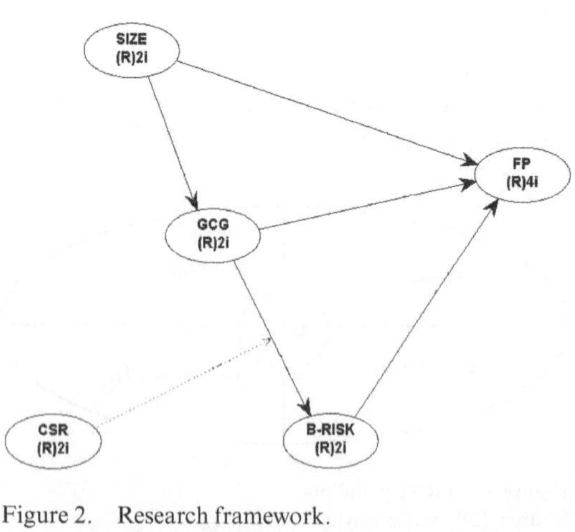

Figure 2. Research framework.

3 RESEARCH METHOD

The research approach used was the quantitative approach which may generalize the data processed to better know the relationship between the variables (Anshori & Iswati, 2009). The population of this research was 143 companies from the manufacturing sector listed on the Indonesian Stock Exchange (BEI) in the period 2014–2015. The sample criteria was that it had to be a company who stated their amount of CSR funds for 2014–2015 and who were consistently listed in BEI. There were 54 company used as a sample in the research collected by documentation and the aforementioned method. The variables used can be seen in Table 1 below.

3.1 *Firm size*

Firm size is how big or small the company is which is measured by the natural logarithm of the total number of employees and the natural logarithm of the total assets.

1. Firm size = Ln (TA)
2. Firm size = Ln (NoE)

Note:
TA : Total Asset
NoE: Number of Employee

3.2 *Good Corporate Governance (GCG)*

Good Corporate Governance is the implementation of good management to do with ethics and company principles. ([28] Pieris dan Nizam, 2007:131). GCG is measured by:

$$\text{Audit Comitee Ratio} = \frac{\textit{Total Independent Audit Comitee}}{\text{Total Audit Comitee}}$$

And,

$$\text{Commissioners Ratio} = \frac{\textit{Total Independent Commissioners}}{\text{Total Commissioners}}$$

Table 1. Type and name of variables.

Hypothesis	Var. independent	Var. mediating	Var. moderating	Variable dependent
H1	*Firm size*	–	–	*Financial performance*
H2	*Firm size*	–	–	GCG
H3	GCG	–	–	*Business risk*
H4	GCG	–	CSR	*Business risk*
H5	GCG	–	–	*Financial performance*
H6	*Business risk*	–	–	*Financial performance*
H7	*Firm size*	GCG	–	*Financial performance*
H8	*GCG*	*Business risk*		*Financial performance*
H9	*Firm size*	GCG and *business risk*		*Financial performance*

Source: The result of data processing, 2016.

3.3 *Business risk*

Business risk is the risk arising when a company encounters liabilities in their operating activities (Brigham dan Houston, 2013) which is measured by the long-term debt ratio to total assets and standard deviation EBIT to total assets.

1. Business risk = LTD/TA
2. Business risk = s EBIT/TA

Note:

EBIT : Earning Before Interest and Tax

3.4 *Corporate Social Responsibility (CSR)*

CSR is corporate responsibility to do with society's welfare in relation to the economic, social, and environmental sectors ([26] Budi, 2007). CSR is measured by CSR disclosure or according to the GRI Index 4.0 indicators, as well as the fund ratio of CSR to total expenses.

1. $CSRD = \Sigma\ ij/Nj_{ij/Nj}$
2. CSR Ratio = CSR fund/total expense

Note :

CSRD : Corporate Social Responsibility Disclosure
: items disclosed by company
Nj : items should be disclose

3.5 *Financial performance*

Performance can described as every change in a company that shows at the end of the company's accounting period ([5] Waseem et al. 2011). Financial performance is measured by ROA, ROE, MtBV, and PER with the equation below.

ROA = net income/total asset
ROE = net income/total equity
MTBV = market price per share/book value per share
PER = market price per share/earnings per share

4 ANALYSIS AND DISCUSSION

The data was analyzed by Partial Least Square (PLS). PLS is one of the analysis methods that can perform measurements and model structuring ([32] Abdillah dan Jogiyanto, 2015). The special advantage is that it can test the complex relationship between many constructs and indicators. It can also be related to different types of measurement. It can even do testing with small abnormal distributions. ([33] Ghozali and Latan, 2014). The PLS analysis was divided in to two:

1. Outer Model Measurement explains the relationship between the indicators with its variables
2. Inner Model or Structural Model Measurement explains the relationship between the independent variables to the dependent variable, also called the hypotheses analysis.

4.1 *Outer model measurement*

The outer model measurement is done through three criteria: convergent validity, discriminant validity, and composite reliability.

4.2 *Convergent validity*

Convergent validity of the outer model can be seen from the loading factor between the indicator and the construct. The criteria is the loading factor of every indicators that should be bigger than 0.70 to be called valid. If the indicators have a loading factor between 0.40–0.70, then the indicator should be analyzed to see the impact of its elimination AVE and composite reliability ([34] Sholihin dan Ratmono, 2013).

From the Table 2, it can be seen that all of the indicators of variable size, GCG, business risk, and CSR have fulfilled the validity convergent because their loading factors are more than 0.70 and have p value less than 0.05. For the indicator of financial performance, just two indicators the validity convergent; ROA and MTBV. PER must be eliminated because it has a loading factor less than 0.40 and the p value is 0.232. ROE needs advanced analysis because its loading factor is between 0.40–0.70, in order to see the impact on AVE and composite reliability changes.

Table 3 shows that AVE and composite reliability before the elimination of any indicator has not exceeded any limit desired which is 0.05 and 0.70 respectively. After PER has been eliminated, AVE and composite reliability increased exceeded the limit desired. Then after the elimination of ROE and PER, the value of AVE and composite reliability increased, and exceeded the limit which is 0.696 and 0.821 respectively. From the results, it suggests that the indicators that should be eliminated are PER and ROE. The Table 4 contains the loading factors, AVE, and the composite reliability of the variables used.

Table 2. Reliability and convergent validity.

Latent variable	Mean	Std Dev.	Loading	P value
Size (composite reliability = 0.912; AVE = 0.839)				
Ln (TA)	28.501	1.544	0.916	<0.001
Ln (NoE)	7.537	1.634	0.916	<0.001
Good Corporate Governance (composite reliability = 0.688; AVE = 0.524)				
RKA	0.34	0.12	0.724	<0.001
RKI	0.39	0.09	0.724	<0.001
Business Risk (composite reliability = 0.775; AVE = 0.633)				
LTD/TA	0.2055	0.3117	0.795	<0.001
EBIT/TA	3.4055	5.4664	0.795	<0.001
CSR (composite reliability = 0.670; AVE = 0.504)				
GRI Index	0.296	0.1263	0.71	<0.001
CSR ratio	0.00282	0.00776	0.71	<0.001
Financial Performance (composite reliability = 0.676; AVE = 0.398)				
ROA	0.0463	0.0875	0.807	<0.001
ROE	0.1326	0.8848	0.635	<0.001
MTBV	29.07	90.76	0.730	<0.001
PER	24.15	97.28	0.069	0.232

Source: The result of data processing using WarpPls, 2017.

Table 3. The comparison AVE and composite reliability.

	AVE	Composite reliability
Before eliminating	0.398	0.676
After eliminating PER	0.530	0.770
After eliminating ROE, PER	0.696	0.821

Source: The data processing using WarpPls, 2017.

Table 4. Results of new combined loadings and cross loading, AVE, and composite reliability.

		Loading factors	P value	AVE	CR
Size	Ln (TA)	(0.916)	<0.001	0.839	0.912
	Ln (NoE)	(0.916)	<0.001		
GCG	RKA	(0.724)	<0.001	0.524	0.688
	RKI	(0.724)	<0.001		
B-Risk	LTD/TA	(0.795)	<0.001	0.633	0.775
	S EBIT/TA	(0.795)	<0.001		
CSR	GRI index	(0.710)	<0.001	0.504	0.670
	CSR Ratio	(0.710)	<0.001		
FP	ROA	(0.834)	<0.001	0.696	0.821
	MTBV	(0.834)	<0.001		

Source: Data processing using WarpPls, 2017.

Table 5. Correlation construct with square root of AVE.

	Size	GCG	B-Risk	CSR	FP
Size	(0.916)	−0.082	−0.166	0.186	0.159
GCG	−0.082	(0.724)	0.214	0.047	0.105
B-Risk	−0.166	0.214	(0.795)	−0.037	−0.098
CSR	0.186	0.047	−0.037	(0.710)	0.034
FP	0.159	0.105	−0.098	0.034	(0.834)

Source: Data processing using WarpPls, 2017.

4.3 *Discriminant validity*

Discriminant validity is assessed by the measurement of the cross-loading with the construct. The loading factors of the correlations with the construct must be greater than the indicators of the other construct ([33] Ghozali dan Latan, 2014). Whereas the diagonal column must be greater than the other columns and rows. Table 5 below shows us that the five variables have fulfilled the discriminant validity.

4.4 *Inner model measurement*

The inner model evaluation used R-square (R2) for measuring how the independent variables can describe the dependent variables. Q-square (Q2) was used to measure the predictive validity for each variable. The role of the relevancy limit for each variable must be greater than 0 or positive to be called relevant.

5 DISCUSSION

5.1 *The effect of firm size on financial performance*

Larger firms have more resources. Having more resources will ease up the process of the corporate management earning a profit reflected by the returns. With a higher profit, investors will respond by having higher demands of the stock that leads to the higher stock prices compared to the book value of the shares. This result is supported by the previous research studies by [32] Wiagustini and Ni Putu (2015); [15] Meilic and I Gede (2014); [14] Izati and Farah (2014) and [5] Waseem et al. (2011) that stated that an increase in total assets may get a positive response from the company and impact by increasing its stock price.

5.2 *The effect of firm size on Good Corporate Governance (GCG)*

The previous research stated that the larger firms would have better corporate governance ([5] Waseem, et al.: 2011). But the empiric result goes against their statement, it showed that firm size had a negative effect on GCG. This may be caused by smaller firm having a fluctuate condition, that can impact on smaller investors who are interested in investing in that company. To overcome this, small companies focus on increasing good corporate governance that makes them more effective at controlling their staff and management. It also makes it easier to build regulations because of its small scope which drives the trust of investors in decision-making.

5.3 *The effect of Good Corporate Governance (GCG) on business risk*

Higher good corporate governance implementation will face higher risks (Lestianingsih, 2008 and [12] Roziq and Herdian, 2012). GCG implementation will underlie the risks that drive the company to manage themselves professionally. GCG is needed to control the business risks of a company. This may cause better corporate governance to face higher risks in order to increase financial performance. Therefore, a company with higher GCG won't be worried about facing higher risks. This statement is supported by the prior research of [12] Roziq and Herdian (2012); [35] Alam and Syed (2013) and Lee (2016) which stated that GCG had a positive effect on business risk.

5.4 *The effect of Good Corporate Governance (GCG) on Financial Performance (FP)*

Independent audit committees and independent commissioners are the staff who have no involvement with corporate ownership so they will not take sides. GCG implementation is intended to set the relationship as being both internal and external. Staff that are independent can increase the trust of investors in its company. GCG will increase the transparency and accountability of management in making financial reports, which is also effective in increasing financial performance. Previous research by [5] Waseem et al (2011); [7] Renny N et al. (2013) and [12] Roziq and Herdian (2012) supported this result with their statement that there was a positive relationship between GCG and financial performance. Meanwhile [15] Meilic and I Gede (2014) and [31] Rahman, Arief dkk. (2015) stated that GCG affected financial performance without being conclusive.

5.5 *The effect of business risk on Financial Performance (FP)*

The higher the company's liabilities, the higher the interest expense that must be paid which influence current profit. Higher interest expenses will lead to decreasing the financial performance that can be measured by ROA and MtBV. This result is congruent with the findings of [32] Wiagustini and Ni Putu (2015) which stated that business risk had a negative effect on financial performance as measured by PER. [12] Roziq and Herdian (2012) and [14] Izati and Farah (2014) concluded that there was no relationship between business risk and financial performance.

5.6 *The effect of firm size on Financial Performance (FP) through Good Corporate Governance (GCG) and business risk*

Table 6 the direct effect on H1 and Table 8 for the indirect effect shows that there is a decreasing value of the ß and p value. The result of the VAF and p value on WarpPls indicates a different result for the 6th hypothesis and 8th for each VAF < 20%

Table 6. Summary of direct effects.

Hypothesis	ß value	*P* value	R^2	Q^2	Conclusion
H1	0.18	0.03**	0.032	0.046	Accepted
H2	0.13	0.08***	0.02	0.025	Accepted
H3	0.27	<0.01*	0.071	0.072	Accepted
H5	0.16	0.05***	0.024	0.032	Accepted
H6	–0.21	0.01**	0.045	0.054	Accepted

Source: The result of data processing using WarpPls, 2017.

Table 7. The result of moderating effect.

Hypothesis	ß value	*P* value	Conclusion
H4	–0.22	<0.01	Accepted

Source: The result of data processing using WarpPls, 2017.

Table 8. Summary of Indirect/Mediating effects.

	Indirect effects				
	ß value	*p* value	VAF	*P* value	Conclusion
H7	Size → FP		–0.6014	0.229	Rejected
	0.17	0.04			
H8	GCG → FP		–0.718	0.389	Rejected
	0.14	0.06***			
H9	Size → FP		–	0.453	Rejected
	0.17	0.04			

***Significant on level $\alpha < 0.1$,
**Significant on level $\alpha < 0.05$,
*Significant on level $\alpha < 0.01$,
Source: The result of data processing using WarpPls, 2017.

and p value is 0.389 and 0.453 respectively which is not significant. This means that the direct effect of firm size on financial performance is greater than the indirect effects. GCG and business risk are not mediating variables between firm size and financial performance. This proves the previous research studies by Meilic dan I Gede (2014); [14] Izati and Farah (2014) and [5] Waseem et al. (2011) which stated that firm size directly effects financial performance.

5.7 *The effect of good corporate governance on financial performance through business risk*

From Table 8, it can be seen that the value of ß decreases from 0.16 to 0.14 and the p value becomes 0.06. The result of the VAF and p value of WarpPls processing shows the opposite number. VAF < 20% indicates that business risk doesn't mediate the relationship of GCG and financial performance. This is supported by p value = 0.229 which is not significant. The result concludes that the direct effect of GCG on financial performance is greater than its indirect effect. Therefore, business risk isn't an intervening variable between good corporate governance and financial performance. [12] Roziq and Herdian (2012) found the same result.

5.8 *The effect of good corporate governance on business risk moderated by CSR*

Table 5 describes how CSR moderates the relationship between GCG and financial performance. The negative result of –0.22 means that higher CSR implementation will decrease or weaken the effect of GCG on financial performance. Companies who commit to implementing CSR have a long-term plan to increase the stakeholder's trust in that company. CSR can build a good relationship between the stakeholder and the corporation which is expected to decrease the business risk. This result has been accepted and supported by Lee (2016) who stated that CSR decreases the effect of GCG on business risk.

6 CONCLUSION

1. Firm size and good corporate governance (GCG) has a positive effect on financial performance. Business risk has a negative effect on financial performance.
2. Firm size has a negative effect on good corporate governance
3. Good corporate governance has a positive effect on business risk
4. Good corporate governance and business risk aren't mediating variables in this research study.

GCG doesn't mediate the relationship between firm size and financial performance, and business risk doesn't mediate GCG and financial performance. GCG and business risk don't mediate the relationship between firm size and financial performance.

REFERENCES

[1] Daniri, M.A. Good Corporate Governance: Konsep Penerapannya dalam Konteks Indonesia. Jakarta: GloriaPrinting, 2005.

[2] Anonim. 2012. Business Ethic. (Online book). Retrieved from: http://2012books.lardbucket.org/books/business-ethics/s17–02-three-theories-of-corporate-so.html accessed on 13th April 2016, 20.27 WIB.

[3] Undang-Undang Nomor 40 Tahun 2007 tentang Perseroan Terbatas Pasal 1 ayat 3.

[4] Peraturan Pemerintah Nomor 47 Tahun 2012 tentang Pelaksanaan Tanggung Jawab Sosial dan Lingkungan Perusahaan.

[5] Waseem, "mohammad yahya" A-H., Alzurqan, S.T., & Al-Sufy, F.J. The Effect of Corporate Governance on the Performance of Jordanian Industrial Companies: An Empirical Study on Amman Stock Exchange. International Journal of Humanities and Social Science. Vol. 1 No. 4 (April 2011): 55–69.

[6] Jo, H., & Harjoto, M.A. Corporate Governance and Firm Value: The Impact of Corporate Social Responsibility. J Bus Ethics 103, 2011, 351–383.

[7] Renny, N., Nurcahyo, B., Sri K.A., & Sugiharti B. Implementation of Good Corporate Governance and Its Impact on Corporate Performance: The mediation Role of Firm Size (Empirical Study of Indonesia). Global Business and Management Research: An International Journal. Vol. 5 No. 2&3, 2013: 91–104.

[8] Ihsan, M., dkk. Corporate Governance and Corporate Social Responsibility Disclosure: Evidence from the US Banking sector. J Bus Ethics 125, 2014: 601–615.

[9] Purwani, T. Pengaruh Good Corporate Governance terhadap Kinerja Perusahaan. Majalah Ilmiah INFORMATIKA. Vol. 1 No. 2 (Mei 2010): 47–60.

[10] Li, H., Jr, S.J., & Yost, K. Corporate Risk and Corporate Governance: Another View. Emerald Managerial Finance. Vol. 39 No. 3, 2013:204–227.

[11] Lee, S., Kim, Y.K., & Kim, K. Corporate Governance, Firm Risk, And Corporate Social Responsibility: Evidence From Korean Firms. The Journal of Applied Business Research. Vol. 32 No. 1. (January-February 2016). 303–316.

[12] Roziq, A., & Danurwenda, H.N. Pengaruh Good Corporate Governance terhadap Corporate Social Responsibility melalui Risiko Bisnis dan Kinerja Keuangan pada Bank Umum Syariah di Indonesia. Jurnal Akuntansi Universitas Jember. Vol. 10 No. 1, 2012.

[13] Kaptiana, D.K., & Asandimitra, N. Pengaruh Struktur Modal, Risiko Bisnis dan Pertumbuhan Penjualan terhadap ROE Perusahaan Manufaktur. Jurnal Ilmiah Manajemen.Volume 1 Nomor 3 (Mei 2013): 713–723.

[14] Izati, C., & Margaretha, F. Factor-faktor yang Mempengaruhi Kinerja Keuangan pada Perusahaan Basic Industry and Chemical di Indonesia. E-Jurnal Manajemen fakultas Ekonomi Universitas Trisakti Vol. 1 No. 2 (September 2014): 21–43.

[15] Meilic, D.A.T., & Wisadha, I.G.S. Pengaruh Good Corporate Governance, Kualitas Laba, dan Ukuran Perusahaan pada Kinerja Perusahaan. E-Jurnal Akuntansi Universitas Udayana. Volume 7 Nomor 3, 2014: 733–746.

[16] Fachrudin, K.A. Analisis Pengaruh Struktur Modal, Ukuran Perusahaan, dan Agency Cost terhadap Kinerja Perusahaan. Jurnal Akuntansi dan Keuangan. Vol. 13 No. 1 (Mei 2011): 37–46.

[17] Brigham E.F. & Houston, J.F. Fundamental of Financial Management. United State of America: Thomson South Western, 2004.

[18] Schoech. Contingency Theory. UTA School of Social Work, Community and Administrative Practice. January 2006: 1–4.

[19] Betts, S.C. Contingency Theory:Science or Technology?. Journal of Business and Economics Research. Volume 1. Number 8, 2003:123–130.

[20] Harahap, S.S. Analisis Kritis dan Laporan Keuangan. Jakarta: PT Raja Grafindo Perkasa, 2009.

[21] Sudana, I.M. Manajemen Keuangan Perusahaan: Teori dan Praktik. Jakarta: Erlangga, 2011.

[22] Gibson, C., Financial Reporting and Analysis: Using Financial Accounting Information. South Western: Cengage Learning, 2009.

[23] Wahyudiono, B. Mudah Membaca Laporan Keuangan. Jakarta: Raih Asa Sukses, 2014.

[24] Gitman, L.J. & Zutter, C.J.. Principle of Managerial Finance. Thirteenth Edition. United States: Printece Hall, 2012.

[25] Brigham E. F & Houston, J.F. Fundamental of Financial Management. United State of America: Thomson South Western, 2004.

[26] Budi, U.H. Corporate Social Responsibility. Jakarta: PT Sinar Grafika, 2007.

[27] Martin F. et al. Beyond Governance Creating Corporate Value through Performance, Confergence and Responsibility. England: John Wiley & Son, Ltd, 2005.

[28] Pieris, J., & Nizam J.W. Etika Bisnis & Good Corporate Governance. Jakarta: Pelangi Cendekia, 2007.

[29] Sedarmayanti. Good Governance (Kepemerintahan yang Baik) dan Good Corporate Governance (Tata kelola Perusahaan yang Baik). Bandung: CV. Mandar Maju, 2007.

[30] Suwito, E., & Herawati, A. 2005. Analisis Pengaruh Karakteristik Perusahaan terhadap Tindakan Perataan Laba yang Dilakukan oleh Perusahaan yang terdaftar di Bursa Efek Jakarta. SNA VIII Solo.

[31] Rachman, A.N., dkk. 2015. Pengaruh Good Corporate Governance dan Financial Leverage terhadap Financial Performance dan Nilai Perusahaan (Studi pada Perusahaan yang Terdaftar di Indeks Sri Kehati Selama Periode 2011–2014). Jurnal Administrasi Bisnis (JAB). Vol. 27. No. 1 (October):1–10.

[32] Abdillah, W., & Jogiyanto. 2015. Partial Least Square (PLS) Alternatif Structural Equation Modeling

(SEM) dalam Penelitian Bisnis. Yogyakarta: Penerbit ANDI. Brigham and Houston. 2013. Dasar-dasar Manajemen Keuangan (Essential of Financial Management). Edisi 11, Buku 2. Jakarta: Salemba Empat.

[33] Ghozali, I., & Latan, H. 2014. Partial Least Square Konsep, Metode, dan Aplikasi Menggunakan Program WarpPLS 4.0. Edisi Kedua. Semarang: Badan Penerbit Universitas Diponegoro.

[34] Sholihin, M., & Ratmono, D. 2013. Analisis SEM-PLS dengan WarpPLS 3.0 untuk hubungan Nonlinier dalam Penelitian Sosial dan Bisnis. Yogyakarta: Penerbit ANDI.

[35] Alam, A. & Syed Z.A.S. Corporate governance and its Impact on Firm Risk. International Journal of Management, Economics and Social Science. Vol. 2(2), 2013:76–98.

[36] Wahyudi, I., & Azheri, B. Corporate Social responsibility, Prinsip, Pengaturan dan implementasi. Malang: Intrans Publishing dan Inspire Indonesia, 2008.

Increasing Management Relevance and Competitiveness – Sukoco et al. (Eds)
© 2018 Taylor & Francis Group, London, ISBN 978-0-8153-7455-8

The effect of good corporate governance on financial performance with capital structure and earnings management as mediating variables

N. Soewarno, B. Tjahjadi & B.D.P. Utomo
Universitas Airlangga, Surabaya, Indonesia

ABSTRACT: This study aimed to examine the effect of Good Corporate Governance on financial performance with the capital structure and earnings management as mediating variable. This study used secondary data from Indonesia Stock Exchange on SOE period 2011–2015. The population in this study were 97 go public SOEs in Indonesia during the period 2011–2015. Sampling technique used was purposive sampling. Of the 97 population, there were 67 state-owned enterprises that matched the criteria to be sampled for this research. Hypothesis testing was done by using Partial Least Squares—with software warpPLS version 5.0. The results of this study showed:1) capital structure mediated the effect of mechanisms of good corporate governance on financial performance; 2) earning management did not mediate the effect of mechanisms of good corporate governance on financial performance; 3) capital structure and earnings management did not mediate the effect of good corporate governance on financial performance.

Keywords: Good Corporate Governance, Financial Performance, Capital Structure, Earnings Management

1 INTRODUCTION

One of the roles of the government to develop the economy of Indonesia could be done by establishing State-Owned Enterprises (SOEs), in which the government as a shareholder has a stake of at least 51%, with the remaining shares could be owned by society (Idris 2016). SOE establishment is intended as agents of development. SOE as agents of development should have a profit motive. SOEs can also be regarded as an organization that is unique because of having two sides that are arguably contradictory. On the one hand, state-owned enterprises as agents of development must be run through tight regulation, but, on the other hand, SOEs must also have a profit motive.

Good corporate governance mechanisms are expected to boost the efficiency and effectiveness of state-owned enterprises, which will lead to increase in financial performance. Financial performance is a major benchmark in assessing whether the company's performance is improved or not, which can be seen from financial statements. Many investors and creditors assess financial performance through financial ratios. If SOEs have the trust of investors and creditors, the investors and creditors will not hesitate to make an investment or a loan that will increase the value of the company.

Good corporate governance not only has a direct impact on financial performance, but also has indirect effect through earnings management as a mediating variable. Good corporate governance is expected to reduce opportunistic actions in SOEs, one of which is the practice of earnings management. Earnings management performed managers will affect the company's financial performance as well as influencing value of its stock price in the market (Ujiyantho and Agus 2007). This is supported by research conducted by Patrick Paulinus, and Nympha (2015) which stated that the size of the board of directors has a significant effect on earnings management. Another study conducted by Jamkarani and Hozi (2016) states that accrual earnings management has an influence on future ROA.

The indirect effect of good corporate governance on financial performance is also related to the capital structure. The relationship of good corporate governance to the capital structure lies in the selection of the company's capital resources. Decision about capital source selection includes a variety of considerations, including whether the company will use internal or external resources. Internal sources may include reserves and retained earnings. If internal resources are already used to their full potential, it is necessary to look for external sources by borrowing from creditors or issuing new shares. Companies using debt will be monitored by creditors, which can lead to better financial performance. Creditors will not lend funds if they see the financial ratios of SOE show poor results and, therefore, companies will try to maintain their financial performance. SOEs will choose financing through debt policy because it has a lower risk compared to issuing stocks and to prevent moral hazard. When managers have a stake in the company, the managers will oversee the company's growth, because it is very important to them as one of the shareholders. In order to get profit, companies definitely need capital, one of which is by using the liability for capital funding (Rahadian and Hadiprajitno 2011).

Capital structure influences practice of earnings management, because, by selecting debts as funding source, SOEs tend to perform earnings management practices to meet the borrowing requirements of creditors. This is supported by research conducted by Shirzad and Haghighi (2015) which states that there is a negative relationship between corporate financial leverage proxied by total debt ratio to accrual earnings management.

This study aimed to examine the mediating effect of capital structure and earning management in the relationship of GCG towards financial performance, in the case on go public SOEs.

2 THEORETICAL FRAMEWORK AND HYPOTHESIS DEVELOPMENT

Good corporate governance is closely related to agency theory. Agency theory is a theory that explains the agency relationship and the problems it creates (Jensen and Meckling 1976). Agency theory is the relationship between the two parties, in which the first party acts as a principal/principals and the second party is called an agent and acts as an intermediary representing a principal in the transaction with third parties. The principal authorizes the agent to carry out transactions on behalf of the principal and is expected to make the best decisions for the principal. With the basic concepts of agency theory, it is to be expected that the agent will be running the company on behalf of the principal, and investors, as a principal, would receive a return on the funds they have invested. Good corporate governance is concerned with how they (investors) are confident that managers will benefit them, confident that the manager will not steal, embezzle or invest in projects that do not make profit, by using the fund or the capital that has been invested by the investor, and also related with how investors control managers (Sam'ani 2008).

2.1 *Capital structure mediates the relationship of good corporate governance on financial performance*

The Board of Directors is responsible for the management of SOEs and achieving their objectives. While the independent commissioner is an independent party chosen by stakeholders and assigned to evaluate the performance of the company, and also takes the decisions to achieve company progress, not for personal or group interests. The stronger the independent commissioner, the greater the capital funding. SOEs will choose financing through debt policy because it has a lower risk compared to issuing stocks and to prevent moral hazard. Independent commissioners also consider that issuing shares will increase interest among shareholders. When managers have a stake in the company, the managers will oversee the company's growth closely and thoroughly, because it is very important to them as one of the shareholders. The manager will choose debt capital financing because it has a smaller company risk and benefits managers as shareholders. Selection of the debt itself will gain control of the creditors, which causes financial performance to be good. Creditors will not lend funds if they see the financial ratios of the SOE show poor results and, therefore, companies will still maintain good financial performance. This research was supported by Rahadian and Hadiprajitno (2014), who state that managerial ownership has positive effect on capital structure. Another study, conducted by Nirajini and Priya (2013), states that there is significant influence between debt equity ratio against financial performance and no significant effect between the debt to asset ratio of the financial performance.

H1: The capital structure mediates the effect of good corporate governance of financial corporate performance.

2.2 *Effect of good corporate governance mechanisms on financial performance management with earnings as a mediating variable*

Conflict of interest between management and owners of the company may lead to earnings management action. Earnings management arises because of the divergence of interests between the agent and the principal or other parties. Earning management can be minimized through multiple mechanisms of corporate governance, including the board of directors, managerial ownership, and independent board. Agency problem appears when there is different interest between owner and agent. The owner wants high company performance so that the market value of the company stock is higher, but management seek in achieving a good company performance for personal gain. Improved financial performance will result in the company's value to rise. It will bring many investors who will invest and allure creditors to lend funding. Investors and creditors use company financial statements and the financial ratios of the SOEs in order to analyze company performance. Patrick, Paulinus, and Nympha (2015) stated that the board size significantly influences earnings management. Meanwhile, according to Jamkarani and Hozi (2016), the accrual earnings management has a significant influence on future ROA.

H2: Earnings management mediates the effect of good corporate governance on financial performance.

2.3 *Effect of good corporate governance mechanisms on financial performance with capital structure and earnings management as a mediating variable*

The directors are responsible to management SOEs in order to achieve their objectives. While the independent commissioner is an independent party chosen by stakeholders and assigned to evaluate the performance of the company. The commissioner takes the decisions to improve the company performance, not for personal or group interests. The stronger the independent commissioner, the investors and creditors will have more trust in the company; therefore, it is easier for the company to get more funding (Rahadian and Hadiprajitno 2014). SOEs will choose financing through debt policy because it has a lower risk compared to issuing stocks and to prevent moral hazard.

SOEs debt to creditors is likely to increase earnings management practices in order to fulfill the borrowing requirements from creditors. It could be stated that the higher the debt, the higher becomes the earning management. Creditors will use financial ratios of the SOE to monitor and evaluate their financial performance. SOEs tend to do earning management to avoid breaching debt covenants as a means of window dressing (Widyaningdyah 2001). Research conducted by Rahadian and Hadiprajitno (2014) states that managerial ownership has a significant positive effect on the capital structure. Research conducted by Shirzad and Haghighi (2015) states that there is significant influence between corporate financial leverage proxied debt to asset ratio to accrual earnings management. Meanwhile, according to Jamkarani and Hozi (2016) also state that the Accrual Earnings management has a significant influence on future ROA.

H3: Capital structure and earnings management mediates the effect of good corporate governance to the financial performance.

3 RESEARCH METHODS

This study used listed state-owned enterprises on the Indonesia Stock Exchange in the period 2011–2015. The sample used in this study is as many as 67 companies.

3.1 *Data*

This study uses secondary data from the annual report of SOEs listed on the Stock Exchange in 2011–2015. Data required in this study were obtained from BEI website at http://www.idx.co.id.

3.2 *Variables*

The independent variable in this study is Good Corporate Governance. Good Corporate Governance consists of the proportion of independent commissioners, the size of the board of directors and managerial ownership in SOEs 2011–2015. The dependent variable in this research is financial performance using ROA and ROE as a proxy. The mediating variables in this study are capital structure and earnings management. Capital structure is measured by the ratio of Debt to Equity and the ratio of Debt to Asset. Earnings management is measured using discretionary accrual and non-discretionary accrual.

3.3 *Methods*

The sample used is purposive sampling method. In this study, the data analysis technique used is the measurement models for outer and inner models and hypothesis testing of direct and indirect influence.

4 ANALYSIS AND DISCUSSION

The object of this research is the financial performance of SOEs listed in the BEI. The population in this study is listed state companies in BEI period 2011–2015, while the sample is determined by purposive sampling and amounted to 67 companies.

4.1 *Descriptive statistical analysis*

Descriptive statistical analysis provides a description of data, which consists of maximum, minimum, average value and standard deviation. Standard deviation is a reflection of the average

Table 1. Table descriptive statistics.

Indikator	N	Min	Maks	Mean	Std. Deviasi
GCG 1	67	0.2900	0.6300	0.4100	0.0908
GCG 2	67	5.0000	11.0000	6.7313	1.7802
GCG 3	67	0.0000	0.0047	0.0005	0.0010
EM 1	67	–0.1170	0.1740	0.0208	0.0634
EM 2	67	–0.1240	0.0370	–0.0255	0.0347
SM 1	67	0.2400	0.9200	0.6001	0.2248
SM 2	67	0.3200	11.4000	3.1050	3.1186
KK 1	67	–0.0500	0.2700	0.0711	0.0666
KK 2	67	–0.0800	0.3800	0.1728	0.0805

deviation from the mean of data. Standard deviation can describe how great is the data variation. If the standard deviation value is much greater than the mean value, the mean value is a poor representation of the overall data. Meanwhile, if the standard deviation is very small compared to the mean value, the mean value can be used as a representation of all the data. Based on test results obtained by descriptive statistics, there were 67 samples from 97 populations. The processed data on descriptive statistics can be viewed as Table 1.

4.2 *Evaluation model measurement (outer model)*

4.2.1 *Validity test (convergent validity)*

The validity of the measurement model can be seen from the correlation between the scores of indicators with a construct score (loading factor) with a value criteria loading factor of each indicator greater than 0.70 it can be said to be valid. Furthermore, for p-value, < 0.05 was considered significant. Sholihin and Ratmono (2013: 66) explained that, in some cases, the terms of loading above 0.70 are often not met.

Therefore, loading between 0.40 to 0.70 should still be considered to be maintained. Furthermore, they also explained that, with the indicator loading < 0.40 removed from the model., deletion indicator with loading between 0.40 to 0.70 could increase AVE, Cronbach's alpha and composite reliability above the limit value. Value restriction for the AVE is 0.50 and Cronbach's alpha and composite reliability are 0.70.

Based on the Table 2, only GCG 3 must delete the indicator because its value is in the position of < 0.40. While the two indicators of earnings management indicate that all indicator values are in position 0.4 < Loading < 0.70, which should be reconsidered with a view to value of AVE, Cronbach's alpha and composite reliability.

Table 2. Results of the combined output loadings and loadings cross.

Indikator	GCG	EM	SM	KK	SE	P-Value
GCG 1	0.895	0.058	−0.082	−0.125	0.091	<0.001
GCG 2	0.909	−0.107	−0.061	0.128	0.090	<0.001
GCG 3	0.292	0.152	0.441	−0.014	0.111	0.005
EM 1	−0.070	0.677	−0.359	−0.035	0.098	<0.001
EM 2	0.070	0.677	0.359	0.035	0.098	<0.001
SM 1	−0.117	0.029	0.967	−0.041	0.089	<0.001
SM 2	0.117	−0.029	0.967	0.041	0.089	<0.001
KK 1	0.021	−0.005	−0.366	0.936	0.090	<0.001
KK 2	−0.021	0.005	0.366	0.936	0.090	<0.001

Table 3. Results output latent variable coefficients.

	GCG	EM	SM	KK
R-square coefficient		0.372	0.058	0.248
Adjusted R-square coefficient		0.362	0.029	0.212
Composite reliability coefficient	0.774	0.629	0.967	0.934
Cronbach's alpha coefficient	0.565	–0.180	0.931	0.859
Average variances extracted	0.571	0.459	0.935	0.877
Full collinearity VIFs	1.439	1.078	1.842	1.261
Q-squared coefficient		0.100	0.362	0.294

Table 4. The output combined loadings and cross loadings after deletion of indicator GCG 3 and EM 2.

Indikator	GCG	EM	SM	KK	SE	P-Value
GCG 1	0.915	0.006	0.012	−0.128	0.090	<0.001
GCG 2	0.915	−0.006	−0.012	0.128	0.090	<0.001
EM 1	0.000	1.000	−0.000	−0.000	0.088	<0.001
SM 1	−0.119	0.007	0.967	−0.040	0.089	<0.001
SM 2	0.119	−0.007	0.967	0.040	0.089	<0.001
KK 1	0.020	−0.013	−0.368	0.936	0.090	<0.001
KK 2	−0.020	0.013	0.368	0.936	0.090	<0.001

Based on the Table 3 for the indicators EM, AVE is still under 0.50, and Cronbach's alpha and composite reliability still below 0.70. Therefore, it only needs to do a deletion in one of the indicators of EM 2.

Based on the Table 4 it shows that the overall indicator meets the criteria.

Based on Table 5, all the indicators meet the AVE value > 0.50. GCG has a value AVE 0.838 > 0.50, EM has a value AVE 1.000 > 0.50, SM has a value AVE 0.935 > 0.50, and KK has a value AVE 0.877 > 0.50. In conclusion all variables have met the criteria.

Table 5. AVE value.

Average variances extracted (AVE)			
Variable	AVE Value	Criteria	Description
GCG	0.838>	0.50	Accepted
EM	1.000>	0.50	Accepted
SM	0.935>	0.50	Accepted
KK	0.877>	0.50	Accepted

Table 6. Loading values latent construct and to other construct indicators.

Indi-kator	Load-ing		Loading value to other construct indicators				
			GCG	EM	SM	KK	Ket
GCG 1	0.915	>		0.006	0.012	−0.128	Accepted
GCG 2	0.915	>		−0.006	−0.012	0.128	Accepted
EM 1	1.000	>	0.000		−0.000	−0.000	Accepted
SM 1	0.967	>	−0.119	0.007		−0.040	Accepted
SM 2	0.967	>	0.119	−0.007		0.040	Accepted
KK 1	0.936	>	0.020	−0.013	−0.368		Accepted
KK 2	0.936	>	−0.020	0.013	0.368		Accepted

Table 7. Latent variable coefficient.

	GCG	EM	SM	KK	Criteria
Composite reliability	0.912	1.000	0.967	0.934	>0.70
Cronbach's alpha	0.807	1.000	0.931	0.859	>0.70

4.2.2 *Discriminant validity*

Discriminant validity is assessed by cross loading of measurement constructs. It can be seen by looking at loading latent constructs to see which would predict a better indicator than the other constructs. If the correlation constructs with the basic measurements (each indicator) is greater than the size of the other constructs, then discriminant validity is met.

These are presented in the Table 6 for ease in reading the data:

4.2.3 *Reliability test*

According to the Table 7, these results show the composite reliability of each construct, GCG with a value of 0.912, EM with a value of 1.000, SM with 0.967 values, and KK with a value of 0.934. The results of Cronbach's alpha also show the GCG with a value of 0.807, EM with a value of 1.000, SM with 0.931 value and KK with a value of 0.859. It can be concluded that all variables have met the criteria of composite reliability and Cronbach's alpha.

4.3 *Evaluation of structural model (inner model)*

The next step is to evaluate the structural (inner models), which includes suitability test model (fit model), path coefficient and R^2. In the test there are three index model fit testing, i.e. average path coefficient (APC), average R-squared (ARS) and the average variance factor (AVIF) with APC criteria and ARS accepting a p-value < 0.05 and AVIF < 5 (Sholihin and Ratmono 2013: 61).

4.4 *Hypothesis test results*

Based on Figure 1 above, it shows that there is a direct effect significance with path coefficients and p-values of GCG to KK amounting to 0.25 and 0.01, respectively, and R value² of 0.06.

Based on Figure 2 above, it shows that the path coefficients and p-values of GCG to KK show no significant effect of 0.057 and 0.318, respectively, and the value of R^2 of 0273, path coefficients and p-values of GCG to SM show a significant influence 0.58 and < 0.001, respectively, and R^2 of 0.338. Then, path coefficients and p-values of SM to KK showed a significant effect of −0.52 and < 0.001, respectively, and R^2 of 0.273. Path coefficients and p-values of GCG to EM showed a significant effect of –0.27 and 0.009, respectively, and the value of R^2 of 0.07. Path coefficients and p-values of EM to KK showed no significant effect of 0.017 and 0.444 ($p > 0.05$), respectively, and R^2 of

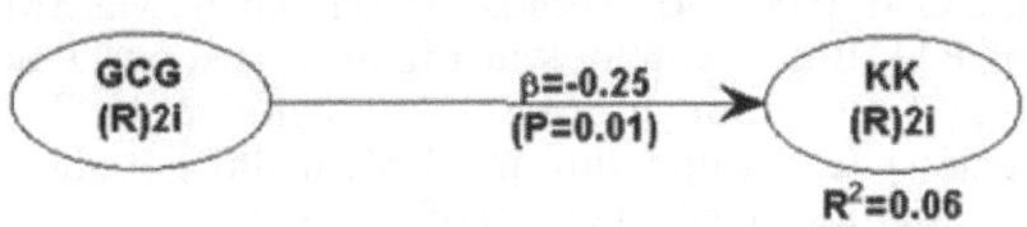

Figure 1. Direct effect.

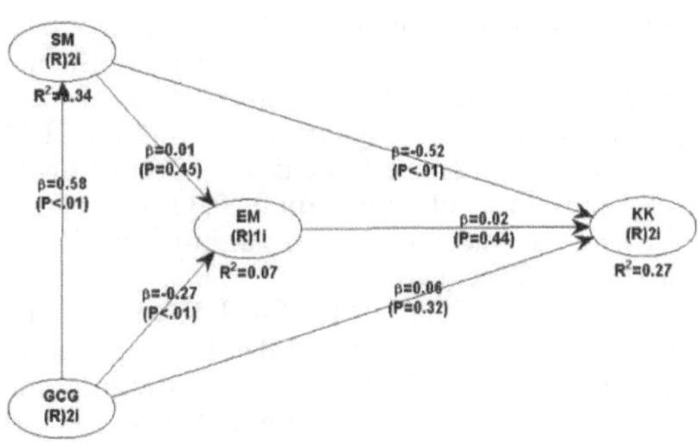

Figure 2. Indirect effect.

Table 8. General SEM result analysis.

Index		P-Value	Criteria	Description
APC	0.244	P = 0.009	p < 0.05	Accepted
ARS	0.227	P = 0.012	p < 0.05	Accepted
AVIF	1.259. Ideally < 3.3		Acceptable if < 5	Accepted

Table 9. P-values of indirect effect for a path with two segments.

	GCG	EM	SM	KK
GCG				
EM	0.463			
SM				
KK	0.003		0.499	

Table 10. P-values of indirect effect for path with three segments.

	GCG	EM	SM	KK
GCG				
EM				
SM				
KK	0.499			

0.27. Path coefficients and p-values of SM to EM showed no significant effect of 0.014 and 0.455 ($p > 0.05$), respectively, and R^2 of 0.07.

Based on Table 9, it shows there are p-values of indirect effect for a path with two segments of GCG to 0.003 households, which can be via SM or EM. But, if you look at Figure 2, it shows that only GCG through SM showed significant effect against KK, while, through EM, it did not show any significant effect ($p > 0.05$).

Based on Table 10, it shows the p-values of indirect effect for path with three segments of GCG to KK amounted to 0.499.

The first hypothesis shows that the direct effect of GCG to KK showed a significant influence which amounted to 0.25 with p-value of 0.01 ($p < 0.05$). But, after entering the SM and EM variables into the model, the direct effect of GCG to KK becomes not significant by 0.32. This allows SM as a full mediating variable, but one should look at the subsequent terms.

The indirect effect of GCG to KK with mediation of Capital Structure (SM) shows a significant indirect effect in that path coefficients and p-values of GCG to SM were 0.58 and < 0.001 ($p < 0.05$), respectively, while path coefficients and p-values of SM to KK amounted to 0.52 and < 0.001 ($p < 0.05$), respectively. This is powered with p-values of indirect effect for a path with two segments and showed significant effect of GCG to KK of 0.003 ($p < 0.05$). Thus, the first hypothesis is accepted that SM has a full mediating relationship with GCG to KK because all requirements have been met. The research proves that directors are responsible for the management of SOEs and achieving their objectives, while the independent commissioner is an independent party chosen by stakeholders and assigned to evaluate the performance of the company, and also takes the decisions to achieve company progress, not for personal or group interests. The stronger the independent commissioner, the greater the capital funding. SOEs will choose financing through debt policy because it has a lower risk compared to issuing stocks and to prevent moral hazard. Independent commissioners also consider that issuing shares will increase interest among shareholders. When managers have a stake in the company, the managers will oversee the company's growth closely and thoroughly, because it is very important to them as one of the shareholders. The manager will choose debt capital financing because it has a smaller company risk and benefits managers as shareholders. Selection of the debt itself will gain control of the creditors, which causes financial performance to be good. Creditors will not lend funds if they see the financial ratios of SOEs show poor results and, therefore, companies will still maintain good financial performance.

The second hypothesis shows that the direct effect of GCG to KK showed a significant influence of 0.25 with p-value of 0.01 ($p < 0.05$). After entering the SM and EM variables into the model, the direct effect of GCG to KK becomes not significant by 0.32. This allows EM as a full mediating variable, but should see next requirement. The indirect effect of GCG to KK with mediation earnings management (EM) showed that the indirect effect is not significant, namely path coefficients and p-values of GCG to EM amounted to −0.27 and 0.009, respectively, while path coefficients and p-values of EM to KK amounted to 0.017 and 0.444 ($p > 0.05$), respectively. Thus, there is no effect of mediation on this hypothesis and the second hypothesis is rejected. The results showed that conflict of interest between management and owners of the company may lead to earnings management action. Earnings management arises because of the divergence of interests between the agent and the principal or other parties. Earning management can be minimized through multiple mechanisms of corporate governance, including the board of directors, managerial ownership, and independent board. Agency problem appears when there is different interest between owner and agent.

In addition, bad image of earnings management means there are no positive responses by investors (Suryono 2016). Earnings management only affects market performance and does not affect the financial performance by attracting investors. Example of earnings management could be shift of revenue to the current period. Thus, the absence of earnings management influences on financial performance and, thus, the earnings management (EM) did not prove to mediate the effect of good corporate governance on financial performance.

The third hypothesis shows that the direct effect of GCG to KK showed a significant influence which amounted to 0.25 with p-value of 0.01. After entering the SM and EM variables into the model, the direct effect of GCG to KK becomes not significant by 0.32. This allows EM and SM as full mediating variables, but should see next requirement. Then, identifying the indirect effect of GCG to SM to EM to KK, the indirect effect is not significant to the track because the track SM to EM path coefficients and p-values of 0.014 and 0.455 ($p > 0.05$), respectively. While the path EM to KK path coefficients and p-values are 0.017 and 0.444 ($p > 0.05$) respectively. It is powered with p-values of indirect effect for paths with three segments and showed no significant effect to the amount of 0.499 ($p > 0.05$). Therefore, SM and EM did not prove to mediate the effect of GCG against KK and the third hypothesis is rejected. The results showed the directors are responsible for management of SOEs in order to achieve their objectives, while the independent commissioner is an independent party chosen by stakeholders and assigned to evaluate the performance of the company. The commissioner takes the decision to improve the company performance, not for personal or group interests. The stronger the independent commissioner, the investors and creditors will have more trust to the company; therefore it is easier for the company to get more funding (Rahadian and Hadiprajitno 2014). SOEs will choose financing through debt policy because it has a lower risk compared to issuing stocks and to prevent moral hazard.

High debt doesn't mean bad news, because it could mean the company's expansion and that leverage (debt to assets) had no effect on earnings management (Hartanto and Nugrahanti 2015). The level of debt does not have effect on earnings management. In addition, bad image of earnings management means there is no positive responses by investors (Suryono 2016). Earnings management only affects market performance and does not affect the financial performance by attracting investors. Example of earnings management could be shift of revenue to the current period. Thus, the absence of earnings management influences on financial performance and, thus, the earnings management (EM) and capital structure did not prove to mediate the effect of good corporate governance on financial performance.

5 CONCLUSION

This study examines the effect of good corporate governance on financial performance of the capital structure and earnings management as intervening variable. The following are the conclusions of this study:

1. The results of this study indicate that capital structure variables proved to have full mediating effect of good corporate governance on financial performance. The results in this study are consistent with research conducted by Nirajini and Priya (2013) and Rahadian and Hadiprajitno (2014).
2. The results of this study indicate that earnings management variables proved to not mediate the effect of good corporate governance on financial performance. The results in this study are consistent with research conducted by Suryono (2016), which states that earnings management as bad news is not responded positively by investors.
3. The results of this study indicate that the variables capital structure and earnings management are not proven to mediate the effect of good corporate governance on financial performance. The results in this study are consistent with research conducted by Hartanto and Nugrahanti (2015), which states leverage or use of high debt does not mean bad news, because there may be expansion efforts in that leverage (debt to assets) has no effect on earnings management, while research conducted by Suryono (2016) states that earnings management as bad news is not responded positively by investors.

6 RECOMMENDATIONS

Based on the above conclusions, the recommendations are as follows:

1. The authorities, such as Association of Public Accountants Indonesia (Certified), should make reporting standards provide limits on the use of methods and accounting principles more effectively to avoid being misused by management.
2. Future study is expected to increase the number of independent variables, such as the audit committee, institutional ownership and foreign ownership. The variable proportion of inde-

pendent commissioners and board size is one of the few independent commissioner characteristics, so that further research can incorporate other characteristics of independent directors, such as competence, educational background and experience.

3. For subsequent research, it can increase the number of dependent variables, such as NPM, PER, PBV.
4. For further research, it is expected to increase the number of samples as well as extend the time of the study.
5. For further research, SOEs should be divided by PSO and non PSO.

REFERENCES

Hartanto, D., & Nugrahanti, Y.W. 2015. Pengaruh Struktur Kepemilikan dan Struktur Modal terhadap Manajemen Laba. *Jurnal Ekonomi dan Bisnis,* 9 no. 1. *Jurnal Universitas Muhammadiyah Sumatera Utara*, 1 no. 1.

Idris, A. 2016. *Ekonomi Publik*. Edisi Pertama. Cetakan Pertama. Yogyakarta: Deepublish.

Jamkarani, R.G., & Hozi, T. 2016. Relationship between Accrual Earnings management and Future Financial Performance. *Medwell Journals Internationals Business Management*, 10 no.6:1013–1019.

Jensen, M.C., & Meckling, W.H. 1976. Theory of the Firm: Managerial Behavior, Agency Cost, and Ownership Structure. *Journal of Financial and Economics*, 4 no.2: 305–360.

Nirajini, A., & Priya, K.B. 2013. Impact of Capital Structure on Financial Performance of the Listed Trading Companies in Sri Lanka. *International Journal of Scientific and Research Publications,* 3 no.5.

Patrick, Amaechi, E., Paulinus, E.C., & Nympha, A.N. 2015. The Influence of Corporate Governance on Earnings Management Practices: A Study of Some Selected Quoted Companies in Nigeria. American *Journal of Economics, Finance and Management*, 1 no. 5:482–493.

Rahadian, A., & Hadiprajitno, P.B. 2014. Pengaruh Good Corporate Governance terhadap Struktur Modal Perusahaan pada Perusahaan Manufaktur di BEI periode 2010–2012. *Diponegoro Journal of Accounting,* 3 no. 2:1–12.

Sam'ani. 2008. *Pengaruh Good Corporate Governance and Leverage* Terhadap Kinerja Keuangan Pada Perbankan YangTerdaftar Di Bursa Efek Indonesia (BEI) Tahun 2004–2007.Tesis. Semarang: Program Pascasarjana Universitas Diponegoro.

Shirzad, A., & Haghighi, R. 2015. The effect of corporative leverage on earnings management in Drug industry. *Research Journal of Finance and Accounting*, 6 no. 17.

Sholihin, M., & Ratmono, A. 2013. Analisis SEM-PLS dengan WarpPLS 3.0 *untuk Hubungan Nonlinier dalam Penelitian Sosial dan Bisnis*. Yogyakarta: CV Andi.

Suryono, Y. 2016. Pengaruh Good Corporate Governance, Ukuran Perusahaan, Leverage Perusahaan, dan Pergantian CEO Terhadap Kinerja Perusahaan Yang Dimediasi Oleh Manajemen Laba. *Jurnal Akuntansi dan Manajemen*, 27 no 2: 75–90.

Ujiyantho, A., & Agus, B. 2007. Mekanisme Corporate Governance, Manajemen Laba dan Kinerja Keuangan. Simposium Nasional Akuntansi X. Makasar.

Widyaningdyah, A.U. 2001. Analisis Faktor-faktor yang Berpengaruh Terhadap Earning Management pada Perusahaan Go Public di Indonesia. *Jurnal Akuntansi dan Keuangan*, 3 no. 2: 89–101.

Increasing Management Relevance and Competitiveness – Sukoco et al. (Eds)

The impact of IFRS adoption on earnings management in the banking and mining sectors

H. Musvosvi
Department of Accounting, University of Fort Hare, East London, South Africa

ABSTRACT: This study investigates whether the Adoption of IFRSs-based standards has an effect on Earnings Management specifically in the Banking and Mining sectors. There is however a limitation of the aftermath effects of IFRS in Emerging Economies and also a continuous elimination of Financial and Mining Industries from the samples of previous studies which motivated this study to investigate the impact of IFRS in the Banking and Mining Industries of the companies on the Johannesburg Stock Exchange. This study therefore used a sample of 12 firms listed on the Johannesburg Stock Exchange in both the Mining and Banking industries for a study period from 2002–2004 Pre-IFRS and 2010–2012 Post-IFRS using the Modified Jones Model. In agreement with previous studies the results indicate that Post-IFRS Earnings Management in both Banking and Mining industries reduced. Additionally the study also finds that there is no significant differences regarding Earnings Management comparing large and small size companies. The findings of this study are useful in providing various stakeholders e.g. JSE, investors, accounting and auditing professionals an additional tool for ensuring that financial reporting matches the real economic value of companies. It also creates an awareness for the non-adopting jurisdictions to adopt IFRS.

Keywords: Banking, Earnings Management, Emerging Markets, IFRS, Mining, Modified Jones Model

1 INTRODUCTION

South Africa was settled by Europeans in 1652 and became a British Colony. By 1828, English was the only official language. In 1910, South Africa was granted colonial self-governance and became the independent Union of South Africa (Prather-Kinsey, 2006). However, as a result of the long association with Britain, South Africa's government and legal system reflect that of the British Common law. South Africa has a long history, stretching back to 1976 of the cooperation with and involvement in the International Accounting Standards Board (IASB) (Coetzee, 2014). The legal framework for corporate reporting in South Africa is governed by the 1973 Companies Act (no. 61). In the mid-1990s South Africa's standard setters agreed to use the International standards as the basis for new standards, adapted for local conditions (Sellami & Slimi, 2016). Johannesburg Stock Exchange (JSE) has been adopting IAS with a lag as early as 1995 and in 2005 required all domestic listers to comply with IFRS (Prather-Kinsey, 2006). In fact As of October 2000, JSE required listed companies to prepare their annual financial statements in accordance with the national law applicable to listed companies and to apply either South African statements of GAAP or International Accounting Standards. The JSE released its final amendments to the listings requirements on 15 May 2003. After this review, the JSE required all listed companies to adopt IFRS in financial years commencing on or after 1 January 2005 (Sellami & Slimi 2016). The effects of IFRS on Earnings Management is a widely researched topic. Many studies on the effects of IFRS on Earnings Management usually eliminate financial institutions and mining industries in their data sample. The argument being that firms in the financial sector and mining sector have characteristics that differ fundamentally from other firms (Cai, Rahman, & Courtenay, 2008; Houqe, van Zijl, Dustan & Karim, 2012; Mnif & Slimi, 2016; Peasnell, Pope, & Young, 2000). Roychowdhury (2006) also alludes that mining industries and financial industries are regulated industries and hence should be eliminated from Earnings Management research. In the following sections this study will discuss the Literature Review in section 2 together with the Hypothesis Development. Section 3 talks about the Methodology employed in this research. Results are discussed in section 4 and Section 5 the Conclusion and Recommendations.

2 LITERATURE REVIEW AND HYPOTHESIS DEVELOPMENT

Motivated by Onalo, Mohd & Ahmad (2014) whose study empirically investigate the effects of IFRS-based standards on Earnings Management specifically in the banking and mining industries. Onalo et al., (2014) study finds that the use of IFRS impacted more significantly and positively on the quality of accounting information of banks than the previous local standards for two countries in their study i.e. Nigeria and Malaysia. The study therefore recommend that globally, IFRSs should be adopted as the standard for the preparation and reporting of financial statements. Other scholars such as Ajit, Malik, and Verma (2013) indicates that industry wise categorization shows that the companies in the line of business viz..., construction and mining etc. are more involved in relatively high levels of Earnings Management. However on the other hand vast of the studies that focus on the effects of IFRS on Earnings Management on non-financial and non-mining industries have found that for example Post IFRS Nnadi, Omoteso, & Yu, (2015) provides evidence on the effects of regulatory environment on financial reporting quality of Hong Kong companies which are cross listed in mainland China. Sellami & Slimi (2016) study on South African non-financial institutions indicates that Post IFRS Earnings Management decreased and these results suggests that mandatory transition to IFRS contribute to an improvement in the quality of accounting information. Dayanandan, Donker, Ivanof & Karahan (2016)'s study empirical evidence shows that IFRS adoption decrease in Earnings Management is lower during the post-IFRS period. However the results hold for firms in Western Europe. Callao & Jarne (2007) results show that Earnings Management has intensified since the adoption of IFRS in Europe. Furthermore Zeghal (2011) mandatory adoption of IFRS has decreased Earnings Management level. Based on the above I formulated the following hypothesis.

H1: Earnings Management in both the Mining and Banking Industry is lower Post IFRS.

Studies show that large companies manipulate Earnings of the company to avoid reporting negative Earnings. Albrecth & Richardson (1990) find evidence that larger firms are less motivated to smooth Earnings than smaller firms. Lee & Choi (2002) also find that company size has a role to play in discriminating between companies that do not manage Earnings to avoid losses. Indicating that small firms tend to manage Earnings more frequently to avoid reporting losses than larger firms. Ali, Noor, Khurshid & Mahmood (2015) study reveals that there is a positive and significant impact of firm size on Earnings Management. Lukani (2013) shows that there is no significant differences concerning Earnings Management initiatives and practices amongst large and small size companies. Burgstahler & Dichev 1997 results show that large firms and small ones manage their Earnings in order to avoid small losses. Furthermore Degeorge & Zeckhauser (1999) indicated that large firms manipulated Earnings of the company in order to avoid negative Earnings.

H2: There is no significant differences regarding Earnings Management comparing large and small size companies.

3 METHODOLOGY

The Dependent variable in this study is Earnings Management. And the Independent Variable is IFRS measured using a dichotomous variable coded as 0 before the year 2005 and 1 after IFRS adoption year i.e. after 2005. Size is also an Independent variable measured using the natural logarithm of Total Assets. The two control variables in this study are growth which is measured as current year sales minus prior year sales multiplied by 100% and Leverage which is measured as the total debt per year divided by total assets per year. The study employs the Modified Jones Model which decomposes total accruals into non-discretionary and discretionary accruals. The Discretionary accruals are then used as a proxy for Earnings Management. The estimating process is as follows:

Step 1

Consistent with previous studies of Earnings Management

Total Accruals are computed as:

$$TA_t = \frac{(\Delta CA_t - \Delta CASH_t - \Delta CL_t - DEP_t)}{(A_t - 1)}$$

where

TA_t = Total Accurals in year t, scaled by total assets as t − 1

ΔCA_t = Change in current assets in year t and t − 1

$\Delta Cash$ = Change in cash and cash equivalents in year t and t − 1

ΔCL_t = Change in current liabilities in year t and t − 1

ΔDCL_t = Change in short-term debt included current liabilities in year t, and t − 1.

Step 2

Dechow, Sloan, and Sweeney (1995) states that the estimates of $\alpha_1, \alpha_2, \alpha_3$ and nondiscretionary accruals during the estimation period (in which no systematic Earnings Management is hypothesized) are those obtained from the original Jones Model. Therefore:

$$\frac{TA_t}{A_t - 1} = \alpha_1\left(\frac{1}{A_t - 1}\right) + \alpha_2\left(\frac{\Delta REV_t}{A_t - 1}\right) + \alpha_3\left(\frac{PPE_t}{A_t - 1}\right)$$

where

TA_t = Total Accruals in year t divided by total assets in year $t - 1$,
ΔREV_t = Revenues in year t less revenues in year $t - 1$ scaled by total assets at $t - 1$.
PPE_t = Gross property plant and equipment in year t, scaled by total assets at $t - 1$,
A_{t-1} = Total assets in year $t - 1$,
α_1, α_2, and α_3 = Ordinary Least Squares (OLS) estimates of α_1, α_2, and α_3.

Step 3

$$NDA_t = \alpha_1\left(\frac{1}{A_t - 1}\right) + \alpha_2(\Delta REV_t - \Delta REC_t) + \alpha_3(PPE_t)$$

where

NDA_t = Nondiscretionary accruals in year t scaled by total assets at $t - 1$
α_1, α_2, and α_3 = Company specific parameters
A_{t-1} = Total assets in year $t - 1$
ΔREV_t = Revenues in year t less revenues in year $t - 1$ scaled by total assets at $t - 1$
PPE_t = Gross property plant and equipment in year t, scaled by total assets $t - 1$.

The discretionary accruals can then be calculated when the nondiscretionary accruals are subtracted from the total accruals. The calculated discretionary accruals are a proxy for the level of Earnings Management that is applied within a company.

Step 4

Regression Equation processed in SPSS reads as follows:

$$DA = \alpha_1 + \alpha_2 IFRS_t + \alpha_3 SIZE_{i,t} + \alpha_4 LEV_{i,t} + \alpha_5 GWTH_{it} + \varepsilon_{i,t}$$
$$DACC_t = TACC_t - NDACC_t$$

where

$TACC_t - NDACC_t$ = discretionary accruals
IFRS = the accounting standard used, (0 = SA GAAP and 1 = IFRS)
ε = An error term
$\alpha_1, \alpha_2, \alpha_3, \alpha_4, \alpha_5$, = Regression coefficients (calculated automatically in SPSS)
t = Year index, range from 2002–2004 and 2010–2012
i = Firm index, using the company key
LEV = Leverage
SIZE = Company Size
GWTH = Growth.

4 RESULTS AND DISCUSSION

Table 1 above show the regression results. Consistent with prior literature Onalo, (2014); Sellami, ((2016) & Callao, (2007) that says that IFRS adoption has a negative impact on Earnings Management this study agrees with that notion as ($p < 0.05$) and also there is a negative coefficient indicating a negative direction for the impact of IFRS on Earnings Management. The possible reason being that IFRS in the financial services sector is more stringent as far as financial reporting is concerned due to the complexity of its products and contracts. As for the mining sector, although IFRS 6 was issued as an accounting standard for the extractive industries, it only covers the recognition, measurement and reporting of expenditure in the Exploration and Evaluation phase of investment, and hence does not include expenditures in either pre or post Exploration and Evaluation (Noel, 2010). Thus it is evident that IFRS 6 only has a limited remit in terms of reducing the diversity in accounting practices amongst firms in the extractive industries, as it does not impact accounting and reporting matters associated with the other three investment stages (Abdo, 2016).

The second hypothesis in this study stated that there is no significant differences regarding Earnings Management comparing large and small size companies. And in agreement the Size variable is not significant ($p > 0.1$).

Table 1. SPSS regression results.

	Unstandadised coefficient		Standadise coefficient		
Model	B	Std. Error	Beta	t	sig
(constant)	0.533	0.291		1.831	0.072
IFRS	−0.340	0.076	−0.489	−4.481	*0.000
LEVERAGE	0.041	0.067	0.065	0.619	0.538
SIZE	−0.013	0.018	−0.080	−0.732	0.467
GROWTH	0.120	0.000	0.103	0.991	0.325

* Significant.

The Control variables in this study both Leverage and Growth show an insignificant relationship with Earnings Management.

5 CONCLUSION AND RECOMMENDATIONS

The aim of the study was to investigate the impact of IFRSs based standards on Earnings Management using a sample of 12 JSE listed Mining and Banking industries. Consistent with previous studies this study finds that IFRS has a negative effect on Earnings Management and that there is no significant differences regarding Earnings Management comparing Large and small size companies. The notable limitation of this study is that the results cannot be generalized to all Emerging Economies as countries differ fundamentally in terms of various institutional characteristics and Economic growth. I suggest that future research consider the impact of other Accounting quality variables over a longer period of time.

REFERENCES

Abdo, H. 2016. Accounting for Extractive Industries: Has IFRS 6 Harmonised Accounting Practices by Extractive Industries? *Australian Accounting Review* 26(4): 346–359.

Ajit, D., Malik, S.A.R.A.T., & Verma, V.K. 2013. Earnings Management in India. *SEBI DRG Study*.

Albrecht, W.D., & Richardson, F.M. 1990. Income smoothing by economy sector. *Journal of Business Finance & Accounting* 17(5): 713–730.

Ali, U., Noor, M.A., Khurshid, M.K., & Mahmood, A. 2015. Impact of Firm Size on Earnings Management: A Study of Textile Sector of Pakistan.

Burgstahler, D., & Dichev, I. 1997. Earnings Management to avoid Earnings decreases and losses. *Journal of accounting and economics 24*(1): 99–126.

Cai, L., Rahman, A.R., & Courtenay, S.M. 2008. The effect of IFRS and its enforcement on Earnings Management: An international comparison.

Callao, S., Jarne, J.I., & Laínez, J.A. 2007. Adoption of IFRS in Spain: Effect on the comparability and relevance of financial reporting. *Journal of International Accounting, Auditing and Taxation* 16(2): 148–178.

Coetzee, S.A., Schmulian, A., & Kotze, L. 2014. Communication apprehension of South African accounting students: The effect of culture and language. *Issues in Accounting Education* 29(4): 505–525.

Dayanandan, A., Donker, H., Donker, H., Ivanof, M., Ivanof, M., & Karahan, G. 2016. IFRS and accounting quality: legal origin, regional, and disclosure impacts. *International Journal of Accounting and Information Management* 24(3): 296–316.

Dechow, P.M., Sloan, R.G., & Sweeney, A.P. 1995. Detecting Earnings Management. *Accounting review*, 193–225.

Degeorge, F., Patel, J., & Zeckhauser, R. 1999. Earnings Management to exceed thresholds. *The Journal of Business* 72(1): 1–33.

Houqe, M.N., van Zijl, T., Dunstan, K., & Karim, A.W. 2012. The effect of IFRS adoption and investor protection on Earnings quality around the world. *The International Journal of Accounting* 47(3): 333–355.

Lee, B.B., & Choi, B. 2002. Company size, auditor type, and Earnings Management. Journal of ForensicAccounting, III, 27–50.

Llukani, T. 2013. Earnings Management and firm size: an empirical analyze in Albanian market. *European Scientific Journal* 9 (16).

Nnadi, M., Omoteso, K., & Yu, Y. 2015. Does regulatory environment affect Earnings Management in transitional economies? An empirical examination of the financial reporting quality of cross-listed firms of China and Hong Kong. In *Neo-Transitional Economics* 245–276. Emerald Group Publishing Limited.

Noël, C., Ayayi, A.G., & Blum, V. 2010. The European Union's accounting policy analyzed from an ethical perspective: The case of petroleum resources, prospecting and evaluation. *Critical Perspectives on Accounting* 21(4): 329–341.

Onalo, U., Lizam, M., & Kaseri, A. 2014. The effects of changes in accounting standards on Earnings Management of Malaysia and Nigeria banks. *European Journal of Accounting Auditing and Finance Research, 2*(8): 15–42.

Peasnell, K.V., Pope, P.F., & Young, S. 2000. Detecting Earnings Management using cross-sectional abnormal accruals models. *Accounting and Business research, 30*(4): 313–326.

Prather-Kinsey, J. 2006. Developing countries converging with developed-country accounting standards: Evidence from South Africa and Mexico. *The international journal of accounting, 41*(2): 141–162.

Roy Chowdhury, S. 2006. Earnings Management through real activities manipulation. *Journal of accounting and economics, 42*(3): 335–370.

Sellami, Y.M., & Slimi, I. 2016. The effect of the mandatory adoption of IAS/IFRS on Earnings Management: Empirical evidence from South Africa. *International Journal of Accounting and Economics Studies, 4*(2): 87–95.

Zéghal, D., Chtourou, S., & Sellami, Y.M. 2011. An analysis of the effect of mandatory adoption of IAS/IFRS on Earnings Management. *Journal of international accounting, auditing and taxation, 20*(2), 61–72.

Increasing Management Relevance and Competitiveness – Sukoco et al. (Eds)
© 2018 Taylor & Francis Group, London, ISBN 978-0-8153-7455-8

Managerial ownership and corporate diversification in the family and non-family businesses

T. Perdana & N. Fitdiarini
Universitas Airlangga, Surabaya, Indonesia

ABSTRACT: The purpose of this research to examine the impact of managerial ownership on firm's level of diversification at family firms and non-family firms listed on the Indonesia Stock Exchange. The samples of this research consisted of 120 samples from 30 family firms and 720 samples from 180 non-family firms listed on the Indonesia Stock Exchange during 2010–2013. Dependent variable was level of diversification and the independent variable used managerial ownership. This research used control variables, such as financial leverage, Return on Assets (ROA), business risk, firm size and institutional ownership. The empirical results of Ordinary Least Square regressions show that managerial ownership has significant impact with positive direction on level of diversification in family firms (family business), while in non-family firms (non-family business) it has significant impact with negative direction.

1 INTRODUCTION

Family companies are a distinct phenomenon in the business world. In Indonesia, 96% or 159,000 out of 165,000 companies are family companies (Pikiran Rakyat 2006). Family firms also have a significant share of the country's revenue. Poza (2010) says that 80%–98% of business in the world is a family business. In addition, family businesses contribute 75% of GDP (Gross Domestic Product) in various countries. Indonesia is also one of the countries that hides a surprising fact about the phenomenon of family business, which is that family business plays a vital role in moving the wheels of the Indonesian economy. The goals of various companies, although with different family ownership structures (family business and non-family business) are the same. Both are business organizations that have a goal to maximize the wealth of shareholders or owners of the company (Sudana 2011: 7). Recent research has indicated that the unique context of family enterprises leads to differences between family and non-family business in terms of strategies, including internationalization strategies, innovation strategies, and acquisition strategies. In addition, Anderson and Reeb (2003) support that there are also differences between family and non-family business within the context of a diversified strategy. According to Hitt, Ireland and Hoskisson (2013: 148), business diversification strategies are corporate-level strategies that focus on actions to gain competitive advantage by selecting and managing different business groups in multiple market industries.

Companies use diversification strategies to achieve value creation through economies of scope, financial economies, or market power (Barney 1991; Montgomery, 1985). In addition to the benefits already mentioned, the diversification strategy also has costs that must be incurred by the company to achieve the expected benefits. These costs include costs associated with the incidence of difficulties related to coordination, asymmetric information and incentive misalignment (Denis, Denis and Yost 2002). Agency problems in the family business arise when the equity ratio of a family shareholder is large enough for effective control within the firm. The family shareholders will be concentrated with the interests of the family alone, not the interests of minority shareholders (Chu 2009). In terms of diversification, it can generate good opportunities for speculation and exploitation of minority shareholders' interests (Claessens et al. 2002). In contrast to what happens in non-family businesses, where the level of diversification tends to be lower than that of family businesses, the diversification strategy that managers use in non-family businesses is an indication of managers acting in their entrenchment. The main shareholder can reduce the opportunistic behavior of the manager by using managerial ownership to solve the problem (Lin et al. 2014).

In non-family businesses, managerial ownership can have a positive impact in reducing conflicts related to agency problems and maximizing corporate value. As argued by Jensen and Meckling (1976), based on agency theory, principals must encourage managers to act in the interests of shareholders by overseeing managers (which would incur agency costs) or by increasing incentive alignment through alternatives that may include managerial ownership or stock options. The interest perspective in agency theory suggests that diversification helps owners, managers and their families to achieve their goals while ensuring the survival of the company (Chen and Yu 2012).

Research on diversification has indeed been done, but few have examined the effect of managerial ownership on future levels of diversification with samples of family and non-family enterprises. In addition, most previous studies have shown that there are different relationships between ownership and diversification structures. This study examines the effect of managerial ownership on the level of corporate diversification, using panel data of annual reports of 30 family firms and 180 non-family enterprises over the period 2010–2013.

2 LITERATURE REVIEW

2.1 *Diversification*

Diversification is one approach to corporate-level corporate strategy. According to Jusuf et al. (2013: 129), diversification is the process of entering one or more different industries with their core or original industries to find ways to use company-specific competencies in increasing value to customers and sustaining competitive advantage. A diversified company operates in one or more industries in an effort to increase long-term profitability. Each industry entered by the company will build an operating division or business unit that is essentially a self-contained company that executes a number of value chain functions required to create and sell products to a particular market. In order to increase profitability, a diversification strategy must enable the company or its business units to stand alone in performing their value chain functions at a lower cost or through businesses that produce higher differentiation and premium prices.

The immediate benefits of implementing a diversified strategy, as expressed by George and Kabir (2011), are companies in a single business unit that can share resources such as brand, managerial capabilities, customer loyalty and technological innovation with other business units. The company's diversification strategy is also capable of creating shareholder value by reducing failures in products, labor and the financial markets (Martin and Sayrak 2003).

Lewellen (1971) argued that diversification can reduce the variance in future cash flows by improving the debt capacity to reduce the possibility of financial distress. A diversified company can reduce taxes and transaction costs by transferring funds from one surplus business unit to a deficit business unit (Bhide 1993). According to Berger and Ofek (1995), this is due to an internal transaction mechanism. For diversified firms, having an internal market to fund the company's capital needs offers valuable benefits. Internally-acquired capital is cheaper than funds raised from external capital markets.

2.2 *Agency theory*

In relation to ownership. there are two types of agency problems, namely:

1. Type I, between management (agents) and shareholders (owners) (Jensen and Meckling 1976). This type often occurs in non-family business.
2. Type II, between majority and minority shareholders (Shleifer and Vishny 1997). This agency problem occurs when managers and owners in a family business are the same (most managers are family members).

In non-family businesses, it makes managers sometimes prefer short-term profits and exhibits behaviors that are inconsistent with shareholders or owners' desires to meet individual benefits (Lin et al. 2014). Even within a family business, diversification can generate good opportunities for speculation and means to exploit the interests of minority shareholders (Claessens et al. 2002). Shleifer and Vishny (1986) said that diversification is very beneficial for managers because it allows them to reduce personal risks, increase power and remuneration and make their roles indispensable.

2.3 *Managerial ownership*

In a non-family business, agency problems can be minimized or even eliminated when the company owner is also the manager of the company because the interests of the manager have been aligned with the interests of the shareholders, i.e. with managerial ownership (Singh and Davidson 2003). In addition, managers can also feel the impact of various decisions taken, including decisions related to diversification strategies. Therefore, the level of diversification in non-family businesses tends to be low due to the supervision of major shareholders through managerial ownership (Lin et al. 2014).

May (1995) supports the argument that managers who invest a large percentage have a strong motive for lowering their personal risk through a diversified strategy. Given these motives, diversification will generate opportunities to achieve family interests by exploiting the interests of minority shareholders (Chu 2009).

2.4 *Incentives alignment and management entrenchment hypothesis*

Incentives alignment hypothesis predicts that managers with larger shareholdings have greater incentives to act in the interests of minority shareholders. According to Lin el al. (2014), the presence of managerial ownership will tend to reduce the opportunistic behavior of managers through diversification strategies. Therefore, based on the theory of incentives alignment hypothesis, non-family business managerial ownership negatively affects the level of corporate diversification.

Hypothesis shows that managers with high managerial ownership have greater control over the company, allowing them to act in their own interests. These problems are in harmony with what happens in the family business. In a family business, high managerial ownership by a manager who is also a member of the family makes him or she act opportunistically and harass minority shareholders. Associated with the diversification strategy, Claessens et al. (2002) state that the strategy generates opportunities for speculation and exploitation of minority shareholders' interests. Therefore, the theory of entrenchment hypothesis is evident in the family business. In addition, it supports a positive relationship between managerial ownership and corporate diversification.

2.5 *Family business*

A family business is a family-owned company and is managed by several family members. Susanto et al. (2007: 4) mentions that, according to business terminology, family companies are divided into two kinds, family-owned enterprise (FOE), and family business enterprise (FBE). In Indonesia, most of the family companies are FBE. However, as the competition and business demands grow, high competencies are needed to manage the company. If the need for such competence is not met by family members, then professionals from outside the circle of family members are required. Therefore, it is not uncommon for family firms to metamorphose from FBE to FOE.

3 RESEARCH MODEL

Below is the research model of the study.

Family Business:

$$DIVi,t+1 = \alpha 0 + \alpha 1 FBOWNi,t + \alpha 2 DEBTi,t + \alpha 3 ROAi,t + \alpha 4 RISKi,t + \alpha 5 SIZEi,t + \alpha 6 INSTi,t + \varepsilon i,t \quad (1)$$

Non-family Business:

$$DIVi, t+1 = \beta 0 + \beta 1\ NFBOWNi, t + \beta 2 DEBTi,t + \beta 3 ROAi,t + \beta 4 RISKi,t + \beta 5 SIZEi,t + \beta 6 INSTi,t + vi, t \quad (2)$$

where DIVi, t + 1: company diversification rate i in period t + 1; FBOWNi,t: managerial ownership of family business in period t; NFBOWNi,t: managerial ownership of non-family businesses in period t; DEBTi,t: financial leverage of firm i in period t; ROAi,t: return on assets of firm i in period t; RISKi t: business risk of company i in period t; SIZEi,t: firm size i in period t; INSTi,t: institutional ownership of investor company i in period t.

4 DATA AND ANALYSIS

Based on data that have been measured, it is necessary to do an analysis to determine the effect of independent variables on the dependent. Here are the results of regression tests in family and non-family business.

The results on the regression table indicate the family business is becoming more diversified and the theory of entrenchment hypothesis arises. In addition to personal interests, managers who are members of the family will also act for the benefit of the family, but, in the end, it is actually miserable minority shareholders.

Table 1. Regression analysis at family business.

Dependent variable	Independent variable	Coef	SE	Sig.
DIV (i,t+1)	(Constant)	–0,653	0,612	0,289
	OWN	–2,019	0,477	0,000
	ROA	–0,925	0,397	0,022
	RISK	–1,278	0,611	0,040
	DEBT	0,096	0,124	0,440
	INST	–0,032	0,127	0,799
	SIZE	0,048	0,020	0,018

Table 2. Regression analysis at non-family business.

Dependent variable	Independent variable	Coef	SE	Sig.
DIV (i,t+1)	(Constant)	1,548	0,187	0,000
	OWN	0,327	0,105	0,002
	ROA	0,022	0,084	0,794
	RISK	0,102	0,039	0,010
	DEBT	0,020	0,023	0,382
	INST	0,003	0,046	0,946
	SIZE	–0,026	0,006	0,000

These results suggest that the theory of incentive alignment hypothesis appear in non-family businesses. Managerial ownership is able to align interests between managers and shareholders. Thus, managers will not adopt unfavorable diversification, or even bring harm to the company (value decreasing).

5 CONCLUSION

Managerial ownership has a significant effect on the positive direction towards the level of diversification within the family business. It can be said that, the greater the share ownership by managers, the greater the level of diversification of the company. Meanwhile, managerial ownership has a significant effect on the negative direction of diversification in non-family business. It can be argued that, the greater the share ownership by managers, the smaller the level of the company's diversification. The results of this study can be a consideration for investors in making decisions by understanding and differentiating the impact of managerial ownership on the level of diversification that companies take in family and non-family companies, so that investors are more careful and can take investment decisions appropriately.

REFERENCES

Anderson, R.C. & Reeb, D.M. 2003. Founding-Family Ownership and Firm Performance: Evidence from the S&P 500. *Journal of Finance*, 58:1301–1328.

Anderson, R.C. & Reeb, D.M. 2003. Founding-Family Ownership, Corporate Diversification, and Firm Leverage. *Journal of Law and Economics*, 46, no. 2:653–684.

Anderson, R.C., Duru, A., & Reeb, D. 2012. Investment Policy in Family Controlled Firms. *Journal of Banking and Finance*, 36:1744–1758.

Andres, C. 2008. Family Ownership, Financing Constraints, and Investment Decisions. *Working Paper*. University of Bonn.

Barney, J. 1991. Firm Resources and Sustained Competitive Advantage. *Journal of Management*, 17 no.1: 99–120.

Berger, P.G. & Ofek, E. 1995. Diversification's Effect on Firm Value. *Journal of Financial Economics*, 37: 39–65.

Chen, C.J. & J.Y. C-M.J. Yu. 2012. Managerial Ownership, Diversification, and Firm Performance: Evidence from Emerging Market. *International Business Review*, 21:518–534.

Chu, W. 2009. Family Ownership and Firm Performance: Influence of Family Management, Family Control and Firm Size. *Asia Pacific Journal Management*, 28: 833–851.

Chua, J.H., Chrisman, J.J., & Sharma, P. 1999. Defining the Family Business by Behavior. *Entrepreneurship: Theory and Practice*, 23, no. 4: 19–39.

Classens, S., Djankov, S., Fan, J., & Lang, L., 2002. Disentangling the incentives and entrenchment effects of large shareholdings. Journal of Finance 57, 2741–2771.

Denis, D.J., Denis, D. K., & Sarin, A. 1997. Agency Problem, Equity Ownership, and Corporate Diversification. *Journal of Finance*, 52 no. 1: 135–160.

Denis, D.J., Denis, D.K., & Sarin, A. 1999. Agency Theory and the Influence of Equity Ownership Structure on Corporate Diversification Strategies. *Strategic Management Journal*, 20, no.11:1071–1076.

Denis, D.J., Denis, D.K., & Yost, K. 2002. Global Diversification, Industrial Diversification, and Firm Value. *Journal of Finance*. Vol. 57, No. 5, pp. 1951–1979.

George, R., & Kabir. (2011). Heterogenity in Business Groups and the Corporate Diversification-Firm Performance Relationship. *Journal of Business Research.*

Hitt, M.A., Ireland, R.D., & Hoskisson, R.E. 2013. *The Management of Strategy: Concepts and Cases*. Canada: South-Western.

Jensen, M.C. & Meckling, W. H. 1976. Theory of the Firm: Managerial Behavior, Agency Cost, and Ownership Structure. *Journal of Financial Economics*, 3: 305–360.

Lewellen, W.G. 1971. A Pure Financial Rationale for the Conglomerate Merger. *Journal of Finance*, 26 no. 2: 521–537.

Lin, T.-J., Chang, L., Hou, C-P., & Chou, P-R. 2014. The Dynamic Relationship between Managerial Ownership and Corporate Diversification: Evidence for Family and Non-Family Business. *International Journal of Economics and Finance*, 6 no.5:84–95.

Martin, J.D. & Akin, S. 2003. Corporate Diversification and Shareholder Value: a Survey of Recent Literature. *Journal of Corporate Finance*, 9:37–57.

Montgomery, C.A. 1985. Product-Market Diversification and Market Power. *Academy of Management Journal*, 28 no.4:789–798.

Montgomery, C.A. 1994. Corporate Diversification. *Journal of Economic Perspectives*, 8 no. 3:163–178.

Poza, E. J. 2004. *Family Business*. Ohio: South-Western.

Sudana, I.M. 2011. *Manajemen Keuangan*. Surabaya: Erlangga.

Shleifer, A., & Vishny, R., 1986. Large shareholders and corporate control. Journal of Political Economy 94, 461–488.

Susanto, A.B., Wijanarko, H., Susanto, P., & Mertosono, S. 2007. *The Jakarta Consulting Group on Family Business*. Jakarta: The Jakarta Consulting Group.

Udaya, J., Wennadi, L.Y., & Lembaga. 2013. *Manajemen Stratejik*. Jakarta: Graha Ilmu.

Villangola, B. & Amit, R. 2004. How Do Family Ownership, Control, and Management Affect Firm Value? *EFA 2004 Maastricht Meetings Paper*, No. 3620.

Wulf, J. 1998. Influence and Inefficiency in the Internal Capital Market: Theory and Evidence. *Unpublished Manuscript, the Wharton School, University of Pennsylvania.*

Increasing Management Relevance and Competitiveness – Sukoco et al. (Eds)
© 2018 Taylor & Francis Group, London, ISBN 978-0-8153-7455-8

CEO gender, corporate finance decisions, and performance

R.H. Setianto & J. Mahbubi
Department of Management, Universitas Airlangga, Surabaya, Indonesia

ABSTRACT: This study aims to determine the effect of CEO gender on corporate financial decisions namely, investment decisions, financing decisions (leverage) and corporate performance. This study is made up from 478 firms year data of 151 manufacturing companies listed on the Indonesia Stock Exchange for the period 2010–2014. By employing linear regression, the results indicate that companies led by female CEOs tend to have lower investment and leverage level compared to those led by male CEOs. On the other hand, female CEOs contribute better to the company's performance compared to male CEOs.

1 INTRODUCTION

Issues on women's emancipation and gender equality are interesting topics around the world, including Indonesia. In the context of Indonesian companies, based on the data from the Indonesia Stock Exchange, there is a growing trend of increasing the level of gender diversity in boards of directors, measured by the ratio of the number of female directors to the total number of directors, In 2011, the average number of female board directors was only 7.52%, while, in 2014, a significant increase was recorded, up to 21.65% of board members in Indonesia were women. More specific research conducted by the Center for Governance, Institutions and Organizations (CGIO) found that 11.6% of directors' positions are held by female directors with the figure for female CEOs standing at 6.5% alone. Further, research conducted by the CGIO contained within the Indonesia Boardroom Diversity Report (2012), concluded that Indonesia tops the list in Asia for the percentage of female directors, with 11.6%, more than Hong Kong, China, Malaysia, and even Singapore.

Regardless of the increasing trend of women on the board of directors, it is undeniable that the gender of the CEO is still often a debate, especially in a country like Indonesia that performs eastern customs. Very conservative companies still claim that top management positions must be held by male directors. But, in its development, the increasing rights of gender equality and women's emancipation movement have changed the paradigm.

This development should not escape the influence of psychological differences between men and women in a financial decision-making company. In Huang and Kisgen's financial and psychological literature (2013: 822), it was found that male directors had a higher overconfidence rate than women in taking corporate financial decisions with a 2% lower return announcement than female directors. This becomes an interesting finding when CEO gender can influence financial decisions and the return, or profitability, of a company.

Increasing numbers of females in the top level of management raises the question of whether there are any differences between male and female CEOs in managing a company. In this paper, we investigate the influence of CEO's gender on corporate financial decisions in Indonesia, namely investment policy and financing policy. Furthermore, this paper also investigates the impact of female CEOs on firms' financial performance.

This study is related to earlier studies that investigated the relation between gender diversity on corporate decision and performance. For instance, a study conducted by Weber and Zulehner (2010) found that increasing gender diversity on the board of directors resulted in increasing acquisitions and performance in Norwegian firms. A more recent study conducted by Faccio et al. (2016) found that women CEOs tend to take on less risk compared to their male counterparts. On the other hand, research conducted by Adams and Ragunathan (2013) and Berger et al. (2014) on the banking industry documented that more women on a board of directors is associated with higher risk than those banks with fewer female board members. While Sila et al. (2016) found no relationship between gender diversity and risk.

This study contributes to the existing literature in that research on this topic has only been done in developed countries like the United States, making this research an exciting new topic to be studied in a country with an emerging economy like Indonesia.

2 DATA AND METHODOLOGY

This study utilizes the data of manufacturing firms listed on the Indonesian Stock Exchange from 2010 to 2014. The selected firms are firms with a CEO tenure of a minimum two years. The transition years are excluded from this study to avoid bias. Most of the data was retrieved from the listed companies' financial reports posted on the Indonesia Stock Exchange (IDX) website.

$$Y_{i,t+1} = \beta_0 + \beta_1 GENDER_{i,t} + \theta x_{i,t} + \varepsilon_{i,t} \quad (1)$$

where, $Y_{i,t+1}$ is the dependent variable, namely, investment policy as measured by ratio of capital expenditure to total asset, financing policy as measured by ratio of debt to total assets, and financial performance as measured by return on asset.

$GENDER_{i,t}$ is a dummy variable which is equal to 1 if firms are headed by female CEOs and/or CFOs, and equal to 0 otherwise. Female CFOs can be considered and included as female CEOs because most of the financial decisions are made by CFOs. This is done to increase the sample of female CEOs in the study, given the small number of female CEOs in Indonesia.

Control variables consist of firm AGE, as a natural logarithm of the number of years since incorporation, and market to book value ratio.

3 RESULTS AND ANALYSIS

3.1 *Descriptive statistics*

The final sample of this study employed 150 manufacturing companies with a total of 478 observations consisting of 73 observations for female CEOs and 405 observations for male CEOs with the following sample description details (Table 1).

As presented in Table 2, average investment level (INV) of manufacturing companies in Indonesia, calculated by the ratio of capital expenditure to total assets, is 0.0745. The average investment made by firms with male CEOs exceeds the industry average overall of 0.068, while the average company's investment with female CEOs is below the industry average as a whole at 0.045. This average difference is significant at the 1% level, indicating that the companies' aggressiveness rate with male CEOs in investment decisions is significantly higher when compared to companies with female CEOs.

Table 1. Sample description.

Gender CEO	Number of firms	Number of observations
Female CEO	7	25
Female CFO	15	48
Male CEO and CFO	128	405
Total	150	478

Table 2. Descriptive statistics.

	Mean		
Variables	Industry	Male	Female
INV	0.0745	0.068	0.045
LEV	0.5504	0.469	0.419
ROA	0.0594	0.050	0.073
AGE	3.477	3.481	3.481
MTB	2.1891	2.51	1.78

For financial leverage (LEV) variables proxied with debt to total asset ratio, both firms with male and female CEOs have an average below the industry average of overall manufacturing firms with a value of 0.5504. Companies with male CEOs have an average of 0.469, while companies with female CEOs have an average of 0.419. This average difference is significant at the 5% level, indicating that companies with female CEOs are significantly less likely to use debt as a source of financing than firms with male CEOs.

Manufacturing companies in Indonesia have an average value of performance (ROA) of 0.0594, calculated with the profitability ratio on return on assets. Companies with female CEOs have a higher average performance than the average firm overall of 0.073, while firms with male CEOs have average performance lower than the average company overall of 0.050. This average difference is significant at the 5% level, indicating that, on average, companies with female CEOs perform significantly better than companies with male CEOs.

Based on the independent sample t-test represented in Table 3, it was found that the average investment made by male CEOs was higher than the average investment of female CEOs, as well as the industry average, but the result was that male CEOs tend to have a lower return on assets. Performance of female CEOs was even below the industry's average performance. This shows an overestimation by a male CEO with a disproportionate return. These findings support Huang and Kisgen (2013), who says that male CEOs are more overconfident than female CEOs. This can happen because the male CEO has a tendency to do individualistic decision-making or make a decision based on himself, which shows high confidence over the decision made.

3.2 *Regression analysis*

Column 1 of Table 4 shows the first model regression results that measure the effect of the CEO gender (GENDER) and the control variables on the firms' investment decision (INV). In this model, the probability value of the independent variable (GENDER) is less than 0.05 with a coefficient of –0.022, indicating that the female CEO has a negative effect on the investment decision of the company (INV). Column 2 shows the effect of CEO gender (GENDER) on corporate financing decisions (LEV). In this model, the significance value of the independent variable (GENDER) is less than 0.05, with a coefficient of –0.047, indicating that the female CEO has a negative effect on the companies' funding decision (LEV). Column 3 shows the effect of CEO gender (GENDER) on company performance (ROA). In this model, the probability value of independent variables (GENDER) is less than 0.05, with a coefficient of 0.023, which indicates that the female CEO has a positive effect on company performance (ROA).

3.3 *CEO gender and investment decisions*

CEO gender has a negative effect on investment decisions. This suggests that female CEOs tend to be more moderate in corporate investment decisions. The results of this study support previous research by Huang and Kisgen (2013) which states that female CEOs tend to execute fewer investment decisions. These results are supported by significant mean difference test results in which firms with female CEOs have a lower average capital expenditure to total assets ratio than company with male CEOs, and with the industry average. Based on the regression coefficient, companies with female CEOs invested 2.2% less than male CEOs.

One possible explanation for this result may be psychological and behavioral factors. Female CEOs are believed to have more cautious behavioral traits, and are risk averse. Previous literature concluded that, in general, female CEOs have more conservative thinking in the sense that they are more likely to invest in less risky portfolios with investment retention behavior. In contrast male CEOs tend to be more aggressive in their investment behavior.

3.4 *CEO gender and financing decisions*

CEO gender has a negative effect on financing decisions. This suggests companies with female CEOs tend to use less debt than firms with male CEOs. This result supports previous research by Huang (2013) which states that companies with female CEOs tend to have lower debt levels. The regression results in Column 2 of Table 4 are in line with the results shown in the independent sample t-test in which companies with female CEOs have a lower debt ratio than companies with male CEOs, and the industry average. Based on the regression coefficient, female CEOs use debt as a source of financing 4.7% less than male CEOs.

A possible explanation for this result, related to the psychological and behavioral corporate factors, is that female CEOs tend to keep a lower level of debt, as debt is one of the risky financing sources i.e. the higher the level of debt, the higher the bankruptcy risk of the company, and there is an inherent risk to debt, namely interest charges and default risk. This explanation is also consistent with the pecking order theory which states that

Table 3. Independent sample t-test.

	Independent sample t-test			
	Equal variances assumed		Equal variances not assumed	
Variables	t	Sig.	t	Sig.
INV	3.24**	0.000	3.85**	0.001
LEV	2.28*	0.023	2.11*	0.038
ROA	–2.53*	0.012	–2.80**	0.006

Notes: **,* indicate significance levels of 1% and 5%, respectively.

Table 4. Regression results.

	Investment (INV)		Financing (LEV)		Performance (ROA)	
Variable	Coeff	*p-value*	Coeff	*p-value*	Coeff	*p-value*
Constant	0.123**	0.000	0.636**	0.000	–0.068**	0.006
GENDER	–0.022**	0.002	–0.047*	0.030	0.023**	0.001
AGE	–0.017*	0.018	–0.050*	0.016	0.025**	0.000
MTB	0.002**	0.001	0.004*	0.034	0.019**	0.000
F	8.315 (0.000)		4.750 (0.003)		112.000 (0.000)	
R^2	0.057		0.033		0.434	
D-W	1.417		1.319		0.824	

Notes: **,* indicate significance levels of 1% and 5%, respectively.

internal funding sources have lower risk than external funding sources.

3.5 *CEO gender and firm performance*

CEO gender has a positive effect on company performance. This indicates that female CEOs have a positive influence on company performance. The results of this study support previous research by Dezso and Ross (2008) which concluded that the participation of women on the board of directors is strongly associated with better corporate performance and higher return. Huang and Kisgen (2013) had similar findings to those obtained by Khan and Vieito (2013), where companies led by women have a higher Return on Assets (ROA).

The regression results in this third model are in line with the results from the independent sample t-test in which companies with female CEOs have a higher ROA ratio than a firm with male CEOs, and the industry average. The regression coefficient indicates that companies with female CEOs have a 2.3% higher performance rate than companies with male CEOs.

This is an interesting result since, in the previous model, we found that companies with female CEOs have a tendency to avoid risk by having a low level of investments along with debt ratio, but the performance, or profitability, of their companies is better than those of male CEOs. This indicates that there are other factors affecting the companies' performance with female CEOs, such as psychological, behavioral, or leadership style. Furthermore, companies with female CEOs tend to be more optimal in managing assets. This, then, contributes to the trend of a higher ROA ratio in companies with female CEOs.

4 CONCLUSIONS

This study empirically examines the relationship between CEO gender and corporate finance decisions for the case of Indonesia. Employing independent sample t-test and regression approaches for the years 2010 to 2014, we find a significant difference between companies with male and female CEOs in terms of investment and leverage level. Companies with a female CEO tend to have lower investment and leverage level. However, results from the independent sample t-test indicate that firms with a female CEO exhibit a higher level of profitability.

Results from regression analysis support the evidence from the independent sample t-test, whereby female CEOs tend to be more conservative as compared to male CEOs in terms of investment decisions. In the context of financing decisions, female CEOs also tend to have a lower level of debt as compared to a company with a male CEO. Interestingly, female CEOs also tend to be more conservative in their investment and financing decisions, and firms with a female CEO have a higher return on asset ratio.

REFERENCES

Adams, R.B., & Ragunathan, V. (2013). *Lehman sisters*. University of New South Wales & University of Queensland Working paper.

Berger, A.N., Kick, T., & Schaeck, K. (2014). Executive board composition and bank risk taking. *Journal of Corporate Finance*, *28*(October 2014), 48–65.

Dezso, C., & Ross, D. (2008). Girl power: Female participation in top management and firm performance. *Working paper No. RHS06104. Robert H. Smith School of Business University of Maryland.*

Faccio, M., Marchica, M.T., & Mura, R. (2016). CEO gender, corporate risk-taking, and the efficiency of capital allocation. *Journal of Corporate Finance*. *39*(August 2016), 193–209.

Huang, J., & Kisgen, D.J. (2013). Gender and corporate finance: Are male executives overconfident relative to female executives? *Journal of Financial Economics*, *108*(3), 822–839.

Khan, W.A., & Vieito., J.P. (2013). CEO gender and firm performance. *Journal of Economics and Business*, *67*(May-June 013), 55–66.

Sila, V., Gonzales, A., & Hegendorff, J. (2016). Women on board: Does boardroom gender diversity affect firm risk?. *Journal of Corporate Finance*, *36*(February 2016), 26–53.

Weber, A., & Zulehner, C. (2010). Female hires and the success of start-up firms. *American Economic Review*, *100*(2), 358–361.

Increasing Management Relevance and Competitiveness – Sukoco et al. (Eds)
© 2018 Taylor & Francis Group, London, ISBN 978-0-8153-7455-8

Empirical testing of the accuracy of various theory models to measure the value of the firm

N.D. Kusumaningrum & I.M. Narsa
Universitas Airlangga, Surabaya, Indonesia

ABSTRACT: This study tested and compared the five most common theory models that are used in determining the value of a firm: the clean surplus approach Feltham *et al.* (1995); the dividend approach (Gordon, 1962); the earning approach (Beaver, 1981); the cash flow approach (Miller *et al.*, 1961); and the capital approach (Tobin, 1971). The statistical test used in the study were using Analysis of Variance; and the post-hoc test. An ANOVA test was used to find the inequality between firm's values derived from the theory models with the actual value of a firm. The post-hoc test is known as one of the best theory models to predict the value of other theory models. This study provides evidence that the results of the calculations against five assessment theory models gave different results and stated that the clean surplus is the best theory model to predict the value of other theory models.

Keywords: clean surplus, dividends, earnings, cash flow, capital, value of a firm

1 INTRODUCTION

The concept of continuity of business, known as 'going concern' (Suwardjono, 2005), is one of the main basic concept in accounting. It assumes that a firm will continue until an unspecified time, but there remains a need for a periodic valuation in order to confirm its intrinsic value and to perform a comparison with it's stock price. In the concept of going concern, certain parties' related business interests need to be protected. Therefore, it is very important to be able to measure the value of a firm appropriately and accurately with a calculation that is consistent, and doesn't change so that it can be easily compared.

The development of such valuation methods are described in Fama (1970), but not all provide continuity between the model of valuation and the purpose of the valuation itself. Thus the valuation models continue to evolve for the better according to Graham *et al.* (1934). Gordon (1962), initiated the dividend discount model, but followed by the cash flow theory by Miller *et al.* (1961), and then by Beaver (1981) model valuations based on earnings: they continue to evolve to this day. Damodaran (2002) states that generally there are three approaches used in performing valuations: relative valuation: contigent claim valuation: and discounted cash flow valuation. Thavikulwat (2004) performed valuations of related corporate value which can be determined through five distinct steps: book value: market value: the value of capital: deductive valuation adjustment: and net worth.

Nugroho *et al.* (2009) research tested three theories that are used in determining the value of a company: the dividend approach (Gordon, 1962): earning approach (Beaver, 1981): and cash flow approach (Miller *et al.*, 1961). It was found that there was a difference in the calculation result from each model, but the difference was not statistically significant. Where the results of this research supported by the research of (Subramanyam *et al.*, 1996).

Researchers are motivated to analyze the associated value of a firm. This research study will test theory models of five approach to quantifying firm value based on the theory models approach by Thavikulwat (2004) and Nugroho *et al.* (2009): the clean surplus approach (Feltham *et al.*, 1995): dividend approach (Gordon, 1962): earning approach (Beaver, 1981): cash flow approach (Miller *et al.*, 1961): capital approach (Tobin, 1971). The researchers of this study seek to compare the result from calculation of the value of a firm with the use of the five theory models the stock price valuation model, order to determine which has the most accuracy among the five model theories. Therefore, the hypotheseis presented in this study are: there is a difference between the values of a firm calculated from the theory models and the actual value of a firm; and one of the theory models is better predicting the value of a firm than the other theory models. The method of research used in this study is to determine if the results of the calculation from the five theory models is better that used in determining the actual value of firm.

2 LITERATURE REVIEW

2.1 *Theory model of the cash flow approach*

Based on the assumption by (Nugroho *et al.*, 2009), to formulate approaches to cash flow using the concept of Miller *et al.* (1961), Equation 1 was used:

$$F_v = \sum_{t=1}^{\infty} \frac{F_t}{(1+r)^t} \tag{1}$$

Notes:
Fv: Value of the firm
Ft: Free cash flow from perioda t
r: Weighted average cost of capital

2.2 *Theory model of the dividend approach*

Gordon (1962) assumes that dividends are rising on a consistent level for an extended period and are not limited. Nugroho *et al.* (2009) simplifyied the equation as followsshown in Equation 2:

$$FV = \sum_{t=1}^{\infty} \frac{D_t}{(1+r)^t} \tag{2}$$

Notes:
FV: Value of the firm
Dt: Devidend period t
r: Cost of capital

2.3 *Theory model of the capital approach*

For capital approach theory model, this research usesd the basic assumptions Tobin (1971) and used a formula approach as shown in Equation 3:

$$Q = \frac{MVE + PS + Debt}{TA} \tag{3}$$

Notes:
MVE: The firm's stock capitalization
PS: The outstanding preferred stock
TA: Total asset at t year
Debt: Total debt at t year
Q: Value of the firm

2.4 *Theory model of the earning approach*

Based on the assumption by (Nugroho *et al.*, 2009), to formulate approaches to profit with concept by (Beaver, 1981), equation 4 was used is:

$$FV = \sum_{t=1}^{\infty} \frac{L_t}{(1+r)^t} \tag{4}$$

Notes:
FV: Value of the firm
Lt: Earnings from period *t*
R: Cost of capital

2.5 *Theory model of the clean surplus approach*

The valuation theory and the explanation of theories and concepts of clean surplus by Feltham *et al.* (1995) were studied. This study then used the approach of the clean surplus theory based on the concept conceived by (Feltham *et al.*, 1995), and was formulated in Equation 5 as follows:

$$FV = B_{jt} + \sum_{i=1} \frac{E_t(ROE_{t+1} - r)B_{t-1})}{(1+r)^i} \tag{5}$$

Notes:
FV: Value of the firm
Bjt: Book of Eequity period t
ROE: Return on equity
r: Weight of average cost of capital

3 METHODOLOGY

This study is a comparative quantitative research to compare the results of the prediction of a firm's value using theory models, with the actual value of a firm. Because this research focuses on the comparative test of each theory model, the sample in this study uses four incorporated companies listed in the four five liquid index on the Indonesia Stock Exchange between 2008 and 2016. These where: PT Astra Argo Lestari; Tbk.; PT Astra International; Tbk. (ASII); PT Bank Central Asia; Tbk. (BBCA); and PT Bank Rakyat Indonesia Persero Tbk. (BBRI).

The data in this study was analyzed using analysis of variance and the post-hoc test with the use of SPSS software version 17.

The data was first tested using a homogeneity test; the Levenne variance test. If the data met the criteria, then the ANOVA test was performed. The post-hoc test was used to find whether the theory model value was different from the model results with other theories.

4 RESULTS AND DISCUSSION

To test the homogeneity variant of the research data, the Levenne variance test was used. The test of homogeneity of variances showed that F-test scored 42,954 with value score of df1 and df2, respectively by 5 and 210 and significant at a 0.05. That result has meaning that the zero hypothesis which states that the variants between groups are the same is rejected. This means that the variants between groups tested did not meet the criteria of homogeneity, as is shown the significance of values 0.000. From the homogeneity of variances results, it can be inferred that the ANOVA test criteria can't be met however, according to Ghozali (2006) this is not fatal, and analysis can still be performed throughout the group as there is still a proportional sample size. Thus, in testing the next step, ANOVA can be used to address the research hypothesis that the value of the firm is not the same between theory model values of the firm and the actual value of the firm.

The parametric difference test used in the study was the ANOVA test, which was used to find the difference between the theory model of value of the firm with the actual value of the firm. The results of testing proved the existence of a difference. This was observed from the ANOVA results, the firm's value had a value variable type III sum of squares of 647.111 with a value of 5 and df mean square values of 129.422 where the value of the F-test is known of 120.490 as well as the significant value of 0.00. Interpretation of the results of the ANOVA test, with the F-test based on the value of 120.490, is supported with a value of 0.00 significant at 5. These results show that there is a difference between the theory models' value of the firm with the actual value of the firm. The value of the type III sum of squares of 647.111, as well as the value of the adjusted R square of 0.735, indicates that the value of the firm's previous prediction of variability can be explained by the variability of corporate values of 73.5%.

After knowing that there is a difference between the results of the prediction model theory of value of the firm with the actual value of the firm, then post-hoc test. The post-hoc test results can be seen in Table 1.

Table 1 outlines the results of the post-hoc test and shows that almost all groups of contrastive values company unless the group of theory model profit approach and cash flow approach was showing the significance of value greater than 0.05 of each post-hoc testing is conducted to test T3 Tamanhe's of 0.9 test of T3 Dunnett's, 0.9, and Games-Howell test of 0.7, where the post-hoc test results showed that the value of the group's significance is insignificant $p > 0.05$. Therefore, it can be interpreted that the theory models with the profit approach and with the cash flow approach has a value of the same company or not unlike, it was meaning the average difference of 2.519. While results for the other groups were significant at 0.05 ($p < 0.05$).

Table 1. Post-hoc result.

Variabel			Sig.*		
I	II	MD	T	D	G
Earning	Capital	3.9	0.0	0.0	0.0
	Clean surplus	–0.8	0.0	0.0	0.0
	Cash flow	–0.2	0.9	0.9	0.7
	Devidend	0.5	0.0	0.0	0.0
	Actual value	–1.5	0.0	0.0	0.0
Capital	Earning	–3.9	0.0	0.0	0.0
	Clean surplus	–4.7	0.0	0.0	0.0
	Cash flow	–4.2	0.0	0.0	0.0
	Devidend	–3.4	0.0	0.0	0.0
	Actual value	–5.4	0.0	0.0	0.0
Clean surplus	Earning	0.8	0.0	0.0	0.0
	Capital	4.7	0.0	0.0	0.0
	Cash flow	0.5	0.0	0.0	0.0
	Devidend	1.3	0.0	0.0	0.0
	Actual value	–0.7	0.0	0.0	0.0
Cash flow	Earning	0.2	0.9	0.0	0.7
	Capital	4.2	0.0	0.0	0.0
	Clean surplus	–0.5	0.0	0.0	0.0
	Devidend	0.7	0.0	0.0	0.0
	Actual value	–1.3	0.0	0.0	0.0
Devidend	Earning	–0.5	0.0	0.0	0.0
	Capital	3.4	0.0	0.0	0.0
	Clean surplus	–1.3	0.0	0.0	0.0
	Cash flow	–0.7	0.0	0.0	0.0
	Actual value	–0.2	0.0	0.0	0.0
Actual Value	Earning	1.5	0.0	0.0	0.0
	Capital	5.4	0.0	0.0	0.0
	Clean surplus	0.7	0.0	0.0	0.0
	Cash flow	1.3	0.0	0.0	0.0
	Devidend	2.0	0.0	0.0	0.0

Notes:
Sig.*: Significant value 5%
MD: Mean difference
T: Tamhane test
D: Dunnett T3 test
G: Games-Howell test

To be able to answer the hypothesis which states that theory models are better at predicting the value of a firm than the other theory models, then based on the magnitude of the average value being different from the results of the post-hoc test in Table 1, it can be shown that the actual value of the firm is clean surplus < cash flow < earnings < dividend < capital.

The post-hoc test results, it can be seen that the clean surplus model approach is the best theory model. These findings also answered the second hypothesis in this study that the theory model with the earning approach is not the best approach model to predict the value of a firm, but rather the clean surplus approach. This finding also disproved previous research results conducted by (Subramanyam *et al.*, 1996) who stated that the theory model to best predict the value of a firm was the profit approach.

5 CONCLUSION

Based on the results of the hypothesis tests, it can be concluded that there is a difference between the approach used in determining the value of a firm and the findings from the calculations, which show that the five assessment theory models give different results. Further to this, the theory model approach of clean surplus by Feltham *et al.* (1995), is the most accurate model to predict the value of a firm.

REFERENCES

Beaver, W.H. (1981). Econometric properties of alternative security return methods. *Journal of Accounting Research*, 163–184.

Damodaran, A. (2002). Investment valuation, 2. *Aufl., New York, 817.*

Fama, E.F. (1970). Multiperiod consumption-investment decisions. *The American Economic Review, 60*(1), 163–174.

Feltham, G.A., et al. (1995). Valuation and clean surplus accounting for operating and financial activities. *Contemporary accounting research, 11*(2), 689–731.

Ghozali, I. (2006). *Aplikasi analisis multivariate dengan program SPSS*: Badan Penerbit Universitas Diponegoro.

Gordon, M. (1962). The Investment, Financing, and Valuation of the Corporation (Homewood, IL: Irwin).

Graham, B., et al. (1934). *Security analysis: Principles and technique:* McGraw-Hill.

Miller, M.H., et al. (1961). Dividend policy, growth, and the valuation of shares. *the Journal of Business, 34*(4), 411–433.

Nugroho, M.P.W., et al. (2009). *Pengujian teori dalam menentukan nilai perusahaan:: Teori Gordon, Beaver dan Miller dan Modigliani.* Universitas Gadjah Mada.

Subramanyam, K., et al. (1996). Going-Concern Status, Earnings Persistence, and Informativeness of Earnings. *Contemporary accounting research, 13*(1), 251–273.

Suwardjono, M. (2005). Accounting Theory: BPFE, Yogyakarta.

Thavikulwat, P. (2004). The architecture of computerized business gaming simulations. *Simulation & Gaming, 35*(2), 242–269.

Tobin, J. (1971). *Essays in economics: macroeconomics* (Vol. 1): Mit Press.

Increasing Management Relevance and Competitiveness – Sukoco et al. (Eds)
© 2018 Taylor & Francis Group, London, ISBN 978-0-8153-7455-8

Determinant variables of the performance rating of banks operating in Indonesia

Sugiarto
Doctoral Management Program, Universitas Pelita Harapan, Tangerang, Indonesia

ABSTRACT: The performance rating of banks operating in Indonesia is determined by quantitative and qualitative aspects. Infobank Research Bureau (2015) classifies banks operating in Indonesia in four categories: very good, good, quite good, and not good. In this study, the performance rating of banks is classified into two groups, namely very good and not very good. Banks that are classified as good, quite good, and not good according to the Bureau of Research Infobank are combined into a group of banks with the rating not very good. This research was conducted to find variables that become significant determining factors for the performance rating of banks operating in Indonesia. The study was conducted using secondary data obtained from Infobank (2015). Overall 99 banks were evaluated. The research variables were Composite Risk Management Profile (RMP_CG), Good Corporate Governance Composite Profile (GCG_CG), Non-Performing Loan (NPL), Net Interest Margin (NIM), Core Capital (CoreCap), Return on Assets (ROA), Return on Equity (ROE), Profit Growth (PrGrowth), and Ratio of Operating Expenses to Operating Income (BOPO). Tests were performed using discriminant analysis. The results obtained indicate that performance classification of banks are affected by variables RMP_CG, NPL, NIM, CoreCap, ROA, ROE, PrGrowth, and BOPO. The accuracy of the predictions of the model is 88.9%. The accuracy of the model categorized is high, so the discriminant model obtained is valid and can be used to classify the performance rating of banks operating in Indonesia.

Keywords: Bank's performance rating, determinant variables

1 INTRODUCTION

The performance rating of banks operating in Indonesia is determined by both quantitative and qualitative aspects. The performance rating of the bank is its status in terms of its condition and quality. Infobank Research Bureau (2015) [1] set a bank's performance using four approaches, including the key financial ratios, growth, composite value of good corporate governance and risk management profile. The approach used by Infobank Research Bureau refers to Bank Indonesia Circular Letter (Surat Edaran Bank Indonesia) [2] and Bank Indonesia Regulation on Rating of Commercial Bank Health Level (Peraturan Bank Indonesia) [3].

The bank's key financial ratio reflects the relative magnitude of two selected numerical values taken from the bank's financial statements. Often used in accounting, there are many standard ratios used to evaluate the overall financial condition of a bank. Financial analysts use a bank's financial ratios to compare the strengths and weaknesses in various banks. ROA and ROE have positive significant effect on public banks' stock prices in Indonesia [4], while banks' stock prices are an indicator of their performance which also influences their reputation. The previous study also regards the Return on Assets (ROA) as a major indicator of a wellmanaged bank [5].

The operational continuity of the Indonesian banking sector will depend on the ability of each banking institution to maintain high competitiveness, one of which is reflected by the bank's ability to maintain its profit growth. The bank's profit growth can reflect the level of operational efficiency as well as the bank's ability to deal with any disruptions that arise, both internally and externally. The results of the previous study [6] found that the high costs generated by these deposits weigh negatively on the performance of banks. From previous research it can be concluded that there are differences in the average NIM on the banks belonging to the classification of different commercial bank business activities [7].

A bank's composite value of good corporate governance reflects the extent to which a bank is able to implement the basic principles of good corporate governance, which consists of transparency, accountability, responsibility, independence and fairness. However, previous research [8] based on global data of banks whose assets exceed 10 billion euros in 2006, found no evidence confirming the widespread belief. Their results do not indicate that banks with higher corporate governance quality rating performed better during the crisis.

A bank's risk management profile reflects its general condition and affects its ability to face a significant negative effect of changes in business conditions and other external factors. A bank's risk management profile reflects its performance in managing risks. The better the performance of the bank's risk management the better the bank's performance. Previous study [9] found that control and credit quality are important variables in determining the performance of a bank.

In respect of the four approaches, Infobank Research Bureau conducted a more detailed breakdown into seven criteria including risk management profile, composite value of corporate governance, capital, asset quality, profitability, liquidity and efficiency.

The weight of each criteria stated in brackets are as follows: ratings profile of risk management (20%), composite value of corporate governance (20%), capital (10%), asset quality (10%), profitability (15%), liquidity (12.5%), and efficiency (12.5%). After the accumulated value, Infobank Research Bureau established the performance of banks operating in Indonesia. Bank performance determination is based on the cumulative value obtained. Banks that received a total value of 81 to 100 get very good rating, a bank with a total value of 66 up to 80 get good rating, banks with a total value of 51 up to 65 get quite good rating, and the banks with a total value of 0 up to 50 get not good rating.

The research focus is on the desire to find variables that become significant determinants for the performance of banks, especially for banks with a very good rating. In this study, the performance rating of banks is classified into two groups, namely very good and not very good. Banks that are classified as good, quite good, and not good according to the Bureau of Research Infobank are combined into a group of banks with the rating not very good.

2 RESEARCH METHOD

The study was conducted using secondary data obtained from Infobank (2015). Overall 99 banks were evaluated. The research variables were Composite risk management profile (RMP_CG), Good Corporate Governance composite profile (GCG_CG), Non-Performing Loan (NPL), Net Interest Margin (NIM), Core capital (CoreCap), Return on Assets (ROA), Return on Equity (ROE), Profit Growth (PrGrowth), and Ratio of Operating Expenses to Operating Income (BOPO). Tests were performed using discriminant analysis.

3 ANALYSIS AND RESULTS DISCUSSION

The Discriminant Analysis Group Statistics of the 99 banks evaluated is shown in Table 1. Of the 99 banks evaluated, 36 banks were classified as not very good (status 0.00) and 63 banks were classified as very good (status 1.00).

Based on tests of equality of group means as shown in Table 2, especially from Sig column, it can be seen that the GCG_CG is the only variable that has sig > 0.05. Thus the performance rating very good or not very good of banks surveyed is not affected by the GCG_CG. The assumption that GCG is considered to influence the bank performance rating because it affects the capacity of bank management as well as determining the continuity

Table 1. Discriminant analysis group statistics.

Group Statistics

Status		Valid N (listwise) Unweighted	Weighted
0.00	RMP_CG	36	36.000
	GCG_CG	36	36.000
	NPL	36	36.000
	NIM	36	36.000
	CoreCap	36	36.000
	ROA	36	36.000
	ROE	36	36.000
	PrGrowth	36	36.000
	BOPO	36	36.000
1.00	RMP_CG	63	63.000
	GCG_CG	63	63.000
	NPL	63	63.000
	NIM	63	63.000
	CoreCap	63	63.000
	ROA	63	63.000
	ROE	63	63.000
	PrGrowth	63	63.000
	BOPO	63	63.000
Total	RMP_CG	99	99.000
	GCG_CG	99	99.000
	NPL	99	99.000
	NIM	99	99.000
	CoreCap	99	99.000
	ROA	99	99.000
	ROE	99	99.000
	PrGrowth	99	99.000
	BOPO	99	99.000

Table 2. Tests of equality of group means.

	Wilks' Lambda	F	df1	df2	Sig.
RMP_CG	0.918	8.716	1	97	0.004
GCG_CG	0.998	0.216	1	97	0.643
NPL	0.766	29.567	1	97	0.000
NIM	0.928	7.505	1	97	0.007
CoreCap	0.955	4.553	1	97	0.035
ROA	0.532	85.380	1	97	0.000
ROE	0.674	46.915	1	97	0.000
PrGrowth	0.867	14.854	1	97	0.000
BOPO	0.544	81.468	1	97	0.000

of a bank's performance whose business activities become more complex. These findings support the findings of previous studies [8]. Savings guaranteed by the Deposit Insurance Agency (Lembaga Penjamin Simpanan, LPS) to the nominal value up to IDR 2 billion, may be one of the arguments that make customers less concerned about GCG. Based on the saving guaranteed by the Deposit Insurance Agency (LPS), banks customers who have savings of less than IDR 2 billion are not too concerned with the condition of bank's GCG because when banks fail, their funds in the bank are still guaranteed by the Deposit Insurance Agency (LPS). Thus the performance rating very good or not very good of banks surveyed are affected by RMP_CG, NPL, NIM, CoreCap, ROA, ROE, PrGrowth, BOPO.

By using unstandardized coefficients selection it will be obtained Canonical Discriminant Function Coefficients as shown at Table 3.

The discriminant model which was formed in connection with the variables that pass the test in the previous stages is:

$$\begin{aligned}\Sigma Score = & -1.709 + 0.027\,\mathrm{RMP}_{cc} - 0.139\,\mathrm{NPL} \\ & + 0.007\,\mathrm{NIM} + 0.000\,\mathrm{CoreCap} \\ & + 1.034\,\mathrm{ROA} - 0.067\,\mathrm{ROE} \\ & + 0.002\,\mathrm{PrGrowth} - 0.016\,\mathrm{BOPO}\end{aligned} \tag{1}$$

Using the discriminant function established further, the classification of performance of banks operating in Indonesia can be traced. The variables included in the model along with their coefficient signs are consistent with the findings of previous studies except for the sign of the coefficient of ROE, which is different from the previous findings [4]. The value of Canonical Discriminant Function Coefficients, which is quite small for CoreCap although still a significant role supporting the findings of the previous research [5], is not as expected by the regulator in the explanations given by [10] and [11], that a high level of capital reduces the risk (bankruptcy) incurred by banks. A bank that has a high level of equity sends a very positive signal to the

Table 3. Canonical discriminant function.

	Function 1
RMP_CG	0.027
NPL	–0.139
NIM	0.007
CoreCap	0.000
ROA	1.034
ROE	–0.067
PrGrowth	0.002
BOPO	–0.016
(Constant)	–1.709

Unstandardized coefficients.

Table 4. Classification results[a]

		Status	Predicted group membership 0.00	1.00	Total
Original	Count	0.00	34	2	36
		1.00	9	54	63
	%	0.00	94.4	5.6	100.0
		1.00	14.3	85.7	100.0

a. 88.9% of original grouped cases correctly classified.

market about the solvency of the bank and its very low credit risk. In addition to the cost of debt being lower, a strongly capitalized bank, compared to a weakly capitalized bank, does not need to borrow as much to finance a given level of assets. Finally, taking the signal theory, the use of equity (more expensive than debt) to finance a project tells the market that the bank is very confident in its projects and their profitability will meet expectations.

Having obtained a discriminant function, further searches of how far the classification is correct were carried out and are shown in Table 4.

The original column shows that there are 34 banks that at the beginning of the data are classified as not very good (0.00), and from the classification of fixed discriminant function in the group that are not very good. Two banks that were originally rated as not very good turned out to be very good.

Likewise, 54 banks originally entered as very good, and still remained at very good, and nine banks that initially entered as very good turned out to be not very good. Thus the prediction accuracy of the model is 88.9%.

Considering that the accuracy of the predictions of the model generated is 88.9% which already exceeds 50%, the accuracy of the model generated can be categorized as high, so the discriminant model obtained is valid and can be used to classify performance ratings of banks operating in Indonesia.

4 CONCLUSION

1. The results obtained indicate that performance rating classification of banks are affected by variables RMP_CG, NPL, NIM, CoreCap, ROA, ROE, PrGrowth, and BOPO.
2. The accuracy of the predictions of the model is 88.9%.
3. The accuracy of the model is categorized as high, so the discriminant model obtained is valid and can be used to classify performance ratings of banks operating in Indonesia.

REFERENCES

[1] Infobank (2015). Rating 118 bank di Indonesia, *Infobank, 437*(XXXVII (411)), pp. 32–37.
[2] Bank Indonesia (2011, October 25). Surat Edaran Bank Indonesia No.13/ 24 /DPNP/2011 perihal Penilaian Tingkat Kesehatan Bank Umum, pp. 1–28.
[3] Bank Indonesia (2011, January 5). Peraturan Bank Indonesia No.13/1/PBI/2011 perihal Penilaian Tingkat Kesehatan Bank Umum, pp. 4–10.
[4] Sugiarto & Adinoto, N. (2016). Determinants identification of public banks stock prices in Indonesia based on fundamental analysis. *International Journal of Applied Business and Economic Research, 14*(6), 4705–4712.
[5] Jeff, L. (1990). Capital adequacy: The benchmark of the 1990's. *Bankers' Magazine, 173*(1), 14–18.
[6] Demirgüç-Kunt, A., Huizinga, H. (1999). Determinants of commercial bank interest margins and profitability: some international evidence. *World Bank Economic Review 13*(2), 379–408.
[7] Sugiarto, (2016). Performance evaluation of Indonesian banks and foreign banks operating in Indonesia related to classification of capital. *Advances in Economics, Business and Management Research, 15, 1st Global Conference on Business, Management and Entrepreneurship (GCBME-16). Atlantis Press*, pp. 104–108.
[8] Beltratti, A., Stulz, R. (2009). Why did some banks perform better during the credit crisis? A cross country study of the impact of governance and regulation. *ECGI's Finance Working Paper, 254.*
[9] Garoui, N., Sessi, F. & Jarboui, A. (2013). Determinants of banks performance: viewing test by cognitive mapping technique (case of biat). *International Journal of Contemporary Economics and Administrative Sciences 3*(1), 22–46.
[10] Bourke, P. (1989). Concentration and other determinants of bank profitability in Europe, North America and Australia. *Journal of Banking and Finance 13*(1), 65–79.
[11] Berger, A. (1995). The profit–structure relationship in banking: tests of market power and efficient structure hypotheses. *Journal of Money, Credit and Banking 27*(2), 404–431.

Increasing Management Relevance and Competitiveness – Sukoco et al. (Eds)
© 2018 Taylor & Francis Group, London, ISBN 978-0-8153-7455-8

Fraud prevention analysis in the financial management of local government

A.A. Nugroho
Universitas Pendidikan Indonesia, Bandung, Indonesia

Y.N. Supriadi
STISIP Yuppentek, Tangerang, Indonesia

ABSTRACT: This research analyzes the role of whistleblowing and competence of human resources in order to prevent early fraud problems. The success of whistleblowing and human resources in prevention and detection of fraud competence is determined by the employees commitment and integrity. The whistleblowing and human resources competence need to understand cheating and types of fraud that may occur in the implementation of government wheels. This research took place at Regional Financial Income Board of Tangerang City and is a quantitative research using data from questionnaires and measured using a Likert scale. The population in this study is all employees of the Regional Financial Income Board of Tangerang City. Sampling was done using a purposive sampling technique, with a sample of 86 respondents. The type of data used in this study is primary data and the data analysis technique using multiple linear regression analysis. The results showed that there is a significant link between whistleblowing and human resource competence on fraud prevention. Together whistleblowing and human resource competence have a simultaneous effect on fraud prevention. Thus, in carrying out the function, government has to work efficiently, especially in the improvement of regional financial statements, because the main role of these variables in its function is present in the prevention of fraud that will attempt to eliminate the causes of the fraud. fraud prevention make it easier to overcome if there has been cheating and make a better local government financial management.

Keywords: Competence of human resources, prevention of fraud, whistleblowing system

1 INTRODUCTION

The current news coverage in the mass media about various corruption cases in Indonesia is a big problem for Indonesia. When measured by corruption levels in the Corruption Perception Index for 2014, Indonesia ranks 107th out of 175 countries, up 2 points and increase 7 point from 2013. Indonesia scores fifth in Southeast Asia after Singapore, Malaysia, the Philippines and Thailand. Alimbudiono & Andono, 2004 said Nevertheless, the score should be appreciated as a result of working with governments, communities and businesses to prevent and combat corruption. The presence of community awareness to conduct whistleblowing is also very effective in revealing the corruption and fraud that occurred. Along with the spirit of regional autonomy comes the basis for all local governments to be able to develop the potential of resource management, in order to generate local revenue sources, it becomes the considering of all local governments how the value of the original opinion of the region continues to increase, so that the purpose of the implementation of the government that the acceleration of the welfare of the community materialized will acieved. The phenomenon of fraud in government in Indonesia has reached a level of concern. There are many stories about fraud cases that have involved irresponsible people, both in the legislative, executive and even judicial ranks. Various efforts have been made by the Government of Indonesia both by empowering maximum law enforcement agencies, such as attorneys, courts, and police. Even in the last decade the government has also established and empowered the Corruption Eradication Commission (KPK) to eradicate corruption in Indonesia. But unfortunately the results are still not in accordance with expectations, in which Indonesia remains one of the 10 most corrupt countries in the world [2].

However, the occurrence of fraud in local financial management becomes a problem that must be improved. The occurrence of fraud in the local government due to internal control factors are absent or weak or carried our loosely and ineffectively. Often employees are employed without consideration of their honesty and integrity. The existence of exploitation is not good, misused or placed with great pressure to achieve the goals and financial goals that lead to fraud. It also Strong allegedly contra management model itself cheating, inefficient and or ineffective and not obeying the applicable laws and regulations. Often government officials are found to have personal problems that cannot be solved, usually financial problems, family health needs or having an excessive lifestyle. Finally, the history or tradition of cheating is inherent from unscrupulous elements [3]. To run the functions of local government, financial factors are very important, because every activity of government organizations, whether public or private, cost money. Natural resources and resources related to the capital are owned by the region. Therefore, each region has its own special emphasis on potentials that can uncover and add to the source of Pendapatan Asli Daerah (PAD). The tendency of accounting fraud has attracted much media attention and has become a prominent and important issue in the eyes of world business players [4]. One of the efforts to realize good financial management capacity is that the government undertakes bureaucratic feasibility so that it can demand that state finance management be conducted cleanly, accountably, and free from corruption, collusion and nepotism. To make it happen, an audit of state financial management is required. Examination is an independent, objective, and professional identification, analysis and evaluation process based on inspection standards to assess the truth, accuracy, credibility and reliability of information on the management and accountability of state finances. The number of findings and complaints from the community about the management of local government finances has been input into a separate record, so that local governments need to reexamine policies in anticipation of it. These findings explain the weaknesses of internal control and non-compliance of entities to legislation. The audit results also provide information on potential losses of countries/regions found in the audit process resulting from misuse and inefficiency of APBN/APBD usage, [5] Errors and fraud practices of local government organizations are still commonly found. The types of fraud that occur in regional government are generally in the form of corruption, other forms of fraud such as misuse of assets and fraud financial reports tend to occur less. Corruption in Indonesia occurs almost all levels of government and almost all areas, such as budget misuse, licensing, bribery, illegal fees and fraud in the procurement of goods/services.

Thus, the public will always make demands for public accountability (transparency and public accountability) to have an impact on the process of development of government management in Indonesia. Transparency and public accountability are two inseparable aspects of the principles of good governance. The implication now becomes a rampant and interchangeable study, the implementation of participatory regional planning, implementation and accountability as a logical consequence. Issues surrounding transparency and accountability cannot be separated from the widespread misuse of authority and misappropriation of funds by unscrupulous employees and officials in government. Transparency and accountability require the media to communicate to the community better and faster. [6] Fraud is a deliberate form of fraud that can result in unnoticed losses by the aggrieved party and provides benefits to the perpetrators of fraud. In this research, the researcher intends to analyze the role of whistleblowing and competence of human resources in order to prevent early fraud problems.

2 THEORETICAL FRAMEWORK

According to Brandon whistleblowing is an action performed by a person or several employees to divulge fraudulent behavior, either committed by the Regional Financial Income Board of Tangerang City or his superiors to other parties. [7] Whistleblowing is generally undertaken in secret (confidential). Disclosure must be made in good faith and not as a personal complaint of a particular Tangerang City Revenue Party policy (grievance) or based on a bad or slanderous will, to detect, minimize and then eliminate cheating or fraud committed by internal organizations.

The reporting system of violations, or as commonly referred to as the whistleblowing system, is a channel for a whistleblower to complain of fraud or violations committed by an internal organization. This system aims to uncover fraud that can harm the organization and prevent more fraud [8]. The application of a whistleblowing system becomes a tool that can be used to prevent corruption or fraud that can occur financial management of revenue of local origin. A whistleblower is a person who reports an unlawful act, especially corruption or fraud, within the organization or institution in which he works. This person usually has sufficient data or evidence of unlawful conduct. The role of whistleblower is very important in exposing an action against the law within the internal organization. However, many people are afraid to complain of fraud, because the risks to be faced can be difficult to avoid, meaning that they may prefer to be silent. These include the threat of being reported himself, the threat of dismissal and the impact on his family. Security guarantees and legal protection against whistleblowers have existed since 2006 with the introduction of the 2006 Law on Witness and Victim Protection. It is one of the motivators for a person to become a whistleblower. A whistleblower, in an effort to uncover an act of fraud either in the Tangerang City Regional Financial Income Board or a government institution, can indeed be driven by various motivations, such as retaliation to dismissal from the District Financial Income Board of Tangerang City where he worked, looking for appreciation, or the intention to create a more ethical environment within the Tangerang City Regional Financial Income Board. What is clear is that a whistleblower has a strong motivation to dare to uncover a criminal scandal against the public.

Whistleblowers have a conscience that gives a strong indication of the importance of a scandal to be revealed. The Supreme Audit Agency of Indonesian Republic (BPK RI) found that problem there is still low quality of financial report information of the region caused by the accounting understanding of the report compiler itself that directly related to the competence of human resources, has not been applied optimally financial accounting system and still weak internal control system. For good local financial management, employees should have competent human resources, supported by accounting education backgrounds, frequently attended education and training, and have experience in finance. [9] There are some problems that need to be studied further, that is whether whistleblowing systems have an effect on theprevention of financial management fraud in receipt of original revenue of Regional Financial Income of Tangerang City, whether competence of human resources influence the prevention of fraud against the financial management revenue of Original Regional Income Town Financial Income Board Tangerang, and whether the whistleblowing system and human resource competence have an effect on the prevention of financial management fraud in receipt of Original Revenue in Regional Finance Income Board of Tangerang City. In order to answer the problem, this study aims to prove empirically the influence of whistleblowing systems and the competence of human resources affect the prevention of financial management fraud revenue of the Original Regional Financial Income Board City Tangerang. This research proposes the hypothesis that one of the benefits of a good whistleblowing system implementation is the emergence of reluctance to commit violation, because of trust in an effective reporting system [10]. The existence of a whistleblowing system is not only a fraud reporting channel, but also a form of supervision. Employees are afraid to cheat because this system can be used by all employees, so fellow employees become mutually supervising of each other and are afraid to report other employees for cheating. This can prevent fraud that will occur within financial management. This shows that a whistleblowing system has an effect on fraud prevention [11].

According to Tjiptoherijanto, to assess the capacity and competence of human resources in implementing a function, including accounting, it must be seen from the level of responsibility and competence of these resources [12]. Responsibility can be seen from or contained in the job description. Job descriptions are the basis for doing a good job. Without a clear job description, the resource cannot perform their duties properly. While the competence of resources can be seen from educational background, training, and from the skills expressed in the execution of tasks. According to Nurillah competence of human resources is the ability of an individual, an organization (institutional), or a system to perform the functions or authority to achieve its objectives effectively and efficiently. Aspects of human resources have potential problems, namely potential labor corruption/fraud are handled by weak internal control system [13].

These findings indicate that the competence of human resources in the government agencies affect the quality of financial statements so that local governments need to create programs/policies to improve human resources. Failure of local government human resources in understanding and applying accounting logic will have an impact on mistakes made in financial statements and mismatch reports with standards established by the government [14].

Based on the definition, the research frame of reference is described in the following figure:

The formulation of hypotheses in this study are:

H1: Whistleblowing Systems influence on prevention of fraud within financial management revenue. Regional Financial Income Board of Tangerang City Competence is the required qualification of an auditor to carry out the audit correctly. In carrying out the audit, an auditor must have ethical personal

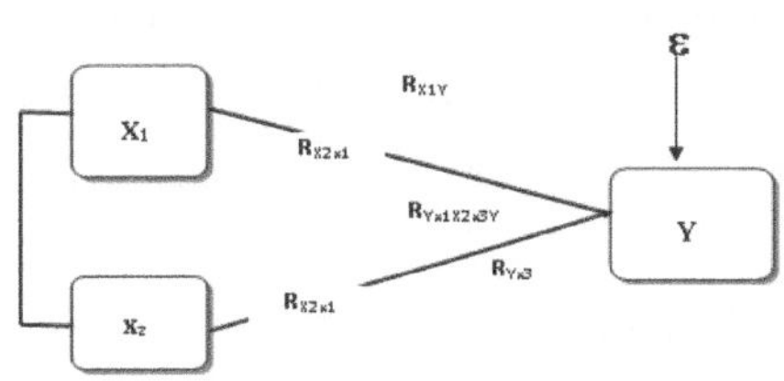

Figure 1. Frame of reference paradigm.

qualities, adequate knowledge, and specialist expertise in their field. The competence of human resources has a significant effect on the detection of fraudulent financial reporting [15]. Based on the theory and previous research, the research hypothesis proposed.

H2: Competence of human resources affect the prevention of financial management of the occurrence of fraud within Regional Financial Income Board of Tangerang City One of the benefits of good whistleblowing systems is the emergence of reluctance to commit abuses, due to the belief in effective reporting systems [16], which shows that whistleblowing systems have an effect on fraud prevention. Competency is a qualification that the auditor. In conducting the audit, an auditor must have good personal quality, sufficient knowledge and specialist expertise in their field and human resource competence has a significant effect on fraudulent financial reporting detection. Based on the theory and previous research, the proposed research hypothesis.

H3: Whistleblowing Systems and competence of human resources have an effect on fraud prevention of the financial management of revenue of Original Revenue in Tangerang City Regional Financial Income Board.

3 RESEARCH METHOD AND ANALYSIS

This research is related to the influence of whistleblowing systems and human resource competence that have a joint and significant effect on fraud prevention. This research uses a human resource management approach. Respondents in this study are employees of the Regional Financial Income Board of Tangerang City. Therefore, the analysis encompassing whistleblowing systems and human resource competencies have an effect simultaneously and significantly on the prevention of fraud.

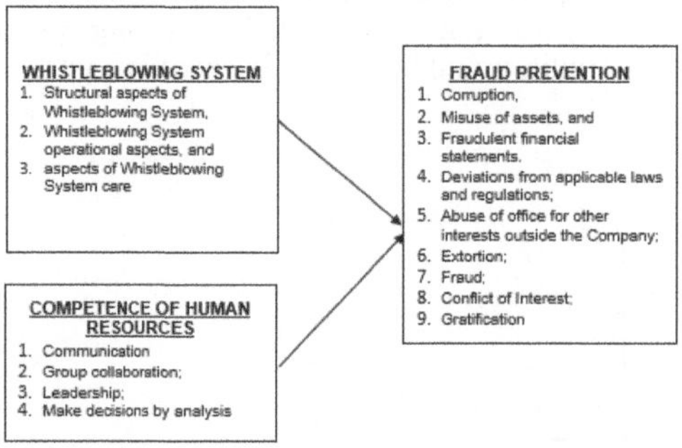

Figure 2. The causal structure of the research.

This research used a descriptive survey and an explanatory survey. The research was conducted using survey method and quantitative data analysis techniques that are causal comparative, a sample size of 86 respondents, research and analysis technique path analysis using SPSS 20.0 software. Based on the conceptual hypothesis, there is a correlation between research variables. Figure 2 shows the research diagram:

4 RESEARCH RESULTS

Based on path analysis using SPSS 20 for Windows, path coefficients are used to recognize the effect between variables and t-calculated values used to test the hypothesis: whistleblowing systems and human resource competencies have joint and significant effect on fraud prevention, which results as follows:

4.1 *F Test result intended to test the significancy of the influence of independent variables on bounded variable, simultaneously*

Value Fcount > F Table that is 11.743 > 3.88, then Ho is rejected and Ha accepted. This indicates that all independent variables (whistleblowing system, competence of human resources fraud prevention) have a significant effect on fraud prevention simultaneously. So the hypothesis reads ‘that a whistleblowing system and the competence of human resources jointly and significantly affect the pre-

Table 1. Summary of structural equation estimation.

Model	Sum of squares	df	Mean square	F	Sig.
1 Regression	423.764	3	141.255	11.743	0.000
Residual	986.376	82	12.029		
Total	1410.140	85			

a. Predictors: (Constant), whistleBlowing_system, competence.
b. Dependent Variable fraud_ prevention.
Source: SPSS. 20.0 Output, 2017.

Table 2. Correlation and determination analysis.

Model	Model summary[b]			
	R	R square	Adjusted R square	Std. Error of the estimate
1	0.548[a]	0.301	0.275	3.46828

a. Predictors: (Constant), whistleBlowing_system, competence
b. Dependent Variable fraud_ prevention
Source: SPSS. 20.0 Output, 2017.

Table 3. T test analysis.

Model	Unstandardlized coefficients		Standardlized coefficients			Collinearity Statistics	
	B	Std. Error	Beta	t	Sig.	Tolerance	VIF
1 (Constant)	12.488	3.539		3.529	0.001		
whistle Blowing_system	0.163	0.087	0.181	1.888	0.063	0.925	1.081
Competence	0.295	0.114	0.332	2.580	0.012	0.515	1.941

a. Dependent Variable: fraud_ prevention
Source: SPSS. 20.0 Output, 2017.

vention of fraud is acceptable'. Where the calculation results of correlation and determination analysis can be summarized into the table below:

Based on the calculation of SPSS. 20.0 for Windows obtained the correlation value of 0.548, while the coefficient of determination obtained is 0.301 or 30.1%. This shows the percentage influence of a whistleblowing system and human resource competencies jointly and significantly affect the prevention of fraud in the District Financial Income Tangerang City 30.1% while the remaining 69.9% is influenced by other variables.

4.2 *Test result T*

Based on the calculation results with the help of SPSS.20.0 for Windows, the value of T arithmetic of 3.529 and T table df 86 for 2,620 significance value of 0.000 > 0.05 was obtained. This means 3,529 > 2,620. Then Ho is rejected and Ha accepted which means there is a significant influence that a whistleblowing system and the competence of human resources jointly and significantly affect the prevention of fraud in the Regional Financial Income Board Tangerang City; thus the hypothesis is proved. The discussion in the table above can be explained as follows: $\hat{y} = \alpha$ x1 x2 so that $\hat{Y}$ = 12.488 0.163 X1 0.295 X2. From the above equation it can be concluded that the influence of a whistleblowing system and human resource competence have a joint and significant effect on the prevention of fraud in Financial Income Board of Tangerang City.

4.3 *Effect of whistleblowing systems on fraud prevention*

The results of the first hypothesis test show that the whistleblowing system variables significantly influence the prevention of fraud shown by the value (sig.) T equal to 1.888 where the whistleblowing variable significance level is greater than 0.63, which means the hypothesis is accepted. This means that the whistleblowing system variable has an effect on fraud prevention. It can be interpreted that the Regional Financial Income Board of Tangerang City, which serve as the object of this research, has justification for the application of whistleblowing system, because it is proven to be able to prevent fraud. Whistleblowing systems must have at least three aspects: structural aspects, operational aspects, and maintenance aspects. From the results of this study, it is essential that employees understand these three aspects that can then influence them to be reluctant to perform fraud and report fraud acts that occur if they find out. A whistleblowing system has a significant effect on fraud prevention. The research was conducted by Regional Finance Income Board of Tangerang City, which has applied a whistleblowing system, while other research by conducted by Tangerang City Financial Income Board which has not applied a whistleblowing system. Its show that Whistleblowing System affects Fraud Prevention. However, according to Titaheluw's research, it is not in accordance with this study, which states that a whistleblowing system is not the only system that can be used in preventing fraud; there are also other factors that can prevent the occurrence of fraud. This indicates that the better the application of a whistleblowing systems, the higher the level of fraud prevention or fraud [17].

4.4 *Effect of human resources competence on fraud prevention*

The results of testing the second hypothesis show that human resource competence has a significant effect on fraud prevention. The analysis results show (sig.) T equal to 2,580, in which the level of significance of human resource competence variable of 2.580 is smaller than 0.013 which means the hypothesis is accepted. It shows the competence of human resources has a significant effect on fraud prevention. Competence of human resources has a significant effect on fraud detection [18].

The competence of human resources positively affects the auditor's ability to detect fraud. To assess the capacity and competence of human resources in performing a function, including accounting, it must be seen from the level of responsibility and competence of human resources. So with the competence of good human resources, the higher the probability that an employee will not commit fraud. This is because the human resources already have knowledge and understanding about fraud prevention. Based on these concepts, it appears that the competence of human resources and fraud prevention is directly proportional; if the better the competence of human resources of the employee, the higher the probability that an employee will not take fraud action. Due to the better the level of competence of human resources, the understanding of fraud and the effort to prevent and detect fraud, the potential for fraud action is smaller. Hence the competence of human resources has a positive and significant impact on fraud prevention.

4.5 *The influence of whistleblowing systems and human resource competence on fraud prevention*

The result of hypothesis examination shown in Table 1, obtained by F counted 11,743 with significant level less than 0,05 0.000. Thus it can be concluded that fraud prevention variables are affected jointly by whistleblowing system variables and human resource competencies. Whistleblowing systems affect fraud prevention, although a whistleblowing system is not the only system that can be used in preventing fraud; there are also other factors that can prevent the occurrence of fraud. Competency is a qualification that the auditor needs to perform an audit properly. In conducting the audit, an auditor must have good personal quality, sufficient knowledge, and specialist expertise in their field. The competence of human resources has a significant effect on fraud detection. This shows the better the application of a whistleblowing system, the higher the prevention rate of fraud or cheating otherwise the higher the level of competence of human resources, the higher the intention to do the whistleblowing level so that the higher the prevention rate of fraud. Taking fraud prevention measures depends not only on the effectiveness of the whistleblowing system alone, but the government agencies should pay attention to the level of competence of good human resources for fraud/fraud prevention. Because of the higher level of human resource competence, the understanding of the whistleblowing system and the prevention of fraud as prevention and fraud detection, the potential for fraud is reduced.

So that whistleblowing system and human resource competence significantly influence fraud prevention. Thus the hope of good governance and clean good governance will be achieved optimally, this will affect the public trust and the goal of social welfare achievement by the government will run well in accordance with the vision and mission of Tangerang city government, especially for the city's financial revenue agency Tangerang ability to work professionally away from fraudulent actions so that this institution becomes an example for other Local Government Work Units.

5 CONCLUSION

Based on the results of research it can be concluded that the application of a whistleblowing system and human resource competence can significantly influence the prevention of fraud. With the implementation of a whistleblowing system and competence in Tangerang City Revenue Agency, which is a container for a whistleblower in preventing or uncovering fraud that occurred in the government.

The application of a whistleblowing system is one form of internal control of Tangerang City Financial Income Board in minimizing and suppressing the risk that may occur. So the higher the application of the whistleblowing system and competence in a Regional Income Board of Tangerang City, the higher the level of fraud prevention in a Regional Financial Income Board of Tangerang City.

The application of a whistleblowing system and competence of human resources in influencing fraud prevention is not too big. It caused by some employees who still doubt that the application of a whistleblowing system will provide assistance in conveying the violations that occur. The Regional Financial Income Board of Tangerang City needs to explain to employees to the details of the protection policy for whistleblower, and the Head of the Agency must also guarantee to whistleblowers that what they report will not be a problem for them. In addition there are still some variables outside the research model that may affect fraud prevention as well as internal control, good governance and proactive fraud auditing.

REFERENCES

Alimbudiono, R.S. & Andono, F.A. (2004). Human resource readiness and its relation with financial responsibility to society. *Jurnal Akuntansi dan Keuangan Sektor Publik*.

Amrizal, Ak, Mm, Cfe. Prevention and detection of fraud by internal auditor. Jakarta.

Bertot, J.C., P.T.J., & Grimes, J.M. (2010). Promoting transparency and accountability through ICTs, social media, and collaborative e-government. Transforming government: People process and policy, 6(1), 78–91.

Brandon, J.R. (1967). Theatre in Southeast Asia. Massachusetts: Cambridge University Press.

Dewi, R. (2012). Journal of fraudulent financial reporting. ForumB isnis & Keuangan I, Bandung.

Komite Nasional Kebijakan Governance (KNKG) (2008). Pedoman Sistem Pelaporan Pelanggaran—SPP (whistleblowing system—WBS). Jakarta: KNKG.

Koswara. (2000). Otonomy and regional taxes. Jogjakarta, Indonesia: PT Gramedia Widiasarana.

Nurillah, A.S. (2014). Impact of human resources, regional financial system application, information technology, and internal control in quality of regional government financial report., Fakultas Ekonomika Dan Bisnis Universitas Diponegoro Semarang.

Octaviari, N.V. (2015). Effect of whistleblowing system employee perception in fraud prevention with ethic behavior as intervening variable on PT Pagilaran. Skripsi. Universitas Negeri Yogyakarta.

Setyaningrum, D. (2012). Analysis of BPK-RI Audit Quality Factors. Journal. Jakarta: Universitas Indonesia.

Sukmaningrum, P.H. (2012). Factors related to regional government financial report. jurnal akuntasi.

Taufik, M. (2008). Effect of work experiences and internal auditor profession to fraud detection ability. Skripsi. Universitas Islam Negeri Syarif Hidayatullah.

Titaheluw, L.C. (2011). Effect of system whistleblowing application to fraud prevention, Fakultas ekonomi, Jurusan akuntansi. Universitas widyatama.

Transparency International (2015). Corruption Perceptions Index 2015. Retrieved from www.transparency.org/cpi2015/results.

Warisno, (2008). Technology of food process. Teknologi Pengolahan dan Yogyakarta: Yayasan Pustaka Nusantara.

Increasing Management Relevance and Competitiveness – Sukoco et al. (Eds)
© 2018 Taylor & Francis Group, London, ISBN 978-0-8153-7455-8

The effect of leverage and profitability on stock return: A study on the mining sector companies listed on the Indonesia stock exchange for the period 2011–2015

Yayan Hendayana
Doctoral Program of Management Science, Universitas Pendidikan Indonesia, Bandung, Indonesia

H. Hari Mulyadi
Universitas Pendidikan Indonesia, Bandung, Indonesia

Zulkifli Musannip Efendi Siregar
Sekolah Tinggi Ilmu Ekonomi Labuhan Batu, Indonesia

Agus Setyo Pranowo
Doctoral Program of Management Science, Universitas Pendidikan Indonesia, Bandung, Indonesia

ABSTRACT: This study aims to examine the effect of leverage represented by debt ratio (DTA) and profitability represented by Return On Assets (ROA) on stock returns in Mining Companies were listed on the Indonesian Stock Exchange (IDX) period 2011–2015. The sample selected nineteen mining sector firms. To prove the influence of independent variables on the dependent variable, the researcher using panel data regression. The result shows that leverage (DTA) partially have a positive effect and significant on stock return. Profitability (ROA) have a positive and significant effect on stock return. Simultaneously leverage (DTA) and profitability (ROA) have a significant effect on stock return. For the next researcher, it is better to add other variables, use samples from other sector companies, and increase the period of observation by adding the most recent research year.

Keywords: Stock Return, Leverage and Probability.

1 INTRODUCTION

Capital markets are one place that sell stocks and interest obligations with the aim that the sale proceeds will be used as an additional fund or to strengthen a company's capital (Fahmi, 2014). For investors, the existence of capital markets expands investment options, so the opportunity to optimize benefits becomes more open.

In efforts to obtain optimum benefit, investors who choose to invest in stocks are faced with the choice to maximize returns on varying levels of risk or minimize risks at varying levels of return. In business there is a classic proposition that bears minimum risk to obtain maximum results (Prawironegoro, 2006).

The mining industry in early 2015 tended to be stagnant. A few mining companies were forced out of business due to the impact of the conditions. However, this does not account for the poor economy all mining entrepreneurs just resigned. The optimism of the mining industry will definitely be revived, with President Joko Widodo promoting the potential of Indonesia in the international forum. Moreover, Indonesia has become one of the largest countries in mining production, especially coal mining.

Table 1 shows that the value of stock returns of companies fluctuated from year to year. To determine the relationship between a company's financial performance with changes in stock prices and the return generated, various studies have been conducted. A previous study by Sunarto (2001) examined the influence of profitability and leverage ratios on stock returns in manufacturing companies listed on the Indonesia Stock Exchange. The research result showed that the Return on Assets (ROAs), Return on Equity (ROE), and the Debt-to-Total Asset (DTA) ratio simultaneously affect *t* stock return. This research is consistent with the result of research conducted by Hapcin Suhairy (2006) entitled "Influence of Profitability Ratio and Leverage to Return of Stock Manufacturing Company at Indonesia Stock Exchange." The result of research shows that the profitability ratio (represented by ROE and ROA) and the

Table 1. Stock return in the mining sector, 2011–2015.

Code	Year 2011	2012	2013	2014	2015
Adaro Energy Tbk	–31.9	–9	–36.6	–0.2	–49
Aneka Tambang (persero) Tbk	–30.1	–17.6	–17.1	–1.3	–64.2
Atlas Resources Tbk	0	–0.7	–43.7	–11	–45.7
Ratu Prabu Energy Tbk	–45.7	–17.5	–30.3	–44.2	51.8
Cita Mineral Investindo Tbk	–0.6	0	23.8	141	0
Citatah Tbk	–2.7	–21.6	10.4	17.5	–18.8
Darma Henwa Tbk	6.9	–39	0	0	0
Elnusa Tbk	–30.3	–24	97.9	116	–63.1
Energy Mega Persada Tbk	40.2	–56.2	–20.5	40.9	–50.5
Garda Tujuh Buana	835	572	–60.3	–76.6	–28.4
Harum Energy Tbk	–19.7	–8.7	–52.3	–39.6	–59.3
Vale Indonesia tbk	–29.9	–23.3	14	41.5	–54.9
Indo Tambangraya Megah Tbk	–28.1	14.4	–28.9	–41.8	–59.9
Resources Alam Indonesia Tbk.	73.9	–60.4	–17.5	–46.1	–56.4
Mitra Investindo Tbk	–5.6	59.9	–10.8	–84.2	–36.7
J Resources Asia Pasifik Tbk	0	157.8	–51.9	57.4	153.7
Tambang Batubara Bukit Asam (persero) Tbk	–24.6	–8.8	–35.6	23.3	–61.1
Petrosea Tbk	35.1	–58.3	–18.4	–19.8	–68.8
Timah (persero) Tbk	–36.8	–4.5	0.2	17.7	–57.6
Average	37.11	23.92	–14.61	4.76	–29.94

Source: Indonesia Stock Exchange.

leverage ratio (represented by DTA) simultaneously affect stock returns, but the profitability ratio only partially significantly affects stock returns, whereas the leverage ratio does not significantly affect stock returns.

The research by Ngaisah (2008) entitled "Influence of Profitability and Leverage Ratios on Stock Return on Companies listed in Jakarta Islamic Index (JII) in 2004–2006." The result of research shows that ROA has no significant effect on stock returns; ROE and DTA partially significantly affect stock returns; and ROA, ROE, and DTA simultaneously influence stock returns.

Research by Fitriadi (2009) entitled "Effect of Profitability, Leverage and Firm Size Against Stock Return of Property Company in Indonesia Stock Exchange Year 2001–2007". The results showed that ROE and DER variables significantly influence stock returns. ROA variable and firm size variable have no significant effect to stock return.

2 LITERATURE REVIEW

2.1 *Stock returns*

In simple terms, a stock refers to a share in the ownership of a company. It represents a claim on the company's assets and earnings. The percentage stake that an investor holds is reflected in the number of shares the investor acquires from the company's stocks. Thus, the more shares that one acquires, the greater his/her ownership rights in the company. When one holds a company's stock, it means that person is one of the many owners (shareholders) of the company and as such s/he has a claim (although usually very small) to everything the company owns. An investor's ownership of shares is represented by a stock certificate—a piece of paper that serves as a proof to ownership (Acheampong & Shibu, 2014).

According to Brigham and Houston (in Acheampong & Shibu, 2014) an ordinary stock simply represents an ownership interest in a corporation. In this modern age of business, however, such certificates are rarely given to the shareholder because the brokerage firms keep these records electronically, known as holding shares "in street name." This is done in an attempt to make the stock easily tradable. Unlike in the past where one had to physically take a share certificate to the brokerage in order to sell shares, now stocks can be easily traded with just a click of the mouse or even a phone call.

Return of expectation is expected return will be obtained by investor in the future whereas return realization is return which have happened which calculated by using historical data. Stock returns can be obtained in the form of dividends and capital gain/loss. Capital gain/loss is the difference more or less than stocks. Dividends are used to measure the performance of stocks based on dividend distribution; the greater the dividend, the more attractive the stock to investors. A higher stock price indicates that the stock is more attractive to investors, because the higher the stock price the greater the capital gain. Return realization used in this study is the capital gain/loss, often also called the actual return (Heryanto, 2016).

2.2 *Leverage*

A leverage ratio proxied by DTA is used in research because it can determine whether the ability of a company's assets to finance operations will use a lot of debt or equity capital. By using debt the owner will get the funds and not lose control of the company (Hartono, (2013).

One of the leverage ratios used by investors is the DTA ratio or the ratio of the comparison of company debts, which is derived from the ratio of total debt divided by total assets (Fahmi, 2014).

Financial risks are linked with funding decisions; this means that they are linked with company selection of a combination of its financial structure. Financial leverage leads to a high degree of risk faced by shareholders, so it increases the likelihood of its inability to service the debt. Therefore, financial policy tries to harmonize between the impact of borrowing and the return on equity, as well as the degree of risk faced by shareholders (Barakat, 2014).

2.3 *Profitability*

Van Horne (in Fardiansyah & Juanda, 2016) stated that there are two types of profitability: the profitability of sales and the profitability of investments. Together, the ratio between these shows the level of efficiency in company operations.

A group's profitability ratio measures the firm's profit to sales figures and the level of a particular asset or investment of the owners (Gitman & Zutter 2012). Profitability ratio is an indicator of a firm's overall efficiency. It is usually used as a measure of earnings generated by a company during a period of time based on its level of sales, assets, capital employed, net worth, and earnings per share. Profitability ratio measures earning capacity of a firm, and it is considered an indicator of its growth, success, and control. Creditors, for example, are interested in the profitability ratio as it indicates a company's capability to meet interest obligations. Shareholders also are interested in the profitability ratio as it indicates the progress and rate of return on their investments (Kabajeh & Dahmash 2012).

3 RESEARCH METHODS

3.1 *Population sample*

The population in this research is mining companies listed on the Indonesia Stock Exchange for the period 2011–2015. A total of 19 mining firms were included in the study sample (Table 2). The sampling method used was purposive sampling. The sampling technique was based on a criterion that considers judgement sampling. Sample selection in this study used the following criteria:

- Companies that were included in the mining sector during the period 2011–2–015.
- Companies that continued listing on the Indonesia Stock Exchange during the period 2011–2015 (never suspended).
- Companies that published financial reports for the period 2011–2015.
- Companies that recorded stock price data (closing price) for the years 2011–2015.

Table 2. Sample population.

No.	Firm	Subsector
1	Adaro Energy Tbk	Coal mining
2	Atlas Resources Tbk	Coal mining
3	Darma Henwa Tbk	Coal mining
4	Garda Tujuh Buana	Coal mining
5	Harum Energy Tbk	Coal mining
6	Indo Tambangraya Megah Tbk	Coal mining
7	Resources Alam Indonesia TBK	Coal mining
8	Tambang Batubara Bukit Asam (persero) Tbk	Coal mining
9	Petrosea Tbk	Coal mining
10	Ratu Prabu Energy Tbk	Oil and gas
11	Elnusa Tbk	Oil and gas
12	Energy Mega Persada Tbk	Oil and gas
13	Aneka Tambang (persero) Tbk	Metals and minerals
14	Cita Mineral Investindo Tbk	Metals and minerals
15	Vale Indonesia tbk	Metals and minerals
16	J Resources Asia Pasifik Tbk	Metals and minerals
17	Timah (persero) Tbk	Metals and minerals
18	Citatah Tbk	Rock mining
19	Mitra Investindo Tbk	Rock mining

Source: Indonesia Stock Exchange.

- Companies with Jakarta Islamic Index stocks.
- Companies with an initial public offering in the year 2011.

3.2 *Data collection technique*

The data used in this research are primary data from secondary sources. Data have been processed further, for example in the form of tables, graphs, diagrams, and pictures, so it is more informative if used by others.

3.3 *Data analysis technique*

This research used descriptive method verification with quantitative data analysis to estimate the influence of several independent variables collectively and individually on dependent variables. The analysis aimed to test the hypothesis applied in researching the effect of leverage and profitability on stock returns of mining companies listed on the Indonesia Stock Exchange, with the consolidated financial statement data of mining companies for the period 2011–2015.

The analytical method used in this study was the panel data regression model. Data processing was performed using the computer program EViews 9.

4 DISCUSSION

4.1 *Descriptive analysis*

Based on the results of the descriptive analysis, stock returns, leverage, and profitability data are presented in Table 3.

Table 3 shows that stock returns has a minimum value of –0.842 and a maximum of 8.35, with a for a mean of 0.042316 and a standard deviation of 1.1492.

Leverage (DTA) has a minimum value of 0.1 and a maximum of 0.772, with a mean of 0.411897 and a standard deviation of 0.161984.

Profitability (ROA) has a minimum value of –0.7213 and a maximum of 0.75, with a mean of 0.061341 and a standard deviation of 0.155176.

4.2 *Testing panel data regression*

Hypothesis test results are presented in Table 4.

Based on Table 4, the regression equation can be written as:

$$\text{Return} = -1.9138087602 + 1.519084\,\text{DTA} + 1.748357\,\text{ROA} + [\text{CX=F}] \quad (1)$$

Table 3. Descriptive analysis results.

	Stock returns	DTA	ROA
Mean	0.042316	0.411897	0.061341
Median	–0.184000	0.400000	0.035000
Maximum	8.350000	0.772000	0.750000
Minimum	–0.842000	0.100000	–0.721300
Standard deviation	1.149215	0.161984	0.155176
Skewness	5.369795	0.394570	–0.148552
Kurtosis	35.89835	2.324523	12.28637
Jarque–Bera test	4740.660	4.271089	341.7028
Probability	0.000000	0.118180	0.000000
Sum	4.020000	39.13020	5.827400
Sum-squared deviation	124.1453	2.466442	2.263484
Observations	95	95	95

Table 4. Results of panel data regression with random effect.

Variable	Coefficient	Standard error (SE)	*t*-Statistic	Probability
C	–0.690636	0.321965	–2.145064	0.0346
DTA	1.519084	0.679869	2.234376	0.0279
ROA	1.748357	0.812411	2.152060	0.0340
Effects specification			Standard deviation (SD)	ρ
Cross-section random			0.500897	0.2024
Idiosyncratic random			0.994372	0.7976
Weighted statistics				
R-squared	0.067687	Mean dependent variable		0.028094
Adjusted *R*-squared	0.047419	SD dependent variable		1.050074
SE of regression	1.024874	Sum-squared resid		96.63382
F-statistic	3.339642	Durbin–Watson statistic		0.947773
Probability (*F*-statistic)	0.039796			
Unweighted statistics				
R-squared	0.020403	Mean dependent variable		0.042316
Sum-squared resid	121.6124	Durbin–Watson statistic		0.753105

Notes: Dependent variable: Stock return. Method: Panel estimated generalized least square (cross-section random effects). Date: 02/08/16. Time: 08:53. Sample: 2011–2015. Periods included: 5. Cross-sections included: 19. Total panel (balanced) observations: 95. Swamy-Arora estimator of component variances. White cross-section standard errors and covariance (corrected for degree pf freedom).
Source: Output EViews.

In Equation (1), white cross-section is added to minimize errors that occur in the usual random effect equation. Coefficient of DTA + 1.519084, mean DTA positive influence on stock returns, and the coefficient of ROA + 1.748357, implying ROA has a positive influence on stock returns.

4.3 *The T-test*

4.3.1 *Effect of leverage (DTA) on stock returns*

Results of t-test showed that leverage (DTA) with regression coefficient β1 = 1.519084. Stock returns have a positive and significant effect, with a 95% confidence level, where the probability of t-statistic (0.0279) is less than $\alpha = 0.05$ or t-test = 2.234376, which is greater than the t-table value of 1.662, which means that H_0 is rejected. The results are consistent with the hypothesis of the study stating that DTA has a partially positive effect on the stock returns of 19 mining companies listed on the Indonesia Stock Exchange for the period 2011–2015.

The regression coefficient of leverage (DTA) to stock returns has a positive value. It shows if leverage (DTA) increases by one unit then stock returns will increase to 1.519084. In other words, if leverage (DTA) increases then stock returns will also increase, and if DTA decreases then stock returns will also decrease.

4.3.2 *Influence of profitability on stock returns*

Results of t-test showed that profitability (ROA) with regression coefficient β2 = 1.748357. Stock returns have a positive and significant effect, with a 95% confidence level, where the probability of t-statistic (0.0340) is less than $\alpha = 0.05$ or t-test = 2.152060, which is greater than the t-table value of 1.662, which means that H_0 is rejected. These empirical findings, according to the research hypothesis, states that profitability has a partially positive effect on stock returns of 19 mining companies listed on the Indonesia Stock Exchange for the period 2011–2015.

The regression coefficient of profitability (ROA) to stock return has a positive value. It shows if profitability (ROA) increases by one unit then stock returns will increase to 1.519084. In other words, if profitability (ROA) increases then the stock returns will also increase, and if ROA decreases then stock returns will also decrease.

4.4 *The F – test*

Table 4 shows that the value of F-statistic from this research model is 3.339642. This value is greater than the F-table value of 3.10 or probability (F-statistic) of 0.039796 less than $\alpha = 0.05$, which means that H_0 is rejected. This means that the variables leverage and profitability simultaneously significantly influence stock returns.

4.5 *Test the coefficient of determination (R-squared)*

Table 4 shows that the R-squared value of the research model obtained using the random effects model is 0.067687. This suggests that stock returns can be explained by the contribution of DTA and ROA amounting to 6.7%, with a 5% level of significance. The remaining 93.3% is explained by other variables outside of the model.

5 CONCLUSION

The following conclusions can be drawn based on the results of this research and discussion about the effect of leverage and profitability on stock returns by using a population sample of mining sector companies listed on the Indonesia Stock Exchange for the period 2011–2015:

- Leverage is represented by DTA and has a regression coefficient value of 1.519084, with a significance value of 0.0279 ($P < 0.05$) and a t-test value of 2.234376, which is greater than the t-table value of 1.662. Thus, it can be concluded that leverage (DTA) significantly influences stock returns.
- Profitability is represented by ROA and has a regression coefficient value of 1.748357, with a significance value of 0.034 ($P < 0.05$) and a t-test value of 2.15206, which is greater than the t-table value of 1.662. Thus, it can be concluded that profitability (ROA) significantly influences stock returns.
- Leverage is represented by DTA and profitability is represented by ROA, which has an F-statistic value of 3.339642 that is greater than the F-table value of 3.10. So, it can be concluded that leverage and profitability simultaneously significantly influence stock returns.

6 RECOMMENDATION

Based on the results of this research, the researcher recommends the following:

- Companies outside this study sample should pay attention to factors of leverage and profitability as these can affect stock returns.
- Investors should pay attention to factors of leverage and profitability before investing in the capital market, so that the expected returns are in accordance with expectations and maximum results are obtained.

- Researchers should add other variables, use samples of companies from other sectors, and increase the period of observation by adding the most recent research year. It is aimed so that the result of his research can also describe in general and broad. In addition, researchers can use different proxies for their independent variables.

ACKNOWLEDGMENTS

The author would like to express gratitude to the Indonesia Stock Exchange for assisting in collecting research data. The author thanks the Indonesian University of Education (Universitas Pendidikan Indonesia, Bandung) and the Airlangga University that facilitated international conferences on the framework of the development of science. The author also thanks the Indonesia Endowment Fund for Education (Lembaga Pengelola Dana Pendidikan) for sponsoring the publication of this article.

REFERENCES

Acheampong, P., Agalega, E., & Shibu, A.K. (2014). The effect of financial leverage and market size on stock returns on the Ghana Stock Exchange: Evidence from selected stocks in the manufacturing sector. *International Journal of Financial Research*, *5*(1), 125–134. https://doi.org/10.5430/ijfr.v5n1p125.

Barakat, A. (2014). The impact of financial structure, financial leverage and profitability on industrial companies shares value (Applied study on a sample of Saudi industrial companies). *Research Journal of Finance and Accounting*, *5*(1), 55–66.

Eugene F. Brigham dan Joel F. Houston, 2006, *Fundamentals of Financial Management*, Salemba Empat, Jakarta.

Fahmi. (2014), *Corporate Finance Management and Capital Market*. Mitra Wacana Media, Jakarta.

Fardiansyah, T., Achsani, N. A., & Juanda, B. (2016). The relationship analysis between profitability ratio and the firm size to the banking stock return after the implementation of PBI no. 14/26/PBI/2012. *Research Journal of Finance and Accounting, 7*(10), 39–50.

Fitriadi, (2009), Effect Of Profitability, Leverage And Firm Size To Stock Return Of Property Company In Indonesia Stock Exchange In 2001–2007, Thesis, Universitas Atmajaya Yogyakarta.

Foroghi, D., & Jahromy, S. M. E. (2015). Impact of profitability on stock returns based on the price, return and differenced models in Tehran Stock Exchange. *International Journal of Applied Business and Economic Research, 13*(2), 955–970.

Gitman, L. J., & Zutter, C. J. (2012). *Principles of Managerial Finance* (13th edn.). Boston: Prentice Hall.

Hapcin, Suhairy. (2006). The Effect of Profitability Ratios And Leverage On Stock Return Of Manufacturing Companies In Indonesia Stock Exchange, Thesis, Fakultas Ekonomi Sumatera Utara, Medan.

Hartono. (2013). *Portfolio Theory And Investment Analysis*, BPFE, Yogyakarta.

Heryanto. (2016). Effect of liquidity and profitability to bank stock. *International Journal of Business and Management*, *1*(1), 17–23.

https://doi.org/10.5430/ijfr.v5n1p125.

Kabajeh, M. A., AL Nu'aimat, S. M., & Dahmash, F. N. (2012). The relationship between the ROA, ROE and ROI ratios with Jordanian insurance public companies market share prices. *International Journal of Humanities and Social Science*, *2*(11), 115–120.

Ngaisah, S. (2008), The Effect of Profitability Ratios And Leverage On Stock Return On Companies Registered In Jakarta Islamic Index (JII) Tahun, 2004–2006. Thesis, Fakultas Syari'ah, Universitas Islam Negri Sunan Kalijaga, Yogyakarta.

Prawironegoro, D. (2006), *Financial Management*, Jakarta: Diadit Media.

Sunarto. 2001. Effect of Profitability Ratios and Leverage Against Stock Return of Manufacturing Companies In BEJ. *GEMA STIKUBANK, Edisi 33, No. 3, Juni 2001, hal. 63–81.*

Van Horne James C, Wachowich Jr. Jhon M (1997) *Principles of Financial Management*. Heru Sutojo Translation, Indonesian Edition, Penerbit Salemba Empat, Jakarta.

Increasing Management Relevance and Competitiveness – Sukoco et al. (Eds)
© 2018 Taylor & Francis Group, London, ISBN 978-0-8153-7455-8

Asymmetric information at first seasoned equity offering in the Indonesian capital market

H. Meidiaswati
Kartini University, Surabaya, Indonesia

Basuki & Andry Irwanto
Universitas Airlangga, Surabaya, Indonesia

ABSTRACT: The aim of this study is to determine whether the Signaling Theory or the Market Feedback Theory has more explaining power regarding the relationship between Initial Public Offering (IPO) and First Seasoned Equity Offering (FiSEO) in the Indonesian capital market. The findings of this study show that asymmetric information exists in the Indonesian capital market related to IPO and FiSEO. The Signaling Theory can explain the speed of FiSEO in the Indonesian capital market. Nevertheless, the Market Feedback Theory has more explaining power than the Signaling Theory in relation to the offering value of the FiSEO. Another finding of this study indicates the influence of the corporate lifecycle on the speed of FiSEO. Further research can be directed to answer the question as to whether FiSEO in Indonesia is pre-planned decisions in timing the market (Baker & Wurgler, 2002) or the impact of the dynamics of the corporate lifecycle (DeAngelo et al., 2010; Hovakimian & Hutton, 2010).

Keywords: IPO, FiSEO, Asymmetric Information, Signaling Theory, Market Feedback Theory

1 INTRODUCTION

First Seasoned Equity Offering (FiSEO) is interesting, as it is generally conducted by a relatively young company with little experience, making it vulnerable to uncertainty. Two interesting theories to be examined with regard to FiSEO are related to the Initial Public Offering (IPO). First, the Signaling Theory (Allen & Faulhaber, 1989; Grinblatt & Hwang, 1989; Welch, 1989, 1996; Chemmanur, 1993) states that good quality companies deliberately signal to the market, in the hope that the market can differentiate good and bad quality companies. To be effective, signals must be accepted and perceived as good and not easily imitated by poor quality companies (Megginson, 1997). According to the Signaling Theory, good quality issuers have, from the beginning, planned to raise funds in stages. According to Jegadeesh et al. (1993), the higher the underpricing: (1) the more likely the company to issue Seasoned Equity Offering (SEO), (2) the greater the number of shares issued during SEO, and (3) the faster the implementation of SEO. In contrast, according to Welch (1996), good quality companies that underprice can take longer to issue FiSEO. A good quality company will issue FiSEO when the market has realized the true value of the company. The magnitude of underpricing does not make a good quality company immediately issue FiSEO, which increases the probability of poor quality companies that imitate underpricing, thus revealing the true value. Issuers can also signal to the market through the selection of underwriters. A reputable underwriter will minimize asymmetric information between the issuer and the investor, and minimize investment risk in the primary market. Markets believe eminent underwriters will not guarantee low quality companies.

The second is the Market Feedback Theory (Garfinkel, 1993; Jegadeesh et al., 1993; Levis, 1995; Spiess & Pettway, 1997; Espenlaub & Tonks, 1998; Van Bommel & Vermaelen, 2003; Hill & Hillier, 2009). According to this theory, aftermarket return also shows the possibility of issuing FiSEO rather than underpricing IPO shares. After the IPO, the market will make a correction on stock price, so the issuer will consider issuing equity (SEO) for subsequent financing needs. The real value realization of the issuer will appear on the 20th or 40th day after the first day of trading (Jegadeesh et al., 1993).

The two theories are interesting because they are derived from asymmetric information. The Signaling Theory is based on a common assumption that many researchers often use asymmetric information, that the issuer has more information about the company than the outsider. In contrast, the Market Feedback Theory believes that investors and markets are more understanding about the value of issuers.

2 LITERATURE REVIEW

IPO is a company's first step into the capital market by selling some of its shares to the public. The collection of funds in the capital markets by publicly listed companies is known by several terms, such as seasoned common stock issuance (Slovin et al., 1994), equity offering following the IPO (Welch, 1996), sequential financing (Chang et al., 2004), or, as Hertzel et al. (2012) term it, staging. Several studies use a fund-raising policy by a company that has gone public as a model to prove underpricing hypotheses of shares at an IPO. Kennedy et al. (2006) summarize at least two theories related to underpricing and seasoned offerings: (1) the Signaling Theory by Allen and Faulhaber (1989), Grinblatt and Hwang (1989), and Welch (1989); and (2) the Market Feedback Theory by Garfinkel (1993), Jegadeesh et al. (1993), Levis (1995), Spiess and Pettway (1997), Espenlaub and Tonks (1998), Van Bommel and Vermaelen (2003), and Hill and Hillier (2009). Underpricing in the primary market is indicated to be the basis for determining company policy when returning to the capital market. The amount of underpricing is expected to be a reference to two types of decisions made by the company when conducting the seasoned offering: (1) time of seasoned financing, and (2) the amount of funds raised during the seasoned offering. Jegadeesh et al. (1993) found a positive relationship between IPO underpricing and the probability and value of subsequent seasoned offerings.

Some researchers indicate underpricing of IPO shares as a signal from the issuer to potential investors (Allen & Faulhaber, 1989; Jegadeesh, 1991). This signaling is done because of the asymmetric information between the issuer and the potential investors, who generally do not know the condition of the company before going public. Asymmetric information encourages issuers to signal to the market about the quality of the company. Signaling is done after the company goes public by underpricing the stock. This signal is expected to be acceptable and perceived by the investor as the agent wishes. After the first day of trading, information about the company will be more open so that the market will react to the information with marked increase in stock market prices after trading in the secondary market.

Based on the time, the return earned in the capital market is divided into two, that is, the income earned during the first day's trading, known as the initial return, and return earned on trading in the secondary market. IPO share earnings on the first day of trading are known as initial returns. The initial return can be calculated using absolute price or adjusting with market earnings (Ahmad-Zaluki & Kect, 2012). Meanwhile, the earnings of shares in the secondary market can be calculated using Cumulative Abnormal Returns (CARs).

There are several theories related to underpricing. One of which is asymmetric information in the distribution of information between market participants, that include: issuers, underwriters and investors (Fabrizio, S. & De Lorenzo, M, 2001; Al-Shammari et al., 2013). Although beneficial to investors, underpricing becomes a cost for issuers because they have to bear a number of potential funds that cannot be realized (leaving money on the table) (Ritter & Welch, 2002). Therefore, only qualified issuers are able and willing to conduct underpricing at the IPO. For investors, underpricing will provide a good experience (Jenkinson, 1990). Good experience at the time of IPO is expected to increase interest in buying shares when raising additional funds.

From the issuer's point of view, the IPO underpricing phenomenon is very detrimental. Underpricing causes losses for issuers because of the large "money left on the table," which creates the company's goal to obtain large funds from the IPO, which is not optimal. Possible indications are that the issuer considers underpricing as the cost of going public or the cost of obtaining funds from the capital market through two subsequent offerings: (1) third offering and (2) SEO (Hertzel et al., 2012). According to the Signaling Theory of good quality, company managers will set an underpriced IPO price to signal that the company's share value is undervalued. They will then make a subsequent offering at a higher price.

According to Jegadeesh (1991), there is a positive relationship between the level of underpricing and the possibility of the company re-raising funds and issuing securities in the market and the amount of funds needed. Jegadeesh et al. (1993) found a positive relationship between IPO underpricing and the possibility of making seasoned offerings, and the tendency to make it within three years after the IPO. Companies that get less funds at the IPO (highly underpriced) will make additional capital faster. Meanwhile, according to Hertzel et al. (2012), many companies recognize that the funds collected during an IPO are not sufficient to fund the expected investment in the future. This insufficiency is anticipated by returning to the stock market.

The Signaling Theory is the result of asymmetric information between the parties that interact. Asymmetric information encourages interested parties to signal to be captured by others as desired by the signal giver. This signaling is expected to benefit the parties, as it minimizes asymmetric information between the parties that interact. Asymmetric information can occur between issuers and investors in the capital market, and issuers can have more information than investors. According to Morse (1981), the main assumption of the Signaling Theory is that management has more complete and accurate information about the value of firms and that foreign investors do not know about factors that affect firm value.

Allen and Faulhaber (1989) assume that the company has information about the quality and prospects that are not known to outside investors. Companies use underpricing as a signal to show their quality and will sell a small portion of their shares at the time of the initial offer.

Initial return influences the speed of seasoned offering (Jegadeesh et al., 1993; Welch, 1996; Crouzet et al., 2003). IPO underpricing is positively related to the speed of conducting SEO and the value of offerings issued during seasoned offerings (Jegadeesh et al., 1993; Crouzet et al., 2003). Conversely, good quality companies that underprice can also take longer to issue FiSEO. Good quality companies will issue SEO when the market has realized the true value of the company (Welch, 1996). Good quality companies show their superiority through the size of underpricing and the length of time FiSEO takes. Welch (1989) and Jegadeesh et al. (1993) stated that the level of underpricing will determine the offering price at SEO. The higher the underpricing of IPO, the higher the stock price during SEO.

In addition to underpricing, issuers can also signal through the selection of underwriters. According to Fernando et al. (2005), the underwriter's reputation can be used as a quality signal of the issuer. A qualified issuer will choose a reputable underwriter (Fernando et al., 2005; Carter et al., 2010; Jones & Swaleheen, 2010). According to Jones and Swaleheen (2010), the company chooses a reputable underwriter to send signals to the market. Reputation of underwriters is also positively associated with underpricing of shares (Carter & Manaster, 1990).

Both theories are derived from asymmetric information between issuers and investors: The Market Feedback Theory assumes that investors (in aggregate) have more information than issuers (Garfinkel, 1993; Levis, 1995, Spiess & Pettway, 1997; Espenlaub & Tonks, 1998; Subrahmanyam & Titman, 1999; Van Bommel & Vermaelen, 2003; Hill & Hillier, 2007). The theory also assumes the market is efficient, so that issuers can observe the market price during the IPO and obtain valuable information from the observation. According to the Market Feedback Theory, underpricing is done to encourage regular investors to disclose information about actual company value. The issuer's investment decisions will depend on market opinion on the value of the company. If the price formed after the IPO is profitable, the issuer will consider returning to the market through the issuance of equity.

Jegadeesh et al. (1993), Welch (1996), Crouzet et al. (2003), and Hertzel et al. (2012) indicate that, to test the underpricing theory, in addition to connecting the level of underpricing of shares with subsequent financing, it is also necessary to examine the stock performance after the IPO. Stock price performance after the IPO can reflect the company's condition more than the initial return. This is because, after the IPO, information related to the issuer will be more publicized, so that investors will get a more complete picture of the issuer. Stock performance after the IPO can be measured from observations in the short run, usually within six days after the IPO (Espenlaub & Tonks, 1998). Stock performance after the IPO can be calculated by two methods of event time approach, that is, CARs and Buy-and-Hold Abnormal Returns (BHARs). Both methods of event time approach have advantages, where CAR is more suitable for calculating short- or medium-term returns, whereas BHAR is more appropriate for calculating long-term returns. According to Jegadeesh et al., (1993), firms with higher CAR tend to implement SEO faster. Meanwhile, according to Welch (1996), the higher the aftermarket performance of IPO shares the shorter the time between IPO and SEO.

According to Jegadeesh et al., (1993), post-IPO CAR is positively related to SEO probability and the value of SEO. Therefore, although the results of Jegadeesh et al. (1993) are consistent with the Signaling Theory, when viewed as a whole, it does not agree in terms of signaling as the main determinant of IPO underpricing. Welch (1989) indicated that even underpricing can be a means of signaling investors; the main objective is to maximize the bid price on the next issue of the stock. Meanwhile, according to Hertzel et al. (2012), underpricing IPO shares is in accordance with the staging hypothesis, because the manager of a good quality company will limit the shares issued at the IPO in order to raise capital through subsequent offering at a higher price. Post-IPO share performance is one of the 'considerations of companies in determining the price of securities to be issued at subsequent offerings.

3 RESEARCH METHOD

This is an explanatory research to analyze the relationship between variables and explain the influence between variables through hypothesis testing. This research uses secondary data from the Indonesia Stock Exchange website, Britama website, Indonesian Capital Market Electronic Library, and The Financial Services Authority (Otoritas Jasa Keuangan). The sample is 128 non-financial companies that conducted IPOs in the Indonesian Stock Exchange during the period 1990–2013 and FiSEO with the following criteria: (1) Companies conducted FiSEO during the observation period; (2) consistently registered with the Indonesian capital market in accordance with its industry during the study period; (3) did not engage in other corporate actions other than FiSEO up to 40 days after the IPO; and (4) the financial statements end on December 31 of each year.

Tests have been conducted with linear regression. The stock's first day of trading return was measured by Market—Adjusted Initial Return (MAIR). Aftermarket returns of 20 and 40 days after the IPO are measured by CAR over the period from trading day 1 to day 20 after the IPO date for CAR20, and during 20 and 40 days' post-IPO period for CAR40. Robustness test is done by dividing the sample into two based on the median, as well as eliminating the data during the economic crises that occurred in Indonesia in the period 1997–98 and 2008–09.

4 EMPIRICAL RESULT

This research shows that the pattern of FiSEO in the Indonesian capital market can be proved by two theories that derive from the asymmetrical theory. Viewed from the speed of FiSEO, the first day's earnings of shares prove the Signaling Theory exists in the Indonesian capital market. This indicates that issuers in the Indonesian capital market have an understanding of the company's value, although limited, and try to inform its value when conducting an IPO. This means that, in the short run, the company is still considering the quality signal with the IPO to determine the timing of funds accumulated through FiSEO, especially on issuers who quickly implement FiSEO. In companies that are slow to perform FiSEO, quality signals are no longer usable. The slower the company performs FiSEO, the more factors that can affect the company's policy of issuing FiSEO, and the quality signal at the time of the IPO is no longer relevant.

These results are consistent with those of Welch (1989), Carter and Manaster (1990), Jegadeesh (1991), and Jegadeesh et al., (1993), in that the speed of a company's FiSEO can be explained by the Signaling Theory and underpricing when IPOs are made by issuers as a signal to investors about the quality of issuers. When investors already know the true value of the stock, then the stock price will move closer to the real value.

The findings of this study differ slightly from those of Jegadeesh et al. (1993), and further support Welch (1996) in terms of the effect of short-term return on the speed of FiSEO. This study shows that the greater the initial return, the longer the issuers conduct FiSEO. One of the reasons for issuers to underprice is to give a signal about the quality of a company, which is difficult to imitate by poor quality companies. Good quality companies show their superiority with daring underpricing and longer waiting time for FiSEO (Welch, 1996). Good quality companies will not be in a hurry to issue FiSEO, as they are financially secure and may already be planning staging emissions (Table 1).

Underwriter Reputation (UnREP) can, in a limited fashion, be used as a proxy for the issuer's quality signals. Further studies are needed to determine whether UnREP is properly used as a signal to implement FiSEO. The review can be done by confirming whether the underwriters during the IPO and FiSEO are the same or changed and how they affect the post-IPO and FiSEO returns. This is to confirm whether the issuer's quality signals include those considered by investors in realizing the issuer's value and are reflected in the short-term post-IPO market performance (Table 2).

Table 1. Regression result for speed of SEOs.

	All SEOs		Quick SEOs		Late SEOs	
Variable	Model 1	Model 2	Model 3	Model 4	Model 5	Model 6
MAIR	0.004**	0.004**	0.005**	0.004**	4.104	0.001
UnREP	–0.004	0.004	0.003	0.002	–0.008	0.002
CAR20	0.002	2.10^{-4}	–0.001	-4.10^{-4}	–0.001	-2.10^{-4}
CAR40	–0.003	–0.002	–0.003	–0.003	5.104	0.002
ROA		0.014		0.005		0.003
Age		0.017**		–0.011**		0.010**
Size		–0.136		–0.014		–0.103
CAPEX		–0.006		0.005		–0.077
DTA		0.005		0.002		–0.002
Constant	1.304	4.166	0.645	0.718	2.010	4.212
R^2	0.044	0.185	0.111	0.233	0.025	0.197

The independent variables are: MAIR (Market Adjusted Initial Return), UnREP (Underwriter Reputation), CAR (Cumulative Abnormal Return), ROA (Return on Assets), CAPEX (Capital Expenditure), DTA (Debt to Total Assets).
*Significant at 10% level.
**Significant at 5% level.

Table 2. Regression result for volume of SEOs.

	All SEOs		Quick SEOs		Late SEOs	
Variable	Model 1	Model 2	Model 3	Model 4	Model 5	Model 6
MAIR	0.002	0.002	0.002	0.002	–0.001	–0.001
UnREP	–0.014	–0.007	–0.025	–0.020	–0.009	0.002
CAR20	0.006**	0.005**	0.003	0.002	0.008**	0.009**
CAR40	–0.007	–0.007	–0.004	–0.005	–0.006	–0.004
ROA		0.011		–0.002		0.006
Age		0.005		–0.020*		0.022
Size		–0.058		0.063		–0.108**
CAPEX		–0.014		–0.004		–0.077
DTA		–0.003		–0.006		–0.004
Constant	1.209	2.707	0.985	–0.059	1.515	4.003
R^2	0.107	0.123	0.111	0.191	0.114	0.184

*Significant at 10% level.
**Significant at 5% level.

The testing of the Market Feedback Theory shows CAR20 affects the value of FiSEO in all samples and groups of companies that are late implementing FiSEO. By the time a company regains funds over a long period of time, quality signals are no longer relevant for consideration. The company, therefore, uses market feedback around the IPO to determine the funds raised through FiSEO. The 40th day earnings are insignificant, indicating that, after the 20th day, the earnings are not used as feedback for issuers for FiSEO decisions.

These results are similar to FiSEO in capital markets of developed countries. This is due to the fact that, although the Indonesian capital market belongs to emerging market capital, the dominance of foreign investors with better investment capability or those more sophisticated (informed) makes information asymmetric, and especially FiSEO policy tends to be the same as phenomena in developed countries. The results of research related to the speed of FiSEO in the Indonesian capital market support findings from Welch (1996). The value-related supply of this study supports the findings of Jegadeesh et al. (1993), Levis (1995), Spiess and Pettway (1997), Espenlaub and Tonks (1998), Van Bommel and Vermaelen (2003), and Hill and Hillier (2007), who argue that the Market Feedback Theory is more able to explain the FiSEO phenomenon.

The results show that aftermarket performance of IPOs becomes an important indication of a company's decision to conduct FiSEO in the Indonesian capital market, as in England (Levis, 1995) and the United States (Jegadeesh et al., 1993). These results are not entirely consistent with those of Garfinkel (1993), Jegadeesh et al. (1993), Levis (1995), Spiess and Pettway (1997), and Espenlaub and Tonks (1998), which state that the influence of signals provided through underpricing is weak, so it does not support the Signaling Theory. In this study, the Signaling Theory can be explained from the current offer value of FiSEO through MAIR, if the short-term income is measured by BHAR. This influence is consistent both with and without control variables. Jegadeesh (1991) and Jegadeesh et al. (1993) stated that the real value of the issuer will appear on the 20th or 40th day after the first trading day of the stock.

This study supports Jegadeesh et al. (1993), Levis (1995), Spiess and Pettway (1997), Espenlaub and Tonks (1998), and Hill and Hillier (2007), who argue that market feedback is more able to explain the FiSEO phenomenon. It means that FiSEO in the Indonesian capital market is similar to FiSEO in developed countries. The uniqueness of the Indonesian capital market is caused by the number of investors, the characteristics of investors, the number of shares traded, market capitalization, and the number and speed of issuers in the SEO. Both capital markets are driving companies issuing strategies to get feedback from the market and utilizing feedback for investment decisions. This occurs because, although the issuer understands the business and its workings, the market has a different mechanism in assessing the issuer. As a new player, issuers use feedback from the market in the form of stock market price movements as a consideration for company policy, especially FiSEO. This result is supported by the condition of the Indonesian capital market dominated by foreign investors who have better knowledge and investment skills than local investors.

At various tests, the firm's age consistently affects FiSEO. These results indicate that the issuer's FiSEO policy in the Indonesian capital market is strongly influenced by the company's maturity, as measured by the company's age, in addition to signal and market feedback considerations as a consequence of information asymmetry.

5 CONCLUSION

The Signaling Theory, proxied by MAIR, can explain the speed of FiSEO in the Indonesian capital market. The greater the value of MAIR, as an indication of the company's quality signal, the longer and more patiently issuers wait to conduct FiSEO. In addition to MAIR, the company's speed of performing FiSEO is influenced by control variables, such as age and firm size. These results indicate that, taking into account age and size, for firms that are in a period of rapid growth and maturity in meeting the needs of development funds or maintaining the company's position externally, FiSEO is one of the alternatives to cover previous capital expenditures, especially companies that are at the growth stage of their life cycle. Companies that are already in the maturity stage tend to use internal funding sources or debt and, therefore, tend to slower FiSEO.

Stock earnings from the 20th day (CAR20) have a significant effect on the value of FiSEO. The effect of CAR20 is strong, because it remains significant with or without control variables. This suggests that, with regard to the magnitude of the offer value at FiSEO, the Market Feedback Theory is better able to explain FiSEO policy than the Signaling Theory. As a market feedback indicator, earnings from the 20th day can better explain the value of the company's offerings at FiSEO compared with earnings from the 40th day. These results indicate that information over 20 days after the IPO is not relevant as a feedback to FiSEO.

Subsequent research can be directed to testing theories using different proxies or measures, as well as testing other theories (other than the Signaling Theory and the Market Feedback Theory) to obtain a broader picture of the theories applicable to FiSEO policies. The lifecycle of a company may be considered as one of the material considerations because the results of testing company age consistently affect the speed and value of FiSEO. It is also interesting to review whether the Signaling Theory and the Market Feedback Theory can explain advanced SEO.

REFERENCES

Ahmad-Zaluki, N.A. & Kect, L. B. 2012. The Investment Performance of Mesdaq Market Initial Public Offerings (IPOs). *Asian Academy of Management Journal of Accounting and Finance*. 8 (1): 1–23.

Allen, F. & Faulhaber, G. R. (1989). Signaling by underpricing in the IPO market. *Journal of Financial Economics*, 23(2), 303–323.

Al-Shammari, H. A., O'Brien, W. R. & Al-Busaidi, Y. H. (2013). Firm internalization and IPO firm performance. *International Journal of Commerce and Management*, 23(3), 242–261.

Baker, M. & Wurgler, J. (2002). Market timing and capital structure. *The Journal of Finance*, 57(1), 1–32.

Carter, R. B. & Manaster, S. (1990). Initial public offerings and underwriter reputation. *Journal of Finance, 45*(4), 1045–1067.

Carter, R. B., Dark, F. H. & Sapp, T. R. A. (2010). Underwriter reputation and IPO issuer alignment 1981–2005. *The Quarterly Review of Economics and Finance, 50*, 443–455.

Chang, S-C., Chen, S-S. & Liu, Y. (2004). Why firms use convertibles: A further test of the sequential-financing hypothesis. *Journal of Banking & Finance, 28*, 1163–1183.

Chemmanur, T. J. (1993). The pricing of initial public offerings: A dynamic model with information production. *Journal of Finance*, 48, 285–304.

Crouzet, F., Ginglinger, E. E. & Vijayraghavan V. (2003). French IPO returns and subsequent security offerings: Signaling hypothesis versus market feedback hypothesis. Working Paper. Paris: University of Paris.

DeAngelo, H., DeAngelo, L. & Stulz, R. M. (2010). Seasoned equity offerings, market timing, and the corporate lifecycle. *Journal of Financial Economics*, 95, 275–295.

Espenlaub, S. & Tonks, I. (1998). Post-IPO directors' sales and reissuing activity: An empirical test Of IPO signalling models. *Journal of Business Finance and Accounting*, 25(9), 1037–1079.

Fabrizio, S. & De Lorenzo, M. (2001). Asymmetric information and the role of underwriter. The prospectus and the analyst in underpricing of IPO. The Italian case. *Social Science Research Network*. https:papers.ssrn.com/sol3/papers.cfm?abstract_id = 279251.

Fernando, C. S., Gatchev, V. A. & Spindt, P.A. (2005). Wanna dance? How firms and underwriters choose each other. *Journal of Finance*, 60, 2437–2469.

Garfinkel, J. (1993). IPO underpricing, insider selling and subsequent equity offerings: Is underpricing a signal of quality? *Financial Management, 22*, 74–83.

Grinblatt, M. & Hwang, C. Y. (1989). Signalling and the pricing of new issues. *The Journal of Finance*, 44, 393–420.

Hertzel, M. G., Huson, M. R. & Parrino, R. (2012). Public market staging: The timing of capital infusions in newly public firms. *Journal of Finance Economics*, 106, 72–90.

Hill, P. & Hillier, D. (2009). Market feedback, investment constraints, and managerial behavior. *European Financial Management*, 15(3), 584–605.

Hovakimian, A. & Hutton, I. (2010). Merger motivated IPOs. *Financial Management,* 39(4), 1547–1573.

Jegadeesh, N. (1991). Seasonality in stock price mean reversion: Evidence from the US and UK. *Journal of Finance*, 46, 1427–1444.

Jegadeesh, N., Weinstein, M. & Welch, I. (1993). An empirical investigation of IPO returns and subsequent equity offerings. *Journal of Financial Economics*, 34(2), 153–175.

Jenkinson, T. J. 1990. Initial public offerings in the United Kingdom, the United States, and Japan, *Journal of the Japanese and International Economies*, 4, 428–449.

Jensen, M. C. & Meckling, W. H. 1976. Theory of the firm: Managerial behavior, agency costs and ownership structure. Journal of Financial Economics, 3(4), 305–360.

Jones, T. L. & us Swaleheen, M. (2010). Endogenous examination of underwriter reputation and IPO returns. *Managerial Finance*, 36(4), 284–293.

Kennedy, D., Ranjini, S. & Vetzal, K. (2006). The implications of IPO underpricing for the firm and insiders. *Journal of Empirical Finance*, 13(1), 49–78.

Levis, M. (1995). Seasoned equity offerings and the short-run and long-run performance of initial public offerings in the UK. *European Financial Management*, 1(2), 125–146.

Megginson, W. (1997). *Corporate finance theory*. United States: Addison-Westley.

Morse, D. (1981). Price and trading volume reaction surrounding earnings announcements: A closer examination. *Journal of Accounting Research*, 19, 374–383.

Ritter, J. R. & Welch, I. (2002). A review of IPO activity, pricing, and allocations, *The Journal of Finance*, 57(4), 1795–1828.

Slovin, M. B, Sushka, M. E. & Bendeck, Y. M. (1994). Seasoned common stock issuance following an IPO. *Journal of Banking and Finance*, 18, 207–226.

Spiess, D. K. & Pettway, R. H. (1997). The IPO and first seasoned equity sale: Issue proceeds, owner/managers' wealth, and the underpricing signal. *Journal of Banking and Finance,* 21(7), 967–988.

Subrahmanyam, A., & Titman, S. (1999). The Going-Public Decision and the Development of Financial Markets. *The Journal of Finance*, 54-(3): 1045–1082.

Van Bommel, J. & Vermaelen, T. (2003). Post-IPO capital expenditures and market feedback. *Journal of Banking and Finance*, 58, 1499–1520.

Welch, I. (1989). Seasoned offerings, imitation costs, and the underpricing of initial public offerings. *Journal of Finance*, 44, 421–449.

Welch, I. (1996). Equity offering following the IPO theory and evidence. *Journal of Corporate Finance*, 2, 227–259.

Increasing Management Relevance and Competitiveness – Sukoco et al. (Eds)
© 2018 Taylor & Francis Group, London, ISBN 978-0-8153-7455-8

Efficiency analysis of economic empowerment program in Surabaya National Amil Zakat Institution using Data Envelopment Analysis method (DEA)

F. Ramadhani & E.F. Cahyono
Universitas Airlangga, Surabaya, Indonesia

ABSTRACT: This study aims to examine the efficiency level of community empowerment programs at Surabaya. National Amil Zakat Instititution. This research uses a non-parametric quantitative approach with Data Envelopment Analysis method. Sampling is taken from three National Amil Zakat Institutions in Surabaya according to specified sample criteria. For the periods 2015 to 2016, the average relative value of economic empowerment programs with Varibale Return to Scale (VRS) assumptions is more efficient than the Constant Reutrn to Scale (CRS) assumptions. This indicates that, in relative terms, the community empowerment program at LAZNAS has achieved only technical efficiency, but is not yet optimal in scale efficiency.

1 INTRODUCTION

One of the most crucial problems in the economic sector experienced by most developing countries, including Indonesia, is poverty. Recorded up to 2016, the the population living below the poverty line as of March 2016 was 28,000,410 people or 10.86% of the Indonesia total population (Statistik 2016). In its efforts to alleviate poverty and inequality in Indonesia, the government has allocated a 2016 Amendment Budget Revised State Budget (APBN-P) of 776.3 trillion (Ministry of Finance,-2016), but it has not been able to fully solve the poverty problem in Indonesia.

Islam has a solution to eradicate poverty, which is by the development of zakat. Zakat is part of the Five Pillars of Islam that must be observed by every Muslim. According to (Al Qardawi 1999) argued that Islam views the poor as something that endangers aqidah, morals, healthy, family, and society.

Zakat aims not only to provide consumptive support the poor, but also to have a broader purpose of, meeting the deficiency in society's needs. Zakat can minimize social disparity, and can also reduce the numbers in of people in ling tem poverty (Huda, Suprayogi et al. 2012).

The majority of the Indonesian population is Muslim, so there is a huge potential of zakat. The results of research by the National Amil Board (BAZNAS) and the Bogor Agricultural Institute (IPB) in 2011 showed that the potential of zakat in Indonesia is estimated to reach IDR-296 trillion annually. The potential of zakat in 2015 was estimated to reach IDR286 trillion, its calculated based on the gross domestic product (GDP). As GDP increases, the potential of zakat also received increases (Brodjonegoro 2016). This data show there to be a great impact in alleviating poverty if zakat funds are absorbed optimally.

Zakat and infaq (altruistic activities) given to mustahiq will serve as a supporter of economic improvement if consumed in productive activities. The utilization of productive zakat actually has a careful planning and implementation concepts, -such as in studying the causes of poverty, including—the least working capital and lack of employment; with the presence of these problems, there is a need for productive zakat development.

Zakat funds and infaq funds (altruistic activities) distributed for productive activities and will be more efficient and effective if implemented by the Surabaya Natinal Amil Zakat Institutitution (LAZ) or Amil Zakat Board (BAZ), because these institutions allocate, utilize and distribute zakat funds professionally They—necessarily provide zakat funds, but also support the *mustahiq* providing training and guidance so that the funds are really distributed optimally and usefully, —so that the *mustahiq* can obtain feasible and independent income. Economic empowerment programs aim to raise the living standard of the poor (minimizing poverty) and can also change a person's enttlitement from zakat recipient (mustahiq) into obligatory zakat (*muzzaki*). To achieve these goals requires the roles and responsibilities of both parties, the parties are the Amil Zakat Institution and the mustahiq for the economic empowerment program to run optimally. Thus, the efficiency of the economic empowerment program becomes important. The more efficient a program or the organization of the Zakat Institute, the greater the positive impact for all parties to realize greater benefit for the people.

Efficiency is the ratio comparison between output and input (Rusydiana et al 2013). Efficiency is one of many parameters that are often used to measure organizational performance. In running an institution, or-, in this case, to run a program, efficiency is required in program management, such as in how much use is made of existing inputs for optimal output achievement.

This research uses a non-parametric Data Envelopment Analysis (DEA) method because this method is the most flexible to measure efficiency. The measurement technique using DEA has two models: CRS (Constant Return to Scale) and VRS (Variable Return to Scale). According to (Rusydiana et al. (2013), the CRS model is an economic efficiency measurement (overall technical efficiency) while the VRS model measures the technical efficiency (pure technical efficiency). A unit is said to be efficient if its value reaches 100%. The farther from 100% or near the nearere to 0%, the more inefficient. Based on the background, the writers intend to examine the "Efficiency Analysis of Economic Empowerment Program in Surabaya National Amil Zakat Institution (LAZNAS) using the Data Envelopment Analysis Method."

2 LITERATURE REVIEW

2.1 *The concept of economic empowerment*

According to Mubyarto (1997:26), empowerment is an effort to build the power of society by encouraging, motivating and awakening public awareness on the potential possessed and then striving to develop it.

Community economic empowerment is in the sense of developing the economic system of society by society and for the benefit of the community itself by developing and increasing the potentials and abilities of society. In addition being supported to—utilize resources efficiently and effectively to encourage economic development of people will increase people's productivity (Maghfiroh 2015).

According to—Raharjo (2014), community economic empowerment has three missions. First, economic and business development missions that have universal economic and business benchmarks, such as production, employment, profit, savings, investment, and export-import. Second, the implementation of ethics and the provisions of Islamic law, which is a must in the economic activities of Muslims. Third, building the Islamic economic powers becomes a source of funds and proponents of da'wah that can be obtained through zakat, infaq, shadaqah, and waqf.

2.2 *Efficiency concept*

Efficiency is the ratio comparison between output and input (Rusydiana et al., 2013:9). In the efficiency concept proposed by Worthington (Tanjung & Devi 2013:320) there are three types of efficiency:

1. *Technical efficiency_* an efficiency that refers to maximizing output with a certain amount of input.
2. *Allocative efficiency_* a combination of efficiency selection between the use of technically efficient inputs to produce the maximum output.
3. *Cost efficiency* or economic efficiency a combination of technical efficiency and allocative efficiency.

2.3 *Efficiency in islamic economics*

Islam greatly recommends efficiency, from the efficiency of time and, financesto not doing and saying anything—futile (not useful) or perfroming actions that can cause harm or evil.

Time efficiency in Islam demands the optimal use of time, so that there is no wasted time.

Allah *Subhanahu Wa Ta'ala* has given a great blessing of age,. for which God is worshipped. Man who wastes age is a loser. Man must be able to use the Time or Age that is given efficiently, as well as believing in Allah SWT, doing good deeds, counseling each other in truth, counseling in patience, not being wasteful and utilizing his money in the right way.

Based on the above verse, the efficiency concept should be set for the performance of the economic empowerment program so that LAZNAS can manage input and output optimally.

2.4 *Data Envelopment Analysis (DEA)*

DEA is a frontier analysis methods using non-parametric techniques to measure the relative efficiency level of an operational unit, through calculating the efficiency value of each unit in a data set. DE used to identify a frontier in evaluating the performance of the investigated entities, hence it iscalled "an envelop" (Cooper, et al. 2006:19).

DEA is designed to measure the relative efficiency of a Decision Making Unit (DMU) by combining multiple inputs and multiple outputs simultaneously. Calculations using DEA will result in the relative efficiency of each DMU, which is the ratio of the number of weighed outputs towards the weighted input. DEA can be formulated as follows (Rusydiana et al.. 2013:21):

$$Efficiency\,of\;DMU = \frac{\sum_{i=1}^{m} \mu_i y_{is}}{\sum_{r=1}^{n} v_r x_{rs}} \quad (1)$$

Remarks:
m = Number of outputs
y_{is} = Total i output produced by organization/DMUs

μ_i = Weight for i output produced by organization/DMUs

n = Number of inputs

X_{rs} = Number of j input used by the organization/DMU s

V_r = Weight of j input given by the organization/DMU s

l = 1,2, ..., m

r = 1,2, ..., n

On the scale, DMU has an variety efficiency score from 0% to 100%. DEA is a frontier analysis using two approach models, the CCR model with C CRS assumption, and the BCC model with Variable to Scale (VRS) assumption variables. Both models are more explicitly detailed as follows (Rusydiana et al, 2013:22).

1. Constant Return to Scale (CRS)

This model was popularized by Charles, Cooper, and Rhodes in 1978 and termed the CCR by using Constant Return to Scale (CRS) assumption. As the name implies, this model assumes that the addition of one unit of input will result in the addition of one unit of output or the addition ratio between input and output additions must be the same. An additional input of x times will increase the output by x times as well. Another assumption is that each DMU operates optimally. (Rusydiana, 2013: 22).

2. Variable to Scale (VRS) variable

This model was developed in 1984 by Bunker, Charnes and Cooper and termed BCC with Return to Scale Variables (VRS) assumption. This model assumes that DMU has not operated optimally, so, in this model, the ratios between input and output additions are not equal (Return to Scale Variable). An additional input of x times will not cause an increase in output by x times as well but may be smaller or greater than x times. (Rusydiana, 2013: 22).

3 RESEARCH METHODS

3.1 *Input and output variables*

Input Variables:

1. Operational Cost of Economic Empowerment Program: Costs incurred by the Amil Zakat Institution as a cost to carry out activities or operations on the economic empowerment program.
2. Personnel Costs of Economic Empowerment Program: Costs incurred by the Amil Zakat Instittution for the salaries of employees or workers in the economic empowerment program.
3. Socialization Cost of Economic Empowerment Program: Costs incurred by the Amil Zakat Institution to introduce or socialize the economic empowerment program by advertising, distributing brochures and others.

Output Variables:

1. Funds accumulated for economic empowerment programs: zakat funds, infaq, and shadaqah that are obtained by Amil Zakat institution for the economic empowerment program
2. Distributed Capital for *mustahiq* in economic empowerment programs: funds distributed or incurred for muzzaki in economic empowerment programs.
3. Number of Mustahiq: Number of Mustahiq who followed or registered in an economic empowerment program.

3.2 *Population and sample*

The population used in this research is the Zakat Institution, which already has a certificate as a National Amil Zakat Institute (LAZNAS) based on Indonesian Ministry of Religious Affair No. 333 Year 2015, using purposive sampling technique.

3.3 *Types and data sources*

This research uses quantitative secondary data type in the form of the financial reports of the Economic Empowerment Program from Amil Zakat Institution from 2015 to 2016. The secondary data used in this study is sourced from the relevant Amil Zakat institutions and websites of the Amil Zakat Institution studied.

3.4 *Data analysis technique*

This research uses DEA technique to measure the efficiency level of economic empowerment programs at by Amil Zakat institution. The processing steps are as follows:

1. Determine the input and output variables based on the approach used.
2. Proces data using DEA with the help of Banxia Frontier Analyst 4 software. There are three stages in the data processing:

A. Table of Efficiency

Shows which DMU is the most efficient, indicating efficiency value by 1 or optimal, whereas it is said to be inefficient if its value is less than 1.

B. Table of Peer Units

Determines what will be done for an inefficient DMU. At this stage, it will be shown how to achieve efficiency by looking at the multiplier on the DMU, which is the reference to achieve the efficiency level.

C. Table of Target Value

Determines how much (percentage) efficiency has been achieved by each DMU, both regarding input and output. At this stage the actual value and targets to be achieved will be shown for each input and output to be efficient.

3. Interpret results of DEA data processing.
At this stage the results of data processing with DEA will be presented. It will also be explained in detail where DMUs are efficient and inefficient, explaining the cause of the DMU inefficiency, and how to improve efficiency by looking at the Multiplier and the target value of the DMU as the reference.

4 RESULTS AND ANALYSIS

4.1 *Efficiency analysis of economic empowerment programs at LAZNAS with VRS assumptions*

Table 1 below shows that, in 2015 to 2016, there were one in three DMUs or 83.3% of LAZNAS, which were technically efficient. When viewed from the overall average, the economic empowerment program at LAZNAS has decreased the efficiency level, which, in 2015,- reached 100% efficiency, then decreased to 85.37% in 2016. Changes in the efficiency value experienced by LAZNAS in the year 2015–2016 can be classified into two categories, namely, the efficiency value was down, and the efficiency value was constant. Yatim Mandiri and LMI (Lembaga Manajemen Infaq) are LAZNAS that can remain constant to maintain performance relatively well. Meanwhile, LAZNAS Nurul Hayat has a decreased efficiency level.

In 2016, LAZNAS Nurul Hayat experienced a significant decrease in efficiency that reached 56.1%, while initially, in 2015 it reached 100% efficiency. Data shows that, in 2016, Nurul Hayat had not succeeded in allocating input and output optimally. LAZNAS Yatim Mandiri and LMI remain consistent achieving 100% full efficiency value in 2015 and 2016, indicating that both LAZNAS had allocated inputs and outputs optimally.

4.2 *Efficiency analysis of economic empowerment programs at LAZNAS with CRS assumptions*

Table 2 shows that, in 2015–2016, there were two out of three economic empowerment programs that were declared to be efficient in technical efficiency and scale, -namely, -LAZNAS LMI for two consecutive years in 2015 and 2016 and Yatim Mandiri in 2016. When viewed from overall means, the economic empowerment program at LAZNAS with CRS assumption experienced an increase in efficiency level, which, in 2015, reached an efficiency rating of 83.6%, and increased to 84.17% in 2016. The change in efficiency values experienced by LAZNAS in 2015–2016 can be classified into three categories, namely, increased efficiency, decreased efficiency and fixed efficiency.

Table 1. Table of efficiency with VRS assumption.

	EMPOWERMENT PROGRAM		
		VRS	
NO	DMU	2015	2016
1	Nurul Hayat	100%	56.1%
2	LMI	100%	100%
3	Yatim Mandiri	100%	100%
	Average	100%	85.37%

Table 2. Table of efficiency with CRS assumption.

	EMPOWERMENT PROGRAM		
		CRS	
NO	DMU	2015	2016
1	Nurul Hayat	68.5%	52.3%
2	LMI	100%	100%
3	Yatim Mandiri	88.3%	100%
	Average	83.6%	84.17%

LMI is one of the three LAZNAS that can maintain its performance very well. From 2015 to 2016, LMI has a 100% efficiency rating, proving that LMI has been technically efficient and scaled. Not many LMIs can achieve 100% efficiency. Yatim Mandiri also proved able to raise the performance of its economic empowerment program so that, in 2016, it was efficient in technical efficiency and scale by obtaining 100% of efficiency value, which shows that Yatim Mandiri has allocated input and output optimally and is in its operational scale, whereas, in 2015, Yatim Mandiri was not yet efficient, with an efficiency rating of 88.3%. However, LAZNAS Nurul Hayat is still declared inefficient and has a decreased efficiency level. In 2015 to 2016 Nurul Hayat's LAZNAS the efficiency level decreased by 16.2%. In 2015, Nurul Hayat had an efficiency value of 68.5%, and this continued to decline until 2016, when its efficiency value was 52.3%. This shows that, in 2015 and 2016, Nurul Hayat has not been successful in correcting the allocation of input and output optimally.

4.3 *Determination of efficiency benchmark*

Determination of efficiency reference aims to determine which DMU or LAZNAS can be used as a benchmark for other LAZNAS that have not achieved efficiency, so that, -subsequently; it can be known how many targets must be met for the economic empowerment program in LAZNAS to reach an efficient level.

The table above shows that the economic empowerment program at LAZNAS Nurul Hayat for the

Table 3. Table of Peer Units: The efficiency reference of 2015–2016 assumes VRS.

	Empowerment program (VRS)		
NO	DMU	Score efficiency	Efficiency benchmark
1	Nurul Hayat 2016	56.1%	LMI 2015 and NH 2015

Table 4. Table of Peer Units: The efficiency reference for 2015–2016 assumes CRS.

	Empowerment program (CRS)		
NO	DMU	Score efficiency	Efficiency benchmark
1	Nurul Hayat 2015	56.1%	LMI 2015 and NH 2015
2	Nurul Hayat 2016	52.3%	LMI 2015
3	Yatim Mandiri	88.3%	LMI 2016 and YM 2016

year 2016 did, not reach the efficiency value, using the economic empowerment program reference at LAZNAS LMI and Nurul Hayat in the year 2015 as its benchmark.

The table above shows that the economic empowerment program at LAZNAS Nurul Hayat in 2015 did not reach the efficiency value, using the economic empowerment program in LAZNAS LMI of 2015 and, also using LAZNAS LMI reference 2015 as its benchmark in 2016 for Nurul Hayat. For Yatim Mandiri in 2015, the reference from LMI Institute and Yatim Mandiri in 2016 are used as its benchmark.

4.4 *Targeting*

Target setting aims to show the number of targets or values to achieved by LAZNAS that have not reached an efficiency of each input and output variables and will also explain the sources of input and output variables that enables economic empowerment program performance in LAZNAS to become inefficient.

The target that Nurul Hayat has to fulfill in order to achieve technically efficient condition from the output side is to increase the collected fund by 78,28%. Nurul Hayat suggest to increase distributed capital by 156.55%; in addition, Nurul Hayat increase the amount of Mustahiq to help empower their economy by as much as 80.79%. Improvements also need to be done from the input side, which is considered too large. Personnel costs should be reduced by 10.02% and socialization costs by 25.3%.

Table 5. Table of value target based on VRS assumption.

	Empowerment program (VRS)			
DMU	Variable	Actual	Target	%
NH 2016	Collected fund	66,908,400	119,284,168	78.28
	Distributed capital	28,351,000	73,048,836	157.66
	Jumlah Mustahiq	28	51	80,79
	Operational cost	15,818,900	15,818900	–
	Personnel cost	20,156,600	18,136,771	10,02
	Socialization cost	2,582,500	1,927,584	25,36

On the CRS (Variable Return to Scale) assumption of the economic empowerment program, in 2015, there were two LAZNAS which experienced inefficiency, Nurul Hayat and Yatim Mandiri, and, in 2016, Nurul Hayat was still not able to improve its performance and was still under efficient. The target that Nurul Hayat had to meet in 2015 was to be able to achieve a technical efficient condition so as to increase the collected fund by 46.5%, while the distributed capital was still not optimal so it must increase by 89.56% and Nurul Hayat must also increase the number of mustahiq by as much as 93.64% b. Cost also needs to be done for cost that are overvalued, so that there is no waste. Personnel costs should be reduced by 24.3% and socialization costs should also be reduced by 93.42%. Nurul Hayat's target to achieve efficiency in both technical and scale conditions in 2016 was by raising 91.23% of collected funds, and the distributed capital also needed to be increased almost threefold by as much as 196.76% because it was still less than optimal and still far from the target. In addition Nurul Hayat also needed to increase the number of mustahiq by as much as double or 101.75%. Meanwhile, the personnel costs are still considered too large and must be reduced by 15.82% and socialization costs should be reduced by as much as 81.57% because it is still considered lavish.

By 2015 Yatim Mandiri had not yet reached efficiency, with a value of 88.3%, so it needs to be improved. The target that must be met by Yatim Mandiri to achieve a technical and scale efficient condition is to increase the collected fund by 13.31% and distributed capital must also be increased by as much as 24.32%. Yatim Mandiri must also increase the number of mustahiq by as much as 13.31% in order to more empower the mustahiq economy. Also, improvement also needs to be done regarding cost, which is considered too

Table 6. Table of value targets based on CRS assumption.

	Empowerment program (CRS)			
DMU	Variable	Actual	Target	%
NH Tahun 2015	Collected fund	27,027,400	39,474,719	46.5
	Distributed capital	13,232,000	25,082,045	89.56
	Jumlah Mustahiq	9	17	93.64
	Operational cost	4,880,400	4,880,400	0
	Personnel cost	6,915,000	5,234,568	24.3
	Socialization cost	2,232,000	146,824	93.42
NH Tahun 2016	Collected fund	66,908,400	127,949,887	91.23
	Distributed capital	28,351,000	81,298,738	186,76
	Amount of Mustahiq	28	56	101.75
	Operational cost	15,818,900	15,818,900	0
	Personnel cost	20,156,500	16,966,868	15.82
	Socialization cost	2,582,600	475,902	81.57
YM Tahun 2015	Collected fund	88,173,125	99,912,951	13.31
	Distributed capital	48,495,219	60,290,633	24.32
	Jumlah Mustahiq	104	118	13.31
	Operational cost	22,043,281	21,927,173	0.53
	Personnel cost	17,634,625	17,634,625	0
	Socialization cost	1,034,625	138,657	86.6

high and is felt to be excessive. Operational costs should be reduced, even if only of 0.53%, and socialization costs by 86.6%.

5 CONCLUSION

1. Based on VRS (Variable Return to Scale) assumption, the economic empowerment program at LAZNAS in 2015–2016 as a whole is relatively efficient. There is one LAZNAS that has not achieved efficiency, which was Nurul Hayat in 2016, but in the other LAZNAS efficiency has been achieved. The other two LAZNAS, LMI and Nurul Hayat, remain consistently efficient from 2015 to 2016.
2. Based on the CRS (Constant Return to Scale) assumption, the economic empowerment program in LAZNAS 2015–2016 is overall balanced. In 2015 there were two inefficient LAZNAS, whereas in 2016 only one LAZNAS experienced inefficiency. There is only one LAZNAS that has achieved consistent efficiency for two years consecutively from 2015 to 2016 that is LMI.

REFERENCES

Al Qardawi, Y. (1999). "FIQHAL ZAKAH."

Brodjonegoro, B. (2016). "Bappenas resmikan pusat kajian strategis. *Bappenas inaugurated the strategic study center*"

Cooper, W.W., et al. (2006). *Introduction to data envelopment analysis and its uses: with DEA-solver software and references*, Springer Science & Business Media.

Huda, N., et al. (2012). "Keuangan Publik Islami: Pendekatan Teoritis dan Sejarah."*("Islamic Public Finance: Theoretical and Historical Approach.") Jakarta: Kencana Prenada Media Grup.*

Maghfiroh, S. (2015). "MODEL MANAJEMEN STRATEGIS PEMBERDAYAAN EKONOMI UMAT MELALUI ZAKAT, INFAK, SEDEKAH (Studi Kasus pada LAZIS Qaryah Thayyibah Purwokerto)." (*"STRATEGIC MANAGEMENT MODEL OF ECONOMIC EMPOWERMENT THROUGH ZAKAT, INFAK, ALMS*)(*Case Study on LAZIS* Qaryah Thayyibah Purwokerto)." *Economic: Jurnal Ekonomi dan Hukum Islam* **5**(2): 81–111.

Ministry of Finance, Republic of Indonesia (2016). Anggaran penerimaan dan belanja negara perubahan, (*State budget revenues and expenditures change*) Ministry of finance.

Mubyarto (1997). "*Ekonomi Pancasila*" (*Pancasila Economics*) Aditya Media.

Raharjo (2014). "Komunitas jurnal pengembangan masyarakat." (Community development journal).

Rusydiana, A.S. and T.S. Conculting (2013). Mengukur Tingkat Efisiensi dengan Data Envelopment Analysis (DEA): Teori dan Aplikasi, (*Measuring Efficiency Level with Data Envelopment Analysis (DEA): Theory and Applications*) SMART Publishing, Katulampa Bogor.

Statistik, B.P. (2016). Presentase penduduk miskin maret *(Percentage of poor population)*.

Tanjung, H. and A. Devi (2013). "Metodologi Penelitian Ekonomi Islam." *(Islamic Economic Research Methodology.) Jakarta: PT Gramata Publishing.*

Increasing Management Relevance and Competitiveness – Sukoco et al. (Eds)
© 2018 Taylor & Francis Group, London, ISBN 978-0-8153-7455-8

Impact of interest rates, money supply, treasury bill and borrowing on exchange rate volatility in Indonesia

Wahyudayanto Utama & Nugraha
Universitas Pendidikan Indonesia, Bandung, Indonesia

ABSTRACT: This research is to find the relationship between USD/IDR Exchange Rate volatility and four macroeconomic factors (Interest Rates, Borrowing, Treasury Bill and Money Supply). The data are taken form Indonesian Reserve Bank period July 2005 until October 2015. The first testing are stationary testing with Augmented Dickey-Fuller (ADF) to test a stationarity nature of data. Furthermore, An initialisation equation is testing with Johansen testing to test his cointegrating properties. Stationary at level stage and Cointegration are absolute requirement for a equation could be formed with VECM method. From this model it can find correlation between Exchange Rate and Trasury Bill. That VECM equation can be used to do simulation that shown an impact of the macroeconomic on Exchange Rate at economic shock condition using the Impulse Response test.

1 INTRODUCTION

The Exchange Rate in Indonesia shows quite extreme fluctuations against some currencies from 2005 to 2015.

The prediction with a model are science that continues to grow especialy at prediction of Exchange Rate. The model of Exchange Rate prediction are divided into two parts (Kamruzzaman et al., 2006:141): (1) Technical Analysis: an analysis based on historical data such as time series analysis or regression analysis; and (2) Fundamental Analysis: an analysis that connected between variable. The Fundamental Analysis is not a knowledge or standard knowledge that connect between macroeconomic variable. Fundamental Analysis can be used to make long-term predictions of the Exchange Rate volatility.

This were like as presented by some researchers. Ramasamy and Abar (2015) stated that the volatility of Exchange Rate are influenced by nine domestic macroeconomic: Interest Rate, Inflation, Balance of Payment (BoP), Employment Rate, Corruption Index, Gross Domestic Product (GDP), Deficit/ Surplus Rate, Tax Rate and Borrowing Rate. Ali et al. (2015) presented a study on the impact of the Interest Rate, Consumer Price Index and Money Supply on the Exchange Rate. The study was conducted in Pakistan and the results of them indicate that the Consumer Price Index has a positive correlation with Exchange Rate volatility. It was also shown that Interest Rates and Money Supply had an impact, as opposed to Exchange Rate volatility. Nchor et al. (2015) also researched about the relationship between Interest Rate, Exchange Rate and Inflation in Ghana, where construction was done using an Autoregressive Distributed Lag Model (ARDL) approach. And the results of research was find that the Interest Rate and Exchange Rates affect Inflation. The several studies above shown that the economic conditions of each country have different characteristics. The research in this paper will look for a connection between Exchange Rate volatility and some of macroeconomic factors.

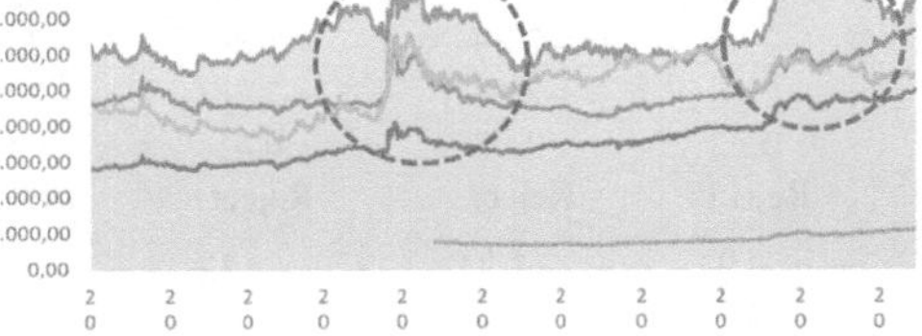

Figure 1. Foreign exchange rate volatility against IDR.

The research objectives are to find a connection between Exchange Rate volatility and some of macroeconomic factors in Indonesia, and to find an influence of macroeconomics against Exchange Rate volatility in economic shock conditions in Indonesia.

2 LITERATURE REVIEW

Baker and Filbeck (2015: 81) presented that risks were consist of several kinds: Market Risk: risks that occurs due to price fluctuations in markets trading; Credit Risk: risks that caused by credit which is divided into two: default risk and recovery risk; Default Risk is the risk of credit based on Credit Rating; Recovery Risk is the process of recovery when the default risk occurs; Operation Risk: risks that occurs due to the business management process; Liquidity Risk: risks that occurs due to changes in asset value because of financial behavior, such as the rise and fall of the value of goods due to Exchange Rate volatility; Country Risk: risks that arises from global trade, for instance, the risk of inflation, or the risks of different labor costs; Systemic Risk: risks that arises from negative issue; Behavior Risk: risks that arises from an irrational decision; Governance Risk: risks that occurs from decision-making at the highest level, where mistakes in making decisions can be a major social impact; Inflation Risk: risks that arising from inflations and Risk Aggregation and Capital Management is the control of all risks.

Exchange Rate it is self when associated with the risk factors above, would affect the Credit Risk, Liquidity Risk, Operational Risk, Country Risk and Behavior Risk.

From the 39 researches about connection between Exchange Rate volatility and macroeconomics in the last five years, It is find that 25 macroeconomics variable influences Exchange Rate volatility (Utama, 2017:34). These macroeconomics varable are:

1. *Interest Rate* – interest rate that issued by the Central Bank of the country.
2. *Inflation* – rate of inflation of a country.
3. *Expenditure Government* – represents all of government expenditures.
4. *Balance of Payment (BoP)* – a systematic organized of all transaction.
5. *Export* – a record of sales of goods from one country to another.
6. *Import* – a record of purchasing goods in a country with other countries.
7. *Employment Rate* – the amount of active labor.
8. *Corruption Index* – the level or index of corruption.
9. *Growth Domestic Production (GDP)* – the average income of people in a country.
10. *Deficit/Surplus* – the amount of deficit or surplus in a country's economy.
11. *Tax Rate* – the average tax revenue.
12. *Borrowing Rate* – the amount of debt.
13. *Foreign Direct Investment (FDI)* – an investment entering a country.
14. *Treasury Bill* – a debt issued by the state.
15. *Money Supply* – the money circulating in a country.
16. *Openness of Economy* – the level of economic openness in the world.
17. *Remittance Amount* – the number of remittance transactions.
18. *Reserve Amount* – a foreign exchange.
19. *Agricultural Production Index* – the agricultural production level of a country.
20. *Industrial Production Index* – the production level of the industry in the country.
21. *Portfolio Index* – the value or price of a particular portfolio.
22. *Producer Price Index* – the average price of goods and services in industry.
23. *Consumer Price Index* – the average price of goods and services consumed by households.
24. *Stock Index* – the average stock trading price.
25. *Commodity Market* – the average price of trading commodities.

We must make a model to describe a connection between Exchange Rate volatility and macroeconomics variable, and for the method we choose the *Vector Error Correction Model (VECM)*.

Table 1. ADF testing.

Stage			LNER	IR	LNBOR	LNMS	LNTB
Level	t-Statistik		–0.54	–2.16	0.35	–1.66	–2.73
	Critical Value	1%	–3.48	–3.48	–3.48	–3.49	–3.49
		5%	–2.89	–2.89	–2.89	–2.89	–2.89
		10%	–2.58	–2.58	–2.58	–2.58	–2.58
	Probabilitas		0.88	0.22	0.98	0.45	0.07
	Decision	<0,05	**Reject**	**Reject**	**Reject**	**Reject**	**Reject**
First Difference	t-Statistik		–8.29	–4.31	–11.34	–3.52	–13.02
	Critical Value	1%	–3.48	–3.48	–3.48	–3.49	–3.49
		5%	–2.89	–2.89	–2.89	–2.89	–2.89
		10%	–2.58	–2.58	–2.58	–2.58	–2.58
	Probabilitas		0.00	0.00	0.00	0.00	0.04
	Decision	<0,05	**Receive**	**Receive**	**Receive**	**Receive**	**Receive**

3 METHOD

3.1 *Research data*

The data used herein is secondary data taken from Central Bank of Indonesia, from July 2005 to October 2015.

3.2 *Initial equation*

Referring to the research that has been done, for initial model it uses an Ordinary Least Square (OLS) model, so the relationship between Exchange Rate and other macroeconomics variable can be expressed as:

$$ER_t = \beta_0 IR_t + \beta_1 MS_t + \beta_2 TB_t + \beta_3 Bor_t \quad (1)$$

When Equation 1 above is used there would be a very large value difference, so the solution of the equation is linearly invalid. According to Tukey (1977: 57) the data had to be exploratory or solved so that it had a value adjacent to transform to the natural log.

$$LnER_t = \beta_0 IR_t + \beta_1 LnMS_t + \beta_2 LnTB_t + \beta_3 LnBor_t \quad (2)$$

Table 2. Unit root test for residual.

Description		t-Statistic	Prob.*
Augmented Dickey-Fuller test statistic		−4.42849	0.0004
Test critical values	1% level	−3.4842	
	5% level	−2.88505	
	10% level	−2.57939	

4 RESULT

4.1 *Stationarity testing*

The stationary test in this research uses the Augmented Dickey-Fuller (ADF) method. This test would test each variable data which it have stationary nature or not. If it is stationary, second question is "in what stage the data is stationary". The results of stationary testing with ADF are shown in Table 1.

The data is stationary at the *First Difference stage.*

4.2 *Residual testing*

This test uses ADF for residual testing.

The residual is stationary at the level stage. It means that the equation is not spurious and has a long run relationship.

4.3 *Lag length criteria for cointegration and unrestricted VAR*

Lag value is choiced from the smallest but outcome most (Udoh et al., 2012: 852).

The result of a Lag Optimal is 12.

4.4 *Johannsen cointegration test*

The cointegrations are shown in Table 4.

4.5 *Vector Error Correction Model (VECM)*

Estimated cointegration equation (cointEq 1) from Table 5 is:

$$LnER_t = -0.004 IR_t + 2.6 LnMS_t - 0.11 LnTB_t - 2.6 LnBor_t \quad (3)$$

Table 3. VAR lag order selection criteria.

Lag	LogL	LR	FPE	AIC	SC	HQ
0	173.4	NA	3.40E-08	−3.008	−2.88632	−2.958439
1	969.6	1507.01	3.56E-14	−16.78	−16.05017	−16.4829
2	1022	95.3426	2.17E-14	−17.28	−15.9409	−16.73426*
3	1048	43.4469	2.17E-14	−17.28	−15.3403	−16.4942
4	1069	34.641	2.35E-14	−17.22	−14.6677	−16.18224
5	1081	18.6582	3.01E-14	−16.99	−13.8314	−15.70657
6	1102	30.13	3.35E-14	−16.91	−13.1502	−15.38591
7	1130	37.21	3.35E-14	−16.96	−12.5865	−15.18289
8	1151	27.6019	3.77E-14	−16.9	−11.922	−14.87902
9	1182	35.6617	3.72E-14	−16.99	−11.4091	−14.72671
10	1217	38.6795	3.42E-14	−17.18	−10.99	−14.66817
11	1252	35.2918	3.24E-14	−17.36	−10.567	−14.60575
12	1322	63.13086*	1.74e-14*	18.15464	−10.7516	−15.15098

Table 4. Johannsen cointegration test.

Unrestricted cointegration rank test (trace)				
Hypothesized		Trace	0.05	
No. of CE(s)	Eigenvalue	Statistic	Critical value	Prob.**
None*	0.448413	161.5782	69.81889	0
At most 1*	0.331305	95.53809	47.85613	0
At most 2*	0.303787	50.86866	29.79707	0.0001
At most 3	0.084582	10.67565	15.49471	0.2322
At most 4	0.007772	0.866112	3.841466	0.352
Unrestricted cointegration rank test (maximum eigenvalue)				
Hypothesized		Max-Eigen	0.05	
No. of CE(s)	Eigenvalue	Statistic	Critical value	Prob.**
None*	0.448413	66.04014	33.87687	0
At most 1*	0.331305	44.66942	27.58434	0.0001
At most 2*	0.303787	40.19301	21.13162	0
At most 3	0.084582	9.80954	14.2646	0.2247
At most 4	0.007772	0.866112	3.841466	0.352

Table 5. Long run relationship VECM.

Cointegration Eq.	CointEq 1
LNER(–1)	1
IR(–1)	0.003981
	–0.01277
	[0.31169]
LNBOR(–1)	2.595759
	–0.20726
	[12.5240]
LNMS(–1)	–2.57578
	–0.15043
	[–17.1230]
LNTB(–1)	0.110531
	–0.06173
	[1.79050]
C	–7.92076

Table 6. Short run relationship VECM.

D(LNER)	D(IR)	D(LNBOR)	D(LNMS)	D(LNTB)
–0.25467	**–2.64146**	**–0.00357**	**0.015464**	**–0.61633**
–0.08842	–0.4901	–0.06614	–0.06058	–0.78279

From Table 6, it is occur correction 25.47%, 264.15%, 0.36% and 61.6% from long run equation in variable exchange rate, Interest Rate, Borrowing and Money Supply.

Table 7. Granger causality test.

Null hypothesis	F-Statistic	Prob.	Decision
IR does not Granger Cause LNBOR	1.65088	0.0924	Accepted
IR does not Granger Cause LNER	1.52217	0.1315	Accepted
IR does not Granger Cause LNMS	2.08759	0.0258	Reject
IR does not Granger Cause LNTB	2.18244	0.0193	Reject
LNBOR does not Granger Cause IR	0.86503	0.5846	Accepted
LNBOR does not Granger Cause LNER	0.89049	0.5596	Accepted
LNBOR does not Granger Cause LNMS	2.16205	0.0206	Reject
LNBOR does not Granger Cause LNTB	1.8715	0.0491	Reject
LNER does not Granger Cause IR	0.80773	0.6417	Accepted
LNER does not Granger Cause LNBOR	1.69731	0.0811	Accepted
LNER does not Granger Cause LNMS	1.77042	0.0658	Accepted

(*Continued*)

Table 7. (*Continued*).

Null hypothesis	F-Statistic	Prob.	Decision
LNER does not Granger Cause LNTB	1.03946	0.4211	Accepted
LNMS does not Granger Cause IR	0.8762	0.5736	Accepted
LNMS does not Granger Cause LNBOR	0.96269	0.4903	Accepted
LNMS does not Granger Cause LNER	1.40756	0.1779	Accepted
LNMS does not Granger Cause LNTB	1.09526	0.3744	Accepted
LNTB does not Granger Cause IR	0.93249	0.5189	Accepted
LNTB does not Granger Cause LNBOR	0.99841	0.4574	Accepted
LNTB does not Granger Cause LNER	5.49254	7.00E-07	Reject
LNTB does not Granger Cause LNMS	0.99709	0.4586	Accepted

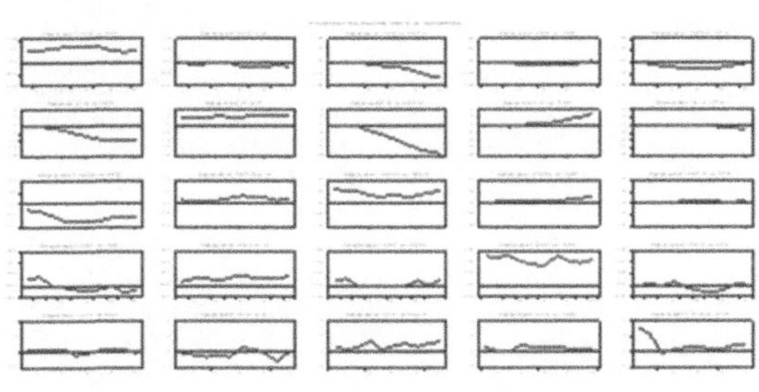

Figure 2. Impulse response analysis.

4.6 *Granger causality*

The results in Table 7 shows that Treasury Bill causes Exchange Rate volatility.

4.7 *Impulse response*

In line 1 of Figure 2, the graph shows when shock economic condition, the variable that influences LnER most, It is self from a past period.

In line 2 of Figure 2, the graph shows that LnER has an opposite effect to IR from the first period, when the shock economic attack IR.

In line 3, if shock economic attack it happen at LnBor then an opposite effect on LnER is happen.

In lines 4 and 5, if shock economic attack it happen at LnTB and LnMS, then it does not have an effect on LnER.

5 CONCLUSION

On the basis of empirical evidence above, it is concluded that Treasury Bill has influence to Exchange Rate, as shown in Granger Causality Test.

In the Impulse Response test, it is shown that the biggest effect of Exchange Rate volatility when shock economic attack itself from past period. On the other hand, the decrease of Borrowing has an opposite effect on the Exchange Rate.

ACKNOWLEDGMENT

The authors would like to thank Telkom University for providing funding for this research.

REFERENCES

Ali, T.M., Mahmood, M.T. & Bashir, T. (2015). Impact of interest rate, inflation and money supply on exchange rate volatility in Pakistan. *World Applied Sciences Journal*, *33*(4), 620–630.

Baker, H.K. and Filbeck, G. (Eds.). (2015). *Investment risk management*. Oxford University Press.

Kamruzzaman, J., Begg, R.K. & Sarker, R.A. (2006). *Artificial neural networks in finance and manufacturing* (p. 141). Idea Group Publishing.

Nchor, D., Darkwah, S.A. & LubošStřelec (2015). Inflation, exchange rates and interest rates in Ghana: An autoregressive distributed lag model. *International Journal of Scientific and Research*, *5*(1).

Ramasamy, R. & Abar, S.K. (2015). Influence of macroeconomic variables on exchange rates. *Journal of Economics, Business and Management*, *3*(2), 276–281.

Tukey, J.W. (1977). *Exploratory data analysis*. Addison-Wesley Publishing Company.

Udoh, E.J., Akpan, S.B., John, D.E. & Patrick, I.V. (2012). Cointegration between exchange rate volatility and key macroeconomic fundamentals: Evidence from Nigeria. *Modern Economy*, *3*(07), 846–855.

Utama, Wahyudayanto. (2017). *Pemodelan fluktuasi nilai mata uang USD/IDR, EUR/IDR, GBP/IDR, JPY/IDR terhadap makro ekonomi dengan metoda vector error correction model (VECM)*. Universitas Pendidikan Indonesia.

Increasing Management Relevance and Competitiveness – Sukoco et al. (Eds)
© 2018 Taylor & Francis Group, London, ISBN 978-0-8153-7455-8

Determinants of non-performing loan comparative study of banks in Indonesia and Nepal

S.K. Singh
Nepal Commerce Campus, Kathmandu, Nepal

I.M. Sudana
Universitas Airlangga, Surabaya, Indonesia

ABSTRACT: The main aim of this study was to find out the effect of macro-economic factors (GDP, Inflation, and Exchange rate) and bank specific factors (Bank size, level of capital, ROA, CAR and NLIR) on the NPL of banks in Indonesia and Nepal. This study used regression analysis to determine the effect of the independent variables consisting of macro-economic factors and bank specific factors. Based on the analysis results, there are three variables (GDP, bank size and NLIR) that have a significant effect on the NPL of Indonesian banks. The variables of GDP and inflation also have a significant effect on the NPL of Nepali banks. In both countries, GDP has a negative and significant effect on NPL but only inflation has a negative and significant effect on NPL only in Nepal. The change in GDP affects both countries but for inflation, banks in Nepal were not affected.

Keywords: macro-economic factors, banks specific factors, Non-performing loan

1 INTRODUCTION

Most of the country's financial intermediaries play a vital role in developing a better economy. Developing countries like Indonesia and Nepal face big challenges and opportunities to improve their financial problems. Banking failures can affect the economy, such as banking failures leading to a banking crisis that is detrimental to the banking sector, which can reduce the flow of credit in the country that ultimately affects the efficiency and productivity of various industrial sectors (Chijoriga, 1998; Brownbridge and Harvey, 1998). The size of NPLs can be affected by various macroeconomic factors and specific factors in the banks themselves (Jimenez and Sauina (2007), Khemraj and Pasha (2009) and Louzisetal (2011). This research used both countries' banking sectors dependent and independent variables throughout, which have a significant effect on NPL. It will more helpful to understanding the variable effects and variable sensitivity in the financial sector of both countries. The reminder of this paper is organized as follows: in the next step, we present the theoretical analysis and develop the hypothesis. The detailed methodology is the third section. The empirical results, discussion and the implications of the findings are in the fourth section. Finally, we have concluded the paper with its limitations and providing some suggestions for future research.

2 THEORETICAL ANALYSIS HYPOTHESIS DEVELOPMENT

2.1 *Non-performing loan*

The main function of a bank is to collect deposits from customers and to lend those deposits to the borrower (Warue, 2013). In the process of lending, it is difficult for banks to predict whether a loan will be paid in full or not. This process creates a default level of risk in lending. Banks therefore use diversification and other credit risk management techniques, such as screening borrowers for the minimization of loan default rates. Consequently, they are able to minimize the levels of NPL.

Banking credit risk comes from non-performing loans (NPLs). It is one of the vital indicators which plays the biggest role in measuring the level of credit risk in banking. Non-performing loans occur when borrowers are experiencing repayment difficulties when it comes to some or all of their obligations to the creditors as agreed upon in earlier contracts. Non-performing loans are measured based on the assessment of the quality of the credit. Non-performing loans can be calculated by using the below formula.

$$Non-performing\ loan = \frac{Non-performing\ loan}{Total\ credit} \quad (1)$$

GDP growth: Worsening economic activity decelerates income and accelerates payment difficulties, and more businesses are adversely affected as a result which will result in a higher default risk. Therefore, the cyclical variable of GDP growth is projected to be negatively related to NPL. Koch and McDonald (2003) suggested that a good economic condition builds the confidence of both the borrower and lender about the investment project and their ability to repay the loans (GDP).

H1: The level of GDP growth has a negative effect on NPL.

2.2 *Inflation*

Inflation: Marco-economic inflation is another macro-economic factor which affects the efficiency of banking activities. Inflation depreciates the value of money which reduces the rate of return in general. The reduction in capital investment negatively affects economic performance (Boyd, Levine et al., 2001). The inflation rate is one indicator that is often used to measure the stability of the price of goods and services. Inflation is defined as the increase in general price level continuously within a certain period.

H2: The inflation rate has a positive effect on NPL.

2.3 *Exchange rate*

Exchange rate: On the other hand, this is one of the external factors that also plays a vital role in banking. It is one of the macro-economic debates in the literature because developing markets and the volatility of the exchange rate is one of the main sources of economic instability (Zameer and Siddiqi, 2010). The volatility in the exchange rates was found to have an important role in inducing banking crises in many countries, by first weakening the economy and then the financial stability (Lindgren, Garcia et al., 1996).

H3: The exchange rate has a negative effect on NPL.

2.4 *Bank size*

This bank specific factor provides a much richer insight in to the determinants of NPL. Even though macro-economic conditions may offer a valuable contribution to explain credit risk at an aggregate level, it is the bank's specific financial situation that will ultimately determine whether it will default on its liabilities. Taking the bank specific variables in to account may provide a clear understanding of the factors that drive NPL. The size of the bank can be judged from the total assets held by the bank. The research conducted by Misra and Dhal (2010) showed that large banks tend to have higher NPLs than smaller banks. This is because large banks tend to lend in large quantities towards large companies with high risk. Small banks have a more rigorous style of management in conducting the screening and monitoring of loans so that the level of NPLs at a small bank is lower. Bank size is usually measured by the total assets. It is a key factor in banking studies. This study has measured bank size by the total number of assets.

H4: Size of the Bank has a negative effect on NPL.

2.5 *Quality of bank management*

The quality of the bank management is an assessment of the ability of the bank's management in relation to its operational activities (Berger and DeYoung 1997). The bank's management is proxied by the ROA ratio. ROA is an effective measurement of performance because it eliminates the problem of size which makes it easier for comparisons to be drawn across multiple firms (Lev and Saunder, 1979). Demsetz and Lehn (1985) suggests that as a way of accounting for profit, ROA may reflect yearly fluctuations in underlying business conditions better than the stock market rates of return. This is because the stock market rates of return reflect expected future developments that may mask current fluctuations in the business conditions.

H5: The quality of the bank's management (ROA) has a negative effect on NPL.

2.6 *The level of capital*

Banks use capital to finance their operations and expansion, and it serves as a cushion to absorb unexpected operating losses (Bichsel and Blum, 2004). When a borrower fails to make some or all of their promised interest and principal payments, these defaulted loans result in losses which can eventually reduce the bank's capital. Hence, banks assume that more risks increase their capital (Altunbas et al. 2007). More capital implies a bigger cushion to avoid failure resulting from a higher level of risk (Ahmad and Ariff, 2007).

H6: The level of capital (CAR) has a negative effect on NPL.

2.7 *Interest rate on loan*

In both countries, the banking sector loans and their interest rate are one the main causes of NPLs in both countries' financial sector. Research conducted by Jimenez and Saurina (2005) and Fofack (2005) showed that when the bank raised the interest rates on loans, the bank had a potential increased credit risk and this lead many companies to not be able to afford to pay the high interest charges. The higher the credit risk, the higher the interest rates prompted by the banks (Sutojo, 2000). An increase in interest rates would worsen the quality of the loans. This can be seen in the high cost of loan interest charged by banks, which will make it more difficult for a company to repay the loan so the bank has the potential to increase the NPL.

H7: The interest rate on loans has a positive effect on NPL.

3 RESEARCH AND METHODOLOGY

3.1 *Sample and data*

This research consisted mostly of commercial banks in Indonesia and Nepal. This sample was selected using purposive sampling method using certain criteria, which consisted of being a commercial bank contained in the Directory of Banks Indonesian and on the Nepal Rastra Bank website from 2003–2012.

3.2 *Variable identification*

3.2.1 *Dependent variable*

Non-performing loan: In this research, the dependent variable is the Non-performing loan (NPL).

3.2.2 *Independent variables*

1. The growth of domestic product (GDP) growth is the indicator of the economic condition of both countries. The data of GDP growth was taken from the annual report of the International Monetary Fund (IMF) statistics for this research.
2. Inflation is the rise in the general price levels continuously within one year. The inflation data was collected from the International Monetary Fund (IMF) report.
3. The exchange rate is the exchange of one currency in each county to U.S. dollars. For this research, all of the exchange rates of each year were taken from the International Monetary Fund (IMF) Report.
4. The size of the bank was assessed by the total assets held by the bank, and it was measured by the Ln (total Assets) equation.
5. The ability of the company to generate profit using their total assets is ROA. The ROA was calculated as Earning after tax (EAT) divided by the total number of assets.
6. The CAR ratio is equity divided by risk weighted assets. Core and supplementary capital are used as a cushion against risk.
7. The interest rate of the loan is the interest rate paid by the borrower to the bank on any loans obtained. The data obtained from the loan interest rate of each banks' annual report made up this factor.

3.3 *Model analysis*

To determine the influence of the macro-economic factors (GDP, inflation and exchange rate) and the bank-specific factors (rate of the loan, the size of the bank, and the bank's management, capital and loan loss provision) of the NPL, this study will use a multiple regression analysis model estimation method by way of the following equation:

$$(NPL)_{i,t} = \beta_0 + \beta_1 (GDP)_t + \beta_2(INF)_t + \beta_3(EX)_t + \beta_4 (Bank\ Size)_{i,t} + \beta_5(ROA)_{i,t} + \beta_6(CAR)_{i,t} + \beta_7 (IRL)_{i,t} + \in_{i,t}$$

4 RESULTS AND DISCUSSION

This research study was conducted on commercial banks registered and listed in the Directory of Banking Indonesia and Nepal Rastra Bank, both of which have gone public or have not gone public since 2003–2012. The description of the statistics for each variable used in the study has been presented in Table 1.

Based on Table 1, it can be seen that the value of the lowest NPL amount of the Indonesian banks was 0.03% and the Nepalese banks lowest amount was 0.10%. This indicates that the banks are able to manage credit well and are selective in providing

Table 1. Descriptive variables of Indonesian and Nepali banking.

Indonesian Banks	N	Minimum	Maximum	Mean	Std. Deviation
Descriptive Statistics of Indonesian banks					
NPL	635	.03	17.56	2.0815	1.51796
GDP	633	4.63	7.16	5.9611	.71384
INFLASI	635	2.78	17.11	6.6885	3.70032
Ex. RTAE	635	9.06	11.52	9.3805	.74243
BANKSIZE	635	17.46	34.09	26.9054	4.48252
ROA	635	.02	15.04	2.6047	1.64648
CAR	635	.15	107.93	21.5826	12.34042
NLIR	635	8.16	30.71	17.7432	5.41337
Descriptive Statistics of Nepali banks					
NPL	106	.10	5.00	1.7368	1.14387
GDP	106	3.40	6.10	4.3426	.87071
Inflation	106	3.96	12.62	7.9164	2.4076
Ex. Rate	106	4.20	4.45	4.3164	.07389
Bank Size	106	23.91	27.54	26.0152	.69055
ROA	106	.03	4.38	1.6529	.85344
CAR	106	8.85	24.75	13.2194	2.65160
NLIR	106	7.20	18.00	11.0217	2.63629

credit to customers in both countries. This is so that there are no non-performing loans incurred by the bank. The highest value for Indonesian banks was 17.56% NPL and as well 8.60%, it shows that there are banks that are included in the bad credit category. The average NPLs of the banks in Indonesia and Nepal amounted to 2.28% and 1.80% respectively. It means that most of the loans were extended by the banks in Indonesia. In term of Nepali Banking, the current credit because of the NPL ratio is below the limit of 5% in accordance with the provisions stipulated by the Bank of Indonesia and Nepal Rastra Bank.

The value of the lowest GDP growth for Indonesia was 4.63%. This means that the decline in Indonesia's economic performance is in line with the weakening of purchasing power. The highest GDP value amounting to 7.16% indicates that Indonesia's economic growth has increased, driven by increased domestic consumption. The average GDP was 5.86%, which indicates that the average economic growth in Indonesia is low. On the other hand, Nepali's lower GDP was 3.40%. This means that the purchasing power of the Nepali rupee is diminishing. The lowest inflation rate in Indonesia was 2.78%. This indicates that the prices of goods and services tends to decrease. The highest inflation rate in Indonesia was 17.11%, which indicates that the increase and decrease of unstable fuel prices affecting the price of goods and services has risen high enough. The lowest value of bank size was 17.46 and the highest bank value amounted to 34.22. The average size of the banks amounted to 26.920. The greater numbers of the total assets of the banks showed that the larger assets were used in the activities to do with the bank's operations. One of the operational activities of a bank is to give credit to the public.

The regression analysis showed that in the context of the Indonesian banking sector, the variables of GDP, inflation, exchange rate ROA and CAR had a negative effect on NPL, but bank size, NLIR had a positive effect on NPL. On the other hand, in terms of the Nepali banking sector, the variables of GDP, inflation, ROA, CAR had a negative effect on the NPL, but bank size, exchange rate and NLIR had a positive effect on NPL. The hypothesis results shows that in relation to the Indonesian banks exchange rate, NLIR has a significant effect on NPL at $\alpha = 5\%$ and GDP has a negative and significant effect at $\alpha = 10\%$. The other variables are insignificant. In the context of Nepali banks, the hypothesis testing showed that only inflation has a negative and significant at $\alpha = 5\%$. When it comes to the other variables, only GDP has a negative effect and significant effect at $\alpha = 10\%$ and the rest of them were not significant. R-square value was used to determine how much the independent variables could explain the variability of the dependent variable. The R-square value in this study amounted to 0.087 for Indonesian banking and the Nepali banking amounted to 0.194. This indicates that 8.7% and 19.4% NPL variability can be explained by the variables of GDP, inflation, exchange rate, bank size, ROA, CAR and the interest rate on loans.

5 CONCLUSION

In the context of the Indonesian banks, growth domestic product (GDP) has a negative effect but is not significant. In terms of Nepal, it has a negative and significant effect on the bank's NPL. It means that in relation to the Indonesian banks, it has no influence but in the context of Nepal, when GDP is high, then the NPLs will be low. When the GDP decreases then NPL will increase, and vice versa. The variable of inflation has a negative relationship with NPL in the Indonesian banks but is not significant. Nepali banks have a negative relationship that is significant on NPL. It shows that inflation has no influence on the Nepali economy but in certain cases, it only effects banking in relation to NPL. For Indonesian banks, the exchange rate has a negative effect but not a significant one and for the Nepali banks, it has a positive effect that is not significant on the bank's NPL also. It clarifies that the exchange rate does not have influence in both countries to do with NPL. The variable of bank size in Indonesia has a positive and significant effect on NPL banks. In Nepal it has a positive effect, but not a significant one. It does make it clear that when in Indonesia a bank's size is big, then the NPL is also high due to there being more debtors and more investment in the sector. The variable of Return on Assets (ROA) of both countries has a negative and not significant effect on NPL. It means that this variable has no effect on both countries' banks. The variable of Capital Adequacy Ratio (CAR) for Indonesia and Nepal have a negative but not significant effect on NPL. It means that both countries' CAR has more influence in relation to the movement of NPL. The variable of interest rate on loans in Indonesia has a positive and significant effect on NPL. On the other hand, the Nepali banks' interest rate on loans is positive but not significant. It means that the interest rate on the loans of both countries plays a crucial role in increasing the NPLs of banks in both countries.

6 SUGGESTION

This research can help to provide information about the factors affecting NPLs impact in both

Indonesian and Nepali banking. Throughout this research, it has been made evident that CEOs, shareholders and financial investors who want to invest in both countries can analyze the impact in the banking market of the stated variables and their associated sensitivity. This study can helpful to the policy makers, practitioners and the researchers to help them to understand better the determinants of NPL in banking management in Indonesia and Nepal.

REFERENCES

Acharya, M. "Development of the Financial System and Its Impact on Poverty Alleviation in Nepal" *Economic Review*, Occassional Paper, Nepal Rastra Bank (15), 2003: 1–32.

Ahmad, N.H. and Ariff, M. "Multi-country Study of Bank Credit Risk Determinants." *The International Journal of Banking and Finance* 5(1), 2007: 135–152.

Angbazo, L. "Commercial Bank Net Interest Margins, Default risk, Interest-rate Risk, and Off-balance Sheet Banking." *Journal of Banking & Finance* 21(1), 1997: 55–87.

Aver, B. "An Empirical Analysis of Credit Risk Factors of the Slovenian Banking System." *Managing Global Transitions* 6(3), 2008: 317–334.

Berger, A.N. and DeYoung, R. "Problem Loans and Cost Efficiency in Commercial Banks." *Journal of Banking & Finance* 21(6), 1997: 849–870.

Brewer, E. "Risk, Regulation, and S & L Diversification into Nontraditional Assets." *Journal of Banking & Finance* 20(4), 1996: 723–744.

Bhattacharya, B. and Roy, T. "Macroeconomic Determinants of Asset Quality of Indian Public Sector Banks: A Recursive VAR Approach." *Journal of Bank Management* 7(1), 2008: 20–40.

Campbell, A. "Bank Insolvency and The Problem of Nonperforming Loans." *Journal of Banking Regulation* 9(1), 2007: 25–45.

Castro, V. "Macroeconomic Determinants of the Credit Risk in the Banking System: The Case of the GIPSI." *Economic Modelling* 31, 2012: 672–683.

Crouhy, M., Galai, D. and Mark, R. *Risk Management*. New Youk, McGraw-Hill, 2000.

Dahal, B. "Experience of the Nepalese Commercial Banks and Challenge Ahead: Nepalese Financial System: Growth and Challenges." *Nepalese Financial System, Nepal Rastra Bank,* 2009: 50–63.

Demetriades, P.O. and Luintel, K.B. "*Banking Sector Policies and Financial*, 1996.

Demirgüç-Kunt, A. and Detragiache, E. "The Determinants of Banking Crises in Developing and Developed Countries. *International Monetary Fund Staff Papers* 45(1), 1998: 81–109.

Ferrari, A., Jaffrin, G. and Shrestha, S. *Access to Financial Services in Nepal World Bank Publications*, 2007.

Fich, E.M. and Shivdasani, A. "Are Busy Boards Effective Monitors?" *Journal of Finance* (2), 2006 689–724.

Gallo, J.G., Apilado, V.P. and Kolari, J.W. "Commercial Bank Mutual Fund Activities: Implications for Bank Risk and Profitability." *Journal of Banking & Finance* 20(10), 1996: 1775–1791.

Hadad, M.D., Santoso, W., Santoso, B., Besar, D.S. and Rulina, I. *Macroeconomic Stress Testing for the Indonesian Banking System,* Loughborough Univ. Banking Centre., M.K., Karels, G.V. and Peterson, M.O. (1994). "Deposit Insurance, Market Discipline and Off-balance Sheet Banking Risk of Large US Commercial Banks." *Journal of Banking & Finance* 18(3), 2006: 575–593.

Jiménez, G. and Saurina, J. "Credit Cycles, Credit Risk, and Prudential Regulation." *International Journal of Central Banking* 2(2), 2006: 65–98.

Jimenez, G., Lopez, J.A., dan Saurina, J. How Does Competition Impact Bank Risk-Taking?. *Federal Reserve Bank of San Fransisco Working Paper* No.23, 2007.

Kalirai, H. and Scheicher, M. "Macroeconomic Stress Testing: Preliminary Evidence for Austria." *Financial Stability Report* 3(1), 2002: 58–74.

Kitua, D.Y. *Application of Multiple Discriminant Analysis in Developing a Commercial Banks Loan Classification Model and Assessment of Significance of Contributing Variables:* A Case of National Bank of Commerce MBA thesis, UDSM,, Dar es Salaam, 1996.

Kashyap, A.K., Rajan, R. and Stein, J.C. "Banks as Liquidity Providers: An Explanation for the Coexistence of Lending and Deposit-taking."*Journal of Finance* 54(1), 2002: 33–73.

Khemraj, Tarron dan Pasha, Sukrishnalall. *The Determinants of Non-Performing Loans: an Econometric Case Study of Guyana. Working Paper,* Financial Stability Unit of the Bank of Guyana, 2009.

Koch, T.W. and McDonald, S.S. *Bank Management* 3rd edition, Sydney, Thomson, 2003.

Laeven, L. and Valencia, F. "*Systemic Banking Crises: A New Database.*" International Monetary Fund Report, Working Paper 08/224, 2008.

Louzis, Dimitrios P., Vouldis, Angelos T., dan Metaxas, Vasilios S. Macroeconomic and Bank Specific Determinants of Non-Performing Loans in Greece: A Comparative Study of Mortgage, Business and Consumer Loans Portofolios. *Journal of Banking and Finance* 36, 2011; 1012–1027.

Ngerebo, T.A. "The Impact of Foreign Exchange Fluctuation on the Intermediation of Banks in Nigeria" (1970–2004). *African Journal of Business Management* 6(11), 2011: 3872–3879.

Pokhrel, D.R. "Banking System Development in Nepal: A Comparative Analysis." Osaka Sangyo University Journal of Economics 7(2), 2006: 215–256.

Richard, E., Chijoriga, M., Kaijage, E., Peterson, C. and Bohman, H. "Credit Risk Management System of a Commercial Bank in Tanzania." International Journal of Emerging Markets 3(3), 2008: 323–332.

Ross, S.A., Westerfield, R.W. and Jordan, B.D. *Fundamental of Corporate Finance* New York, USA, McGraw-Hill Companies Inc, 1998.

Salas, V. and Saurina, J. "Credit Risk in Two Institutional Regimes: Spanish Commercial and Savings Banks." *Journal of Financial Services* Research 22(3), 2002: 203–224.

Saunders, A. and Cornet, M.M. *Financial Institutions Management. A Risk Management Approach*. Boston, McGraw-Hill Irwin, 2008.

Increasing Management Relevance and Competitiveness – Sukoco et al. (Eds)
© 2018 Taylor & Francis Group, London, ISBN 978-0-8153-7455-8

Bank specific variable and credit risk analysis on Islamic banking in the world

K.A. Effendi
Department of Management, Universitas Pendidikan Indonesia, Bandung, Indonesia
Department of Management, Widyatama University, Bandung, Indonesia

N. Nugraha
Department of Management, Universitas Pendidikan Indonesia, Bandung, Indonesia

ABSTRACT: The purpose of this study is to examine the Bank Specific Variable (BSV) factors which affect credit risk in Islamic banking. The research method is explanatory research and uses secondary data derived from Islamic bank financial statements. The results of this study show the existence of a significant negative effect on the Capital Adequacy Ratio (CAR) and Financing Quality (FQL) to credit risk. There is a significant positive effect on Financing Expansion (FEXP) on credit risk and no significant effect on Return on Assets (ROA) on credit risk in Islamic banking. The results of this study contrast with previous studies. The cause is the difference of the object under study, the year of data collection and the amount of data used. The impact of this study is to provide information for the prevention of credit risk that will impact on the sustainability of the Islamic banking business.

Keywords: BSV, credit risk, Islamic banking

1 INTRODUCTION

The global financial crisis in 2008, which many economists have called the worst economic or financial crisis since the great depression in the 1930s, due to excessive lending and negligence by banks in the long run, has increased the importance of credit risk management. The risk is inherent in everything that operates commercially, but for banks and financial institutions, credit risk is an important factor that needs to be managed. Credit risk is the possibility that the borrower or counter party will fail to fulfill its obligations in accordance with agreed terms. Credit risk arises from bank transactions with loans to companies, individuals, and other banks or financial institutions (Gontarek, 1999). Credit risk is also defined as the potential of bank borrowers to fail to meet their obligations in accordance with approved requirements (Islamic Financial Services Board, 2009). Therefore, it can be concluded that credit risk is a risk that is the bank's responsibility if the debtor cannot pay the credit. Credit risk also exists in Islamic banks because they manage financing.

Islamic banks, just like conventional banks, also benefit by providing facilities to their customers. In order to gain profit, there are several contracts in Islamic banking. The contracts are classified in two categories: financing contracts (*murabaha, ijarah, istisna, salam*, etc.) and investment contracts (*mudarabah, musharakah*). Every contract in Islamic banking has many risks, but the main one is credit risk *"on mudarabah contracts and musharakah this risk is called 'risk of capital reduction'"* (Islamic Financial Services Board, 2009). Many researchers argue that despite resistance to the crisis, Islamic banks have a higher risk level of credit risk than conventional banking. Research shows that the success of a financial institutions depends on its strength against external risks and the capacity to survive in difficult economic situations so that it will remain profitable for shareholders. Akkizidis and Khandelwal (2008) also argue that risk management in Islamic banking institutions created by the Islamic Financial Services Board (IFSB) is regulated in the form of prudential principles. IFSB has recognized the importance of effective risk management. They recognize the importance of risk management due to the challenges of Islamic law that must be enforced and international pressure on Islamic banking. But the fact is that Islamic banks do not yet have the right risk management tools to handle risks.

Some literature highlights the impact of the bank specific factor (BSV) on problematic loans (credit risk). Several researchers in the banking literature examine the relationship between BSV and credit risk. In particular, Berger and DeYoung (1997), Fischer et al. (2001), Jiménez and Saurina (2004) and Ahmad and Ariff (2007), among others, concentrated their research on the effects of BSV on banking credit risk. How et al. (2005) measured credit risk on Islamic and conventional banks in Malaysia. The previous research has shown that sharia banks faced credit risks just like conventional banks. Ahmad, N.H. & Ahmad, S.N. (2004) research showed that both Islamic and conventional banks faced several similarities and differences in dealing with credit risk. Credit risk from both banks are influenced by leverage, financing costs and weighted asset risks that show a positive effect on credit risk. However, the credit risk of these banks is influenced by other factors as well, such as management efficiency, regulatory capital and the provision of bad loans. Management efficiency and capital rules are positively related to credit risk in Islamic banks, while they are negatively associated with conventional banks. Furthermore, the findings based on 23 commercial banks with a dual banking system claimed that commercial banks in Malaysia with an Islamic banking side faced lower credit risk compared to conventional banking. These findings are consistent with those of Chazi, A. & Syed, L.A.M. (2010) which suggested that a dual banking system typically holds a larger amount of capital which reduces credit risk due to capital diversification. This study examined credit risks from Islamic and conventional banks during the global financial crisis. They used ratio analysis techniques and 2005–2008 data from 14 countries. The above findings lead to the conclusion that Islamic banking with lower credit risk indicates better capitalization. Return on Assets (ROA) and Return on Equity (ROE) of Islamic banks are found to be less stable than conventional banks. Further findings indicate that Islamic banks faced a lower bankruptcy risk compared to conventional banks during periods of financial crisis. In addition, Beck, T. & Feyen, E. (2013) compared credit risk from Islamic banks with conventional banks using the ratio of gross loan loss reserves, loan provision losses for gross and non-performing loans of gross loans as a proxy of asset quality. These findings suggested that non-performing loans and the provision of loan losses from Islamic banks are lower than conventional banks, so that the credit risk of Islamic banks is lower and the quality of assets is better than conventional banks. Based on the results, the researchers aimed to determine what BSV factors are that affect credit risk in Islamic banking.

2 METHODOLOGY

The research method used is hypothesis testing or explanatory research. This research uses secondary data derived from Islamic bank financial statements from 2009–2016, from five countries and 28 Islamic banks namely Saudi Arabia, United Arab Emirates, Malaysia, United Kingdom, and Indonesia.

The variables of this research is X_1: Capital Adequacy Ratio (CAR), X_2: Profitability—Return on Asset (ROA), X_3: Financing Quality (FQL), X_4: Financing Expansion (FEXP), and Y: Credit Risk—Non-Performing Financing (NPF).

The formulas:

$$CAR = Total\ Capital/Risk\ Weighted\ Assets \quad (1)$$

$$ROA = Net\ after\ tax/Total\ Asset \quad (2)$$

$$FQL = Loan\ Loss\ Provision/Total\ Asset \quad (3)$$

$$FEXP = Total\ Financing/Total\ Assets \quad (4)$$

$$NPF = Total\ NPF/Total\ Financing \quad (5)$$

The test is a panel data regression testing using Eviews 9. There are four regression model of panel data namely: Common effect, fixed effect, fixed effect with cross section weight and random effect. There are three test models named chow test, hausman test and lagrange multiplier test. Chow test to choose the common effect or fixed effect model, Hausman test to choose the random effect or fixed effect model and Lagrange multiplier test to choose common effect or random effect, the last test used when the result of chow test and hausman test is not aligned. Below is a hypothesis for model test:

- The first model is a *chow test* that is h_0: Common effect and h_a: Fixed effect.
- The second model is a *hausman test* that is: h_0: Random effect and h_a: Fixed effect.
- The third model is *lagrange multiplier* test that is ho: Common effect and ha: Random effect.
- If p-value > 0,05 then accept h_0 and if p-value < 0,05 then reject h_0.

The next step is to read the results of the panel data regression which is the best model, whether it is common effect, fixed effect, fixed effect with cross section weight and random effect.

3 RESULTS AND DISCUSSION

3.1 *Correlation*

Table 1 summarizes the correlation values for all the variables used. This test is performed to identify some variables that have a high correlation with correlation value above 0.8. If there is a correlation value above 0.8, then between variables there are multicollinearity.

The test result in Table 1 shows all variables have a correlation value below 0.8. This means that all the variables are free of multicollinearity. If all variables are free from multicollinearity, then the research is continued.

3.2 *Estimation results*

Table 2 shows the estimation of the effect of BSV on credit risk. The analysis was performed using balanced panel data from 2009 to 2016 from 28 Islamic banks in the world with 223 observations. According to White (1980), a cross-section is used to adjust standard error for potential heteroscedasticity. Table 2 is a summary of the model selection test consisting of the Chow test to find out which model will be selected, whether pooled ols or fixed effect, and the Hausman test to determine which model will be selected, whether random effect or fixed effect. The results of the estimation are presented in Table 2:

Based on the estimation result in Table 2, it can be concluded that the fixed effect model with GLS-Weights is cross-section weights. The goodness of fit in the model of 0.7424 or 74.24% (R-square) means that all variables can affect the credit risk of 74.24% and the rest is influenced by other variables not included in this research. Besides, because of the high goodness of fit value, the selection of the fixed effect model as the best panel data regression model is also due to the result of chow and hausman test which obtained p-value <0,05 as shown in Tables 3 and 4 below.

Table 3 shows the probability result is 0.0000, This explains that h_0 is rejected so that the result obtained is a fixed effect model better than the common effect model. Therefore, according to the results of Chow testing, the model used is a fixed effect model.

The results in Table 4 indicate conformity with the previous test, ie h_0 rejected because the probability value <0.05, then the result obtained is a fixed effect model is better than the random effect model.

Table 1. Pairwise correlation matrix of variables.

	CR	CAR	ROA	FQL	FEXP
CR	1.0000				
CAR	0.0496	1.0000			
ROA	−0.1399	−0.1904	1.0000		
FQL	0.2649	−0.4831	0.0586	1.0000	
FEXP	−0.1270	−0.3350	−0.0113	−0.0247	1.0000

Table 3. Chow test.

Redundant fixed effects tests Equation: Untitled Test cross-section fixed effects			
Effects test	Statistic	d.f.	Prob
Cross-section F	18.65	−27,19	0.0000

Table 4. Hausman test.

Correlated random effects—Hausman test Equation: Untitled Test cross-section random effects			
Test summary	Chi-Sq. statistic	Chi-Sq. d.f.	Prob
Cross-section random	35.69	4	0.0000

Table 2. Estimation results.

	Dependent variable: credit risk							
	Pooled ols		Fixed effect		Fixed effect		Random effect	
Independent variable	Coef	Prob	Coef	Prob	Coef	Prob	Coef	Prob
C	0.04	0.09	0.19	0.00	0.10	0.00	0.13	0.00
CAR	0.1	0.03	−0.2	0.00	−0.05	0.01	−0.1	0.02
ROA	−0.3	0.05	0.05	0.71	0.02	0.68	−0.1	0.54
FQL	−0.0	0.38	−0.2	0.00	−0.08	0.00	−0.1	0.00
FEXP	0.8	0.00	0.91	0.00	0.8	0.00	0.70	0.00
R^{2*}	0.1288		0.6018		0.7424		0.1268	
DW*	0.8454		1.8317		1.4302		1.3643	
DV*	no		Yes		Yes		no	
GLSW*	no weights		no weights		cross-section weights		no weights	

Note: R^2 is R-square, DW is Durbin Watson, DV is Dummy Variables and GLSW is GLS-Weights.

This shows that the fixed effect model is the most appropriate model in regression testing in this study and is evidenced by the harmonized results of the Chow test, the Hausman test, and the comparison test between pooled ols, fixed effect and random effect.

The result of the data panel regression with cross-section weight fixed effect model is that the variable of capital adequacy ratio, financing quality, and financing expansion have significant influence on credit risk. CAR and FQL have a negative effect, while FEXP has a positive effect on credit risk. While the profitability variable on return on assets has no significant effect on credit risk, this means that the high or low profit earned has no effect on credit risk in Islamic banking.

The coefficient value of CAR has a negative relation of 0.05 to credit risk, meaning that for every 1% increase in the capital adequacy ratio, then the credit risk will decrease by 5%. The coefficient value of FQL has a negative relation of 0.08 to credit risk, meaning that for every 1% increase in the financing quality ratio, then the credit risk will decrease by 8%. The coefficient value of FEXP has a positive correlation of 0.8 to credit risk, meaning that for every 1% increase in the expansion ratio of financing, then the credit risk will also increase by 80%. In this case, the biggest factor affecting credit risk is financial expansion. Because the financing expansion intended in this study is the expansion of financing taken from the capital, so the capital used will be greater than before and give more influence to the occurrence of credit risk in Islamic banking.

This research is in line with the findings of Misman et al. (2015) and Haryono et al. (2016) which found a significant negative effect on CAR on credit risk. This is because bank capital is an important variable used by banks to manage credit risk levels. Each bank has an obligation to provide minimum capital to maintain the stability and health of the bank, as well as to minimize credit risk in the banking sector. This indicates that more capital adequacy owned by Islamic banks will help Islamic banks reduce their credit risk. This implies that higher capital and prudential management policies can reduce the level of problem financing in Islamic banks because bank capital is an important variable that banks use to manage credit risk. Variable Financing Quality in this study have a significant negative effect on credit risk. This is not in line with the research of Misman et al (2015) which found that there was a significant positive effect on credit risk. The results of this study as expected because of the decline in quality of financing has the potential to increase the risk of financing failure. The different findings one of the causes is the number of observations, the more the number of obsevation will result in better findings.

The financing expansion variable has a significant and positive influence on credit risk, which is inversely related to the findings of Rahman and Shahimi (2010) and Misman et al. (2015) who found a significant negative relationship. The positive impact of these positive have a corresponding relationship because if too much spend on financing, can cause credit risks to increase. This is because in addition to financing, funds are also needed for the provision of capital adequacy to maintain the health of Islamic banks.

Furthermore, ROA represents the bank's profitability which shows how profitable the bank's assets are in generating revenue. Thus, it can be seen that banks with a high ROA are considered to have effective credit risk management because they can manage their loan portfolio, thereby decreasing the allowance for credit losses. But the finding in this research is that ROA has no significant effect on credit risk, which is not in line with the research of Haryono et al. (2016) who found a significant positive influence of ROA on credit risk. The cause of the difference of these findings could be due to the observation units used, Possibly given that Haryono et al.'s research only concerned Indonesia whereas this research covered five different countries representing the world's Islamic banking sector. Therefore, ROA in Islamic banking in the world does not give a significant influence on credit risk.

4 IMPACT

In this study, the researchers obtained findings that the BSV had a significant influence on the occurrence of credit risk in Islamic banks in five countries, namely Saudi Arabia, United Arab Emirates, Malaysia, United Kingdom, and Indonesia. BSV capital (CAR) and financing quality (FQL) have a negative effect on credit risk. This provides information to Islamic banking in these five countries to maintain their capital adequacy ratio and the quality of their financing distribution to stay within certain limits set in each central bank. If an Islamic bank has CAR and FQL is low or minimal, then the impact on the credit risk of Islamic banks will increase. This will threaten the business continuity in Islamic banking. This is the case with the Financing Expansion (FEXP) which has a positive effect on credit risk. The information that can be obtained is that the expansion must be done based on a mature calculation, in terms of cost, capital and interests. If there is high expansion then the impact is an increase in credit risk. This happens because if Islamic banks spend too much on financing, especially on the financing of strict quality control. This will disrupt the use of capital, because in addition to being used for financing, capital is also required for the provision of capital adequacy to maintain the health of Islamic banks.

5 CONCLUSION

The conclusions obtained in this research are the existence of a significant negative effect on the ratio of capital adequacy and quality of financing to credit risk in Islamic banking in the world. And there is a significant positive influence on financing expansion to credit risk and no significant influence on ROA on credit risk in Islamic banking in the world. This research can provide advice for policy makers, risk managers and academics to add new findings in science and knowledge to better manage risk and minimize credit risk by increasing capital adequacy in order to maintain the health of Islamic banks, and to better manage the quality of financing with apply 5C (character, capacity, capital, colleteral, and condition) and limit the maximum financing is 80% of total assets, in order to minimize the risk of Islamic banking credit.

ACKNOWLEDGMENT

Thank you to the Financial Funding Management Agency (LPDP) of Indonesia's finance ministry which contributed sponsorship for international conferences at the Global Conference on Business, Management and Entrepreneurship (GCBME) 2017.

REFERENCES

Ahmad, N.H. & Ahmad, S.N. (2004). Key factors influencing credit risk of Islamic bank: A Malaysian case. *The Journal of Muamalat and Islamic Finance Research, 1*, 65–80.

Ahmad, N.H. & Ariff, M. (2007). Multi-Country study of bank credit risk determinants. *International Journal of Banking and Finance, 5*(1), 135–152.

Akkizidis, I. & Khandelwal, S.K. (2008). *Financial risk management for Islamic banking and finance.* Published by Palgrave Macmillan. ISBN: 9780230598751. DOI: 10.1057/9780230598751.

Beck, T. & Feyen, E. (2013). Benchmarking financial systems: Introducing the financial possibility frontier. *World Bank Policy Research working paper 6615.*

Berger, A.N. & DeYoung, R. (1997). Problem loans and cost efficiency in commercial banks. *Journal of Banking & Finance, 21*(6), 849–870.

Chazi, A. & Syed, L.A.M. (2010). Risk exposure during the global financial crisis: the case of Islamic banks. *International Journal of Islamic and Middle Eastern Finance and Management, 3*(4), 321–333, https://doi.org/10.1108/17538391011093261.

Fischer, K.P., Gueyie, J., & Ortiz, E. (2001). Risk-taking and charter value of commercial banks from the Nafta countries. *The International Journal of Finance, 13*(1).

Gontarek, W. (1999). *Looking after loans, credit risk—Loans, credit risk supplement to risk magazine.* published by www.incisivemedia.com.

Haryono, Y., Ariffin, N.M., & Hamat, M. (2016). Factors affecting credit risk in Indonesian Islamic banks. *Journal of Islamic Finance, 5*(1), 12–25.

How, J.C.Y., Karim Abdul, M. & Verhoeven, P. (2005). Islamic financing and bank risks: The case of Malaysia. *Thunderbird International Business Review, 47*(1).

Islamic Financial Services Board. (2009). *Guiding principles on shari'ah governance systems for institutions offering Islamic financial services.* ISBN: 978-983-44579-5-2.

Jiménez, G. & Saurina, J. (2004). Collateral, type of lender and relationship banking as determinants of credit risk. *Journal of Banking and Finance, 28*(9), 2191–2212.

Khan, T. & Ahmed, H. (2001). Risk management: An analysis of issues in Islamic financial industry. *Occasional Paper No. 5, Islamic Research and Training Institute, Islamic Development Bank,* Jeddah.

Misman, F.N., Bhattib, I., Loub, W., Samsudina, S. & Rahman, N.H.A. (2015). Islamic banks credit risk: A panel study. *Paper presented at the International Accounting and Business Conference, IABC.*

Rahman, A.A. & Shahimi, S. (2010). Credit risk and financing structure of Malaysian Islamic banks. *Journal of Economic Cooperation and Development, 3*(31), 83–105.

White, Halbert. (1980). A heteroskedasticity-consistent covariance matrix estimator and a direct test for heteroskedasticity. *The Econometric Society, 48* (4), 817–838. doi: 10.2307/1912934.

Green business

Increasing Management Relevance and Competitiveness – Sukoco et al. (Eds)
© 2018 Taylor & Francis Group, London, ISBN 978-0-8153-7455-8

When and how does the business become green? Green knowledge consequence for management and organization

Susminingsih
IAIN Pekalongan, Pekalongan, Indonesia

K. Chandra Kirana & Sri Hermuningsih
University of Sarjanawiyata Tamansiswa, Yogyakarta, Indonesia

ABSTRACT: Purpose—This study aims to combine the literature on green business and sustainability of batik business into management and organization framework. This research seeks to build and to elaborate the relationship of anthropological business problem, green knowledge, green management and green organization. Design/methodology/approach—The research focuses on Indonesian entrepreneur who have the experience of information of batik business and their green knowledge. This study undertakes an anthropological study by means of observation, interview and documentation method. The informant is chosen by purposive sampling technique. Findings—The paper finds that the extant literature in the field of business and management heavily concerned green knowledge practices within Small and Medium-sized Enterprises (SMEs). Originality/value—The paper is benefit to academics and managers to consider green knowledge when they meet environment challenge. Since sustainability is important to all SMEs, to enhance understanding of when and how to cope with green management and green organization as green knowledge consequence is necessary. Paper Type: Research paper.

Keywords: business, green knowledge consequence, green management and green organization

1 INTRODUCTION

The enterprise's sustainability depends heavily on the capability of the enterprise's manager in adapting with the environmental changes tend to be uncertain (Lee, 2009). The business environment become a big issue which continues to cling to enterprises management, both on large scale enterprises and small and medium scale enterprises. This business challenge could mean change for both the organization and management (Georg & Fussel 2000; Harris and Crane, 2002).

The adaptation process towards a business challenge for an enterprise organization is a learning process (Millard, 2011). Innovations on every sector are finally carried out, whether on process innovation, product innovation, management innovation, organization innovation, marketing innovation, and so on. Every innovation aims to maximize profit and reduce expense. Efficiency becomes output innovation (Millard, 2011). The efficiency on human and natural including environmental preservation into a market icon to date.

2 ORGANIZATIONAL LEARNING

The discussions about organizational learning (OL) have keept developing during the last few years, especially concerning dealing with business challenges (Hooper, et al. 2000; Hansen, et al. 2005; Rome & Wijen, 2005). Cognition or aspects of understanding for the first time indicate a contact for entrepreneurs who face challenges. This makes behavior aspect to be a response form towards a business issue. Sometimes, both aren't sequentially happen, and even contrary. There are times when business response occurs reflexively and there are times when it is a continuation of learning outcomes (Fiol and Lyles, 1985).

3 GREEN KNOWLEDGE

Knowledge is very important especially when human have to make a decision that involves many factors: mental, cultural, theoretical models which are all come from the human experiences that are generally involved in an organization. Resource efficiency become a central issue since the industrial world is confronted with the depletion of various resources and also the emergence of a number of problems resulting from the industrial environment itself. Resources consists of capital/financial, labor, technology, as well as the business environment change challenge such as market orientation, consumer satisfaction, business competition techniques, environment pollution. The combination of these various condition become a requirement for a businessman when making a business orientation change. A number of indicators for knowledge about management get appreciated and drive businesses toward sustainability (Millard, 2011). Various methods to efficient business have achieved a lot such as replacing materials with the environment friendly ones, in line with green movements, as well as replacing techniques with faster ones and ones with a lower pollutant level.

4 METHOD

The location of this research is Pekalongan City, Central Java. The research subjects are Batik SMEs taken one from each in Java. This study is a qualitative study using phenomenon approach and case studies in Pekalongan City. The method used is descriptive, meaning that researchers provide overview systematically, factually and accurately on the facts and the characteristics of certain populations. The case study method is also used in this study in order to analyze in detail the current situation and interaction environment of organizational such as Batik SMEs.

The analytical tool used as a source of analysis in this study is phenomenon approach. The phenomenon approach used as a basis for determining some of the functions that are supposed to encourage the performance of Batik SME in Pekalongan City, Central Java, which uses natural dyes produced from leaves, roots, and certain shaved wood phenomena encountered. This research is classified as empiric-rational-inductive research.

The primary data are obtained from the field while the secondary data are obtained from journal and official reports about the number of SMEs.

5 RESULT

The information obtained showed that the batik industry was also experiencing various business turbulences. Much research has been conducted done and verified that Green human resources, which states that one's leadership in managing enterprises and organization's members are vital in making a number of enterprise innovations (Chen, 2011). With regards to the price, motif, expensive material, market orientation, competition, etc. basically, those conditions became a common dilemma, because the sustainability of the batik industry has been counterproductive with the waste it generates. The more dynamic the batik business is, the more chronic the waste it generates. The poor environment coupled with water contamination on both color and odor, makes the society, government, and businessmen conduct experiments to switch to natural dyes. The environment pollution level because of batik waste is quiet unsettling because of the used chemical dye chemical contents. Among the natural dyes used are: **Turmeric** (*curcuma domestica val*), the part used are its rhizomes and root tubers which can produce yellow dye. ***Secang* plant** (*Caesaslpinia Sapapan Lin*), the part used is its tree bark to produce red dye. ***Tingi*** (*Ceriops Condolleana*); ***jambal*** (*Pelthopherum pterocarpum*); ***tegeran*** (*Cudrania Javanensis*), the part used are its tree bark and wood to produce *soga* dye on batik. **Shallot** (*Allium Ascalonicium L*), the part used is its outer skin to produce brownish orange dye. **Mimosa** (*Mimosa Pudica*), the part used are its flowers and leaves to produce greenish yellow dye. **Coconut** (*Cocos Nucifera*), the part used is its coconut huskto produce brownish beige dye. ***Andong*** (*Cardyline Futicosa Backer*), the part used are its leaves to produce green dye. **Noni** (*Morinda Citrifolia*), the part used is its rood to produce red dye. **Mango** (*Mangitera Indica Lina*), the part used is its tree bark to produce green dye. **Indigo** (*Indigofera Tinctoria*), the part used are its leaves and tree branches to produce blue dye. **Teak** (*Tectona Grandis L*), the part used are its young leaves to produce brownish red dye. **Tea** (*Camelia Sinensis*), the part used are its old leaves to produce brown dye. **Avocado** (*Persea*), the part used are its leaves to produce brownish green dye.

The batik consumer's orientation has shifted to natural dye batik. It is understood that the go green movement in both local and overseas consumer has affected the batik consumer's interest. Since nature conservation came to the world's attention, in batik industry the switch from synthetic dye to natural dye is the solution. Five main principal of environment friendly dye concept are: **Rethink**, where businessmen rethink when are going to keep using non environmental friendly materials. This includes resource conservation such as fabric, wax, and other materials as the fuel to melt the wax. **Reduce**, which reduces the water containment after the use of natural dye. Besides to reducing the pollution, the amount of synthetic dye consumption can be reduced when batik businessmen use leaves/roots/fruit peels which are often discarded. **Recovery**, which is polluted environment recovery. Today, the attention towards the existence of Waste water Treatment Plant (WWTP), is not the responsibility of the Pekalongan City government alone, but also the home industries, or also known as individual WWTP. From the waste treatment plant before released to a river, the waste is first processed to eliminate pollutant levels. **Reuse**, which is achieved by innovating residues. Some of batik businessmen have already applied by turning cement paper, wood, coconut shell, and jeans fabric into batik media. **Recycle**, by recycling wax residues to be reused.

On the technical side, the batik business in Pekalongan is also innovative. Previously, batik is processed by two main technique, which were written and stamped, or combined. Both techniques require a great deal of time, so that the market demand often cannot be supplied in a short period of time. On the marketing side, efforts are made both through various national scale exhibition events such as *Pekan Batik Nasional (PBN)* and an international scale exhibition, which is the International Pekalongan Batik Week. Since Pekalongan City is inaugurated as The World City of Batik and Creative City World by UNESCO, the interest from both society and businessmen towards batik has increased. The Pekalongan City local government in cooperation with the central government has developed the batik business through series of programs that are applied by an institution which called the *Dewan Kerajinan Nasional Daerah (Dekranasda)* or Regional National Crafts Council together with the ministry of industry and trade.

6 DISCUSSION

Innovation is often interpreted as something done by the company to add value, both directly for the business and indirectly for the consumer, with a dual purpose, which is to make the consumer satisfied and loyal, and also to maintain the existence of the business (Kamaruddeen, et al. 2009; Gibbon et al, 1994; Lyons et al., 2007; Dembowski, 2013). From the Green Knowledge typology, the belief that comes from the Giver of Belief makes human sure about the happenings, including in business, and forms a positive mindset. The term green refers to a situation that is secure, pleasant, peaceful, co-operative, tolerant, mutual respect, and the need for each other (coexistence). These values are often became the basis of a green innovation, in order to both response the environment and as a proof of the business' proactive attitude to maximize its profit and efficiency (Wong, 2012; Johnstone et al., 2010, Porter and van der Linde, 1995). For a businessman, efficiency became the next green innovation orientation. Doing the right thing, became a principle of every business needed to fulfill the organization and consumer's needs. The urge to survive and provide the consumer's needs become the main motivator, while in the same time they have to be wary of the demands for environmental safety. Often, environmental damage; pollution, health, social-cultural level are related with industry. The environment safety standard such as energy saving become a reference of a production process and urges the production process to adapt by applying process development and innovation (Chiou et al. 2011; Eggers, et al., 2013). Individual greening occurs because a person experiences environmental awareness. Green organizations also play a role in the operation of green knowledge.

Human self-awareness, as a part of other human communities, supports mutual respect, esprit de corps, mutual care, and the need for relationships with each other.

7 CONCLUSION

Industry is often placed face-to-face with environment, includes relation and consumer. Although the industry as an organization would be a relation and a consumer for the environment. The term green is the businessman's way to accommodate the knowledge is in the form of both parties co-operative relationship or interplay. The batik industry is inversely proportional with the environment condition. The presence of pollution that is not keep occurring, encourages the government and businessmen to innovate to minimize the negative impact, while in the same time increasing the resource efficiency. The innovating attitude in the green knowledge theory is a result of organizational learning process, both as a proactive response and action. The green knowledge principle that based on peaceful situation, tolerant, partnership, and care, stimulates the businessmen to have a change in both management and organizational relationship in their work team.

REFERENCES

Chen, Y.S. (2011). "Green Organizational Identity: Sources and Consequence", *Management Decision*, Vol. 49, No. 1. pp. 384–404.

Chiou, T.Y., Chan, H.K. Lettice, F. and Chung, S.H. (2011). "The Influence of Greening the Suppliers and Green Innovation on Environmental Performance and Competitive Advantage in Taiwan", *Transportation Research Part E*, Vol. 47 No. 6 November, pp. 822–836.

Demboski, F.L. (2013), "The Roles of Benchmarking, Best Practices & Innovation in Organizational Effectiveness", *The International Journal of Organizational Innovation*, Vol. 5, No. 3, January, pp. 6–20.

Eggers, F., Kraus, S., Hughes, M., Laraway, S., & Snycerski, S. (2013). "Implications of Customer and Entrepreneurial Orientation for SME Growth". *Management Decision,* 51 (3), 524–546.

Fiol, M.C., & Lyles. (1985). Organizational Learning, *Academy of Management Review,* 10 (4), pp. 803–813.

Georg, S., Fussel, L. (2000). "Making Sense of Greening and Organizational Change", *Business Strategy and the Environmental,* 9, 175–185.

Gibbons, H.R., Limoges, C., Nowotny, H., Schwartzman, S., Scott, P., and Trow, M. (1994). *The New Production of Knowledge.* London: Sage.

Harris, L.C., Crane, A. (2002). "The Greening of Organizational Culture, Management Views on the Depth, Degree and Diffusion of Change", *Journal of Organizational Change Management,* Vol. 15. No. 3, pp. 214–234.

Hansen, OE., Sondergard, B., Holm. J., and Kerndrup, S. (2005). "Creation and Communication of Environmental Knowledge within and between Communities of Practice". In I. Oehme, and U. Seebacher (Eds), *Corporate Sustainability: Theoretical Perpectives and Practical Approaches,* Muchen, Wien: Profil.

Hooper, P., Jukes, S., & Stubbs, M. (2000). "SME Environmental Performance and the Business Support Network Network: Problem-Solving not Panacea". Paper presented at *The Business Strategy and the Environmental Conference,* Leeds, 18–19 September.

Johnstone, N., Hascic, I. and Popp, D. (2010). "Renewable Energy Policies and Technological Innovation: Evidence Based on Patent Counts", *Environmental and Resource Economics,* Vol. 45, No. 1., pp. 133–155.

Kamaruddeen, A.M., Yusof, N.A., Said, I. (2009). "A Proposed Framework for Measuring Firm Innovativeness in the Housing Industry", *International Journal of Organization Innovation,* Vol. 2, No. 2. pp. 101–132.

Lee, K., (2009), "Why and How to Adopt Green Management into Business Organizations?", *Management Decision,* Vol. 47, No. 7. pp. 1101–1121.

Lyons, R.K., Chatman, J.A., & Joyce, C.K., (2007). "Innovation in Services: Corporate Culture and Invesment Banking". *California Management Review,* 50(1), 174–191.

Millard, D. (2011), "Management Learning and the Greening of SMEs: Moving Beyond Problem-Solving", *Jerman Journal of Research in Human Resource Management,* 25 (2), pp. 178–195.

Porter, M. and van der Linde, C. (1995), "Toward a New Conception of Environment-Competitiveness Relationship", *Journal of Economic Perspective,* Vol. 9, No. 4, pp. 97–118.

Roome, N., & Wijen, F. (2005). "Stakeholder Power and Organizational Learning", *Corporate Environmental Management,* 10, pp. 69–76.

Wong, K.S., (2012), "The Influence of Green Product Competitiveness on the Success of Green Product Innovation, Empirical Evidence from the Chinese Electrical and *Electronic* Industry", *European Journal of Innovation Management,* Vol. 15, No. 4, pp. 468–490.

Increasing Management Relevance and Competitiveness – Sukoco et al. (Eds)
© 2018 Taylor & Francis Group, London, ISBN 978-0-8153-7455-8

The role of financial technology for the agricultural sector in Indonesia: Case study of I-Grow FinTech company

T. Widiastuti, R. Sukmana & I. Mawardi
Universitas Airlangga, Surabaya, Indonesia

Wahyuningsih
Universitas Indonesia, Depok, Indonesia

I.W. Indrawan
International Islamic University of Malaysia, Malaysia

ABSTRACT: The agricultural sector is a strategic sector because it is directly related to the food security of a nation. Indonesia as an agricultural country has good potential in agriculture, especially after the development of many technologies that support the production process in this field. The development of technology in this era of globalization not only includes production technology, but has also penetrated the financial sector. The concept of Financial Technology (FinTech) is about providing capital for the business actors, including farmers, to expand and increase their production output. This research used the qualitative approach to explore more about the role of FinTech based on crowdfunding, with a focus on the company I-Grow, the first FinTech company with a vision to maintain a sustainable and balanced agricultural sector. The results showed that as one of the FinTech companies in the field of agriculture, I-Grow has been able to present a sustainable and profitable alternative to financing the agricultural sector. I-Grow's success rests on its ability to be an intermediary between investors and the agricultural actors, as well as its encouragement for more efficient and transparent business schemes.

Keywords: Agricultural Sector, Financial Technology, I-Grow

1 INTRODUCTION

Indonesia is an agricultural country. Agriculture and the rural sector has a strategic role in relation to national development (Ashari & Saptana, 2005). The agricultural sector still plays a very strategic role in the national economy. This sector remains a main source of income and livelihood for the majority of the population, helping contribute to the Gross Domestic Product and foreign exchange resources, as well as being the supplier of raw materials and markets to the industrial sector. In fact, additionally, the role of the agricultural sector cannot be replaced by other sectors as a source of food (Batubara, 2007; Asaad, 2011).

The agricultural sector is known as a business sector that is quite risky, causing the interest of financial institutions to fund the business sector to be relatively low. Several studies show that the proportion of banking credit for agriculture is still far below the financing for industry, trade, restaurants and hotels, transportation, and other economic sectors (Tsabita, 2013).

On the topic of economic growth, real Research and Development (R&D) activities that produce technological innovations are often touted as the primary engine of growth in an advanced economy (Chou, 2007). One evidence to support the above statement is the emergence of technological innovations in the financial service sector that enable people to receive financial services without physically coming into the financial institution's office. Examples of this type of Financial Technology (FinTech) include mobile banking, Internet banking, electronic money and crowdfunding. For instance, with crowdfunding scheme, we can connect the money holders directly to certain investments or donation beneficiaries by using smartphone applications.

From above explanation, it is an opportunity to learn and innovate in the agricultural sector by integrating it with FinTech. Currently, number of researches that focus on agriculture amounts to more than 100,000 studies. In comparison, researches related to FinTech is still less than 1,000 studies. However, there has not been any research that discusses FinTech and agriculture. Whereas, a FinTech company focusing on this sector has begun to emerge since 2013, not only in Indonesia (four companies) but also abroad (one company).

This paper aims to fill the gap through an exploration about the role of FinTech as a sustainable financing instrument through field research, and is associated with a review of the previous studies related to FinTech. Therefore, the research question asked in this study is how the concept and role of I-Grow as a green business entity in Indonesia is based on a crowdfunding scheme.

2 LITERATURE REVIEW

2.1 *Financial technology*

FinTech is a term that refers to an integration of ICT (Information and Communication Technology) and financial services, or an ICT-based financial services (G. Li et al., 2017:2). There are three elements that make up FinTech services. They are supporting technology, organization and incoming investments (Zavolokina et al., 2016:77). The mechanism of FinTech is described below.

Furthermore, there are a number of services provided by FinTech as follows (G. Li et al., 2017:2):

1. Practical and cheap remittance service. Analysis of financial data, both for individual customers and companies.
2. Financial software that can improve the performance of customer financial analysis to be more efficient.
3. Platform; the term for the provision of easy and secure transaction services.

The presence of FinTech is currently driven by a number of factors, as presented by Puschmann (Puschmann, 2017). First, the development of IT

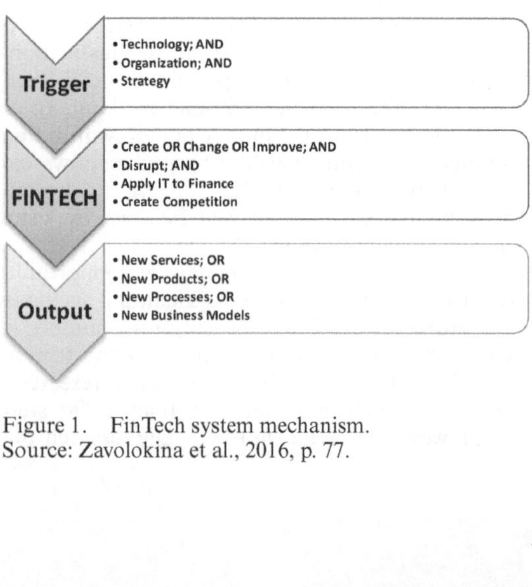

Figure 1. FinTech system mechanism.
Source: Zavolokina et al., 2016, p. 77.

such as social media, cloud computing and the Internet has enabled people to automate their businesses. In addition, an advanced IT presence has enabled the existence of business schemes with truly new products and services, apart from the conventional ones. In the financial sector, the birth of crowdfunding is a tangible example of changes in financial services as an impact of IT development.

Second, there has been a change in consumer behavior. Consumers today tend to have such a high level of interaction with IT and Internet devices. This encourages financial service providers to be able to provide self-service facilities for customers with IT access.

Third, are the changes in the ecosystem of the financial industry. Today, conventional banking and insurance have adjusted their business volumes and tend to focus on particular segment specializations.

Fourth, changes in regulations. A number of countries, such as the United Kingdom, Singapore and Hong Kong, provide regulations that encourage the growth of FinTech. Such a rule may be an incubation center for digital financial services and the provision of model assistance to businesses in the FinTech field.

Fintech has some advantages. First, a company engaged in FinTech is able to provide practical and diverse financial services for their consumers, with an Internet basis that can be accessed anywhere and at any time. Moreover, FinTech uses certain algorithms that can make financial services available 24 hours a day (G. Li et al., 2017). Second, FinTech does not present the value of the business using the digitalization framework alone. Instead, FinTech is a tool that is capable of combining available resources (organizations, environments and strategies) to create added value from existing businesses (Zavolokina et al., 2016). Third, FinTech enables the consumers to obtain financial services with easy and fast access, attractive interest rates and guaranteed transparency of the transactions (Wood & Steiner, 2016).

Despite the advantages, FinTech also has several weaknesses. The most concerning weakness is regarding the security aspect for transactions and information submitted over the Internet network. This condition happens along with rampant hacking cases that occur on the Internet. Among the forms of security threats to the transactions through FinTech are 'CSRF (Cross-Site Request Forgery), DDOS attack and Session hijacking' (G. Li et al., 2017).

2.2 *Crowdfunding*

The term crowdfunding refers to a fund-raising mechanism for investment from a large number of investors using Internet media, either with a donation scheme, or lending or equity participation, and is aimed at a business or social campaign.

Crowdfunding allows for investments to be made by a large number of people without having minimum and maximum limits for investing. Crowdfunding is believed can bring huge amounts of investment and profit levels. Thus, SMEs (small medium enterprises) and startups are starting to use crowdfunding as the source of their business financing (Zilgalvis, 2014). In addition, the crowdfunding scheme is not just an alternative financing scheme for SMEs and startups. Also, the crowdfunding scheme enables entrepreneurs to be more confident in opening up their businesses thus improving the economy of the community.

There are two key factors that drive the emergence of the crowdfunding scheme. First, innovations in the field of IT. Second, the global financial crisis has created higher prudence in traditional financial institutions in relation to lending. Despite a keen interest, a number of risks lurk in crowdfunding practices. Among these are fraud, potential loss of all investments resulting from business losses, investment liquidation, complexity from anti-money laundering regulations, intellectual property protection challenges, platform failures, uneven information access and a lack of secondary markets (Zilgalvis, 2014). Therefore, it is advisable for entrepreneurs seeking funding through a crowdfunding scheme to open up with detailed business plans and forecasting for future finances, preparing the investors who are ready to invest at the start of the campaign along with management that are ready to manage campaigns and funds earned (Wood & Steiner, 2016).

2.3 *Agricultural financing*

Agriculture is a fundamental economic activity because it plays an important role in the production of the food of a country (Son et al., 2017). One of problems in the agricultural sector is entities that control the value chain of the agricultural sector, leading to there being only a handful of agribusiness companies, while the majority of people are living in agriculture-based ground-level businesses and are vulnerable to poverty (Miller & Jones, 2010). In addition, loan providers for farmers often do not pay attention to the condition of the farmers' business environment, which tends to be uncertain and is not oriented toward increasing the value chain of the agricultural business. Therefore, a proper financing mechanism is needed to encourage the farmers' production and competition.

A study by Novak et al. (2016) mentioned a number of potential sources of financing in agriculture. First, financing by an individual derived from an excess of household income, after deducting household expenses. This source of financing was very good if people's income increased, but must be supported by a stable economic condition. Second, investments were coming from a legal entity to expand its business. Third, there was financing that came from project-based government spending. Government alignments are important because most farmers will find it difficult to compete without the government's assistance. However, limited government fiscal space means that a source of funding from the state should be combined with other funding sources. Fourth, loans from commercial banks. Loans from commercial banks for agriculture unfortunately had a number of constraints, such as farmers who generally did not have collateral, high interest rates, uncertain government subsidies and agricultural business high risks. So, for this sector it was difficult to obtain bank loans. Fifth, investment from institutional investors that act as an alternative to financing the funds alone. Sixth, multinational companies such as McDonald's, KFC and Pepsi, had been investing in agricultural companies which become their raw material suppliers. Seventh, international funding agencies such as the World Bank and the International Monetary Fund (Novak et al., 2016).

However, the above funding sources only provide capital and do not solve the agricultural value chain problems. Therefore, a mechanism that can encourage the strengthening of the agricultural value chain is needed. There are three factors that can drive improvement of the value chain in a given economic sector, including agriculture. First, proper regulation that deals with production standards, input and output arrangements, and good priorities in infrastructure development are needed. Optimum financial inclusion is characterized by the integration of stakeholders in the business, which is conducted through a proprietary scheme or a detailed contract in order to increase the access to input for farmers and eliminate some components of the cost. Third, implementation of strict contract transactions in order to avoid illegal actions, such as dismissal or an alteration of contracts unilaterally and defaulted due to negligence (Miller & Jones, 2010).

2.4 *Previous studies*

There are a number of studies that have reviewed agricultural financing innovations. A study by Son et al. (2017) initiated a financing model called the PMF (Production Mutualization Fund) Model, which aimed to improve the capability of the agricultural value chain so that better bankability of agricultural businesses can be achieved. The model was a form of equity financing sourced from public or private funds, with the aim of improving bankability and sustainability of agricultural enterprises through improvement of the value chain. This model required contribution from all involved parties. The private sector as main investor provides capital for the agricultural business. The government is also involved as a financier and provides easy access to bureaucracy. The government and the private sector, in channeling their capital from a Special Purpose Vehicle (SPV), is tasked with building infrastructure for farmers and overseeing production and cost flow, so that unnecessary costs can be cut, as well as providing training and knowledge transfer for the farmers to increase their income and skills capacity.

The second study was conducted by Novak et al. (2016) that identified a number of potential sources of financing for the agricultural sector in the Ukraine, such as bank financing and government financing. This study concluded that there are seven investment mechanisms that can serve as a catalyst for agricultural development, but it needs to be further studied to determine the best financing method.

The third study by Zhao et al. (2017) involved conducting a survey on the impact of financing for farming families in Lishui City, Zhejiang Province, China. This study concluded that a variety of funding sources, both governmental and institutional, had a positive influence on the income of farming families. However, various sources of financing have different functions, so it is very important that the source of financing is still maintained for better management of the farmers' businesses.

3 RESEARCH METHODOLOGY

This study was conducted using the qualitative approach, which is a research approach that does not need generalization for any of the findings or results (Kaelan, 2012). The qualitative research approach is conducted to explore a new discovery found in the research field, which has a relationship with the main objective that is expected to be covered. To be certain, this research used field research as the specific tool.

Data collection in this research was done through a literature study and interviews. The literature items used in this paper are concerned with crowdfunding and FinTech, as well as the website of I-Grow as the study case of this paper. Meanwhile, an interview was conducted with I-Grow's founder, Mr. Andreas Senjaya, through an online chat application named *WhatsApp.*

The data collected will be analyzed in several steps. First, data reduction will be done by classifying information based on the issues involved. After that, data presentation will be provided by graphical presentation and the researcher will propose a model which accommodates the findings from the informant. Lastly, there will be concluding remarks as the answer to the problem statements, as well as recommendations for future research studies to be conducted.

4 FINDINGS AND DISCUSSION

4.1 *Description of I-Grow*

I-Grow is a startup business that aims to create an efficient production mechanism and investment in organic farming with a good economic scale. I-Grow was founded in 2013 by Andreas Senjaya, a student at the Faculty of Computer Science in the University of Indonesia. I-Grow acts as an intermediary actor, connecting investors with farmers and landowners to participate in selling the agricultural products they produced to end users. I-Grow has a vision to preserve life on earth and to create fair and equitable food security for all people.

There are several advantages offered by I-Grow. First is the level of profitable investment. I-Grow operates on a profit-sharing scheme and each year has a 13–24% profit rate for the investors. Second, I-Grow has been contributing in relation to utilizing idle land, but has economic potential to empower landowners and farmers in relation to planting areas. Third, I-Grow does not only encourage a food-oriented increase in commercial activity as a business focus. Instead, I-Grow also encourages green activities and environmental conservation in the planting areas. I-Grow seeks to create domestic food security by involving investors to empower farmers, to utilize unemployed land and to encourage reforestation in planting areas. Some of the commodities planted by I-Grow can be seen in the following Table.

Investment in I-Grow has several phases. The phases are described below.

I-Grow is currently running well and has an investors and partners network as follows.

The success of I-Grow had been recognized internationally, as evidenced by the following awards.

1. Top 2 in World Summit Awards
2. 1st Winner from Payments Dragons' Den
3. 1st Winner from Tech in Asia
4. 21st Best from Disrupt 100
5. 5th Best from Ummah Wide
6. 1st Winner in G-Startup Worldwide Jakarta
7. 2nd Winner in Startup Istanbul
8. Top 25 from Australia Awards

Table 1. I-Grow commodities & investment values.

Name of plantation	Investment value of a tree (IDR)	Return rate (% per annum)
Breadfruit	1,500,000	10–15
Coconut	2,500,000	12–15
Avocado	2,500,000	15
Deli Honey Guava	1,500,000	7–20
Cassava	15,000,000	16
Fragrant Root	10,000,000	15
Banana	12,500,000	15–20
Peanut	14,900,000	18–26
Longan	2,500,000	12–46
Durian	5,000,000	19–47
Palm Date	5,000,000	10–20
Olive	3,500,000	15–20

Source: https://www.igrow.asia/.

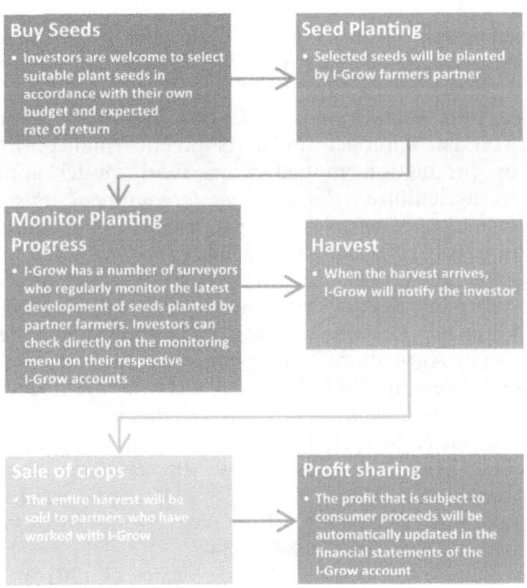

Figure 2. Workflow mechanism in I-Grow.

Table 2. I-Grow network data.

Indicator	Data
Land Planted	1,247 hectares
Trees Planted	11,014,276 trees
Investors	19,872 people
Farmers	2,300 farmers
Absorbed Carbon Dioxide	358,804 kg CO_2

Source: https://www.igrow.asia/.

9. Top 20 in ASEAN (Association of South East Asia Nations) Impact Challenge
10. Top 5 in Innovation 4 Impact
11. Top 40 in K-Startup Grand Challenge 2016.

4.2 *Discussion and analysis*

Previous studies regarding agricultural financing were focused on funding sources that came from the government and institutional private companies. I-Grow, as a startup company, is a breakthrough in maintaining agricultural financing.

Based on a study by G. Li et al. (2017:2), I-Grow can be regarded as a startup company with FinTech services that is oriented toward creating a 'platform'. This platform is created to ensure secure and easy transactions for stakeholders. In this case, I-Grow created a linkage between urban investors and rural farmers. This scheme is essentially a typical financial inclusion scheme that enables farmers to access financial services, involving reasonable cost and time (Wahid, 2014).

This scheme has several advantages compared to other agricultural financing sources, such as government grants or loans from private companies. First, I-Grow has been able to provide a profitable investment scheme to the investors. With a variety of personal investors, I-Grow and farmers will not become dependent on certain parties for maintaining the financing of their agriculture business. Second, the investment scheme with a profit-sharing contract will not burden the farmers. It is different from a loan that will become a liability and cost for farmers, while a profit-sharing contract will protect farmers from financial exploitation. On the other hand, investors will also get a higher return as farmers' performance increases. Third, the supervision mechanism run by I-Grow will provide remote supervision for investors.

This will ensure fulfillment of farming standards as well as all parties' participation in the business process. It is parallel with Miller and Jones (2010) who stated the above requirements as being the key to success in creating improvement in the value chain of a given economic sector. In other words, I-Grow has driven improvements in the agricultural sector in Indonesia.

5 CONCLUSION AND RECOMMENDATION

I-Grow as a startup has been able to present a sustainable and profitable alternative to financing for agriculture. I-Grow's success relies on I-Grow's ability to be an intermediary medium between investors and agricultural actors, and encourages more efficient and transparent business schemes. Not merely providing profitable investments for investors, it has an impact on the farmers' economy, especially to do with raising capital for their farms and is essentially a kind of financial inclusion. I-Grow has also been able to improve the value chain in the agricultural sector through remote supervision provided by I-Grow's surveyors.

Further research studies may take on an empirical analysis on the performance of such startups which use a crowdfunding scheme to maintain agricultural financing. An assessment on their efficiency, effectiveness and the impact on the economic, social and environmental aspects is important to enhance the startup's performance, as well as enacting the sound regulations on startups with a real impact on society.

REFERENCES

Books and Journals

Adimihardja, A. (2006). Strategi Mempertahankan Multifungsi. Pertanian di Indonesia. *Jurnal Litbang Pertanian (*The strategy of Defending multifunctional agriculture in Indonesia. *Journal of Agricultural) R & D, 25*(3), 99–105. Retrieved from http://pustaka.litbang.pertanian.go.id/publikasi/p3253064.pdf.

Asaad, M. (2011). Peningkatan Peranan Perbankan Syariah untuk Pembiayaan Usaha Pertanian. *Jurnal Miqot* (The increased role of Islamic banking for financing agriculture business. *Journal Miqot), 35*(1), 113–127. Retrieved from http://download.portalgaruda.org/article.php?article=392238&val=8601&title=peningkatan%20peranan%20perbankan%20syariah%20untuk%20pembiayaan%20usaha%20pertanian.

Ashari, A. & Saptana, S. (2005). Prospek pembiayaan syariah untuk sektor pertanian. *Jurnal Forum Penelitian Agro Ekonomi* (Sharia financing Prospects for the agricultural sector. *Journal of Economic Research Forum Agro), 23*(2), 132–147. Retrieved at April 4, 2017 from http://pse.litbang.pertanian.go.id/ind/pdffiles/FAE23-2e.pdf.

Badan Perencanaan Pembangunan Nasional. (2012). Langkah menuju ekonomi hijau: Langkah dan memulainya (The National Development Planning Board. (2012) steps towards a green economy: steps and get started). Retrieved from http://www.bappenas.go.id/index.php/download_file/view/7197.

Badan Pusat Statistik. (2016). Indikator pasar tenaga kerja Indonesia Agustus 2016. Jakarta: Badan Pusat Statistik (The Central Bureau of Statistics. (2016). Indicators of the labor market Indonesia August 2016. Jakarta: Central Bureau of Statistics).

Batubara, M.M. (2007). Peran lembaga permodalan dalam pembiayaan sektor agribisnis ditingkat pertanian rakyat di Sumatera Selatan. *Jurnal Fordema* (The role of capital in agribusiness sector financing the present farming people in South Sumatra. *Journal Fordema), 7*(1), 69–76, Retrieved from http://www.perpustakaan.kemenkeu.go.id/FOLDERJURNAL/kredit%20agribisnis.pdf.

Chou, Y.K. (2007). Modeling financial innovation and economic growth: Why the financial sector matters to the real economy. *The Journal of Economic Education, 38*(1), 78–90.

Kaelan. 2012. *Metode Penelitian Kualitatif Interdisipliner*. Yogyakarta: Paradigma.

Li, G., Dai, J.S., Park, E.M. & Park, S.T. (2017). A study on the service and trend of Fintech security based on text-mining: Focused on the data of Korean online news. *Journal of Computer Virology and Hacking Techniques*, 1–7. Retrieved from https://doi.org/10.1007/s11416-016-0288-9.

Li, L., Peng, M., Jiang, N. & Law, R. (2017). An empirical study on the influence of economy hotel website quality on online booking intentions. *International Journal of Hospitality Management, 63*, 1–10. Retrieved from https://doi.org/10.1016/j.ijhm.2017.01.001.

Miller, C. & Jones, L. (2010). *Agricultural value chain finance. Tools and lessons*. Food and Agriculture Organization of the United Nations and Practical Action Publishing, p. 195.

Novak, I., Verniuk, N. & Novak, Y. (2016). Structuring of sources of attracting capital to agricultural production as a prerequisite for the formation of an effective investment. Mechanism in the agricultural sector, *159*, 29–33.

Puschmann, T. (2017). Fintech. *Business & Information Systems Engineering*, (2017) 59(1), 69–76. Retrieved from https://doi.org/10.1007/s12599-017-0464-6.

Son, V.N., Schinckus, C. & Chong, F. (2017). A post-Marxist approach in development finance: PMF or production mutualisation fund model applied to agriculture. *Research in International Business and Finance, 40*, 94–104. Retrieved from https://doi.org/10.1016/j.ribaf.2016.12.008.

Tsabita, K. (2013). Analisis Risiko Pembiayaan Syariah pada Sektor Pertanian, Kasus: BPRS Amanah Ummah, Leuwiliang, Bogor. Unpublished Thesis, Bogor Agricultural University.

Wahid, Nusron. 2014. *Keuangan Inklusif. Membongkar. Hegemoni Keuangan*. Jakarta: Gramedia.

Wood, G. & Steiner, J. (2016). Trustless Computing—The What Not the How. In *Banking Beyond Banks and Money* (pp. 133–144). Springer International Publishing. Retrieved from https://doi.org/10.1007/978-3-319-42448-4.

Zavolokina, L., Dolata, M. & Schwabe, G. (2016). The FinTech phenomenon: Antecedents of financial innovation perceived by the popular press. *Financial Innovation, 2*(1), 16. Retrieved from https://doi.org/10.1186/s40854-016-0036-7.

Zhao, F., Yan, S.R., Peng, H., Yan, H.P., & Xiao, J.Z. (2017). An empirical research on the influence of Chinese rural financial reform on cultivation of new agricultural business entities. *Journal of Discrete Mathematical Sciences and Cryptography, 20*(1), 389–405. Retrieved from https://doi.org/10.1080/09720529.2016.1183314.

Zilgalvis, P. (2014). The need for an innovation principle in regulatory impact assessment: The case of finance and innovation in Europe. *Policy and Internet, 6*(4), 377–392. Retrieved from https://doi.org/10.1002/1944-2866.POI374. http://www.unep.org/greeneconomy/Portals/88/EMPLOYMENT.pdf.

URL

https://www.igrow.asia/.

Increasing Management Relevance and Competitiveness – Sukoco et al. (Eds)
© 2018 Taylor & Francis Group, London, ISBN 978-0-8153-7455-8

Gintingan in the Subang district of West Java: An implementation of local wisdom in sustainable development in Indonesia

Kurniawan Saefullah
Faculty of Economics and Business, Universitas Padjadjaran, Bandung, Indonesia

ABSTRACT: The role of culture in development has been considered a critical point in sustainable development. Woodley et al. (2006) state that the absence of the cultural factor in development leads to unsuccessful development programs. In this context, Marsden (1994), along with Warren et al. (1995), has previously highlighted the importance of using an emic approach in development. *Gintingan* is an example of a local institution in the Sundanese Region of West Java, Indonesia, which is based on local culture and wisdom. The tradition represents an indigenous form of mutual-aid institution which is influenced by the Sundanese worldviews of *tritangtu* and local wisdom of *silih asah, silih asih and silih asuh* (Irawan 1999). By using qualitative approaches through observation and literature studies, this paper attempts to describe how *gintingan* has been implemented by local people in the Subang district of West Java, including its role in sustainable community development.

Keywords: Culture & Development; Emic Approach; Local Institution; Gintingan; Sustainable Community Development

1 INTRODUCTION

Shaffer et al. (2006) addressed the importance of analyzing community in development. While some economists have been discussing the study of a nation state (macro level) including individual consumers and firms (micro level), some economists have left out the important middle ground between the two levels: *community*. Therefore, they suggest an analysis at the community level of development, where various development problems occur. For instance, the problem of poverty mainly related to people and their environment at the community level, both in urban and rural areas.

The attention to community in development brought us to the concept of sustainable development. The concept of sustainable development, first introduced in the Brundtland Report 'Our Common Future', a report by the World Commission on Environment and Development in 1987. It is a development attempt to alleviate poverty, create equitable living standards, satisfy the basic needs of all peoples, and ensure that there are no irrevocable damages to natural resources and nature. It also highlights the connection between economic aspects of the people with any other social and environmental factors in order to make development sustainable. The report of the IUCN Renowned Thinkers Meeting in 2006 recommended that development plans, policy and implementation include economic, social and environmental factors. Development objectives should be achieved *equitably* (where balances between economic and social are fulfilled), *viable* (where balances between economic and environment are accomplished), and *bearable* (where balances between social and environment are not omitted). The concept of green business and green economics are also part of themes discussed in sustainable development. It is, therefore, no surprise that the United Nations launched its post-2015 development agenda, namely Sustainable Development Goals (SDGs). As the successor of the previous Millennium Development Goals (MDGs), the United Nations' SDGs attempt to not only empower institutional approach, including business and public services, to achieve development objectives, but also to ensure that the achievement could be sustainably realized. Various current problems today i.e. incidents of poverty, deforestation, floods, poor water sanitation, are some examples of how development objectives were achieved without compromising the balance between economic, social and environmental factors (Swisher et al., 2009; Marsden, 1994; and Warren et al. 1995).

Marsden (1994) and Warren et al. (1995) have underlined the importance of cultural inclusion in sustainable development. Every community has its own culture. Culture refers to what a community of people thinks, says, does and makes: its customs, language, material artefacts and shared systems of attitudes and feelings. Development policies therefore, should be approached based on people's culture in the community and not by a single prescription of development. Marsden (1994) states that 'it is now commonplace to hear that there are many paths to development. Each built on a different cultural base and using different tools, techniques and organizations. The assumptions underlying the view that it would be sufficient to transfer western technology and expertise no longer hold'. Warren et al. (1995) suggest an *emic* (insider view) approach in development rather than an *etic* (outsider view) approach. Their view is supported by Woodley et al. (2006) who argued that 'despite the fact that development planners aim to optimize development and reduce disparity between the rich and the poor, they often do so without acknowledging the indigenous people's food, livelihood systems and culture'.

As a country that has hundreds of ethno-cultural groups, Indonesia is rich in cultural traditions, which have been implemented for many generations throughout the country. The tradition encompasses socio-cultural aspects of the community, to economy, politics, health-care, as well as education, including various forms of local institutions. In terms of social interaction, *gotong royong* has been implemented in Indonesia as a cultural interaction where people in the community, mutually help each other to attain particular shared goals. *Gotong royong* represents communalism culture in Indonesian people. *Gotong royong* has been transpiring in various traditions and institutions in many ethno-cultural groups in Indonesia (Taylor & Aragon, 1991 and Rochmadi, 2012). One of the local traditions which is based on *gotong royong* is *gintingan*, a socio-economic and cultural institution in the Sundanese region of the district of Subang, West Java, Indonesia. The tradition has been implemented for almost half a century by the local people of Subang (Irawan, 1999 and Prasetyo, 2012).

There has been various research conducted that aim to understand the relationship between culture and development. Yet, the study that attempts to explore the link between culture and economic development, particularly in Sundanese culture remains scarce. Therefore, this paper tries to fill the gap in the existing literature and research by focusing the research on Sundanese culture. Specifically, this paper aims to demonstrate empirical evidence on how a local institution, in this context *gintingan*, integrates culture and development. Its mechanism, cosmological reasoning (known as local wisdom) and historical background, as well as its contribution to sustainable community development are discussed. By using qualitative approaches through observation and literature studies, this paper attempts to describe the importance cultural inclusion has in development. Business institutions and public institutions, including policy makers, should be aware of how important, local wisdom and socio-cultural factors should be accommodated in future business and development plans or policies.

2 METHODS

This paper uses a case study approach to demonstrate how a local socio-economic institution of *gintingan* was established, conceptualized and implemented in the Subang district of West Java, Indonesia. A case study is an exploration of a *bounded system* or a case (or multiple cases) over time through detailed, in depth, data collection involving multiple sources of information rich in context (Creswell, 1998).

As part of doctoral research at Leiden Ethnosystems and Development (LEAD) Programme, Leiden University, the author uses descriptive analysis through the Leiden Ethnosystems approach. This approach involves a combination of three analyses: 1) the Participant View (PV), known also as an *emic* approach; 2) the Historical Dimension (HD) where historical (including cosmological) perspective is elaborated in the analysis and 3) a comparative analaysis among sample villages was applied as an implementation of Field Ethnological Studies (Slikkerveer, 1999). In this paper, two sample villages of the Subang district of West Java province were studied in mid-2012, combining non-participative observations, in-depth interviews and a literature study.

3 RESULTS

3.1 *Subang, Sundanese cosmology and practices*

Subang is one of the districts in the West Java Province of Indonesia, where people's livelihood in the community is influenced by Sundanese culture. Sundanese is the second largest ethno-cultural group in Indonesia with the total number of inhabitants circa 46 million people, spread throughout Indonesia, although most of them live in West Java and Banten Province. Sundanese people, including the local people of Subang, have a cosmological view, named as *tritangtu*. *Tritangtu* is a Sundanese term which is derived from *tri* = three and *tangtu* = realms/components. The Sundanese cosmology of *tritangtu* influences the Subang people's livelihoods, including socio-cultural activities as well as economic activities and institutional forms. The Sundanese believe that human well-being, as a development objective, will only be achieved through a harmonious life balance between humans, the environment, and sacred/spiritual beings. The three factors: human, environment and sacred/spiritual beings are the three components of *tritangtu*. This triadic structure is acknowledged as part of the Sundanese life structure (Djunatan, 2011 and Wijaya, 2009). From the interviews with two elderly people (Pak Haji Ade in Sukamelang village & Pak Wali in Cimanglid village), the cosmology of *tritangtu* has been transpired by Sundanese in various forms of daily activities and principles of life. In terms of landscape arrangements, Sundanese divides into three divisions: *tonggoh* or *hulu* (highland), *lebak* (midland) and *hilir* (lowland). The highland is meant for any creature other than humans to live. In fact, this landscape division has an implicit Sundanese value which relates to water management. Since water flows from the highland to the lowland, the highland area should be kept free from any human activities to ensure that the waters flowing from the highland are clean in order that any beings who live in the lowland can enjoy clean water. In terms of social interaction, Sundanese divides also in the principles of interaction into three components, which is also known as Sundanese wisdom: harmonious life between human and human (*silih asuh*), harmonious life between human and the earth/environment (*silih asih*), and harmonious life between human and spiritual beings (*silih asah*). Silih means reciprocal. It shows that, in terms of social interaction, the Sundanese believe that well-being in social life will only be achieved by implementing reciprocal interactions with humans, spiritual beings and the environment: in giving attention, respect, support, as well as other forms of interaction (Irawan, 1999).

3.2 *Gintingan: Concept and practices*

In terms of socio-economic life, Sundanese also implements the principle of reciprocity in various activities. In Subang, the reciprocity can be seen through a community institution, named as *gintingan*. *Gintingan* is a local initiative by people in the community in which a household which has a very pressing economic problem (*hajat*) receives contributions from other community members, so their needs can be economically and socio-culturally fulfilled. *Gintingan* can be defined as a traditional socio-economic and cultural system, or community-managed institution, which is based on mutual help (*gotong royong*), using mutual rotation systems (*arisan*) where a ceremony (wedding etc.) is used as a medium of the socio-economic transaction.

The term *'gintingan'* was taken from the word *gantang or ginting*: scale measures of rice/paddy. One gantang measures about 10 liters of rice. Meanwhile, Wijaya (2009) relates the term *gintingan* with *gentenan* which means reciprocity.

Earlier research has defined *gintingan* in various ways. Irawan (1999) defined *gintingan* as *'Pola hajatan dengan penggunaan sistem arisan'* (mechanism of the ceremony using mutual help-rotation systems), whereas Prasetyo (2012) defined gintingan as *'Sistem Ekonomi tradisional berupa simpanan kredit beras melalui hajatan'* (traditional economic systems where the credit and saving of rice is implemented through specific ceremony). The household which has large needs (*hajat*) and wishes to conduct a ceremony (*hajatan*) act as a debtor while people in the community, who are contributing to the household, act as creditors. The medium of exchange in this mechanism is a *gantang* of rice or 10 liters of paddy rice.

The practice of *gintingan* can be explained as follows: if a household in the community has an economic problem or a very important need (*hajat*), for instance a wedding ceremony, this household will inform his/her community leader about their need for other people's contributions. The community leader then informs all community members of the request from the household. Together with the community leader and the community members, the household sets the date of the ceremony or ritual (*hajatan*), representing the time period when the people in the community can start contributing to the household. To support the process of collecting the contributions, the leader usually establishes an organizing committee (community-managed institution). The organizing committee then arranges the planning of the ceremony (*hajatan*), both technical and non-technical preparations, as well as implementation.

The organizing committee usually divides the tasks among community members, and determines the person who will be responsible for collecting and administering the contributions (treasurer) as well as the wedding organizer who prepares the cultural event related to the wedding ceremony the household wishes to conduct. All the people in the community will then contribute to the household, based on a specific measure. Considering that the tradition uses paddy rice as the form of contribution, a *gantang* or scale for rice measure is used. One *gantang* is equal to 10 liters of paddy rice. People can contribute one or more *gantang*, depending on their ability.

As an illustrative example, 200 households in the community contribute to this needy household, and each of the households contributes one *gantang* of paddy rice. The household in need will receive at least approximately 2000 liters of paddy rice. If we calculate the amount of collected paddy rice with the price of one liter of paddy rice, say 15,000 rupiah per liter, the total amount collected for the household would be about 30 million rupiah. This collected paddy rice, received from the community, will be used by the household to fulfill their needs. Based on the author's observation in the two villages, the money generally was used to pay for the wedding ceremony, which had already been planned.

The needy household will document every single contribution by the community members and there is no finite time period to repay the contributions. Only if another household has a similar need or problem, then the repayment can be done in a similar way.

4 DISCUSSION

As discussed, development is a multidisciplinary branch of social science, which addresses various topics on how people and their society attempt to achieve well-being. It encompasses economic aspects of the society as well as other interrelated factors, including politics, socio-cultural, and, health and education. However, some development planners have been focusing more on the economic aspects of development rather than any other aspects of the human being. The particular focus has been elaborated on by Leys (2005) in his article 'The Rise and Fall of Development Theory'.

The importance of balancing economic aspects of development with social and ecology has been discussed by many authors. It involves not only the roles of business institutions, but also public service institutions, i.e. government agencies and policy makers. Numerous efforts have been made by development planners as well as private institutions in order to achieve development objectives. However, as Woodley et al. (2006) mentioned earlier, the exclusion of cultural aspects in development lead to unsuccessful development programs.

A similar argument could also be identified in the context of the microfinance role in alleviating poverty. As acknowledged by many development policy makers and micro-business entities, microfinance has a role to play in poverty alleviation. The Grameen Bank of Muhammad Yunus, the Bank Rakyat Indonesia in Indonesia and the Self-Help Group in India, are among some of the success stories, documented by Obaidullah (2008). Various works have indicated that microfinancing contributes a positive impact on the income of the borrowers, with an increase of 30% compared to that of those who do not take credit from microfinance. The positive impact of microfinancing not only affects the economic aspects of people, but also shows an improvement in the nutrition of the people, a decrease in gender disparities, and increased welfare of rural people (Obaidullah, 2008; SMERU Research Institute, 2005).

The role microfinance in poverty alleviation reveals success stories as well as critics. Hume and Mosley (1996), Bateman (2010) and Brouwer and Dijkema (2002) are among the authors who criticize the microfinance role in combating poverty. Bateman (2010) criticizes the glorification of microfinance instead of assisting poor people to become independently economically active. There is a tendency that microfinance has become commercialized by investors who are expecting huge returns through investing in microfinance institutions. Extremely poor people are seen as unbankable and thus, not profitable. Therefore, commercialization of microfinance tends to limit microfinance services to economically active people only. This tendency of limiting microfinance services to extremely poor people is supported by the findings of Hume and Mosley (1996) as also discussed by Brouwer and Dijkema (2002). According to them, successful microfinance in contributing to poverty reduction is particularly effective in improving the status of the middle and upper segments of the poor. Clients below the poverty line or the extremely poor were worse off after borrowing than before. As a result, only economically active people could access microfinance institutions and services. The extremely poor people couldn't use microfinance as a solution to their economic problems. It is not surprising that Fernando (2004) claims that, instead of eliminating poverty, microfinance is in fact perpetuating it. Fernando argued that *"The users of microfinance are generally those who are living within poverty lines, and those who are among the poorest in the society remain neglected and invisible by the microfinance. The requirement set by microfinance cannot be fulfilled by the poorest or extremely poor groups in the society"*. Microfinance then becomes 'exclusive' to poor people, particularly the extremely poor, as they are not bankable, do not have any collateral, and have no income generating activities. They are predicted to be unable to repay any possible 'borrowed money' from microfinance institutions.

This discourse has supported the argument by Woodley et al. (2006) who stated that the exclusion of cultural factors as part of the social dimension of sustainable development, has led to the failure of the microfinance role in development. The challenge, therefore, is that there is a need for evidence based research on how culture could be accommodated within development, particularly at the community level. *Gintingan* is an example of how a local institution plays its role in community development. It integrates cultural aspects of the people with socio-economic development. According to Slikkerveer (2007), gintingan can be classified as an Integrated Microfinance Institution.

The practice of *gintingan* has not only improved the lives of people in the community in financial or material terms, but also in terms of social and human interaction. In terms of social, the community may maintain the culture of "care" whereas, similar culture is rarely found nowadays in urban areas. Modern institutions which are based on impersonal communication and economic transactions have replaced the social cohesion as is still implemented in rural areas.

5 CONCLUDING REMARK

The *gintingan* tradition in the Subang district of West Java province has shown that socio-cultural dimensions can be integrated with the economic aspect of development. The tradition has demonstrated that not only is a bottom-up approach effective to involve people in development at the community level, but it is also effective in the implementation of self-sustained development as people were able to use their internal resources to solve their economic problem by implementing mutual help and mutual contribution (*gotong royong*), based on Indonesian culture, particularly Sundanese. It is expected that this paper will give valuable input to the government and policy makers, in applying a bottom-up development approach, where it is necessary to include community participation and the cultural perspective of local people. Nevertheless, further research is still required, particularly in the practices of culturally based institutions in supporting sustainable development, as well as how culturally based institutions could comply with the challenge of globalization.

ACKNOWLEDGMENT

The author would like to thank his supervisor, Prof. L. J. Slikkerveer and the Leiden Ethnosystems and Development (LEAD) Programme of Leiden University who have supported the research. In addition, the author would like to extend greater appreciation to the Indonesian Government, in particular the Directorate General of Higher Education, Ministry of Higher Education, Research and Technology (previously under the Ministry of Education and Culture) who has supported the author during his PhD research from 2011 to 2013. Similar gratitude is given to the Faculty of Economics and Business, University of Padjadjaran, Bandung Indonesia who gave permission to the author in pursuing his doctoral study at Leiden University.

REFERENCES

Bateman, M. (2010). *Why doesn't microfinance work?: The destructive rise of local neoliberalism*. London: Zed Books.

Brouwer, A.W., Dijkema, D. (2002). *Microfinance dilemma: The case of Bandung, Indonesia*. EC Paper No. 124 Rijksuniversiteit Groningen, The Netherlands. Retrieved from https://www.rug.nl/research/portal/files/3058685/EC124download.pdf.

Creswell, J.W. (1998) *Qualitative inquiry and research design: Choosing among five traditions*. London: Sage.

Djunatan, S. (2011). *The principle of affirmation: An ontological and epistemological ground of interculturality*. Doctoral dissertation. Erasmus University of Rotterdam, Rotterdam.

Fernando, N.A. (2004). Microfinance outreach to the poorest: A realistic objective? *Focal point for microfinance*. (Asian Development Bank). March 2004.

Hulme, D., Mosley, P. (1996). Finance against poverty. London and New York: Routledge.

Irawan, E. (1999). *Sistem Gintingan dalam hajatan terhadap kelangsungan ekonomi dan perkembangan kesenian tradisional di daerah kabupaten Subang*. Laporan Penelitian. [Gintingan System in ceremonies and its contributions to support traditional arts and culture in Subang district. Research's Report]. STISI Bandung, unpublished.

Leys, C. (2005). *The rise and fall of development theory*. In M. Edelman & A. Haugerud (Eds.), *The anthropology of development and globalization*. New Jersey: Blackwell Publishing.

Marsden, D. (1994). *Indigenous management and the management of indigenous knowledge*. In S. Wright, (Ed.), *Anthropology of organizations*. London: Routledge.

Obaidullah, M. (2008). *Role of microfinance in poverty alleviation: Lessons from experiences in selected IDB members countries*. 1st edition. IRTI-IDB.

Prasetyo, J.E. (2012). *Komersialisasi Sosial di Pedesaan: Studi Terhadap Modal Sosial Gantangan di Tiga Desa Miskin di Kabupaten Subang*. [Social commercialization in rural area of Subang district: A study on social capital of 'Gantangan' in three poor villages. (Master's thesis)]. Institut Pertanian Bogor.

Rochmadi, N. (2012). Gotong Royong sebagai 'Çommon Identity' dalam kehidupan bertetangga Negara-Negara ASEAN. ['Gotong Royong' as a common identity of daily life in ASEAN Countries]. *Jurnal Forum Sosial*. Malang: Universitas Negeri Malang.

Shaffer, R., Deller, S., Marcouiller, D. (2006). Rethinking community economic development, *Economic Development Quarterly*, *20*(1), 59–74.

Slikkerveer, L.J. (1999). Ethnoscience, 'TEK', and its application to conservation. In D.A. Posey (Ed.), *Cultural and spiritual values of biodiversity: A complementary contribution to the global biodiversity assessment* (pp. 167–260). London: Intermediate Technology Publications Ltd.

Slikkerveer, L.J. (2007). Integrated microfinance management and health communication in Indonesia, *Cleveringa Lecture Series*. Jakarta: Trisakti School of Management/Sekar Manggis Foundation.

SMERU Research Institute (2005). *The socio-economi impact of a microcredit program in Sulawesi, 13* (Jan–Mar).

Swisher, M.E., Rizola, S., Stern, J. (2009). *Sustainable community development*. Florida: IFAS Extension, University of Florida.

Taylor, P.M., Aragon, L.V. (1991). *Beyond the Java Sea: Art of Indonesia's Outer Islands (p. 10)*. New York: Abrams Inc.

Warren, D.M., Slikkerveer, L.J., Brokensha, D. (Eds.). (1995). *The cultural dimension of development: Indigenous knowledge systems*. London: Intermediate Technology Publications.

Wijaya, K. (2009). Kondangan sistem 'Narik Gintingan' dalam perspektif sosiologi hukum islam: studi kasus di desa Citrajaya kecamatan Binong kabupaten Subang. [Cerremony system of 'Narik Gintingan' from the perspective of islamic sociology]. Undergraduate thesis, UIN Sunan Kalijaga Jogjakarta.

Woodley, E., Crowley, E., Dey de Pryck, J., & Carmen, A. (2006). *Cultural indicators of indigenous peoples' food and agro-ecological systems* (Paper on the 2nd Global Consultation on the Right to Food and Food Security for Indigenous Peoples). Nicaragua: SARD Initiative.

World Comission on Environment and Development (WCED). (1987). Our Common Future—The Brundtland Report, New York: United Nations.

Author index

For Product Safety Concerns and Information please contact our
EU representative GPSR@taylorandfrancis.com Taylor & Francis
Verlag GmbH, Kaufingerstraße 24, 80331 München, Germany